Lecture Notes in Computer Science 5807

Commenced Publication in 1973
Founding and Former Series Editors:
Gerhard Goos, Juris Hartmanis, and Jan van Leeuwen

Jacques Blanc-Talon   Wilfried Philips
Dan Popescu   Paul Scheunders (Eds.)

Advanced Concepts for Intelligent Vision Systems

11th International Conference, ACIVS 2009
Bordeaux, France, September 28–October 2, 2009
Proceedings

 Springer

Volume Editors

Jacques Blanc-Talon
DGA/D4S/MRIS
CEP/GIP
16 bis, avenue Prieur de la Côte d'Or, 94114 Arcueil, France
E-mail: blanc@etca.fr

Wilfried Philips
Ghent University
Department of Telecommunication and Information Processing
St.-Pietersnieuwstraat 41, 9000 Gent, Belgium
E-mail: philips@telin.UGent.be

Dan Popescu
CSIRO ICT Centre
P.O. Box 76, Epping, Sydney NSW 1710, Australia
E-mail: dan.popescu@csiro.au

Paul Scheunders
University of Antwerp
Universiteitsplein 1, Building N, 2610 Wilrijk, Belgium
E-mail: paul.scheunders@ua.ac.be

Library of Congress Control Number: 2009934966

CR Subject Classification (1998): I.5, I.2.10, I.4, I.3, I.2

LNCS Sublibrary: SL 6 – Image Processing, Computer Vision, Pattern Recognition, and Graphics

ISSN   0302-9743
ISBN-10   3-642-04696-7 Springer Berlin Heidelberg New York
ISBN-13   978-3-642-04696-4 Springer Berlin Heidelberg New York

springer.com

© Springer-Verlag Berlin Heidelberg 2009
Printed in Germany

Typesetting: Camera-ready by author, data conversion by Scientific Publishing Services, Chennai, India
Printed on acid-free paper   SPIN: 12766079   06/3180   5 4 3 2 1 0

Preface

This volume collects the papers accepted for presentation at the 11th International Conference on Advanced Concepts for Intelligent Vision Systems (ACIVS 2009). Following the first meeting in Baden-Baden (Germany) in 1999, which was part of a large multiconference, the ACIVS conference then developed into an independent scientific event and has ever since maintained the tradition of being a single track conference. ACIVS 2009 attracted computer scientists from 25 different countries, mostly from Europe, but also from Australia, New-Zealand and Japan, and from the USA and Mexico.

Although ACIVS is a conference on all areas of image and video processing, submissions tend to gather within certain major fields of interest. As was the case last year, about a quarter of the selected papers deal with image and video coding and processing, including filtering and restoration and low-level analysis. Topics related to biometrics (including face recognition), tracking, pattern recognition and scene understanding all remain well represented. Noteworthy are the growing number of papers related to medical applications and color processing and the papers related to the Technovision projects. We would like to thank the invited speakers Steve Sangwine (University of Essex, UK) and Jordi Inglada (CNES, France) for enhancing the technical program with their presentations.

A conference like ACIVS would not be feasible without the concerted effort of many people and support of various institutions. The paper submission and review procedure was carried out electronically and a minimum of three reviewers were assigned to each paper. From 115 submissions, 43 were selected for oral presentation and 25 as posters. A large and energetic Program Committee, helped by additional referees (about 110 people) – listed on the following pages – completed the long and demanding reviewing process. We would like to thank all of them for their timely and high-quality reviews. Also, we would like to thank our sponsors, DGA, Philips Research, Barco, Eurasip, the IEEE Benelux Signal Processing Chapter and the Flemish FWO Research Community on Audiovisual Systems, for their valuable support.

Last but not least, we would like to thank all the participants who trusted in our ability to organize this event for the 11th time. We hope they attended a stimulating scientific event and enjoyed the atmosphere of the ACIVS social events in the city of Bordeaux.

July 2009

J. Blanc-Talon
W. Philips
D. Popescu
P. Scheunders

Organization

ACIVS 2009 was organized by SEE (Société de l'Electricité, de l'Electronique et des Technologies de l'Information et de la Communication) and Ghent University.

Steering Committee

Jacques Blanc-Talon	DGA, Bagneux, France
Wilfried Philips	Ghent University - IBBT, Ghent, Belgium
Dan Popescu	CSIRO, Sydney, Australia
Paul Scheunders	University of Antwerp, Wilrijk, Belgium

Organizing Committee

Alain Appriou	ONERA, Châtillon, France
Frédéric Barbaresco	THALES, Limours, France
Jacques Blanc-Talon	DGA, Bagneux, France
Pierre Melchior	ENSEIRB, Talence, France
Béatrice Valdayron	SEE, Paris, France

Sponsors

ACIVS 2009 was sponsored by the following organizations:

- Philips Research
- DGA
- The IEEE Benelux Signal Processing Chapter
- Eurasip
- Barco
- DSP Valley
- The FWO Research Community on Audiovisual Systems (AVS)

Program Committee

Hamid Aghajan	Stanford University, USA
Marc Antonini	Université de Nice Sophia Antipolis, France
Kenneth Barner	University of Delaware, Newark, USA
Ismail Ben Ayed	GE Healthcare, London, Canada
Jenny Benois-Pineau	LaBRI, Talence, France
Laure Blanc-Feraud	INRIA, Sophia-Antipolis, France
Philippe Bolon	University of Savoie, Annecy, France

Don Bone   Canon Information Systems Research
                                      Australia, Sydney, Australia
Salah Bourennane   Ecole Centrale de Marseille, France
Marco Cagnazzo   ENST, Paris, France
Umberto Castellani   Università degli Studi di Verona, Italy
Jocelyn Chanussot   INPG, Grenoble, France
Pamela Cosman   University of California at San Diego, La Jolla,
                                      USA
Yves D'Asseler   Ghent University, Belgium
Jennifer Davidson   Iowa State University, Ames, USA
Arturo de la Escalera Hueso   Universidad Carlos III de Madrid, Leganes,
                                      Spain
Touradj Ebrahimi   Ecole Polytechnique Fédérale de Lausanne,
                                      Switzerland
Don Fraser   University of New South Wales, Canberra,
                                      Australia
Edouard Geoffrois   DGA, Arcueil, France
Jerome Gilles   DGA/CEP, Arcueil, France
Georgy Gimel'farb   The University of Auckland, New Zealand
Markku Hauta-Kasari   InFotonics Center Joensuu, Finland
Mark Holden   Canon Information Systems Research
                                      Australia, Sydney, Australia
Dimitris Iakovidis   University of Athens, Greece
Frédéric Jurie   CNRS - INRIA, Saint Ismier, France
Arto Kaarna   Lappeenranta University of Technology,
                                      Finland
Konstantinos Karantzalos   National Technical University of Athens,
                                      Greece
Andrzej Kasinski   Poznan University of Technology, Poland
Soo-Kyun Kim   Paichai University, Korea
Ron Kimmel   Technion-Israel Institute of Technology, Haifa,
                                      Israel
Richard Kleihorst   VITO, Belgium
Nikos Komodakis   University of Crete, Greece
Murat Kunt   EPFL, Lausanne, Switzerland
Hideo Kuroda   Nagasaki University, Japan
Olivier Laligant   IUT Le Creusot, France
Kenneth Lam   The Hong Kong Polytechnic University,
                                      Hong Kong, China
Patrick Lambert   Polytech' Savoie, Annecy-le-Vieux, France
Peter Lambert   Ghent University, Ledeberg-Ghent, Belgium
Yue Li   CSIRO ICT Centre, Sydney, Australia
Xavier Maldague   Université de Laval, Québec, Canada
Joseph Mariani   Université Paris VI, Paris XI, Orsay, France
Gérard Medioni   USC/IRIS, Los Angeles, USA

Alfred Mertins	Universität zu Lübeck, Germany
Amar Mitiche	INRS, Montréal, Canada
Rafael Molina	Universidad de Granada, Spain
Adrian Munteanu	Vrije Universiteit Brussel, Belgium
Henri Nicolas	LaBRI, Talence, France
Frank Nielsen	Ecole Polytechnique - Sony CSL, Palaiseau, France
Michel Paindavoine	Université de Bourgogne, Dijon, France
Sankar Pal	Indian Statistical Institute, Kolkata, India
Nikos Paragios	Ecole Centrale de Paris, Chatenay-Malabry, France
Jussi Parkkinen	University of Joensuu, Finland
Fernando Pereira	Instituto Superior Técnico, Lisbon, Portugal
Stuart Perry	Canon Information Systems Research Australia, Sydney, Australia
Aleksandra Pizurica	Ghent University - IBBT, Belgium
Gianni Ramponi	Trieste University, Italy
Paolo Remagnino	Kingston University, UK
Luis Salgado Alvarez de Sotomayor	Universidad Politécnica de Madrid, Spain
Guna Seetharaman	AFRL, Rome, USA
Hugues Talbot	ESIEE, Noisy-le-Grand, France
Frederic Truchetet	Université de Bourgogne, Le Creusot, France
Ewout Vansteenkiste	Ghent University - IBBT, Ghent, Belgium
Peter Veelaert	University College Ghent, Ghent, Belgium
Gerald Zauner	Fakultät für Technik und Umweltwissenschaften, Wels, Austria
Djemel Ziou	Sherbrooke University, Sherbrooke, Canada

Reviewers

Hamid Aghajan	Stanford University, USA
Sandrine Anthoine	University of Nice, France
Marc Antonini	Université de Nice Sophia Antipolis, France
Mohamed Bahgat	University of Cairo, Egypt
Doru Balcan	Carnegie Mellon University, Pittsburgh, PA, USA
Dimitris Bariamis	University of Athens, Greece
Abdel Belaïd	INRIA, Nancy, France
Ismail Ben Ayed	GE Healthcare, London, Canada
Jenny Benois-Pineau	LaBRI, Talence, France
Laure Blanc-Feraud	INRIA, Sophia-Antipolis, France
Jacques Blanc-Talon	DGA, Bagneux, France
Philippe Bolon	University of Savoie, Annecy, France
Don Bone	Canon Information Systems Research Australia, Sydney, Australia

Salah Bourennane	Ecole Centrale de Marseille, France
Patrick Bouthemy	IRISA/INRIA, Rennes, France
Marco Cagnazzo	ENST, Paris, France
Umberto Castellani	Università degli Studi di Verona, Italy
Jocelyn Chanussot	INPG, Grenoble, France
Tse-wei Chen	National Taiwan University, Taiwan
Euijin Choo	Korea University, Korea
Pamela Cosman	University of California at San Diego, La Jolla, USA
Yves D'Asseler	Ghent University, Belgium
Matthew Dailey	Asian Institute of Technology, Klong Luang, Thailand
Frédéric Dambreville	CEP, Arcueil, France
Jennifer Davidson	Iowa State University, Ames, USA
Johan De Bock	Ghent University - IBBT, Belgium
Arturo de la Escalera Hueso	Universidad Carlos III de Madrid, Leganes, Spain
Xavier Descombes	INRIA Sophia Antipolis, France
Bernadette Dorizzi	INT, Evry, France
Arno Duijster	University of Antwerp, Belgium
Laurent Dupont	Nancy University, France
Karen Egiazarian	Tampere University of Technology, Tampere, Finland
Don Fraser	University of New South Wales, Canberra, Australia
Andre Galligo	Nice University, France
Basilis Gatos	Demokritos, Athens, Greece
Jan-Mark Geusebroek	University of Amsterdam, The Netherlands
Jerome Gilles	DGA/CEP, Arcueil, France
Georgy Gimel'farb	The University of Auckland, New Zealand
Markku Hauta-Kasari	InFotonics Center Joensuu, Finland
Mark Holden	Canon Information Systems Research Australia, Sydney, Australia
Dimitris Iakovidis	University of Athens, Greece
Claudia Iancu	National University of Ireland, Galway, Ireland
Ianir Ideses	Tel Aviv University, Israel
Robin Jaulmes	DGA, Paris, France
Frédéric Jurie	CNRS - INRIA, Saint Ismier, France
Arto Kaarna	Lappeenranta University of Technology, Finland
Konstantinos Karantzalos	National Technical University of Athens, Greece
Andrzej Kasinski	Poznan University of Technology, Poland
Soo-Kyun Kim	Paichai University, Korea
Richard Kleihorst	VITO, Belgium
Nikos Komodakis	University of Crete, Greece

Table of Contents

Technovision

Fundamental Mathematical Techniques

Image Processing, Coding and Filtering

Image and Video Analysis

Computer Vision

Tracking

Color, Multispectral and Special-Purpose Imaging

Medical Imaging

Biometrics

Evaluation of Interest Point Detectors for Non-planar, Transparent Scenes

Chrysi Papalazarou[1], Peter M.J. Rongen[2], and Peter H.N. de With[1,3]

[1] Eindhoven University of Technology,
5600 MB Eindhoven
The Netherlands
[2] Philips Healthcare
5680 DA Best
The Netherlands
[3] CycloMedia Technology
4180 BB Waardeburg
The Netherlands

Abstract. The detection of stable, distinctive and rich feature point sets has been an active area of research in the field of video and image analysis. Transparency imaging, such as X-ray, has also benefited from this research. However, an evaluation of the performance of various available detectors for this type of images is lacking. The differences with natural imaging stem not only from the transparency, but -in the case of medical X-ray- also from the non-planarity of the scenes, a factor that complicates the evaluation. In this paper, a method is proposed to perform this evaluation on non-planar, calibrated X-ray images. Repeatability and accuracy of nine interest point detectors is demonstrated on phantom and clinical images. The evaluation has shown that the Laplacian-of-Gaussian and Harris-Laplace detectors show overall the best performance for the datasets used.

Keywords: Interest point detection, features, X-ray, evaluation, depth estimation.

1   Introduction

Interest point detection is the first step in many high-level vision tasks, either directly or through intermediate tasks like surface reconstruction, self-calibration, etc. Much research has been devoted to the task of interest point detection as a discipline, and many detection algorithms have been proposed. Several researchers have addressed the performance of subsets of these detectors in a number of evaluation papers [1,2,3,4,5].

In this paper, we examine a special type of content, namely transparency images, more specifically X-ray images made with a rotating C-arm. This imaging system resembles a moving camera system with known calibration parameters. A comparison of the configurations of a pinhole camera model and an X-ray source-detector system is shown in Figure 1. The evaluation of these images

J. Blanc-Talon et al. (Eds.): ACIVS 2009, LNCS 5807, pp. 1–11, 2009.

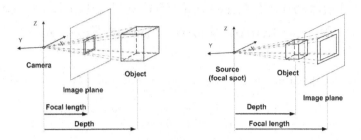

Fig. 1. Comparison of configuration between camera (left) and X-ray system (right)

is challenging for two main reasons: (1) the transparency creates overlapping structures that can mislead the detection (a problem dual to occlusions in natural imaging), and (2) scenes imaged with a rotating C-arm do not comply with the planarity demand. The transparency, along with the high noise content and relatively low contrast of X-ray, complicates the detection step itself. The non-planarity forces us to consider a different evaluation scheme than what is usually applied in generic imaging.

Most evaluations of interest point detection have been performed either on planar (or assumed to be planar) scenes, or on objects with a known configuration. An exception is [5], where intersecting epipolar constraints are used between triplets of calibrated views: reference, test, and auxiliary view. However, that work is motivated by object recognition applications, and uses evaluation criteria described from a large feature database. In our work, we propose an evaluation method that does not assume planarity, and uses multiple views, along with the calibration information, to create a reference model for each sequence. Thus, no prior statistical knowledge or database creation is needed, and the detectors can be evaluated per dataset. Additionally, in our approach the error in the reference set creation is taken into account by comparing the detectors under controlled error conditions, as will be further explained later.

The evaluation does not create an absolute ground truth, and thus we cannot conclude on the ability of the detectors to capture the true position of interest points. It is our opinion, however, that since such a ground truth cannot be obtained for complex scenes, a relative comparison can serve to select the best detection scheme for a given task. This evaluation is tuned to the application for which the detection step is used, namely the creation of a sparse depth map using feature point correspondences. The goal of the evaluation is to identify the detector or detectors that provide the most rich and robust feature points, under various imaging conditions.

The remainder of this paper is structured as follows: first, the proposed evaluation method is described and justified in Section 2. Next, the interest point detectors used are briefly introduced (Section 3) and some implementation details given (Section 4). The experiments performed on a number of phantom and clinical images are described, and the results of the evaluation presented in Section 5, followed by conclusions in Section 6.

2   Description of the Evaluation Scheme

In scenes that can be considered planar (e.g. faraway landscapes), a typical method of interest point evaluation comprises the following steps: (1) detection of N points $\mathbf{x}_i$, $i = 1..N$ on the image, (2) 2D transformation of the image with a known transform (e.g. affine), such that the ground-truth position of the feature points on the second image $\tilde{\mathbf{x}}'_i$ can be predicted, (3) detection of points in second image $\mathbf{x}'_i$, (4) measurement of the error $|\tilde{\mathbf{x}}'_i - \mathbf{x}'_i|$. The planarity of the scene allows the application of one global 2D transformation that determines the displacement of all image points. If this assumption does not hold, world points that are in different depths will undergo different transformations, such that no single homography will exist that will describe their position.

A more general approach, employing invariance methods for the evaluation of corner extraction, has been proposed by [4]. These invariants assume specific configurations of the object, e.g. polyhedrals, to construct a manifold that constrains the true positions of corners. Although it is also possible to use objects of a known configuration for X-ray, for example, a dodecahedron phantom (the X-ray equivalent of a checkerboard pattern), we opted to perform the evaluation on anatomical phantom images without any ground truth. There are two main motivations behind this:

1. It is precisely the performance of the detectors in "real" (or similar to real) images that we want to assess. A detector that performs well on an artificial pattern does not necessarily preserve its performance for more complex (clinical) content. This is especially important, as the different properties of medical X-ray images are motivating this research.
2. The configuration of a model object contains some inherent errors (e.g. size, placement), which in the case of depth estimation may be in the order of the errors that we want to measure, preventing its use as an absolute ground truth. An example of this is shown in Figure 2 showing the predicted position

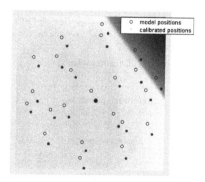

Fig. 2. Comparison between predicted (theoretical) positions of lead bullets of dodecahedron phantom, with the positions extracted after calibration

of points on a dodecahedron phantom, which is assumed to be positioned at the iso-center. The predicted positions are overlaid on the original image, and compared with the position obtained from calibration. Since calibration is performed assuming accurate 2D detection, it is clear that the inherent error in the model interferes with any attempt to measure the absolute accuracy.

Instead, we construct an evaluation method which is inspired by the final task of 3D localization of the feature points. In this method, a subset of the available views is used to create a reference set of interest points for each detector. This is done by tracking corresponding feature points in successive views, and using these correspondences to obtain their 3D coordinates. The 3D back-projection step is performed by using a combination of intersection and resection, as described in [6], and by employing the available calibration parameters. Next, the reference points are projected onto each of the frames to be tested.

Two evaluation criteria are routinely employed in interest point detection (see e.g. [1], [7]): repeatability and accuracy. Here, we have modified their definition in compliance with the rest of our scheme. Thus, an interest point is considered to be repeated when its distance to the nearest projected reference point is smaller than a threshold. We define repeatability in this framework as the ratio between the number of repeated points and the size of the reference set. Accuracy is then expressed as the Euclidian distance between the matched points and corresponding reference points. The evaluation scheme is outlined in Figure 3.

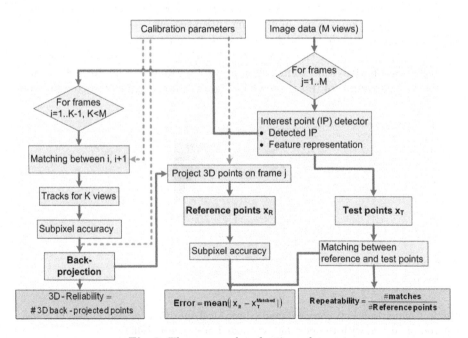

Fig. 3. The proposed evaluation scheme

The creation of the reference set contains an error, since the true position of the points is neither known in 2D, nor in 3D. This is an inherent limitation introduced by the non-coplanarity of the feature points. To control the effect of this error, we employ a selection on the reference points based on their 2D re-projection error. A point with a large re-projection error in the reference set is considered unstable and rejected. This introduces an additional evaluation criterion in our scheme: the number of points that can be back-projected with a small re-projection error, which indicates the detector's ability to select suitable points. This metric is further on termed as the detector's "3D reliability". Under the assumption that the 3D error is reflected on the 2D re-projection error, this metric also implies that the influence of the 3D error is normalized between the different detectors. This means that the evaluation of detectors is performed among points that have similar re-projection errors, thus enabling a fair relative comparison on the grounds of 2D repeatability and accuracy. The different sources of error are illustrated in Figure 4.

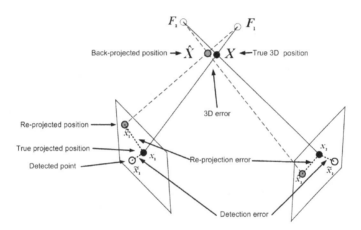

Fig. 4. Illustration of the different error types

3   Suitable Interest Point Detection

In this work, we start from a definition of a suitable interest point as *a point that can be reliably linked to a specific world point*. It is of no special importance whether the point examined is expressed as a corner, a blob, or in any other form. The specific characteristics of the neighborhood also do not play an important role, as long as this neighborhood (or some description of it) allows the point to be reliably tracked, in a way that is consistent with its world position. This definition bears a resemblance to the notion of "good features to track" by Shi *et al.* [8], in the sense that the task defines the quality of the features. Our approach incorporates the additional demand that, as we are ultimately aiming at recovering 3D structure, 3D constraints stemming from the application (i.e. calibration parameters and physical limitations in world position) are also considered.

To this end, we have tested a number of interest point detectors known from literature. These include: (1) the conventional Harris corner detector [9], (2) the morphology-based SUSAN detector [10], (3) Laplacian-of-Gaussian [11], (4) multi-scale Harris, (5) Determinant of Hessian [12], (6) normalized curvature [11], (7) Harris-Laplace [13], (8) Ridge corner points [14] [15], and (9) Ridgeness features transformed with the Euclidian distance transform.

The evaluation presented here concentrates as much as possible to the task of detection itself. Therefore, all other steps of the evaluation, including matching, sub-pixel estimation and back-projection, are kept the same for the different detectors tested. This excludes combinations of detectors and descriptors from this evaluation, such as e.g. the popular SIFT transform [16]. The detection part of SIFT and its successors [12], [17] uses an approximation of the Laplacian-of-Gaussian, which is included in this evaluation. The main power of SIFT, however, lies in the description of the feature points that allows for a different matching scheme. The evaluation of description schemes is not within the scope of this paper.

4   Implementation Details of the Detectors

In the following, we provide some implementation aspects and settings of the detectors. The main consideration during the implementation has been to tune all detectors as well as possible to the high noise content and low contrast of X-ray images, which makes the tradeoff between the number of detected feature points and their stability more difficult than in the case of natural images.

4.1   Parameter Settings

The Harris detector was used with smoothing $\sigma = 2$ and the k factor was chosen equal to 0.08. For SUSAN, we used the original implementation provided in [10]. The multi-scale Gaussian derivatives were calculated for a number of successive scales, defined as: $\sigma_k^D = s \cdot \sigma_0 \cdot q^{k-1}$, where n_{sc} is the number of scales and q the factor between them. The parameter s defines the relation between integration and derivation scale. We used $s = 0.7$, $q = 1.3$, $\sigma_0 = 1.5$ pixels and $n_{sc} = 9$ for detectors (4) through (7), as indicated above. For detectors (8) and (9) (ridge features) we used larger scales, $\sigma_0 = 5$ and $q = 1.5$, to capture the coarser elongated structures. For detector (9), the same ridgeness feature representation is used as for (8), and a binary mask is created for each scale by a soft histogram-based thresholding. Then, the Euclidian distance transform is applied to the mask image and this is used as the feature representation. This operation aims at capturing high-curvature points on the centerlines of coarse ridges.

4.2   Maxima Selection

Each of the detectors provides a feature representation of the image, from which the most prominent points are selected. We select the 500 largest extrema as feature points. This ensures comparability between the detectors and does not affect the repeatability measurement in our scheme. For the case of multi-scale features, scale-space maxima are used [16], where the neighborhood for the maxima selection is larger for small scales, to avoid concentration of noisy feature points very close to each other. We use the empiric relation $nb = \lceil \sigma_{n_{sc}} \cdot \sigma_0 / \sigma_k^2 \rceil$ to obtain appropriate neighborhood sizes.

For all tested detectors, a selection is applied to the candidate feature points. Points located on significant edges, where the localization is expected to be poor, are rejected by examining the ratio of the Eigenvalues of the Hessian matrix in a patch of size 3σ around the candidate point, as in [16]. A final rejection is applied to points with a low rms value of the Eigenvalues, as these points correspond to little or no local structure. The parameters of this selection were the same for all detectors.

4.3   Matching

In the experiments, we used a combination of correlation-based matching and geometric constraints. Candidate matches are searched for in a block of the target image, defined by the epipolar constraints [18] and a clipping volume that restricts the 3D position of the features. The epipolar constraints are specified using the known calibration parameters, while the clipping volume constraint stems from the configuration of the X-ray system, where the object is always positioned between the X-ray source and the detector.

4.4   Sub-pixel Accuracy

The accuracy of the detected interest points is extended by applying spline interpolation on the feature representations. For multi-scale detectors, the interpolation is applied in the 3D volume of the feature representation, using a patch of size equal to the scale of the feature. The sub-pixel accuracy is not used in the matching step, as that would involve a heavy computational cost due to dense interpolation of the feature representations. Instead, it is applied after the matching to obtain better accuracy in the back-projection step.

5   Experimental Results

The above-described evaluation was applied on two sequences of phantom images and two of clinical images, examples of which are shown in Figure 5. The sequences were made using an X-ray system equipped with a rotational C-arm and were 122 frames long. For each sequence, sub-sequences were selected to create the reference set, where the length of the sub-sequence was chosen such that a minimum number of 10 points is back-projected with an error below a predetemined tolerance. This tolerance was varied as part of the evaluation. Different sub-sequences of 20 frames (6 in total) were used to create the reference points. The number of reference points for the different datasets is shown in Figure 6.

After the reference set was created, two parameters were varied: the tolerance in the creation of the reference points (back-projection error), and the threshold

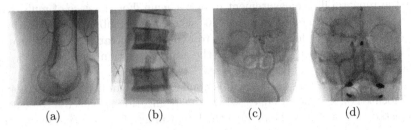

Fig. 5. Examples of the data. Phantom images: (a) Knee phantom with wires, (b) Chest phantom with catheter. (c), (d): Clinical images of head angiograms.

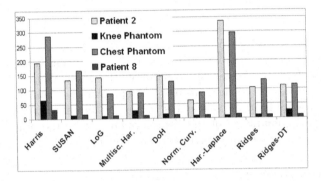

Fig. 6. Number of back-projected points for a back-projection error tolerance of 5 pixels and a matching distance of 5 pixels

of the matching (termed recall-precision in [19]). The repeatability and accuracy were measured for each frame in the sequence, excluding the ones used for the reference creation, and averaged over the number of sub-sequences. The results are shown in Figures 7 and 8. In Figure 6, the difference in the number of back-projected points among datasets is evident. Since the same parameters were used in all sequences, this reflects the relative sensitivity of all the tested detectors to the content. The 2 sequences for which many points can be tracked within a small sub-sequence, are the chest phantom and the first of the clinical sequences. In those, however, the points are less repeated over the entire sequence, as can be seen in Figure 7. The other two sequences, knee phantom and second clinical sequence, achieve a far smaller number of 3D points, but a larger repeatability. This is possibly due to the fact that in these sequences high-contrast objects (the wires in the first and the tooth implants in the second) are visible throughout the sequence and can be found reliably. For both sequences, the Laplacian-of-Gaussian scores high, while they individually achieve maximum performance with the Determinant-of-Hessian and single-scale Harris, respectively. The other two datasets (chest and clinical 2) respond best to Harris-Laplace, but here also the LoG scores high. However, the repeatability scores in this case lie almost a factor of 2 below the knee and clinical 1 datasets.

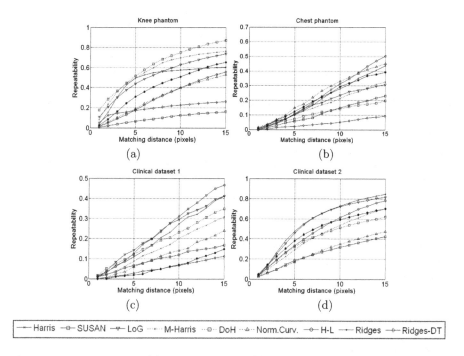

Fig. 7. Repeatability for: (a) Knee phantom, (b) Chest phantom (c) Sequence 1 of head angiograms (d) Sequence 2 of head angiograms

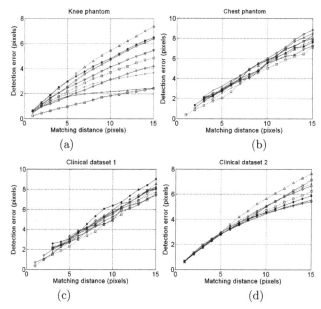

Fig. 8. Accuracy for: (a) Knee phantom, (b) Chest phantom (c) Sequence 1 of head angiograms (d) Sequence 2 of head angiograms

In the accuracy (2D error) measurements, the chest phantom and clinical 1 datasets show little variation between detectors, with a slightly better performance (lower error) of the Determinant-of-Hessian. The detection error increases approximately linearly with matching tolerance, as expected from the evaluation scheme: increases in the matching threshold are added to the mean detection error. In the knee and clinical 2 datasets, again the LoG scores well (best score in clinical 2). In the knee dataset, the Harris and SUSAN detectors score surprisingly well, Harris even better than its multi-scale version. This may be explained from the content of the sequence. It is mainly the points on the wires that can be tracked and back-projected reliably in this sequence. Their high contrast and distinctiveness, along with the relatively smooth background, enable the morphology-based SUSAN detector to achieve good accuracy; however, its low repeatability for the same dataset excludes it from being the best option. Additionally, it must be noted that the single-scale detectors only perform well when the kernel size is tuned to the size of the detected objects. This may be the reason that SUSAN and Harris score much lower in e.g. the chest sequence, where objects of different scales are present.

6   Conclusions

This paper has presented an analysis of feature point evaluation for non-planar scenes captured by a rotating X-ray system. We have addressed the implications of the non-planarity and proposed an evaluation method to overcome them. While the proposed method cannot guarantee absolute error measurements, the creation of a reference set from the image data with a controlled back-projection error serves to make these measurements comparable. This allows for the selection of the best detection algorithm for a given task. In the context of sparse depth estimation, a good feature point detector should: (1) lead to a reliable back-projection for as many points as possible, (2) allow the establishment of reliable correspondences under projective transformation of the image, and (3) localize the detected points accurately.

According to these criteria, we have found the Laplacian-of-Gaussian and Harris-Laplace detectors to score overall high in repeatability for the 4 datasets used. Little variation occurred between the multi-scale detectors in terms of localization accuracy. The variation between results for different types of content implies an interesting future topic: to investigate the response of these, or more, detectors for different types of clinical images, as this may potentially allow content-dependent selection of the detection method for each clinical application.

References

1. Schmid, C., Mohr, R., Bauckhage, C.: Evaluation of interest point detectors. International Journal of Computer Vision 37(2), 151–172 (2000)
2. Remondino, F.: Detectors and descriptors for photogrammetric applications. In: ISPRS III (2006)

3. Mokhtarian, F., Mohanna, F.: Performance evaluation of corner detectors using consistency and accuracy measures. Computer Vision and Image Understanding 102(1), 81–94 (2006)

4. Heyden, A., Rohr, K.: Evaluation of corner extraction schemes using invariance methods. In: International Conference on Pattern Recognition, vol. 1, p. 895 (1996)

5. Moreels, P., Perona, P.: Evaluation of features detectors and descriptors based on 3d objects. International Journal of Computer Vision 73(3), 263–284 (2007)

6. Chen, Q., Medioni, G.G.: Efficient iterative solution to m-view projective reconstruction problem. In: CVPR, pp. 2055–2061 (1999)

7. Farin, D.: Automatic video segmentation employing object/camera modeling techniques. PhD thesis (2005)

8. Shi, J., Tomasi, C.: Good features to track. In: IEEE Computer Society Conference on Computer Vision and Pattern Recognition, CVPR 1994, pp. 593–600 (1994)

9. Harris, C., Stephens, M.: A combined corner and edge detection. In: Proc. of 4th Alvey Vision Conference, pp. 147–151 (1988)

10. Smith, S.M., Brady, J.M.: Susan-a new approach to low level image processing. International Journal of Computer Vision, 45–78 (1997)

11. Lindeberg, T.: Feature detection with automatic scale selection. International Journal of Computer Vision 30, 79–116 (1998)

12. Bay, H., Tuytelaars, T., Van Gool, L.: Surf: Speeded up robust features. In: Leonardis, A., Bischof, H., Pinz, A. (eds.) ECCV 2006. LNCS, vol. 3951, pp. 404–417. Springer, Heidelberg (2006)

13. Mikolajczyk, K., Schmid, C.: An affine invariant interest point detector. In: Heyden, A., Sparr, G., Nielsen, M., Johansen, P. (eds.) ECCV 2002. LNCS, vol. 2350, pp. 128–142. Springer, Heidelberg (2002)

14. Shilat, F., Werman, M., Gdalyahn, Y.: Ridge's corner detection and correspondence. In: Computer Vision and Pattern Recognition, p. 976 (1997)

15. Maintz, J.B.A., van den Elsen, P.A., Viergever, M.A.: Evaluation of ridge seeking operators for multimodality medical image matching. IEEE Transactions on Pattern Analysis and Machine Intelligence 18(4), 353–365 (1996)

16. Lowe, D.G.: Distinctive image features from scale-invariant keypoints. Int. J. Comput. Vision 60, 91–110 (2004)

17. Mikolajczyk, K., Schmid, C.: Scale & affine invariant interest point detectors. International Journal of Computer Vision 60(1), 63–86 (2004)

18. Hartley, R.I., Zisserman, A.: Multiple View Geometry in Computer Vision, 2nd edn. Cambridge University Press, Cambridge (2004)

19. Mikolajczyk, K., Schmid, C.: A performance evaluation of local descriptors. IEEE Trans. Pattern Anal. Mach. Intell. 27(10), 1615–1630 (2005)

On the Evaluation of Segmentation Methods for Wildland Fire

Steve Rudz[1,2], Khaled Chetehouna[2], Adel Hafiane[2], Olivier Sero-Guillaume[1], and Hélène Laurent[2]

[1] LEMTA (UMR 7563 CNRS/INPL/UHP), 2 avenue de la Forêt de Haye - 54504 Vandoeuvre les Nancy cedex, France
[2] ENSI de Bourges, Institut PRISME UPRES EA 4229, 88 boulevard Lahitolle, 18020 Bourges Cedex, France

Abstract. This paper focuses on the study of fire color spaces and the evaluation of image segmentation methods commonly available in the literature of wildland and urban fires. The evaluation method, based on the determination of a segmentation quality index, is applied on three series of fire images obtained at the usual scales of validation of forest fire models (laboratory scale, fire tunnel scale and field scale). Depending on the considered scale, different methods reveal themselves as being the most appropriate. In this study we present the advantages and drawbacks of different segmentation algorithms and color spaces used in fire detection and characterization.

Keywords: Wildland fire, Color spaces, Segmentation methods, Evaluation.

1 Introduction

Fire has been and continues to be a threat to humans and ecosystems. Recent large or costly fires have occurred in both the wildlands and in the wildland-urban interface. The forest fires that occurred in France in 2003, in Greece in 2007 and in Australia in 2009 have shown that, in spite of the extensive worldwide research that has been carried out during the past decades, there still remain many issues to be addressed by the scientific community, to provide better guidance to managers and decision makers. It is necessary to conduct theoretical and experimental research to improve the understanding and ability to predict the behavior of free-burning wildland fires. Usually, the experimental research is carried out in three scales which are the laboratory, the fire tunnel and the field scales. The experiments made at these scales give entrance parameters such as the rate of spread, the physical and the geometrical characteristics of flames needed for the validation of the propagation models of forest fires [1].

Several experimental methods classified in two categories have been developed. The first group concerns discrete measures and typically consists in the use of a thermocouples set [2] or in the equidistant positioning of threads perpendicular to the fire spread direction [3]. The second class concerns continuous methods

J. Blanc-Talon et al. (Eds.): ACIVS 2009, LNCS 5807, pp. 12–23, 2009.

and involves the use of heat flux sensors [4,5] and the computer vision. Using this last technique, recent examples in the literature [6,7,8] have shown promising possibilities for determining the position, the rate of spread and some geometric properties of forest fires such as flame height, flame inclination angle and fire base contour. Indeed, Martinez-de Dios et al. [6] have presented a computer vision technique for forest fire perception to measure the fire front position, the flame height and inclination angle and the fire base width. Their system processes images from visual and infrared cameras in order to compute a 3D perception model of the fire and is applied in fire experiments at field scale. Chetehouna et al. [7] have used an image processing method based on Direct Linear Transformations of visual images, for computing the positions and the rate of spread for a linear flame front propagating on a flat surface in laboratory fire experiments. Rossi and Akhloufi [8] have presented a new framework for 3D modeling of flames in order to compute dynamic fire characteristics like its position, orientation, dimension and heading direction.

The determination of geometrical characteristics of fire front depends on the image segmentation accuracy. Many segmentation methods based on different approaches have been developed for wildland and urban fire images [6,7,8,9,10,11]. Most of these methods use the discriminative properties in the color spaces to obtain the fire regions in the image. Generally, models are obtained in specific color space to represent fire zones in the image; the thresholding is a common technique used to segment the fire regions based on such models. Indeed, a 3D Gaussian model in the RGB color space has been used in [8] to verify preliminary k-means segmentation in the YUV color space. Chen et al. [9] have combined RGB and saturation to build three decision rules to detect fire regions in images. Ko et al. [10] have proposed a RGB probability model built from dynamic fire scenes. Celick and Demirel [11] have presented a generic color model in YCbCr color space for flame pixel classification. These different works on fire image segmentation have shown good performances, but it is unclear which method is more appropriate and how its performance depends on the different experiment scales. In fact, up to now, there is no benchmark for testing and comparing the proposed methods. In the image processing domain, many works have been performed during the last decades to solve the crucial problem of the evaluation of image segmentation results [12,13,14,15,16]. Hafiane et al. [14] have notably proposed a supervised evaluation criterion to quantify the quality of segmentation algorithms. Based on an human expert evaluation, this criterion have shown best performances comparing to classical evaluation criteria.

In this paper, we propose a study of fire in color spaces and an evaluation of well-known segmentation methods for fire images. Our evaluation uses the criterion proposed in [14] for fire images obtained from three types of experiments (laboratory, fire tunnel and prescribed burning). The aim is to benchmark the fire image segmentation allowing better fire detection and determination of flame characteristics. The paper is organized as follows: the next section presents the fire regions in different color spaces; section 3 describes the segmentation techniques used for fire scenes; the evaluation method for segmentation quality measure is detailed in section 4; finally, experiments and evaluation results are presented in section 5.

2   Fire in Color Spaces

As mentioned in previous section, the fire segmentation methods use different color spaces, but it is difficult to know which one is better. The purpose of this section is to present fire properties in color spaces such as RGB, YUV, HSI and YCbCr used in fire field images. Figure 1(a) illustrates an example of prescribed burning images and figure 1(b) shows fire regions manually cropped by human expert. The isolated fire images are decomposed into three components according to the used color space where histogram is computed for each component. For more robustness, we average the histograms over 10 fire images. In this part all considered images correspond to the field scale.

(a)   (b)

Fig. 1. (a) Example of field fire image (prescribed burning), (b) human expert segmentation of fire zone

The histograms in RGB color space are given on figure 2 (a)(b)(c). The Red channel has about 50% fire pixels at the highest value 255. On the Green channel, there are a Gaussian distribution ($\mu = 154.8, \sigma = 48.4$) and a peak, eight times higher than the highest point of the Gaussian, with a maximum value 255. On the Blue channel, there is a typical Gaussian distribution ($\mu = 122, \sigma = 38.8$) with a maximum value 135. Here, the condition that the fire pixels correspond to $I_R \geq I_G > I_B$ used in [9] is verified.

The second color space studied for fire is the HSI (Hue-Saturation-Intensity). This model is based on human color perception. The channel H takes values from 0° to 360°, the channel S between 0 and 100% and the channel I from 0 to 255. Because of the range of colors from red to yellow for fire, we expect that flame pixels are distributed from 0° to 70° on the channel H. The part of the Hue distribution from 300° to 360°, which represents colors from pink to red, is also interesting. We can indeed consider that this range of angles corresponds to fire occluded by a thin smoke. The Saturation channel S is a typical Gaussian distribution ($\mu = 33.4, \sigma = 13.3$) as shown in figure 2(e). On the Intensity channel I, figure 2(f), there is also a Gaussian model ($\mu = 175.6, \sigma = 36$).

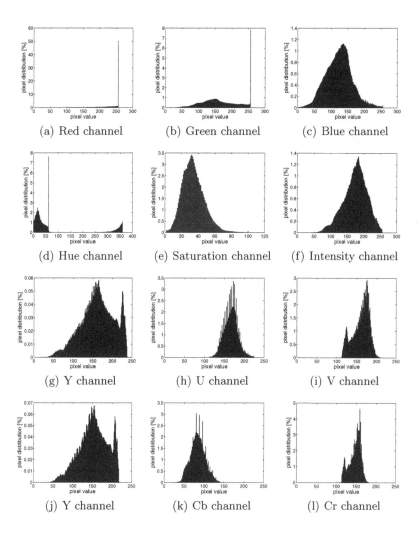

Fig. 2. Histograms of fire region at field scale in different color spaces: (a)(b)(c) for RGB space, (d)(e)(f) for HSI space, (g)(h)(i) for YUV space and (j)(k)(l) YCbCr space

The YUV and the YCbCr color spaces histograms are shown in figures 2 (g)-(l). We can notice that they have a similar tendency because they both rely on an analog system with different scale factors. Channel Y is the luminance component and Cb and Cr are the blue-difference and red-difference chroma components. The idea of this last color space is to separate luminance from chrominance because human eye is more sensitive to brightness information (luminance) than to color information (chrominance). On the two chrominance channels, Cb and Cr, the fire pixels distribution is Gaussian with respectively $(\mu = 98.6, \sigma = 18.3)$ and $(\mu = 161.1, \sigma = 14.5)$. The luminance channel Y for both YCbCr and YUV is characterized by the addition of two Gaussian distributions. Finally, the U and V are Gaussian like distributions with respectively ($\mu = 196.2, \sigma = 16.8$) and ($\mu = 190.8, \sigma = 20.2$).

Each color space presents interesting characteristics in fire color images, but it is difficult to know which space is more appropriate for segmentation. The next section describes fire segmentation methods that use the described color spaces. In the experiment part, we show the advantage of each one.

3   Segmentation Methods

Recent works [8]-[11] have shown promising possibilities for fire pixels detection using different ways of segmentation. Before to proceed to their supervised evaluation, we detail in this section these four approaches and present their models of fire thresholding segmentation.

3.1   Method 1

This algorithm based on a combination of YUV and RGB color spaces has been elaborated by Rossi and Akhloufi [8]. The authors claim that the V channel is interesting for finding fire region and use a k-means clustering on this channel to find two areas in the image: fire and non-fire. The authors assume that the biggest region in the clustered V channel is the fire. They thereafter use a 3D Gaussian model in RGB color space to compute a reference model for color classification of fire pixels. The 3D Gaussian model is defined by the following mean and standard deviation:

$$\begin{cases} \mu = (\mu_R, \mu_G, \mu_B) \\ \sigma = \max(\sigma_R, \sigma_G, \sigma_B) \end{cases} \tag{1}$$

where μ_i is the mean value for channel i and σ_i its standard deviation, $i \in \{R, G, B\}$. Each pixel is represented by its color component $I = (I_R, I_G, I_B)$ and is declared as fire-pixel or not fire-pixel by mean of the equation:

$$\begin{cases} \parallel I(x,y) - \mu \parallel \leq c \times \sigma : I(x,y) \text{ is fire-pixel} \\ Otherwise \qquad\qquad\quad : I(x,y) \text{ is not fire-pixel} \end{cases} \tag{2}$$

here $\parallel \cdot \parallel$ is the Euclidean norm and c is a constant.

3.2   Method 2

The second method is the one developed by Chen et al. [9]. This algorithm is based on three decision rules:

$$\begin{cases} \text{condition 1}: I_R(x,y) > R_T \\ \text{condition 2}: I_R(x,y) \geq I_G(x,y) > I_B(x,y) \\ \text{condition 3}: I_S(x,y) \geq (255 - I_R(x,y))\frac{S_T}{R_T} \end{cases} \tag{3}$$

where $I_R(x,y)$, $I_G(x,y)$ and $I_B(x,y)$ represent pixel values in R, G and B channels. S is the saturation channel and R_T, S_T are respectively two thresholds for R and S channels. The pixel is affected to the fire region or not using the following conditions:

$$\begin{cases} \textit{if } (\text{rule 1}) \text{ and } (\text{rule 2}) \text{ and } (\text{rule 3}) = \textit{true} \\ \textit{then} : I(x,y) \text{ is fire-pixel} \\ \textit{else} : I(x,y) \text{ is not fire-pixel} \end{cases} \tag{4}$$

This method for fire-pixel detection combines RGB space with the saturation channel of HSI color space. According to their various experimental results, the authors propose values range from 55 to 65 and 115 to 135 respectively for S_T and R_T.

3.3   Method 3

This method corresponds to the algorithm of Ko et al. [10] which is based on a RGB probability model. This model assumes the independence of RGB channels distributions for each pixel, so the Gaussian probability distribution is estimated as follows:

$$p_i(x,y) = \frac{1}{\sqrt{2\pi}\sigma_i} \exp\left(\frac{(I_i(x,y) - \mu_i)^2}{2\sigma_i^2}\right), \; i \in \{R, G, B\} \tag{5}$$

In this equation $I_i(x,y)$ is the color value for the ith color channel in a fire image, μ_i is the mean value of I_i and σ_i is the standard deviation of I_i. To declare a pixel as fire candidate, a threshold τ is used and the following condition is proposed:

$$\begin{cases} p\left(I(x,y)\right) = p_R\left(I_R(x,y)\right) \times p_G\left(I_G(x,y)\right) \times p_B\left(I_B(x,y)\right) \\ \textit{if } p\left(I(x,y)\right) > \tau \\ \textit{then} : I(x,y) \text{ is fire-pixel} \\ \textit{else} : I(x,y) \text{ is not fire-pixel} \end{cases} \tag{6}$$

The authors do not give any experimental value for the threshold τ. The main difficulty of their algorithm is to choose this parameter because the probabilities $p_i(x,y)$ highly depend on the environmental conditions.

3.4   Method 4

The fourth algorithm has been proposed by Celick and Demirel [11]. This algorithm uses the YCbCr color space and is based on five decision rules:

$$\begin{cases} I_Y(x,y) > I_{Cb}(x,y) \\ I_{Cr}(x,y) > I_{Cb}(x,y) \\ \mid I_{Cb}(x,y) - I_{Cr}(x,y) \mid \geq \tau \\ I_Y(x,y) > \mu_Y \text{ and } I_{Cb}(x,y) < \mu_{Cb} \text{ and } I_{Cr}(x,y) > \mu_{Cr} \\ I_{Cb} \geq fu\left(I_{Cr}\right) \cap I_{Cb} \leq fd\left(I_{Cr}\right) \cap I_{Cb} \leq fl\left(I_{Cr}\right) \end{cases} \tag{7}$$

where (x,y) is the location of a pixel, μ_i is the mean value for channel i, $fu(I_{Cr})$, $fd(I_{Cr})$ and $fl(I_{Cr})$ are three polynomial functions whose intersections contain fire area in the Cr-Cb plane. According to authors, the best value of threshold τ is 40. The fire region is defined if all the rules of equation (7) are verified, else the candidate fire pixel is declared in no-fire zone.

4   Segmentation Evaluation

As previously exposed, the image segmentation step remains a prolific domain if we consider the number of works published in that area. So far, no method has revealed itself as being efficient for all cases. Depending on the acquisition conditions, the following treatments and the aimed interpretation objectives, different approaches can be more or less suited to a considered application. This variety often makes it difficult to evaluate the efficiency of a proposed method and places the user in a tricky position face to this question: which method is the more accurate for my specific application ?

Two major approaches for evaluation can be found in the literature. The first one gathers the so called unsupervised evaluation criteria [13,16]. These criteria call for no specific knowledge about the content or associated significance of the image and require no expert assessment. They are based on the computation of statistics from some chosen characteristics attached to each pixel or group of pixels and have therefore the major advantage of being easily computable. The second approach gathers the so called supervised evaluation criteria which are computed from a dissimilarity measure between a segmentation result and a ground truth of the same image, often obtained according to an expert judgement [14,15]. Even if these criteria inherently depend on the confidence in the ground truth, they are widely used for many applications. In such case, the ability of a segmentation method to favor a subsequent interpretation and understanding of the image is taken into account. As for our application, expert assessment was available, we collected ground truths. In order to fit the expert diagnosis as close as possible, we consequently focused in this paper on supervised evaluation dedicated to region-based segmentation.

We use a quality index to evaluate segmentation results [14]. This criterion consists in measuring the overlap between the segmentation result and the reference. It takes into account geometric aspects (localization) of the segmented classes. The over- and under-segmentations are also penalized.

Let C_i be the set of pixels in the image belonging to the class i, C_i^{Ref} and C_j^{Seg} are two classes from the reference image, I^{Ref}, and the segmentation result, I^{Seg}, respectively. The *matching index* M_I is defined as a weighted overlap ratio over all classes:

$$M_I = \sum_{j=1}^{NC_{Seg}} \frac{Card(C_{i*}^{Ref} \cap C_j^{Seg})}{Card(C_{i*}^{Ref} \cup C_j^{Seg})} \rho_j \qquad (8)$$

where $i^* = \underset{i=1}{\overset{NC_{Ref}}{\operatorname{argmax}}}(Card(C_i^{Ref} \cap C_j^{Seg}))$ is the class index of the class in the ground truth with the largest overlap (pixel-by-pixel basis) compared to one class in the segmentation result, C_j^{Seg}, NC_{Ref} and NC_{Seg} are the number of classes in the reference and segmented images respectively (in our application, $NC_{Ref} = NC_{Seg} = 2$, fire or not-fire class). ρ_j is a size-based weighting factor that controls the influence of each class so that smaller classes have less influence than the larger ones,

$$\rho_j = \frac{Card(C_j^{Seg})}{Card(I^{Seg})} \tag{9}$$

However, Eq. 8 does not appropriately take into account the region spatial homogeneity (ie. fragmentation or merges) of the regions constituting each class. Each region of the reference and of the segmentation result is labeled; using the number of connected regions in the reference and segmented images, the following weight function is defined to penalize over- and under-segmentation errors:

$$\eta = \begin{cases} NR_{Ref}/NR_{Seg} & if \quad NR_{Seg} \geq NR_{Ref} \\ log(1 + NR_{Seg}/NR_{Ref}) & otherwise \end{cases} \tag{10}$$

where NR_{Ref} and NR_{Seg} are the number of connected regions in the reference and segmented images respectively. The log term allows to more penalize a presence of slight under-segmentation in comparison with a presence of slight over-segmentation. The final evaluation criterion $\mathcal{H}$ is then given by the following equation:

$$\mathcal{H} = \frac{M_I + m \times \eta}{1 + m} \tag{11}$$

where m is a weighting coefficient which controls the importance of the over- or under-segmentation errors in the judgment.

This evaluation method has been compared to criteria from the literature: the Vinet's measure [18], the Hamming's criterion [19], the three Yasnoff's criteria [20] and the two Martins's criteria [21]. The used criterion yields the closest results to human judgment. For our application, $m = 0.5$ provides an adequate tradeoff between the two parameters, M_I and η, contributing to the evaluation measure.

5 Experiments and Results

As indicated above, the different fire images are obtained at the three usual scales of validation of forest fire models. The first series of images is extracted from a video of fire carried out in the laboratory of the firefighters departmental School of Sancoins in France. For these tests, a visual camera (30 images/second, 640×480 pixels) is used to film the flame spread over straw in a combustion table with an effective burning surface of 2 m^2. The second series of experiments is realized in the fire tunnel of CEREN laboratory situated in south of France (Marseille) where *Quercus coccifera* shrubs are used as combustible. The different color images of size 2448×3264 pixels are cropped from two fire videos taken by visual cameras at different locations. The field experiments of fire were realized in Vigan (south of France) in 2007 on vegetation constituted of heterogeneous shrubs. A typical size for such prescribed burning is fifty meters long (size of the plot to be burnt). The forest fire color images of size 1600×1200 pixels are obtained from a video taken by a fixed camera. The segmentation methods

Table 1. Mean quality evaluation of the four tested segmentation methods at different scales

	Method 1	Method 2	Method 3	Method 4
Laboratory scale	69.0	9.0	**82.6**	43.8
Fire tunnel scale	30.4	**65.3**	51.7	60.6
Field scale	32.0	**79.3**	36.9	42.9

parameters are set as follows: method 1 ($c = 2$), method 2 ($R_T = 125$, S_T=60), method 3 (τ=0.003) and method 4 (for laboratory scale τ=0.05, for tunnel and field scales τ=40).

For the laboratory scale, method 3 is better than the others as shown in table 1. The threshold value for this method was fixed according to our experiments because authors [10] do not recommend any value for τ. The method 1 also gives good results because, in this case, the k-means segmentation into two parts is clearly appropriate. However, the fire has been over-segmented, which points out the fact that the checking, operated after the k-means segmentation, is not enough efficient for this scale. The method 2 does not give good results because the camera sensor is saturated in most part of the fire. It means that $I_R = I_G = I_B$. According to the present criterion $I_R \geq I_G > I_B$, this method can not work in such a configuration. The method 4 is also penalized by the saturation problem of the camera sensor because when $I_R = I_G = I_B, I_{Cb} = I_{Cr}$, Celik's rule ($|I_{Cr} - I_{Cb}| \geq \tau$) needs to have a very low threshold τ, which is eighty times lower than the one given in [11]. Figure 3 shows samples of original image, ground truth and segmentation results for the laboratory scale.

Figure 4 shows for one original image in fire tunnel scale, the corresponding ground truth and the obtained segmentation results. Results presented in table 1 show that method 2 yields the best performances. This method works properly

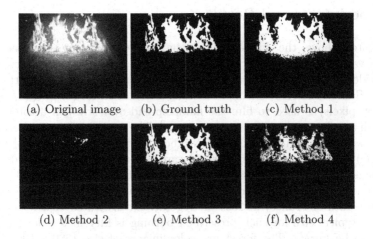

(a) Original image   (b) Ground truth   (c) Method 1

(d) Method 2   (e) Method 3   (f) Method 4

Fig. 3. Examples of segmentation results for laboratory scale

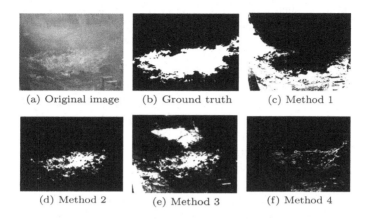

(a) Original image   (b) Ground truth   (c) Method 1

(d) Method 2   (e) Method 3   (f) Method 4

Fig. 4. Examples of segmentation results for fire tunnel scale

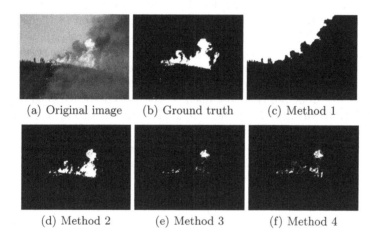

(a) Original image   (b) Ground truth   (c) Method 1

(d) Method 2   (e) Method 3   (f) Method 4

Fig. 5. Examples of segmentation results for field scale

because there is no problem of camera saturation. The criterion $I_R \geq I_G > I_B$, which allows to detect fire, can then be applied efficiently. The method 4 is ranked in the second place in this evaluation and can also work properly because the camera saturation effect is not important. The method 1 is the last ranked one because, in the tunnel scale, the k-means over the channel V is not able to separate the fire region in the image because no-fire region has similar values in V channel. In that case, the RGB learning strategy applied thereafter on the selected clustered region is not significant of what fire is in RGB color space.

Figure 5 shows for one original image in field scale the corresponding ground truth and the obtained segmentation results. As shown in table 1, method 2 is closer to the ground truth segmentation than the others. The score of the segmentation quality index is about 79.3 %, outperforming method 4, method

3 and method 1. In such kind of fire images, the separation of fire regions can be easily performed in RGB color space. Therefore, like for the tunnel scale, the three rules of method 2 are verified by most fire pixels.

6   Conclusion

Over the last decades, several segmentation methods have been developed to detect the flame region in a fire scene. In this paper, we have attempted to evaluate four segmentation methods available from the wildland and urban fires literature using supervised evaluation. The principal steps of this study can be summarized in three parts. The first one concerns the study of the fire pixels distribution in different color spaces for images obtained at the field scale. This study made it possible to show the validity of the second criterion of method 2 [9] which presents better performances in fire tunnel and field scales. The second part concerns the segmentation evaluation criterion which was claimed in a previous study [14] to yield the closest results to human judgment. In the last part, we evaluate the performances of different segmentation methods at three experiment scales. The results show that method 3 of Ko et al. [10] is the most appropriate at laboratory scale with a quality index of 82.6 %. The segmentation method of Chen et al. [9] gives the best performances at tunnel and field scales with a quality index equal to respectively 65.3 % and 79.3 %. We will first of all compare the fire front positions obtained by the method of Ko et al. [10] with those obtained by the heat fluxes method [22] for fire experiments carried out on combustion table. Secondly, even if method 2 is the best for fire tunnel and field scales, the quality index shows that all methods need improvement. The existing methods remain quiet simple and further development needs to be proposed. We plan to investigate this research area and at least to confront the region approach with the contour one. All these improvements allowing prediction of the fire front positions can help firefighters to optimize the distribution of their fighting means.

References

1. Séro-Guillaume, O., Ramezani, S., Margerit, J., Calogine, D.: On large scale forest fires propagation models. International Journal of Thermal Sciences 47(6), 680–694 (2008)
2. Zhou, X., Weise, D., Mahalingamx, S.: Experimental measurements and numerical modeling of marginal burning in live chaparral fuel beds. Proceedings of the Combustion Institute 30, 2287–2294 (2005)
3. Santoni, P.A., Simeoni, A., Rossi, J.L., Bosseur, F., Morandini, F., Silvani, X., Balbi, J.H., Cancellieri, D., Rossi, L.: Instrumentation of wildland fire: Characterisation of a fire spreading through a Mediterranean shrub. Fire Safety Journal 41(3), 171–184 (2006)
4. Chetehouna, K., Séro-Guillaume, O., Sochet, I., Degiovanni, A.: On the experimental determination of flame front positions and of propagation parameters for a fire. International Journal of Thermal Sciences 47(9), 1148–1157 (2008)

5. Silvani, X., Morandini, F.: Fire spread experiments in the field: Temperature and heat fluxes measurements. Fire Safety Journal 44(2), 279–285 (2009)
6. Martinez-de Dios, J.R., Arrue, B.C., Ollero, A., Merino, L., Gómez-Rodríguez, F.: Computer vision techniques for forest fire perception. Image and Vision Computing 26(4), 550–562 (2008)
7. Chetehouna, K., Zarguili, I., Séro-Guillaume, O., Giroud, F., Picard, C.: On the two ways for the computing of the fire front positions and the rate of spread. Modelling, Monitoring and Management of Forest Fires. WIT Transactions on Ecology and the Environment 119, 3–12 (2008)
8. Rossi, L., Akhloufi, M.: Dynamic fire 3D modeling using a real-time stereovision system. In: International Joint Conferences on Computer, Information, and Systems Sciences, and Engineering (CIS2E 2008), December 5-13 (2008)
9. Chen, T., Wu, P., Chiou, Y.: An early fire-detection method based on image processing. In: Proceeding of International Conference on Image Processing, ICIP 2004, pp. 1707–1710 (2004)
10. Ko, B.C., Cheong, K.H., Nam, J.Y.: Fire detection based on vision sensor and support vector machines. Fire Safety Journal 44(3), 322–329 (2009)
11. Celik, T., Demirel, H.: Fire detection in video sequences using a generic color model. Fire Safety Journal 44(2), 147–158 (2009)
12. Zhang, Y.J.: A survey on evaluation methods for image segmentation. Pattern Recognition 29(8), 1335–1346 (1996)
13. Chabrier, S., Emile, B., Rosenberger, C., Laurent, H.: Unsupervised performance evaluation of image segmentation. EURASIP Journal on Applied Signal Processing, Special issue on performance evaluation in image processing, 1–12 (2006)
14. Hafiane, A., Chabrier, S., Rosenberger, C., Laurent, H.: A new supervised evaluation criterion for region based segmentation methods. In: Blanc-Talon, J., Philips, W., Popescu, D., Scheunders, P. (eds.) ACIVS 2007. LNCS, vol. 4678, pp. 439–448. Springer, Heidelberg (2007)
15. Unnikrishnan, R., Pantofaru, C., Hebert, M.: Toward objective evaluation of image segmentation algorithms. IEEE Transactions on Pattern Analysis and Machine Intelligence 29(6), 929–944 (2007)
16. Zhang, H., Fritts, J.E., Goldman, S.A.: Image segmentation evaluation: A survey of unsupervised methods. Computer Vision and Image Understanding 110(2), 260–280 (2008)
17. Chabrier, S., Laurent, H., Emile, B.: Psychovisual evaluation of image segmentation results. In: IEEE Conference on Signal Processing, ICSP (2006)
18. Vinet, L.: Segmentation et mise en correspondance de regions de paires dimages stereoscopiques, Ph.D. dissertation, Universite de Paris IX Dauphine, Juillet (1991)
19. Huang, Q., Dom, B.: Quantitative methods of evaluating image segmentation. In: International Conference on Image Processing (ICIP 1995), Washington, DC, USA, vol. 3, pp. 53–56 (1995)
20. Yasnoff, W.A., Mui, J.K., Bacus, J.W.: Error measures for scene segmentation. Pattern Recognition 9, 217–231 (1977)
21. Martin, D., Fowlkes, C., Tal, D., Malik, J.: A database of human segmented natural images and its application to evaluating segmentation algorithms and measuring ecological statistics. In: International Conference on Computer Vision (ICCV), July 2001, pp. 416–423 (2001)
22. Rudz, S., Chetehouna, K., Séro-Guillaume, O.: Determination of the Flame Fire Front Characteristics by Means of a Flame Model and Inverse Method. In: Proceedings of 6th Mediterranean Combustion Symposium, Corsica, pp. 7–11 (2009)

2D Face Recognition in the IV^2 Evaluation Campaign

Anouar Mellakh[1], Anis Chaari[2], Souhila Guerfi[2], Johan Dhose[3],
Joseph Colineau[3], Sylvie Lelandais[3], Dijana Petrovska-Delacrètaz[1],
and Bernadette Dorizzi[1]

[1] Institut TELECOM,TELECOM & Management SudParis
9 Rue Charles Fourier,Evry, France
[2] Laboratoire IBISC-CNRS FRE 3190
Université dEvry, 91020 Evry Cedex, France
[3] THALES, RD
128, 91767 Palaiseau Cedex, France
{mohamed.anouar_mellakh,Dijana.Petrovska,
Bernadette.Dorizzi}@it-sudparis.eu,
{anis.chaari,souhila.guerfi,sylvie.lelandais}@ibisc.fr,
{Johan.dhose,joseph.colineau}@thalesgroup.com

Abstract. In this paper, the first evaluation campaign on 2D-face images using the multimodal IV^2 database is presented. The five appearance-based algorithms in competition are evaluated on four experimental protocols, including experiments with challenging illumination and pose variabilities. The results confirm the advantages of the Linear Discriminant Analysis (LDA) and the importance of the training set for the Principal Component Analysis (PCA) based approaches. The experiments show the robustness of the Gabor based approach combined with LDA, in order to cope with challenging face recognition conditions. This evaluation shows the interest and the richness of the IV^2 multimodal database.

Keywords: Database, 2D face recognition, evaluation campaign, appearance-based algorithms.

1 Introduction

In the last two decades, a lot of work has been done in the field of face recognition [1]. Despite the huge progresses done in algorithmic performance and a better understanding of how face recognition works, face recognition approaches are still very sensitive to adverse conditions. Recent evaluation campaigns, like FRVT2002 [2], FRGCv2 [3], and FRVT2006 [4] confirm this tendency, and show that despite the good performance of 2D face algorithms in controlled environments, the majority of the proposed algorithms are not robust to more challenging conditions, including degraded acquisition conditions and pose variations. The IV^2 face database has been designed to allow evaluations of biometric algorithms in adverse conditions, including variabilities related to image quality,

J. Blanc-Talon et al. (Eds.): ACIVS 2009, LNCS 5807, pp. 24–32, 2009.

pose, expressions and illumination. The paper is organized as follows. In Sect. 2 the multimodal IV² database and the 2D-face evaluation protocols used in this evaluation campaign are presented. The submitted algorithms and their results are reported in Sect. 3. Sect. 4 ends up with conclusions and perspectives from the 2D-face IV² evaluation campaign.

2 The IV² Database and the 2D Face Evaluation Protocols

Besides the 2D-face images in the IV² database, audio-video sequences, 2D face stereoscopic data, 3D-face laser scans and near infra-red iris images are also present, allowing to further exploit multimodality[5]. The IV^2 database contains 315 subjects with one session data where 77 of them also participated to a second session. From this database, a subset of 52 subjects has been distributed as a development set while an evaluation package, different from the development, has also been defined including evaluation protocols.

Acquisition Protocol

Following a *one variability at a time strategy*, the following variabilities are present: image resolution, pose, expression and illumination. During each acquisition session, a high and a low resolution video sequence are captured simultaneously. The subject starts by reading some sentences, then looks at the left, right, up and down. At the end of this acquisition step, two audio-video sequences are available. In Fig.1(a-b) examples of still images acquired with the high quality digital camera and the low quality webcam are shown. At this step the acquisition continues using only the high resolution DV camera, with an automatic light intensity variation. The face images used for the illumination evaluation protocol are extracted from these high resolution sequences.

(a)   (b)

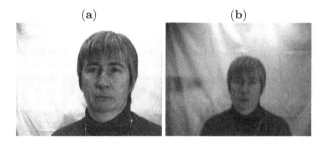

Fig. 1. Examples of still images extracted from the talking face sequences: (a) with the high quality digital camera and (b) with the low quality web camera

2D Evaluation Protocols

For this first evaluation campaign, only one still image per subject was used for enrollment and one still image for the test phase. All the enrollment images

Table 1. Description of test images according to the evaluation protocol (N stands for Number)

Experiment	Experiment 1	Experiment 2	Experiment 3	Experiment 4
Sessions	Mono-session	Mono-session	Mono-session	Multisession
Quality	high	high	low	high
Expression Variation	small	No	No	No
Illumination Variation	No	Yes	No	No
N. Intra tests	2595	2502	1654	1796
N. Inter tests	2454	2362	1598	1796

are frontal, with high resolution, taken under maximum illumination and with neutral expressions. Table 1 gives a description of the test images according to the corresponding protocol.

The 2D-face evaluation campaign for IV^2 was conducted in September 2007, on the same way as the NIST speaker evaluation: each team conducted a list of tests with no indication on their type (intraclass or interclass). The protocols were constructed in order to have the same number of client and impostors tests. This strategy allows having equivalent FAR(False Acceptance Rate) and FRR(False Rejection Rate) distributions.

3   Submitted Algorithms

All submitted algorithms use the appearance-based approaches. IBISC-1&2 and BioSecure are based on Eigenfaces [6]. IBISC-3 and IT-SudParis are based on Fisherfaces [7]. The general idea of Eigenfaces and Fisherfaces is to represent a face in a reduced dimensional space Φ by $x = \sum_{i=1}^{n} \alpha_i V_i$ where x is the face vector in the input space and V_i the vectors in the new space Φ. The reduced space Φ is computed in different manners for the two approaches, as described in 3.1 and 3.2.

3.1   Principal Component Analysis (PCA) Based Systems

IBISC-1&2 and BioSecure are based on the Eigenfaces approach, proposed by Turk and Pentland [6]. The purpose of this approach is to find the projection axes that maximize the variance of the input space. Considering the covariance matrix $C = \sum_{i=1}^{N} (x_i - \overline{x})(x_i - \overline{x})^T$, for the input samples $X = [x_1, x_2...x_N]$, and solving the eigen problem $C\Phi = \Phi\Lambda$ leads to the computation of an orthogonal basis Φ that describes the face space in the different variance directions Λ.

A reduced projection space is obtained by keeping the axes with the maximum of variances (highest eigenvalues), and the projected vector on the reduced space is considered as the new representation.

Biosecure Reference System[BioSecure]. It was developed by *Boğaziçi University* and it uses the standard Eigenface approach[6]. The face space is built using the images from the world set of the BANCA database [8] (30 subjects, 10 images per subject with 3 different quality images, namely controlled, degraded and adverse). The dimensionality of the reduced space is selected such as 99% of the variance of the training data is kept. The *Cosine* norm is used to measure the distance between the projected vectors of the test and enrollment images.

PCA [IBISC[1]-1]. The face space is built using 152 face images from 50 subjects of the IV²(all images are taken from the controlled illumination sequences with high resolution camera). They are taken from the disjoint development part of IV² not used for evaluation. All the projection axes are kept. The $L1$ norm is used to measure the distance between two projected vectors.

Modular PCA [IBISC-2]. In order to address the problem of face recognition including facial expressions, illumination and pose variability, Pentland and al. [9] have proposed to implement a modular PCA on different facial regions. The main idea of this approach is that facial regions are affected differently through variable conditions. For example, facial expressions affect mouth more than other facial regions. The facial regions, from which classifiers are built, are illustrated in Fig. 2. For each face region (eyes, nose and mouth) a reduced space is built and the $L1$ distance between the projections of each region is computed. A weighted sum of the different region distances is used to compute the global face distance.

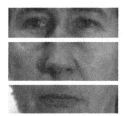

Fig. 2. Examples of different facial regions used to build the modular PCA classifiers

3.2 Linear Discriminant Analysis

The purpose of Linear Discriminant Analysis (LDA) is to look for axes, in the data space, that best discriminate the different classes. In other words, for some given independent parameters, the LDA creates a linear combination of those parameters that maximizes the distances between the means of the different classes and minimizes at the same time the distances between samples of the same class.

---

[1] Laboratoire d'Informatique, Biologie Intégrative et Systèmes Complexes, Université d'Evry, France.

LDA based on intensity image[IBISC-3]. The face projection space was built using 156 face images from 52 subjects of the IV2 developpment part. All computed axes are used to reduce the dimensionality of the input space. For all the classes in the sample space,, two kinds of measures are defined, the within-class scatter matrix:

$$S_w = \sum_{j=1}^{c} \sum_{i=1}^{N_j} (x_i^j - \mu_j)(x_i^j - \mu_j)^T \tag{1}$$

with x_i^j the ith sample of class j, μ_j the mean of class j, c the number of classes and N_j the number of all training samples of class j. The second measure is the between-class scatter matrix:

$$S_b = \sum_{j=1}^{c} (\mu_j - \mu)(\mu_j - \mu)^T \tag{2}$$

with μ_j the mean of class j and μ the mean of all samples. The purpose of LDA is to select the linear subspace Φ, which maximizes the ratio of the quotient [7]:

$$\Gamma(T) = \frac{|T^T S_b T|}{|T^T S_w T|} \tag{3}$$

The optimal projection matrix Φ which maximizes $\Gamma(T)$ can be obtained by solving a generalized eigenvalue problem $S_b \Phi = S_w \Phi \Lambda$ that is equivalent to solve $S_w^{-1} S_b \Phi = \Lambda \Phi$. The maximization of $\Gamma(T)$ is possible if the S_w matrix is non singular. However, in the face recognition experiments, data are always under represented. Usually, the size of the face image vector is much greater than the number of samples in the learning database which leads to a *Small Sample Size* problem. Thus, the within scatter matrix S_w is singular and we cannot compute directly Φ. The solution proposed in [7] and [10] is to carry a PCA data reduction upstream the LDA, so that the new within scatter matrix is not singular.

LDA Gabor approach [IT-SudParis[2]]. The representation of the face image is obtained by the convolution of this face image with the family of Gabor filters, defined by $IG_{s,o} = I \otimes G_{s,o}$, where $IG_{s,o}$ denotes the convolution result corresponding to the Gabor filter at a certain orientation o and scale s, and $G_{s,o}$ is given by

$$G(x,y) = \frac{1}{2\pi\sigma\beta} e^{-\pi \left[\frac{(x-x_0)^2}{\sigma^2} + \frac{(y-y_0)^2}{\beta^2} \right]} e^{i[\xi_0 x + \nu 0 y]}$$

with (xo, yo) the center of the filter in the spatial domain, ξ_0 and $\nu 0$ the spatial frequency of the filter, σ and β the standard deviation of the elliptic Gaussian

---

[2] Institut TELECOM,TELECOM & Management SudParis, Evry, France.

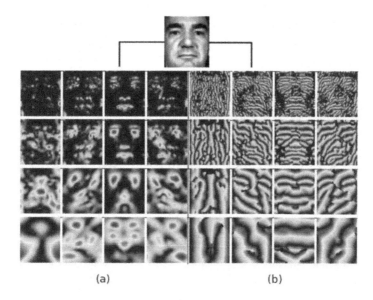

(a)   (b)

Fig. 3. Results of a convolution of a face image with a family of 16 Gabor filters (4 orientations (horizontal) et 4 scales (vertical)). Set (a) represent the magnitude and (b) the phases of the convolutions.

along x and y. $IG_{s,o}$ is a complex number. Its magnitude is denoted $M(IG_{s,o})$ and its phase $P(IG_{s,o})$ [Fig 3].

Most of the works using the Gabor features for face recognition are based on the magnitude part of the Gabor features[11,12].

In this section, the experiments are conducted using a fusion of the magnitude and the phase features [13], motivated by the fact that the useful information is located on the phase part. When normalized face images are considered, some parts do not contain any texture that could be analyzed by the lower scales of the Gabor filters. For these regions, the Gabor analysis gives $Real(IG_{s,o}) \sim 0$ and $Im(IG_{s,o}) \sim 0$. Even if its values are very near to 0, the magnitude part of the convolution is not affected by this problem but the phase part becomes undetermined for these specific regions.

To bypass the undetermined forms, we propose to select the informative regions, by thresholding the magnitude at each analysis point:

$$P(IG_{s,o}(x,y)) = \begin{cases} 0, \text{ if } M(IG_{s,o})(x,y) < Th \\ P(IG_{s,o}(x,y)) = \arctan(\frac{Im(IG_{s,o}(x,y))}{Real(IG_{s,o}(x,y))}), \text{ else.} \end{cases}$$

where (x,y) are the coordinates of the analysis point. The Gabor filtering is applied on normalized faces with histogram equalization (16 Gabor filters are used with 4 scales and 4 orientations). The magnitude ($M(IG_{s,o})$) and the corrected phase) at each scale/orientation are then down-sampled, normalized to zero mean and unit variance, and transformed to a vector by concatenating the

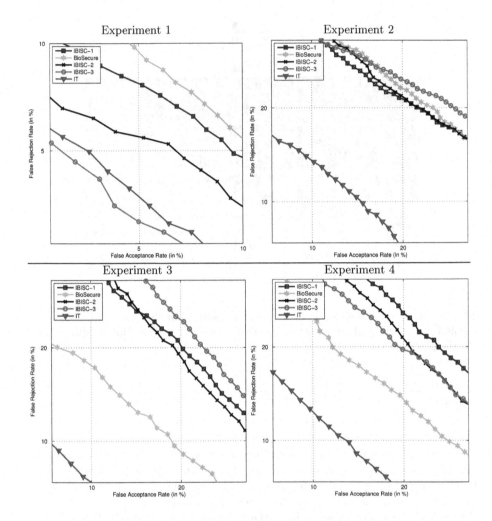

Fig. 4. Det curves of the experiments presented in Table 1

columns. This new feature vector is used as an input for the LDA algorithm [7] in order to get a more discriminative representation.

3.3   Results

The results of the submitted systems, for the four experiments, are reported as Detection Error Trade of (DET) curves in Figures 4, and in terms of Equal Error Rates in Table 2 (with confidence level of 95% the EER lies in the confidence interval of (±X) see [14] for more details).

For Experiment 1 , all submitted algorithms give relatively good results: only data from one session is used and the enrollment and test images are chosen

Table 2. Equal Error Rates of the submitted systems, with associated confidence intervals

Participants	Experiment 1	Experiment 2	Experiment 3	Experiment 4
IBISC-1(PCA)	6,7 (±0.8)	20,7 (±1.3)	22.2 (±1.6)	20,1 (±1.6)
BioSecure(PCA)	7,3 (±0.8)	21,6 (±1.4)	16,3 (±1.4)	13,6 (±1.4)
IBISC-2(Mod PCA)	5,3 (±0.7)	20,7 (±1.4)	20,5 (±1.5)	19,5 (±1.6)
IBISC-3(LDA)	**3,7** (±0.6)	22,5 (±1.4)	19,7 (±1.5)	21,7 (±1.7)
IT(LDA Gabor)	4,2 (±0.6)	**12,0** (±1.1)	**11,3** (±1.2)	**8,3** (±1.1)

with a maximum illumination, and small expression variations. The DET curve of Exp1 shows that the performance of the systems span from 3 to 7% of EER. In this evaluation, the LDA based approaches perform better than the PCA based ones. These results confirm the state of the art showing a better performance for LDA than PCA. Note also that the small expression variations (specially mouth movement) don't affect these appearance-based approaches.

For the other experiments, the Gabor based approach outperforms the other algorithms (12% vs ~20%) of EER for Exp2, (11.3% vs ~(16%-22%)) for Exp3 and (8,3% vs 13%-22%) for Exp4. In the case of illumination variations (Exp2) the performance of all the algorithms based on image intensity as direct input, decrease dramatically. The approach based on the combined Gabor features is more robust. This difference in performance is due to the fact that Gabor filtering allows a local frequency analysis of the texture at different scales and orientations.

For Exp3 and Exp4, we denote differences in performance between the two algorithms based on PCA (IBISC-1 and BioSecure). The PCA reduction space for BioSecure Reference system was built using different sets of images (controlled, degraded and adverse), so these variations are better handled, in the test set, by this algorithm which leads to better performance. The performance of the modular PCA in degraded scenarios is equivalent to the global PCA. This can be explained by the fact that the regions used to learn the different spaces of the local classifiers correspond only to one type of faces taken under a maximum illumination with a high resolution camera.

4   Conclusions and Perspectives

In this paper five appearance based methods are evaluated on the IV^2 database. The results confirm the state of art: the LDA performs well in controlled scenarios, the choice of the training set for PCA analysis is very important for the quality of algorithms generalization and performance quickly decrease with the wide range of variabilities to be handled. The LDA applied to a Gabor transformation of face, is more robust than the classical gray scale approach. In the presented 2D face evaluations (using only still images), only a small subset of the recorded multimodal data in the IV^2 database is exploited. Future work concentrates on preparing more data for new experiments, including video sequences, and multimodal data. These 2D face evaluations have shown the contribution of this database for new evaluations in adverse real life conditions.

Acknowledgments. This work has been realized during the Techno Vision program and has been supported by the French Research Department and the Ministry of Defense.

References

1. Jain, A.K., Li, S.Z.: Handbook of Face Recognition. Springer, Secaucus (2005)
2. Phillips, J., Grother, P., Micheals, R.J., Blackburn, D.M., Tabassi, E., Bone, J.M.: Frvt 2002: Evaluation report. Technical report, NIST (March 2003)
3. Phillips, J., Flynn, P.J.: Overview of the face recognition grand challenge. In: CVPR (June 2005)
4. Jonathon Phillips, P., et al.: Frvt 2006 and ice 2006 large-scale results. Technical report, NIST (March 2007)
5. Website of iv^2 project (2006-2007), http://iv2.ibisc.fr/
6. Turk, M., Pentland, A.: Eigenfaces for recognition. Journal of Cognitive Neuroscience 3(1), 71–86 (1991)
7. Belhumeur, P.N., Hespanha, J.P., Kriegman, D.J.: Eigenfaces vs fisherfaces: Recognition using class specific linear projection. In: Proc. of the 4th ECCV, pp. 45–58 (April 1996)
8. Bailly-Bailliére, E., et al.: The banca database and evaluation protocol. In: Kittler, J., Nixon, M.S. (eds.) AVBPA 2003. LNCS, vol. 2688, pp. 625–638. Springer, Heidelberg (2003)
9. Pentland, A.P., Moghaddam, B., Starner, T.E.: View-based and modular eigenspaces for face recognition. In: CVPR, pp. 84–91 (1994)
10. Swets, D.L., Weng, J(J.): Using discriminant eigenfeatures for image retrieval. IEEE Transactions on PAMI 18(8), 831–836 (1996)
11. Liu, C.J.: Capitalize on dimensionality increasing techniques for improving face recognition grand challenge performance. IEEE Transactions PAMI 28(5), 725–737 (2006)
12. Zhou, M., Wei, H.: Face verification using gabor wavelets and adaboost. In: ICPR, pp. I:404–I:407 (2006)
13. Dijana Petrovska Delacretaz, D., Chollet, G., Dorizzi, B.: Guide to Biometric Reference Systems and Performance Evaluation. Springer, Heidelberg (2009)
14. Wayman, J.L.: Confidence interval and test size estimation for biometric data. In: Proc. IEEE AutoID 1999, pp. 177–184 (October 1999)

Background Subtraction Techniques: Systematic Evaluation and Comparative Analysis*

Sonsoles Herrero and Jesús Bescós

Video Processing and Understanding Lab (VPULab)
Universidad Autónoma de Madrid
E-28049 Madrid, Spain
{Sonsoles.Herrero,J.Bescos}@uam.es

Abstract. Moving object detection is a critical task for many computer vision applications: the objective is the classification of the pixels in the video sequence into either foreground or background. A commonly used technique to achieve it in scenes captured by a static camera is Background Subtraction (BGS). Several BGS techniques have been proposed in the literature but a rigorous comparison that analyzes the different parameter configuration for each technique in different scenarios with precise ground-truth data is still lacking. In this sense, we have implemented and evaluated the most relevant BGS techniques, and performed a quantitative and qualitative comparison between them.

1 Introduction

The segmentation of moving objects in video sequences is a critical low level task in many application areas such as video compression, video surveillance, video indexing, etc. It provides a classification of the pixels in a video sequence into foreground or background of the scene. There are many different techniques for video segmentation depending on the type of the video sequence and the objectives of the application. The most commonly used technique in scenes captured by static cameras is Background Subtraction (BGS): it is based on the modeling of the background of the scene and the extraction of the moving objects (foreground) by somehow *subtracting* the modeled background from the current frame.

BGS techniques are defined by the background model and the foreground detection process. According to [1], the background model is described by three aspects: the initialization, the representation and the update process of the scene background. A correct initialization allows to acquire a background of the scene without errors. For instance, techniques that analyze video sequences with presence of moving objects in the whole sequence should consider different initialization schemes to avoid the acquisition of an incorrect background of the scene. The representation describes the mathematical techniques used to model the value of each background pixel. For instance, unimodal sequences (where background pixels variation follows an unimodal scheme) need more simple models to describe the background of the scene than

---

* Work supported by the Spanish Government (TEC2007-65400 – SemanticVideo), the Spanish Administration agency CDTI (CENIT-VISION 2007-1007) and the Comunidad de Madrid (S-0505/TIC-0223 - ProMultiDis-CM).

J. Blanc-Talon et al. (Eds.): ACIVS 2009, LNCS 5807, pp. 33–42, 2009.

the multimodal ones (where background pixels, due to scene dynamism, vary following more complex schema). The update process allows to incorporate specific global changes in the background model, such as those owing to illumination and viewpoint variation. Additionally, these techniques usually include pre-processing and post-processing stages to improve final foreground detection results.

There are many classifications of BGS techniques in the literature[2][3][4], according to different criteria.. However, some authors agree on a classification depending on the complexity of the analyzed video sequence and on the type of representation of the background model.

According to complexity a first division could distinguish between controlled and non-controlled environments, the former including simple techniques (e.g., based on frame differences[5], running average[6], median filtering[3]), and the latter, targeting sequences captured in changing environments due to camera noise, illumination and changing viewpoints, including more complex ones. In this case, depending on the background dynamism we can divide techniques into unimodal (e.g., those using a simple Gaussian distribution[7] or a Chi-Square one[8]) and multimodal (e.g., based on mixtures of Gaussians[9][10], on the mean-shift algorithm [11], on Kernel Density Estimation[12][13] or on Hidden Markov Models[14]).

According to the model representation, existing techniques can be classified into basic, parametric and non-parametric. The former refers to more or less heuristic approaches (e.g, frame differencing, temporal mean or median, running average). Parametric ones try to fit pixel variation to well-known probability distributions. Finally, non-parametric techniques try to estimate a precise distribution via histogram or kernel-based approaches.

In this paper, we present a comparative evaluation of the most relevant BGS techniques on a representative set of scenarios. As each technique includes one or several parameters, we have first obtained the best set of parameters for every scenario, according to some selected quality measures. Then, we have applied all the techniques to all the considered sequences in order to obtain a quantitative and qualitative evaluation of their performance. In this sense, Section 2 presents the selected BGS techniques and their most relevant parameters. Section 3 discusses the evaluation methodology to compare the selected techniques describing the dataset, the quality metrics, and the selection of technique parameters. Section 4 shows the evaluation results. Finally, section 5 presents the conclusion of this work.

2   Selected Techniques

In this section, we briefly describe the selected BGS techniques, classified according to the model representation, just in order to identify their most relevant parameters and implementation details that might diverge from the referenced work.

2.1   Basic Models

Frame differencing (FD) [5]: also known as temporal difference, this method uses the previous frame as background model for the current frame. Setting a threshold, τ , on the squared difference between model and frame decides on foreground and background. This threshold is the analyzed parameter.

Median filtering (MF) [3]: uses the median of the previous N frames as background model for the current frame. As FD, a threshold τ on the model-frame difference decides. This threshold is the only analyzed parameter. This method claims to be very robust, but requires memory resources to store the last N frames.

2.2 Parametric Models

Simple Gaussian (SG) [7]: represents each background pixel variation with a Gaussian distribution. For every new frame, a pixel is determined to belong to the background if it falls into a deviation, σ, around the mean. The parameters of each Gaussian are updated with the current frame pixel by using a running average scheme[6], controlled by a learning factor α. The initial deviation value, σ_o, and α are the analyzed parameters.

Mixture of Gaussians (MoG) [9]: represents each background pixel variation with a set of weighted Gaussian distributions. Distributions are ordered according to its weight; the more relevant (until the accumulated weight gets past a threshold, τ) are considered to model the background; the remaining model the foreground. A pixel is decided to belong to the background if it falls into a deviation, σ, around the mean of any of the Gaussians that model it. The update process is only performed on the Gaussian distribution that describes the pixel value in the current frame, also following a running average scheme with parameter α. The initial Gaussians deviation value, σ_o, the threshold τ, and α are the analyzed parameters.

Gamma method (G) [8]: in practice represents each background pixel with a running average of its previous values. The decision on a pixel belonging to the background is performed by summing up the square differences between pixel values of a square spatial window centred in the considered pixel frame and the corresponding background model values, and setting a threshold τ over it. A theoretical development, based on the assumption that the pixel variation follows a Gaussian, concludes that the thresholded function follows a Chi-square distribution, which bases the threshold selection, in fact a probability. This threshold is the analyzed parameter.

2.3 Non-Parametric Models

Histogram-based approach (Hb) [15]: represents each background pixel variation with a histogram of its last N values, which is re-computed every L frames ($L \ll N$). A threshold τ is set on each normalized histogram (hence being different for each pixel), so that incoming pixels with values over the threshold are considered to be background. The value of the threshold is the analyzed parameter.

Kernel Density Estimation (KDE) [12] estimates the probability density function (*pdf*) of each pixel for each frame, via averaging the effect of a set of kernel functions (typically Gaussian) centred at each pixel value for the N previous frames. A pixel is determined to belong to the background if its probability of belonging to the modeled distribution is higher that a threshold τ, which is the only analyzed parameter.

3 Evaluation Methodology

The methodology used to compare the BGS techniques includes: selection of a data-set, selection of adequate quality metrics, experimental tests to obtain the parameters values that best perform for each technique and each sequence type, and comparative analysis of the results obtained for each technique in every case. This section describes the first three steps; Section 4 focuses on comparative results.

3.1 Data-Set Selection and Description

We have chosen to use the dataset described in [16], as it includes a representative set of high-quality uncompressed video sequences and the associated ground-truth. The dataset sequences are classified according to different criteria (e.g., textural complexity, apparent velocity, object structure...). In our work, just two of these criteria have been considered relevant: background situation (indoor, outdoor) and background dynamism (unimodal, multimodal). A summary of the selected test sub-sequences and criteria is shown in Fig. 1. Detailed information can be found in [16].

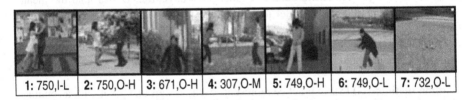

Fig. 1. Selected test sub-sequences and criteria from the cVSG dataset. Lower data indicates sequence ID: number of frames considered, background situation (**I**ndoor/**O**utdoor) – background dynamism (**L**ow/**M**edium/**H**igh). All frame sizes are 720x576.

3.2 Performance Evaluation Metrics

In order to evaluate the selected techniques, we have selected the precision (P) and recall (R) measures for foreground ($P1, R1$) and background ($P0, R0$) detection:

$$P0 = TN/(TN + FN), \ R0 = TN/(TN + FP) \tag{1}$$

$$P1 = TP/(TP + FP), \ R1 = TP/(TP + FN),$$

where TP indicates the number of foreground pixels correctly detected, TN the number of background ones correctly detected, FP the number of foreground pixels wrongly detected as background and FN the number of background ones wrongly detected as foreground. Additionally, the F-score measure has been selected to combine P and R measures for foreground ($F1$) and background ($F0$) results:

$$F0 = 2 \cdot P0 \cdot R0/(P0 + R0), \ F1 = 2 \cdot P1 \cdot R1/(P1 + R1) \tag{2}$$

Table 1. Analyzed parameters for each technique (FD, MF, SG, etc.), including the range (format [init_value:step:end_value]) or set (format: [value,value,...]) of tested values for each sequence (ID) and the resulting optimum value (Opt)

ID	FD		MF		SG				G	
	τ	Opt	τ	Opt	α	Opt	σ_o	Opt	τ	Opt
1	[20:20:160]	140	[10:10:90]	20	$[10^{-8},5.10^{-8},$ $10^{-7},5.10^{-7},$ $10^{-6},5.10^{-6},10^{-5}]$	10^{-6}	[1:3:18]	6	$[10^{-7},10^{-5}$ $,10^{-3}]$	10^{-5}
2	[50:50:800]	450	" "	60	$[10^{-4},5.10^{-4},$ $10^{-3},5.10^{-3},$ $10^{-2},5.10^{-2},10^{-1}]$	10^{-2}	[30:5:55]	35	" "	10^{-5}
3	[20:20:320]	180	" "	20	" "	10^{-3}	[1:3:18]	10	" "	10^{-7}
4	[20:20:160]	40	" "	10	" "	5.10^{-2}	[30:5:55]	35	" "	10^{-3}
5	[20:20:160]	40	" "	10	" "	5.10^{-4}	[1:3:18]	5	" "	10^{-7}
6	[20:20.160], [2:2:20]	20	" "	10	$[10^{-8},5.10^{-8},$ $10^{-7},5.10^{-7},$ $10^{-6},5.10^{-6},10^{-5}]$	10^{-6}	[1:3:18]	6	" "	10^{-7}
7	[20:20:160]	40	" "	10	" "	10^{-5}	[1:3:18]	5	" "	10^{-3}

ID	Hb		KDE		MoG					
	τ	Opt	τ	Opt	α	Opt	σ_o	Opt	τ	Opt
1	[.75:.05:.95]	.75	[.25:.05:.5]	.009	$[10^{-7},5.10^{-7},$ $10^{-6},5.10^{-6},$ $10^{-5},5.10^{-5},10^{-4}]$	5.10^{-5}	[24:2:34]	28	[.75:.05:.95]	.90
2	[.75:.05:.95]	.75	[.25:.05:.5]	.005	$[10^{-4},5.10^{-4}$ $10^{-3},5.10^{-3},$ $10^{-2},5.10^{-2},10^{-1}]$	10^{-2}	[20:5:50]	40	" "	.85
3	[.75:.05:.95]	.75	[.25:.05:.5]	.005	" "	5.10^{-3}	[10:5:40]	30	" "	.90
4	[.75:.05:.95]	.85	[.25:.05:.5]	.009	" "	5.10^{-3}	[5:5:35]	15	" "	.95
5	[.75:.05:.95]	.85	[.25:.05:.5]	.009	" "	10^{-3}	[5:5:35]	20	" "	.85
6	[.75:.05:.95]	.85	[.25:.05:.5]	.009	" "	10^{-4}	[24:2:34]	32	" "	.85
7	[.75:.05:.95]	.90	[.25:.05:.5]	.009	" "	10^{-3}	[2:2:18]	4	" "	.95

3.3 Selection of Optimum Parameters for Each Technique

In order to find optimum values for each parameter of the selected techniques, we have performed an exhaustive search for each test sequence, previously defining for each case either a test range and a searching step or a set of test values (according to values used by other authors[17][18]), which reasonably guarantee to find a global quality maximum. When more than one parameter is analyzed, we have followed a *one at a time* scheme, searching for its optimum value while setting *reasonable* values for the others, and then setting this parameter to the obtained optimum while searching for other parameter's optimum.

The criterion to find the optimum values was to maximize the average of the F-score measures for foreground and background, $F0$ and $F1$. The test ranges/values and the obtained results for each technique and sequence are compiled in Table 1.

4   Experimental Results

In this section, experimental results of the selected BGS techniques are presented and compared, first from an efficiency point of view, and then from a quality point of view, both quantitatively and qualitatively.

Table 2. Average processing time (in seconds per frame) required by each technique for each sequence

ID	FD	MF	SG	G	MoG	KDE	Hb
1	0.0305	0.0303	0.0212	0.012	5.2900	1.070	13.3929
2	0.0251	0.0277	0.0306	0.017	4.9800	1.121	13.8902
3	0.0283	0.0288	0.0269	0.015	8.3839	0.523	13.7242
4	0.0301	0.0311	0.0292	0.011	3.5975	1.081	13.5353
5	0.0276	0.0298	0.0292	0.011	3.5975	2.975	13.4074
6	0.0296	0.0308	0.0295	0.012	4.1171	4.357	13.5050
7	0.0298	0.0308	0.0292	0.011	3.8724	4.292	14.0642
Mean	0,0287	0,0299	0,0279	0,0127	4,8341	2,2027	13,6456

4.1   Efficiency Considerations

Table 2 compiles average processing time per frame and global average values for each technique and sequence. It should be noted that the selected techniques have been fully implemented in MatLab; hence, efficiency data should be considered in a relative way.

The computational load is high for KDE and Hb due to the need to estimate the *pdf* using the last values of each pixel. Simple techniques like FD and MF present the lowest computational cost. The G method has been implemented with some improvements that speed-up the spatial window-based analysis, resulting in low computational cost. Also notice the high variation that some techniques experiment depending on the analyzed sequence.

Table 3. Performance metrics (in percentage) of the selected techniques for each sequence. The better results, in terms of the F-score, for each sequence are highlighted in bold.

ID	FD						MF						SG					
	P0	P1	R0	R1	F0	F1	P0	P1	R0	R1	F0	F1	P0	P1	R0	R1	F0	F1
1	92.2	58.9	98.3	22.1	95.2	32.2	96.5	86.6	98.9	66.5	97.7	72.2	97.1	89.8	99.1	72.5	98.1	80.2
2	91.4	30.2	96.2	15.5	93.7	20.5	93.9	59.8	97.0	41.7	**95.4**	**49.1**	91.0	70.6	99.6	8.2	95.1	14.8
3	95.6	48.9	94.6	54.5	95.1	51.6	97.5	44.1	90.8	75.8	94.1	55.8	92.0	66.8	99.5	9.8	95.6	17.1
4	88.2	30.9	92.9	20.3	90.5	24.5	91.1	44.1	91.5	42.7	91.3	43.4	92.8	36.1	83.9	58.6	88.1	44.7
5	89.6	32.9	94.4	20.1	91.9	25.0	93.4	50.8	93.1	52.4	93.3	51.6	92.6	68.0	97.2	42.9	**94.8**	**52.6**
6	93.5	68.3	99.1	22.3	96.2	33.6	98.5	61.7	95.3	84.1	96.9	71.7	98.8	87.1	98.8	86.9	**98.8**	**87.1**
7	99.2	72.0	99.7	44.1	99.5	54.7	99.5	89.9	99.9	66.9	99.7	76.7	99.4	60.7	99.5	56.7	99.4	58.6

ID	G						MoG						KDE					
	P0	P1	R0	R1	F0	F1	P0	P1	R0	R1	F0	F1	P0	P1	R0	R1	F0	F1
1	99.3	97.8	99.8	93.7	**99.5**	**95.7**	98.8	90.2	99.0	88.7	98.9	89.4	94.3	39.0	91.9	48.2	93.1	43.1
2	92.8	99.9	99.9	27.9	96.3	43.6	93.0	52.2	96.8	32.3	94.9	39.8	93.2	25.6	87.6	39.7	90.3	31.1
3	93.0	54.6	99.2	22.8	95.5	32.2	96.7	51.5	93.9	66.8	**95.3**	**58.1**	96.7	37.4	89.1	68.4	92.7	48.4
4	93.7	48.8	90.0	61.4	**91.8**	**54.4**	89.7	50.9	95.6	29.5	92.5	37.4	88.7	28.4	89.3	27.3	89.0	27.9
5	97.2	51.3	89.5	81.2	93.2	62.9	95.8	57.2	92.8	70.1	**94.3**	**63.0**	91.1	37.1	92.1	34.1	91.6	35.5
6	99.6	90.4	99.1	95.6	**99.3**	**92.9**	99.4	85.8	98.6	93.1	**99.0**	**89.3**	94.7	49.5	96.5	38.9	95.5	43.6
7	99.9	65.1	99.3	97.2	**99.6**	**77.9**	99.8	85.6	99.8	86.5	**99.8**	**86.0**	99.6	33.0	97.8	74.0	98.7	45.7

ID	Hb					
	P0	P1	R0	R1	F0	F1
1	94.8	89.3	99.4	49.4	97.0	63.7
2	94.1	44.8	94.1	44.4	94.1	44.6
3	94.3	48.5	95.9	39.8	95.1	43.7
4	88.8	45.3	95.7	22.6	92.1	30.1
5	91.0	50.8	95.9	30.7	93.4	38.3
6	97.7	90.2	99.3	74.5	98.5	81.6
7	99.1	73.5	99.8	39.1	99.5	51.0

4.2 Quantitative Analysis

Detailed detection results are shown in Table 3. Data indicate that the G technique overall obtained the best results for all type of sequences, which mainly reinforces the underlying idea of considering a spatial window instead of performing a pixel-wise decision. Apart from it, for high background dynamism sequences (IDs 2, 3 and 5) and for the medium one (ID 4), MF and MoG performed specially well; it is noteworthy the good behavior of the MF technique, not specifically designed to cope with multimodality. For low dynamism sequences (IDs 1, 6 and 7) parametric approaches, while being particularly designed for multimodal situations, generally obtained the best results. It can also be observed that the detection results in the more dynamic sequences present low foreground detection accuracy for all the techniques.

4.3 Qualitative Analysis

Although objective results provide rigorous conclusions on each technique behavior, we consider that some other subjective aspects might help to form an impression of

Table 4. Subjective apreciation of three aspects of the analyzed techniques: very-good (↑↑), good (↑), medium (↕), bad (↓), very-bad (↓↓)

	FD	MF	SG	G	MoG	KDE	Hb
Object-mask quality	↓↓	↓	↑	↑↑	↑↑	↕	↓
Background noise	↕	↕	↓	↓	↓	↑	↑
Parameter setting	↑↑	↑↑	↕	↓	↓	↓	↑

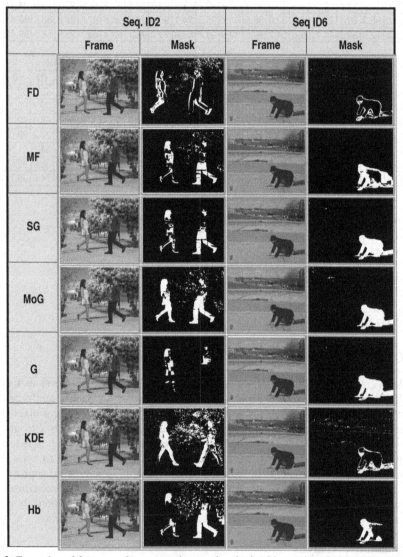

Fig. 2. Examples of frames and segmentation masks obtained by each technique. The left columns show frame 204 of the multimodal sequence ID 2, and the right ones show frame 279 of the unimodal sequence ID 6.

their overall performance. In this sense, Table 4 compiles our subjective appreciation of the visual quality of the object segmentation mask, the level of noise that contains the segmented background, and the easiness to fix the technique parameters.

Additionally, Fig. 2 shows for each technique two illustrative frames along with the obtained segmentation masks. Frames belong to the multimodal sequence ID 2 and to the unimodal one ID 6. The multimodal samples have more background pixels incorrectly detected than the unimodal ones for all the techniques, mainly due to the difficulty of characterizing the complex dynamics of the background. Its also possible to observe that parametric approaches obtain better masks for unimodal and multimodal backgrounds with low or medium dynamism than the simple and non-parametric ones; this is so because for these types of background, the percentage of background pixels presenting multimodality is low compared to that of unimodal pixels and object pixels.

5 Conclusions

In this paper, we have presented an evaluation of the most representative BGS techniques. Firstly, the most relevant parameters of each technique have been identified and their optimum values have been computed in the tests performed. Secondly, the accuracy of the foreground and background detection has been quantitative compared for all the selected techniques. Finally, a qualitative evaluation has been performed analyzing several subjective aspects of each technique.

As a conclusion of the comparative study, parametric techniques present the best accuracy in in-door unimodal sequences and out-door sequences with low percentage of multimodality. The drawbacks of these techniques are their difficulty in the parameter adjustment and the complexity of the mathematical models employed. On the other hand, non-parametric techniques present results with less accuracy and they are very sensitive to the probability density function estimation process (kernel selected, number of previous pixel samples analyzed...) requiring high computational and memory resources. Additionally, it is crucial to study the parameters of any background segmentation technique, to identify the most relevant and sensitive ones.

References

[1] Cristani, M., Bicego, M., Murino, V.: Multi-level background initialization using Hidden Markov Models. In: First ACM SIGMM Int. workshop on Video surveillance, pp. 11–20 (2003)
[2] Piccardi, M.: Background subtraction techniques: a review. In: SMC 2004, vol. 4, pp. 3099–3104 (2004)
[3] Cheung, S.-C., Kamath, C.: Robust techniques for background subtraction in urban traffic video. In: Panchanathan, S., Vasudev, B. (eds.) Proc. Elect Imaging: Visual Comm. Image Proce. (Part One) SPIE, vol. 5308, pp. 881–892 (2004)
[4] Cucchiara, R.: People Surveillance, VISMAC Palermo (2006)
[5] Ewerth, R., Freisleben, B.: Frame difference normalization: an approach to reduce error rates of cut detection algorithms for MPEG videos. In: ICIP, pp. 1009–1012 (2003)

[6] Tang, Z., Miao, Z., Wan, Y.: Background Subtraction Using Running Gaussian Average and Frame Difference. In: Ma, L., Rauterberg, M., Nakatsu, R. (eds.) ICEC 2007. LNCS, vol. 4740, pp. 411–414. Springer, Heidelberg (2007)

[7] Wren, A., Darrell, P.: Pfinder: Real-time tracking of the human body. PAMI (1997)

[8] Cavallaro, A., Steiger, O., Ebrahimi, T.: Semantic video analysis for adaptive content delivery and automatic description. IEEE Transactions on Circuits and Systems for Video Technology 15(10), 1200–1209 (2005)

[9] Stauffer, G.: Adaptive background mixture models for real-time tracking. In: CVPR (1999)

[10] Carminati, L., Benois-Pineau, J.: Gaussian mixture classification for moving object detection in video surveillance environment. In: ICIP, pp. 113–116 (2005)

[11] Comaniciu, D.: Mean shift: a robust approach toward feature space analysis. IEEE Transactions on Pattern Analysis and machine Intelligence 24(5), 603 (2002)

[12] Elgammal, A.M., Harwood, D., Davis, L.S.: Non-parametric model for background subtraction. In: Vernon, D. (ed.) ECCV 2000. LNCS, vol. 1843, pp. 751–767. Springer, Heidelberg (2000)

[13] Zivkovic, Z., Van Der Heijden, F.: Efficient adaptive density estimation per image pixel for the task of background subtraction. Pattern Recognition Letters 27(7), 773–780 (2006)

[14] Stenger, B., Ramesh, V., Paragios, N., Coetzee, F., Buhmann, J.M.: Topology Free Hidden Markov Models: Application to Background Modeling. In: Eighth Int. Conf. on Computer Vision, ICCV 2001, vol. 1, pp. 294–301 (2001)

[15] Mittal, A., Paragios, N.: Motion-based background subtraction using adaptive kernel density estimation. In: Proceedings of the Int. Conf. Comp. Vision and Patt. Recog., CVPR, pp. 302–309 (2004)

[16] Tiburzi, F., Escudero, M., Bescós, J., Martínez, J.M.: A Corpus for Motion-based Video-object Segmentation. In: IEEE International Conference on Image Processing (Workshop on Multimedia Information Retrieval), ICIP 2008, SanDiego, USA (2008)

[17] El Baf, F., Bouwmans, T., Vachon, B.: Comparison of Background Subtraction Methods for a Multimedia Application. In: 14th International Conference on systems, Signals and Image Processing, IWSSIP 2007, Maribor, Slovenia, pp. 385–388 (2007)

[18] Parks, D.H., Fels, S.S.: Evaluation of Background Subtraction Algorithms with Post-Processing. In: IEEE Fifth International Conference on Advanced Video and Signal Based Surveillance, AVSS 2008, pp. 192–199 (2008)

Kolmogorov Superposition Theorem and Wavelet Decomposition for Image Compression

Pierre-Emmanuel Leni, Yohan D. Fougerolle, and Frédéric Truchetet

Université de Bourgogne, Laboratoire LE2I, UMR CNRS 5158,
12 rue de la fonderie, 71200 Le Creusot, France

Abstract. Kolmogorov Superposition Theorem stands that any multivariate function can be decomposed into two types of monovariate functions that are called inner and external functions: each inner function is associated to one dimension and linearly combined to construct a hash-function that associates every point of a multidimensional space to a value of the real interval $[0, 1]$. These intermediate values are then associated by external functions to the corresponding value of the multidimensional function. Thanks to the decomposition into monovariate functions, our goal is to apply this decomposition to images and obtain image compression.

We propose a new algorithm to decompose images into continuous monovariate functions, and propose a compression approach: thanks to the decomposition scheme, the quantity of information taken into account to define the monovariate functions can be adapted: only a fraction of the pixels of the original image have to be contained in the network used to build the correspondence between monovariate functions. To improve the reconstruction quality, we combine KST and multiresolution approach, where the low frequencies will be represented with the highest accuracy, and the high frequencies representation will benefit from the adaptive aspect of our method to achieve image compression.

Our main contribution is the proposition of a new compression scheme: we combine KST and multiresolution approach. Taking advantage of the KST decomposition scheme, the low frequencies will be represented with the highest accuracy, and the high frequencies representation will be replaced by a decomposition into simplified monovariate functions, preserving the reconstruction quality. We detail our approach and our results on different images and present the reconstruction quality as a function of the quantity of pixels contained in monovariate functions.

1 Introduction

The Superposition Theorem is the solution of one of the 23 mathematical problems conjectured by Hilbert in 1900. Kolmogorov has proved that continuous multivariate functions can be expressed as sums and compositions of monovariate functions. The KST, reformulated and simplified by Sprecher in [11], [12], can be written as:

J. Blanc-Talon et al. (Eds.): ACIVS 2009, LNCS 5807, pp. 43–53, 2009.
© Springer-Verlag Berlin Heidelberg 2009

Theorem 1 (Kolmogorov superposition theorem). *Every continuous function defined on the identity hypercube, $f : [0,1]^d \longrightarrow \mathbb{R}$, can be written as sums and compositions of continuous monovariate functions as:*

$$f(x_1, ..., x_d) = \sum_{n=0}^{2d} g_n \Big(\sum_{i=1}^{d} \lambda_i \psi(x_i + b_n) \Big), \tag{1}$$

with ψ continuous function, λ_i and b constants. ψ is called inner function and g external function.

Coordinates $x_i, i \in [\![1, d]\!]$ of each dimension are combined into a real number by a hash function (obtained by linear combinations of inner functions ψ) that is associated to corresponding value of f for these coordinates by the external function g.

Igelnik has presented in [5] an approximating construction that provides flexibility and modification perspectives over the monovariate function construction. Using Igelnik's approximation network, the image can be represented as a superposition of layers, *i.e.* a superposition of images with a fixed resolution. The constructed network can be reduced to a fraction of the pixels of the whole image: the smaller the tiles, the larger the quantity of information. We study the reconstruction quality using monovariate functions containing only a fraction of the original image pixels. To improve the reconstruction quality, we apply this decomposition on images of details obtained by a wavelet decomposition: external functions obtained from the decomposition of images of details can be simplified, providing better reconstruction quality than larger tile sizes.

The structure of the paper is as follows: we present the decomposition algorithm in section 2. In section 3, we present the results of gray level image decompositions, and combine the KST decomposition with wavelets to improve the reconstruction. In the last section, we present our conclusions and several promising research perspectives.

Our contributions include improvements and modifications of Igelnik's algorithm for image decomposition, the characterization of the obtained continuous decomposition, and the determination of the reconstruction quality as a function of the quantity of information contained in monovariate functions.

2   Algorithm

We briefly describe the algorithm proposed by Igelnik, and we invite the interested reader to refer to [5] and [4] for a detailed description of the algorithm. The first step is the definition of a disjoint tilage over the definition space $[0,1]^d$ of the multivariate function f. To entirely cover the space, several tilage layers are generated by translation of the first layer, as illustrated in Figure 1. For a given tilage layer n, d inner functions ψ_{ni} are randomly generated: one per dimension, independently from function f. The functions ψ_{ni} are sampled with M points, that are interpolated by cubic splines. The convex combination of these internal functions ψ_{ni} with real, linearly independent, and strictly positive values λ_i is the argument of external function g_n (one per dimension). Finally, the external function is constructed, using multivariate function values at the centers of hypercubes. To optimize network construction, each layer is weighted by coefficients a_n and summed to approximate the multivariate function f.

With this scheme, the original equation 1 becomes:

$$f(x_1, ..., x_d) \simeq \sum_{n=1}^{N} a_n g_n \left(\sum_{i=1}^{d} \lambda_i \psi_{ni}(x_i) \right). \tag{2}$$

Remark 1. In the equation 1, one internal function ψ is defined for the whole network, and the argument x_i is translated for each layer n of a constant b_n. In this algorithm, one inner function ψ is defined per dimension (index i) and layer (index n).

The tilage is then constituted with hypercubes C_n obtained by cartesian product of the intervals $I_n(j)$, defined as follows:

Definition 1.

$$\forall n \in [\![1, N]\!], j \geqslant -1, I_n(j) = [(n-1)\delta + (N+1)j\delta, (n-1)\delta + (N+1)j\delta + N\delta],$$

where δ is the distance between two intervals I of length $N\delta$, such that the function f oscillation is smaller than $\frac{1}{N}$ on each hypercube C. Values of j are defined such that the previously generated intervals $I_n(j)$ intersect the interval $[0, 1]$, as illustrated in Figure 1.

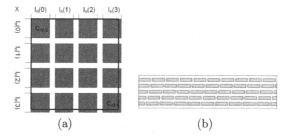

(a)   (b)

Fig. 1. (a) Cartesian product of intervals I to define a disjoint tilage of hypercubes C. (b) Superposition of translated disjoint tilages.

2.1   Inner Functions Construction ψ_{ni}

Each function ψ_{ni} is defined as follows: generate a set of j distinct numbers y_{nij}, between Δ and $1 - \Delta$, $0 < \Delta < 1$, such that the oscillations of the interpolating cubic spline of ψ values on the interval δ is lower than Δ. j is given by definition 1. The real numbers y_{nij} are sorted, *i.e.*: $y_{nij} < y_{nij+1}$. The image of the interval $I_n(j)$ by function ψ is y_{nij}. This discontinuous inner function ψ is sampled by M points, that are interpolated by a cubic spline, as illustrated in Figure 3(a). We obtain two sets of points: points located on plateaus over intervals $I_n(j)$, and points M' located between two intervals $I_n(j)$ and $I_n(j+1)$, that are randomly placed. Points M' are optimized during the network construction, using a stochastic approach (see [5]).

Once functions ψ_{ni} are constructed, the argument $\sum_{i=1}^{d} \lambda_i \psi_{ni}(x)$ of external functions can be evaluated. On hypercubes $C_{nij_1,\ldots,j_d}$, it has constant values $p_{nj_1,\ldots,j_d} = \sum_{i=1}^{d} \lambda_i y_{nij_i}$. Every random number y_{nij_i} generated verifies that the generated values p_{nij_i} are all different, $\forall i \in [\![1, d]\!], \forall n \in [\![1, N]\!], \forall j \in \mathbb{N}, j \geqslant -1$.

Fig. 2. Example of function ψ sampled by 500 points that are interpolated by a cubic spline

2.2   External Function Construction g_n

The function g_n is defined as follows:

- For every real number $t = p_{n,j_1,\ldots,j_d}$, function $g_n(t)$ is equal to the Nth of values of the function f at the center of the hypercube $C_{nij_1,\ldots,j_d}$, noted A_k.
- The definition interval of function g_n is extended to all $t \in [0, 1]$. Two points B_k and B'_k are placed in A_k neighborhood, such that $t_{B_k} < t_{A_k} < t_{B'_k}$. The placement of points B_k and B'_k in the circles centered in A_k must preserve the order of points: $\ldots, B'_{k-1}, B_k, A_k, B'_k, B_{k+1}, \ldots$, *i.e.* the radius of these circles must be smaller than half of the length between two consecutive points A_k. Points B'_k and B_{k+1} are connected with a line defined with a slope r. Points A_k and B'_k are connected with a nine degree spline s, such that: $s(t_{A_k}) = g_n(t_{A_k})$, $s(t_{B'_k}) = g_n(t_{B'_k})$, $s'(t_{B'_k}) = r$, and $s^{(2)}(t_{B'_k}) = s^{(3)}(t_{B'_k}) = s^{(4)}(t_{B'_k}) = 0$. Points B_k and A_k are connected with a similar nine degree spline. The connection condition at points A_k of both nine degree splines give the remaining conditions. This construction ensures the function continuity and the convergence of the approximating function to f (proved in [5]). Figure 3(b) illustrates this construction.

The external function has a "noisy" shape, which is related to the global sweeping scheme of the image: Sprecher and *al.* have demonstrated in Ref.[13] that using internal functions, space-filling curves can be defined. The linear combination of inner functions associates a unique real value to every couple of the multidimensional space $[0, 1]^d$. Sorting these real values defines a unique path through the tiles

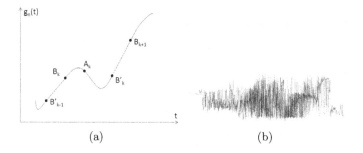

(a)   (b)

Fig. 3. (a) Plot of g_n. Points B, A and B' are connected by a nine degree spline. Points B' and B are connected by lines. (b) Example of function g_n for a complete layer of Lena decomposition.

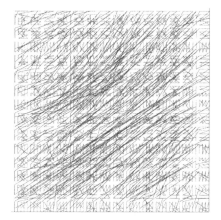

Fig. 4. Igelnik's space filling curve

of a layer: the space filling curve. Figure 4 illustrates an example of such a curve: the pixels are swept without any neighborhood property conservation.

2.3   Network Stochastic Construction

The construction of monovariate functions requires some parameters to be optimized using a stochastic method (ensemble approach, see [4]): the weights a_n associated to each layer, and the placement of the sampling points M' of inner functions ψ that are located between two consecutive intervals. To optimize the network convergence, three sets of points are constituted: a training set D_T, a generalization set D_G, and a validation set D_V. N layers are successively built. To add a new layer, K candidate layers are generated with the same plateaus y_{nij}, which gives K new candidate networks. The difference between two candidate layers is the set of sampling points M' located between two intervals $I_n(j)$ and $I_n(j+1)$, that are randomly chosen. We keep the layer from the network with the smallest mean squared error that is evaluated using the generalization set D_G. The weights a_n are obtained by minimizing the difference between the approximation given by the network and the image of function f for the points of the training set D_T. The algorithm is iterated until N layers are constructed. The validation error of the final network is determined using validation set D_V, i.e. by applying the approximated function to D_V.

To determine coefficients a_n, the difference between f and its approximation $\tilde{f}$ must be minimized:

$$\|Q_n a_n - t\|, \; noting \; t = \begin{bmatrix} f(x_{1,1}, ..., x_{d,1}) \\ ... \\ f(x_{1,P}, ..., x_{d,P}) \end{bmatrix}, \tag{3}$$

with Q_n a matrix of column vectors q_k, $k \in [\![0, n]\!]$ that corresponds to the approximation ($\tilde{f}$) of the kth layer for points set $\big((x_{1,1}, ..., x_{d,1}), ..., (x_{1,P}, ..., x_{d,P})\big)$ of D_T:

$$Q_n = \begin{bmatrix} \begin{bmatrix} \tilde{f}_0(x_{1,1}, ...x_{d,1}) \\ ... \\ \tilde{f}_0(x_{1,P}, ...x_{d,P}) \end{bmatrix}, ..., \begin{bmatrix} \tilde{f}_n(x_{1,1}, ...x_{d,1}) \\ ... \\ \tilde{f}_n(x_{1,P}, ...x_{d,P}) \end{bmatrix} \end{bmatrix}.$$

An evaluation of the solution $Q_n^{-1}t = a_n$ is proposed by Igelnik in Ref.[4]. The coefficient a_l of the column vector $(a_0, ..., a_n)^T$ is the weight associated to layer l, $l \in [\![0, n]\!]$. Figure 5 presents an overview of a network constituted of 5 tilage layers.

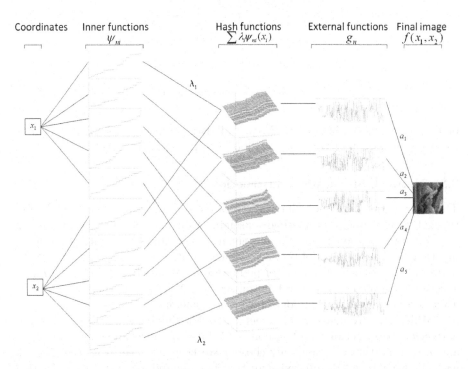

Fig. 5. Overview of a 5 tilage layer network

3   Results

The algorithm presented in the previous section can be used to decompose gray level images (seen as bivariate functions). Each pixel corresponds to a tile of the bidimensional space $[0, 1]^d$, where the bivariate function has a constant value. By changing the parameters δ and N, the size of the tilage can be adjusted, *i.e.* the number of tiles per layer. The tile size directly determines the number of pixels of the original image that are utilized for the network construction: pixel values located on the center of tiles are utilized to construct external functions g_n. Decreasing the number of pixels from the original image in external functions (*i.e.* increasing tile size) leads to a partial use of the original image pixels. To characterize the compression properties of the network, we represent the number of pixels of the original image that are contained in the network as a function of PSNR reconstruction, by training the network with a 100x100 pixels image to reconstruct a 100x100 pixels image. Figure 6 presents several reconstructions obtained using between 100% and 15% of the pixels from original image, and figure 8 (dot line) details the obtained PSNR. Figure 7 presents the reconstuction

(a)   (b)   (c)   (d)

Fig. 6. Lena reconstruction, using 100%(a), 70%(b), 40%(c), 15%(d) of original image pixels

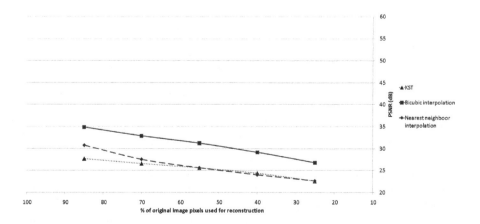

Fig. 7. PSNR of image reconstruction as a function of the number of pixels utilized to define external functions

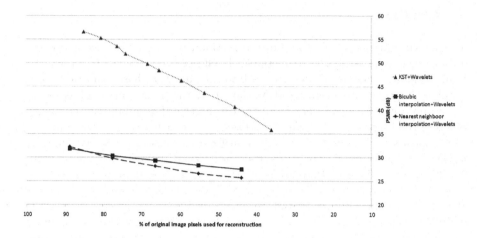

Fig. 8. PSNR of image reconstruction using wavelets as a function of the number of pixels utilized to define external functions

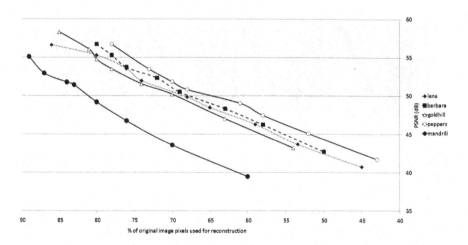

Fig. 9. PSNR of five classical image reconstruction

using KST and reconstructions obtained using bicubic and nearest neighboor interpolation of an image containing only a fraction of original image pixels.

We combine our decomposition scheme with a multiresolution approach to improve the reconstruction quality: a wavelet decomposition leads to 4 sub-images, one is a low-frequencies image, and three contains high frequencies. Our goal is to decompose the images of details using small tiles, and, taking advantage of the limited contrast, to replace values in external functions to reduce the number of pixels from the original image required to the external functions construction (as if larger tiles were used). An interesting property of this approach is that the decomposition of the images of details (high frequencies) leads to simple external

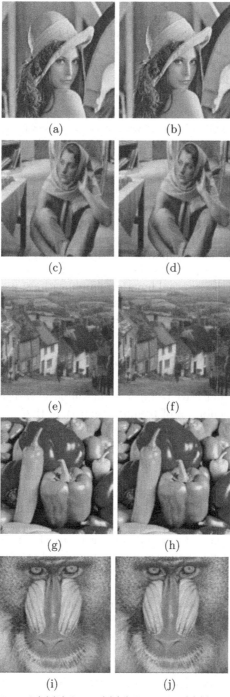

Fig. 10. Reconstruction of (a)(b) lena, (c)(d) barbara, (e)(f) goldhill, (g)(h) peppers and (i)(j) mandrill, using about 50% and 80% (respectively) of the number of original image pixels

functions, with limited oscillations. Computing the mean value for every external function and replacing the values located at a distance from the mean value smaller than the standard deviation allows to decrease the number of pixels retained for the network construction. Precisely, the smallest tile size (a tile = a pixel) is utilized to decompose an image of details, and is reduced up to only 15% of pixels after external function simplification. We compare this simplification approach with well known image interpolation techniques: we reconstruct 100x100 images of details obtained with wavelets decomposition using bicubic and nearest neighboor interpolation with only a fraction of the original image pixels. Figure 8 details the obtained PSNR for Lena: the reconstruction PSNR is higher and above 30dB for up to a 60% compression rate, and no visible artefacts can be seen (see figure 10). Figure 9 presents the compression and associated reconstruction PSNR for five images: Lena, Goldhill, Peppers, Barbara, and Mandrill. The reconstruction PSNR is higher and above 40 dB for up to 65% compression rate. Figure 10 presents the results obtained on these five images with two external functions simplification (high and low compression rates). We observe that the reconstruction is not visibly altered. The irregular repartition of measures is due to the external function simplifications: measures are realized with regular simplification criteria over external functions, but the simplification of external functions obtained is image dependent, so the compression ratio.

4   Conclusion and Perspectives

We have dealt with multivariate function decomposition using KST. We have presented our implementation of Igelnik's algorithm, that provides control over the size of tiles, which determines the quantity of pixels from the decomposed image that are utilized and contained in the network. Using this size reduction, we have proposed a compression approach, that has been proved adapted to the decomposition of subimages of details obtained from a wavelet decomposition. Due to the simple representation of the high frequencies, the monovariate functions can be simplified: the three images of details can be replaced by a decomposition into simplified monovariate functions, preserving the reconstruction quality. We have presented the results of our approach, applied to various gray level images and different simplification parameters of external functions.

Our principal contribution is the presentation of a compression method, combining KST decomposition and wavelets decomposition simplification: the decomposition of an image into continuous monovariate functions, that relies on a superposition of tilage layers, that can be used to compress an image, and the reconstruction and compression rate improved by applying this decomposition to wavelet image decomposition.

From these results, several perspectives can be pointed out: further developments of this approach are required to obtain a complete compression method, i.e. the size of the compressed image has to be evaluated, which implies the development of an adapted quantization. The second perspective is the addition of encryption and authentication to this compression scheme: considering the direct decomposition of an image into monovariate functions, one can remark that definitions of external and internal monovariate functions are independent. Moreover, internal functions are required to re-arrange external functions and reconstruct the image. Can internal functions be used as a signature or as an encryption key? And finally, a multiresolution approach can be considered: layers of a network can have different tilage densities, so the image could be progressively reconstructed, with an increasing resolution, by progressively superposing the layers.

References

1. Brattka, V.: Du 13-ième problème de Hilbert à la théorie des réseaux de neurones: aspects constructifs du théorème de superposition de Kolmogorov. L'héritage de Kolmogorov en mathématiques. Éditions Belin, Paris, pp. 241–268 (2004)
2. Braun, J., Griebel, M.: On a constructive proof of Kolmogorov's superposition theorem. Constructive Approximation (2007)
3. Hecht-Nielsen, R.: Kolmogorov's mapping neural network existence theorem. In: Proceedings of the IEEE International Conference on Neural Networks III, New York, pp. 11–13 (1987)
4. Igelnik, B., Pao, Y.-H., LeClair, S.R., Shen, C.Y.: The ensemble approach to neural-network learning and generalization. IEEE Transactions on Neural Networks 10, 19–30 (1999)
5. Igelnik, B., Parikh, N.: Kolmogorov's spline network. IEEE transactions on neural networks 14(4), 725–733 (2003)
6. Igelnik, B., Tabib-Azar, M., LeClair, S.R.: A net with complex weights. IEEE Transactions on Neural Networks 12, 236–249 (2001)
7. Köppen, M.: On the training of a Kolmogorov Network. In: Dorronsoro, J.R. (ed.) ICANN 2002. LNCS, vol. 2415, p. 474. Springer, Heidelberg (2002)
8. Lagunas, M.A., Pérez-Neira, A., Nájar, M., Pagés, A.: The Kolmogorov Signal Processor. LNCS, vol. 686, pp. 494–512. Springer, Berlin (1993)
9. Moon, B.S.: An explicit solution for the cubic spline interpolation for functions of a single variable. Applied Mathematics and Computation 117, 251–255 (2001)
10. Sprecher, D.A.: An improvement in the superposition theorem of Kolmogorov. Journal of Mathematical Analysis and Applications 38, 208–213 (1972)
11. Sprecher, D.A.: A numerical implementation of Kolmogorov's superpositions. Neural Networks 9(5), 765–772 (1996)
12. Sprecher, D.A.: A numerical implementation of Kolmogorov's superpositions ii. Neural Networks 10(3), 447–457 (1997)
13. Sprecher, D.A., Draghici, S.: Space-filling curves and Kolmogorov superposition-based neural networks. Neural Networks 15(1), 57–67 (2002)

Theorems Relating Polynomial Approximation, Orthogonality and Balancing Conditions for the Design of Nonseparable Bidimensional Multiwavelets

Ana M.C. Ruedin

Departamento de Computación, Facultad de Ciencias Exactas y Naturales,
Universidad de Buenos Aires
Ciudad Universitaria, Pab. I. CP 1428, Ciudad de Buenos Aires
ana.ruedin@dc.uba.ar

Abstract. We relate different properties of nonseparable quincunx multiwavelet systems, such as polynomial approximation order, orthonormality and balancing, to conditions on the matrix filters. We give mathematical proofs for these relationships. The results obtained are necessary conditions on the filterbank. This simplifies the design of such systems.

Keywords: multiwavelets, nonseparable, polynomial reproduction, quincunx, balancing.

1 Introduction

In the search for wavelet transforms having appropriate properties, according to specific image processing applications, different types of wavelets have been approached.

Separable 2D wavelet systems produce subbands that capture image details in the vertical and horizontal directions, which does not agree with our visual system, whereas nonseparable bidimensional wavelets give a more isotropic treatment of the image [1, 2, 3, 4, 5].

Multiwavelets, related to time–varying filterbanks, are a geralization of the wavelet theory, in which the approximation subspaces are the linear span of more than one scaling function [6, 7, 8, 9]. They offer a greater degree of freedom in the design of filters.

There has been a growing interest in unifying both research lines, and construct nonseparable bidimensional multiwavelets [4, 10]. For these constructions, the quincunx lattice has been frequently chosen, because downsampling/ upsampling operations on this lattice are isometric contractions/ dilations of the plane [11, 12, 13, 14, 15].

In this paper we deal with different properties imposed upon nonseparable 2D multiwavelet systems, and show how they translate into conditions on the matrix filters. Several results give restrictions on the eigenvalues and eigenvectors

J. Blanc-Talon et al. (Eds.): ACIVS 2009, LNCS 5807, pp. 54–65, 2009.

of the sums of the (lowpass) matrix filters having their index on one of the cosets $(S_i^{(00)})$, and on the eigenvalues/eigenvectors of the sum of all (lowpass) matrix filters $(S^{(00)})$ as well as on the kernel of the sum of all (highpass) matrix filters $(T^{(00)})$. Several results concern vectors v_{00}, v_{10}, v_{01}, v_{20}, v_{11} and v_{02} which play a fundamental role in approximating polynomials. Some results given in [11] without proof, such as Lemmas 2 and 3, and Theorem 1, are revised and proofs are given. Lemma 4 and Theorem 2 are original contributions.

In Section II definitions and formulae are given for nonseparable quincunx multiwavelets. In Section III necessary conditions are deduced on the matrix filters, after imposing orthogonality and polynomial approximation conditions. In Section IV order 1 and 2 balancing conditions are defined, and originate conditions over matrices constructed with matrix filters $(S^{(00)}, S^{(01)}$ and $S^{(10)}$, and similar constructions where the indices are restricted to each coset). Concluding remarks are given in Section V, and a new example of a nonseparable multiwavelet system on the quincunx grid, having polynomial approximation order 2 and balancing order 2, is given in the appendix.

2 A Nonseparable Bidimensional Mutiwavelet System and Desired Properties

In this setting, both the refinable function and the wavelet, are function vectors of 2 components, that is, they are determined by 2 functions.

2.1 A Nonseparable Bidimensional Multiscaling Function

The multiscaling function $\Phi = [\Phi_1 \ \Phi_2]^T$, spans the approximation spaces V_j.

We consider 2 possible dilation matrices : D_1, a reflection or symmetry followed by an expansion of the real plane in $\sqrt{2}$, and D_2, a rotation followed by an expansion of the real plane in $\sqrt{2}$. Both matrices have singular values $\sigma_k = \sqrt{2}$ and determinant $|D| = 2$.

$$D_1 = \begin{bmatrix} 1 & 1 \\ 1 & -1 \end{bmatrix} \qquad D_2 = \begin{bmatrix} 1 & -1 \\ 1 & 1 \end{bmatrix}$$

Given an image x, we define the downsampling operation with D as:
$y = x \downarrow D \quad \Leftrightarrow \quad y_n = x_{Dn} \ (n \in Z^2)$. This operation reflects and contracts the image.

Both D_1 and D_2 induce a decomposition of the set Z^2 into $|D| = |\det(D)| = 2$ cosets Γ_0 and Γ_1:

$$Z^2 = \Gamma_0 \cup \Gamma_1 \ ; \ \Gamma_0 = \{DZ^2\} \ ; \ \Gamma_1 = \left\{ DZ^2 + \begin{bmatrix} 1 \\ 0 \end{bmatrix} \right\}. \tag{1}$$

Φ_1 and Φ_2 are 2 functions, defined over R^2, that verify the following dilation or refinable equation (written in vector form in Eq. (2); written in detail in Eq. (3)):

$$\Phi(x) = \sum_{k \in \Lambda \subset Z^2} H^{(k)} \Phi(Dx - k), \tag{2}$$

```
      O ×
    O × O ×
  O × O × O ×
    O × O ×
      O ×
```

Fig. 1. Part of a quincunx lattice with 2 cosets

$$\begin{bmatrix} \Phi_1(x) \\ \Phi_2(x) \end{bmatrix} = \sum_{k \in \Lambda} \left[H^{(k)} \right] \begin{bmatrix} \Phi_1(Dx - k) \\ \Phi_2(Dx - k) \end{bmatrix}, \tag{3}$$

where $H^{(k)}$ are 2×2 matrices (matrix filters), with indices in Λ. In Fig. (1) are drawn pairs of integers belonging to both cosets: those in Γ_0 are drawn with circles and those in Γ_1 are drawn with crosses. Both cosets conform a quincunx lattice.

2.2   A Nonseparable Bidimensional Multiwavelet

The number of wavelets is 2. The equation for the multiwavelet is:

$$\Psi(x) = \sum_{k \in \Lambda} G^{(k)} \Phi(Dx - k). \tag{4}$$

where $G^{(k)}$ are 2×2 matrices (matrix filters). We choose matrices $G^{(k)}$ having the same indices $k \in \Lambda$, as $H^{(k)}$. The entries of matrices $H^{(k)}$ and $G^{(k)}$ are the parameters to be determined in the choice or design of a multiwavelet. We ask for given properties on the multiscaling function and the multiwavelet. These properties are reflected on conditions over the entries of $H^{(k)}$ and $G^{(k)}$, and will make things easier.

2.3   Analysis and Synthesis Processes

The analysis scheme (see Fig. (2)) has 2 inputs (2 images), and outputs 2 branches from the lowpass and 2 branches from the highpass operations. The corresponding formulae are given below.

$$c_{\cdot,k}^{(-1)} = \frac{1}{\sqrt{|D|}} \sum_{j \in Z^2} H^{(j - Dk)} c_{\cdot,j}^{(0)} \tag{5}$$

$$d_{\cdot,k}^{(-1)} = \frac{1}{\sqrt{|D|}} \sum_{j \in Z^2} G^{(j - Dk)} c_{\cdot,j}^{(0)}. \tag{6}$$

$$c_k^{(0)} = \frac{1}{\sqrt{2}} \left[\sum_{j \in Z^2} \left(H^{(k - Dj)} \right)^T c_{\cdot,j}^{(-1)} + \sum_{j \in Z^2} \left(G^{(k - Dj)} \right)^T d_{\cdot,j}^{(-1)} \right] \tag{7}$$

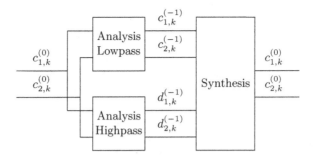

Fig. 2. Analysis-synthesis scheme

2.4   Compact Support

Φ_1 and Φ_2 are compactly supported multiscaling functions, whose supports are contained in a set $S \subset R^2$, that depends on D and Λ, and verifies

$$S = \bigcup_{k \in \Lambda \subset Z^2} D^{-1} \{S + k\} = D^{-1} \{S + \Lambda\}.$$

It may be shown that the supports of Ψ_1 and Ψ_2 are also compact.

2.5   Polynomials in the Linear Span of the Integer Translates of Φ

The smoothness of a scaling function, and the degree of the polynomials it can reproduce, are related [16]. We say that $\Phi(x)$ has polynomial approximation order s if any polynomial $p(x)$ of degree $\leq s$ can be written as a linear combination of the integer translates of Φ_1 and Φ_2, i.e.

$$p(x) = \sum_{k \in Z^2} \alpha_k^T \, \Phi(x + k) \tag{8}$$

where α_k is a column vector of 2 elements.

To abridge notation, we call $S_i^{(j,\ell)}$ the sum of all matrices $H^{(k)}$, whose indices $k = (k_1, k_2)$ belong to coset Γ_i, multiplied by $k_1^j \, k_2^\ell$; and we call $S^{(j,\ell)}$ the same sum over both cosets:

$$S_i^{(j\,\ell)} = \sum_{k \in \Gamma_i} k_1^j k_2^\ell \, H^{(k)}, \qquad S^{(j\,\ell)} = \sum_{k \in \Gamma_0 \cup \Gamma_1} k_1^j k_2^\ell \, H^{(k)} = S_0^{(j\,\ell)} + S_1^{(j\,\ell)}. \tag{9}$$

We list the conditions for polynomial approximation, given in [17] for compactly supported functions:

$$v_{00}^T = v_{00}^T \, S_i^{(00)}, \tag{10}$$

$$v_{10}^T = -v_{00}^T S_i^{(10)} + (d_{11} \, v_{10} + d_{12} \, v_{01})^T \, S_i^{(00)}, \tag{11}$$

$$v_{01}^T = -v_{00}^T S_i^{(01)} + (d_{21} v_{10} + d_{22} v_{01})^T S_i^{(00)}, \tag{12}$$

$$v_{20}^T = v_{00}^T S_i^{(20)} - 2(d_{11} v_{10} + d_{12} v_{01})^T S_i^{(10)}$$
$$+ \{ d_{11}^2 v_{20} + 2 d_{11} d_{12} v_{11} + d_{12}^2 v_{02} \}^T S_i^{(00)}, \tag{13}$$

$$v_{11}^T = v_{00}^T S_i^{(11)} - (d_{21} v_{10} + d_{22} v_{01})^T S_i^{(10)} - (d_{11} v_{10} + d_{12} v_{01})^T S_i^{(01)}$$
$$+ \{ d_{11} d_{21} v_{20} + (d_{12} d_{21} + d_{11} d_{22}) v_{11} + d_{11} d_{22} v_{02} \} S_i^{(00)}, \tag{14}$$

$$v_{02}^T = v_{00}^T S_i^{(02)} - 2(d_{21} v_{10} + d_{22} v_{01})^T S_i^{(01)}$$
$$+ \{ d_{21}^2 v_{20} + 2 d_{21} d_{22} v_{11} + d_{22}^2 v_{02} \}^T S_i^{(00)}. \tag{15}$$

Vectors $v_{00}, v_{10}, v_{01}, v_{20}, v_{11}$ and v_{02} are vector columns of 2 entries.

If there exists a vector $v_{00} \neq [0,0]$ that verifies Eq. (10) for $i = 0, 1$, then contants belong to the span of the multiscaling function.

If there exist vectors $v_{00}, v_{10}, v_{01}, v_{00} \neq [0,0]$, that verify Eqs. (10–12) for $i = 0, 1$, then Φ has polynomial approximation order 1.

If there exist vectors $v_{00}, v_{10}, v_{01}, v_{20}, v_{11}$ and $v_{02}, v_{00} \neq [0,0]$, that verify Eqs. (10–15) for $i = 0, 1$, then Φ has polynomial approximation order 2.

Remark 1. Vectors $v_{00}, v_{10}, v_{01}, v_{20}, v_{11}$ and v_{02} play a fundamental role in approximating polynomials. Once they are known, it is possible to calculate α_k of Eq. (8).

For instance ($x = (x_1, x_2)$):

$$1 = v_{00}^T \sum_{k=(k_1,k_2)} \Phi(x - k)$$

$$x_1 = \sum_{k=(k_1,k_2)} [k_1 v_{00} + v_{10}]^T \Phi(x - k)$$

$$x_2 = \sum_{k=(k_1,k_2)} [k_2 v_{00} + v_{01}]^T \Phi(x - k)$$

$$x_1^2 = \sum_{k=(k_1,k_2)} [k_1^2 v_{00} + 2 k_1 v_{10} + v_{20}]^T \Phi(x - k)$$

$$x_1 x_2 = \sum_{k=(k_1,k_2)} [k_1 k_2 v_{00} + k_1 v_{01} + k_2 v_{10} + v_{11}]^T \Phi(x - k)$$

$$x_2^2 = \sum_{k=(k_1,k_2)} [k_2^2 v_{00} + 2 k_2 v_{01} + v_{02}]^T \Phi(x - k).$$

2.6   Orthonormality Conditions

Orthonormality conditions over the multiscaling funtion and the multiwavelet are:

$$\langle \Phi_i(x-k), \Phi_j(x-l) \rangle = \partial_{i,j} \, \partial_{k,l} \quad i=1,2 \;\; j=1,2 \quad k,l \in Z^2 \tag{16}$$

$$\langle \Psi_i(x-k), \Psi_j(x-l) \rangle = \partial_{i,j} \, \partial_{k,l} \quad i=1,2 \;\; j=1,2 \quad k,l \in Z^2 \tag{17}$$

$$\langle \Phi_i(x-k), \Psi_j(x-l) \rangle = 0 \quad i=1,2 \;\; j=1,2 \quad k,l \in Z^2 \tag{18}$$

These conditions induce the following conditions over matrices $H^{(k)}$ and $G^{(k)}$, that ensure that the whole system is an orthonormal filterbank. This filterbank determines the multiwavelet transform as well as its inverse transform. The orthogonality conditions guarantee stability of image processing operations.

$$\sum_{k \in \Lambda \subset Z^2} H^{(k)} \left[H^{(k+Dj)} \right]^T = \begin{cases} |D| \; I & \text{if} \quad j=(j_1,j_2)=(0,0) \\ 0 & \text{if} \quad j=(j_1,j_2) \neq (0,0) \end{cases} \tag{19}$$

$$\sum_{k \in \Lambda \subset Z^2} G^{(k)} \left[G^{(k+Dj)} \right]^T = \begin{cases} |D| \; I & \text{if} \quad (j_1,j_2)=(0,0) \\ 0 & \text{if} \quad (j_1,j_2) \neq (0,0) \end{cases} \tag{20}$$

$$\sum_{k \in \Lambda \subset Z^2} G^{(k)} \left[H^{(k+Dj)} \right]^T = 0 \quad \forall \, j \in Z^2 \tag{21}$$

3   Properties Reflected on Filters

Lemma 1. *If a multiscaling function has polynomial approximation order s, and $|r| \leq s$, then all r moments of multiwavelets Ψ_1, Ψ_2 vanish, that is, for $i=1,2$,*

$$\int \int x_1^{r_1} \, x_2^{r_2} \, \Psi_i(x_1,x_2) \, dx_1 dx_2 = 0 \qquad 0 \leq |r| = r_1 + r_2 \leq s.$$

Lemma 2. *A multiscaling function (Φ_1, Φ_2), and a multiwavelet (Ψ_1, Ψ_2) verify:*

1. $S^{(00)} \begin{bmatrix} \int \Phi_1 \\ \int \Phi_2 \end{bmatrix} = |D| \begin{bmatrix} \int \Phi_1 \\ \int \Phi_2 \end{bmatrix}$,

2. $T^{(00)} \begin{bmatrix} \int \Phi_1 \\ \int \Phi_2 \end{bmatrix} = |D| \begin{bmatrix} \int \Psi_1 \\ \int \Psi_2 \end{bmatrix}$, *where* $T^{(00)} = \displaystyle\sum_{k \in \Gamma_0 \cup \Gamma_1} G^{(k)}$.

Proof: The proof is carried out by integrating Eqs. (2) and (4).

Remark 2. $|D| = 2$ for the dilation matrices considered. Then $\lambda = 2$ is an eigenvalue of $S^{(00)}$.

Lemma 3. *If (Φ, Ψ) verify orthonormality conditions (Eqs. (16), (18), (17)), and constants lie in the span of $\{\Phi(x - k)\}$, then the following results may easily be proved.*

1. *Both matrices $S_1^{(00)}$ and $S_2^{(00)}$ have eigenvalue $\lambda = 1$ and v_{00} is the left eigenvector associated to $\lambda = 1$.*

2. $v_{00}^T S^{(00)} = 2 v_{00}^T.$

3. $1 = v_{00}^T \sum\limits_{k \in Z^2} \Phi(x - k).$

4. $v_{00}^T = \left[\int \Phi_1(x)dx, \int \Phi_2(x)dx\right].$

5. $S^{(00)} v_{00} = |D| v_{00}.$

6. $\int \Psi_i(x)dx = 0 \quad for\ i = 1, 2.$

7. $T^{(00)} v_{00} = \begin{bmatrix} 0 \\ 0 \end{bmatrix}.$

4   Further Desired Properties

4.1   Balancing Φ_1 and Φ_2

When processing a constant signal one may get unbalanced values at the 2 outputs of the lowpass branch, if no additional conditions are set on the multiwavelet system. This annoying fact suggested the idea of balanced multiwavelets [18, 19]. Multiwavelets are (order 1) balanced if the the lowpass branch preserves 2 equal constant images and the highpass branch annihilates them.

Definition 1. *A multiwavelet system is said to be (order 1) balanced if*

$$c_{\cdot,k}^{(0)} = \begin{bmatrix} 1 \\ 1 \end{bmatrix} \ \forall\ k \in Z^2 \iff \begin{cases} c_{\cdot,k}^{(-1)} = a_1 \begin{bmatrix} 1 \\ 1 \end{bmatrix} \ \forall k \in Z^2; \ where\ a_1\ is\ constant > 0 \\ d_{\cdot,k}^{(-1)} = \begin{bmatrix} 0 \\ 0 \end{bmatrix} \ \forall k \in Z^2 \end{cases}.$$

Theorem 1. *If the multiwavelet system is order 1 balanced, orthonormality conditions are verified, and $|D| = 2$, then*

1. $a_1 = \sqrt{2},$

2. $S^{(00)} \begin{bmatrix} 1 \\ 1 \end{bmatrix} = 2 \begin{bmatrix} 1 \\ 1 \end{bmatrix},$

3. $\begin{bmatrix} 1 & 1 \end{bmatrix} S_i^{(00)} = \begin{bmatrix} 1 & 1 \end{bmatrix} for\ i = 0, 1.$

Proof: First replace

$$c_k^{(0)} = \begin{bmatrix} 1 \\ 1 \end{bmatrix}, \quad c_k^{(-1)} = a_1 \begin{bmatrix} 1 \\ 1 \end{bmatrix},$$

in Eq.(6)

$$S^{(00)} \begin{bmatrix} 1 \\ 1 \end{bmatrix} = a_1 \sqrt{|D|} \begin{bmatrix} 1 \\ 1 \end{bmatrix}.$$

Next, replace

$$c_k^{(0)} = \begin{bmatrix} 1 \\ 1 \end{bmatrix}, c_k^{(-1)} = a_1 \begin{bmatrix} 1 \\ 1 \end{bmatrix}, \quad \text{and } d_k^{(-1)} = \begin{bmatrix} 0 \\ 0 \end{bmatrix}$$

in Eq. (7). Note that for fixed k, $k - Dj$ belongs to the same coset, so that

$$\begin{bmatrix} 1 \\ 1 \end{bmatrix} = \frac{a_1}{\sqrt{|D|}} \sum_{j \in \Gamma_i} H_j^T \begin{bmatrix} 1 \\ 1 \end{bmatrix}.$$

Transpose to obtain

$$\begin{bmatrix} 1 & 1 \end{bmatrix} S_i^{(00)} = \frac{\sqrt{|D|}}{a_1} \begin{bmatrix} 1 & 1 \end{bmatrix}$$

sum over both cosets, and observe that

$$\begin{bmatrix} 1 & 1 \end{bmatrix} S^{(00)} = 2 \frac{\sqrt{|D|}}{a_1} \begin{bmatrix} 1 & 1 \end{bmatrix}.$$

It follows that 2×2 matrix $S^{(00)}$ has the following eigenvalues i) $a_1 \sqrt{|D|}$, ii) $2\frac{\sqrt{|D|}}{a_1}$, iii) $|D|$ (lema 2). At least 2 of these eigenvalues must be equal. Recall that $|D| = 2$, and conclude that $a_1 = \sqrt{2}$. The rest of the proof is trivial.

Remark 3. If a multiwavelet system is order 1 balanced, then is has polinomial approximation order 0. The reverse does not hold.

In [20] order 2 balancing was defined for 1D multiwavelets. We now extend the definition to 2D multiwavelets and for any dilation matrix D. Any discretized order 1 polynomial is to be preserved by the lowpass analysis branch, while detail coefficients are to be 0. Since one step of the analysis branch rotates or reflects an image, we expect the 2D discretized order 1 polynomial to be rotated or reflected. Accordingly, we set

Definition 2. *A multiwavelet system is (order 2) balanced if*

- *it is (order 1) balanced,*
- *for every $k = (k_1, k_2) \in Z^2$, for $m = 1, 2$, and for some $a_2 > 0$, it verifies*

$$c_k^{(0)} = k_m \begin{bmatrix} 1 \\ 1 \end{bmatrix} \Longleftrightarrow \begin{cases} c_k^{(-1)} = a_2 (Dk)_m \begin{bmatrix} 1 \\ 1 \end{bmatrix} \\ d_k^{(-1)} = \begin{bmatrix} 0 \\ 0 \end{bmatrix} \end{cases}$$

Theorem 2. *If a multiwavelet orthonormal system is order 2 balanced, and* $|D| = 2$ *, then theorem 1 holds, and*

1. $a_2 = \sqrt{2}$,
2. $S^{(10)} \begin{bmatrix} 1 \\ 1 \end{bmatrix} = \begin{bmatrix} 0 \\ 0 \end{bmatrix}$,
3. $S^{(01)} \begin{bmatrix} 1 \\ 1 \end{bmatrix} = \begin{bmatrix} 0 \\ 0 \end{bmatrix}$,
4. $\begin{bmatrix} 1 & 1 \end{bmatrix} S_i^{(\bar{1}0)} = \begin{bmatrix} 0 & 0 \end{bmatrix}$ *for* $i = 0, 1,$,
5. $\begin{bmatrix} 1 & 1 \end{bmatrix} S_i^{(01)} = \begin{bmatrix} 0 & 0 \end{bmatrix}$ *for* $i = 0, 1$.

Proof: Replace

$$c_j^{(0)} = j_m \begin{bmatrix} 1 \\ 1 \end{bmatrix} \quad \text{and} \quad c_k^{(-1)} = a_2 (Dk)_m \begin{bmatrix} 1 \\ 1 \end{bmatrix}$$

in Eq.(6), change variables $j - Dk = l$, and obtain

$$a_2 (Dk)_m \begin{bmatrix} 1 \\ 1 \end{bmatrix} = \frac{(Dk)_m}{\sqrt{|D|}} \sum_l H^{(l)} \begin{bmatrix} 1 \\ 1 \end{bmatrix} + \frac{1}{\sqrt{|D|}} \sum_l l_m H^{(l)} \begin{bmatrix} 1 \\ 1 \end{bmatrix},$$

which is equivalent to

$$\sqrt{|D|} \left(a_2 - \frac{2}{\sqrt{|D|}} \right) (Dk)_1 \begin{bmatrix} 1 \\ 1 \end{bmatrix} = S^{(10)} \begin{bmatrix} 1 \\ 1 \end{bmatrix}, \quad \text{when } m = 1,$$

and to

$$\sqrt{|D|} \left(a_2 - \frac{2}{\sqrt{|D|}} \right) (Dk)_2 \begin{bmatrix} 1 \\ 1 \end{bmatrix} = S^{(01)} \begin{bmatrix} 1 \\ 1 \end{bmatrix}, \quad \text{when } m = 2.$$

Matrices $S^{(10)}$ and $S^{(01)}$ cannot have an eigenvector associated to an eigenvalue that depends on k. Therefore $\left(a_2 - \frac{2}{\sqrt{|D|}} \right)$ must be zero, and we have proved 2 and 3.

Now replace

$$c_k^{(0)} = k_m \begin{bmatrix} 1 \\ 1 \end{bmatrix}, \quad c_j^{(-1)} = a_2 (Dj)_m \begin{bmatrix} 1 \\ 1 \end{bmatrix}, \quad \text{and} \quad d_j^{(-1)} = \begin{bmatrix} 0 \\ 0 \end{bmatrix}$$

in the Eq.(7),

$$k_m \begin{bmatrix} 1 \\ 1 \end{bmatrix} = \frac{a_2}{\sqrt{|D|}} \sum_{j \in Z^2} \left(H^{(k - Dj)} \right)^T (Dj)_m \begin{bmatrix} 1 \\ 1 \end{bmatrix}.$$

Set $l = k - Dj$, which belongs to the same coset for fixed k. Transpose and apply (3) of theorem 1, to obtain

$$\begin{bmatrix} 1 & 1 \end{bmatrix} S_i^{(10)} = \begin{bmatrix} 0 & 0 \end{bmatrix} \quad \text{when } m = 1,$$

and

$$\begin{bmatrix} 1 & 1 \end{bmatrix} S_i^{(01)} = \begin{bmatrix} 0 & 0 \end{bmatrix} \quad \text{when } m = 2.$$

Lemma 4. *If the following conditions hold:*

- *the multiwavelet system is orthonormal,*
- *we have polynomial order approximation 1,*
- *the system is order 2 balanced*
- $|D| = 2$

then vectors v_{10} and v_{01} of Eqs. (11)-(15) verify

$$[v_{10}^T] \begin{bmatrix} 1 \\ 1 \end{bmatrix} = [v_{01}^T] \begin{bmatrix} 1 \\ 1 \end{bmatrix} = 0$$

Proof: Sum Eq. (11) for $i = 0, 1$, and obtain

$$2v_{10}^T = -v_{00}^T S^{(10)} + (d_{11}v_{10} + d_{12}v_{01})^T S^{(00)}.$$

Right multiply this equality by $\begin{bmatrix} 1 \\ 1 \end{bmatrix}$, apply (2) from theorem 1 and (3) from theorem 2; deduce

$$v_{10}^T \begin{bmatrix} 1 \\ 1 \end{bmatrix} = (d_{11}v_{10} + d_{12}v_{01})^T \begin{bmatrix} 1 \\ 1 \end{bmatrix}.$$

Similarly, applying Eq. (12) we obtain

$$v_{01}^T \begin{bmatrix} 1 \\ 1 \end{bmatrix} = (d_{21}v_{10} + d_{22}v_{01})^T \begin{bmatrix} 1 \\ 1 \end{bmatrix}.$$

We deduce the following

$$\begin{bmatrix} v_{10}^T \\ v_{01}^T \end{bmatrix} \begin{bmatrix} 1 \\ 1 \end{bmatrix} = D \begin{bmatrix} v_{10}^T \\ v_{01}^T \end{bmatrix} \begin{bmatrix} 1 \\ 1 \end{bmatrix}.$$

If vector $\begin{bmatrix} v_{10}^T \\ v_{01}^T \end{bmatrix} \begin{bmatrix} 1 \\ 1 \end{bmatrix}$ is not zero, this means that it is an eigenvector of D associated to eigenvalue $\lambda = 1$, which is absurd. (Both dilation matrices have eigenvalues greater than 1 in absolute value). Then

$$[v_{10}^T] \begin{bmatrix} 1 \\ 1 \end{bmatrix} = [v_{01}^T] \begin{bmatrix} 1 \\ 1 \end{bmatrix} = 0$$

5 Conclusions

We have given several theorems which translate some properties imposed upon nonseparable 2D quincunx multiwavelet systems on conditions on their filters. These conditions are necessary, and thus simplify the design of such systems. Some equalities which we have arrived at have already been used in the construcion of 2D multiwavelets [21, 12], thus showing their utility.

In the Appendix, we give the coefficients of new example of a nonseparable multiwavelet associated to D_2, having polinomial approximation order 2 and balancing order 2.

This work was supported by Agencia Nacional de Promoción Científica y Técnica, Préstamo BID-PICT 26001, and Universidad de Buenos Aires X199.

References

[1] Cohen, A., Daubechies, I.: Non-separable bidimensional wavelet bases. Revista Matematica Iberoamericana 9, 51–137 (1993)

[2] Kovacevic, J., Vetterli, M.: Nonseparable multidimensional perfect reconstruction filter banks and wavelet bases for R^n. IEEE Trans. Inf. Theor. 38, 533–555 (1992)

[3] Lawton, W., Lee, S., Shen, Z.: Stability and orthonormality of multivariate refinable functions. SIAM J. Math. Anal. 28, 999–1014 (1997)

[4] Karoui, A., Vaillancourt, R.: Nonseparable biorthogonal wavelet bases of $L^2(\Re^n)$. CRM Proceedings and Lecture Notes American Math. Society 18, 135–151 (1999)

[5] Ji, H., Riemenschneider, S., Shen, Z.: Multivariate compactly supported fundamental refinable functions, duals and biorthogonal wavelets. Studies in Applied Mathematics (to appear)

[6] Strela, V., Heller, P., Strang, G., Topiwala, P., Heil, C.: The application of multiwavelet filterbanks to image processing. IEEE Transactions on Image Processing 8, 548–563 (1999)

[7] Plonka, G., Strela, V.: Construction of multiscaling functions with approximation and symmetry. SIAM Journal of Mathematical Analysis 29, 481–510 (1998)

[8] Keinert, F.: Wavelets and Multiwavelets, vol. 42. Chapman and Hall/CRC Press, Boca Raton (2003)

[9] Ghouti, L., Bouridane, A., Ibrahim, M.: Improved image fusion using balanced. multiwavelets. In: Proc. Eusipco. (2004)

[10] Tay, D., Kingsbury, N.: Design of nonseparable 3-d filter banks wavelet bases using transformations of variables. IEE VISP 143, 51–61 (1996)

[11] Ruedin, A.: Balanced nonseparable orthogonal multiwavelets with two and three vanishing moments on the quincunx grid. In: Wavelet Appl. Signal Image Proc. VIII. Proc. SPIE, vol. 4119, pp. 519–527 (2000)

[12] Ruedin, A.M.C.: Construction of nonseparable multiwavelets for nonlinear image compression. Eurasip J. of Applied Signal Proc. 2002(Issue 1), 73–79 (2002)

[13] Feilner, M., Van De Ville, D., Unser, M.: An orthogonal family of quincunx wavelets with continuously adjustable order. IEEE Transactions on Image Processing 14, 499–510 (2005)

[14] Van De Ville, D., Blu, T., Unser, M.: Isotropic polyharmonic b-splines: Scaling functions and wavelets. IEEE Transactions on Image Processing 14, 1798–1813 (2005)

[15] Chen, Y., Adams, M., Lu, W.: Design of optimal quincunx filter banks for image coding. EURASIP J. Appl. Signal Process. 147 (2007)

[16] Ron, A.: Smooth refinable functions provide good approximation orders. SIAM J. Math. Anal. 28, 731–748 (1997)

[17] Cabrelli, C., Heil, C., Molter, U.: Accuracy of lattice translates of several multidimensional refinable functions. J. of Approximation Theory 95, 5–52 (1998)

[18] Lebrun, J., Vetterli, M.: Balanced multiwavelets: Theory and design. IEEE Transactions on Signal Processing 46, 1119–1125 (1998)

[19] Selesnick, I.: Balanced multiwavelet bases based on symmetric fir filters. IEEE Trans. on Signal Processing 48, 184–191 (2000)

[20] Lebrun, J., Vetterli, M.: High order balanced multiwavelets. IEEE Proc. ICASSP 3, 1529–1532 (1998)

[21] Ruedin, A.M.C.: Polyphase filter and polynomial reproduction conditions for the construction of smooth bidimensional multiwavelets. In: Blanc-Talon, J., Philips, W., Popescu, D., Scheunders, P. (eds.) ACIVS 2007. LNCS, vol. 4678, pp. 221–232. Springer, Heidelberg (2007)

Appendix

Here we list the coefficients for a nonseparable multiwavelet system associated to D_2, having compact support, an orthogonal filterbank, polinomial approximation order 2 and balancing order 2.

In matrix $\overline{\Lambda}$ are the indices Λ in column form. In matrix C are given the coefficients of matrices $H^{(k)}$, each one in a row. In matrix F are given the coefficients of matrices $G^{(k)}$, each one in a row.

$$\overline{\Lambda} = \begin{bmatrix} 0 & 2 & 1 & 0 & -1 & -1 & 0 & 1 & 2 & 2 & 1 & 0 & -1 & 1 & -2 & 1 & 0 & 3 \\ 2 & 1 & 1 & 1 & 1 & 0 & 0 & 0 & 0 & -1 & -1 & -1 & -1 & -2 & 0 & 2 & -2 & 0 \end{bmatrix}$$

$$H^{\Lambda(:,j)} = \begin{bmatrix} C_{j,1} & C_{j,2} \\ C_{j,3} & C_{j,4} \end{bmatrix} \qquad G^{\Lambda(:,j)} = \begin{bmatrix} F_{j,1} & F_{j,2} \\ F_{j,3} & F_{j,4} \end{bmatrix} \qquad j = 1 \ldots 18$$

$$C = $$

$-9.202072757022481e-02$	$2.121899192614539e-01$	$-3.954725777710372e-03$	$3.050732143493001e-02$
$-7.514465457226407e-02$	$-1.501198529490192e-02$	$-1.055600014863127e-01$	$7.919401379307994e-02$
$2.460078960178408e-01$	$-3.907089057367634e-01$	$1.814878127692222e-01$	$9.642684711734541e-03$
$2.704598063764237e-01$	$-1.036152467300218e-01$	$3.087840985649198e-02$	$1.953288706290261e-01$
$-1.530481771535136e-02$	$-3.117590584517424e-02$	$-1.078231488603165e-01$	$1.645398796955068e-01$
$-2.071836316067843e-02$	$3.153589099329080e-01$	$2.769471157640822e-01$	$1.313029309495921e-01$
$4.705170528571775e-01$	$2.883840216082162e-01$	$-5.648270794827338e-02$	$8.001126592296544e-01$
$5.384949499360149e-01$	$-2.677240547008755e-02$	$-5.248038262864768e-01$	$5.089069539892260e-01$
$-1.098696199273217e-01$	$-6.480835609334244e-02$	$-7.987014322355679e-02$	$-1.735189889779463e-02$
$-1.283581452772623e-02$	$1.148935249705596e-01$	$3.023278178921931e-01$	$4.924442294682076e-02$
$5.591668901351264e-01$	$1.268323175693516e-01$	$-1.336342718906081e-01$	$9.236548328909892e-01$
$2.742083986591646e-01$	$-2.696188942210803e-01$	$3.851203344633379e-01$	$4.134243672301164e-01$
$3.577543562728547e-01$	$2.319272460242027e-01$	$1.783650995479739e-01$	$5.576340198106872e-04$
$4.714311538824083e-02$	$1.331442953827208e-02$	$-2.657088765319778e-01$	$-2.227748180438723e-01$
$1.248084116957960e-03$	$-1.768774007528323e-01$	$2.903056921572946e-02$	$-1.691414875928634e-01$
$6.254136413863719e-02$	$1.289583247181990e-02$	$1.329864586040654e-01$	$-1.463323343540613e-01$
$-4.174993394180103e-01$	$-1.957627405350867e-01$	$-7.118275776066309e-03$	$8.876751117895430e-02$
$-8.414900602936709e-02$	$-4.144395632526846e-02$	$1.706516469685593e-02$	$-8.294635339676434e-03$

$$F = $$

$1.469604538230460e-01$	$-3.428603302933819e-01$	$-3.583577518720671e-02$	$3.621465911922494e-02$
$1.397840966690090e-01$	$7.920507701229568e-03$	$1.907563895686445e-01$	$-1.777873684399306e-01$
$-4.243151058685026e-01$	$6.182331681731801e-01$	$-2.740288641186419e-01$	$-2.122964778213926e-01$
$1.872393466305442e-01$	$-5.003615108316620e-01$	$1.746023684365583e-01$	$-4.484226745759814e-01$
$-3.662432660878706e-02$	$2.989259410207614e-01$	$6.031718019893548e-02$	$1.100726469376281e-02$
$-8.837327683184504e-03$	$2.114829305693812e-01$	$1.374182290378853e-02$	$4.115264812759586e-02$
$-2.292458776303935e-01$	$4.420477634215208e-01$	$-3.362872183265151e-01$	$8.831836106093453e-02$
$-1.521330446123482e-01$	$-5.667383271306479e-01$	$7.458334877191681e-01$	$4.579633516003656e-01$
$1.904958480463601e-01$	$1.063175625001106e-01$	$1.178308886333611e-01$	$5.634380344158274e-03$
$-1.089102014479069e-01$	$-5.696786989913417e-02$	$1.347825398652045e-01$	$-1.632899811267440e-02$
$8.344824036845477e-02$	$3.584449420872980e-02$	$-5.848449791641036e-01$	$-1.775830776602824e-01$
$2.217608309711699e-01$	$-1.080667840937730e-01$	$1.589459749817733e-01$	$2.001630663883931e-01$
$2.440978779548018e-01$	$1.421112346207536e-01$	$6.023353642819543e-02$	$-1.255965358762427e-02$
$-7.331425054931233e-03$	$-2.222257570720376e-01$	$-1.217984611517955e-01$	$-1.007376266873097e-01$
$4.806097735073317e-03$	$-1.319127320230592e-01$	$1.306868860809642e-01$	$-6.631543195587963e-02$
$-1.241666543750311e-01$	$6.783963670916784e-01$	$-2.584331521488268e-01$	$3.238149150401827e-01$
$-2.570311385404774e-01$	$-1.079552704607635e-01$	$1.879453792989767e-01$	$5.017189737227958e-02$
$1.300023069124928e-01$	$6.741784154038612e-02$	$-7.767912982991730e-02$	$-2.409242445182481e-03$

$$v_{00} = [\, 1 \;\; 1 \,]$$

$$v_{10} = [\, -8.350716093319319e-009 \;\; 8.372684095179815e-009 \,]$$

$$v_{01} = [\, -6.133153913787786e-009 \;\; 6.133363256302630e-009 \,]$$

Mixtures of Normalized Linear Projections

Ahmed Fawzi Otoom[1], Oscar Perez Concha[1],
Hatice Gunes[1,2], and Massimo Piccardi[1]

[1] School of Computing and Communications
University of Technology, Sydney (UTS), Sydney, Australia
{afaotoom,oscarpc,haticeg,massimo}@it.uts.edu.au
[2] Department of Computing
Imperial College London, London, UK
hgunes@doc.ic.ac.uk

Abstract. High dimensional spaces pose a challenge to any classification task. In fact, these spaces contain much redundancy and it becomes crucial to reduce the dimensionality of the data to improve analysis, density modeling, and classification. In this paper, we present a method for dimensionality reduction in mixture models and its use in classification. For each component of the mixture, the data are projected by a linear transformation onto a lower-dimensional space. Subsequently, the projection matrices and the densities in such compressed spaces are learned by means of an Expectation Maximization (EM) algorithm. However, two main issues arise as a result of implementing this approach, namely: 1) the scale of the densities can be different across the mixture components and 2) a singularity problem may occur. We suggest solutions to these problems and validate the proposed method on three image data sets from the UCI Machine Learning Repository. The classification performance is compared with that of a mixture of probabilistic principal component analysers (MPPCA). Across the three data sets, our accuracy always compares favourably, with improvements ranging from 2.5% to 35.4%.

Keywords: Dimensionality reduction, Linear transformation, Normalization, Object classification.

1 Introduction

Object recognition is one of the fundamental problems in computer vision. In any object recognition task, features are first extracted from the images of objects of interest. Then, a classifier is learned using the chosen feature representation. However, in many cases, the feature set tends to be high in dimensionality, posing a serious challenge to the learning process. High dimensional feature sets combined with limited samples can lead to a "curse of dimensionality" problem [1].

A fundamental approach to mitigate this problem is to apply dimensionality reduction before building the classifier. A well known technique for reducing the dimensionality is Principle Component Analysis (PCA) [2]. In PCA, the data in the high dimensional space are transformed by an orthogonal projection

J. Blanc-Talon et al. (Eds.): ACIVS 2009, LNCS 5807, pp. 66–76, 2009.

into a lower dimensional space. This transformation is performed in a way that maximizes the variance of the projected data. In the reduced space, clustering analysis, density modeling and classification are carried out often with higher classification accuracy than in the original space.

PCA has also been articulated as a maximum likelihood solution for a latent variable model, widely known as Probabilistic PCA (PPCA) [3]. However, confusion should be avoided between the use of PCA and PPCA in supervised learning. PCA is commonly applied to data from all classes to find a compressed representation sacrificing the minimum amount of information; density modelling for each class later occurs on the compressed data. PPCA is instead applied separately to data from each class to directly model their density with maximum likelihood. In PPCA, a P-dimensional observed data vector y can be described in terms of a D-dimensional latent vector x as:

$$y = Wx + \mu + \epsilon \qquad (1)$$

where W is a P x D matrix describing a linear transformation and ϵ is an independent Gaussian noise with a spherical covariance matrix $\sigma^2 I$. Factor analysis (FA) [4] is closely related to PPCA, except that the noise is assumed to have a diagonal covariance matrix. Mixture models that extend the above methods have also been proposed including: mixture of PCA [5], MPPCA [6], and mixture of FA [7].

Differently from the above approaches, in [8], we proposed a method for dimensionality reduction within a mixture model. At each iteration of an EM process and within each of the mixture components, the class' data are projected by a linear transformation in a way that maximizes the log-likelihood of the data, in that component, for that particular class. The method proved capable of very high accuracy in an initial evaluation [8]. However, two main issues may arise: firstly, the component densities across the mixture model and across different classes can be different in scale. Secondly, the projection matrix may tend to zero leading to a singularity problem. Hence, it is crucial to propose a solution to avoid these problems; in this case, we propose the normalization of the transformation matrix.

In this paper, we experiment with different normalization methods with the aim of finding the best method for normalizing the projection matrix over three 'hard' image data sets from the UCI repository [9]. Moreover, we propose an approach for an effective initialization of our EM algorithm and we measure its sensitivity to the initialization of the projection matrix. Finally, we compare the performance of our method with that of MPPCA.

This paper is organized as follows: in section 2, we present the proposed method, the different normalization techniques, and the initialization stage. In section 3, we explain the experiments conducted to validate our approach and compare our results with that of MPPCA and the best reported results in the literature. Finally, in section 4, we draw our conclusions and discuss future work.

2   Approach and Methodology

As we mentioned in the previous section, PCA provides a mean to compress a set of samples into a lower dimensionality space by an orthogonal transformation. In analogy with this concept and as an extension to it, we propose to compress a set of samples by a linear transformation that is not restricted to be orthogonal.

In this section, we present the proposed method and the formulas for the projection matrix and the mixture parameters. We also raise the main concerns surrounding the implementation of the projection process, and suggest solutions to address these concerns. Moreover, we discuss the initialization of the EM algorithm and the projection matrices.

2.1   Mixture of Normalized Linear Projections (MNLiP)

We consider y as a multivariate random variable within a high, P-dimensional space, and Ω as a $D \times P$ real matrix with $D << P$. We define the lower, D-dimensional space as $x = \Omega y$ and the density function $p(x)$ in such a compressed space can be modelled as:

$$p(x) = p(\Omega y) = f(y) \qquad (2)$$

$f(y)$ is not a proper density in the y-space, but is a probability function that repeats the probability density $p(x)$ for all points y satisfying $x = \Omega y$. For instance, if $p(x)$ is Gaussian, $f(y)$ has the shape of a Gaussian "ridge", i.e. a D-dimensional Gaussian function that repeats itself along the direction of $x = \Omega y$, in the y-space.

While this dimensionality reduction carries an inevitable loss of information, we hope that it could also mollify the curse of dimensionality inherent with the high dimensionality of y-space. Our approach is inspired by an analogy with sensor measurements, where x can be seen as a view of y made available by a sensor. If the representation power of x is adequate, it permits to successfully study properties of y. In general, if we have an array (mixture) of M sensors, this can offer a richer representation of y than a single sensor. Let us call $f(y|l)$ the score function for the $l - th$ sensor in the array, where $l = 1..M$; it holds that:

$$f(y|l) = p(\Omega_l y|l) \qquad (3)$$

where we assume that each sensor has its own independent view of y, expressed by Ω_l [10].

Let us now assume that we have a way to estimate a discrete distribution, $p(l)$, stating the *quality* of the $l - th$ sensor at explaining the y data. From Bayes theorem, we obtain:

$$f(y, l) = f(y|l)p(l) = p(\Omega_l y|l)p(l) \qquad (4)$$

By marginalising over l, we obtain the probability function $f(y)$ for the sensor array case:

$$f(y) = \sum_{l=1}^{M} f(y, l) = \sum_{l=1}^{M} f(y|l)p(l) = \sum_{l=1}^{M} p(\Omega_l y|l)p(l) \qquad (5)$$

which closely recalls the general density of a mixture distribution. By assuming that the individual sensor densities are Gaussian, and noting $\alpha_l = p(l)$ we obtain:

$$f(y) = \sum_{l=1}^{M} \alpha_l \mathcal{N}(\Omega_l y | \mu_l, \Sigma_l) \tag{6}$$

where the $\mathcal{N}(\Omega_l y | \mu_l, \Sigma_l)$ terms are the densities of the data in the compressed spaces. Moreover, the weights, α_l, the means, μ_l, and the covariance matrices, Σ_l are the parameters of a mixture distribution fit over the l-th compressed space for $l = 1..M$.

Once an $f(y)$ density is learnt for each c class, $c = 1..C$, maximum likelihood classification can be simply attained as:

$$c^* = \arg \max_c (f(y|c)) \tag{7}$$

In [8], we have presented in details the derivation of the re-estimation formula for the transformation matrix (or, with slightly stretched language, projection), Ω_l. We considered Ω_l as $P, D \times 1$ column vectors, $\Omega_l = (w_j)_l, j = 1..P$, and we update it column by column, rather than the whole matrix at once. For example, the re-estimation formula for $(w_1)_l$ is the following:

$$(w_1)_l = \frac{\sum_{i=1}^{N}(-(w_2^g)_l y_{i2} - ... - (w_P^g)_l y_{iP} + \mu_l^g) y_{i1} p(l|y_i, \theta^g)}{\sum_{i=1}^{N} y_{i1}^2 p(l|y_i, \theta^g)} \tag{8}$$

where N is the number of samples, $(w_j^g)_l, j = 2..P$ are the other columns' "old" values, θ^g represent the model's old parameters, and $p(l|y_i, \theta^g)$ is the *responsibility* of the l-th component for the y_i sample [2]. We define our responsibilities as:

$$p(l|y_i, \theta^g) = \frac{\alpha_l^g \mathcal{N}(\Omega_l y_i | \mu_l^g, \Sigma_l^g)}{\sum_{k=1}^{M} \alpha_k^g \mathcal{N}(\Omega_k y_i | \mu_k^g, \Sigma_k^g)} \tag{9}$$

the computation of such responsibilities constitutes the E-step in the EM algorithm. The responsibility reflects the *quality* of the l-th component in projecting and explaining the original observation. Similarly to Eq. 8, we derived the re-estimation formulas for the remaining column vectors. The re-estimation formulas for the other mixture parameters, which are calculated in the M-step, remain as in the conventional EM:

$$\alpha_l = \frac{1}{N} \sum_{i=1}^{N} p(l|y_i, \theta^g) \tag{10}$$

$$\mu_l = \frac{\sum_{i=1}^{N} \Omega_l y_i p(l|y_i, \theta^g)}{\sum_{i=1}^{N} p(l|y_i, \theta^g)} \tag{11}$$

$$\Sigma_l = \frac{\sum_{i=1}^{N}(\Omega_l y_i - \mu_l)(\Omega_l y_i - \mu_l)^T p(l|y_i, \theta^g)}{\sum_{i=1}^{N} p(l|y_i, \theta^g)} \tag{12}$$

Two important issues may occur as a result of the projection step:

- the component densities across the mixture model and across different classes, can be different in scale. By this, we mean that the linearly transformed space (the x-space) does not have a defined scale; therefore, likelihood $p(x)$ can be made arbitrarily larger or smaller by changes to the scale of x.
- as a consequence of this and the maximum-likelihood target, the scale of x may tend to 0 along iterations to endorse high values of $p(x)$. In turn, this implies that the projection matrix may also tend to zero (an undesirable solution that we call degenerate or singular hereafter).

In order to avoid these problems, we propose the normalization of the projection matrix at each step of the EM algorithm. By equating the concept of norm to that of scale, this will make the densities of equal scale across the different components, and also across different classes. Further, this will avoid Ω_l reaching the degenerate solution and act as a likelihood regularization. Therefore, after each EM step, we normalize Ω_l as follows:

$$\Omega_l = \frac{\Omega_l}{Norm(\Omega_l)} \qquad (13)$$

In section 3, we experiment with four different normalization techniques in order to choose the best for avoiding the aforementioned problems. The four methods are:

- L2 Norm (L2): the norm is equal to the largest singular value of Ω_l.
- L1 Norm (L1): the norm is equal to the largest column sum of Ω_l.
- Infinite Norm (Inf): the norm is equal to the largest row sum of Ω_l.
- Frobenius Norm (Fro): the norm is equal to the $\sqrt{\sum diag(\Omega_l^T \Omega_l)}$.

Thus, MNLiP searches for possible solutions over the likelihood space. Every time a solution is provided by the maximization step of EM, we normalize the projection matrix Ω_l in order to keep it on an equal scale. The expectation-maximization steps become therefore expectation-maximization-normalization steps. An obvious disadvantage of this approach is that the new normalized solution might or might not have higher likelihood than the previous normalized solution. For this reason, we monitor the evolution of the likelihood along the iterations and elicit ad-hoc convergence criteria.

2.2 Initialization Phase

In this section, we discuss the initialization strategy for the EM algorithm of MNLiP. It is widely-known that the parameters' values traversed by the EM algorithm during learning (and the likelihood value achieved at convergence) strongly depend on the parameters' initial values. Different approaches have been proposed for dealing with this issue, including: initialization by clustering; running multiple starts and choosing the solution that provides the highest log-likelihood; split-and-merge operations; and others [11]. For our approach, we choose to apply a deterministic initialization to ensure repeatable results at each run. Namely, we decided to initialize the projection matrix, Ω, by the orthonormal transformation provided by PCA, selecting either the *largest* or the *smallest eigenvectors* (i.e. the eigenvectors associated with the largest and smallest eigenvalues, respectively). Projecting the data by the largest eigenvectors transforms them into a space where their variance is maximized and, under the hypothesis that their distribution is Gaussian, the likelihood is minimum amongst all orthonormal projections. Conversely, projecting them with the minimum eigenvectors transforms them into a space where their variance is minimized and likelihood is maximum [12]. Initializing with the largest eigenvectors forces EM to explore a large region of the parameter space before convergence, thus giving it the possibility to find better solutions. On the other hand, initializing with the minimum eigenvectors typically permits a much faster convergence of the EM algorithm.

In section 3, we present the results of classification based on the two different approaches and show how our algorithm is not significantly sensitive to the selection of the eigenvectors for the initial projection matrix. As the data per class are projected to each of the components, the initial parameters of the EM algorithm are chosen as follows:

- The initial mean μ_l and covariance matrix Σ_l of each component are computed directly from the projected data of that component.
- The initial priors α_l for $l = 1..M$, are chosen to be equal across all the components.

3   Experiments and Analysis

This section presents the steps we followed to evaluate the performance of our classifier (MNLiP) over several well known data sets. It also presents comparative results to help position the performance of our approach. In the following, we describe these main tasks: 1) selection of the data sets used for our experiments, 2) experiments and classification results and, 3) discussion and comparison of the results.

3.1   Images Data Sets

The image data sets that we have utilized for the experiments were selected from the *UCI Machine Learning Repository* [9], which is extensively used by the pattern recognition community. Therefore, results can be easily compared with other algorithms provided in the literature. In particular, we selected three data sets:

1. *Vehicles*, which, given the silhouette of four types of vehicles must distinguish between four categories: bus, van and two types of cars, *Opel* and *Saab*.
2. *Wisconsin Prognostic Breast Cancer (WPBC)*, which has the purpose of predicting the recurrence of breast cancer given certain measurements. The measurements represent data from a digitized image of a fine needle aspirate (FNA) of a breast mass and they describe characteristics of the cell nuclei present in the image.

3. The *Optical handwritten Digits* (*OpticDigit*) data set represents handwritten digits from 0 to 9. The feature vectors contain integers that symbolize the number of "on" pixels counted in the 4x4 non overlapping blocks resulting from the division of original image of the digit in 32x32 bitmaps. This gives an input matrix of 8x8 where each element is an integer in the range 0..16.

The reason why we opted for these data sets is that they are all high dimensional, yet different from each other, not only in the number of instances or features (as Table 1 shows), but also in the nature of the measurements and the feature representation. For example, the features in *Vehicles* represent shapes that are measured from the silhouettes (compactness, circularity, elongatedness, ...); *WPBC* data set measures also shape and texture of the cell nuclei present in the image of breast mass (compactness, area, perimeter, concavity, symmetry, ...); and finally, *OpticDigit* presents on/off pixels in a digital image of a handwritten digit. Thus, the selected data sets offer a wide range of diversity to inform the comparative analysis.

Table 1. Comparative summary of the data sets used

Data set	# Features (P)	# Instances	# Classes
Vehicle	18	846	4
OpticDigit	64	5620	10
WPBC	33	198	2

3.2 Experiments

This section presents the results obtained with the proposed method over the data sets presented above. In addition, the results were directly compared with those provided by MPPCA since this approach can be seen as the most closely comparable:

- in both methods, component distributions are Gaussian, maximum likelihood is the target, and the EM algorithm is used for learning;
- both methods offer a dimensionality reduction approach, promising to deliver higher accuracy in classification tasks.

Nevertheless, it is important to highlight the main differences between our algorithm and MPPCA: MNLiP projects every class (original data, P-dimensional) independently into a reduced space (D-dimensional), and subsequently represents each class separately with a probabilistic model in this projected space. The classification is carried out by taking a new datum, projecting such datum as many times as class-models we have, and finally evaluating such projected datum in each of the class-probabilistic models presented in the reduced space. Conversely, MPPCA learns the class densities directly in the original space, but under a dimensionality constraint. Therefore, the first main difference is that MPPCA models the data in the original space, whereas our model does it in the reduced one. The second main difference is that MPPCA determines the optimal solution as an orthonormal projection. Our method, instead, enjoys greater freedom because it attains a solution as an affine projection.

In addition, the results were also contrasted with the best reported results in the literature independently of the classification approach that was used therein.

The classifiers were all trained in a supervised way. The accuracy is computed as the percentage of the number of instances correctly classified against the whole number of instances using 5-fold cross validation (CV). We opted for the 5-fold cross validation because it provides a fair balance between the large bias of the hold-out method and the larger variance and computational load of 10-fold cross validation and the leave-one-out method.

The initialization for the mixture model and Ω_l transformation matrices for each class is as follows:

- The number of mixture components (M) and reduced dimensions (D) were manually selected.
- The transformation matrices for each class $\Omega^{[0]}$ were computed by using PCA eigenvectors of the covariance matrix of the original data $(P$ dimensional). As said before, we experimented with two types of initialization: selecting either the largest or the smallest consecutive eigenvectors so that $\Omega_l = \Omega^{[0]}$, $l = 1..M$. For example, if we have a case with two components per class (M=2) and a reduced space of three dimensions (D=3), we select the three first eigenvectors for the first $\Omega_1^{[0]}$ and the three consecutive ones for $\Omega_2^{[0]}$.
- Transformed data: $x_l^{[0]} = \Omega_l^{[0]} y$, $l = 1..M$.
- Covariance type in the reduced space: full.
- Means, $\mu_l^{[0]}$, and variances, $\Sigma_l^{[0]}$, $l = 1..M$: computed from transformed data.
- Equal prior for each of the components, $\alpha_l^{[0]} = \frac{1}{M}$, $l = 1..M$.

As we pointed out before, the normalization step does not guarantee monotonic increase of the likelihood; hence, we must select a maximum number of iterations to stop. Following a trial and error approach, we observed that accuracy was stable when selecting 250 and 5 iterations with the maximum and minimum eigenvector initialization, respectively. For MPPCA, instead, accuracy stability was empirically achieved after 200 iterations. Also, we tried several combinations of reduced dimensions (D) and number of components (M), having the highest accuracy and more stable results with D=3 and M=2.

Table 2 shows the results of 5-fold cross-validation over the various data sets for MPPCA and for the proposed classifier (MNLiP) with different normalization methods and initialization strategies.

In order to further prove the comparative performance of our method, we show the highest reported accuracy results in the literature for the three UCI data sets in Table 3.

Table 2. Results for the proposed algorithm for different norms (L2-norm, L1-norm, Fro-norm and Inf-norm) and initialization (maximum and minimum eigenvectors). The last column shows the results for MPPCA. Results are obtained by 5-fold CV and are represented in terms of accuracy (%).

Classifier	MNLiP max init.				MNLiP min init.				MPPCA
Norms	L2	L1	Fro	Inf	L2	L1	Fro	Inf	
Data set									
Vehicle	99.9	100.0	99.9	99.9	100.0	100.0	100.0	100.0	72.3
WPBC	100.0	100.0	100.0	100.0	100.0	100.0	100.0	100.0	64.6
OpticDigit	99.7	93.5	99.7	99.8	99.9	99.9	99.9	99.9	97.4

Table 3. Detailed list of the highest accuracy reported in the literature for the Vehicle, WPBC and optic digit data sets. *: MNLiP.

Data set	Source	Validation method	Classification approach	(%)
Vehicle	*	5-fold CV	MNLiP	100
	[13]	10-fold CV	Modified SVM	91.7
WPBC	*	5-fold CV	MNLiP	100
	[14]	Leave-one-out	SVM	91.0
OpticDigit	*	5-fold CV	MNLiP	99.9
	[15]	Hold-Out	Nearest neighbor	99.2

3.3 Results Comparison

First of all, we analyze the results of our algorithm in terms of different normalizations of the projection matrices Ω (see table 2). Though we try to establish a rank among norms, the results do not show any trend that allow us to conclude that certain normalization techniques outperform others. For example, in the case of *OpticDigit* with maximum eigenvector initialization of the projection matrix, the minimum accuracy value corresponds to the L1-norm (93.5%). Nevertheless, the L1-norm presents a simlialr accuracy result to the other normalization methods of (99.9%), in the same instance with minimum eigenvectors initialization. Something similar could be said about the Inf-norm, which presents the highest result in the case of maximum initial eigenvectors of the projection matrix (99.8%) but presents a simlialr accuracy result to the other normalization methods of (99.9%), in the same instance with minimum eigenvectors initialization. For the rest of the data sets, the results are very similar and all with very high accuracy.

Secondly, in terms of initialization of the projection matrix Ω, we can conclude that both methodologies are very similar in performance, only obtaining a result below the average for the maximum eigenvector initialization with L1-norm in *OpticDigits* (93.5%). This confirms that our algorithm is not significantly sensitive to the choice of the initial projection matrix Ω. However, the processing time needed by the training stage is dramatically different, since the algorithm with maximum eigenvectors initialization employs 250 iterations against only 5 of the minimum. Such a marked difference makes us opt for the minimum eigenvectors initialization. The reason for the much faster stabilization of the latter is that its orthonormal projection is typically closer in values to the final affine projection.

By comparing our results with those provided by MPPCA (see table 2), we can see that there is a major improvement for the *Vehicle* data set (72.3% in MPPCA vs. 100% in MNLiP) and *WPBC* (64.6% in MPPCA vs. 100% in MNLiP). For *OpticDigit*, we can observe a slight improvement, from the 97.4% of MPPCA to the best case of 99.9% for our algorithm.

Finally, if we contrast these results against the best reported in the literature (see Table 3), MNLiP obtains the best performance for all the three data sets. Again, the greatest improvement is achieved over *Vehicle* (100% vs. 91.7%) and *WPBC* (100% vs. 91.0%), whereas a minor improvement is obtained for the *OpticDigit* (99.9% vs. 99.2%). Yet, for this data set the margin for improvement is minimal and MNLiP almost saturates it.

Overall, we can conclude that MNLiP always reports a remarkably higher accuracy over the compared classification methods for all the image data sets under study.

4   Conclusions

In this paper, we have presented a major extension to a dimensionality reduction approach previously introduced by these authors in [8]. Our approach provides Gaussian mixture models with a novel EM algorithm capable of learning optimal projection matrices along with the other mixture model parameters. In contrast to PCA or MPPCA that exploit orthonormal linear projections, our method proposes the use of affine projections, thus enjoying greater freedom in the choice of the transformation values. Nevertheless, in the absence of normalization, our approach reports two potential limitations: the Gaussian components do not have a defined scale; and the projection matrix may tend to converge to a degenerate, singular solution. To avoid both problems, we proposed the normalization of the projection matrix within each iteration of the EM by using four types of norms: L2-norm, L1-norm, Inf-norm and Fro-norm. In addition, we proposed initialization strategies for the projection matrix based on the largest and smallest eigenvectors of the covariance matrix of the raw data.

The experiments carried out over three well known image data sets (*Vehicle*, *WPBC* and *OpticDigit*) show that the four normalization techniques offer comparable results. Therefore, we can not conclude that any outperforms the others. However, though the accuracy is largely independent of the initialization of the projection matrix Ω, it is the initialization with the smallest eigenvectors that leads to the best trade-off between high accuracy and number of iterations.

Furthermore, the comparison of our algorithm against MPPCA, which is the most closely resembling approach in the literature, shows the significantly increased performance of our algorithm, with major improvements of more than 27% and 35% on the *Vehicle* and *WPBC*, respectively, and a slight yet significant improvement of more than 2% for *OpticDigit*. Moreover, our results also outperform the best results reported to date over all the tested data sets.

Acknowledgment

The authors wish to thank the Australian Research Council and iOmniscient Pty Ltd that have partially supported this work under the Linkage Project funding scheme - grant LP0668325.

References

1. Bellman, R.: Adaptive Control Processes - A Guided Tour. Princeton University Press, Princeton (1961)
2. Bishop, C.M.: Pattern Recognition and Machine Learning. Springer, Heidelberg (2006)
3. Tipping, M.E., Bishop, C.M.: Probabilistic principal component analysis. Journal of the Royal Statistical Society: Series B (Statistical Methodology) 61(3), 611–622 (1999)
4. Bartholomew, D.J.: Latent Variable Models and Factor Analysis. Charles Griffin & Co. Ltd., London (1987)
5. Hinton, G.E., Dayan, P., Revow, M.: Modeling the manifolds of images of handwritten digits. IEEE Transactions on Neural Networks 8(1), 65–74 (1997)
6. Tipping, M.E., Bishop, C.M.: Mixtures of probabilistic principal component analyzers. Neural Computation 11(2), 443–482 (1999)
7. Ghahramani, Z., Hinton, G.E.: The em algorithm for mixtures of factor analyzers. Technical Report CRG-TR-96-1, University of Toronto (1997)
8. Piccardi, M., Gunes, H., Otoom, A.F.: Maximum-likelihood dimensionality reduction in gaussian mixture models with an application to object classification. In: 19th IEEE International Conference on Pattern Recognition, Tampa, FL, USA (2008)
9. Asuncion, A., Newman, D.J.: UCI machine learning repository (2007)
10. Kittler, J.V.: Combining classifiers: A theoretical framework. Pattern Analysis and Applications 1(1), 18–27 (1998)
11. Figueiredo, M.A.F., Jain, A.K.: Unsupervised learning of finite mixture models. IEEE Transactions on Pattern Analysis and Machine Intelligence 24(3), 381–396 (2002)
12. Bolton, R.J., Krzanowski, W.J.: A characterization of principal components for projection pursuit. The American Statistician 53(2), 108–109 (1999)
13. Zhong, P., Fukushima, M.: A regularized nonsmooth newton method for multi-class support vector machines. Technical report, Department of Applied Mathematics and Physics, Kyoto University (2005)
14. Mangasaria, O.L., Wild, E.W.: Nonlinear knowledge-based classification. Technical Report 06-04, Data Mining Institute (2006)
15. Keysers, D., Gollan, C., Ney, H.: Local context in non-linear deformation models for handwritten character recognition. In: International Conference on Pattern Recognition, vol. 4, pp. 511–514 (2004)

A New Feasible Approach to Multi-dimensional Scale Saliency

Pablo Suau* and Francisco Escolano

Robot Vision Group, Departamento de Ciencia de la Computación e IA,
Universidad de Alicante, Spain
{pablo,sco}@dccia.ua.es

Abstract. In this paper, we present a multi-dimensional extension of an image feature extractor, the scale saliency algorithm by Kadir and Brady. In order to avoid the curse of dimensionality, our algorithm is based on a recent Shannon's entropy estimator and on a new divergence metric in the spirit of Friedman's and Rafsky estimation of Henze-Penrose divergence. The experiments show that, compared to our previous existing method based on entropic graphs, this approach remarkably decreases computation time, while not significantly deterioring the quality of the results.

Keywords: multi-dimensional data, scale saliency, KD-partition.

1 Introduction

Low-level extraction of features on images is a well studied topic in the field of computer vision, mainly due to its importance as first step in many vision applications. This type of features range from earlier ones like interest points and edges [18][8] to more recent affine covariant features [14]. Affine features represent highly salient regions which are invariant to a set of transformations, and have been proved to be useful in different applications, like baseline stereo [13] or object classification [19]. Our work is based on the scale saliency feature extractor by Kadir and Brady [5], which models saliency in terms of unpredactibility by means of Information Theory. It is commonly applied to problems like robot localization [16] and object recognition [3].

Unlike other affine feature extraction algorithms, scale saliency may also be applied to color images and even higher dimensional data. Pixel intensity pdf is estimated from histograms; thus the algorithm can extract salient features from color images using 2D and 3D histograms. Extension to higher dimensions is straightforward. However, this extension is conditioned by the curse of dimensionality, and as a consequence, scale saliency is not appropriate for multi-dimensional data. Recent approaches generalize scale saliency in order to deal with color and texture information [22], but they are very specific and its application to higher dimensional data is not direct. This problem motivated our

---

* We would like to thank Dan Stowell for providing us with information about his entropy estimation algorithm. This work was funded by the Ministerio de Educación y Ciencia through project TIN2008-04416.

J. Blanc-Talon et al. (Eds.): ACIVS 2009, LNCS 5807, pp. 77–88, 2009.

previous work [21], in which we introduced a multi-dimensional version of the scale saliency algorithm, based on entropic graphs [15]. It works like the original Kadir and Brady algorithm; only entropy and interscale divergence estimations were modified in order to decrease the complexity order from exponential to linear with respect to data dimensions.

Our naturally scalable approach allowed us to report results on data up to 31 dimensions. The same results were impossible to obtain in the case of the original scale saliency algorithm, due to its exponentially increasing time and spatial requirements. It in this paper we introduce a revision of our previous work. Entropy estimation is based on the recent method by Stowell *et al.*: KD-partition [20]. Regarding interscale divergence, we designed a new metric inspired both by Friedman and Rafsky's estimation of the Henze-Penrose Divergence [15] and KD-partition. These modifications provide an outstanding improvement to the execution time of our feature extraction algorithm, while not significantly deteriorating its quality. The result is a time-efficient multi-dimensional scale saliency algorithm which is opened to new areas of application. This paper is structured as follows: section 2 summarizes the scale saliency algorithm by Kadir and Brady. Section 3 reviews entropy estimation from entropic graphs, summarizes the KD-partition method and introduces the new divergence metric. Section 4 shows the proposed multi-dimensional scale saliency algorithm. Finally, experimental results are reported in section 5, and conclusions are outlined in section 6.

2 Scale Saliency

Our work is based on the scale saliency algorithm by Kadir and Brady [5], which extracts isotropic regions from images (for an anisotropic generalization, see [7]). These regions, also known as image features, represent the visually salient parts of the image, that is, those parts on the image that are uncommon or unpredictable with respect to their neighborhood. This is the idea behind the work by Gilles [4], that introduces Shannon's entropy as an adequate measure of unpredictability. Given a pixel x and its neighborhood R_x, local entropy is defined as:

$$H_{R_x} = -\sum_i P_{R_x}(i) \log_2 P_{R_x}(i) .$$

(1)

where $P_{R_x}(i)$ is the probability of region R_x containing intensity i. The main drawback of this approach is the limited range of scales in which salient features may be detected. Furthermore, extracted features tend to be unstable.

The scale saliency algorithm extends this idea adding the property of scale invariability. Scales s are represented as different R_x sizes. The algorithm estimates Shannon's entropy for all pixels x and scales s between a minimum scale s_{min} and a maximum scale s_{max} (Eq. 2). Kadir and Brady define unpredictable as rare, and as a consequence, they consider that only those features that are salient over a limited range of scales are salient features. Thus, for each pixel x, the algorithm only selects those scales that satisfy Eq. 3. Entropy is weighted at each of these peak scales by means of Eq. 4, producing saliency values (Eq. 5). Finally, pixels and scales with highest $Y(s_p, x)$ are selected as the most salient features.

$$H(s, x) = -\sum_i P_{s,x}(i) \log_2 P_{s,x}(i) . \tag{2}$$

$$S_p = \{s : H(s-1, x) < H(s, x) < H(s+1, x)\} . \tag{3}$$

$$W(s, x) = \frac{s^2}{2s-1} \sum_i |P_{s,x}(i) - P_{s-1,x}(i)| . \tag{4}$$

$$Y(s_p, x) = H(s_p, x) W(s_p, x) . \tag{5}$$

In the case of color images or multi-dimensional data (several values assigned to each pixel), the algorithm is also applied following these steps [6]. However, pdfs in Eq. 2 and Eq. 4 are obtained from intensity frequency histograms. Therefore, time and spatial complexity exponentially increases with data dimensions.

3   Multi-dimensional Entropy Estimation

The idea behind our approach is to apply an alternative entropy estimation metric for which complexity does not exponentially increases with data dimensions. It is a natural extension of the original algorithm and may be applied in the case of high dimensional data (see section 5). Shannon's entropy estimation has been widely studied in the past [1]. These methods are usually classified as "plug-in", if an estimation of the pdf is plugged into the entropy estimation formulas, and "non plug-in", if they bypass the pdf estimation and estimate the entropy directly from the samples.

In a previous work [21] we made use of a non plug-in method: Shannon's entropy estimation from Rényi α-entropy and entropic graphs. In order to estimate entropy from a set of m dimensional samples $X_n = \{x_1, \ldots, x_n\}$, a minimal length graph spanning X_n is built. Examples of this type of graphs are Minimal Spanning Trees (MSTs) and K-Nearest Neighbors Graphs (KNNGs). In the case of KNNGs, we denote by $M(X_n)$ the possible set of edges $e_{ij} = (x_i, x_j)$ in the class of graphs built from X_n, where each vertex is connected to other K vertices in the graph. The total power weighted KNNG length is given by

$$L_\gamma(X_n) = \min_{M(X_n)} \sum_{e \in M(X_n)} |e|^\gamma . \tag{6}$$

with $\gamma \in (0, d)$ and being $|e|$ the euclidean distance between connected graph vertices. A consistent estimator of the α-entropy of X_n is given by

$$H_\alpha(X_n) = \frac{d}{\gamma} \left[\ln \frac{L_\gamma(X_n)}{|e|^\alpha} - \ln \beta \right] . \tag{7}$$

being $\alpha = (d-\gamma)/\gamma$ and β a constant bias criterion independent of X_n. Eq. 7 approximates Shannon's entropy when $\alpha = 1$. But, although Eq. 7 is only defined for $\alpha \in [0, 1[$, it can be asymptotically estimated [17]. An alternative Shannon's entropy estimation from KNNGs was proposed by Leonenko et al. [10]. For any k, the estimation is given by

$$H_k = \frac{1}{n} \sum_{i=1}^n \log \xi_{i,k} . \tag{8}$$

where

$$\xi_{i,k} = (n-1)\exp[-\psi(k)]V_m(\rho_{i,k})^m \ . \tag{9}$$

being ψ the digamma function, V_m the volume of the m-dimensional unit ball and $\rho_{i,k}$ the distance from sample i to its k-nearest neighbor.

Recall that the advantage of the entropy estimators summarized in this section is that they can be directly plugged into Eq. 2, bypassing the pdf estimation based on histograms. In order to complete the scale saliency algorithm, a substitute for Eq. 4 must be defined. In our previous work we proposed the Friedman and Rafsky's estimation of the Henze-Penrose divergence [15]. It shares with the Rényi α-entropy estimation their underlying data structure. Therefore, entropy weighting and estimation are performed simultaneously. Furthermore, in both cases the time complexity is also slightly affected by dimensionality. Given two sample sets X and O, the Friedman and Rafsky's divergence is obtained from the proportion of edges of the MST (or the KNNG) built from $X \cup O$ that link a sample from X with a sample from O (see [21] for more details).

In spite of the remarkably complexity improvement over the original scale saliency algorithm, practical execution time of the algorithm is still high (see section 5.1). Building a KNNG for each pixel at each scale is computationally expensive, even if a semidynamic graph structure is used to update the KNNG for the same pixel in different scales [2]. Most of this computational burden is due to distance calculations. This fact motivated us to propose a new multidimensional scale saliency approach based on a recent entropy estimation algorithm that no requires distances [20]. Our new approach is completed with a new divergence measure in the spirit of Friedman and Rafsky's method, but inspired by this entropy estimation algorithm.

3.1   KD-Partition Based Entropy Estimation

In this subsection we summarize the KD-partition based entropy estimation by Stowell et al. [20], that we adopted for our algorithm. Although it is a non plug-in estimation based on sample spacing, its main advantage is that it does not require the computation of any distance. It relies on a recursive and adaptive rectilinear data partition, similar to the one applied when building a kd-tree. The samples are splitted into a set $A = \{A_1, \ldots, A_p\}$ of disjoint m-dimensional volumes, and entropy is estimated from the proportion of samples in each volume with respect to the total number of samples:

$$H = \sum_{i=1}^{p} \frac{n_i}{n} \log\left(\frac{n}{n_i}\mu(A_i)\right) \ . \tag{10}$$

In Eq. 10, n is the total number of samples, n_i is the amount of samples in A_i, and $\mu(A_i)$ is the volume of A_i.

The adaptive partition algorithm works as follows (for further details, see [20]). The first recursive call is applied to an only initial volume that contains all the samples. An axis is selected, and the sample median value along that axis med_d is used to split the data into two new disjoint volumes, with approximately equal probability: samples which value in the selected axis is greater than med_d will be assigned to A_i and the rest to A_j. After updating the limits of volumes A_i and A_j, the algorithm is recursively applied to both. In each new recursive call a different axis is selected in order to partition the data. The recursion termination is produced when two conditions are met: a given partition level is reached, and sample uniformity in the current volume is high. After partition, entropy is estimated from Eq. 10.

3.2 KD-Partition Based Divergence Estimation

In this subsection we introduce a new and simple divergence metric, inspired by Friedman and Rafsky's test, but adapted to the entropy estimation algorithm explained above. Recall that in Friedman and Rafsky's test a MST (or KNNG) is built over the samples of the two distributions X and O; then the divergence is given by the inverse of the proportion of edges connecting pairs of samples (x_i, o_j). The idea behind this test is to consider the divergence as a function of proximity between samples gathered from different distributions. Our divergence metric translates this idea to the context of KD-partition based entropy estimation: given the two distributions X and O, we apply the KD-partition schema to split their samples into a set A of volumes, and then divergence is estimated as a function of the difference of samples from X and O in all these regions:

$$D(X\|O) = \sum_{i=1}^{p} \left| \frac{\frac{n_{x,i}}{N_x} - \frac{n_{o,i}}{N_o}}{2} \right| . \tag{11}$$

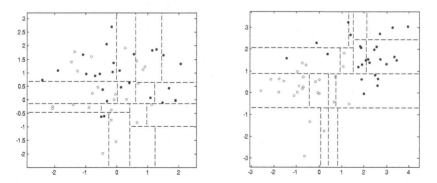

Fig. 1. Two examples of divergence estimation for the case of two Gaussian densities. Left: both densities share the same mean parameter ($D(X\|O) = 0.3462$). Right: the mean of the two densities is different. The amount of regions that contain samples extracted from an only distribution is higher ($D(X\|O) = 0.7692$).

where N_x and N_o are the total number of samples in X and O, and $n_{x,i}$ and $n_{o,i}$ are the amount of samples from both distributions in A_i. This is a normalized divergence, in the sense that its value lies in the range $[0, 1]$ for any pair of distributions. An example is shown in Fig. 1.

4   The Multi-dimensional Scale Saliency Algorithm

Our multi-dimensional scale saliency approach is shown in Algorithm 1. In order to generalize the original algorithm [5] to higher scales, it makes use of the entropy estimator based on KD-partition and also our divergence metric. The input of the algorithm is the set of m features extracted for each pixel on the image; it may be gradient or color information (for instance, the intensity of the three RGB bands), intensity values on a pixel through a set of video frames, or any other multidimensional information. The algorithm is straightforward, and the only remarkable comment should be made about interscale divergence (line 4). Due to the fact that $X_{i-1} \subset X_i$, we may reuse the KD-partition made during entropy estimation in order to calculate $D(X_{i-1}||X_i)$ in this step. The output of the algorithm is a set saliencies in an array HW that must be ordered; then a subset of these will be selected as the most salient features of the image.

Input: A m-dimensional array I containing m features for each pixel of the image
Output: An array HW containing weighted entropy values for all pixels on image at each scale
foreach *pixel x of image* **do**
 foreach *scale s_i between s_{min} and s_{max}* **do**
  (1) Create a m-dimensional sample set $X_i = \{x_i\}$ from the local neighborhood of pixel x at scale s_i in I;
  (2) Apply KD-partition to X in order to estimate entropy $H(s_i)$
  if $i > s_{min} + 1$ **then**
   if $H(s_{i-2}) < H(s_{i-1}) > H(s_i)$ **then**
    (* Entropy peak *)
    (4) KD-partition divergence: $W = \frac{s^2}{2s-1} D(X_{i-1}||X_{i-2})$;
    (5) $HW(s_{i-1}, x) = H(s_{i-1}) \cdot W$;
   end
   else
    | (6) $HW(s_{i-1}, x) = 0$;
   end
  end
 end
end

Algorithm 1. Multi-dimensional scale saliency from entropic graphs.

5   Experimental Results

This section discusses several experimental results aimed to compare our approach with the original scale saliency algorithm. Our execution time experiments demonstrate not only that the time complexity decreases its order from exponential to linear with respect to data dimensions, but also that our approach runs extremely faster than our previous implementation [21]. As can be seen from our repeatability experimental results, these improvements do not significally deteriorate the quality of our feature extractor.

5.1   Execution Time

The Bristol Hyperspectral Images Database[1] was used to test the effect of data dimensionality on the studied algorithms (the original scale saliency algorithm, our previous implementation [21] and the approach introduced in this paper). The image database consists of 29 images built from 31 spectrally filtered images with a resolution of 256x256. Thus, every pixel on the image is represented by a 31 dimensional vector. Our algorithm can directly cope with this input. We modified the code of the original implementation by Kadir and Brady[2] in order to make it able to receive images with more than 3 dimensions as input. The results shown in Fig. 2 were obtained calculating the average execution time of the 29 images on a standard computer as we added image bands, from 1 to 31. Histogram quantization was necessary in the case of the Kadir and Brady scale saliency algorithm, due to the exponential increase of spatial complexity. On the contrary, entropy estimation from KNNGs or KD-Partitions do not require intensity quantization.

As expected, the execution time of Kadir and Brady algorithm exponentially increases, due to the fact that the complexity of this algorithm is $O(n^m)$. This is not the case of the other two tested algorithms. The expected complexity of the approach in [21] is $O(kn + n \log n)$, while the KD-partition estimation complexity is $O(n \log n)$. Their execution time increases linearly with the number of dimensions. The noticeably lower execution time of KD-partition scale saliency makes it a feasible method for processing high dimensional data on images. It is impossible to apply Kadir and Brady scale saliency to this data due to time and spatial requirements. And although KNNG scale saliency solves this issue, its time requirements are still excessive.

Fig. 2 compares results for two different scale ranges. This factor strongly affects the performance of KNNG scale saliency, but KD-partition scale saliency seems to scale better under different values of s_{min} and s_{max}. However, scale range still impacts on KDP time efficiency. During Kadir and Brady algorithm, pdf estimation in higher scales is built over those at lower scales. Nevertheless, in KD-partition scale saliency, iterations corresponding to higher scales do not use any information from lower ones. A dynamic KD-partition schema would minimize the impact of scale range in our approach.

---

[1] http://psy223.psy.bris.ac.uk/hyper/
[2] http://www.robots.ox.ac.uk/~timork/salscale.html

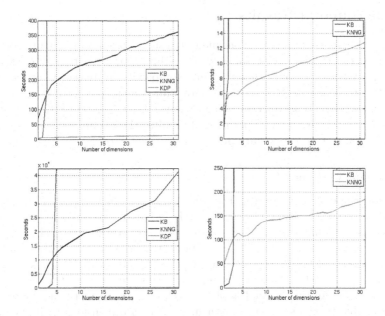

Fig. 2. Comparison of the average computation time between Kadir and Brady scale saliency (KB), KNNG based scale saliency (KNNG) and our approach (KDP), when 1 to 31 bands of the Bristol database images are processed. Top row: $s_{min} = 5$, $s_{max} = 8$ and KB grayscale values quantized to 64 histogram bins. Low row: $s_{min} = 5$, $s_{max} = 20$ and KB grayscale values quantized to 32 histogram bins. In both cases, the right column shows KDP execution times in detail, compared to KB.

5.2   Detector Quality

We tested our algorithm using the well known dataset employed in most feature extractors performance surveys [14] in order to compare its quality with respect to the original Kadir and Brady implementation. The experiment tests the repeatability of the extracted features, that is, the average amount of corresponding regions detected in images under different image conditions. Results shown in Fig. 3 were obtained with an overlap threshold of 40% (two features are considered to match if their ratio of intersection is over 40% after size normalization). In all cases, the range of scales was set between $s_{min} = 3$ and $s_{max} = 20$, and the 1% of most salient features were extracted. In the case of Kadir and Brady algorithm, the histogram quantization was set to 16 bins (as set in the code provided by the authors).

In general our approach provides similar results when compared to the color Kadir and Brady results. As one may expect, our repeatability is slightly lower since our method is based on estimation from sample spacing. However, in general it overcomes the grayscale scale saliency repeatability. There are two sequences for which our approach's repeatability is remarkably low. JPEG compression yields homogeneous regions, that in the case of the KD-partition algorithm produce a higher amount of zero volume partitions. A possible solution is adding random gaussian noise to all pixel values. This noise assures higher entropy estimation

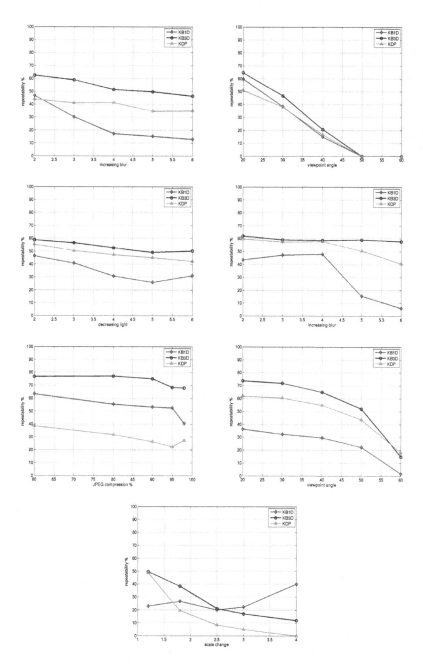

Fig. 3. Repeatability test results for all image groups in the experiment dataset (*bikes*, *graf*, *leuven*, *trees*, *ubc*, *wall* and *bark*), except for *boat* sequence, that consists of grayscale images. The three tested methods are: grayscale Kadir and Brady scale saliency (KB1D), RGB Kadir and Brady scale saliency (KB3D) and our approach using RGB as input (KDP).

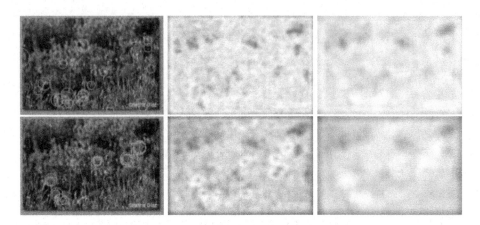

Fig. 4. Color and grayscale saliency comparison. Top: features extracted from grayscale intensities, and entropy estimation for $s = 5$ and $s = 10$. Bottom: features extracted from color intensities, and entropy estimation for $s = 5$ and $s = 10$. In all cases, brighter intensities represent higher entropies. Adding color information helps to search salient objects in this highly textured image.

reliability from entropic graphs in presence of zero length edges [15]. Low repeatability is also present in *bark* sequence, that tests scale changes. Nonetheless, color scale saliency by Kadir and Brady also fails in this test. Surprisingly, color information seem to deteriorate repeatability results with scale changes.

5.3 Discussion and Applications

Although our algorithm can be applied to process color images, the original scale saliency algorithm performs better at lower dimensionalities. Thus, we should look for applications in which the high dimensionality of data makes impossible the usage of histograms for entropy estimation. It is the case of video processing, in which we can consider a video sequence as a multi-band image. Each pixel represents as a multi-dimensional vector containing all the pixel values through the video sequence. Then, scale saliency applied to this type of image may look for spatio-temporal subwindows (similar to the features extracted by Laptev algorithm [9]). Regarding still images, Fig. 4 gives an insight on how additional features may help in processes like object recognition or image registration. A recent image registration approach by Torralba *et al.* [11] uses dense sampled 128D SIFT features [12] as input. Our algorithm can process all pixels in a 256x256x128 image for scales between $s_{min} = 3$ and $s_{max} = 20$ in less than 8 minutes, on a standard computer.

6 Conclusions and Future Work

A new and feasible approach to multi-dimensional scale saliency has been presented. The two main steps of the algorithm, entropy estimation and interscale computation, are based on a recent entropy estimator (the KD-partition estimator) and on a new divergence metric inspired by the Friedman and Rafky's test. Compared to our previous KNNG method, execution time noticeably decreases, allowing its practical application to computer vision problems. By the other hand, the quality of the feature extraction is not strongly affected.

Our future work is addressed to study the impact of high-dimensional data on several computer vision problems. In the case of robot mapping, multi-dimensional scale saliency may help to analyze video sequences in order to search informative transitions in the map. We are also interested in studying how additional features may improve image registration or categorization.

References

1. Beirlant, E., Dudewicz, E., Gyrofi, L., Van der Meulen, E.: Nonparametric entropy estimation. International Journal on Mathematical and Statistical Sciences 6(1), 17–39 (1996)
2. Bentley, J.L.: K-d trees for semydinamic point sets. In: Proceedings of the 6th Annual ACM Symposium on Computational Geometry, pp. 187–197 (1990)
3. Fergus, R., Perona, P., Zisserman, A.: Object Class Recognition by Unsupervised Scale-Invariant Learning. In: Proceedings of the 2003 IEEE Conference on Computer Vision and Pattern Recognition, vol. 2, pp. 264–271 (2003)
4. Gilles, S.: Robust Description and Matching of Images. PhD thesis, University of Oxford (1998)
5. Kadir, T., Brady, M.: Scale, Saliency and Image Description. International Journal of Computer Vision 45(2), 83–105 (2001)
6. Kadir, T., Boukerroui, D., Brady, M.: An analysis of the Scale Saliency algorithm, Technical report (2003)
7. Kadir, T., Zisserman, A., Brady, M.: An Affine Invariant Salient Region Detection. In: Pajdla, T., Matas, J.G. (eds.) ECCV 2004. LNCS, vol. 3021, pp. 228–241. Springer, Heidelberg (2004)
8. Konishi, S., Yuille, A.L., Coughlan, J.M., Zhu, S.C.: Statistical Edge Detection: Learning and Evaluation Edge Cues. IEEE Transactions on Pattern Analysis and Machine Intelligence 25(1), 57–74 (2003)
9. Laptev, I.: On Space-Time Interest Points. International Journal of Computer Vision 64(2/3), 107–123 (2005)
10. Leonenko, N., Pronzato, L., Savani, V.: A class of Rényi estimators for multidimensional densities. Annals of Statistics 36(5), 2153–2182 (2008)
11. Liu, C., Yuen, J., Torralba, A.: Dense Scene Aligment Using SIFT Flow for Object Recognition. In: The 2009 IEEE Conference on Computer Vision and Pattern Recognition (to appear, 2009)
12. Lowe, D.: Distinctive Image Features from Scale-Invariant Keypoints. International Journal of Computer Vision 60(2), 91–110 (2004)
13. Matas, J., Chum, O., Urban, M., Pajdla, T.: Robust Wide Baseline Stereo from Maximally Stable Extremal Regions. In: Proceedings of the 13th British Machine Vision Conference, pp. 384–396 (2002)
14. Mikolajczyk, K., Tuytelaars, T., Schmid, C., Zisserman, A., Matas, J., Schaffalitzky, F., Kadir, T., Gool, L.V.: A comparison of affine region detectors. International Journal of Computer Vision 65(1/2), 43–72 (2005)

15. Neemuchwala, H., Hero, A., Carson, P.: Image registration methods in high-dimensional space. International Journal of Imaging Systems and Technology 16, 130–145 (2006)
16. Newman, P., Cole, D., Ho, K.: Outdoor SLAM Using Visual Appearance And Laser Ranging. In: Proceedings of the 2006 IIIE International Conference on Robotics and Automation, pp. 1180–1187 (2006)
17. Peñalver, A., Escolano, F., Sáez, J.M.: EBEM: An entropy-based EM algorithm for gaussian mixture models. In: Proceedings of the 18th International Conference on Pattern Recognition (2), pp. 451–455 (2006)
18. Schmid, C., Mohr, R.: Local Grayvalue Invariants for Image Retrieval. IEEE Transactions on Pattern Analysis and Machine Intelligence 19(5), 530–535 (1997)
19. Sivic, J., Russell, B., Efros, A., Zisserman, A., Freeman, W.: Discovering objects and their location in images. In: Proceedings of the tenth IEEE International Conference on Computer Vision, vol. 1, pp. 370–377 (2005)
20. Stowell, D., Plumbley, M.D.: Fast multidimensional entropy estimation by K-D partitioning. In: IEEE Signal Processing Letters (To be published)
21. Suau, P., Escolano, F.: Multi-dimensional Scale Saliency Feature Extraction Based on Entropic Graphs. In: Proceedings of the 4th International Symposium on Visual Computing (2), pp. 170–180 (2008)
22. Zhang, M., Lu, Z., Shen, J.: A Robust Salient Region Extraction Based on Color and Texture Features. International Journal of Computer Science 3(3), 142–148 (2008)

Attributed Graph Matching Using Local Descriptions

Salim Jouili, Ines Mili, and Salvatore Tabbone

LORIA UMR 7503 - University of Nancy 2
BP 239, 54506 Vandoeuvre-lès-Nancy Cedex, France
{salim.jouili,mili,tabbone}@loria.fr

Abstract. In the pattern recognition context, objects can be represented as graphs with attributed nodes and edges involving their relations. Consequently, matching attributed graphs plays an important role in objects recognition. In this paper, a node signatures extraction is combined with an optimal assignment method for matching attributed graphs. In particular, we show how local descriptions are used to define a node-to-node cost in an assignment problem using the Hungarian method. Moreover, we propose a distance formula to compute the distance between attributed graphs. The experiments demonstrate that the newly presented algorithm is well-suited to pattern recognition applications. Compared with well-known methods, our algorithm gives good results for retrieving images.

1 Introduction

Recently, graphs become commonly used as an adequate representations for documents, and many recognition problems can be formulated as an attributed graph matching problem, where nodes of the graphs correspond to local features of the document and edges correspond to relational aspects between features. Therefore, attributed graphs matching imply establishing correspondences between nodes of two graphs as consistently as possible. In the last decades, there have been many researches on defining efficient and fast graph matching algorithms [8]. The major approaches for matching attributed graphs include edit distance minimization [10,2,3], spectral approach [7], Bayesian approaches [1], probing technique [6], and probabilistic relaxation [13]. According to [11], for most of these approaches, the attributed graph matching is implemented following 2-steps procedure: Firstly, similarities between every pair of nodes in two graphs, forming a distance matrix, are computed using a predefined measure. Secondly, the matching between nodes is based on the distance matrix using an approximate algorithm such as the bipartite matching [3]. Therefore, the attributed graph matching problem is mathematically formulated as an assignment problem.

In this paper, we propose a new efficient algorithm for matching and computing the distance between attributed graphs. We introduce a new *vector-based node signature* as a local description in the attributed graph (AG). Each node

J. Blanc-Talon et al. (Eds.): ACIVS 2009, LNCS 5807, pp. 89–99, 2009.

is associated with a vector where components are a collection of degrees, the attributes of the node and the incident edge attributes. To compute a distance between two node signatures, we use the Heterogeneous Euclidean Overlap Metric (HEOM) which handles numeric and symbolic attributes. Afterwards, using the node signatures and the HEOM distance, a cost matrix is constructed. The cost matrix describes the matching costs between nodes in two graphs, it is a (n,m) matrix where n and m are the sizes of the two graphs. An element (i,j) in this matrix gives the distance between the ith node signature in the first graph and the jth node signature in the second graph. To find the optimum matching, we consider this problem as an instance of the assignment problem, which can be solved by the Hungarian method [14]. We also introduce a new metric to compute the distance between graphs.

The remainder of this paper is organized as follow: in the next section (§2), local descriptions for graphs and the distance between these local descriptions are described. The proposed matching algorithm is described and the distance between two graphs is also introduced. This algorithm is used to find correct node-to-node correspondences between two graphs, and to retrieve graphs in data-sets (Section 3). In Section 4, we have compared our method with the Umeyama [12] and the Zass's probabilistic [13] methods for the matching task and with the BGMEDG [3] for the retrieving task.

2   Local Descriptions of AG

In this paper, we present an algorithm for reducing the problem of graph matching to a bipartite graph matching problem by means of node signatures. We have taken inspiration from literature, to use an assignment-based algorithm for graph matching [3,9,18,19] by making use of a new node signature. To compute the distance between graphs, a framework is proposed in this section to extract node signatures and compute distance between these signatures.

2.1   Node Signatures

In the literature, the major part of proposed AG matching algorithms deal with global-based representation of graphs. Then, the graph is handled as one entity which can be only one vector[6], a matrix [7] or a string [15]. In few previous work, the concept of node signature has been introduced in [20,19,17], where the node signatures have been computed by making use of spectral approach, decomposition approach and random walks approach. We can remark that these methods using node signatures describe the graph locally.

In this paper, we propose also a local-based descriptions instead of global-based description of graphs. Henceforth, each graph is represented by a set of local descriptions which are related to the node features and used to compute the node-to-node distance. In the following, we denote the local descriptions as node signatures. Contrary to previous works, our node signature is a simple vector and computed straightforwardly from the adjacency matrix.

In order to construct a signature for a node in an attributed graph, we use all available information into the graph and related to this node. These information are the node attribute(s), the node degree and the attributes of the incident edges to this node. The collection of these informations should be refined into an adequate structure which can provides distances between different node signatures. In this perspective, we define the node signature as a set composed by three subsets which represent the node attribute, the node degree and the attributes of the incident edges to this node. Given a graph G = (V, E, A) where V is the vertex set, E is the edge set, and A is the attribute set that contains unary attribute a_i (linked to each node n_i) and binary attribute a_{ij} (linked to each edge $e_k = (n_i, n_j) \in E$). The node signature is formulated as follows:

$$Ns(n_i) = \{\{a_i\}, d^o(n_i), \{a_{ij}\}_{\forall n_j \in E}\}$$

Where $n_i \in V$, $\{a_i\}$ is the attribute of the node n_i, $d^o(n_i)$ gives the degree of n_i, and $\{a_{ij}\}$ is the set of the attributes of the incident edges to n_i.

The set of these node signatures (vectors) describing nodes in an attributed graph is a collection of local descriptions. So, local changes of the graph will modify only a subset of vectors while leaving the rest unchanged.

2.2 Distance Metric between Node Signatures

Classically, to determine the similarity between two entities in multidimensional feature space, a distance metric is required. Although several distance metrics have been proposed [22], the most commonly used metrics are suitable only for either symbolic *or* numeric attributes. These include the *Euclidean* and *Manhattan* distance metrics for numeric attributes, and the *Overlap* distance for symbolic attributes. In our case, the node signature can be expected to encounter a spectrum of different types of attributes including numeric and symbolic data that require more complex metrics. Wilson and al. [22] review a list of well-known metrics based on heterogenous distance function which handle multiple data type. We can classify these metrics into two family. On the one hand, the distances based on the value difference metric (e.g. *Heterogeneous Value Difference Metric*) and on the other hand the Euclidean-based distance (e.g. *Heterogeneous Euclidean Overlap Metric*). Since the metrics in the first family are only used in the classification context and need a learning phase, by introducing class information into the distance formula. Therefore, we use the second family i.e. *Heterogeneous Euclidean Overlap Metric* (HEOM) to compute the distance between two node signatures. The HEOM uses the *overlap* metric for symbolic attributes and the normalized Euclidean distance for numeric attributes. The overall distance between two heterogeneous node signatures *i* and *j* is given by the function HEOM(*i,j*):

$$HEOM(i, j) = \sqrt{\sum_{a=0}^{A} \delta(i_a, j_a)^2} \qquad (1)$$

Here a refers to one attributes of A and $\delta(i_a, j_a)$ is defined as:

$$\delta(i_a, j_a) = \begin{cases} 1 & \text{if } i_a \text{ or } j_a \text{ are missing} \\ Overlap(i_a, j_a) & \text{if } a \text{ is symbolic} \\ rn\_diff_a(i_a, j_a) & \text{if } a \text{ is numeric} \end{cases}$$

Missing attribute values are handled by returning an attribute distance of 1 (a maximal distance) even if of the attribute values is missed. The function $Overlap$ and the rang-normalized difference rn_diff_a are defined as:

$$Overlap(i_a, j_a) = \begin{cases} 0 & \text{if } i_a = j_a \\ 1 & \text{otherwise} \end{cases}$$

$$rn\_diff_a(i_a, j_a) = \frac{|i_a - j_a|}{range_a}$$

The value $range_a$ is used to normalize the attributes. This normalization scales the attributes down to the point where differences are almost less than one [22]. Therefore, we can remark that the definition of δ guarantees a value in the interval [0 1].

3   Proposed AG Matching Algorithm

3.1   Algorithm

As described in Section 1, two attributed graphs can be matched by using the 2-steps procedure [11]. In the proposed algorithm, we adopt the use of node signatures and an assignment problem. Note that, the distances between node signatures and the Hungarian method [14] (for solving the assignment problem) correspond to the first and the second steps of the 2-steps procedure, respectively. We improve this 2-steps procedure, by adding a new step which consists in computing the distance between the attributed graphs in a metric framework.

So, in a first step, distances between every pair of nodes in two attributed graphs are computed using the distance defined in the previous section. These distances form a cost matrix which defines a node-to-node assignment for a pair of graphs. This task can be seen as an instance of the assignment problem which is the second step in our algorithm. The assignment problem can be solved by the Hungarian method, running in $O(n^3)$ time[14] where n is the size of the biggest graph. The permutation matrix P, obtained by applying the Hungarian method to the cost matrix, defines the optimum matching between two given graphs. As third step, based on the permutation matrix P, we define a matching function M as follow :

$$M(x_i) = \begin{cases} y_j, & \text{if } P_{i,j}=1 & \text{(2a)} \\ 0, & \text{else} & \text{(2b)} \end{cases}$$

where x_i and y_j are the nodes, respectively, in the first and the second graph. Using this matching function we compute the distance between two attributed graphs. Before introducing the distance formula we denote by:

- $|M|$: the size of the matching function M which is the number of matching operations. In any case, when two attributed graphs are matched the number of the matching operations is the size of the smaller one.
- $\hat{M} = \sum D_n(\text{Ns}(x), \text{Ns}(M(x)))$: the matching cost which is the sum of the matching operation costs, for two attributed graphs matched by M.

We define the distance between two attributed graphs g_i and g_j as follows:

$$D(g_i, g_j) = \frac{\hat{M}}{|M|} + ||g_i| - |g_j|| \tag{3}$$

This distance represents the matching cost normalized by the matching size, and is increased by the difference of sizes of the two graphs ($|g_i|$ is the size of the graph g_i i.e. number of nodes). We can demonstrate that this distance is a metric satisfying non-negativity, identity of indiscernible, and symmetry triangle inequality conditions.

3.2   Attributed Graph Matching Example

Here, we present an example of attributed graph matching in order to clarify the proposed algorithm. Figure 1 shows two attributed graphs to be matched, g_1 with four nodes and g_2 with five nodes, and each node in the two graphs is attributed by two symbolic attributes and each edge by a numeric attribute. First, The node signatures in the two graphs must be computed. Using the previous definition, the graph g_1 has the following node signatures:

$$g_1:\{ \text{Ns}(n_{1_1})=\{\{\mathbf{a,b}\},\mathbf{2}, \{0.5,\ 0.3\}\},$$
$$\text{Ns}(n_{1_2})=\{\{\mathbf{b,b}\},\mathbf{2}, \{0.5,\ 0.1\}\},$$
$$\text{Ns}(n_{1_3})=\{\{\mathbf{c,d}\},\mathbf{2}, \{0.9,\ 0.1\}\},$$
$$\text{Ns}(n_{1_4})=\{\{\mathbf{d,e}\},\mathbf{2}, \{0.9,\ 0.3\}\}\}$$

and the graph g_2 has the following node signatures:

$$g_2:\{ \text{Ns}(n_{2_1})=\{\{\mathbf{t,y}\},\mathbf{3}, \{0.5,\ 0.3,\ 0.3\}\},$$
$$\text{Ns}(n_{2_2})=\{\{\mathbf{x,x}\},\mathbf{3}, \{0.5,\ 0.3,\ 0.2\}\},$$
$$\text{Ns}(n_{2_3})=\{\{\mathbf{y,z}\},\mathbf{3}, \{1.3,\ 0.7,\ 0.2\}\},$$
$$\text{Ns}(n_{2_4})=\{\{\mathbf{z,z}\},\mathbf{3}, \{1.5,\ 0.7,\ 0.3\} \}$$
$$\text{Ns}(n_{2_5})=\{\{\mathbf{s,r}\},\mathbf{4}, \{1.5,\ 1.3,\ 0.3,\ 0.3\}\}\}$$

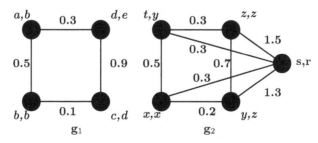

Fig. 1. Two attributed graphs

Next, we compute the cost matrix between nodes in the two graphs g_1 and g_2 making use of the distance described in §2. For example, the distance between the node signatures of n_{1_1} and n_{2_1} is given by:

$$\text{HEOM}(n_{1_1}, n_{2_1}) = \sqrt{\sum_{a=0}^{5} \delta(n_{1_1 a}, n_{2_1 a})^2} = 1.7578$$

The computed cost matrix C between all the node signatures in g_1 and g_2 is:

	n_{2_1}	n_{2_2}	n_{2_3}	n_{2_4}	n_{2_5}
n_{1_1}	1.7578	1.7578	2.0221	2.0320	2.2764
n_{1_2}	2.0011	2.0011	2.0276	2.0374	2.2959
n_{1_3}	2.0055	2.0055	2.0144	2.0199	2.2804
n_{1_4}	2.0044	2.0055	2.0189	2.0144	2.2696

and then the permutation matrix P, obtained by applying the hungarian algorithm to the cost matrix is:

	n_{2_1}	n_{2_2}	n_{2_3}	n_{2_4}	n_{2_5}
n_{1_1}	1	0	0	0	0
n_{1_2}	0	1	0	0	0
n_{1_3}	0	0	1	0	0
n_{1_4}	0	0	0	1	0

Therefore, the correspondences between nodes in g_1 and g_2 can be established from P, and the distance between g_1 and g_2 is:

$$D(g_1, g_2) = \frac{1.7578 + 2.0011 + 2.0144 + 2.0144}{4} + |5 - 4| = 2.9469.$$

4   Experimental Results

In this section, we provide some experimental results of the new attributed graph matching method. We check our method with two kinds of graphs attributes : graphs with only numeric attributes(weighted graphs) and graphs with symbolic and numeric attributes. We start with a matching problem using real world data and numeric attributes. The aim here is to evaluate how the new algorithm recovers the node-to-node matching under structural changes and to compare it with the well-known Umeyama method [12] and the Zass's algorithm [13]. Afterward, we evaluate our graph distance by performing a graph retrieval task. Here, we provide a comparison with the method published by Riesen and al. [3] for two different data sets (images and molecules).

4.1   Node-to-Node Matching

We provide a comparison between our algorithm, the Umeyama method for inexact graph matching [12] and the Zass's probabilistic method [13] because both methods provide a explicit correspondence between nodes in two graphs using Hungarian Method [14].

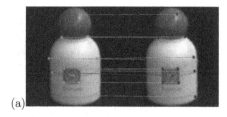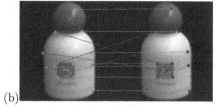

(a)   (b)

Fig. 2. (a) Correspondences with our algorithm. (b) Correspondences with the Umeyama algorithm (green lines correspond to correct correspondences and red lines to false ones).

The Umeyama [12] method matches nodes between two graphs by performing eigendecomposition of their adjacency matrices. The authors compute the permutation matrix that brings the nodes of the graph into correspondence by applying the Hungarian Method [14] on the outer-product of the left singular vectors of the adjacency matrices. This method works only for graphs with same numbers of nodes.

Zass and al. [13] derived the graph matching problem in a probabilistic framework, which is solved via convex optimization and based on an algebraic relation between the hyperedges, the global optimum of the matching is found via an iterative successive projection algorithm.

Firstly, to provide a comparison with the Umeyama's algorithm, we have selected 23 images from the same class in the COIL-100 database [21] which contains the same number of corner points. Here, we are concerned with matching the Delaunay triangulations of corner-features, where each edge is weighted by a numeric attribute representing the Euclidean distance between two points. We use the Harris corner detector [16] to extract point features. Figure 2 (image of 50th object rotated in 320° and in 325°) shows the correspondences between the corners as lines between the two images using our algorithm (Fig.2(a)) and the Umeyama algorithm (Fig.2(b)). The results of the comparison are summarized in Table 1. From these results, our new method provides higher correct correspondence rate from the compared algorithms. Contrary to the Umeyama method our algorithm deals with graphs with different sizes and take into account both numeric and symbolic attributes. In the next section, we repeat this set of experiments using graphs with different sizes.

Table 1. Comparison of the two Matching Algorithms (CCR: correct correspondence rate)

Algorithms	Correct correspondences	False correspondences	CCR
Umeyama	2120	916	69.83%
Zass	2222	814	73.19%
Our method	2525	511	**83.17%**

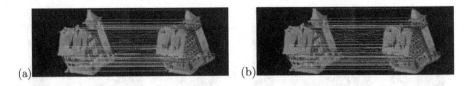

Fig. 3. (a) Correspondences with our algorithm. (b) Correspondences with the Zass algorithm (green lines correspond to correct correspondences and red lines to false ones).

Table 2. Comparison of the two Matching Algorithms (CCR: correct correspondence rate)

Algorithms	Correct correspondences	False correspondences	CCR
Zass	1474	1162	55.92%
Our method	1658	978	**62.90%**

Secondly, we use the CMU/VASC model-house sequence database which contains 9 images corresponding to different camera viewing directions. The graphs are obtained by the Delaunay triangulations based on the Harris [16] corner points. Figure 3 shows an example of the results obtained when we match two images using our method and the Zass method. From these results, it is clear that the new method returns considerably better matches (see table 2).

From the two previous set of experiments, our method has shown good flexibility and robustness among different data sets. In fact, in the model-house sequence database there are clearly significant structural differences in the graphs in comparison to the selected subset from the COIL-100 database. For these two graph sets our new method provides good results.

4.2   Graph Retrieval

Here, the retrieval performance is evaluated on four databases from the IAM graph database repository [4]:

- The COIL-RAG database (7200 images, 72 classes) consists of COIL-100 database where images are transformed into region adjacency graphs. Each region corresponds to a node linked with attributes specifying the color histogram, and adjacent regions correspond to the edges which are attributed with the length of the common border.
- The Mutagenicity database consists of 4337 graphs (2 classes) representing molecular compounds, the nodes represent the atoms labeled with the corresponding chemical symbol and edges by valence of linkage.
- The Letter database (3000 graphs, 15 classes) involves graphs that represent distorted letter drawings. Each distorted letter correspond to a graph by representing lines by edges and ending points of lines by nodes. The nodes are labeled by two-dimensional attribute giving its position.

– The GREC database [5](1100 images, 22 classes) which consists of graphs representing symbols from architectural and electronic drawings. Here the ending points (ie corners, intersections and circles) are represented by nodes which are connected by undirected edges and labeled as lines or arcs.

In Table 3, we synthesize the types of the attributes (symbolic or numeric) present in the edges and the nodes of the graphs in each database. For example, the graphs in the GREC database are composed by symbolic and numeric attributes assigned to the nodes and the edges.

Table 3. Synthesis of attributes types in the used databases.(E: Edge, N: Node)

	COIL-RAG	Mutagenicity	Letter	GREC
Symbolic		N		E,N
Numeric	E,N	E	N	E,N

In these experiments, the receiver-operating curve (ROC) is used to measure retrieval performances. The ROC curve is formed by Precision rate against Recall rate. Precision rate is the ratio of the number of correct images to the number of retrieved images. Recall is the ratio of the number of correct images to the total number of correct images in the database. We provide a comparison between our method and the Riesen and al. method [3] which consider (as our approach) the graph matching as an instance of an assignment problem. However, in their method (called BGMEDG) a bipartite graph matching is proposed to compute the edit distance of graphs. More precisely, the method computes the edit distance between two graphs based on a bipartite graph matching by means of the Hungarian algorithm and provides only sub-optimal edit distance results. Therefore, this algorithm requires predefined cost functions to define the node-to-node and edge-to-edge costs. Then, the Hungarian algorithm is applied to this matrix to find an edit path which consists in the minimum-cost node assignment.

Figure 4 shows the Precision-Recall curves obtained by applying the new method and the BGMEDG method on the different databases. The cost functions of the BGMEDG method have been defined empirically. These results note that our method outperforms the BGMEDG on three databases among four. Especially, the results on the GREC database, when nodes and edges contain combined symbolic and numeric attributes, demonstrate that our node signatures are flexible and robust against different type of attributes. However, our method fails on the Mutagenicity database, but the performance is quite similar to the other approach.

Finally, we can note that the extracted node signatures provide good structural local descriptions of the graphs. In addition, when both nodes and edges are labeled by combined symbolic and numeric attributes, the concept of node signature becomes more significant and its stored information becomes more discriminant.

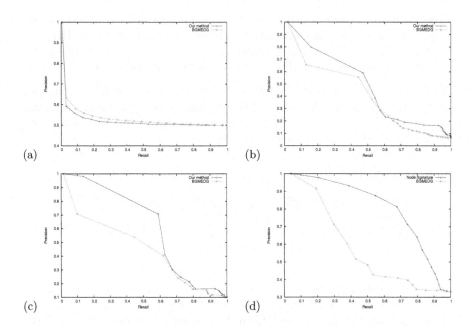

Fig. 4. Precision-Recall curves on different databases :(a) Mutagenicity. (b) Letter. (c) COIL-RAG. (d) GREC.

5   Conclusion

In this work, we propose a new attributed graph matching technique based on node signatures describing local information in the graphs. We construct a cost matrix based on the distance between each pair of nodes in two graphs. To compute the distance between two graphs defined with symbolic and numeric attributes we have used the *Heterogeneous Euclidean Overlap Metric*. The optimum matching is computed using the Hungarian algorithm and based on a proposed metric graph distance. Experimentally, we have proved that our method performs node-to-node correspondences between two graphs, and provides good results to retrieve different kind of images represented by attributed graphs.

Acknowledgments. This research is partially supported by the French National Research Agency project NAVIDOMASS referenced under ANR-06-MCDA-012 and Lorraine region.

References

1. Myers, R., Wilson, R.C., Hancock, E.R.: Bayesian Graph Edit Distance. IEEE Trans. Pattern Anal. Mach. Intell. 22(6), 628–635 (2000)
2. Neuhaus, M., Bunke, H.: Edit distance-based kernel functions for structural pattern classification. Pattern Recognition 39(10), 1852–1863 (2006)

3. Riesen, K., Bunke, H.: Approximate graph edit distance computation by means of bipartite graph matching. Image Vis. Comput. (2008), doi:10.1016/j.imavis.2008.04.004

4. Riesen, K., Bunke, H.: IAM Graph Database Repository for Graph Based Pattern Recognition and Machine Learning. In: IAPR Workshop SSPR & SPR, pp. 287–297 (2008)

5. Dosch, P., Valveny, E.: Report on the Second Symbol Recognition Contest. In: Proc. 6th IAPR Workshop on Graphics Recognition, pp. 381–397 (2005)

6. Lopresti, D., Wilfong, G.: A fast technique for comparing graph representations with applications to performance evaluation. International Journal on Document Analysis and Recognition 6(4), 219–229 (2004)

7. Shi, J., Malik, J.: Self Inducing Relational Distance and Its Application to Image Segmentation. In: Burkhardt, H.-J., Neumann, B. (eds.) ECCV 1998. LNCS, vol. 1406, pp. 528–543. Springer, Heidelberg (1998)

8. Conte, D., Foggia, P., Sansone, C., Vento, M.: Thirty Years of Graph Matching in Pattern Recognition. Int'l J. Pattern Recognition and Artificial Intelligence 18(3), 265–298 (2004)

9. Jouili, S., Tabbone, S.: Graph matching using node signatures. In: Torsello, A., Escolano, F., Brun, L. (eds.) GbRPR 2009. LNCS, vol. 5534, pp. 154–163. Springer, Heidelberg (2009)

10. Sanfeliu, A., Fu, K.-S.: A Distance Measure between Attributed Relational Graphs for Pattern Recognition. IEEE Transactions on Systems, Man and Cybernetics 13, 353–362 (1983)

11. Kim, D.H., Yun, I.D., Lee, S.U.: A New Attributed Relational Graph Matching Algorithm Using the Nested Structure of Earth Mover's Distance. In: 17th International Conference on Pattern Recognition, pp. 48–51 (2004)

12. Umeyama, S.: An eigendecomposition approach to weighted graph matching problems. IEEE Trans. Pattern Anal. Mach. Intell. 10(5), 695–703 (1988)

13. Zass, R., Shashua, A.: Probabilistic graph and hypergraph matching. In: IEEE Conference on Computer Vision and Pattern Recognition, pp. 1–8 (2008)

14. Kuhn, H.W.: The Hungarian method for the assignment problem. Naval Research Logistic Quarterly 2, 83–97 (1955)

15. Robles-Kelly, A., Hancock, E.R.: Graph edit distance from spectral seriation. IEEE Trans. Pattern Anal. Mach. Intell. 27(3), 365–378 (2005)

16. Harris, C., Stephens, M.: A combined corner and edge detection. In: Proceeding of the 4th Alvey Vision Conference, pp. 189–192 (1988)

17. Gori, M., Maggini, M., Sarti, L.: Exact and Approximate graph matching using random walks. IEEE Trans. Pattern Anal. Mach. Intell. 27(7), 1100–1111 (2005)

18. Gold, S., Rangarajan, A.: A graduated assignment algorithm for graph matching. IEEE Trans. Pattern Anal. Mach. Intell. 18(4), 377–388 (1996)

19. Shokoufandeh, A., Dickinson, S.: Applications of Bipartite Matching to Problems in Object Recognition. In: Proceedings of ICCV Workshop on Graph Algorithms and Computer Vision, September 21 (1999)

20. Eshera, M.A., Fu, K.S.: A graph distance measure for image analysis. IEEE Trans. Syst. Man Cybern. 14, 398–408 (1984)

21. Nene, S.A., Nayar, S.K., Murase, H.: Columbia Object Image Library (COIL-100), Technical report, Columbia Univ. (1996)

22. Wilson, D.R., Martinez, T.R.: Improved heterogeneous distance functions. Journal of Artificial Intelligence Research 6(1), 1–34 (1997)

A Template Analysis Methodology to Improve the Efficiency of Fast Matching Algorithms

Federico Tombari, Stefano Mattoccia, Luigi Di Stefano,
Fabio Regoli, and Riccardo Viti

Department of Electronics Computer Science and Systems (DEIS)
Advanced Research Center on Electronic Systems (ARCES)
University of Bologna, Italy
{federico.tombari,stefano.mattoccia,luigi.distefano}@unibo.it,
{fabio.regoli,riccardo.viti}@studio.unibo.it
www.vision.deis.unibo.it

Abstract. Several methods aimed at effectively speeding up the block matching and template matching tasks have been recently proposed. A class of these methods, referred to as exhaustive due to the fact that they optimally solve the minimization problem of the matching cost, often deploys a succession of bounding functions based on a partitioning of the template and subwindow to perform rapid and reliable detection of non-optimal candidates. In this paper we propose a study aimed at improving the efficiency of one of these methods, that is, a state-of-the-art template matching technique known as *Incremental Dissimilarity Approximations* (IDA). In particular, we outline a methodology to order the succession of bounding functions deployed by this technique based on the analysis of the template only. Experimental results prove that the proposed approach is able to achieve improved efficiency.

1 Introduction and Previous Work

Template matching and block matching are two classical image analysis problems that occur in countless vision applications. Template matching is widely deployed for tasks such as quality control, defect detection, robot navigation, face and object recognition, edge detection. On the other hand, block matching is a common approach adopted, e.g., for the purpose of motion estimation in video compression, so as to reduce temporal redundancy in video sequences.

Template matching and block matching inherently rely on a matching cost that, once minimized (or maximized, in case a similarity measure is deployed) allows locating the position of the template in the search space. Commonly used matching costs are those derived from the L_p norm:

$$\delta_p(x,y) = ||I_s(x,y) - T||_p^p = \sum_{i=1}^{M}\sum_{j=1}^{N}|I(x+i,y+j) - T(i,j)|^p \qquad (1)$$

where T is the template to be found and $I(x,y)$ is the image *subwindow* at location (x,y), both of size $M \times N$, while $|| \cdot ||_p$ denotes the L_p norm. If $p = 1$

J. Blanc-Talon et al. (Eds.): ACIVS 2009, LNCS 5807, pp. 100–108, 2009.

then $\delta_p(x, y)$ is the *Sum of Absolute Differences* (SAD), while by taking $p = 2$ it becomes the *Sum of Squared Differences* (SSD).

Since this task is usually computationally expensive, several methods have been recently proposed with the aim of rendering this minimization procedure more efficient. Within them, a class of methods is referred to as exhaustive since they optimally solve the problem by guaranteeing that the minimum they find is always the global one [2], [4], [5], [3], [7], [6], [8], [9]. One of the first exhaustive methods ever proposed is *Partial Distortion Elimination* (PDE) [9], which simply terminates the computation of the SAD function once the error becomes higher than the current minimum. Then, Li and Salari [1] proposed a method that deploys the triangular inequality to rapidly detect non-optimal candidates based on the SAD measure. Successive proposals tried to improve Li and Salari's performance by using partitioning schemes and relying on several more sophisticated bounding functions computed on corresponding parts of the template and subwindow.

Some of these techniques apply an iterative refinement of the bounding function based either on multilevel schemes [4], [7] or on the concept of partial cost [2], [9]. It is interesting to note that very few investigations have been performed so far on which parts of the template and subwindow should be analyzed first during this iterative process. As a matter of facts, the majority of these methods simply analyses the partitions in a sequential manner. In [10] an improvement of the PDE method is proposed that relies on the analysis of the image subwindow $I(x, y)$ in order to detect the regions of the subwindow where the matching cost should be computed first.

In this paper, we propose an analysis aimed at improving the performance of a state-of-the-art template matching technique known as *Incremental Dissimilarity Approximations* (IDA) [2]. In particular, we present here a strategy to optimally select on which parts of the template and subwindow the matching cost should be computed first. A relevant aspect is that the analysis is carried out on the template only, so that it can be regarded as an offline stage of the algorithm and therefore does not yield any computational overhead at runtime. The paper is structured as follows. Section 2 reviews the IDA technique, while Section 3 describes the proposed approach. Then, 4 presents experimental results aimed at assessing the improvements yielded by the proposed method.

2   The IDA Algorithm

The IDA technique is an exhaustive technique that aims at speeding up template matching based on matching costs derived from the L_p norm and relies on the *triangular inequality*:

$$||I_s(x, y) - T||_p^p \geq \left| ||I_s(x, y)||_p - ||T||_p \right|^p \tag{2}$$

Hence, the right-hand term, hereinafter recalled as $\beta_p(x, y)$, is a lower-bound of $\delta_p(x, y)$. Let's now consider a partitioning of the template and the image subwindow into r disjoint regions. In order to increase the computational efficiency, IDA deploys regions made out of successive rows and characterized by equal

number of rows, n (under the assumption that N is a multiple of r). Let the
partial bound term computed between rows (ρ, θ) be defined as:

$$\beta_p(x,y)|_\rho^\theta = \left| \|I_s(x,y)\|_p \right|_\rho^\theta - \|T\|_p \Big|_\rho^\theta \Big|^p =$$
$$\Big| \Big[\sum_{i=1}^{M} \sum_{j=\rho}^{\theta} |I(x+i, y+j)|^p \Big]^{\frac{1}{p}} - \Big[\sum_{i=1}^{M} \sum_{j=\rho}^{\theta} |T(i,j)|^p \Big]^{\frac{1}{p}} \Big|^p \tag{3}$$

and the *partial dissimilarity* term between rows (ρ, θ) be defined as:

$$\delta_p(x,y)|_\rho^\theta = \|I_s(x,y) - T\|_p^p \Big|_\rho^\theta = \sum_{i=1}^{M} \sum_{j=\rho}^{\theta} |I(x+i, y+j) - T(i,j)|^p \tag{4}$$

It is possible to compute (3) on each of the r regions defined on the template
and image subwindow and to sum up these terms:

$$\beta_{p,r}(x,y)|_1^N = \sum_{t=1}^{r} \beta_p(x,y)|_{(t-1)\cdot n+1}^{t\cdot n} \tag{5}$$

so as to yield a lower bound of the $\delta_p(x,y)$ function which is *tighter* than (2),
i.e.:

$$\delta_p(x,y) \geq \beta_{p,r}(x,y)|_1^N \geq \beta_p(x,y) \tag{6}$$

The bounding property of function $\beta_{p,r}(x,y,n)|_1^N$ can be deployed in order to
select rapidly non-optimal candidates thanks to the following sufficient condition:

$$\beta_{p,r}(x,y)|_1^N > \delta_m \tag{7}$$

where δ_m is the minimum of the distance function *found so far*. If inequality
(7) holds, then the current candidate can not be the one yielding the global
minimum due to the left inequality in (6); thus, the algorithm can proceed with
the next candidate saving the computations needed for $\delta_p(x,y)$.

In the case that (7) is not verified, IDA determines a more efficient sufficient
condition characterized by a bounding function closer to the actual value of
the $\delta_p(x,y)$ function. This is done by computing the partial dissimilarity term
associated with the first region and then using it to replace the corresponding
partial bound term in $\beta_{p,r}(x,y)|_1^N$:

$$\gamma_{p,(r-1)}(x,y) = \delta_p(x,y)|_1^n + \beta_{p,(r-1)}(x,y)|_{n+1}^N \tag{8}$$

yielding an associated sufficient condition analogous to (7). Should this new
condition be not verified either, the algorithm would continue checking other
sufficient conditions characterized by increasing efficiency by substituting, at
generic step i, the $i-th$ partial bound term with its corresponding partial
dissimilarity term. Overall, the algorithm can test up to r increasingly tighter
sufficient conditions, associated with bounding functions

$$\beta_{p,r}|_1^N, \gamma_{p,(r-1)}, \gamma_{p,(r-2)}, \cdots, \gamma_{p,1} \tag{9}$$

Should no one of these conditions be verified, the algorithm would complete the computation of the dissimilarity function by calculating the partial dissimilarity term associated with the last region and then compare $\delta_p(x, y)$ to δ_m. Thanks to this scheme, the IDA algorithm has proved to achieve notable speed-ups compared to state-of-the-art techniques [2].

3   The Proposed Ordering Approach

As pointed out in the previous Section, the IDA algorithm exploits a succession of increasingly tighter bounding function based on the substitution of the partial bound term with the partial dissimilarity term on the current region. This is done by following a naive *top-down* scheme that starts computing the first partial dissimilarity on the first region and sequentially follows down to the last region (*forward substitution*). The rationale beyond this work is to propose a more clever approach to order the computation of the partial dissimilarity terms on the r regions upon some criteria based on the characteristics of the data. In particular, since we don't want to increase the computational burden of the algorithm, the proposed approach should rely on the analysis of the template only, so that the computation of the best ordering of the partition could be seen as a negligible offline stage of the process, that has to be computed once for each template used in the search.

The intuitive assumption, supported by experimental analysis, is that on those areas of the template where the signal is stronger, the partial bound term tends to be less tight to the corresponding partial dissimilarity term. Hence, as a general rule the partial dissimilarity term should be computed first on those regions denoted by the highest presence of signal (i.e. non-uniform regions). In our approach, to measure the amount of signal present on the t-th region, we use a very basic indicator such as the intensity variance:

$$\sigma_t(x, y) = \frac{1}{M \cdot n} \cdot \sum_{i=1}^{M} \sum_{j=(t-1)\cdot n+1}^{t \cdot n} (T(i,j) - \mu_t(x, y))^2 \qquad (10)$$

T (r=4)	IDA standard:	Proposed approach:
$\sigma_1 = 5$	1st	4th
$\sigma_2 = 10$	2nd	3rd
$\sigma_3 = 23$	3rd	1st
$\sigma_4 = 16$	4th	2nd

Fig. 1. Example showing the proposed ordering scheme compared to the original IDA ordering scheme on a template partitioned into 4 regions (i.e. $r = 4$.)

μ_t being the mean intensity value computed on the region:

$$\mu_t(x, y) = \frac{1}{M \cdot n} \cdot \sum_{i=1}^{M} \sum_{j=(t-1)\cdot n+1}^{t\cdot n} T(i, j) \qquad (11)$$

The computation of (10) on all the r regions of the template allows to derive the following order rule: the first region on which the partial dissimilarity term is computed in case the first sufficient condition (7) does not hold is the one referring to the template region with the highest variance. Then, successive partial dissimilarity terms are computed following a decreasing variance order of the corresponding template region. The last partial dissimilarity term, that completes the computation of the dissimilarity term, is computed on the template region yielding the lowest variance. Fig. 1 shows an example that highlights the different region ordering between the original IDA algorithm and the proposed approach.

Overall, since the variance of the template regions can be computed offline, the only computational overhead introduced at runtime by the proposed scheme compared to the original IDA approach is given by the access to the index vector that stores the partition ordering for the template being used. This small overhead has been experimentally demonstrated to be negligible, as it will also evident from the results presented in the next Section. Furthermore, it is worth pointing out that the proposed scheme could be extended to all template matching and block matching methods that include a successive refinement of the bounding term, e.g. as it is the case of [4], [7], [9].

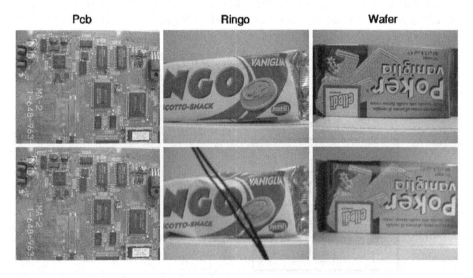

Fig. 2. The dataset used for experimental results. Upper row: images where the templates are extracted from. Lower row: reference images where the templates have to be located.

4   Experimental Results

This section presents experimental results aimed at assessing the capabilities of the proposed ordering scheme to speed up the IDA technique. As shown in Fig. 2, the dataset for testing is composed by three images, where templates are extracted from (upper row in the Figure), and three reference images where the extracted templates have to be located (lower row in the Figure). All reference

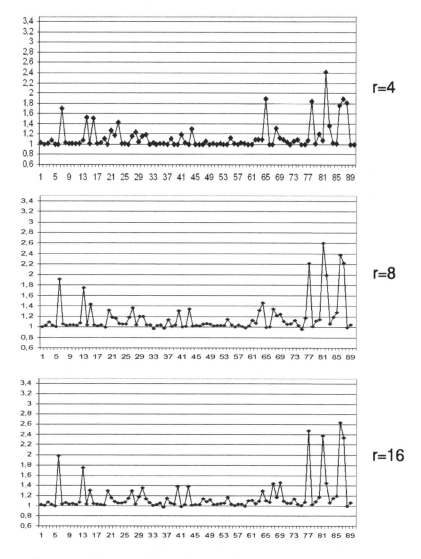

Fig. 3. Comparison between the speed-ups yielded by the proposed ordering strategy and those yielded by the conventional IDA approach (forward substitution) with different values of r. Numbers on the horizontal axis identify different template matching instances.

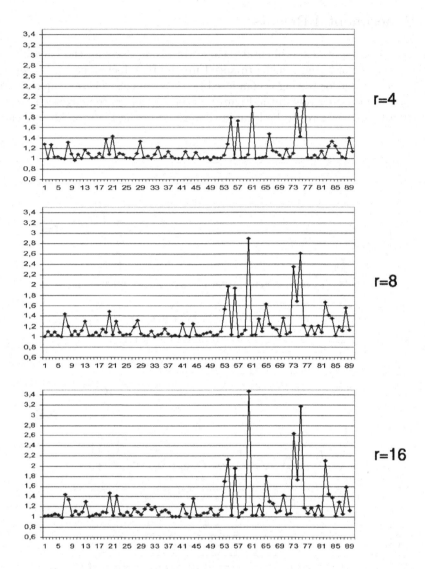

Fig. 4. Comparison between the speed-ups yielded by the proposed ordering strategy and those yielded by the conventional IDA approach (backward substitution) with different values of r. Numbers on the horizontal axis identify different template matching instances.

images are sized 640×480 while all extracted templates are 64×64. As it can be seen from the Figure, distortions between the templates and the image come from different sources such as artificial noise (*Pcb*), different view point and image defocus (*Ringo*), different view point and occlusions (*Wafer*). A total of 30 templates are randomly extracted from each image, using a fixed threshold on the variance of the intensities to reject uniform templates: hence, overall a total

Fig. 5. Templates yielding the highest speedups between IDA with the proposed ordering scheme and the standard IDA algorithm in the forward and backward substitution cases

of 90 template matching instances are tested for each comparison. All execution times were measured on a PC with a 2.0 GHz P4 CPU. All template matching algorithms are based on the SSD measure.

Figure 3 shows the ratio between the speedups with respect to the Full Search algorithm yielded by IDA with the proposed partition ordering and those yielded by IDA with the conventional *forward* substitution (i.e. partial distances are computed starting from the first partition to the last one) for the typical values of the partition parameter r (i.e. 4, 8, 16) suggested in [2]. Analogously, Figure 4 shows the ratio between the speedups yielded by the proposed ordering strategy and those yielded by IDA deploying a *backward* substitution (from the last part to the first one) for the same values of the partition parameter r as in Fig. 3.

As it can be seen from the two Figures, the proposed ordering scheme is effective in improving the efficiency of the IDA algorithm with respect to a naive approach (i.e. forward or backward substitution). In particular, it is important to note that on the considered dataset the reported speed-ups are never significantly lower than 1 (the minimum speed-up being 0.96), while they range up to 3.4. In addition, Table 1 reports the mean speed-ups yielded by IDA deploying the proposed ordering scheme compared to the Full Search algorithm, using the same values of parameter r as in the Figures 3, 4, that demonstrates the notable efficiency of the overall technique.

To complete our experimental analysis, we also show, in Fig. 5, the 10 templates yielding the highest speedups in the results reported in Figures 3 and 4 (i.e., 5 for the forward substitution case and 5 for the backward substitution case). It is interesting to note that, in the first case, these templates show

Table 1. Speed-ups yielded by IDA deploying the proposed scheme vs. Full-Search

Dataset	r=4	r=8	r=16
Pcb	18.3	27.4	31.6
Ringo	69.0	84.8	76.9
Wafer	30.0	49.0	48.2

low-textured areas in the upper areas, with most of the signal concentrated in the middle-low part. This confirms the intuition that starting to compute the partial dissimilarity terms with the forward substitution method yields less effective sufficient conditions compared to the proposed ordering approach, thus the majority of non-optimal candidates requires the computation of more partial dissimilarity terms, that render the whole technique slower. An analogous situation occurs in the backward substitution case, where this time the low-textured regions are those in the lower part of the templates.

5   Conclusions

This paper presented an ordering method for the partitioning scheme deployed by an exhaustive template matching technique known as IDA. The experimental results presented in this paper allow us to conclude that the proposed scheme is an effective way to improve the capabilities of the IDA algorithm, since it is able to achieve notable speed-ups compared to the naive scheme embedded in the original IDA algorithm, and in the worst case it performs as well as the original IDA algorithm. We look forward to applying the proposed approach to other methods such as PDE or [7].

References

1. Li, W., Salari, E.: Successive elimination algorithm for motion estimation. IEEE Trans. on Image Processing 4(1), 105–107 (1995)
2. Tombari, F., Mattoccia, S., Di Stefano, L.: Full search-equivalent pattern matching with Incremental Dissimilarity Approximations. IEEE Trans. on Pattern Analysis and Machine Intelligence (PAMI) 31(1), 129–141 (2009)
3. Mahmood, A., Khan, S.: Early termination algorithms for correlation coefficient based block matching. In: Proc. Int. Conf. on Image Processing (ICIP 2007), vol. 2, pp. 469–472 (2007)
4. Wei, S.D., Lai, S.H.: Efficient Normalized Cross Correlation Based on Adaptive Multilevel Successive Elimination. In: Yagi, Y., Kang, S.B., Kweon, I.S., Zha, H. (eds.) ACCV 2007, Part I. LNCS, vol. 4843, pp. 638–646. Springer, Heidelberg (2007)
5. Pan, W.H., Wei, S.D., Lai, S.H.: Efficient NCC-Based Image Matching in Walsh-Hadamard Domain. In: Forsyth, D., Torr, P., Zisserman, A. (eds.) ECCV 2008, Part III. LNCS, vol. 5304, pp. 468–480. Springer, Heidelberg (2008)
6. Alkhansari, M.G.: A fast globally optimal algorithm for template matching using low-resolution pruning. IEEE Trans. Image Processing 10(4), 526–533 (2001)
7. Gao, X.Q., Duanmu, C.J., Zou, C.R.: A multilevel successive elimination algorithm for block matching motion estimation. IEEE Trans. Image Processing 9(3), 501–504 (2000)
8. Hel-Or, Y., Hel-Or, H.: Real-time pattern matching using projection kernels. IEEE Trans. Pattern Analysis and Machine Intelligence 27(9), 1430–1445 (2005)
9. Bei, C.D., Gray, R.M.: An improvement of the minimum distortion encoding algorithm for vector quantization. IEEE Trans. on Communication 33, 1132–1133 (1985)
10. Montrucchio, B., Quaglia, D.: New Sorting-Based Lossless Motion Estimation Algorithms and a Partial Distortion Elimination Performance Analysis. IEEE Trans. on Circuits and Systems for Video Technology 15(2) (2005)

Enhanced Low-Resolution Pruning
for Fast Full-Search Template Matching

Stefano Mattoccia, Federico Tombari, and Luigi Di Stefano

Department of Electronics Computer Science and Systems (DEIS)
Advanced Research Center on Electronic Systems (ARCES)
University of Bologna, Italy
{federico.tombari,stefano.mattoccia,luigi.distefano}@unibo.it
www.vision.deis.unibo.it

Abstract. Gharavi-Alkhansari [1] proposed a full-search equivalent algorithm for speeding-up template matching based on L_p-norm distance measures. This algorithm performs a pruning of mismatching candidates based on multilevel pruning conditions and it has been shown that, under certain assumptions on the distortion between the image and the template, it is faster than the other full-search equivalent algorithms proposed so far, including algorithms based on the Fast Fourier Transform. In this paper we propose an original contribution with respect to Gharavi-Alkhansari's work that is based on the exploitation of an initial estimation of the global minimum aimed at increasing the efficiency of the pruning process.

1 Introduction

Template matching aims at locating a given template into an image. To perform this operation the *Full-search* (FS) algorithm compares the template with all the template-sized portions of the image which can be determined out of it. Hence, a *search area* can be defined in the image where the subimage candidates are selected and compared, one by one, to the template. In order to perform the comparison and select the most similar candidate, a function measuring the degree of similarity - or distortion - between template and subimage candidate is computed. A popular class of distortion functions is defined from the distance based on the L_p norm:

$$\delta_p(X, Y_j) = ||X - Y_j||_p = \Big(\sum_{i=1}^{N} |x_i - y_{j,i}|^p \Big)^{\frac{1}{p}} \tag{1}$$

with X being the template and Y_j the generic subimage candidate, both seen as vectors of cardinality N, and with $|| \cdot ||_p$ denoting the L_p norm, $p \geq 1$. With $p = 1$ we get the *Sum of Absolute Differences* (SAD) function, while by taking $p = 2$ and squaring (1) we get the *Sum of Squared Distances* (SSD) function.

The method proposed in [1] is a very fast FS-equivalent algorithm, yielding notable computational savings also compared to FFT-based algorithms. This

J. Blanc-Talon et al. (Eds.): ACIVS 2009, LNCS 5807, pp. 109–120, 2009.

method, referred to as *Low Resolution Pruning* (*LRP*), applies several sufficient conditions for pruning mismatching candidates in order to carry out only a fraction of the computations needed by the full search approach.

By analysing the LRP algorithm we devised some modifications aimed at improving the overall performance of the approach. In particular, we devised three different full-search equivalent algorithms, conceptually based on the same idea but deploying different strategies of application. The common point of the three algorithms is to perform a fast initial estimation of the global minimum and consequently trying to exploit this knowledge so as to speed-up the matching process.

2   LRP Method

As in [1], we will refer to the template vector as $X = \{x_1, \cdots, x_N\}$, of cardinality N, and to the K candidate vectors against whom X must be matched as $Y_1, \cdots, Y_K$. Each vector will have the same cardinality as the template vector, i.e. $Y_j = \{y_{j,1}, \cdots, y_{j,N}\}$. In [1], a transformation is introduced, represented by a $N \times N'$ matrix, A, which replaces those elements of a vector corresponding to a block of pixels of size $\sqrt{M} \times \sqrt{M}$ with a single element equal to the sum of those elements. Hence, the resulting vector of the transformation will have cardinality $N' = \frac{N}{M}$ (from this point of view the transformation denoted by A acts as a binning operator). By applying this transformation on the template vector X and on a generic candidate vector Y_j the new vectors $\bar{X}$ and $\bar{Y}_j$ are obtained:

$$\bar{X} = AX \tag{2}$$

$$\bar{Y}_j = AY_j \tag{3}$$

The matrix p-norm, defined in [1] as:

$$||A||_p = \sup_{x \neq 0} \frac{||AX||_p}{||X||_p} = M^{\frac{p-1}{2p}} \tag{4}$$

induces the following inequality:

$$||A||_p \cdot ||X||_p \geq ||\bar{X}||_p \tag{5}$$

By applying the transformation defined by A to the template X and the generic candidate Y_j equation (5) is rewritten as:

$$||A||_p \cdot \delta_p(X, Y_j) \geq \delta_p(\bar{X}, \bar{Y}_j) \tag{6}$$

By introducing a threshold, D, which is obtained by computing δ_p on a *good* candidate Y_b:

$$D = ||A||_p \cdot \delta_p(X, Y_b) \tag{7}$$

a pruning condition can be tested for each candidate Y_j:

$$\delta_p(\bar{X}, \bar{Y}_j) > D \tag{8}$$

If (8) holds, then Y_j does not represent a better candidate compared to Y_b due to (6). Y_b is obtained by performing an exhaustive search between $\bar{X}$ and the K transformed candidates $\bar{Y}_1, \cdots, \bar{Y}_N$ and by choosing the candidate which leads to the global minimum.

The basic LRP approach described so far is extended in [1] by defining several levels of resolution and, correspondingly, a transformation matrix for each pair of consecutive levels. Given $T + 1$ levels of resolution, with level 0 being the full resolution one and level T being the lowest resolution one, first the transformation is iteratively applied in order to obtain the several versions of the vectors at reduced cardinality. Each element is obtained by summing corresponding M elements of its upper resolution level (usually, at the lowest level each vector is made out of a single element, which coincides with the sum of all the full-resolution elements). That is, at level t the cardinality of vector Y_j is reduced from N (original size) to $\frac{N}{M^t}$. We will refer to X^t and Y_j^t as the template and candidate vectors transformed to level t.

After this initial step, the basic LRP is iterated T times, starting from the lowest resolution level (i.e. T). At generic step t first the initial candidate is determined by searching between those candidates not pruned so far in the current level (i.e. t) and by choosing the one which leads to the minimum distance, i.e. Y_b. Then, the threshold D^t is computed as:

$$D^t = ||A||_{p,t} \cdot \delta_p(X, Y_b) \tag{9}$$

with the transformation matrix p-norm $||A||_{p,t}$ being as:

$$||A||_{p,t} = M^{\frac{t \cdot (p-1)}{2p}} \tag{10}$$

Finally the pruning test is applied at each left candidate of the current level t:

$$\delta_p(X^t, Y_j^t) > D^t \tag{11}$$

As it can be easily inferred, the strength of the method is to prune the majority of candidates at the lower levels, based on the fact that computing $\delta_p(X^t, Y_j^t)$ requires less operations than computing $\delta_p(X, Y_j)$.

3   Enhanced-LRP Algorithms

Since LRP is a data dependent technique, the choice of Y_b determines the efficiency of the sufficient conditions and the performance of the algorithm. Our idea consists in rapidly finding a better guess of Y_b compared to that found by the LRP algorithm. If Y_b could be conveniently initialized previously to the matching process, the algorithm could benefit of it by deploying a more effective threshold D^t as well as by reducing the number of evaluated candidates at each iteration holding in the same time the property of finding the global minimum (i.e. exhaustiveness).

Hence, we propose to determine an estimation of the global minimum, $\tilde{Y}_b$, by means of any non-exhaustive algorithm which is able to perform this operation at a small computational cost compared to that of the whole LRP algorithm. The choice of the non-exhaustive algorithm can be made between a number of methods proposed so far in literature, which reduce the search space in order to save computations (i.e. [2], [3], [4], [5]). In our implementation, which will be used for the experimental results proposed in this paper, we have chosen a standard two-stage coarse-to-fine algorithm. More precisely, at start-up image and template are sub-sampled by means of a binning operation, then the FS algorithm is launched on the reduced versions of image and template and a best candidate at sub-sampled resolution is determined. Finally, the search is refined in a neighborhood of the best match that has been found at full resolution, still by means of the FS algorithm, and $\tilde{Y}_b$ is initialized as the candidate referred to the best score obtained.

The use of a non-exhaustive method for estimating $\tilde{Y}_b$ requires a fixed overhead. Nevertheless, this method is more likely to find a candidate closer to the global minimum compared to the Y_b found by the LRP algorithm, especially at the lowest levels of resolution, where candidate vectors are reduced up to a very few elements (typically up to one at the lowest level). Once $\tilde{Y}_b$ has been determined by means of a fast non-exhaustive algorithm, we propose three different strategies for exploiting this information in the LRP framework, thus leading to three different algorithms, referred to as ELRP 1, ELRP 2 and ELRP 3. It is important to point out that, despite the use of a non-exhaustive method for the estimation of $\tilde{Y}_b$, the three proposed algorithms are all exhaustive since they all guarantee that the best candidate found is the global minimum. This is due to the fact that the proposed algorithms throughout the template matching process use the same bounding functions as LRP (i.e. 9, 11) but plugging in different candidates. Hence if a candidate is pruned by any of the conditions applied by the ELRP algorithms, then it is guaranteed to have a score higher than that of the global minimum.

3.1   ELRP 1

The non-exhaustive algorithm applied at the beginning gives us a candidate, $\tilde{Y}_b$, and its distance from the template X computed at highest level (i.e. level 0), $\delta_p(X, \tilde{Y}_b)$. Hence, at each step t, the first threshold D^t is determined by means of $\tilde{Y}_b$:

$$D^t = ||A||_{p,t} \cdot \delta_p(X, \tilde{Y}_b) \tag{12}$$

Then each candidate Y_j is tested with the pruning condition:

$$\delta_p(X^t, Y_j^t) > D^t \tag{13}$$

If (13) holds, candidate Y_j is pruned from the list. Thanks to this approach, differently from [1], at the lower level we avoided to execute an exhaustive search in order to initialize Y_b. Nevertheless, if $\tilde{Y}_b$ has been initialized badly, its use along the several pruning levels would result to bad efficiency of the pruning conditions, yielding to poor performance of the algorithm. Hence, at each level t, subsequently to the pruning test, an updating procedure of candidate $\tilde{Y}_b$ is

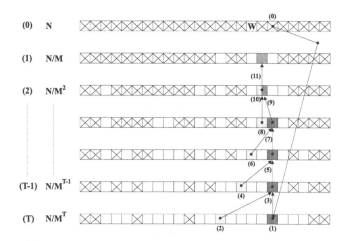

Fig. 1. A graphical visualization of the ELRP 1 algorithm. Each layer represents one of the $T + 1$ levels of the algorithm, while each block represents a candidate at a particular level of resolution. Gray squares correspond to candidate $Y_{b,l}$, while black squares correspond to candidate $\tilde{Y}_b$, each one at its respective stage of the algorithm. The candidate corresponding to the global minimum is denoted by letter W, while at each stage the pruned candidates are denoted with a crossed box.

applied. In particular, we search for the candidate still left in the list L with the minimum distance:

$$Y_{b,l} = \arg \min_{Y_j^t \in L} \{\delta_p(X^t, Y_j^t)\} \tag{14}$$

Then, if $Y_{b,l}$ and $\tilde{Y}_b$ don't coincide, they are compared by looking at their distance at highest resolution, and the candidate which concurs for the minimum distance is selected as the new $\tilde{Y}_b$ to be used for next step:

$$\tilde{Y}_b = \arg \min_{Y = \tilde{Y}_b, Y_{b,l}} \{\delta_p(X, Y)\} \tag{15}$$

It is worth noting that the determination of $Y_{b,l}$ in (14) only requires l additional tests, with l being the number of candidates still left in the list after the application of the pruning condition, since the term $\delta_p(X^t, Y_j^t)$ is already computed for the pruning test (13). Hence, it is expected that ELRP 1 holds the potential to speed-up the LRP method since, compared to LRP, the search space in which to search for the minimum is reduced by all the candidates already pruned by (13). Nevertheless, there might be some cases in which the effectiveness of the bounding threshold deployed by ELRP 1 (12) is lower than the corresponding one of LRP: this aspect, together with the need of an initial overhead to estimate $\tilde{Y}_b$, can cause overall a slower performance of ELRP 1 compared to LRP.

Figure 1 shows a graphical description of the ELRP 1 algorithm. At each level there are K candidates, represented by the squares. Going bottom up, thanks to the elimination conditions applied some candidates are iteratively pruned at each level (denoted by the crossed boxes), while the others are propagated up to the top level, where the exhaustive search is determined on the left vectors and the best candidate is found (denoted by W). At start-up, i.e. step (0), candidate $\tilde{Y}_b$ is determined by means of the non-exhaustive technique and used to prune the candidates at level T. Then, at each level, after applying the pruning condition (13) on the candidates still in the list, the two vectors $\tilde{Y}_b$ and $Y_{b,l}$ (respectively, the black and the gray squares) are compared and the best between the two at highest level (i.e. 0) is chosen (15) as $\tilde{Y}_b$ for the upper level.

3.2 ELRP 2

As outlined in Section 2, at each step t the LRP algorithm performs an exhaustive search between the candidates left in the list in order to determine Y_b as the candidate which corresponds to the minimum distance, so that it can be used for the computation of the threshold D^t. Conversely, method ELRP 1 reduces this search at each step by means of $\tilde{Y}_b$ and a strategy for updating $\tilde{Y}_b$ by means of $Y_{b,l}$. A different approach is devised by keeping the exhaustive search performed between the candidates left at the lower level. With this approach, at each step t we first determine Y_b as the candidate yielding the minimum score at level t between the candidates left in the list. Then, $\tilde{Y}_b$ is updated as:

$$\tilde{Y}_b = \arg \min_{Y = \tilde{Y}_b, Y_b} \{\delta_p(X, Y)\} \tag{16}$$

It is worth to note that also this approach contains a strategy which allows for using a different candidate in case $\tilde{Y}_b$ is estimated badly by the initial non-exhaustive step. This is performed by means of the comparison in (16). It is also important to point out that, thanks to (16), the bounding terms deployed by ELRP 2 are guaranteed being always more (or, at worst, equally) effective compared than the corresponding ones devised by LRP. In terms of performance, this guarantees that in the worst case ELRP 2 will be slower than LRP only for the amount of time needed to carry out the estimation of $\tilde{Y}_b$, which, as previously mentioned, has to be small compared to the overall time required by the algorithm.

3.3 ELRP 3

In this third approach, we propose to change the rule by which the candidates are tested. Each candidate Y_j is compared (13) against all the possible pruning conditions which can be determined until either it is pruned, or the last level (i.e. level 0) is reached, which means the distance between X and Y_j must be computed. Of course, the succession of the pruning conditions follows the original algorithm, going from the lowest level (i.e. level T) up to the highest one. Hence, each candidate will be individually tested against up to T pruning conditions.

This approach allows to devise an updating procedure as follows. At the beginning of the algorithm, the thresholds D^t are computed at each level by means of $\tilde{Y}_b$. When a candidate Y_j can not be skipped by any of the T conditions applied, the actual distance $\delta_p(X, Y_j)$ must be computed and the best candidate is updated as:

$$\tilde{Y}_b = \arg \min_{Y=\tilde{Y}_b, Y_j} \{\delta_p(X, Y)\} \tag{17}$$

Furthermore, the algorithm does not need anymore to keep a list where to store the candidates which have not been pruned *so far*, with extra savings for what means operations and memory requirements.

4 Experimental Results

This section compares the results obtained using the ELRP 1, ELRP 2 and ELRP 3 algorithms described in Section 3 with those yielded by the LRP algorithm. In the situation considered in [1], i.e. images affected by artificial noise, LRP yields notable speed-ups with respect to the FS algorithm. Nevertheless, we are also interested in testing the algorithms with more typical distortions found in real-world applications, i.e. those generated by slight changes in illumination and position. Thus, we carry out two experiments.

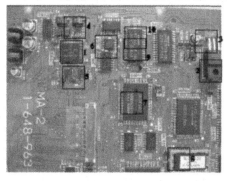

Fig. 2. The reference image used in Experiment 1 (top, left) and 2 (top, right). Bottom: the 10 templates used in the experiments are highlighted by black boxes.

In the first experiment 10 templates are extracted from an image as shown in fig. 2 (bottom), then the reference image is chosen as an image taken at a different time instant from a close-by position and with slightly different illumination conditions (see Figure 2, top left). Hence, the distortions between the templates and the reference image are generated by slight changes in pose and illumination, which can be regarded as the typical distortions found in real template matching scenarios. Then, in order to complete the experimental framework, we propose another experiment where the proposed algorithms are tested in the same conditions as in [1], that is, artificial noise is added to the image where the templates where extracted from (see Figure 2, top right). In particular, the introduced distortion is represented by i.i.d. double exponential (Laplace) distributed noise with parameters $\sigma = 10$ and $\mu = 0$. The 10 templates are the same as in experiment 1 (Figure 2, bottom).

To be coherent with the experimental framework proposed in [1], each template used for the two experiments is of size 64×64. This allows to have $M = 4 = 2 \times 2$, and the number of pruning levels $T = 6$. For the same reason, we use here the SSD function (i.e. $p = 2$). All the algorithms deploy incremental calculation techniques (i.e. [6]) for efficient computation of the transformed candidates at each level of resolution. Finally, the benchmark platform was a Linux workstation based on a *P4 3.056 GHz* processor; the algorithms were implemented in *C* and compiled using *Gcc* with optimization level *O3*.

Table 1. Measured speed-ups against FS in Experiment 1

Template	LRP	ELRP1	ELRP2	ELRP3
T1	11.3	17.9	16.4	17.9
T2	26.0	43.8	35.8	47.9
T3	7.1	9.9	9.5	9.8
T4	5.0	9.9	9.7	9.8
T5	18.2	28.6	25.2	29.8
T6	11.4	25.5	22.8	26.4
T7	13.1	25.0	22.2	25.7
T8	22.1	27.7	24.4	28.9
T9	11.5	12.8 *	14.2 *	24.0 *
T10	11.6	11.0 *	11.5 *	17.2 *
Mean	13.7	21.2	19.2	23.7
St.Dev.	6.5	11.0	8.4	11.2

Table 1 and Table 2 show the speed-ups (i.e. ratios of measured execution times) yielded by *LRP, ELRP 1, ELRP 2* and *ELRP 3* with regards to the FS SSD-based algorithm. As for the ELRP algorithms, the execution times include also the initial non-exhaustive step. Table 1 is relative to the dataset of experiment 1, while Table 2 shows the results concerning experiment 2. Furthermore, in the two tables symbol * is used to highlight those cases where the non-exhaustive algorithm applied at the first step does not find the global minimum: overall, this happens in 3 cases out of 20. Nevertheless, though already

Table 2. Measured speed-ups against FS in Experiment 2

Template	LRP	ELRP1	ELRP2	ELRP3
T1	25.7	30.0	25.9	31.6
T2	36.5	39.5	32.7	42.7
T3	20.8	24.6	22.0	25.7
T4	20.8	23.9	21.5	24.9
T5	16.4	18.5	17.0	18.8
T6	21.8	25.0	22.2	26.2
T7	21.2	23.9	21.1	24.6
T8	24.7	32.5	28.1	34.8
T9	15.0	11.1 *	14.4 *	12.6 *
T10	14.6	15.5	14.5	15.6
Mean	21,8	24,5	21,9	25,8
St.Dev.	6,4	8,3	5,8	9,0

specified previously, we remind here that even in the cases marked with an $*$ the three ELRP algorithms are always guaranteed to find the global minimum. Finally, the two tables also report the mean speed-up and its standard deviation yielded by each algorithm over the dataset.

Table 1 shows that in most cases the ELRP algorithms yield notable speed-ups compared to LRP, while in the less favorable cases the behavior of the two classes of algorithms can be regarded as equivalent. In particular, as it can be inferred from Table 1, ELRP 1 and 2 are able to determine computational savings compared to LRP in 9 cases out of 10 while, for what means ELRP 3, it is always faster than LRP. Hence, ELRP 3 can be regarded as the most efficient algorithm in the considered template matching scenario. This can also be inferred by the mean speed-ups, which for all ELRPs is notably higher compared to that of LRP, and it is highest for ELRP3. Nevertheless, the standard deviation yielded by the ELRPs is also higher than that of LRP.

As for Experiment 2, Table 2 shows that even if the computational advantages of ELRPs with respect to LRP are less evident when artificial noise is the only distortion, they are still present. For instance, ELRP 1 and 3 yield to computational savings compared to LRP in 9 cases out of 10. Instead, ELRP 2 obtains results comparable to LRP, being faster in 6 cases out of 10 and with speed-ups often similar to those of the original technique. Overall, compared to LRP, the reported mean speed-ups are higher for ELRP 1 and ELRP 3, and almost equivalent for ELRP 2.

To complement previous results, Table 3 and Table 4 report the percentages of candidates skipped by the conditions applied at each pruning level $P_6, \cdots, P_t, \cdots, P_1$, with the last column showing the total percentage of skipped candidates. By looking at these tables, it can be seen that often the pruning conditions applied at the lowest levels by LRP results not to be effective: i.e., overall the first condition prunes less than 1.0% in 14 cases out of 20. Thus, the pruning load is pushed on the higher levels, which increases the total number of operations required by LRP. Conversely, in the ELRP algorithms the corresponding conditions are usually much more effective due to the estimation of

Table 3. Efficiency of the pruning conditions used by the algorithms in Experiment 1

T	Alg	$P_6\%$	$P_5\%$	$P_4\%$	$P_3\%$	$P_2\%$	$P_1\%$	$P_{TOT}\%$
T1	LRP	9.2	13.8	11.3	60.0	4.7	0.9	100.0
	ELRP1	49.7	13.9	16.4	14.6	4.5	0.9	100.0
	ELRP2	49.7	13.9	16.4	14.6	4.5	0.9	100.0
	ELRP3	49.7	13.9	16.4	14.6	4.5	0.9	100.0
T2	LRP	53.5	23.8	6.0	16.6	0.0	0.0	100.0
	ELRP1	92.9	4.2	2.2	0.7	0.0	0.0	100.0
	ELRP2	92.9	4.2	2.2	0.7	0.0	0.0	100.0
	ELRP3	92.9	4.2	2.2	0.7	0.0	0.0	100.0
T3	LRP	2.9	0.5	30.9	37.7	25.0	3.0	100.0
	ELRP1	11.7	9.6	20.0	41.5	16.9	0.3	100.0
	ELRP2	11.7	9.6	20.0	41.5	16.9	0.3	100.0
	ELRP3	11.7	9.6	20.0	41.5	16.9	0.3	100.0
T4	LRP	0.4	0.0	6.8	27.8	63.6	1.4	100.0
	ELRP1	8.8	6.6	30.5	37.7	15.5	0.8	100.0
	ELRP2	8.8	6.6	30.5	37.7	15.5	0.8	100.0
	ELRP3	8.8	6.6	30.5	37.7	15.5	0.8	100.0
T5	LRP	0.3	11.4	72.1	13.8	2.4	0.0	100.0
	ELRP1	27.6	37.7	30.4	4.1	0.1	0.0	100.0
	ELRP2	27.6	37.7	30.4	4.1	0.1	0.0	100.0
	ELRP3	27.6	37.7	30.4	4.1	0.1	0.0	100.0
T6	LRP	0.2	0.3	15.3	82.8	1.4	0.0	100.0
	ELRP1	15.4	27.6	52.3	4.6	0.1	0.0	100.0
	ELRP2	15.4	27.6	52.3	4.6	0.1	0.0	100.0
	ELRP3	15.4	27.6	52.3	4.6	0.1	0.0	100.0
T7	LRP	8.8	0.1	65.2	17.6	7.3	1.1	100.0
	ELRP1	57.0	15.5	15.7	10.0	1.6	0.2	100.0
	ELRP2	57.0	15.5	15.7	10.0	1.6	0.2	100.0
	ELRP3	57.0	15.5	15.7	10.0	1.6	0.2	100.0
T8	LRP	0.0	2.3	95.1	2.7	0.0	0.0	100.0
	ELRP1	14.3	42.3	40.8	2.7	0.0	0.0	100.0
	ELRP2	14.3	42.3	40.8	2.7	0.0	0.0	100.0
	ELRP3	14.3	42.3	40.8	2.7	0.0	0.0	100.0
T9	LRP	0.9	5.6	7.3	85.9	0.3	0.0	100.0
	ELRP1	15.1	10.3	22.3	45.6	6.7	0.0	100.0
	ELRP2	15.1	10.3	22.3	52.0	0.3	0.0	100.0
	ELRP3	29.7	28.6	28.1	12.9	0.6	0.1	100.0
T10	LRP	0.0	1.4	41.8	48.4	8.4	0.0	100.0
	ELRP1	7.0	6.0	16.1	63.3	7.4	0.1	100.0
	ELRP2	7.0	6.0	30.2	49.3	7.5	0.0	100.0
	ELRP3	13.4	21.5	31.6	32.2	1.3	0.1	100.0

candidate $\tilde{Y}_b$. This happens also when the initial step does not find the global minimum, which means that $\tilde{Y}_b$ still represents a better estimation of the best match (as regards the matching score) with respect to those used by LRP for the initial pruning conditions. For instance, in the worst case the first condition prunes 4.7%. Nevertheless, in a few cases the better effectiveness of the initial pruning conditions does not imply a speed-up with respect to LRP due to the computational overhead associated with the initial search.

For what means the behavior of the 3 proposed algorithms, ELRP 2 is the one which obtains the most similar performance compared to the original algorithm.

Table 4. Efficiency of the pruning conditions used by the algorithms in Experiment 2

T	Alg	$P_6\%$	$P_5\%$	$P_4\%$	$P_3\%$	$P_2\%$	$P_1\%$	$P_{TOT}\%$
T1	LRP	4.3	82.1	6.7	5.0	1.7	0.1	100.0
	ELRP1	76.2	10.3	6.7	5.0	1.7	0.1	100.0
	ELRP2	76.2	10.3	6.7	5.0	1.7	0.1	100.0
	ELRP3	76.2	10.3	6.7	5.0	1.7	0.1	100.0
T2	LRP	86.5	9.3	1.5	2.3	0.4	0.0	100.0
	ELRP1	93.5	2.2	1.5	2.3	0.4	0.0	100.0
	ELRP2	93.5	2.2	1.5	2.3	0.4	0.0	100.0
	ELRP3	93.5	2.2	1.5	2.3	0.4	0.0	100.0
T3	LRP	0.1	11.0	79.9	9.0	0.0	0.0	100.0
	ELRP1	24.1	23.1	43.8	9.0	0.0	0.0	100.0
	ELRP2	24.1	23.1	43.8	9.0	0.0	0.0	100.0
	ELRP3	24.1	23.1	43.8	9.0	0.0	0.0	100.0
T4	LRP	0.0	2.8	89.3	7.7	0.2	0.0	100.0
	ELRP1	19.3	18.8	54.0	7.7	0.2	0.0	100.0
	ELRP2	19.3	18.8	54.0	7.7	0.2	0.0	100.0
	ELRP3	19.3	18.8	54.0	7.7	0.2	0.0	100.0
T5	LRP	0.0	2.8	75.6	18.4	3.0	0.1	100.0
	ELRP1	17.8	23.1	37.6	18.4	3.0	0.1	100.0
	ELRP2	17.8	23.1	37.6	18.4	3.0	0.1	100.0
	ELRP3	17.8	23.1	37.6	18.4	3.0	0.1	100.0
T6	LRP	0.0	5.5	90.8	3.6	0.1	0.0	100.0
	ELRP1	9.5	29.5	57.2	3.6	0.1	0.0	100.0
	ELRP2	9.5	29.5	57.2	3.6	0.1	0.0	100.0
	ELRP3	9.5	29.5	57.2	3.6	0.1	0.0	100.0
T7	LRP	0.1	77.9	11.0	7.7	2.9	0.5	100.0
	ELRP1	65.1	12.9	11.0	7.7	2.9	0.5	100.0
	ELRP2	65.1	12.9	11.0	7.7	2.9	0.5	100.0
	ELRP3	65.1	12.9	11.0	7.7	2.9	0.5	100.0
T8	LRP	0.0	26.8	73.1	0.1	0.0	0.0	100.0
	ELRP1	15.2	64.9	19.8	0.1	0.0	0.0	100.0
	ELRP2	15.2	64.9	19.8	0.1	0.0	0.0	100.0
	ELRP3	15.2	64.9	19.8	0.1	0.0	0.0	100.0
T9	LRP	0.1	0.1	66.7	30.3	2.7	0.1	100.0
	ELRP1	4.7	2.7	9.0	80.8	2.7	0.1	100.0
	ELRP2	4.7	2.7	59.5	30.3	2.7	0.1	100.0
	ELRP3	17.7	14.1	25.4	34.0	8.1	0.5	100.0
T10	LRP	0.0	0.0	55.9	42.7	1.4	0.0	100.0
	ELRP1	9.4	18.1	28.4	42.7	1.4	0.0	100.0
	ELRP2	9.4	18.1	28.4	42.7	1.4	0.0	100.0
	ELRP3	9.4	18.1	28.4	42.7	1.4	0.0	100.0

In particular, it is able to obtain notable speed-ups in Experiment 1, not counterparted by particular negative performances. These results confirm the trend exposed in Section 3, that is the performance of ELRP 2 compared to LRP is lower bounded by the computational weight of the non-exhaustive overhead needed to initialize $\tilde{Y}_b$, which ought to be small. This can be seen by considering that in the worst case, i.e. T2 of Experiment 2, the speed-up of LRP to ELRP 2 is just 1.1. Even when the non-exhaustive initial step can not find the global minimum (i.e. the *-cases in the tables) the behavior of the algorithm turns out to be at worst very close to that of LRP. In addition, it is also interesting to note that tables 3, 4 confirm that the aggregated candidates pruned by ELRP 2 at each conditions are always equal or higher than those pruned respectively by the conditions devised by LRP.

On the other hand, experimental results demonstrate that the strategies deployed by ELRP 1 and ELRP 3 are more effective than that of LRP since they both are able to obtain higher benefits in terms of computational savings compared to ELRP 2 on the average. In particular, ELRP 3 is the algorithm which yields the highest speed-ups and whose behavior is always favorable compared to LRP along the considered dataset, with the exception of a single instance where the speed-up obtained by ELRP 3 is slightly less than that of LRP. Hence, it can be regarded as the best algorithm, especially if the distortions between image and template are those typically found in real template matching applications.

5   Conclusions

We have shown how the LRP technique described in [1] can be enhanced by means of three different full-search equivalent algorithms (referred to as ELRP 1, ELRP 2 and ELRP 3), which deploy an initial estimation of a good candidate to be used in the pruning process. The proposed algorithms are able to yield significant speed-ups compared to the LRP technique in an experimental framework where distortions between templates and reference images are represented by changes in pose and illumination as well as by artificial noise. The variations proposed in our work do not increase the memory requirements of the original algorithm. Besides, it comes natural to expect that further improvements can be obtained if a more efficient non-exhaustive technique is used to determine the initial candidate, $\tilde{Y}_b$, in spite of the naive method we implemented for our tests.

References

1. Gharavi-Alkhansari, M.: A fast globally optimal algorithm for template matching using low-resolution pruning. IEEE Trans. Image Processing 10(4), 526–533 (2001)
2. Goshtasby, A.: 2-D and 3-D image registration for medical, remote sensing and industrial applications. Wiley, Chichester (2005)
3. Barnea, D., Silverman, H.: A class of algorithms for digital image registration. IEEE Trans. on Computers C-21(2), 179–186 (1972)
4. Li, W., Salari, E.: Successive elimination algorithm for motion estimation. IEEE Trans. on Image Processing 4(1), 105–107 (1995)
5. Wang, H., Mersereau, R.: Fast algorithms for the estimation of motion vectors. IEEE Trans. on Image Processing 8(3), 435–439 (1999)
6. Mc Donnel, M.: Box-filtering techniques. Computer Graphics and Image Processing 17, 65–70 (1981)

A Novel Approach to Geometric Fitting of Implicit Quadrics*

Mohammad Rouhani and Angel D. Sappa

Computer Vision Center, Edifici O Campus UAB
08193 Bellaterra, Barcelona, Spain
{rouhani,asappa}@cvc.uab.es

Abstract. This paper presents a novel approach for estimating the geometric distance from a given point to the corresponding implicit quadric curve/surface. The proposed estimation is based on the height of a tetrahedron, which is used as a coarse but reliable estimation of the real distance. The estimated distance is then used for finding the best set of quadric parameters, by means of the Levenberg-Marquardt algorithm, which is a common framework in other geometric fitting approaches. Comparisons of the proposed approach with previous ones are provided to show both improvements in CPU time as well as in the accuracy of the obtained results.

1 Introduction

Fitting a curve or surface to a given cloud of points is a fundamental problem in computer vision and geometric modelling. It has been an active topic during the last two decades [1,2]. The appearance of new sensors, which allow to obtain a large amount of 3D data in a reduced time, and the need to process all this information efficiently have opened new challenges looking for efficient fitting approaches.

Although there are many tools in Computer Aided Design to represent curves and surfaces, the implicit representation is more efficient since it avoids the parametrization problem (i.e., difficulties arise especially when one should face up to unorganized cloud of points). The surface is described as the set of points $\mathbf{X}$ satisfying the equation $f(\mathbf{c}, \mathbf{X}) = 0$; where $\mathbf{c}$ is the set of parameters. This set of points is also referred as *zero set* of f. Although different function spaces could be used for the implicit representation (e.g., B-Spline functions [2,3], and radial basis functions [4]) in the current work the implicit polynomial case is considered.

Having represented the surface as an implicit polynomial, the fitting problem can be modelled as an optimization problem: *finding the set of parameters that minimize some distance measures between the given set of points and the fitted*

---

* This work has been partially supported by the Spanish Government under project TRA2007-62526/AUT; research programme Consolider-Ingenio 2010: MIPRCV (CSD2007-00018); and Catalan Government under project CTP 2008ITT 00001.

J. Blanc-Talon et al. (Eds.): ACIVS 2009, LNCS 5807, pp. 121–132, 2009.

curve or surface. The most natural way to define the distance is to measure the deviation of the function values from the expected value (i.e., zero) at each given point. This measure criterion is referred in the literature as *algebraic distance* [5,6].

Another distance measure, referred as *orthogonal* or *geometric distance*, is defined as the shortest distance from the given point to the fitting surface. On the contrary to the algebraic distance, this distance has a direct link to the geometry of the data, and its final result makes sense as a consequence. Although this definition of the distance is complete and leads us to the best fitting result, it has a nonlinear nature with the model parameter, that discourages its use. On the other hand, since there is no closed formula to compute the shortest distance, two strategies have been proposed in the literature: (*a*) compute the orthogonal distance by means of an iterative approach (e.g., [2,7]); and (*b*) compute an approximation to this distance and use it as the residual value of the point (e.g., [8,9]).

Algebraic and geometric distances are two different viewpoints for the fitting problem. Although both of them could be exploited for some optimization models leading to the optimal parameters in their own sense, the frameworks they use are different. Algebraic fitting methods are based on quadratic optimization model (least square) giving a *non-iterative* unique solution, while the geometric ones are based on some non-linear models giving the solution through *iterative* algorithms.

The current work proposes a novel technique for an efficient estimation of the geometric distance, from a given point p to the corresponding implicit quadric fitting surface. This distance is computationally efficient as well as a reliable approximation. This geometric criterion is later on used in an optimization framework. The rest of the paper is organized as follows. Section 2 describes the problem and introduces related work. The proposed technique is presented in section 3. Section 4 gives experimental results and comparisons. Finally, conclusion and future work are presented in section 5.

2   Related Work

In this section, the two major approaches in surface fitting: *algebraic* and *geometric*, are presented in more details to show the motivations of the proposed approach. Furthermore, a brief introduction to the optimization method used in the current work is also given.

Fitting problems aim at fining a curve or surface *close* to a given cloud of points $\mathbf{X} = \{p_i\}_{i=1}^n$. Before explaining the meaning of *close* we should define the implicit surface we want to find. Without loss of generality let us consider the quadratic implicit surfaces:

$$f_{\mathbf{c}}(x, y, z) = c_1 x^2 + c_2 y^2 + c_3 z^2 + c_4 xy + c_5 xz \qquad (1)$$
$$+ c_6 yz + c_7 x + c_8 y + c_9 z + 1 = 0,$$

where $\mathbf{c} = (c_1, ..., c_9)^T$ is the vector we are searching for. This implicit representation provides us many facilities; e.g., for closed surfaces we can easily find out whether a point is inside or outside of the surface just through checking the sign of f at the given point.

2.1   Algebraic Approaches

Since the implicit representation is used, a point is on the surface if and only if the output of f_c in (1) is zero at the given point. It leads us to define the following optimization criterion, which is known as algebraic approach:

$$\sum_X f_c^2(x, y, z). \tag{2}$$

This minimization problem is also equivalent to the overdetermined system $Mc = b$, where M is the monomial matrix computed at given points, and $\mathbf{b}$ is a column vector containing -1. Regardless to these different viewpoints, the optimal solution could be computed through least square solutions:

$$\mathbf{c} = (M^T M)^{-1} M^T b. \tag{3}$$

Algebraic distance has a simple formulation and a straightforward solution that is not iterative. Unfortunately, this method could fail for real world data set, where there is no information about the distribution of noise. As an illustration Fig. 1(a) shows how this method, despite its simplicity, fails to fit a cloud of points[1] picked from a spherical patch. Here the algebraic method tries to put the value of implicit function close to zero, and because of this *algebraic criterion* the curvature of the data, which is an important *geometric* property, is missed.

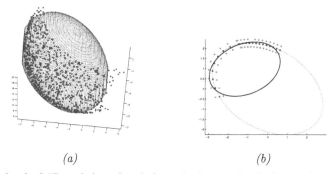

(a)   *(b)*

Fig. 1. (*a*) A cloud of 3D real data fitted through the simple algebraic approach (3). Some clusters of points are inside the surface and some outside. (*b*) Result of the 3L algorithm [6] (solid line). Since the data points are not uniformly distributed it fails to fit them; while, in this case, the simple algebraic (3) is able to give the exact solution (dotted line).

Two common problems, inherent to algebraic approaches, are (*a*) computational instability of the zero set; and (*b*) lack of geometric sense in this procedure. However, the non-iterative framework of algebraic approaches has attracted the attention of many researchers. For instance, focussing on the instability problem, Hezer et al. [5] analyze the sensitivity of the zero set to small coefficient

---

[1] K2T structured light camera system, University of South Florida.

changes and minimize an upper bound of the error in order to have a more stable output. In addition to the instability problem, algebraic method does not have any geometric meaning. Indeed what is happening inside the procedure is just to minimize a quadratic optimization function—which is equivalent to an overdetermined system of equations. Keren et al. [10] try to constrain the surface parameter space in order to obtain a geometrically reasonable output. Blane et al. [6] and Tasdizen et al. [11] in parallel researches propose to add some geometric concept inside the optimization problem.

In [11] they try to maintain the estimated gradient value at each data points while they fit the data. In [6] Blane et al. add two complementary sets to the given data set, which are a shrunken and an expanded version of the original data set (this method is referred as 3L algorithm, which stands for 3 level set). After finding these complementary sets through local regression, they try to find an implicit function not only gaining zero in the original data set, but achieving +1 and -1 respectively in the shrunken and expanded sets. Although it is a robust and widely used approach in the literature, it could fail for some simple cases even in 2D. Figure 1(b) shows a set of non-uniformly distributed points on an ellipse. Because of two other supplementary sets, the 3L algorithm tried to find a compromise between all three sets, so fails to fit the right ellipse. In the figure the dotted line ellipse corresponds to the output of 3L, while the solid line one is the output of simple algebraic (3), which manages to fit it.

2.2   Geometric Approaches

In addition to algebraic methods, there is another category based on geometric distance—or an approximation of it—usually referred as *geometric approach*. In this case the distance between a point and the surface is usually defined as the shortest distance between this point and its correspondence on the surface. Thus, in general case of geometric methods we have the following optimization problem:

$$min_{\mathbf{c}}(\sum_{i=1}^{n} min_{\hat{p}_i} d(p_i, \hat{p}_i)), \tag{4}$$

where each $\hat{p}_i$ is the correspondence of p_i on the surface.

Theoretically, both unknown surface parameters and the correspondences must be found simultaneously, but practically this problem is tackled by first assuming an initial surface, and then refine it till convergence is reached. So, the fitting problem is split up into two stages: 1) point correspondence search; and 2) surface parameter refinement. The first stage deals with the inner part of (4), while the second one concerns about the outer one.

Point correspondence search: Regarding to the first stage, we need to find the correspondence for each data point. For this purpose, two different strategies have been proposed in the literature: (a) finding the shortest distance by solving a non-linear system (e.g., [2,7]); and (b) computing an estimation of the shortest distance (e.g., [8,9]).

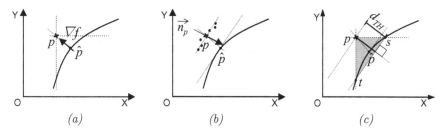

Fig. 2. Orthogonal distance estimation between p and a quadric curve. (*a*) The shortest distance is found using the iterative method proposed by [7]. (*b*) An estimation of the curve orientation, through applying PCA in a local neighborhood, used by [9]. (*c*) Distance estimation based on the proposed approach (i.e., by finding the Triangle Height, d_{TH}).

In [7] Ahn et al. propose the *direct method* to find the correspondence (or foot-point) on the surface, which is based on its geometric properties. This foot-point, $\hat{p}$, is somewhere on the surface satisfying $f(\hat{p}) = 0$. Furthermore, the line connecting the data point with the foot-point must be parallel to the ∇f at the foot-point, where ∇ is the gradient operator (see Fig. 2(*a*)). In other words, the equation $\nabla f \times (\hat{p} - p) = 0$ must be satisfied. Merging these two conditions, the following system of equations must be solved:

$$\begin{pmatrix} f_c \\ \nabla f_c \times (\hat{p} - p) \end{pmatrix} = \mathbf{0}. \tag{5}$$

This equation could be solved by the Newton method for a non-linear system of equations.

Although this method is precise enough, and even covers some well-known method in the literature, like [12] and [13], it is quite time-consuming due to the iterations. Fig. 3 illustrate the iterative approach leading to the approximated foot-point. In each iteration, the point moves to a lower level curve till reaching the zero level curve. Simultaneously, the gradient direction at each iteration is adapted to be parallel to the connecting line.

Instead of computing the real shortest distance, [9] proposes some estimation avoiding iteration. For the correspondence problem they proposed to restrict the search along the estimated normal direction. The estimated normal at each data point is computed by using principal components analysis (PCA). Precisely speaking, the covariance matrix of a set of points in the neighborhood is computed at first, and then its smallest eigenvector[2] is adopted as the orientation. (Fig. 2(b) shows an illustration in 2D space).

After finding the correspondence set for the given data set, the surface parameters should be refined through some minimization. However, on the contrary to algebraic approaches where least square method gives a unique and direct solution, geometric approaches need a different framework for finding the optimal set

---

[2] Eigenvector associated with the smallest eigenvalue.

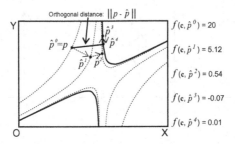

Fig. 3. Orthogonal distance computed by means of the iterative approach proposed in [7]. Solid curve correspond to the $f(\mathbf{c}, \mathbf{X}) = 0$, while dotted ones show the level curves obtained after each iteration of (5); $\hat{p}$ converges to the curve after four iterations.

of parameters. Next section presents one of the most well-known optimization frameworks adopted by most of geometric approaches.

Surface parameters refinement: As a result from the previous stage the set of points $\{\hat{p}_i\}_{i=1}^n$, corresponding to every p_i in $\mathbf{X}$ has been found. Hence, now an optimization framework is used to refine the surface parameter. LevenbergMar- quardt algorithm (LMA) is a well-known method in non-linear optimization [14], which in some sense interpolates between the GaussNewton algorithm and the gradient descent.

In order to handle LMA, the value of the functional (inner part of (4)) and its partial derivatives, which is expressed in the Jacobian matrix, should be provided. Since each $\hat{p}_i$ lies on the surface, every distance $d(p_i, \hat{p}_i)$ can be easily expressed as a function of surface parameters:

$$d_i(\mathbf{c}) = \|p_i - \hat{p}_i\|^2, \tag{6}$$

more precisely, equation $f(\mathbf{c}, \hat{p}_i) = 0$ provides a link between surface parameters and $\{\hat{p}_i\}_{i=1}^n$ set, and distances as a consequence. This relationship is used to compute the Jacobian matrix:

$$J_{ij} = \frac{\partial d_i}{\partial c_j} = -\frac{\partial d_i}{\partial \hat{p}_i} \frac{\partial f / \partial c_j}{\partial f / \partial \hat{p}_i}. \tag{7}$$

Having estimated the geometric distance (6) and its Jacobian matrix (7), it is easy to refine the surface parameter through LMA as follows:

$$c^{t+1} = c^t + \beta \triangle c,$$
$$(J^T J + \lambda diag(J^T J))\triangle c = J^T D, \tag{8}$$

where β is the refinement step; $\triangle c$ represents the refinement vector for the surface parameters; λ is the damping parameter in LMA; and the vector $D = (d_1(\mathbf{c}^t), ..., d_n(\mathbf{c}^t))^T$ corresponds to the distances. Parameter refinement (8) must be repeated till convergence is reached.

3   Proposed Approach

So far, the geometric approaches have been concerned about the best *direction* (i.e., the shortest distance) in each data point toward the surface. Taubin [12] approximate this direction with the gradient vector of the level set passing through the data point. Ahn et al. [7] present different optimization models in order to reach a better approximation of the best direction. They show that the method used by Taubin is a special case of their general method.

In the current work, a novel estimation of the geometric distance is presented, which despite other approaches, is not based on a single direction. First a tetrahedron is constructed, and then the geometric distance is approximated with the tetrahedron height segment; this tetrahedron is easily defined by the given point and three intersections satisfying $f_c(x, y_p, z_p) = 0$, $f_c(x_p, y, z_p) = 0$ and $f_c(x_p, y_p, z) = 0$, where (x_p, y_p, z_p) is the given point. Fig. 2(c) shows an illustration for the 2D case; the 3D case in depicted in Fig. 4(a).

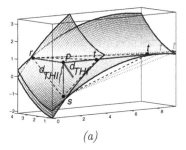
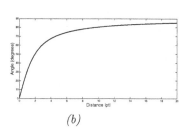

(a)   (b)

Fig. 4. Transition from a tetrahedron height vector to a triangle height vector. (a) Illustration of two surfaces with their corresponding intersection points (planar triangular patch (r, s, t)). (b) Angle between tetrahedron height segment and (pt) segment, as a function of distance $|pt|$.

In the particular case tackled in this work, since the fitted surface is defined by an implicit quadric equation $f_c(x, y, z) = 0$, the intersection points can be easily found by solving some quadratic equations. Each equation gives two roots, the closest one to the data point is selected as the vertex of the tetrahedron.

A direct formula to describe the proposed distance can be found. Let r, s and t be the three intersections with a quadric surface, which create a triangular planar patch (see Fig. 4(a)). Since the volume of the tetrahedron is defined as the product of the area of each base by its corresponding height, three pairs of expressions lead us to the same value. Hence, the height of the tetrahedron, d_{TH}, could easily be computed from the following relationship:

$$(|rs \times rt|.|d_{TH}|)/6 = (|pr|.|ps|.|pt|)/6 = v, \tag{9}$$

where $\times$ refers to the cross product operator between two vectors. Similar relationship can be found in the 2D case, but by using the area of the triangle instead of the volume.

Note that in the extreme cases, when intersections with some of the directions $(1, 0, 0)$, $(0, 1, 0)$, $(0, 0, 1)$ cannot be found, the 3D case becomes into: i) the 2D case (two intersections); ii) only one intersection, which has been used in [8]; or iii) the point p is an outlier since none of the three directions intersects the implicit quadric surface. Transitions between different cases are smoothly reached; Fig. 4(a) shows an illustration where one of the vertices of the triangular patch (r, s, t) moves away from current position up to the extreme—i.e., no intersection between vertex t and the implicit surface can be found[3]; the smooth transition from the tetrahedron height segment orientation to the triangle height segment orientation can be appreciated in the illustration of Fig. 4(b).

This proposed measurement criterion can be exploited in a fitting framework. Indeed, the function $\sum d_i^2$ could be a good optimization model for the surface fitting, where each d_i is the proposed distance, d_{TH}, for the point p_i in the data set. Based on (9), this function has a nonlinear relationship with the surface parameters. Hence, for this part a nonlinear optimization method is needed to find the best set of parameters.

In the current work, the LMA is adopted, which has been presented in section 2.2. As mentioned above, the Jacobian matrix, which shows the sensitivity of each d_i with respect to the parameter vector, needs to be computed. For this purpose (9) could be used to describe d_{TH} based on the surface parameters, and consequently we have:

$$D_j|d_{TH}| = (|rs \times rt|.D_j v - v.D_j|rs \times rt|)/|rs \times rt|^2, \qquad (10)$$

where $D_j = \partial/\partial c_j$. All these terms are based on the coordinates of the intersections, and since every intersection r, s, and t is implicitly related to the parameter vector, the derivations could be easily computed like (7).

4   Experimental Results

Two major approaches, the *algebraic* and *geometric* one, with their extensions have been presented. Algebraic methods are quite fast, but unfortunately the structure of the data is neglected. On the other hand, geometric methods are more afraid of the geometry of the data, as the name implies, but they are quite slow. The proposed method, which belongs to the geometric category, is implemented and compared with the most important methods in the literature.

In the two dimensional case, a set of points picked from an ellipse with a non-uniform distribution is used. Fig. 1(b) presents the result from the 3L algorithm [6], which fails to fit the right ellipse, even though the case is not noisy. However, the simple algebraic (3) manages to fit it, but the point is that the 3L algorithm is supposed to include more geometric information than the least square approach.

Fig. 5(a) depicts the result of the proposed method for the same set of points. Both algebraic and proposed method converge to a similar result, but problems

---

[3] These experiments have been performed by applying smooth changes in the geometry of the surface, which correspond to smooth changes in the parameter space.

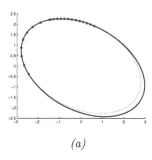
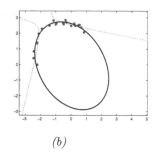

(a)   (b)

Fig. 5. Fitting a 2D set of points picked non-uniformly from an ellipse. (a) Without noise: Algebraic (dotted line) and proposed method (solid line) both reach similar results. (b) Noisy data case: Algebraic method (dotted line) misses the elliptic structure, while the proposed approach (solid line) reaches a good result.

arise when some noise is added to the points. Fig. 5(b) highlights the robustness of the proposed method to noise; whereas the algebraic one missed the elliptic structure of the data, and fitted the patch as a split hyperbola. Fitzgibbon et. al. [15] proposed a fitting method just for 2D elliptic cases based on algebraic approaches. From this simple example, one can understand the hardship for algebraic methods when the function space is bigger than the quadratic one.

The proposed approach has been also compared with the state of the art by using real range images obtained with the the K2T structured light camera system, University of South Florida. A first data set, from a spherical object, is presented in Fig. 1(a). It contains 1000 points, and as indicated in that figure, the algebraic method fails to fit the right sphere; since this approach is just trying to put the *algebraic* value of the quadratic function closer to *zero*, a wrong result is achieved. Fig. 6 shows the result obtained by the proposed method, when the same set of points is considered. In this case a sphere with a bigger radius covering the whole data set has been used as an initialization. The whole process took 4.26 sec. in a 3.2GHz Pentium IV PC with a non-optimized Matlab code. The other geometric method, proposed by [7], reaches similar result but 10 times slower. Since at each parameter refinement iteration there are additional iterations to find the foot-points.

Fig. 7 shows a 3D patch picked from a cylinder corrupted by a Gaussian noise. This patch was generated and rotated in a synthetic way. Three different methods are compared based on the accumulated real distances from the points to the achieved surface, computed by using [7]. Fig. 7(a) and (c), respectively, show the results of the 3L algorithm [6] and the proposed method. Both images show similar result, one concave and the other one convex though. The first one has an accumulated real distance of 28.90 and the proposed one has an accumulated distance of 5.45, which is more than five times smaller. Fig. 7(b) shows the result from another geometric approach [7]. This result has the lowest distance (5.24), and it is still a cylinder, but it took more than five times compared with the proposed algorithm.

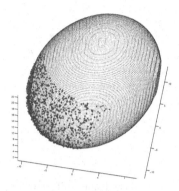

Fig. 6. Fitting real 3D data through the proposed approach

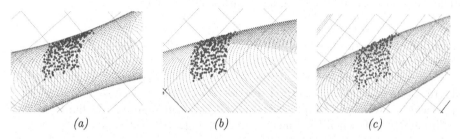

(a)   (b)   (c)

Fig. 7. Fitting of the 3D patch of a cylinder disrupted by gaussian noise for: (a) the 3L algorithm[6]; (b) the geometric method proposed by [7]; (c) the proposed method

In the last example another comparison is presented. This time a part of a noisy ellipsoid is used as an input of both algebraic and geometric approaches. Fig. 8(a) illustrates how the simple algebraic method (3) misses the elliptic structure of the patch, and gives a hyperboloid. This example shows the importance of using geometric clues. Fig. 8 (b) and (c) illustrate the 3L results, with different parameters. As mentioned in section 2.1, the 3L algorithm, as the name stands for, needs two other data sets that are offsets of the original one. Here, the offsets are constructed with different user defined parameters, which show the amounts of translation. Fig. 8(c) shows the result of the 3L method with a smaller parameter; so as we continue to squeeze the offset, the result makes more sense, but unfortunately after a while on, since the data is noisy, three level sets merged together and the whole procedure collapses. Finally, Fig. 8(d)) depicts the result of the proposed method, which manages to fit the data and maintain the elliptic curvature as well. It should be mentioned that, the proposed distance estimation does not need any parameter adjustment. The result from [7] is skipped, because it obtains quite the same result but with a slower convergence.

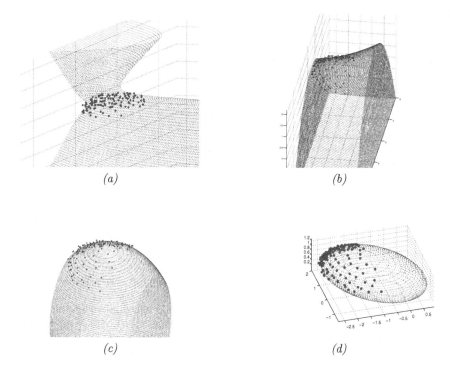

(a)   *(b)*

(c)   *(d)*

Fig. 8. Fitting 3D points picked from an ellipsoid with a non-uniform distribution. Final results from: (*a*) the simple algebraic method (3); (*b*) and (*c*) the results of the 3L algorithm [6] with different set parameters; and (*d*) proposed method.

5   Conclusions

This paper presents a throughout study of state of the art fitting methods. Furthermore, a novel geometric distance estimation is proposed. Despite other geometric estimations, which are based on one direction to find the foot-point associated to each data point, the proposed one is based on three different directions; hence it does not need any iterations. This approximation value has been used with a LMA optimization framework. In that framework an iterative approach finds the best set of surface parameters. Compared with other geometric methods, instead of relying on a costly iterative approach to find the foot-points, a direct way is proposed. As a conclusion, it can be said that even though several algorithms have been proposed for quadric fitting there is a trade off between CPU time and accuracy of surface parameters for selecting the best one; this trade off get more evident when it is increased the number of points to be fitted or the percentage of noise. The only concern arises in the proposed method when no intersection could be found for some data points; however, the proposed method is flexible enough to apply there other direction instead of the coordinate axis. Future work will study this possibility.

References

1. Besl, P., Jain, R.: Segmentation through variable-order surface fitting. IEEE Trans. on Pattern Analysis and Machine Intelligence 10(2), 167–192 (1988)
2. Aigner, M., Jutler, B.: Gauss-newton-type technique for robustly fitting implicit defined curves and surfaces to unorganized data points. In: IEEE International Conference on Shape Modelling and Application, pp. 121–130 (2008)
3. Yang, Z., Deng, J., Chen, F.: Fitting unorganized point clouds with active implicit b-spline curves. Visual Computing 21(1), 831–839 (2005)
4. Carr, J., et al.: Reconstruction and representation of 3d objects with radial basis functions. SIGGRAPH, 67–76 (2001)
5. Helzer, A., Barzohar, M., Malah, D.: Stable fitting of 2d curves and 3d surfaces by implicit polynomials. IEEE Trans. on Pattern Analysis and Machine Intelligence 26(10), 1283–1294 (2004)
6. Blane, M., Lei, Z., Civil, H., Cooper, D.: The 3l algorithm for fitting implicit polynomials curves and surface to data. IEEE Trans. on Pattern Analysis and Machine Intelligence 22(3), 298–313 (2000)
7. Ahn, S., Rauh, W., Cho, H., Warnecke, H.: Orthogonal distance fitting of implicit curves and surfaces. IEEE Trans. on Pattern Analysis and Machine Intelligence 24(5), 620–638 (2002)
8. Chen, C., Hung, Y., Cheng, J.: Ransac-based darces: A new approach to fast automatic registration of partially overlapping range images. IEEE Trans. on Pattern Analysis and Machine Intelligence 21(11), 1229–1234 (1999)
9. Gotardo, P., Bellon, O., Boyer, K., Silva, L.: Range image segmentation into planar and quadric surfaces using an improved robust estimator and genetic algorithm. IEEE Trans. on Systems, Man, and Cybernetics Part B: Cybernetics 34(6), 2303–2316 (2004)
10. Keren, D., Gotsman, C.: Fitting curves and surfaces with constrained implicit polynomials. IEEE Trans. on Pattern Analysis and Machine Intelligence 21(1), 476–480 (1999)
11. Tasdizen, T., Tarel, J., Cooper, D.: Improving the stability of algebraic curves for applications. IEEE Trans. Image Processing 9(3), 405–416 (2000)
12. Taubin, G.: Estimation of planar curves, surfaces, and nonplanar space curves defined by implicit equations with applications to edge and range image segmentation. IEEE Trans. on Pattern Analysis and Machine Intelligence 13(11), 1115–1138 (1991)
13. Sampson, P.D.: Fitting conic sections to very scattereda data: An iterative refinement of the bookstein algorithm. Computer Graphics and Image Processing, 18, 97–108 (1982)
14. Fletcher, R.: Practical Methods of Optimization. Wiley, New York (1990)
15. Fitzgibbon, A., Pilu, M., Fisher, R.: Direct least square fitting of ellipses. IEEE Trans. on Pattern Analysis and Machine Intelligence 21(5), 476–480 (1999)

Two-Level Bimodal Association for Audio-Visual Speech Recognition

Jong-Seok Lee and Touradj Ebrahimi

Multimedia Signal Processing Group
Ecole Polytechnique Fédérale de Lausanne (EPFL)
CH-1015 Lausanne, Switzerland
{jong-seok.lee,touradj.ebrahimi}@epfl.ch
http://mmspg.epfl.ch

Abstract. This paper proposes a new method for bimodal information fusion in audio-visual speech recognition, where cross-modal association is considered in two levels. First, the acoustic and the visual data streams are combined at the feature level by using the canonical correlation analysis, which deals with the problems of audio-visual synchronization and utilizing the cross-modal correlation. Second, information streams are integrated at the decision level for adaptive fusion of the streams according to the noise condition of the given speech datum. Experimental results demonstrate that the proposed method is effective for producing noise-robust recognition performance without a priori knowledge about the noise conditions of the speech data.

1 Introduction

In the field of speech-based human-computer interaction, it becomes important to utilize the acoustic and the visual cues of speech simultaneously for effective recognition of spoken language by computers. Audio-visual speech recognition (AVSR) systems which additionally observe lip movements along with acoustic speech have been proposed and shown to produce enhanced noise-robust performance due to the complementary nature of the two modalities [1]. The speakers' lip movements contain significant cues about spoken language and, besides, they are not affected by acoustic noise. Therefore, the visual speech signal is a powerful information source for compensating for performance degradation of acoustic-only recognition systems in noisy environments.

How to integrate the two modalities is an important issue in constructing AVSR systems showing good recognition performance. Generally, approaches for this can be classified into two broad categories: The first one is early integration (EI), or feature fusion, in which the features from the two signals are concatenated to form a composite feature vector and then inputted to a recognizer [2]. The other one is late integration (LI), or decision fusion, where independent recognition results for the two feature streams are combined at the final decision stage [3,4]. Each approach has its own advantages against the other one. For example, constructing an AVSR system based on the EI approach is relatively simple, while, in the LI approach, it is easy to

J. Blanc-Talon et al. (Eds.): ACIVS 2009, LNCS 5807, pp. 133–144, 2009.

implement an adaptive weighting of the two modalities according to the noise condition of the given speech data for noise-robust recognition performance [5].

Since the acoustic speech signal and the visual observation of the lip movements are two complementary aspects of the speech production process, there apparently exist strong cross-modal correlation which can be extracted from temporally aligned streams of the two signals and used for noise-robust recognition. On the other hand, it is known that temporal asynchrony is involved in the audio-visual correlation structure. Unfortunately, either of the two integration approaches does not model well such characteristics of audio-visual speech: The EI approach temporally correlates the two feature streams but assumes perfect synchrony between them. In the LI approach, conditional independence of one stream upon the other one is assumed and their temporal correlation is largely ignored, so that the complementary nature of the two modalities is considered only at the decision level.

In this paper, we propose a new integration method which explicitly exploits the cross-modal correlation of audio-visual speech and, thereby, enhances performance of AVSR. Our method associates the acoustic and the visual information in two levels: First, by using the canonical correlation analysis (CCA), each feature vector is projected to a new space where the correlation between the projected features is maximized, and the resultant features are concatenated for feature-level integration. In order to consider the asynchronous characteristics of the two signals, the correlation analysis is conducted with features of multiple frames. Second, decision-level association is performed between the streams of the acoustic data and the data integrated at the feature level, which adaptively combines the streams for robustness of recognition over various noise conditions. Experimental results demonstrate that the proposed method significantly enhances noise-robustness in comparison to conventional EI and LI techniques in diverse noise conditions.

The rest of the paper is organized as follows: The following section overviews existing researches related to our work. Section 3 describes the proposed system using two-level association. In Section 4, the performance of the proposed method is demonstrated via experiments on isolated-word recognition tasks. Finally, concluding remarks are given in Section 5.

2 Related Work

2.1 Audio-Visual Information Fusion

The primary goal of AVSR, i.e. robust recognition over various noise conditions, is achieved only by an appropriate information fusion scheme. Successful audio-visual information fusion should take advantage of the complementary nature of the two modalities to produce a synergetic performance gain. On the other hand, the integrated recognition performance may be even worse than the performance of any modality if the integration is not performed properly, which is called "attenuating fusion" [1].

As briefly explained in the introduction, EI and LI are the two main categories for audio-visual integration. In the former approach, the feature vectors of the two signals are concatenated and fed into a recognizer. This scheme has an advantage of simplicity. In the latter approach, the features of each modality are independently processed by the corresponding recognizer and then the outputs of the two recognizers are integrated for the final decision. Although which approach is more suitable is still arguable, there are advantages of using LI over EI for implementing noise-robust AVSR systems. First, it is easy to adaptively control relative contributions of the two modalities to the final decision with the LI approach because the modalities are processed independently. Such an adaptive control scheme is effective for producing noise-robust recognition performance over various noise conditions [3,4,5]. Second, while the EI approach assumes a perfect synchrony of the modalities, the LI approach allows flexibility for modeling the temporal relation of the acoustic and the visual signals. Previous studies suggest that audio-visual speech is not perfectly synchronized but there exist asynchronous characteristics between them: For some pronunciations, the lips and the tongue start to move up to several hundred milliseconds before the actual speech sound is produced [6]. It was demonstrated that the lips move to their initial position about 200 ms before the onset of the acoustic speech signal [7]. Also, audio-visual speech does not require precise synchrony and there exists an intersensory synchrony window during which the performance of human speech perception is not degraded for desynchronized audio-visual signals [8].

A drawback of LI is that the audio-visual correlation is not fully utilized for recognition due to separate processing of the two signals. In this paper, we solve this problem by feature-level association of the acoustic and the visual features. Previous researches for utilizing the audio-visual correlation are reviewed in the following subsection.

2.2 Audio-Visual Correlation Analysis

Previous researches on analysis of the audio-visual correlation have done mostly for speaker recognition and speaker detection. Fisher and Darrell [9] proposed a speaker association method used in multi-speaker conversational dialog systems, where an information theoretic measure of cross-modal correspondence is derived based on a probabilistic multimodal generation model so that the highly correlated part in a video sequence with the speech signal can be detected. In [10], an audio-visual feature combination method was introduced to improve speaker recognition performance; the two feature vectors are transformed by using CCA to utilize the audio-visual correlation. The idea of transforming the feature vectors of the acoustic and the visual modalities can be also found in other work: Bredin and Chollet [11] used the co-inertia analysis to measure audio-visual correspondence and showed that their method can be used to detect replay attacks in bimodal identity verification. Slaney and Covell [12] proposed a linear projection method to measure the degree of synchronization between the acoustic and the image data based on CCA.

Researchers found that it is necessary to consider asynchronous characteristics of the acoustic and the visual modalities when the cross-modal correlation of the two modalities is analyzed. Bregler and Konig [2] showed that the mutual information between them reaches the maximum when the visual signal is delayed up to 120 milliseconds. Based on this result, Eveno and Basacier [13] allowed a delay between the two signals up to 80 milliseconds in defining a liveness score for audio-visual biometrics. Sargin *et al.* [10] experimentally showed that feature combination with asynchrony of 40 milliseconds produces the largest cross-modal correlation and the best speaker recognition performance.

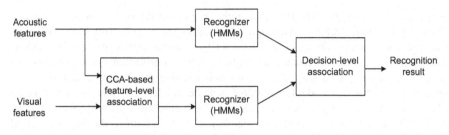

Fig. 1. Proposed system architecture

3 Proposed System

3.1 Overall System

The overall structure of our AVSR system is shown in Fig. 1. First, compact features are extracted from each signal. Then, the feature-level association takes place to combine the two feature streams with considering correlations and synchronization of the two modalities. The combined and the acoustic features are separately fed into the corresponding recognizers which are composed of hidden Markov models (HMMs). We observed that, since the feature-level association does not consider relative importance (or reliability) of the acoustic and the visual modalities, the integrated features produce worse performance than the audio-only ones for low-noise conditions while the recognition performance by using them is better than that by the visual-only ones for high-noise conditions. Therefore, the acoustic features are utilized again at the decision step in order to improve recognition performance especially for low-noise conditions. The decision-level association adaptively fuses the outputs of the two recognizers according to the noise condition of the speech signal, which produces the final recognition result.

3.2 Acoustic Feature Extraction

From the acoustic speech, we extract the popular Mel-frequency cepstral coefficients (MFCCs) [14]. While a window function having the length of 25 ms proceeds by 10 ms at a time, the 12-th order MFCCs and their temporal derivatives (delta terms) are extracted. To reduce channel distortions contained in the speech, the cepstral mean subtraction method is applied [14].

3.3 Visual Feature Extraction

The images in the database used in this paper contain the face region around the speakers' lips. From the grayscale images, the visual features are obtained as follows [15]: First, variations within and across images such as illuminations and skin color of the speakers are reduced by left-to-right brightness balancing and pixel value normalization. Then, the two mouth corners are detected by applying thresholding. The lip region is cropped based on the found corners, and then normalized so that rotation- and scale-invariant lip region images are obtained. Next, for each pixel point, the mean pixel value over an utterance is subtracted to reduce unwanted variations across image sequences. Finally, 12-dimensional features are obtained by applying the principal component analysis (PCA) to the mean-subtracted images. Also, their delta terms are computed and used together as in the acoustic features.

3.4 Feature-Level Association

The first step for feature-level association is to make the two feature vector sequences have the same frame rate. The acoustic feature sequence usually has a higher rate than the visual one. Thus, we perform interpolation of the visual features by using cubic splines to obtain the acoustic and the visual features of the same frame rate (100 Hz in our case).

Let $\mathbf{x}_t$ and $\mathbf{y}_t$ be the N_A-dimensional acoustic feature vector and the N_V-dimensional visual one after interpolation at time t, respectively. In order to consider the correlation between them, CCA is performed with $\mathbf{x}_t$ and $\mathbf{y}_{t-\tau:t+\tau}=[\mathbf{y}_{t-\tau}, \mathbf{y}_{t-\tau+1}, ..., \mathbf{y}_{t+\tau}]$ which is the collection of the visual feature vectors within a window having the length of $2\tau+1$. The parameter τ determines the length of the window. In this paper, we use a symmetric window for simplicity. Correlation analysis for multiple frames has the following implications: First, it can simultaneously deal with various degrees of audio-visual asynchrony which may be different for different pronunciations. Second, the correlation between neighboring frames is considered and thus dynamic characteristics of speech can be captured. It is known that such inter-frame correlation is important for noise-robust human speech understanding [16].

The objective of CCA is to find the two transformation matrices H_A and H_V for $\mathbf{x}_t$ and $\mathbf{y}_{t-\tau:t+\tau}$, respectively, which maximize the correlation of the transformed features $\mathbf{u}_t$ and $\mathbf{v}_t$:

$$
\begin{aligned}
\mathbf{u}_t &= H_A^T \mathbf{x}_t, \\
\mathbf{v}_t &= H_V^T \mathbf{y}_{t-\tau:t+\tau} .
\end{aligned}
\tag{1}
$$

Specifically, the first columns of H_A and H_V are obtained by solving the following maximization problem:

$$
\mathbf{h}_{A1}, \mathbf{h}_{V1} = \arg\max_{\mathbf{h}_A, \mathbf{h}_V} \frac{E\left[(\mathbf{h}_A^T \mathbf{x}_t)(\mathbf{h}_V^T \mathbf{y}_{t-\tau:t+\tau}) \right]}{\sqrt{E\left[(\mathbf{h}_A^T \mathbf{x}_t)^2 \right] E\left[(\mathbf{h}_V^T \mathbf{y}_{t-\tau:t+\tau})^2 \right]}} .
\tag{2}
$$

The solution of the above problem, which can be found by solving an eigenvalue problem, forms the first pair of canonical basis vectors. Then, the second pair is obtained for the residuals in the same manner after the components along the first basis vectors are removed from the original data. This procedure is iteratively applied so that the extracted basis vectors compose the transformation matrices H_A and H_V. The dimension of $\mathbf{u}_t$ and $\mathbf{v}_t$, N, is given by the minimum between the dimensions of $\mathbf{x}_t$ and $\mathbf{y}_{t-\tau:t+\tau}$, i.e. $N=\min\{N_A, (2\tau+1)N_V\}$. The columns of H_A and H_V, $\{\mathbf{h}_{Ai}\}$ and $\{\mathbf{h}_{Vi}\}$, $i=1,2,...,N$, form a set of orthonormal basis vectors for each data. More details of a general description of CCA can be found in [17].

The two transformed feature vectors, $\mathbf{u}_t$ and $\mathbf{v}_t$, are concatenated for feature-level association. Since continuous HMMs having Gaussian mixture models with diagonal covariance matrices are used for recognition, the concatenated features are transformed further by using the maximum likelihood linear transform (MLLT) [18] so that each component of the feature vector is uncorrelated with each other.

3.5 Decision-Level Association

The decision-level association is performed by a weighted sum of the outputs of the two recognizers (i.e. HMMs): For a given audio-visual datum O, the recognized utterance u^* is given by [3,4]

$$u^* = \arg\max_i \left\{ \gamma \log P(O \mid \lambda_A^i) + (1 - \gamma) \log P(O \mid \lambda_{AV}^i) \right\}, \tag{3}$$

where λ_A^i and λ_{AV}^i are the HMMs for the acoustic and the feature-level associated features of the i-th class, respectively, and $\log P(O \mid \lambda_A^i)$ and $\log P(O \mid \lambda_{AV}^i)$ are their outputs, i.e. log-likelihoods. The weighting factor γ, whose value is between 0 and 1, determines how much each recognizer contributes to the final recognition result. It is necessary to generate an appropriate value of γ for each given audio-visual datum to produce noise-robust recognition performance. For this, we use the neural network-based method [19] where a feedforward neural network (NN) receives the "reliability" measures of the two recognizers as its inputs and produces an appropriate weighting factor as its output.

The reliability of each data stream can be measured from the corresponding HMMs' outputs. When the acoustic speech does not contain noise, the acoustic HMMs' outputs show large differences, which implies large discriminability between the classes. On the contrary, the differences become small for data containing much noise. Among various possible definition of the reliability measure based on this observation, we use the following one which has been shown to produce the best performance [5,20]:

$$S = \frac{1}{C-1} \sum_{i=1}^{C} \left\{ \max_j \log P(O \mid \lambda^j) - \log P(O \mid \lambda^i) \right\}, \tag{4}$$

where C is the number of classes. In other words, the reliability of a data stream is defined by the average difference between the maximum log-likelihood and the other ones computed from the HMMs for the stream.

The NN is trained so as to model the input-output mapping between the two reliabilities and the proper integration weight so that it works as an optimal weight estimator. Training is done by the following steps: First, we calculate the reliabilities of the two recognizers' outputs for the training data of a few selected noise conditions. We use ∞ dB, 20 dB, 10 dB and 0 dB speech data corrupted by white noise. Then, for each datum, the weight value for correct recognition, which appears as an interval, is searched exhaustively. For a low-noise condition, a relatively large interval of the weight produces the correct recognition results because of large differences between the HMMs' outputs; when the speech contain much noise, the interval of the weight for correct recognition becomes small. Finally, the NN is trained with the pairs of the reliabilities and the found weight values. When a test datum of unknown noise condition (which may not be considered during training) is presented, the NN produces an estimated proper weight for the datum via its generalization capability.

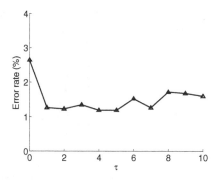

Fig. 2. Recognition performance in error rates (%) with respect to the value of τ for clean audio-visual speech data

4 Experiments

The performance of the proposed method is demonstrated via experiments on the isolated-word audio-visual speech database which contains sixteen Korean city names [19]. For each word, three utterances of 56 speakers (37 males and 19 females) are recorded. It should be noted that the database includes more significant amounts of data for speaker-independent recognition experiments than many of the previously reported databases [21,22,23].

The acoustic signal is recorded at the rate of 32 kHz, which is downsampled to 16 kHz for feature extraction. The 12-th order MFCCs and their delta terms are extracted, as explained in Section 3.2. The visual signal contains the face region around the speakers' mouths and is recorded at the rate of 30 Hz. Twelve features based on PCA and their delta terms are extracted for each frame (Section 3.3).

The recognition task is performed in a speaker-independent manner. To increase reliability of the experiments, we use the jackknife method where the data of 56 speakers are divided into four parts and we repeat the experiments four times with the data of three parts (42 speakers) for training and the remaining part (14 speakers) for test.

For simulating noisy conditions, we chose four real-world noise data from the NOISEX-92 database [24]: white noise (WHT), F-16 cockpit noise (F16), factory noise (FAC) and operation room noise (OPS). Each noise signal is added to the clean acoustic speech to produce speech data of various signal-to-noise (SNR) values.

For recognizers, left-to-right continuous HMMs are used. We use the whole-word model which is a standard approach for small vocabulary recognition tasks. The number of states in each HMM is set to proportional to the number of the phonetic units of the corresponding word. We use three Gaussian functions for the Gaussian mixture model in each state.

4.1 Results of Feature-Level Association

In the correlation analysis method presented in Section 3.4, it is necessary to determine an appropriate window size τ. We determine its value by examining recognition

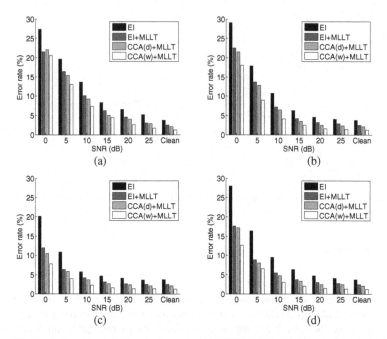

Fig. 3. Comparison of EI techniques for (a) WHT, (b) F16, (c) FAC and (d) OPS

performance for clean speech. Fig. 2 shows the recognition error rate with respect to the value of τ. In the figure, $\tau=0$ means that CCA is performed for perfectly synchronized audio-visual features without using the temporal window. It is observed that, by using τ larger than 0, we can obtain reduced error rates compared to the case of $\tau=0$. This implies that considering audio-visual asynchrony by using the temporal window in CCA improves recognition performance. The best performance is obtained when $\tau=5$, which is used through our experiments henceforce.

Next, we compare various EI techniques including the proposed one. In Fig. 3, the proposed method explained in Section 3.4 (noted by "CCA(w)+MLLT") is compared with three other methods: "EI" means the conventional feature fusion method where concatenated acoustic and visual feature vectors are used for recognition. "EI+MLLT" indicates the case where MLLT is additionally applied to the "EI" features for modeling with diagonal covariance matrices in HMMs. "CCA(d)+MLLT" is a variant of the method presented in [10]; in this method, CCA is performed with desynchronized features (i.e. $\mathbf{x}_t$ and $\mathbf{y}_{t-\tau}$) and the transformed features are concatenated for recognition. For fair comparison, we additionally applied MLLT to the projected features. Here, the amount of the time delay is set to four as in [10].

From the figure, it is observed that the proposed method shows the best performance over various conditions. Although the recognition performance is improved by modeling asynchrony by using a relative delay between the two data sequences (i.e. "CCA(d)+MLLT") in comparison to the case without considering the delay ("EI+MLLT"), the fixed delay is not sufficient for modeling the asynchrony and thus "CCA(d)+MLLT" is outperformed by our method considering asynchrony over multiple frames.

4.2 Results of Two-Level Association

Table 1 shows the performance of the proposed AVSR system in comparison to that of unimodal and conventional bimodal recognition systems. For the case of LI, the decision-level adaptive fusion method explained in Section 3.5 is used. Note that the visual-only recognition is not influenced by acoustic noise and thus constant for all noise conditions. On the other hand, the performance of the audio-only recognition is significantly degraded when the acoustic signal contains much noise. From the results of bimodal recognition (i.e. EI, LI and the proposed method), it is observed that using bimodal information reduces the error rate significantly for low SNR conditions compared to the audio-only recognition. However, EI has a defect that its performance for high SNRs is worse than that of the audio-only recognition because EI does not control proper amounts of relative contributions of the two modalities according to the noise condition. For the same reason, EI is always outperformed by LI which adaptively adjusts the degrees of the relative contributions of the modalities. Finally, the proposed method shows the best performance among the unimodal and the bimodal recognition schemes. On average for all conditions, the relative error reduction by the proposed method over LI is 45.2%.

Table 1. Performance of unimodal and bimodal recognition in error rates (%)

Noise	SNR (dB)	Video-only	Audio-only	EI	LI	Proposed
Clean			0.9	3.8	1.2	0.3
WHT	25		2.3	5.2	1.6	0.6
	20		5.8	6.5	2.7	1.4
	15		14.7	8.3	4.5	3.1
	10		29.5	13.6	8.5	6.5
	5		51.5	19.6	13.7	12.9
	0		74.2	27.4	19.7	21.4
F16	25		1.1	4.0	1.2	0.6
	20		1.4	4.5	1.4	0.6
	15		3.2	6.3	1.8	1.1
	10		10.9	10.8	4.5	2.4
	5		35.9	17.8	9.4	7.3
	0	22.0	81.6	29.1	19.5	18.8
FAC	25		1.0	3.7	1.2	0.4
	20		1.0	4.1	1.3	0.4
	15		1.5	4.7	1.5	0.5
	10		2.9	5.7	2.3	0.9
	5		9.3	10.8	4.0	2.1
	0		45.3	20.1	9.7	6.0
OPS	25		1.0	4.1	1.2	0.4
	20		1.6	4.8	1.3	0.6
	15		2.8	6.3	1.9	0.6
	10		9.0	9.5	3.5	1.5
	5		32.3	16.3	8.3	4.6
	0		80.8	27.9	19.2	12.6

5 Conclusion

We have proposed a two-level association method for AVSR in which audio-visual correlation and asynchrony are considered at the feature level and the adaptive fusion of the multimodal information is performed at the decision stage. The experimental results demonstrated that the proposed correlation analysis over multiple frames can effectively exploit the audio-visual correlation present in an asynchronous manner. Moreover, it was shown that the proposed two-level association method consistently produces improved robustness over various noise conditions in comparison to the conventional unimodal and bimodal recognition schemes. An advantage of the proposed method is that it does not require a priori knowledge about the noise condition of the given audio-visual datum for robust recognition performance.

While a temporal window of a fixed length was used in our correlation analysis and its effectiveness was shown through the experiments, using a window having an utterance-dependent length may be more beneficial because an appropriate window length may vary for each utterance. Such a variable window length can be determined via statistical and linguistic analysis of audio-visual speech or optimization through training. Further study in this direction would be desirable.

Investigating the validity of the proposed method for diverse recognition tasks would be also desirable. For example, connected-word or continuous speech recognition tasks can be considered, whereas this paper addressed an isolated word recognition task. In such cases, there exist unmanageably many possible word or phoneme sequence hypotheses to be considered for the decision-level association. Solutions for this could be to consider only N-best hypotheses from each data stream and test 2N combined pairs [7], or to incorporate the adaptive weighting scheme into joint modeling of the streams by using complex models such as multi-stream HMMs [4]. Also, while we simulated the noisy conditions by adding noise to the clean speech, it would be interesting to examine with speech data recorded in noisy environments how the Lombard effect affects the performance of the proposed method, especially the correlation analysis performed in the feature-level association.

Another possibility of audio-visual association other than the feature-level and the decision-level associations is to analyze and exploit the audio-visual correlation at the signal level. This could lead to acoustic speech enhancement performed prior to feature extraction [25] and be used in conjunction with the proposed AVSR scheme.

Acknowledgments. The research leading to these results has received funding from the European Community's Seventh Framework Programme (FP7/2007-2011) under grant agreement no. 216444 (PetaMedia), and the Swiss NCCR Interactive Multimodal Information Management (IM2).

References

1. Chibelushi, C.C., Deravi, F., Mason, J.S.D.: A Review of Speech-Based Bimodal Recognition. IEEE Trans. Multimedia 4, 23–37 (2002)
2. Bregler, C., Konig, Y.: 'Eigenlips' for Robust Speech Recognition. In: Proc. ICASSP, Adelaide, Australia, pp. 669–672 (1994)

3. Rogozan, A., Deléglise, P.: Adaptive Fusion of Acoustic and Visual Sources for Automatic Speech Recognition. Speech Commun. 26, 149–161 (1998)

4. Dupont, S., Luettin, J.: Audio-Visual Speech Modeling for Continuous Speech Recognition. IEEE Trans. Multimedia 2, 141–151 (2000)

5. Lee, J.-S., Park, C.H.: Adaptive Decision Fusion for Audio-Visual Speech Recognition. In: Mihelič, F., Žibert, J. (eds.) Speech Recognition, Technologies and Applications, I-Tech, Vienna Austria, pp. 275–296 (2008a)

6. Benoît, C.: The Intrinsic Bimodality of Speech Communication and the Synthesis of Talking Faces. In: Taylor, M.M., Nel, F., Bouwhuis, D. (eds.) The Structure of Multimodal Dialogue II, pp. 485–502. John Benjamins, Amsterdam (2000)

7. Meyer, G.F., Mullligan, J.B., Wuerger, S.M.: Continuous Audio-Visual Digit Recognition using N-Best Decision Fusion. Information Fusion 5, 91–101 (2004)

8. Conrey, B., Pisoni, D.B.: Auditory-Visual Speech Perception and Synchrony Detection for Speech and Nonspeech Signals. J. Acoust. Soc. Amer. 119, 4065–4073 (2006)

9. Fisher III, J.W., Darrell, T.: Speaker Association with Signal-Level Audiovisual Fusion. IEEE Trans. Multimedia 6, 406–413 (2004)

10. Sargin, M.E., Yemez, Y., Erzin, E., Tekalp, A.M.: Audiovisual Synchronization and Fusion using Canonical Correlation Analysis. IEEE Trans. Multimedia 9, 1396–1403 (2007)

11. Bredin, H., Chollet, G.: Audiovisual Speech Synchrony Measure: Application to Biometrics. EURASIP J. Advances in Signal Processing 2007, 11 pages, Article ID 70186 (2007)

12. Slaney, M., Covell, M.: FaceSync: A Linear Operator for Measuring Synchronization of Video Facial Images and Audio Tracks. In: Leen, T.K., Dietterich, T.G., Tresp, V. (eds.) Advances in Neural Information Processing Systems, vol. 13, pp. 814–820. MIT Press, Cambridge (2001)

13. Eveno, N., Besacier, L.: Co-Inertia Analysis for "Liveness" Test in Audio-Visual Biometrics. In: Proc. Int. Symposium on Image and Signal Processing and Analysis, Zagreb, Croatia, pp. 257–261 (2005)

14. Huang, X., Acero, A., Hon, H.-W.: Spoken Language Processing: A Guide to Theory, Algorithm, and System Development. Prentice Hall, Upper Saddle River (2001)

15. Lee, J.-S., Park, C.H.: Training Hidden Markov Models by Hybrid Simulated Annealing for Visual Speech Recognition. In: Proc. IEEE Int. Conf. Systems, Man, Cybernetics, Taipei, Taiwan, pp. 198–202 (2006)

16. Hermansky, H.: Exploring Temporal Domain for Robustness in Speech Recognition. In: Proc. Int. Congress on Acoustics, Trondheim, Norway, pp. 61–64 (1995)

17. Hardoon, D.R., Szedmak, S., Shawe-Taylor, J.: Canonical Correlation Analysis: An Overview with Application to Learning Methods. Dept. Comput. Sci., Univ. London, UK, Tech. Rep. CSD-TR-03-02 (2003)

18. Gopinath, R.A.: Maximum Likelihood Modeling with Gaussian Distributions for Classification. In: Proc. ICASSP, Seattle, USA, pp. 661–664 (1998)

19. Lee, J.-S., Park, C.H.: Robust Audio-Visual Speech Recognition based on Late Integration. IEEE Trans. Multimedia 10, 767–779 (2008b)

20. Lewis, T.W., Powers, D.M.W.: Sensor Fusion Weighting Measures in Audio-Visual Speech Recognition. In: Proc. 27th Australasian Conf. Computer Science, Dunedin, New Zealand, pp. 305–314 (2004)

21. Movellan, J.R.: Visual Speech Recognition with Stochastic Networks. In: Tesauro, G., Touretzky, D., Leen, T. (eds.) Advances in Neural Information Processing Systems, vol. 7, pp. 851–858. MIT Press, Cambridge (1995)

22. Chibelushi, C.C., Gandon, S., Mason, J.S.D., Deravi, F., Johnston, R.D.: Design Issues for a Digital Audio-Visual Integrated Database. In: Proc. IEE Colloq. Integrated Audio-Visual Processing for Recognition, Synthesis, Communication, London, UK, pp. 7/1–7/7 (1996)
23. Pigeon, S., Vandendrope, L.: The M2VTS Multimodal Face Database (Release 1.00). In: Proc. Int. Conf. Audio- and Video-based Biometric Authentication, Crans-Montana, Switzerland, pp. 403–409 (1997)
24. Varga, V., Steeneken, H.J.M.: Assessment for Automatic Speech Recognition: II. NOISEX 1992: A Database and an Experiment to Study the Effect of Additive Noise on Speech Recognition Systems. Speech Commun. 12, 247–251 (1993)
25. Rivet, B., Girin, L., Jutten, C.: Mixing Audiovisual Speech Processing and Blind Source Separation for the Extraction of Speech Signals from Convolutive Mixtures. IEEE Trans. Multimedia 15, 96–108 (2007)

Level Set-Based Fast Multi-phase Graph Partitioning Active Contours Using Constant Memory

Filiz Bunyak and Kannappan Palaniappan*

Department of Computer Science,
University of Missouri-Columbia, Columbia, MO 65211 USA

Abstract. We present multi-phase FastGPAC that extends our dramatic improvement of memory requirements and computational complexity on two-class GPAC, into multi-class image segmentation. Graph partitioning active contours GPAC is a recently introduced approach that elegantly embeds the graph-based image segmentation problem within a continuous level set-based active contour paradigm. However, GPAC similar to many other graph-based approaches has quadratic memory requirements. For example, a 1024x1024 grayscale image requires over one terabyte of working memory. Approximations of GPAC reduce this complexity by trading off accuracy. Our FastGPAC approach implements an exact GPAC segmentation using constant memory requirement of few kilobytes and enables use of GPAC on high throughput and high resolution images. Extension to multi-phase enables segmention of multiple regions of interest with different appearances. We have successfully applied FastGPAC on different types of images, particularly on biomedical images of different modalities. Experiments on the various image types, natural, biomedical etc. show promising segmentation results with substantially reduced computational requirements.

1 Introduction

PDE-based segmentation methods such as active contours attract a considerable interest particularly in biomedical image analysis because of their advantages such as mathematical description of the underlying physics phenomena, subpixel precision, and direct extension to higher dimensions [7, 20]. Active contours can use edge-based or region-based information. Recent research is increasingly focusing on the use of statistical region-based image energies introduced in [5, 6, 12, 13, 21]. This interest is partly due to larger basin of attraction in region-based energies compared to edge-based energies. Some efficient edge-based and region-based image energy terms can be found in [8].

Image segmentation can also be formulated as a graph-partitioning problem [3, 9, 10, 16, 19]. The common theme underlying these approaches is formation of a weighted graph where each vertex corresponds to an image pixel or region. Edge weight between two vertices of the graph represents the similarity/dissimilarity between two corresponding pixels/regions. This graph is partitioned by minimizing some application specific cost function which is usually summation of the weights of the edges that

---

* This work is partially supported by a United States National Institutes of Health grant, NIBIB award R33 EB00573.

J. Blanc-Talon et al. (Eds.): ACIVS 2009, LNCS 5807, pp. 145–155, 2009.

are cut. Graph cut approaches have strong connections to active contours and level sets. The segmentation energies optimized by graph cuts combine boundary regularization with region-based properties in the same fashion as Mumford-Shah style functionals [3]. When image segmentation problem is formulated as the best bi-partitioning of the image into two regions A and B, minimum cut technique minimizes a cost function defined as:

$$cut(A, B) = \sum_{u \in A, v \in B} w(u, v) \tag{1}$$

In a recent paper [17], Sumengen and Manjunath have introduced a framework called graph partitioning active contours (GPAC), that uses the equivalent energy functional in the continuous domain written as:

$$E_{CR} = \int\int_{R_i(\mathcal{C}(t)))} \int\int_{R_o(\mathcal{C}(t))} w(p_1, p_2) dp_1 dp_2 \tag{2}$$

where $\mathcal{C}$ is a curve, t is the time parameter of the evolution of $\mathcal{C}$, R_i and R_o are the interior and exterior of this curve, p_1 and p_2 are points such that $p_1 \in R_o$, $p_2 \in R_i$, and $w(p_1, p_2)$ is a dissimilarity measure between points p_1 and p_2. The pair of double integrals reflect the integration over a 2D region defined by $R_r(x, y)$.

This approach combines advantages of pairwise pixel (dis)similarity-based cost functions with flexibility of the variational methods [2]. But heavy computational and memory requirements prevent the technique's direct application to large images. Some *approximations* of the GPAC algorithm have been proposed in [17] and [2] to alleviate this problem by partitioning the input image into regular blocks or into "superpixels" and by calculating the dissimilarities at block or superpixel level respectively.

In this paper we present multi-phase FastGPAC that extends our recent dramatic improvement [4] of both memory requirements and computational complexity of two-class GPAC [17], into multi-class image segmentation. This new algorithm makes use of GPAC possible for segmentation of high throughput and high resolution images as in biomedical and geospatial applications. In Section 2, we give an overview of the graph partitioning active contours (GPAC). In Section 3, we present our efficient distribution-based reformulation. In Section 4, we extend our approach to multi-phase segmentation. Experimental results and conclusion are presented in sections 5,6.

2   Overview of Graph Partitioning Active Contours

The across-region cuts energy function (Eq. 2) that maximizes the dissimilarity between regions is not straightforward to extend to multi-class segmentation. In [2], Bertelli *et al.* reformulate this energy function in terms of pairwise dissimilarity within the regions:

$$E_{WR}(\mathcal{C}) = \int\int_{p_2 \in R_i(\mathcal{C})} \int\int_{p_1 \in R_i(\mathcal{C})} w(p_1, p_2) dp_1 dp_2 + \int\int_{p_2 \in R_o(\mathcal{C})} \int\int_{p_1 \in R_o(\mathcal{C})} w(p_1, p_2) dp_1 dp_2 \tag{3}$$

Here we use the latter (within regions) formulation. For 2-phase, both energy functions: Eq. 2 and Eq. 3 result in the same curve evolution equation (see [2] for proof).

Curve evolution corresponding to Eq. 3 can be done explicitly using snake-like active contours or implicitly using level set-based active contours. Level set-based approach provide advantages such as eliminating the need to reparameterize the curve and automatic handling of topology changes [15].

In level set-based active contours, a curve C ($C = \partial r$, boundary of an open set $r \in \Omega$) is represented implicitly via a Lipschitz function $\phi : \Omega \mapsto \mathbb{R}$ by $C = \{(x, y)|\phi(x, y) = 0\}$, and the evolution of the curve is given by the zero-level curve of the function $\phi(t, x, y)$ [5]. Ω represents the whole image domain, r represents inside of the curve C (foreground). , $(\Omega \setminus r)$ represents outside of the curve C (background). The function ϕ is positive inside and negative outside of the curve C. Heaviside function:

$$H(\phi) = \begin{cases} 1 \text{ if } \phi > 0 \\ 0 \text{ } elsewhere \end{cases}$$

is used as an indicator function for the points inside and outside of C. Using level set representation Eq. 3 is written as:

$$E = \iint_\Omega \iint_\Omega w(p_1, p_2) H(\phi(p_1)) H(\phi(p_2)) dp_1 dp_2$$
$$+ \iint_\Omega \iint_\Omega w(p_1, p_2) \Big(1 - H(\phi(p_1))\Big) \Big(1 - H(\phi(p_2))\Big) dp_1 dp_2 \quad (4)$$

Steepest descent minimization of Eq. 4 leads to the curve evolution equation:

$$\frac{\partial \phi(p_2)}{\partial t} = \delta(\phi(p_2))[\iint_\Omega w(p_1, p_2) \Big(1 - H(\phi(p_1))\Big) dp_1$$
$$- \iint_\Omega w(p_1, p_2) H(\phi(p_1))] \quad (5)$$

discretized as:

$$\frac{\Delta \phi(p_2)}{\Delta t} = \delta_\epsilon(\phi(p_2)) \Big[\sum_{p_1 \in R_o(C)} w(p_2, p_1) - \sum_{p_1 \in R_i(C)} w(p_2, p_1) \Big] \quad (6)$$

where δ_ϵ is discretized delta function. We refer to the expression inside the brackets as region variability term (RV). For regularization, mean curvature flow which adds to the variational cost function a term proportional to the length of the zero level set contour is used [5]:

$$\mu \cdot Length(C) = \mu \cdot \iint_\Omega |\nabla H(\phi(p))| dp = \mu \cdot \iint_\Omega \delta(\phi(p)) |\nabla \phi(p)| dp \quad (7)$$

curve evolution corresponding to this term is:

$$\frac{\partial \phi}{\partial t} = \mu \delta(\phi) \text{ div } \frac{\nabla \phi}{|\nabla \phi|} = \mu \delta \mathcal{K} \quad (8)$$

Regularization term is discretized as described in [5, 14].

The computational bottleneck in GPAC algorithm is the calculations of the regional sums in Eq. 6 that measure the (dis)similarity of each image point p_1 to every points in regions $R_o(\mathcal{C})$ and $R_i(\mathcal{C})$ respectively. For an image of size N^2, this results in $O(N^2 \times N^2)$ pixel-to-pixel dissimilarity computation operations. To avoid recomputation at each contour evolution iteration, these dissimilarities are pre-computed once and kept in memory as a look-up table. For an image of size N^2, this results in a symmetric dissimilarity matrix $\mathbf{W}$ with N^2 rows and N^2 columns, where an element $W(i,j)$ is $w(p_i, p_j)$, dissimilarity of pixels p_i and p_j. Number of such dissimilarities kept in this method is $N^4/2$. Since even for small images $\mathbf{W}$ becomes quite large and hard to fit in memory (1TB for a $1K \times 1K$ image and 2 bytes per $w(p_1, p_2)$), approximations are proposed in [17] and in [2] by partitioning the input image into blocks or into "superpixels" respectively.

3   Fast Graph Partitioning Active Contours (FastGPAC)

While pairwise pixel similarity-based cost functions are powerfull, direct implementation of GPAC is quite costly. For an N^2-pixel image, computational complexity and memory requirements of the look-up table $\mathbf{W}$ are both $O(N^4)$, since (dis)similarity of each N^2 pixels to each N^2 pixels is computed and stored. Use of the original GPAC algorithm for high resolution or high throughput image analysis is not feasible because of these high memory requirements and computational complexity. In this section, we summarize our fast graph partitioning active contours (FastGPAC) approach that dramatically reduces the computational complexity and the memory requirements of GPAC to $O(N^2)$ and $O(1)$ respectively by reducing the 2D regional sums in Eq. 6 into 1D distribution sums. Detailed complexity analysis for GPAC and FastGPAC can be found in [4].

For feature-based (dis)similarity measures $w(p_1, p_2)$ that does not involve spatial distance between pixels p_1, p_2. $w(p_1, p_2)$ can be re-written as:

$$w(p_1, p_2) \equiv D(F(p_1), F(p_2)) \tag{9}$$

where $F(p)$ is a feature extracted at point $p(x, y)$, and D is a dissimilarity measure defined on F (i.e. for absolute grayscale intensity difference, $w(p_1, p_2) = |I(p_1) - I(p_2)|$, feature $F(p)$ is grayscale intensity $I(p)$ and the dissimilarity measure D is L_1 metric.)

Theorem 3.1 (GPAC Region Sum Theorem). For cases where the dissimilarity measure $w(p_1, p_2)$ is feature-based (does not involve spatial distance between pixels), the 2D regional sums, $\sum_{p_1 \in R_r} w(p_2, p_1)$ (for $R_r = R_i$ or R_o) can be reduced to 1D sums independent of the spatial size or shape of the regions $R_r(\mathcal{C})$.

$$\sum_{p_1 \in R_r} w(p_1, p_2) \equiv \sum_{j=0}^{L-1} h_r(j) \times D(F(p_2), j) \tag{10}$$

where $\mathbf{h_r}$ is the histogram of the feature F in the rth region R_r, $D()$ is a (dis)similarity measure, L is number of bins in $\mathbf{h}$, and $h_r(j) = \sum_{p_1 \in R \wedge F(p_1)=j} 1$ is the jth bin of $\mathbf{h_r}$

corresponding to the number of points $p_1 \in R_r$ whose feature $F(p_1) = j$. In the more general case, $D(F(p_2), j)$ is replaced by $D(F(p_2), C(j))$ where $C(j)$ is a representative value for the histogram bin $h(j)$.

Proof. This equality is derived by grouping the points p into feature class bins $F(p) = j$, and by separating the original sum into two nested sums as follows:

$$\sum_{p \in R_r} w(p_2, p_1) \equiv \sum_{p_1 \in R_r} D(F(p_2), F(p_1)) = \sum_{j=0}^{L-1} \sum_{p_1 \in R_r \wedge F(p_1)=j} D(F(p_2), F(p_1))$$

$$= \sum_{j=0}^{L-1} D(F(p_2), j) \times \underbrace{\sum_{p_1 \in R_r \wedge F(p_1)=j} 1}_{h(j)}$$

$$= \sum_{j=0}^{L-1} D(F(p_2), j) \times h(j) \tag{11}$$

In this case the discretized region variability term becomes:

$$\sum_{p_1 \in R_o(\mathcal{C})} w(p_2, p_1) - \sum_{p_1 \in R_i(\mathcal{C})} w(p_2, p_1)$$

$$= \sum_{j=0}^{L-1} h_o(j) \times D(F(p_2), j) - \sum_{j=0}^{L-1} h_i(j) \times D(F(p_2), j)$$

$$= \sum_{j=0}^{L-1} [h_o(j) - h_i(j)] \times D(F(p_2), j) \tag{12}$$

and the curve evolution equation in 6 transforms into:

$$\frac{\Delta\phi(p_2)}{\Delta t} = \delta_\epsilon(\phi(p_2)) \left[\sum_{j=0}^{L-1} [h_o(j) - h_i(j)] \times D(F(p_2), j) \right] \tag{13}$$

4   Extension of FastGPAC into Multi-phase Segmentation

The two phase segmentation scheme described above segments the image into two: foreground and background, and is appropriate for segmentation of single class objects/appearances from a single class background. However images often contain multiple classes of objects or multiple regions of interests with different appearances. Various approaches can be used to extend 2-phase segmentation to deal with multiple classes such as hierarchical 2-phase segmentations or N-level sets where each class is assigned a level set. In [18], Chan and Vese presented a multi-phase extension of their two-phase level set image segmentation algorithm [5]. The multi-phase approach enables efficient partitioning of the image into n classes using just $log(n)$ level sets without leaving any gaps or having overlaps between level sets. This ensures that each pixel is properly

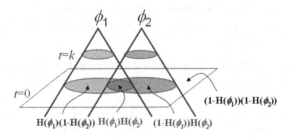

Fig. 1. A four-phase level set partitioning, with two level set functions ϕ_1 and ϕ_2. $H(\phi_1)$ and $H(\phi_2)$ are the Heaviside functions associated with each level set function.

assigned to a unique class during the segmentation process. Figure 1 illustrates the 4-phase (2 level set) case.

In [2], GPAC is extended to multi-phase in a way similar to Vese and Chan's multi-phase extension [18]. In this scheme, the n-phase energy function becomes:

$$E = \sum_i^n \iint_\Omega \iint_\Omega w(p_1, p_2)\chi_i(p_1)\chi_i(p_2)dp_1 dp_2 \qquad (14)$$

χ_i is the indicator function that takes value of 1 for phase i, and 0 otherwise. $k = log_2 n$ level set functions are used to represent n phases. 4-phase (2 level set) GPAC energy function is written as:

$$\begin{aligned}
E_{WR} &= \iint_\Omega \iint_\Omega w(p_1, p_2)[\chi_1(p_1)\chi_1(p_2)]dp_1 dp_2 \\
&+ \iint_\Omega \iint_\Omega w(p_1, p_2)[\chi_2(p_1)\chi_2(p_2)]dp_1 dp_2 \\
&+ \iint_\Omega \iint_\Omega w(p_1, p_2)[\chi_3(p_1)\chi_3(p_2)]dp_1 dp_2 \\
&+ \iint_\Omega \iint_\Omega w(p_1, p_2)[\chi_4(p_1)\chi_4(p_2)]dp_1 dp_2 \qquad (15)
\end{aligned}$$

where the indicator functions χ_{1-4} for the four regions are:

$$\chi_1(p) = H(\phi_1(p))H(\phi_2(p)); \qquad \chi_2(p) = H(\phi_1(p))(1 - H(\phi_2(p)))$$
$$\chi_3(p) = (1 - H(\phi_1(p)))H(\phi_2(p)); \quad \chi_4(p) = (1 - H(\phi_1(p)))(1 - H(\phi_2(p)))$$

Curve evolution for this 4-phase energy function is then:

$$\begin{aligned}
\frac{\partial \phi_1(p_2)}{\partial t} &= \delta(\phi(p_2))\Big\{ H(\phi_2(p_2))\Big[\iint_\Omega w(p_1, p_2)\chi_3(p_1)dp_1 - \iint_\Omega w(p_1, p_2)\chi_1(p_1)dp_1 \Big] \\
&+ (1 - H(\phi_2(p_2)))\Big[\iint_\Omega w(p_1, p_2)\chi_4(p_1)dp_1 - \iint_\Omega w(p_1, p_2)\chi_2(p_1)dp_1 \Big] \Big\} \\
\frac{\partial \phi_2(p_2)}{\partial t} &= \delta(\phi(p_2))\Big\{ H(\phi_2(p_2))\Big[\iint_\Omega w(p_1, p_2)\chi_2(p_1)dp_1 - \iint_\Omega w(p_1, p_2)\chi_1(p_1)dp_1 \Big] \\
&+ (1 - H(\phi_2(p_2)))\Big[\iint_\Omega w(p_1, p_2)\chi_4(p_1)dp_1 - \iint_\Omega w(p_1, p_2)\chi_3(p_1)dp_1 \Big] \Big\} \qquad (16)
\end{aligned}$$

Note that the normalization and regularization terms are ignored for simplicity of the notation, otherwise these terms needs to be included.

Although FastGPAC is initially defined for binary (2-phase) segmentation [4], GPAC region sum theorem equally applies to the regional sums in Eq. 16. As in the 2-phase case the 2D regional sums $\sum_{p_1 \in R_r} w(p_2, p_1)$ are reduced to 1D sums independent of the spatial size or shape of the regions R_r. In n-phase case R_r refers to the n regions/classes defined by $k = log(n)$ level sets. In 2-phase these regions correspond to R_i, R_o, in 4-phase these regions correspond to $\chi_1, .., \chi_4$ defined above. FastGPAC transforms the 4-phase curve evolution equation Eq. 16 into its more efficient form:

$$\frac{\Delta \phi_1(p_2)}{\Delta t} = \delta_\epsilon(\phi_1(p_2)) \Big\{ H(\phi_2(p_2)) \sum_{j=0}^{L-1} [h_3(j) - h_1(j)] D(F(p_2), j)$$

$$+ (1 - H(\phi_2(p_2))) \sum_{j=0}^{L-1} [h_4(j) - h_2(j)] D(F(p_2), j) \Big\} \tag{17}$$

$$\frac{\Delta \phi_2(p_2)}{\Delta t} = \delta_\epsilon(\phi_2(p_2)) \Big\{ H(\phi_1(p_2)) \sum_{j=0}^{L-1} [h_2(j) - h_1(j)] D(F(p_2), j)$$

$$+ (1 - H(\phi_1(p_2))) \sum_{j=0}^{L-1} [h_4(j) - h_3(j)] D(F(p_2), j) \Big\} \tag{18}$$

where $h_1, .., h_4$ denotes the regional histograms corresponding to the regions $\chi_1, .., \chi_4$. While the actual number of operation in FastGPAC increases linearly with number of phases, complexity order remains the same since N^4 point-to-point dissimilarity computation is reduced to N^2 pixel to n histograms dissimilarity computation, where n is number of phases.

5 Experimental Results

In this section we compare original GPAC [1] and FastGPAC results in terms of computational time and similarity of the segmentation masks. And we present sample two-phase and multi-phase FastGPAC segmentation results for different imaging applications and modalities including natural scenery, various biomedical imagery (MRI, histopathology, fluorescent microscopy), and geospatial images.

In order to make a fair comparison regardless of coding optimizations, GPAC code by Luca Bertelli [1] is used as a base for the FastGPAC code. Both programs (original GPAC [1] and our FastGPAC) are written as a combination of Matlab and C functions. Both programs are tested on Intel Xeon 5140 dual core with dual processor machines with 10 GB RAM . While [2] extends the original 2-phase GPAC to multi-phase, the source code we use for original GPAC [1] is a 2-phase segmentation code, thus the speed-up and mask similarity are given for 2-phase GPAC and FastGPAC results. As discussed in Section 4, similar speed-ups with a constant factor are expected for multi-phase FastGPAC versus multi-phase GPAC.

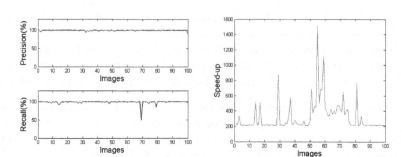

Fig. 2. Quantitative FastGPAC vs. GPAC comparison results on the Berkeley Segmentation Dataset [11]. a) Segmentation mask similarity in terms of recall and precision. b) Speed-up obtained by FastGPAC.

Fig. 3. Sample 2-phase FastGPAC segmentation results for images 42049, 253027,227092, 302008, 376043 from Berkeley segmentation dataset [11]. First row: original image, second row: foreground region.

Figure 2 shows quantitative comparison results on the Berkeley Segmentation Dataset [11]. Detailed complexity analysis for 2-phase GPAC and FastGPAC can be found in our recent paper [4]. Segmentation results for selected images are shown in Figure 3. For both programs input images are converted from RGB color space into YC_bC_r color space and resized to 241×146 pixels (because of the original GPAC's memory requirements). The luma component Y is scaled into [0-100], chroma components C_b and C_r are scaled into [0-200] ranges. Parameters $\mu = 4000$, $\lambda_1 = \lambda_2 = 1$, ($\epsilon = 0.001$, $\delta_t = 0.5$ for level set) are used for both programs. Segmentation similarity (Figure 2a) is measured in terms of recall and precision defined as below:

$$\text{recall} = \frac{|Mask_G \cap Mask_F|}{|Mask_G|}, \qquad \text{precision} = \frac{|Mask_G \cap Mask_F|}{|Mask_F|} \qquad (19)$$

where $Mask_G$, $Mask_F$ are GPAC and FastGPAC segmentation masks respectively. Mean precision and recall of the FastGPAC masks compared to corresponding GPAC masks are 99% and 98.3% respectively. The deep minimum (around 70 in x-axis) corresponds to the image #96073 where the background and foreground color distributions

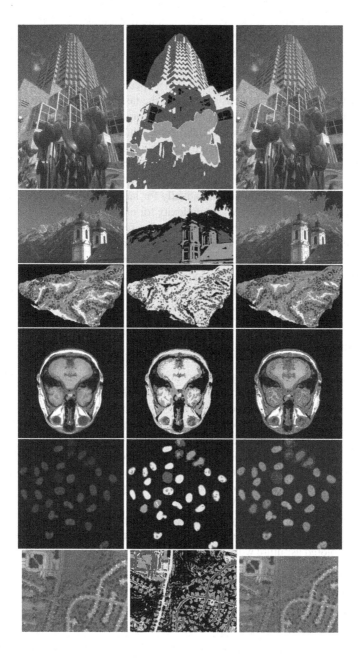

Fig. 4. Sample segmentation results for different imaging applications and modalities including natural scenery (rows 1,2), various biomedical imagery (histopathology (row 3), MRI (rows 4), fluorescent microscopy (row 5)), and geospatial images (row 6). First column: original image, second column: segmentation mask, third column:segmentation contours superimposed on the original image, first phase as red, second phase as green lines.

are very similar and texture is the distinctive feature that should be used for segmentation. For this image both GPAC and FastGPAC programs used with only color features fail dramatically producing segmentation masks far from the desired mask. Figure 2b shows speed-up obtained for images of the same dataset. FastGPAC results in an average of $322\times$ speed-up in elapsed time and $226\times$ speed-up in CPU time. CPU time is the time for which the CPU was busy executing the task. It does not take into account the time spent in disk I/O. Because of its large memory requirements, $O(N^4)$ for an image of size N^2, GPAC uses more virtual memory than FastGPAC increasing its disk access and elapsed time. For larger image sizes the difference between CPU time and elapsed time becomes even larger. These speed-up numbers illustrate that even for quite small images there is a significant timing difference between original GPAC and Fast-GPAC algorithms, which increases dramatically for larger images considering $O(N^2)$ complexity for FastGPAC vs. $O(N^4)$ complexity for original GPAC.

FastGPAC's dramatic improvements in memory requirements and computational complexity enable use of GPAC on high throughput and high resolution images (e.g. biomedical and geospatial). Figure 4 presents sample multi-phase segmentation results for different imaging applications and modalities including natural scenery (rows 1,2), various biomedical imagery (histopathology (row 3), MRI (rows 4), fluorescent microscopy (row 5)), and geospatial images (row 6).

6   Conclusion and Future Works

We present a fast formulation of graph partitioning active contours (GPAC) that combines accuracy and dramatic speed-up. The new formulation reduces memory requirements from $O(N^4)$ to $O(1)$ and computational complexity from $O(N^4)$ to $O(N^2)$ for an $N \times N$ image. We further extend this fast formulation from two-phase segmentation to multi-phase segmentation, enabling segmentation of multiple regions of interests with different appearances. FastGPAC algorithm provides flexibility of the GPAC algorithm enabled by possibility of using different image features and different dissimilarity measures while being computationally feasible for large images, high spatial resolutions, and long image sequences. We have successfully applied FastGPAC to biomedical, geospatial and natural imagery. Experiments show promising segmentation results. Additional speedup can be obtained through parallelization on GPU or Cell processors, and will be explored as future work.

References

1. Bertelli, L.: GPAC implementation,
   http://vision.ece.ucsb.edu/~lbertelli/soft_GPAC.html
2. Bertelli, L., Sumengen, B., Manjunath, B., Gibou, F.: A variational framework for multiregion pairwise similarity-based image segmentation. IEEE Trans. on Patt. Anal. Mach. Intell. 30(8), 1400–1414 (2008)
3. Boykov, Y., Funka-Lea, G.: Graph cuts and efficient n-d image segmentation. Int. J. Comp. Vision 70(2), 109–131 (2006)
4. Bunyak, F., Palaniappan, K.: Efficient segmentation using feature-based graph partitioning active contours. In: Int'l Conf. Computer Vision (September 2009)

5. Chan, T., Vese, L.: Active contours without edges. IEEE Trans. Image Proc. 10(2), 266–277 (2001)
6. Cohen, L.: On active contour models and balloons. Comput. Vis., Graphics, Image Processing 53, 211–218 (1991)
7. Dejnozkova, E., Dokladal, P.: Embedded real-time architecture for level-set-based active contours. EURASIP Journal on Applied Signal Processing 2005(17), 2788–2803 (2005)
8. Jacob, M., Blu, T., Unser, M.: Efficient energies and algorithms for parametric snakes. IEEE Trans. Image Process. 13(9), 1231–1244 (2004)
9. Kolmogorov, V., Zabin, R.: What energy functions can be minimized via graph cuts? IEEE Trans. Patt. Anal. Mach. Intell. 26(2), 147–159 (2004)
10. Malcolm, J., Rathi, Y., Tannenbaum, A.: A graph cut approach to image segmentation in tensor space. In: IEEE Conf. Comp. Vision and Patt. Rec., pp. 1–8 (2007)
11. Martin, D., Fowlkes, C., Tal, D., Malik, J.: A database of human segmented natural images and its application to evaluating segmentation algorithms and measuring ecological statistics. In: Proc. 8th Int'l Conf. Computer Vision, July 2001, vol. 2, pp. 416–423 (2001)
12. Paragios, N., Deriche, R.: Geodesic active regions for motion estimation and tracking. In: Proc. Int. Conf. Computer Vision, Corfu, Greece, pp. 688–694 (1999)
13. Ronfard, R.: Region-based strategies for active contour models. Int. J. Comput. Vision 13, 229–251 (1994)
14. Rudin, L., Osher, S., Fatemi, E.: Nonlinear total variation based noise removal algorithms. Phys. D 60, 259–268 (1992)
15. Sethian, J.: Level Set Methods and Fast Marching Methods: Evolving Interfaces in Computational Geometry. In: Fluid Mechanics, Computer Vision, and Materials Science. Cambridge University Press, Cambridge (1999)
16. Shi, J., Malik, J.: Normalized cuts and image segmentation. IEEE Trans. Patt. Anal. Mach. Intell. 22(8), 888–905 (2000)
17. Sumengen, B., Manjunath, B.S.: Graph partitioning active contours (GPAC) for image segmentation. IEEE Trans. Patt. Anal. Mach. Intell., 509–521 (April 2006)
18. Vese, L., Chan, T.: A multiphase level set framework for image segmentation using the Mumford and Shah model. Int. J. Computer Vision 50(3), 271–293 (2002)
19. Wu, Z., Leahy, R.: An optimal graph theoretic approach to data clustering: Theory and its application to image segmentation. IEEE Trans. Patt. Anal. Mach. Intell. 15(11), 1101–1113 (1993)
20. Wang, X., He, W., Metaxas, D., Matthew, R., White, E.: Cell segmentation and tracking using texture-adaptive snakes. In: Proc. IEEE Int. Symp. Biomedical Imaging, Washington, DC, April 2007, pp. 101–104 (2007)
21. Zhu, S., Yuille, A.: Region competition: Unifying snakes, region growing, and bayes/mdl for multiband image segmentation. IEEE Trans. Patt. Anal. Mach. Intell. 18, 884–900 (1996)

Image Quality Assessment Based on Edge-Region Information and Distorted Pixel for JPEG and JPEG2000

Zianou Ahmed Seghir[1] and Fella Hachouf[2]

[1] Department of computing science, University of Mentouri Constantine, Road of Ain El Bey,
25000 Constantine, Algeria
zianou_ahmed_seghir@yahoo.fr
[2] Electronic Department, University of Mentouri Constantine, Road of Ain El Bey, 25000
Constantine, Algeria
Tel.: 031-61-42-07 poste 31; Fax: 031-61-42-07
fhachouf@wissal.dz

Abstract. The main objective of image quality assessment metrics is to provide an automatic and efficient system to evaluate visual quality. It is imperative that these measures exhibit good correlation with perception by the human visual system (HVS). This paper proposes a new algorithm for image quality assessment, which supplies more flexibility than previous methods in using the distorted pixel in the assessment. First, the distorted and original images are divided into blocks of 11×11 pixels, and secondly, we calculate distorted pixels then visual regions of interest and edge information are computed which can be used to compute the global error. Experimental comparisons demonstrate the effectiveness of the proposed method.

Keywords: Image Quality Assessment, Mean structural similarity Index (MSSIM), Difference Mean Opinion Score (*DMOS*), distorted pixel.

1 Introduction

Image quality evaluation [4, 11-14] is of fundamental importance for numerous image and video processing applications, such as compression, communication, printing, analysis, registration, restoration and enhancement, where the goal of quality assessment algorithms is to automatically assess the quality of images or videos in agreement with human quality judgments. Over the years, several researchers are looking for new quality measures, better adapted to human perception. It is important to evaluate the performance of these algorithms in a comparative setting and analyze the strengths and weaknesses of these methods.

Image quality assessment methods can be classified into subjective and objective methods. The first approach of image quality assessment is subjective quality testing which is based on many observers that evaluate image quality. These tests are time consuming and have a very strict definition of observational conditions.

The second approach is the objective image quality testing based on mathematical calculations. The objective quality evaluation is easier and faster than the subjective one because observers are not needed. One of the properties required for an image quality criterion is that it should produce objective scores well correlated with

J. Blanc-Talon et al. (Eds.): ACIVS 2009, LNCS 5807, pp. 156–166, 2009.

subjective quality scores produced by human observers during quality assessment tests. Some of them use a human visual model (HVS) [5-6]. These HVS models can model only parts of human vision that we need (e.g. spatial resolution, temporal motion, color fidelity, color resolution...). A majority of these models requires a tested image and its corresponding matching reference in order to determine the perceptual difference between them.

Most of the objective image quality assessment techniques in the available literature are error-based methods. These methods use pixel based difference metrics like, Signal to Noise Ratio (SNR) and Peak Signal to Noise Ratio (PSNR). However, in many cases these metrics may not correlate [1] well with the perceived visual quality. The majority of the proposed perceptual quality assessment models have followed a strategy of modifying the mean squared error (MSE) measure so that errors are penalized in accordance with their visibility [4].

In this work, the problem of image quality evaluation with reference image is reduced to edge information, visual region and distorted pixel. The experiment is carried out using sets of original images with its deformed versions from LIVE image quality database [3]. The performance of the proposed quality metric is compared with the Gradient-based Structural Similarity (GSSIM) [8], Visual region of interest Weighted Quality Index (VroiWQI) [9] and PSNR.

The paper is organized as follows. Some algorithms of image quality measures are presented in Section 2. Proposed image quality measure is defined next. Performance of the proposed measure will be illustrated by examples involving images with different types of distortion in Section 4, followed by the conclusion.

2 Related Work

Most of the efforts in the research have been focused on the problem of image quality assessment. We present some image quality assessment metrics that are based on the HVS error sensitivity paradigm and those based on arbitrary signal fidelity criteria. The mean squared error (MSE) computed by averaging the squared intensity differences of distorted and reference image pixels, along with the related quantity of peak signal-to-noise ratio (PSNR). MSE and PSNR are widely used because they are simple to calculate, have clear physical meanings, and are mathematically easy to deal with for optimization purposes (MSE is differentiable, for example). But they are not very well matched to perceived visual quality [1]. In [2, 4, 7] Zhou Wang proposed a new philosophy of the Structural Similarity Index (SSIM) for image quality measurement based on the assumption that the HVS is highly adapted to extract structural information from the viewing field. MSSIM includes three parts: Luminance Comparison $l(x, y)$, Contrast Comparison $c(x, y)$ and Structure Comparison $s(x, y)$. However, MSSIM fails in measuring badly blurred images [4]. In [8], they have proposed an improved quality assessment called Gradient-based Structural Similarity (GSSIM) based on the edge information as the most important image structure information. The Sobel operators are used to obtain the edge information due to its simplicity and efficiency. They have used this measure in determination edge information where the contrast comparison $c(x, y)$ and structure comparison $s(x, y)$ in [7] are replaced by with the gradient-based contrast comparison $c_g(x, y)$ and structure comparison $s_g(x, y)$

respectively. This measure is very interesting in using edge information with MSSIM but, it cannot use for measuring quality of the region information. In [9] a visual region of interest weighted quality index is introduced. The index is based on weighted quality indices of local regions that capture structural distortion in the local regions between the test image and the original image. Weights are assigned in accordance with Visual regions of interest, characterized by the entropy of the region which emphasizes the texture variance in that region. Equation (1) gives the expression for VroiWQI.

$$\text{VroiWQI} = \sum_{i=1}^{M} \sum_{i=1}^{N} [E] * [\text{SSIM}] / \sum_{i=1}^{M} \sum_{i=1}^{N} [E] \tag{1}$$

Where $[E]$ is the subset matrix of normalized entropy values E. Weighted Quality Index not interested in using edge information.

Motivated with these studies, in this paper, an edge-region and distorted pixels measure is proposed which doesn't exploit a priori knowledge about the distorted image and the types of artifacts.

3   Proposed Method

Original image is denoted by *Original(mm,nn)* and distorted image is denoted by *Distorted(mm,nn)*. Both images have *mm×nn* pixels. Thus, the images are partitioned into overlapped 11× 11 blocks (see Fig.1.), where the overlapping area is on one pixel. At each step, the local statistics is calculated within the block. The choice of 11×11 overlap is motivated by the subdivision the image on local 8×8 square window, often exhibits undesirable "blocking" artifacts problem [4]. Thus, this kind of problem is hidden, or mostly disappeared, when the partition superior on 8× 8 block of pixel is used. Let bk_j and bk_i be blocks of distorted image and original image respectively.

3.1   Distorted Pixels and Displacement Measure

In the first step, we identify distorted pixels. All blocks of 11×11 pixels are divided into non-overlapped 3×3 sub-blocks (see Fig.1.). With such a partitioning approach, any kind of artifacts creates pixel distortions from neighborhood pixels is calculated. The mean of each sub-block (sbk_{jsub}) of the deformed image is calculated. Let Mf_i be the mean of pixels of a sub-block (sbk_{jsub}) of the distorted image and Xf_i its intensities. This mean can be estimated as follows:

$$Mf_i = \frac{1}{9} \sum_{i=1}^{9} Xf_i \tag{2}$$

The same procedure is applied on the original image. This one has also a mean M_i and X_i its intensities. For each sub-block (sbk_{isub}) of the original image, the mean is calculated.

$$M_i = \frac{1}{9} \sum_{i=1}^{9} X_i \tag{3}$$

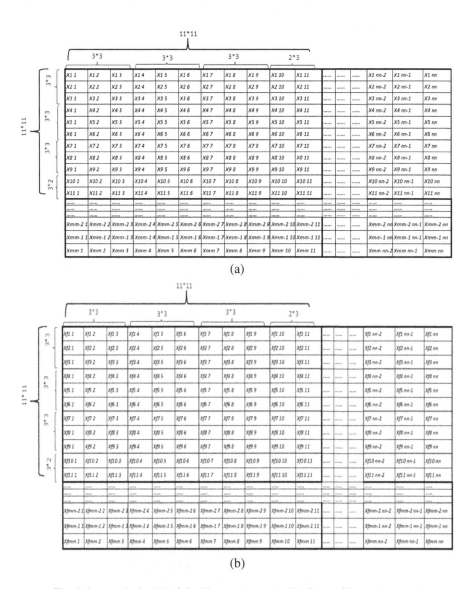

Fig. 1. Image pixels: (a) original image (mm×nn), (b) distorted image (mm×nn)

The difference measure DM between the two sbk_{isub} and sbk_{jsub} can be estimated as follows:

$$DM = \sqrt{\frac{1}{9}\sum_{i=1}^{9}\left(Mf_i - X_i\right)^2 + \left(M_i - Xf_i\right)^2} \qquad (4)$$

The distorted pixels measurement Id between the two bk_i and bk_j is defined by:

$$Id = \frac{1}{A} \sum_{i=1}^{A} DM_i \qquad (5)$$

where A ($A = 11*11/3*3$) is the total number of partially overlapping sub-blocks within block of 11×11 pixel. All Id can be arrayed in a $(m \times n)$ matrix $id_{global} = [Id_{i,j}]$ ($1 \le i \le m = mm/11$ and $1 \le j \le n = nn/11$).

3.2 Visual Regions of Interest

In this stage we have used the same function developed in [9] where the regions in the original image is modeled by computing the similar entropy "e" in each block of 11 x 11 pixels of the original image, using equation (6), where h_i is a random variable indicating intensity, $p(h_i)$ is the histogram of the intensity levels in a region, K is the number of possible intensity levels. K varies from 0 to 255 for gray scale images.

$$e = -\sum_{i=i}^{K} p(h_i) \log_2 p(h_i) \qquad (6)$$

All e can be arrayed in a $(m \times n)$ matrix $E = [e_{i,j}]$ ($1 \le i \le m = mm/11$ and $1 \le j \le n = nn/11$), where each element $e_{i,j}$ is the similar entropy of the block.

In this step, the formula for measuring the region structure comparison measures is as follows:

$$s_r(bk_i, bk_j) = e_{ij} * s(bk_i, bk_j) \qquad (7)$$

Where $s(bk_i, bk_j) = (\sigma_{bki\,bkj} + C_3)/(\sigma_{bki}\,\sigma_{bkj} + C_3)$, $C_3 = C_2/2$ where $C_2 = (K_2 L_2)$, $K_2 \ll 1$, L_2 is the dynamic range of the pixel values (255 for 8-bit grayscale images), σ_{bki} and σ_{bkj} are the standard deviation of blocks bk_i and bk_j respectively, $\sigma_{bki\,bkj}$ is the covariance of blocks bk_i and bk_j.

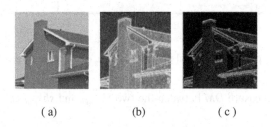

    (a)   (b)   (c)

Fig. 2. (a) Original House image (b) Simulated image showing the Visual regions of interest map (c) and Simulated image showing the edge information

Fig.2 displays the original "House" image (512 x 512) and its normalized entropy map E (64x64), with a value of 1 indicating the region of highest interest represented as white, and a value of 0 indicating the region of lowest interest as black. The other levels of the image ranging from white to black represent the Visual regions with descending level of interest.

3.3 Edge Information

In the [8] an improved quality assessment called Gradient-based Structural Similarity (*GSSIM*) is proposed based on the edge information as the most important image structure information. The Sobel operators are used to obtain the edge information due to its simplicity and efficiency. We set *Xorg* and *Ydist* represent the gradient map of the original image and the distorted one respectively, and let bk_i' and bk_j' be blocks (theirs size 11*11 pixels) of *Xorg* and *Ydist* respectively.

This measure is used in determination edge information where the contrast comparison $c(bk_i, bk_j)$ and structure comparison $s(bk_i, bk_j)$ in [7] are replaced by with the gradient-based contrast comparison $c_g(bk_i', bk_j')$ and structure comparison $s_g(bk_i', bk_j')$ respectively.

Fig.2 shows the original "House" image (512 x 512) and its transformed using Sobel operators. In our proposed measure, we have used only structure comparison $s_g(bk_i', bk_j')$ where its formula is as follows:

$$s_g\left(bk_i', bk_j'\right) = \frac{\sigma_{bk_i' bk_j'} + C_3}{\sigma_{bk_i'}\sigma_{bk_j'} + C_3} \tag{8}$$

where $\sigma_{bk_i'}$ and $\sigma_{bk_j'}$ are the standard deviation of blocks bk_i' and bk_j' respectively, $\sigma_{bk_i' bk_j'}$ is the covariance of blocks bk_i' and bk_j'.

3.4 Global Error

Finally, the edge-region and distorted pixels structural similarity (*ERDMSSIM*) is described as follows

$$ERDMSSIM\left(bk_i, bk_j\right) = \left[l\left(bk_i, bk_j\right)\right]^\alpha \cdot \left[c\left(bk_i, bk_j\right)\right]^\beta \cdot \left[s_{ER}\left(bk_i, bk_j\right)\right]^\gamma$$
$$+ \omega * pie\left(bk_i, bk_j\right) \tag{9}$$

Where: $pi(bk_i, bk_j) = Id_{i,j}$, $s_{ER}(bk_i, bk_j) = (s_g(bk_i', bk_j') + s_r(bk_i, bk_j))/2$, $\omega \ll 1$. We set $\alpha = \beta = \gamma = 1$.

The overall error measure of the original image and a distorted one are calculated as sum of *ERDMSSIM* (bk_i, bk_j); the normalized measure is defined as

$$ERDMSSIM\left(Original, Distorted\right) = \frac{1}{2 * Eb}\sum_{i=1}^{M} ERDMSSIM\left(bk_i, bk_j\right) \tag{10}$$

Where $Eb = (mm*nn)/11*11$ is the total number of blocks.

This measure is closer to "*zero*" when the image has the best quality and closer to the "*one*" in the other case.

Furthermore, *ERDMSSIM* is intended for color image. This later is divided on three images: red, blue and green. For each one, the measures defined before are calculated. The latest measure means *ERDMSSIM*, is divided on three. So, *ERDMSSIM* for color image is equal *ERDMSSIM* for red image plus *ERDMSSIM* for blue image plus *ERDMSSIM* for green image divided by three.

4 Experiment Results

To verify the effectiveness of the proposed method, experiments are performed on the Live Image Quality Assess Database Release2 [3] of the Laboratory for Image & Video Engineering in the University of Texas at Austin. The database consists of twenty-nine high resolution 24-bits/pixel RGB color images, distorted using five distortion types: JPEG2000, JPEG, White noise in the RGB components, Gaussian blur in the RGB components, and bit errors in JPEG2000 bit stream using a fast-fading Rayleigh channel model. Each image was distorted with each type, and for each type the perceptual quality covered the entire quality range.

We tested the proposed method on available images in the LIVE database. And, we have compared the performance of our algorithm against PSNR, VroiWQI and GSSIM. Tables 1, 2 and 3 summarize the validation results. Fig.3 shows original images and its transformed images.

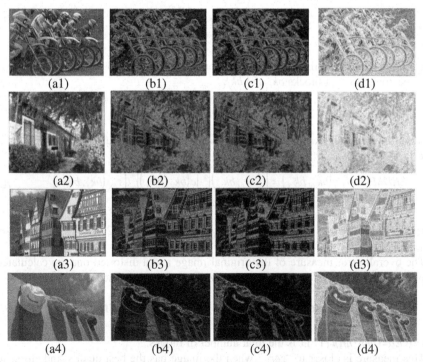

Fig. 3. (a) Original image (b) Simulated image showing the edge information of original image (c) Simulated image showing the edge information of distorted image (d) and Simulated image showing the Visual regions of interest map of original image

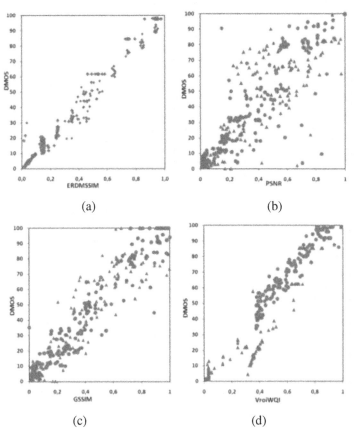

Fig. 4. Scatter plots of *DMOS* versus model prediction for JPEG2000, JPEG. (a) *ERDMSSIM* (b) PSNR (c) GSSIM (d) VroiWQI.

In order to provide quantitative measures on the performance of our proposed *ERDMSSIM* quality assessment method, we follow the standard performance evaluation procedures employed in the video quality experts group (VQEG) FR-TV Phase II test [10]. We performed non-linear mapping between the objective and subjective scores [10]. Five-parameter (β_1, β_2, β_3, β_4 and β_5) non-linear mapping is used to transform the set of quality ratings by the objective quality metrics to a set of predicted *DMOS* values denoted *DMOS*ₚ. Non-linear mapping is chosen over linear mapping to account for the non-linear characteristics of subjective scores at the extremes of test ranges. The mapping function is a logistic function with additive linear term given in Equation 11.

$$DMOS_p = \beta_1 \, \text{logistic}\left(\beta_2,(VQR-\beta_3)\right) + \beta_4 + \beta_5 \tag{11}$$

$$\text{logistic}\,(\tau,VQR) = \frac{1}{2} - \frac{1}{1+\exp(VQR\,\tau)} \tag{12}$$

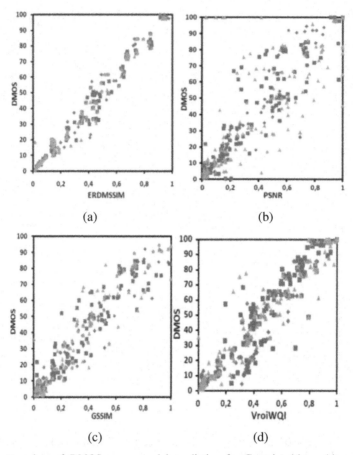

Fig. 5. Scatter plots of *DMOS* versus model prediction for Gaussian blur, white noise, and Fastfading distorted images. (a) *ERDMSSIM* (b) PSNR (c) GSSIM (d) VroiWQI.

where *VQR* is the quality rating by the objective method (*ERDMSSIM*, VroiWQI, GSSIM or PSNR.) and β_1, β_2, β_3, β_4, β_5 are chosen for best fit. The fitting (optimization of β parameters) was done with MATLAB's *fminsearch* function.

After the non-linear mapping, the following metrics are using in calculation between the subjective and objective scores:

- Metric 1: non-linear regression correlation coefficient (*CC*).
- Metric 2: Spearman rank-order correlation coefficient (*ROCC*).
- Metric 3: Outlier ratio (*OR*) of "outlier-points" to total points *N*.
- Metric 4: root mean square error (*RMS*).
- Metric 5: mean absolute error (*MAE*).

The simulation results for all the distorted images are shown in Fig.4, Fig.5, table1, table 2 and table 3. The tables show the quantitative measures of the performance of *ERDMSSIM*, VroiWQI, GSSIM and PSNR. Five metrics are used to measure these

Table 1. Performance comparison of image quality assessment methods (PSNR, GSSIM, VroiWQI, and the ERDMSSIM) on JPEG distorted images

Method	CC	ROCC	MAE	RMS	OR
GSSIM	0.9009	0,6169	5,097	5,887	0,063
PSNR	0.8688	0,6163	5,891	5,891	0,085
VroiWQI	0.8921	0.7982	5.991	5.954	0.062
ERDMSSIM	0.9425	0,9024	5,093	5,080	0,060

objective models. The correlation coefficient (*CC*) after non-linear regression means the correlation degree between each model and *DMOS*, and the larger *CC* value means the better accuracy. The spearman rank-order correlation coefficient (*ROCC*), it is considered as a measure of prediction monotonicity, larger *ROCC* value means the better monotonicity. The mean absolute error (*MAE*), root mean squared error (RMS) and outlier ratio (*OR*) are measures of prediction consistency, smaller value means better performance. Fig.4 and Fig.5 show the scatter plots of Difference Mean Opinion Score (*DMOS*) versus *ERDMSSIM*, PSNR, VroiWQI and GSSIM. Tables 1, 2 and 3 show that the *ERDMSSIM*, even in its simplest form, is competitive with all methods presented in this paper. The comparative results between PSNR, VroiWQI and GSSIM show that *ERDMSSIM* results are consistent with the subjective scores much better than GSSIM, VroiWQI and PSNR.

The GSSIM combines three factors: loss of correlation, luminance distortion and contrast distortion. The value computed by that measure is not convenient in subjective evaluation.

In this test, proposed image quality measure produces results that are in good agreement with subjective visual quality of corresponding images. From the validation result listed above, our algorithm *ERDMSSIM* has a better correspondence to human judgment. The results in Tables 1 and 2 show that *ERDMSSIM* gives notably superior values over GSSIM, VroiWQI and PSNR.

Table 2. Performance comparison of image quality assessment methods (PSNR, GSSIM, VroiWQI, and the ERDMSSIM) for JPEG2000 images

Method	CC	ROCC	MAE	RMS	OR
GSSIM	0.8830	0,8456	4,654	5,7140	0,075
PSNR	0.8590	0,6198	8,916	8,9169	0,085
VroiWQI	0.8526	0.7541	4.745	5.6920	0.065
ERDMSSIM	0.9058	0,9208	4,700	5,0240	0,042

Table 3. Performance comparison of image quality assessment methods (PSNR, GSSIM, VroiWQI, and the ERDMSSIM) for Gaussian blurs, white noise, and Fastfading distorted images

Method	CC	ROCC	MAE	RMS	OR
PSNR	0.7690	0,7523	5,4480	6,4230	0,069
VroiWQI	0.8752	0.8821	4.8670	5.7180	0.063
GSSIM	0.8626	0,8766	4,9850	5,8179	0,062
ERDMSSIM	0.9137	0,9010	4,1280	5,0892	0,045

5 Conclusion

In this paper, we have introduced a novel image quality assessment based on distorted pixels. First, the distorted and original images are divided into blocks of 11×11 pixels, then we calculate distorted pixels, which can be used to compute the whole error. The performance of the proposed metric is found to be better than previously metrics which does not use the distorted pixels in calculation.

We are continuing efforts into improving the *ERDMSSIM* by introducing other attribute in the measurement. Extending the *ERDMSSIM* to incorporate new distances could further improve performance. We are hopeful that this new approach will give new insights into visual perception of quality.

References

1. Girod, B.: What's wrong with mean-squared error. In: Watson, A.B. (ed.) Digital Images and Human Vision, pp. 207–220. The MIT Press, Cambridge (1993)
2. Wang, Z., Bovik, A.C.: Universal image quality index. IEEE Signal Processing Letters 9, 81–84 (2002)
3. Sheikh, H.R., Wang, Z., Cormack, L., Bovik, A.C.: LIVE image quality assessment database (2005),
   http://www.cns.nyu.edu/~zwang/files/research/quality_index/
4. Wang, Z., Bovik, A.C., Sheikh, H.R., Simocelli, E.P.: Image quality assessment: From error measurement to structural similarity. IEEE Trans. Image Processing 13(4), 600–612 (2004)
5. Daly, S.: The Visible Difference Predictor: An Algorithm for the Assessment of Image Fidelity. Digital Images and Human Vision, 179–206 (1993)
6. Osberger, W.: Perceptual Vision Models for Picture Quality Assessment and Compression Aplications. Queensland University of Technology, Brisbane (1999)
7. Wang, Z., Lu, L., Bovik, A.C.: Video Quality Assessment Based on Structural Distortion Measurement. Signal Processing: Image Communication 19(2), 121–132 (2004)
8. Chen, G.H., Yang, C.L., Xie, S.L.: Gradient-Based Structural Similarity for Image Quality Assessment. In: ICIP 2006, pp. 2929–2932 (2006)
9. Venkata Rao, D., Sudhakar, N., Ramesh Babu, I., Pratap Reddy, L.: Image Quality Assessment Complemented with Visual Regions of Interest. In: ICCTA 2007, pp. 681–687 (2007)
10. VQEG: Final Report from the video quality experts group on the validation of objective models of video quality assessment, FR-TV Phase II (August. 2003),
    http://www.vqeg.org/
11. Puzicha, J., Hofmann, T., Buhmann, J.: Non-parametric similarity measures for unsupervised texture segmentation and image retrieval. In: Proc. CVPR 1997, pp. 267–272 (1997)
12. Puzicha, J., Rubner, Y., Tomasi, C., Buhmann, J.: Empirical evaluation of dissimilarity measures for color and texture. In: Int. Conf. on Computer Vision, Corfu., Greece, September 1999, vol. 2, pp. 1165–1173 (1999)
13. Basseville, M.: Distance measures for signal processing and pattern recognition. Signal Process 18, 349–369 (1989)
14. West, J.M., Fitzpatrick, M.Y., Wang, B.M., Dawant, C.R., Maurer, et al.: Comparison and evaluation of retrospective intermodality brain image registration techniques. Journal of Computer Assisted Tomography 21(4), 554–566 (1997)

Fast Multi Frames Selection Algorithm Based on Macroblock Reference Map for H.264/AVC

Kyung-Hee Lee and Jae-Won Suh

Chungbuk National University, College of Electrical and Computer Engineering,
12 Gaeshin-dong, Heungduk-gu, Chongju, Korea
khlee82@cbnu.ac.kr, sjwon@cbnu.ac.kr

Abstract. The variable block size motion estimation (ME) and compensation (MC) using multiple reference frames is adopted in H.264/AVC to improve coding efficiency. However, the computational complexity for ME/MC increases proportional to the number of reference frames. In this paper, we propose a new efficient reference frame selection algorithm to reduce the complexity. The proposed algorithm selects suitable reference frames by employing the spatial and temporal correlation of video sequence. The experimental results show that the proposed algorithm decreases video encoding time while keeping the similar visual quality and bit rates.

Keywords: Fast Multi frame Selection, Motion Estimation, Macroblock Reference Map, Mode Decision.

1 Introduction

The fast growth of digital transmission services has generated a great deal of interest in the transmission of video signals over a band-limited channel. The bandwidth constraint necessitates the use of efficient coding schemes to compress the video data, such as H.26x and MPEG-x series. The H.264/AVC standard [1] is the most advanced video coding standard developed by the Joint Video Team (JVT) of ISO/IEC MPEG and ITU-T VCEG. This standard taking various new coding techniques gains more beneficial effect of the coding performance than previous coding standards. Newly adapted methods are 4×4 integer discrete cosine transform (DCT), spatial prediction for intra macroblock (MB), variable block size ME/MC with multiple reference frames, loop filter, context-based adaptive binary arithmetic coding (CABAC), and so on.

The improvement of coding efficiency mainly comes from the close prediction for residual image. The variable block size ME/MC based on quarter pixel accuracy considerably reduces the prediction errors. In addition, the use of multiple reference frames for ME/MC increases the prediction accuracy. However, the computational complexity for ME/MC increases proportional to the number of reference frames.

In the literature, numerous algorithms have been proposed to reduce the complexity of multiple reference frame ME (MRF-ME). They can be classified into

J. Blanc-Talon et al. (Eds.): ACIVS 2009, LNCS 5807, pp. 167–175, 2009.

three main categories: fast ME, fast skip MRF-ME, and reference frame selection (RFS). Many fast ME algorithms have been proposed is to reduce the search points by exploiting the temporal and spatial correlation between the reference frames [2][3][4]. Su et al. [3] adopted the continuous motion tracking technique to guess a good initial search point for quick convergence but still required searching all reference frames. Fast skip MRF-ME is to find the criteria to escape MRF-ME. Huang et al. [5] analyzed the available information of intra and inter prediction from the previous frame and decided to keep on searching one more reference frame or to terminate. RFS algorithm discriminates the number of reference frames according to the statistical data [6][7][8]. Wu et al. [8] take use of spatial correlation to reduce the number of reference frames for large size modes, while utilizing spatial correlation to get rid of the unnecessary ones for small size modes.

In this paper, we propose an effective RFS algorithm without a significant loss of visual quality and a big increment of bit-rates. In section 2, we briefly introduce a general inter mode decision method and analyze the effects of MRF-ME. Section 3 explains the proposed algorithm based on MB reference map. In section 4, we summarize the simulation results. Finally, we draw conclusions in section 5.

2   Mode Decision for H.264/AVC

To take advantage of temporal redundancy, H.264/AVC adapts variable block size ME/MC with multiple reference frames for inter mode prediction.

2.1   Multiple Reference Frame Motion Estimation

Each MB can be divided into a block partition of sizes 16×16, 16×8, 8×16, or 8×8 pixels, called MB partition. The 8×8 block can be partitioned further into 8×4, 4×8, or 4×4 pixels, called submacroblock(SMB) partition as shown in Figure 1(a). MB partitions in the current frame refer to previously encoded and stored reference frames for ME/MC as shown in Figure 1(b). The order of ME is notified inside the MB partition. During this process, the overhead called the reference parameter (REF) is required to signal which frame is referred. Therefore, the REF must be transmitted for each mode 16×16, 16×8, and 8×16. If 8×8 is selected for current MB, the REF is coded only once for each 8×8 SMB. It means that all SMB partitions must refer to the same frame.

2.2   Best Inter Mode Selection

The best inter MB mode is chosen by considering a Lagrangian cost function, which includes distortion and rates. For each mode, a partition can use 16 reference frames for ME/MC, and then selects the reference frame and motion vector (MV) which minimize the value J in cost function Eq. (1).

$$J(MV, REF|\lambda_{motion}) = SAD(s, r(MV, REF)) + \\ \lambda_{motion} \cdot (R(m(REF) - p(REF))) + (REF)) \tag{1}$$

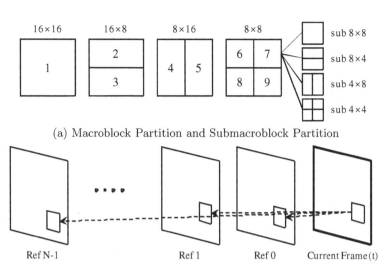

(a) Macroblock Partition and Submacroblock Partition

(b) Multiple Reference Frame Motion Estimation

Fig. 1. Inter Modes and Motion Estimation

where $m(REF)$ denotes the MV in the reference frame considered, $p(REF)$ denotes the predicted MV from the neighbors, and λ_{motion} is the Lagrange multiplier. $R(m(REF) - p(REF))$ means the bit rates for encoding the difference between two MVs, REF notifies the reference frame to be used, and SAD is used as distortion measure, which is computed as Eq. (2)

$$SAD(s, r(m)) = \sum_{x \in H, y \in V}^{H,V} |s(x, y) - r(x - m_x, y - m_y)| \qquad (2)$$

where $s(x, y)$ and $r(x - m_x, y - m_y)$ mean the original video signal and predicted video signal, respectively. H and V are the horizontal and vertical dimensions of the examined partition, such as 16, 8, or 4. The m_x, m_y are the current MV being considered.

2.3 The Effects of MRF-ME

The advantage of MRF-ME is that it can further reduce the temporal redundancy in the video sequences by considering more than one reference frames. As shown in Figure 2, if many reference frames are used for inter mode prediction, we can get the high peak signal to noise ratio (PSNR) and the low bit rates.

However, the computational complexity for ME/MC increases proportional to the number of reference frames. ME/MC is the most computationally intensive function block in the video codec. The increased computational complexity penalizes the benefit of coding efficiency. In addition, the probability to be selected as the best reference frame goes into a decline with the increasing interval between the current frame and reference frame as shown in Table 1. Table 1

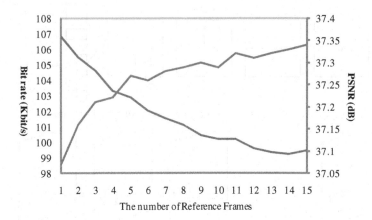

Fig. 2. The Number of Reference Frames for MRF-ME vs. Bit rate and PSNR

Table 1. Distribution of Best Reference Frame

Sequence (CIF)	Ref 0	Ref 1	Ref 2	Ref 3	Ref 4
Crew	81.12	10.92	4.18	1.93	1.84
Football	87.78	5.53	3.37	1.81	1.51
Foreman	72.19	12.91	8.70	3.28	2.92
Highway	62.83	15.53	11.86	5.68	4.10
News	83.70	7.48	5.28	1.79	1.75
Silent	83.99	6.79	4.89	2.02	2.31
Mother & Daughter	79.92	9.00	6.23	2.15	2.70

shows the statistical probability distribution of best reference frame. The number of the Table indicates the probability of choosing the best reference frame during MRF-ME with 5 reference frames. The reason is that correlation between frames decreases according to their interval. Therefore, we need some fast reference frame selection algorithm to reduce the computational complexity.

3   Proposed Algorithm

3.1   MB Reference Map

The results of previous discussion show that investigating all reference frames is a time consuming task in almost all cases. The proposed method selects suitable reference frames according to the results of the first prediction with 16×16 block.

In the first stage, ME with 16×16 block is performed on the whole N reference frames. After finishing this process, we can get the MV sets $\{MV_{Ref0}, MV_{Ref1}, ..., MV_{RefN}\}$ for the 16×16 block and determine the one having minimal RD cost from Eq. (1). During this process, we can obtain SAD sets $\{SAD^i_{Ref0}, SAD^i_{Ref1},$

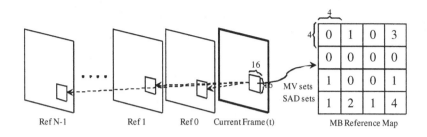

Fig. 3. Generation of MB Reference Map

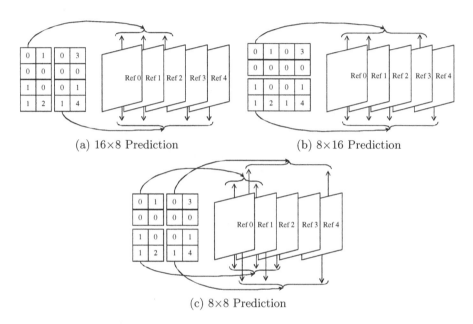

(a) 16×8 Prediction

(b) 8×16 Prediction

(c) 8×8 Prediction

Fig. 4. Reference Frame Selection

..., $SAD^i_{RefN}|i = 1, 2, ..., 16\}$ for 4×4 block unit between current frame and reference frame. Among the SAD sets, the reference frame number generating the smallest SAD is used for MB reference map as shown in Figure 3.

3.2 Reference Frame Selection

Next, the MB reference map is used for RFS about remaining blocks 16×8, 8×16, 8×8. The MB reference map indicates which reference frame should be selected for ME. If MB reference map of current MB is the same as Figure 3, the first 16×8 block ME is done with 0, 1st and 2nd reference frames and the second 16×8 block ME is done with 0, 1st, 3th and 4th reference frames as shown in Figure 4(a). The remaining ME process is similar to that of 16×8 block.

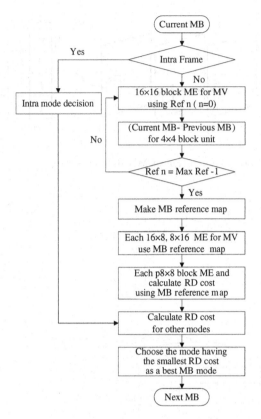

Fig. 5. Flowchart of Proposed Algorithm

The flowchart of the proposed algorithm is illustrated in Figure 5. It is summarized as follows:

1. ME with 16×16 block for multi reference frames
2. Calculate SAD for 4×4 block using the MV for every reference frame
3. Make the MB reference map
4. ME for remaining blocks according to MB reference map

4   Experimental Results

Analysis has been performed in JVT reference software JM14.1 on seven video sequences in QCIF and CIF format. Simulation conditions are summarized into Table 2.

Our proposed algorithm was compared with Wu *et al.* [8] algorithm under the same conditions. Figure 6 shows the example of the RD curves of different reference frame selection methods. (a) and (b) are the test results of Foreman QCIF and CIF, respectively. The RD curves for the other test sequences are

Table 2. Simulation Conditions

Parameters	Condition
Profile	main
Rate Distortion Optimization	Enable
Sequence Types	IPPP (150 frames)
Frame Rate	15 fps
Search Range	16
Quantization Parameters	28, 32, 36, 40
Number of Reference Frames	5

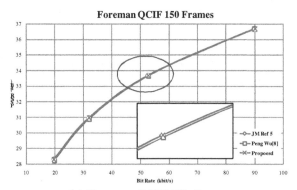

(a) Foreman QCIF RD Curve

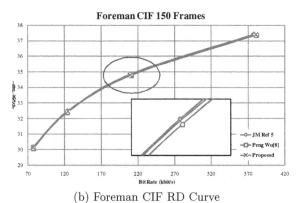

(b) Foreman CIF RD Curve

Fig. 6. Rate Distortion Curves

similar. From RD curves, we can say that the coding efficiency of the propose algorithm is similar to that of full search algorithm in JM14.1.

In addition, we used several measures from Eq. (3) to Eq. (5) for evaluating the performance of the proposed algorithm. We summarized the simulation results in Table 3. We tested all sequences for various QP and took an average.

$$\triangle PSNR = PSNR_{new\_method} - PSNR_{JM} \tag{3}$$

Table 3. Performance comparison of reference frame selection algorithms

Sequence		QCIF			CIF		
		ΔP	ΔB	ΔT	ΔP	ΔB	ΔT
Crew	Wu *et al.*[8]	−0.01	0.33	−26.20	−0.01	0.17	−37.59
	Proposed Alg.	−0.01	0.24	−33.40	0.00	0.14	−34.29
Football	Wu *et al.*[8]	0.00	0.37	−23.26	−0.01	0.13	−33.54
	Proposed Alg.	0.00	0.37	−35.05	−0.01	0.12	−35.05
Foreman	Wu *et al.*[8]	−0.06	0.26	−33.39	0.00	0.33	−39.30
	Proposed Alg.	−0.02	0.07	−36.39	0.01	0.05	−32.67
Highway	Wu *et al.*[8]	−0.06	0.46	−36.26	−0.06	0.47	−43.83
	Proposed Alg.	−0.01	−0.60	−39.53	0.01	−0.03	−35.75
News	Wu *et al.*[8]	−0.02	0.46	−41.57	−0.03	0.01	−47.00
	Proposed Alg.	−0.02	0.46	−47.38	−0.01	−0.02	−45.97
Slient	Wu *et al.*[8]	−0.03	0.24	−41.97	−0.01	0.30	−49.01
	Proposed Alg.	0.00	0.27	−48.49	−0.01	0.20	−46.01
Mother & Daughter	Wu *et al.*[8]	−0.02	0.41	−42.07	−0.03	−0.29	−50.15
	Proposed Alg.	0.00	0.20	−41.16	−0.02	−0.61	−41.82

$$\Delta Bits = \frac{Bit_{new\_method} - Bit_{JM}}{Bit_{JM}} \times 100(\%) \tag{4}$$

$$\Delta Time = \frac{Time_{new\_method} - Time_{JM}}{Time_{JM}} \times 100(\%) \tag{5}$$

The proposed algorithm achieves good performances for the three measurements. In QCIF sequences, the encoding time was reduced by 33.40% ∼ 48.49% with negligible loss in PSNR and small increment of bit-rates compared with JM14.1. In CIF sequences, the encoding time reduction was 32.67% ∼ 46.01%. Although the encoding time reduction ratio of the proposed algorithm is worse than that of Wu *et al.* [8], the bit rates increment is small.

5   Conclusions

In this paper, we proposed a simple and effective fast multi reference frame selection scheme to reduce computational complexity for H.264/AVC. First, the results of 16×16 ME with full reference frames is analyzed. Then, MB reference map is made by the calculated SAD for 4×4 unit. Finally, we can easily decide reference frame of 16×8, 8×16, and 8×8 block according to the MB reference map. Experimental results showed that our approach can noticeably reduce the coding complexity while achieves similar visual quality as conventional full reference frames algorithm.

Acknowledgement

This work was supported by the Korea Science and Engineering Foundation (KOSEF) grant funded by the Korea government(MEST) (NO.R01-2008-000-20485-0).

References

1. Information Technology-Coding of Audio-Visual Objects-part 10: Advanced Video Coding, Final Draft International standard, ISO/IEC FDIS 14496-10 (March 2005)
2. Tourapis, A.M., Au, O.C., Liou, M.L.: Highly Efficient Predictive Zonal Algorithms for Fast Block Matching Motion Extimation. IEEE Trans. Circuit and Systems for Video Technology 12(3), 934–947 (2002)
3. Su, Y., Sun, M.T.: Fast Multiple Reference Frame Motion Estimation for H.264/AVC. IEEE Trans. Circuit and Systems for Video Technology 16(3), 447–452 (2006)
4. Sun, Q., Chen, X.H., Wu, X., Yu, L.: A Content-adaptive Fast Multiple Reference Frames Motion Estimation in H.264. In: IEEE International Symposium, Circuits and Systems, pp. 3651–3654 (2007)
5. Huang, Y.W., Hsieh, B.Y., Chien, S.Y., Ma, S.Y., Chen, L.G.: Analysis and Complexity Reduction of Multiple Reference Frames Motion Estimation in H.264/AVC. IEEE Trans. Circuit and Systems for Video Technology 16(4), 507–522 (2006)
6. Li, X., Li, E.Q., Chen, Y.K.: Fast Multi-Frame Motion Estimation Algorithm with Adaptive Search Strategies in H.264. In: IEEE International Conference, Acoustics, Speech and Signal Processing, vol. 3, pp. 369–372 (2004)
7. Shen, L., Liu, Z., Zhang, Z., Wang, G.: An Adaptive and Fast Multiframe Selection Algorithm for H.264 Video Coding. IEEE Signal Processing Letters 14(11), 836–839 (2007)
8. Wu, P., Xiao, C.B.: An Adaptive Fast multiple Reference Frames Selection Algorithm for H.264/AVC. In: IEEE International Conference, Acoustics, Speech and Signal Processing, pp. 1017–1020 (2008)
9. http://iphome.hhi.de/suehring/tml/download/old_jm/jm14.1.zip

Highlight Removal from Single Image

Pesal Koirala, Markku Hauta-Kasari, and Jussi Parkkinen

Department of Computer Science and Statistics
University of Joensuu, Finland
pkoirala@cs.joensuu.fi

Abstract. The highlight removal method from the single image without knowing the illuminant has been presented. The presented method is based on the Principal Component Analysis (PCA), Histogram equalization and Second order polynomial transformation. The proposed method does not need color segmentation and normalization of image by illuminant. The method has been tested on different types of images, images with or without texture and images taken in different unknown light environment. The result shows the feasibility of the method. Implementation of the method is straight forward and computationally fast.

Keywords: PCA, Histogram equalization, Dichromatic reflection model, Polynomial transformation.

1 Introduction

The aim of this study is to remove the highlight from single color image without having prior illumination information and without doing clustering of color. In this study we tested our method in variety of images with texture, without texture, with one or two color images and multicolored images and the images taken in different environment and the images directly downloaded from the web. The proposed method is based on principal component analysis and histogram equalization of first principal component. The first principal component refers to the principal component corresponding to largest eigen value. Second principal component was selected or rejected depending on the fidelity ratio of corresponding eigen values as in most of the cases it was found that second PC carries some part of specular component. However still some specular component remains in first PC. The effect of specular component in first PC is diffused by applying histogram equalization. By setting threshold value in the fidelity ratio of second largest value, it was found that weather second PC is part of specular component or not. Finally the image was reconstructed using histogram equalized first PC and selected other PC according to threshold. However reconstructed image shifts color value. The original color was achieved applying second order polynomial transformation by the basis function calculated from the diffuse detected part to the reconstructed image. The work flow of the method has been shown in Fig. 5.

J. Blanc-Talon et al. (Eds.): ACIVS 2009, LNCS 5807, pp. 176–187, 2009.

1.1   Previous Work

There are a lot of previous works in that field. Shafer [9] proposed the dichromatic reflection model for color image. In that method the diffuse component and specular component was separated based on the parallelogram distribution of colors in RGB space. The method extended by Klinker et al. [6] showed the T-shaped color distribution containing reflectance and illumination color vectors. The experiment was performed in the lab environment and It is very difficult to extract T-shaped cluster for real images due to noise factor. polarization filter was used to separate reflection components from gray level images [2]. The polarization filter method was extended in RGB color images to find the highlight depending on the principal that in the dielectric material the specular component is polarized and diffuse component is not polarized [8]. This method is also suitable for multicolored texture image but needs additional polarization filter which may not be practical for all the cases. Tan et al. [1] proposes highlight removal method without doing color segmentation and using ploarization filter. Tan method is also suitable for multicolored texture images. This method proposed specular free image (SF) which is devoid of specular effect but retains exact geometrical information. However there is shift of color value. By using logarithmic differentiation between specular free image and input image, the highlight free pixels were successfully detected. Then the specular component of each pixels were removed locally involving a maximum of only two pixels. Similarly Shen et al. [5] proposed chromaticity based specularity removal method in a single image even with out any local interactions between neighboring pixels and without color segmentation. This method is based on solving the least square problem of the dichromatic reflection model on a single pixel level. However both of the methods [1] [5] require previous information of illumination. The information of illumination can be approximated by using existing color constancy algorithm [4]. The accuracy of the result in both methods depends on the accuracy of the estimated illuminant source. Illumination constrained inpainting method was described in reference [14]. This method is based on the assumption that the illumination color is uniform through the highlight. This method is suitable for texture surface. But it is computationally slow. The highlight removal method in spectral image was proposed in reference [3]. This method does not require illuminant estimation. The method [3] uses mixture model of Probabilistic PCA to detect highlight affected part and diffuse part in the image. Finally the highlighted detected part mapped across the first eigen vector of diffused part was used to remove highlight during reconstruction process by PCA. The specular free spectral image was obtained by using Orthogonal Subspace Projection [10]. In that method the projector maps the radiance spectrum R to the subspace orthogonal to the illumination spectrum.

2   Highlight Detection

The highlight detected area in the given image is calculated on the single pixel level, based on the difference between the original image and the modified specular free image (MSF)[5]. The MSF is calculated by adding the mean of minimum of RGB color value of original image to the specular free image (SF) as shown in Eq.(2). The specular free image is calculated by subtracting the minimum of RGB color value in each pixel level as shown in Eq.(1).

$$SF_i(x,y) = I_i(x,y) - min(I_1(x,y), I_2(x,y), I_3(x,y)) \qquad (1)$$

$$MSF_i(x,y) = SF_i(x,y) + \overline{I}_{min} \qquad (2)$$

In Eq.(1) and Eq.(2) SF and MSF are specular free image and modified specular free image. Similarly $I_i(x,y)$ is the value of ith color channel at (x,y) pixel position of original image I. The subscript i ranges from 1 to 3 corresponding to Red, Green and Blue channel.

Threshold value should be set in the difference between original and MSF image to classify each pixel in the group of highlight and highlight free part.

$$pixel = \begin{cases} \text{highlight} & \text{if } d_i(x,y) > th \text{ for all i} \\ \text{diffuse} & \text{otherwise} \end{cases}$$

Where $d_i(x,y) = I_i(x,y) - MSF_i(x,y)$

The average value of the minimum of the color channel has been used as threshold [5]. However to set the accurate threshold value is the challenging task. In this experiment threshold value has been set after visual assessment of classification results of each image. The result of highlight detection of pear is shown in Fig.1. The different threshold values we used have been listed in Table 1.

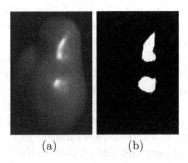

(a)   (b)

Fig. 1. Highlight detection (a) Original Image (b) Black is diffuse part and white is highlight part

3 Highlight Removal

3.1 Dichromatic Reflection Model

Shafer et al. [9] described dichromatic reflection model for modeling the reflectance of dielectric objects. The model suggests that the reflection can be represented by the linear combination of diffuse and specular components. Based on this model the intensity of the image for single illumination case is defined as in Eq.(3).

$$I(x,y) = K_d(x,y) \int_\omega R(\lambda,x,y)S(\lambda)q(\lambda) + K_s(x,y) \int_\omega S(\lambda)q(\lambda) \qquad (3)$$

Where $I(x,y)$ is the color vector of red, green and blue colors at pixel position (x,y) of the image. q is the camera sensor sensitivity of each color. K_d and K_s are the weighting factors for diffuse and specular reflections respectively. The weighting factors are dependent on the geometric structure of the surface. $R(\lambda)$ is the diffuse reflectance at pixel position (x,y) and $S(\lambda)$ is the spectral power distribution of the illuminants which is independent of geometry of the surface. λ represents each wavelength which lies within visible range ω. Here the specular reflection is not considered since it is assumed that specular reflection is equal to the spectral power distribution of light source. $\int_\omega$ represents the summation with in the visible range ω. Eq.(3) is rewritten in simple form as in Eq.(4).

$$I(x,y) = K_d(x,y)I_d(x,y) + K_s(x,y)I_s(x,y) \qquad (4)$$

Where $I_d(x,y) = \int_\omega R(\lambda,x,y)S(\lambda)q(\lambda)$ and $I_s(x,y) = \int_\omega S(\lambda)q(\lambda)$. The $I_s(x,y)$ can simply be written as I_s since it is independent of surface geometry. As a result it can be said that specular component is the result of scaling of the illuminant color.

3.2 Principal Component Analysis

Here our goal is to remove specular part (highlight) from the image without using illuminant information. In our work we have used Principal Component Analysis [11] to describe image as the linear combination of different components. RGB image can be represented by three principal components weighted by three eigen vectors since it has three color channels. The eigen vectors were calculated from the correlation matrix of the given image and sorted according to descending order of eigen values. The image representation by Principal component is shown in Eq.(5).

$$I = VP \qquad (5)$$

Where I is the given image in matrix form of size $L*N$, L is number of color channels, here it is 3 for RGB image and N is the number of pixels in the image. Similarly $V = [V_1 V_2 V_3]$ is the matrix of size $L*L$ consisting L principal component vectors so each vector is of size $L*1$ and $P = [P_1; P_2; P_3]$ is principal component of size $L*N$ since L is number of principal component vectors chosen. Each principal component has size $1*N$. The sign ; is used to separate rows. Without loss of generality Eq.(5) is rewritten in the form as in Eq.(6).

$$I = V_1 P_1 + V_2 P_2 + V_3 P_3 \qquad (6)$$

Where V_i and P_i are principal component vectors and corresponding principal components respectively. We assume that one of the principal components may

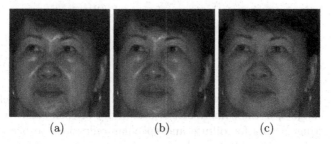

(a)   (b)   (c)

Fig. 2. Highlight removal (a)Original Image (b)Result without using histogram equalization (c) Result with using histogram equalization

contain the part of specular reflection. In experiment we found that in most of the cases second principal component corresponding to second largest eigen value contains the part or whole of the specular reflection. However it is not always true. The threshold value should be set in the fidelity ratio of second largest eigen value to detect weather second largest principal component contains specular component.

$$\text{Second PC} = \begin{cases} \text{diffuse component} & \text{if } f_2 > th \\ \text{specluar component} & \text{otherwise} \end{cases}$$

Where f_2 is the fidelity ratio of second largest eigen value and th is the threshold. Here we have set the value of th equal to 2. The fidelity ratio of the jth eigen value are calculated as the ratio of ith eigen value to the sum of total eigen values as shown in Eq.(7).

$$f_j = \frac{\sigma_j}{\sum\limits_{i=1}^{L} \sigma_i} 100 \tag{7}$$

Where σ_j is the jth eigen value. If the second principal component was detected as Specular component it was not used in reconstruction process otherwise it was used. Table 1 lists the fidelity ratio of each eigen value and selected principal components according to it for reconstruction process for different samples. Nevertheless in experiment it was found that the first principal component still contains some specular part. To diffuse the specular affect remained in first principal component; histogram equalization [12] was applied in the first principal component normalized between 0 to 1. Accordingly the Eq.(6) is rewritten in Eq.(8).

$$\tilde{I} = V_1 P_h + V_2 P_2 + V_3 P_3 \tag{8}$$

Where P_h is histogram equalized principal component and $\tilde{I}$ is the reconstructed image. The middle part of the right side is included or removed in reconstruction according to fidelity ratio of second largest eigen vector. The effect of histogram equalization in final result has been illustrated in Fig. 2.

3.3   Polynomial Transformation

The reconstructed image by PCA $\tilde{I}$ is the image without highlight but the color of the image is changed. The original color of the image without highlight is obtained by using second order polynomial transformation. The main problem is to find the weight function for polynomial transformation. The weight function is calculated using transformation between detected diffuse part of original image and corresponding part of reconstructed image as shown in Eq.(9). The diffuse part was detected according to the rule as described in section *Highlight detection*.

$$I_d = W\tilde{M}_d \qquad (9)$$

In Eq.(9) I_d is diffuse detected part in original image and its size is $L * N$, here L is number of channels which is 3 for RGB image and N is number of diffuse detected pixels. $\tilde{M}_d$ is the second order polynomial extension of corresponding diffuse detected part $\tilde{I}_d$ of reconstructed image $\tilde{I}$. Reconstructed diffuse detected part is $I_d = [R \quad G \quad B]^T$ where R, G and B are the vectors containing red, green and blue color values. Now $\tilde{M}_d = [R \quad G \quad B \quad R*G \quad R*B \quad G*B \quad R*R \quad G* G \quad B*B]^T$. $[]^T$ is transpose of matrix. As a result the size of the basis function W is $3 * 9$ and size of $\tilde{M}_d$ is $9 * N$. The basis function W can be calculated by using least square pseudo inverse matrix calculation as shown in Eq.(10).

$$W = I_d[\tilde{M}_d^T \tilde{M}_d]^{-1}\tilde{M}_d^T \qquad (10)$$

Where $[]^{-1}$ is the inverse of matrix. The calculated basis function W is employed to the whole of the reconstructed image $\tilde{I}$ as shown in Eq.(11) to achieve accurate diffuse image D. In Eq.(11) M is the second order polynomial extension of reconstructed image $\tilde{I}$.

$$D = W\tilde{M} \qquad (11)$$

Fig. 3 and Fig. 4 shows the result of polynomial transformation applied to the PCA reconstructed image. The same polynomial method can be directly applied to specular free image to get original color. In that case $\tilde{I}$ is the specular free image calculated as described in [1][5]. The result of the output depends on the

Table 1. Fidelity ratio analysis f_1, f_2 and f_3 are fidelities of firt to third largest eigen value. Fifth column shows the PC selected in reconstruction process. Threshold is the threshold value for specular detection.

Image	Fidelity ratio			PC selected	Threshold
	f_1	f_2	f_3		
Pear	98.697	1.225	0.078	1st and 3rd	0.1
Face	99.552	0.392	0.057	1st and 3rd	0.3
Yellow ball	98.049	1.248	0.7032	1st	0.3
Green ball	99.606	0.380	0.015	1st	0.1
Hat	83.6973	12.9819	3.321	1st, 2nd and 3rd	0.3
Fish	90.6494	7.4925	1.8581	1st, 2nd and 3rd	0.3

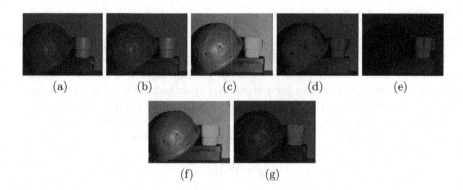

Fig. 3. Highlight removal (a) Original image (b)Reconstructed image by first PC (c) by histogram equalized first PC (d)by second PC (d)by third PC (e) by histogram equalized first PC and second and third PC (f) Image after second order polynomial transformation. Reconstructed results by second and third PC have been scaled to visualize.

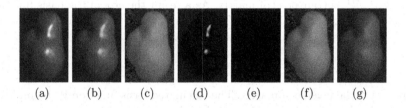

Fig. 4. Highlight removal (a) Original image (b)Reconstructed image by first PC (c) by histogram equalized first PC (d)by second PC (d)by third PC (e) by histogram equalized first PC and third PC (f) Image after second order polynomial transformation. Reconstructed results by second and third PC have been scaled to visualize.

specular free image. Sometime specular free image calculated without normalization gets the gray or black highlight in the specular detected region even after removing achromatic color. In that case accurate diffuse color can not be achieved. However it does not hamper just to detect highlight so in that case PCA based method is the good solution.

4   Results and Discussions

Dichromatic reflection model describes the reflection of the surface as a linear combination of specular and diffuse reflection components [9]. The scaling factor of the diffuse and specular reflection depends on the geometric properties of the surface therefore each component should be separated pixel wise. So multiple image of the same surface is the easy solution. However practically it might not be feasible since in most of the cases as we should remove highlight or specular part from the given single image. The polarizing filter might be the solution but

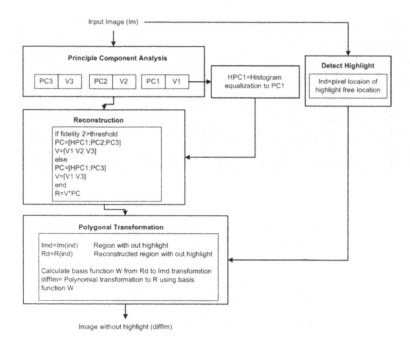

Fig. 5. Block diagram describing method to remove highlight from image

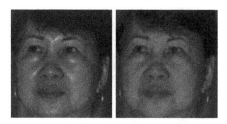

Fig. 6. Face image with highlight and Image reconstructed without highlight

extra hardware should be installed in the camera and it might not be feasible in the case provided that we have already image from other sources. Different methods have been described to separate highlight and body reflection. Most of them are based on color segmentation and known light source information. The accuracy of the highlight removal depends on the accuracy of color segmentation. In the case of unknown light source, the chromaticity of light source can be estimated by color constancy algorithm and the result depends on the estimated value and the correct estimation of illuminant color from single image is always the problem.

In this research we employed linear principal component to remove highlight since dichromatic reflection model is the linear relationship between diffuse and specular component. As we know that in three channel color image, the image

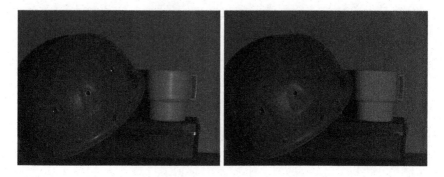

Fig. 7. Hat image with highlight and Image reconstructed without highlight

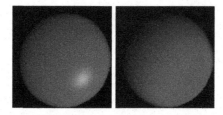

Fig. 8. Green ball image with highlight and Image reconstructed without highlight

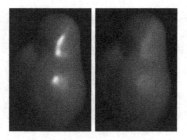

Fig. 9. Pear image with highlight and Image reconstructed without highlight

Table 2. Average S-CIELAB color difference Δ E between the diffuse detected part of original image and final image after polynomial transformation. D is the standard deviation of S-CIELAB color difference.

	Pear	Face	Yellow ball	Green ball	Hat	Fish
Δ E	0.954	0.354	2.802	4.036	0.415	0.445
D	2.877	0.801	5.526	4.529	1.275	1.673

can be separated to three different components by using PCA. Here we assume that one of the three components might contain the highlight component. After separating image in three components, we found that in most of the cases

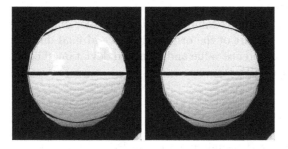

Fig. 10. Yellow ball image with highlight and Image reconstructed without highlight

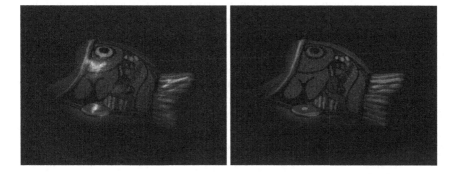

Fig. 11. Fish image with highlight and Image reconstructed without highlight

principal component across second highest variance separates some of the highlight effect of the image. However it might not be true for all the images. Fig. 3 and Fig. 4 show both cases without highlight and with highlight in scond principal component respectively. We tested more than twenty different images from uniformly color distributed images to multicolored textured images, we found that by setting the threshold value of fidelity ratio corresponding to second largest eigen value , it can be detected weather second principal components carries highlight. We got feasible result setting threshold value equal to 2. The eigen value analysis for some samples has been listed in Table 1. The second principal component lesser than threshold value has not been included in reconstruction process. However in most of the cases it was found that still first principal component carries some specular part as well as most of diffuse part. To diffuse the specular effect, the histogram equalization was applied to the first principal component. However the reconstructed result using above described method by PCA gives the image without highlight but there is shift of color. The original color was estimated by using basis function calculated from second order polynomial transformation of diffuse detected part of reconstructed image and original image. The final result obtained applying the polynomial transformation to the reconstructed image using histogram equalized first principal component and other component is promising as shown in Fig. 6-11. In our knowledge there is no ready evaluation method. Here we applied the spatial extension of color difference foumula S-CIELAB color difference forumula [13] in the diffuse detected part of the original image and final diffuse image. Average S-CIELAB color difference value and standard deviation of color difference have been shown in Table 2.

5   Conclusions

The highlight removal technique based on Principal Component Analysis was proposed. In the proposed method, histogram equalization was applied to first principal component of the images. In the experiment, it was found that in most of the cases second principal component carries large portion of the highlight. However it was not true for all the cases. So second principal component was included only if the fidelity ratio of second largest eigen vector is greater than threshold value otherwise rejected . The color of the reconstructed image gets shifted due to histogram equalization in first principal component. However reconstructed image is free of highlight. The color of the reconstructed image was corrected by using second order polynomial transformation. The weight vector of the polynomial transformation was obtained by using the transformation of the pixels of reconstructed image to the original image corresponding to highlight free pixels in original image. The accuracy of the result was evaluated by using S-CIELAB color difference formula in highlight free area. The method was tested in different types of images without considering camera noise and illuminant type. The result obtained is quite promising.

References

1. Tan, R.T., Ikeuchi, K.: Seperating Reflection Components of Textured Surfaces Using a Single Image. IEEE Transactions on Pattern Analysis and Machine Intelligence 27, 178–193 (2005)
2. Wolff, L.B., Boult, T.: Constraining object features using polarization reflectance model. IEEE Trans. on Pattern Analaysis and Machine Intelligence 13(7), 635–657 (1991)
3. Bochko, V., Parkkinen, J.: Highlight Analysis Using a Mixture Model of Probabilistic PCA. In: Proceedings of the 4th WSEAS International Conference on Signal Processing, Robotics and Automation, Salzburg, Austria Article No. 15 (2005) ISBN:960-8457-09-2
4. Lee, H.-C.: Method for computing the scene illuminant chromaticity from specular highlights. J. Opt. Soc. Am. 3, 1694–1699 (1986)
5. Shen, H.-L., Zhang, H.-G., Shao, S.-J., Xin, J.H.: Chromaticity-based Seperation of reflection components in a single image. Pattern Recognition 41, 2461–2469 (2008)
6. Klinker, G.J., Shafer, S.H., Kanade, T.: The measurement of Highlights in Color Images. Int'l J. Computer Vision 2, 7–32 (1990)
7. Schluns, K., Koschan, A.: Global and Local Highlight Analysis in Color Images. In: Proceedings of CGIP 2000, First International Conference on Color in Graphics and Image Processing, Saint-Etienne, France, October 1-4, pp. 300–304 (2000)

8. Nayar, S.K., Fang, X.S., Boult, T.: Separation of reflection components using color and polarization. Int. J. Computer Vision 21, 163–186 (1997)
9. Shafer, S.A.: Using color to seperate reflection components. Color Res. App. 10, 210–218 (1985)
10. Fu, Z., Tan, R.T., Caelli, T.M.: Specular Free Spectral Imaging Using Orthogonal Subspace Projection. In: Proceedings of the 18th International Conference on Pattern Recognition (2006)
11. Jolliffe, I.T.: Principal Component Analysis. Springer series of statistics. Springer, Heidelberg (2002)
12. Gonzalez, R.C., Woods, R.E.: Digital Image Processing, 2nd edn. Prentice-Hall, Englewood Cliffs (2002)
13. Zhang, X., Wandell, B.: A Spatial Extension of CIELAB for Digital Color Image Reproduction,
    http://white.stanford.edu/~brian/scielab/scielab3/scielab3.pdf
14. Tan, P., Lin, S., Quan, L., Shum, H.-Y.: Highlight Removal by Illumination-Constrained Inpainting. In: Proceeding of the ninth IEEE International Conference on Computer Vision (ICCV 2003), vol. 2 (2003)

Parameter Estimation in Bayesian Super-Resolution Image Reconstruction from Low Resolution Rotated and Translated Images

Salvador Villena[1,*], Miguel Vega[1], Rafael Molina[2],
and Aggelos K. Katsaggelos[3]

[1] Dpto. de Lenguajes y Sistemas Informáticos,
Universidad de Granada, Granada 18071, Spain
[2] Dpto. de Ciencias de la Computación e Inteligencia Artificial,
Universidad de Granada, Granada 18071, Spain
[3] Department of Electrical Engineering and Computer Science,
Northwestern University, Evanston, IL 60208-3118, USA

Abstract. This paper deals with the problem of *high-resolution* (HR) image reconstruction, from a set of degraded, under-sampled, shifted and rotated images, utilizing the variational approximation within the Bayesian paradigm. The proposed inference procedure requires the calculation of the covariance matrix of the HR image given the LR observations and the unknown hyperparameters of the probabilistic model. Unfortunately the size and complexity of such matrix renders its calculation impossible, and we propose and compare three alternative approximations. The estimated HR images are compared with images provided by other HR reconstruction methods.

Keywords: High resolution images, Bayesian paradigm, Variational inference, covariance matrix calculation.

1 Introduction

We use the term Super-Resolution (SR) to denote the process of obtaining an HR image, or a sequence of HR images, from a set of LR images [1]. Following the Bayesian framework we focus in this paper on the reconstruction of HR images from a set of downsampled, rotated, and shifted LR images, (see [1] and the references therein, [2] and [3]).

In this paper we assume that the translation and rotation registration parameters are known or previously estimated and examine the difficulties in estimating the HR image, the noise, and the prior parameters in the Bayesian framework. Bayesian methods rely on image models that encapsulate prior image knowledge and avoid the ill-posedness of the image restoration problems. In this paper a prior model based on the $\ell 1$ norm of vertical and horizontal first order differences

* This work was supported in part by the Comisión Nacional de Ciencia y Tecnología under contract TIC2007-65533 and the Consejería de Innovación, Ciencia y Empresa of the Junta de Andalucía under contract P07-TIC-02698.

J. Blanc-Talon et al. (Eds.): ACIVS 2009, LNCS 5807, pp. 188–199, 2009.

of image pixel values is introduced. At a second level, hyperpriors on the model parameters are introduced and finally, the HR image as well as the parameters are estimated under the Bayesian paradigm, utilizing a variational approximation. The whole estimation process requires the calculation of the inverse of a high dimensional matrix which can not be easily calculated. Part of this paper is devoted to examining the adequacy of several approximate matrix inversion methods to our SR task.

The paper is organized as follows. In section 2 we discuss the Bayesian model and in section 3 the Bayesian inference we use. The different approximations to matrix inversion considered are described in section 4. Experimental results are described in section 5. Finally, section 6 concludes the paper.

2   Bayesian Modeling

Consider a set $\mathbf{g} = (\mathbf{g}_1^t, \dots, \mathbf{g}_U^t)^t$ of $U \geq 1$, observed LR images each with $P = N_1 \times N_2$ pixels. Our aim is to reconstruct a $p = M_1 \times M_2$ HR image $\mathbf{f}$, where $M_1 = L \times N_1$ and $M_2 = L \times N_2$, from the set $\mathbf{g}$ of LR observed images using the Bayesian paradigm. We assume all images, $\mathbf{f}$ and $\mathbf{g}_q$, $q = 1, \dots, U$, to be lexicographically ordered.

In this paper we assume that each LR observed image $\mathbf{g}_q$, for $q = 1, \dots, U$, is a noisy, downsampled, blurred, rotated through a known angle γ_q, and shifted by a known displacement $\mathbf{d}_q$, version of the HR image.

Let us now study the joint probability distribution $p(\Theta, \mathbf{f}, \mathbf{g})$ that is expressed, within the Hierarchical Bayesian paradigm (see [4]), in terms of the hyperprior model $p(\Theta)$ on the hyperparameters Θ, the prior model $p(\mathbf{f}|\Theta)$ and the degradation model $p(\mathbf{g}|\mathbf{f}, \Theta)$ as

$$p(\Theta, \mathbf{f}, \mathbf{g}) = p(\Theta)p(\mathbf{f}|\Theta)p(\mathbf{g}|\mathbf{f}, \Theta) . \tag{1}$$

2.1   Prior Model

The prior model we use in this paper is

$$p(\mathbf{f}|\alpha^h, \alpha^v) = \frac{1}{Z(\alpha^h, \alpha^v)} \times \exp\left\{ - \sum_{i=1}^{p} [\alpha^h \parallel \Delta_i^h(\mathbf{f}) \parallel_1 + \alpha^v \parallel \Delta_i^v(\mathbf{f}) \parallel_1] \right\}, \tag{2}$$

where $\Delta_i^h(\mathbf{x})$ and $\Delta_i^v(\mathbf{x})$ represent the horizontal and vertical first order differences at pixel i, respectively, α^h and α^h are model parameters, and $Z(\alpha^h, \alpha^v)$ is the partition function that we approximate as

$$Z(\alpha^h, \alpha^v) \propto (\alpha^h \alpha^v)^{-p}. \tag{3}$$

2.2   Degradation Model

A 2-D image translation $\mathbf{d}$ followed by a rotation through an angle γ is defined by

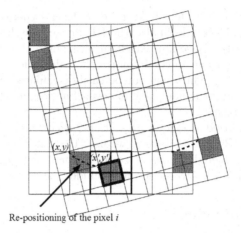

Re-positioning of the pixel i

Fig. 1. Illustration of the global original and rotated grids

$$\begin{pmatrix} x' \\ y' \end{pmatrix} = \begin{pmatrix} \cos(\gamma) & -\sin(\gamma) \\ \sin(\gamma) & \cos(\gamma) \end{pmatrix} \begin{pmatrix} x \\ y \end{pmatrix} + \mathbf{d}, \tag{4}$$

where $(x'y')^t$ are the new coordinates and $(x\ y)^t$ the old ones.

When this geometric transformation is globally applied to a discrete image, the vertices of its corresponding centered pixel grid fall into subpixel regions of the rotated grid (see Fig. 1). Since we do not know the exact new pixel observations, an approximation, such as a nearest neighbor or a bilinear interpolation is usually applied, see [5], [2] and [3]. In this paper we use bilinear interpolation. Thus if we denote by $\mathbf{f}'$ the discrete image obtained after applying a translation $\mathbf{d}$ followed by a rotation with angle γ to the discrete image $\mathbf{f}$, we have $\mathbf{f}' = \mathbf{R}_{(\mathbf{d},\gamma)}\,\mathbf{f}$, where $\mathbf{R}_{(\mathbf{d},\gamma)}$ is a $p \times p$ real matrix.

The process to obtain the observed, displaced and rotated LR images $\mathbf{g}_q$, $q = 1, \ldots, U$ from $\mathbf{f}$ can thus be modeled as

$$\mathbf{g}_q = \mathbf{DHR}_{(\mathbf{d}_q,\gamma_q)}\mathbf{f} + \epsilon_q = \mathbf{C}_q\mathbf{f} + \epsilon_q, \tag{5}$$

where ϵ_q represents the acquisition noise, assumed to be additive white Gaussian with variance β^{-1} and $\mathbf{C}_q$ is the $P \times p$ matrix

$$\mathbf{C}_q = \mathbf{DHR}_{(\mathbf{d}_q,\gamma_q)}, \tag{6}$$

where $\mathbf{H}$ is a $p \times p$ matrix modeling sensor integration as a uniform blurring of size L, and $\mathbf{D}$ is a $P \times p$ downsampling matrix.

Finally for the set of U observations $\mathbf{g} = (g_1^t, \ldots, g_U^t)^t$ we have

$$p(\mathbf{g}|\mathbf{f}, \beta) \propto \beta^{\frac{UP}{2}} \exp\left[-\frac{\beta}{2} \sum_{q=1}^{U} \|\mathbf{g}_q - \mathbf{C}_q\mathbf{f}\|^2 \right]. \tag{7}$$

2.3   Hyperprior Model

Our prior knowledge on the different model parameters $\theta \in \Theta$, is modeled using

$$p(\Theta) = \prod_{\theta \in \Theta} p(\theta), \tag{8}$$

where $p(\theta)$ are gamma hyperpriors

$$p(\theta) = \Gamma(\theta | a_\theta^o, b_\theta^o), \ \forall \ \theta \in \Theta. \tag{9}$$

The gamma distribution has the form

$$\Gamma(\theta \mid u, v) = \frac{v^u}{\Gamma(u)} \theta^{u-1} \exp[-v\theta], \tag{10}$$

where $\theta > 0$, $u > 0$ and $v > 0$ with mean $\mathbf{E}[\theta] = u/v$ and variance $\mathbf{var}[\theta] = u/v^2$.

Our set of model parameters is then $\Theta = (\alpha^h, \alpha^v, \beta)$, and the joint distribution is given by

$$p(\Theta, \mathbf{f}, \mathbf{g}) = p(\Theta)p(\mathbf{f}|\alpha^h, \alpha^v)p(\mathbf{g}|\mathbf{f}, \beta), \tag{11}$$

where $p(\Theta)$, $p(\mathbf{f}|\alpha^h, \alpha^v)$ and $p(\mathbf{g}|\mathbf{f}, \beta)$ are defined respectively in Eqs. (8), (2) and (7) above.

3   Bayesian Inference

Bayesian inference on the unknown HR image $\mathbf{f}$ and hyperparameters given the observed $\mathbf{g}$ is based on the posterior probability distribution

$$p(\Theta, \mathbf{f}|\mathbf{g}) = \frac{p(\Theta, \mathbf{f}, \mathbf{g})}{p(\mathbf{g})}. \tag{12}$$

Since $p(\Theta, \mathbf{f}|\mathbf{g})$ of Eq. (12) can not be found in closed form, because $p(\mathbf{g})$ can not be calculated analytically, we apply variational methods to approximate this distribution by the distribution $q(\Theta, \mathbf{f})$ minimizing the Kullback-Leibler (KL) divergence, which is given by [6,7]

$$C_{KL}(q(\Theta, \mathbf{f})\|p(\Theta, \mathbf{f}|\mathbf{g})) = \int q(\Theta, \mathbf{f}) \log \left(\frac{q(\Theta, \mathbf{f})}{p(\Theta, \mathbf{f}|\mathbf{g})} \right) d\Theta d\mathbf{f}$$

$$= \int q(\Theta, \mathbf{f}) \log \left(\frac{q(\Theta, \mathbf{f})}{p(\Theta, \mathbf{f}, \mathbf{g})} \right) d\Theta d\mathbf{f} + \text{const} = \mathcal{M}(q(\Theta, \mathbf{f}), \mathbf{g}) + \text{const}, \tag{13}$$

and is always non negative and equal to zero only when $q(\Theta, \mathbf{f}) = p(\Theta, \mathbf{f}|\mathbf{g})$.

Due to the form of the prior proposed in Eq. (2) the above integral can not be evaluated, but we can however majorize the $\ell 1$ prior by a function which renders the integral easier to calculate. The majorization to be applied here to our prior model is conceptually similar to the one applied in [8] to the TV prior.

Our prior can be rewritten in the more convenient form

$$p(\mathbf{f}|\alpha^h, \alpha^v) \propto (\alpha^h \alpha^v)^p \times \exp\left\{-\sum_{i=1}^{p}\left[\alpha^h\sqrt{(\Delta_i^h(\mathbf{f}))^2} + \alpha^v\sqrt{(\Delta_i^v(\mathbf{f}))^2}\right]\right\}. \quad (14)$$

Let us consider the following inequality, also used in [9], which states that, for any $w \geq 0$ and $z > 0$

$$\sqrt{w} \leq \frac{w+z}{2\sqrt{z}}. \quad (15)$$

Let us define, for $\mathbf{f}$, $\mathbf{u}^h$ and $\mathbf{u}^v$, where $\mathbf{u}^h$ and $\mathbf{u}^v$ are any p-dimensional vectors $\mathbf{u}^h \in (R^+)^p$, $\mathbf{u}^v \in (R^+)^p$ with components $\mathbf{u}_i^h$ and $\mathbf{u}_i^v$, $i = 1, \ldots, p$, the following functional

$$\mathbf{M}(\alpha^h, \alpha^v, \mathbf{f}, \mathbf{u}^h, \mathbf{u}^v) = (\alpha^h \alpha^v)^p \times$$
$$\exp\left\{-\sum_{i=1}^{p}\left[\alpha^h \frac{(\Delta_i^h(\mathbf{f}))^2 + \mathbf{u}_i^h}{2\sqrt{\mathbf{u}_i^h}} + \alpha^v \frac{(\Delta_i^v(\mathbf{f}))^2 + \mathbf{u}_i^v}{2\sqrt{\mathbf{u}_i^v}}\right]\right\}. \quad (16)$$

Now, using the inequality in Eq. (15) and comparing Eq. (16) with Eq. (14), we obtain $p(\mathbf{f}|\alpha^h, \alpha^v) \geq c \cdot \mathbf{M}(\alpha^h, \alpha^v, \mathbf{f}, \mathbf{u}^h, \mathbf{u}^v)$. As it will be shown later, vectors $\mathbf{u}^h$ and $\mathbf{u}^v$ are quantities that need to be computed and have an intuitive interpretation related to the unknown image $\mathbf{f}$. This leads to the following lower bound for the joint probability distribution

$$p(\Theta, \mathbf{f}, \mathbf{g}) \geq c \cdot p(\Theta)\mathbf{M}(\alpha^h, \alpha^v, \mathbf{f}, \mathbf{u}^h, \mathbf{u}^v)p(\mathbf{g}|\mathbf{f}, \beta)$$
$$= \mathbf{F}(\Theta, \mathbf{f}, \mathbf{g}, \mathbf{u}^h, \mathbf{u}^v), \quad (17)$$

Hence, by defining

$$\tilde{\mathcal{M}}(q(\Theta, \mathbf{f}), \mathbf{g}, \mathbf{u}^h, \mathbf{u}^v) = \int q(\Theta, \mathbf{f}) \log\left(\frac{q(\Theta, \mathbf{f})}{\mathbf{F}(\Theta, \mathbf{f}, \mathbf{g}, \mathbf{u}^h, \mathbf{u}^v)}\right) d\Theta d\mathbf{f}, \quad (18)$$

and using Eq. (17), we obtain for $\mathcal{M}(q(\Theta, \mathbf{f}), \mathbf{g})$, defined in Eq. (13),

$$\mathcal{M}(q(\Theta, \mathbf{f}), \mathbf{g}) \leq \min_{\{\mathbf{u}^h, \mathbf{u}^v\}} \tilde{\mathcal{M}}(q(\Theta, \mathbf{f}), \mathbf{g}, \mathbf{u}^h, \mathbf{u}^v). \quad (19)$$

Therefore, by finding a sequence of distributions $\{q^k(\Theta, \mathbf{f})\}$ that monotonically decreases $\tilde{\mathcal{M}}(q(\Theta, \mathbf{f}), \mathbf{g}, \mathbf{u}^h, \mathbf{u}^v)$ for fixed $\mathbf{u}^h$ and $\mathbf{u}^v$, a sequence of an ever decreasing upper bound of $C_{KL}(q(\Theta, \mathbf{f})||p(\Theta, \mathbf{f}|\mathbf{g}))$ is also obtained due to Eq. (13). Furthermore minimizing $\tilde{\mathcal{M}}(q(\Theta, \mathbf{f}), \mathbf{g}, \mathbf{u}^h, \mathbf{u}^v)$ with respect to $\mathbf{u}^h$ and $\mathbf{u}^v$, generates vector sequences $\{\mathbf{u}^{hk}\}$ and $\{\mathbf{u}^{vk}\}$ that tightens the upper-bound for each distribution $q^k(\Theta, \mathbf{f})$. Therefore, the sequence $\{q^k(\Theta, \mathbf{f})\}$ is coupled with the sequences $\{\mathbf{u}^{hk}\}$ and $\{\mathbf{u}^{vk}\}$. We use the following iterative algorithm to approximate the posterior distribution of image and hyperparamneters and tighten the upper-bound.

Algorithm 1. *Posterior image distribution and parameter estimation using* $q(\Theta, \mathbf{f}) = q(\Theta)q(\mathbf{f})$.
Given $q^1(\Theta)$, *an initial estimate of* $q(\Theta)$, *and* $\{\mathbf{u}^{h^1}, \mathbf{u}^{v^1}\} \in (R^+)^{2p}$, *for* $k = 1$, *2, ... until a stopping criterion is met:*

1. *Find*

$$q^k(\mathbf{f}) = \arg\min_{q(\mathbf{f})} \tilde{\mathcal{M}}(q(\mathbf{f})q^k(\Theta), \mathbf{g}, \mathbf{u}^{h^k}, \mathbf{u}^{v^k}) \tag{20}$$

2. *Find*

$$\{\mathbf{u}^{h^{k+1}}, \mathbf{u}^{v^{k+1}}\} = \arg\min_{\{\mathbf{u}^h, \mathbf{u}^v\}} \tilde{\mathcal{M}}(q^k(\mathbf{f})q^k(\Theta), \mathbf{g}, \mathbf{u}^h, \mathbf{u}^v) \tag{21}$$

3. *Find*

$$q^{k+1}(\Theta) = \arg\min_{q(\Theta)} \tilde{\mathcal{M}}(q^k(\mathbf{f})q(\Theta), \mathbf{g}, \mathbf{u}^{h^{k+1}}, \mathbf{u}^{v^{k+1}}) \tag{22}$$

Set $q(\Theta) = \lim_{k\to\infty} q^k(\Theta)$, $q(\mathbf{f}) = \lim_{k\to\infty} q^k(\mathbf{f})$.

To calculate $q^k(\mathbf{f})$, we observe that differentiating $\tilde{\mathcal{M}}(q(\mathbf{f})q^k(\Theta), \mathbf{g}, \mathbf{u}^{h^k}, \mathbf{u}^{v^k})$ in Eq. (20) with respect to $q(\mathbf{f})$ and setting it equal to zero, we obtain

$$q^k(\mathbf{f}) = \mathcal{N}\left(\mathbf{f} \mid \mathbf{E}_{q^k(\mathbf{f})}[\mathbf{f}], \mathbf{cov}_{q^k(\mathbf{f})}[\mathbf{f}]\right), \tag{23}$$

with

$$\mathbf{cov}_{q^k(\mathbf{f})}^{-1}[\mathbf{f}] = \mathbf{E}_{q^k(\Theta)}[\beta] \sum_{q=1}^{U} \mathbf{C}_q^t \mathbf{C}_q + \mathbf{E}_{q^k(\Theta)}[\alpha^h] \Delta_h^t \mathbf{W}(\mathbf{u}^{h^k}) \Delta_h$$
$$+ \mathbf{E}_{q^k(\Theta)}[\alpha^v] \Delta_v^t \mathbf{W}(\mathbf{u}^{v^k}) \Delta_v \tag{24}$$

and $\mathbf{E}_{q^k(\mathbf{f})}[\mathbf{f}]$ given by

$$\mathbf{E}_{q^k(\mathbf{f})}[\mathbf{f}] = \mathbf{cov}_{q^k(\mathbf{f})}[\mathbf{f}] \ \mathbf{E}_{q^k(\Theta)}[\beta] \sum_{q=1}^{U} \mathbf{C}_q^t \mathbf{g}_q. \tag{25}$$

In Eq. (24) Δ^h and Δ^v represent $p \times p$ convolution matrices associated respectively with the first order horizontal and vertical differences, and $\forall \mathbf{u} \in (R^+)^p$, $\mathbf{W}(\mathbf{u})$ is the diagonal $p \times p$ matrix with entries

$$\mathbf{W}(\mathbf{u})_{ii} = \frac{1}{\sqrt{\mathbf{u}_i}} \text{ for } i = 1, \ldots, p. \tag{26}$$

The matrices $\mathbf{W}(\mathbf{u}^{h^k})$ and $\mathbf{W}(\mathbf{u}^{v^k})$ can be interpreted as spatial adaptivity matrices since they control the amount of horizontal and vertical smoothing at each pixel location depending on the strength of the intensity variation at that pixel, as expressed by the horizontal and vertical intensity gradients, respectively.

To calculate $\mathbf{u}^{d^{k+1}}$, for $d \in \{h, v\}$, we have from Eq. (21) that

$$\mathbf{u}^{d^{k+1}} = \arg\min_{\mathbf{u}} \sum_{i=1}^{p} \frac{\mathbf{E}_{q^k(\mathbf{f})}\left[(\Delta_i^d(\mathbf{f}))^2\right] + \mathbf{u}_i}{\sqrt{\mathbf{u}_i}} \tag{27}$$

and consequently

$$\mathbf{u}^{d^{k+1}}_i = \mathbf{E}_{\mathbf{q}^k(\mathbf{f})}\left[(\Delta^d_i(\mathbf{f}))^2\right] \text{ for } i = 1,\ldots,p. \tag{28}$$

It is clear from Eq. (28) that vectors $\mathbf{u}^{d^{k+1}}$, for $d \in \{h, v\}$, are functions of the spatial first order horizontal and vertical differences of the unknown image $\mathbf{f}$ under the distribution $\mathbf{q}^k(\mathbf{f})$ and represent the local spatial activity of $\mathbf{f}$.

Finally, differentiating the right hand side of Eq. (22) with respect to $\mathbf{q}(\Theta)$ and setting it equal to zero we find that

$$\mathbf{q}^{k+1}(\Theta) \propto \exp\left\{\mathbf{E}_{\mathbf{q}^k(\mathbf{f})}\left[\ln \mathbf{F}(\Theta, \mathbf{f}, \mathbf{g}, \mathbf{u}^{h^{k+1}}, \mathbf{u}^{v^{k+1}})\right]\right\}. \tag{29}$$

Thus we obtain

$$\mathbf{q}^{k+1}(\Theta) = \mathbf{q}^{k+1}(\alpha^h)\mathbf{q}^{k+1}(\alpha^v)\mathbf{q}^{k+1}(\beta), \tag{30}$$

where $\mathbf{q}^{k+1}_h(\alpha^h)$, $\mathbf{q}^{k+1}_v(\alpha^v)$ and $\mathbf{q}^{k+1}(\beta)$ are respectively the gamma distributions

$$\mathbf{q}^{k+1}_d(\alpha^d) = \Gamma\left(\alpha^d \Big| p + a^o_{\alpha^d}, \sum_i \sqrt{\mathbf{u}^{d^{k+1}}_i} + b^o_{\alpha^d}\right) \tag{31}$$

for $d \in \{h, v\}$ and

$$\mathbf{q}^{k+1}(\beta) = \Gamma\left(\beta \Big| \frac{PU}{2} + a^o_\beta, \frac{\mathbf{E}_{\mathbf{q}^k(\mathbf{f})}\left[\sum_{q=1}^U \|\mathbf{g}_q - \mathbf{C}_q\mathbf{f}\|^2\right]}{2} + b^o_\beta\right). \tag{32}$$

So we have

$$\mathbf{E}_{\mathbf{q}^{k+1}_d(\alpha^d)}\left[\alpha^d\right] = \frac{p + a^o_{\alpha^d}}{\sum_i \sqrt{\mathbf{u}^{d^{k+1}}_i} + b^o_{\alpha^d}}, \tag{33}$$

$$\mathbf{E}_{\mathbf{q}^{k+1}(\beta)}\left[\beta\right] = \frac{\frac{UP}{2} + a^o_\beta}{\frac{1}{2}\mathbf{E}_{\mathbf{q}^k(\mathbf{f})}\left[\sum_{q=1}^U \|\mathbf{g}_q - \mathbf{C}_q\mathbf{f}\|^2\right] + b^o_\beta}. \tag{34}$$

It is possible to express the inverses of these means in the more meaningful forms

$$\frac{1}{\mathbf{E}_{\mathbf{q}^{k+1}_d(\alpha^d)}\left[\alpha^d\right]} = \gamma_{\alpha^d}\frac{1}{\alpha^d_o} + (1 - \gamma_{\alpha^d})\frac{\sum_i \sqrt{\mathbf{u}^{d^{k+1}}_i}}{p} \tag{35}$$

and

$$\frac{1}{\mathbf{E}_{\mathbf{q}^{k+1}(\beta)}\left[\beta\right]} = \gamma_\beta\frac{1}{\beta_o} + (1 - \gamma_\beta)\frac{\mathbf{E}_{\mathbf{q}^k(\mathbf{f})}\left[\sum_{q=1}^U \|\mathbf{g}_q - \mathbf{C}_q\mathbf{f}\|^2\right]}{UP}, \tag{36}$$

where

$$\gamma_{\alpha^d} = \frac{a^o_{\alpha^d}}{p + a^o_{\alpha^d}} \text{ and } \gamma_\beta = \frac{a^o_\beta}{UP/2 + a^o_\beta}. \tag{37}$$

These mean values are convex linear combinations of the inverses of the means of the hyperpriors $\alpha_o^d = \frac{a_o^{0^d}}{b_o^{0^d}}$ and $\beta_o = \frac{a_\beta^0}{b_\beta^0}$, and their corresponding ML estimates. γ_{α^d} and γ_β take values in $[0, 1)$, and can be interpreted as the confidence on the parameter values.

Equation (25) can be solved iteratively utilizing the *Conjugate Gradient* (CG) method without the need of explicitly obtaining the full covariance matrix of Eq. (24), but estimation of $\mathbf{u}$ in Eq. (28) and evaluation of Eq. (36) requires the evaluation of

$$\mathbf{E}_{\mathbf{q}^k(\mathbf{f})}\left[(\Delta_i^d(\mathbf{f}))^2\right] = \left(\Delta_i^d(\mathbf{E}_{\mathbf{q}^k(\mathbf{f})}[\mathbf{f}])\right)^2 + \mathbf{E}_{\mathbf{q}^k(\mathbf{f})}\left[\left(\Delta_i^d(\mathbf{f} - \mathbf{E}_{\mathbf{q}^k(\mathbf{f})}[\mathbf{f}])\right)^2\right], \quad (38)$$

where

$$\mathbf{E}_{\mathbf{q}^k(\mathbf{f})}\left[\left(\Delta_i^d(\mathbf{f} - \mathbf{E}_{\mathbf{q}^k(\mathbf{f})}[\mathbf{f}])\right)^2\right] = \mathbf{tr}\left(\mathbf{cov}_{q^k(\mathbf{f})}[\mathbf{f}]\Delta_i^{d\,t}\Delta_i^d\right), \quad (39)$$

and

$$\mathbf{E}_{\mathbf{q}^k(\mathbf{f})}\left[\|\,\mathbf{g}_q - \mathbf{C}_q\mathbf{f}\,\|^2\right] = \|\,\mathbf{g}_q - \mathbf{C}_q\mathbf{E}_{\mathbf{q}^k(\mathbf{f})}[\mathbf{f}]\,\|^2 + \mathbf{tr}\left(\mathbf{cov}_{q^k(\mathbf{f})}[\mathbf{f}]\mathbf{C}_q^t\mathbf{C}_q\right), \quad (40)$$

respectively, and whose exact evaluation would require to evaluate the full covariance matrix. This problem can be solved utilizing different approximation methods described in the next section.

4 Approximate Matrix Inversion Methods

We have to calculate $\mathbf{tr}\left[\mathbf{cov}_{q^k(\mathbf{f})}[\mathbf{f}]\mathbf{V}\right]$ where $\mathbf{cov}_{q^k(\mathbf{f})}[\mathbf{f}]^{-1}$ has been defined in Eq. (24), and $\mathbf{V}$ is $\mathbf{V} = \Delta_i^{d\,t}\Delta_i^d$, or $\mathbf{C}_q^t\mathbf{C}_q$ (See Eqs. (39) and (40)).

Based on the properties of the matrix $\mathbf{cov}_{q^k(\mathbf{f})}[\mathbf{f}]^{-1}$ we have selected and described here the following approximation methods to estimate $\mathbf{cov}_{q^k(\mathbf{f})}[\mathbf{f}]$: Jacobi or diagonal preconditioning, Circulant preconditioning, and *Factorized Sparse Approximate Inverse* (FSAI) [10]. The description of each of these methods has been completed with their corresponding approximations of $\mathbf{tr}[\mathbf{cov}_{q^k(\mathbf{f})}[\mathbf{f}]\mathbf{V}]$.

4.1 Jacobi Preconditioning

Jacobi preconditioning approximates $\mathbf{cov}_{q^k(\mathbf{f})}[\mathbf{f}]$ by the inverse of its diagonal. This is the simplest and faster approximation. Using this approach we have

$$\mathbf{tr}[\mathbf{cov}_{q^k(\mathbf{f})}[\mathbf{f}]\mathbf{V}] \approx \sum_{i=1}^{p} \mathbf{V}_{ii}\mathbf{cov}_{q^k(\mathbf{f})}[\mathbf{f}]_{ii}. \quad (41)$$

4.2 Circulant Preconditioning

A block semi-circulant approximation of $\mathbf{cov}_{q^k(\mathbf{f})}[\mathbf{f}]^{-1}$ and $\mathbf{C}_q^t\mathbf{C}_q$, can be defined with the help of $\mathbf{C}_q \approx \overline{\mathbf{C}}_q = \mathbf{DH}\overline{\mathbf{R}}(\mathbf{d}_q, \gamma_q)$, where $\overline{\mathbf{R}}(\mathbf{d}_q, \gamma_q)$ is the convolution matrix obtained by averaging the convolution filters associated to each row of $\mathbf{R}(\mathbf{d}_q, \gamma_q)$, that is,

$$\overline{\mathbf{R}}(\mathbf{d}_q, \gamma_q)_{i\,1} = \frac{1}{p} \sum_{l=1}^{p} \mathbf{R}(\mathbf{d}_q, \gamma_q)_{\{(l+i-1) \bmod p\}\,l}. \tag{42}$$

Therefore, the matrix $\mathbf{cov}_{q^k(\mathbf{f})}[\mathbf{f}]^{-1}$ can be approximated by a matrix $\mathbf{O}$ defined as

$$\mathbf{O} = \mathbf{E}_{q^k(\Theta)}[\beta] \left(\sum_{q=1}^{U} \overline{\mathbf{C}}_q^t \overline{\mathbf{C}}_q \right) + \mathbf{E}_{q^k(\Theta)}[\alpha^h] z(\mathbf{u}^{hk}) \Delta_h^t \Delta_h$$

$$+ \mathbf{E}_{q^k(\Theta)}[\alpha^v] z(\mathbf{u}^{vk}) \Delta_v^t \Delta_v, \tag{43}$$

with $z(\mathbf{u}) = \frac{1}{p} \sum_i \frac{1}{\sqrt{\mathbf{u}_i}}, \forall \mathbf{u} \in (R^+)^p$.

Then, $\mathbf{O}$ is a block semi-circulant approximation of $\mathbf{cov}_{q^k(\mathbf{f})}[\mathbf{f}]^{-1}$ and

$$\mathbf{tr}[\mathbf{O}^{-1} \Delta_i^{dt} \Delta_i^d] = \frac{1}{p} \mathbf{tr}[\mathbf{O}^{-1} \Delta^{dt} \Delta^d]$$

and $\mathbf{tr}[\mathbf{O}^{-1} \overline{\mathbf{C}}_q^t \overline{\mathbf{C}}_q]$ can be calculated in the frequency domain.

4.3   FSAI Method

Finally we consider the Cholevsky factorization of the *symmetric definite positive* (SPD) matrix $\mathbf{cov}_{q^k(\mathbf{f})}[\mathbf{f}]^{-1} = \mathbf{L}\mathbf{L}^T$. The idea behind FSAI is to find a lower triangular matrix $\mathbf{G}$ with $\mathbf{Q}$ sparsity pattern (arrangement of nonzero elements in an sparse matrix that it must be specified a priori and such that $\mathbf{Q} \subseteq \{(i,j) : i \leq j\}$), that minimizes the Frobenius norm $\|\mathbf{I} - \mathbf{L}\mathbf{G}\|_F$, where the Frobenius norm of an $A_{N \times M}$ matrix is

$$\|A\|_F = \sqrt{\sum_{i=1}^{N} \sum_{j=1}^{M} |A_{ij}|^2}.$$

In [10] the following algorithm to find $\mathbf{G}$ is proposed:

Algorithm 2

- *Step 1: Compute a lower triangular matrix $\hat{\mathbf{G}}$ with sparsity pattern $\mathbf{Q}$, such that $(\hat{\mathbf{G}} \mathbf{cov}_{q^k(\mathbf{f})}[\mathbf{f}]^{-1})_{i,j} = \mathbf{I}_{i,j}, \forall (i,j) \in \mathbf{Q}$.*
- *Step 2: Calculate $\mathbf{D} = (\mathrm{diag}(\hat{\mathbf{G}}))^{-1}$ and $\mathbf{G} = \mathbf{D}^{\frac{1}{2}} \hat{\mathbf{G}}$.*

Note that in step 1 $\hat{\mathbf{G}}$ is computed by rows: each row requires the solution of a small local SPD linear system, the size of which is equal to the number of nonzero allowed in that row. A common choice for the sparsity pattern is to allow non-zeros in $\mathbf{Q}$ only in positions corresponding to non-zeros in the lower triangular part of $\mathbf{cov}_{q^k(\mathbf{f})}[\mathbf{f}]^{-1}$ [11]. Finally we approximate $\mathbf{tr}[\mathbf{cov}_{q^k(\mathbf{f})}[\mathbf{f}]\mathbf{V}]$ by $\mathbf{tr}[\mathbf{G}\mathbf{V}\mathbf{G}^T] = \sum_{i=1}^{p} \sum_{j=1}^{i} \sum_{k=1}^{i} \mathbf{G}_{ij} \mathbf{V}_{jk} \mathbf{G}_{ik}$.

5 Experimental Results

A number of experiments have been carried out using synthetic LR images that allow us to measure the quality of the HR image reconstructed with the proposed Algorithm 1 (henceforth $\ell 1$) using different preconditioning techniques.

We show results for the image set of LR images obtained from the HR images in Fig. 2a and Fig. 3a. Sequences of 16 rotated, displaced and downsampled, by a factor of 4, images have been obtained and Gaussian noise of 30 dB and 40 dB was added. Reconstructions utilizing the different preconditioning methods have been performed and their quality has been numerically measured utilizing the peak signal-to-noise ratio (PSNR), and the *Structural Similarity Index Measure* (SSIM) defined in [12], whose maximal value, corresponding to equal images, is $+1$.

The proposed algorithm was ran until the criterion

$$\|\mathbf{f}^k - \mathbf{f}^{k-1}\|^2 / \|\mathbf{f}^{k-1}\|^2 < 10^{-4} \tag{44}$$

was satisfied, where $\mathbf{f}^k$ denotes image point estimate for the k iteration step. Gamma hyperpriors parameter values a_θ^o and b_θ^o, $\forall \theta \in \Theta$ (see Eq. (9)) were determined experimentally for each image.

Table 1 shows a numeric comparison of the results obtained utilizing the different preconditioning methods and the reconstruction using a SAR prior. Figure 2b shows one of the 40 db LR observed images. Figure 2c shows the HR reconstruction obtained by using Jacobi's approximation (the other two approximations produced very similar reconstruction, see also table 1). Figure 2d displays the reconstruction using a SAR prior.

Finally, Fig. 3b shows one of the 30 dB LR observed images. Figure 3c shows the HR reconstruction obtained by using Jacobi's approximation and Fig. 3d displays the reconstruction using a SAR prior.

Table 1. PSNR and SSIM values of (2a) and (3a) images for 16 observed images

Image	Method	SNR 30 dB		SNR 40 dB	
		PSNR	SSIM	PSNR	SSIM
(2a)	Jacobi	24.1	0.76	29.3	0.90
	FSAI	23.5	0.75	28.6	0.89
	Circulant	23.3	0.79	28.5	0.91
	SAR	20.9	0.61	26.4	0.81
(3a)	Jacobi	31.0	0.89	34.4	0.94
	FSAI	30.8	0.88	34.3	0.94
	Circulant	30.7	0.88	34.5	0.93
	SAR	28.8	0.82	31.8	0.94

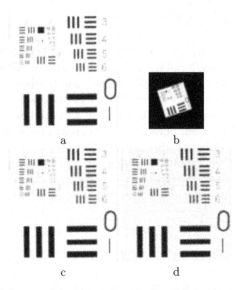

a   b

c   d

Fig. 2. (a) Original image, (b) one of the 16 40 dB LR observed images from the sequence, (c) HR reconstruction using Jacobi matrix approximation and (d) the reconstruction using SAR prior

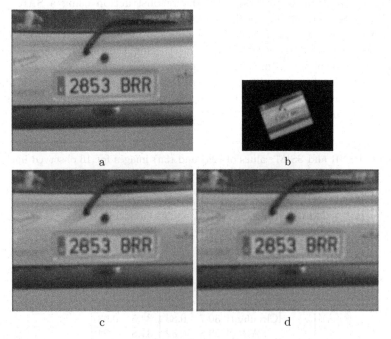

a   b

c   d

Fig. 3. (a) Original image, (b) One of the 16 30 dB LR observed images from the sequence, (c) HR reconstruction using Jacobi matrix approximation and (d) the reconstruction using SAR prior

6   Conclusions

The Bayesian high-resolution image reconstruction method proposed in [13] has been extended to consider arbitrary displacements and rotations. Several matrix inversion techniques have been considered in our algorithm implementation, from which similar results are obtained. The utilization of a prior based on the $\ell 1$ norm of horizontal and vertical differences in images gives results better than the utilization of a SAR prior.

References

1. Katsaggelos, A., Molina, R., Mateos, J.: Super resolution of images and video. In: Synthesis Lectures on Image, Video, and Multimedia Processing. Morgan & Claypool (2007)
2. Tipping, M.E., Bishop, C.M.: Bayesian image super-resolution. In: Becker, S., Thrun, S., Obermayer, K. (eds.) Advances in Neural Information Processing Systems, vol. 15, pp. 1279–1286. MIT Press, Cambridge (2003)
3. Pickup, L.C., Capel, D.P., Roberts, S.J., Zisserman, A.: Bayesian methods for image super-resolution. The Computer Journal (2007)
4. Molina, R., Katsaggelos, A.K., Mateos, J.: Bayesian and regularization methods for hyperparameter estimation in image restoration. IEEE Transactions on Image Processing 8, 231–246 (1999)
5. Hardie, R.C., Barnard, K.J., Bognar, J.G., Armstrong, E.E., Watson, E.A.: High-resolution image reconstruction from a sequence of rotated and translated frames and its application to an infrared imaging system. Society of Photo-Optical Instrumentation Engineers 37(1), 247–260 (1998)
6. Kullback, S., Leibler, R.A.: On information and sufficiency. Annals of Math. Stat. 22, 79–86 (1951)
7. Kullback, S.: Information Theory and Statistics. Dover Publications, New York (1959)
8. Babacan, S., Molina, R., Katsaggelos, A.: Parameter estimation in tv image restoration using variational distribution approximation. IEEE Trans. on Image Processing 17(3), 326–339 (2008)
9. Bioucas-Dias, J., Figueiredo, M., Oliveira, J.: Total-variation image deconvolution: A majorization-minimization approach. In: ICASSP 2006 (2006)
10. Kolotilina, L.Y., Yeremin, A.Y.: Factorized sparse approximate inverse preconditioning: I. theory. SIAM J. Matrix Anal. Appl., 45–58 (1993)
11. Benzi, M.: Preconditioning techniques for large linear systems: A survey. J. Comput. Phys. 182, 418–477 (2002)
12. Wang, Z., Bovik, A.C., Sheikh, H.R., Simoncelli, E.P.: Image quality assessment: From error measurement to structural similarity. IEEE Trans. on Img. Proc. 13(4), 600–612 (2004)
13. Molina, R., Vega, M., Abad, J., Katsaggelos, A.K.: Parameter Estimation in Bayesian High-Resolution Image Reconstruction with Multisensors. IEEE Transactions on Image Processing 12(12), 1655–1667 (2003)

A New Approach to Sparse Image Representation Using MMV and K-SVD

Jie Yang, Abdesselam Bouzerdoum, and Son Lam Phung

School of Electrical, Computer and Telecommunications Engineering
University of Wollongong, Wollongong, NSW 2522, Australia

Abstract. This paper addresses the problem of image representation based on a sparse decomposition over a learned dictionary. We propose an improved matching pursuit algorithm for Multiple Measurement Vectors (MMV) and an adaptive algorithm for dictionary learning based on multi-Singular Value Decomposition (SVD), and combine them for image representation. Compared with the traditional K-SVD and *orthogonal matching pursuit* MMV (OMPMMV) methods, the proposed method runs faster and achieves a higher overall reconstruction accuracy.

1 Introduction

Signal representation is important for efficient signal processing, data compression, pattern recognition and machine learning. The problem of how to select a set of basis vectors for efficient representation of signals in a given dataset has been extensively investigated in the past [1,2]. This problem can be described mathematically as follows: given an original signal $\mathbf{y}$ in an n-dimensional space and a set of basis vectors, find, within a preset tolerance, a compact representation of $\mathbf{y}$ using the subspace spanned by the basis vectors. The development of pursuit algorithms such as *orthogonal matching pursuit* [5] from *compressed sensing* [3,4], with the capability to find a sparse representation, has offered new approaches for tackling the aforementioned problem. Using an over-complete dictionary D consisting of k basis vectors or *atoms*, the original signal can be decomposed by solving the following system of linear equations:

$$\mathbf{y} = D\mathbf{x} \qquad (1)$$

In the past, the K-SVD approach has been proposed for dictionary-based learning for a sparse representation [6,7,8]. However, this approach has a number of problems in dealing with high-dimensional signals. First, K-SVD depends heavily on a pursuit algorithm to calculate the sparse coefficients. Second, it updates the dictionary atom-by-atom during each iteration. Furthermore, the K-SVD requires large storage because the computed non-zero coefficients reside in different locations.

To overcome the K-SVD disadvantages, we propose a new approach to signal representation that is based on the concept of Multiple Measurement Vectors (MMV) [9], [10]. MMV aims to find a solution where most nonzero elements

J. Blanc-Talon et al. (Eds.): ACIVS 2009, LNCS 5807, pp. 200–209, 2009.

are clustered in a few rows. The proposed method requires significantly less storage compared to K-SVD. Furthermore, it allows the simultaneous update of several atoms, which leads to faster convergence and better reconstruction accuracy. Here, the new method is applied to a simulated data and the problem of image representation and its performance is assessed in terms of reconstruction accuracy and convergence speed.

The paper is organized as follows. Section 2 provides background information on compressed sensing and K-SVD algorithm. Section 3 presents the proposed approach based on Multiple Measurement Vectors. Section 4 gives an analysis of the proposed approach in an image representation task. Section 5 presents concluding remarks.

2   Background

This section reviews the basic concepts of compressed sensing and discusses two existing algorithms, namely *orthogonal matching pursuit*(OMP) and K-SVD.

2.1   Compressed Sensing

Compressed sensing (CS) aims to find a sparse solution to the problem in (1), where most of the elements of the solution vector $\mathbf{x}$ are zero [3, 4]. Compressed sensing algorithms can be divided into two broad categories: (i) Single Measurement Vector (SMV) [5], [11] where the solution is a vector; and (ii) Multiple Measurement Vectors (MMV) [9], [10] where the solution is a two-dimensional array, or matrix.

In SMV, the problem can be formulated as:

$$\text{minimize} \, \|\mathbf{x}\|_0 \, , \text{ subject to } \, \mathbf{y} = D\mathbf{x} \tag{2}$$

where $\mathbf{y} \in \mathbb{R}^n$ is an observable (measurement) vector, $D \in \mathbb{R}^{n \times k}$ is a known dictionary containing k basis vectors or atoms, and $\|\mathbf{x}\|_0$ denotes the number of nonzero elements in $\mathbf{x}$. This problem can be solved by several approaches, including greedy algorithms such as Orthogonal Matching Pursuit [5], and non-convex local optimization such as FOCUSS algorithm [11].

On the other hand, the aim in MMV is to

$$\text{minimize} \, \|X\|_0 \, , \text{ subject to } \, Y = DX \tag{3}$$

where $Y \in \mathbb{R}^{n \times m}$ is a matrix comprising multiple measurement vectors, X is the solution matrix $(X \in \mathbb{R}^{k \times m})$, and $\|X\|_0$ denotes the number of non-empty rows in X. A non-empty row has at least one non-zero entry. The OMP technique and its variants developed for SMV have been extended to tackle MMV [9].

In this paper, we focus on the Orthogonal Matching Pursuit for MMV algorithm (OMPMMV) proposed in [10]. The steps of this iterative algorithm are summarized in Table 1. In this algorithm, $\mathcal{S}_t$ denotes the set of selected atoms after the t-th iteration, and R_t represents the residual error, obtained by using $\mathcal{S}_t$ for signal reconstruction.

Table 1. OMPMMV algorithm [10]

1. Initialize $S_0 = \emptyset$ (empty set) and $R_0 = Y$.
2. Repeat steps 3 to 6 until convergence.
3. Compute $A = D^T R_{t-1}$.
4. Select from D the column (or atom) $\mathbf{d}_i^t$, which
corresponds to the row A_i with the largest magnitude in A.
5. Update the set of selected atoms: $S_t = S_{t-1} \bigcup \mathbf{d}_i^t$.
6. Update the residual $R_t = Y - S_t X_t$,
where $X_t = [S_t^T S_t]^{-1} S_t^T Y$.

2.2 K-SVD Method

Consider an $n \times m$ matrix Y, comprising m measurement vectors, and a known fixed dictionary $D \in \mathbb{R}^{n \times k}$. The problem of finding a compact signal representation can be expressed as

$$\text{minimize } S_m(X), \text{ subject to } Y = DX \qquad (4)$$

where $S_m(X)$ is a sparsity measure of X. In [6,7,8], $S(X)$ is defined in terms of the l^0-norm for columns $\mathbf{x}_i$ of X. In K-SVD method, each column $\mathbf{y}_i$ of Y is extracted and the traditional SMV method is applied on the pair $(\mathbf{y}_i, D)$ to obtain a solution in the form of

$$\widehat{\mathbf{x}}_i = \underset{\mathbf{x}_i}{\text{argmin}} \, \|\mathbf{x}_i\|_0, \text{ subject to } \mathbf{y}_i = D\mathbf{x}_i \qquad (5)$$

Note that K-SVD assumes that the dictionary D is unknown so it calculates D as well. Hence, the optimization problem in (5) becomes

$$\left(\widehat{D}, \widehat{X}\right) = \underset{D,X}{\text{argmin}} \, \{S_m(X) + \|Y - DX\|_F^2\}, \qquad (6)$$

where $\|.\|_F^2$ denotes the Frobenius norm.

The main advantage of K-SVD is that it not only finds a sparse solution for each column of X, but also updates simultaneously the dictionary D via SVD. The reader is referred to [6,7,8] for a wide range of applications of K-SVD.

3   MMV-Based Signal Representation

To describe the proposed MMV-based approach to signal representation, we first give some definitions:

Definition 1. Given a matrix X, its *sparse I rank* $S_1(X)$ is the largest number of non-zero entries in any column of X.

Definition 2. Given a matrix X, its *sparse II rank* $S_2(X)$ is the number of non-empty rows in X. A non-empty row must have at least one non-zero entry.

It is clear that the K-SVD method uses *sparse I rank* as its optimization criterion. In this paper, we propose a new approach to address the problem in (6), using the *sparse II rank* $S_2(X)$. The problem is now formulated as

$$\left(\widehat{D}, \widehat{X}\right) = \underset{D,X}{\text{argmin}} \ \{S_2(X) + \|Y - DX\|_F^2\} \tag{7}$$

The K-SVD method treats the columns of Y independently. By contrast, our approach considers all columns simultaneously; therefore, it is able to update multiple columns in the dictionary at each iteration. To solve the MMV problem, we propose a new MMV pursuit algorithm, called Enhanced Orthogonal Matching Pursuit or EOMP. This algorithm improves upon the the traditional OMPMMV shown in Table 1 in two ways: (i) it selects more than one atom at each iteration; (ii) it keeps a compact solution by discarding irrelevant atoms. The steps of the EOMP algorithm are summarized in Table 2 below.

Table 2. Enhanced Orthogonal Matching Pursuit Algorithm

Input
   matrix $Y \in \mathbb{R}^{n \times m}$,
   matrix $D \in \mathbb{R}^{n \times k}$,
   maximum number of selected atoms K_{max},
   thresholds λ and γ.
Ouput
   matrix $X \in \mathbb{R}^{k \times m}$
Procedure
1. *Initialization*
   residual error: $R_0 = Y$,
   set of selected atoms: $\mathcal{S} = \emptyset$.
2. *Subset Selection*
   Find atom $\mathbf{d}_i$ in D so that $\|\mathbf{c}_i\|_q \geq \lambda \ \underset{j=1, j \neq i}{\overset{k}{\sup}} \ \|\mathbf{c}_j\|_q$, where $\mathbf{c}_i = (R_{t-1})^T \mathbf{d}_i$ and $q > 1$.
   Add selected atoms to $\mathcal{S}$: $\mathcal{S} = \mathcal{S} \bigcup \mathbf{d}_i$.
3. *Atom Extraction*
   3.1 Discard $\mathbf{d}_i$ if its coherence satisfies $|\langle \mathbf{d}_i, \mathbf{d}_k \rangle| \leq \gamma$, for all $\mathbf{d}_k \in \mathcal{S}$, where $i \neq k$.
   3.2 If $|\mathcal{S}| > K_{max}$, delete $(|\mathcal{S}| - K_{max})$ atoms with the lowest scores $\|\mathbf{c}_i\|_q$.
4. *Solution Update*
   Find X that minimizes $\|\mathcal{S}X - Y\|_F^2$.
   Update the residual error $R_t = Y - \mathcal{S}X$.
5. *Stopping Criterion*
   If the number of columns in $\mathcal{S}$ is equal to K_{max}, stop.
   Otherwise, go to Step 2.

Remark 1. The thresholds λ and γ control the size of S for the orthogonal projection, and they play an important role in EOMP. Our method does not recycle the same atoms like OMPMMV does. A larger λ means more atoms will be selected at each iteration. When $\lambda = 1$, EOMP behaves like the traditional OMPMMV. Furthermore, EOMP eliminates similar atoms; the threshold γ determines how many atoms should be discarded. In contrast, OMPMMV keeps all the atoms found, even if they are highly correlated; this tends to slow down convergence of OMPMMV. In this paper, we use $\lambda = 0.8$ and $\gamma = 0.45$.

Remark 2. Suppose that at the t-th iteration, EOMP selects m_1 atoms, but only m_2 of them are kept for the update Step, where $m_1 \geq m_2$. The complexity of EOMP is

$$O(kp_1 + m_1(m_1 - 1)/2 + m_2p_2) \tag{8}$$

where p_1 is the cost of multiplying R_{t-1} and an atom, and p_2 is the cost of *Solution Update* step. The three terms in (8) correspond to the three steps of *Subset Selection*, *Atoms Extraction*, and *Solution Update*. Subset Selection step involves k atoms in D. Atoms Extraction step needs to compare m_1 selected atoms. Solution Update step requires solving a linear equation with m_2 coefficients. By comparison, OMPMMV has, at the t-th iteration, a complexity of $O(kp_1 + m_2p_2)$. However, OMPMMV needs m_2 iterations to find m_2 atoms whereas EOMP may require only one or two iterations to locate the possible candidates.

Remark 3. For comparison purposes, we select the parameters of EOMP so that it uses the same amount of storage as the K-SVD method. The maximum number of selected atoms K_{max} can then be calculated as

$$K_{max} = \left\lfloor \frac{c \times a \times N_s + b \times a \times N_s}{c \times N_s + b} \right\rfloor \tag{9}$$

where c is number of bits required to store a coefficient, a is the maximum number of selected atoms in K-SVD, N_s is the number of columns in the target image, and b is the number of bits required to store a coefficient index.

Generally the nonzero elements in the solution obtained by EOMP are clustered in a few rows; therefore, we can update more than one atom in D at each iteration. To aid the explanation, we next define an operator called *svds*. By the singular value decomposition, a matrix $A \in \mathbb{R}^{m \times n}$ can be written as

$$A = U\Sigma V^T \tag{10}$$

where $U \in \mathbb{R}^{m \times m}$ and $V \in \mathbb{R}^{n \times n}$ are orthogonal matrices. Given a positive integer k, we define the *svds* operator as

$$svds(A, k) = \{U_k, \Sigma_k, V_k^T\} \tag{11}$$

where U_k is the first k columns in U, Σ_k is a diagonal matrix of size $k \times k$, and V_k^T is the first k columns in V^T.

The EOMP strategy for updating the dictionary D and the coefficients matrix is shown in Table 3.

Next we propose an improved K-SVD algorithm that combines the Enhanced OMP, presented in Table 2, and the Dictionary Update Strategy, presented in Table 3. This algorithm, called IK-SVD, is shown in Table 4.

Table 3. Dictionary Update Strategy

At iteration t, perform Steps 1 to 4:
1. Select N atoms from D^{t-1} that correspond to non-empty rows $\{X_s^{t-1}\}$ in X^{t-1}:
   $$D_s^{t-1} = \{\mathbf{d}_i^{t-1} \in D^{t-1} \mid \text{column } \mathbf{x}_i^{t-1} \neq \mathbf{0}\}.$$
   where N is a predefined integer and $\mathbf{x}_i^{t-1}$ is the i-th row in X^{t-1}.
2. Calculate the error due to D_s^{t-1}:
   $$E_s^{t-1} = Y - \sum_{\mathbf{d}_i^{t-1} \in D_s^{t-1}} \mathbf{d}_i^{t-1} \mathbf{x}_i^{t-1}.$$
3. Apply the $svds$ operator to E_s^{t-1} to compute X_s^t and D_s^t:
   $$\{U_N, \Sigma_N, V_N^T\} = svds(E_s^{t-1}, N), \text{ and } D_s^t = U_N, X_s^t = \Sigma V_N^T.$$
4. Repeat Steps 1 to 3 until all non-empty rows in X^{t-1} have been processed.

Table 4. Improved K-SVD algorithm for signal representation (IK-SVD)

Input:
   matrix Y in $\mathbb{R}^{n \times m}$,
   maximum number of selected atoms K_{max},
   thresholds λ and γ, and
   maximum number of iterations T_{max}.
Output:
   coefficient matrix X of size $k \times m$,
   dictionary D of size $n \times k$.
Procedure:
1. Initialize a random dictionary D^0 and coefficient matrix X_a.
2. Repeat Steps 3 and 5 for $t = 1, 2, ..., T_{max}$.
3. Apply EOMP algorithm (Table 2) on $\{Y, D^{t-1}\}$ to obtain X_b.
4. Set $X_{t-1} = X_a$ or $X_{t-1} = X_b$, to give the smallest reconstruction error:
   $$\|Y - D_{t-1}X_{t-1}\|$$
5. Apply Dictionary Update Strategy (Table 3)
   on $\{Y, D^{t-1}, X^{t-1}\}$ to obtain D^t and X_a.

Remark 4. The main difference between the proposed IK-SVD algorithm and the traditional K-SVD algorithm is that a more optimal coefficient matrix is selected from the two outputs produced by the EOMP step (Step 3) and the Dictionary Update step (Step 5). This leads to better convergence for the IK-SVD.

4   Experiments and Analysis

In this section, we analyze the performance of the proposed algorithm, and compare it with the traditional K-SVD algorithm. First, we test the convergence of the proposed method using a simulated data set. Second, we evaluate the proposed algorithm and the K-SVD on an image representation task. To measure the error between the original signal and the reconstructed signal, we use the Peak Signal-to-Noise Ratio (PSNR):

$$PSNR = 20 \log_{10}(255/RMSE), \tag{12}$$

where $RMSE$ denotes the root-mean-square error between columns of Y and Y^*.

4.1   Convergence Analysis

A signal Y is created in the range of $[-1, 1]$. It has a dimension of 50. White Gaussian noise is added; the signal-to-noise ratio (SNR) has values of 10dB, 20dB, and 30dB. The dictionary D has initially 50 atoms, each of which is normalized to a unit l^2-norm. The total number of training iterations is set to 30.

In this experiment, we examine the effects of three factors on the K-SVD and the proposed method: (i) the number of selected atoms K_{max}, (ii) the size of dictionary k, and (iii) the number of samples m in Y. We vary one factor while keeping the rest the same. For the K-SVD, we apply OMP algorithm to find the sparse coefficients in each column of the solution X. The number of coefficients ranges from 8 to 12. For the proposed IK-SVD, we use $\lambda = 0.8$ and $\gamma = 0.45$.

Table 5. Comparison of K-SVD and IK-SVD on simulated signals with white Gaussian noise

(K_{max}, k, m)	Execution Time (s)			PSNR (db)		
$(8, 50, 1000)$	SNR=10	SNR=20	SNR=30	SNR=10	SNR=20	SNR=30
K-SVD	46.54	46.70	47.80	66.68	69.25	70.66
IK-SVD (proposed)	10.52	10.72	10.98	68.78	71.90	72.28
$(12, 50, 1000)$	SNR=10	SNR=20	SNR=30	SNR=10	SNR=20	SNR=30
K-SVD	85.96	86.48	89.09	64.11	65.47	65.74
IK-SVD (proposed)	12.35	12.24	13.11	67.16	69.60	70.36
$(12, 70, 1000)$	SNR=10	SNR=20	SNR=30	SNR=10	SNR=20	SNR=30
K-SVD	92.42	92.46	92.46	64.17	65.27	65.56
IK-SVD (proposed)	15.71	16.89	17.37	64.92	65.96	66.88
$(12, 70, 2000)$	SNR=10	SNR=20	SNR=30	SNR=10	SNR=20	SNR=30
K-SVD	174.52	174.64	174.76	63.69	64.91	65.25
IK-SVD (proposed)	28.03	28.43	28.79	65.18	66.36	66.91

Table 5 shows the execution time and the reconstruction error for both K-SVD and IK-SVD methods, at different noise levels. In terms of execution time, IK-SVD method runs between 3.6 and 6.9 times faster than the K-SVD. The improvement is most significant when the number of selected atoms $(K_{max})$and the number of signal samples (m) are high. An explanation for this result is that, at each iteration, the proposed method can update multiple atoms in D. In addition, the IK-SVD takes less time to find an $S_2(X)$ solution compared to the traditional OMP method used in K-SVD. In terms of reconstruction error,

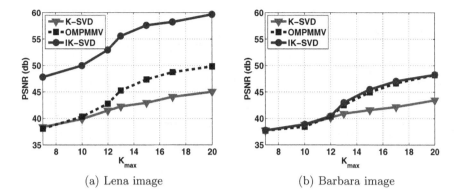

(a) Lena image   (b) Barbara image

Fig. 1. Comparison of K-SVD, OMPMMV, and IK-SVD in image representation task: PSNR of reconstructed images

the IK-SVD method has higher PSNRs compared to the K-SVD in all cases. In summary, incorporation of MMV into K-SVD method improves significantly the performance of signal representation.

4.2 Application to Imaging Representation

In this experiment, we apply the IK-SVD algorithm on two images: *Barbara* and *Lena*. The size of these images is 512×512 pixels. First, each image is partitioned into non-overlapping blocks of size $M \times N$ pixels, where $M = N = 8$. A matrix Y is formed for training, by randomly selecting among these blocks; each block forms one column in Y. We apply both the K-SVD and IK-SVD methods on Y to extract two dictionaries. The dictionary size is set to $8 \times M \times N$. We also implement the OMPMMV method for comparison.

For K-SVD, we set the maximum number of atoms (K_{max}) in the range from 7 to 20. For IK-SVD and OMPMMV, the maximum number of atoms (K_{max}) is adaptively computed as in (9), so that the same amount of storage is used by EOMP and K-SVD. We run the test 20 times. The PSNR and execution time are shown in Fig. 1 and Fig. 2, respectively.

Fig. 1 and Fig. 2 show that even OMPMMV is better than that of K-SVD. The only difference between them is that OMPMMV uses $S_2(X)$, whereas K-SVD uses $S_1(X)$. This demonstrates the advantage of the MMV-based scheme. Compared to the proposed algorithm IK-SVD, OMPMMV algorithm needs more computation time to converge. This is because IK-SVD can select several atoms from D at each step. Also, the result shows that when the maximum number of atoms K_{max} increases, the accuracy of all algorithms is enhanced. However, the IK-SVD method has a lower reconstruction error than the K-SVD and OMP-MMV. When K_{max} increases from 10 to 20, K-SVD execution time increases sharply, whereas IK-SVD appears more stable and robust.

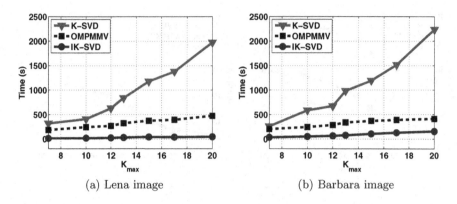

(a) Lena image   (b) Barbara image

Fig. 2. Comparison of K-SVD, OMPMMV, and IK-SVD in image representation task: Execution time

5 Conclusion

This paper addresses the problem of sparse decomposition for signal representation. To date, K-SVD is the state-of-the-art method for solving this problem. We have proposed here a new method that is based on Multiple Measurement Vectors (MMV), which offer a better trade-off between computational accuracy and storage requirement. The proposed method uses an enhanced MMV pursuit algorithm (EOMP) to find a minimal-$S_2(X)$ solution and the multi-singular value decomposition to accelerate processing. Experimental results indicated that the new method runs 3.6 to 6.9 times faster, and has lower reconstruction error, compared to the existing K-SVD algorithm.

References

1. Wickerhauser, M.V.: Adapted wavelet analysis from theory to software. A. K. Peters, Ltd., Natick (1994)
2. Donoho, D.L.: On Minimum Entropy Segmentation, pp. 233–269. Academic Press, Inc., New York (1994)
3. Haupt, J., Nowak, R.: Signal Reconstruction From Noisy Random Projections. IEEE Transactions on Information Theory 52, 4036–4048 (2006)
4. Rauhut, H., Schnass, K., Vandergheynst, P.: Compressed Sensing and Redundant Dictionaries. IEEE Transactions on Information Theory 54, 2210–2219 (2008)
5. Tropp, J.A., Gilbert, A.C.: Signal Recovery From Random Measurements Via Orthogonal Matching Pursuit. IEEE Transactions on Information Theory 53, 4655–4666 (2007)
6. Aharon, M., Elad, M., Bruckstein, A.: K-SVD: An Algorithm for Designing Overcomplete Dictionaries for Sparse Representation. IEEE Transactions on Signal Processing 55, 4311–4322 (2006)
7. Elad, M., Aharon, M.: Image Denoising Via Sparse and Redundant Representations Over Learned Dictionaries. IEEE Transactions on Image Processing 15, 3736–3745 (2006)

8. Mairal, J., Elad, M., Sapiro, G.: Sparse Representation for Color Image Restoration. IEEE Transactions on Image Processing 17, 53–69 (2008)
9. Cotter, S.F., Rao, B.D., Kjersti, E., Kreutz-Delgado, K.: Sparse solutions to linear inverse problems with multiple measurement vectors. IEEE Transactions on Signal Processing 53, 2477–2488 (2005)
10. Chen, J., Huo, X.: Theoretical Results on Sparse Representations of Multiple-Measurement Vectors. IEEE Transactions on Signal Processing 54, 4634–4643 (2006)
11. Rao, B.D., Engan, K., Cotter, S.F., Palmer, J., Kreutz-Delgado, K.: Subset selection in noise based on diversity measure minimization. IEEE Transactions on Signal Processing 51, 760–770 (2003)

3D Filtering of Colour Video Sequences Using Fuzzy Logic and Vector Order Statistics

Volodymyr Ponomaryov, Alberto Rosales-Silva, and Francisco Gallegos-Funes

National Polytechnic Institute of Mexico, ESIME, Av. Santa Ana, 1000,
Col. San Fco- Culhuacan, 04430, Mexico-city, Mexico
{Ponomaryov,vponomar}@ipn.mx

Abstract. Novel approach designed in this paper permits the suppression of impulsive noise in multichannel video sequences. It employs the fuzzy logic and vector order statistic methods to detect motion and noise presence during spatial-temporal processing neighbouring video frames, preserving the edges, fine details, as well as colour properties. Numerous simulation results have justified it excellent performance in terms of objective criteria: Pick Signal-to-Noise Ratio (PSNR), Mean Absolute Error (MAE) and Normalized Colour Difference (NCD), as well as in subjective perception by human viewer.

1 Introduction

Images and video sequences are acquired by sensor of different nature, so, the quality of data can be degraded because of non-ideality of a sensor or during transmission process where a noise is introduced. Standard processing operations: edge detection, image segmentation, pattern recognition in noise presence can present low quality results. So, the image pre-processing stage is a principal part in any computer vision application and includes reducing image noise without degrading its quality.

There are known many algorithms that are employed for impulsive noise suppression in two dimensions (2D), for example some proposed in [1-6]. The aim of this work is to design a novel scheme that permits to realize the processing in 2D, as well as and in 3D, demonstrating better performance in terms of objective and subjective criteria. A novel filtering scheme employs fuzzy logic and vector order statistic theory in processing of video sequences, and as it is justified, proposed approach can efficiently suppress impulsive noise generated in communication channel, guaranteeing better edge and fine preservation and chromaticity characteristics.

Novel scheme, named as 2D Fuzzy Two Step Colour Filter, gathering the fuzzy set theory and vector order statistics has demonstrated the ability to outperform existed filters as one can see analyzing the simulation results.

There are other 2D algorithms that are also implemented and used in this paper as comparative ones: INR filter [1], AMNF, AMNF2 (Adaptive Non-Parametric Filters) [2]; AMNF3 (Adaptive Multichannel Non-Parametric Vector Rank M-type K-nearest Neighbour Filter) [3]; GVDF (Generalized Vector Directional Filter) [4]; CWVDF (Centred Weighted Vector Directional Filters) [5]; and, finally, VMF_FAS (Vector

J. Blanc-Talon et al. (Eds.): ACIVS 2009, LNCS 5807, pp. 210–221, 2009.
© Springer-Verlag Berlin Heidelberg 2009

Median Filter Fast Adaptive Similarity) [6]. These techniques demonstrated the better results among a lot of other existed and are used as comparative ones. Developing mentioned novel 2D filter, we also present a novel 3D filtering approach employing a correlation between neighbour frames. Here, the information from previous or/and future frames can be also available, but the efficient employment of the several neighbour frames should be found during processing, taking into account a motion between frames. A lot of proposals have been presented in video denoising, in spatial, temporal and spatio-temporal denoising [7-15].

Let draw a brief review of several video denoising algorithms. Paper [7] exposes a motion-compensated 3D locally adaptive minimum mean squared error filter in processing the video sequences using the intelligent pixel aggregation algorithm. Novel video denoising algorithm for Gaussian noise in the wavelet transform (WT) domain is introduced in [8] permitting usage of local correlations between the wavelet coefficients of video sequence in space and time. The technique based on the transform in the local 3D variable-sized windows is designed in [9]. For every spatial position in each a frame, the block-matching algorithm is employed to collect highly correlated blocks from neighbouring frames. The final estimate is a weighted average of the overlapping local ones. An image sequence algorithm for noise suppression that is similar to before mentioned is proposed in [10]. Another technique [11] involves two low-complexity filters for Gaussian noise reducing. A new algorithm, in which the local variance of Gaussian noise is estimated in the homogeneous cubes for the 3-D video signal, is employed in paper [12]. Novel temporal denoising filter multihypothesis motion compensated filter is developed for removing of Gaussian noise in a video signal [13]. In the paper [14], the video denoising is realized in the WT domain, where the motion estimation/compensation, temporal filtering, and spatial smoothing are undertaken. Recently in [15], a new fuzzy-rule-based algorithm for noise suppression of video sequences corrupted with Gaussian noise is exposed. The method constitutes a fuzzy-logic-based improvement of a detail and the motion adaptive multiple class averaging filter. Proposed fuzzy motion and detail adaptive video filter (FMDAF) has shown excellent ability in suppression of Gaussian noise.

In this paper, introducing 3D scheme in filtering the video sequences contaminated by impulsive noise, we also realize the adaptation of several 2D algorithms in filtering of 3D video data: MF-3F (Median Filter that exploits three frames); VGVDF, VVMF (Video Vector Median Filter) [16], which applies the directional techniques as an ordering criterion; VVDKNNVMF (Video Vector Directional K-nearest Neighbour Vector Median Filter) [16], where the ideas of vector order statistics are employed. Additionally, we have implemented the KNNF (K-nearest neighbour filter) [17]; VATM (Video Alpha Trimmed Mean) [17]; and VAVDATM (Video Adaptive Vector Directional Alpha Trimmed Mean) [18] that connects the directional techniques procedures with adaptive and order statistics techniques.

First, in novel approach, during the spatial stage of processing for proposed algorithm, each a frame is filtered in every R, G, and B channel, employing fuzzy logic and vector order statistic methods together. Second, the filtered frames are processed in the next, temporal stage of the algorithm detecting the noise and movement levels by proposed fuzzy-directional method, employing the filtered spatial frame (t-1) and next one (t). As a final step, the present frame is filtered applying the fuzzy rules based on direction information, which realises the suppression of a noise in a current frame. Numerical simulations demonstrate that novel framework outperforms several mentioned above filtering approaches in processing the video colour sequences. It has been investigated the contaminated by impulsive noise test colour images: "Lena", "Peppers", "Baboon". "Parrots" (320x320 pixels in RGB space, 24 bits), and video sequences: "Flowers" and "Miss America" (QCIF format, 176x144 pixels in each a frame).

2 Fuzzy Two Step Colour Filter

Let introduce the absolute differences named as *gradients* and *angle divergence* (directions) that represent the level of similarity among different pixels. This permits the usage of its values in probe of two hypothesises: the central pixel is a noise one or it is noisy free pixel. To resolve this, let calculate in each a window for each a direction (*N, E, S, W, NW, NE, SE, SW*), in respect to the central pixel, the "*gradient*" $\left| x_c^\beta(i,j) - x^\beta(i+k, j+l) \right| = \nabla_{(k,l)}^\beta x(i,j)$, where $(i,j) = (0,0)$. Here, index β shows different *R*, *G*, and *B* channels of colour frame, and (k,l) represent each one of the eight mentioned directions with values: $\{-1,0,1\}$ (see Fig.1). Similar to [19, 20], let introduce not only one "*basic gradient*" for any direction, but also four "*related gradient*", with (k,l) from values $\{-2,-1,0,1,2\}$. Function ∇_γ^β shows the gradient values for each a direction, and parameter γ marks any chosen direction. For example, for the "*SE*" direction (Fig.1), the gradients are as follows: $\nabla_{(1,1)}^\beta x(0,0) = \nabla_{SE(basic)}^\beta$,

$\nabla_{(0,2)}^\beta x(i-1, j+1) = \nabla_{SE(rel1)}^\beta$, $\nabla_{(2,0)}^\beta x(i+1, j-1) = \nabla_{SE(rel2)}^\beta$, $\nabla_{(0,0)}^\beta x(i-1, j+1)$

$= \nabla_{SE(rel3)}^\beta$, and $\nabla_{(0,0)}^\beta x(i+1, j-1) = \nabla_{SE(rel4)}^\beta$.

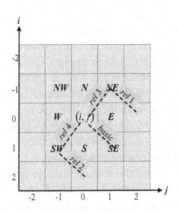

Fig. 1. *Basic* and *related* directions for *gradients* and *angle divergence* values

Let introduce the *angle divergence* for each a channel in such a way where we omit two of three channels in the case of each a colour frame. For example, in the "SE" direction, the "*basic*" and "*related*" vectorial (angular) values can be written as:

$\theta^{\beta}_{(0,2)} x(i-1, j+1) = \theta^{\beta}_{SE(rel1)}$, $\theta^{\beta}_{(2,0)} x(i+1, j-1) = \theta^{\beta}_{SE(rel2)}$, $\theta^{\beta}_{(0,0)} x(i-1, j+1) = \theta^{\beta}_{SE(rel3)}$,

and $\theta^{\beta}_{(0,0)} x(i+1, j-1) = \theta^{\beta}_{SE(rel4)}$. The basic *angle divergence* in the "SE" direction between pixels (0,0) and (1,1) for given channel β (Fig.1) is calculated as follows:

$$\theta^{\beta}_{\gamma=SE(basic)} = \arccos\left[\frac{2(255)^2 + x^{\beta}_{(0,0)} \cdot x^{\beta}_{(1,1)}}{\left(2(255^2) + \left(x^{\beta}_{(0,0)}\right)^2\right)^{1/2} \cdot \left(2(255^2) + \left(x^{\beta}_{(1,1)}\right)^2\right)^{1/2}}\right]. \quad (1)$$

Figure 1 exposes the employed pixels in processing procedure in the chosen SE direction for the *basic* and *related* components.

Let introduce fuzzy sets: BIG (B) and SMALL (S) that permit estimating the noise presence in a central pixel for window 5×5. A big membership degree (near to value one) in the S set shows that the central pixel is free of noise, and large membership degree in the B set shows that central pixel is noisy one with large probability. The Gaussian membership functions are used to calculate membership degrees for fuzzy gradient and fuzzy angle values:

$$\mu_{\nabla^{\beta}_{\gamma=SE(basic)}(SMALL,BIG)} = \begin{cases} 1, & \text{if } \left(\nabla^{\beta}_{\gamma} < med2, \nabla^{\beta}_{\gamma} > med1\right) \\ \left(\exp\left(-\left\{\frac{\left(\nabla^{\beta}_{\gamma} - med2\right)^2}{2\sigma_1^2}\right\}\right), \exp\left(-\left\{\frac{\left(\nabla^{\beta}_{\gamma} - med1\right)^2}{2\sigma_1^2}\right\}\right)\right), & otherwise \end{cases}, \quad (2)$$

where values $med1 = 60$, $med2 = 10$, $\sigma_1^2 = 1000$;

$$\mu_{\theta^{\beta}_{\gamma}(SMALL,BIG)} = \begin{cases} 1, if & (\theta^{\beta}_{\gamma} \leq med4, \quad \theta^{\beta}_{\gamma} \geq med3) \\ \left(\exp\left[-\left\{\frac{(\theta^{\beta}_{\gamma} - med4)^2}{2\sigma_2^2}\right\}\right], \quad \exp\left[-\left\{\frac{(\theta^{\beta}_{\gamma} - med3)^2}{2\sigma_2^2}\right\}\right]\right), & otherwise, \end{cases} \quad (3)$$

and values $med3 = 0.615$, $med4 = 0.1$, $\sigma_2^2 = 0.8$. The values in equations (2)-(3) were found during numerical simulations according to the best values for PSNR and MAE criteria.

3 Fuzzy Rules in Two Dimensions

Let present novel fuzzy rules applied for gradient values and angular values in each a channel.

Fuzzy Rule 1_2D introduces the membership level of $x^{\beta}_{(i,j)}$ in the set BIG for any γ direction: **IF** (∇^{β}_{γ} is B AND $\nabla^{\beta}_{\gamma(rel1)}$ is S, AND $\nabla^{\beta}_{\gamma(rel2)}$ is S, AND $\nabla^{\beta}_{\gamma(rel3)}$ is B,

AND $\nabla^\beta_{\gamma(rel4)}$ is B) AND $\left(\theta^\beta_\gamma$ is B AND $\theta^\beta_{\gamma(rel1)}$ is S, AND $\theta^\beta_{\gamma(rel2)}$ is S, AND $\theta^\beta_{\gamma(rel3)}$ is B, AND $\theta^\beta_{\gamma(rel4)}$ is B) **THEN** fuzzy gradient-angular value $\nabla^{\beta F}_\gamma \theta^{\beta F}_\gamma$ is BIG. The operator AND= $\min(A,B)$ outside of the parenthesis, and inside of the parenthesis A AND $B=A*B$.

Fuzzy Rule 2_2D presents the *noisy factor* gathering eight fuzzy gradient-directional values that are calculated for each a direction as: *IF* fuzzy gradient-angular values $\nabla^{\beta F}_N \theta^{\beta F}_N$ is B OR $\nabla^{\beta F}_S \theta^{\beta F}_S$ is B, OR $\nabla^{\beta F}_E \theta^{\beta F}_E$ is B, OR $\nabla^{\beta F}_W \theta^{\beta F}_W$ is B, OR $\nabla^{\beta F}_{SW} \theta^{\beta F}_{SW}$ is B, OR $\nabla^{\beta F}_{NE} \theta^{\beta F}_{NE}$ is B, OR $\nabla^{\beta F}_{NW} \theta^{\beta F}_{NW}$ is B, OR $\nabla^{\beta F}_{SE} \theta^{\beta F}_{SE}$ is B **THEN noisy factor** r^β is BIG. The operation OR in rule 2 is introduced as $\max(A,B)$

The noisy factor r^β is employed as a threshold to distinguish among a noisy pixel and a free noise one. So, if $r^\beta \geq R^\beta_0$, it is applied the filtering procedure employing the fuzzy gradient-angular values as weights, in opposite case, the output is formed as unchanged central pixel: $y^\beta_{out} = x^\beta_{(i,j)}$.

For $r^\beta \geq 0.3$ (the value $R^\beta_0 = 0.3$ was chosen in numerical simulations according to the best values for PSNR and MAE criteria), the fuzzy weights are used in the standard negator function ($\varsigma(x)=1-x, \quad x\in[0,1]$) defined as $\rho(\nabla^{\beta F}_\gamma \theta^{\beta F}_\gamma)=1-\nabla^{\beta F}_\gamma \theta^{\beta F}_\gamma$, where $\nabla^{\beta F}_\gamma \theta^{\beta F}_\gamma \in [0,1]$; so, this value origins the fuzzy membership value in a new fuzzy set defined as "NO BIG" (noise free). Introducing the fuzzy weight for central pixel in NO BIG fuzzy set as follows: $\rho(\nabla^{\beta F}_{(0,0)} \theta^{\beta F}_{(0,0)})=3\sqrt{1-r^\beta}$, finally, the ordering procedure is defined in the spatial filtering algorithm as follows:

$$x^\beta_{\dot\gamma} = \left\{ x^\beta_{SW}, \ldots, x^\beta_{(i,j)}, \ldots, x^\beta_{NE} \right\}, x^{\beta(1)}_{\dot\gamma} \leq x^{\beta(2)}_{\dot\gamma} \leq \cdots \leq x^{\beta(9)}_{\dot\gamma} \overset{implies}{\Rightarrow}$$

$$\rho\left(\nabla^{\beta F}_\gamma \theta^{\beta F}_\gamma\right)^{(1)} \leq \rho\left(\nabla^{\beta F}_\gamma \theta^{\beta F}_\gamma\right)^{(2)} \leq \cdots \leq \rho\left(\nabla^{\beta F}_\gamma \theta^{\beta F}_\gamma\right)^{(9)},$$

where $\dot\gamma = (N, E, S, W, (i,j), NW, NE, SE, SW)$ permitting to remove the values more outlying from the central pixel (i,j).

So, the filtering algorithm, which applies the fuzzy *gradient-angular* values, selects one of the neighbour pixels from the j_{th} ordered values or central component permitting to avoid the smoothing of a frame.

4 Three Dimensional Filtering

4.1 Fuzzy Colour Filter in Three Dimensions

Let introduce 3D procedure employing the above presented filtering procedure as a first step in the initial frame of a video sequence (spatial stage). After the temporal stage of the algorithm, the mentioned spatial algorithm should be used again to suppress non-stationary noise left during the temporal stage of the procedure. Employing two neighbour frames (past and present) of a video sequence permits to calculate the movement and noise fuzzy levels of a central pixel. Here, a 5x5x2 sliding window, which is formed by *past* and *present* frames, is employed, and the difference values between these frames are calculated:

$$\lambda^{\beta}_{(k,l)}\left(A(i,j),B(i,j)\right)=\left|A(i+k,j+l)-B(i+k,j+l)\right|,\qquad(4)$$

where $A(i,j)$ are pixels in *t-1* frame of video sequence, and $B(i,j)$ show the pixels in *t* frame, with indexes $(k,l)\in\{-2,-1,0,1,2\}$.

Using values $\lambda^{\beta}_{(k,l)}$ in Eq. (4)) denominated as *gradient difference values*, we obtain an *error frame*. Now, let calculate the *absolute difference gradient values* of a central pixel in respect to its neighbour ones for a 5x5x1 window processing. The *absolute difference gradient values* are calculated in the next equation for the *SE (basic)* direction only. The same procedure should be repeated for all other *basic* and *related* values in any direction:

$$\nabla'^{\beta}_{(1,1)}\lambda(0,0)=\nabla'^{\beta}_{SE(basic)},\text{ where }\nabla'^{\beta}_{SE(basic)}=\left|\lambda^{\beta}_{(0,0)}-\lambda^{\beta}_{(1,1)}\right|,\qquad(5)$$

As in 2D framework, let calculate the *absolute difference angular values* of a central pixel in respect to its neighbour ones as an *angle divergence* value among *t-1* and *t* frames as follows:

$$\phi^{\beta}_{(k,l)}\left(A(i,j),B(i,j)\right)=\arccos\left[\frac{2(255)^2+A(i+k,j+l)\cdot B(i+k,j+l)}{\left(2(255^2)+(A(i+k,j+l))^2\right)^{1/2}\cdot\left(2(255^2)+(A(i+k,j+l))^2\right)^{1/2}}\right]\quad(6)$$

Using *angle divergence* value $\phi^{\beta}_{(k,l)}$, we present the *absolute angular divergence* ones:

$$\nabla''^{\beta}_{(1,1)}\phi(0,0)=\nabla''^{\beta}_{SE(basic)},\text{ where }\nabla''^{\beta}_{SE(basic)}=\left|\phi^{\beta}_{(0,0)}-\phi^{\beta}_{(1,1)}\right|,\qquad(7)$$

The same reasoning done for $\nabla'^{\beta}_{SE(basic)}$ in respect to $\nabla^{\beta}_{SE(basic)}$ is realized also for $\nabla''^{\beta}_{SE(basic)}$ value. Let employ the same Gaussian membership functions for fuzzy values as in the equations (2)-(3) introducing the *fuzzy gradient-angular difference values*. The numerical experiments realized in this case have given the values for function in eq. (3): $med4=0.01$, $med3=0.1$ according to the best PSNR and MAE criteria results.

4.2 Fuzzy Rules in 3D Filtering

Fuzzy rules used to characterize the movement and noise levels in central pixel components are defined as follows:

Fuzzy Rule 1_3D determines the *FIRST 3D fuzzy gradient-angular difference value* as $\left(\nabla'^{\beta F}_{\gamma}\nabla''^{\beta F}_{\gamma}\right)_{FIRST}$: *IF* $\left(\nabla'^{\beta}_{\gamma}\text{ is B AND }\nabla'^{\beta}_{\gamma(rel1)}\text{ is S, AND }\nabla'^{\beta}_{\gamma(rel2)}\text{ is S, AND }\right.$ $\nabla'^{\beta}_{\gamma(rel3)}$ is B, AND $\nabla'^{\beta}_{\gamma(rel4)}$ is B) AND $\left(\nabla''^{\beta}_{\gamma}\text{ is B AND }\nabla''^{\beta}_{\gamma(rel1)}\text{ is S, AND }\nabla''^{\beta}_{\gamma(rel2)}\text{ is S,}\right.$

AND $\nabla''^{\beta}_{\gamma(rel3)}$ is B, AND $\nabla''^{\beta}_{\gamma(rel4)}$ is B) **THEN** $\left(\nabla'^{\beta F}_{\gamma}\nabla''^{\beta F}_{\gamma}\right)_{FIRST}$ is BIG. This rule characterizes the *movement and noise confidence* in a central pixel by neighbour fuzzy
values in any γ direction. Operation AND= $\min(A,B)$ outside of parenthesis.

Fuzzy Rule 2_3D defines the *SECOND 3D fuzzy gradient-angular difference value* as $\left(\nabla'^{\beta F}_{\gamma}\nabla''^{\beta F}_{\gamma}\right)_{SECOND}$: **IF** $\left(\nabla'^{\beta}_{\gamma}\right.$ is S AND $\nabla'^{\beta}_{\gamma(rel1)}$ is S, AND $\nabla'^{\beta}_{\gamma(rel2)}$ is S)
OR $\left(\nabla''^{\beta}_{\gamma}\right.$ is S AND $\nabla''^{\beta}_{\gamma(rel1)}$ is S, AND $\nabla''^{\beta}_{\gamma(rel2)}$ is S) **THEN** $\left(\nabla'^{\beta F}_{\gamma}\nabla''^{\beta F}_{\gamma}\right)_{SECOND}$ is
SMALL. This rule characterizes the *no movement confidence* in a central pixel in
any γ direction. Operation OR= $\max(A,B)$; also, the operation AND= $A*B$ inside
of parenthesis for fuzzy rules 1 and 2 presented above.

Fuzzy Rule 3_3D defines the *fuzzy 3D noisy factor* r^{β} : **IF** $\left(\left(\nabla'^{\beta F}_{SE}\nabla''^{\beta F}_{SE}\right)_{FIRST}\right.$ is B
OR $\left(\nabla'^{\beta F}_{S}\nabla''^{\beta F}_{S}\right)_{FIRST}$ is B, OR, $\cdots$, OR $\left(\nabla'^{\beta F}_{N}\nabla''^{\beta F}_{N}\right)_{FIRST}$ is B) **THEN** r^{β} is BIG.
This Fuzzy Rule permits to calculate the *fuzzy noisy factor* and estimate the move-
ment and noise level in a central component using the fuzzy values determined for all
directions.

Fuzzy Rule 4_3D defines the *no movement 3D confidence factor* η^{β} : **IF**
$\left(\left(\nabla'^{\beta F}_{SE}\nabla''^{\beta F}_{SE}\right)_{SECOND}\right.$ is S OR $\left(\nabla'^{\beta F}_{S}\nabla''^{\beta F}_{S}\right)_{SECOND}$ is S, OR $\cdots$, OR $\left(\nabla'^{\beta F}_{N}\nabla''^{\beta F}_{N}\right)_{SECOND}$ is
S) **THEN** η^{β} is SMALL.

The parameters r^{β} and η^{β} can be effectively applied in the decision: if a central
pixel component is noisy, or is in movement, or is a free one of both mentioned
events. Fuzzy Rules from 1_3D to 4_3D determine the novel algorithm based on the
fuzzy parameters. It should be chosen the *j*-th component pixel, which satisfies to
proposed conditions, guaranteeing that edges and fine details should be preserved
according to ordering criterion in the selection of the nearest pixel according to fuzzy
measure matter to the central pixel in *t-1* and *t* frames.

Enhancement of noise suppression capabilities of the filter can be realized at the final step via application of the FTSCF-2D that permits decreasing the influence of the
non-stationary noise left by temporal filter. Some modifications of the FTSCF-2D
applied after the FTSCF-3D should be realized because of the non-stationary nature
of noise.

5 Numerical Simulation

Performance of the filters is measured under different commonly used criteria, such
as: PSNR, MAE [21], and NCD [16, 22, 23]. Lena, Baboon, Peppers, Parrots,
etc. colour images with different texture propertied were used to evaluate 2-D algorithms. Also, Miss America and Flowers video colour sequences were investigated to
justify robustness of the designed 3D filtering scheme in varying texture of a video
sequence. The frames of the video sequences were contaminated by impulsive noise
with different intensity in each a channel.

Table 1 presents PSNR criterion values for 2D designed algorithm against other existed ones exposing the better values in the case of low and middle noise intensity. The best performance is presented by designed algorithm until 15% of noise intensity for Lena and until 10% for Baboon and Peppers colour images guaranteeing the robustness of novel framework because of different texture and chromaticity properties of the mentioned images.

Table 1. PSNR criterion values for Lena, Baboon, and Peppers images, accordingly

(%) Noise	FTSCF-2D	AVMF	VMF	AMNF3	CWVDF	VMF_FAS	INR
0	**37,12**	31,58	30,47	29,45	33,05	*36,46*	31,71
2	**35,55**	31,31	30,3	29,34	32,15	*34,88*	31,58
5	**33,99**	30,95	30,07	29,21	31,24	*31,85*	31,45
10	**31,50**	30,10	29,46	28,93	29,04	28,80	*30,93*
20	26,86	27,83	27,58	*28,18*	24,3	24,8	**29,03**
0	*29,19*	24,44	24,15	23,76	24,96	**30,14**	27,44
2	*28,64*	24,39	24,11	23,71	24,67	**29,27**	27,25
5	**27,85**	24,27	24,02	23,64	24,16	*27,22*	27,01
10	**26,60**	23,97	23,78	23,48	23,14	25,29	*26,39*
20	*23,72*	22,88	22,79	23,09	20,67	22,47	**24,95**
0	**38,06**	31,55	30,88	29,47	32,87	*35,49*	32,56
2	**35,61**	31,28	30,68	29,25	31,47	*33,39*	32,10
5	**33,64**	30,81	30,30	29,02	29,75	31,19	*31,54*
10	**31,09**	29,80	29,44	28,71	27,34	29,01	*30,81*
20	26,07	27,30	27,19	*27,82*	22,12	24,45	**28,41**

Table 2. MAE criterion values for Lena, Baboon, and Peppers mages, accordingly

(%) Noise	FTSCF-2D	AVMF	VMF	AMNF3	CWVDF	VMF_FAS	INR
0	*0,41*	1,89	4,08	4,84	2,63	**0,26**	4,35
2	*0,62*	2,09	4,17	4,92	2,83	**0,54**	4,37
5	**0,91**	2,39	4,29	5,04	3,10	*1,19*	4,41
10	**1,48**	2,97	4,57	5,22	3,82	*2,35*	4,53
15	**2,17**	*3,63*	4,92	5,46	4,87	3,709	4,7
20	**3,11**	*4,41*	5,41	5,74	6,38	5,0	4,98
0	*2,14*	6,97	8,55	10,46	5,42	**0,94**	7,54
2	*2,42*	7,1	8,59	10,57	5,82	**1,4**	7,63
5	**2,87**	7,36	8,701	10,73	6,42	*2,54*	7,77
10	**3,67**	7,87	8,96	11,02	7,65	*4,06*	8,09
15	**4,63**	8,59	9,43	11,36	9,17	*5,83*	8,50
20	**5,83**	9,49	10,11	11,75	10,99	*7,69*	8,99
0	*0,31*	1,51	2,86	4,17	1,32	**0,2**	3,62
2	**0,52**	1,68	2,96	4,27	1,63	*0,56*	3,68
5	**0,82**	1,97	3,14	4,42	2,15	*1,14*	3,75
10	**1,38**	2,49	3,49	4,66	3,20	*2,07*	3,9
15	**2,16**	*3,13*	3,95	4,92	4,82	3,7	4,18
20	**3,13**	*3,92*	4,53	5,26	6,92	4,84	4,47

Table 2 exposes that the best performance in preservation of the edges and fine details for mentioned images is demonstrated by designed method permitting to avoid the smoothing in wide range of noise intensity. Fig.2 exposes subjective perception for image Parrots showing better preservation for edges, fine details and chromaticity characteristics in the case when designed filter is employed.

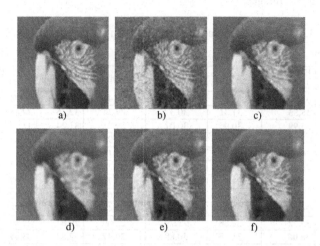

Fig. 2. Zoomed image region of image Parrots a) original, b) contaminated by impulsive noise of 10% intensity, c) Designed FTSCF-2D, d) AMNF3, e) VMF_FAS, f) INR

Table 3. Average NCD values for Flowers video colour sequence

(%) Noise	FTSCF_3D	MF_3F	VVMF	VVDKNN VMF	VGVDF	VAVD ATM	VATM	KNNF
0	**0,003**	0,014	0,014	0,015	0,016	0,011	0,014	*0,006*
5	**0,004**	0,014	0,014	0,016	0,016	0,012	0,014	*0,008*
10	**0,006**	0,015	0,015	0,017	0,016	0,012	0,015	*0,010*
15	**0,007**	0,015	0,015	0,017	0,016	*0,013*	0,015	*0,013*
20	**0,009**	0,016	0,016	0,018	0,017	*0,014*	0,016	0,017
25	**0,010**	0,017	0,017	0,019	0,018	*0,015*	0,017	0,022
30	**0,012**	0,018	0,018	0,020	0,020	*0,017*	0,018	0,027

Table 4. Average MAE values for Miss America video colour sequence

(%) Noise	FTS CF-3D	MF_3F	VVMF	VVDKN N VMF	VGVD F	VAVD ATM	VATM	KNNF
0	**0,04**	2,46	2,50	2,91	2,99	*0,82*	2,52	1,49
5	**0,37**	2,51	2,54	3,11	2,91	*1,11*	2,57	1,91
10	**0,74**	2,59	2,61	3,28	2,87	*1,41*	2,65	2,67
15	**1,18**	2,70	2,71	3,43	2,85	*1,71*	2,76	3,84
20	**1,76**	2,86	2,85	3,60	2,89	*2,044*	2,92	5,47
30	**3,58**	3,35	3,31	4,39	*3,28*	2,85	3,44	10,11
40	**6,91**	4,42	**4,33**	6,78	4,712	*4,35*	4,73	16,22

The capabilities of the designed algorithm in 3D processing are also exposed in following tables and figures. NCD criterion values, which are presented in the Table 3, characterizes the preservation in the chromaticity properties, justifying that the best performance in wide range of noise corruption in Flowers video sequence was obtained by novel 3D framework. It is known that this video sequence is characterized by variable texture and high diversity in colour distributions, so, this confirms

Table 5. Average NCD values for Miss America video colour sequence

(%) Noise	FTSCF-3D	MF_3F	VVMF	VVDKNN VMF	VGVDF	VAVD ATM	VATM	KNNF
0	**0,000**	0,009	0,009	0,011	0,011	*0,003*	0,009	0,006
5	**0,002**	0,009	0,009	0,011	0,011	*0,004*	0,009	0,007
10	**0,003**	0,010	0,009	0,012	0,010	*0,005*	0,010	0,010
15	**0,005**	0,010	0,010	0,012	0,010	*0,006*	0,010	0,014
20	*0,008*	0,010	0,010	0,012	0,010	**0,007**	0,010	0,020
30	0,016	*0,012*	*0,012*	0,015	*0,012*	**0,010**	*0,012*	0,038

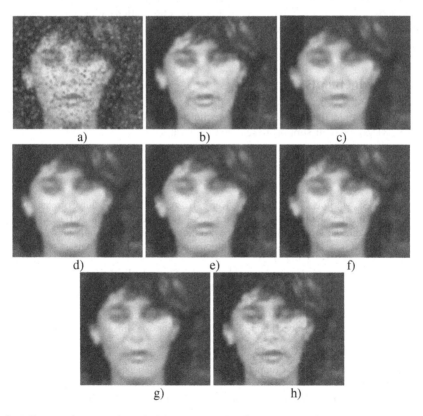

Fig. 3. a) Zoomed image region of 10th Miss America frame contaminated by impulsive noise of 15% intensity, b) Designed FTSCF-3D, c) MF_3F; d) VVMF, e) VGVDF, f) VAVDATM; g) VATM; h) KNNF

the robustness of the proposed framework. Similar numerical results (Tables 4 and 5) in less detailed video sequences, such as Miss America show that the designed algorithm demonstrates the best filtering performance (MAE and NCD values) for low and middle noise levels until 20% of noise intensity.

Subjective perception by human viewer can be observed in Figure 3 showing better performance of the designed 3D framework in comparison with known methods.

This figure presents the zoomed filtered Miss America frame, where novel algorithm preserves better the edges, fine details, and chromaticity properties against other filters.

6 Conclusion

The proposed framework has demonstrated the better performance in noise suppression for multichannel video sequences in comparison with existed filtering techniques. Novel 3D filtering approach outperforms known 2D and/or 3D filtering techniques as numerous simulation results justify. Fuzzy set theory together with vector order statistics technique, which are exploited in the designed algorithm, have demonstrated the better preservation of the edges, fine details and chromaticity characteristics in multichannel images and sequences in terms of objective criteria, as well as subjective perception by human viewer.

Acknowledgements

The authors would thank National Polytechnic Institute of Mexico and CONACYT (project 8159) for their support to realize this work.

References

1. Schulte, S., Morillas, S., Gregori, V., Kerre, E.: A New Fuzzy Color Correlated Impulse Noise Reduction Method Trans. on Image Proc. 16(10), 2565–2575 (2007)
2. Plataniotis, K.N., Androutsos, D., Vinayagamoorthy, S., Venetsanopoulos, A.N.: Color Image Processing Using Adaptive Multichannel Filters. IEEE Transactions on Image Processing 6(7), 933–949 (1997)
3. Ponomaryov, V.I., Gallegos-Funes, F.J., Rosales-Silva, A.: Real-time color imaging based on RM-Filters for impulsive noise reduction. Journal of Imaging Science and Technology 49(3), 205–219 (2005)
4. Trahanias, P.E., Venetsanopoulos, A.N.: Vector Directional Filters. A new class of multichannel image processing Filters. IEEE Trans. on Image Processing 2, 528–534 (1993)
5. Lukac, R., Smolka, B., Plataniotis, K.N., Venetsanopoulos, A.N.: Selection Weighted Vector Directional Filters. Comput. Vision and Image Understanding 94, 140–167 (2004)
6. Smolka, B., Lukac, R., Chydzinski, A., Plataniotis, K.N., Wojciechowski, W.: Fast Adaptive Similarity Based Impulsive Noise Reduction Filter. Real-Time Imaging 9(4), 261–276 (2003)
7. Yin, H.B., Fang, X.Z., Wei, Z., Yang, X.K.: An Improved Motion-Compensated 3-D LLMMSE Filter With Spatio–Temporal Adaptive Filtering Support. IEEE Trans. on Circuits and Syst. for Video Techn. 17(12), 1714–1727 (2007)

8. Varghese, G., Wang, Z.: Video Denoising using a Spatiotemporal Statistical Model of Wavelet Coefficient. In: Proc. of the IEEE ICASSP Int. Conf., pp. 1257–1260 (2005)
9. Rusanovskyy, D., Dabov, K., Egiazarian, K.: Moving-Window Varying Size 3D Transform-Based Video Denoising. In: Proc. of IEEE Int. Conf. VPQM 2006, Scottdale, USA, pp. 1–4 (2006)
10. Protter, M., Elad, M.: Image Sequence Denoising via Sparse and Redundant Representations. IEEE Trans. on Image Procces 18(1), 27–35 (2007)
11. Sen, D., Swamy, M.N.S., Ahmad, M.O.: Computationally fast techniques to reduce AWGN and speckle in videos. IET Image Process 1(4), 319–334 (2007)
12. Ghazal, M., Amer, A., Ghrayeb, A.: A Real-Time Technique for Spatio–Temporal Video Noise Estimation. IEEE Trans. on Circuits and Syst. For Video Techn. 17(12), 1690–1699 (2007)
13. Guo, L., Au, O.C., Ma, M., Liang, Z.: Temporal Video Denoising Based on Multihypothesis Motion Compensation. IEEE Trans. on Image Proc. (2009)
14. Jin, F., Fieguth, P., Winger, L.: Wavelet Video Denoising with Regularized Multiresolution Motion Estimation. EURASIP Journal on Applied Signal Processing, Art. ID 72705 1–11 (2006)
15. Mélange, T., Nachtegael, M., Kerre, E.E., Zlokolica, V., Schulte, S., De Witte, V., Pižurica, A., Philips, W.: Video Denoising by Fuzzy Motion and Details Adaptive Averaging. Journal of Electron. Imaging 17 (2008) 0430051-19
16. Ponomaryov, V.: Real-time 2D-3D filtering using order statistics based algorithms. Journal of Real-Time Image Processing 1(3), 173–194 (2007)
17. Zlokolica, V., Philips, W., Van De Ville, D.: A new non-linear filter for video processing. In: Proc. of the third IEEE Benelux Signal Processing Symposium (SPS-2002), Leuven, Belgium, pp. 221–224 (2002)
18. Ponomaryov, V., Rosales-Silva, A., Golikov, V.: Adaptive and vector directional processing applied to video colour images. Electronics Letters 42(11), 623–624 (2006)
19. Schulte, S., De Witte, V., Nachtegael, M., Van del Weken, D., Kerre, E.: Fuzzy two-step filter for impulse noise reduction from color images. IEEE Trans. Image Processing 15(11), 3567–3578 (2006)
20. Zlokolica, V., Schulte, S., Pizurica, A., Philips, W., Kerre, E.: Fuzzy logic recursive motion detection and denoising of video sequences. Journal of Electronic Imaging 15(2), 23008 (2006)
21. Bovik, A.: Handbook of Image and Video Processing. Academic Press, San Diego (2000)
22. Prat, W.K.: Digital Image Processing, 2nd edn. Wiley, New York (1991)
23. Plataniotis, K.N., Venetsanopoulos, A.N.: Color Image Processing and Applications. Springer, Berlin (2000)

A Performance Comparison of De-convolution Algorithms on Transmission Terahertz Images

Yue Li[*], Li Li, Juan Tello, Dan Popescu, and Andrew Hellicar

CSIRO ICT Centre, Marsfield, NSW, Australia
yue.li@csiro.au

Abstract. Terahertz imaging has found applications in many fields, to explore these applications we have built a coherent, transmission terahertz imaging system at 186 GHz. De-convolution algorithms were tested for improving the image's resolution beyond the diffraction limit of the imaging system. Tested algorithms include the Wiener, Tikhonov, and Richardson-Lucy algorithms. Their performances are discussed and compared in this paper. Experimental results have demonstrated that coherent de-convolution algorithms are capable of improving the resolution of images formed with this imaging system.

1 Introduction

Many terahertz imaging systems have been proposed in the literature [1]-[13]. We have built two coherent terahertz imaging systems. One is at 610 GHz [14] and another is at 186 GHz [15]. Since de-convolution algorithms can improve the image's resolution beyond the diffraction limit of an imaging system, de-convolution algorithms have been tested for improving the resolutions of images formed using these two systems. The 610 GHz system only measures the power of the received signal because it is difficult to measure the phase of received signals at this frequency. As a result, coherent de-convolution algorithms (such as the Wiener and Tikhonov) cannot be used on these images and the incoherent Richardson-Lucy algorithm was tested to evaluate its performances on a coherent imaging system. Experimental results shown in [14] have demonstrated that, even though the resolution has been improved there are some artifacts in the processed images. On the other hand, both magnitude and phase of received signals are measured in the 186 GHz system and the coherent Wiener de-convolution algorithm has been tested. Experimental results have shown that the Wiener de-convolution algorithm can significantly improve the resolution of images with minimum artifact [16]. In this paper, we present testing results of the Tikhonov algorithm and the incoherent Richardson-Lucy algorithms on images acquired using the 186 GHz system, and compare their performances with that of the Wiener algorithm.

2 Imaging System

The setup of the coherent terahertz imaging system at 186 GHz is shown in Fig. 1. The 186 GHz continuous wave, generated by a signal generator and a 12x multiplier, is

---

[*] Corresponding author.

J. Blanc-Talon et al. (Eds.): ACIVS 2009, LNCS 5807, pp. 222–229, 2009.

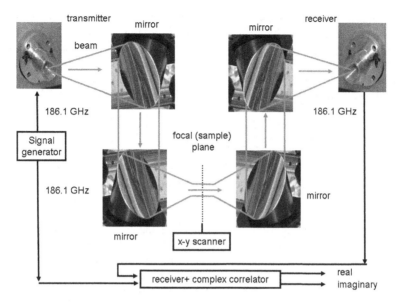

Fig. 1. The transmission terahertz imaging system at 186 GHz

transmitted from a stepped horn. Two parabolic mirrors are used to focus the transmitted wave onto the sample, and the wave that passes through the sample is collected and focused by two more parabolic mirrors onto another stepped horn used as the receiver. The received signal is amplified by a purpose-built receiver [17] and cross-correlated with the transmitted signal using a purpose-built complex correlator [15]. A complex image of the sample is generated by mechanically raster scanning the sample.

3 De-convolution Methods

The imaging process of the coherent terahertz imaging system can be modeled as,

$$g(x, y) = h(x, y) \otimes f(x, y) + n(x, y), \tag{1}$$

where $\otimes$ denotes the two-dimensional convolution. $f(x, y)$ in (1) is the complex sample-response to the incident wave at (x, y); its magnitude is related to the attenuation (scattering and absorption) properties of the sample, and its phase is related to the thickness and refractive index of the sample. $h(x, y)$ in (1) is the complex point-spread function (the beam) of the imaging system. The width of $|h(x, y)|$ determines the resolution of the imaging system. Since the beam width has a finite size, different parts of the transmitted wave can pass through sample regions that have different propagation speeds and/or thicknesses, resulting in constructive or deconstructive interference, which is the characteristic property of a coherent imaging system. $g(x, y)$ in (1) is the formed complex image of the sample, and $n(x, y)$ is the additive complex noise. The Wiener de-convolution algorithm can be expressed in the spatial frequency domain as:

$$\hat{F}(u, v) = \left[\frac{|H(u, v)|^2}{|H(u, v)|^2 + S_N(u, v) / S_f(u, v)} \right] \frac{G(u, v)}{H(u, v)}, \tag{2}$$

where G and H are the two-dimensional spatial Fourier transform of g and h respectively. S_N and S_f are the spatial power-spectrum-density function of the noise n and the sample response f, respectively. The left-hand side of Eq. (2) is the spatial spectrum of the de-convolved image, and the de-convolved image is its 2-dimensional inverse Fourier transform. S_n and S_f need to be estimated before the algorithm can be applied.

The Tikhonov de-convolution algorithm can be expressed in the spatial frequency domain as:

$$\hat{F}(u,v) = \left[\frac{|H(u,v)|^2}{|H(u,v)|^2 + \gamma(u^2 + v^2)} \right] \frac{G(u,v)}{H(u,v)}, \tag{3}$$

where γ is the regulation parameter. The Tikhonov de-convolution algorithm is a variation of the Wiener algorithm. The Wiener and Tikhonov algorithms are not iterative.

The Richardson-Lucy algorithm [18]-[20] is for incoherent imaging systems and tested here for comparison. This algorithm only uses the power of the formed image, which corresponds to the rate of received number of photons. It assumes that photon noises dominate the image power and the additive Gaussian noises can be ignored. From (1) and ignoring the Gaussian noise, the mean of the received power $m(x, y)$ is:

$$m(x, y) = |g(x, y)|^2 = |h(x, y) \otimes f(x, y)|^2. \tag{4}$$

For an incoherent imaging system, the mean of the image power can be expressed as

$$m(x, y) = |g(x, y)|^2 = |h(x, y)|^2 \otimes |f(x, y)|^2 \tag{5}$$

Equation (4) can be reduced to (5) if the sample-response $f(x, y)$ is random-like. The image power at pixel (i, j) satisfies the Poisson distribution:

$$P[q(i, j)] = e^{-m(i,j)} \frac{m(i, j)^{q(i,j)}}{q(i, j)!}, \tag{6}$$

where $q(i, j)$ is the measured power at pixel (i, j). The Richardson-Lucy method is a Maximum Likelihood algorithm for Poisson distribution. From (6), the log likelihood function L is:

$$L = \sum_{i=1}^{I} \sum_{j=1}^{J} \{-m(i, j) + q(i, j) \ln m(i, j)\}, \tag{7}$$

where terms that are independent of $f(i, j)$ are ignored. By setting the partial derivative of L with respect to $f(i, j)$ to zero and use the Picard iteration,

$$d^{s+1}(i, j) = d^s(i, j) \sum_{i=1}^{I} \sum_{j=1}^{J} \left[\frac{q(i, j)}{\sum_{k=1}^{K} \sum_{l=1}^{L} a(i - k, j - l) d^s(k, l)} a(i - k, j - l) \right], \tag{8}$$

where s is the iteration index, $a(i, j) = |h(i, j)|^2$ and $d(i, j) = |f(i, j)|^2$. The solution can be derived iteratively. In each iteration step, two convolutions are required.

4 Experimental Results

The point-spread function of the imaging system is approximated with the complex image of a 1-mm pinhole. The magnitude and phase images of the 1-mm pinhole are shown in Figs. 2(a) and (b) respectively. The step size of the x-y scanner was 0.1 mm. One can see that the magnitude image has a Gaussian-like main-lobe but it is not circular. The -3 dB full width of the main-lobe in the horizontal and vertical directions is about 1.3 mm and 1.7 mm, respectively. The phase value in the phase image is random in low magnitude regions due to noises and is smooth within the main-lobe. This pinhole image is actually the convolution between the true point spread function and the pinhole aperture. Therefore, using a smaller pinhole is an advantage. However, 1-mm diameter was the minimum required to ensure adequate signal to noise ratio.

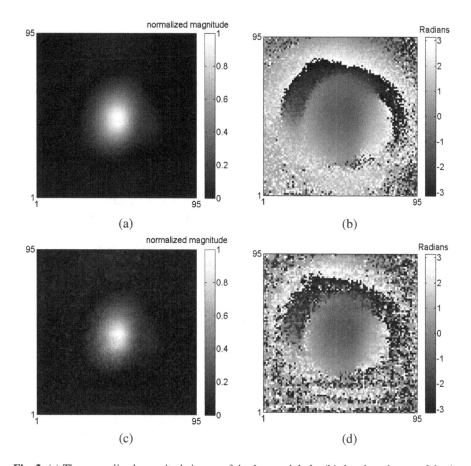

Fig. 2. (a) The normalized magnitude image of the 1-mm pinhole. (b) the phase image of the 1-mm pinhole. (c) and (d) the de-convolved magnitude and phase images of the 1-mm pinhole respectively, using the Wiener algorithm. The step size of the x-y scanner is 0.1 mm in both directions.

The de-convolved (using the Wiener algorithm) point spread function from the pinhole aperture is shown in Figs. 2(c) and (d). The -3 dB full width of the main-lobe in the horizontal and vertical directions has only been improved to about 1.1 mm and 1.5 mm, respectively. Therefore, the 1-mm pinhole size actually has less effect on the beamwidth than one would be expected. This can be simply proved by convolving a disk function with a two-dimensional Gaussian function. On the other hand, the noises become stronger in the de-convolved point spread function. Experimental results have indicated that using the de-convolved point spread function is actually worse than using the original point spread function, due to more noises. Therefore, only results using the original point-spread function are presented below.

A chocolate bar (Fig. 3) was used as the imaging target in this experiment. Terahertz imaging has actually been proposed for quality control of chocolate production [21].

Fig. 3. The chocolate bar being imaged

The magnitude and phase images of the chocolate bar are shown in Figs. 4 (a) and (b), respectively. In the original magnitude image, the letters are darker than the back ground since the letters are thicker (more attenuation). Along the edges of the letters the magnitude is smaller than that in the letters at some locations. This is due to a combination of scattering and interference (phase changes caused by thickness variations). Note that there are some vertical lines in the magnitude image, which are artifacts in the imaging system. In the original phase image, the phase values at the letter and the background are different due to thickness changes. By measuring the phase difference between the letters and the background areas, the refractive index of the chocolate bar can be estimated from the letter height. The interference between waves within the beam coming from the background areas and the letters usually reduces the phase differences and an improvement of resolution should decrease the interference effect and increase the measured phase difference.

De-convolution results using the Wiener and Tikhonov algorithms are shown in Figs. 4(c)-(f). The noise-to-signal-ratio $S_N(u, v) / S_f(u, v)$ for the Wiener algorithm was approximated with a constant, and its value as well as the value of the regulation parameter γ for the Tikhonov algorithm was optimized by visual inspection. The performances of the two algorithms are very similar for this image, as a result of the minor difference between equations (2) and (3). The processed magnitude image exhibits better defined letter boundaries and a higher letter/background contrast. In the processed phase image, the phase difference between the letter and the background has been increased, indicating an improved resolution. Since the geometry and refractive index of the chocolate bar are unknown, it is difficult to perform a quantitative analysis on the improvement of image quality after processing. However, processing results have clearly shown that the original magnitude and phase images are a smoothed version of the processed images. On the other hand, some processing artifacts can also be seen in the processed images.

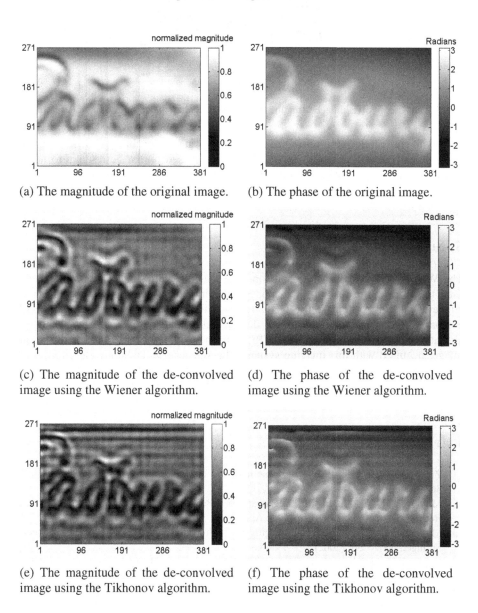

(a) The magnitude of the original image.   (b) The phase of the original image.

(c) The magnitude of the de-convolved image using the Wiener algorithm.   (d) The phase of the de-convolved image using the Wiener algorithm.

(e) The magnitude of the de-convolved image using the Tikhonov algorithm.   (f) The phase of the de-convolved image using the Tikhonov algorithm.

Fig. 4. De-convolution results. The step size of the x-y scanner is 0.1 mm in both directions. $S_n /$ $S_f = 0.003$ for the Wiener algorithm and $\gamma = 0.001$ for the Tikhonov algorithm.

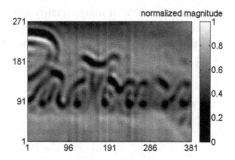

Fig. 5. The de-convolved image using the incoherent Richardson-Lucy algorithm. 20 iterations.

The de-convolution result using the Richardson-Lucy algorithm is shown in Fig. 5. The optimal number of iterations was determined based on the best signal to noise ratio in the processed image, and it was found to be 20. The de-convolution result is not as good as those using the two other algorithms due to the fact that the imaging system is coherent.

5 Summary

The Wiener, Tikhonov, and Richardson-Lucy de-convolution algorithms have been used to improve the resolution of images acquired using a coherent, transmission terahertz imaging system at 186 GHz. Their performances have been evaluated and compared. Experimental results have demonstrated that the Wiener and Tikhonov algorithms perform similarly and the Richardson-Lucy algorithm is much worse on images acquired with this imaging system. The Wiener and Tikhonov algorithms are capable of improving the resolution of images acquired with this imaging system. A testing phantom will be designed and manufactured for quantitative analysis of the improvement in future research.

References

1. Zhang, X.-C.: Terahertz wave imaging: horizons and hurdles. Phys. Med. Biol. 47, 3667–3677 (2002)
2. Mittelman, D.M., Gupta, M., Neelamani, R., Baraniuk, R.G., Rudd, J.V., Koch, M.: Recent advances in terahertz imaging. Appl. Phys. B 68, 1085–1094 (1999)
3. Mittleman, D.: THz Sensing and Imaging Technology. Springer Series in Optical Sciences. Springer, New York (2002)
4. Siegel, P.H.: Terahertz technology. IEEE Trans. Microw. Theory Tech. 50(3), 910–928 (2002)
5. Siegel, P.H.: THz technology: An overview. Int. J. High Speed Electron. Syst. 13(2), 351–394 (2003)
6. Hu, B., Nuss, M.: Imaging with Terahertz Waves. Optics Letters 20(16), 1716–1718 (1995)
7. Nishizawa, J.: Exploring the terahertz range. J. Acoust. Soc. Jpn. 57, 163–169 (2001)

8. Zhang, X.-C.: Pulsed systems, electro-optic detection, and applications. In: Int. School of Solid State Physics, 36th Workshop: Physics and Technology of THz Photonics, Erice, Italy, July 20–26 (2005)

9. Zhong, H., Redo, A., Chen, Y., Zhang, X.-C.: THz Wave Standoff Detection of Explosive Materials. In: Proceedings of SPIE, vol. 6212 (2006)

10. Dickinson, J.C., et al.: Terahertz Imaging of Subjects with Concealed Weapons. In: Proceedings of SPIE, vol. 6212 (2006)

11. Kemp, M.C., et al.: Security Applications of Terahertz Technology. In: Proceedings of SPIE, vol. 5070 (2003)

12. Woodward, R.M., et al.: Terahertz Pulse Imaging of ex vivo Basal Cell Carcinoma. Journal Invest Dermatol. 120, 72–78 (2003)

13. Dobroiu, A., Yamashita, M., Ohshima, Y.N., Morita, Y., Otani, C., Kawase, K.: Terahertz imaging system based on a backward wave oscillator. Appl. Opt. 43(30), 5637–5646 (2004)

14. Li, Y., Li, L., Hellicar, A., Guo, Y.J.: Super-resolution reconstruction of Terahertz images using the Richardson-Lucy algorithm. In: SPIE Defense + Security conference, 6949-17 (March 2008)

15. Hellicar, A., Tello, J., Li, Y., Brothers, M., Rosolen, G., Hay, S., Li, L.: Active imaging at 187 GHz. In: IEEE 2008 international conference on Radar, September 2-5, pp. 183–187 (2008)

16. Li, Y., Tello, J., Li, L., Popescu, D., Hellicar, A.: A Transmission THz Imaging System and Image De-convolution. In: 2009 IEEE International Symposium on Antennas and Propagation and the 2009 USNC/URSI National Radio Science Meeting, North Charleston, SC, USA, June 1-5 (2009)

17. Archer, J.W., Shen, M.G.: 176 – 200 GHz receiver module using indium phosphide and gallium arsenide MMICs. Microwave and Optical Technology Letters 42, 458–462 (2004)

18. Lettington, A.H., Dunn, D., Rollason, M.P., Alexander, N.E., Yallop, M.R.: Use of constraints in superresolution of passive millimetre-wave images. In: SPIE Proceedings, vol. 5077, pp. 100–109 (2004)

19. Lucy, L.B.: An iterative technique for the rectification of observed distributions. Astron. J. 79, 745–759 (1974)

20. Richardson, W.H.: Bayesian-based iterative method of image restoration. Journal of the optical society of America 62(1), 55–59 (1972)

21. Joerdens, C., Koch, M.: Detection of foreign bodies in chocolate with pulsed terahertz spectroscopy. Optical Engineering 47(3), 037003 (2008)

Content-Based Annotation of User Generated Videos on a Mobile Platform

Hristina Pavlovska, Tomislav Kartalov, and Zoran Ivanovski

Faculty of Electrical Engineering and Information Technologies,
University Ss Cyril and Methodius,
Karpos II bb POB 574, 1000 Skopje, Macedonia
hpavlovska@gmail.com, {kartalov,zoran.ivanovski}@feit.ukim.edu.mk
http://www.dipteam.feit.ukim.edu.mk

Abstract. This paper focuses on the problems of video annotation of outdoor user generated low bit-rate videos. An effective algorithm for estimating percentage of artificial (man-made) and natural content in a video frame is presented. The algorithm is based on edge information from the luminance frame only and it is intended to be executed on a mobile platform in an acceptable time frame. The experiments, performed on a large set of user generated videos, adhere with human perception of artificial and natural content.

Keywords: Video annotation, feature extraction, content-based classification, content-based video analysis.

1 Introduction

User generated videos have great diversity in content, recording conditions and environment, recording equipment, and applied video editing. The unpredictable variability of the content is what makes them attractive for content-based analysis. The variability of the other parameters renders the analysis very difficult.

Different approaches and techniques have been developed for content-based video classification. In most of the cases videos are considered as a sequence of images and the problem is analyzed as an image classification problem. The majority of the algorithms are designed for high quality images and videos, running on a desktop computer with sufficient resources.

This paper considers content-based classification of user generated low bit-rate videos. The focus of attention is on the broad class of outdoor videos recorded by low-performance handheld cameras, such as cameras integrated in mobile phones. In the proposed algorithm, artificial (man-made) vs. natural content is classified in a given video sequence (in Section 3 definitions of the concepts artificial and natural are presented). The algorithm is intended to be performed on a mobile platform in an acceptable time frame. Considering that the video could originate from different sources, i.e. it could be recorded using embedded camera on a mobile platform or downloaded from another source (e.g. YouTube) the

J. Blanc-Talon et al. (Eds.): ACIVS 2009, LNCS 5807, pp. 230–241, 2009.

classification procedure should be robust to compression artifacts and independent of coding parameters encoded in the bitstream. The reason for the latter is two-fold: first, many mobile platforms use hardware video decoder that outputs decoded YUV sequence and coding parameters are unavailable, and, second, often downloaded video is transcoded and compression artifacts do not correlate with coding parameters in the bitstream.

The proposed algorithm estimates the percentage of artificial and natural content in a given video frame. The algorithm has low computational complexity, as well as memory requirements. It uses decoded YUV video sequence as input. The classification is based on edge information from the luminance (Y) frame only. The process of feature extraction, as well as preprocessing and postprocessing, is implemented using integer arithmetic operations only. Evaluation of the performance of different classifiers was performed in order to examine their usability on a mobile platform. The performance of the algorithm when applied on a single image is comparable to the algorithms intended to be used with good quality images, published in the literature. When applied on low bit-rate video, it shows robustness and high consistency with human perception of artificial and natural content. The outcome of the proposed video annotation algorithm can be beneficial in video retrieval and management, as well as for video editing.

This paper is organized as follows: Section 2 briefly discusses some related work on image classification in the literature. Section 3 presents the definitions of the concepts artificial and natural. Section 4 describes the algorithm for video annotation in detail. The experimental results obtained using the proposed algorithm are presented in Section 5. And finally Section 6 contains the conclusions.

2   Related Work

The problem of content-based classification of images and video has been analyzed and researched from many different aspects. Different approaches to video classification have been developed, such as retrieval by example, video summarizing and video indexing or labelling [1]. The authors in [2], [3] have conducted experiments with 8 human subjects to classify a set of images. Subjects were asked to group 171 color images into meaningful categories without giving them explicit criteria for judgment. According to the results, a hierarchical classification is considered in which at highest level is indoor/outdoor classification, followed by city/landscape classification. The type of information used for classification is also subject of extensive analysis in the literature. The edges in an image give significant information for the artificial/natural classification problem. Given an accurate edge map, one can easily recognize the image content or overall scene. Authors in [2], [3], have performed analysis of color and texture image characteristics and how discriminative they are for the city/landscape image classification. Their analysis suggests usage of descriptors that are based on edges rather than those based on color. Building edge direction histogram [2], [3], [4], [5], is the most common edge-based technique for feature extraction. Man-made objects usually have dominant presence of vertical and horizontal edges, whereas the natural scenes usually have edges that are randomly distributed in different directions. Texture description in terms of an edge direction histogram is relatively simple and easy to compute. Another group of edge-based techniques depend upon information about the spatial distribution of edges in the image. Edge coherence vector, [2], [3] is used in context of distinguishing between edges forming structures and arbitrary arranged edge pixels. In [6] the Local Edge Pattern histogram is obtained by applying Canny edge operator on the input image and coding the output edge map with values representing local pattern formed by the edges. Local Dominant Orientation distribution-LDO, proposed in [7], is describing the global structure of the input image. It is based on the distribution of the orientation of the image gradient and its energy. The orientations are obtained by use of second oriented derivatives of Gaussian filters. In [8], edge analysis is suggested as a technique for calculating texture descriptor in order to detect man-made objects. First, straight edge detection with the Burns operator is applied to the image. Then, analysis of the perceptual organization of the edges is performed. This includes hierarchical extraction of straight line segments, conjunctions, parallel lines, and polygons. All algorithms in the previous mentioned work attempt to assign a unique label to images. The authors in [9], [10], take different approach and introduce organization of the database based on concepts like degree of naturalness, openness, roughness and etc. These concepts are used to order pictures along the relevant semantic axes. The same authors have shown that different image categories, among which are man-made/natural categories, have different spectral signatures. The signatures are used for image classification in eight different classes.

3   Definition of the Categories Artificial / Natural

The following definitions for the context classes are exploited:

- Scenes with artificial (man-made) content - this class consider image samples taken in urban environment, with meaningful artificial objects like cars, buildings and other architectural structures.
- Scenes with natural content - this class consider image samples taken in natural environment with typically natural elements like vegetation, water, soil, sand and image samples without meaningful presence of artificial elements.

Examples of image samples typical for the two considered classes are displayed in Fig. 1. As it can be noticed, the label natural is given to the image samples that contain urban street. Although there is man-made object in the image (avenue with cross-walk), the global attention in the image is on the city park, or the alley of palm trees. If the images were taken from the same urban street, but in front of car traffic they would be labeled artificial. The reason for this kind of labelling is in the fact that the overall structure in the image forms the human perception of the given scene, regardless of the origin of the particular objects present.

a) Artificial content   b) Natural content

Fig. 1. Examples of image samples for two content classes: a) artificial and b) natural

4   Algorithm Description

Video classification is achieved by making decisions for individual frames. The algorithm is applied separately on image blocks rather than on the whole frame. This kind of approach allows estimation of percentage of the artificial and natural content present in the scene. The size of the image blocks represents compromise between the possibility to have content belonging to only one class and having enough data (detected edges) to make a reliable decision. Image blocks that are one quarter of the video frame are used in the here presented work.

The algorithm is consisted of preprocessing phase, feature extraction, classification and post-processing phase.

4.1   Preprocessing Phase

In the preprocessing phase, frame selection is applied on the input video sequence depending on the classification task. If the outcome of the classification is used in video editing, then decision should be made for every video frame. For approximate description of the video content along the timeline, the decision could be made for smaller set of frames. According to the opinion of group of observers, three frames per second is the minimum processing frame rate for relatively robust content description of the user generated videos.

The compression process produces visible artifacts, mostly in the form of blocking effect, introducing excessive presence of regular structure in the video frame. To solve this problem, very simple and effective deblocking procedure [13] is applied, only in the vicinity of the 8×8 block borders.

4.2   Feature Vector Calculation

In highly compressed videos color is often distorted and suffer from artifacts. Also, hand held devices, like mobile phones, have cameras with very differently adjusted white balance, rendering the color-based classification of videos with different origin very difficult. Although the same statement can be given for the luminance component, the edge information is still preserved and less affected by the white balance adjustment. Because of that, our research is focused on edge-based techniques for feature extraction applied on the luminance component of the image. In the proposed algorithm edge direction histogram is ised as feature vector. To our knowledge, this technique was used with high quality images, but it wasn't researched enough for low bit-rate videos. For edge extraction, modification of the widely used Canny edge detection algorithm [14] is used.

Edge Detection Algorithm. In the here developed algorithm, the initial stage of canny edge detection which includes filtering out the noise in the original image is skipped. For computing the x and y gradient values, difference between adjacent pixels is calculated instead of image convolution with a Gaussian. Differing from [14], spatially adaptive low threshold is applied in order to extract candidates edge pixels, and fixed high threshold for extracting strong edges. Edge detection is performed through the following three stages:

Stage 1: Extraction of Candidates Edge Pixels. The pixels extracted at this level will be further analyzed for being part of the strong edges and are refered to as candidates edge pixels. First, the gradient of the luminance in x and y direction, G_x and G_y, is calculated. The gradient magnitudes are approximated with the sum of the absolute values of the estimated gradients in both directions. The map of candidates edge pixels is calculated by thresholding the gradient magnitudes with the following adaptive threshold:

$$T_d = T + c \cdot Blockact \tag{1}$$

where *Blockact* is block activity and $T = 6$ and $c = 0.0122$ are constant coefficients whose values are obtained experimentally. The block activity is calculated by summing the gradient magnitudes for non-overlapping 8×8 image blocks, following the mostly used pattern in video compression. For each of the extracted candidates edge pixels an edge direction is being calculated as arcus tangens of the ratio of G_x and G_y. The map of edge orientations is then uniformly quantized in four levels (0, 45, 90 and 135 degrees). In order to lower the computational complexity, the calculation of the edge direction and its quantization is implemented using look-up table.

Stage 2: Non-maximum Suppression. In order to get minimal response, the non-maximum suppression procedure is applied. A search is carried out in the output candidate edge map of the previous stage to extract edge pixels with gradient magnitude that is local maximum in the gradient direction.

Stage 3: Selection of Strong Edge Pixels and Edge Connecting. Pixels with large gradient magnitude are more likely to correspond to strong edges, building the image structure. Therefore a relatively high threshold is applied on the gradient magnitudes of the edge pixels extracted in the previous stage. The threshold value is empirically set to $T_h = 34$. The rest of the edge pixels are marked as "weak edge pixels". There is a possibility that weak edge pixels are part of the contours building the image structure, but were blurred in the compression process. Hence, edge connecting is performed by putting a 3×3 window over the map of "strong edges" and marking as strong the weak edge pixels that are inside the window. The procedure is applied iteratively. The tests that were performed showed that the minimum number of iterations for which the final edge map has enough edge information for describing the image content is three. The outcome of this stage is final binary edge map used for calculation of feature vector.

Edge Direction Histogram Calculation. In low bit-rate videos the edges are blurred to some extent due to the compression. Therefore the number of possible edge directions in a given edge map is expected to be lower. As a result the intervals forming the edge direction histogram is lowered, in order to reduce the amount of necessary calculations without loss of the overall accuracy of the algorithm. A set of experiments were performed using uniform quantization of the angle space of $180°$. The optimal accuracy was achieved using 8 quantization levels. Hence, for every image block a vector of 8 feature elements is used, representing its edge direction histogram. The feature elements are normalized with the number of detected edge pixels.

4.3   Classification

For the purpose of developing and testing the algorithm a video database consisting of user generated outdoor videos was created. Most of the video sequences were downloaded from YouTube. The quality varies from low to medium and the video resolutions are QCIF and QVGA. Various video frames were selected from this database in order to form training and test sets.

Training Set. For the purpose of developing the algorithm video database of 205 outdoor videos was created, from which the video frames used for training were hand-picked. Care was taken that frames with similar or overly dark content are avoided,as well as the frames with insignificant amount of edges. A total of 443 frames were chosen and divided in image blocks. The image blocks that were not sound representatives of a class (like blocks containing both artificial and natural objects) were discarded. The final training set consists of 784 image blocks, with equal parts from each class.

Test Set. For evaluation of the algorithm video database of 122 outdoor videos was created, from which 566 video frames were randomly chosen and divided in blocks. Image blocks with similar or overly dark content were discarded. Each image block was given a label artificial or natural based on the mean opinion of 4 observers. The final test set consists of 1069 image blocks from which 689 were labelled as natural and 380 as artificial. According to the observers, image blocks that contain crowd or close-ups of human faces were given label natural although this kind of content isn't considered in the training process.

Training and Classification. Two most frequently used classification techniques were implemented and tested: k-nearest neighbors (k-nn) and Support Vector Machines (SVM). The training and classification procedures will be explained in detail in the following subsections.

Alongside the two classes, artificial and natural, a new class is introduced labelled as "unknown". If a given image block doesn't have enough extracted edges it is very unreliable to classify its content; hence, all image blocks that have percentage of edge pixels lower than specified threshold P% are labelled as unknown. The value for P% is empirically set to 3%. This kind of approach resulted in 1.84% test samples from the class artificial and 7.69% test samples from the class natural classified as unknown. In the calculation of the accuracies presented in Section 5, the number of unknown samples is not included.

SVM-based Classification. For SVM-based training and classification, the *libSVM* [11] library is used. The c-SVM with Radial Basis Function (RBF) k ernel was chosen, with penalty parameter C and kernel parameter γ. For optimal selection of the SVM parameters, grid search was performed on C and γ using 10-fold cross validation. The final SVM model contains 144 support vectors.

k-nn Classification. In the training procedure of the k-nn classifier, k-means clustering of the feature vectors calculated from the training samples was performed, and the centroids were used as a training set. Different number of clusters and distance measures were tested. The number of clusters was set to 150, and cityblock metric was chosen as a distance measure.

One can expect that each cluster should have feature vectors of only one class. In practice, some of the clusters are not homogeneous, which makes labelling of the centroids difficult. This is solved with introducing a class label "ambiguous". If more than P1% of the clusters members are from one class, then the centroid is labeled as feature vector for the dominant class (artificial or natural); otherwise the centroid is labeled as a feature vector for the ambiguous class. The value of P1% is chosen empirically and set to 70%. This kind of centroid labelling yielded 83 labels artificial, 62 labels natural and 5 labels ambiguous.

For classifying the test samples, k-nn classification is used with cityblock distance measure and majority rule of the nearest neighbors.

Decision Forming. The classification outputs on block level are combined to describe the video frame content as percentage of artificial and natural. In order to solve the problem of small movements of the objects in the scene from one image block to other, fifth image block is introduced, positioned in the center of the frame with size equal to one quarter of the image. This new image block is overlapping with the existing blocks, thus enabling consistent decision for the objects that are positioned near the center of the image. The additional block doesn't require significant amount of calculations since its edge direction histogram can be calculated from the parts of the edge direction histograms of the other four blocks. The fifth image block has equal contribution in calculating the percentage of artificial and natural content in the given video frame.

Table 1. Test results obtained using different k in k-nn

k	Artificial		Natural	
	True (%)	Ambiguous (%)	True (%)	Ambiguous (%)
1	79.28	4.74	89.31	3.63
3	77.36	2.37	91.03	1.31
5	78.72	1.05	90.66	0.58
7	76.84	0	90.27	0
9	77.37	0	90.13	0
11	76.58	0	89.84	0

4.4 Post-Processing

The post-processing is applied on the decisions for the video frames in order to increase the consistency of the decisions inside the time interval of one second. Namely, the artificial/natural content in user generated videos can not abruptly change inside the time interval of one second. To cancel out the outliers and to somewhat smoothen the sequence of decisions made for the video frames, median filtering along the time line is applied. The support of the filter is equal to the number of video frames that were classified for one second of video.

5   Experimental Results

In order to evaluate the performance of the algorithm described in Section 4, two series of experiments were conducted. In the first series the performance of the algorithm applied on image blocks using both classifications techniques, SVM and k-nn, was evaluated. For these experiments the test set described in previous section was used, consisted of 1069 image blocks, 689 labeled as natural and 380 labeled as artificial. When SVM was used as classifier, 78.28% of the image blocks with artificial content and 92.92% of the image blocks with natural content were correctly classified. As it can be noticed, the accuracy of the classification of the image blocks with natural content is higher than the accuracy achieved with image blocks showing artificial content. This is a consequence of the noise added to the image in the recording and compression process. The noise is corrupting the regularity of the structure, which is the main measure for artificial content in the scene. For the natural content, irregular distribution of the edges is expected, irregularity being emphasized by addition of the noise.

A series of tests were performed for k-nn classification with different values for k. The results are shown in Table 1. As it can be seen, classification accuracy reaches its maximum for k=5 or k=1. In case of k=5 the number of ambiguous samples is significantly decreased but the computational complexity in comparison to k=1 is considerably higher. In the calculation of the k-nn accuracies presented in Section 5, the number of ambiguous samples is not included.

Table 2. Comparative results for the SVM and k-nn classifications (k=1)

Label	SVM	k-nn (k=1)
True Artificial (%)	78.28	79.28
True Natural (%)	92.92	89.31
Ambiguous Artificial (%)	/	4.74
Ambiguous Natural (%)	/	3.63

Fig. 2. A subset of misclassified test samples

Table 2 shows comparative results obtained using SVM-based and k-nn classification algorithms. The two classification algorithms give very similar results, except that the SVM algorithm doesn't yield ambiguous samples. The classification accuracies of both algorithms are similar to those published in the literature. For the classification problem city vs. landscape in [2], k-nn classification accuracy of 91.7% is published. The results were obtained on database of 2716 good quality images using edge direction histogram with 73 elements as feature vector, in contrast of 8 elements of here proposed feature vector. For retrieving good quality images that have man-made objects [8], accuracy of 84.26% on 245 images with man-made objects and accuracy of 79.72% on 130 images without man-made objects are published.

Fig. 2 shows examples for inaccurately classified test samples. Some of the samples are misclassified due to loss of strong edges as a result of heavy compression, first column, or the origin of the content, e.g. man-made objects in archeological sites, panorama city shots and artificial objects covered by green, second and third column. The presence of mostly irregularly textured regions results in misclassification of highly textured buildings and housetops, fourth column in Fig. 2. The fifth column of Fig. 2 shows samples that are incorrectly

Table 3. Complexity of the feature extraction (operations per pixels)

Multiplications	Additions	abs()	Comparisons	Total
0.02	3.05	2	12.74	17.81

Table 4. Complexity for the classifiers (operations per feature vector)

Classifier	Multiplications	Additions	abs()	exp()	Comparisons	Total
SVM	1440	2305	/	144	1	3890
1-nn	0	2250	1200	/	150	3600

classified because they are not considered in the training set, for example close-ups of artificial objects and samples with artificial content taken from bird's eye view. Both SVM and k-nn, show non-robust classification of trees, animals and close-ups of human due to the presence of strong vertical edges, last column.

The second series of experiments address the overall video annotation precision while processing each video frame. The algorithm is tested on 122 user generated videos from which the test set was created. In Fig. 3 examples of annotated videos obtained using SVM classification, are presented. It can be observed that the first three video sequences are annotated more accurately. The percentage of artificial content truthfully follow the content changes in the scene. The last video sequence illustrates the problem of presence of humans in the scene. It is expected that the algorithm should classify the origin (artificial/natural) of the environment in which the user has recorded the video, without taking into consideration human figures in the scene. In that sense, significant presence of humans in the scene has negative influence on the classification accuracy.

5.1   Computational Complexity

In Table 3 the complexity of the feature extraction phase is summarized. The numbers represent average number of operations per pixel, calculated over the complete test video set. It should be emphasized that all arithmetic operations are integer operations. The complexity of the SVM-based classification and k-nn ($k=1$) classification of each feature vector is given in Table 4. The SVM engine from the libSVM [11] library was used; hence, the implementation is not optimized for mobile platform and the arithmetic operations are applied on floating point numbers. The k-nn classifier is implemented using integer arithmetic operations only and from the presented number of operations it can be concluded that in combination with proposed feature extraction is easily applicable on a mobile platforms available today. The total running time of the algorithm (implemented in C) on a computer with a 1.73GHz Intel Centrino CPU and 1GB of RAM is 11.7 sec for YUV video file with QVGA resolution and 663 frames (approximately 58 frames/sec). This includes reading the video, deblocking, feature extraction and classification.

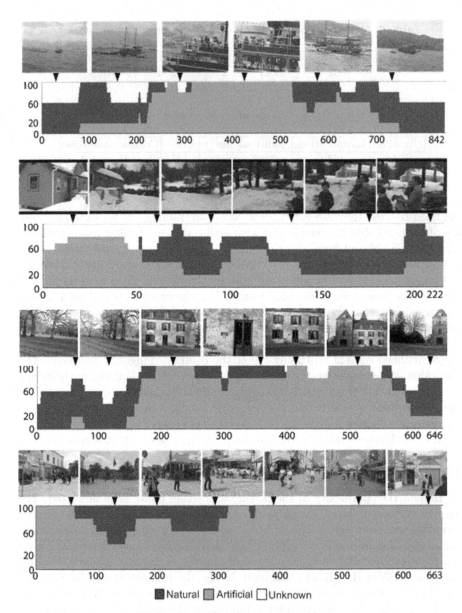

Fig. 3. Examples of annotated videos

6   Conclusions

The proposed algorithm demonstrates that robust and consistent results in annotation of low bit-rate user generated videos can be achieved based on utilization of luminance texture information only. Its computational simplicity and low storage requirements enables its application for efficient video annotation on a mobile platform. The outcome of the algorithm could be used for interactive video editing and/or retrieval. The experimental results presented here show that the decisions made by the algorithm are highly consistent with human perception of artificial and natural content.

Acknowledgments. The results were obtained in the course of a research project commissioned and funded by NXP Software B.V., Eindhoven.

References

1. Roach, M., Mason, J., Evans, N., Xu, L.-Q.: Recent trends in video analysis: a taxonomy of video classification problems. In: Proceedings Internet and Multimedia Systems and Applications, pp. 348–354 (2002)
2. Vailaya, A., Jain, A.K., Zhang, H.J.: On Image Classification: City Images vs. Landscapes. In: IEEE Trans. on Pattern Recognition, pp. 1921–1936 (1998)
3. Vailaya, A., Figueiredo, M.A.T., Jain, A.K., Zhang, H.J.: Image Classification for Content-Based Indexing. In: IEEE Trans. on Image Processing, pp. 117–130 (2001)
4. Vogel, J., Schiele, B.: Natural Scene Retrieval based on a Semantic Modeling Step. In: Third International Conference on Image and Video Retrieval, Dublin (2004)
5. Gorkani, M.M., Picard, R.W.: Texture Orientation for sorting photos at a Glance. In: Proceedings of the 12th IAPR International Conference, pp. 459–464 (2004)
6. Cheng, Y.-C., Chen, S.-Y.: Image classification using color, texture and regions. In: Image and Vision Computing, pp. 759–776 (2001)
7. Dugue, G., Oliva, A.: Classification of scene photographs from local orientations features. In: Pattern Recognition Letters, pp. 1135–1140 (2000)
8. Iqbal, Q., Aggarwal, J.K.: Retrieval by classification of images containing large manmade objects using perceptual grouping. In: Pattern Recognition (2002)
9. Torralba, A., Oliva, A.: Semantic organization of scenes using discriminant structural templates. In: Proceedings of International Conference on Computer Vision, pp. 1253–1258 (1999)
10. Oliva, A., Torralba, A.: Modeling the shape of the scene: A holistic representation of the spatial envelope. International Journal of Computer Vision (2001)
11. LIBSVM: a library for support vector machines, `http://www.csie.ntu.edu.tw/~cjlin/libsvm`
12. Stauder, J., Sirot, J., Borgne, H., Cooke, E., O'Connor, N.E.: Relating visual and semantic image descriptors. In: Proceedings of European Workshop EWIMT (2004)
13. Petrov, A., Kartalov, T., Ivanovski, Z.: Blocking effect reduction in low bitrate video on a mobile platform. To be presented on IEEE ICIP 2009 (2009)
14. Canny, J.: Relating visual and semantic image descriptors. In: IEEE Transactions on pattern analysis and machine intelligence, pp. 679–698 (1986)

Dynamic Texture Extraction and Video Denoising

Mathieu Lugiez[1,2], Michel Ménard[1], and Abdallah El-Hamidi[2]

[1] L3i - Université de La Rochelle
[2] MIA - Université de La Rochelle

Abstract. According to recent works, introduced by Y.Meyer [1] the decomposition models based on Total Variation (TV) appear as a very good way to extract texture from image sequences. Indeed, videos show up characteristic variations along the temporal dimension which can be catched in the decomposition framework. However, there are very few works in literature which deal with spatio-temporal decompositions. Thus, we devote this paper to spatio-temporal extension of the spatial color decomposition model. We provide a relevant method to accurately catch Dynamic Textures (DT) present in videos. Moreover, we obtain the spatio-temporal regularized part (the geometrical component), and we distinctly separate the highly oscillatory variations, (the noise). Furthermore, we present some elements of comparison between several models in denoising purpose.

1 Introduction

Decomposing an image into meaningful components appears as one of major aims in recent development in image processing. The first goal was image restoration and denoising; but following the ideas of Yes Meyer [1], in the Total Variation minimization framework of L. Rudin, S. Osher and E. Fatemi [2], image decomposition into geometrical and oscillatory components grants access to the textured part of an image, rejected by the previous model. We only cite, among many others, most recent works which we appear like most relevant and useful papers. In this way, reader can refer to the work of Aujol et al. [3] [4], Aujol and Chambolle [5], Aujol and Kang [6], Vese and Osher [7], Gilles [8] and more recently Bresson and Chan [9], Duval et al. [10] and Aubert et al. [11].

We are aiming to decompose videos into three components, regular one, the geometry **u**, oscillating one **v**, representative of texture and highly oscillating one, the noise **w** (see Fig.1 for a grayscale image decomposition example). So, we deal with color image sequences in extending to time existing reliable models. Moreover, through the texture component, we attempt to determinate the dynamics present in sequences, which will be suited for future work on Dynamic Texture (DT).

After have introduced different minimization functionals and a DT definition, we present the color spatio-temporal decomposition framework and subsequently their implementation. Then, we show some significant results, in particular the dynamicity of DT and comparing the denoising ability of the different models.

J. Blanc-Talon et al. (Eds.): ACIVS 2009, LNCS 5807, pp. 242–252, 2009.
© Springer-Verlag Berlin Heidelberg 2009

1.1 Decomposition Models

In 2001, Y. Meyer in [1] has proposed an extension of the famous image restoration model proposed by Rudin, Osher and Fatemi [2], based on the BV^1 space:

$$\inf_{u \in BV} F^{ROF}(u) \left(J(u) + \frac{1}{2\lambda} \|f - u\|_{L^2}^2 \right) \tag{1}$$

where f is the original image and the parameter λ controls the L_2-norm of the residual part $f - (u + v + w)$.

He has suggested an appropriate space (G^2) to model oscillating signals (i.e texture and noise), close to the dual space of BV. Aujol et al. in [3] solve the Meyer algorithm, and propose the following minimization functional:

$$\inf_{(u,v) \in BV \times G / f = u+v} F^{A2BC}(u,v) \left(J(u) + J^*(u) + \frac{1}{2\lambda} \|f - u - v\|_{L^2}^2 \right) \tag{2}$$

where J^* is the Legendre-Fenchel transform[3]of J, so J is the indicator function on $G_\eta = v \in G / \|v\|_G \leq \eta^4$.

To decompose image sequences in suitable components we propose to extend the Aujol-Chambolle [5] decomposition model. It rely on dual norms derived from BV, G and E^5spaces. Authors propose to minimize the following discretized functional:

$$\inf_{(u,v,w) \in X^3 / f = u+v+w} F^{AC}(u,v,w) = \underbrace{J(u)}_{\substack{\text{Regularization:}\\ \text{TV}}} + \underbrace{J^*\left(\frac{v}{\eta}\right)}_{\substack{\text{Texture}\\ \text{extraction}}} + \underbrace{B^*\left(\frac{w}{\delta}\right)}_{\substack{\text{Noise extraction by}\\ \text{wavelet shrinkage}}}$$

$$+ \underbrace{\frac{1}{2\lambda} \|f - u - v - w\|_X^2}_{\text{Residual part}} \tag{3}$$

where X is the Euclidian space $\mathbb{R}^{N \times N}$. J^* and B^*, are the Legendre-Fenchel transform of respectively J and B. See Fig.1 for an image decomposition example through F^{AC}.

1.2 Repetitivity in Video and Dynamic Texture (DT)

A new issue in texture analysis is its extension to the temporal dimension, a field known as Dynamic Texture Analysis. In DTA, the notion of self-similarity

---

[1] $BV(\Omega)$ is the subspace function $u \in L^1(\Omega)$ such that the following quantity, the total variation of u, is finite: $J(u) = sup\left\{\int_\Omega u(x)div(\xi(x))dx\right\}$ such that $\xi \in C_c^1(\Omega, \mathbb{R}^2), \|\xi\|_{L^\infty(\Omega)} \leq 1$

[2] G, is a Banach space, composed of all distributions v: $v = \partial_1 g_1 + \partial_2 g_2 = div(g)$ with g_1 and $g_2 \in L^\infty(\mathbb{R}^2)$ endowed with the following norm $\|v\|_G = inf\{\|g\|_{L^\infty(\Omega, \mathbb{R}^2)}/v = div(g), g = (g_1, g_2), |g(x)| = \sqrt{(|g_1|^2 + |g_2|^2)(x)}\}$

[3] $F^*(v) = sup_u(\langle u, v\rangle_{L^2} - F(u))$, where $\langle ., .\rangle_{L^2}$ stands for the L^2 inner product.

[4] i.e: $J^*\left(\frac{v}{\eta}\right) = 0$ if $v \in G_\eta$, $+\infty$ elsewhere

[5] E is a Banach space to model very oscillating patterns: $E = \dot{B}_{-1,\infty}^\infty$ dual space of $\dot{B}_{1,1}^1$.

Fig. 1. Grayscale image decomposition with AC functional. From top to bottom and left to right: Texture component (v_{AC}), original noisy image, noise component (w_{AC}) and regular or geometrical part (u_{AC}).

central to conventional image textures is extended to the spatio-temporal domain. DT typically results from processes such as water flows, smoke, fire, flag blowing in the wind or moving escalator. Important tasks are thus detection [12], segmentation [13], synthesization and perceptual characterization [14] of DT.

Image sequences present variations along time dimension. These variations could be, purely temporal (led blinking), spatial in movement (a leaf waving into wind like as shown in Fig.2:(1)), periodic or pseudo-periodic (like an escalator or the low frequencies dues to quasi periodic anemone contractions as shown in Fig.2:(3)) or spatio-temporal (flowing water and wavelets as shown in Fig.2:(2)). To properly catch all this spatio-temporal variation (i.e DT) and effectively separate them from spatio-temporal structures we consider a video as an pseudo 3-D image, i.e a volume, so that we can apply 2-D image algorithms correctly extended to the 2-D+t case. Indeed, straight spatial (i.e frame by frame) point of view is not sufficient to rightly discern patterns presenting dynamic process or movement. Moreover since static informations are redundant in a sequence, and since we take into account temporal variations, we grant to decomposition process to be more accurate and efficient for discerning the geometry and texture.

2   Spatio-temporal Extension

2.1   Spatio-temporal Structure and Discretization

We assume that we have a given image sequence $f \in L^2(\Omega)$, where Ω is an open and bounded domain on $\mathbb{R}^3$, with Lipschitz boundary. In order to recover u, v and w from f, we propose:

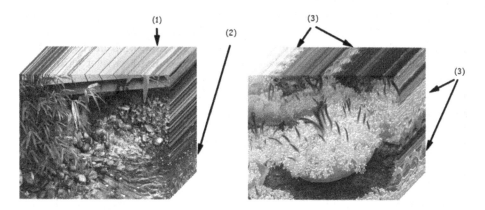

Fig. 2. 2D+t block of two dynamic textures. Here, a dynamic texture is seen as a data cube. One can clearly see at (1) leaves blowing in wind: a spatial texture in movement, at (2) flowing water and wavelets: spatio-temporal texture and at (3) spatio-temporal low frequencies dues to periodic anemone contractions.

- an extended discrete version of gradient vector: $|\nabla u|_{xyt}$ given by:

$$(\nabla \mathbf{u})_{i,j,k} = \left((\nabla \mathbf{u})^x_{i,j,k}, (\nabla \mathbf{u})^y_{i,j,k}, (\nabla \mathbf{u})^t_{i,j,k}\right) \tag{4}$$

where,

$$(\nabla \mathbf{u})^t_{i,j,k} = \begin{cases} \mathbf{u}_{i,j,k+1} - \mathbf{u}_{i,j,k-1} & \text{if } k < N \\ 0 & \text{if } k = 1 \text{ or } N \end{cases}$$

- an extended discrete total variation definition:

$$J(\mathbf{u}) = \int_\Omega \sqrt{\sum_{c=R,G,B} |((\nabla \mathbf{u})^x_{i,j,k})_c|^2 + |((\nabla \mathbf{u})^y_{i,j,k})_c|^2 + \alpha|((\nabla \mathbf{u})^t_{i,j,k})_c|^2} dxdydt$$

$$\tag{5}$$

We introduce the constant α to maintain homogeneity between space and time components. The quantization steps can be different along space and time dimensions. In practice, we often set it to one, but user can tune it.

- an adapted definition of G: inspired by [7] for the vectorial RGB case, extended to the third dimension:

Definition 1. *Let G denote the Banach space consisting of all generalized vector-valued functions* $\mathbf{v}(x,y,t) = (v_R(x,y,t), v_G(x,y,t), v_B(x,y,t))$ *which can be written as:*

$$v(x,y,t) = (div\,\boldsymbol{g_R}, div\,\boldsymbol{g_G}, div\,\boldsymbol{g_B}) \tag{6}$$

$$\boldsymbol{g_{x,c}}, \boldsymbol{g_{y,c}}, \boldsymbol{g_{t,c}} \in L^\infty(\mathbb{R}^3), c = R, G, B \ ,$$

induced by the norm $\|\boldsymbol{v}\|_*$ *defined as the lower bound of all L^∞ norms of functions* $|\boldsymbol{g}|$, *where* $|\boldsymbol{g}| = \sqrt{|\boldsymbol{g_R}|^2 + |\boldsymbol{g_G}|^2 + |\boldsymbol{g_B}|^2} = \sqrt{\sum_{c=R,G,B} ((\boldsymbol{g_{x,c}})^2 + (\boldsymbol{g_{y,c}})^2 + (\boldsymbol{g_{t,c}})^2)}$, *and where the infinitum is computed over all decompositions (6) of* $\boldsymbol{v}$.

- **an adapted shrinkage scheme:** In [15], authors use a connection given by Weickert in [16] between wavelet shrinkage and non linear diffusion filtering to introduce the noise component in color image decomposition model. Indeed, by considering an explicit discretization and relating it to wavelet shrinkage, Weickert gives shrinkage rules where all channels are coupled. The formula states a general correspondence between a shrinkage function $W_{ST}(S_\theta(w_j^i, \delta))$ and the total variation diffusivity of an explicit nonlinear diffusion scheme. So, in order to steer the evolution of all three channels in spatio-temporal domain, the following shrinkage function W_{ST}, relying on weight of S_θ for the wavelet coefficient w_i^j, is proposed:

$$S_\theta(w_i^j) = w_i^j \left(1 - 39\theta \left(\sqrt{\sum_i c * (w_{R,i}^j)^2 + c * (w_{Gi}^j)^2 + c * (w_{Bi}^j)^2} \right)^{-1} \right) \quad (7)$$

where w_j^i is the wavelet coefficient, j the resolution and $c = 1$ if $i \in \{x, y, t\}$, $c = 2$ if $i \in \{xy, xt, yt\}$ and $c = 4$ if $i = xyt$. The soft wavelet thresholding functional W_{ST} for a given wavelet coefficient, with threshold δ is given by:

$$W_{ST}(S_\theta(w_i^j), \delta) = \begin{cases} S_\theta(w_i^j) - \delta & if \ S_\theta(w_i^j) \geq \delta \\ 0 & if \ |S_\theta(w_i^j)| \leq \delta \\ S_\theta(w_i^j) + \delta & if \ S_\theta(w_i^j) \leq -\delta \end{cases} \quad (8)$$

2.2 Numerical Implementation

Thanks to recent advances in color image processing ([10] and [9]), motivating by the well known Chambolle's projection [17], we are able now to use a projected gradient algorithm computing the solution of this dual formulation problem extended to time. So we dispose of an efficient way to numerically solve the different minimization problem induced by the extended functional (3), using fixed point method: $\mathbf{P}^0 = 0$, and

$$\mathbf{P}_{i,j,k}^{n+1} = \frac{\mathbf{P}_{i,j,k}^n + \tau(\nabla(div(\mathbf{P}^n) - \frac{\mathbf{f}}{\lambda}))_{i,j,k}}{max(1, |\mathbf{P}^n + \tau(\nabla(div(\mathbf{P}^n) - \frac{\mathbf{f}}{\lambda}))_{i,j,k}|_2)} \quad (9)$$

with $\tau < \frac{\lambda}{\eta}$ to ensure the convergence of the algorithm [9].

In order to compute the solution of problem (1) we propose the following numerical scheme adapted to the vectorial formulation (Eq.(4) - (9)) according to spatio-temporal point of view:

$$\mathbf{u}_{ROF} = \mathbf{f} - P_{G_\lambda}(\mathbf{f})$$
$$\mathbf{v}_{ROF} = P_{G_\lambda}(\mathbf{f})$$

To solve the problem (2), following Aujol et al. [3], we adapted the solution to the vectorial and spatio-temporal (Eq.(4) - (9)) case and propose the following algorithm:

1. Initialization: $\mathbf{u}_0 = 0$, $\mathbf{v}_0 = 0$
2. Iterations:

$$\tilde{\mathbf{v}}_{\text{A2BC}} = P_{G_\eta}(\mathbf{f} - \mathbf{u}_{\text{A2BC}})$$
$$\tilde{\mathbf{u}}_{\text{A2BC}} = \mathbf{f} - \mathbf{u}_{\text{A2BC}} - \tilde{\mathbf{v}}_{\text{A2BC}} - P_{G_\lambda}(\mathbf{f} - \tilde{\mathbf{v}}_{\text{A2BC}})$$

3. Repeated until:

$$max(|\tilde{\mathbf{u}}_{\text{A2BC}} - \mathbf{u}_{\text{A2BC}}|, |\tilde{\mathbf{v}}_{\text{A2BC}} - \mathbf{v}_{\text{A2BC}}|) \le \epsilon$$

So, to resolve the minimization problem (3) we propose to follow the numerical scheme of Aujol and Chambolle [5] adapted to vectorial formulation (Eq.(4) - (9)):

1. Initialization: $\mathbf{u}_0 = 0$, $\mathbf{v}_0 = 0$, $\mathbf{w}_0 = 0$
2. Iterations:

$$\tilde{\mathbf{w}}_{\text{AC}} = P_{\delta B_E}(\mathbf{f} - \mathbf{u}_{\text{AC}} - \mathbf{v}_{\text{AC}})$$
$$= \mathbf{f} - \mathbf{u}_{\text{AC}} - \mathbf{v}_{\text{AC}} - W_{ST}(\mathbf{f} - \mathbf{u}_{\text{AC}} - \mathbf{v}_{\text{AC}}, \delta)$$
$$\tilde{\mathbf{v}}_{\text{AC}} = P_{G_\eta}(\mathbf{f} - \mathbf{u}_{\text{AC}} - \tilde{\mathbf{w}}_{\text{AC}})$$
$$\tilde{\mathbf{u}}_{\text{AC}} = \mathbf{f} - \mathbf{u}_{\text{AC}} - \tilde{\mathbf{v}}_{\text{AC}} - \tilde{\mathbf{w}}_{\text{AC}} - P_{G_\lambda}(\mathbf{f} - \tilde{\mathbf{v}}_{\text{AC}} - \tilde{\mathbf{w}}_{\text{AC}})$$

3. Repeated until:

$$max(|\tilde{\mathbf{u}}_{\text{AC}} - \mathbf{u}_{\text{AC}}|, |\tilde{\mathbf{v}}_{\text{AC}} - \mathbf{v}_{\text{AC}}|, |\tilde{\mathbf{w}}_{\text{AC}} - \mathbf{w}_{\text{AC}}|) \le \epsilon$$

3 Numerical Results: Static versus Dynamic Decomposition (SD vs DD)

All images and results are computed from DynTex [18], a dynamic texture database which provides a diverse high-quality DT. DynTex sequences come from natural scenes presenting a wide variety of moving process. Such diversity grants user to identify and emphasize a lot of aspects in testing purpose.

3.1 Dynamic Texture Extraction

To analyze the influence of the dynamic property of the texture we present a comparison between the two methods of decomposition, SD versus DD, (both computed with same parameters). We can easily see that time impact in result: water in Fig.3 is well regularized and fluid aspect is well represent into the $\mathbf{v}_{\text{AC}}$ component. The regularization is more robust to illumination and movement constraints.

Moreover, if user tunes parameters to obtain a stronger regularization, our algorithm is able to catch wider waves into spatio-temporal texture component: see around the circumference of fountain in Fig.3, small wavelets are well catched in $\mathbf{v}_{\text{AC}}$ than wider waves. It's a matter of deep in spatio-temporal texture extraction, which our algorithm is able to deal with, like shown in Fig.4.

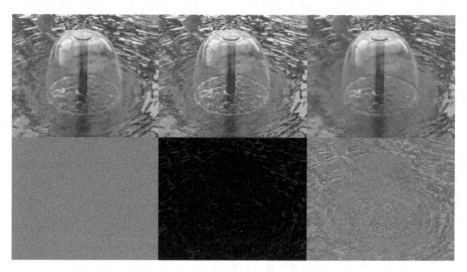

Fig. 3. Left: the geometrical component, $\mathbf{u}_{AC}$, in SD (top) and its texture component $\mathbf{v}_{AC}$ (bottom). Center and top: the original image, bottom: Difference between the static and dynamic $\mathbf{v}_{AC}$ components. Right: the geometrical component in DD (top) and its dynamic texture $\mathbf{v}_{AC}$ (bottom).

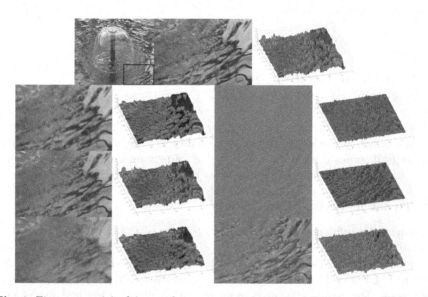

Fig. 4. First row: original image from sequence 6487310 of DynTex, the ROI and a visualization of ROI. Second row: SD of ROI with $\lambda = 140$, $\eta = 140$ from left to right $\mathbf{u}_{AC}$ component and its visualization, since $\mathbf{v}_{AC}$ component and its visualization. Third row, DD of the ROI with $\lambda = 10$ and $\eta = 10$ (weak regularization and texture extraction). Fourth row, DD of the ROI with $\lambda = 140$ and $\eta = 140$ (strong regularization and texture extraction). We can see than SD is not able to deal with dynamicity, moreover, in DD user can catch different scales of waves in the decomposition process.

Fig. 5. From left to right, the geometrical component, $\mathbf{u}_{AC}$, in classic color decomposition (top) and its texture and noise component $\mathbf{v}_{AC}$ (bottom). The original image (center and top), the time influence in calculus of divergence of $\mathbf{v}_{AC}$ component (center and bottom). Then our new dynamic decomposition components (right).

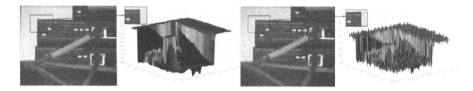

Fig. 6. From left to right, an original image from the sequence 64cc610 of DynTex, the noised version (gaussian noise with void mean and $\sigma = 20$, SNR=14.53, PSNR=21.18), and a visualization of ROI

We present, in Fig.5, a part of a decomposed sequence of flowing water under wood bridge. We can see the static aspect of $\mathbf{u}_{AC}$ component, regularized in space and in time. It seems to be freezed, although texture component, $\mathbf{v}_{AC}$, present a real dynamic. Only moving things or objects presenting dynamicity are taken in account in the temporal divergence part of $\mathbf{v}_{AC}$ component.

The third part of texture component play a key role in our process, movement information is well captured. In this way we obtain the dynamicity present in video through oscillations along time dimension. These results will be useful for future work on dynamic texture characterization.

3.2   Video Denoising

We present in this section some elements of comparison between the different models in denoising purpose. Fig.6 to 9 present the decomposition of one image, pick up from a sequence of eight images, noised separately (and decomposed

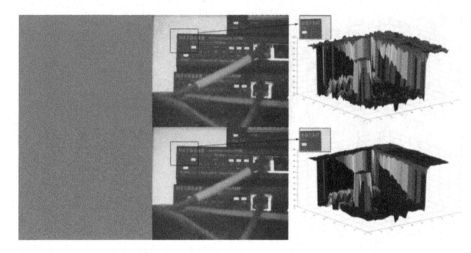

Fig. 7. ROF decomposition with $\lambda = 25$. Top: SD, bottom: DD. Left the v_{ROF} component, center u_{ROF} and right a visualization of ROI. We have a SNR equal to 23.03 and a PSNR equal to 29.54 with SD and respectively 29.09 and 35.59 with DD

Fig. 8. A2BC decomposition with $\lambda = 10$ and $\eta = 25$. Top: SD, bottom: DD. Left the v_{A2BC} component, center u_{A2BC} and right a visualization of ROI. We have a SNR equal to 24.56 and a PSNR equal to 31.12 with SD and respectively 29.57 and 36.08 with DD.

conjointly in the DD process). We present the result of denoising process of the different models. One can easily see that DD clearly outperform SD whatever the model. Moreover the AC functional give the better results even if the texture component catch a part of noise in the decomposition process.

Fig. 9. AC decomposition with $\lambda = 10$, $\eta = 15$ and $\delta = 45$. Top: SD, bottom: DD. Left the v_{AC} component, center u_{AC} and right a visualization of ROI. We have a SNR equal to 25.10 and a PSNR equal to 31.60 with SD and respectively 30.24 and 36.74 with DD.

In the case of very noisy sequence, ($\sigma = 50$, SNR=10.85 and PSNR=17.49), computed with exactly the same parameters and the same sequence, we have:

- ROF: for SD we obtain a SNR=16.40 a PSNR=22.90 and for DD we have respectively 21.04 and 27.55.
- A2BC: for SD we obtain a SNR=18.32 a PSNR=24.83 and for DD we have respectively 25.23 and 31.73.
- AC: for SD we obtain a SNR=20.58 a PSNR=27.12 and for DD we have respectively 26.91 and 33.42.

4   Discussion

We have investigate in the present paper the spatio-temporal extension of color decomposition models through projection approach. One can see that taking into account variations along the temporal axe appears as a useful and innovative way to catch the dynamic texture present in videos. Moreover this extension provide a useful tool for video denoising, indeed dynamic model clearly outperform classical decomposition, reinforcing the denoising ability of TV based models. So, we provide an efficient tool to separate dynamic texture, structure and noise in image sequence.

References

1. Meyer, Y.: Oscillating Patterns in Image Processing and Nonlinear EvolutionEquations: The fifteenth dean jacqueline B. Lewis Memorial Lectures. American Mathematical Society, Boston (2001)
2. Rudin, L., Osher, S., Fatemi, E.: Nonlinear total variation based noise removal. Physica D 60, 259–269 (1992)

3. Aujol, J.F., Aubert, G., Blanc-Féraud, L., Chambolle, A.: Image decomposition into a bounded variation component and an oscillating component. Journal of Mathematical Imaging and Vision 22(1), 71–88 (2005)
4. Aujol, J.F., Gilboa, G., Chan, T., Osher, S.: Structure-texture image decomposition - modeling, algorithms, and parameter selection. International Journal of Computer Vision 67(1), 111–136 (2006)
5. Aujol, J.F., Chambolle, A.: Dual norms and image decomposition models. International Journal of Computer Vision 63(1), 85–104 (2005)
6. Aujol, J.F., Kang, S.H.: Color image decomposition and restoration. J. Visual Communication and Image Representation 17(4), 916–928 (2006)
7. Vese, L.A., Osher, S.J.: Color texture modeling and color image decomposition in a variational-PDE approach. In: SYNASC, pp. 103–110. IEEE Computer Society, Los Alamitos (2006)
8. Gilles, J.: Noisy image decomposition: A new structure, texture and noise model based on local adaptivity. J. Math. Imaging Vis. 28(3), 285–295 (2007)
9. Bresson, X., Chan, T.: Fast minimization of the vectorial total variation norm and applications to color image processing. In: SIAM Journal on Imaging Sciences, SIIMS (submitted 2007)
10. Duval, V., Aujol, J.F., Vese, L.: A projected gradient algorithm for color image decomposition. Technical report, CMLA Preprint 2008-21 (2008)
11. Aubert, G., El-Hamidi, A., Ghannam, C., Ménard, M.: On a class of ill-posed minimization problems in image processing. Journal of Mathematical Analysis and Applications 352(1), 380–399 (2009); Degenerate and Singular PDEs and Phenomena in Analysis and Mathematical Physics
12. Dedeoglu, Y., Toreyin, B.U., Gudukbay, U., Cetin, A.E.: Real-time fire and flame detection in video. In: IEEE International Conference on Acoustics, Speech, and Signal Processing (ICASSP 2005), vol. II, pp. 669–673 (2005)
13. Chetverikov, D., Péteri, R.: A brief survey of dynamic texture description and recognition. In: 4th International Conference on Computer Recognition Systems (CORES 2005), Advances in Soft Computing, Poland, pp. 17–26. Springer, Heidelberg (2005)
14. Péteri, R., Chetverikov, D.: Dynamic texture recognition using normal flow and texture regularity. In: Marques, J.S., Pérez de la Blanca, N., Pina, P. (eds.) IbPRIA 2005. LNCS, vol. 3523, pp. 223–230. Springer, Heidelberg (2005)
15. Dubois, S., Lugiez, M., Péteri, R., Ménard, M.: Adding a noise component to a color decomposition model for improving color texture extraction. In: 4th European Conference on Colour in Graphics, Imaging, and Vision. Espagne, Barcelona (2008)
16. Weickert, J., Steidl, G., Mrázek, P., Welk, M., Brox, T.: Diffusion filters and wavelets: What can they learn from each other? In: Paragios, N., Chen, Y., Faugeras, O. (eds.) Handbook of Mathematical Models in Computer Vision, pp. 3–16. Springer, Heidelberg (2006)
17. Chambolle, A.: An algorithm for total variation minimization and its applications. JMIV 20, 89–97 (2004)
18. Péteri, R., Huiskes, M., Fazekas, S.: Dyntex: A comprehensive database of dynamic textures (2008), http://www.cwi.nl/projects/dyntex/

Unsupervised Detection of Gradual Video Shot Changes with Motion-Based False Alarm Removal

Ralph Ewerth and Bernd Freisleben

Department of Mathematics and Computer Science, University of Marburg
Hans-Meerwein-Str. 3, D-35032 Marburg, Germany
{ewerth,freisleb}@informatik.uni-marburg.de

Abstract. The temporal segmentation of a video into shots is a fundamental prerequisite for video retrieval. There are two types of shot boundaries: abrupt shot changes ("cuts") and gradual transitions. Several high-quality algorithms have been proposed for detecting cuts, but the successful detection of gradual transitions remains a surprisingly difficult problem in practice. In this paper, we present an unsupervised approach for detecting gradual transitions. It has several advantages. First, in contrast to alternative approaches, no training stage and hence no training data are required. Second, no thresholds are needed, since the used clustering approach separates classes of gradual transitions and non-transitions automatically and *adaptively* for each video. Third, it is a generic approach that does not employ a specialized detector for each transition type. Finally, the issue of removing false alarms caused by camera motion is addressed: in contrast to related approaches, it is not only based on low-level features, but on the results of an appropriate algorithm for camera motion estimation. Experimental results show that the proposed approach achieves very good performance on TRECVID shot boundary test data.

Keywords: Video indexing, gradual transition detection, shot boundary detection, gradual video shot changes, video retrieval.

1 Introduction

A video sequence typically consists of a large number of shots that have been put together during a production process either to tell a story or to communicate some kind of information (e.g., news or documentary). A shot is the fundamental processing unit in video retrieval applications, and most indexing and retrieval algorithms rely on a correct temporal segmentation of a video into shots. The task of shot boundary detection is to perform a temporal segmentation of a given video into single shots and to recognize two types of transitions: abrupt shot changes ("cuts") and gradual transitions. If a shot abruptly follows a preceding shot, it is called a *cut*; if transitional frames are inserted between two shots, then it is called a *gradual transition*. The most common gradual transitions are fades (in and out), dissolves, and wipes. Although most shot changes in videos are abrupt, the percentage of gradual transitions might be large for some video collections and genres. The frequency of gradual transitions

J. Blanc-Talon et al. (Eds.): ACIVS 2009, LNCS 5807, pp. 253–264, 2009.

varies noticeably for different video domains. For example, in the test sets for the shot boundary detection task of the TRECVID [12] evaluations from 2003 to 2007, the percentage of gradual transitions is between 10% and 51% [14]. Hence, it is obvious that the correct detection of gradual shot boundaries is as important as cut detection for some applications.

Several high-quality algorithms have been proposed for detecting cuts, but the detection of gradual transitions is a surprisingly difficult problem in practice. For example, recall and precision of the best approaches evaluated at TRECVID in the years from 2005 to 2007 [12] are about 10-20% lower than for cut detection. There are three main reasons: 1.) Several types of gradual transitions exist: dissolve, fade-in and fade-out, wipe, and many other effects that eventually use motion or 3D-effects; 2.) A gradual transition can be of arbitrary length, it ranges from one frame up to dozens of frames; 3.) Often, the shot content changes slightly due to camera or object motion, causing many false alarms for state-of-the-art gradual transition detectors.

In recent years, two kinds of approaches for gradual transition detection have emerged. The first type of approaches is based on different detectors for different transition types. There are proposals for specialized dissolve detectors (e.g., [8, 9, 10, 11]), fade detectors (e.g., [11, 16]), and wipe detectors (e.g., [11, 13]). The other class of approaches relies on the application of a general gradual transition detector (e.g., [1, 2, 3, 4, 17, 18, 19]). While the use of specialized detectors promises to find corresponding effects with a higher accuracy, the development, adaptation and training efforts are higher for this kind of approach. In addition, it is not clear how to deal with transition types that do not fall into one of the classes of available detector types.

In this paper, we present a generic unsupervised approach for gradual transition detection in videos. The idea of the proposed approach is to view a gradual shot change as an abrupt shot change at a lower temporal resolution. Therefore, in contrast to most related approaches (e.g., [1, 8, 17, 18]), subsampled time series of frame dissimilarities are considered. Given a time series with a frame distance m that is subsampled accordingly by the factor m, a gradual transition of length $L{\leq}m$ should be represented by an isolated peak in the time series - as it is the case for a cut at the original temporal resolution (especially, if L<<m). Using a temporal sliding window for the subsampled time series, a feature vector is created for frame positions where the maximum peak is in the middle of the window. These feature vectors are passed to a k-means clustering algorithm that basically takes place in the same manner as in our previously proposed cut detection approach [5]. The frame positions of the beginning and the end of a transition are refined optionally. Since fades are well recognizable due to the appearance of monochrome frames, the proposed approach is supplemented by a fade detector. This is the only specialized transition detector in the proposed approach. In the context of gradual transition detection, no sophisticated algorithms for detecting sequences of camera motion reliably have been utilized to remove false alarms (to the best of our knowledge). Consequently, we also present a novel false alarm removal scheme based on our high-quality camera motion estimation approach [6]. Experimental results demonstrate the very good performance of our approach.

The paper is organized as follows. In Section 2, related work for gradual transition detection is discussed. Our approach to unsupervised gradual transition detection is presented in Section 3. Experimental results on TRECVID shot boundary test data are shown in Section 4. Section 5 concludes the paper and outlines areas for future work.

2   Related Work

As mentioned above, one kind of approaches for gradual transition detection consists of specialized gradual transition detectors for fades, dissolves, and wipes. For example, Hanjalic [8] has presented a specialized dissolve detector, and Lienhart [9, 10] and Truong et al. [16] have presented specialized approaches for dissolves and fades. Liu et al. [11] have proposed a successful approach relying on specialized detectors. Their shot boundary detector is based on different detectors for cuts, fades (in and out), dissolves, short dissolves and wipes. Each detector is realized via a finite state machine (FSM) with either four or five different states. Overall, sixteen different functions are used to decide whether a state is kept or left, these functions are evaluated based on threshold parameters. The video is analyzed frame by frame using the FSMs, and state changes are based on comparing one or more features with pre-defined or adaptive thresholds. For cut and dissolve detection, a support vector machine (SVM) is applied to verify transition candidates. Eighty-eight intra- and inter-frame features are extracted; the inter-frame features are extracted for a frame distance of 1 and 6. The intra-frame features measure the histogram mean, variance, skewness, flatness, dynamic range and edge ratio in horizontal and vertical direction. The inter-frame features measure the difference for these features for two different frames, histogram distance in HSV space, but also include motion features and measures for matching error and matching ratio of two frames. For dissolve verification, another set of specialized features is used, including predominantly variance (of brightness) and edge features. The features are extracted from a region of interest (i.e., the frame border is ignored). This approach belonged to the best approaches at TRECVID 2007: recall was 70.9% and precision was 80.2% for gradual transition detection (f1-measure: 75.3).

   Bescós [1] has analyzed several frame disparity functions for shot boundary detection. The metrics are evaluated based on the measure of divergence, an index that describes the separability of two classes. Regarding gradual transitions, Bescos shows that divergence between transition and non-transition class increases when the frame distance is increased from 1 up to at least the transition length L, whereas the metric choice is not crucial for divergence. Bescos describes a model for gradual transitions that has the following characteristics: First, in the time series with frame distance n ($n \geq L$, where L is transition length) the frame center of the sliding window should have a maximum value. Second, the peak should be reached gradually. For such frame positions, a three-dimensional feature vector is created that captures the properties of a typical triangular pattern (for $n=L$) caused by a gradual transition in a time series with frame distance $n>1$. Results are reported for a subset of the MPEG-7 test set (460 grad. transitions): 87% recall and 66% precision for gradual transitions.

   Chua et al. [3] have proposed a unified approach to detect cuts and gradual transitions by using a temporal multi-resolution approach. It is realized by applying a wavelet transform to frame histograms and other measures. The authors use histogram differences as well as a coarse representation of MPEG motion vectors. First, they detect candidates from the set of local maxima and then they apply an adaptive thresholding technique. Finally, they use support vector machines to find an optimal classification of cuts and non-cuts. The final version of their approach [4] includes motion information as well as a refinement approach with support vector machines and achieves a recall of 89% and a precision of 88% for gradual transitions on the MPEG-7 video test set. However, results at the TRECVID 2002 evaluation are significantly worse: 38% recall and 47% precision for gradual transitions [2].

Yeo and Liu [17] have suggested a general approach to detect gradual transitions. Frame dissimilarities are measured with a temporal distance of $k>1$, where k must exceed the duration of the longest transition (e.g., $k=40$). Then, the idea is to detect plateaus with sloping sides in such time series, which is achieved similarly to cut detection using a local threshold. The authors report a recall of about 90% and a precision of about 75% for 19 gradual transitions in five test videos.

Zheng et al. [20] have proposed a shot boundary detection framework that is based on a cut detector, a fade detector and a gradual transition detector. Several features are extracted from both the compressed and the uncompressed domain: mean and standard deviation of pixel intensities for fade detection, color histogram, pixel-wise difference measures for cut and gradual transition detection, and motion vector information that is used for gradual transition detection only. The fade detector is based on monochrome frame detection and tracking using several pre-defined thresholds. To detect long gradual transitions, Yuan et al. [18, 19] have extended the previous FSM-based approach of Zheng et al. [20] via a graph partition model for temporal video shot segmentation in which a graph is built based on multi-pair frame similarity measures. Within a sliding window, frame similarity is measured for all frame pairs. While each frame is considered as a node in a graph, these similarity values are considered as the related edge weights. The graph partition model tries to divide this graph in two subgraphs A and B by optimizing an objective function: the association between the two subgraphs has to be minimized, whereas the association in a subgraph has to be maximized. Yuan et al. have incorporated the graph partition model into the original framework and have substituted some components of [20] by using a support vector machine for cut detection and gradual transition detection. One SVM is trained for cut detection, three SVMs are trained for gradual transition detection for different temporal resolutions using the TRECVID test sets of 2003 and 2004. At TRECVID 2007, a motion detector was added [19]. This approach belonged to the best two approaches for gradual transition detection (recall: 73.3%, precision: 71.8%, f1: 72.5).

3   Unsupervised Gradual Transition Detection

The proposed approach for gradual transition detection consists of three main components: a fade detector, the unsupervised gradual transition detector, and a false alarm removal method based on camera motion estimation. The general gradual transition detection process is preceded by fade detection [16], since fades can be detected more easily than arbitrary gradual transitions. Afterwards, frame dissimilarities are measured at several frame distances. Finally, a state-of-the-art approach for camera motion estimation is used to remove false alarms.

One of the main ideas is to view a gradual shot change as an abrupt shot change at a lower temporal resolution. Therefore, in contrast to other approaches, temporally subsampled time series of frame dissimilarities are considered for frame distances greater than 1. Some previous approaches for gradual transition detection have considered frame dissimilarity measures at different frame distances, too, but they retained the original temporal resolution in these measurements [1, 8, 9, 17]. Chua et al.

[4] obtained a moderate subsampling of factor 4 using the wavelet transform that is applied to the original time series of dissimilarity values. It is typical for gradual transitions that they cause a plateau pattern in such measurements, as first observed by Yeo and Liu [17]. However, such plateau patterns can also be caused by motion, and in practice they rarely take the ideal shape that is assumed in theory. Thus, these plateau patterns are much harder to detect than isolated peaks. This is the main motivation for the subsampling in our approach. Given a time series with a frame distance m that is subsampled by factor m, a gradual transition of length $L \leq m$ (especially for $L \ll m$, e.g. $L \leq m/2$) should be represented by an isolated peak in the time series - as it is the case for a cut at the highest temporal resolution.

Based on this observation, different feature vectors are created for several temporal resolutions (i.e., for several frame distances). These feature vectors are then clustered using the k-means algorithm. The number of k clusters is known in advance: a transition cluster and a non-transition cluster, i.e. $k=2$. Clustering has the advantage that no training data is needed for classifying gradual transitions, as it is required for supervised learning approaches. Furthermore, clustering adaptively yields different "decision rules" to separate transitions and non-transitions for different videos, in contrast to a supervised learning approach. Finally, false alarms are removed based on the results of a high-quality motion estimation algorithm. The main algorithmic steps of our proposed approach are now described in more detail.

1) Fade Detection. The fade detector is realized according to the proposal of Truong et al. [16]. First-order and second-order differences are computed for mean and variance of frame luminance. A smoothing filter is applied to reduce the impact of noise. First, monochrome frames are detected by checking whether the variance of a frame is below a threshold. If so, then the subsequent (preceding) frames are analyzed in order to find a fade-in (fade-out). The first assumption is that the sign of the smoothed first-order luminance mean does not change during the fading process. As long as this is the case, the second-order differences of the variance curve are analyzed: It has been observed that there is a large negative spike near the start of a fade-out or the end of a fade-in in the second-order difference luminance variances. To detect such spikes, the subsequent (preceding) values of the smoothed second-order variance differences are checked for such spikes (indicating start or end frame of fade transition) until the sign of the smoothed first-order luminance mean changes.

2) Gradual Transition Detection. After fade detection, the detection of gradual transitions of arbitrary type takes place. First, frame dissimilarities are extracted for several frame distances (e.g., 5, 10, 15, 20, 30, 40, 50). Then, feature vectors are created based on the frame dissimilarity measurements. These feature vectors are then passed to the clustering process that produces two clusters: a "transition" cluster and a "non-transition" cluster. These steps are described in detail below.

2.1) Measuring Frame Dissimilarities. First, frame dissimilarities are computed based on histograms of approximated DC-frames [17] in RGB color space with 512 bins. These dissimilarities are computed for certain temporal frame distances Δt. To detect gradual transitions, frames are compared at a higher temporal distance, for example up to 50 frames. For this reason, a histogram based metric is more suited to compute frame dissimilarities than a motion compensated pixel-based comparison that is more sensitive to object and camera motion. A subsampled set of frame dissimilarity values is obtained for a temporal resolutions Δt by:

$$D(\Delta t, offset) = \{d_{0,\Delta t}, d_{1,\Delta t}, ..., d_{i,\Delta t}, ..., d_{n/\Delta t, \Delta t}\} \tag{1}$$

where $\Delta t \in N \backslash \{0\}$, and $d_{i,\Delta t}$ is the dissimilarity value for the frames $i*\Delta t + offset$ and $(i+1)*\Delta t + offset$, for all frames with $(i+1)*\Delta t \le maxFrameNumber$. As mentioned above, the idea is to view a gradual shot change as a cut at a lower temporal resolution. Therefore, each time series of dissimilarity values with frame distance Δt is subsampled by the factor Δt. If a gradual transition of length L (this could be a cut of "length 0" as well) starts at position n, this transition should be represented in all time series with $L \le \Delta t$ (especially for $L << \Delta t$, e.g. $L \le \Delta t/2$) by a peak in the dissimilarity measurements. The variable offset allows shifting a subsampled time series. This can be useful to also capture transitions with a length of nearly Δt that start in the middle of two measurement time points: Such transitions will not yield an isolated peak in the time series but will produce two similar neighbored peaks of lower height.

2.2) Creating Feature Vectors. The feature vectors are now created similarly to the task of cut detection and consist of the same two components: *max'* and *sec'*. The value *max'* represents the maximum dissimilarity value in the middle of a temporal sliding window, it is normalized for each time series using the corresponding maximum of the series. The feature *sec'* describes the ratio of the second largest and the maximum dissimilarity in the sliding window. Different time series are obtained for the combinations of Δt and *offset*. For each temporal resolution Δt_i, the basic sliding window size of $2m+1$ is set separately based on the parameter x: $m = max(x*\Delta t_0 /\Delta t_i, c)$, where t_0 is the finest temporal resolution, i.e. $t_0 < \Delta t_i$, c is a constant and controls the minimum size for m (e.g., $c=2$). The parameter x represents the length of the sliding window at the finest temporal frame resolution, that is x represents the sliding window duration that is (nearly, except for rounding errors and the minimum window size c) equal for all temporal resolutions. By computing m separately for each Δt, fewer dissimilarity values are taken into account at lower temporal resolutions due to the preceding subsampling. The sliding window is not extended since at lower temporal resolutions the probability increases that neighbored cuts and transitions could be within the sliding window and affect the usefulness of the parameter *sec'*.

2.3) Clustering Gradual Transition Candidates. The feature vectors are clustered using k-means with $k=2$. The clusters are initialized with two artificial feature vectors which represent either an ideal transition or non-transition. This also helps to prevent a degraded result in case when there are no transitions in a video.

At least three strategies are possible to cluster the time series: 1.) Clustering can be conducted separately for each time series Δt including potentially time series for different offsets. 2.) Clustering can be conducted for each time series separately for each combination of the parameters Δt and offset. 3.) A third possibility is to process the feature vectors of all time series in one clustering process. The latter requires a reasonable normalization across the several temporal resolutions. In our approach, the feature vectors are normalized according to the maximum value of the corresponding time series. In the first two cases, the clustering result must be merged afterwards.

2.4) Postprocessing the Gradual Transition Cluster(s). After k-means clustering, the members of the gradual transition cluster(s) (there are several clusters if clustering has been applied at least for each Δt separately) must be processed further. First, all transitions are removed whose frame interval includes a cut according to the cut detection results. Second, there might be feature vectors in one "transition" cluster or in the "transition" clusters of different clusterings that have a frame overlap. Two possibilities are considered to merge the frame interval of the transitions: union and intersection.

False alarms are removed if the start frame and the end frame are too similar, which is the case when the dissimilarity value between start and end frame is below a threshold. Therefore, the average and standard deviation are computed for the "cuts" cluster (the result of the unsupervised cut detection process) with respect to histogram dissimilarity. Then, the threshold for false alarm removal is defined as:

$$thresh = dissim_{avg}(cuts) - \alpha \cdot dissim_{stddev}(cuts) \tag{2}$$

A transition of length 1 is considered as a false alarm if the dissimilarity value at the start position in the time series $D(\Delta t, 0)$ with $\Delta t=1$ is below $thresh$.

Furthermore, a transition interval can be refined optionally. Therefore, the beginning of the transition is shifted forward frame by frame: If the dissimilarity of the new (start) frame and the end frame is equal or above to the dissimilarity value of the original start frame and end frame, the current frame is considered as the new transition start and the resizing process stops.

3) False Alarm Removal via Camera Motion Analysis. To enhance gradual transition detection, camera motion estimation is applied to a video, too. For this purpose, the camera motion estimation approach that we have proposed in a previous paper [6] is used. The camera motion estimation algorithm returns a number of frame intervals where camera motion has been detected separately for the following motion types: pan (horizontal camera movement), tilt (vertical camera movement), and zoom in/out. Again, several strategies are possible to employ these results for false alarm removal. First, each combination of these motion types or a single motion type can be considered for false alarm removal. Furthermore, several cases are possible when a gradual transition has to be considered as a false alarm:

1. Frame interval of gradual transition is completely covered by motion interval.
2. The frame interval of the gradual transition and the motion interval intersect.
3. False alarm removal is applied on a frame basis: The frames that also exhibited motion are removed from the gradual transition.

Empirical results have shown that the first strategy works best in practice.

4 Experimental Results

The unsupervised gradual transition detection approach was tested on TRECVID shot boundary test sets. At TRECVID 2005, our unsupervised approach without camera motion belonged to the top approaches of 21 institutes: our best run achieved a recall of 72.2% and precision of 69.1%, yielding an f1-measure of 70.6. Only three institutes submitted runs at TRECVID 2005 that outperformed our approach in terms of statistical significance [15].

In this section, we report results on the TRECVID 2007 shot boundary test set that consists of 17 videos. Several experiments have been conducted to investigate the impact of different parameters. Regarding feature vector representation and the clustering strategy, we have already shown [7] that these factors do not have a significant impact on the detection result.

First, results for several single-used frame distances (6, 10, 20, 30, 40, 50) in conjunction with different sliding window sizes are presented in Table 1. Using only a single frame distance yields moderate f1-values up to 59.0, for example for a frame

Table 1. Performance for gradual transition detection on TRECVID 2007 test set for different single frame distances and different window sizes

Frame distance, window size parameter x	Recall [%]	Precision [%]	F1
6, 1	70.9	2.2	4.3
6, 3	58.7	19.5	29.3
6, 6	51.9	44.4	47.9
6, 9	43.7	60.4	**50.7**
6, 12	36.9	65.5	47.2
6, 24	1.9	80.0	3.7
10, 1	72.3	6.9	12.6
10, 3	53.4	33.0	40.8
10, 5	45.6	44.8	45.2
10, 6	45.6	48.0	**46.8**
10, 9	29.1	61.9	39.6
10, 12	23.8	71.0	35.6
10, 24	13.3	73.6	22.5
20, 1	72.3	17.3	27.9
20, 2	66.5	46.0	54.4
20, 3	59.2	53.7	**56.3**
20, 6	37.4	76.2	50.2
20, 12	21.4	80.0	33.8
30, 1	70.4	20.6	31.9
30, 2	58.7	44.2	50.4
30, 3	46.6	59.3	**52.2**
30, 6	35.4	76.8	48.5
30, 12	11.2	88.5	19.9
30, 24	8.3	70.8	14.9
40, 1	65.0	32.8	43.6
40, 2	54.4	64.4	**59.0**
40, 3	42.2	69.0	52.4
40, 6	18.9	78.0	30.4
40, 12	13.1	79.4	22.5
40, 24	0.5	25.0	1.0
50, 1	64.1	38.2	47.9
50, 2	50.0	57.2	**53.4**
50, 3	36.4	72.8	48.5
50, 6	17.0	77.8	27.9
50, 12	18.0	77.1	29.2

Table 2. Performance for gradual transition detection on TRECVID 2007 test set for a combination of frame distances and different window sizes

Frame distances (window size parameter x)	Fade detection	False Alarm Removal Histogram-Based	False Alarm Removal Motion (Pan)	Recall [%]	Precision [%]	F1
6, 10 (6)	No	No	No	69.9	13.9	23.2
6, 10 (9)	No	No	No	64.6	31.7	42.5
6, 10 (12)	No	No	No	61.6	39.7	**48.3**

distance of 40 in conjunction with a sliding window size of 2. In another experiment, the usefulness of combining several frame distances in one clustering process has been investigated. The related results are presented in Table 2 - Table 6. The combination of frame distances itself did not improve performance (e.g., see Table 2).

However, the incorporation of fade detection and false alarm removal improves the results considerably (Table 3 – Table 6). In particular, false alarm removal based on horizontal camera motion (pan) improves the detection results significantly; precision is increased by an absolute value of 30% for some test cases (e.g., see Table 4, 4th row; or Table 5, third row). Using pan detection for additional false alarm removal yields a very good f1-value of 71.6. The incorporation of vertical camera motion (tilt) improved the results as well (by 24% in terms of precision), but was inferior compared to pan. Considering detected camera zoom sequences or using all camera motion types did not improve the detection quality (see Table 4), but the reasons have not been analyzed yet.

In Table 5, results for some other combinations of frame distances are presented. Here, also, best results were obtained, if fade detection, histogram-based false alarm removal and pan-based false alarm removal were used. Results for using six frame distances are displayed in Table 6. Again, false alarm removal based on pan improves the precision significantly and yields the best results, while recall remains stable at the same time.

Overall, the proposed unsupervised approach achieves a very good performance compared to the best approaches at TRECVID 2007. Only two institutes [11, 19] have submitted runs (with f1=75.3 and f1=72.5, respectively, see also Section 2) at TREC-VID 2007 that outperformed our best result (in terms of f1-measure: 71.6) reported in

Table 3. Performance for gradual transition detection on TRECVID 2007 test set for a combination of frame distances with different window sizes and false alarm removal strategies

Frame distances (window size parameter x)	Fade detection	False Alarm Removal Histogram-Based	False Alarm Removal Motion	Recall [%]	Precision [%]	F1
6, 10, 20 (6)	No	No	No	91.3	2.5	4.9
6, 10, 20 (6)	No	**Yes**	No	75.7	28.0	40.9
6, 10, 20 (9)	No	No	No	87.9	7.4	13.6
6, 10, 20 (9)	**Yes**	**Yes**	**Pan**	73.8	58.7	**65.4**

Table 4. Performance for gradual transition detection on TRECVID 2007 test set for a combination of frame distances and different motion-based false alarm removal strategies

Frame distances (window size parameter x)	Fade detection	False Alarm Removal Histogram-Based	False Alarm Removal Motion	Recall [%]	Precision [%]	F1
6, 10, 20 (12)	No	No	No	79.1	17.2	28.3
6, 10, 20 (12)	No	Yes	No	72.3	41.2	52.5
6, 10, 20 (12)	Yes	Yes	No	74.6	41.1	53.0
6, 10, 20 (12)	Yes	Yes	Pan	72.8	70.4	**71.6**
6, 10, 20 (12)	Yes	Yes	Tilt	70.9	64.6	67.6
6, 10, 20 (12)	Yes	Yes	Zoom	45.1	60.0	51.5
6, 10, 20 (12)	Yes	Yes	All	43.7	65.7	52.5

Table 5. Performance for gradual transition detection on TRECVID 2007 test set for different combinations of frame distances, window sizes, fade detection, and false alarm removal

Frame distances (window size parameter x)	Fade detection	False Alarm Removal Histogram-Based	False Alarm Removal Motion (Pan)	Recall [%]	Precision [%]	F1
6, 30, 50 (12)	No	Yes	No	76.7	27.1	40.0
6, 30, 50 (12)	Yes	Yes	No	77.2	26.8	39.8
6, 30, 50 (12)	Yes	Yes	Yes	75.2	55.6	**63.9**
30, 40, 50 (2)	No	No	No	71.8	35.0	47.1
30, 40, 50 (2)	Yes	No	No	74.3	34.9	47.5
30, 40, 50 (2)	Yes	Yes	No	69.9	40.0	50.9
30, 40, 50 (2)	Yes	Yes	Yes	73.3	56.3	**63.7**
30, 40, 50 (1)	No	No	No	82.0	15.6	26.2

Table 6. Performance for gradual transition detection on TRECVID 2007 test set. Fade detection and histogram-based false alarm removal is used in all cases.

Frame distances (window size parameter x)	False Alarm Removal Motion (Pan)	Recall [%]	Precision [%]	F1
6, 10, 20, 30, 40, 50 (12)	No	78.6	23.7	36.4
6, 10, 20, 30, 40, 50 (12)	Yes	77.7	52.8	62.9
6, 10, 20, 30, 40, 50 (24)	No	79.6	29.1	42.6
6, 10, 20, 30, 40, 50 (24)	Yes	78.2	59.0	67.3
6, 10, 20, 30, 40, 50 (24)	No	78.2	34.5	47.9
6, 10, 20, 30, 40, 50 (30)	Yes	75.7	62.7	68.6
6, 10, 20, 30, 40, 50 (36)	Yes	75.2	65.7	**70.1**
6, 10, 20, 30, 40, 50 (40)	Yes	75.2	66.8	**70.8**
6, 10, 20, 30, 40, 50 (50)	Yes	70.4	70.0	**70.2**

this paper, but the performance differences are not significant in a statistical sense (at an alpha level of 0.05). To check this, we have conducted a significance test based on partial randomization according to Smeaton et al. [15]. In contrast to our approach, Liu et al.'s approach [11] uses a number of specialized detectors, and several parameters have to be set in the corresponding finite state automata. Yuan et al.'s approach [19] makes use of supervised learning and employs a number of SVMs that have to be trained in advance, which is disadvantageous compared to our unsupervised approach. The advantage of the proposed approach is that neither specialized detectors are required nor training data are needed, while it can achieve very good performance at the same time.

4 Conclusions

In this paper, an unsupervised approach for gradual transition detection has been proposed. The main idea of the approach is to detect gradual transitions by frame dissimilarity measurements at a lower temporal resolution. At lower resolutions, a gradual transition has a similar appearance as cuts in the original temporal resolution. Hence, our unsupervised cut detection approach can also be used for gradual transition detection and has been adapted for this purpose in several ways. To remove false alarms, a state-of-the-art camera motion estimation approach has been used. Experimental results for the presented approach have demonstrated that the approach achieves competitive performance compared to currently best approaches, while our unsupervised approach offers several advantages: First, no training data is needed to learn a model for gradual transitions. Second, the clustering process achieves a decision adaptively for each video in contrast to approaches based on supervised learning or threshold-based approaches. Third, only one specialized transition detector is employed in the approach. Finally, no threshold parameters have to be involved for decision making.

There are several areas for future work. For example, the integration of additional features should be investigated; in particular, multiple pair-wise frame dissimilarity measurements within a sliding window should be analyzed. Furthermore, the selection of frame distances and sliding window sizes should be performed automatically and adaptively for each video. Finally, the temporal subsampling via wavelet analysis is an interesting area for future work.

Acknowledgments. This work is financially supported by the Deutsche Forschungs-gemeinschaft (German Research Foundation, SFB/FK615, Project MT).

References

1. Bescos, J.: Real-Time Shot Change Detection Over Online MPEG-2 Video. IEEE Transactions on Circuits and Systems for Systems and Video Technology 14(4), 475–484 (2004)
2. Chandrashekhara, A., Feng, H.M., Chua, T.-S.: Temporal Multi-Resolution Framework for Shot Boundary Detection and Keyframe Extraction. In: Proceedings of the Eleventh Text Retrieval Conference (TREC 2002), pp. 492–496 (2002), http://trec.nist.gov//pubs/trec11/index.track.html#video
3. Chua, T.-S., Kankanhalli, M., Lin, Y.: A General Framework for Video Segmentation Based on Temporal Multi-Resolution Analysis. In: Proc. of International Workshop on Advanced Image Technology, Fujisawa, Japan, pp. 119–124 (2000)

4. Chua, T.-S., Feng, H.M., Anantharamu, C.: An Unified Framework for Shot Boundary Detection via Active Learning. In: Proc. of IEEE International Conference on Acoustics, Speech and Signal Processing 2003, Hong Kong, Band II, pp. 845–848. IEEE Press, Los Alamitos (2003)

5. Ewerth, R., Freisleben, B.: Video Cut Detection without Thresholds. In: Proc. of 11th Int'l Workshop on Signals, Systems and Image Processing, Poznan, Poland, pp. 227–230 (2004)

6. Ewerth, R., Schwalb, M., Tessmann, P., Freisleben, B.: Estimation of Arbitrary Camera Motion in MPEG Videos. In: Proceedings of the 17th International Conference on Pattern Recognition, Cambridge, UK, vol. I, pp. 512–515. IEEE Press, Los Alamitos (2004)

7. Ewerth, R.: Robust Video Content Analysis via Transductive Learning Methods. Doctoral thesis (2008), http://archiv.ub.uni-marburg.de/diss/z2008/0478/

8. Hanjalic, A.: Shot Boundary Detection: Unraveled and Resolved? IEEE Transactions on Circuits and Systems for Video Technology 12, 533–544 (2002)

9. Lienhart, R.: Comparison of Automatic Shot Boundary Detection Algorithms. In: Image and Video Processing VII 1999, SPIE Proc., vol. 3656(29), pp. 290–301.a (1999)

10. Lienhart, R.: Reliable Transition Detection in Videos: A Survey and Practitioner's Guide. International Journal of Image and Graphics 3, 469–486 (2001)

11. Liu, Z., Zavesky, E., Gibbon, D., Shahraray, B., Haffner, P.: AT&T Research at TRECVID 2007. In: TREC Video Retrieval Online Proceedings (2007), http://www-nlpir.nist.gov/projects/tvpubs/tv7.papers/att.pdf (April 2, 2009)

12. TRECVID: TREC Video Retrieval Evaluation (March 27, 2009), http://www-nlpir.nist.gov/projects/t01v

13. Petersohn, C.: Wipe Shot Boundary Determination. In: Proceedings of IS&T/SPIE Electronic Imaging 2005, Storage and Retrieval Methods and Applications for Multimedia, San Jose, CA, USA, pp. 337–346 (2005)

14. Smeaton, A., Over, P.: TRECVID-2007: Shot Boundary Detection Task Summary (2007), http://www-nlpir.nist.gov/projects/tvpubs/tv7.slides/tv7.sb.slides.pdf (March 27, 2009)

15. Smeaton, A., Over, P., Doherty, A.: Video Shot Boundary Detection: Seven Years of TRECVid Activity. In: Computer Vision and Image Understanding (in press, 2009) (accepted manuscript) (March 26, 2009), ISSN 1077-3142, dio: 10.1016/j.cviu.2009.03.011 (2009)

16. Truong, B.T., Dorai, C., Venkatesh, S.: New Enhancements to Cut, Fade, and Dissolve Detection Processes in Video Segmentation. In: Proc. of ACM Multimedia, pp. 219–227 (2000)

17. Yeo, B.L., Liu, B.: Rapid Scene Analysis on Compressed Video. IEEE Transactions on Circuits and Systems for Video Technology 5(6), 533–544 (1995)

18. Yuan, J., Wang, H., Xiao, L., Zheng, W., Li, J., Lin, F., Zhang, B.: A Formal Study of Shot Boundary Detection. IEEE Transaction on Circuits and Systems for Video Technology 17(2), 168–186 (2007)

19. Yuan, J., Guo, Z., Lv, L., Wan, W., Zhang, T., Wang, D., Liu, X., Liu, C., Zhu, S., Wang, D., Pang, Y., Ding, N., Liu, Y., Wang, J., Zhang, X., Tie, X., Wang, Z., Wang, H., Xiao, T., Liang, Y., Li, J., Lin, F., Zhang, B., Li, J., Wu, W., Tong, X., Ding, D., Chen, Y., Wang, T., Zhang, Y.: THU and ICRC at TRECVID 2007. In: Online Proc. of TRECVID Conference Series 2007, April 2 (2009), http://www-nlpir.nist.gov/projects/tvpubs/tv.pubs.org.html

20. Zheng, W., Yuan, J., Wang, H., Lin, F., Zhang, B.: A Novel Shot Boundary Detection Framework. In: Proceedings of the SPIE. Visual Communications and Image Processing, vol. 5960, pp. 410–420 (2005)

VISRET – A Content Based Annotation, Retrieval and Visualization Toolchain

Levente Kovács, Ákos Utasi, and Tamás Szirányi

Distributed Events Analysis Research Group
Computer and Automation Research Institute, Hungarian Academy of Sciences
Kende u. 13-17, 1111 Budapest, Hungary
{levente.kovacs,utasi,sziranyi}@sztaki.hu
http://web.eee.sztaki.hu

Abstract. This paper presents a system for content-based video retrieval, with a complete toolchain for annotation, indexing, retrieval and visualization of imported data. The system contains around 20 feature descriptors, a modular infrastructure for descriptor addition and indexing, a web-based search interface and an easy-to-use query-annotation-result visualization module. The features that make this system differ from others is the support of all the steps of the retrieval chain, the modular support for standard MPEG-7 and custom descriptors, and the easy-to-use tools for query formulation and retrieval visualization. The intended use cases of the system are content- and annotation-based retrieval applications, ranging from community video portals to indexing of image, video, judicial, and other multimedia databases.

1 Introduction

In the field of content-based multimedia indexing and retrieval research, there are some systems that provide model-based retrieval possibilities in one way or the other. The performance of these systems is highly dependent on the effectiveness of categorization and classification algorithms they contain, yet the most important part from a user's point of view is the ease of use of the query interface and the relevancy of the first N results presented. Easily understandable visualization is also a feature that is usually neglected, which is a mistake, since if the results' relevancy cannot be easily judged the users cannot help in refining the relevancy of these results - which in turn would be important for the researchers.

In this work we present a system that provides a toolset for aspects of storage and retrieval of video data: a tool for annotating videos, scenes, shots, frames and regions, a content server with a flexible backend for descriptor and content import, a user frontend for textual and model-based query formulation and result viewing, and a result visualization module that can present the retrieval results in 2D and 3D with images and point clouds, and provides an interface for creating visual queries based on simple clicking through graphs and videos. As a whole, the system can be used to store and index annotated or non-annotated

J. Blanc-Talon et al. (Eds.): ACIVS 2009, LNCS 5807, pp. 265–276, 2009.
© Springer-Verlag Berlin Heidelberg 2009

video content, perform retrievals based on textual and model-based queries, and visualize the results. We will present all the modules, including the indexing server, and most of the feature descriptors we use.

2   Related Works

We know of some image/video searching solutions, some based on content interpretation, others based on textual searches among annotations (created by hand, by speech-to-text, or from the context of the original source).

The Simplicity engine [1] is one of the most widely known content-based search engines used by many institutions and web sites. It is based on classification of low level features, based mostly on wavelet feature extractors and region matching. The Amico library [2] provides access to a multimedia collection where every element has been imported with complete catalog and metadata information by the partners, and searches are performed over these associated data. [3] provides content-based search based on color and texture content. The VideoQ engine [4] besides textual search provides an intuitive interface to draw an arrangement of regions and colors as a query sketch and provides results which match these sketches. [7] is an image search engine where hashes - fingerprints - are extracted from uploaded images and compared to stored hashes of indexed web images. It is sensitive to rotation and heavy scaling though, and it does not use any content-based features. [8] combines extensive manual tagging and machine learning strategies to categorize movies into classes of mood, tone, structure, also including tagging information like awards and user flags. Other popular image and video search engines like [5,6], although backed by large companies, still do not provide real content based search possibilities. Their services currently rely heavily on textual annotations, some coming from speech-to-text engines, some from manual work, and from text extraction around the video from its original context. Most of these systems exploits only a limited amount - or none - content-based features for retrieval, and this is one of the main issues we try to address here.

The Visret system that we present in this paper - and the tools it consists of - is both similar and different to some of the above engines. Similar in that it provides textual and content-based search possibilities over a video pool. Different in that it has a modular support for standard and non-standard - i.e. new, custom - feature descriptors, all background processing is automatic (feature extractions, indexing), contains versatile annotation and visualization tools, and provides visual query, search and browse possibilities. The main advantage of the presented framework is its flexibility and versatility, its modular architecture provides easy ways of managing, testing, adding new descriptors, and the visual query interface gives more freedom of browsing.

3   The Visret System

The Visret toolchain is a set of backend, fronted, descriptor, indexing, retrieval and visualization tools that when put together, can cover the full process of storage and content-based retrieval of video data. The elements of the system are as follows, for their arrangements see Fig. 1:

- Annotation tool: This tool is a pre-processor for the content server. It contains automatic shot/scene segmentation, and a series of aids for annotating scenes, shots, frames, objects of a video. It can also be extended with modules, e.g. automatic face recognition and annotation. It is an applications running on Microsoft Windows (XP or higher).
- Database and server backend: It provides an administrative interface for importing videos into the database, and adding descriptor modules to the server. The available descriptors all run automatically for the videos and their results get stored in the database. It is implemented as a set of Enterprise JavaBean and Message-Driven Bean modules of a Java EE application on a Sun Glassfish container server and IBM DB2 database server.
- Descriptors: Descriptors are written as separate executables - based on a common template -, and then are imported into the server backend. All imported descriptors are automatically run over the existing videos, and all new imported videos are fed through the descriptors automatically. New ones can easily be added, one just needs to write one conforming to the given template, and provide a metric associated to the new descriptor.
- Indexer: The indexing service builds index trees for all the features and provides a socket-based access for the server to perform content-based queries.
- Web based retrieval interface: An interface for formulating textual queries for searching among annotated contents, and model images for searching based on content similarity. Results are presented in relevancy order, can be played and associated annotations can be viewed. It runs as a JavaServer Faces web module of the JAVA EE application on a Sun Glassfish application server.
- Visualization tool: A tool for viewing 2D distribution of images for any 2 selected descriptors, and 3D point cloud distributions for any 3 selected descriptors, with color-based visualization of associated categories. Any image can be selected as a query, annotations can be viewed and edited, new categories can be assigned and existing ones can be edited. It is currently an application running on Microsoft Windows (XP or higher) but we are working on integrating it into the server frontend as a JavaScript (AJAX) based web application.

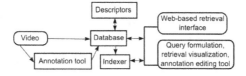

Fig. 1. The Visret toolchain architecture

3.1   Annotation

The VIND (Video INDexer) application is a tool for automatic segmentation of videos into scenes and shots, producing an XML output of the video details. It also provides a set of tools for assigning textual annotations to parts of videos (to the whole video, to scenes, to shots, to frames and objects of a frame). It can be extended with feature extractors, e.g. it automatically extracts representative frames of shots and human faces on frames of a shot, which also get stored in the XML output. The video and the produced annotation can be imported into the database. The most important features of the annotation tool are:

- Automatic shot change detection (cuts, fades, wipes).
  - For this purpose we use shot, fade and wipe detections developed for our archive film restoration system [20]. As an example, shot changes are detected by an optical flow analysis method, based on the analysis of motion estimation errors among frames, For the basic cut detector let $E_{i,t,t+1} = \|b_{,t} - b_{i,t+1}\|$ be the error (e.g. mean square error) between a block b_i of frame t and the same block, being motion compensated from the next frame $t + 1$, that is $b_{i,t+1} - V_{x,y}(b_{i,t})$, $V_{x,y}$ being the motion vector of the ith block, and let $D_i = 1$ if $E_{i,t,t+1} > \gamma$ and 0 otherwise (where γ is a constant). If $\sum_{i=0}^{N} D_i > \varepsilon$ (ε usually is half or two-thirds of the number of blocks) then we signal a shot boundary. This method runs in multiples of real-time on decompressed video frames.
- Automatic representative frame extraction for shots.
  - Representative frames are selected by color histogram analysis. Since in the browsing and retrieval visualization tool these will be the frames standing for each segmented shot, they need to be some average of the shot frames. We chose a color-based selection, for speed and generally good performance. The r-frame will be the one closest to the average histogram of a shot, i.e. $R_i = \underset{j=1...N}{\operatorname{argmin}} \|p_j - \overline{p}\|$, where N is the number of shots, i is the location of the representative frame in shot number j, $p_j(n) = \frac{c_n}{c}$, c is the frame pixels, c_n is a histogram color.
- Automatic face detection (based on [14]).
- Highly visual tools for point-and-click editing (i.e. re-positioning) of scene, shot, and representative frame locations.
- Tools for aiding textual annotation of video structure elements, i.e. whole video, scenes (group of shots), shots, frames, regions (objects), by free text or by pre-defined word collections.

Fig. 2 left shows a screenshot of the main annotation window, with a video loaded, shots detected and displayed in browsing mode. Fig. 2 right shows the region annotation dialog, where rectangular and ellipsoid regions can be defined and textually annotated for further reference and search.

3.2   Indexing

For indexing of the imported video content we need feature descriptors. The descriptors we use are either standard MPEG-7 ones, or ones that we have

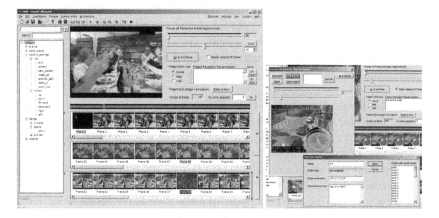

Fig. 2. Left: The main window of the annotation tool, with a loaded video, detected shots, annotation tools. Right: The region (rectangular or ellipsoid) definition and annotation dialog of the annotation tool.

developed. These descriptors are modules added to the server backend, and they automatically run for each imported video, their output being stored in the database, along the corresponding frames and shots of the videos. Some of them run on frames (usually on the representative frames of a shot), others run on image sequences (e.g. motion-based descriptors) which are run for each stored video shot. Each descriptor has an associated distance metric, which is used to tell how one content element relates to the others. Indexing is done based on these descriptors and their metrics. Some of the descriptors we use are:

- AverageColor: extracts color samples from frame regions (blocks).
- AverageMotion: extracts representative motion directions from frame blocks.
- ColorLayout, ColorStructure, DominantColor, EdgeHistogram, Homogenous-Texture, ScalableColor: MPEG-7 color, edge and texture descriptors [9].
- ColorSegments: color segmentation based on MeanShift [12] classification.
- DayNight: a boolean descriptor, decides whether a frame is a day/night shot, based on color distribution and lighting conditions.
- Focus: a relative focus map extractor based on a blind deconvolution approach [10], for obtaining focused areas as a base for indexing [15].
- GrasSky: measures the percentage of grass-like green and sky-like blue color distributions on frames.
- MotionActivity: MPEG-7 motion descriptor, extracts motion-specific information on a region-based approach.
- SiftPoints: SIFT (Scalable Invariant Feature) [11] descriptor, extracts the 128-dimensional features for the SIFT points found on the frame.
- Skin: a Boolean descriptor, decides whether a frame contains skin colors or not; it is based on a statistical learning of possible skin colors.

The indexer builds index-trees for each of the descriptors. The trees we use are customized BK-trees [13], which we will call BK*-trees. The indexer exists as a separate entity, providing a socket-based interface for submitting queries. This is so because we wanted the content server be able to constantly work on newly imported videos, while new indexes are only built once or twice a day and providing the last index structure between re-runs. Thus, both the content server and the indexing service can run in parallel, providing uninterrupted service.

The reason we do not use KD-trees [21] is because KD-trees are best suited for partitioning high dimensional spaces, while our solution build index trees for each descriptor (i.e. dimension), each one having its own metric and distance functions. This is how we can easily combine a lot of different feature descriptors, without the need for common normalization (i.e. joint equal contribution or some logistic regression).

This structure can be used to build quickly searchable index trees for any descriptor which has a metric. We build these trees for every descriptor we use, separately. The query service will then pick up these index trees and perform queries upon them, when requested by the retrieval interface. Naturally, these trees are only able to generate results for a single descriptor at a time, but all of them can be used when performing multi-dimensional queries.

Traditionally BK-trees have been used for string matching algorithms. Essentially they are representations of point distributions in discrete metric spaces. That is, if we have feature points with an associated distance metric, then we can populate a BK*-tree with these points in the following way:

1. Pick one of the points as the root node, R.
2. Each node will have a constant number of M child nodes.
3. A point P_j will be placed into the child node N_i ($i = 0...M - 1$), if $i \cdot \frac{d}{M} < d(P_i, P_j) < (i + 1) \cdot \frac{d}{M}$, where d is the maximum distance that two points can have (respective the associated metric) and P_j is P_i's parent node. Thus, a node will contain a point if its distance from the parent falls into the interval specified above; each node representing a difference interval $[i \cdot d/M; (i + 1) \cdot d/M]$.
4. Continue recursively until there are no more points left to insert.

The performance of these trees is high; results are generated and ordered in 100-3000ms (depending on the features used in a query, Intel Core2 CPU at 2.4GHz) over the ~7000 video shots that we currently have in our database. Our video collection consists of video captures from television broadcasts (news, nature films, cartoons, movie clips, ads, etc.) and surveillance cameras.

However, multi-dimensional queries can also be formulated, by selecting multiple features by which the results should be generated, and the results are retrieved from the hypercube cut out from the N-dimensional space of these features, where the lengths of the cube's sides are determined by user-editable window sizes (which is equivalent with the threshold value t below, as a control mechanism regarding the number of returned results, i.e. a simple more or less choice, based on a relative scale between 0 and 1). See Fig. 3.

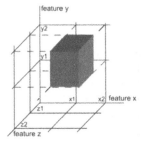

Fig. 3. Retrieving points from a cube of 3D space defined by 3 feature axes

Given a content-based query (Q), the trees are searched for entries similar to the model image or video shot:

1. If $d_0 = d(Q, R) < t$ (t is user-adjustable), the root R element is a result.
2. Let N_i be the children of node P_j ($P_0 = R$), and let $d_k = d(N_k, P_j)$ for the child N_k where

$$\begin{cases} k \cdot \frac{d}{M} \in [d_{j-1} - t, d_{j-1} + t] & \text{or} \\ (k+1) \cdot \frac{d}{M} \in [d_{j-1} - t, d_{j-1} + t] & \text{or} \\ k \cdot \frac{d}{M} \leq d_{j-1} - t \text{ and } (k+1) \cdot \frac{d}{M} \geq d_{j-1} + t \end{cases} \quad (1)$$

   then if $d_k < t$ the element from child N_k is a result.
3. Repeat step 2 recursively until the whole tree is visited.
4. Sort all the results in the increasing order of their d distances and return the ordered result list.

3.3 Retrieval

The retrieval over the stored video content can be done in two ways. First, textual queries can be formulated, when we search among the annotations, and display matching results. Logical combinations (and, or) of full or partial words can be used as query strings. Secondly, model images can be provided either by uploading a query image, or selecting one of the results of a textual query. Results are provided by the indexing service presented above, and results are presented for the user in the order of relevance, i.e. matches with lower distance are put at the front.

Fig. 4 shows two samples of model-based queries and first N results, where two query images have been provided, and the results have been generated by using two features (a color based and an edge based, combined). The resulting images can be clicked on, then the video shots they are associated with pop up and can be played, their annotations can be viewed, and new queries can be formulated by using the specific shot/frame as the model. Fig. 10 shows elements of the retrieval web interface.

We do not wish to detail the retrieval performance of the descriptors in this paper. The performance of the MPEG-7 descriptors we use are known from practical uses and from many literature sources [18,19]. The performance of our relative focus-based descriptor has been detailed in [15]. The evaluation of the other descriptors, and the performance increases of their combined use will be the subject of another paper. For a quick example though, we included Fig. 5, which shows comparison data for six example content-based retrievals. The six retrievals contain single, and combined queries in the following order: 2 (two features), 1 (single feature), 1 (single feature), 2 (two features), 3 (three features), 2 (two features). In the left diagram we show how the precision of the retrievals behave when the in-class precision is measured: if the query image shows a football field with players, the results should also have such a content. The right diagram shows how the prevision of the same retrievals change, when the feature content's precision is measured: if the the query contains a certain color and edge/texture content, the results should also have such a content. The category recognition [16,17] step is what our current on-going research is focused on.

Fig. 4. Top: Query images. Bottom: Results.

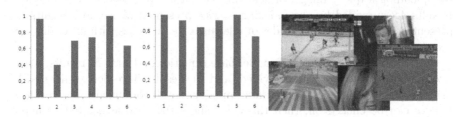

Fig. 5. Precision values for 6 queries. Left: in-class precision, middle: descriptor precision, right: sample query images.

3.4 Visualization

Besides presenting the results in decreasing order of relevance to the user on the web interface above, we created a tool which provides a flexible way for browsing among database shots and images, easily selecting query shots/images, performing textual queries, viewing/editing/assigning annotations and categories to shots/images, 2D and 3D visualization of results and images belonging to a specific category. The main window of the tool is in Fig. 6.

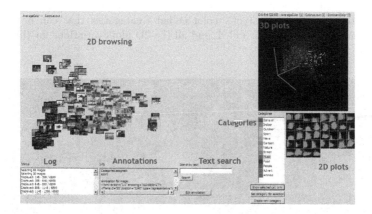

Fig. 6. Main window of the visualization tool, with a subset of the representative frames

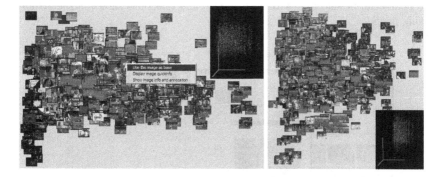

Fig. 7. Selecting any displayed image (left) to be the query, and re-arrange the images with the new image as the base (right)

The most important functions this tool provides are:

– Display the representative frames in a 2D browsing mode where the two axes can be any combination of the available descriptors.
– Images can be zoomed and dragged around.

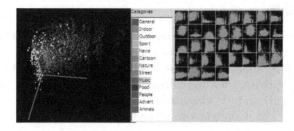

Fig. 8. Left: 3D plot of frame distributions for 3 specific features, different colors mean different categories. Right: List of - color coded - categories that can be assigned, displayed, and new ones can be added; and all the 2D plots variations for the selected features.

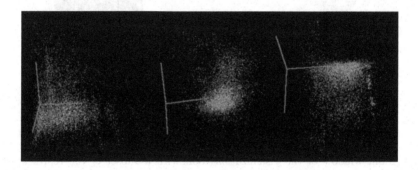

Fig. 9. 3 samples for displaying 3D point cloud distributions of images, any of the descriptors can be selected to be one of the 3 axes. 3D plots can be rotated, zoomed, tilted; points can be selected (with click&move) and selections shown in the 2D image browsing pane.

Fig. 10. Search web interface. Left-to-right: user search window; view video data and annotation; administrative interface with imported videos and descriptors.

- Select any of the displayed images, use them as a query image for a content-based retrieval and re-display the images in a form where this new query image is the base of the 2D representation (Fig. 7).
- View and edit the annotation of any selected image.

- Assign categories to a selection of images, add new categories, edit categories (Fig. 8).
- Display a 3D point cloud of the images (Fig. 9) where colors represent different categories; the axes of the 3D plot can be any combination of the available descriptors; the 3D plots can be zoomed, rotated, points can be selected (larger yellow points in the plot), any selection of images from the 2D view can be displayed in the 3D view as well.
- Display all 2D combinations of descriptor pairs for easy selection (simple point&click) to change the image display perform text queries on the annotations, and the result frames will be displayed in the 2D view.

3.5   Conclusions, Future Work

The system we presented contains a series of tools aiding the import, processing, indexing and querying a video database, and the visualization of the results. For each imported video the descriptors are run automatically, and every newly added descriptor is also automatically run for all previously imported videos, indexing is also automatic. What the system is lacking, is a high level categorization algorithm, which would learn features specific for certain categories, and then automatically classify newly imported videos and shots into the learnt categories. This certainly is a highly desired feature, that we are working on. Still, in its current form, the architecture provides an easy platform for testing new descriptors, already usable for general video retrieval tasks - e.g. judicial media search in one of our projects -, and the performance of the retrieval engine is in the range of milliseconds. We are also working on extending it to support standalone images besides videos, and importing Corel, Microsoft and other image databases into our data pool.

The system can easily be extended with additional descriptors, and the addition of other modalities - e.g. audio - can also easily be done without modifying the elements of the system. We are also working on integrating the visualization tool into the web interface as an AJAX application, and making an instance of the system publically accessible as a community video server.

Acknowledgments. Our work has been partially supported by the JUMAS EU FP7 project, and by the Hungarian Scientific Research Fund under grant number 76159.

References

1. Wang, J.Z., Li, J., Wiederhold, G.: SIMPLIcity: Semantics-sensitive Integrated Matching for Picture LIbraries. IEEE Trans. on Pattern Analysis and Machine Intelligence 23(9), 947–963 (2001)
2. The Art Museum Image Consortium, http://www.amico.org/
3. IBM's Query by Image Content, IBM QBIC, http://wwwqbic.almaden.ibm.com/
4. Chang, S.F., Chen, W., Meng, H.J., Sundaram, H., Zhong, D.: VideoQ: An Automatic Content-Based Video Search System Using Visual Cues. In: Proceedings of ACM Multimedia (1997)

5. Google video search, http://video.google.com/
6. Yahoo video search, http://video.search.yahoo.com/
7. Tineye, http://tineye.com/
8. Jinni, http://www.jinni.com/
9. Manjunath, B.S., Ohm, J.R., Vasudevan, V.V., Yamada, A.: Color and Texture Descriptors. IEEE Tr. on Circuits and Systems for Video Technology 2(6), 703–715 (2001)
10. Kovács, L., Szirányi, T.: Focus Area Extraction by Blind Deconvolution for Defining Regions of Interest. IEEE Tr. on Pattern Analysis and Machine Intelligence 29(6), 1080–1085 (2007)
11. Lowe, D.G.: Object recognition from local Scale-Invariant Features. In: Proceedings of ICCV, pp. 1150–1157 (1999)
12. Comaniciu, D., Meer, P.: Mean Shift: A Robust Approach Toward Feature Space Analysis. IEEE Tr. on Pattern Analysis and Machine Intelligence 24(5), 603–619 (2002)
13. Burkhard, W., Keller, R.: Some Approaches to Best-Match File Searching. In: Proceedings of CACM (1973)
14. Viola, P., Jones, M.: Robust Real-Time Face Detection. International Journal of Computer Vision (IJCV) 57(2), 137–154 (2004)
15. Kovács, L., Szirányi, T.: Evaluation of Relative Focus Map Based Image Indexing. In: Proceedings of CBMI, pp. 181–191 (2007)
16. Ion, A., Stanescu, L., Burdescu, D., Udristoiu, S.: Mapping Image Low-Level Descriptors to Semantic Concepts. In: Proceedings of ICCGI, pp. 154–159 (2008)
17. Fergus, R., Perona, P., Zisserman, A.: Weakly Supervised Scale-Invariant Learning of Models for Visual Recognition. Int. J. Comput. Vision 71(3), 273–303 (2007)
18. Annesley, J., Orwell, J., Renno, J.P.: Evaluation of MPEG7 Color Descriptors for Visual Surveillance Retrieval. In: Proceedings of ICCCN, pp. 105–112 (2005)
19. Ojala, T., Maenpaa, T., Viertola, J., Kyllonen, J., Pietikainen, M.: Empirical Evaluation of MPEG-7 Texture Descriptors with A Large-Scale Experiment. In: Proceeedings of the Workshop on Texture Analysis in Machine Vision, pp. 99–102 (2002)
20. Czúni, L., Hanis, A., Kovács, L., Kránicz, B., Licsár, A., Szirányi, T., Kas, I., Kovács, G., Manno, S.: Digital Motion Picture Restoration System for Film Archives (DIMORF). SMPTE Motion Imaging Journal, 170–178 (May/June 2004)
21. Friedman, J.H., Bentley, J.L., Finkel, R.A.: An Algorithm for Finding Best Matches in Logarithmic Expected Time. ACM Trans. on Mathematical Software 3(3), 209–226 (1977)

Combination of Attributes in Stereovision Matching for Fish-Eye Lenses in Forest Analysis

P. Javier Herrera[1], Gonzalo Pajares[1], María Guijarro[2], J. Jaime Ruz[3], and Jesús M. De la Cruz[3]

[1] Dpto. Ingeniería del Software e Inteligencia Artificial, Facultad de Informática, Universidad Complutense, 28040 Madrid, Spain
[2] Centro Superior de Estudios Felipe II, Ingeniería Técnica en informática de Sistemas 28300 Aranjuez, Madrid, Spain
[3] Dpto. Arquitectura Computadores y Automática, Facultad de Informática, Universidad Complutense, 28040 Madrid, Spain
pjherrera@pdi.ucm.es, pajares@fdi.ucm.es,
mguijarro@cesfelipesegundo.com,
{jjruz,jmcruz}@dacya.ucm.es

Abstract. This paper describes a novel stereovision matching approach by combining several attributes at the pixel level for omni-directional images obtained with fish-eye lenses in forest environments. The goal is to obtain a disparity map as a previous step for determining distances to the trees and then the volume of wood in the imaged area. The interest is focused on the trunks of the trees. Because of the irregular distribution of the trunks, the most suitable features are the pixels. A set of six attributes is used for establishing the matching between the pixels in both images of the stereo pair. The final decision about the matched pixels is taken by combining the attributes. Two combined strategies are proposed: the Sugeno Fuzzy Integral and the Dempster-Shafer theory. The combined strategies, applied to our specific stereo vision matching problem, make the main finding of the paper. In both, the combination is based on the application of three well known matching constraints. The proposed approaches are compared among them and favourably against the usage of simple features.

Keywords: Sugeno Fuzzy Integral, Dempster-Shafer theory, fish-eye stereo vision, Stereovision matching, omni-directional forest images.

1 Introduction

One important task in forests maintenance is to determine the volume of wood in an area for different purposes, including the control of growth of the trees. This task can be carried out by stereovision systems. Fish-eye lenses allow imaging a large sector of the surrounding space with omni-directional vision. This justifies its use.

According to [1] we can view the classical problem of stereo analysis as consisting of the following steps: image acquisition, camera modelling, feature acquisition, image matching, depth determination and interpolation. The key step is that of image

J. Blanc-Talon et al. (Eds.): ACIVS 2009, LNCS 5807, pp. 277–287, 2009.

matching. This is the process of identifying the corresponding points in two images that are cast by the same physical point in the 3-D space. This paper is devoted solely to the matching one. Two sorts of techniques have been used for matching: area-based and feature based [2, 3].

Area-based stereo techniques [4] use correlation between brightness (intensities) patterns in the local neighbourhood of a pixel in one image with brightness patterns in the local neighbourhood of the other image. Also statistical textures can be considered under this category. Feature-based methods [5] use set of pixels with similar attributes, colour, gradient (module and direction) or Laplacian. These are the six attributes available to be used in our matching procedure.

Figure 1(a) displays one omni-directional image (let's say the left one) of the stereo pair captured with a camera equipped with a fish-eye lens. Figure 1(b) displays the signed and expanded area on Figure 1(a). In Figure 1(c) the corresponding area in the right image of the stereo pair is displayed. The different locations of the tree's crowns with respect each camera of the stereovision system produce an important lighting variability between both areas. This is applicable to the whole image. Moreover, as mentioned before, our interest is only focused on the matching of the trunks because they contain basically the wood. One could think about the matching of features such as the trunks themselves, perhaps by exploiting their forms and apparent orientation towards the centre of the image. But this is a complex task because depending on the sun position there are trunks fully and partially illuminated or in shade, this can be observed in the right or left semicircles in the image of figure 1a, respectively. Additionally, only exact vertical trees with respect the image system are imaged oriented toward the centre, but this rarely occurs, i.e. radial explorations do not follow exactly the trunks. Because of this difficulty the segmentation of the trunks as features has been postponed for future research. This is the reason by which this paper is focused on the matching at the pixel level.

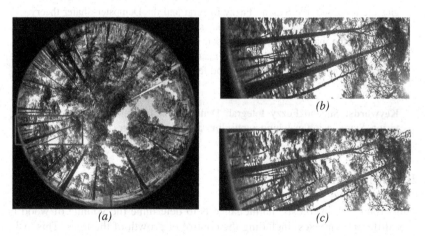

Fig. 1. (a) Omni-directional left image; (b) left expanded area; (c) corresponding right expanded area

The following three stereovision constraints can be applied for solving the matching problem. *Epipolar*: derived from the system geometry, given a pixel in one image its correspondence will be on the called epipolar line. *Similarity*: matched pixels display similar attributes or properties. *Uniqueness*: a pixel in the left image must be matched to a unique pixel in the right one.

Given a pixel in the left image, we apply the epipolar constraint for determining a list of candidates, which are potential matches, in the right image. Each candidate becomes an alternative for the first pixel. We also apply the similarity constraint based on the six attributes mentioned above, obtaining six similarity measures. The final decision about the correct match, among the list of candidates, is made according to the support that each candidate receives by combining the similarity measures. Two strategies are used for the combination: the Sugeno Fuzzy Integral (SFI) paradigm and the Dempster-Shafer (DES) theory. The unique selection made in SFI or DES implies the application of the uniqueness constraint. The combined SFI and DES strategies make the main contribution of this paper. The proposed approaches are compared among them and favourably against the usage of individual attributes catalogued as area-based and feature-based correspondence techniques.

This work is organized as follows. Section 2 describes the design of the matching process; including a brief overview of the SFI paradigm and DES theory. Section 3 describes the results obtained by using the combined SFI and DES approaches, and comparing these results with those obtained by considering the attributes individually. Section 4 presents the conclusions and future work.

2 Design of the Matching Process

2.1 Epipolar: System Geometry

Figure 2 displays the stereo vision system geometry [6]. The 3D object point P with world coordinates with respect to the systems (X_1, Y_1, Z_1) and (X_2, Y_2, Z_2) is imaged as (x_{i1}, y_{i1}) and (x_{i2}, y_{i2}) in image-1 and image-2 respectively in coordinates of the image system; α_1 and α_2 are the angles of incidence of the rays from P; y_{12} is the baseline measuring the distance between the optical axes in both cameras along the y-axes; r is the distance between image point and optical axis; R is the image radius, identical in both images.

According to [7], the following geometrical relations can be established,

$$r = \sqrt{x_{i1}^2 + y_{i1}^2} \; ; \; \alpha_1 = (r90°)/R \; ; \; \beta = tg^{-1}\left(y_{i1}/x_{i1}\right) \tag{1}$$

Now the problem is that the 3D world coordinates (X_1, Y_1, Z_1) are unknown. They can be estimated by varying the distance d as follows,

$$X_1 = d\cos\beta; \quad Y_1 = d\sin\beta; \quad Z_1 = \sqrt{X_1^2 + Y_1^2}\Big/\tan\alpha_1 \tag{2}$$

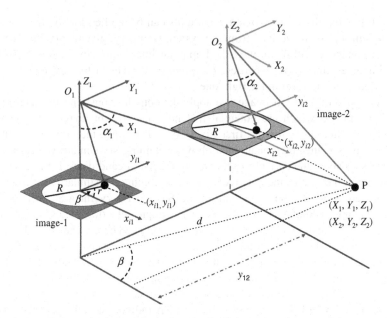

Fig. 2. Geometric projections and relations for the fish-eye based stereo vision system

From (2) we transform the world coordinates in the system $O_1X_1Y_1Z_1$ to the world coordinates in the system $O_2X_2Y_2Z_2$ taking into account the baseline as follows:

$$X_2 = X_1; \quad Y_2 = Y_1 + y_{12}; \quad Z_2 = Z_1 \tag{3}$$

Assuming no lenses radial distortion, we can find the imaged coordinates of the 3D point in image-2 as [7],

$$x_{i2} = \frac{2R\arctan\left(\sqrt{X^2+Y^2}\big/Z_2\right)}{\pi\sqrt{\left(Y_2/X_2\right)^2+1}}; \quad y_{i2} = \frac{2R\arctan\left(\sqrt{X^2+Y^2}\big/Z_2\right)}{\pi\sqrt{\left(X_2/Y_2\right)^2+1}} \tag{4}$$

Because of the system geometry, the epipolar lines are not concentric circumferences and this fact is considered for matching. Figure 3 displays four epipolar lines, in the third quadrant of the right image, which have been generated by the four pixels located at the positions marked with the squares, which are their equivalent locations in the left image.

Using only a camera, we capture a unique image and each 3D point belonging to the line $\overline{O_1P}$, is imaged in (x_{i1}, y_{i1}). So, the 3D coordinates with a unique camera cannot be obtained. When we try to match the imaged point (x_{i1}, y_{i1}) into the image-2 we follow the epipolar line, i.e. the projection of $\overline{O_1P}$ over the image-2. This is equivalent to vary the parameter d in the 3-D space. So, given the imaged point (x_{i1}, y_{i1}) in the image-1 (left) and following the epipolar line, we obtain a list of m

potential corresponding candidates represented by (x_{i2}, y_{i2}) in the image-2 (right). The best match is associated to a distance d for the 3D point in the scene, which is computed from the stereo vision system. Hence, for each d we obtain a specific (x_{i2}, y_{i2}), so that when it is matched with (x_{i1}, y_{i1}) d is the distance for the point P. Different measures of distances during different time intervals (years) for specific points in the trunks, such as the ends or the width of the trunk measured at the same height, allow determining the evolution of the tree and consequently its state of growth and also the volume of wood. This requires that the stereovision system is placed at the same position in the 3D scene and also with the same camera orientation (left camera North and right camera South).

Fig. 3. Epipolar lines in the right image generated from the locations in the left image marked with the squares

2.2 Similarity: Attributes for Area and Feature-Based

Each pixel l in the left image is characterized by its attributes; one of such attributes is denoted as A_l. In the same way, each candidate i in the list of m candidates is described by identical attributes, A_i. So, we can compute differences between attributes of the same type A, obtaining a similarity measure for each one as follows,

$$s_{iA} = \left(1 + |A_l - A_i|\right)^{-1}; \quad i = 1,...,m \qquad (5)$$

$s_{iA} \in [0,1]$, $s_{iA} = 0$ if the difference between attributes is large enough (minimum similarity), otherwise if they are equal ($s_{iA} = 1$, maximum similarity).

As mentioned before, in this paper we use the following six attributes for describing each pixel: a) correlation; b) texture; c) colour; d) gradient magnitude; e) gradient direction and f) Laplacian. Both first ones are area-based computed on a 3×3 neighbourhood around each pixel through the correlation coefficient [8,9,10] and standard deviation [11] respectively. The four remaining ones are considered as feature-based [5]. The colour involves the three red-green-blue spectral components (R,G,B) and the absolute value in the equation (5) is extended as the sum of absolute differences as $|A_l - A_i| = \sum_H |H_l - H_i|$, $H = $ R,G,B. It is a similarity measurement for colour images [9], used satisfactorily in [10] for stereovision matching. Gradient (magnitude and direction) and Laplacian are computed by applying the first and second derivatives [11], over the intensity image after its transformation from the RGB plane to the HSI (hue, saturation, intensity) one. The gradient magnitude has been used in [5,10] and the direction in [5]. Both, colour and gradient magnitude have been linearly combined in [10] producing satisfactory results as compared with the Middlebury test bed [3]. The coefficients involved in the linear combination are computed by testing reliable correspondences in a set of experiments carried out during a previous stage. Based on the conclusions reported in [10], the combination of attributes appears as a suitable approach. SFI and DES can cope specifically with the combination of attributes because they are specifically designed for classifier combination [12]. With a little adjusting they can be used for combining attributes in stereovision matching. They allow making a decision about a unique candidate (uniqueness constraint). This justifies their choice in this paper. We give details about them in section 2.3.

Given a pixel in the left image and the set of m candidates in the right one, we compute the following similarity measures for each attribute A: s_{ia} (correlation), s_{ib} (colour), s_{ic} (texture), s_{id} (gradient magnitude), s_{ie} (gradient direction) and s_{if} (Laplacian). The identifiers in the sub indices identify the attributes according to these assignments. The attributes are the six described above, i.e. $\Omega \equiv \{a,b,c,d,e,f\}$ associated to correlation, texture, colour, gradient magnitude, gradient direction and Laplacian.

2.3 Uniqueness: Combined Strategies

Now we must match each pixel l in the left image with the best of the potential candidates (uniqueness). This is a decision that can be made through the combined SFI paradigm and the DES theory. We describe briefly both approaches.

2.3.1 SFI: Sugeno Fuzzy Integral Paradigm
This paradigm allows combining the individual similarities, which are computed through the equation (5). The SFI requires the computation of the relevance assigned for each attribute, from which we can compute the so-called *fuzzy densities*. This is solved by computing the $\lambda - fuzzy$ measure using the data [12]. The calculation starts with selecting a set of six fuzzy values, g^a, g^b, g^c, g^d, g^e, g^f, each one representing the individual relevance of the associated attribute in Ω.

The value of λ needed for calculating the fuzzy densities g is obtained as the unique real root greater than -1 of the polynomial,

$$\lambda + 1 = \prod_{j \in \Omega} \left(1 + \lambda g^j\right) \tag{6}$$

The individual relevancies for each attribute are computed from the data, as described later in the section 3.1.

Once the g^a, ... g^f are obtained and λ is found, the SFI works as follows:

1. For a given pixel l in the left image, we compute the similarities through the equation (5) between l and every candidate i, with $i = 1,...,m$, obtaining a

column vector as: $[s_{ia}, s_{ib}, s_{ic}, s_{id}, s_{ie}, s_{if}]^T$; without lost of generality assume that s_{ia} is the highest similarity value and s_{if} the lowest. This vector is arranged under this criterion, i.e. $s_{ia} > s_{ib} > s_{ic} > s_{id} > s_{ie} > s_{if}$.

2. Arrange the above fuzzy values correspondingly with the mentioned arrangement, i.e. $g^a, g^b, g^c, g^d, g^e, g^f$ and set the first fuzzy density $g(a) = g^a$.

3. Compute the remaining fuzzy densities,

$$g(b) = g^b + g(a) + \lambda g^b g(a)$$
$$g(c) = g^c + g(b) + \lambda g^c g(b)$$
$$\dots\dots\dots\dots\dots$$
$$g(f) = g^f + g(e) + \lambda g^f g(e)$$

(7)

4. Calculate for each candidate i, the support to be matched with l as,

$$\mu_i(l) = \max_{h \in \Omega}\{\min\{s_{ih}, g(h)\}\}$$

(8)

5. The decision about the best match is made by selecting the maximum support $\mu_i(l)$ among all candidates, but only if this value is greater than a threshold, set to 0.5 in this paper, after trial and error.

2.3.2 DES: Dempster-Shafer Theory

The Dempster-Shafer theory owes its name to works by the both authors in [13] and [14], the method as it is applied in our approach is as follows [12]:

1. In our stereovision matching problem a pixel l is matched correctly or incorrectly. Hence, we identify two classes, which are the class of true matches and the class of false matches, w_1 (true) and w_2 (false). Given a set of samples from both classes, we compute the similarities of the matches belonging to each class according to (5) and build a 6-dimensional mean vector, where its components are the mean values of their similarities, i.e. $\overline{v}_j = \left[\overline{s}_{ja}, \overline{s}_{jb}, \overline{s}_{jc}, \overline{s}_{jd}, \overline{s}_{je}, \overline{s}_{jf}\right]^T$; $\overline{v}_1$ and $\overline{v}_2$ are the mean for w_1 and w_2 respectively. This is carried out during a previous phase, equivalent to the training one in classification problems.

2. Given a candidate i from the list of m candidates for l, we compute the 6-dimensional vector x_i, where its components are the similarity values obtained according to (5) between l and i, i.e. $x_i = \left[s_{ia}, s_{ib}, s_{ic}, s_{id}, s_{ie}, s_{if}\right]^T$. Then we calculate the proximity Φ between each component in x_i and each component in $\overline{v}_j$ based on the Euclidean norm $\|\cdot\|$, equation (9).

$$\Phi_{jA}(x_i) = \frac{\left(1 + \|s_{iA} - \overline{s}_{jA}\|^2\right)^{-1}}{\sum_{k=1}^{2}\left(1 + \|s_{iA} - \overline{s}_{kA}\|^2\right)^{-1}} \quad \text{where } A \in \Omega$$

(9)

3. For every class w_j and for every candidate i, we calculate the belief degrees,

$$b_j^i(A) = \frac{\Phi_{jA}(x_i)\prod_{k \neq j}(1-\Phi_{kA}(x_i))}{1-\Phi_{jA}(x_i)\left[1-\prod_{k \neq j}(1-\Phi_{kA}(x_i))\right]} \; ; \; j = 1,2 \qquad (10)$$

4. The final degree of support that candidate i, represented by x_i, receives for each class w_j taking into account that its math is l is given by,

$$\mu_j(x_i) = \prod_{A \in \Omega} b_j^i(A) \qquad (11)$$

5. We chose as the best match for l, the candidate i with the maximum support received for the class of true matches (w_1), i.e. $\max_i\{\mu_1(x_i)\}$ but only if it is greater than a threshold set to 0.5 in this paper after experimentation, as in the SFI approach.

3 Results

The system is based on the scheme of the figure 2, with a baseline of 1 meter. The cameras are equipped each one with Nikon FC-E8 fisheye lens, with an angle of 183°. The valid colour images in the circle contain 6586205 pixels.

The tests have been carried out with twenty pairs of stereo images. We use four of them for computing the relevance of each attribute for SFI, from which the fuzzy densities can be obtained, and the mean vectors $\bar{v}_1$ and $\bar{v}_2$ for DES. At a second stage, we apply the SFI and DES approaches pixel by pixel for the remainder sixteen stereo pairs, as described respectively in subsections 2.3.1 and 2.3.2.

Our interest consists of determining the disparity of the trees trunks located in an area of 25 m^2 around the stereo vision system.

The disparity is the absolute difference value in sexagesimal degrees, taking into account the imaged circle, between the pixel in the left image and its matched pixel in the right one.

We have available the information of disparities provided by the end users. Thus, for each pixel in a trunk we know its correct disparity value according to this expert knowledge; which allows us to compute the percentage of error. For each one of the sixteen pairs of stereo images used for testing, we compute the disparity error for the trunks and then average these errors among the sixteen pairs of stereo images.

3.1 Computing the Relevancies in SFI and the Mean Vectors for DES

As mentioned before, SFI and DES are suitable for combining classifiers. Both require a previous training to learn some parameters. In classification, SFI learns the relevance for each classifier, so that, during the combination, every classifier intervenes with a specific different weight on the final decision. In our combined SFI stereovision matching approach, we also compute the relevance of each attribute for determining its specific contribution to the decision through the fuzzy densities. The original DES combiner uses decision templates for comparing the new patterns to be classified, in our stereovision matching approach the decision templates are replaced by the mean vectors $\bar{v}_1$ and $\bar{v}_2$. As in [10], although with a different criterion, these vectors and the relevancies are determined by considering a number of reliable true and false matches obtained from the set of four pairs of stereo images used for this purpose. This is carried out as follows, for each pixel in the left images, we compute the disparity with respect its matched pixel in the right ones, but considering each one of the six attributes separately through the equation (5). So, we compute the averaged percentage of error for the four pairs of stereo images and for each attribute, based on the expert knowledge available about the disparities in the trunks. These percentages are: $p_a = 28$ (correlation), $p_b = 10$ (colour), $p_c = 14$ (texture), $p_d = 9$ (gradient magnitude), $p_e = 30$ (gradient direction) and $p_f = 27$ (Laplacian). So, the individual relevancies are computed as $g^h = p_h / \sum_k p_k$, $h, k = a,b,c,d,e,f$. Finally, the fuzzy values are exactly the following: $g^a = 0.150$, $g^b = 0.179$, $g^c = 0.187$, $g^d = 0.189$, $g^e = 0.145$ and $g^f = 0.152$. As one can see, the most relevant attribute is the gradient magnitude.

Also, considering the true and false matches under the expert knowledge, we compute for each attribute the similarity values according to equation (5) and average them for true and false matches, obtaining: $\bar{v}_1 = [0.81, 0.85, 0.92, 0.96, 0.79, 0.80]^T$ and $\bar{v}_2 = [0.12, 0.11, 0.08, 0.07, 0.11, 0.10]^T$ respectively.

3.2 SFI and DES Performances

As before, for each pixel in each one of the sixteen pairs of stereo images, available for testing, we obtain its disparity considering the six attributes separately by applying the equation (5) and a maximum similarity criterion among the m candidates and also by applying the SFI and DES approaches based on maximum supports, given by equations (8) and (11) respectively.

Fig. 4. (*a*) Left image; (*b*) expanded area; (*c*) disparity map obtained by the SFI approach

Figures 4(a) and 4(b) are the same that Figures 1(a) and 1(b) respectively. Figure 4(c) displays the disparity map obtained by the SFI approach in the area. The colour bar shows the disparity level values according to the colour. The disparity map obtained by DES is very similar.

Table 1 displays the averaged percentage of error based on the similarity for the six individual attributes used separately, identified as: (s_a, s_b, s_c, s_d, s_e, s_f). The averaged percentage of error obtained with both, SFI and DES decision making approaches are also displayed. The standard deviations are included.

Table 1. Averaged percentage of errors and standard deviations obtained through maximum similarity criteria for each attribute separately and the SFI and DES decision making approaches

Averaged percentage of error and standard deviations															
s_a		s_b		s_c		s_d		s_e		s_f		DES		SFI	
%	σ	%	σ	%	σ	%	σ	%	σ	%	σ	%	σ	%	σ
30	2.9	16	1.3	18	1.7	14	1.1	35	3.6	32	3.1	**11**	**1.6**	**11**	**1.3**

From results in table 1, one can see that both SFI and DES obtain similar results and outperform the individual similarity based approaches. This means that the combination of similarities between attributes improve the results obtained by using similarities separately. The best individual similarity results are obtained through the similarities provided by the gradient magnitude attribute (s_d). This implies that it is the most relevant attribute. This agrees with its relevance obtained in section 3.1, as it has turned out to be the most relevant attribute.

4 Concluding Remarks

In this paper we have proposed a strategy for stereovision matching, with omni-directional images, in a system equipped with fish-eye lenses. The method applies three well-known constraints (*epipolar*, *similarity* and *uniqueness*) by combining area-based and feature-based matching attributes. For each pixel in the left image a list of possible candidates in the right image is obtained for determining its corre-spondence. The similarity between attributes establishes measures for the matching between each left pixel and its candidates. Under the SFI paradigm and the DES the-ory, we combine the similarities between six attributes and make a decision for choos-ing the unique candidate, if any, for each left pixel. The proposed combined strategies obtain similar results and outperform the methods that use similarities separately.

Although the results achieved can be considered satisfactory, they could be im-proved by applying additional constraints such as *smoothness* or *ordering*, which have been used for matching in conventional stereovision systems.

The proposed combined approaches can be applied to any environment for stereo-vision matching, i.e. obviously classical ones with images captured with lenses under perspective projection. The unique modification consists in the computation of the epipolar lines, which determine where the candidate pixels must be located. In classical stereovision system they are straight and horizontal lines.

Acknowledgements

The authors wish to acknowledge to the Council of Education of the Autonomous Community of Madrid and the Social European Fund for the research contract with the first author. Also to Dr. Fernando Montes, from the Escuela Técnica Superior de Ingenieros de Montes at the Politechnical University of Madrid and to Dra. Isabel Cañellas from the Forest Research Centre (CIFOR, INIA) for his support and the imaged material supplied. To the DPI2006-15661-C02-01 project, a part of the research has been granted by it. Finally, to the anonymous three referees for their valuable comments and suggestions.

References

1. Barnard, S., Fishler, M.: Computational Stereo. ACM Computing Surveys 14, 553–572 (1982)
2. Cochran, S.D., Medioni, G.: 3-D Surface Description from binocular stereo. IEEE Trans. Pattern Anal. Machine Intell. 14(10), 981–994 (1992)
3. Scharstein, D., Szeliski, R.: A taxonomy and avaluation of dense two-frame stereo correspondence algorithms. Int. J. Computer Vision 47(1-3), 7–42 (2002), http://vision.middlebury.edu/stereo/
4. Tang, L., Wu, C., Chen, Z.: Image dense matching based on region growth with adaptive window. Pattern Recognit. Lett. 23, 1169–1178 (2002)
5. Lew, M.S., Huang, T.S., Wong, K.: Learning and feature selection in stereo matching. IEEE Trans. Pattern Anal. Machine Intell. 16, 869–881 (1994)
6. Abraham, S., Förstner, W.: Fish-eye-stero calibration and epipolar rectification. Photogrammetry and Remote Sensing 59, 278–288 (2005)
7. Schwalbe, E.: Geometric Modelling and Calibration of Fisheye Lens Camera Systems. In: Proc. 2nd Panoramic Photogrammetry Workshop, Int. Archives of Photogrammetry and Remote Sensing, vol. 36, Part 5/W8 (2005)
8. Barnea, D.I., Silverman, H.F.: A Class of Algorithms for Fast Digital Image Registration. IEEE Trans. Computers 21, 179–186 (1972)
9. Koschan, A., Abidi, M.: Digital Color Image Processing. Wiley, Chichester (2008)
10. Klaus, A., Sormann, M., Karner, K.: Segmented-Based Stereo Matching Using Belief Propagation and Self-Adapting Dissimilarity Measure. In: Proc. of 18th Int. Conference on Pattern Recognition, vol. 3, pp. 15–18 (2006)
11. Pajares, G., de la Cruz, J.M.: Visión por Computador: Imágenes digitales y aplicaciones, RA-MA (2007)
12. Kuncheva, L.: Combining Pattern Classifiers: Methods and Algorithms. Wiley, Chichester (2004)
13. Dempster, A.P.: A generalization of Bayesian inference. Journal of the Royal Statistical Society B 30, 205–247 (1968)
14. Shafer, G.: A Mathematical Theory of Evidence. Princeton University Press, Princeton (1976)

Image Categorization Using ESFS: A New Embedded Feature Selection Method Based on SFS

Huanzhang Fu[1], Zhongzhe Xiao[1],
Emmanuel Dellandréa[1], Weibei Dou[2], and Liming Chen[1]

[1] Université de Lyon, CNRS
Ecole Centrale de Lyon, LIRIS, UMR5205, F-69134, France
{huanzhang.fu,zhongzhe.xiao,
emmanuel.dellandrea,liming.chen}@ec-lyon.fr
[2] Tsinghua National Laboratory for Information Science and Technology, Department
of Electronic Engineering, Tsinghua University, Beijing, 100084, P.R. China
douwb@mail.tsinghua.edu.cn

Abstract. Feature subset selection is an important subject when training classifiers in Machine Learning (ML) problems. Too many input features in a ML problem may lead to the so-called "curse of dimensionality", which describes the fact that the complexity of the classifier parameters adjustment during training increases exponentially with the number of features. Thus, ML algorithms are known to suffer from important decrease of the prediction accuracy when faced with many features that are not necessary. In this paper, we introduce a novel embedded feature selection method, called ESFS, which is inspired from the wrapper method SFS since it relies on the simple principle to add incrementally most relevant features. Its originality concerns the use of mass functions from the evidence theory that allows to merge elegantly the information carried by features, in an embedded way, and so leading to a lower computational cost than original SFS. This approach has successfully been applied to the domain of image categorization and has shown its effectiveness through the comparison with other feature selection methods.

Keywords: Image Categorization, Feature Selection, Evidence Theory.

1 Introduction

When a classification problem has to be solved, the common approach is to compute a wide variety of features that will carry as much as possible different information to perform the classification of samples. Thus, numerous features are used whereas, generally, only a few of them are relevant for the classification task. Including the other in the feature set used to represent the samples to classify, may lead to a slower execution of the classifier, less understandable results, and much reduced accuracy [1]. In this context, the objective of feature selection is three-fold: improving the prediction performance of the predictors,

J. Blanc-Talon et al. (Eds.): ACIVS 2009, LNCS 5807, pp. 288–299, 2009.

providing faster and more cost-effective predictors, and gaining a deeper insight into the underlying processes that generated the data.

Thus, a feature selection method aims at finding the most relevant features. There exist considerable works in the literature on the question. Interesting overviews include [2][3]. However, the relevance notion is not perfectly defined and may depend on the feature selection method. One of these definitions [4] is to consider that a feature f is relevant if it is incremental useful to a learning algorithm L with respect to a feature subset S: the accuracy that L produces an hypothesis using the feature set $f \cup S$ is higher than the accuracy achieved only using S. In the case of classification problems, the accuracy can be the correct classification rate.

Feature selection methods can be categorized into three main categories according to the dependence to the classifiers: filter approaches, wrapper approaches and embedded approaches [5].

Filter methods include Relief method [6], Focus algorithm [7], Orthogonal Forward Selection [8], and normally evaluate the statistical performance of the features over the data without considering the proper classifiers. The irrelevant features are filtered out before the classification process [1]. Their main advantage is their low computational complexity which makes them very fast. Their main drawback is that they are not optimized to be used with a particular classifier as they are completely independent of the classification stage.

Wrapper methods on the contrary evaluate feature subsets with the classification algorithm in order to measure their efficiency according to the correct classification rate [2]. Thus, feature subsets are generated thanks to some search strategy, and the feature subset which leads to the best correct classification rate is kept. Among algorithms widely used, we can mention Genetic Algorithm (GA) [9][10], Sequential Forward Selection (SFS) [11], Sequential Floating Selection [12] and Oscillating Selection [13]. The computational complexity is higher than the one of filter methods but selected subsets are generally more efficient, even if they remain sub-optimal [14].

In embedded feature selection methods, similarly to wrapper methods, feature selection is linked to the classification stage, this link being in this case much stronger as the feature selection in embedded methods is included into the classifier construction. Some examples of such method are recursive partitioning methods for decision trees such as ID3 [15], C4.5 [16][17] and CART [18], or the recently proposed recursive feature elimination (RFE) approach, which is derived based on the support vector machine (SVM) theory and has shown its good performance for the gene selection [19][20]. Embedded methods offer the same advantages as wrapper methods concerning the interaction between the feature selection and the classification. Moreover, they present a better computational complexity since the selection of features is directly included in the classifier construction during training process.

In our work, we introduce a new embedded feature selection method we have developed and called ESFS, inspired from the wrapper method SFS since it relies on the simple principle to add incrementally most relevant features, and making use of the term of mass function which is introduced from the evidence theory which allows elegantly to merge feature information in an embedded way, leading to a lower computational cost than original SFS. This approach has been evaluated on the problem of image classification and has shown its effectiveness comparing to other feature selection methods.

The rest of this paper is organized as follows. In section 2, we introduce the evidence theory on which our feature selection method is based, and detailed in section 3. Experimental results are presented in section 4. Finally, conclusions and perspectives are drawn in section 5.

2   Overview of the Evidence Theory

In our feature selection scheme, the term "belief mass" from the evidence theory is introduced into the processing of features.

Dempster and Shafer wanted in the 1970's to calculate a general uncertainty level from the Bayesian theory. They developed the concept of "uncertainty mapping" to measure the uncertainty between a lower limit and an upper limit [21]. Similar to the probabilities in the Bayesian theory, they presented a combination rule of the belief masses (or mass function) $m()$.

The evidence theory was completed and presented by Shafer in [22]. It relies on the definition of a set of n hypotheses Ω which have to be exclusive and exhaustive. In this theory, the reasoning concerns the frame of discernment 2^{Ω} which is the set composed of the 2^n subsets of Ω. In order to express the degree of confidence we have in a source of information for an event A of 2^{Ω}, we associate to it an elementary mass of evidence $m(A)$.

The elementary mass function or belief mass which presents the chance of being a true statement is defined as:

$$m : 2^{\Omega} \rightarrow [0,1] .$$ (1)

which satisfies:

$$m(\Phi) = 0 \ and \ \sum_{A \subseteq 2^{\Omega}} m(A) = 1 .$$ (2)

The belief function is defined if it satisfies $Bel(\Phi) = 0$ and $Bel(\Omega) = 1$ and for any collection $A_1...A_n$ of subsets of Ω

$$Bel(A_1 \cup ... \cup A_n) \geq \sum_{I \subseteq \{1...n\}, I \neq \phi} (-1)^{|I|+1} Bel(\cap_{i \in I} A_i) .$$ (3)

The belief function shows the lower bound on the chances, and it corresponds to the mass function with the following formulaes

$$Bel(A) = \sum_{B \subseteq A} m(B) \ \forall \ A \subset \Omega .$$ (4)

$$m(A) = \sum_{B \subseteq A} (-1)^{|A-B|} Bel(B) .$$ (5)

where $|X|$ means the number of elements in the subset X.

The doubt function is defined as $Dou(A) = Bel(\bar{A})$ and the upper probability function is defined as $Pl(A) = 1 - Dou(A)$. The true belief in A should be between $Bel(A)$ and $Pl(A)$.

The Dempster's combination rule can combine two or more independent sets of mass assignments by using orthogonal sum. For the case of two mass functions, let m_1 and m_2 be mass functions on the same frame Ω, the orthogonal sum is defined as $m = m_1 \oplus m_2$, to be $m(\Phi) = 0$, and

$$m(A) = K \sum_{X \cap Y = A} m_1(X) \bullet m_2(Y) . \tag{6}$$

$$K = \frac{1}{1 - \sum_{X \cap Y = \phi} m_1(X) \bullet m_2(Y)} . \tag{7}$$

For the case with more than two mass functions, let $m = m_1 \oplus ... \oplus m_n$. It satisfies $m(\Phi) = 0$ and

$$m(A) = K \sum_{\cap A_i = A} \prod_{1 \leq i \leq n} m_i(A_i) . \tag{8}$$

$$K = \frac{1}{1 - \sum_{\cap A_i = \phi} \prod_{1 \leq i \leq n} m_i(A_i)} . \tag{9}$$

This definition of mass functions from the evidence is used in our model in order to represent the source of information given by each feature, and to combine them easily and to consider them as a classifier whose recognition value is given by the mass function.

3   ESFS Scheme

Recall that an exhaustive search of the best subset of features, leading to explore a space of 2^n subsets, is impractical, we turn to a heuristic approach for the feature selection. The SFS is selected as the basic of our feature selection. For this classifier dependent sub-optimal selection method, we have provided in this work two innovations. First, the range of subsets to be evaluated in the forward process is extended to multiple subsets for each size, and the feature set is reduced according to a certain threshold before the selection in order to decrease the computational burden caused by the extension of the subsets in the evaluation. Second, since the SFS is a classifier dependent method, the concept of belief masses which comes from the evidence theory is introduced to consider the feature as a classifier which leads to an embedded feature selection method.

3.1   Method Overview

Heuristic feature selection algorithm can be characterized by its stance on four basic issues that determine the nature of the heuristic search process. First, one must determine the starting point in the space of feature subsets, which influences the direction of search and operators used to generate successor states. Second decision involves the organization of the search. As an exhaustive search in a space of 2^n feature subsets is impractical, one needs to rely on a more realistic approach such as greedy methods to traverse the space. At each point of the search, one considers local changes to the current state of the features, selects one and iterates. The third issue concerns the strategy used to evaluate alternative subsets of features. Finally, one must decide on some criterion for halting the search. In the following, we bring our answers to the previous four questions.

The SFS algorithm begins with an empty subset of features. The new subset S_k with k features is obtained by adding a single new feature to the subset S_{k-1} which performs the best among the subsets with $k-1$ features. The correct classification rate achieved by the selected feature subset is used as the selection criterion. In the original algorithm of SFS, there are totally $n * (n+1)/2$ subsets which need to be evaluated and the optimal subset may be missing in the searching.

In order to avoid departure too far from the optimal performance, we proposed an improvement of the original SFS method by extending the subsets to be evaluated. In each step of forward selection, instead of keeping only one subset for each size of subsets, a threshold is set according to the compromise between the performance and the computational burden (which is decided according to the performance from experiments with a small amount of data in our work) and all the subsets with the performance above the threshold are kept to enter the evaluation in the next step. Since remaining multiple subsets in each step may lead to heavy computational burden, only the features selected in the first step (subsets with single feature), thus having the best abilities to discriminate among classes that occur in the training data, are used in the evaluation in posterior steps. As the features are added to the potential subsets one by one in the SFS process, the forward process of creating a feature subset with size k can be seen as a combination between two elements: a subset with size $k-1$ and a single feature. Thus, if we consider each subset as a feature itself, the process of creating a new feature subset can be interpreted as generating a new feature from two features.

A wrapper feature selection scheme such as the SFS needs to specify a classifier in order to evaluate improvement of classification accuracy as feature selection criterion. In our case, the classifier used in this feature selection method is simply based on the belief masses of the features which are modeled from the distribution of the features for each class obtained from the training data. The belief masses of samples in the testing set are calculated with the model of the belief masses. The class with the highest belief mass is then taken as the output of the classification. This classifier is repeated for every subset in evaluation for searching the best feature subset. The procedure is detailed in the next subsection.

3.2 Feature Selection Procedure

The feature selection procedure is introduced in this section with its four steps.

Step 1: Calculation of the belief masses of the single features.

Before the feature selection starts, all features are normalized into $[0, 1]$. For each feature,

$$Fea_n = \frac{Fea_{n0} - min(Fea_{n0})}{max(Fea_{n0}) - min(Fea_{n0})} . \tag{10}$$

where Fea_{n0} is the set of original value of the nth feature, and Fea_n is the normalized value of the nth feature.

By definition of the belief masses, the mass can be obtained by different ways which can represent the chance for a statement to be true. In this paper, the PDFs (probability density functions) of the features computed from the training data are used to represent the masses of the single features.

The curves of PDFs of the features are obtained by applying polynomial interpolation to the statistics of the distribution of the feature values from the training data.

Taking the case of a 2-class classifier as example, the classes are defined as subset A and subset A^C. First, the probability densities of the features in each of the 2 subsets are estimated from the training samples by the statistics of the values of the features in each class. We define the probability density of the kth feature Fea_k in subset A as $Pr_k(A, f_k)$ and the probability density in subset A^C as $Pr_k(A^C, f_k)$, where the f_k is the value of the feature Fea_k .According to the probability densities, the masses of feature Fea_k on these two subsets can be defined as

$$m_k(A, f_k) = \frac{Pr_k(A, f_k)}{Pr_k(A, f_k) + Pr_k(A^C, f_k)} . \tag{11}$$

$$m_k(A^C, f_k) = \frac{Pr_k(A^C, f_k)}{Pr_k(A, f_k) + Pr_k(A^C, f_k)} . \tag{12}$$

where at any possible value of the kth feature f_k, $m_k(A, f_k) + m_k(A^C, f_k) = 1$.

In the case of N classes, the classes are defined as $A_1, A_2, ..., A_N$. The masses of feature F_k of the ith class A_i can be obtained as

$$m_k(A_i, f_k) = \frac{Pr_k(A_i, f_k)}{\sum_{n=1}^{N} Pr_k(A_n, f_k)} . \tag{13}$$

which satisfies

$$\sum_{i=1}^{N} m_k(A_i, f_k) = 1 . \tag{14}$$

Step 2: Evaluation of the single features and selection of the initial set of potential features.

When the distribution model of the belief masses of the single features for the different classes have been extracted from the training data, the single features are evaluated by passing the distribution model derived from the training data. For each sample, its belief mass value can be extracted from feature mass functions. The samples are assigned to the class which has the highest belief mass and thus performances of correct classification rates can be obtained.

Within this process, the single features can then be ordered according to the correct classification rate given by mass functions and thus the best features can be selected.

The features are ordered in descending order according to the correct classification rates $R_{single}(F_k)$ as $\{F_{s1}, F_{s2}, ..., F_{sN}\}$, where N means the total number of features in the whole feature set.

In order to reduce the computational burden in the feature selection, an initial feature set FS_{ini} is constructed with the best K features in the re-ordered feature set according to a certain threshold in classification rates as $FS_{ini} = \{F_{s1}, F_{s2}, ..., F_{sK}\}$.

The threshold of the classification rates is decided according to the best classification rate as:

$$R_{single}(F_{s\_K}) \geq thres_{\_1} * R_{best\_1} . \tag{15}$$

where $R_{best\_1} = R_{single}(F_{s\_1})$. In our work of image classification, the threshold value $thres_{\_1}$ is set to 0.7 according to a balance between the overall performance and the calculation time by experiments. This threshold may vary with different problems, and around 100 features are kept in our applications above the threshold of 0.7.

Only the features selected in the set FS_{ini} will attend in the latter steps of feature selection process. The elements (features) in FS_{ini} are seen as subsets with size 1 at the same time.

Step 3: Combination of features for the generation of the feature subsets.

For the iterations with subsets with size $k(k \geq 2)$, the generation of a subset is converted into the creation of a new feature by using an operator of combination from two original features, and the subsets are selected according to a threshold similar to the case with single features for each size of subsets.

We note the set of all the feature subsets in the evaluation with size k as FS_k and the set of the selected subsets with size k as FS_k'. Thus, FS_1 equals to the original whole feature set, and $FS_1' = FS_{ini}$. From $k = 2$, the set of the feature subsets FS_k is noted as:

$$FS_k = Combine(FS_{k-1}', FS_{ini}) = \{Fc0_{1\_k}, Fc0_{2\_k}, ..., Fc0_{N_k\_k}\} . \tag{16}$$

where the function "Combine" means to generate new features by combining features from each of the two sets FS_{k-1}' and FS_{ini} with all the possible combinations except the case in which the element from FS_{ini} appears in the original features during the generation process of the element from FS_{k-1}'; $Fc0_{n\_k}$ represents the generated new features; and N_k is the number of elements in the set FS_k.

The creation of a new feature from two features is implemented by combining the contribution of the belief masses of the two features, making use of an operator of combination. The combining process works as follows.

Assume that N classes are considered in the classifier. For the ith class A_i, the pre-processed mass m^* for the new feature $Fc0_{t\_k}$, which is generated with Fc_{x_k-1} from FS_{k-1}' and Fs_y from FS_{ini}, $Fc0_{t\_k} = Combine(Fc_{x\_k-1}, Fs_y)$, is calculated as

$$m^*(A_i, fc0_{t\_k}) = T(m(A_i, fc_{x\_k-1}), m(A_i, fs_y)) . \tag{17}$$

where f_x is the value of the feature F_x, and $T(x, y)$ is an operator of combination that corresponds to a t-norm operator, being a generalization of the conjunctive 'AND' [27]. The sum of m^*s may not be 1 according to different operators. In order to meet the definition of belief masses, the m^*s can then be normalized as the masses for the new feature:

$$m(A_i, fc0_{t\_k}) = \frac{m^*(A_i, fc0_{t\_k})}{\sum_{n=1}^{N} m^*(A_n, fc0_{t\_k})} . \tag{18}$$

The performance of the combined new feature may be better than both two features in the combination. However, the combined new feature may even performance worse than any of the two original features, which will be eliminated in the selection.

The correct classification rates of the combined new features can be obtained with the belief masses by assigning the class with the highest belief mass to the data samples, and the combined new features can then be ordered in descending order according to the correct classification rates as with the single features:

$$FS_k = \{Fc0_{1\_k}, Fc0_{2\_k}, ..., Fc0_{N_k\_k}\} = \{Fc_{1\_k}, Fc_{2\_k}, ..., Fc_{N_k\_k}\} . \tag{19}$$

The best feature with size k is noted as $Fc_{best\_k} = Fc_{1\_k}$, and the recognition rate of feature Fc_{best_k} is recorded as R_{best_k}.

Similar to the selection of FS_{ini} in the evaluation of the single features, a threshold is set to select a certain number of subsets with size k to take part to the next step of forward selection. The set of the subsets remained is noted as

$$FS'_k = \{Fc_{1\_k}, Fc_{2\_k}, ..., Fc_{N_{0k}\_k}\} . \tag{20}$$

which satisfies $R(Fc_{N_{0k}\_k}) \geq thres\_k * R_{best\_k}$. In order to simplify the selection, the threshold value $thres\_k$ is set in our work to the same value as 0.7 in every step without any adaptation to each step.

Step 4: Stop criterion and the selection of the best feature subset.

The stop criterion of ESFS occurs when the best classification rate begins to decrease while increasing the size of the feature subsets. In order to avoid missing the real peak of the classification performance, the forward selection stops when the classification performance continues to decrease in two steps, $R_{best\_k} < min(R_{best\_k-1}, R_{best\_k-2})$.

4   Experimental Results

The feature selection method proposed in previous section has been evaluated on the problem of image classification.

4.1 Dataset

Our experiments are performed on the SIMPLIcity dataset [25]. It is a subset of the COREL database, formed by 10 image categories, each containing 100 images. For the purpose of validating our ESFS based image categorization approach, 6 categories containing totally 600 images have been chosen in our experiments: Beach, Building, Bus, Flower, Horse, and Mountain. Some sample images are presented in Fig. 1.

Fig. 1. Some sample images from SIMPLIcity dataset (from top to bottom, from left to right, they belong to Beach, Building, Bus, Flower, Horse and Mountain)

4.2 Feature Extraction

A total number of 1056 features have been computed to represent each image sample from SIMPLIcity dataset. The corresponding feature set thus includes Color Auto-Correlogram (CAC), Color Coherence Vectors (CCV), Color Moments (CM), Edge Histogram (EH), Grey Level Co-occurrence Matrix (GLCM) and Texture Auto-Correlation (TAC), which belong to 3 groups respectively: Color features, Texture features and Shape features. The high number of features as compared to the relatively low number of samples available for training classifiers strongly suggests the use of a feature selection method to improve classification accuracy.

4.3 Results

Four groups of experiments have been made on SIMPLIcity dataset: one with all the features without selection, the second with features selected with filter methods, such as fisher filter [23] and principal component analysis (PCA) [26], the third with features selected using a wrapper method, such as SFS, and the last with the best features selected by ESFS.

Five types of one step global classifiers are tested: Multi-layer Perceptron (Neural Network, marked as MP in the following text), Decision Tree (C4.5),

Linear Discriminant Analysis (LDA), K-Nearest Neighbors (K-NN), and multi-class SVM (C-SVC). Each classifier is tested with several parameter configurations, and only the best results are kept. The experiments are carried out on TANAGRA platform [24] with 4-folds cross-validation. The experimental results are listed in Table 1.

Table 1. Comparison between the results without feature selection and with the features selected by different methods

Classification rate	C4.5	LDA	K-NN	MP	C-SVC
No Selection	69.4%	56.8%	80.0%	79.7%	87.3%
Fisher Filter	68.9%	89.2%	79.8%	83.2%	82.9%
PCA	68.3%	85.7%	52.1%	80.5%	51.9%
SFS	69.4%	88.2%	79.5%	80.6%	81.2%
ESFS	**70.8%**	**90.4%**	**83.0%**	**87.1%**	**87.3%**

The features selected by the embedded method ESFS are actually working in a filter way on the several classifiers in this experiment. The results show that for all of the classifiers tested in this experiment, the features selected by ESFS work better than both the original features without selection and the features selected by other methods. We can observe from the table that for certain classifiers, such as K-NN and MP, the superiority of our ESFS is very obvious and presented an improvement from 4% to 8% in the classification rate as compared to other methods. For the other classifiers, ESFS also performed efficiently and showed its advantage. Moreover, focusing in C-SVC, we found that the classification rate of feature selection methods decreased gravely as compared to that of "No Selection" except in the case of ESFS, which performed the same as "No Selection". This phenomenon is probably due to the high ability of SVM in solving the small dataset, high dimensional pattern recognition problems and even in this case, our ESFS approach has still maintained the highest performance. Thus, these experimental results have shown that ESFS is able to select the most discriminative features for the problem of image classification. Moreover, if we compare the computational cost between original SFS and ESFS, as the first one works as a wrapper feature selection method, a training of the classifier (MP for example) needs to be performed for each possible combination of features, at each step of the SFS process, whereas ESFS carry its own classifier thanks to mass functions which are used both for feature combination and decision value, and thus do not need any training during the selection process. So, the computational cost of ESFS is much lower than the one of SFS. Experiments presented previously have been realized on a PC computer equipped with Intel Core Duo T7200/2GHz and 2GB memory using Windows XP system. In this case, the selection process with ESFS takes around 50 minutes whereas the selection by SFS lasts from 8 hours for C-SVC to two weeks for MP.

5   Conclusion and Future Work

In this paper, we have presented a novel feature selection method, ESFS, which relies on the simple principle to add incrementally most relevant features. For this purpose, each feature is represented by a mass function from the evidence theory, which allows to merge the information carried by features in an embedded way, and so leading to a lower computational cost than wrapper method. Experimental results on the problems of image classification shown that selecting relevant features improves the classification accuracy, and for this purpose, ESFS, used as a filter selection method, performs better than the traditional filter method, namely Fisher and PCA algorithm, and wrapper method, namely SFS.

We envisage in our future work to use ESFS as the basis of a hierarchical classifier, which will be represented by a binary classification tree where ESFS will be nodes. The purpose of this hierarchical structure is to allow to better separate classes by first separating classes far away from each other and then concentrating on closer classes. Moreover, thanks to ESFS, each subclassifier could have at its disposal its own feature set.

Acknowledgment

This work is partly supported by the ANR under the project Omnia ANR-07-MDCO-009.

References

1. Hall, M.A., Smith, L.A.: Feature Subset Selection: A Correlation Based Filter Approach. In: International Conference on Neural Information Processing and Intelligent Information Systems, pp. 855–858. Springer, Heidelberg (1997)
2. Kohavi, R., John, G.H.: Wrappers for Feature Subset Selection. Artificial Intelligence 97(1-2), 273–324 (1997); Special issue on relevance
3. Guyon, I., Elisseff, A.: An Introduction to Variable and Feature Selection. Journal of Machine Learning Research 3, 1157–1182 (2003)
4. Blum, A., Langley, P.: Selection of Relevant Features and Examples in Machine Learning. Artificial Intelligence 97, 245–271 (1997)
5. Kojadinovic, I., Wottka, T.: Comparison Between a Filter and a Wrapper Approach to Variable Subset Selection in Regression Problems. In: European Symposium on Intelligent Techniques, Aachen, Germany, September 14-15 (2000)
6. Arauzo-Azofra, A., Benitez, J.M., Castro, J.L.: A Feature Set Measure Based on Relief. In: Proceedings of the 5th International Conference on Recent Advances in Soft Computing, pp. 104–109. Nottingham (2004)
7. Almuallim, H., Dietterich, T.G.: Learning with Many Irrelevant Features. In: Proceedings of the 9th National Conference on Artificial Intelligence, pp. 547–552. AAAI Press, San Jose (1991)
8. Mao, K.Z.: Orthogonal Forward Selection and Backward Elimination Algorithms for Feature Subset Selection. IEEE Transactions on Systems, Man, and Cybernetics, Part B: Cybernetics 34(1), 629–634 (2004)

9. Yang, J.H., Honavar, V.: Feature Subset Selection Using a Genetic Algorithm. IEEE Intelligent Systems 13(2), 44–49 (1998)
10. Huang, J.J., Cai, Y.Z., Xu, X.M.: A Hybrid Genetic Algorithm for Feature Selection Wrapper Based on Mutual Information. Pattern Recognition Letters 28(13), 1825–1844 (2007)
11. Whitney, A.W.: A Direct Method of Nonparametric Measurement Selection. IEEE Transactions on Computers 20(9), 1100–1103 (1971)
12. Pudil, P., Novovičová, J., Kittler, J.: Floating Search Methods in Feature Selection. Pattern Recognition Letters 15(11), 1119–1125 (1994)
13. Somol, P., Pudil, P.: Oscillating Search Algorithms for Feature Selection. In: Proceedings of the 15th International Conference on Pattern Recognition, pp. 406–409 (2000)
14. Spence, C., Sajda, P.: The Role of Feature Selection in Building Pattern Recognizers for Computer-aided Diagnosis. In: Proceedings of SPIE. Medical Imaging 1998: Image Processing, vol. 3338, pp. 1434–1441 (1998)
15. Quinlan, J.R.: Induction of Decision Trees. Machine Learning 1(1), 81–106 (1986)
16. Quinlan, J.R.: C4.5: Programs for Machine Learning. Morgan Kaufmann Series in Machine Learning (1993)
17. Quinlan, J.R.: Improved Use of Continuous Attributes in C4.5. Journal of Artificial Intelligence Research 4, 77–90 (1996)
18. Breiman, L., Friedman, J.H., Olshen, R., Stone, C.J.: Classification and Regression Trees. Chapman & Hall/CRC, Boca Raton
19. Guyon, I., Weston, J., Barnhill, S., Vapnik, V.: Gene Selection for Cancer Classification using Support Vector Machines. Machine Learning 46(1-3), 389–422 (2002)
20. Rakotomamonjy, A.: Variable Selection Using SVM-based Criteria. Journal of Machine Learning Research 3, 1357–1370 (2003)
21. Dempster, A.P.: A Generalization of Bayesian Inference. J. Royal Statistical Soc. Series B 30 (1968)
22. Shafer, G.: A Mathematical Theory of Evidence. Princeton University Press, Princeton (1976)
23. Narendra, P.M., Fukunaga, K.: A Branch and Bound Algorithm for Feature Selection. IEEE Transactions on Computers 26(9), 917–922 (1977)
24. Rakotomalala, R.: TANAGRA: A free software for the education and the research. In: Actes de EGC 2005, RNTI-E-3, vol. 2, pp. 697–702 (2005)
25. Wang, J.Z., Li, J., Wiederhold, G.: SIMPLIcity: Semantics-Sensitive Integrated Matching for Picture Libraries. IEEE Transactions on Pattern Analysis and Machine Intelligence 23(9), 947–963 (2001)
26. Jolliffe, I.T.: Principal Component Analysis. Springer series in statistics (2002)
27. Schweizer, B., Sklar, A.: Probabilistic Metric Spaces. North Holland, New York (1983)

Pattern Analysis for an Automatic and Low-Cost 3D Face Acquisition Technique

Karima Ouji[1], Mohsen Ardabilian[1], Liming Chen[1], and Faouzi Ghorbel[2]

[1] LIRIS, Lyon Research Center for Images and Intelligent Information Systems,
Ecole Centrale de Lyon. 36, av. Guy de Collongue, 69134 Ecully, France
[2] GRIFT, Groupe de Recherche en Images et Formes de Tunisie,
Ecole Nationale des Sciences de l'Informatique, Tunisie

Abstract. This paper proposes an automatic 3D face modeling and localizing technique, based on active stereovision. In the offline stage, the optical and geometrical parameters of the stereosensor are estimated. In the online acquisition stage, alternate complementary patterns are successively projected. The captured right and left images are separately analyzed in order to localize left and right primitives with sub-pixel precision. This analysis also provides us with an efficient segmentation of the informative facial region. Epipolar geometry transforms a stereo matching problem into a one-dimensional search problem. Indeed, we employ an adapted, optimized dynamic programming algorithm to pairs of primitives which are already located in each epiline. 3D geometry is retrieved by computing the intersection of optical rays coming from the pair of matched features. A pipeline of geometric modeling techniques is applied to densify the obtained 3D point cloud, and to mesh and texturize the 3D final face model. An appropriate evaluation strategy is proposed and experimental results are provided.

Keywords: Active stereovision, Amplitude analysis, Biometry, Plastic surgery, Sub-pixel sampling, Dynamic programming, Face segmentation.

1 Introduction

3D acquisition techniques have been applied in several fields such as biometry and facial animation or for aesthetic and plastic surgery, in surgical operation simulation, medical tracking, digital design of facial conformer and custom prosthesis, for example. Among 3D scanning techniques, two main groups are to be distinguished: passive methods and active ones. The techniques in which special lights are not used are called passive methods [1,2,3]. They use only information contained in the images of the scene. Otherwise, methods which use a controlled source of light such as laser or a coded light to recover the 3D information are called active methods. Lights intervene to extract dimensional information and to provide more precise reconstruction than passive methods. Active approaches can be 3D non-contact scanners like laser triangulation based ones. Here, laser rays coming out of a light source hit the object and are captured by a camera

J. Blanc-Talon et al. (Eds.): ACIVS 2009, LNCS 5807, pp. 300–308, 2009.

at different angles, using a rotating mirror. These devices capture highly accurate reconstructions. However, they are expensive and their output is usually noisy, requiring manual editing. In addition, they suffer from the surfaces reflection which generates small unreal variations in the surface of the scanned object [4,5].

The second solution is a structured light based approach in which special light is directed onto the object to be scanned, like the techniques presented in [7,8,9]. This process helps to solve the correspondence problem. When one pattern of light is projected onto the scene to be measured, depth information is extracted by analyzing the pattern deformations. If a set of light patterns is projected, extracting the codeword assigned to each pixel in the images allows the range image to be formed[4]. In this paper we propose a fully automatic and low cost 3D acquisition approach based on active stereovision. It uses a calibrated binocular stereo system assisted by a structured light source to recover 3D geometry. The proposed approach has the advantage of acquiring many images per second without any special synchronization between light source and cameras. It is especially appropriate for the acquisition of a 3D video sequence of non-textured surfaces like the human face or body.

The remainder of the paper is organized as follows: Section (2) describes our 3D reconstruction technique. In Section (3), the automatic face segmentation and primitives extraction process is detailed. In the section (4), we emphasize our evaluation strategy and first results of the developed technique and section (5) concludes the paper.

2   Overview of the Proposed Technique

Our 3D acquisition technique uses a calibrated binocular stereo system assisted by a structured light source. It is a low cost technique which retrieves depth information through a fully automatic procedure. It employs a particular pattern projected with a non invasive light source to deal with non textured surfaces like the human face or body. This provides us with left and right primitives for a given face with sub-pixel precision. The proposed stereo sensor is illustrated in figure 1.

We first calibrate the left and right cameras in order to extract their optical characteristics and geometrical parameters. Second, two complementary patterns with alternate black and white stripes are projected onto the face. The images are rectified through epipolar geometry transformation. Thus corresponding points necessarily have the same Y-coordinate, in rectified images.

Epipolar geometry transforms a stereo matching problem into a unidimensional search problem. Indeed, we employ an adapted, optimized dynamic programming algorithm to pairs of primitives which are already located [4,10]. Continuity, uniqueness and ordering constraints are taken into account within our algorithm. Also, the maximum disparity range is computed regarding the maximum and minimum of depth and geometry of our stereo system. This represents a disparity limit constraint which improves the stereo matching process.

In this paper, we propose to resolve the matching problem through an automatic process for each epiline separately. An amplitude analysis of gray level

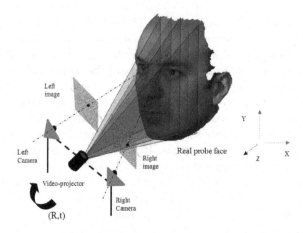

Fig. 1. Proposed stereo sensor

curves provides us with an automatic extraction of left and right primitives with a sub-pixel resolution for each epiline. An efficient 2D segmentation of the informative facial part is also guaranteed by amplitude analysis. Since left and right facial data are sparse and successful stripes projected on a probe face are similar, we propose to search for a reference stripe and to localize it on both left and right images. The light illuminating the facial surface produces some more highly contrasted stripes than others. These stripes are recorded identically by the right and left cameras. The more highly contrasted stripe is identified in the right and left images and used as a reference stripe for more effective stereo matching. The reference stripe should be invariant to lighting and serves mainly as a constraint to enhance the dynamic programming optimization process.

3D geometry is recovered by computing the intersection of optical rays coming from the pair of matched features. A pipeline of geometric modeling techniques is applied to densify the obtained 3D point cloud, and to mesh and texturize the 3D final face model. The stereo matching algorithm, optic triangulation and geometric modeling techniques employed to obtain a 3D reconstructed face are described in more detail in [6]. The next section will focus on primitives extraction and the face segmentation principle based on amplitude analysis. It is the initialisation work for the automatic stereo matching process and 3D information retrieval.

3   Pattern Analysis for Automatic Primitives Extraction and Face Segmentation

The key step in stereo-based approaches is the matching problem that focuses on establishing correspondences between snapshots. In our approach, we rectify images by applying epipolar geometry transformation. This operation reduces the complexity of the matching problem from a bidimensional to a unidimensional search problem. Indeed, matched primitives necessarily have the same Y-coordinate, in rectified images.

(a) Left Image

(b) Inversed Left Image

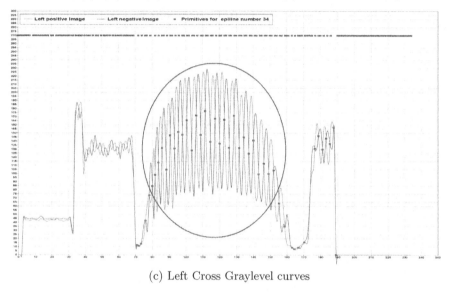

(c) Left Cross Graylevel curves

Fig. 2. Automatic Left Sub-Pixel Sampling Process

Left and right primitives are distinguished by projecting, successively, negative and positive patterns of light on the face. A positive pattern contains black and white stripes and a negative one inverses black stripes position and white ones. For each epiline, we propose to represent and study gray level variation curves corresponding to both a left positive epiline and a left negative one. Figure 2 presents left positive and negative curves and their intersecting points for a given epiline. Pixels which are on the red circle make up the informative facial part. Also, a representation and a study of gray level variation curves is performed for both the right positive epiline and the right negative one. For both left and right sides, intersection points are chosen as the left and right primitives to be matched. This process lets us localize left and right primitives with sub-pixel precision.

Given left and right primitives, our aim is to provide an automatic segmentation of the facial region and to localize automatically a reference stripe for stereo matching. In other words, we need to compute the horizontal coordinate of a reference stripe in both left and right sides.

When the pattern is projected, we try to insure a strong contrast on the informative facial area and a weak contrast on the background of the scanned face as shown in figure 2. The idea is to profit from contrast variation in order to segment given 2D face images and retrieve the informative facial part. Also, it helps us to extract a reference stripe and to carry out a complete automatic 3D face acquisition process.

The facial region from the left and right images is extracted for each epiline separately. The segmentation process aims to extract primitives situated on the facial region for each epiline . Thus, we compute the maximum and minimum for both positive and negative left curves. The amplitude value is computed as the difference between each maximum on the positive left curve with its corresponded minimum computed by the negative left curve, as shown in figure 3. A sliding window is then employed on all amplitude values to identify the first and the last primitives which delimit the face for left images.

The maximum and minimum for both positive and negative right curves are also determined. We calculate the amplitude value between each maximum on the positive right curve with its corresponded minimum computed by the negative right curve as shown in figure 4. A sliding window is employed on all amplitude values to identify the first and the last primitives which delimit the face for right images.

For each epiline, the sliding window identifies the first primitive on the facial region as the first primitive situated after the biggest ascending jump of the amplitude values. The last primitive on the facial region is identified by the sliding window as the first primitive situated before the biggest descending jump of the amplitude values. Sliding window employs first and last primitives computed for the previous epiline to enhance the efficiency of the first and last primitives delimiting the facial region on the current epiline.

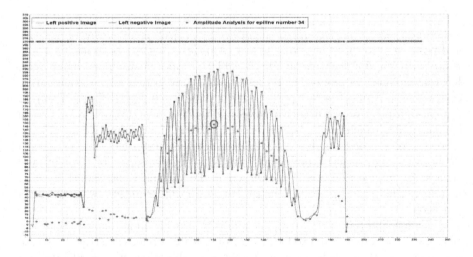

Fig. 3. Amplitude Analysis for Left reference stripe localization

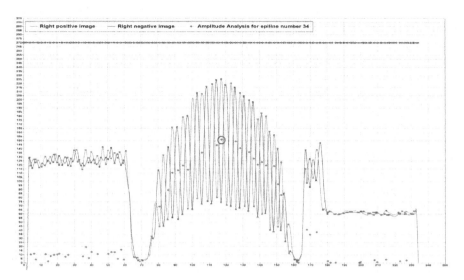

Fig. 4. Amplitude Analysis for Right reference stripe localization

A 2D segmentation step lets us match only primitives which are situated on the facial surface. Thus the matching algorithm is faster, which means it is possible to create a video sequence of a 3D face model in real time. Also, the 2D facial segmentation step minimizes spike generation on the final 3D face model.

To extract a reference stripe, we propose to identify it on one epiline and proceed to localize it on all epilines by using a contour-following principle. To identify a reference stripe on a given epiline, its horizontal coordinate on both left and right sides needs to be computed. The reference stripe coordinate on the left side is localized by the coordinate of the maximum and minimum couple for which the amplitude value is biggest. Amplitude analysis to localize the left reference stripe for a given epiline is illustrated in figure 3. The point which is on the red circle constitutes the reference stripe position for the left side.

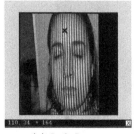

(a) Left Image

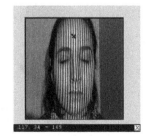

(b) Right Image

Fig. 5. Reference stripe localized on a given epiline

The reference stripe coordinate on the right side is localized by the coordinate of the maximum and minimum couple for which the amplitude value is biggest. Amplitude analysis to localize the right reference stripe for a given epiline is illustrated in figure 4. The point which is on the red circle constitutes the reference stripe position for the right side.

Figure 5 shows the reference stripe position on the left and right sides for current epiline and validates the premise that the left and right positions found correspond to the same stripe on the left and right sides.

4   Evaluation and Experimental Results

Precision computation of 3D scanning technology is based on studying the shape variation between a scanned object and a real one in terms of a given geometric decriptor such as perimeter, surface or curvature. We especially need to study the relation between 3D acquisition system resolution and precision. In fact, raising the number of 3D points calculated from an optical triangulation step provides us with a scanned object nearer to its real shape.

We propose to analyze too the influence of improving camera resolution on the 3D acquisition system resolution. Studying the relation between system resolution and camera resolution and also the relation between camera resolution and system precision is important to evaluate a 3D scanning system. Indeed, the better the camera resolution, the greater the number of 2D points determined from the sampling step. As a result, the number of 3D points computed from optical triangulation is greater. This means that the precision of the 3D acquisition system is higher. So, the 3D model provided by the proposed technique is more faithful to real facial shape. Also, a study of the influence of stripe width on scanning system resolution and precision helps to evaluate the quality of the system. An example of a 3D reconstructed face is illustrated in figure 6.

At present, a plane with a non-reflective surface is used to evaluate the proposed approach. The plane's 3D model is first reconstructed. Second, its theoretical

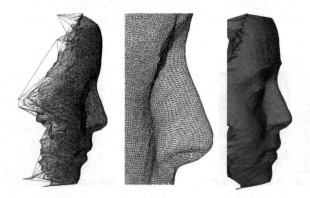

Fig. 6. Final 3D reconstructed model

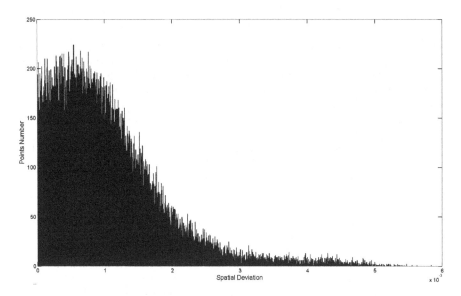

Fig. 7. Spatial Deviation Distribution for a 3D plane scan

equation is calculated using all its 3D point cloud. An orthogonal distance vertex between plane and all its 3D points is created. Such a vertex provides us with global and local information about the efficiency of our 3D reconstruction process.

A mean deviation of 0.0011 mm and a maximum deviation of 0.0058 mm are determined between the scanned 3D point cloud and the plane's theoretical equation. Figure 7 presents the spatial deviation distribution.

5 Conclusion

In this paper, a fully automatic and low cost facial acquisition technique is proposed based on an amplitude analysis of gray level curves. Amplitude analysis provides 2D automatic primitives extraction and segmentation of the informative facial part. As a result, stereo matching includes only primitives which are situated on the facial surface. Thus the matching algorithm is faster, which means a video sequence of a 3D face model can be created in real time.

In our future work, we propose to extend the proposed technique to a 3D video acquisition technique and to evaluate this technique with a phantom object of a known dimension. Moreover, computation of geometric descriptors on a reconstruted face such as curvature or geodesics can be envisaged for biometric and medical purposes.

Acknowledgments. This research is supported in part by the ANR under the French project FAR3D ANR-07-SESU-004.

References

1. Kolev, K., Cremers, D.: Integration of Multiview Stereo and Silhouettes Via Convex Functionals on Convex Domains. In: Forsyth, D., Torr, P., Zisserman, A. (eds.) ECCV 2008, Part I. LNCS, vol. 5302, pp. 752–765. Springer, Heidelberg (2008)
2. Liu, Z., Zhang, Z., Jacobs, C., Cohen, M.: Rapid Modeling of Animated Faces From Video. Journal of Visualization and Computer Animation 12, 227–240 (2001)
3. D'Apuzzo, N.: Modeling human faces with multi-image photogrammetry. In: Proceedings of SPIE, San Jose, California (2002)
4. Ben Amor, B., Ardabilian, M., Chen, L.: Efficient and low-cost 2.5D and 3D face photography for recognition. In: IEEE International Conference on Signal-Image Technology and Internet-based Systems, Yaounde, Cameroun (2005)
5. Blais, F.: Review of 20 years of range sensor development. Journal of Electronic Imaging 13, 231–240 (2004)
6. Ben Amor, B., Ardabilian, M., Chen, L.: An Improved 3D Human Face Reconstruction Approach Based on Cubic Splines Models. In: IEEE Int. Symposium on 3D Data Processing Visualization and Transmission, North Carolina (2006)
7. Garcia, E., Dugelay, J.L., Delingette, H.: Low Cost 3D Face Acquisition and Modeling. In: ITCC, Las Vegas (2001)
8. Zhang, L., Curless, B., Seitz, S.M.: Rapid shape acquisition using color structured light and multipass dynamic programming. In: IEEE Int. Symposium on 3D Data Processing Visualization and Transmission, Padova (2002)
9. Narasimhan, S.G., Koppal, S.J., Yamazaki, S.: Temporal Dithering of Illumination for Fast Active Vision. In: Forsyth, D., Torr, P., Zisserman, A. (eds.) ECCV 2008, Part IV. LNCS, vol. 5305, pp. 830–844. Springer, Heidelberg (2008)
10. Ohta, Y., Kanade, T.: Stereo intra- and interscanline search using dynamic programming. IEEE Trans. PAMI. 7, 139–154 (1985)
11. Ouji, K., Ben Amor, B., Ardabilian, M., Chen, L., Ghorbel, F.: 3D Face Recognition using R-ICP and Geodesic Coupled Approach. In: IEEE International MultiMedia Modeling, Sophia-Antipolis (2009)

Bayesian Pressure Snake for
Weld Defect Detection

Aicha Baya Goumeidane[1], Mohammed Khamadja[2], and Nafaa Naceredine[1]

[1] Welding and NDT Research Centre, Route de Delly Brahim
Cheraga, Algiers, Algeria
ab_goumeidane@yahoo.fr
[2] SP_Lab, Electronics Department, Mentouri University,
Constantine, Algeria
m_khamadja@yahoo.fr

Abstract. Image Segmentation plays a key role in automatic weld defect detection and classification in radiographic testing. Among the segmentation methods, boundary extraction based on deformable models is a powerful technique to describe the shape and then deduce after the analysis stage, the type of the defect under investigation. This paper describes a method for automatic estimation of the contours of weld defect in radiographic images. The method uses a statistical formulation of contour estimation by exploiting statistical pressure snake based on non-parametric modeling of the image. Here the edge energy is replaced by a region energy which is a function of statistical characteristics of area of interest.

Keywords: Snake, images segmentation, pdf estimation, Radiographic images, Non Destructive Inspection.

1 Introduction

Non-destructive testing (NDT) is a branch of engineering concerned with methods of detecting defects in objects without altering the object in any way [1]. Radiography inspection is one of the most important, versatile and widely accepted NDT methods for inspection of weld structures [2],[3]. Radiographic inspection involves the use of penetrating gamma or X-radiation to examine the weld defects and internal features [3].

Conventionally, weld radiographs are checked and interpreted by human experts. However, interpretation of weld radiographs by humans is very subjective, inconsistent, labor-intensive and sometimes biased [4],[5]. Therefore, various automated inspection techniques for weld radiographs were attempted worldwide over the past years.

Computer vision is a key factor for the implementation of total quality within the different processes in industrial automation. Companies that use this technology acquire a competitive advantage because it leads to increased production, an improvement in the quality of products, and a decrease in manufacturing costs as well [6]. The process that allows automated computer vision is known as Automatic Visual Inspection, and its objective is to determine whether a product lies inside or outside the

J. Blanc-Talon et al. (Eds.): ACIVS 2009, LNCS 5807, pp. 309–319, 2009.
© Springer-Verlag Berlin Heidelberg 2009

range of acceptance for a determined manufacturing process. To this end, different techniques for digital image processing are used [7]. Automatic Visual Inspection is a denomination that encompasses a large group of analyses and algorithms that are divided by a series of processing stages among which are; image formation, pre-processing, segmentation, extraction of characteristics and classification.

Segmentation is one of the initial stages within the Automatic Visual Inspection process. Its application allows the initial separation of regions of interest which are subsequently classified. Segmentation is often considered the most complex task in the processing of images [4]. Research in this area is copious but specific to the material being analyzed. In the case of the present investigation, different strategies and methods have been evaluated that centre on the detection of defects in welding images. Segmentation consists of partitioning the image into disjoint regions, where each region is homogenous with respect to a given property, such as texture, grey level, type of colour, etc. with the purpose of separating regions of interest for their posterior recognition [4]Thus, the segmentation problem can be approached with different methods, which generally can be categorized into two types of techniques; those oriented towards the detection of edges, and those oriented towards region detection.

The boundary-based segmentation (which is often referred as edge-based) relies on the generation of a strength image and the extraction of prominent edges, while the region-based segmentation relies on the homogeneity of spatially localized features and properties.

Early approaches for boundary-based image segmentation have used local filtering techniques such as edge detection operators [8],[9]. These approaches are a compromise between simplicity, with accompanying light computational cost and stability under noise, but have difficulty in establishing the connectivity of edge segments. This problem has been confronted by employing variational methods (Active contour).

Active contour or snake model is recognized to be one of the efficient tools for 2D/3D image segmentation, and quickly gained searchers interest following their debut in 1987 [10]. Broadly speaking a snake is a curve which has the ability to evolve (under the influence of internal forces going from within the curves itself and external forces computed from the image data) to match the contour of an object in the image.

The bulk of the existing works in segmentation using active contours models can be categorized into two basic approaches: edge-based approach, and region-based one. The edge-based approaches are called so because the information used to drawn the curves to the edges is strictly along the boundary. Hence, a strong edge must be detected in order to drive the snake (active contour). This obviously causes poor performance of the snake in weak gradient fields. Also, this adds the constraint that the snake must be initially placed near the object of interest, otherwise it might fall into the wrong minima in the gradient field. That is, the approaches laying on this technique are adapted for a certain class of problems, but they fail in the presence of noise. Several improvements have been proposed to overcome these limitations but still they fail in numerous cases [11],[12].

With the region- based ones [13],[14]the inner and the outer region defined by the snake are considered and, thus, they are well- adapted to situation for which it is difficult to extract boundaries from the target. We can note that such methods, which are region-based are computationally intensive since the computations are made over a region (whereas they are made over a boundary in edge-based methods)[15].

In this paper we aim to extract boundaries of weld defects from radiographic images by trying a statistical formulation of active contour estimation by exploiting a statistical pressure snake based on non-parametric modeling of the image.

This paper is organized as follows: in Sec.2 we introduce the mathematic foundation of active contour. In Sec.3 we present how is achieved the detection process. Sec.4 is dedicated to experimental results. We draw the main conclusions in Sec.5

2 Snakes

The active contour model for image segmentation, more communally known as snakes, are characterized by a parametric representation of a contour C(s) which evolves towards certain image features under a force. C(s) is defined as:

$$C(s) = [x(s), y(s)]', s = [0, 1]$$

More precisely, the model moves to minimize the energy

$$E(C) = \int_0^1 \left(E_{int}(C(s)) + E_{Im\,g}(C(s)) + E_{Ext}(C(s)) \right) ds \tag{1}$$

E_{Int} represents the energy of the contour resulting from the internal forces that maintain a certain degree of smoothness and even control point spacing along the curvature of the contour. E_{Img} is the energy content resulting from image forces. Image forces are responsible for driving the contour toward certain image features, such as edges, and are computed based on the image data. Finally, E_{Ext} represents the energy resulting from the external forces, which may or may not be applied, from a high-level source such as a human operator or other high-level mechanisms to maintain certain characteristics of the contour. Allowing the snake to change its shape and position minimizes the total energy of the contour.

In the model proposed by Cohen et al. [16], a pressure force $f(s)$ is added to the snake force as a second external force to push the curve outward or inward. In this way, the curve is considered as a balloon that has been inflated or deflated. Eq.(2) represents the pressure force, where $\vec{n}$ is the normal unit vector to the curve at the point s.

$$f(s) = k.\vec{n}(s) \tag{2}$$

However this formulation leads to the fact that these forces must be initialized to push out or push in, a condition that mandates careful initialization, but has the attractive propriety of pushing any point of the curve forwards or backwards. One has just to choose the appropriate weight of the pressure force k [12].

Hence, a statistical approach to the pressure snake introduced above, resolves the problem of the weight k. Indeed the snake introduced by [17] uses a first order statistic to drive their pressure model and then, the pressure force is given by:

$$f(s) = \left(1 - \frac{|I(s) - \mu|}{k\sigma}\right) \vec{n}(s) \tag{3}$$

μ and σ are the mean and the standard deviation of a user-defined seed region.. It is obvious from Equation (3) that this model assumes a Gaussian distribution for the seed area. From Equation (3), we see that a positive pressure is applied if the distance between the image intensity and the mean is within $k\sigma$ and negative pressure is applied otherwise. Hence, the accurate selection of k is required to obtain good snake performance. It also implies that a negative pressure will be applied to the snake if the local image intensity is outside the $k\sigma$ region, even if that local intensity is vastly different from the background intensity.

A more accurate bayes-based formulation of the statistical pressure force which seems to be more adequate was introduced [17], [18], [19]. This force is given by:

$$f(s) = \left(p(x/B) - p(x/O)\right)\vec{n}(s) \tag{4}$$

where $p(x|O)$ and $p(x|B)$ are the conditional probability density functions of the object and the background respectively. This model overcomes the disadvantages of the previous pressure model of Eq. (3). The model does not make assumptions on the *pdf* of the features of the object.

Also, the model takes into consideration the *pdf* of the background. The problem is reduced to that of accurately estimating both $p(x|O)$ and $p(x|B)$, particularly in the case of non-simple *pdf*s.

3   Weld Defect Detection

To make use of the Bayesian pressure model of Eq. (4), one should have a good estimation of the density function of the image data model. E. Parzen [20] proposed a method to non-parametrically estimating the probability density function from a set of training examples, the image data points in our case.

3.1   Parzen-Window Density Estimation

Parzen-window density estimation is essentially a data-interpolation technique [21]. Given an instance of the random sample, X, Parzen-windowing estimates the Probability Density Function *pdf* P(X) from which the sample was derived. It essentially superposes *kernel* functions placed at each observation. In this way, each observation x_i contributes to the *pdf* estimate. For n observations $\{x_i\}_{i=1}^n$ the Parzen-window estimate is defined as:

$$\hat{P}(x) = \frac{1}{n}\sum_{i=1}^{n}\frac{1}{h}K(\frac{x-x_i}{h}) \tag{5}$$

where $K(x)$ is the window function or kernel in the d-dimensional space such that :

$$\int K(x)dx = 1 \tag{6}$$

and $h>0$ is the window width or bandwidth parameter that corresponds to the width of the kernel. The bandwidth h is typically chosen based on the number of available observations n. The Gaussian *pdf* is a popular kernel for Parzen-window density estimation, being infinitely differentiable and thereby lending the same property to the Parzen-window *pdf* estimate P(X). Indeed the radiographic images are well described by Gaussian distributions [14], that is what motivates us to use Gaussian kernel to have more accurate estimate of the *pdf*. The Gaussian kernel is given by:

$$K(z) = \frac{1}{2\pi} \exp\left(-\frac{z^2}{2}\right) \qquad (7)$$

3.2 Bandwidth Selection

Different kernels generate different shapes of the estimated density. The most important parameter is the so-called bandwidth h, and can be optimized, for example, by cross-validation [22]. The cross-validation method minimizes the integrated squared error. This measure of discrepancy is based on the squared differences $\left\{\hat{f}_h(x) - f(x)\right\}^2$. Averaging these squared deviations over a grid of points $\{x_i\}_{i=1}^n$ leads to:

$$\frac{1}{n}\sum_{i=1}^n \left\{\hat{f}_h(x_i) - f(x_i)\right\}^2 \qquad (8)$$

Asymptotically, if this grid size tends to zero, we obtain the integrated squared error:

$$\int \left\{\hat{f}_h(x) - f(x)\right\}^2 dx \qquad (9)$$

In practice, it turns out that the method consists of selecting a bandwidth that minimizes the cross-validation function.

$$\int \hat{f}_h^2 - 2\sum_{i=1}^n \hat{f}_{h,i}(x_i) \qquad (10)$$

Where $\hat{f}_{h,i}$ is the density estimate obtained by using all data points except for the i-th observation. Both terms in the above function involve double sums. Computation may therefore be slow. There are many other density bandwidth selection methods. Probably the fastest way to calculate this is to refer to some reasonable reference distribution. The idea of using the Normal distribution as a reference, for example, goes back to [23]. The resulting choice of h is called the rule of thumb.

For the Gaussian kernel and a Normal reference distribution, the rule of thumb is to choose:

$$h_G = 1.06 \hat{\sigma} n^{-1/5} \qquad (11)$$

where $\hat{\sigma} = \sqrt{n^{-1}\sum_{i=1}^n (x_i - \bar{x})^2}$ denotes the sample standard deviation. This choice of h_G optimizes the integrated squared distance between the estimator and the true density.

3.3 Snake Progression

Under the hypothesis of conditional independence, we make the model progress by achieving a density estimation at each iteration inside and outside the closed contour S representing the snake (respectively $\hat{p}(x \mid x \in Inside)$ and $\hat{p}(x \mid x \in Outside)$). For each image pixel x falling on a snake node s, $p(x|Inside)$- $p(x|Outside)$ is computed. This will tell if the pixel under investigation should, with respect to the two estimated densities, belong to the set of the image pixels consisting the inside of the curve S or those consisting the outside part of *S*. Hence, if *p(x|Inside)- p(x|Outside)* is positive, it generates a positive pressure and the curve will be inflated and if the result is a negative one, the generated pressure will deflate the snake. Therefore, the curve *S* deforms to perform an aggregation of all the pixels that most likely, belong to the same region, beginning from the initial seed consisting of the pixels inside the initial contour, until achieving the gathering of all the pixels of the defect under investigation.

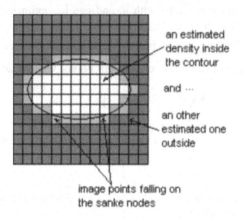

Fig. 1. An example of an observed image and the snake

4   Experimental Results

We have achieved detecting using a non optimized Matlab language on some defect radiographic images. A sample of these images is given below.

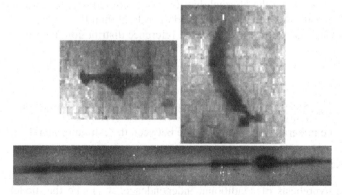

Fig. 2. Test images

Fig. 3. Detected defect

Fig. 4. Background

An example of the computed histogram and the estimated *pdf* performed by Parzen windowing at the last iteration algorithm (detected defect and its background shown above), are illustrated in the figures below.

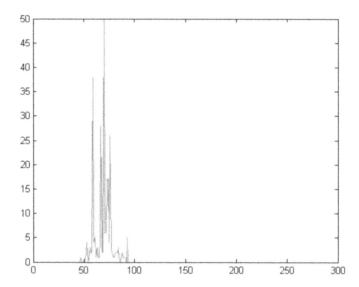

Fig. 5. Histogram of the detected defect

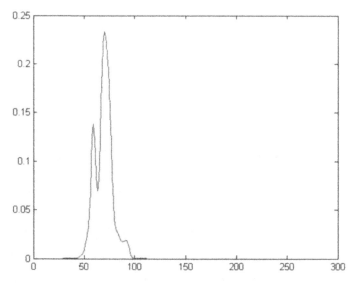

Fig. 6. Estimated *pdf* of the detected defect

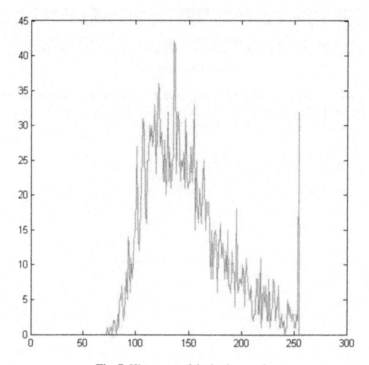

Fig. 7. Histogram of the background

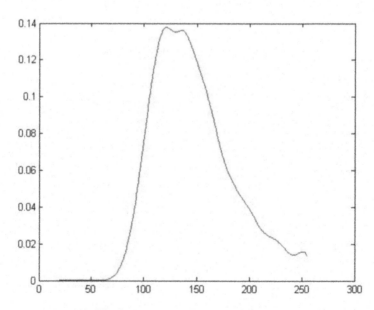

Fig. 8. Estimated *pdf* of the background

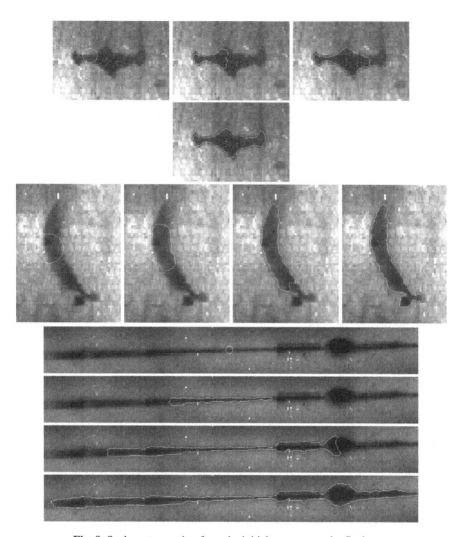

Fig. 9. Snakes progression from the initial contours to the final ones

The results of the snake behaviour are illustrated for the tree test images in Fig.9, where each snake progresses from an initial contour represented by a circle crossing the defect. No assumptions were made, about the images statistics or the defects shapes and statistics, to drive the snake to the defect contours. These snakes show a satisfactory detection of boundaries for three different defect shapes. Indeed this pressure snake shows a good behavior by progression from its initial state and getting closer to the real defect contour till fitting the defect shape in the final state.

To validate these results, we compare them with those obtained by the Maximum likelihood snake developed in [24]. From the point of view of the final contour the two approaches give approximately the same results as shown in Fig.10. However when we checked the execution time, we saw the Bayesian pressure snake is faster

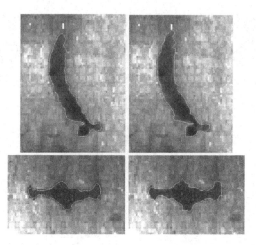

Fig. 10. The comparison of the snakes' results. At left the Bayesian pressure model, at right the Maximum Likelihood one.

then the one developed in [24] even the later gained in progression speed comparatively to the original one [13].

5   Conclusion and Further Works

We have described a new approach for weld defects boundary extraction in radiographic images, based on a statistical pressure snake. Experiments on radiographic images have shown the ability of the model to give a good estimation of the contours by fitting almost concavities. There are several advantages of the approach. First, it does not depend of finding strong gradient fields in the image. Also, the non-parametric estimation approach alleviates the requirement of initializing the function parameters in the case of parametric estimation. Third, the approach takes an advantage from the very accurate estimates of the pdf s obtained by Parzen windows. We mention here that in the case of NDT, the radiographic images may have very similar defect and background pdfs, this because of the small contrast between the background and the weld defect regions, the pronounced granularity due to digitization and the type of film used in industrial radiographic testing and the presence of background gradient of image, characterizing the thickness variation of the irradiated component part. For all these reasons this model can fail, but also all the algorithm based on Bayes theory and all those based on the detection of strong edges to drive the model. For further work we want to model other feature that can differentiate the defects from the background.

References

1. Lawrence, E.B.: Non-destructive Testing Handbook. In: Radiography and Radiation Testing, vol. 3. American Society for Non-destructive Testing (1985)
2. Hayes, C.: The ABC's of Non-destructive Weld Examination. Welding Journal 76(5), 46–51 (1997)

3. De Carvallo, A., et al.: Evaluation of the relevant features of Welding Defects in Radiographic Inspection. Materials Research 6(3), 427–432 (2003)
4. Schwartz, C.: Automatic Evaluation of Welded Joints using Image Processing. In: Conference Proceeding of American Institute of Physics, vol. 657(1), pp. 689–694 (2003)
5. Liao, T.W., Ni, J.: An Automated Radiographic NDT System for Weld Inspection. Part I. Weld Extraction. NDT&E Int. 29(3), 157–162 (1996)
6. González, R., Woods, R.E.: Digital Image Processing. Addison Wesley, USA (1992)
7. Newman, T.S., Jain, A.K.: A survey of automated visual inspection. Computer Vision and Image Understanding 61(2), 231–262 (1995)
8. Canny, J.: A computational approach to edge detection. IEEE Transactions on Pattern Analysis and Machine Intelligence 8, 769–798 (1986)
9. Deriche, R.: Using Canny's Criteria to Derive a Recursively Implemented Optimal edge Detector. International Journal of Computer Vision 1, 167–187 (1987)
10. Kass, M., Witkin, A., Terzopoulos, D.: Snakes: Active Contour Models. Int'l J. Computer Vision, 321–331 (1988)
11. Xu, C., Prince, J.: Snakes, shapes, and gradient vector flow. IEEE Transactions on Images Processing 7(3), 359–369 (1998)
12. Goumeidane, A.B., Khamadja, M., Nacereddine, N., Mekhalfa, F.: Parametric Active Contour for Weld Defects Boundary Extraction in Radiographic testing. In: Proc. of the 8th QCAV SPIE, vol. 63560R (2007)
13. Jardim, S.M.G.V.B., Figuerido, M.A.T.: Segmentation of Fetal Ultrasound Images. Ultrasound in Med. & Biol. 31(2), 243–250 (2005)
14. Nacereddine, N., Hamami, L., Ziou, D.: Probabilistic Deformable Model For Weld Defect Contour Estimation in Radiography. Machine Graphics & Vision 3(4), 547–556 (2006)
15. Chesnaud, C., Réfrégier, P., Boulet, V.: Statistical Region Snake-Based Segmentation Adapted to Different Physical Noise Models. IEEE trans. on PAMI 21(11), 1145–1157 (1999)
16. Cohen, L.D., Cohen, I.: Finite-Element Methods for Active Contour Models and Balloons for 2D and 3D Images. IEEE Trans. Pattern Analysis and Machine Intelligence 15(11), 1131–1147 (1993)
17. Ivins, J., Porrill, J.: Active region models for segmenting medical images. In: Proceedings of the IEEE Internation Conference on Image Processing (1994)
18. Abd-Almageed, W., Smith, C.E.: Mixture models for dynamic statistical pressure snakes. In: IEEE International Conference on Pattern Recognition, Quebec City, Canada (2002)
19. Abd-Almageed, W., Ramadan, S., Smith, C.E.: Kernel Snakes: Non-parametric Active Contour Models. In: IEEE international conference on systems, man and cybernetics, Washington (2003)
20. Parzen, E.: On the estimation of a probability density function and the mode. Ann. Math. Statistics 33, 1065–1076 (1962)
21. Duda, R., Hart, P., Stork, D.: Pattern Classification. Wiley, Chichester (2000)
22. Härdle, W.: Smoothing Techniques, With Implementations in S. Springer, New York (1991)
23. Silverman, B.W.: Density Estimation for Statistics and Data Analysis. Monographs on Statistics and Applied Probability, vol. 26. Chapman and Hall, London (1986)
24. Goumeidane, A.B., Khamadja, M., Nacereddine, N., Mekhalfa, F.: Statistical Deformable Model Based Weld Defect Contour Estimation in Radiographic Inspection. In: Proceedings of the International Conference on Computational Intelligence for Modelling, Control and Automation (CIMCA 2008), pp. 420–425. IEEE Computer Society, Los Alamitos (2008)

Parallel Blob Extraction Using the Multi-core Cell Processor

Praveen Kumar[1], Kannappan Palaniappan[1,*], Ankush Mittal[2],
and Guna Seetharaman[3]

[1] Dept. of Computer Science, Univ. of Missouri, Columbia, MO 65211, USA
[2] Dept. of Elec. and Comp. Eng., Indian Inst. of Tech. Roorkee, 247667, India
[3] Air Force Research Laboratory, Information Directorate, Rome NY 13441, USA

Abstract. The rapid increase in pixel density and frame rates of modern imaging sensors is accelerating the demand for fine-grained and embedded parallelization strategies to achieve real-time implementations for video analysis. The IBM Cell Broadband Engine (BE) processor has an appealing multi-core chip architecture with multiple programming models suitable for accelerating multimedia and vector processing applications. This paper describes two parallel algorithms for blob extraction in video sequences: binary morphological operations and connected components labeling (CCL), both optimized for the Cell-BE processor. Novel parallelization and explicit instruction level optimization techniques are described for fully exploiting the computational capacity of the Synergistic Processing Elements (SPEs) on the Cell processor. Experimental results show significant speedups ranging from a factor of nearly 300 for binary morphology to a factor of 8 for CCL in comparison to equivalent sequential implementations applied to High Definition (HD) video.

1 Introduction

Real-time applications of image and video processing algorithms have seen explosive growth in number and complexity over the past decade driven by demand from a variety of consumer, scientific and defense applications, combined with the wide availability of inexpensive digital video cameras and networked computing devices. Video object detection forms a core stage of visual computing in a number of applications like video surveillance [1], visual biometrics, activity analysis in video [8], smart rooms for video conferencing, visual effects for film, content-based spatial queries [13], tracking of geospatial structures in satellite imagery [17], and segmentation of cells in biomedical imagery [2], all of which have high computational loads, storage and bandwidth requirements. A critically challenging goal for many of these applications is (near) real-time processing frame rates of 20 to 30 fps (frames per second) and high definition (HD) or better spatial image resolution.

---

* This work was partially supported by U.S. Army Research Lab/Leonard Wood Institute award LWI-181223 and U.S. National Institute of Health award R33 EB00573.

New architectures and parallelization strategies for video analysis are being developed due to the increased accessibility of multi-core, multi-threaded processors along with general purpose graphics processing units. For example, IBM's Cell Broadband Engine (BE) is based on an architecture made of eight SPEs delivering an effective peak performance of more than 200 GFlops, using very wide data-paths and memory interchange mechanisms. A good exposition of scientific computing and programming on the Cell BE is provided in[4]. Details of implementing scientific computing kernels and programming the memory hierarchy can be found in [15] and [6], respectively. The potential benefits of multi-core processors can only be harnessed efficiently by developing parallel implementations optimized for execution on individual processing elements requiring explicit handling of data transfers and memory management. The process of refactoring legacy code and algorithms – originally optimized for sequential architectures – to modern multicore architectures invariably requires insight and reanalysis which opens the door for creative innovations in algorithm design, data structures and application specific strategies as demonstrated in this paper.

Research efforts from both academia and industry have shown the strength of the Cell BE for video processing and retrieval [16,9], compression [7,11] and other computer vision applications [5]. However there is not much work reported on parallelizing algorithms/operations for video object detection and extraction on the Cell processor. We have implemented a variety of image and video analysis algorithms including motion estimation, blob segmentation and feature extraction in the context of object detection and tracking using multi-core systems at varied levels of scene complexity and workload. In this paper, we describe our parallel implementation of the morphological processing and connected components labeling (CCL) algorithms for blob extraction optimized for the Cell processor. The rest of the paper is organized as follows: Section 2 gives a brief overview of the moving blob segmentation algorithm and discuss the computation and memory characteristics. Section 3 and 4 gives the detailed description of the proposed parallel implementation for morphological operations and CCL algorithms respectively. Section 5 describes the performance evaluation of our implementation and the speedup achieved followed by the conclusions.

2 Moving Blob Extraction Algorithm

The multistage algorithm for extracting blobs or objects that are moving with respect to their background is briefly outlined below:

1. Motion estimation and detection of foreground/moving regions. This step forms the bulk of computation which varies depending on the complexity and robustness of the motion-estimation algorithm used. We use flux tensor computation [1,3] which consists of (separable) 3-D convolutions for calculating spatio-temporal derivatives, followed by 3-D weighted integration to compute the flux tensor trace. Then, a threshold opertation is applied to create a binary image or mask corresponding to moving regions. In our previous work [12], we parallelized this step on Cell BE and our implementation was benchmarked to process 58 frames/second on HD frame size (1920 × 1080).

2. Consolidation, filtering and elimination using binary morphology. Morphological operations "opening" and "closing" are applied to clean-up spurious responses to detach touching objects and fill in holes for single objects. Opening is erosion followed by dilation and closing is dilation followed by erosion. More details on basic erosion and dilation operator is explained in section 3 in the context of parallel implementation. Opening is applied to remove small spurious flux responses, and closing would merge broken responses. There is high degree of parallelism in this step, and it is computationally expensive step as these operators have to be applied in several passes on the whole image. Therefore, faster parallel implementation is not only intuitive but indispensable for real-time processing.

3. Detection of connected components and postprocessing. In principle, the binary image resulting from Step 2 must have one connected region for each separately moving object. These regions or blobs must be uniquely labeled, in order to uniquely characterize the object pixels underlying each blob. Since there is spatial dependency at every pixel, it is not straightforward to parallelize it. Although the underlying algorithm is simple in structure, the computational load increases with image size and the number of objects – the equivalence arrays become very large and hence the processing time [10]. Furthermore, with all other steps being processed in parallel with high throughput, it becomes imperative to parallelize this step and to avoid it from becoming a bottleneck in the processing stream.

4. Compute image statistics for each blob/object including: bounding box, centroid, area, perimeter etc.

3   Parallel Implementation of Binary Morphological Dilation and Erosion

Morphological operations process an input image by applying a structuring element and producing an output image, where each computed pixel is based on a comparison of the corresponding pixels drawn from the structuring element and the input image. The most basic morphological operations are dilation and erosion; and, both opening and closing are compound operations based on successive application of dilation and erosion. Dilation adds pixels to the boundaries of objects in an image, while erosion removes pixels along object boundaries. The rule for dilation is that the value of the output pixel is the maximum value of all the pixels in the input pixel's neighborhood. In a binary image, if any of the pixels is set to the value 1, the output pixel is set to 1. The rule for erosion is that the value of the output pixel is the minimum value of all the pixels in the input pixel's neighborhood. In a binary image, if any of the pixels is set to 0, the output pixel is set to 0. This is described mathematically as:

$$A \oplus B = \{z | (\hat{B})_z \cap A \neq \emptyset\} \tag{1}$$

$$A \ominus B = \{z | (B)_z \subseteq A\} \tag{2}$$

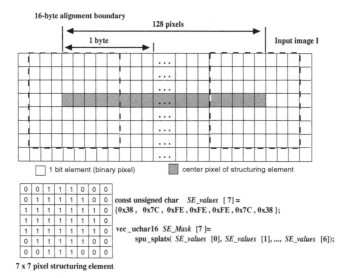

Fig. 1. Structuring element representation and processing on input image

where $\hat{B}$ is the reflection of set B and $(B)_z$ is the translation of set B by point z as per the set theoretic definition.

In a recent paper [14], the authors describe their parallel implementation of morphology using the Cell processor for the OpenCV environment. However, this implementation uses one byte to represent each pixel and thus can process only 16 pixels simultaneously by utilizing the 128-bit SIMD SPE computing unit. Our implementation, for blob processing using a binary input image, represents each pixel by a single bit (packed as bytes) and utilizes bitwise AND/OR SIMD comparison operations to process 128 pixels simultaneously. However, this requires an appropriate bit manipulation strategy for pixel based data access (i.e., bit by bit). The Cell BE processor is optimized for loading data from the local store that is aligned into 128-bit or 16 byte vector cache lines. Thus, it became a challenge to move the required data from local store to the SPU registers.

The data is packed in aligned byte vectors and we execute specialized instructions from SIMD intrinsic library to execute shuffle (*spu_shuffle*) or bit rotate operations (*spu_rlqw*) to access pixel data that is located on arbitrary alignment or the boundary of the 16 byte alignment. The *spu_shuffle* combines the bytes of two vectors as per an organization pattern defined in third vector. The required alignment pattern are stored in static look-up tables in the SPU local store. Figure 1 shows the processing of input image by structuring element and its construction with an example of 7×7 pixel elliptical shaped element. Each row of structuring element is represented using one byte element with appropriate bit pattern stored in a array *values* and which is replicated to 16 byte vector array *Mask* to operate on 128 pixel data of I at once. Figure 2 a) shows how to access a 16 byte aligned vector data (*current*) and its neighbor vector data with one byte shift in left (*previous*)

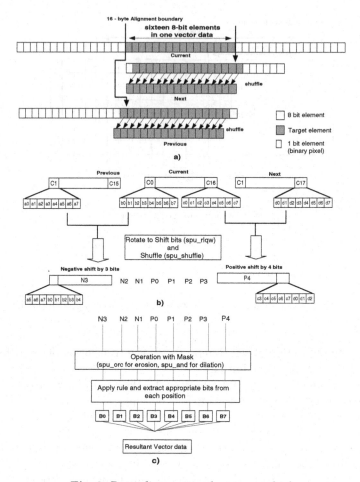

Fig. 2. Data alignment and access method

and right (*next*) direction. Figure 2 b) shows how to get further bit by bit access using bit rotate and shuffle operations and the subsequent comparison operations.

4   Parallel Implementation of CCL

Connected Components Labeling (CCL) scans an image and groups its pixels into components based on pixel connectivity. In the first step, the image is scanned pixel-by-pixel (from top to bottom and left to right) in order to identify connected pixel regions, i.e. regions of adjacent pixels which share the same set of intensity values and temporary labels are assigned. CCL works on binary or graylevel images and different measures of connectivity (4-connectivity, 8-connectivity etc.) are possible. For our blob segmentation, the input is binary image and 8-connectivity measure is considered. After completing the scan, the

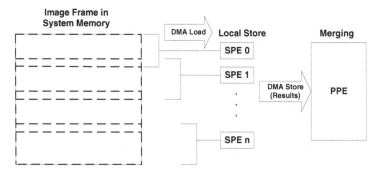

Fig. 3. Parallelization model for connected components labeling on the IBM Cell BE

equivalent label pairs are sorted into equivalence classes and a unique label is assigned to each class. In the final step, a second scan is made through the image, during which each label is replaced with its associated equivalence class label.

The proposed CCL parallelization approach for the Cell architecture belongs to the class of divide-and-conquer algorithms. The PPE runs the main process which divides the image into multiple regions and allocates the labeling task to multiple threads running on SPE's then merges the results from each SPE to generate the final label across the entire image. Each SPE performs DMA data loading from the system memory and labels the allocated region independently. The data can be partitioned into blocks of rows, columns or tiles. Dividing the image data into tiles would increase the number of cases required for the algorithm to handle during merging. Division of the image into blocks of columns allows only one row per DMA transfer requiring a list of DMA request for fetching the entire data. Therefore, dividing the image into blocks of rows is preferred because a bulk of data (several rows) can be transferred per DMA request issue. Some components may span multiple regions, so to ensure that such components get a correct equivalence label in the merge step, each region allocated to one SPE has just one overlapping row with top and bottom adjacent regions. Figure 3 shows the main phases of our parallelization approach.

The resultant array of local labels within each region is put back into main memory through DMA store operation. The PPE uses a list of pointers $Region[i]$ to point to arrays that maintain the local labels with respect to SPE_i. Initially, index for each array element is the local label before equivalence resolution whereas the array element itself is the local label after equivalence resolution in the corresponding regions. Since the labeling starts from value 1, the array location for index 0 is used to store the total number of distinct labels after resolution of equivalence class of labels. To connect each region with its neighboring regions to generate the actual label within the entire image, the PPE updates the array elements in $Region[i]$ by adding the total labels T that reached at the end of $Region[i-1]$. Figure 4 depicts the an example of list of labels for $Region[i]$ which shows that local label 1, 2 and 5 are equivalent with local label 1 and their global label within the entire image is $T+1$; local label 3, 4, and 6 are equivalent with local label 2 and their global label is $T+2$ where T is the total labels reached

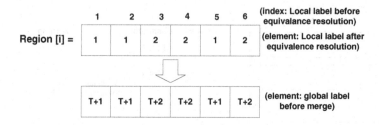

Fig. 4. An example of list of labels in Region[i]

at the end of $Region[i-1]$. While updating the labels in the global list we also need to resolve equivalences of pixel labels for the overlapping row between regions. To do this we use a list of pointers, $OverlapBottom[i]$ and $OverlapTop[i]$ to store the local labels for the overlapping pixel in the bottom and the top row respectively, of the region processed by SPE_i. Now for any pixel k in the overlapping row between regions i and $i-1$, the local labels as calculated by SPE_i and SPE_{i-1} are stored in $OverlapTop[i][k]$ and $OverlapBottom[i-1][k]$ which should be equivalent. We use this information to resolve equivalence of labels across different regions during merge phase of algorithm.

PPE Implementation. The part of the proposed algorithm implemented on the PPE side is presented in Algorithm 1. In the beginning, four buffers are created: $Frame, Region, OverlapTop$ and $OverlapBottom$. These buffers are used to store the frame pixels to be sent to the SPEs and the results obtained from each SPE. The image is divided into N (=number of available SPE's) regions with an overlap of one row at the top and bottom of the region with the adjacent region. The first region and the last region does not have any overlap at the top and bottom respectively. Correspondingly, the address locations in the buffers is determined and send as control block to the SPE thread. The SPE performs DMA operations to load the input data and store the results at these locations. PPE waits for the SPE to finish computing and notify the total number of local labels through mailbox communication. Then it updates the labels by going through each $Region[i]$ one by one, adding the total labels reached till previous region and resolving the equivalence by calling merge function.

SPE Implementation. On the SPE side, the first stage of the algorithm is essentially like any standard sequential algorithm which scans the allocated region of the image pixel by pixel, assigning a temporary label to a new pixel and marks the labels of connected pixels as equivalent. However, the algorithm used to resolve the equivalence class is implemented in a way that utilizes the SIMD instructions. The standard sequential algorithm which efficiently resolves the equivalence class of labels using $Union\text{-}Find$ algorithm by trying to minimize the height of the search tree is not ideal for an SPE implementation which delivers most of its computational capacity by issuing vectorized SIMD instructions.

Algorithm 1. Parallel Connected Components Labeling: PPE side

1: Allocate $Frame, Region, OverlapTop, OverlapBottom$ and control block cb buffer

2: Divide image into N regions along with the overlap
3: **for** each SPE thread i **do**
4:    Create thread i to run on SPE i
5:    Load the control blocks $cb[i]$ with the corresponding address location for $Frame, Region, OverlapTop, OverlapBottom$ buffer to the thread
6: **end for**
7: **for** each SPE thread i **do**
8:    Get Total number of local labels from SPE i mailbox into $Labels[i]$
9:    Wait for thread joining and destroy the context
10: **end for**
11: Initialize total number of labels $T \leftarrow 0$
12: **for** each region i **do**
13:    **for** each label index $j = 1$ to $Labels[i]$ **do**
14:       $Region[i][j] \leftarrow T + Region[i][j]$
15:    **end for**
16:    $T \leftarrow T + Region[i][0]$
17:    **if** region is not first **then**
18:       Call $Merge(i, T, Region, OverlapTop, OverlapBottom)$ function to update global labels and value of T
19:    **end if**
20: **end for**

The choice of an algorithm for implementing an application on SPE depends more on how the operations can be grouped for issuing in SIMD fashion to utilize the 128-bit SIMD units which can operate on 16 8-bit integers, eight 16-bit integers, four 32-bit integers, or four single precision floating-point numbers in a single clock cycle. Hence, we choose an alternative algorithm that resolves equivalences by expressing equivalent relations as a binary matrix and apply the Floyd-Warshall algorithm to obtain transitive closure as shown in Algorithm 2. An interesting point to note in this algorithm is that although it takes $O(n^3)$ OR operations, these can be implemented very efficiently on SPE's using SIMD bitwise OR operations reducing approximately 16 separate OR operations to one packed OR operation. The corresponding vectorized code on SPE side follows:

Listing 1.1. SIMDized SPE Code for Equivalence-Class Resolution

```
for (j=1;j<n;j++){
   for (i=1;i<n;i++){
      if (T[i*n+j]==1){
      vec_uchar16* v1=(vec_uchar16*) &T[i*n];
      vect_uchar16* v2=(vect_uchar16 *) &T[j*n];
         for (k=1;k<size/16;k++){
            v1[k]=spu_or(v1[k],v2[k]);}
} } }
```

Algorithm 2. Floyd-Warshall Algorithm for Equivalence Resolution of Classes

---

Start with $T \leftarrow A$
$n \leftarrow no.of labels$
for each j from 1 to n **do**
  for each i from 1 to n **do**
    if $T(i,j) = 1$ **then**
      for each k from 1 to n **do**
        $T(i,k) = T(i,k) OR T(j,k)$
      end for
    end if
  end for
end for

Due to memory constraints on the local store, only a portion of the image data can be brought into the local store at a time. This required the implementation to handle the spatial dependancy on the previous row pixel, whenever a new block of rows is fetched. This was done by using two arrays *OverlapTop* and *OverlapBottom* to store the labels of the pixels in the top and bottom row for the current block of rows. The bottom row from the previous block of rows needs to be combined with the first row from the next block to check pixel connectivity; likewise the *OverlapBottom* array for the current block of rows is updated to propagate information to the next block of rows. Finally when the scan is complete, *OverlapTop* and *OverlapBottom* arrays are sent to the PPE for use in merging labels in the adjacent block regions. The SPE also sends out the array of labels after resolving label equivalences in the buffer *Region*[i].

5   Experimental Results

We evaluated and measured the execution time of our implementation of morphological processing and connected components labeling on the SONY PS-3 which has only six active Cell SPE processors out of eight. In our experiments with morphological processing, we compared our performance with that reported in Cell OpenCV.The experiment was conducted by using all the 6 SPE's and varying the size and shape of the structuring element. Table 1 shows the measured execution time of one dilation or erosion operation averaged over 10 executions when the input image size is 1024×768. The original code implemented only on the PPE represents the sequential performance baseline and the optimized code implemented on the SPEs represents the parallel performance achieved on the multicore Cell.

An interesting point to note is that for a given size of structuring element, regardless of the structuring element shape our implementation has roughly constant cost, whereas the sequential and OpenCV implementations become significantly slower as reflected in Table 1. This is because our representation of the structuring element uses the same number of bits for a given window size irrespective of shape which has a dramatic impact on the morphology computation

Table 1. Comparison of execution time of one Erosion/Dilation operation and showing speed up with respect to the sequential implementation

Structuring Element		PPE original optimized code(ms)	Proposed SPE code		Cell OpenCV performance (ms)	
Size	Shape		Time (ms)	Speedup	Time (ms)	Speedup
7 x 7	Ellipse	89.806	0.311	289.6	0.973	92.4
5 x 5		47.74	0.290	164.6	0.562	84.9
3 x 3		16.324	0.261	62.5	0.308	52.9
7 x 7	Rectangle	24.235	0.310	78.2	0.337	71.9
5 x 5		18.782	0.280	67.1	0.289	64.9
3 x 3		14.341	0.260	55.2	0.276	51.9

for elliptical structuring elements. As shown in Table 1, our implementation successfully achieved very high speed up ratios (ranging from about 55 times to 290 times faster for different workload sizes) outperforming the reported Cell OpenCV benchmarks. The speedup increased for larger sized structuring elements i.e., as the amount of computation increased.

For evaluating our implementation of the connected components labeling algorithm, we compared the performance with different versions of the sequential and parallel code. We implemented sequential code using *Union-Find* algorithm (called *sequential_UnionFind*) and *Floyd-Warshall* algorithm (called *sequential_FW*) for execution only on the PPE. The experimental results for proposed parallel connected components labeling algorithm are presented with and without SIMD instructions for resolution of equivalence class labels, called *parallel_CCL* and *parallel_CCL_SIMD* respectively, with execution on PPE and all 6 SPE's. Figure 5 shows the results for four different implementations of the CCL algorithm on different sized images, with the number of regions set to 250 and the total amount of foreground pixels set to 30% for all images. It was observed that *sequential_FW* gave better performance than *sequential_UnionFind*

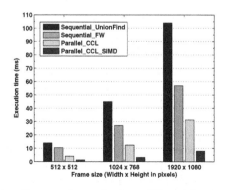

Fig. 5. Execution time per frame for four different implementations of CCL

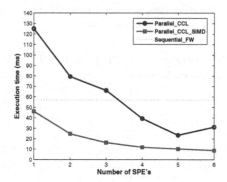

Fig. 6. Variation in parallel CCL performance across different number of SPEs

probably because branch instructions and recursions in *sequential_UF* code are not efficiently supported for execution. The average speedup for the parallel implementation without using SIMD instructions is about 2 times, increasing to 8 times with SIMD instructions. Figure 6 shows how the parallel performance scales as the number of SPES is varied. It can be observed that the execution time for the parallel implementation without SIMD instructions is greater than the serial execution time up to 3 SPEs due to the overhead of thread creation, data communication, merging the results, etc. which does not scale up linearly for a low number of SPE cores. Moreover the variation is not smooth as the total time is bounded by the maximum of the execution time over all SPEs. By varying the number of SPE's, the data partitioning area/boundary changes, which can cause increase or decrease in the number of regions and foregrounds pixels to be processed by any SPE depending on the distribution pattern in the image. This also explains the unexpected increase in the execution time for 6 SPE's as compared to 5. However, the optimized performance using SIMD instructions is always superior to the sequential version and scales up consistently with increasing number of SPE's.

6   Conclusions

This paper describes parallel algorithms for binary image morphology and connected components labeling suitable for SPMD multi-core architectures such as the Cell processor. The binary morphology operations were optimized for execution on the Cell SPE by representing each pixel as a single bit (packed into bytes) and utilizing bitwise comparison using AND/OR SIMD operations to process 128 pixels simultaneously. Novel bit level data access and alignment techniques for Cell BE were proposed in this context. The parallelization approach for the proposed CCL Cell implementation required a customized data partitioning and merging algorithm split between the SPEs and the PPE respectively using a fast SIMD version of the Floyd-Warshall equivalence resolution algorithm that was superior to the standard Union-Find search algorithm. Our implementation using 6 SPEs achieves a speedup of up to 290 times for processing erosion/dilation operation using 7×7 pixel-sized elliptical structuring element with input images of 1024×768 and a speed up of about 8 times for connected components labeling on input images of 1920×1080 with 250 regions and 30% foreground pixels. Our future work will examine implementations on other multi-core architectures like GPUs as well as parallelizing other video processing tasks like normalized cross-correlation for image registration.

References

1. Bunyak, F., Palaniappan, K., Nath, S., Seetharaman, G.: Flux tensor constrained geodesic active contours with sensor fusion for persistent object tracking. J. Multimedia 2(4), 20–33 (2007)

2. Bunyak, F., Palaniappan, K., Nath, S.K., Baskin, T.I., Dong, G.: Quantitative cell motility for *in vitro* wound healing using level set-based active contour tracking. In: Proc. 3rd IEEE Int. Symp. Biomed. Imaging (ISBI), April 2006, pp. 1040–1043 (2006)

3. Bunyak, F., Palaniappan, K., Nath, S.K., Seetharaman, G.: Geodesic active contour based fusion of visible and infrared video for persistent object tracking. In: IEEE Workshop Applications of Computer Vision (WACV 2007), page Online (2007)

4. Buttari, A., Luszczek, P., Kurzak, J., Dongarra, J., Bosilca, G.: A rough guide to scientific computing on the Playstation 3. Technical Report UT-CS-07-595, Innovative Computing Laboratory, University of Tennessee Knoxville (2007)

5. Chen, T.P., Budnikov, D., Hughes, C.J., Chen, Y.-K.: Computer vision on multicore processors: Articulated body tracking. In: IEEE Int. Conf. Multimedia and Expo., pp. 1862–1865 (2007)

6. Fatahalian, K., Knight, T.J., Houston, M., Erez, M., Horn, D.R., Leem, L., Park, J.-Y., Ren, M., Aiken, A., Dally, W.J., Hanrahan, P.: Sequoia: Programming the memory hierarchy. In: Proc. ACM/IEEE Conf. Supercomputing (2006)

7. Hidemasa, M., Munehiro, D., Hiroki, N., Yumi, M.: Multilevel parallelization on the Cell/B.E. for a motion JPEG 2000 encoding server. In: Proc. 15th Int. Conf. Multimedia, pp. 942–951 (2007)

8. Kolekar, M.H., Palaniappan, K., Sengupta, S., Seetharaman, G.: Semantic concept mining based on hierarchical event detection for soccer video indexing. J. Multimedia (2009)

9. Liu, L., Kesavarapu, S., Connell, J., Jagmohan, A., Leem, A., Paulovicks, L., Sheinin, B., Tang, V.L., Yeo, H.: Video analysis and compression on the STI Cell Broadband Engine processor. In: IEEE Int. Conf. Multimedia and Expo. (2006)

10. Manohar, M., Ramapriyan, H.K.: Connected component labeling of binary images on a mesh connected massively parallel processor. Computer Vision, Graphics, and Image Processing 45(2), 133–149 (1989)

11. Momcilovic, S., Sousa, L.: A parallel algorithm for advanced video motion estimation on multicore architectures. In: Int. Conf. Complex, Intelligent and Software Intensive Systems, pp. 831–836 (2008)

12. Palaniappan, K., Kumar, P., Ersoy, I., Davis, S.R., Bunyak, F., Linderman, M., Seetharaman, G., Linderman, R.: Parallel flux tensor for real-time moving object detection. Submitted to International Conference on Image Processing (2009)

13. Shyu, C.R., Klaric, M., Scott, G., Barb, A., Davis, C., Palaniappan, K.: GeoIRIS: Geospatial information retrieval and indexing system – content mining, semantics, modeling, and complex queries. IEEE Trans. Geoscience and Remote Sensing 45(4), 839–852 (2007)
14. Sugano, H., Miyamoto, R.: Parallel implementation of morphological processing on cell/be with opencv interface. In: 3rd Int. Symp. Communications, Control and Signal Processing, pp. 578–583 (2008)
15. Williams, S., Shalf, J., Oliker, L., Kamil, S., Husbands, P., Yelick, K.: Scientific computing kernels on the Cell processor. Int. J. Parallel Progrm. 35, 263–298 (2007)
16. Yu, J., Wei, H.: Video processing and retrieval on cell processor architecture. In: Ma, L., Rauterberg, M., Nakatsu, R. (eds.) ICEC 2007. LNCS, vol. 4740, pp. 255–262. Springer, Heidelberg (2007)
17. Zhou, L., Kambhamettu, C., Goldgof, D., Palaniappan, K., Hasler, A.F.: Tracking non-rigid motion and structure from 2D satellite cloud images without correspondences. IEEE Trans. Pattern Analysis and Machine Intelligence 23(11), 1330–1336 (2001)

Quality Fusion Rule for Face Recognition in Video

Chao Wang, Yongping Li, and Xinyu Ao

The center for Advanced Detection and Instrumentation, Shanghai Institute of Applied Physics,
Chinese Academy of Science, 201800 Shanghai, China
{wangchao,ypli,aoxinyu}@sinap.ac.cn

Abstract. Face recognition in video is confronted with many problems: varying illumination, pose and expression. Their compensation algorithms may produce much noise and make face abnormal, which degrade the face image quality. In this paper, motivated by human cognitive process, a quality fusion rule is designed to reduce the influence of compensated face image quality that may affect recognition performance. Combined with video features and the recognition contribution degrees of compensated face image, the rule fuses the recognition result of every face video frame to opt best result. In this paper, quality fusion rule for illumination compensation is mainly involved. In the experiment, the proposed quality fusion rule is evaluated on a face video database with varied illumination. In contrast to other state-of-the-art methods, the novel approach has better recognition performance.

1 Introduction

Face recognition systems, when used in conjunction with Closed-Circuit Television (CCTV) surveillance video, are expected to offer a partially accurate means to identify potential terrorists and criminals. They operate by comparing video captured faces against law enforcement databases.

However, in many real mass transit places, the recognition result is not satisfying. For example, the face recognition system set up in Logan Airport of Boston, had never correctly identified a single face in its database of suspects, let alone resulted in any arrests. Research [1] shows that face recognition systems sometimes failed to recognize people after some time has elapsed, because of changes in environmental illumination and face pose and expression. Correspondingly, some compensation algorithms [2-4] were proposed in recent years. But the compensated results also have several defects, include (i) much noise may be added in it and (ii) the faces may change abnormally, which lead to the quality decline of face image.

Many research results have shown that quality measures as auxiliary information can improve the face recognition performance. Adler et al. [5] employed log-linear fit of quality to genuine scores, for which quality measures are continues. However, the scores and quality measures may result in a more complex classifier, thus having a higher chance of overfitting the training data. Josef Kittler and Norman Poh [6] proposed a fusion paradigm where the quality measures are quantized into a finite set of discrete quality states. The scores are achieved by the posteriori probability of a quality state given the observed quality measures.

J. Blanc-Talon et al. (Eds.): ACIVS 2009, LNCS 5807, pp. 333–342, 2009.

In this paper, a quality fusion rule is presented in details and experimental results show its superiority when compared with other existed approaches. The rest of paper is organized as follow: Motivated by human brain cognitive system [7], an illumination quality fusion rule is proposed in Section 2. Experiments are presented in Section 3, and finally, the conclusion and discussion are given in Section 4.

2 Illumination Quality Fusion Rule

2.1 Illumination Classification

Based on Lambert's illumination model [8] and the theory of linear illumination subspace [9], Lee et al. [10] concluded that the face illumination space can be expressed well by five to nine face illumination images, as this number of images results in the lowest error rate for face recognition.

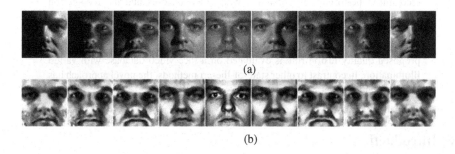

(a)

(b)

Fig. 1. Samples of cropped faces in YaleB face database. The azimuth angles of the lighting of images from left to right column are: -85o, -70o, -50°, -35°, 0°, 35°, 50°, 70° and 85°, respectively. The corresponding elevation angles are: 20°, -35°, -40°, 15°, 0°, 15°, -40°, -35° and 20°, respectively. Note: (0°,0°) is regarded as even illumination (central image). (a) original images; (b) illumination compensation result.

In this paper, nine face images are chosen as the face illumination subspace in which to realize the illumination compensation. According to the position of light source, the nine face images can be selected from (φ, θ): (0°,0°), (68°,-90°), (74°,108°), (80°,52°), (85°,-42°), (85°,-137°), (85°,146°), (85°,-4°), (51°,67°). φ is the azimuth angle and θ is the elevation angle. In our approach, the YaleB database (*Yale University, 2001*) is used as reference, which includes ten persons; everyone has sixty four frontal face images with different lighting conditions. Nine kinds of angles are selected from the frontal faces of the YaleB database, which are close to φ and θ. The angles are listed as follows: (-85°,20°), (-70°,-35°), (-50°,-40°), (-35°,15°), (0°,0°), (35°,15°), (50°,-40°), (70°,-35°), (85°,20°) (the angles set is called LSP Set in this paper, the order is unchanged, see Fig. 1(a)). So the lighting conditions can be divided into nine categories rather than sixty four categories, which can reduce the computational complexity.

2.2 Generation of Weights

Illumination compensation [2] can improve face recognition in varying illumination, but it also produces much noise (for example, see Fig. 1(b)). Face images already compensated illumination can be graded according to their image quality. Each grade corresponds to a weight.

In this paper, we present two approaches to calculate the weights. One is principal component analysis (PCA) algorithm and cosine distance (CSD), where PCA belongs to global feature approaches; the other is active appearance model (AAM) [11] and bidimensional regression (BDR) [12], where AAM involves geometry feature approaches.

2.2.1 Generation of Weights via PCA and CSD

We select YaleB face database to obtain the weights. For the database, there are ten persons. Each person has a frontal and even illumination face image (see Fig. 2). The ten face images are used as training data to calculate PCA space. All the 640 samples, which are divided into nine categories according to their illumination direction, are regarded as testing data.

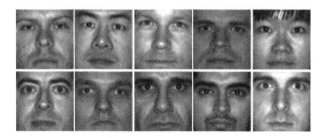

Fig. 2. Normal face images in YaleB database

Let u_j represents the training feature vector of the jth person and $v_{j_i}^{k}$ $\left(i=1,\cdots,9; j=1,\cdots,10; k=1,\cdots,C_i^j\right)$ represents the kth testing feature vector of the jth person under the ith illumination, where $i=1,\cdots,9$ are in correspondence with the order of LSP Set and C_i^j represents the number of the testing samples of the jth person under the ith illumination (Here $C_i^j=7$ ($i=1,\cdots,9$ and $i\neq5$, $j=1,\cdots,10$), $C_5^j=8$ ($j=1,\cdots,10$)).

Then cosine distance (CSD) can be used to calculate the weights. The corresponding formula is as follows:

$$w_{PCi}^{j} = \sum_{k=1}^{C_i^j} \left| v_{j_i}^{k} \cdot u_j \middle/ \left\| v_{j_i}^{k} \right\| \left\| u_j \right\| \right| \middle/ C_i^j \tag{1}$$

$$w_{PCi} = \sum_{j=1}^{10} w_{PCi}^{j} \middle/ 10 \tag{2}$$

where $w_{PC_i}^{\ j}$ represents the weight value of the jth person under the ith illumination, w_{PC_i} represents the weight value under the ith illumination (via PCA and CSD).

2.2.2 Generation of Weights via AAM and BDR

For this approach, we also use YaleB face database to obtain the weight values. A set of geometry feature points (GFPs) is extracted from each image by AAM (see Fig. 3).

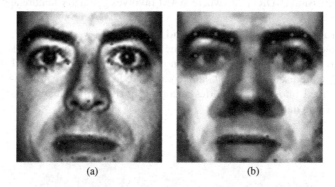

(a)   (b)

Fig. 3. (a) GFPs map of the face under light source $(0°,0°)$; (b) GFPs map of the face under light source $(-35°,15°)$

Let $Z_{j_i}^{\ k} = \left(x_{j_i}^{\ k}, y_{j_i}^{\ k}\right)$ $\left(i = 1,\cdots,9; j = 1,\cdots,10; k = 1,\cdots,C_i^{\ j}\right)$ represents the kth 2D GFPs testing feature vector of the jth person under the ith illumination, where $x_{j_i}^{\ k}$ denotes the abscissa vector of GFPs, $y_{j_i}^{\ k}$ denotes the ordinate vector of GFPs, i and $C_i^{\ j}$ are the same meaning with that in Eq. (11) and (12). $Z_{j_i}^{\ k}$ is similar to $v_{j_i}^{\ k}$, but $Z_{j_i}^{\ k}$ is a 2D vector, the elements of which represent geometric position coordinates of feature points.

BDR can be viewed as a mechanism for comparing the degree of resemblance between two planar configurations of points and, more generally, for comparing the geometric configurations of independent and dependent 2D variables. Therefore, we can calculate the similarity between any two 2D vectors by BDR. The weight value equals to the similarity, which is described as follows:

$$w_{ABi}^{\ j} = \sum_{k=1}^{C_i^j} BDR\left(Z_{j_i}^{\ k}, u_j\right)\Big/C_i^{\ j} \tag{3}$$

$$w_{ABi} = \sum_{j=1}^{10} w_{ABi}^{\ j}\Big/10 \tag{4}$$

where $BDR(\cdot)$ represents BDR calculation, $w_{AB_i}^{\,j}$ represents the weight value of the jth person under the ith illumination, w_{AB_i} represents the weight value under the ith illumination (via AAM and BDR).

2.3 Design of Rule

From the perspective of human brain cognitive system, face recognition in video is different from face recognition in still. For face image, we can only utilize the face information from the still and make a recognition judgment, even though we cannot make certain our decision. For face video sequences, the cognition is a gradual process, which includes affirmation or negation ..., and to the final confirmation. Actually, it is similar to a process from fuzzy to clear.

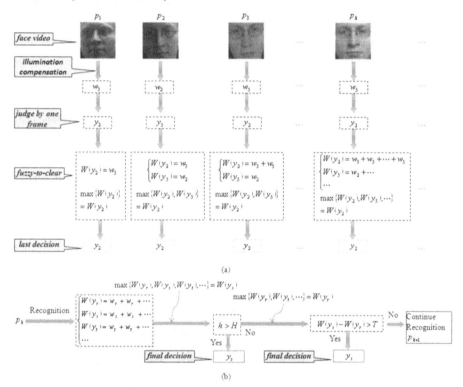

Fig. 4. Quality fusion rule (a) fusion process; (b) decision scheme

We simulate the human brain cognitive process to design a quality fusion rule for face recognition in video. Let p_h denotes the hth face video frame, $p_1, p_2, p_3, \cdots$ are continuous in time; w_i represents the weight value under the ith illumination (see Eq. (2, 4)); y_l represents the lth class; $W(y_l)$ represents the weight sum of getting the recognition result y_l. The fusion rule can be described in Fig. 4.

As shown in Fig. 4(a), wrong decision may be made "*just by one frame*". If face video features are used, correct recognition rate would increase. More results are gained in the following experiments section.

Besides, identification cognitive process does not always accompany the whole face video sequences (see Fig. 4(b)). The "*last decision*" can be verified by the "*decision scheme*". H and T are the thresholds, which can be appointed empirically.

2.4 Other Quality Fusion Rule

Similar with illumination quality fusion rule, the proposed quality fusion rule can be applied to other compensation algorithms, such as face pose compensation and face expression compensation.

For example, the face expression can be classified into several categories: sad, laugh, normal, rage and so on. We compensate these expressions with pertinence. Then a corresponding quality fusion rule can also be designed for it.

3 Experimental Evaluation

3.1 Face Video Database

The face video database, which is composed by IIT-NRC face video database [13] and UO face video database [14], contains 15 individuals totally. Each individual has a normal frontal face image and two video sequences: the image is for training (see Fig. 5(a)), and the video is for testing (see Fig. 5(b)). In some video sequences, the definition of face or environmental illumination changes constantly so that our quality fusion rule can be evaluated effectively.

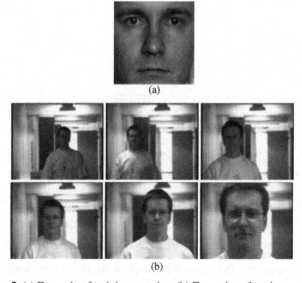

Fig. 5. (a) Example of training samples; (b) Examples of testing samples

In this paper, varying pose is not considered. So a frontal face detection algorithm (the deflection angel of head is confined to about $-15° - 15°$) is applied to process the video sequences.

3.2 Experiments on Illumination Quality Fusion

In this section, in the beginning, we can calculate two kinds of weights: the weights gained by PCA+CSD and the weights gained AAM+BDR. Then both of them are compared.

With the weights, the quality fusion rule can be combined with the illumination compensation. In order to manifest the performance of the fusion rule, it is compared with other exist methods from the literatures.

All of the experiments of the section are evaluated on the face video database. Each person has only one normal frontal face image as training sample.

3.2.1 Determination of Weights

According to the scheme (mentioned in Section 2.2), two kinds of weight values can be gained for each lighting source categories. The results are in listed in Table 1.

Table 1. Weights of quality fusion rule

Class (Order of LSP Set)	Weight (PCA+CSD)	Weight (AAM+BDR)
1	0.625	0.675
2	0.750	0.800
3	0.825	0.875
4	0.925	0.950
5	1.0	1.0
6	0.900	0.925
7	0.850	0.900
8	0.750	0.800
9	0.650	0.675

As shown in Table 1, for each class, the weight values gained by AAM+BDR are all bigger than those gained by PCA+CSD. They illuminate that the features, which are extracted from low quality face image by AAM, are abound with more effective information. In other words, compared with PCA representation, we can locate the feature points in low quality face image accurately by means of AAM. In addition, the weights generation is evaluated on the same face pose, which is more helpful to AAM.

Then we evaluate Scheme I (weights generated by PCA and CSD) and Scheme II (weights generated by AAM and BDR) on the face video database. In "*judge by one frame*" step (see Fig. 4), there are two processes: feature extraction and classification. We use NNR as classification algorithm. For Scheme I, PCA is taken as feature extraction algorithm and the distance measure of NNR is CSD; for Scheme II, AAM is taken as feature extraction algorithm and the distance measure of NNR is BDR. These algorithms are all in corresponding with the algorithms which are used to generate weights. The recognition rates are calculated by "*final decision*". The comparison result is shown in Fig. 6.

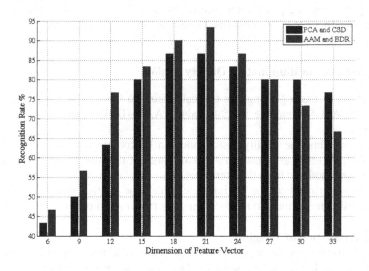

Fig. 6. Comparison of weights generations between PCA&CSD and AAM&BDR

By the means of the columns shown in Fig. 6, when the dimension of feature vector is less than or equal to 27, the value of Column 2 (AAM and BDR) is greater than or equal to that of Column 1 (PCM and CSD); after the abscissas point 27, the value of Column 2 is lower than that of Column 1. The peak value of recognition rate appears in Column 2 at the abscissas point 21. When the dimension of feature vector is small, AAM can locate the main key feature points accurately, which gains more effective information than PCA representation. When the dimension is big, the location accuracy of feature points would decrease gradually. Because the face pose and expression varies slightly in face video (the deflection angel of head is limited about $-15° - 15°$), which lead that more feature points are located in wrong position. Different from PCA, the importance of feature points for AAM are equal, which means that we cannot evaluate the importance of the feature points coordinates by the value size.

3.2.2 Comparison with Other Methods

In order to represent the effect of the quality fusion rule, the illumination compensation [2] with none, Adler's quality fusion rule [5], Poh's quality fusion rule [6] and the proposed quality fusion rule are compared on face video database (see Fig. 7). Here we adopt Scheme II (weights generate by AAM and BDR). The feature extraction algorithm and classification algorithm use AAM and NNR(BDR) respectively.

As seen from Fig. 7, the recognition rates with the proposed rule are higher than others at peak. Adler's method think quality measures should be continuous, which form a more complex classifier. With the increase of the feature vector dimension, the overfitting problem is more serious. Poh's approach only classifies the illumination into two categories: good illumination and bad illumination, unless there are more training data due to its probability calculation. In addition, unlike the proposed rule, they don't consider the video features. We can conclude that the proposed quality fusion rule can improve face recognition in video.

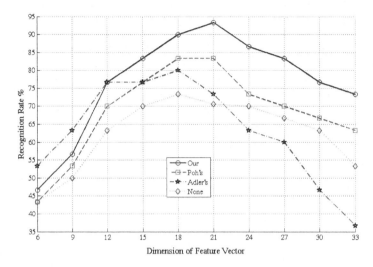

Fig. 7. Comparison results

4   Conclusions and Future Directions

In this paper, we introduce a novel quality fusion rule for face recognition in video. For the rule, motivated by the human brain cognitive system, the features of face video sequences are involved. There are some future works we intend to continue our investigation on the improvements. Firstly, we evaluate the proposed quality fusion rule on pose compensation and expression compensation. Another possible improvement we are considering is to make further improvement of the quality fusion rule by simulating the human brain cognitive function, such as the nonlinear of the system.

Furthermore, the face video database we used for experiments is not big enough to evaluate our algorithm sufficiently. A mass of video sequences for more than 50 target persons captured in subway gating view is on the progress.

Acknowledgment

This project is supported by the National High Technology Research and Development Program (HTRDP) of China, Grant No.: 2008AA01Z124.

References

1. Boston Globe, Face recognition fails in Boston airport (July 2002)
2. Wang, C., Li, Y.: An efficient illumination compensation based on plane-fit for face recognition. In: The 10th International Conference on Control, Automation, Robotics and Vision, pp. 939–943 (2008)

3. Huisman, P., van Munster, R., Moro-Ellenberger, S., Veldhuis, R., Bazen, A.: Making 2D face recognition more robust using AAMs for pose compensation. In: Proceedings of the 7th International Conference on Automatic Face and Gesture Recognition, pp. 108–113 (2006)
4. Mpiperis, I., Malassiotis, S., Strintzis, M.G.: Expression Compensation for Face Recognition Using a Polar Geodesic Representation. In: Third International Symposium on 3D Data Processing, Visualization, and Transmission, June 2006, pp. 224–231 (2006)
5. Adler, A., Dembinsky, T.: Human vs. automatic measurement of biometric sample quality. In: Canadian Conference on Electrical and Computer Engineering, May 2006, pp. 2090–2093 (2006)
6. Poh, N., Heusch, G., Kittler, J.: On Combination of Face Authentication Experts by a Mixture of Quality Dependent Fusion Classifiers. In: Haindl, M., Kittler, J., Roli, F. (eds.) MCS 2007. LNCS, vol. 4472, pp. 344–356. Springer, Heidelberg (2007)
7. Haxby, J.V., Hoffman, E.A., Gobbini, M.I.: The distributed human neural system for face perception. Trends in Cognitive Sciences 4, 223–233 (2000)
8. Wang, Y.-h., Ning, X.-j., Yang, C.-x., Wang, Q.-f.: A method of illumination compensation for human face image based on quotient image. Information Sciences 178(12), 2705–2721 (2008)
9. Hallinan, P.: A low-dimensional representation of human faces for arbitrary lighting conditions. In: Proc. IEEE Conference on Computer Vision and Pattern Recognition, pp. 995–999 (1994)
10. Lee, K., Jeffrey, H., Kriegman, D.: Acquiring linear subspaces for face recognition under variable lighting. IEEE Transactions on Pattern Analysis and Machine Intelligence 27(5), 1–15 (2005)
11. Cootes, T.F., Edwards, G.J., Taylor, C.J.: Active appearance models. IEEE Transactions on Pattern Analysis and Machine Intelligence 23, 681–685 (2001)
12. Friedman, A., Kohler, B.: Bidimensional Regression: Assessing the Configural Similarity and Accuracy of Cognitive Maps and Other Two-Dimensional Data Sets 8(4), 468–491 (2003)
13. Gorodnichy, D.O.: Video-based framework for face recognition in video. In: Second Workshop on Face Processing in Video (FPiV 2005) in Proceedings of Second Canadian Conference on Computer and Robot Vision (CRV 2005), Victoria, BC, Canada, May 9-11, pp. 330–338 (2005)
14. Martinkauppi, B., Soriano, M., Huovinen, S., Laaksonen, M.: Face video database. In: Proc. First European Conference on Color in Graphics, Imaging and Vision (CGIV 2002), Poitiers, France, April 2-5, pp. 380–383 (2002)

Decorrelation and Distinctiveness Provide with Human-Like Saliency

Antón Garcia-Diaz, Xosé R. Fdez-Vidal, Xosé M. Pardo, and Raquel Dosil

Universidade de Santiago de Compostela, Grupo de Visión Artificial,
Departamento de Electrónica e Computación, Campus Sur s/n,
15782 Santiago de Compostela, Spain
{anton.garcia,xose.vidal,xose.pardo,raquel.dosil}@usc.es

Abstract. In this work, we show the capability of a new model of
saliency, of reproducing remarkable psychophysical results. The model
presents low computational complexity compared to other models of the
state of the art. It is based in biologically plausible mechanisms: the
decorrelation and the distinctiveness of local responses. Decorrelation of
scales is obtained from principal component analysis of multiscale low
level features. Distinctiveness is measured through the Hotelling's T^2
statistic. The model is conceived to be used in a machine vision system,
in which attention would contribute to enhance performance together
with other visual functions. Experiments demonstrate the consistency
with a wide variety of psychophysical phenomena, that are referenced
in the visual attention modeling literature, with results that outperform
other state of the art models.

Keywords: saliency, bottom-up, attention, eye-fixations.

1 Introduction

The Human Visual System (HVS) has to face a huge computational complexity, as has been shown in visual search experiments [1]. It confronts this challenge through the selection of information. A key role in this selection process
is played by the visual attention mechanisms, including the data-driven ones,
leading to the so called bottom-up saliency. There is an increasing interest in
the understanding of this attentional component and the appraisal of its relative
importance in relation to the top-down, knowledge-based mechanisms. Correspondingly, an increasing number of approaches to its computational modeling
is coming up. There exists as well, an evident interest in the application of these
models in the solution of technical problems requiring active vision approaches,
like robotics, image compression or object recognition.

Many of the models for bottom-up saliency proposed in the literature are
based on abundant evidences from psychophysical experimentation. Nothdurft
[2] has proposed that local feature contrast generally attracts gaze. In the same
direction, Zetchsche [3] points out to the local contribution to the structure content as driving attention. In general, most models of bottom-up saliency assume

J. Blanc-Talon et al. (Eds.): ACIVS 2009, LNCS 5807, pp. 343–354, 2009.
© Springer-Verlag Berlin Heidelberg 2009

that local distinctiveness is the basis for data-driven attention. Following this direction, the already classic model of Itti & Koch [4] proposed the iteration of center-surround competition processes to reach a powerful computational model of saliency. With a similar approach Le Meur et al. [5] posed a scheme using a multiscale and multioriented decomposition, along with contrast sensitivity, visual masking, center-surround competition and perceptual grouping. Recently, a different set of approaches to bottom-up saliency has been proposed based on similarity and local information measures. In these models local distinctiveness is obtained either from self-information [6][7], mutual information [8][9], or from dissimilarity [10], using different decomposition and competition schemes.

In a previous work [11] we studied the combination of scale information decorrelation with center-surround (c-s) differences. There, we compared the obtained performance in visual search experiments with the model of Itti & Koch [4]. In that approach only achromatic information was taken into account. Moreover, that model was unable to correctly reproduce some important psychophysical phenomena tackled here.

In this paper we propose a more efficient, simple and light approach to the problem of modeling bottom-up saliency. It is based solely in the decorrelation of scale information without the use of c-s differences. Hence, we turn back to the proposal of Olshausen & Field about the need of taking into account the decorrelation of neural responses, when considering the behavior of a population of neurons, subject to stimuli of a natural image [12]. That means considering neurons collectively, instead of individually. This is believed to be closely related to the important role of Non Classical Receptive Fields (NCRF) in the functioning of HVS. Therefore, we start from a classic multiscale decomposition on two main feature dimensions: local orientation energy and color. We obtain the decorrelated responses applying PCA to the multiscale features. Then, we measure the statistical distance of each feature to the center of the distribution as the Hotelling's T^2 distance. Finally, we apply normalization and Gaussian smoothing to gain robustness. The resulting maps are firstly summed, delivering local energy and color conspicuities, and then they are normalized and averaged, producing the final saliency map.

It is worth noting that we start -like probably most models- from a controlled decomposition, which retains important information. Thus, it is suitable for combination with top-down modulation approaches, like the incorporation of contextual influences or learning and recognition mechanisms. Unlike in the model of Bruce & Tsotsos [7], who use a decomposition based on independent components of patches from natural images, in our model it is very simple to actuate on (and from) scales, orientations or color components.

This approach reproduces a wide variety of psychophysical results, all of them closely related to the attentional function of the HVS. Hence, we will show how the model matches the nonlinearity against orientation contrast; the efficient (parallel) and inefficient (serial) search, the orientation asymmetry, the presence-absence asymmetry and Weber's law, the influence of background on color asymmetries, and the capability in the prediction of eye fixation data. Therefore the model achieves a degree of validation that outperforms other state of the art models.

The paper is organized as follows. Section 2 describes the bottom-up saliency model. In Section 3, experiments and results are presented and discussed. Finally, Section 4 summarizes the paper.

2   Model

The input image is codified using the Lab color model. In this way, each pixel is described by one luminance component (L), and two color opponent components: red/green (a) and blue/yellow (b). Unlike other implementations of saliency [8][13], this election is based on a widely used psychophysical standard. We decompose the luminance image by means of a Gabor-like bank of filters, in agreement with the standard model of V1. Since orientation selectivity is very weakly associated with color selectivity, the components a and b simply undergo a multiscale decomposition. Hence, we employ two feature dimensions -in the sense proposed by Wolfe [14]-: color and local energy. By decorrelating the multiscale responses, extracting from them a local measure of variability, and further performing a local averaging, we obtain a unified and efficient measure of saliency.

2.1   Local Energy and Color Maps

Luminance is filtered with a bank of log Gabor filters [15], constructed in the frequency domain. The transfer function of a log Gabor filter takes the expression:

$$logGabor(\rho, \alpha; \rho_i, \alpha_i) = e^{-\frac{(\log(\rho/\rho_i))^2}{2(\log(\sigma_{\rho i}/\rho_i))^2}} e^{-\frac{(\alpha - \alpha_i)^2}{2(\sigma_\alpha)^2}}. \tag{1}$$

where (ρ, α) are polar frequency coordinates and (ρ_i, α_i) is the central frequency of the filter.

While the Gabor filter is non-zero for negative frequencies and presents a non-zero DC component, giving rise to artifacts, the log Gabor does not present this problem. Besides, it presents a symmetric profile in a logarithmic frequency scale. Hence, in a linear frequency scale it shows a long tail towards the high frequencies, providing a more localized impulse response. The impulse response is a complex valued function (with no analytical expression), whose components are a couple of functions in phase quadrature, f and h. Hence, the response of a log Gabor filter with scale s and orientation o to a luminance image L is:

$$(L * logGabor_{so})(x, y) = L * f_{so}(x, y) + L * h_{so}(x, y) i. \tag{2}$$

The modulus of the complex response of this filter is a measure of the local energy of the input associated to the frequency band with scale s and orientation o [16][17] .

$$e_{so}(x, y) = \sqrt{(L * f_{so})^2 + (L * h_{so})^2}. \tag{3}$$

Regarding the color dimension, we obtain a multiscale representation both for a and b, from the responses to a bank of log Gaussian filters.

$$logGauss(\rho) = e^{-\frac{(\log(\rho))^2}{2(\log(2^n \sigma))^2}}. \tag{4}$$

Thus, for each scale and color opponent component we get a real valued response map:

$$Resp_{s\,a}(x,y) = (a * logGauss_s)(x,y)$$

$$\tag{5}$$

$$Resp_{s\,b}(x,y) = (b * logGauss_s)(x,y)$$

The parameters used here were: 4 scales spaced by one octave, 4 orientations (for local energy), minimum wavelength of 4 pixels, angular standard deviation of $\sigma_\alpha = 37.5°$, and a frequency bandwidth of 2 octaves.

2.2   Distinctiveness from Decorrelation

Variability and richness of structural content have been proven as driving attention in psychophysical experiments [3]. Here we have chosen a measure of distance between local and global structure to represent distinctiveness. But before estimating such distance, we need to preprocess the low level representation. Observations from neurobiology show decorrelation of neural responses, as well as an increased population sparseness in comparison to what can be expected from a standard Gabor-like representation [18]. To decorrelate the multiscale information of each sub-feature (orientations and color components) we perform a PCA on the corresponding set of scales. Preliminary tests using ICA instead of PCA, in order to reach higher order decorrelation, have not improved the results, while showing a higher computational cost. We don't discard however this possibility. To further extract the statistical distance at each point we make use of the Hotelling's T^2 statistic. Being x_{ij} a feature corresponding to scale i and pixel j, with $i=\{1,...,S\}$ and $j =\{1,...,N\}$, we compute the statistical distance $T^2{}_j$ of each pixel in the decorrelated coordinates

$$\mathbf{X} = \begin{pmatrix} x_{11} & \cdots & x_{1N} \\ \vdots & \vdots & \vdots \\ x_{S1} & \cdots & x_{SN} \end{pmatrix} \rightarrow (PCA) \rightarrow \mathbf{T}^2 = \left(T_1^2, \cdots, T_N^2\right). \tag{6}$$

T^2 is defined as follows, where $\mathbf{x_j}$ is a multiscale feature vector with S components and $\mathbf{W}$ is the covariance matrix.

$$T_j^2 = (\mathbf{x_j} - \bar{\mathbf{x}})^\mathrm{T}\mathbf{W}^{-1}(\mathbf{x_j} - \bar{\mathbf{x}}). \tag{7}$$

This provides an efficient mechanism for the deployment of pop-out effects, widely observed in psychophysics experiments, by means of a multivariate measure of the distance from a feature vector associated to a point in the image to the average feature vector of the global scene, that is, a measure of the local feature contrast.

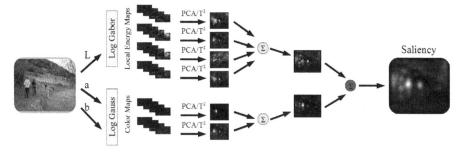

Fig. 1. Bottom-up Saliency Model

Final Map. The final saliency is obtained normalizing, smoothing and summing the extracted maps, first within each feature dimension and next with the resulting local energy conspicuity and color conspicuity maps. This provides with a unique value of saliency for each point of the image.

Computational Complexity. Two types of operations have been used. Firstly, filtering for decomposition and smoothing, has been realized as the product of the transfer functions of the input and the filters, using the Fast Fourier Transform (FFT) and its inverse (IFFT). This means a computational complexity of $O(k\ N \log(N) + N)$, being k the number of operations, a constant independent of the image, and N the number of pixels of the image. Secondly, a PCA has been performed with a complexity of $O(S^3 + S^2 N)$, being S the number of scales (dimensionality) and N the number of pixels [19]. In our case, as the number of scales is relatively small and remains constant, we are interested in the dependency on the number of pixels, being $O(N)$. The overall complexity of the algorithm, against the resolution of the image, is hence established by the use of the FFT, being $O(N \log(N))$.

3 Experimental Results and Discussion

We focus here in showing the consistency of the model with a number of outstanding psychophysical results related to bottom-up attention in the HVS. Most of these experiments are yet classic in literature related to visual attention. All of them have been employed to validate any of the state of the art models cited here. They are related to different behaviors observed in the study of human attention: nonlinearity against orientation contrast, efficient (parallel) and inefficient (serial) search, orientation asymmetry, presence-absence asymmetry and Weber's law, and influence of background on color asymmetries. Finally a ROC analysis shows how the model predicts eye fixations better than other models of the state of the art on an open access image dataset.

We start proving the nonlinear behavior of the model against orientation contrast. Hence, examining figure 2 we see how saliency increases quickly from 10° to 30°-35°, an then it remains constant at a saturation value. This is in agreement

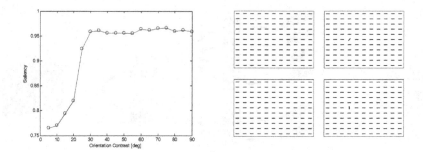

Fig. 2. Nonlinearity of saliency against orientation contrast. Four example images are shown.

with the already classic psychophysical experiment conducted by Nothdurft [20]. Other models like the proposed by Harel et al. [10] or Bruce and Tsotsos [7] do not reproduce this result on our images. At least with the code publicly provided by the authors, using the default configuration. This is also the case of the model of Itti and Koch [4][8].

Other main issue in the validation of a saliency model is related to the reproduction of the results of efficient search of certain feature singletons and the inefficient search of conjunction singletons. Of course, it is also very important what features give rise to this behavior. Thereby, we can see in figure 3 four typical examples to illustrate all of this and the corresponding saliency produced by our model. The first one is an image provided by Bruce, together with the code of his model of saliency [7], reproducing a typical example collected by Wolfe [14]. As we see, character "2" does not stand out among the fives, because it has not any different feature to produce pop-out nor parallel search. However, the tilted "5" does stand out, due to the unique orientation that it presents. In the same way, the red "5" stands out due to its unique color, and the smaller "5" stands out due to its unique size.

The three remaining images are also typical examples of color (second image) and orientation (third image) pop-out -this used by Itti & Koch [4]-, and serial search for a target differing from distractors in a unique conjunction of color and orientation (fourth image).

We show now how the saliency provided by the model allows to explain several psychophysical phenomena known as search asymmetries [21]. A couple of stimuli differing in a simple feature exhibit different detection times depending on which is the target and which is the distractor. Actually, this term encompasses phenomena of very different nature. It has been pointed, in most cases, that the name itself is not suitable. The reason is that the underlying assumption of symmetric design of the experiment is wrong.

Orientation asymmetry seems to be however a real asymmetry, not related at all to an asymmetric design of the experiment. This asymmetry really indicates the existence of four privileged canonical orientations [21]. Thus the HVS is observed to present a different behavior depending on the orientation, therefore

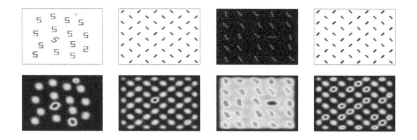

Fig. 3. Four examples related to efficient and inefficient search [14]

arising the asymmetry. Given that we have assumed the existence of four canonical orientations (like many other models), it should not be surprising that the model provides with the expected result. In this sense, we see in figure 4 that the relative saliency of a target tilted 80° within vertical distractors is clearly higher than that of a vertical target within 80° tilted distractors, so much so that in the first case occurs a pop-out, inexistent in the second case. Hence, the result provided by the model perfectly matches the observed in psychophysical experiments.

The model reproduces also the asymmetric behavior exhibited by the HVS when target and distractors only differ in the presence or absence of a simple element or feature. In the figure 4 we see two examples typically used to illustrate this fact. As we can see, when the target is the stimulus (circle, dash) with the additional vertical bar present, a pop-out is observed. However when the vertical bar is present in the distractors and absent in the target, there is no pop-out. This is again in agreement with the observed behavior of the HVS. The explanation in the frame of our model matches up with a fact pointed out by Zetchsche [3]: saliency is directly related to the structure content in the image. Therefore, the absence of structure doesn't contribute at all to the increase of saliency, but to its decrease. Or in other words, presence is not a feature. Then, this is not a true asymmetry since the underlying experiment design is not symmetric.

Another consequence of this presence/absence behavior is the so called Weber's law. This law states that an increase in the relative length in a given dimension gives place to a proportional increase of saliency [21]. In figure 5 we

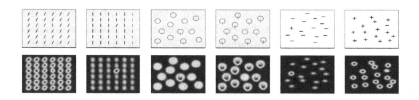

Fig. 4. In the upper row: images used to reproduce the orientation asymmetry (two first), and the presence-absence asymmetry (four remaining). In the lower row the corresponding saliencies are shown.

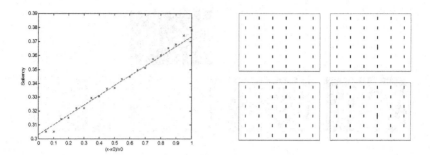

Fig. 5. Saliency against relative increase in length exhibits a linear behavior. Four of the 20 displays used are also shown.

show four examples of the 20 images used to test this behavior in our model. The results provided present a very good match with the Weber's law. As we can see, saliency is linear respect to the relative extension of the target. This result is also reproduced by the models proposed by Harel et al. [10] or Gao et al [8] . The model of Bruce and Tsotsos does not reproduce so well this linear behavior. Except for Gao et al. these comparisons have been made with the code publicly provided by the authors, using the default configuration. On the other hand, the model of Itti and Koch fails in reproducing this law [4][8].

Other important psychophysical result obtained by Rosenholtz et al. [22], shows the way in which background properties influence the color search asymmetries. Consider two stimuli of the same luminance differing only in color. These asymmetries consist in observing a different detection time in a visual search task when target and distractors are exchanged. In this context Rosenholtz et al observed that background properties (color and luminance) have direct effects on these asymmetry, to the point to be reversed, generated or suppressed. This challenges the denomination of asymmetry given to these phenomena, since it implies to ignore the existence of the background, that breaks in fact the assumed asymmetry, explaining the results. In figure 6 we can see an example in which the model reproduces this asymmetry and its reversal under a change in background color, in the same way that was observed by Rosenholtz et al. Unlike Bruce and Tsotsos [7] -who employed images elaborated by their selves- we use here reproductions of the images employed by Rosenholtz et al. in their experiments [22]. Hence, in the figure 6 we can see how on a gray background the redder stimulus is more salient, explaining the lower detection time in visual search reported by Rosenholtz et al.. Meanwhile, when the color of the background is changed to red, the situation is reversed and the less red target becomes more salient than the redder target. This is in agreement with the detection time observed by Rosenholtz et al. in the experiments.

Moreover, our model predicts a higher relative saliency of the redder target in the gray background than the less red target in the red background, again in agreement with the reported search detection times. Note that this is an asymmetry -both in experimental and model results-, not an antisymmetry. In

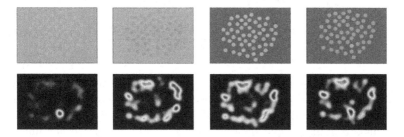

Fig. 6. Example of color asymmetry reversal by a change in color background

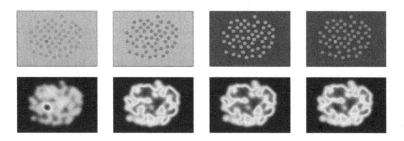

Fig. 7. Example of color asymmetry suppression by a change in color background

contrast, in the example provided by Bruce and Tsotsos [7], their model seems to show an antisymmetric behavior. This criticism must be taken with caution since they employed their own images, similar but still different to those used in experiments with humans.

We have also observed, in agreement with human behavior, an influence of the contrast of stimuli relative to background in the magnitude of the asymmetry. But it remains out of the scope of this work to quantitatively measure of this effect. On the other hand, Rosenholtz et al. found that changes in color background can also generate or suppress a color asymmetry. In figure 7 we see how the result provided by our model matches well with this behavior of the HVS.

On a gray background, a bluer target is more salient than a less blue target, in agreement with the observed lower detection time. Meanwhile, on a red background the asymmetry almost disappears, with only a slightly higher saliency of the less blue target compared to the bluer. This result appears to be consistent again with the results reported by Rosenholtz et al. [22].

The model of Bruce and Tsotsos, which capable of capturing an antisymmetry (more than an asymmetry), on images of their own -not the ones used in psychophysical experiments- is not, however, able to reproduce correctly other important results like the suppression or generation of an asymmetry by a change in background color. On the other hand, their model provides with a measure of saliency much less graded than the model proposed here.

Table 1. AUC values obtained from ROC analysis

T^2-Based	AIM	Gao et al.
0.791	0.789	0.769

Other state of the art models, like the model by Gao et al [8] or the model by Harel et al [10], have not shown either the capability of reproducing these results. The model proposed by Rosenholtz et al. has been specifically designed to explain these results. It remains questionable how it would capture other important results like orientation or size pop-out, or its capability of reproducing other psychophysical results with images constructed in different color spaces. In this sense, it is worth noting that we have used the Lab color space to decompose the image, which is different to the one employed by Rosenholtz et al. to synthesize their images. And this is very interesting, since even the stimuli symmetry may disappear when the color space to represent them is replaced. Therefore, we think that it could be interesting to do experiments similar to these but with stimuli that are symmetric in different color spaces, to see what computational models reproduce better the ensemble of results.

Finally we compare the performance of the model in predicting human eye fixations through ROC analysis. We use an open access image dataset, published by Bruce & Tsotsos. It is made up of 120 images, and of the corresponding fixation data for 20 different subjects. A detailed description of the eye-tracking experiment can be found in [6]. We can see in table 1 the obtained AUC value, that outperforms those obtained by the models of Bruce & Tsotsos and Gao et al. on the same image dataset.

The way in which ROC analysis is performed is often not explicit. In fact, they have been compared AUC values computed in different manners. We have opted here, like many authors [9][10][23], for computing a ROC curve for each image and next averaging the result. Bruce and Tsotsos [7] compute instead a unique curve for all of the images. Results are, in fact, very close using both methods, at least with this dataset. There are also several approaches in treating uncertainty. Hence, Harel et al. or Gao et al. do not provide with it. Bruce and Tsotsos use a procedure [24] that does not reflect the inter-scene variance, and only affects in practice the third decimal value. We think that this requires a deeper analysis, in the line pointed in [25]. It would be worth checking the influence of the type of scene in the result. In fact, the images in this dataset present mainly urban or indoor scenes, which lack of representativity of possibles contexts. We leave this task for a future work since it remains out of the scope of this paper, given the extension required.

4   Conclusions

We have shown the predictive capabilities of a simple model of bottom-up saliency, that resorts to the decorrelation of the responses to a Gabor-like bank of filters. The decorrelation of neural responses, biologically plausible, is thought to be related to the influence of NCRF, when V1 cells are subjected to natural stimuli [12][18].

Our model agrees with an important set of psychophysical phenomena. To our knowledge, none of the models of the state of the art cited here, have been validated with all of these results at once. On the other hand these results are highly relevant references in the literature related to visual attention [14][20][21][22]. Moreover, all of them have served to support the validity of any of the referred models.

Hence, our model suitably reproduces the nonlinear behavior against orientation contrast; the efficient search phenomena on orientations, color and size, as well as the inefficient search of conjunctions of orientation and color; the orientation asymmetry; the presence/absence asymmetry and the Weber's law; and the influence of background in color search asymmetries (we expect that a quantitative comparison would reinforce this assessment). Finally by means of a ROC analysis we can claim that our model predicts human fixations better than other models of the state of the art on an open access image dataset.

On the other hand the computational complexity of our model is O(N log(N)). This value clearly improves the ones achieved by other models. For instance Harel et al. report a computational complexity of $O(N^4)$ for their model.

Finally, our model, like that of Bruce & Tsotsos [7], avoids any parameterization of the process, beyond the initial decomposition of the image. However, we maintain an initial decomposition which is ordered and suitable for the incorporation, from the beginning, of top-down influences. This tunable design, in the line of many other approaches, makes the model more suitable for machine vision purposes.

Acknowledgments. This work has been granted by the Spanish Government (TIN2006-08447), and by the Government of Galicia (PGIDIT07PXIB206028PR).

References

1. Tsotsos, J.K.: Computational foundations for attentive Processes. In: Itti, L., Rees, G., Tsotsos, J.K. (eds.) Neurobiology of Attention, pp. 3–7. Elsevier Academia Press, Amsterdam (2005)
2. Nothdurft, H.C.: Salience of Feature Contrast. In: Itti, L., Rees, G., Tsotsos, J.K. (eds.) Neurobiology of Attention, pp. 233–239. Elsevier Academia Press, Amsterdam (2005)
3. Zetzsche, C.: Natural Scene Statistics and Salient Visual Features. In: Itti, L., Rees, G., Tsotsos, J.K. (eds.) Neurobiology of Attention, pp. 226–232. Elsevier Academia Press, Amsterdam (2005)
4. Itti, L., Koch, C.: A saliency-based search mechanism for overt and covert shifts of visual attention. Vision Research 40, 1489–1506 (2000)
5. Le Meur, O., Le Callet, P., Barba, D., Thoreau, D.: A coherent computational approach to model bottom-up visual attention. IEEE Transactions on Pattern Analysis and Machine Intelligence 28, 802–817 (2006)
6. Bruce, N., Tsotsos, J.K.: Saliency Based on Information Maximization. Advances in Neural Information Processing Systems 18, 155–162 (2006)

7. Bruce, N., Tsotsos, J.K.: Saliency, attention, and visual search: An information theoretic approach. Journal of Vision 9(3), 1–24 (2009)
8. Gao, D., Mahadevan, V., Vasconcelos, N.: On the plausibility of the discriminant center-surround hypothesis for visual saliency. Journal of Vision 8, 13 (2008)
9. Gao, D., Mahadevan, V., Vasconcelos, N.: The discriminant center-surround hypothesis for bottom-up saliency. In: Proceedings of the Neural Information Processing Systems (NIPS) Conference, Vancouver, Canada (2007)
10. Harel, J., Koch, C., Perona, P.: Graph-Based Visual Saliency. Advances in Neural Information Processing Systems 19, 545–552 (2007)
11. Garcia-Diaz, A., Fdez-Vidal, X.R., Pardo, X.M., Dosil, R.: Local energy variability as a generic measure of bottom-up salience. In: Yin, P.-Y. (ed.) Pattern Recognition Techniques, Technology and Applications, pp. 1–24. In-Teh, Vienna (2008)
12. Olshausen, B.A., Field, D.J.: How Close Are We to Understanding V1? Neural Computation 17, 1665–1699 (2005)
13. Itti, L., Koch, C., Niebur, E.: A model of saliency-based visual attention for rapid scene analysis. IEEE Transactions on Pattern Analysis and Machine Intelligence 20(11), 1254–1259 (1998)
14. Wolfe, J.M., Horowitz, T.S.: What attributes guide the deployment of visual attention and how do they do it? Nature Reviews. Neuroscience 5(6), 495–501 (2004)
15. Field, D.J.: Relations Between the Statistics of Natural Images and the Response Properties of Cortical Cells. Journal of the Optical Society of America A 4(12), 2379–2394 (1987)
16. Kovesi, P.: Invariant Measures of Image Features from Phase Information. Ph.D. Thesis, The University or Western Australia (1996)
17. Morrone, M.C., Burr, D.C.: Feature Detection in Human Vision: A Phase-Dependent Energy Model. Proceedings of the Royal Society of London B 235, 221–245 (1988)
18. Vinje, W.E., Gallant, J.L.: Sparse coding and decorrelation in primary visual cortex during natural vision. Science 287, 1273–1276 (2000)
19. Sharma, A., Paliwal, K.K.: Fast principal component analysis using fixed-point algorithm. Pattern Recognition Letters 28, 1151–1155 (2007)
20. Nothdurft, H.C.: The conspicuousness of orientation and motion contrast. Spatial Vision 7 (1993)
21. Treisman, A., Gormican, S.: Feature analysis in early vision: Evidence from search asymmetries. Psychological Review 95, 15–48 (1988)
22. Rosenholtz, R., Nagy, A.L., Bell, N.R.: The effect of background color on asymmetries in color search. Journal of Vision 4, 224–240 (2004)
23. Tatler, B.W., Baddeley, R.J., Gilchrist, I.D.: Visual correlates of fixation selection: Effects of scale and time. Vision Research 45, 643–659 (2005)
24. Cortes, C., Mohri, M.: Confidence intervals for the area under the ROC curve. In: Advances in Neural Information Processing Systems 17: Proceedings of The 2004 Conference, p. 305. MIT Press, Cambridge (2005)
25. Fawcett, T.: An introduction to ROC analysis. Pattern recognition letters 27, 861–874 (2006)

Intelligent Vision: A First Step – Real Time Stereovision

John Morris, Khurram Jawed, and Georgy Gimel'farb

Electrical and Computer Engineering and Computer Science,
The University of Auckland, New Zealand

Abstract. We describe a real time stereo vision system capable of processing high resolution (1Mpixel or more) images at 30 fps with disparity ranges of 100 pixels or more. This system has a fast rectification module associated with each camera which uses a look up table approach to remove lens distortion and correct camera misalignment in a single step. The corrected, aligned images are passed through a module which generates disparity and occlusion maps with a latency of two camera scan line intervals. This module implements a version of the Symmetric Dynamic Programming Stereo (SDPS) algorithm which has a small, compact hardware realization, permitting many copies to be instantiated to accommodate large disparity ranges. Snapshots from videos taken in our laboratory demonstrate that the system can produce effective depth maps in real time. The occlusion maps that the SDPS algorithm produces clearly outline distinct objects in scenes and present a powerful tool for segmenting scenes rapidly into objects of interest.

Keywords: Stereovision, real time, dynamic programming.

1   Introduction

As a first step towards reproducing, at least in some limited form, the capabilities of the human eye-brain combination, we describe here a binocular vision system which is capable of converting high resolution (at least 1Mpixel) images streaming from a pair of cameras into depth maps in real time, which we define as the common video rate of 30fps because, at that rate, human systems 'see' continuous motion. The system uses reconfigurable circuits (FPGAs) to achieve the parallelism necessary to perform the large numbers of (albeit simple) computations needed for matching the two images to determine depth. It includes pre-processor modules which remove distortion and correct for camera misalignment in real time. A full system, capable of processing 1Mpixel images at 30 fps with disparity range, $\Delta > 100$ pixels, comfortably fits on a 'medium' size FPGA, which means that the core correspondence algorithm - a basic version of Gimel'farb's Symmetric Dynamic Programming Stereo (SDPS) algorithm[1] - can be enhanced further to improve matching performance, for example with adaptive matching to enhance tolerance for noise.

The applications for this system are diverse and range from collision avoidance and path planning for moving vehicles through motion capture (for tracking

J. Blanc-Talon et al. (Eds.): ACIVS 2009, LNCS 5807, pp. 355–366, 2009.

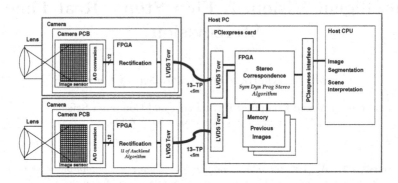

Fig. 1. Full System Block diagram: incorporating smart cameras with FPGAs which may be programmed to rectify images for any particular optical configuration

individuals and special effects in movies) to security applications (intelligent monitoring of dynamic environments and biometrics). To be effective, though, we must have accurate depth measurements, which implies a need for large disparity ranges - $\Delta > 100 \rightarrow 1\%$ depth accuracy without calling on subpixel matching techniques. This, in turn, requires high resolution images and we set a target - to be able to process images of $> 10^6$ pixels at 30 fps.

Once depths have been measured, an intelligent system still has to interpret the scene and determine the system response - direction to travel, velocity to be set, alarms to be raised, *etc.* Our approach, which uses FPGAs for the simple, repetitive and highly parallel basic image processing, leaves a host general-purpose processor to apply all its power to interpretation and decision making and is a good match of technology to problem: FPGA for the very large number of simple and regular calculations needed to correct images, match them and determine depths and conventional processor for the global and irregular processing needed to recognize features and threats and determine strategy.

A diagram of our full system is shown in Figure 1. Here, we discuss the stereo matching section in detail and show some results obtained from a prototype on an FPGA development card with a pair of CameraLink cameras to be attached directly to the FPGA - see Section 5.

1.1   Related Work

Correction of images by distortion removal and rectification has been extensively discussed. It is usual to assume a simple radial distortion model plus tangential distortion to allow for misalignment of lenses with optical axes [2]. The major focus has been on devising simple and efficient techniques to quantify distortion model parameters. Gribbon *et al.* discuss an lookup table based FPGA implementation [3]: our system adds correction of camera misalignments.

Several hardware stereo systems have been described. Commercial systems which will handle up to 640×480 images appear to be mainly based on correlation algorithms although the Census algorithm[4] has also been used. Dynamic programming algorithms have also been implemented: Cox's algorithm[5] was simulated achieving 64fps for 640×480 pixel images and $\Delta = 128$ pixels[6]. Gong and Yang match 256×256 images at up to 20fps using a GPU[7]. Park and Jeong also implemented a dynamic programming algorithm (Trellis) which could process 320×240 images with $\Delta = 128$[8]. They have also demonstrated a belief propagation algorithm for small images and low disparity range[9,10].

2   Image Pre-processing

For efficient matching, the lens distortion introduced by real lenses and optical systems must be removed. Aligning cameras so that the epipolar lines are collinear with scan lines simplifies the matching algorithm's search for corresponding pixels and allows efficient streaming of pixels through the disparity calculators - see Figure 6.

Our approach is simple and fast: rather than compute ideal image positions from distortion models (*e.g.* the commonly used radial distortion model[2]), in the calibration step, we derive a table of displacements from ideal image positions to distorted image positions. These displacements are stored in lookup tables which address distorted image pixels. This procedure is simple and fast, but, for high resolution images (> 1Mpixel), the lookup tables use more memory than state-of-the-art FPGAs provide. Therefore, noting that the distortion curves are invariably smooth, we used reduced tables, interpolating as necessary. Without introducing any significant error, in our prototype, we reduced a 1024×768 entry table to one with 65×65 entries. Since the displacements from ideal positions to real (distorted) image positions generated by distortions and mechanical misalignment may simply be added, we generate a single table for each camera which fully corrects images to those produced by a canonical (parallel optical axes perpendicular to the baseline, parallel image planes with collinear scan lines) configuration in a single step. Our rectification module, shown in Figure 2, performs two bilinear interpolations: the first uses the reduced lookup tables (one for x and one for y displacements) to generate the address of the desired pixel in the distorted image. Since this address is not conveniently integral, a second interpolation step derives the desired pixel intensity from intensities of its four neighbours in the distorted image.

Ideally the lookup table memory would have four ports (four values are used in each bilinear interpolation) but current FPGAs only provide three ports. We took advantage of the small size of the reduced lookup tables and simply replicate them to make a four-port memory. This is simple and fast and avoids more complex circuitry which re-uses previously fetched lookup table entries.

Since our rectifier needs to buffer a number of scan lines determined by the largest displacement in the lookup tables, it adds a latency of several scan lines. We set up a 'worst-case' scenario by aligning the cameras rather crudely: this

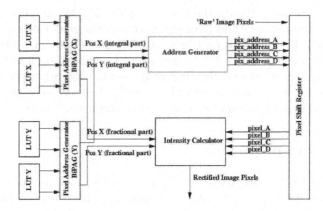

Fig. 2. Rectification module: Pixel Address Generator interpolates lookup table entries to generate distorted image addresses; Address Generator converts a these addresses to addresses in the pixel shift register for four neighbours; Intensity Calculator calculates intensity by bilinear interpolation

Table 1. Rectification module resources for various configurations; scanline length = 1024 pixels; LE - logic elements; DSP = number of DSP blocks

Pixel size (bits)	Scan lines	Logic (LEs)	Regs	DSP	Memory (bits)
12	64	1167	309	27	1,877,064
12	32	963	287	27	1,090,632
12	16	931	277	27	697,416
12	8	895	267	27	500,808
10	64	1003	283	26	1,614,920
10	32	933	272	26	959,560
10	16	902	263	26	631,880
10	8	869	253	26	468,040
8	64	901	259	23	1,342,776
8	32	878	249	23	828,000
8	16	349	239	23	566,344
8	8	901	259	23	435,272

All configurations will fit on a small Altera Cyclone FPGA.

required 64 scan lines to be buffered and contributed significantly to the amount of memory required to implement our system. Table 1 shows the resources needed to implement the rectifier on a Altera Cyclone FPGA - which will be used in our final system. Table 2 (in Section 5) details resources needed for the full system prototype from which the results in this paper are derived. Note that there is a clear benefit to using quality lenses and mechanical design: the number of scan lines which need to be buffered can be significantly reduced which leads to a concomitant reduction in latency and memory resources needed.

3   Stereo Correspondence

In terms of matching quality, the best performing algorithms employ global optimization which makes them slow and adds latencies of at least one frame interval: Scharstein's site provides the latest scores[11]! Thus they are unsuited to real time applications. Correlation algorithms are simple, regular and optimize by averaging over local neighbourhoods. However, to leverage the high degrees of inherent parallelism that they posses, very large numbers of adders are needed, leading to relatively large circuits[12]. They also match poorly when compared to other techniques[11]. Dynamic programming algorithms, on the other hand, optimize over scan lines, making them very suited to systems which stream pixels from cameras, and have better matching performance[11].

Our system uses Gimel'farb's Symmetric Dynamic Programming Stereo (SDPS) algorithm[1] which has good performance and very importantly, reduces the size of the predecessor array - an unavoidable cost of a dynamic programming approach. It also uses only the last two cost array columns so that the disparity calculator blocks (see Figure 5) are compact and fast.

3.1   Symmetric Dynamic Programming Stereo (SDPS)

The SDPS algorithm places a virtual Cyclopæan eye midway between the left and right cameras. In this view, transitions between disparity levels must pass

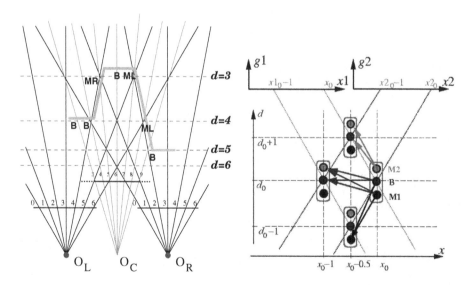

Fig. 3. Camera configuration, showing part of the Cyclopæan image seen by the virtual Cyclopæan camera (centre) and a scene object profile. Visibility states (ML, B or MR) are marked on the profile.

Fig. 4. A set of 'cells' representing points in the Cyclopæan image. Each cell stores costs for three visibility states. The arrows show permitted transitions and dataflow for cost calculation in SDPS. Equations 1, 2 and 3 use the same links.

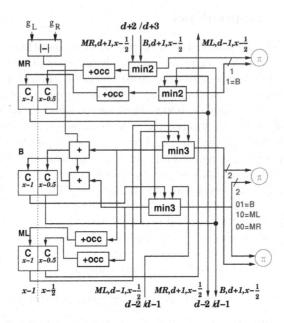

Fig. 5. Disparity calculator for disparities, d and $d+1$. $\frac{\Delta}{2}$ such blocks are instantiated and compute in parallel - see Figure 6.

through monocularly visible states (see Figure 3). Thus SDPS naturally detects occlusions and our system outputs them. Results (see Figure 7), show occlusions neatly outlining objects in the scene: we expect that the occlusion map will prove extremely useful as a very fast way to outline and identify scene objects: it is a very simple map whose elements have only three values - the possible visibility states: B - Binocularly visible; MR - Monocular right (visible only by the right camera) and ML - Monocular left.

Figure 3 shows the canonical arrangement, with a Cyclopæan image (CI) in the centre (dotted rays). A simple profile is shown, with the visibility state of each point on the profile marked. From Figure 3, it is readily seen that any change in disparity along a profile will be accompanied by at least one ML or MR point for each unit change in disparity. This is illustrated in the occlusion maps (see Figure 7) in which it can be seen that the width of the 'outlines' of scene objects is related to the object's separation from its background: foreground objects well separated from the background have broad outlines.

3.2   SDPS Procedure

SDPS matches scan line by scan line, so only one line of image pixels is processed at a time: images are processed as pixels stream from cameras and only Δ pixels from each image are buffered[1]. Thus, we process a one-dimensional array of pixels

---

[1] Rectification requires far more! See Section 2.

from the left, $\mathbf{g^L} = \{g_i^L | i = 0..w - 1\}$ and the right, $\mathbf{g^R} = \{g_i^R | i = 0..w - 1\}$, images. These pixels are used to 'construct' a Cyclopæan image line:

$$\mathbf{g} = \{g_x | x = 0, 1, 2, 3, .., 2w - 1\}$$

Note that $\mathbf{g}$ has twice as many points as $\mathbf{g^{L|R}}$ and that we have chosen to use integral indices rather than the half-integral ones used by Gimel'farb[1]. The corresponding actual image points for a point, x, in the Cyclopæan image in state, B (binocularly visible), at disparity, d, are:

$$x_L = \frac{x + d}{2} \qquad x_R = \frac{x - d}{2}$$

Pixels in the Cyclopæan image with even indices, $x = 0, 2, \ldots$ have even disparities and those with odd indices, $x = 1, 3, \ldots$, odd disparities[1].

In a conventional DP approach, we build two arrays of dimension $6w\Delta$. The cost array, $\mathbf{C}$, has elements, $c_{x,d,s}$, which represent the best cost for a 'path' from the left-most pixel ($x = 0$) to pixel x in the Cyclopæan image ending at disparity, d, with visibility state, $s \in \{MR, B, ML\}$. A predecessor array, π, holds references to the predecessor of each state in the cost array: the final list of disparities is built by a 'back-track' module which works backwards through the predecessor array. Back-tracking contributes the maximum 2 scan lines of latency: note again that this is generally inconsequential compared to latencies introduced in the rectification module *cf.* Section 2.

Each major step has two phases, (e) even indices in the Cyclopæan image (which correspond to even disparities) are considered and (o) odd indices in the Cyclopæan image are computed. To compute new values, c_{dxB}, we use an intensity mismatch between the corresponding pixels for disparity d, *i.e.* $g_{\frac{x+d}{2}}^L$ and $g_{\frac{x-d}{2}}^R$

$$dI(x, d) = |g_{\frac{x+d}{2}}^L - g_{\frac{x-d}{2}}^R|$$

Any function of the difference between pixels could be used but the current implementation shows good results from the simple absolute difference. The cost to reach a binocularly visible point is:

$$c_{x,d,B} = dI(x, d) + \min(c_{x-1,d-1,ML}, c_{x-2,d,B}, c_{x-2,d,MR}) \qquad (1)$$

Costs to reach monocularly visible states are:

$$c_{x,d,ML} = occ\_term + \min(c_{x-1,d-1,ML}, c_{x-2,d,B}, c_{x-2,d,MR}) \qquad (2)$$

$$c_{x,d,MR} = occ\_term + \min(c_{x-1,d+1,MR}, c_{x-1,d+1,B}) \qquad (3)$$

In each case, the state of the cost selected by the min operator is stored in the predecessor array, π. In the back-track stage, since the previous x value, x_{pr}, and disparity, d_{pr}, are uniquely defined by and easily computed from the current, s, and previous, s_{pr}, visibility states, only s_{pr} need be stored in $\pi_{x,d,s}$. Figure 5 shows the circuit for cost evaluation: note that only a handful of small adders are needed - pixels range from 8-12 bits and costs do not need more than 14 bits. The size of the cost registers and associated adders could be limited by subtracting the minimum cost (or some constant value) from each register in the inactive cycle, but this circuit is already sufficiently compact to handle large disparity ranges (see Table 2) in available FPGAs, so this optimization was not implemented.

At line end, a back-track module starts from $\pi(2w - \Delta, argmin_{d,s}(c_{2w-\Delta,d,s}))$ and generates the disparity values for this scan line. Disparities are naturally produced in reverse order, *i.e.* right $\rightarrow$ left when the normal scan is left $\rightarrow$ right: but subsequent host processing is likely to be global and able to work with a scans generated in any order, so we do not incur the additional delay for returning it to the left $\rightarrow$ right order of the pixel stream. In our test programs, the host simply unpacks data packets, which contain corrected left and right pixel data, disparity values and visibility state (from which the occlusion map is formed) and uses the host's efficient memory hierarchy to place data as required for subsequent visualization or storage.

4   FPGA Implementation

Figure 6 shows the major elements of the implementation and their connections. Pixels stream from the two cameras into a pair of FIFOs (not shown)

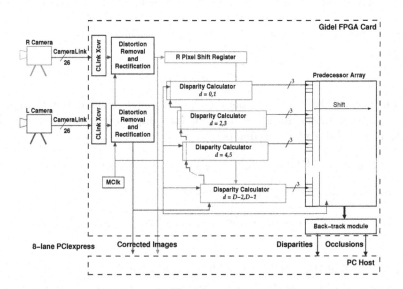

Fig. 6. Prototype system architecture: the section enclosed in the upper dashed boundary fits on a single FPGA

which ensure that the two cameras are perfectly synchronized[2]. The rectification modules then buffer enough pixels for rectification to start. Once the buffers are full, corrected pixels for each camera are emitted synchronously to the correspondence module. This consists of $\Delta/2$ calculator blocks (see Figure 6 and Figure 5). By feeding the left and right pixel streams in opposite directions through the calculator blocks, we ensure that, in each calculation cycle, the needed pixels are present in the correct calculator block.

5   Results

The results shown in this section were obtained with a prototype of the final system based on a Gidel Procstar III card with CameraLink interface and an Altera Stratix III FPGA. Sentech CL83A monochrome cameras (1024×768 pixel frames at 30fps) were directly interfaced to the FPGA. The FPGA card sits on an 8-lane PCIexpress bus in a host PC.

Table 2. Selection of resource requirements

Pixel (bits)	Scan line (pixels)	Scan line buffer	Δ pixels	Logic Utilization	ALUT out of 113600	Registers 113600	Memory (10^6 bits) 5.6
8	1024	64	40	23%	17840	12204	3.5
8	512	128	40	22%	17736	12189	3.4
8	1024	64	64	28 %	24056	14315	3.6
8	1024	64	100	39%	17966	17966	3.8
10	1024	8	40	22%	17736	12350	1.9
10	1024	8	128	48%	41284	20645	2.3
12	1024	8	128	48%	42215	21194	2.5
12	1024	8	256	89%	83364	371406	3.2

5.1   Resources

The space required to implement a circuit is a key metric: it determines how large a problem can be solved in parallel by replication of fundamental circuit blocks. It is also related to the speed of the circuit: large circuits have long, slower interconnects and cannot be clocked as fast as small compact ones.

Table 2 shows the resources required on the Altera FPGA for the *full system* - CameraLink interface, rectification module and correspondence module - for a selection of configuration parameters - number of bits per pixel, number of scan lines buffered to rectify images and disparity range. The figure in 'Logic utilization' column is a rough guide to the fraction of the FPGA's resources used by the circuit. In this case, the target FPGA, an Altera 142,000 logic element

---

[2] Despite our best efforts, the Sentech cameras intransigently refused to synchronize to better than 70μs with hardware triggers.

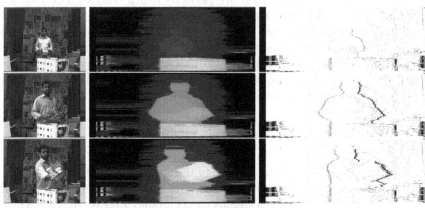

Box: Our model moves forward and places a box ($\Delta = 40$).

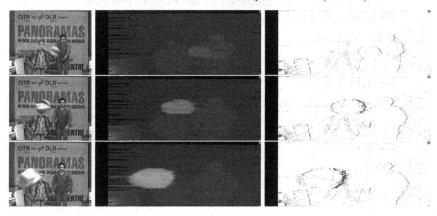

Ball: Figure at the rear (gently) tosses a basketball towards us ($\Delta = 80$).

Fig. 7. Snapshots from video sequences captured in our laboratory: from left to right - left image; disparity map (white represents larger d - closer, black smaller d - farther); occlusion map (grey - ML, right occlusion, white - B, binocular, black - MR, left occlusion). Note that, in the Cyclopæan view, images have twice as many pixels per scan line. Videos with false colour maps (better contrast) and additional sequences may be seen here:

http://www.cs.auckland.ac.nz/~jmor159/HRPG/RT/index.html

FPGA, is relatively small in 2009 technology: so it is clear that our system is easily implemented and does not 'stretch' today's technology. Our final system will separate the rectification circuitry into two small FPGAs (see Figure 1) and result in even smaller utilization factors.

The only resource which taxes today's technology is memory. Most of this is needed to buffer scan lines in the rectification module and the number of lines buffered is large for some of the examples - note that for 64 or 128 buffered scan lines, more than 3×10^6 bits of memory are needed, whereas for 8 buffered scan lines, memory use is significantly smaller. With good mechanical alignment this can be reduced to less than 10: lens distortion contributes 2-3 lines at most. The numbers for 8 buffered scanlines represent systems which use good lenses and are carefully aligned.

Thus the SDPS algorithm is very efficient in terms of resource usage and allows us to either achieve better depth resolution (with higher disparity ranges) or add enhanced adaptive [13] or colour based matching schemes to systems based on available technology.

5.2 Disparity and Occlusion Maps

Selected images from video sequences of some simple choreographed scenes appear in Figure 7. The first sequence shows our actor walking forward and placing a box in front of him. The actor becomes lighter as he approaches. Note that an outline of the main scene objects is clearly visible in the occlusion maps - even when he is not clearly visible in the disparity map. However, this is mainly an illusion due to low image contrast: there is a clear disparity difference! In the second sequence, our actor gently lobs a basketball towards the cameras: it is tracked in flight at 30fps: it becomes lighter as if moves forward. For these images, the disparity range was increased to 80.

6 Conclusions

Since we are still a long way from reproducing the flexibility of human vision, practical systems need to be configured for particular applications. Reconfigurable smart cameras allows a wide range of optical configurations to be handled as demonstrated by the sample configurations in Table 1. The lookup table based approach used in our rectifier is not only fast, it makes no assumptions about the distortion model or mechanical misalignment other than that the curves mapping ideal pixel positions to distorted image positions are smooth. Thus lenses with high distortions, *e.g.* fish-eye lenses and other complex optical systems, will present no problems: although larger lookup tables may be needed, memory requirements are not likely to stress current technology. In the worst case, we can use banks of external memory, that we will routinely add to our final system to permit frame-to-frame optimizations to be added, for larger lookup tables. The benefit from good quality lenses and attention to mechanical design is shown in the resource usage tables and the longer latencies induced by low grade optics and poor alignment - latencies of 60 or more scan lines ($\sim$ 2 ms for 1Mpixels at 30 fps) can be reduced to < 10 scan lines or $\lesssim 300\mu$s.

The SDPS algorithm has a very simple, compact hardware realization which enables our system to produce accurate depth measurements. Small disparity calculator blocks allow disparity ranges > 200 to be implemented on readily available hardware. Preliminary results have been obtained from 1024×768 images with $\Delta = 80$, but synthesis results show that much larger Δ values are possible. Simulations indicate our system will exceed our target of 1Mpixel images processed at 30fps for $\Delta = 100$. Futhermore, FPGA resource utilization is so low, that there is considerable space to add improvements to the basic SDPS algorithm which will improve matching performance.

The combination of disparity map and occlusion map is potentially very important for fast scene understanding: interpretation software can use several strategies to identify objects and their relative importance, for example, an object with a broad 'outline' in the occlusion map is well separated from the background - and possibly extremely important!

References

1. Gimel'farb, G.: Intensity-based computer binocular stereo vision: signal models and algorithms. Int. J. Imaging Systems and Technology 3, 189–200 (1991)
2. Zhang, Z.: A flexible new technique for camera calibration. IEEE Trans. Pattern Analysis and Machine Intelligence 22(11), 1330–1334 (2000)
3. Gribbon, K.T., Johnson, C.T., Bailey, D.G.: A real-time fpga implementation of a barrel distortion correction algorithm with bilinear interpolation. In: Proc. Image and Vision Computing, New Zealand, pp. 408–413 (2003)
4. Zabih, R., Woodfill, J.: Non-parametric local transforms for computing visual correspondence. In: Eklundh, J.-O. (ed.) ECCV 1994. LNCS, vol. 800, pp. 151–158. Springer, Heidelberg (1994)
5. Cox, I.J., Hingorani, S.L., Rao, S.B., Maggs, B.M.: A maximum likelihood stereo algorithm. Computer Vision and Image Understanding 63, 542–567 (1996)
6. Sabihuddin, S.: Dense stereo reconstruction in a field programmable gate array, Master's thesis, University of Toronto (June 2008), http://hdl.handle.net/1807/11161
7. Gong, M.L., Yang, Y.H.: Real-time stereo matching using orthogonal reliability-based dynamic programming. IEEE Trans. Image Processing 16(3), 879–884 (2007), http://dx.doi.org/10.1109/TIP.2006.891344
8. Park, S., Jeong, H.: Real-time stereo vision FPGA chip with low error rate. In: MUE, pp. 751–756. IEEE Computer Society, Los Alamitos (2007)
9. Park, S., Jeong, H.: A high-speed parallel architecture for stereo matching. In: Bebis, G., Boyle, R., Parvin, B., Koracin, D., Remagnino, P., Nefian, A., Meenakshisundaram, G., Pascucci, V., Zara, J., Molineros, J., Theisel, H., Malzbender, T. (eds.) ISVC 2006. LNCS, vol. 4291, pp. 334–342. Springer, Heidelberg (2006)
10. Park, S., Jeong, H.: A fast and parallel belief computation structure for stereo matching. In: IMSA 2007: IASTED European Conference on Proceedings of the IASTED European Conference, pp. 284–289. ACTA Press, Anaheim (2007)
11. Scharstein, D., Szeliski, R.: Stereo Vision Research Page (2005), http://cat.middlebury.edu/stereo/data.html
12. Yi, J., Kim, J., Li, L., Morris, J., Lee, G., Leclercq, P.: Real-time three dimensional vision. In: Yew, P.-C., Xue, J. (eds.) ACSAC 2004. LNCS, vol. 3189, pp. 309–320. Springer, Heidelberg (2004)
13. Morris, J., Gimel'farb, G.: Real-time stereo image matching system. NZ Patent Application 567986, May 2 (2008)

Engineering of Computer Vision Algorithms
Using Evolutionary Algorithms

Marc Ebner

Eberhard Karls Universität Tübingen
Wilhelm-Schickard-Institut für Informatik
Abt. Rechnerarchitektur, Sand 1, 72076 Tübingen
marc.ebner@wsii.uni-tuebingen.de
http://www.ra.cs.uni-tuebingen.de/mitarb/ebner/welcome.html

Abstract. Computer vision algorithms are currently developed by looking up the available operators from the literature and then arranging
those operators such that the desired task is performed. This is often a
tedious process which also involves testing the algorithm with different
lighting conditions or at different sites. We have developed a system for
the automatic generation of computer vision algorithms at interactive
frame rates using GPU accelerated image processing. The user simply
tells the system which object should be detected in an image sequence.
Simulated evolution, in particular Genetic Programming, is used to automatically generate and test alternative computer vision algorithms.
Only the best algorithms survive and eventually provide a solution to
the user's image processing task.

1 Introduction

Software development of computer vision algorithms is usually quite difficult.
In several other fields, e.g. developing graphical user interfaces, the customer
is able to specify how the product should look and how it should react to the
user's input. In most cases, developing the software is rather straight forward
were it not for communication problems between the customer and the software
development company. The difficulty lies in understanding the customer and
finding out what the customer actually wants. However, in the field of Computer
Vision, for many difficult problems it is not known how the problem may be
solved at all.

Suppose that the task is to program a software which recognizes different
objects. The customer would be able to provide images which show the object
which should be recognized. The task of the software engineer would be to write
a piece of software which recognizes these objects in an image sequence taken by
a video camera. The software engineer would then develop the required software
in his lab and take the software and equipment to the site where it should be
used. Quite often, the software developed in the lab may behave different when
installed outside the lab.

J. Blanc-Talon et al. (Eds.): ACIVS 2009, LNCS 5807, pp. 367–378, 2009.

This may be due to different lighting conditions. A computer vision algorithm usually depends on the given environment. Different algorithms may be needed when there is little light available compared to when there is a lot of light available and consequently there is little noise in the data. Development of computer vision software is usually a tedious process with many iterations of testing and modification.

In the field of evolutionary computation [1], where simulated evolution is used to find optimal parameters for a given problem, methods have been developed to automatically evolve computer programs. This field is called Genetic Programming (GP) [2,3]. Currently, it is not possible to evolve large scale software such as a word processor through Genetic Programming. However, Genetic Programming has been used very successfully to evolve variable sized structures for problems such as analog and digital circuit design [4], antenna design [5], robotics or design of optical lenses [6].

With this contribution, we will show how the software development of computer vision algorithms may be automated through the use of Genetic Programming. Until recently, it was very difficult to evolve computer vision algorithms due to the enormous computational resources which are required. With the advent of powerful programmable graphics hardware it is now possible to accelerate this process such that computer vision algorithms can be evolved interactively by the user. This considerable reduces development times of computer vision algorithms.

The paper is structured as follows. First we will have a look at the field of evolutionary computer vision in Section 2. Section 3 shows how Genetic programming may be used evolve computer vision algorithms. GPU accelerated image processing is described in Section 4. A case study of an experimental system which is used to evolve computer vision algorithms is described in Section 5. Section 6 gives some conclusions.

2   Evolutionary Computer Vision

Evolutionary algorithms can be used to search for a solution which is not immediately apparent to those skilled in the art or to improve upon an existing solution. They work with a population of possible solutions. Each individual of the population represents a possible solution to the given problem. The solution is coded into the genetic material of the individuals. Starting from the parent population a new population of individuals is created using Darwin's principle "survival of the fittest". According to this principle, only those individuals are selected which are better than their peers at solving the given problem (usually above average individuals are selected). The selection is usually performed probabilistically. Above average individuals have a higher probability of getting selected than individuals which only perform below the population average. The selected individuals will breed offspring. Those offspring are usually not identical to their parents. Genetic operators such as crossover and mutation are used to recombine and change the genetic material of the parents. This process continues until a sufficient number of offspring have been created. After this, the cycle repeats for another generation of individuals.

In the field of evolutionary computer vision, evolutionary algorithms are used to search for optimal solutions for a variety of computer vision problems. Early work on evolutionary computer vision was started by Lohmann in the 1990s. He showed how an method can be evolved which computes the Euler number of an image using an Evolution Strategy [7].

Initially, evolutionary algorithms were used to evolve low-level operators such as edge detectors [8], feature detectors [9,10], or interest point detectors [11]. They were also used to extract geometric primitives [12] or to recognize targets [13]. Evolutionary algorithms may of course also be used to evolve optimal operators for the task at hand [14]. Poli noted in 1996 that Genetic Programming would be particularly useful for image analysis [15]. Johnson et al. have used Genetic Programming successfully to evolve visual routines which detect the position of the hand in a silhouette of a person [16].

Evolutionary computer vision has become a very active research area in the last couple of years. Current work still focuses on the evolution of low-level detectors [17]. However, research questions such as object recognition [18] or camera calibration [19] are also addressed. Due to the enormous computational requirement, most experiments in evolutionary computer vision are performed off-line. Experiments in evolutionary computer vision can take from one day to several days or even weeks depending on the difficulty of the problem. Once an appropriate solution has been found, it may of course be used in real time. Recently, it has become increasingly apparent that the graphical processing unit (GPU) can be used to speed up general processing done by the central processing unit (CPU). Computer vision algorithms are particularly amenable to GPU acceleration due to the similarity between the computations required for image processing and those performed by the GPU when rendering an image.

3   Genetic Programming for Automated Software Evolution

Evolutionary Algorithms are quite frequently used for parameter optimization. However, for automatic software induction we need to apply Genetic Programming, an evolutionary method which is used to evolve variable sized structures in general and computer programs in particular [2,3]. Genetic Programming can either be used to evolve a computer algorithm from scratch or to improve upon an existing solution. The genetic operators are used to arrange the program instructions contained in the individual such that over the course of evolution the individual performs its intended function.

A computer vision algorithm usually consists of a sequence of image processing operators which are known from the literature. These operators are applied to an input image or to a sequence of images. If one wants to solve a new computer vision problem one has to decide in what order and with which parameters the operators should be applied. For many difficult problems, this is an experimental process. Genetic Programming can be used to automate this process. Here, Genetic Programming is used to automatically search the space of possible image

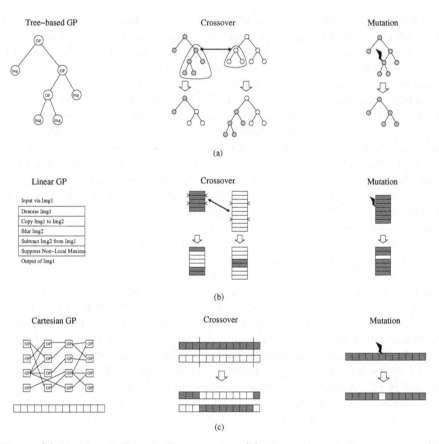

Fig. 1. (a) Tree-based Genetic Programming (b) Linear Genetic Programming (c) Cartesian Genetic Programming

processing operators. The instructions of the computer program correspond to image processing operators.

Current research on Genetic Programming focuses on three main paradigms: tree-based GP, linear GP and Cartesian GP. The three paradigms are illustrated in Figure 1. Tree-based Genetic Programming works with a representation where the individuals are represented by trees. The internal nodes of the tree are the instructions of the program [20]. The external nodes hold the input to the program. If this representation is used for evolutionary computer vision, the external nodes represent the input image and the nodes operate on the entire image. The genetic operators crossover and mutation are used to manipulate the structure of the individual. When the crossover operator is applied, two individuals are selected from the population and two randomly selected sub-trees are exchanged between the two parent individuals. When the mutation operator is applied to create an offspring, a node is selected at random and is replaced with a newly generated sub-tree.

Linear GP uses a linear sequence of instructions [21]. The instructions operate on a set of registers. The input to the program is supplied via the registers. The instructions are used to modify the content of the registers. The output of the program is read out from the output registers. Again, genetic operators such as crossover and mutation are used to manipulate the linear sequence of instructions. If this representation is used for evolutionary computer vision, then the registers represent the entire image or a pixel from the image.

Cartesian Genetic Programming works with a representation where the operators or functions are arranged into a $n \times m$ matrix [22]. The input is provided on the left hand side of the matrix. The operator located in a given column can process the data which is available from any previous column. The output is read out from one or more output nodes on the right hand side of the matrix.

4 GPU Accelerated Image Processing

Evolution of computer vision algorithms at interactive rates is only possible with hardware acceleration. Current PCs are equipped with powerful graphics hardware which can be used to accelerate the image processing operations. The graphics hardware is even used to perform computations which are completely unrelated to computer graphics. It has successfully been used to implement algorithms such as sorting, searching, solving differential equations, matrix multiplications or computing the fast Fourier transform. Owens et al. [23] give a detailed survey on general-purpose computation on graphics hardware. Different applications such as the simulation of reaction-diffusion equations, fluid dynamics, image segmentation, ray tracing or computing echoes of sound sources have all been implemented on the GPU.

Several different packages are available which facilitate the development of GPU accelerated algorithms. Buck et al. [24] have developed a system for general-purpose computation on programmable graphics hardware by using the GPU as a streaming coprocessor. The Compute Unified Device Architecture (CUDA) package is available from Nvidia [25]. With CUDA it is possible to use the GPU as a massively parallel computing device. It is programmed using a C like language.

Image processing operators can be readily mapped to the programming paradigm which is used when rendering images. Hence, several researchers have used the GPU to implement computer vision algorithms. Fung et al. [26] implemented a projective image registration algorithm on the GPU. A hierarchical correlation based stereo algorithm was implemented by Yang and Pollefeys [27,28]. Fung and Mann [29] showed how simple image operations such as blurring, down-sampling and computing derivatives and even a real-time projective camera motion tracking routine can be mapped to the GPU programming paradigm. Fung et al. [30] have developed a computer vision software OpenVIDIA which can be used to develop computer vision algorithms on the GPU.

We now have a look at how the GPU can be used to evolve computer vision algorithms at interactive rates. Current graphics hardware is highly optimized for rendering triangles [31]. In computer graphics, a triangle is defined by its three vertices in three-dimensional space. Additional information such as normal vector, material properties or texture coordinates are usually stored with each vertex. The graphics hardware then maps this triangle onto a two-dimensional plane with discrete pixels. This usually occurs in several stages. The three-dimensional coordinates are first transformed into eye coordinates, i.e. relative to the camera. The coordinates lying within the view frustum are then further transformed into a unit cube. This has the advantage that clipping becomes easier. The rasterizer maps all coordinates within the unit cube to the discrete raster positions of the output image.

The information which is required to color the pixel within a triangle are obtained by interpolating data from the vertices. Originally, the steps taken by the GPU to render a triangle was fixed. It could not be modified by the user. This changed in 1999, when programmable stages were introduced into the graphics pipeline [23]. With modern graphics hardware it is now possible to execute small programs, called vertex and pixel shaders, which perform various computations either per vertex or per pixel in order to determine the color or shader of a vertex or pixel. The code of the vertex shader is usually used to transform the coordinates of the vertex into the unit cube, the clip space. At this stage, all data which is required by the pixel shader is set up. This data includes the normal vector or texture coordinates both of which are specified per vertex. The

```
Texture Declaration
    uniform sampler2D textureColor;
    float sx=1.0/width; float sy=1.0/height;
Blur Shader
    gl_FragColor.rgb=texture2D(textureColor,gl_TexCoord[0].st,3);
Gradient Shader
    vec2 dx[4]={vec2(-sx,.0),vec2(.0,sy),vec2(sx,.0),vec2(.0,-sy)};
    vec4 color,delta;
    float gradient=0.0;
    color=texture2D(textureColor,gl_TexCoord[0].st,0);
    for (int i=0;i<4;i++) {
        delta=color-texture2D(textureColor,gl_TexCoord[0].st+dx[i],0);
        gradient+=dot(delta,delta);
    }
    gl_FragColor.rgb=2*sqrt(gradient);
Laplacian Shader
    vec4 color;
    vec2 dx[4]={vec2(-sx,.0),vec2(.0,sy),vec2(sx,.0),vec2(.0,-sy)};
    color=4*texture2D(textureColor,gl_TexCoord[0].st,0);
    for (int i=0;i<4;i++)
        color-=texture2D(textureColor,gl_TexCoord[0].st+dx[i],0);
    gl_FragColor=5*color;
```

Fig. 2. Shader code which was used to create the output images shown in Figure 3. This demonstrates how easily computer vision operators can be implemented using the OpenGL Shading Language.

Input Image   Blur Shader   Gradient Shader   Laplacian Shader

Fig. 3. Output images generated using the four pixel shaders shown in Figure 2

rasterizer interpolates this data. It is then available for each pixel of the triangle. The code of the pixel shader is basically used to compute the color of each pixel using the interpolated data for every pixel of the triangle.

The shader programs (vertex and pixel shaders) are set up to process four-dimensional 32-bit floating-point vectors. These vectors are four-dimensional because four-dimensional homogeneous coordinates are used to process three-dimensional Cartesian coordinates. These vectors are also used to store the color components red, green and blue together with a transparency value.

When pixel and vertex shaders were first introduced, they had to be programmed using a special kind of assembly language. The commands from this assembly language were mostly dedicated to performing various computations which are frequently needed during the lighting computation when coloring a pixel. A drawback of this approach was that the code was difficult to port to a different graphics card. Later, high-level C-like languages appeared, e.g. Cg [32], developed by Nvidia, and the Open Graphics Library Shading Language (OpenGLSL) [33]. With these C-like languages it is now considerably easier to write pixel and vertex shaders which can be executed on a variety of different graphics cards. The code written for the vertex and pixel shaders is compiled by the graphics driver wherever it is executed.

We will be using the OpenGL Shading Language to program the vertex and pixel shaders. Image processing operations are mapped to the GPU by sending four vertices to the GPU. These vertices constitute a quad which represents our image. The pixel shader is used to perform the image processing operation in parallel for all pixels of the input image. The input image is stored in a texture which is made available to the pixel shader through texture operations. Figure 2 shows the OpenGLSL code for three different image operators (Blur, Gradient, Laplacian). The output of these three pixel shaders for a sample image is shown in Figure 3.

The blur shader uses the mip mapping mechanism of OpenGLSL to compute a blurred input image. The mip mapping mechanism is usually used to downsample textures. The blur shader can be implemented with a single line of code. The gradient shader reads adjacent pixels of the texture, computes the differences and sums up the squared differences over all three color channels. The Laplacian shader reads out the center and surrounding pixels. It then computes the differences between these two. The output of the Laplacian falls within the range [-1,1]. It is therefore mapped to [0,1] for display. These three examples show how easy it is to use the GPU for computer vision applications.

5   Evolving Computer Vision Algorithms Interactively

We have created an object recognition vision system which allows the user to automatically evolve computer vision algorithms at interactive rates. The system is equipped with a video camera from which input images are gathered. Alternatively, the system can also process images from video sequences. The user specifies the object which should be recognized using the mouse pointer. The user keeps pressing the mouse button as long as the object is located underneath the mouse pointer. This is the teaching input used by the system.

Our system works with a parent population of μ individuals. Initially, these individuals are generated entirely at random. The output of the three best individuals is always shown on the screen as shown in Figure 4. The task of the evolved computer programs is to locate the object, which was specified by the user, as closely as possible. The pixel with the largest response, where the RGB colors are interpreted as a 24-bit number, is taken as the position of the object. If several pixels have a response of 0xFFFFFF, then the center of gravity is computed.

The Cartesian Genetic Programming paradigm [22] is used as a representation for the individuals. Each individual consists of a set of connected nodes. For each node, we have to specify the function which is computed by this node. We also have to specify how a given node is connected to previous nodes. This set of connected nodes is not evolved directly. Instead, one works with a linear representation which can be readily mapped to the set of connected nodes. The first number specifies the function computed by the first node. The second number specifies the first argument which can be used be this node and the third number specifies the second argument. The fourth number specifies the function of the second node and so on. The functions which are available to the individuals are taken directly from the OpenGL shading language. The representation is fully described by Ebner [34].

Fig. 4. System overview. The input image is shown in the upper left hand corner. The remaining three images show the output of the best three individuals of the population. The teaching input (specified by the user using the mouse) is the yellow marker. The three rectangular markers (shown in red, green, and blue) show the position located by the best three individual.

bus stop sign

ducks in a pond

interest point

Fig. 5. Results obtained with three evolved object detectors. The three rectangular markers (in red, green and blue) show the position of the object located by the three best individuals of the population. The best output (shown in red) corresponds closely to the object or part of the image which should be located.

Starting from the parent individuals, we create offspring by using the crossover operator with a probability of 70%. In other words, 70% of the offspring are created by recombining the genetic material of parent individuals. The remaining 30% of the offspring are created by simply reproducing a parent individual. For a mutation, a randomly chosen byte is either decreased by one or increased by one or the entire string is mutated with a mutation probability of $2/l$ where l is the length of the string in bits, i.e. on average, we will have two mutations per offspring. In addition to those offspring which are generated from the parent population, the same number of individuals are also generated at random. This allows for a continuous influx of new genetic material.

Individuals are evaluated by computing the distance between the position, which is specified by the user, and the position which is returned by the individual. This is our error measure or fitness function. Since our input is dynamically changing, we also re-evaluate the parent individuals. We then sort the μ parents and λ offspring according to fitness.

The best μ individuals are selected as parents for the next generation among both parents and offspring. This is a so called $(\mu + \lambda)$ Evolution Strategy. Note that we are working with a redundant representation. Two individuals which differ in their genetic representation can actually compute the same function. That's why only one individual for every fitness value is considered for selection. This is an effective method of diversity maintenance in our context. We then repeat this process of reproduction, variation and selection for every input image.

Our system, consisting of an Intel Core 2 CPU running at 2.13GHz and a GeForce 9600GT/PCI/SEE2 graphics card, achieves a frame rate of 4 Hz while evaluating 23 individuals, each processing an input image of size 320x240, for each generation. The speedup is 17 if two high level operators followed by a 2×2 matrix of simpler operators are used compared to an all software implementation of the same algorithm. The speedup increases to 24.6 if four high level operators are used.

This system was tested on several different image sequences (shown in Figure 5). Object detectors which have been evolved so far, include ducks in a pond, traffic signs as well as an interest point on a building. An object detector which is able to locate the object with a reasonably small error was evolved in less than 120 generations, i.e. within 30 seconds with a frame rate of 4Hz. Manually writing these detectors would have taken considerably longer. As the graphics hardware gets more powerful, we will be able to evolve increasingly complex detectors.

6   Conclusions

With current advances in computer graphics hardware it is now possible to automatically generate computer vision algorithms at interactive rates. This reduces development times considerable and also allows laymen, not having any previous experience with the programming of computer vision algorithms, to automatically generate such algorithms. This is a step towards the programming of computers by telling them what the user wants and without explicitly telling the computer exactly what to do.

References

1. Eiben, A.E., Smith, J.E.: Introduction to Evolutionary Computing. Springer, Berlin (2007)
2. Koza, J.R.: Genetic Programming. In: On the Programming of Computers by Means of Natural Selection. The MIT Press, Cambridge (1992)
3. Banzhaf, W., Nordin, P., Keller, R.E., Francone, F.D.: Genetic Programming - An Introduction: On The Automatic Evolution of Computer Programs and Its Applications. Morgan Kaufmann Publishers, San Francisco (1998)

4. Koza, J.R., Bennett III, F.H., Andre, D., Keane, M.A.: Genetic Programming III. Darwinian Invention and Problem Solving. Morgan Kaufmann Publishers, San Francisco (1999)
5. Linden, D.S.: Innovative antenna design using genetic algorithms. In: Bentley, P.J., Corne, D.W. (eds.) Creative Evolutionary Systems, pp. 487–510. Morgan Kaufmann, San Francisco (2002)
6. Koza, J.R., Al-Sakran, S.H., Jones, L.W.: Automated re-invention of six patented optical lens systems using genetic programming. In: Proc. of the 2005 Conf. on Genetic and Evolutionary Computation, pp. 1953–1960. ACM, New York (2005)
7. Lohmann, R.: Bionische Verfahren zur Entwicklung visueller Systeme. PhD thesis, Technische Universität Berlin, Verfahrenstechnik und Energietechnik (1991)
8. Harris, C., Buxton, B.: Evolving edge detectors with genetic programming. In: Koza, J.R., Goldberg, D.E., Fogel, D.B., Riolo, R.L. (eds.) Genetic Programming, Proc. of the 1st Annual Conf., pp. 309–314. The MIT Press, Cambridge (1996)
9. Rizki, M.M., Tamburino, L.A., Zmuda, M.A.: Evolving multi-resolution feature-detectors. In: Fogel, D.B., Atmar, W. (eds.) Proc. of the 2nd American Conf. on Evolutionary Programming, pp. 108–118. Evolutionary Programming Society (1993)
10. Andre, D.: Automatically defined features: The simultaneous evolution of 2-dimensional feature detectors and an algorithm for using them. In: Kinnear Jr., K.E. (ed.) Advances in Genetic Programming, pp. 477–494. The MIT Press, Cambridge (1994)
11. Ebner, M.: On the evolution of interest operators using genetic programming. In: Poli, R., Langdon, W.B., Schoenauer, M., Fogarty, T., Banzhaf, W. (eds.) Late Breaking Papers at EuroGP 1998: the 1st European Workshop on Genetic Programming, Paris, France, pp. 6–10. The University of Birmingham, UK (1998)
12. Roth, G., Levine, M.D.: Geometric primitive extraction using a genetic algorithm. IEEE Trans. on Pattern Analysis and Machine Intelligence 16(9), 901–905 (1994)
13. Katz, A.J., Thrift, P.R.: Generating image filters for target recognition by genetic learning. IEEE Trans. on Pattern Analysis and Machine Int. 16(9), 906–910 (1994)
14. Ebner, M., Zell, A.: Evolving a task specific image operator. In: Poli, R., Voigt, H.-M., Cagnoni, S., Corne, D.W., Smith, G.D., Fogarty, T.C. (eds.) EvoIASP 1999 and EuroEcTel 1999. LNCS, vol. 1596, pp. 74–89. Springer, Heidelberg (1999)
15. Poli, R.: Genetic programming for image analysis. In: Koza, J.R., Goldberg, D.E., Fogel, D.B., Riolo, R.L. (eds.) Genetic Programming 1996, Proc. of the 1st Annual Conf., Stanford University, pp. 363–368. The MIT Press, Cambridge (1996)
16. Johnson, M.P., Maes, P., Darrell, T.: Evolving visual routines. In: Brooks, R.A., Maes, P. (eds.) Artificial Life IV, Proc. of the 4th Int. Workshop on the Synthesis and Simulation of Living Systems, pp. 198–209. The MIT Press, Cambridge (1994)
17. Trujillo, L., Olague, G.: Synthesis of interest point detectors through genetic programming. In: Proc. of the Genetic and Evolutionary Computation Conf., Seattle, WA, pp. 887–894. ACM, New York (2006)
18. Treptow, A., Zell, A.: Combining adaboost learning and evolutionary search to select features for real-time object detection. In: Proc. of the IEEE Congress on Evolutionary Computation, Portland, OR, vol. 2, pp. 2107–2113. IEEE, Los Alamitos (2004)

19. Heinemann, P., Streichert, F., Sehnke, F., Zell, A.: Automatic calibration of camera to world mapping in robocup using evolutionary algorithms. In: Proc. of the IEEE Int. Congress on Evolutionary Computation, San Francisco, CA, pp. 1316–1323. IEEE, Los Alamitos (2006)
20. Koza, J.R.: Artificial life: Spontaneous emergence of self-replicating and evolutionary self-improving computer programs. In: Langton, C.G. (ed.) Artificial Life III: SFI Studies in the Sciences of Complexity Proc., vol. XVII, pp. 225–262. Addison-Wesley, Reading (1994)
21. Nordin, P.: A compiling genetic programming system that directly manipulates the machine code. In: Kinnear Jr., K.E. (ed.) Advances in Genetic Programming, pp. 311–331. The MIT Press, Cambridge (1994)
22. Miller, J.F.: An empirical study of the efficiency of learning boolean functions using a cartesian genetic programming approach. In: Banzhaf, W., et al. (eds.) Proc. of the Genetic and Evolutionary Computation Conf., pp. 1135–1142. Morgan Kaufmann, San Francisco (1999)
23. Owens, J.D., Luebke, D., Govindaraju, N., Harris, M., Krüger, J., Lefohn, A.E., Purcell, T.J.: A survey of general-purpose computation on graphics hardware. In: Eurographics 2005, State of the Art Reports, pp. 21–51 (2005)
24. Buck, I., Foley, T., Horn, D., Sugerman, J., Fatahalian, K., Houston, M., Hanrahan, P.: Brook for GPUs: Stream computing on graphics hardware. In: Int. Conf. on Comp. Graphics and Interactive Techniques (ACM SIGGRAPH), pp. 777–786 (2004)
25. NVIDIA: NVIDIA CUDA. Compute Unified Device Architecture. V1.1 (2007)
26. Fung, J., Tang, F., Mann, S.: Mediated reality using computer graphics hardware for computer vision. In: Proc. of the 6th Int. Symposium on Wearable Computers, pp. 83–89. ACM, New York (2002)
27. Yang, R., Pollefeys, M.: Multi-resolution real-time stereo on commodity graphics hardware. In: Proc. of the IEEE Conf. on Computer Vision and Pattern Recognition, pp. 211–218. IEEE, Los Alamitos (2003)
28. Yang, R., Pollefeys, M.: A versatile stereo implementation on commodity graphics hardware. Real-Time Imaging 11(1), 7–18 (2005)
29. Fung, J., Mann, S.: Computer vision signal processing on graphics processing units. In: Proc. of the IEEE Int. Conf. on Acoustics, Speech, and Signal Processing, 2004, vol. 5, pp. 93–96. IEEE, Los Alamitos (2004)
30. Fung, J., Mann, S., Aimone, C.: OpenVIDIA: Parallel GPU computer vision. In: Proc. of the 13th annual ACM Int. Conf. on Multimedia, Singapore, pp. 849–852. ACM, New York (2005)
31. Akenine-Möller, T., Haines, E.: Real-Time Rendering, 2nd edn. A K Peters, Natick (2002)
32. Fernando, R., Kilgard, M.J.: The Cg Tutorial. In: The Definitive Guide to Programmable Real-Time Graphics. Addison-Wesley, Boston (2003)
33. Rost, R.J.: OpenGL Shading Language, 2nd edn. Addison-Wesley, Upper Saddle River (2006)
34. Ebner, M.: A real-time evolutionary object recognition system. In: Vanneschi, L., Gustafson, S., Moraglio, A., Falco, I.D., Ebner, M. (eds.) EuroGP 2009. LNCS, vol. 5481, pp. 268–279. Springer, Heidelberg (2009)

Shape Recognition by Voting on Fast Marching Iterations

Abdulkerim Capar and Muhittin Gokmen

Istanbul Technical University, Computer Engineering Department,
34469 Ayazaga, Istanbul Turkiye
{capar,gokmen}@itu.edu.tr

Abstract. In this study, we present a Fast Marching (FM) - Shape Description integrated methodology that is capable both extracting object boundaries and recognizing shapes. A new speed formula is proposed, and the local front stopping algorithm in [1] is enhanced to freeze the active contour near real object boundaries. GBSD [2] is utilized as shape descriptor on evolving contour. Shape description process starts when a certain portion of the contour is stopped and continues with FM iterations. Shape description at each iteration is treated as a different source of shape information and they are fused to get better recognition results. This approach removes the limitation of traditional recognition systems that have only one chance for shape classification. Test results shown in this study prove that the voted decision result among these iterated contours outperforms the ordinary individual shape recognizers.

Keywords: Fast Marching, Shape Descriptor, Decision fusion.

1 Introduction

We present a variational framework that integrates the statistical boundary shape models into a Level Set system that is capable of both segmenting and recognizing objects. Level Sets is a promising implicit contour based segmentation method, introduced by Osher and Sethian [3]. Fast marching method is also proposed by Sethian [4] to overcome the high computational requirements of level sets. Although ordinary level sets has the complexity of $O(N^3)$ ($O(N^2)$ for narrow band) fast marching method can be implemented with $O(N)$ complexity [5].

Incorporation of shape knowledge on the segmenting contour is not a new idea [6,7]. Integration of statistical shape variation into the level set methods was first proposed by Leventon et.al. [8] and then several researchers worked on this area [9,10,14]. Cremers et al. [11,12] first presented a variational integration of nonlinear shape statistics into a Mumford-Shah [13] based segmentation process. Cremers [18] has also presented a study to tackle the challenge of learning dynamical statistical models for implicitly represented shapes. He obtained good results of tracking deformable objects like walking person.

There are major differences between these studies and this work: (1) the evolving front (see Fig. 2) is always forced to have the prior shape in the studies.

J. Blanc-Talon et al. (Eds.): ACIVS 2009, LNCS 5807, pp. 379–388, 2009.

However, we stop the front near object boundaries, (2) it is stated that, the proposed method does not work when the number of prior object classes is more than one [14]. However, our system is capable to segment and recognize different classes of characters, (3) previous researchers obtained the shape statistics from the whole map of level set values; however we employ only the front itself for shape description, (4) previously proposed systems need high calculation power because they have two optimization stages, one is for minimization of image based energies, and other is for minimizing shape based energies. On the other hand, our system has one optimization step for minimizing both energies.

Capar and Gokmen [1] represented a concurrent shape segmentation and description system which constructs the base of this study. In this study we have developed a new system which has better segmentation and recognition capabilities. A new speed function is defined for Fast Marching system. The local contour stopping algorithm presented in [1] is also improved with new constrains. The shape descriptor is replaced with GBSD [2], which is a powerful gradient based shape descriptor. Main contribution of the work is to develop a new segmentation-recognition approach which can be applied to any active contour based object segmentation system. Using more than one segmentation results for shape identification is the base of the approach. It has following advantages comparing with traditional object recognition approaches;

- In traditional recognition systems misrecognitions mostly occur because of poor segmentations. An object cannot be easily recognized if we cannot extract it from the background properly. In this study, many segmentation results are employed as input of classifiers to reduce the bad effects of segmentation on recognition.
- In traditional recognition systems only one recognition chance exists for a single object, but we can obtain many decision results while the active contour is capturing the shape. We have showed in Section 4 that voting among these results raises the recognition performance comparing with single decision cases.
- We have feedback mechanism between segmentation and description. This feedback provides better segmentation and recognition results.

2   Fast Marching Methods

The goal of the Level Set method is to track the motion of the interface as it evolves with a known speed [15]. Fast Marching (FM) method is very fast versions of the level set methods with some limitations, that is curve propagation speed F must be of constant sign and the curve must be evolve in one direction. If the speed value is always of constant sign FM method guarantees that one image element is passed only one time by the front. Therefore we can use the arrival time $T(x, y)$ of the front as it crosses the point (x, y) to represent the position of the front. These arrival time values can be calculated based on the well-known equation: $Distance = Time * Rate$. Than we have

$$1 = F\frac{dT}{dx} \Rightarrow |\nabla T|F = 1 \tag{1}$$

The approximate solution of Eq. 1 on a 2D grid is given as in [4]

$$max(D_{ij}^{-x}T,0)^2 + min(D_{ij}^{+x}T,0)^2 + max(D_{ij}^{-y}T,0)^2 + min(D_{ij}^{+y}T,0)^2 = \frac{1}{F_{ij}^2} \quad (2)$$

where $D_{ij}^{-x}T = \frac{T_{i,j}-T_{i-1,j}}{\Delta x}$ and $D_{ij}^{+x}T = \frac{T_{i+1,j}-T_{i,j}}{\Delta x}$. Eq. 2 states that the time difference between neighbor points cannot exceed the inverse of the speed. It also guaranties the one way evolution of the curve, from smaller values to larger values. Modeling the speed function is the most critical step to slow down the front near real object boundaries.

2.1 New Speed Function

A speed function that is inversely proportional with the gradient magnitude and proportional with local boundary curvature is defined in [1]. This is a common formula which assumes that the gradients are spreaded homogeneously accross the image. This assumption is mostly invalid in real world, in terms of physical corruption of objects and imaging noise. Consider Fig. 1 that illustrates the gradient of two cross-sections on the same shape boundary. The blue cross-section is on an edge with a large intensity transition while the red one lies on an edge with small intensity transition. If we use only the gradient magnitudes, the evolving front never passes on these two regions at the same time, because of the imbalance gradient on edge pixels. This is a critical problem on locating the real object boundaries.

To overcome this limitation, second derivatives (Laplacians) are also embedded into the speed formula. With the help of Laplacians, we can determine the location of gradient peaks, which are probable edges. Recall that, laplacian goes to zero while edge intensity transition is increasing.

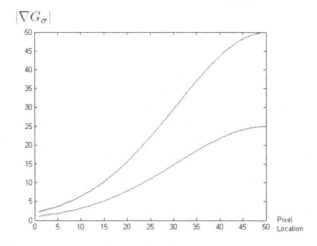

Fig. 1. Two gradient cross-sections on an image. y-axis shows gradient magnitude and x-axis shows cross-section pixel location.

Gradients and laplacians are utilized to formulate the front speed as

$$F = \begin{cases} \frac{\beta|\nabla^2 G_\sigma * I|}{1+\alpha|\nabla G_\sigma * I|} & |\nabla G_\sigma * I| \geq 0 \\ \frac{1}{1+\alpha|\nabla G_\sigma * I|} & otherwise \end{cases} \tag{3}$$

where $|\nabla G_\sigma|$ and $\nabla^2 G_\sigma$ show the gradient and Laplacian operators respectively. β and α are positive constants that control the weight of gradient and Laplacian terms. Laplacian term provides speeding up the front on the regions with high gradient changes when gradients do not reach peaks. It also slows down the front around the gradient peaks.

2.2   Enhanced Front Stopping Algorithm

Contrast differences along shape boundaries (Fig. 1) prevent the global fitting of the fast marching contour on true shape boundary points. That is because different gradient magnitudes produce different speed values and different speed values cause different arrival time values. A local node freezing process is needed to handle these differences and fixing the active contour near the true object boundary points. A local contour stopping algorithm was proposed in [1] which trusts only the local gradient magnitudes to decide whether an active node should be fixed or not.

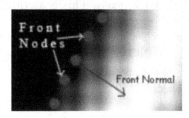

Fig. 2. Demonstration of evolving nodes and the front normal on image gradient map

In this work we improved the algorithm in [1] by adding new constrains. The proposed algorithm tends to freeze the nodes one by one, when the node is on a grid with a high-enough gradient (hysteresis thresholding [16]) and when the gradient is a local maximum toward the normal of the evolving curve (Fig. 2). We have also a smoothness condition to stop the node: If the number of fixed trial points in the 8-neighborhood of the node is more than two then we label it as fixed trial point.

3   Shape Recognition

Integration of shape descriptors into the Fast Marching process is accomplished during front stopping section. We employed the recently proposed boundary based shape descriptor named as GBSD.

3.1 Gradient Based Shape Descriptor

Gradient Based Shape Descriptor (GBSD) [2] is a boundary based shape descriptor which could be applied to both binary and grayscale images. The steerable [17] G-Filters [19] are used to obtain gradient information at different orientations and scales, and then aggregate the gradients into a shape signature. The signature derived from the rotated object is circularly shifted version of the signature derived from the original object. This property is called the circular-shifting rule [20]. The shape descriptor is defined as the Fourier transform of the signature.

We use the complex gradient shape signature $H(\Gamma)$ which is defined as

$$H\left(\Gamma\right) = \begin{bmatrix} D^{\theta_0} + jD^{\theta_0 + \frac{\pi}{2}} \\ D^{\theta_0} + jD^{\theta_0 + \frac{\pi}{2}} \\ \vdots \\ D^{\theta_0} + jD^{\theta_0 + \frac{\pi}{2}} \end{bmatrix} \tag{4}$$

where $D^{\theta}(x_i, y_i) = \left(I * G^{\theta}\right)(x_i, y_i)$ is the steerable filter response at the boundary point (x_i, y_i) and $\theta_0 = 0$. $G^{\theta}(x_i, y_i)$ is the θ rotated version of the Gradient filter $G^{\theta=0}(x_i, y_i)$.

3.2 FM - GBSD Integration

Fast Marching trial points $x_t(k)$ [4] constitute the shape contour. There are two types of trial points in this study: "fixed" trial points $x_f(k)$ and "Moving" trial points $x_m(k)$ such that

$$x_t(k) = x_f(k) \bigcup x_m(k). \tag{5}$$

Shape signatures $u(t)$ are obtained by a linear process over the boundary points (see Eqn. 4), then

$$u_t(t) = u_f(t) \bigcup u_m(t) \tag{6}$$

Fourier Descriptors of shape signature is calculated as

$$\begin{aligned} a_n &= \frac{1}{N} \sum_{t=0}^{N-1} u_t(t) exp(\frac{-j2\pi nt}{N}) \\ &= \frac{1}{N}[U_f + U_m] \\ &= \frac{1}{N}\{\sum_{t=0}^{F-1} u_f(t) exp(\frac{-j2\pi nt}{N}) + \sum_{t=F}^{N-1} u_m(t) exp(\frac{-j2\pi nt}{N})\} \end{aligned} \tag{7}$$

where F and N shows the number of fixed trial points and all trial points.

The formulation in Eq. 7 has the advantages that calculation complexity is decreased since the fixed term is stable and it does not change rapidly. New fixed points are simply added to U_f and calculation for old fixed points is not repeated.

Another point is to determine the starting time of shape description as the front is getting closer to the real shape boundary. Number of fixed trial points is a good parameter to start description, since it increases while the contour getting closer to real edges. We start shape description process when the number of fixed trial points is greater than number of moving points.

3.3   Classification with Voting

Recognition methods mostly suffered from segmentation errors, which are especially important for boundary based classifiers. A general segmentation system produces only one result for a single shape. However, the proposed Fast Marching based object segmentation - recognition technique is able to create more than one object boundary outcomes, which can be combined to improve classification performance. It is also useful while working with limited number of train samples. We can increase the number of train samples with utilizing different boundary contours for the same shape.

Consider that we have collected M shape descriptor vectors $[a^0, a^1, ..., a^{M-1}]$, M decision results $[r^0, r^1, ..., r^{M-1}]$ and M confidence values $[c^0, c^1, ..., c^{M-1}]$, where $0 < c^i < 1$ at the end of FM iterations. These shape decisions are fused with decision voting which constructs the decision label histogram of r^i and selects the maximum number as final decision (majority voting). The experimental works on classification and performance reports can be found in Section 4. The 1 - nearest neighbour method is selected as classifier.

4   Experimental Work

We utilize the license plate character dataset to measure the recognition performance of the proposed segmentation-recognition system. The database contains 8321 grayscale digit characters segmented from the real vehicle license plates. About the half of the characters in the database, namely 4121 digits, is used in training, and the remaining 4200 digits are kept for testing. The Fast Marching front stopping algorithm (Section 2.2) is applied to prepare the boundary contours in training and testing set. Evolving boundary contours are collected

Fig. 3. 10 Selected boundary contour samples

Table 1. Recognition rates when using single train and single test samples for each character. Numbers 1,2,..,10 indicates the selection order index (See Fig. 3).

Train	Test Index									
Index	10	9	8	7	6	5	4	3	2	1
10	96.82	96.67	95.96	95.28	94.08	91.29	88.38	86.52	85.92	84.75
9	96.8	96.77	96.16	95.81	94.29	91.83	89.39	87.11	86.45	85.43
8	96.7	96.34	96.22	95.83	94.95	92.87	90.0	87.03	85.94	85.48
7	96.42	96.37	96.04	95.86	95.05	93.4	91.67	89.26	88.02	87.34
6	96.42	96.42	96.14	95.91	95.78	94.82	93.15	90.56	89.21	88.48
5	96.6	96.27	96.19	96.09	96.01	95.86	94.85	93.25	91.29	90.81
4	96.29	96.22	96.11	96.06	95.89	95.99	95.94	95.33	94.16	93.53
3	96.29	96.09	95.89	95.76	95.81	95.56	96.19	95.86	95.81	95.73
2	96.39	96.11	95.96	95.37	95.02	94.19	94.64	95.38	95.94	95.91
1	96.39	96.06	95.81	95.3	94.67	93.5	93.04	94.19	95.91	96.09

through FM iterations. We have large number contours for each character; therefore, we need to select a certain number of contours. Naturally, the contour samples, which include big number of fixed trial points, have more recognition potential. For that reason, the selection starts when the fixed point percentage exceeds 50% and continues until global front freeze. We have selected 10 contour samples uniformly in this defined period for each character (See Fig. 3).

In traditional classification schemes, there is only one chance to classify a pattern in contrast to proposed system. We have 10 samples for each pattern (Fig. 3) in training and testing. Table 1 exposes the recognition rates with single training sample and single testing sample for each character pattern as in traditional methods.

Let i and j indicates the selected sample index of training and testing patterns respectively. We can easily see on Table 1 that, success rates increases while $|i-j|$ decreases. As you see on the table, rates are bigger along the left diagonals, where $|i-j|$ is near zero. Another result, which is extracted from Table 1, is that recognition rates are better for big sample indexes i and j. That is because these sample contours have more fixed nodes than others have, so they are near the real object boundaries. Now we have more than one sample for each pattern both in training and testing set. Therefore we need to merge these information sources. We accomplished three test mechanisms as follows:

Test1. This test is proceed to measure the effect of augmented train set with evolving contour samples. We utilized all 10 training samples and made test on single test samples. Recognition rates are shown at Table 2. Recognition

Table 2. Testing with augmented training set

	Test Index									
Train	10	9	8	7	6	5	4	3	2	1
Select All	97.08	96.87	96.7	96.67	96.62	96.42	96.75	96.42	96.47	96.49

Table 3. Testing with augmented testing set

Test	Train Index									
	10	9	8	7	6	5	4	3	2	1
Select Best	98.75	98.8	98.68	98.5	98.5	98.65	98.65	98.65	98.63	98.63

Table 4. Recognition rates with voting

Test	Train Index								
	10	9	8	7	6	5	4	3	2
Voting	97.56	97.51	97.28	97.2	96.98	97.13	96.77	96.82	96.8

performance is obviously better than the results in Table 1, which means that training set augmentation property of the proposed technique increases the success rate.

Test2. Second test is to show the advantage of test set augmentation. We use single training samples and test on whole 10 testing samples. A character is accepted to be classified right when any sample is right. Recognition rates are listed on Table 3. However, this type of test cannot be used in real problems, it is only for demonstrating the classification power in these augmented test samples.

Test3. Third test is actually a special combination of first two tests. In this test, each test sample classification result is threaded as a different source of decision and a simple decision voting is accomplished. Notice that, this type of test can be used in any real world classification problem. We investigate the recognition performance while changing the sample number for each training & testing pattern (Table 4). Naturally, the performance is getting better while the sample number is increasing. We obtained at most 97.56 % recognition rate when we combine all 10 samples together. Note that, the results in this voting test is

Fig. 4. Segmentation result on corrupted characters, left column: input images, middle column: Canny edge detection results, right column: results of the proposed system

much better than the single sample number test in Table 1, which reaches 96.82% at maximum. It proves that the proposed segmentation - recognition system is more successful than the traditional single sample recognition systems.

One of the main problems of the character segmentation is degradation of the images by noise or physical effects. As an example, paints or mugs on the license plate surface causes such problems. The proposed system is also capable of solving such problems by incorporating shape information into the front stopping conditions. Segmentation results of the Canny Edge Detection [16] method and the proposed method are illustrated in Fig. 4. As seen in the results, our system can capture the object boundaries better in spite of the noise around the characters.

5   Conclusion

Shape identification systems mostly suffer from the object segmentation problems. Moreover, segmentation errors are more dangerous for boundary based shape recognizers than other type of recognizers. This study proposed a new approach to setup a shape recognition system working with multiple segmentation outputs of Fast Marching Algorithm. These outputs are threaded as different sources of decision and they are fused to have final decision. With the help of our experiments we showed that this decision fusion approach outperforms other traditional -single decision- shape recognizers.

We have chosen a simple majority voting approach as decision approach. That is because we aim to show the advantage of using multiple decision results against single decision. Other more complicated fusion techniques will be investigated in future work.

References

1. Capar, A., Gokmen, M.: Concurrent segmentation and recognition with shape-driven fast marching methods. In: Proc. ICPR, Hong Kong, vol. 1, pp. 155–158 (2006)
2. Capar, A., Kurt, B., Gokmen, M.: Gradient-based shape descriptors. Machine Vision and Applications (2008), doi:10.1007/s00138-008-0131-5
3. Osher, S., Sethian, J.A.: Fronts propagating with curvaturedependent speed: Algorithms based on the Hamilton-Jacobi formulation. Journal of Computational Physics, 12–49 (1988)
4. Sethian, J.A.: A Fast Marching level set method for monotonically advancing fronts. Proc. Nat. Acad. Sci. 93(4), 1591–1595 (1996)
5. Yatziv, L., Bartesaghi, A., Sapiro, G.: O(N) implementation of the fast marching algorithm. Journal of Computational Physics 212(2), 393–399 (2006)
6. Wang, Y., Staib, L.: Boundary finding with correspondence using statistical shape models. In: Proc. CVPR, pp. 338–345 (1998)
7. Staib, L., Duncan, J.: Boundary finding with parametrically deformable contour methods. IEEE PAMI 14(11), 1061–1075 (1992)
8. Leventon, M., Grimson, W., Faugeras, O.: Statistical Shape Infuence in Geodesic Active Contours. In: Proc. CVPR, pp. 316–323 (2000)

9. Chen, Y., Tagare, H., Thiruvenkadam, S., Huang, F., Wilson, D., Gopinath, K., Briggsand, R., Geiser, E.: Using Prior Shapes in Geometric Active Contours in a Variational Framework. IJCV 50(3), 315–328 (2002)

10. Gastaud, M., Barlaud, M., Aubert, G.: Combining Shape Prior and Statistical Features for Active Contour Segmentation. IEEE Transactions on Circuits And Systems for Video Technology 14(5), 726–734 (2004)

11. Cremers, D., Tischhaauser, F., Weickert, J., Schnörr, C.: Diffusion Snakes: Introducing Statistical Shape Knowledge into the Mumford-Shah Functional. IJCV 50(3), 295–313 (2002)

12. Cremers, D., Kohlberger, T., Schnörr, C.: Shape Statistics in Kernel Space for Variational Image Segmentation. Pattern Recognition, Special Issue on Kernel and Subspace Methods in Computer Vision 36(9), 1929–1943 (2003)

13. Mumford, D., Shah, J.: Optimal approximations by piecewise smooth functions and associated variational problems. Comm. Pure Appl. Math. 42, 577–685 (1989)

14. Paragios, N., Rousson, M.: Shape Priors for Level Set Representations. In: European Conference in Computer Vision, pp. 78–92 (2002)

15. Sethian, J.A.: Level Set Methods and Fast Marching Methods. Cambridge University Press, New York (1999)

16. Canny, J.: A computational approach to edge detection. IEEE Transactions on Pattern Analysis and Machine Intelligence 8(6), 679–698 (1986)

17. Freeman, W.T., Adelson, E.H.: The Design and Use of Steerable Filters. IEEE Transactions on Pattern Analysis and Machine Intelligence 13, 891–906 (1991)

18. Cremers, D.: Dynamical Statistical Shape Priors for Level Set-Based Tracking. IEEE Trans. Pattern Anal. Mach. Intell. 28(8), 1262–1273 (2006)

19. Gokmen, M., Jain, A.K.: $\lambda\tau$-Space Representation of Images and Generalized Edge Detection. IEEE Transactions on Pattern Analysis and Machine Intelligence 19(6), 545–563 (1997)

20. Capar, A., Kurt, B., Gokmen, M.: Affine-Invariant Gradient Based Shape Descriptor. In: Gunsel, B., Jain, A.K., Tekalp, A.M., Sankur, B. (eds.) MRCS 2006. LNCS, vol. 4105, pp. 514–521. Springer, Heidelberg (2006)

Unusual Activity Recognition in Noisy Environments

Matti Matilainen, Mark Barnard, and Olli Silvén

University of Oulu, Department of Electrical and Information Engineering,
Machine Vision Group
{matti.matilainen,olli.silven}@ee.oulu.fi,
mark.barnard@surrey.ac.uk
http://www.ee.oulu.fi/mvg/

Abstract. In this paper we present a method for unusual activity recognition that is used in home environment monitoring. Monitoring systems are needed in elderly persons homes to generate automatic alarms in case of emergency. The unusual activity recognition method presented here is based on a body part segmentation algorithm that gives an estimation of how similar the current pose is compared to the poses in the training data. As there are arbitrary number of possible unusual activities it is impossible to train a system to recognize every unusual activity. We train our system to recognize a set of normal poses and consider everything else unusual. Normal activities in our case are walking and sitting down.

Keywords: Computer vision, body part segmentation, unusual activity recognition.

1 Introduction

Unusual activity recognition has many possible applications in automatic surveillance. We are concentrating on monitoring elderly people in home environments to generate automatic alarms when unusual activity is detected. There are other solutions for making alarms such as passive infrared sensors, accelerometers, and pressure pads. These kinds of sensors must be worn all the time so the automatic video monitoring approach is much more comfortable to the person using it.

The problem with computer vision based systems is that they usually have to be trained for each installation location separately. This increases the cost of the system significantly. In domestic environments the furniture causes difficult occlusions. We have developed a solution that requires neither training nor adjustment of parameters in a new location. Our system uses only one uncalibrated camera. The features and statistical methods we used to model the actions work very well in very noisy environments and under occlusions.

Unusual activity recognition is addressed in several publications. Chowdhury and Chellappa [1] tracked the persons and then classified the actions to normal/unusual based on the trajectories. They obtained a set of basis shapes from the training trajectories. The unknown activities were recognized by projecting

J. Blanc-Talon et al. (Eds.): ACIVS 2009, LNCS 5807, pp. 389–399, 2009.

onto those basis shapes. Salas et al. [2] also used only the trajectories of objects. They presented a method that detects forbidden turns and red light infringements in vehicular intersections. Nait-Charif et al. [3] trained Gaussian Mixture Models (GMMs) for recognizing inactivity zones from overhead camera. When the person monitored becomes inactive outside the inactivity zone it is considered unusual activity. Mahajan et al. [4] used several layers of finite state machines (FSM) to model the activities. They label an unknown activity unusual if the logical layer FSM fails to recognize it. Töreyin et al. [5] calculated the height and widht ratios of bounding boxes. This sequence was wavelet transformed and used as features in HMM based classification to discriminate between walking and falling over. The method has problems telling the difference between sitting down and falling over so they also analyzed the audio tracks of the videos to find high amplitude sounds produced by falling over.

In statistical pattern recognition the patterns are D dimensional feature vectors that can be considered as points in D dimensional feature space. Each class forms a cluster of points into the feature space. The unknown sample vectors can be classified to some of these classes depending on how close it is to the corresponding cluster. If the distributions in the training data are the same as in real world the classifier performs optimally. The classifier needs enough training data to be able to generalize enough to recognize patterns it has never seen before. If there is not enough training data the classifier cannot recognize anything but the patterns that are included in the training data. This is called overfitting. If the models used are complex they need lots of training data. In some problems there is need for a very large training set that requires labelling. Labelling video data can be very time consuming. Sometimes it is impossible to label the required data by hand.

Synthetic training data can be used instead of hand labelled data. We propose the use of artificial training data to generate a large number of training examples. The synthetic data was created through motion capture. We captured sequences with 5 test subjects. From these sequences we rendered a training database of over 50000 frames. In each frame the body parts are automatically labelled by color. It would be impossible to label this much data by hand.

Synthetic training data has been used many applications. Varga and Bunke [6] created a method for generating synthetic training data from hand written text. They applied geometrical transforms and thinning/thickening operations to the text lines. Heisele and Blanz [7] used morphable models for creating more training data from a small set of face images. They built a 3D model from the example image and then rendered it under varying lighting conditions and from different viewing angles.

In Section 2 we present our unusual activity recognition method. We are using Hidden Markov Models and Gaussian Mixture Models to segment the body parts from background subtracted silhouette images. The body part segmentation algorithm gives an estimation of how well the given silhouette corresponds to the ones in the training data. This information is used at higher level to detect the unusual activities. The experiments conducted are described in Section 3 and discussed in Section 4.

2   Our Approach

Our unusual activity recognition method builds on the body part segmentation algorithm proposed by Barnard et al. [8]. Before body part segmentation a background subtraction algorithm is applied to each frame. Figure 1 illustrates some example frames where the body parts are segmented. The frames are from five different sources. Each is shot with different equipment and the person performing the actions is different in each frame. The resolution and lightning conditions varies. The first column is the original input frame. The second column shows the result of background subtraction. The third column is the final result. In some of the frames the arms are very close to the body and they are correctly recognized. There is also some noise that causes the limbs to be cut out from the silhouette. The silhouette edges are often distorted by varying lightning conditions and shadows that cause the background subtraction to fail.

The body part segmentation algorithm uses Hidden Markov Models (HMMs) [9] and GMMs. These statistical models need a lot of labelled training data to avoid overfitting. We trained the models only with synthetic training data. The synthetic training data was created through motion capture. In the motion capture process 5 subjects (3 male and 2 female) were used. 16 optical markers

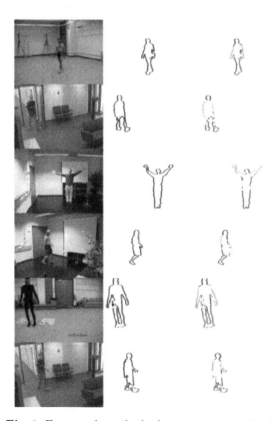

Fig. 1. Frames where the body part segmentation is applied

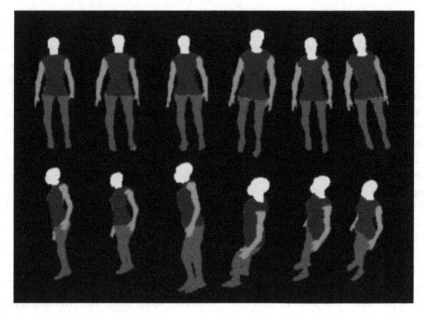

Fig. 2. Examples from the training data. The labelled 3D model rendered from 12 different viewing angles with different offsets.

were attached to each person and the markers were tracked with three cameras. The marker trajectories were used to animate a 3D model. The 3D model had each body part labelled with different colors. This way we had to label the model only once to create a training database of over 50000 frames. Some example frames are shown in Figure 2. The model is rendered from different viewing angles. Labelling that much data by hand is very time-consuming. We can re-render the synthetic training data from new viewing angles, lighting conditions and with added occlusions automatically. We also used some data from the CMU motion capture database. The motion capture process is discussed in detail in [8].

We used shape context features proposed by Belongie et al. [10] to represent the silhouette edges. The shape context features have been used in shape matching and defining the aligning transformation between two objects.

The silhouette edge is sampled at regular intervals. For each sampled edge point the distance and direction to each other edge point that fall under the maximum distance is calculated. These are stored in a histogram. Belognie et al. used a log-polar histogram. In log-polar histogram the spacing is equal in logarithmic space. The log-polar histogram is illustrated on the left of Figure 3. We conducted experiments using modified features [11]. Instead of log-polar histogram we used weighted radial bins as illustrated on the right of Figure 3. The distance of the radial bin from the center is given by,

$$d(r) = \begin{cases} \frac{R}{2N} & \text{if } \frac{R}{3} < r < \frac{2R}{3} \\ \frac{R}{N} & \text{else} \end{cases} \tag{1}$$

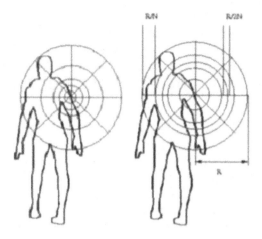

Fig. 3. Illustration of the original and weighted bins

where N is the number of radial bins with equal spacing and R is the overall radius of the shape context descriptor. This way the middle radial bins are emphasized and the locality of the descriptor is maintained.

A GMM was trained for each body part from the shape context features. The GMMs form the states of a HMM. We consider each silhouette outline as a sequence of shapes corresponding to body parts (Head, Arms, Legs and Body). Using an HMM we can constrain the shape recognition by taking into account the transitions between different body parts using Viterbi decoding [9]. The state transition matrix is estimated from the labeled training data. The state transitions are illustrated in Figure 4.

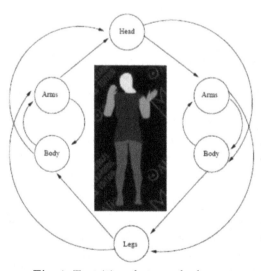

Fig. 4. Transitions between body parts

The body part segmentation algorithm outputs the label (head, body, arms or legs) for each silhouette edge pixel and the likelihood. We calculated the average likelihood over all the edge pixels. When the person is in a pose that is not present in the training data the average likelihood drops. The pose is then considered abnormal. The average likelihood of the pose is given by,

$$L = \frac{1}{m} \sum_{i=1}^{m} l_i \qquad (2)$$

where L is the average likelihood, m is the number of pixels in the silhouette and l_i is the likelihood of the i th pixel.

We used three sequences containing walking (normal activity) and falling over (unusual activity) as the training set to find the statistically optimal threshold for unusual poses. These sequences were not included in the testing set. The average likelihoods for walking and falling over were 55.0 (standard deviation 7.5) and 21.0 (standard deviation 9.3) respectively. The threshold was set to 39.5. This sequence of thresholded likelihoods can be used for higher level recognition.

We propose the use of majority voting over large number of consecutive decisions because the actions occur over a period of time. This way the influence of single frames with incorrect decisions is not significant. When the majority voting window moves through the signal it works like a low pass filter. If the decision is made from only one fame at the time then a large number of false alarms are going to be raised. The false alarms are not as harmful as a missed unusual activity but to keep the system running robustly they must be removed.

This method can be used with several cameras if the whole room can not be covered with a single camera. The frames from each camera can be concatenated to a single buffer and the method can be applied to all the frames in the buffer.

3   Experiments

In our experiments we used 16 test sequences that were shot from only one viewing angle. 14 of the sequences introduce a person walking, falling over and getting up. In one of the sequences the person walks then sits down and then gets up. In the last sequence the person walks around the room. These sequences without any unusual activities are used to test if the method gives false alarms. Test sequences were recorded in different locations using different hardware to get more variations in the data. We used both male and female subjects.

The same models and parameters were used during each test. The models were trained using only synthetic training data that was created through motion capture.

We also tested the method with majority voting over 50 previous frames. If the average likelihood in over 50% of the frames is below the threshold then the activity is unusual. The frame rate of the sequences varies from 10 fps to 20fps resulting in a buffer from 5.0s to 2.5s respectively. If there is at least 1 frame that is classified as unusual in the walking sequence then a false alarm

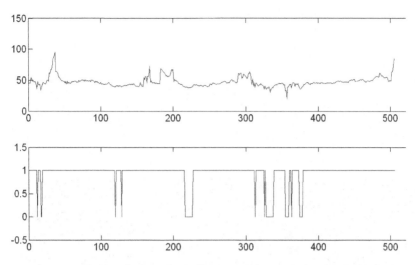

Fig. 5. Average likelihood plot of a walking sequence and the thresholded sequence

has been made. Without any higher level decisions the system is prone to false alarms. There were 5 false alarms in the walk sequences (16 sequences total) without the voting method. There were no false alarms when using the voting method. All the fall over activities were detected correctly with and without the voting. The Figure 5 shows one average likelihood plot of a walking sequence. The second plot is the thresholded sequence where 1 and 0 means normal and unusual activity respectively. There are several frames where the likelihood drops below the threshold so a false alarm would have been generated. If the voting method is applied to this sequence no false alarms are generated.

The majority voting can be applied over any number of frames from different cameras. In addition to the 16 single camera tests we ran tests with International Conference on Distributed Smart Cameras (ICDSC, *http://wsnl2.stanford.edu/ icdsc09challenge/*) videos (four viewing angles) and our own motion capture videos (three viewing angles) that were not used in the training. We chose to use

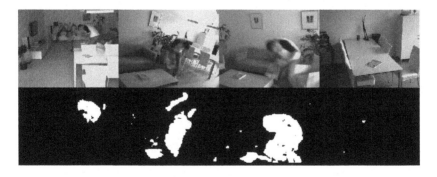

Fig. 6. ICDSC frames with corresponding background subtracted frames

a buffer of 10 frames from each video stream resulting in a buffer of 40 and 30 frames from ICDSC and motion capture videos respectively. Figure 6 illustrates frames from each of the four cameras of the ICDSC videos. In these sequences the

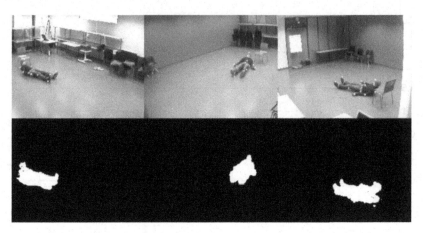

Fig. 7. Frames from our motion capture database

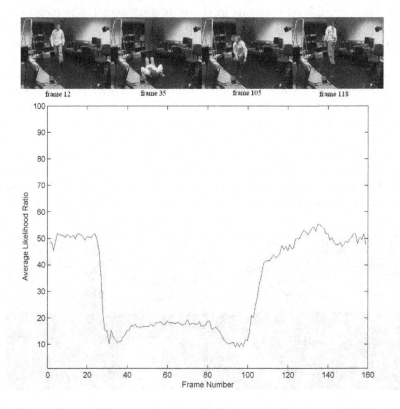

Fig. 8. Frames from a fall over sequence and the corresponding average likelihood plot

background subtraction failed. The person in the sequence moves static objects in the scene and is badly occluded by furniture. The voting method raised one false alarm in this sequence. There were no false alarms in the motion capture video and correct alarm was raised when the person fell over. Figure 7 shows frames from the motion capture sequence where the person has fallen over.

Our experiments show that the voting method reduces the overall frame classification rate but it is acceptable because it is not necessary that every single frame is recognized correctly if the alarms are raised correctly.

4   Discussion

In the testing data 93.41% of the frames were classified correctly when using the statistically optimal threshold. Most of the misclassified frames were the ones where the person was falling over or getting up. Figure 8 shows few frames of a falling over sequence from the test data and the corresponding average likelihood ratio plot. An example sit down sequence is illustrated in Figure 9. In the sit down sequence the likelihood drops when the activity is changing from walking to sitting but it still over the threshold. The average likelihood drops sharply below the threshold when the person falls over.

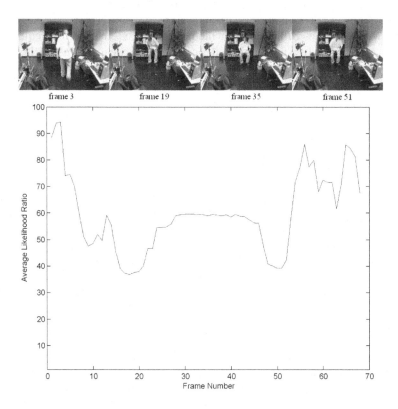

Fig. 9. Frames from a sit down sequence and the corresponding average likelihood plot

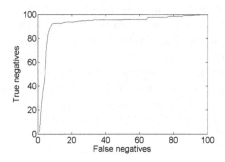

Fig. 10. The receiver operator characteristic

We ran the tests using different thresholds. The receiver operator characteristic (ROC) curve is plotted in Figure 10. In the ROC curve the true negatives (correctly recognized walking) are plotted against false negatives (missed unusual activity). It is important to have a low false negative rate because missing an unusual activity in a monitoring application such as this could be disastrous. Whereas the false positives are not as critical as false negatives it is crucial to keep them as low as possible to have the system running robustly.

The system we presented here has a lot of applications. It can be used in elderly persons homes to monitor for medical concerns. It does not require any sensors to be worn by the monitored person. It is cheap to install in a new location because the training is done only once and the trained models can be used in each installation location.

5   Conclusions

We have presented a solution for unusual activity recognition that uses a body part segmentation algorithm to determine how similar an unknown pose is compared to the ones in the training data. If the pose is close enough compared to the trained models it is considered normal. The unknown activity sequences were processed with majority voting window to ignore the single frames where the recognition was not correct. The body part segmentation algorithm was trained using only synthetic training data we created through motion capture.

We have showed that the solution works in very noisy environments. The models were trained only once and the same models were used in all the test cases. The test sequences were shot in different locations and with different equipment.

References

1. Chowdhury, A., Chellappa, R.: Factorization Approach for Activity Recognition. In: Computer Vision and Pattern Recognition Workshop, vol. 4(4), p. 41 (2003)
2. Salas, J., Jiménez, H., González, J., Hurtado, J.: Detecting Unusual Activities at Vehicular Intersections. In: IEEE International Conference on Robotics and Automation, pp. 864–869 (2007)

3. Nait-Charif, H., McKenna, S.J.: Activity Summarisation and Fall Detection in a Supportive Home Environment. In: International Conference on Pattern Recognition, pp. 323–326 (2004)
4. Mahajan, D., Kwatra, N., Jain, S., Kalra, P., Banerjee, S.: A framework for activity recognition and detection of unusual activities. In: Proceedings of Indian Conference on Computer Vision, Graphics and Image Processing, pp. 15–21 (2004)
5. Töreyin, U.B., Dedeoglu, Y., Cetin, A.E.: HMM Based Falling Person Detection Using Both Audio and Video. In: Signal Processing and Communications Applications, pp. 1–4 (2006)
6. Varga, T., Bunke, H.: Generation of synthetic training data for an hmm-based handwriting recognition system. In: Proceedings International Conference on Document Analysis and Recognition, p. 618 (2003)
7. Heisele, B., Blanz, V.: Morphable models for training a component-based face recognition system. In: Computer Vision and Patern Recognition, p. 1055 (2004)
8. Barnard, M., Matilainen, M., Heikkilä, J.: Body Part Segmentation of noisy human silhouette. In: International Conference on Multimedia and Expo., pp. 1189–1192 (2008)
9. Rabiner, L.R.: A tutorial on Hidden Markov Models and Selected Applications in Speech Recognition. Proceedings of the IEEE 77(2), 257–286 (1989)
10. Belongie, S., Malik, J., Puzicha, J.: Shape matching and object recognition using shape contexts. IEEE Transactions on Pattern Analysis and Machine Intelligence 24(4), 509–522 (2002)
11. Barnard, M., Heikkilä, J.: On bin configuration of shape context descriptors in human silhouette classification. In: International Conference on Advanced Concepts for Intelligent Vision Systems, pp. 850–859 (2008)

Real-Time Center Detection of an OLED Structure

Roel Pieters, Pieter Jonker, and Henk Nijmeijer

Dynamics and Control Group, Department of Mechanical Engineering
Eindhoven University of Technology, PO Box 513, 5600 MB Eindhoven
{r.s.pieters,p.p.jonker,h.nijmeijer}@tue.nl

Abstract. The research presented in this paper focuses on real-time image processing for visual servoing, i.e. the positioning of a x-y table by using a camera only instead of encoders. A camera image stream plus real-time image processing determines the position in the next iteration of the table controller. With a frame rate of 1000 fps, a maximum processing time of only 1 millisecond is allowed for each image of 80x80 pixels. This visual servoing task is performed on an OLED (Organic Light Emitting Diode) substrate that can be found in displays, with a typical size of 100 by 200 μm. The presented algorithm detects the center of an OLED well with sub-pixel accuracy (1 pixel equals 4 μm, sub-pixel accuracy reliable up to ± 1 μm) and a computation time less than 1 millisecond.

1 Introduction

Present day measurement and positioning systems are pushing the limits regarding positioning accuracy and fabrication time. For this, visual servoing is a method that broadens the area for intelligent embedded vision systems (see for instance [3], [5] and [2]). In literature, control in visual servoing is a research topic characterized by various classifications and formats. An extensive review can be found in [5]. Image processing algorithms for this are described e.g. in [8], while vision systems that use image processing to obtain 1 ms visual feedback with a massively parallel architecture are presented in [10] and [6]. However, the combination of image processing and high performance visual servoing in real-time, *without* massively parallel processing is rather new. This combination, with an emphasis on real-time image processing embed in smart cameras, is presented in this paper.

In visual servoing, the measurement loop between product and sensor is cut short by placing a camera directly on the production head. This means that the measuring system now no longer relies on encoders for positioning but solely on the camera. The most limiting factor in this is the balance between a high sampling rate and the size of the image to extract useful information. An equilibrium is found for our OLED application characterized by positioning at micrometer scale and a frame rate of 1 kHz (1000 fps) by using an ROI of 80 × 80 pixels, whereas 1 pixel equals 4 μm. The product to be controlled is in our case a substrate (see figure 1), consisting of a 2D repetitive pattern of OLED 'wells' or

J. Blanc-Talon et al. (Eds.): ACIVS 2009, LNCS 5807, pp. 400–409, 2009.

'cups' which need to be filled (printed) with a polymer substance by an industrial inkjet printer. Each OLED has a typical size of 100×200 μm that should be filled by a slightly larger droplet with an accuracy of maximum 10 μm. As the measurements are taken at 1 kHz, this results in a maximum effective computation time of 1 ms. The captured 80×80 pixels then contain 3 OLED structures. For visualization purposes, this paper deals with images of 100×200 pixels and thus nine OLED cups. The method we present here is split into an on-line step and an off-line step. The off-line step does an initial calibration of the substrate to ensure a margin of alignment with respect to the camera. If necessary, this can be accompanied by a shading correction if the grey-level uniformity is out of bound, and a height adjustment of the camera if the image is out of focus. The on-line step consists of the actual movement of the camera over the substrate from which images are taken at a fixed rate of 1 kHz. The OLED cups are then extracted with a Difference of Gaussian filter which separates the cups from their surroundings. Subsequent morphological operations Erosion and Dilation remove noise. From the resulting blobs the outlines are drawn by following the contours and an area calculation leaves only the nine largest structures. A larger rectangular box is drawn around each structure and used as an ROI (region of interest) on the original image to determine the center of gravity, which gives the center of each cup. Also on-line, a measure of focus can be calculated, as well as an extra orientation calculation with the resulting found cup centers. This paper is organized as follows: Section 2 describes the algorithms used in the off-line step in detail. The algorithms used in the on-line step are explained in Section 3. Results of the performed experiments are given in Section 4. Finally, conclusions and future work are given in Section 5.

The long-term goal of our project 'Fast Focus On Structures' (FFOS) is to develop an intelligent visual servoing system that can be used for various industrial applications such as industrial inkjet printing. This paper mainly focuses on the embedded image processing task for visual servoing, being the extraction of highly accurate positions and orientations (poses) for the control of an x-y table. The motion control side of this project can be found in [2].

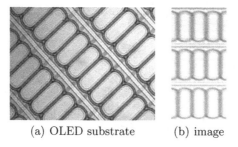

(a) OLED substrate   (b) image

Fig. 1. OLED substrate. High resolution image of OLED substrate (a). The OLED images are rendered in grey scale with, in our case, nine OLEDs per image. The size of this image is 100×200 pixels (b). Image (a) taken from OTB Group.

2 Off-Line Step

The off-line step is used for the calibration of the camera with regard to the OLED substrate. The start point on the substrate for the on-line step should be found and some calibration criteria should be checked. A single image is used to determine if a correction in alignment, depth of focus and shading is necessary. Since in this phase timing is not essential, the image can be as large as the camera allows. This check can be done at several locations on the substrate and with several image sizes.

2.1 Histogram of Gradient Orientations

The orientation of the complete OLED substrate / complete display should be determined with an accuracy of $\pm 1\,°$. This is done to ensure a roughly correct alignment with respect to the initial camera frame. The camera orientation angle can only be corrected up to 5 degrees in the on-line stage, as the center detection algorithm in the on-line stage is only guaranteed between [-5:5] degrees (see section 3). The orientation of the entire OLED is determined by calculating the histogram of gradient orientations from the OLED image, which is convoluted with two different 3 x 3 Sobel kernels:

$$S_x = \begin{bmatrix} 1 & 0 & -1 \\ 2 & 0 & -2 \\ 1 & 0 & -1 \end{bmatrix}, \qquad S_y = \begin{bmatrix} 1 & 2 & 1 \\ 0 & 0 & 0 \\ -1 & -2 & -1 \end{bmatrix} \qquad (1)$$

These resulting gradient approximations are then used to calculate the gradient direction in every pixel:

$$\Theta = \arctan\left(\frac{G_y}{G_x}\right) \qquad (2)$$

where G_x and G_y is the result of the image convoluted with S_x and S_y respectively. This gradient calculation has an accuracy of $\pm 1\,°$, due to the inaccurate

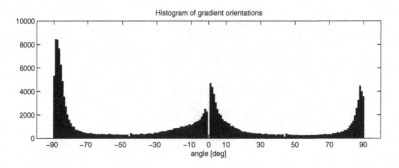

Fig. 2. Histogram of gradient orientations. Image gradients are calculated using 3x3 Sobel kernels. The two peaks represent the vertical (biggest peak) and horizontal edge of the OLED grid structure.

approximation of the image gradient. From the gradient directions a histogram is constructed which depicts peaks in horizontal (x) and vertical (y) directions (see figure 2). These peaks depict the horizontal and vertical edges of the OLED grid.

When the resulting gradient exceeds a threshold (i.e. $|\Theta| > 5°$), the camera orientation should be adjusted or the OLED structure should be repositioned.

2.2   Shading Correction

Depending on the choice and design of the final vision system (i.e. camera, lens, lighting, etc) a *shading correction* can be done off-line and on-line. On-line correction is possible due to its relatively low computation time. The shading is estimated e.g. by morphological filtering [13], where a smoothed version (Gaussian) of the input image is subtracted from the original input image. This smoothed version is the estimate of the background (see figure 3). The standard deviation (sigma) of the 9×9 Gaussian smoothing kernel is determined from the standard deviation of the input image.

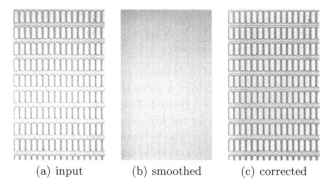

(a) input	(b) smoothed	(c) corrected

Fig. 3. Shading correction. Figure (a) shows the original input image. Figure (b) shows the smoothed version of (a). Figure (c) shows the image corrected for shading.

2.3   Depth of Focus

A sharp focus on the OLED substrate is needed to ensure a reliable pose calculation for each cup. For this a sharpness of focus measure is used. As an image with sharp focus has more high-frequency content than a blurry and badly focused image, a Laplacian operator is used that responds to high-frequency variations of image intensity and produces maximum values when the image is perfectly in focus. Since the terms in the Laplacian can have opposite signs which can cancel each other, a modified Laplacian is used [11]:

$$\nabla_m^2 I = \left| \frac{\partial^2 I}{\partial x^2} \right| + \left| \frac{\partial^2 I}{\partial y^2} \right| \tag{3}$$

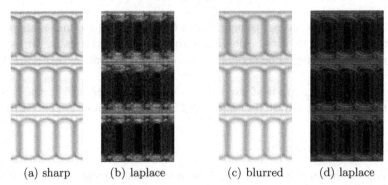

(a) sharp   (b) laplace   (c) blurred   (d) laplace

Fig. 4. Depth of focus. Figure (a) and (b) show the sharp image with its Laplacian. The sum of the sharp Laplacian is 0.3813. Figure (c) and (d) show a blurred image (sharp image convoluted with 5 x 5 Gaussian) with its Laplacian. The sum of the non-sharp Laplacian is 0.1903, which is significantly less. Note that even with the blurred image still all OLED centers are found.

with $I = I(x, y)$ an input image. The normalized measure of focus is then defined as the normalized sum of all values in the modified Laplacian:

$$F_{Mn} = \sum_{i=0}^{n} \sum_{j=0}^{m} \nabla_M^2 I * \frac{1}{128mn} \qquad (4)$$

with n and m the width and height of an image and 128 the normalization factor. When this sum deviates too much from a given threshold (i.e. $F_{Mn} < T_M$), then the height of the camera should be adjusted. This could be done manually or by means of a routine which searches for the highest F_{Mn}. The measure of focus can be calculated off-line but even on-line due to its relatively low computation time. Extensive experimentations with various substrates have to indicate whether an on-line implementation is necessary.

3   On-Line Step

In the on-line step computation time is an important issue. The available single millisecond should be used as effectively as possible. However, some margin should be left to correctly close the computations and to cope with possible delay. To reach the required 1 kHz sampling rate the largest possible image is 80×80 pixels. This contains three OLED cups horizontally separated. To visualize the operations, for this paper we used an image of 100×200 pixels, i.e. nine OLED cups.

3.1   Difference of Gaussians

The images are processed in scale space; an image is represented as a single-parameter family of smoothed images, parameterized by the size of the smoothing kernel, i.e. a low pass filter. It is defined as the function, $L(x, y, \sigma)$, which is produced by convolving a variable-scale Gaussian, $G_\sigma(x, y)$, with an input image, $I(x, y)$:

$$L(x, y, \sigma) = G_\sigma(x, y) * I(x, y), \tag{5}$$

where $*$ represents the convolution in x and y, and

$$G_\sigma(x, y) = \frac{1}{2\pi\sigma^2} e^{-\frac{x^2 + y^2}{2\sigma^2}} \tag{6}$$

with σ the variance (width) of the Gaussian kernel.

Blobs can now be found using scale-space extrema in the Difference-of-Gaussian function $(D(x, y, \sigma))$ convoluted with the input image:

$$\begin{aligned} D(x, y, k, \sigma) &= (G_{k\sigma}(x, y) - G_\sigma(x, y)) * I(x, y) \\ &= L(x, y, k\sigma) - L(x, y, \sigma) \end{aligned} \tag{7}$$

where the difference of two nearby scales is separated by a constant multiplicative factor k [9], [7]. This is equivalent to a band-pass filter that preserves frequencies that lie in the range of both images.

This function is computationally simple - only convolution and subtraction - and the pixel accuracy remains the same before and after computation, i.e. there is no scaling down. After blob-detection, the image is binarized with blobs equal to '1' and the background equal to '0' (see figure 5a).

As can be seen in figure 5a numerous blobs are detected, where some blobs are artifacts of neighboring OLEDs or line segments of the substrate. Also noise can be seen at either side of the OLEDs, which potentially could disturb future computations, such as the contour following. To remove this noise and most of the line segments, the binary image is eroded and subsequently dilated with a 3×3 square structuring element.

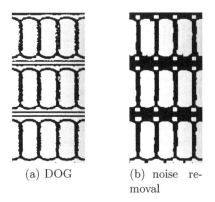

(a) DOG   (b) noise re-
                     moval

Fig. 5. Subtraction of structural element. Figure (a) shows the result after blob-detection (Difference of Gaussians). Figure (b) shows the result after twice erosion and dilation for removal of noise and line segment artifacts.

3.2 Boundary Following

After blob-detection and noise removal the OLED cups and some line segment artifacts (figure 5b) are left. We now follow the boundaries of each binary blob. From the upper left pixel in the binary image a row-wise search is made to find the first '1'. When found, this contour is followed in a counter-clockwise manner (see figure 6b), where each contour point is stored into memory as a Freeman chain code (FCC) [4]. FCC is a compact way to represent a contour of an object. It is basically a sequence of directions of the steps taken when following the boundary of a contour (see figure 6a). Each blob is described in this way until the end of the image is reached (figure 7a).

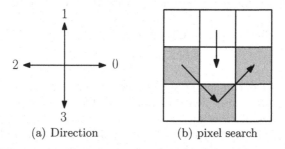

(a) Direction   (b) pixel search

Fig. 6. Boundary following. Figure (a) shows the direction notation for 4-connectivity detection. Figure (b) shows the pixel neighborhood search for 4-connectivity (counter-clockwise) starting from direction '3' (arrow down).

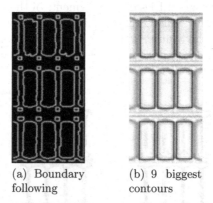

(a) Boundary   (b) 9 biggest
following   contours

Fig. 7. Figure (a) shows the result after boundary following. From this binary image, the nine biggest contours are kept. Figure (b) shows the rectangles (ROIs) which are drawn around each of the nine contours and are used for center of gravity calculation in the input image.

3.3 Center of Gravity

The area of each contour is then calculated and only the nine largest contours are kept which represent the nine OLED cups (figure 7b). A slightly larger ROI is then set around each contour and used as an ROI in the *original* input image to finally calculate the center of gravity. Since the OLED structure is symmetric and we assume there are no significant lighting variations over the OLED, this is also the *center* of the OLED (figure 8a).

4   Experiments and Results

Since the lighting over one OLED (100 by 200 μm) does not change significantly, the algorithm is invariant to lighting or shading differences. The detection of the blobs is invariant to orientation, however, the calculation of the center is not. After the contours are found a rectangle is drawn around it. When the substrate is rotated slightly ($|\alpha_I| > 10°$, with α_I the rotation angle of the OLED substrate), the rectangle does not cover the OLED cup completely anymore (see figure 8b). For this, a lower limit is set in orientation error by correcting a false offset in the off-line step. A more accurate orientation can be calculated in the on-line step by simple triangulation. Each maximum and minimum center point for each row and column on a 3×3 OLED grid is known and can be used to calculate the orientation relatively accurate ($\pm 0.4°$):

$$\tan \alpha_I = \frac{\Delta y}{\Delta x}. \tag{8}$$

with Δ the difference between successive points in x- and y-direction. This can then be used to correct a rotational offset.

Since the center of gravity is a calculation not rounded off to integers, the accuracy of the complete algorithm is sub-pixel, with each pixel being 4 μm in height and width. However, since the precise accuracy is difficult to determine (see e.g. [1]), and the actuation of the x-y table could be limited to a certain precision, the sub-pixel accuracy is said to be reliable up to ± 1 μm. The accuracy specification (maximum 10 μm) has therefore been largely met. Extensive experiments with different substrates under various conditions (i.e. lighting) should give a better proof of performance.

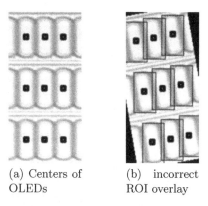

(a) Centers of OLEDs   (b)   incorrect ROI overlay

Fig. 8. Result of algorithm. Figure (a) shows the centers of the nine OLED cups. Figure (b) shows an incorrect ROI overlay when the substrate exceeds an orientation of 10°.

The on-line algorithm is controlled by the timer of the camera, which is set to stream images at a fixed rate (1 [kHz]). Whenever a frame is done and send to the computer, a callback ensures immediate processing on the obtained image. The computation time of the entire on-line algorithm is less then 2 milliseconds, hence each OLED center detection takes about 2/9 milliseconds. The experiments have been carried out under Real-time Linux Ubuntu 8.10 in combination with C/C++ code on a standard notebook with 2 GB of RAM and a 2.4 GHz Intel Core 2 Duo CPU.

5   Conclusions and Future Work

The presented real-time center detection algorithm shows to be a suitable candidate for the computation of center coordinates of an OLED substrate in a visual servoing framework. The algorithm is split in an off-line step for calibration and an on-line step for real-time image processing. Off-line, orientation alignment is checked using a histogram of gradient orientations and a measure of focus is calculated using the Laplacian operator. On-line, the algorithm combines blob-detection, boundary following and center-of-gravity calculation to obtain sub-pixel accuracy (1 pixel equals 4 μm, sub-pixel accuracy reliable up to ± 1 μm).

With an image of 80 x 80 pixels the computation time is less than 1 millisecond per image, making 1 kHz visual servoing possible. Since the algorithm is controlled with the timer of the camera, the main source of delay is due to image processing. The variation of this delay is highly platform dependent. Therefore, further research should be carried out to gain more knowledge in this. Also for future research, an industrial variant will be implemented on an FPGA to cope with delay and to obtain even faster computation. Testing on an actual (moving) setup will provide insight into more complex effects such as delay, lighting influences, abnormalities in alignment, surface inequality, vibrations, etcetera. These effects and their possible solutions can then be subjected to a more close investigation. This will also give insight in the necessity for on-line shading correction and depth of focus adjustment as well as a more precise positioning accuracy.

Acknowledgement

This research was supported by SenterNovem - IOP Precision Technology - Fast Focus On Structures (FFOS).

References

1. van Assen, H.C., Egmont-Petersen, M., Reiber, J.H.C.: Accurate Object Localization in Gray Level Images using the Center of Gravity Measure; Accuracy versus Precision. IEEE Transactions on Image Processing 11(12), 1379–1384 (2002)
2. de Best, J.J.T.H., van de Molengraft, M.J.G., Steinbuch, M.: Direct Dynamic Visual Servoing at 1 kHz by Using the the Product as One Dimensional Encoder. In: 7th IEEE International Conference on control and Automation, New Zealand (submitted 2009)

3. Czajewski, W., Staniak, M.: Real-time Image Segmentation for Visual Servoing. In: Beliczynski, B., Dzielinski, A., Iwanowski, M., Ribeiro, B. (eds.) ICANNGA 2007. LNCS, vol. 4432, pp. 633–640. Springer, Heidelberg (2007)
4. Freeman, H.: Computer processing of line-drawing images. Computing Surveys 6(1), 57–97 (1974)
5. Hutchinson, S., Hager, G.D., Corke, P.I.: A tutorial on visual servo control. IEEE Trans. on Robotics and Automation 12(5), 651–670 (1996)
6. Ishii, I., Nakabo, Y., Ishikawa, M.: Target tracking algorithm for 1ms visual feedback system using massively parallel processing. In: Proc. IEEE Int. Conf. on Robotics and Automation, pp. 2309–2314 (1996)
7. Kanters, F.M.W.: Towards Object-based Image Editing. Phd thesis, Eindhoven University of Technology (2007)
8. Loncaric, S.: A Survey of Shape Analysis Techniques. Pattern Recognition 31(8), 983–1001 (1998)
9. Lowe, D.G.: Distinctive Image Features from Scale-Invariant Keypoints. International Journal of Computer Vision 60(2), 91–110 (2004)
10. Nakabo, Y., Ishikawa, M., Toyoda, H., Mizuno, S.: 1 ms Column Parallel Vision System and It's Application of High Speed Target Tracking Robotics and Automation. In: Proc. IEEE Int. Conf., vol. 1, pp. 650–655 (2000)
11. Riaz, M., Park, S., Ahmad, M.B., Rasheed, W., Park, J.: Generalized Laplacian as Focus Measure. In: Bubak, M., van Albada, G.D., Dongarra, J., Sloot, P.M.A. (eds.) ICCS 2008, Part I. LNCS, vol. 5101, pp. 1013–1021. Springer, Heidelberg (2008)
12. Rodriguez, J., Ayala, D.: Erosion and Dilation on 2D and 3D Digital Images: A new size-independent approach. In: 6th International Fall Workshop on Vision, Modeling and Visualization, pp. 143–150 (2001)
13. Young, I.T.: Shading Correction: Compensation for Illumination and Sensor Inhomogeneities. In: Robinson, J.P., et al. (eds.) Current Protocols in Cytometry, pp. 2.11.1–2.11.12. John Wiley and Sons, Inc., Chichester (2000)

Comparing Feature Matching for Object Categorization in Video Surveillance

Rob G.J. Wijnhoven[1,2] and Peter H.N. de With[2,3]

[1] ViNotion B.V., 5612 AZ Eindhoven, The Netherlands
[2] Eindhoven University of Technology, Eindhoven, The Netherlands
[3] CycloMedia Technology B.V., 4180 BB Waardenburg, The Netherlands

Abstract. In this paper we consider an object categorization system using local HMAX features. Two feature matching techniques are compared: the MAX technique, originally proposed in the HMAX framework, and the histogram technique originating from Bag-of-Words literature. We have found that each of these techniques have their own field of operation. The histogram technique clearly outperforms the MAX technique with 5–15% for small dictionaries up to 500–1,000 features, favoring this technique for embedded (surveillance) applications. Additionally, we have evaluated the influence of interest point operators in the system. A first experiment analyzes the effect of dictionary creation and has showed that random dictionaries outperform dictionaries created from Hessian-Laplace points. Secondly, the effect of operators in the dictionary matching stage has been evaluated. Processing all image points outperforms the point selection from the Hessian-Laplace operator.

Keywords: video surveillance, object categorization, classification, HMAX framework, histogram, bag-of-words, random, Hessian-Laplace.

1 Introduction

Analysis tools have become an indispensable part of a security system with surveillance cameras due to the amount of video data processed by a security operator. The analysis and understanding of scenes starts typically with motion analysis and tracking of objects of interest. A further step is to classify objects in a number of predetermined categories.

Various approaches have been evaluated for object classification. The *Bag-of-Words (BoW)* model was first adopted from text-recognition literature by Csurka *et al.* in [1] for object categorization and has become a popular method for object classification [2,3,4,5,6]. The feature vector stores a histogram containing the number of appearances for each visual feature in a visual dictionary. Riesenhuber and Poggio [7] have proposed a biologically plausible system for object categorization, called *HMAX*. Conceptually, this system works in a comparable way to the BoW model. However, instead of storing a histogram of occurrences of the dictionary features, the distance value of the best match is stored for each feature. Where BoW models typically consider image points selected by *Interest Point Operators (IPOs)*, the HMAX model considers all image

J. Blanc-Talon et al. (Eds.): ACIVS 2009, LNCS 5807, pp. 410–421, 2009.

points. For both the BoW and the HMAX model, the dimensionality of the final feature vector is equal to the number of visual words. Although both methods have been presented and analyzed separately, an absolute comparison for the same dataset has not been published. The purpose of our comparison is to identify the best technique and consider relevant system aspects.

In this paper, we study an object categorization system based on a visual dictionary of local features and compare two techniques for feature vector generation. We show that each technique has a preferred field of operation, depending on the dictionary size. Aiming at an embedded implementation with limited computation power, choosing the best technique of the two for the actual field of operation gives a performance gain of up to 15% for a similar dictionary size and computational complexity.

The remainder of this paper is as follows. Section 2 describes the categorization system and the two compared feature matching techniques. Section 3 presents results on the comparison of the MAX and histogram techniques for both the visual dictionary creation and dictionary matching. Conclusions and recommendations for future work are given in Section 4.

2   System Description

The categorization system consists of several steps which are depicted in Figure 1. During the training stage, images from the training set (1a in Figure 1) are processed by an *Interest Point Operator* (IPO) (Block 2) to obtain characteristic locations in the image. Typically, IPOs find points that correspond to corner-points or blob-like structures. Several operators have been compared and evaluated in [8,9]. Next, descriptions of the local regions around the interest points are generated in Block 3. These local image descriptions are called *features*. A dictionary is created by selecting appropriate features (Block 4) and storing them in the visual dictionary (Block 5). After creating the visual dictionary, it is matched with each training image (Block 6) to generate a *feature vector*. This matching stage is referred to as the *feature matching* stage. Finally, a *classifier* (Block 7) uses these vectors for the training/test images to learn/determine the true object class.

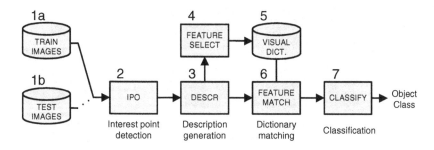

Fig. 1. System overview of the object categorization system

This paper concentrates particularly on the feature matching stage and evaluates two techniques for creation of the feature vector: the *MAX* and the *histogram* techniques. The MAX technique originates from the HMAX system, which is an overall framework for object categorization. Within this framework, we vary the feature matching technique applied and replace the original MAX technique with the histogram technique from the BoW models. Let us first describe the HMAX framework.

2.1   HMAX Framework

Since humans are good at object classification, it is reasonable to look into biological and neurological findings. Based on results from Hubel and Wiesel [10], Riesenhuber and Poggio have developed the "HMAX" model [11] that has been extended recently by Serre [12,13] and optimized by Mutch and Lowe [14]. We have implemented the model proposed by Serre up to the second processing layer [15]. The operation of the HMAX algorithm will now be addressed.

The algorithm is based on the concept of a feed-forward architecture, alternating between simple and complex layers, in line with the findings of Hubel and Wiesel [10]. The first layer implements simple edge detectors by filtering the gray-level input image with Gabor filters of several orientations and sizes to obtain rotation- and scale-invariance. The filters are normalized to have zero mean and a unity sum of squares. At each scale, the image is filtered in multiple orientations, resulting in so-called *S1 features*. For our experiments, we used the parameters as proposed by Serre *et al.* [13].

Continuing in the first layer, but as a succeeding step, the edge-filtered images are processed in the *C1 layer* to obtain invariance in local neighborhoods. This invariance will be created in both the spatial dimensions and in the dimension of scale. In order to obtain spatial invariance, the maximum is taken over a local spatial neighborhood around each pixel and the resulting image is sub-sampled. Because of the down-sampling, the number of resulting *C1 features* is much lower than the number of S1 features obtained in the preceding step. As an illustration, the resulting S1 and C1 feature maps for the input image of a bus at low-filtering scale are shown in Figure 2.

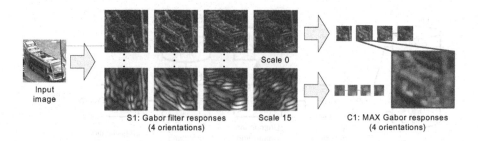

Fig. 2. HMAX feature space example (note: graylevel offset)

The second layer in the processing chain of the model matches stored dictionary C1 features with the C1 feature maps. The resulting matching scores are stored in the *S2 feature map*. The dictionary features are extracted from training images at a random scale and spatial location, at the C1 level. This random extraction is in accordance with Serre's [16] findings and has been confirmed by the authors [17]. Each feature contains all four orientations. Serre proposes to extract features at four different sizes: 4×4, 8×8, 12×12 and 16×16 elements. In our implementation, we use 5×5 features to enable a symmetric pixel neighborhood surrounding a central pixel and avoid large block sizes since in an evaluation they showed to be less important for categorization. Furthermore, for the computing of the subsequent *C2 layer*, for each dictionary feature, the match response with the smallest distance is extracted from the S2 feature map and stored in the final feature vector. This is done by taking the maximum S2 feature response over all scales and all spatial locations. Therefore, the final feature vector has a dimensionality equal to the number of dictionary features used.

The described HMAX framework is now linked to the system overview of Figure 1. In Block 2 involving interest point detection, all image positions at all scales are considered and referred to as the *AllPoints IPO*. In the description generation step (Block 3), the S1 and C1 feature maps are calculated. The dictionary matching stage (Block 6) computes the resulting S2 and C2 feature responses.

2.2   Bag-of-Words System: Histograms

Several systems for object recognition employ the *Bag-of-Words (BoW)* model using local features. Within this model, SIFT features [18] are broadly accepted [1,2,3]. The system is based on a dictionary of visual features (like the HMAX C1 features). The feature vector stores a histogram containing the number of appearances for each visual feature in the dictionary.

Conceptually, the HMAX system works in a comparable way to the BoW model. However, instead of storing a histogram of occurrences of the dictionary features in the BoW case, the best matching score for each feature is stored (*C2* value). The dimensionality of the final feature vector is, as in the BoW case, equal to the number of visual words.

As applied in literature [1,2,3,5,6,19], each considered position in the input image is compared to each dictionary feature and is *Vector Quantized (VQ)* to the most similar dictionary feature. The resulting feature vector stores the histogram value for each feature, representing the number of appearances for that feature, normalized to the total number of considered image points.

Because not every local image description is similar to a local feature in the visual dictionary, the vector quantization can result in a coarse quantization. This leads to noise in the feature vector, which is an inherently known degradation, as the local image description has a low matching score to every dictionary feature. Therefore, we propose a slightly different histogram technique. Instead of applying a *hard* quantization, we propose a more *soft* quantization, where increasing the histogram value of the most similar dictionary feature with unity is replaced by increasing the value by the corresponding matching score (distance). Therefore, the negative influence of image points that are not similar to any dictionary feature, is reduced. In the upcoming comparison, we refer to this technique as the *Matching Score (MS)*, in contrast to the original *Vector-Quantization (VQ)*.

2.3 Dictionary Creation

As proposed by Serre *et al.* [16], creation of the visual dictionary is best done by random sampling of features from images of natural scenery. Although this is counter intuitive, the authors have previously confirmed these results [17]. Applying interest point operators for dictionary creation is not useful within the HMAX framework. The difference in distinctiveness of the dictionary between dictionaries created from natural images, or images from the training set is however, insignificant. For the following experiments, we extract the visual dictionary from the training set. Although previous work [17] has shown that IPOs were not useful in the default HMAX framework, it is not clear if these findings hold when different feature matching techniques are applied. Furthermore, previously only dictionaries of 1,000 features were considered, while we enlarge the scale of operation to smaller and larger dictionaries.

2.4 Dictionary Matching

There are several ways to match the visual dictionary to an input image. In literature, typically interest point operators are used to select points that correspond to structures in the image (e.g. [2,3,4]). In contrast to considering the local image contents, random sampling can be applied, or all image points can be considered (grid-like sampling). It has been found that for dictionary matching, random and grid-like sampling can outperform interest point operators [4,5,6]. The original HMAX model applies a grid-like sampling, where all image points at all considered scales are matched with the dictionary (referred to as the *AllPoints* technique). The authors have previously compared several interest point operators for dictionary matching in the HMAX framework for a single dictionary size [17]. The computational complexity of the system (after dictionary creation) is linear to the number of considered image points. For embedded applications with limited computation power, methods that consider more image positions (like grid-like sampling) can therefore be inappropriate. Therefore, we investigate the effect on classification performance for visual dictionary matching on both the AllPoints and the Hessian-Laplace technique.

3   Experiments

First, we commence with defining the difference between training and testing and the performance measurement criterion. Given a set of *object classes* and an image containing one object, the task of object categorization is to determine the

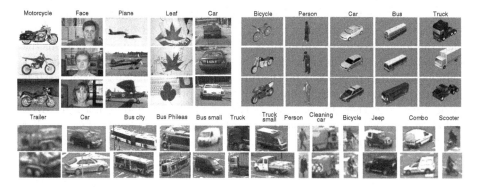

Fig. 3. Example images from datasets Caltech 5 (top-left), Wijnhoven2008 (top-right) and Wijnhoven2006 (bottom)

correct object-class label of the visualized object. The operation of object categorization systems is divided in two phases: training and testing. During training, the system learns from the *training set*, consisting of a number of example images for each object class. The performance of the algorithm is determined as the percentage of correctly labeled objects from the *test set*, averaged over all object classes.

We define the following datasets used for the evaluation. Three different categorization datasets are processed using the categorization system as presented in Section 2: a low-resolution dataset extracted from an hour of surveillance video (*Wijnhoven2006*, 13 classes), a synthetic traffic dataset (*Wijnhoven2008*, 5 classes), and the Caltech-5 dataset[1] (5 classes) containing faces, cars, leafs, planes and motorbikes. See Figure 3 for a visual overview.

Using these datasets, we create the visual dictionary in different ways and evaluate its influence on the performance of the MAX and histogram techniques. Next, the visual dictionary is matched to image points selected by different interest point operators and we measure the resulting performance of the same two feature matching techniques.

3.1 Dictionary Creation: Random vs. Hessian-Laplace

In this experiment we investigate two ways of creating the visual dictionary: random sampling and sampling around Hessian-Laplace interest points. In both cases, we create the initial large dictionary by sampling from images from the training set. To generate the final visual dictionary, a fixed number of features is randomly extracted from this initial set. Feature matching is applied with the techniques as discussed in Section 2: MAX and histogram. During dictionary matching, all image points are processed (*AllPoints* operator). A *Nearest Neighbor (NN)* classifier is used for the final classification.

---

[1] http://www.robots.ox.ac.uk/~vgg/data/data-cats.html

The results are visualized in Figure 4 and lead to several conclusions. First, we consider random dictionary generation (solid lines). It can be seen that for small dictionaries of up to 500 features, the histogram technique outperforms the MAX technique and obtains a gain of 5–15% in classification performance. For dictionaries larger than 500–1,000 features, the MAX technique is preferred. It is interesting to see that both techniques have their preferred field of operation and outperform each other. The computational complexity is equal for both the MAX and histogram techniques and is linear to the number of dictionary features. For computationally constrained systems, the histogram is clearly preferred, while for unconstrained systems, the MAX technique should be used.

Within the experiment, we have employed a vector quantization in the histogram creation procedure. To this end, we compare two cases: the *hard* Vector Quantization (VQ) and the *soft* Matching Score (MS) techniques, as discussed in Subsection 2.2. Figure 4 shows the results of these experiments. Overall, the VQ technique gives an improvement of a few percent in the classification score. Within the range of 50–500 features, there is no significant improvement, or even a small loss. For very small dictionaries of 10–20 features, the VQ technique gives a clear improvement. This is likely due to the large number of points assigned to only a small number of dictionary bins (features), so that the score per bin is always significant and the influence of noise is decreased.

The differences in performance between the histogram and the MAX techniques can be explained by considering that the histogram technique stores the *distribution* of features over the image, whereas MAX only stores the *best response*. This makes the MAX technique very sensitive to variations in the maximum feature appearances. Moreover, when making histograms for large dictionaries, the number of dictionary features approaches the number of image positions, resulting in sparse, noisy histograms, which make the histogram approach less attractive.

Second, we compare dictionary generation using random selection and extraction around Hessian-Laplace interest points. Figure 4 shows that the results of the Hessian-Laplace technique (dashed lines) follow the results of the random technique (solid lines), with an overall lower performance of 5–10%. Towards large dictionaries, the performance of the Hessian-Laplace technique decreases drastically. Over the complete range of dictionary sizes, the random selection outperforms the Hessian-Laplace technique. A marginal exception are the very small dictionaries with 10–20 features, where the Hessian-Laplace slightly outperforms random selection. The conclusion holds for both the MAX technique and the histogram techniques. Thus, random dictionary creation is preferred over using the Hessian-Laplace technique.

In previous work [17], the authors have already shown that for the HMAX framework, dictionary generation using random sampling outperforms the Hessian-Laplace operator. Previously, this conclusion was drawn for a fixed dictionary size. In the current experiments, we generalize this conclusion for a much larger field of operation. Our measurements show occasional exceptions for this conclusion when using very small dictionaries of less than 50 features.

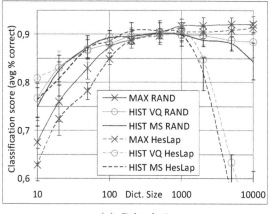

(a) Caltech 5.

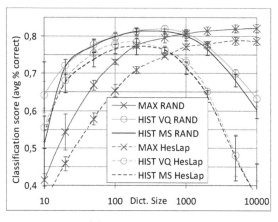

(b) Wijnhoven2006.

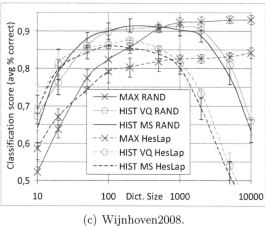

(c) Wijnhoven2008.

Fig. 4. Dictionary creation: Random and Hessian-Laplace (Matching: AllPoints)

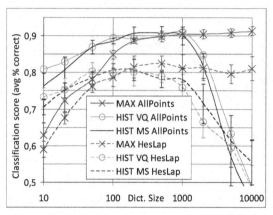

(a) Caltech 5.

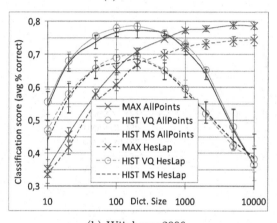

(b) Wijnhoven2006.

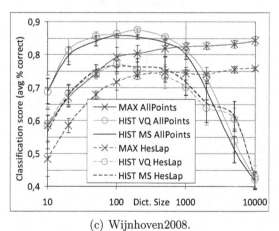

(c) Wijnhoven2008.

Fig. 5. Dictionary matching: AllPoints and Hessian-Laplace (Creation: Hessian-Laplace)

3.2   Dictionary Matching: AllPoints vs. Hessian-Laplace

In this experiment, as a preparation step, we first create dictionaries by HMAX features sampled around Hessian-Laplace interest points (It would have been more logical to exploit a random selection of features for the visual dictionary, but at the time of writing this article, those results were not yet available). Secondly, using these created dictionaries, we vary the interest point operator and measure the performance of dictionary matching. Both the *AllPoints* technique (considering all image points at all scales) and the Hessian-Laplace technique are evaluated for the interest point detection (Block 2 in Figure 1).

The results are shown in Figure 5. As can be seen, the AllPoints technique outperforms the Hessian-Laplace technique as an interest point operator in the dictionary matching procedure. The AllPoints performance is approximately 5–10% higher than the Hessian-Laplace performance. For the MAX technique, the authors have previously [17] shown that applying the Hessian-Laplace technique for dictionary matching results in lower performance. However, only a fixed size dictionary of 1,000 features was considered. The current results generalize the conclusions for the total dictionary size range.

For the histogram techniques, similar results can be seen: the performance of the Hessian-Laplace matching is generally lower that matching with all image points. Only for larger dictionaries, these conclusions are not valid. For very large dictionaries of 5,000 or more features, applying the Hessian-Laplace operator results in comparable or slightly higher classification performance.

In a secondary case of experiments, we have employed a vector quantization in the histogram creation procedure. To this end, we compare two cases: the *hard* Vector Quantization (VQ) and the *soft* Matching Score (MS) techniques, as discussed in Subsection 2.2. The results of these experiments can be seen in Figure 5. For the AllPoints matching, the VQ technique gives an improvement of a few percent in the classification score, for which no direct explanation can be given at this moment. For the Hessian-Laplace matching, a similar gain occurs for small dictionaries, but at some point, the performance of the VQ technique is slightly less than the MS processing. This decrease is explained by the creation of a more sparse histogram because Hessian-Laplace results in less image points than the AllPoints method. The authors expect that the quantization increases the noise in an already sparse distribution, leading to a performance decrease.

4   Conclusions

In this paper, we have addressed several aspects of an object categorization system using local HMAX features. Two feature matching techniques have been compared: the MAX technique, originally proposed in the HMAX framework, and the histogram technique originating from Bag-of-Words literature. The applied matching techniques are used for feature vector creation.

In the first experiment, two different ways of generating the visual dictionary were evaluated: extracting features at random and extracting around Hessian-Laplace interest points. In the second experiment, the interest point operators were varied in the dictionary matching stage. The AllPoints and the Hessian-Laplace interest point operators have been evaluated. We have found that for all experiments, each of these techniques have their own field of operation. The histogram technique clearly outperforms the MAX technique with 5–15% for small dictionaries up to 500–1,000 features. For larger feature sets, the MAX technique takes over and has superior performance. The computational complexity of both the MAX and the histogram technique is linear to the number of dictionary features and the number of matched image points (interest points). Aiming at an embedded implementation (surveillance), the histogram technique is favored over the MAX technique.

For the histogram dictionary matching, we have compared both the often used *hard vector Quantization (VQ)* technique and the proposed *soft Matching Score (MS)* technique for the histogram creation. Overall, VQ tends to give a small improvement in classification score.

We have compared different techniques for dictionary generation. Random extraction is preferred over extraction around Hessian-Laplace interest points, which typically results in a decrease in classification performance of 5–10%. These results are in line with earlier work of the authors [17] and is generalized in this paper to a large range of dictionary sizes.

Furthermore, the second experiment (comparing AllPoints and Hessian-Laplace for dictionary matching) shows that matching with the AllPoints operator outperforms the Hessian-Laplace interest point operator with 5–10%. This is in line with earlier findings [4,5,6]. This conclusion is a generalization of earlier work of the authors [17] which has been expanded here to a large range of dictionary sizes.

In the current experiments, the dictionaries were created using random selection from the initially large set that was constituted by random sampling or extraction around Hessian-Laplace points. Feature selection methods can be used that result in more distinctive visual dictionaries. Recent work of the authors [20] shows that this can result in a significant boost in classification performance.

References

1. Csurka, G., Dance, C.R., Fan, L., Willamowski, J., Bray, C.: Visual categorization with bags of keypoints. In: Proc. European Conference on Computer Vision (ECCV) (May 2004)
2. Sivic, J., Russell, B.C., Efros, A.A., Zisserman, A., Freeman, W.T.: Discovering objects and their location in images. In: Proc. IEEE Int. Conf. on Computer Vision (ICCV), October 2005, vol. 1, pp. 370–377 (2005)
3. Sudderth, E.B., Torralba, A., Freeman, W.T., Willsky, A.S.: Learning hierarchical models of scenes, objects, and parts. In: Proc. IEEE Int. Conf. on Computer Vision (ICCV), October 2005, vol. 2, pp. 1331–1338 (2005)
4. Fei-Fei, L., Perona, P.: A bayesian hierarchical model for learning natural scene categories. In: Proc. IEEE Conf. on Computer Vision and Pattern Recognition (CVPR), vol. 2, pp. 524–531. IEEE Computer Society, Washington (2005)
5. Jurie, F., Triggs, B.: Creating efficient codebooks for visual recognition. In: Proc. IEEE Int. Conf. on Computer Vision (ICCV), October 2005, pp. 604–610 (2005)

6. Nowak, E., Jurie, F., Triggs, B.: Sampling strategies for bag-of-features image classification. In: Leonardis, A., Bischof, H., Pinz, A. (eds.) ECCV 2006. LNCS, vol. 3954, pp. 490–503. Springer, Heidelberg (2006)
7. Riesenhuber, M., Poggio, T.: Hierarchical models of object recognition in cortex. Nature Neuroscience 2(11), 1019–1025 (1999)
8. Schmid, C., Mohr, R., Bauckhage, C.: Evaluation of interest point detectors. International Journal of Computer Vision 37(2), 151–172 (2000)
9. Mikolajzyk, K., Tuytelaars, T., Schmid, C., Zisserman, A., Matas, J., Schaffalitzky, F., Kadir, T., Van Gool, L.: A comparison of affine region detectors. Int. Journal on Computer Vision (IJCV) 65(1), 43–72 (2005)
10. Ullman, S., Vidal-Naquet, M., Sali, E.: Visual features of intermediate complexity and their use in classification. Nature Neuroscience 5, 682–687 (2002)
11. Riesenhuber, M., Poggio, T.: Models of object recognition. Nature Neuroscience 3, 1199–1204 (2000)
12. Serre, T., Wolf, L., Poggio, T.: Object recognition with features inspired by visual cortex. In: Proc. of Computer Vision and Pattern Recognition (CVPR), June 2005, pp. 994–1000 (2005)
13. Serre, T., Wolf, L., Bileschi, S., Riesenhuber, M., Poggio, T.: Robust object recognition with cortex-like mechanisms. Trans. Pattern Analysis and Machine Intelligence (PAMI) 29(3), 411–426 (2007)
14. Mutch, J., Lowe, D.G.: Multiclass object recognition with sparse, localized features. In: Proc. IEEE Conf. on Computer Vision and Pattern Recognition (CVPR), June 2006, vol. 1, pp. 11–18 (2006)
15. Wijnhoven, R., de With, P.H.N.: Patch-based experiments with object classification in video surveillance. In: Blanc-Talon, J., Philips, W., Popescu, D., Scheunders, P. (eds.) ACIVS 2007. LNCS, vol. 4678, pp. 285–296. Springer, Heidelberg (2007)
16. Serre, T.: Learning a Dictionary of Shape-Components in Visual Cortex: Comparison with Neurons, Humans and Machines, Ph.D. thesis, Massachusetts Institute of Technology Computer Science and Artificial Intelligence Laboratory (April 2006)
17. Wijnhoven, R., de With, P.H.N., Creusen, I.: Efficient template generation for object classification in video surveillance. In: Proc. of 29th Symposium on Information Theory in the Benelux, May 2008, pp. 255–262 (2008)
18. Lowe, D.G.: Distinctive image features from scale-invariant keypoints. Int. Journal of Computer Vision (IJCV) 60(2) (January 2004)
19. Crandall, D.J., Huttenlocher, D.P.: Weakly supervised learning of part-based spatial models for visual object recognition. In: Leonardis, A., Bischof, H., Pinz, A. (eds.) ECCV 2006. LNCS, vol. 3951, pp. 16–29. Springer, Heidelberg (2006)
20. Creusen, I., Wijnhoven, R., de With, P.H.N.: Applying feature selection techniques for visual dictionary creation in object classification. In: Proc. Int. Conf. on Image Processing, Computer Vision and Pattern Recognition (IPCV) (July 2009)

Self Organizing and Fuzzy Modelling
for Parked Vehicles Detection

Lucia Maddalena[1] and Alfredo Petrosino[2]

[1] ICAR - National Research Council
Via P. Castellino 111, 80131 Naples, Italy
lucia.maddalena@na.icar.cnr.it
[2] DSA - University of Naples Parthenope
Centro Direzionale, Isola C/4, 80143 Naples, Italy
alfredo.petrosino@uniparthenope.it

Abstract. Our aim is to distinguish moving and stopped objects in
digital image sequences taken from stationary cameras by a model based
approach. A self-organizing model is adopted both for the scene background and for the scene foreground, that can handle scenes containing
moving backgrounds or gradual illumination variations, helping in distinguishing between moving and stopped foreground regions. The model
is enriched by spatial coherence to enhance robustness against false detections and fuzzy modelling to deal with decision problems typically
arising when crisp settings are involved. We show through experimental
results and comparisons that good accuracy values can be reached for
color video sequences that represent typical situations critical for vehicles stopped in no parking areas.

Keywords: moving object detection, background subtraction, background modeling, foreground modeling, stopped object, self organization,
neural network.

1 Introduction

Stopped object detection in an image sequence consists in detecting temporally
static image regions indicating objects that do not constitute the original background but were brought into the scene at a subsequent time, such as abandoned
and removed items, or illegally parked vehicles.

Great interest in the stopped object detection problem has been given by the
PETS workshops held in 2006 [11] and in 2007 [12], where one of the main aims
has been the detection of *left luggage*, that is luggage that has been abandoned
by its owner, in movies taken from multiple cameras. Another example of strong
interest in the considered problem is given by the *i-LIDS bag and vehicle detection challenge* proposed in the AVSS 2007 Conference [24], where the attention
has been driven on abandoned bags and parked vehicles events, properly defined.

A broad classification of existing approaches to the detection of stopped objects
can be given as *tracking-based* and *non tracking-based* approaches. In *tracking-
based* approaches, where the stopped object detection is obtained on the basis of

J. Blanc-Talon et al. (Eds.): ACIVS 2009, LNCS 5807, pp. 422–433, 2009.
© Springer-Verlag Berlin Heidelberg 2009

the analysis of object trajectories through an application dependent event detection phase. These include most of the papers in [11,12]. *Non tracking-based* approaches include pixel- and region-based approaches aiming at classifying pixels/ objects without the aid of tracking modules, and include [6,15,16,21,23].

Our approach to the problem is non tracking-based. The problem is tackled as *stopped foreground subtraction*, that, in analogy with the background subtraction approach, consists in maintaining an up-to-date model of the stopped foreground and in discriminating moving objects as those that deviate from such model. Both background subtraction and stopped foreground subtraction have the common issue of constructing and maintaining an image model that adapts to scene changes and can capture the most persisting features of the image sequence, i.e. the background and stationary foreground, respectively. For such modeling problem we adopt visual attention mechanisms that help in detecting features that keep the user attention, based on a self-organizing neural network.

One of the main issues to be pursued in background subtraction is the uncertainty in the detection caused by the cited background maintenance issues. Usually, crisp settings are needed to define the method parameters, and this does not allow to properly deal with uncertainty in the background model. Recently several authors have explored the adoption of fuzzy approaches to tackle different aspects of detecting moving objects. In [30] an approach using fuzzy Sugeno integral is proposed to fuse texture and color features for background subtraction, while in [2,3] the authors adopt the Choquet integral to aggregate the same features. In [26] a fuzzy approach to selective running average background modeling is proposed, and in [1] the authors model the background by the Type-2 Fuzzy Mixture of Gaussian Model proposed in [31].

The approach we propose is based on the background and the foreground model automatically generated by a self-organizing method without prior knowledge of the pattern classes. An automatic and data dependent fuzzy mechanism is introduced into the update phase for further reinforcing into the background model the contribution of pixels that belong to it. The approach consists in using biologically inspired problem-solving methods to solve motion detection tasks, typically based on visual attention mechanisms. The aim is to obtain the objects that keep the users attention by referring to a set of predefined features.

The paper is organized as follows. In Section 2 we describe a model-based pixelwise procedure allowing to discriminate foreground pixels into stopped and moving pixels, that is completely independent on the background and foreground models adopted. In Section 3 we describe the model for both background and foreground modeling that we adopted in our experiments, that is a variation of a previously presented model for background modeling. Section 4 presents results obtained with the implementation of the proposed approach, while Section 5 includes concluding remarks.

2 Stopped Foreground Detection

In this section we propose a model-based approach to the classification of foreground pixels into stopped and moving pixels. A foreground pixel is classified as *stopped* if it holds the same color features for several consecutive frames; otherwise it is classified as *moving*.

Assuming we have a model BG_t of the image sequence background, we compute a function $E(x)$ of color feature occurrences for pixel $I_t(x)$ as follows

$$E(x) = \begin{cases} \min(\tau_s, E(x) + 1) & \text{if} \quad I_t(x) \notin BG_t \wedge I_t(x) \in FG_t \\ \max(0, E(x) - 1) & \text{if} \quad I_t(x) \notin BG_t \wedge I_t(x) \notin FG_t \\ \max(0, E(x) - k) & \text{if} \quad I_t(x) \in BG_t \end{cases} \quad (1)$$

where model FG_t of the sequence foreground is iteratively built and updated using image pixels $I_t(x)$ for which $E(x) > 0$.

Every time pixel $I_t(x)$ belongs to the foreground model ($I_t(x) \in FG_t$), $E(x)$ is incremented, while it is decremented if it does not belong to the foreground model. The maximum value τ_s for $E(x)$ corresponds to the *stationarity threshold*, i.e. the minimum number of consecutive frames after which a pixel assuming constant color features is classified as stopped. The value for τ_s is chosen depending on the desired responsiveness of the system.

On the contrary, if pixel $I_t(x)$ is detected as belonging to the background ($I_t(x) \in BG_t$), $E(x)$ is decreased by a factor k. The decay constant k determines how fast $E(x)$ should decrease, i.e. how fast the system should recognize that a stopped pixel has moved again. To set the alarm flag off immediately after the removal of the stopped object, the value of decay should be large, eventually equal to τ_s. Pixels $I_t(x)$ for which $E(x)$ reaches the stationarity threshold value τ_s are classified as stopped, and therefore the set ST_t defined as

$$ST_t = \{FG_t(x) : E(x) = \tau_s\}$$

supplies a model for the stopped objects, while the remaining part of FG_t represents moving objects.

The described procedure is completely independent on the model adopted for the scene background and foreground. The model that we have adopted for the background and the foreground will be described in the following section.

3   Background and Foreground Update

Relying on recent research in this area [18,19], for background and foreground modeling a self-organizing neural network, organized as a 3-D grid of neurons, is built up. Each neuron computes a function of the weighted linear combination of incoming inputs, with weights resembling the neural network learning, and can be therefore represented by a weight vector obtained collecting the weights related to incoming links. An incoming pattern is mapped to the neuron whose set of weight vectors is most similar to the pattern, and weight vectors in a neighborhood of such node are updated.

Specifically, for each pixel $p_t = I(x)$ we build a neuronal map consisting of L weight vectors $c^l(p_t), l = 1, \ldots, L,$. Each weight vector $c^l(p_t)$ is represented in the HSV colour space, that allows to specify colours in a way that is close to

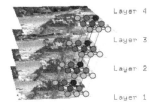

Layer 4

Layer 3

Layer 2

Layer 1

Fig. 1. A simple image (left) and the modeling neuronal map with $L = 4$ layers (right)

human experience of colours, and is initialized to the HSV components of the corresponding pixel of the first sequence frame $I_0(p_t)$. The complete set of weight vectors for all pixels of an image I with N rows and M columns is organized as a 3D neuronal map $\tilde{B}$ with N rows, M columns, and L layers. An example of such neuronal map is given in Fig. 1, which shows that for each pixel $p_t = I_t(x)$ (identified by one of the colored circles in the sequence frame on the left) we have a weight vector $\tilde{B}_t(x) = (c^1(x), c^2(x), \dots, c^L(x))$ (identified by correspondingly colored circles in the model layers on the right).

By subtracting the current image from the background model $\tilde{B}$, each pixel p_t of the t-th sequence frame I_t is compared to the current pixel weight vectors to determine if there exists a weight vector that matches it. The best matching weight vector is used as the pixel's encoding approximation, and therefore p_t is detected as foreground if no acceptable matching weight vector exists; otherwise it is classified as background.

Matching for the incoming pixel $p_t = I_t(x)$ is performed by looking for a weight vector $c^b(p_t)$ in the set $\tilde{B}_t(x) = (c^1(p_t), \dots, c^L(p_t))$ of the current pixel weight vectors satisfying:

$$d(c^b(p_t), p_t) = \min_{i=1,\dots,L} d(c^i(p_t), p_t) \leq \varepsilon \qquad (2)$$

where the metric $d(\cdot)$ and the threshold ε are suitably chosen as in [18].

The best matching weight vector $c^l(p_t) = \tilde{B}_t(x)$ belonging to layer l and all other weight vectors in a $n \times n$ neighborhood N_{p_t} of $c^l(p_t)$ in the l-th layer of the background model $\tilde{B}$ are updated $\forall x \in N_{p_t}$ according to selective weighted running average:

$$\tilde{B}_t^l(x) = (1 - \alpha_t(x))\tilde{B}_{t-1}^l(x) + \alpha_t(x)I_t(x) \qquad (3)$$

where $\alpha_t(x)$ is a learning factor, later specified, belonging to [0,1] and depends on scene variability. If the best match $c^b(p_t)$ satisfying eq. (2) is not found, the background model $\tilde{B}$ remains unchanged. Such selectivity allows to adapt the background model to scene modifications without introducing the contribution of pixels not belonging to the background scene.

Spatial coherence is also introduced in order to enhance robustness against false detections. Let $p = I(x)$ the generic pixel of image I, and let N_p a spatial square neighborhood of pixel $p \in I$. We consider the set Ω_p of pixels belonging to N_p that have a best match in their background model according to eqn. (2), i.e.

$$\Omega_p = \{q \in N_p : d(c^b(q), q) \leq \varepsilon\}.$$

In analogy with [8], the *Neighborhood Coherence Factor* is defined as:

$$NCF(p) = \frac{|\Omega_p|}{|N_p|}$$

where $|\cdot|$ refers to the set cardinality. Such factor gives a relative measure of the number of pixels belonging to the spatial neighborhood N_p of a given pixel p that are well represented by the background model $\tilde{B}$. If $NCF(p) > 0.5$, most of the pixels in such spatial neighborhood are well represented by the background model, and this should imply that also pixel p is well represented by the background model. Values for $\alpha_t(x)$ in eq. (3) are therefore expressed as

$$\alpha_t(x) = M(p_t)\, \alpha(t)\, w(x), \quad \forall x \in N_{p_t}, \tag{4}$$

where $w(x)$ are Gaussian weights in the neighborhood N_{p_t}, $\alpha(t)$ represents the learning factor, that is the same for each pixel of the t-th sequence frame, and $M(p_t)$ is the crisp hard-limited function

$$M(p_t) = \begin{cases} 1 & \text{if } NCF(p_t) \geq 0.5 \\ 0 & \text{otherwise} \end{cases} \tag{5}$$

The background updating rule is formulated in terms of a production rule of the type: if (condition) then (action), incorporating knowledge of the world in which the system works, such as knowledge of objects and their spatial relations. When the condition in the production rule is satisfied, the action is performed. Both condition and action are described in linguistic terms and a numeric method should be adopted to represent the vagueness inherent in these labels effectively. In particular, the flexibility and power provided by fuzzy set theory for knowledge representation makes fuzzy rule-based systems very attractive when compared with traditional rule-based systems. In our case, the uncertainty resides in determining suitable thresholds in the back- ground model. According to this way of reasoning, the fuzzy background subtraction and update algorithm for the generic pixel $p_t \in I_t$ can be stated through a fuzzy rule-based system as follows:

Fuzzy rule-based background subtraction and update algorithm

> if $(d(c_m(p_t), p_t)$ is `low`) and $(NCF(p_t)$ is `high`) then
>   Update $\tilde{B}_t$
> endif

Let $F_1(p_t)$ the fuzzy membership function of $d(c_m(p_t), p_t)$ to the fuzzy set `low` and $F_2(p_t)$ the fuzzy membership function of $NCF(p_t)$ to the fuzzy set `high`; the fuzzy rule becomes:

$$\alpha_t(x) = F_1(p_t)\, F_2(p_t)\, \alpha(t)\, w(x) \tag{6}$$

In order to take into account the uncertainty in the background model deriving by the need of the choice of a suitable threshold ε in eqn. (2), $F_1(p_t)$ is chosen as a saturating linear function given by

$$F_1(p_t) = \begin{cases} 1 - \dfrac{d(c_m(p_t), p_t)}{\varepsilon} & \text{if } d(c_m(p_t), p_t) \leq \varepsilon \\ 0 & \text{otherwise} \end{cases} \tag{7}$$

The function $F_1(p_t)$, whose values are normalized in $[0, 1]$, can be considered as the membership degree of p_t to the background model: the closer is the incoming sample p_t to the background model $C(p_t) = (c_1(p_t), c_2(p_t), \ldots, c_{n^2}(p_t))$, the larger is the corresponding value $F_1(p_t)$. Therefore, incorporating $F_1(p_t)$ in eq. (6) ensures that the closer is the incoming sample p_t to the background model, the more it contributes to the background model update, thus further reinforcing the corresponding weight vectors.

Also spatial coherence introduced through eqn. (5) can be formulated with a fuzzy approach. Indeed, we can observe that the greater is $NCF(p)$, the greater majority of pixels in N_p are well represented by the background model, and the better the pixel p can be considered as represented by the background model. Therefore we modify eq. (4) as follows:

$$\alpha_t(x) = F_2(p_t) \, \alpha(t) \, w(x), \tag{8}$$

where $F_2(p_t)$ is given as

$$F_2(p_t) = \begin{cases} 2 * NCF(p_t) - 1 & \text{if } NCF(p_t) \geq 0.5 \\ 0 & \text{otherwise} \end{cases} \tag{9}$$

and can be considered as the membership degree of pixel p_t to the background model.

The described model $\tilde{B}_t$ has been adopted for both the background model BG_t and the foreground model FG_t described in Section 2 for the classification of stopped and moving pixels.

4   Experimental Results

Experimental results for the detection of stopped objects using the proposed approach have been produced for several image sequences. Some of them are here described; some others can be found in the Supplement Material [20].

In Fig. 2 some frames are shown for sequence *Dataset1*, belonging to the publicly available *PETS 2001* dataset (ftp://ftp.pets.reading.ac.uk/pub/PETS2001). Here a blue car parks (from frame 700 till the sequence end in frame 2688), while a white van stops on the street side for about 600 frames (from frame 990 till to frame 1590). Choosing as stationarity threshold $\tau_S = 1500$, the presented approach allows to correctly detect the blue car as stationary, from frame 2160 till to the sequence end (green/red pixels indicate moving/stopped pixels, respectively). The white van, instead, is correctly detected as a non-stationary object, since it stops

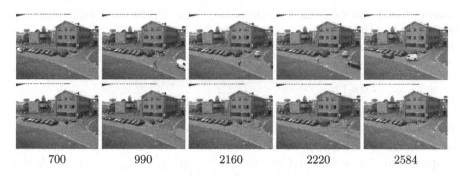

700   990   2160   2220   2584

Fig. 2. Sequence *Dataset1*: selected original frames (first line), and corresponding stopped objects detection (second line). The blue car parks in frame 700, and it is detected as stationary after about $\tau_S = 1500$ frames (starting with frame 2160), till to the sequence end. The white van stops on the street side for about 600 frames (from frame 990 till to frame 1590), and therefore it is not detected as a stationary object.

for less than 1500 frames. It should be observed that the availability of the stationary model ST_t allows to clearly disambiguate moving cars passing in front of the stopped blue car, as in frame 2584.

In order to compare our results with those obtained by other existing approaches, we further consider parked vehicle sequences, named *PV-easy*, *PV-medium*, and *PV-hard*, belonging to the publicly available *i-LIDS 2007* dataset (ftp://motinas.elec.qmul.ac.uk/pub/iLids/), that have corresponding annotated ground truths provided for the AVSS 2007 contest [24]. Such scenes represent typical situations critical for moving object detection in outdoor sequences. Specifically, all the scenes present strong shadows cast by objects on the ground, light positional instability caused by small movements of the camera due to the wind, and strong and long-lasting illumination variations due to clouds covering and uncovering the sun. Experimental results showing the behavior of the adopted 3D neural model in such situations can be found in [20].

Concerning our specific purpose of detecting stopped objects, the considered i-LIDS scenes are devoted to detecting vehicles in no parking areas, where the street under control is more or less crowded with cars, depending on the hour of the day the scene refers to. The no parking area adopted for the AVSS 2007 contest [24] is defined as the main street borders, and the stationarity threshold is defined as $\tau_S = 1500$. This means that an object is considered irregularly parked if it stops in the no parking area for more than 60 seconds (scenes are captured at 25 fps).

Results obtained for sequence *PV-medium* are reported in Fig. 3, where we report only stationary pixels (in red), and not moving pixels that would overlap to stopped objects, hiding such detection results. The empty scene available at the beginning of the sequence (starting from frame 469) allows to train a quite faithful background model. As soon as the dark car stops (starting from frame 700), the function $E(x)$ described in Section 2 starts incrementing for

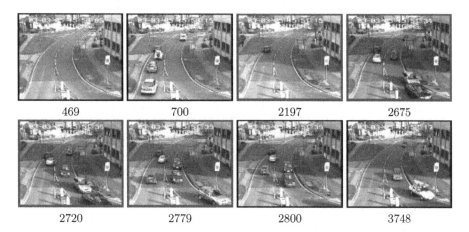

Fig. 3. Detection of stopped objects in sequence *PV-medium*. The car first stops in frame 700. The first stationary object is detected in frame 2197; further stationary pixels are later detected, even if the stopped object is occluded by foreground pixels (e.g. in frame 2720, where the white car covers the stopped car). The car is detected as stopped till to frame 2779, and no more stopped objects are detected till to frame 3748 (end of the sequence).

pixels belonging to the car; such pixels are inserted into the foreground model FG_t and used for the model update. After approximately $\tau_S{=}1500$ frames, $E(x)$ reaches the stationarity threshold τ_S, thus signaling the first stopped object (frame 2197). From this moment till to the end of the stopped car event, the stopped object model allows to distinguish moving objects from the stopped object, as for example in frame 2720, where the white car covers the stopped car. When the car leaves again (from frame 2779), the part of the scene uncovered by the car is again recognized as belonging to the background model, and previously stopped pixels are deleted from the stopped object model.

It should be stressed that illumination conditions have changed quite a bit between the stopping and the leaving of the car. Therefore the actual background area uncovered by the car is very different from the background area that was modeled before the car stop, appearing as subject to a cast shadow. Our background model recognized that area again as background since it includes a mechanism, similar to the one adopted in [18], for detecting shadows and incorporating them into the background model. Specifically, shadow pixels are detected adopting the argument proposed in [7] and are incorporated into the background model according to eq. (3).

Moreover, it should be clarified that we do not identify the whole car, but only its part belonging to the no parking area, since, as suggested for the AVSS 2007 contest, we restrict our attention only to the street including the no parking area (masking out the remaining part of the scene).

Analogous qualitative results can be observed for the other considered *i-LIDS* sequences, as reported in [20].

Table 1. Comparison of ground truth (GT) stopped object event start and end times (in minutes) with those computed with our approach and with different approaches reported in [4,14,17,28], for considered sequences. Related absolute errors $(\varepsilon_O, \ldots, \varepsilon_D)$ are expressed in seconds; total error is computed as the sum of absolute errors over the three sequences.

Sequence	Event	GT	Our	ε_O	A	ε_A	B	ε_B	C	ε_C	D	ε_D
PV-easy	Start	02:48	02:45	3	02:48	0	02:46	2	02:52	4	02:52	4
"	End	03:15	03:19	4	03:19	4	03:18	3	03:19	4	03:16	1
PV-medium	Start	01:28	01:28	0	01:28	0	01:28	0	01:41	13	01:43	15
"	End	01:47	01:51	4	01:55	8	01:54	7	01:55	8	01:47	0
PV-hard	Start	02:12	02:12	0	02:12	0	02:13	1	02:08	4	02:19	7
"	End	02:33	02:34	1	02:36	3	02:36	3	02:37	4	02:34	1
Total error				12		15		16		37		28

We compared results obtained with our approach with those obtained with other approaches for the same sequences. Specifically we considered results obtained by four tracking-based approaches to the detection of stopped objects in the following denoted as: Method **A**, by Boragno et al. [4], who employ a DSP-based system for automatic visual surveillance where block matching motion detection is coupled with MOG-based foreground extraction; Method **B**, by Guler et al. [14], who extend a tracking system, inspired by the human visual cognition system, introducing a stationary object model where each region represents hypotheses stationary objects whose associated probability measures the endurance of the region; Method **C**, by Lee et al. [17], who present a detection and tracking system operating on a 1D projection of images; and Method **D**, by Venetianer et al. [28], who employ an object-based video analysis system featuring detection, tracking and classification of objects.

In Table 1 we report stopped object event start and end times provided with the ground truth and those computed with all considered approaches. Corresponding absolute errors show that generally our approach compares favorably to the other approaches, independently from scene traffic density, and this is still more evident if we consider the total error over the three considered sequences. It should be emphasized that, since our approach to stopped object detection is pixel-based and no region-based post-processing is performed in order to identify objects, in our case a stopped object event starts as soon as a single pixel is detected as stopped and ends soon as no more stopped pixels are detected.

Computational complexity of the proposed algorithm, both in terms of space and time, is $O(LNM)$, where L is the number of layers used for background and foreground models and $N \times M$ is the image dimension. To complete our analysis, in Fig. 4 we report execution times (in msecs/frame) for color image sequences acquired at a frequency of 25 frames per second, varying the spatial resolution and the number L of background and foreground model layers. Image sequences with Small (180x144), Medium (360x288), and High (720x576)

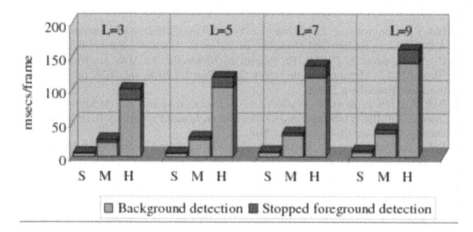

Fig. 4. Execution times (in msecs/frame) for the proposed algorithm on color image sequences with Small (S), Medium (M), and High (H) resolution, varying the number L of background and foreground model layers

resolution have been obtained by subsampling sequence *PV-medium*. Timings have been obtained by prototype implementations in C programming language on a Pentium 4 with 2.40 GHz and 512 MB RAM, running Windows XP operating system, and do not include I/O. The plot shows that only for high resolution sequences the frame rate is not sufficient to obtain real-time processing (about 40 msecs/frame). Nonetheless, we can observe that the stopped foreground detection times represent a small percentage (around 15%) of total execution times. Therefore, stopped foreground detection can be considered a useful and inexpensive by-product of background subtraction.

5   Conclusions

The paper reports our approach to the problem of *stopped foreground subtraction*, consisting in maintaining an up-to-date model of the stopped foreground and in discriminating moving objects as those that deviate from such model. For such modeling problem we adopt visual attention mechanisms that help in detecting features that keep the user attention, based on a 3D self-organizing neural network, without prior knowledge of the pattern classes. The aim is to obtain the objects that keep the user attention in accordance with a set of predefined features, by learning the trajectories and features of moving and stopped objects in a self-organizing manner. Such models allow to construct a system able to detect motion and segment foreground objects into moving or stopped objects, even when they appear superimposed.

References

1. Baf, F.E., Bouwmans, T., Vachon, B.: Type-2 Fuzzy Mixture of Gaussians Model: Application to Background Modeling. In: Bebis, G., Boyle, R., Parvin, B., Koracin, D., Remagnino, P., Porikli, F., Peters, J., Klosowski, J., Arns, L., Chun, Y.K., Rhyne, T.-M., Monroe, L. (eds.) ISVC 2008, Part I. LNCS, vol. 5358, pp. 772–781. Springer, Heidelberg (2008)
2. Baf, F.E., Bouwmans, T., Vachon, B.: A Fuzzy Approach for Background Subtraction. In: IEEE International Conference on Image Processing, ICIP 2008, San Diego, California, USA (October 2008)
3. Baf, F.E., Bouwmans, T., Vachon, B.: Fuzzy Integral for Moving Object Detection. In: IEEE International Conference on Fuzzy Systems, FUZZ-IEEE 2008, Hong-Kong, China, June 1-6, pp. 1729–1736 (2008)
4. Boragno, S., Boghossian, B., Black, J., Makris, D., Velastin, S.: A DSP-based system for the detection of vehicles parked in prohibited areas. In: [24]
5. Cheung, S.-C., Kamath, C.: Robust Techniques for Background Subtraction in Urban Traffic Video. In: Proceedings of EI-VCIP, pp. 881–892 (2004)
6. Collins, R.T., Lipton, A.J., Kanade, T., Fujiyoshi, H., Duggins, D., Tsin, Y., Tolliver, D., Enomoto, N., Hasegawa, O., Burt, P., Wixson, L.: A System for Video Surveillance and Monitoring. The Robotics Institute, Carnegie Mellon University, Tech. Rep. CMU-RI-TR-00-12 (2000)
7. Cucchiara, R., Piccardi, M., Prati, A.: Detecting moving objects, ghosts, and shadows in video streams. IEEE Trans. Pattern Anal. Mach. Intell. 25(10), 1–6 (2003)
8. Ding, J., Ma, R., Chen, S.: A Scale-Based Connected Coherence Tree Algorithm for Image Segmentation. IEEE Transactions on Image Processing 17(2), 204–216 (2008)
9. Elhabian, S.Y., El-Sayed, K.M., Ahmed, S.H.: Moving Object Detection in Spatial Domain using Background Removal Techniques - State-of-Art. Recent Patents on Computer Science 1, 32–54 (2008)
10. Elgammal, A., Duraiswami, R., Harwood, D., Davis, L.S.: Background and Foreground Modeling Using Nonparametric Kernel Density Estimation for Visual Surveillance. Proceedings of the IEEE 90(7), 1151–1163 (2002)
11. Ferryman, J.M. (ed.): Proceedings of the 9th IEEE International Workshop on PETS, New York, June 18 (2006)
12. Ferryman, J.M. (ed.): Proceedings of the 10th IEEE International Workshop on PETS, Rio de Janeiro, Brazil, October 14 (2007)
13. Fisher, R.B.: Change Detection in Color Images,
http://homepages.inf.ed.ac.uk/rbf/PAPERS/iccv99.pdf
14. Guler, S., Silverstein, J.A., Pushee, I.H.: Stationary objects in multiple object tracking. In: [24]
15. Herrero-Jaraba, E., Orrite-Urunuela, C., Senar, J.: Detected Motion Classification with a Double-Background and a Neighborhood-based Difference. Pattern Recognition Letters 24, 2079–2092 (2003)
16. Kim, K., Chalidabhongse, T.H., Harwood, D., Davis, L.S.: Real-time Foreground-Background Segmentation using Codebook Model. Real-Time Imaging 11, 172–185 (2005)
17. Lee, J.T., Ryoo, M.S., Riley, M., Aggarwal, J.K.: Real-time detection of illegally parked vehicles using 1-D transformation. In: [24]
18. Maddalena, L., Petrosino, A.: A Self-Organizing Approach to Background Subtraction for Visual Surveillance Applications. IEEE Transactions on Image Processing 17(7), 1168–1177 (2008)

19. Maddalena, L., Petrosino, A., Ferone, A.: Object Motion Detection and Tracking by an Artificial Intelligence Approach. International Journal of Pattern Recognition and Artificial Intelligence 22(5), 915–928 (2008)
20. Maddalena, L., Petrosino, A.: Further Experimental Results with Self Organizing and Fuzzy Modelling for Parked Vehicles Detection. Tech. Rep. No. RT-DSA-UNIPARTHENOPE-09-03, Dept. of Applied Sciences, University of Naples Parthenope (2009), http://www.dsa.uniparthenope.it
21. Patwardhan, K.A., Sapiro, G., Morellas, V.: Robust Foreground Detection in Video Using Pixel Layers. IEEE Transactions on PAMI 30(4) (2008)
22. Piccardi, M.: Background Subtraction Techniques: A Review. In: Proceedings of IEEE Int. Conf. on Systems, Man and Cybernetics, pp. 3099–3104 (2004)
23. Porikli, F., Ivanov, Y., Haga, T.: Robust Abandoned Object Detection Using Dual Foregrounds. EURASIP Journal on Advances in Signal Processing (2008)
24. Proceedings of 2007 IEEE Conference on Advanced Video and Signal Based Surveillance (AVSS 2007). IEEE Computer Society (2007)
25. Radke, R.J., Andra, S., Al-Kofahi, O., Roysam, B.: Image Change Detection Algorithms: A Systematic Survey. IEEE Transactions on Image Processing 14(3), 294–307 (2005)
26. Sigari, M.H., Mozayani, N., Pourreza, H.R.: Fuzzy Running Average and Fuzzy Background Subtraction: Concepts and Application. Int. J. of Computer Science and Network Security 8(2), 138–143 (2008)
27. Toyama, K., Krumm, J., Brumitt, B., Meyers, B.: Wallflower: Principles and Practice of Background Maintenance. In: Proceedings of the Seventh IEEE Conference on Computer Vision, vol. 1, pp. 255–261 (1999)
28. Venetianer, P.L., Zhang, Z., Yin, W., Lipton, A.J.: Stationary target detection using the objectvideo surveillance system. In: [24],
29. Wren, C., Azarbayejani, A., Darrell, T., Pentland, A.: Pfinder: Real-Time Tracking of the Human Body. IEEE Transactions on PAMI 19(7), 780–785 (1997)
30. Zhang, H., Xu, D.: Fusing Color and Texture Features for Background Model. In: Wang, L., Jiao, L., Shi, G., Li, X., Liu, J. (eds.) FSKD 2006. LNCS (LNAI), vol. 4223, pp. 887–893. Springer, Heidelberg (2006)
31. Zeng, J., Xie, L., Liu, Z.: Type-2 Fuzzy Gaussian Mixture Models. Pattern Recognition 41(12), 3636–3643 (2008)

Rapid Detection of Many Object Instances

Suwan Tongphu, Naddao Thongsak, and Matthew N. Dailey

Computer Science and Information Management
Asian Institute of Technology
{Suwan.Tongphu,Naddao.Thongsak,mdailey}@ait.ac.th

Abstract. We describe an algorithm capable of detecting multiple object instances within a scene in the presence of changes in object viewpoint. Our approach consists of first calculating frequency vectors for discrete feature vector clusters (visual words) within a sliding window as a representation of the image patch. We then classify each patch using an AdaBoost classifier whose weak classifier simply applies a threshold to one visual word's frequency within the patch. Compared to previous work, our algorithm is simpler yet performs remarkably well on scenes containing many object instances. The method requires relatively few training examples and consumes 2.2 seconds on commodity hardware to process an image of size 640×480. In a test on a challenging car detection problem using a relatively small training set, our implementation dramatically outperforms the detection performance of a standard AdaBoost cascade using Haar-like features.

Keywords: Object detection, keypoint descriptors, clustering, visual words, bags of keypoints, AdaBoost.

1   Introduction

Many applications in areas as diverse as biomedical imaging, manufacturing, image retrieval, video surveillance, and autonomous search and rescue would benefit from robust single-image object detection. A large number of approaches have been proposed. Here we focus on methods capable of detecting and accurately localizing *multiple instances* of a given object category in a *single static image*. These methods are obviously applicable to problems such as cell counting in biomedical imaging, in which only a single image is available. However, the methods are also extremely useful for problems involving multiple target tracking with a fixed or moving video camera, since such trackers need to be initialized based on the first video frame. Depending on the tracking application, it may also be necessary to detect and track new instances as they appear in the scene.

When the goal is to detect and localize each instance of an object class in a static image, the typical approach is to run a sliding window over the image, independently classify each image patch, then try to combine multiple detections in the same region. *Template matching*, in which the image patch is normalized then compared to a bank of training examples, is perhaps the simplest method based on this approach. More sophisticated approaches that apply local filters

J. Blanc-Talon et al. (Eds.): ACIVS 2009, LNCS 5807, pp. 434–444, 2009.

and discriminative classifiers, e.g., the Viola and Jones Haar-like feature Ad-aBoost cascade [1], achieve impressive performance in applications such as face detection, in which the object has important features such as eyes in particular relative locations. Many improvements on the Viola and Jones approach have been proposed; for example, Huang et al. [2] use a more flexible yet efficient local filter set and a decision tree structure tailored to face detection under arbitrary in-plane and out-of-plane rotation. However, these approaches may not be ideal for detecting objects with more variable appearance, such as cars, people, buildings, and so on, unless a prohibitively enormous training set is used.

Methods that are more flexible, attempting to perform classification while explicitly allowing for changes in the precise spatial relationships between object parts, can be roughly grouped into those based on *image patch analysis* and *sparse feature analysis*.

Image patch analysis assumes that the target object is composed of a flexible configuration of many small image patches. Mohan et al. [3] propose a component-based method for detecting humans under clutter and occlusion. They train separate support vector machines (SVMs) to detect parts of the entire object (arms, legs, etc.) in restricted regions of the detection window, then train a higher-level SVM to impose geometric constraints among the constituent parts. Keysers et al. [4] first detect interest points, extract image patches around the interest points, scale each patch to a common size, then map each patch to a cluster ID. Finally, the authors apply Breuel's RAST (Recognition by Adaptive Subdivision of Transformation Space) algorithm [5] to find the best rotation, translation, and scale aligning the points on a test image with the matching points on a gallery image.

Sparse feature analysis, on the other hand, uses interest point descriptors that are robust to changes of viewpoint, scale and orientation to increase detection performance. Kim and Dayhot [6] propose a component-based object detection method using SURF [7] and two types of SVMs. After SURF feature extraction, the first SVM filters out points unlikely to lie on objects of interest, and the second bank of SVMs classifies the feature descriptors into likely object components. Finally, the algorithm applies geometrical constraints between candidate components prior to final classification. Csurka et al. [8] introduced the idea of categorizing *bags of keypoints* in a way similar to the way text classification systems categorize bags of words. The authors extract keypoints using the Harris affine detector [9] and compute SIFT descriptors [10] for those keypoints. They then perform vector quantization on the descriptors using a k-means model, and, for purposes of classification, construct a feature summarizing the frequency of occurrence of each keypoint cluster across the image. Finally, they use naive Bayes or a SVM to classify frequency vectors. Das et al. [11] extend this idea to object detection. They use probabilistic latent semantic analysis (PLSA) with a bag-of-visual-words image patch model. SIFT features within a region of interest (ROI) are mapped to discrete visual words obtained during training, visual word occurrence vectors are mapped to a latent topic representation with PLSA. Poor candidate objects are filtered out using various appearance and contextual constraints, and an SVM-based classifier is used to map strong candidate regions to object classes. Although the algorithm performs well on images with multiple object instances, it does not run in real time. Zickler and colleagues [12,13] map observed PCA-SIFT features to cluster centers derived at training time then use each PCA-SIFT feature's scale and orientation to vote for an object center point. The votes from the different feature points are clustered to obtain a final set of object centers. One benefit of the voting approach is that it does not require sliding a detection window over every possible object location and scale. Virtually all sparse feature based techniques can benefit from low-dimensional representations of the descriptors, obtained through general unsupervised dimensionality reduction of standard descriptors [14,13] or discriminatory descriptor learning [15].

In both the image patch and sparse feature approaches, a variety of ways to model geometric constraints between object parts have been proposed. Fergus et al.'s generative model [14] designates one feature point as the "landmark" and models dependent features (which can be occluded) with respect to the landmark feature in a star configuration. Crandall et al. [16] propose an image patch based k-fan model that generalizes the bag-of-patches model ($k = 0$) that does not model spatial configuration and the star model ($k = 1$) that relates each dependent feature to one parent landmark. Higher order models relate dependent features to k parent nodes. All of the generative spatial models simplify computation relative to fully connected models by making various conditional independence assumptions about object parts.

In this paper, we introduce a new object detection algorithm based on sparse features. Our method is similar to other methods based on bags of keypoints [8,11]. We use the basic sliding window approach, mapping feature descriptors to discrete visual words then calculating frequency vectors for those visual words within each window. We then classify each patch using an AdaBoost classifier whose weak classifier simply applies a threshold to one visual word's frequency within the patch. Compared to the previous object detection work, the algorithm is simpler yet performs remarkably well on scenes containing many object instances. The method requires relatively few training examples and in our current implementation consumes 2.2 seconds on commodity hardware to process images of size 640×480. In a test on a challenging car detection problem using a relatively small training set, our implementation dramatically outperforms the detection performance of a standard AdaBoost cascade using Haar-like features.

2   Rapid Multiple-Instance Object Detection

2.1   Overview

Before providing the details of the proposed method, we give a rough overview of the architecture. Fig. 1 provides a schematic overview of our method, which consists of a training and a testing stage.

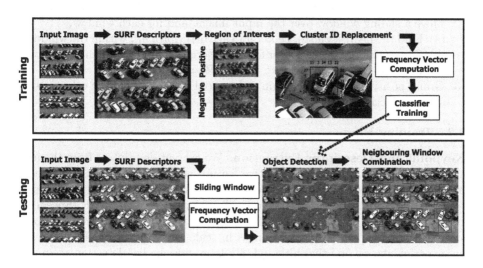

Fig. 1. System overview of the proposed method, showing training and testing flow

The training stage is performed only once and aims to learn a representation of the target object. The following algorithm describes the steps in the training process:

1. For any image I_i, we extract a set D_i of N_i SURF descriptors, where $D_i = \{d_{i,j}\}, 1 \leq j \leq N_i$.
2. From a set of training images, we collect and cluster the SURF descriptors into C groups using the k-means algorithm.
3. From a separate set of training images, for each example object of interest, we create a mask from the object's square bounding box by hand. We find the descriptors $d_{i,j}$ in D_i lying within the mask region, and map each descriptor to the nearest cluster center

$$\underset{c_k \in C}{\operatorname{argmin}} d(d_{i,j}, c_k)$$

where $d(\cdot, \cdot)$ is the Euclidean distance between the input feature point and the input cluster center. We then construct a frequency vector summarizing the cluster centers or "visual words" found within the mask region.
4. From the same of training images, we label negative regions that do not contain the object of interest or only contain partial objects of interest, then construct negative frequency vectors in the same manner as for the positive locations.
5. We train an AdaBoost classifier using a threshold on the frequency of a single visual word as the weak classifier.

In the testing stage, for image I_i, we perform the following steps:

1. Extract a set D_i of N_i SURF descriptors, where $D_i = \{d_{i,j}\}, 1 \leq j \leq N_i$.

2. Move a sliding window over the input image, and for each window,
   (a) Find the nearest cluster center for each descriptor $d_{i,j}$ within the window.
   (b) Compute a frequency vector for the descriptors found within the window.
   (c) Pass the frequency vector to the AdaBoost classifier.
3. Group positive detections within a threshold distance θ of each other into a single detection.

2.2 Training Phase

Keypoint and Descriptor Extraction. We extract descriptors from the image and use them as the representative feature vectors instead of using image pixels directly. In our experiments, we actually consider two different feature descriptors: SIFT (Scale Invariance Feature Transform) [10] and SURF (Speeded-Up Robust Feature) [7]. These feature descriptors provide rich information about local texture that is tolerant to changes in scale and orientation. However, in our experiments, we find that although SIFT provides higher detection accuracy than SURF, because of its fine-scale processing which aims to achieve scale invariance, the multilevel image pyramid computation requires much more time. We therefore primarily use faster the SURF descriptor. Extracting SURF descriptors involves computing keypoints as local maxima of an approximation to the determinant of the local Hessian matrix, assigning scales to keypoints, computing a dominant orientation, then extracting Gaussian-weighted local gradient information in a square window around the keypoint.

Visual Word Representation. In this step, all descriptors extracted from training images are grouped together in order to construct word terms. More specifically, we use k-means to cluster descriptors into many groups which have similar characteristics. We determine the optimal number of classes k experimentally. Following previous research, we call each class a "visual word."

Regions of Interest. For training, we manually label square image regions as either containing a target object or background. A region is considered positive if and only if it covers most of the object's components. Partial objects are treated as negative examples. From the feature descriptors within each square ROI, we find the nearest cluster centers, which are used in the next step. The bounding box typically contains a small background region or parts of other objects along with the object of interest, so the extracted descriptors are typically somewhat noisy.

Frequency Vector. In this step, we count the frequency of occurrence of each visual word in each positive- or negative-labeled square ROI. That is, a k-bin histogram of the SURF descriptors in each labeled window is computed. The vectors are separated into positive and negative training examples, which are used as input to the classifier training procedure.

Classification Model. The positive and negative example frequency vectors are passed to the AdaBoost (Adaptive Boosting) [17] binary classifier training procedure. The strong classifier produced by AdaBoost is constructed from many weak classifiers. In each iteration of the training process, the best candidate weak classifier is selected according to its ability to classify the weighted training set, and on each iteration, the weights of the training examples are updated to give incorrectly classified examples higher weight. In this work, we use a standard monolithic AdaBoost classifier, but a cascade structure similar to that of Viola and Jones might help to speed up the detection process.

2.3   Testing Phase

Keypoint and Descriptor Extraction. As in the training phase, we extract SURF descriptors from the input image. We insert the descriptors into a kd-tree to speed up search time. We then move a sliding window over the entire scene, and for each window, we extract the descriptors within that window using the kd-tree.

Visual Word Representation. Using the visual word model created during training, we map the detected keypoints to visual words as previously described.

Visual Word Frequency Vector for ROI. In this step, the frequency of occurrence of each visual word term within a particular detection window is counted. As during training, we generate a k-bin feature frequency vector. This k-dimensional vector is used to represent an image patch and is used as input to the classifier. As is the case for training ROIs, the frequency vector will typically contain some additive noise in the form of keypoints from the background region within the ROI.

Classification. At this point, we use the AdaBoost classifier from the training stage. We pass the feature frequency vector for each detection window location through the classifier. Clearly, if one detection window position contains an object of interest, nearby detection window locations will also contain the object of interest. Also, since detection window locations close to a positive object location will often contain the same or a very similar set of keypoints, we will typically obtain several positive detections in the neighborhood of a target object. We thus combine neighboring windows into a single detection using a distance threshold.

3   Evaluation

3.1   Experimental Design

In this section, we describe an experimental evaluation of our method on the task of car detection in a surveillance video acquired from a large parking lot. We mounted the camera on a building above the parking lot and captured 9 hours of data in three sessions on 3 different days. An example frame from the test video is shown in Fig. 2.

Fig. 2. Test image extracted from surveillance video for day 3

From the three sessions, we selected the first two days' video data as training data and the third day's video data as test data. In the training data, we manually labeled the location of each car as a positive example and also labeled a large number of background and partial car patches as negative examples. We obtained about 3,000 positive and 7,000 negative training windows through this process. As test data, we simply selected one frame from the third day's surveillance video and labeled the positive locations as ground truth. Fig. 2 shows this frame.

In a first experiment, as a baseline for comparison, we evaluated a standard Viola and Jones AdaBoost cascade using Haar-like features [1] on our car detection dataset. In a second experiment, we compared two different versions of our detection algorithm, one using SURF descriptors and one using SIFT descriptors. In all cases, we used the same training set and the same (separate) test image. We predicted that SURF would outperform SIFT in terms of run time performance and that our sparse feature-based method would outperform the Haar-like feature-based method in terms of accuracy, given the relatively small training set.

3.2 Experiment 1 Results

We built the baseline AdaBoost cascade using the `haartraining` utility from OpenCV [18]. We used a minimum hit rate threshold of 0.995 and a maximum false positive rate of 0.5 for each stage. The trained cascade contained 10 stages

Fig. 3. Detection results for the baseline AdaBoost cascade using Haar-like features

comprised of a total of 234 weak classifiers and had an overall hit rate and false positive rate of 0.996 and 0.249, respectively.

After training, we tested the final classifier on the test image (Fig. 2). We adapted the OpenCV `facedetect` demo to use the single known detection scale for the test data. The detection results are shown in Fig. 3 and the first row of Table 1.

3.3   Experiment 2 Results

We used the Hess implementation [19] of SIFT and the ETH implementation [20] of SURF. We extracted 570,000 128-dimensional SIFT feature descriptors and 320,000 SURF feature descriptors at both 64 and 128 dimensions from the 24 images in the clustering training set, and for each of the three feature sets, we built a model consisting of $k = 30$ clusters. We then computed feature frequency vectors for 3,000 positive and 7,000 negative windows in the training set images. Using these data, we built AdaBoost frequency vector classifiers using OpenCV's [18] generic AdaBoost implementation.

Using the same approach to sliding a constant-scale detection window over the test image as described for Experiment 1, we obtained the results shown in Figure 4 and the last three rows of Table 1.

Fig. 4. Results from proposed object detection algorithm using 128-dimensional SURF descriptors

Table 1. Car detection results. The test scene (Fig. 2) contains 49 target objects. The feature extraction, classification, and overall times are measured in seconds. For bag-of-keypoint methods, feature extraction time includes keypoint extraction and cluster center mapping; classification time includes detection window scanning, frequency vector computation, and AdaBoost-based classification.

Detector	Dims	Hits	Misses	FPs	Time (features)	Time (classification)	Time (overall)
Haar cascade	n/a	29	20	20	n/a	n/a	0.25
Bag of SIFT	128	40	9	4	8.78	0.89	9.66
Bag of SURF	128	37	12	6	1.65	0.54	2.19
Bag of SURF	64	24	25	16	1.40	0.70	2.10

4   Discussion and Conclusion

Examining the results of experiments 1 and 2, we find that the bag-of-keypoints approaches using SIFT or 128-dimensional SURF descriptors perform quite well in terms of detection rates and false positive rates. We also observe that extracting 128-dimensional SURF descriptors takes much less compute time than extracting SIFT descriptors. Although the detection accuracy of SURF is not quite as high as that of SIFT, we find it acceptable.

In comparison to the Haar cascade, our method is much more robust at the cost of a ninefold increase in compute time (0.25 seconds for the Haar cascade compared to 2.2 seconds for the 128-dimensional SURF keypoint based method). We can attribute the increased accuracy of the bag-of-keypoints approach to its rotation invariance, its robustness to non-rigid deformations of the object model, and its insensitivity to lighting conditions. Although it may be possible to dramatically increase the performance of the Haar cascade, the required training set would be prohibitively large, and the resulting detector would necessarily be more complex and most likely slower.

One limitation of our method is that it requires sufficient texture; it does not perform well on objects with color similar to the background. In future work, we will investigate directions to solve this issue. First, we aim to find alternative image features which are robust to the uncluttered object's color. Secondly, we will investigate spatial modeling of the relationships among object components in order to increase detection performance.

The other main limitation is that the run time performance is not as fast as it should be: practical use in real-time systems would in most cases require speedup by a factor of at least 4. We will further optimize our implementation in future work. Through algorithmic improvements and processor architecture-specific optimizations, a significant speedup should be possible. Cascading the AdaBoost classifier would improve classification time (the current classifier is monolithic). In some applications, it is possible to detect objects of interest only once then apply a tracking algorithm like the one proposed in [21]. Instead of detecting objects in every incoming frame, we would perform full detection only on key frames and then use a simpler appearance-based tracker for the intermediate frames. Another possible optimization is dimensionality reduction for the SURF feature descriptor using PCA or a discriminative dimensionality reduction method. This would speed up the nearest neighbor computation required for mapping features to visual words.

We are currently exploring applications of the proposed method in video surveillance systems and in unmanned aerial vehicle (UAV) missions.

Acknowledgments

S. Tongphu and N. Thongsak were supported by graduate fellowships from the Royal Thai Government.

References

1. Viola, P., Jones, M.: Robust real-time face detection. International Journal of Computer Vision 57(2), 137–154 (2004)
2. Huang, C., Ai, H., Li, Y., Lao, S.: High-performance rotation invariant multi-view face detection. IEEE Transactions on Pattern Analysis and Machine Intelligence 29(4), 671–686 (2007)

3. Mohan, A., Papageorgiou, C., Poggio, T.: Example-based object detection in images by components. IEEE Transactions on Pattern Analysis and Machine Intelligence 23, 349–361 (2001)

4. Keysers, D., Deselaers, T., Breuel, T.: Optimal geometric matching for patch-based object detection. Electronic Letters on Computer Vision and Image Analysis 6, 44–54 (2007)

5. Breuel, T.M.: Implementation techniques for geometric branch-and-bound matching methods. Computer Vision and Image Understanding 90, 294 (2003)

6. Kim, D., Dahyot, R.: Face components detection using SURF descriptors and SVMs. In: International Machine Vision and Image Processing Conference, pp. 51–56 (2008)

7. Bay, H., Ess, A., Tuytelaars, T., Gool, L.V.: Speeded-up robust features (SURF). Computer Vision and Image Understanding 110(3), 346–359 (2008)

8. Csurka, G., Dance, C., Fan, L., Willamowski, J., Bray, C.: Visual categorization with bags of keypoints. In: Proceedings of the ECCV International Workshop on Statistical Learning in Computer Vision (2004)

9. Mikolajczyk, K., Schmid, C.: An affine invariant interest point detector. In: Heyden, A., Sparr, G., Nielsen, M., Johansen, P. (eds.) ECCV 2002. LNCS, vol. 2350, pp. 128–142. Springer, Heidelberg (2002)

10. Lowe, D.: Object recognition from local scale-invariant features. In: Proceedings of the International Conference on Computer Vision, ICCV (1999)

11. Das, D., Masur, A., Kobayashi, Y., Kuno, Y.: An integrated method for multiple object detection and localization. In: Proceedings of the 4th International Symposium on Advances in Visual Computing (ISVC), pp. 133–144 (2008)

12. Zickler, S., Veloso, M.: Detection and localization of multiple objects. In: Proceedings of the IEEE-RAS International Conference on Humanoid Robots, pp. 20–25 (2006)

13. Zickler, S., Efros, A.: Detection of multiple deformable objects using PCA-SIFT. In: Proceedings of the National Conference on Artificial Intelligence (AAAI), pp. 1127–1133 (2007)

14. Fergus, R., Perona, P., Zisserman, A.: A sparse object category model for efficient learning and exhaustive recognition. Proceedings of the IEEE Computer Society Conference on Computer Vision and Pattern Recognition (CVPR) 1, 380–387 (2005)

15. Hua, G., Brown, M., Winder, S.A.J.: Discriminant embedding for local image descriptors. International Journal of Computer Vision, 1–8 (2007)

16. Crandall, D., Felzenszwalb, P., Huttenlocher, D.: Spatial priors for part-based recognition using statistical models, pp. 10–17 (2005)

17. Freund, Y., Schapire, R.: A decision-theoretic generalization of on-line learning and an application to boosting. In: Vitányi, P.M.B. (ed.) EuroCOLT 1995. LNCS, vol. 904, pp. 23–37. Springer, Heidelberg (1995)

18. OpenCV Community: Open source computer vision library version 1.1, C source code (2008), http://sourceforge.net/projects/opencvlibrary/

19. Hess, R.: SIFT feature detector, C source code (2006), http://web.engr.oregonstate.edu/~hess/index.html

20. Bay, H., van Gool, L., Tuytelaars, T.: SURF version 1.0.9 (2006), C source code, http://www.vision.ee.ethz.ch/~surf/

21. Okuma, K., Taleghani, A., Freitas, N.D., Freitas, O.D., Little, J.J., Lowe, D.G.: A boosted particle filter: Multitarget detection and tracking. In: Pajdla, T., Matas, J(G.) (eds.) ECCV 2004. LNCS, vol. 3021, pp. 28–39. Springer, Heidelberg (2004)

Concealed Object Perception and Recognition Using a Photometric Stereo Strategy

Jiuai Sun, Melvyn Smith, Abdul Farooq, and Lyndon Smith

Machine Vision Laboratory, Faculty of Environment and Technology
University of the West of England, Bristol, BS16 1QY, UK
{jiuai2.sun,melvyn.smith,abdul2.farooq,lyndon.smith}@uwe.ac.uk

Abstract. Following a review of current hidden objects detection techniques in a range of security applications, a strategy based on an innovative, low-cost photometric stereo technique is proposed to reveal concealed objects. By taking advantage of information rapidly acquired under different illumination conditions, various enhanced real time images can be produced, free from the confusion of textured camouflage. The extracted surface normals can be used for the calculation of curvature and flatness attributes, and providing clues for subsequent hidden object detection and recognition tasks. Experiments on both simulated and real data have verified the strategy is useful for stealthy objects detection and may provide another modality of data for current monitoring system. The results demonstrate good potential application in the detection of concealed objects in security and military applications through the deployment of image enhancement and augmented reality devices.

Keywords: concealed object, perception, enhancement, photometric stereo.

1 Introduction

Screening for and detecting the presence of suspicious or dangerous concealed objects in mass transport environments, such as airport, rail or subway systems has become recognized as an important and difficult task. The need to find suitable tools able to help to protect the public has become even more poignant following recent terrible terrorist attacks. The right detection strategies will help to identify potential dangers before incidents arise. Unfortunately, few techniques have emerged with any potential to effectively deliver satisfactory information in a practical manner. Amongst recent developments backscatter X-ray and millimeter wave/Terahertz technologies are two of the most promising imaging methods [1].

The backscatter X-ray technique creates high resolution images by detecting an X-ray beam reflected from a scanned body. Scanners can penetrate as much as a few millimeters into solid steel by taking advantage of the good penetration capability of high energy X-ray radiation. Since the anatomical details of the person scanned can be reproduced and visualized from this technique, the

J. Blanc-Talon et al. (Eds.): ACIVS 2009, LNCS 5807, pp. 445–455, 2009.

employment of X-ray imaging technique may raise privacy issues. In addition, although manufacturers claim the emitted dosage is minimal, ionizing radiation problems associated with the technique present a potential health hazard [2].

Millimeter wave/Terahertz technology works within the millimetre wave spectrum and generates images from non-ionizing radio frequency energy, emitted passively or reflected actively from the scanned body. The technology can distinguish the difference between a warmer human body and cooler weapons. So it can be used to detect metal guns and knives concealed beneath clothing. However, the radio frequency energy used can only penetrate light clothing materials. It may not be sensitive enough for the objects concealed under thick leather clothes, for example, or hidden within body cavities. Therefore the technique is limited by its low penetration capability. It has been suggested that improved results may be obtained to identify more challenging concealed objects when combined with other sensor modalities in controlled situation [3].

Both backscatter X-ray and millimeter wave/Terahertz technologies have significant practical limitations for detecting concealed objects. Both involve relatively high-cost technology and each need some collaboration from the subject during a whole body scanning procedure. Often a physical pat-down or body scan may prove uncomfortable or impractical. In addition, the expectation of a check procedure may make existing techniques and strategies open to the defeat by those who may find way to circumvent the threat. In such cases a concealed detection and monitoring approach may work more effectively.

Remote controlled close-circuit television cameras offer opportunity for concealed subject monitoring. Cameras working with the right optics are able to acquire detailed information from large crowed public areas, where a single operator may monitor several screens, keeping operational costs low. However, although an experienced operator can pick up and track potential certain threats, concealing strategies or the lack of automated threat identification can confuse the human eye and decrease the power of this strategy [4], [5].

We propose a new strategy with the potential capability to enhance the performance of current monitoring or surveillance systems, either fixed or portable. Images from same systems but with the addition of structured illumination can recover surface normal information which can be used to produce albedo free rendered images, and detect subtle surface features caused by concealed threats, such as weapons, under the clothing or any other camouflaged cover. The concealed object can be metallic and plastic or ceramic in the form of handguns and knives or explosives, which may not be detectable with any one of the sensing modalities mentioned above. The imaging method proposed makes use of available resources and provides an enhanced quality of information, so may work as an add-on function for existing surveillance systems. Finally the technique is non-invasive and does not violate human privacy.

In following we will first explain the principle of the photometric stereo method, which our strategy is mainly based on, and demonstrate its capability for separating surface reflectance from a highly complex environment to reveal hidden subtle shapes. We show how the technique is able to enhance the visibility of a concealed object surface by producing synthetically rendered or shading images under optimised illumination conditions. We demonstrate how the extracted surface normal map is transformed into a curvature and flatness domain for the purpose of automated detecting or recognition. Finally the effectiveness of the proposed strategy is verified and demonstrated through a real practical scenario.

2   Perception of Objects Free from Reflectance Effects

The appearance of a Lambertian surface (note that the assumption of a Lambertian reflectance is not limiting as even specular surfaces contain a dominative Lambertian component) is primarily related to both the surface reflectance and the 3D shape of object. When covered with a complicated textured reflectance (albedo or color, in general), any concealed objects may be hard to find as appear to become 'embedded in the background'. If there are no further assumptions about the surface, it will be challenging to decompose object shape from only one luminance image.

However, if more than one image of the same scene is provided, a technology called photometric stereo can be adopted to separate the reflectance from the shape of the object(s). From the pure surface shape information, artificial shaded images can be rendered with uniform reflectance. As such the resulting variation of intensity is only related to surface shape information, which can be used to extend the visibility beyond normal human vision and to allow the scene to be perceived more easily.

2.1   The Principle of Photometric Stereo

Assuming a Lambertian surface illuminated by a single distant light source, the observed image intensity I at each pixel can be written as the product of the composite albedo ρ(a combination of light source intensity λ and intrinsic reflectance of surface material k) and the cosine value of the incidence angle θ_i between the incidence light direction, expressed as a unit column vector $l = (l_x, l_y, l_z)^T$, and the surface normal, expressed as a unit column vector $N = (N_x, N_y, N_z)^T$:

$$I = \rho \cos(\theta_i) = \rho(l \cdot N) \tag{1}$$

If there is no prior knowledge of the object surface, $m(m \geqslant 3)$ images are needed to fully recover the surface reflectance and shape of the object. Correspondingly m equations like (1) can be written as the following linear system of equations, i.e.

$$I = \rho(L \cdot N) \tag{2}$$

where I is a vector composed by a stack of intensity values $[I_1, I_2, \cdots, I_m]^T$ and L is the illumination matrix $[l_1, l_2, \cdots, l_m]^T$. When the matrix L is known and of at least rank 3, the reflectance and the surface normal can be calculated from the linear equations (2) by a linear least-squares method as:

$$\rho = |(L^T L) \cdot L^T \cdot I| \tag{3}$$

$$N = ((L^T L) \cdot L^T \cdot I)/\rho \tag{4}$$

Most previous photometric stereo work has mainly placed emphasis on accurately recovering the shape of objects [6], [7]. The usefulness of the shaded image with the reflectance information removed in the context for detection of stealthy or concealed objects has not been considered. Next we will demonstrate how perception can be enhanced through producing virtual shaded images.

2.2 Visual Enhancement from Different Illumination Setting

As described in the last section, the reflectance image and shaded image of an object can be separated from luminance images through the principle of photometric stereo. After obtaining surface normal information, numerous synthetically shaded images can be produced by setting virtual lighting conditions [8], [9], [10]. To reveal the surface shape details more clearly, a uniform illumination and homogeneous scene surface are assumed. So the composite albedo can be approximated as a constant E and a shaded image is generated as:

$$I = E\cos\theta_i = E(l \cdot N) \tag{5}$$

where, l is simulated illumination direction which can also be represented by using tilt angle (ϕ, ranging from $0 \sim 360\,°$) and slant angle (φ, ranging from $0 \sim 90\,°$), i.e. $l = (\cos\phi\cos\varphi, \sin\phi\cos\varphi, \sin\varphi)^T$.

The artificially shaded images rendered in such way are free from the confusion of textured reflectance (i.e. camouflage) due to the constant E representing the composite albedo. As such, the rendered shaded images are composed from the object's shape information only. The perception of the object's shape is largely enhanced when compared to the same scene camouflaged by some complicated covering.

There are various images corresponding to different combination of tilt and slant. This mimics the actions that a human may perform to get a best view of an interesting object surface by moving lighting around the object. Such a capability offers an operator the capability to improve the possibility to revealing hidden objects by interacting with a virtual representation of the real scene. We have created a virtual lighting environment able to change slant and tilt angles, and illumination intensity in either interactive or automatic modes.

Figure 1 shows an example in which a toy gun, a knife and a grenade are hidden under a textured cloth. From the acquired luminance image (figure 1(a)) which represents that perceived by the human eye, or conventional surveillance camera, it is not easy to identify the objects hidden under the cloth. However, they become significantly more obvious in the synthetic rendered images as shown in figure 1(b) and 1(c), which correspond to different illumination setting. So in addition to monitoring conventional images acquired from a camera(s) directly, the rendered images provide an additional very different modality of data which can reveal details difficult to find using other normal approaches.

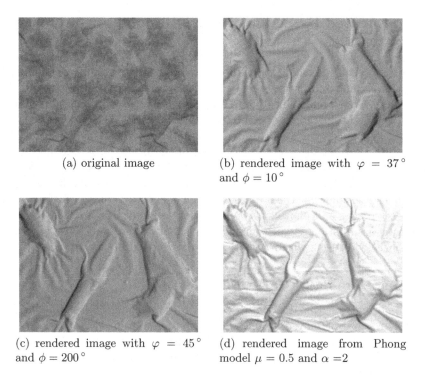

(a) original image

(b) rendered image with $\varphi = 37°$ and $\phi = 10°$

(c) rendered image with $\varphi = 45°$ and $\phi = 200°$

(d) rendered image from Phong model $\mu = 0.5$ and $\alpha = 2$

Fig. 1. One of the acquired images (a) and synthetically rendered images with differing light conditions and reflection model

2.3   Visual Enhancement through Highlighting

The Lambertian model used for shape rendering in a virtual environment is a basic approximation to the real world. Some other reflection models (such as Phong and Torrance-Sparrow models) are more realistic rendering approaches, as they consider effects like highlighting, shadowing and viewpoint. Adding realistic highlights can help to enhance the visual appearance of objects. Here the Phong lighting model is taken as an example to demonstrate how fine details can become more apparent.

The simple Phong reflection model [11] is expressed from the following equations:

$$I = E(\boldsymbol{l} \cdot \boldsymbol{N}) + hightlights \tag{6}$$

$$hightlights = \mu(\boldsymbol{R} \cdot \boldsymbol{V})^{\alpha} \tag{7}$$

Where highlights are related to viewer direction $\boldsymbol{V}$, specular reflection direction ($\boldsymbol{R}$) and a specular reflection constant (μ). The parameter α expresses the shininess of the object's material. Figure 1(d) shows one result of adding a specular or shiny reflectance function to the surface shown in figure 1(c). It gives another impression and draws attention to the form and detail of the objects hidden beneath the cloth.

3 Automated Detection Objects through Surface Normal Patterns

The use of surface normal information has been found useful to enhance the perception of hidden objects by rendering shaded images with optimised illumination and surface reflectance parameters. Such information may also be used to realize the automated detection of concealed or anomalous objects.

As the following detection or recognition procedure will be made using surface normal information, the geometrical shape of the object(s) is assumed distinguishable, i.e. the objects are concealed partially or the shape of the object(s) are conserved even though the object(s) are fully covered. To simplify the problem, we also assume that the objects can be modelled by some basic shapes, like cylinders, spheres and planes or a combination of these elements. This is not an unrealistic assumption as such 'man-made' shapes often tend to be associated with concealed objects within a more randomised natural background.

3.1 Curvature Based Object Detection

Surface normals recovered using photometric stereo change when the observed object is rotated or moved around. So the representation of surface normal is not invariant and may not be a good choice for the detection task. However, the curvatures of an object's surface, calculated from the surface normals, can reveal certain characteristics of interest. Some examples of curvatures extracted from range data have previously been demonstrated as successful in recognition and segmentation applications [12], [13].

When compared to the curvatures obtained from range data, it is more cost effective and robust to calculate curvatures from surface normal data as there is only one differentiation procedure to be carried out. The Gaussian curvature (K) and mean curvature (H) are two parameters frequently used, which can be determined through the following equations:

$$K = \frac{rt - s^2}{(1 + p^2 + q^2)^2} \tag{8}$$

$$H = \frac{(1 + q^2)r - 2pqs + (1 + p^2)}{2(1 + p^2 + q^2)^{(1.5)}} \tag{9}$$

where $p = N_z/N_x$, $q = N_z/N_y$,$r = \partial p/\partial x$, $s = \partial q/\partial y$ and $t = \partial p/\partial y$, N_x , N_y and N_z are the three components of the surface normal $\boldsymbol{N}$.

The Gaussian curvature is an intrinsic property of an object's surface, which is viewpoint invariant and relates only to dimensional information [14]. Specifically the Gaussian and mean curvatures of a plane, a sphere and a cylinder can be represented as $(0, 0)$, $(1/R^2, -1/R)$ and $(0, -1/2R)$, where R is the radius. For objects which can be modelled by the combination of these basic regular geometrical parts (i.e. a cylinder, a sphere, a plane, or those with known modelling parameters), there exist distinct indices in the HK space that is spanned by the mean and Gaussian curvature [15], [16].

Figure 2 presents a procedure to detect a simulated sphere, a plane and a cylinder on a flat surface through surface normal information. Figure 2(a) shows the original geometrical shape of the objects and Figure 2(b) is a synthesised image with camouflage texture and some noise added. The mean curvature of the scene is calculated as representative in figure 2(c), because of its robustness to the noise. The areas of the sphere and cylinders in the curvature map have different constant values from that of the flat background and the rectangle shaped plane in the top-right of the scene. Based on the distinguishing feature within the curvature map, the sphere and cylinder can be picked up and segmented from the background as shown in figure 2(d).

3.2 Flatness Based Object Detection

Although the curvature map can provide an ability to identify/separate objects with simple or complicated shapes, the differentiation procedures involved in the calculation makes the method computational costly and sensitive to noise. The noise may break down the method for some complicated surfaces. This can be found from Figure 2(c), where the difference between interested objects and background is not very obvious, even the object is very simple. This causes difficulty for subsequent detection or recognition tasks.

Based on the observation that the angle between surface normals of two neighbouring pixels in flat areas tends to be smaller than that in curved areas, a novel feature called surface flatness is proposed for classification of different areas across the scene. Similar to the definition of curvature, the flatness describes the variation of surface normal and measures how a geometric surface deviates from being flat. It is also rotation invariant because the angle between surface normal does not change for different viewpoints. Moreover, only simple multiplication and addition steps are required for calculation of flatness. This dramatically decreases the total calculation time and also increases the robustness of the classification, and so provides another efficient descriptor of an object surface.

To calculate the flatness an averaging procedure is firstly applied on the recovered surface normals. With the averaged surface normal N_a, the flatness is calculated as the dot product of the original surface normal N_o and the extracted averaged information N_a, i.e.

$$flatness = N_{low} \cdot N_o \qquad (10)$$

If we consider the direction variation of surface normals in terms of frequency, the scene can be readily divided into different flatness regions, corresponding to various frequencies, i.e. flat areas have low frequencies, while the higher frequencies relate to large variation of surface normal directions. Figure 2(e) shows the flatness map of the same scene calculated using curvatures. Here we find that the flatness map offers a more robust method of distinction the object features from background than that of curvature map as shown in figure 2(c). Figure 2(f) is a segmented result from the calculated flatness map.

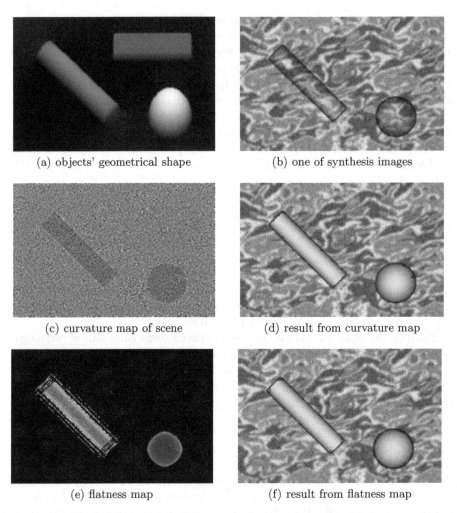

(a) objects' geometrical shape   (b) one of synthesis images

(c) curvature map of scene   (d) result from curvature map

(e) flatness map   (f) result from flatness map

Fig. 2. Simulated objects and their detection through curvature and flatness calculations

4   Experiments

In this section a real scenario is used to evaluate the effectiveness of the photometric stereo based strategy for revealing hidden objects. A dummy is used to represent a human who has four cylinder shaped objects (20mm diameter) about the waist and one rectangular box on the chest. The objects are concealed under a T-shirt which possesses a coloured texture acting as a camouflage. The imaging elements are built using standard low-cost off-the-shelf components, which include an AVT Marlin camera ($F146C$) with a compact Schneider XNP 1.4/17 high-resolution lens, and four Canon flash guns (430 EX).

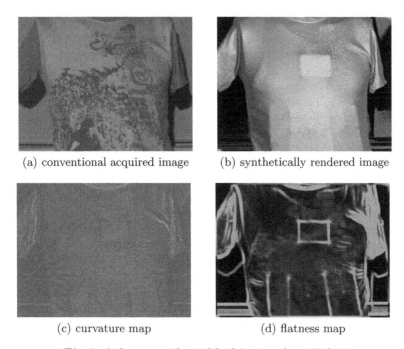

(a) conventional acquired image   (b) synthetically rendered image

(c) curvature map   (d) flatness map

Fig. 3. A dummy with stealth objects under a T-shirt

Figure 3 (a) shows one of the conventional images acquired from the camera, where it is difficult to see the details of the objects hidden under the T-shirt, largely due to the disruptive texture printed on the cloth. However, after separating the confusing reflectance information from the surface and synthetically rendering the scene using a uniform lighting condition and constant albedo with altered specular reflectance, we obtain a very different impression, as shown in the virtual view of figure 3(b). Here subtle details produced by the objects under the clothing are clearly revealed.

Figure 3(c) and (d) show the calculated curvature and flatness maps of the same scenario. As expected the result obtained using curvature has a very low ratio of signal to noise, which is caused by a limited tolerance of the curvature to the noise present in the original acquired images. On the other hand the flatness map can successfully reflect details where there are large variations of the surface normals, i.e. around the edges of the concealed box and cylinders.

5   Conclusions

A photometric stereo based strategy is proposed for the detection of concealed objects as an add-on function to current monitoring or surveillance systems. The new strategy has the capability to separate the surface reflectance or albedo to reveal true 3D shape information. The combined effect is to suppress surface colour and to enhance or make more apparent the 3D quality of the surface. The approach is low cost, needing only the addition of some of extra illumination. By rendering shaded images free from albedo effects, subtle geometrical details become visible as the resultant virtual images are related only to the surface normal information. The direction and intensity of the synthetic illumination used in the virtual image can be altered interactively allowing optimal results to be achieved. The photometric stereo strategy proposed is different from those conventional image-based monitoring methods where the scene is a mixture of texture and shape information and easily affected by the environmental aspects.

We have also demonstrated the potential usefulness of extracted surface normal data for subsequent recognition tasks. Curvature and flatness concepts are developed and verified from simulated and real data. Both curvature and flatness maps can be used to detect interesting or suspicious objects, although the use of flatness was found to be more robust and efficient.

As photometric stereo is based on surface information rather than the material characteristics of objects, unlike other competing methods it will work for almost any material (either metal or non-metal) as long as the object tends to alter the external geometrical structure of the surface. The proposed strategy offers good advantage where the scene background or foreground may be complex and cluttered. In addition the approach does not require harmful radiation and is non-invasive and cost effective. The technique has shown promising results in close range applications in an indoor environment and has potential application as either a fixed system or portable wearable device (analogies to current night vision goggles but intensifying 3D shape rather than image intensity). Future work will explore potential for application in outdoor environments with more challenging objects. We will also aim to achieve automated recognition using 'signatures' associated with more complex, potentially threatening objects so that automated searching for the presence of these predefined signatures within flatness or curvature maps can be implemented.

References

1. Costianes, P.J.: An Overview of Concealed Weapons Detection for Homeland Security. In: Proceedings of the 34th Applied Imagery and Pattern Recognition Workshop, pp. 2–6 (2005)
2. Paulter, N.G.: Guide to the Technologies of Concealed Weapon and Contraband Imaging and Detection, National Institute of Justice Guide 602-00, U.S. Dept. of Justice (2001)
3. Committee on Assessment of Security Technologies for Transportation, National Research Council: Assessment of Millimeter-Wave and Terahertz Technology for Detection and Identification of Concealed Explosives and Weapons. The National Academies Press (2007)
4. Nieto, M.: Public Video Surveillance: Is It an Effective Crime Prevention Tool? California Research Bureau, CRB-97-005 (1997)
5. Bigdeli, A., Lovell, B.C., Sanderson, C., Shan, T., Chen, S.: Vision Processing in Intelligent CCTV for Mass Transport Security. In: IEEE Workshop on Signal Processing Applications for Public Security and Forensics, pp. 1–4 (2007)

6. Sun, J., Smith, M.L., Smith, L.N., Midha, P.S., Bamber, J.C.: Object Surface Recovery Using a Multi-light Photometric Stereo Technique for Non-Lambertian Surfaces Subject to Shadows and Specularities. Image and Vision Computing 25(7), 1050–1057 (2007)
7. Woodham, R.J.: Photometric Method for Determining Surface Orientation from Multiple Images. Optical Engineering 19(1), 139–144 (1980)
8. Malzbender, T., Wilburn, B., Gelb, D., Ambrisco, B.: Surface Enhancement Using Real-time Photometric Stereo and Reflectance Transformation. In: Eurographics Symposium on Rendering, pp. 245–250 (2006)
9. Cignoni, P., Scopigno, R., Tarini, M.: A Simple Normal Enhancement Technique for Interactive Non-photorealistic Renderings. Computers and Graphics 29, 125–133 (2005)
10. Rusinkiewicz, S., Burns, M., DeCarlo, D.: Exaggerated Shading for Depicting Shape and Detail. ACM Transactions on Graphics (Proc. SIGGRAPH) 25(3), 1199–1205 (2006)
11. Phong, B.T.: Illumination for Computer Generated Pictures. Communications of the ACM 18(6), 311–317 (1975)
12. Arman, F., Aggarwal, J.K.: Model Based Object Recognition in Dense Range Images - A Review. ACM Computing Surveys 25(1), 125–145 (1993)
13. Trucco, E., Fisher, R.B.: Experiments in Curvature Based Segmentation of Range Data. IEEE Transaction on PAMI 17(2), 177–182 (1995)
14. Angelopoulou, A., Williams, J., Wolff, L.: A Curvature Based Descriptor Invariant to Pose and Albedo Derived from Photometric Data. In: Proceedings of the IEEE conference on Computer Vision and Pattern Recognition, pp. 165–171 (1997)
15. Besl, P., Jain, R.: Three-dimensional Object Recognition. Computing Surveys 17(1), 75–145 (1985)
16. Pan, X., Lane, D.M.: Representation and Recovery of 3D Curved Objects Using Generalized Cylinders and the Extended Gaussian Image. Pattern Recognition Letters 20, 675–687 (1999)

Tracking 3D Orientation through Corresponding Conics

Alberto Alzati[1], Marina Bertolini[1], N. Alberto Borghese[2], and Cristina Turrini[1]

[1] Dipartimento di Matematica
Università degli Studi di Milano
Via Saldini 50 I20133 Milano Italy
[2] Dipartimento di Scienze dell'Informazione
Università degli Studi di Milano
Via Comelico 39 I20133 Milano Italy

Abstract. We propose here a new method to recover the 3D orientation of a rigid body by matching corresponding conics embedded in the object itself. The method is based on writing the projective equations of the conics and rearranging them in a suitable way. This leads to a very simple linear system. Results from simulated experiments show good accuracy and suggest that this method could be used for instance in augmented reality surgery to effectively track surgery instruments inside the operating room.

Keywords: Axial rotation, painted markers, computer assisted and virtual surgery, navigation systems, multi-camera motion tracking, computer vision, conics and quadrics.

1 Introduction

One of the most exciting application fields of computer vision is nowadays represented by augmented reality surgery. In this domain, the surgeon can view the operating theater on a single monitor that shows the current body part under surgery with superimposed archive images, as well as the instruments that are being utilized by the surgeon. To achieve this, a reliable and accurate tracking of the surgery instruments is required. This allows substantial improvement in the accuracy of the surgery with obvious benefits for the patients [3],[4]. The most diffused prototypes of this kind of systems are produced by Northern Digital and are based on active or passive markers tracking, the second solution being the preferred one as it is not sensitive to ferromagnetic material that is common inside a surgical room. Moreover, higher accuracy can be achieved [5]. Trackers of the last type are based on capturing the motion of a set of markers attached to the instruments, through a set of video cameras. From the markers motion the six degrees of freedom (*dof*) of the instrument can be computed in real-time at video rate. While an instrument's translation and rotation around axes orthogonal to the instrument's axis could be determined via markers attached on the instrument's axial itself, axial rotation remains a difficult parameter to determine. A common solution is to resort to a set of supports to displace the markers with respect to the instrument axis as in figure 1.a (1). However, such a structure occupies quite a large volume and limits the freedom of the surgeon. For this reason, a different solution has been proposed in [6] and [7], where a

J. Blanc-Talon et al. (Eds.): ACIVS 2009, LNCS 5807, pp. 456–461, 2009.

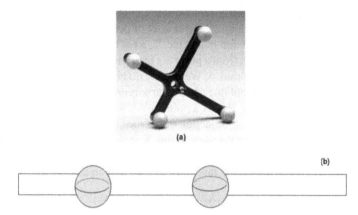

Fig. 1. A typical structure carrying eccentrical markers used in [5] is shown in panel (a). The set-up proposed in the present paper is shown in panel (b).

stripe is painted on the surface of at least one of a set of at least two markers attached on the instrument's axis as in figure 1.b (1). This prevents increasing the instrument's size and therefore helps in making capturing less intrusive. The procedure is based on reconstructing the 3D position of all the points that belong to the stripe; from the points position the orientation of the stripe over the marker and therefore the axial rotation can be derived. Such a procedure requires that many points of the stripe are visible to achieve a high accuracy. We propose here an alternative solution that is based firstly on fitting the images of the stripe points to a suitable conic, and, by matching the conics over different cameras, recovering the stripe orientation. With this procedure, the stripe can be made as small as possible and fewer points may be required as a more robust identification of the pattern can be achieved describing its shape analytically through a conic.

2 Notation and Background Material

First of all we fix the mathematical set up. $\mathbb{E}^3$ denotes the $3-$dimensional real euclidean space. Once an euclidean frame is chosen, coordinate vectors $\mathbf{X}$ of points of $\mathbb{E}^3$ are written as columns, thus their transpose, with the notation of homogeneous coordinates, are $\mathbf{X}^T = (X_1, X_2, X_3, X_4)$, where the corresponding affine coordinates are $(X_1/X_4, X_2/X_4, X_3/X_4)$. We will denote by $\Lambda_{a,b,c} \subseteq \mathbb{E}^3$ the plane, not passing through the origin, with equation $aX_1 + bX_2 + cX_3 = X_4$.

We recall that a conic curve $\overline{\gamma} \subseteq \mathbb{E}^3$ is given by the intersection of a quadric surface Q with a plane Λ. In particular, for a given conic $\overline{\gamma}$ and for a point V not in Λ, it is always possible to get $\overline{\gamma}$ as the intersection of Λ with the quadric cone Γ_V projecting $\overline{\gamma}$ from V.

Once an euclidean frame is chosen in Λ, with homogeneous coordinates $\mathbf{y}^T = (y_1, y_2, y_3)$, $\overline{\gamma}$ is represented by the equation $\mathbf{y}^T \cdot M_{\overline{\gamma}} \cdot \mathbf{y}$ for a suitable 3×3 symmetric matrix $M_{\overline{\gamma}}$. Analogously a quadric Q in $\mathbb{E}^3$ is represented by an equation $\mathbf{X}^T \cdot M_Q \cdot \mathbf{X}$ for a suitable 4×4 symmetric matrix M_Q.

For the convenience of the reader, we fix our notation for cameras, in the context of euclidean reconstruction. As usual, a scene is a set of points $\mathbf{X} \in \mathbb{E}^3$. Once a frame is fixed both in the euclidean space and in a plane Σ, a *camera* is represented as a central projection P of points in 3-space, from a point not in Σ, the center C_P, onto $\mathbb{E}^2 = \Sigma$, or equivalently by a 3×4 matrix of rank 3. We usually do not make any formal distinction between the projection *map* P and one of its matrix representations, for which we use the same symbol P. Accordingly, if $\mathbf{X}$ is a point in $\mathbb{E}^3$, we denote the coordinates of its image in Σ by $P\mathbf{X}$. The center of projection C_P is the right annihilator of P. As usual two different images $\mathbf{y}'$ and $\mathbf{y}$ of the same point $\mathbf{X}$ under different projections P and P' are *corresponding points*.

We recall that ([1]) any projection matrix P_i can be written as

$$P_i = \Delta_{f_i} \cdot [O_i| - O_i \cdot C_i] = [\Pi_i|\mathbf{v_i}],$$

where $\Delta_{f_i} = \begin{pmatrix} f_i & 0 & 0 \\ 0 & f_i & 0 \\ 0 & 0 & 1 \end{pmatrix}$, f_i is the focal length, O_i is a suitable 3×3 rotation matrix and C_i is the vector of the coordinates of the center C_{P_i}.

Given a conic γ in the plane Σ and a point V not belonging to Σ, the matrix representing the quadric cone Γ_V projecting γ from V is $M_{\Gamma_V} = P^T M_\gamma P$, where P is any camera with center $C_P = V$, and M_γ is the matrix representing the conic γ on Σ as described above.

3 Reconstruction of a Conic from Three or More Views

Here we show how to reconstruct a conic in $\mathbb{E}^3$ from three or more views. Though a reconstruction method for a conic from two views has been described in previous papers (e.g. in [2], where the solution needs also a quadratic equation and [8]), here we propose a different and very simple algorithm to get the result via a overdetermined linear system in four unknowns.

First of all we show how to get the equation of a given conic $\overline{\gamma}$ defined as the intersection of a quadric $\overline{Q}$ and a plane $\Lambda = \Lambda_{a,b,c}$ in terms of the homogeneous coordinates (y_1, y_2, y_3) of a fixed frame on Λ. Let N be the 4×3 matrix the columns of which are given by the vectors of the homogeneous coordinates in $\mathbb{E}^3$ of the points whose local coordinates in Λ are: $(1, 0, 0), (0, 1, 0)$ and $(0, 0, 1)$. The relation between homogeneous coordinates of the same point in $\mathbb{E}^3$ and in Λ are given by: $(X_1, X_2, X_3, X_4)^T = N \cdot (y_1, y_2, y_3)^T$. Hence the equation of $\overline{\gamma}$ in Λ is $(y_1, y_2, y_3) \cdot N^T \cdot M_{\overline{Q}} \cdot N \cdot (y_1, y_2, y_3)^T = 0$, in other words one has $M_{\overline{\gamma}} = N^T \cdot M_{\overline{Q}} \cdot N$.

In particular, when $\Lambda = \Lambda_{a,b,c}$, we can choose $N^T = \begin{pmatrix} 1 & 0 & 0 & a \\ 0 & 1 & 0 & b \\ 0 & 0 & 1 & c \end{pmatrix}$.

Let $\overline{\gamma} = \overline{Q} \cap \Lambda_{a,b,c}$ be a conic and consider k projection matrices $\{P_i\}$, with $i = 1 \ldots k \geq 3$. In the sequel we will show how to determine (a, b, c), and hence $\Lambda_{a,b,c}$, from $\gamma_i := P_i(\overline{\gamma})$. Notice that, once $\Lambda_{a,b,c}$ is known, one also gets $\overline{\gamma}$ as the intersection of $\Lambda_{a,b,c}$ with anyone of the quadric cones given by the matrices $P_i^T \cdot M_{\gamma_i} \cdot P_i$, and the orientation of $\Lambda_{a,b,c}$.

Even if our method works for any $k \geq 3$, here, for sake of simplicity, from now on we will assume $k = 3$. Since the three γ_i, with $i = 1, 2, 3$, are images of the same conic $\bar{\gamma}$, the three quadric cones, given by the matrices $P_i{}^T \cdot M_{\gamma_i} \cdot P_i$, have to cut the same conic on the plane $\Lambda_{a,b,c}$. Therefore we get the following two relations among 3×3 symmetric matrices:

$$N^T \cdot P_1^T \cdot M_{\gamma_1} \cdot P_1 \cdot N = \rho_1 N^T \cdot P_2^T \cdot M_{\gamma_2} \cdot P_2 \cdot N, \tag{1}$$

$$N^T \cdot P_3^T \cdot M_{\gamma_3} \cdot P_3 \cdot N = \rho_3 N^T \cdot P_2^T \cdot M_{\gamma_2} \cdot P_2 \cdot N, \tag{2}$$

where ρ_1 and ρ_3 are unknown constants.

The matrices at the left hand side of both equations 1 and 2, can be written respectively as:

$$L_i = A_i + (a, b, c)^T \cdot B_i^T + B_i \cdot (a, b, c) + (a, b, c) \cdot d_i \cdot (a, b, c)^T,$$

with $i = 1, 3$ where A_i is a suitable 3×3 symmetric matrix, B_i is a suitable vector, $d_1 = \mathbf{v_1}^T \cdot M_{\gamma_1} \cdot \mathbf{v_1}$ and $d_3 = \mathbf{v_3}^T \cdot M_{\gamma_3} \cdot \mathbf{v_3}$.

Now we choose the frame in $\mathbb{E}^3$ in such a way that the camera P_2 has center in the origin, which implies $\mathbf{v_2}^T = (0, 0, 0)$. The reason is that, with this choice, the right hand sides $\rho_i R$ of both equations do not contain the unknowns a, b, c (look at $P_2 \cdot N$) From equations 1 and 2 it follows:

$$d_3 L_1 - d_1 L_3 = (d_3 \rho_1 - d_1 \rho_3) R. \tag{3}$$

The matrix equation 3 is linear in the unknowns a, b, c and $r := d_3 \rho_1 - d_1 \rho_3$. We get an overdeterminated linear system of six equations in a, b, c and r.

An algorithm to determine $\Lambda_{a,b,c}$ given three matrices M_{γ_i} is implemented in MATLAB® and it is available by the authors.

4   Simulated Experiments and Results

To assess the accuracy of the proposed method we have carried out a set of simulated experiments. We have set-up three virtual cameras on the same plane, with centers at the vertexes of a right isosceles triangle, with legs of approximately 200 mm. The cameras aimed to a point Z distant approximately 400 mm from them. A conic is then created on a plane whose distance from Z is approximately 45 mm farther with respect to the cameras, simulating that the object is at the boundary of the working volume.

The conic is then projected over the image plane of the three cameras, each having a focal length equal to 50 mm. This procedure produces on the image plane of the cameras ellipses with diameter, δ, less than 35 mm long. We have verified that the orientation of the plane identified with the present method matches the true orientation.

Uniformly distributed noise was then added to the conics parameters with different amplitude: $N2D = 0.05, 0.01$ and 0.001 of the parameters size, that produces a maximum displacement of the conics on the image plane respectively of $\delta/35$, $\delta/350$ and $\delta/700$ that is compatible with the quantization error in actual vision systems.

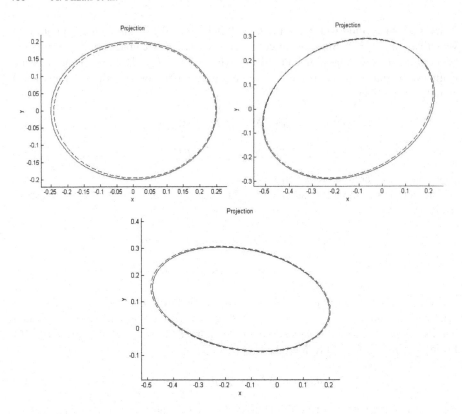

Fig. 2. Conics γ_i with added noise (dashed) in case $N2D = 0.05$

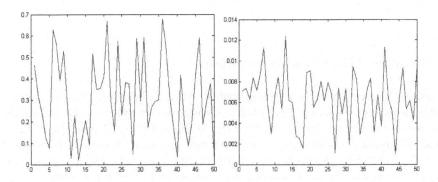

Fig. 3. Amplitude, in degrees, of the angle between the true normal vector of the plane $\Lambda_{a,b,c}$ and the normal vector determined with our method, when $N2D = 0.05$ of the parameters size (on the left) and when $N2D = 0.001$ (on the right). Data refers to 50 different noise realizations.

Results obtained with the different error rates are reported in figure 3 and show that the method is quite robust, achieving an accuracy of 0.313 ± 0.187, with maximum error of 0.7, (respectively 0.071 ± 0.032, with maximum error of 0.16, and 0.006 ± 0.003, with maximum error of 0.012) degrees (mean $\pm$ standard deviation) in the estimate of the axial rotation in case $N2D = 0.05$ (respectively $N2D = 0.01$ and 0.001).

Similar results can be obtained for the other orientation parameters. However, given the set-up in figure 1 (b), the orientation of the plane allows to compute the axial orientation of the surgical instrument which is the most difficult parameter to be determined and also the parameter that required to build offset devices like the one in figure 1 (a).

5 Discussion and Conclusion

The method is based on using a structure like the one suggested in figure 1 (b), that minimally modifies the surgical instrument. From the practical point of view, a possible problem can be that each camera can survey the curve under a limited angle, thus making the estimate of the curves on the image planes unreliable. To avoid this, one possibility can be to make the markers with transparent material. In this way the entire curve becomes visible and one can check the angle between the image plane of each camera and the position (axis) of the instrument in order to avoid quasi-degenerate situations. Results show that this method could be further developed to be used in augmented reality surgery to effectively track surgery instruments inside the operating room.

References

1. Hartley, R., Zissermann, A.: Multiple View Geometry. Cambridge Univ. Press, Cambridge (2000)
2. Quan, L.: Conic Reconstruction and Correspondence from Two Views. IEEE-PAMI 18 (1996)
3. Novotny, P.M., Stoll, J.A., Vasilyev, N.V., Del Nido, P.J., Dupont, P.E., Howe, R.D.: GPU Based Real-time Instrument Tracking with Three Dimensional Ultrasound. In: Larsen, R., Nielsen, M., Sporring, J. (eds.) MICCAI 2006. LNCS, vol. 4190, pp. 58–65. Springer, Heidelberg (2006)
4. Bajka, M., Tuchschmid, S., Streich, M., Fink, D., Székely, G., Harders, M.: Evaluation of a New Virtual-Reality Training Simulator for Hysteroscopy Surgical Endoscopy (2008), doi:10.1007/s00464-0
5. http://www.ndigital.com/medical/products.php
6. Borghese, N.A., Frosio, I.: MI.S.S., Micro Surgery Simulator. In: Proc. 7th Optical 3D Measurement Techniques Conference, Vienna (2005)
7. Frosio, I., Bolognesi, F., Borghese, N.A.: Compact tracking of surgical instruments. IEEE Trans. PAMI (submitted)
8. Sun, T.L.: Conics enhanced vision approach for easy and low-cost 3D tracking. Pattern Recognition 37 (2004)

Parallel Region-Based Level Set Method with Displacement Correction for Tracking a Single Moving Object

Xianfeng Fei[1,3,*], Yasunobu Igarashi[2], and Koichi Hashimoto[1]

[1] Graduate School of Information Science, Tohoku University,
6-6-01 Aramaki Aza Aoba, Aoba-ku, Sendai 980-8579, Japan
{sandra_fei,koichi}@ic.is.tohoku.ac.jp
[2] Graduate School of Information Science, Nara Institute of Science and Technology,
8916-5 Takayama, Ikoma, Nara 630-0192 Japan
igalab1@is.naist.jp
[3] College of Electrical Engineering, Guizhou University, Guiyang, Guizhou,
550003, China
http://www.ic.is.tohoku.ac.jp/ja/index.php?FrontPage

Abstract. We proposed a parallel level set method with displacement correction (DC) to solve collision problems during tracking a single moving object. The major collision scenarios are that the target cell collides with other cells, air bubbles, or a wall of the water pool where cells swim. These collisions result in detected contour of the target spreading to the other obstacles which induces target missing and tracking failure. To overcome this problem, we add displacement correction to the procedure of boundary detection once the collision occurs. The intensity summation of inside detected contour is utilized to determine whether collision occurs. After the collision is detected, we translate the current level set function according to the displacement information of target cell. To clarify the ability of our proposed method, we try cell (paramecium) tracking by visual feedback controlling to keep target cell at the center of a view field under a microscope. To reduce computational time, we implement our proposed method in a column parallel vision (CPV) system. We experimentally show that the combination of our proposed method and CPV system can detect the boundary of the target cell within about 2 [ms] for each frame and robustly track cell even when the collision occurs.

Keywords: boundary tracking, parallel image processing, level set method, displacement correction.

1 Introduction

Microorganism observation tasks require keeping a single object in the middle of visual field under microscopes. This is an object tracking problem from the point of view of the computer vision community. It is therefore desirable to track cell

---

* Corresponding author.

J. Blanc-Talon et al. (Eds.): ACIVS 2009, LNCS 5807, pp. 462–473, 2009.
© Springer-Verlag Berlin Heidelberg 2009

boundary, leading to estimate the position of the object. The model for boundary detection is originally proposed by Kass et al., called snake or active contour [1]. The snake is a parametric curve that minimizes its energy with respect to two forces, one controls the smoothness of the curve and another attracts the curve towards the boundary. The original snake must be placed close to the object to guarantee success. Moreover, the classical energy functional of snakes can not directly deal with changes in topology. The need for topological changes lead to the development of geodesic active contours [2], [3], [4] or level set method (LSM) [5], [6], [7]. Based on curve evolution approach, the evolving contours of these models naturally split and merge. These models are computationally expensive and mostly applied to static images. To reduce the computational cost, the authors group has developed a single moving cell tracking system by using parallel region based LSM and visual servoing [8], [9], [10], [11]. However, our used tracking model is not robust for collision problems like target cell colliding with obstacles such as lots of other cells, air bubbles, or a wall of the water pool where cells swim. In our previous model, parallel region based LSM is in charge of cell boundary detection. When above collision problems occurs, cell boundary detection becomes inaccurate. Detected boundary is not only around target cell but also spreads to other obstacles. With these detection errors accumulating, detected contour switches from target to other obstacles and the tracking fails in the end. Therefore, we propose a new parallel and region-based LSM with displacement correction to solve such collision problems. Once collision is detected, we utilize displacement information of moving target to correct inaccurate boundary detection which makes detected contour not to spread to other obstacles but only around target. To decrease the computational time, we implement this combination of the region-based LSM and displacement correction into a column parallel vision (CPV) system, which is developed by Ishikawa's group and Hamamatsu Photonics K.K. [12], [13]. CPV system consists of a high speed camera and a parallel image processor. We demonstrate that our proposed method can detect and track boundaries of a single moving paramecia, a kind of protozoa, within about 2 [ms] under a microscope. Especially, we prove the ability of collision handling of our proposed model by showing the tracking result when target paramecium collides with other paramecia, air bubble, or the wall of pool.

2   Materials and Methods

2.1   Model of a General LSM

Consider a 2D deformable contours $C(x, y, t)$ in a 2D image. Let Ω be the region that $C(x, y, t)$ encloses (Fig. 1A). $C(x, y, t)$ is implicitly represented as a 3D level set function $\phi(x, y, t)$ [5]. The zero level set $\{(x, y) | \phi(x, y, t) = 0\}$ represents a computed 2D contour $C(x, y, t)$ on the 2D image at any time (Fig. 1B). The level set function ϕ is Lipschitz continuous and satisfies following conditions:

$$\begin{cases} \phi(x, y, t) = 0, & \text{if } (x, y) \in C \\ \phi(x, y, t) > 0, & \text{if } (x, y) \in \Omega \\ \phi(x, y, t) < 0, & \text{if } (x, y) \in \bar{\Omega}. \end{cases} \quad (1)$$

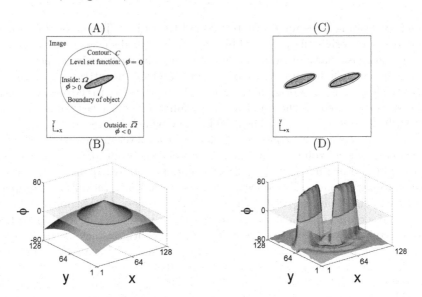

Fig. 1. (A) A relationship among a boundary of an object in an image, a level set function ϕ and a contour C. (B) A sample shape of a monomodel level set function ϕ whose zero level set correspond to the contour C in (A). (C) Two objects and two contours in the image. (D) A bimodel level set function which represents two contours in (C).

The evolution of the level set function ϕ from an initial value is defined to minimize an energy function E by variational approach:

$$\frac{\partial \phi}{\partial t} = -\frac{\partial E}{\partial \phi}. \tag{2}$$

The initial value of ϕ is arbitrary as far as eq. (1) is guaranteed.

2.2   Model of Parallel Region-Based LSM

To decrease the computational complexity and the computational time of general LSM, we propose a new level set energy function based on Chan-Vese Model (CV model) as follows [14]:

$$E = E_{in} + E_{out} \tag{3}$$

$$E_{in} = \frac{\alpha}{2} \int |\nabla \phi|^2 dxdy \tag{4}$$

$$\begin{aligned} E_{out} &= \beta\{\lambda_1 F_1(\phi) + \lambda_2 F_2(\phi)\} \\ &= \beta \int \lambda_1 |I - I_{in}|H(\phi) - \lambda_2 |I - I_{out}| \left[1 - H(\phi)\right] dxdy, \end{aligned} \tag{5}$$

where the integral interval here and hereafter are referred to the whole image. E_{in} and E_{out} denote internal and external energy functions, respectively. α and β are weight parameters of E_{in} and E_{out}, respectively. $I(x, y)$ indicates the image intensity at the position (x, y). Instead of image gradient term ∇I, region-based information I_{in} and I_{out} are used in eq. (5) which represent average intensities of inside and outside C, respectively:

$$I_{in}(\phi) = \frac{\int I H(\phi) dx dy}{\int H(\phi) dx dy}, I_{out}(\phi) = \frac{\int I(1 - H(\phi)) dx dy}{\int (1 - H(\phi)) dx dy}. \tag{6}$$

λ_1 and λ_2 are fitting parameters of inside and outside C, respectively. $H(\phi)$ is the Heavisdie function and $\delta(\phi)$ is the one-dimensional Dirac function, defined as follows:

$$H(\phi) = \begin{cases} 1, & \phi \geq 0 \\ 0, & \phi < 0. \end{cases} \qquad \delta(\phi) = \frac{d}{d\phi} H(\phi). \tag{7}$$

The evolution of the level set function ϕ is described by a following equation:

$$\frac{\partial \phi}{\partial t} = \alpha \nabla^2 \phi - \beta \delta(\phi) \left(\lambda_1 |I - I_{in}| - \lambda_2 |I - I_{out}| \right). \tag{8}$$

Our modifications of CV model are summarized as follows:

Modification 1: For the simplification, considering the architecture of CPV system (see the subsection 2.5), we replace $|\nabla H(\phi)|$ in CV Model with $|\nabla \phi|^2$ in eq. (4). If we use $|\nabla H(\phi)|$ in E_{in}, the cuverture $\kappa(\phi)$ will appears in the the the Euler-Lagarange equation of CV model as

$$\kappa(\phi) = \frac{\phi_{xx} \phi_y^2 - 2 * \phi_x \phi_y \phi_{xy} + \phi_{yy} \phi_x^2}{(\phi_x^2 + \phi_y^2)^{3/2}}. \tag{9}$$

Whereas $|\nabla \phi|^2$ results in $\nabla^2 \phi$ appearing in the Euler-Lagarange equation of ϕ.

$$\nabla^2 \phi = \phi_{xx} + \phi_{yy}. \tag{10}$$

Compare the form of eq. (9) with eq. (10), this modification simplify the calculation of the Euler-Lagarange equation of ϕ dramatically. With the limitation of local memory size of CPV system, it is impossible to implement operations like division, square root within such short sampling interval as 2 [ms]. Therefore this simplification makes our model to be able to implement in parallel. $|\nabla \phi|^2$ is the square of the gradient magnitude of ϕ, if we consider ϕ is a description of a 2D membrane (as the Figure 1C), $|\nabla \phi|^2$ represents the elastic potential energy of this membrane. The value of E_{in} becomes small when a spatial change of ϕ becomes small. Therefore, the new E_{in} still has the smoothing ability for ϕ.

Modification 2: Also for the simplification, we replace $(I - I_{in})^2$ and $(I - I_{out})^2$ in CV Model with $|I - I_{in}|$ and $|I - I_{out}|$ in eq. (5), respectively. Therefore, square operation has turned into absolute value operation which can be implemented in CPV system just by using bit operation directly. The bit operation is more easily to be implemented in CPV system than multiplication. Apparently, E_{out}

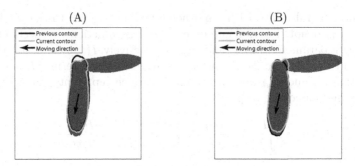

Fig. 2. A diagram of displacement correction (DC). The vertical black ellipse denotes a tracking target cell and horizontal one denotes an obstacle. The black curve denotes previous contour, gray curve denotes current contour. The length of black line with arrow denotes the magnitude of displacement, the arrow denotes the direction of moving. (A) Before DC: The gray curve spread out and cover both target cell and a bit of obstacle. (B) After DC: Moving black curve of (A) to the position of (B) according to the displacement information.

still can obtain its minimum value $E_{out} = 0$ when $|I - I_{in}| \approx 0$ and $|I - I_{out}| \approx 0$. At this time C is on the boundary of the object. So E_{out} also has the ability of boundary detection.

Modification 3: For implementation, first, we discretize the Dirac function $\delta(\phi)$ as

$$\delta(\phi) \approx \frac{1}{1 + |\phi|}. \tag{11}$$

If we utilize $\delta(\phi)$ as

$$\delta(\phi) = \begin{cases} 1, & \phi = 0 \\ 0, & \phi \neq 0, \end{cases} \tag{12}$$

Except for the pixel of $\phi = 0$, the rest of pixels can not update their ϕ which make the convergence of our model slowly. Now with form of eq. (11), the range of ϕ where $\delta(\phi) \neq 0$ is extended which can speed up the convergence of our model. Second, we define h as the discrete space step and $(x_i, y_i) = (ih, jh)$ as the grid points of the image, respectively. Let Δt be the discrete time step and n be the iteration number.

By utilizing above modifications, eq. (8) can be approximately transformed into

$$\frac{\phi_{i,j}^{n+1} - \phi_{i,j}^n}{\Delta t} = \alpha \frac{\phi_{i+1,j}^n + \phi_{i-1,j}^n + \phi_{i,j+1}^n + \phi_{i,j-1}^n - 4\phi_{i,j}^n}{8}$$
$$- \beta \frac{1}{1 + |\phi_{i,j}^n|} [\lambda_1 |I_{i,j} - I_{in}(\phi^n)|$$
$$- \lambda_2 |I_{i,j} - I_{out}(\phi^n)|]. \tag{13}$$

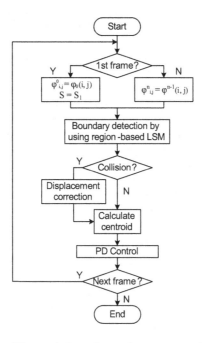

Fig. 3. A flow chart of our proposed model

2.3   Displacement Correction

Firstly, we define some variables: ϕ_n denotes ϕ of nth frame. ϕ_{n-m} denotes ϕ of $(n-m)$th frame. S denotes intensity summation of detected contour inside and is initialized as intensity summation of detected contour inside of the first frame S_1. S_{th} is threshold constant. To solve collision problem, we propose the displacement correction defined by following two steps:

- **collision detection**: When collision occurs, detected contour spreads from target to obstacles and the intensity summation inside contour changes obviously. Therefore, during the evolution, if $|S - S_1| > S_{th}$, we consider it as collision occurring.
- **contour translation**: If collision happens at nth frame, we do not update ϕ_n in terms of eq. (13) directly, whereas we translate previous ϕ_{n-m} from the status of black contour in Fig. 2A to the status of black contour in Fig. 2B. The magnitude and direction of the translation are the magnitude and direction of moving paramecium's displacement, respectively. Then ϕ_n updated as shifted ϕ_{n-m}.

After displacement correction, the black contour in Fig. 2B as current contour is more accurate compared with the gray contour in Fig. 2B. This displacement correction amends boundary detection error caused by collision.

2.4 Implementation of the Parallel Region-Based LSM with Displacement Correction

The proposed LSM for each frame is implemented as following computational steps (Fig. 3):

Step 1: Initialize ϕ as $\phi_0(i,j) = 64 - |I(i,j) - 64| + |I(i,j) - 64|$ for the 1st frame, or as ϕ in the previous frame for each of other frames. Besides record the summation of inside intensity as S_1 for the 1st frame, or as S for each other frames. Generally, set $\alpha = \beta = \lambda_1 = \lambda_2 = 1$, $n = 0$, $m = 4$, respectively.

Step 2: Read the image data I from the camera part into the processor part in the CPV system. (see the subsection 2.5)

Step 3: Compute E_{in} including $\nabla^2 \phi$ by using neighbor connections of the CPV system. (see the subsection 2.5)

Step 4: Compute E_{out} including I_{in} and I_{out} by using the summation circuit of the CPV system. (see the subsection 2.5)

Step 5: Calculate ϕ according to eq. (13) and save it as temporary variable ϕ_{temp}.

Step 6: Check whether collision happens which is $S - S_1 > S_{th}$, where $S_{th} = 250$ is a specified threshold constant. If yes, translate ϕ_{n-m} according to magnitude and direction of displacement. After displacement correction, update ϕ with new ϕ_{n-m}. If no, update ϕ with ϕ_{temp}.

Step 7: Calculate the centroid of contour according to ϕ.

Step 8: Controlling stage by using PD control based on centroid.

Step 9: Check whether there is a next frame. If yes, go back to the Step 2. If no, stop computing.

2.5 Architecture of CPV System

We implement our proposed model in CPV system produced by Hamamatsu Photonics K.K. [12], [13], [15]. CPV system consists of camera, processor and controller parts (Fig. 4A). The camera part includes 128×128 photo-detectors (PDs). The processor part includes 128×128 programmable processing elements (PEs) and one summation circuit. The frame rate of CPV system is 1 [kHz]. The instruction cycle of CPV system is 12.5[MHz]. The image data in PD array is transmitted to PE array through 128 lines AD converter (ADC) in parallel.

PE array can realize a parallel processing in each pixel of the image. A single instruction multiple data stream (SIMD) program is adopted on all PEs. The inner structure of the PEs is based on the S^3pE architecture, which has a bit serial ALU, 512 bits local memory and 4-neighbor connection. By using ALU, we can realize simple operations such as logical and, logical or, logical exclusive or between register A and B. The local memory of each PE can be allocated for intermediate variable in our program. Unfortunately, limited size of local memory constrains the complexity of algorithm that can be implemented in CPV system. With the 4-neighbor connection, we can access the up, down, left and right elements of each element in parallel. This is convenient for us to to capture local features such as Laplace operator $\nabla^2 \phi = (\phi_{i+1,j}^n + \phi_{i-1,j}^n + \phi_{i,j+1}^n +$

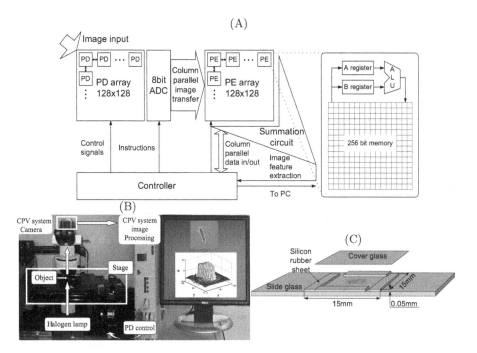

Fig. 4. (A) A schematic architecture of CPV system. (B) A photograph of experimental equipments. Arrows indicate light and information flows. (C) A structure of a water pool where paramecia swim.

$\phi_{i,j-1}^{n} - 4\phi_{i,j}^{n})/8$. The summation circuit (SC) is connected with all PEs to extract global image features such as I_{in} and I_{out}. The controller part sends instructions for the camera and the processor parts and works as an interface of a column parallel data input/output with the PE array. This controller is also connected with a PC (CPU: Intel Pentium 4 HT, 3.00 GHz; RAM: 3.00 GHz, 3 GB; OS: Windows XP) which takes charge in program downloading, program starting, program stopping and image displaying. The image intensity and level set function ϕ are represented with unsigned 8 and signed 16 bit integer, respectively. The bit depth of each PE, PD and SC are all 8.

2.6   System Set-Up

As shown in Fig. 4B, the camera part of CPV system is mounted on the top of an upright microscope (BX51, OLYMPUS). This camera captures blight field images of moving paramecia whose background light is transmitted from a halo-gen lamp at the bottom of microscope. The visual field of the camera is X: 384 [μm], Y: 384 [μm] through a 20-times objective lens (N.A 0.75, UAPO, OLYMPUS). Paramecia swim in a water pool on a slide glass. The average body length of paramecia is about 200 μm. The average speed of paramecia is about 1 [mm/s]. The water pool is enclosed with a glass slide, a cover glass and silicon rubber sheets (Fig. 4C. The size of the water pool is X: 15 [mm], Y: 15 [mm], Z: 0.05 [mm]. The slide glass is fixed on a XY automated stage (MR-J3-10A1, HEPHAIST, Stroke: X axis 80 [mm], Y axis 30 [mm], Resolution: positioning accuracy XY axis 2.5 [μm], Maximum speed: 10 [mm/s]). This stage is controlled using PD control based on visual servoing.

3   Experimental Results

3.1   Result of the Collision Problems

To examine the performance of collision handling of our model, firstly, we conduct experiments of tracking a single paramecium by using proposed model. At the beginning, we wait for a paramecium entering the visual field where no garbage or other obstacle exists. At the moment that we recognize one paramecium is entering (it is called as "target paramecium"), tracking starts and tracking result is recorded in movies (see attached movies). Fig. 3.1A, Fig. 3.1C and Fig. 3.1E are consecutive result image sequences from tracking movies. Fig. 3.1B, Fig. 3.1D and Fig. 3.1F are corresponding simulation results by using general LSM without displacement correction. The white curves in these figures represent zero level sets.

Fig. 3.1A is the result of tracking a single paramecium among lots of paramecia. At 63085 ms, target paramecium without collision is in the middle of visual field. At 67845 ms, target paramecium collides with other paramecia, however detected contour do not expand on another and target paramecium keep being in the middle. At 72605 ms, even with such high density of paramecium, the detected contour still stop around target paramecium and tracking still proceeds successfully. Compared with Fig. 3.1B, the calculated contours spread over all paramecia in the visual field which causes target paramecium lost and tracking failure.

Fig. 3.1c is the result of tracking a single paramecium around an air bubble. From 6800 ms to 7000 ms, target paramecium swims towards the air bubble, at 7200 ms, target paramecium collides with the air bubble, after that this paramecium swims outwards from the air bubble. During the entire process of collision between target paramecium and air bubble, target paramecium is in the middle of visual field all the time which means tracking is successfully. Instead, in Fig. 3.1d, the air bubble is detected as target object by accumulated error. These false detections result in tracking target shifting from the paramecium to the air bubble and tracking failure.

Fig. 3.1e is the result of tracking a single paramecium around a wall of the water pool where paramecia swim. Similar to situation of Fig. 3.1c, even the collision between target paramecium and wall occurs at 2150 ms, the target tracking is still successful around the wall. Conversely, in Fig. 3.1f, the wall is detected as target as well which results in the centroid of target shifting to the wall and tracking stop over the wall.

3.2   Computational Time of Proposed Model

To show how our model reduce computational time, we investigate average computational time for each frame from 14 image sequences (n=50000). The average

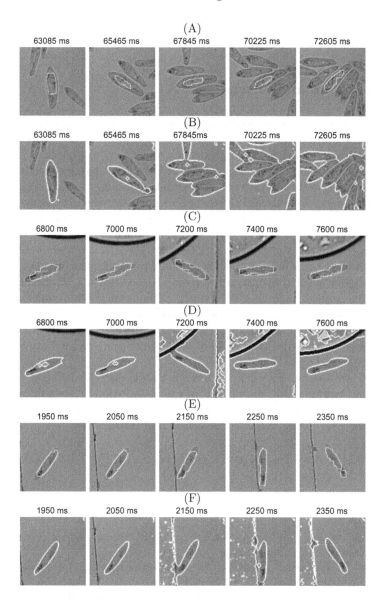

Fig. 5. Contours of target paramecium detected by using our proposed model in CPV system (A) colliding with others (C) colliding with air bubble (E) colliding with the wall. Contours of target paramecium calculated by using region-based LSM. (B) colliding with others (D) colliding with air bubble (F) colliding with the wall.

time for 1st frame T1 is 2.32 [ms] and the average time for other frames T2 is 1.16 [ms]. This reduction is probably because ϕ is initialized as ϕ of the last frame and the position change of paramecium between consecutive frames is very small. The average time for each iteration T3 is 1.02 [ms]. These results represent that our model can reduce the amount of the computational time for each frame to about 2 [ms] with solving the collision problems.

4   Conclusion and Discussion

In order to keep tracking a single paramecium even when collision occurs, we present a novel approach combining parallel region-based level set method with displacement correction for tracking moving paramecium in a sequence of images. A modified region-based level set method is used to detect paramecium in general way. Meanwhile, we estimate if collision situation occurs in each frame. When collision happens, we utilize displacement correction to reduce detection error to keep calculated contour only around target. Experimental results show that our proposed model can detect and track a moving target paramecium successfully even when the target collides with lots of other paramecia, an air bubble, or a wall (Fig. 3.1). It turns out that our model more robust for the collision problem than self-window algorithm or modified region-based LSM [16], [8]. Displacement correction is implemented in CPV system without much computational time increase, we still can detect and track boundaries of moving target paramecia within about 2 [ms] for each frame even collision happens. This computational time in CPV system was about 1/40 of time of the same method implemented in the non-parallel PC.

However, we also find if target paramecium collides with obstacles at very high acceleration, tracking will fail caused by calculated contour splitting into two parts. Therefore, it is an interesting future work to investigate how to preserve topology changes during boundary detection and tracking.

Acknowledgments. This work was partly supported by SORST of JST.

References

1. Kass, M., Witkin, A., Terzopoulos, D.: Snakes: Active contour models. International Journal of Computer Vision 1, 321–331 (1988)
2. Caselles, V., Kimmel, R., Sapiro, G.: Geodesic active contours. International Journal of Computer Vision 22(1), 61–79 (1997)
3. Paragios, N., Deriche, R.: Geodesic active regions for motion estimation and tracking. In: The Proceedings of the Seventh IEEE International Conference on Computer Vision, 1999, vol. 1, pp. 688–694 (1999)
4. Paragios, N., Deriche, R.: Geodesic active contours and level sets for the detection and tracking of moving objects. IEEE Transactions on Pattern Analysis and Machine Intelligence 22, 266–280 (2000)
5. Osher, S., Sethian, J.A.: Fronts propagating with curvature dependent speed: Algorithms based on hamilton-jacobi formulations. Journal of Computational Physics 79, 12–49 (1988)
6. Osher, S., Fedkiw, R.P.: Level set methods: an overview and some recent results. Journal of Computational Physics 169, 463–502 (2001)

7. Malladi, R., Sethian, J.A., Vemuri, B.C.: A fast level set based algorithm for topology-independent shape modeling. Journal of Mathematical Imaging and Vision 6(2), 269–289 (1996)
8. Fei, X., Igarashi, Y., Hashimoto, K.: 2d tracking of single paramecium by using parallel level set method and visual servoing. In: Proceedings of the 2008 IEEE/ASME International Conference on Advanced Intelligent Mechatronics, pp. 752–757 (2008)
9. Oku, H., Ogawa, N., Hashimoto, K., Ishikawa, M.: Two-dimensional tracking of a motile micro-organism allowing high-resolution observation with various imaging techniques. Review of Scientific Instruments 76, 034301-1–034301-8 (2005)
10. Oku, H., Ishikawa, M., Theodorus, Hashimoto, K.: High-speed autofocusing of a cell using diffraction patterns. Optics Express 14, 3952–3960 (2006)
11. Ogawa, N., Oku, H., Hashimoto, K., Ishikawa, M.: Microrobotic visual control of motile cells using high-speed tracking system. IEEE Transactions of Robotics 21, 704–712 (2005)
12. Nakabo, Y., Ishikawa, M., Toyoda, H., Mizuno, S.: 1ms column parallel vision system and it's application ofhigh speed target tracking. In: Proceedings of the 2000 IEEE International Conference on Robotics and Automation, vol. 10, pp. 650–655 (2000)
13. Ishikawa, M., Ogawa, K., Komuro, T., Ishii, I.: A cmos vision chip with simd processing element array for 1ms image processing. In: Dig. Tech. Papers of 1999 IEEE Int. Solid-State Circuits Conf. (ISSCC 1999), pp. 206–207 (1999)
14. Chan, T.F., Vese, L.A.: Active contours without edges. IEEE Transactions on Image Processing 10, 266–277 (2001)
15. Komuro, T., Ishii, I., Ishikawa, M.: Vision chip architecture using general-purpose processing elements for 1ms vision system. In: Proceedings of IEEE International Workshop on Computer Architecture for Machine Perception, pp. 276–279 (1997)
16. Ishii, I., Ishikawa, M.: Self windowing for high-speed vision. Systems and Computers in Japan 32, 51–58 (2001)

Lane Detection and Tracking Using a Layered Approach

Amol Borkar, Monson Hayes, and Mark T. Smith

Georgia Institute of Technology, Atlanta, GA, USA
{amol,mhh3}@gatech.edu
Kungliga Tekniska Högskolan, Stockholm, Sweden
msmith@kth.se

Abstract. A new night-time lane detection system that extends the idea of a *Layered Approach* [1] is presented in this document. The extension includes the incorporation of (1) Inverse Perspective Mapping (IPM) to generate a bird's-eye view of the road surface, (2) application of Random Sample Consensus (RANSAC) to rid outliers from the data, and (3) Kalman filtering to smooth the output of the lane tracker. Videos of driving scenarios on local city roads and highways were used to test the new system. Quantitative analysis shows higher accuracy in detecting lane markers in comparison to other approaches.

Keywords: Lane detection, matched filtering, inverse perspective mapping, Hough transform, RANSAC, Kalman filter.

1 Introduction

In 2002, the Secretary for the Transport Ministry of Malaysia cited 4.9% of traffic related accidents as fatal [2]. The Ministry of Public Safety of China reported 667,507 traffic related accidents in 2003 also as fatal [3]. In multiple studies performed by the National Highway Traffic Safety Administration (NHTSA), driver distractions were reported to be the primary cause of over 20% of the traffic related incidents. Traffic accidents account for a vast majority of fatalities world wide; consequently, improving public safety on roads has become an attractive area to research.

Lane change assistance is an interesting area of automotive research and development. A vital element of lane change assistance is the lane detection module. This particular module needs to be robust to a variety of roads conditions. By constantly monitoring the position of a car within a lane, collisions due to unintentional lane departure caused by driver distractions, fatigue, or driving under the influence of a controlled substance could be avoided.

In this document, some of the challenges in designing a robust lane detection system are addressed. Following the introduction, prominent methods of lane detection are surveyed and their weaknesses are highlighted. Then, the proposed system is introduced and its core elements are described in detail. The performance of this system is then evaluated using data sets recorded on local

J. Blanc-Talon et al. (Eds.): ACIVS 2009, LNCS 5807, pp. 474–484, 2009.

roadways. Quantitative analysis is used to compare the results to other lane detection approaches. Finally, the conclusion and future work is presented.

2   Prior Research

Lane detection is a critical component of most vision-based Driver Assistance (DA) systems; consequently, it is under constant investigation. One of the most popular methods of lane detection involves the use of the Hough transform [4,5,6,7,8,9]. At first, a Canny edge detector is used to produce a binary edge image. The Hough transform is then computed to extract the locations of straight lines in this binary image. It is assumed that the best fitting line generally corresponds to a lane marker boundary. Another commonly used technique is the *Middle-to-Side* approach [10,11,12]. In this approach, the search for a lane marker pixel begins in the middle of image and the search moves outward until the first edge pixel is found on each side. While both, the Hough transform, and *Middle-to-Side* approaches generally yield good result in detecting lane markers, their performance is largely affected in the presence of dominant cracks, surface material changes or tar patches on the road surface. The use of color segmentation to detect lane markers has also been explored [13,14,15,16]. Common implementations necessitate transforming the image from RGB into alternate color spaces like HSI, YCbCr [13] or into custom color spaces as shown in [14,16] to reduce the complexity in segmenting lane markers. Unfortunately, colored illumination from various light sources largely affects the color segmentation algorithms reducing the effectiveness in successfully detecting lane markers. Finally, methods relying on artificial neural networks have also been used to execute lane detection [17,18]. However, most machine learning systems tend to perform well only when there exists a fairly large amount of overlap between the testing and training data which is difficult to achieve in this particular application.

As lane detection is a crucial component of most camera-based DA systems, it needs to be robust to almost any road condition. Most of the systems described above require the lane markers to bear very strong contrast with respect to the road surface. In addition, road surfaces should be free of artifacts such as cracks, arrows, or similar markers. Regrettably, these conditions are unlikely to exist on the road network in most big cities. It is clear from above that the feature extraction stages in existing implementations are unable to satisfactorily distinguish between surface artifacts and lane markers; therefore, there is need to develop an improved technique to detect lane markers that is able to cope with the variety of road conditions that exist around the world.

3   Methodology

Fig. 1 shows the design model of the new night-time lane detection system. Lane detection using a *Layered Approach* [1] is extended with the incorporation of the (1) Inverse Perspective Mapping (IPM) for image transformation, (2) application of RANSAC for outlier elimination, and (3) Kalman filtering for prediction and

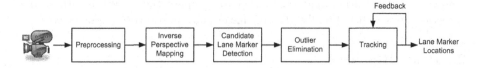

Fig. 1. Design model of the new lane detection system

smoothing. The following sections will detail each component of this improved system.

3.1 Preprocessing

First, temporal blurring is used to generate an *Average Image*. The *Average Image* is an outcome of computing the average between the current and past frames. This type of temporal smoothing helps connect dashed lane markers giving them the appearance of a near continuous line [1]. The *Average Image* is created using the equation below

$$AverageImage = \sum_{i=0}^{\infty} \frac{Image[n - \Delta i]}{N} \qquad (1)$$

Due to their sparseness, detecting dashed lane markers in a single image can be difficult. The temporal blurring enhances the image allowing the dashed lane markers to appear as connected lines; as a result, the lane markers become easier to detect. The average image is then transformed into a grayscale image using a standard pixel-wise transformation [19] shown in Eq. (2). Intermediate results of preprocessing are shown in Fig. 2.

$$\hat{I}(x,y) = 0.299 \cdot Red(x,y) + 0.587 \cdot Green(x,y) + 0.114 \cdot Blue(x,y) \qquad (2)$$

3.2 Inverse Perspective Mapping (IPM)

Next, IPM is used to transform the captured images from a camera perspective to a bird's-eye view. A forward-looking camera will capture images in which

(a) Original image.　　(b) Temporal blurred image.　　(c) Grayscale image.

Fig. 2. Intermediate results of preprocessing

lane markers are not parallel and have line widths that vary as a function of the distance from the camera. This property is evident in Fig. 3a. With IPM, lane detection now becomes a problem of locating a pair of near constant width parallel lines that are generally separated by a predetermined fixed distance [2,20,21,22]. Using various camera calibration parameters such as height from the ground, field of view, and, inclination, a mapping between pixels in the image plane to world plane can be recovered as shown in Fig. 3b.

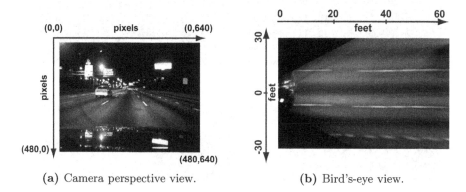

(a) Camera perspective view.   (b) Bird's-eye view.

Fig. 3. Inverse perspective mapping transforms a camera perspective image into a bird's-eye view image

3.3   Candidate Lane Marker Detection

Next, the bird's-eye view image is converted to binary using an adaptive threshold [1,23]. Every binary image is split into two halves and it is assumed that each half contains one lane marker. The bottom half of the birds-eye view image is shown in Fig. 4a. Then, ten highest scoring lines are found in each half image using the low-resolution Hough transform [1] as shown in Fig. 4b. Each line is sampled along its length into a finite set of points at specific columns in the image represented by the green bars in Fig. 4c. For illustration purposes, the sampled points of only one line are shown in Fig. 4d. The equivalent location of sample points is recovered in the grayscale image as shown in Fig. 4e.

Fig. 4f shows that the 1-D intensity profile of a lane marker has a Gaussian-like shape within the window represented in yellow. Based on this property, matched filtering is then performed using a Gaussian kernel as its template. To find the approximate center of each line, a one-dimensional matched filter is applied at each sample point of the line as portrayed in Fig. 4g. The processes of sampling and matched filtering are repeated for the remain nine lines. Finally, the pixels with the largest correlation coefficient in the specific columns that exceed a minimum threshold are selected as the best estimates of the center of the lane marker as indicated by the red plus signs in Fig. 4h.

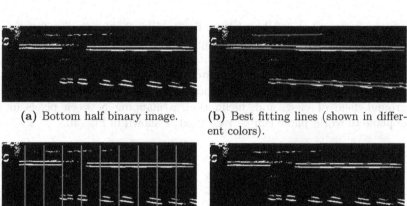

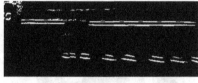

(a) Bottom half binary image.

(b) Best fitting lines (shown in different colors).

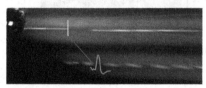

(c) Specific columns where the sampling occurs.

(d) Line sampled along its length.

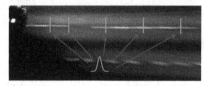

(e) Correspondence in the grayscale image.

(f) 1-D intensity profile of a lane marker within the yellow window.

(g) Search windows centered at sample points for matched filtering.

(h) Best lane marker estimates within each column.

Fig. 4. Intermediate stages for estimating ideal lane marker locations

3.4 Outlier Elimination and Data Modeling

Upon finding the ideal lane marker locations in each column, Random Sample Consensus (RANSAC) is applied to these points. The RANSAC algorithm uses an iterative method to estimate parameters for fitting a mathematical model to a set of observed data which may contain outliers [24,25]. After rejecting the outliers, Linear Least Squares Estimation (LSE) is used to fit a line on the inliers. The fitted line is then parameterized in terms of ρ and θ where ρ is the distance from the origin (top left corner pixel) to the line and θ is the angle as indicated in Fig. 5 (generally is close to $90°$).

3.5 Tracking

The Kalman filter is used to predict the parameters of each line. The state vector $\mathbf{x}(n)$ and observation vector $\mathbf{y}(n)$ are defined as

Fig. 5. Model fitting and line parametrization

$$\mathbf{x}(n) = \mathbf{y}(n) = \left[\, \rho(n)\ \dot{\rho}(n)\ \theta(n)\ \dot{\theta}(n)\,\right]^{T} \qquad (3)$$

where ρ and θ define the line orientation and $\dot{\rho}$ and $\dot{\theta}$ are the derivatives of ρ and θ that are estimated using the difference in ρ and θ between the current and previous frame. The state transition matrix A is

$$A = \begin{bmatrix} 1 & 1 & 0 & 0 \\ 0 & 1 & 0 & 0 \\ 0 & 0 & 1 & 1 \\ 0 & 0 & 0 & 1 \end{bmatrix} \qquad (4)$$

and the matrix C in the measurement equation is the identity matrix. The covariance matrix used in the Kalman filter is constant and diagonal since the noise in the state and measurement equations is assumed to be white and uncorrelated with the others processes. The variance of each noise process is estimated off-line using frames in which accurate estimates of the lanes were being produced. The Kalman filter recursively predicts the parameters in the state vector from the previously available information [26,27].

In the case of lane markers not being detected, the matrix C is set to zero

$$\hat{x}(n|n-1) \rightarrow \hat{x}(n|n) \qquad (5)$$

forcing the Kalman filter to rely purely on its prediction as shown in Eq. (5).

4   Experimental Analysis

4.1   Hardware

A forward facing Firewire color camera is installed below the rear-view mirror so that it has a clear view of the road ahead. The camera interfaces with an Intel based computer running Windows XP and video from the camera is recorded at 30fps onto removable hard disks. Pictures of the hardware setup are shown in Fig. 6.

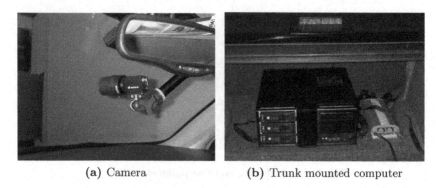

(a) Camera   (b) Trunk mounted computer

Fig. 6. Hardware setup

4.2   Results

The videos were recorded at various times at night to portray a diversity of illumination and traffic conditions that one would encounter in the real world [1]. It should be noted that defining a ground truth for the data is extremely tedious; hence, it is commonly avoided. Consequently, detections were qualitative and based purely on visual inspection by single user. The following rules were used to quantify the results into the different categories: i) a correct detection occurs when more than 50% the of lane marker estimate is overlaid on a lane marker in the scene, ii) an incorrect detection occurs when the estimate is overlaid on something else other than a lane marker, and iii) a missed detection occurs when no estimate is presented when a relevant lane marker is visible. Despite

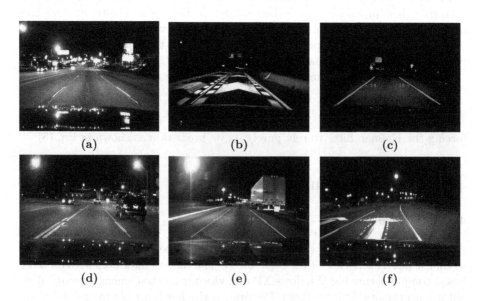

(a)   (b)   (c)

(d)   (e)   (f)

Fig. 7. Examples of accurate lane detection

the presence of navigational text, cracks, tar patches and skid marks on the road, the proposed system is still able to locate lane markers accurately as shown in Fig. 7. In addition, the distance to each lane marker relative to the host vehicle is also calculated.

However, there were a few instances of incorrect lane detections as well. The most common cause of wrong detections being the absence of lane markers due to age and wear on local city roads. This occasionally lead to the detection and tracking of false signals such as cracks as shown in Fig. 8a and 8b. Bumps on road surface would rarely unsettle the measured lane locations. Fortunately in Fig. 8c, the benefit of using the Kalman filter is that it is able to settle within a couple of milliseconds after passing the bump on the road.

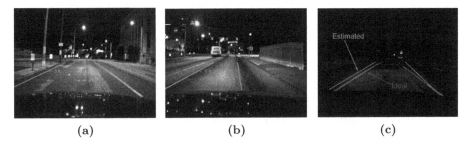

(a)   (b)   (c)

Fig. 8. Examples of inaccurate lane detection

Table 1 shows a comparison of performance between the proposed system and other lane detection implementations that use the Hough transform, *Middle-to-Side* or *Layered Approach* [1]. The results are quantified in terms of accuracy per minute which allows normalization of the results when data is captured using cameras with different frame rates. The data set used for testing consisted of over 10 hours of video of driving scenarios on the local city roads and highways. The detection rates of left and right markers were averaged to produce the numbers in Table 1.

As expected, the first two implementations using a *Layered Approach* displayed overall good performance in detecting and classifying the lane markers correctly. In comparison, the Hough transform and *Middle-to-Side* approaches did not fare as well. The lack of performance is contributed by (1) Canny edge detector, and (2) lane marker classification stages. First, the Canny edge detector uses an adaptive global threshold to convert the gradient edge image to binary [28]. This may prohibit the detection of weak edges such as slightly worn out lane markers in the presence of dominant edges in the image. Additionally, the methods used to classify lane markers pixels namely Hough transform and the outward search are unable to tell if a binary pixel belongs to an actual lane marker or it is noise due to voting. This results in lane marker estimates always being presented which further leads to the 0% missed detection rate that is compensated by the high incorrect detection rate. On the other hand, the adaptive local threshold used in the *Layered Approach* modifies its threshold value locally

Table 1. Performance comparison between different lane detection implementations

Lane Detection Implementation	Road Type	Traffic	Average Detection Rate Per Minute		
			Correct	Incorrect	Misses
	Isolated	Light	98.67%	1.08%	0.25%
	Highway	Moderate	99.58%	0%	0.42%
Proposed System	Metro	Light	97.11%	2.48%	0.41%
	Highway	Moderate	98.22%	1.78%	0%
	City	Variable	87.21%	8.18%	6.61%
	Isolated	Light	91.72%	3.31%	5.17%
	Highway	Moderate	90%	6.24%	3.76%
Layered Approach [1]	Metro	Light	91.47%	6.65%	1.87%
	Highway	Moderate	90.21%	9.11%	0.68%
	City	Variable	79.32%	10.15%	10.53%
	Isolated	Light	90.5%	9.5%	0%
	Highway	Moderate	88.85%	11.41%	0%
Middle-to-Side	Metro	Light	92.15%	7.85%	0%
	Highway	Moderate	90.5%	9.5%	0%
	City	Variable	82.05%	17.95%	0%
	Isolated	Light	85.85%	14.15%	0%
	Highway	Moderate	94.22%	5.78%	0%
Hough Transform	Metro	Light	86.48%	13.52%	0%
	Highway	Moderate	80.99%	19.01%	0%
	City	Variable	66.07%	33.93%	0%

based on neighborhood pixel intensities which in turn allows detection of weak edges [1,23]. In addition, the predetermined threshold enables the matched filtering stage to verify the candidacy of a pixel as part of a lane marker and helps in rejecting noise [1].

5   Conclusions

An extension of a *Layered Approach* to lane detection [1] is presented in this document. The idea of appending (1) Inverse Perspective Mapping (IPM), (2) RANSAC, and (3) Kalman filtering to the original system has shown innovation in technology as well as considerable performance gain. The data set used to test the accuracy of the proposed system was recorded on Interstate highways and city streets in and around Atlanta, GA. Even in the presence of a diversity of road surface features such as cracks, navigational text, skid marks and tar patches, the proposed system was able to yield performance that was superior to other implementations as portrayed in Table 1.

6   Future Work

Lane Departure Warning (LDW) is an immediate application of lane detection which is undergoing implementation. This is an application of extreme interest as drivers tend to fall asleep on the steering wheel, potentially leading to a collision. In addition, shadow removal techniques and RANSAC for curve fitting will be used to allow day time operability and better model fitting. Finally, algorithms will be ported to C++ to facilitate a real-time system.

References

1. Borkar, A., Hayes, M., Smith, M., Pankanti, S.: A layered approach to robust lane detection at night. In: 2009 IEEE Workshop on Computational Intelligence in Vehicles and Vehicular Systems, pp. 51–57 (2009)
2. Muad, A.M., Hussain, A., Samad, S.A., Mustaffa, M.M., Majlis, B.Y.: Implementation of inverse perspective mapping algorithm for the development of an automatic lane tracking system. In: 2004 IEEE Region 10 Conference, TENCON 2004, vol. 1, pp. 207–210 (2004)
3. Zheng, N.N., Tang, S., Cheng, H., Li, Q., Lai, G., Wang, F.Y.: Toward intelligent Driver-Assistance and safety warning systems. IEEE Intelligent Systems 19(2), 8–11 (2004)
4. Bahgat, M.: A simple implementation for unmarked road tracking. In: 14th IEEE Mediterranean Electrotechnical Conference, pp. 929–934 (2008)
5. Lin, C.C., Hsieh, H.W., Huang, D.C., Lin, C.W., Liao, Y.S., Chen, Y.H.: Development of a Multimedia-Based vehicle lane departure warning, forward collision warning and event video recorder systems. In: Ninth IEEE International Symposium on Multimedia Workshops (ISMW 2007), pp. 122–129 (2007)
6. Schreiber, D., Alefs, B., Clabian, M.: Single camera lane detection and tracking. In: Proceedings of the IEEE Intelligent Transportation Systems, pp. 1114–1119 (2005)
7. Assidiq, A., Khalifa, O., Islam, R., Khan, S.: Real time lane detection for autonomous vehicles. In: International Conference on Computer and Communication Engineering, pp. 82–88 (2008)
8. Aly, M.: Real time detection of lane markers in urban streets. In: IEEE Intelligent Vehicles Symposium, Eidenhoven, pp. 7–12 (2008)
9. Wang, C.C., Huang, S.S., Fu, L.C.: Driver assistance system for lane detection and vehicle recognition with night vision. In: 2005 IEEE/RSJ International Conference on Intelligent Robots and Systems (IROS 2005), pp. 3530–3535 (2005)
10. Wang, H., Chen, Q.: Real-time lane detection in various conditions and night cases. In: Proceedings of the IEEE Intelligent Transportation Systems Conference, pp. 17–20 (2006)
11. Kai, N., Kezhong, H.: THMR-V: an effective and robust high-speed system in structured road. In: IEEE International Conference on Systems, Man and Cybernetics, vol. 5, pp. 4370–4374 (2003)
12. Ieng, S.S., Tarel, J.P., Labayrade, R.: On the design of a single lane-markings detector regardless the on-board camera's position. In: Proceedings of the IEEE Intelligent Vehicle Symposium, pp. 564–569 (2003)
13. Sun, T.Y., Tsai, S.J., Chan, V.: HSI color model based Lane-Marking detection. In: IEEE Intelligent Transportation Systems Conference, pp. 1168–1172 (2006)
14. Cheng, H., Jeng, B., Tseng, P., Fan, K.: Lane detection with moving vehicles in the traffic scenes. IEEE Transactions on Intelligent Transportation Systems 7(4), 571–582 (2006)

15. Li, Q., Zheng, N., Cheng, H.: An adaptive approach to lane markings detection. Proceedings of the IEEE Intelligent Transportation Systems 1, 510–514 (2003)
16. Chin, K.Y., Lin, S.F.: Lane detection using color-based segmentation. In: Proceedings of the IEEE Intelligent Vehicles Symposium, pp. 706–711 (2005)
17. Pomerleau, D.A.: ALVINN: an autonomous land vehicle in a neural network. Morgan Kaufmann Publishers Inc., San Francisco (1989)
18. Pomerleau, D.: Neural network vision for robot driving. Kluwer International Series in Engineering and Computer Science, pp. 53–72 (1997)
19. Hoffmann, G.: Luminance models for the grayscale conversion (March 2002), http://www.fho-emden.de/~hoffmann/gray10012001.pdf
20. Sehestedt, S., Kodagoda, S., Alempijevic, A., Dissanayake, G.: Robust lane detection in urban environments. In: IEEE/RSJ International Conference on Intelligent Robots and Systems, pp. 123–128 (2007)
21. Shu, Y., Tan, Z.: Vision based lane detection in autonomous vehicle. Fifth World Congress on Intelligent Control and Automation 6, 5258–5260 (2004)
22. Bertozzi, M., Broggi, A.: GOLD: a parallel real-time stereo vision system for generic obstacle and lane detection. IEEE Transactions on Image Processing 7(1), 62–81 (1998)
23. Davies, E.R.: Machine Vision: Theory, Algorithms, Practicalities, 3rd edn. Morgan Kaufmann, San Francisco (2004)
24. Hartley, R., Zisserman, A.: Multiple View Geometry in Computer Vision, 2nd edn. Cambridge University Press, Cambridge (2004)
25. Fischler, M.A., Bolles, R.C.: Random sample consensus: a paradigm for model fitting with applications to image analysis and automated cartography. Communications of the ACM 24(6), 381–395 (1981)
26. Hayes, M.H.: Statistical Digital Signal Processing and Modeling. Wiley, Chichester (1996)
27. Brookner, E.: Tracking and Kalman Filtering Made Easy. Wiley Interscience, Hoboken (1998)
28. Canny, J.: A computational approach to edge detection. IEEE Transactions on pattern analysis and machine intelligence, 679–698 (1986)

Temporal Templates for Detecting the Trajectories of Moving Vehicles

Hugo Jiménez and Joaquín Salas

Instituto Politécnico Nacional
Cerro Blanco 141, Querétaro, México
hugojh@gmail.com, salas@ieee.org

Abstract. In this study, we deal with the problem of detecting the trajectories of moving vehicles. We introduce a method, based on the spatio-temporal connectivity analysis, to extract the vehicles trajectories from temporal templates, spanned over a short period of time. Temporal templates are conformed with the successive images differences. The trajectories are computed using the centers of the blobs in the temporal template. A Kalman filter for a constant value with emphasis in the measurement uncertainty is used to smooth the result. The algorithm is tested extensively using a sequence took from tower overlooking a vehicular intersection. Our approach allow us to detect the vehicles trajectories without the need to construct a background model or using a sophisticated tracking strategy for the moving objects. Our experiments show that the scheme we propose is reliable, and fast.

Keywords: Vehicles Trajectories, Traffic Surveillance, Tracking Flow, Temporal Templates.

1 Introduction

As the complexity of urban problems grows, there is the urgent need to monitor and survey them either as a prophylactic way to prevent damage or as a forensic tool to figure out what happened. In this context, cameras are seen as a convenient source of information because a number of reasons including the richness of data they provide and the price drop they have experienced. More and more cameras are now being installed rising the need to filter the caudal of information leaving out only what really requires human intervention. A strong pull for their use is provided by increasing computer power and advanced algorithms. Of special importance are the cameras pointing out to areas of vehicular traffic because they may be effective to speed up the transportation velocity, and to reduce the time response to such emergencies as car crashes[8]. In these cases, time is of the essence for causes that include the enormous resources lost in traffic jams or the urgency of people to receive diligent treatment.

In this study, we are interested on the problem of detecting the trajectories of moving vehicles. This is a cornerstone issue that is the basis for higher order traffic analysis, including the adaptive models of paths (specific features of the

J. Blanc-Talon et al. (Eds.): ACIVS 2009, LNCS 5807, pp. 485–493, 2009.

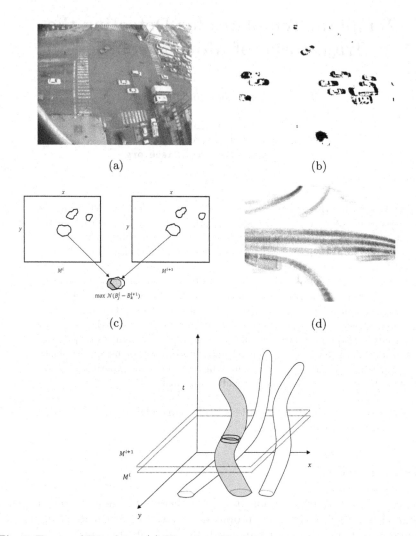

Fig. 1. Temporal Templates. (a) The original image sequence is processed to extract the interframe differences (b). (c) The matching blobs (B_j^i, B_k^{i+1}) correspond to the ones with larger intersecting area $\mathcal{N}(B_j^i \cap B_k^{i+1})$. In 2-D (d), this defines the trajectories that each vehicle follows. In 3-D (e), it is easier to distinguish each vehicle trajectory.

scene) and routes(frequently used pathways)[16], the early detection of unusual activity[22], and the collection of traffic flow statistics[18]. Due to its importance, in terms of both human life and economic impact, there has been considerable interest in the problem. Some researchers [4,15,17] estimate a model of the background[19] to detect moving objects by subtraction. Then, based on correspondence[21], size, and direction of motion, the matching feature in the next frame is associated with the current object. In these approaches, two important aspects to consider are the need to keep an updated model of the

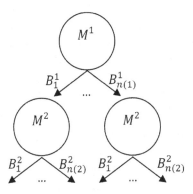

Fig. 2. Schematic about how the greedy deep first search spatiotemporal analysis is carried out. Each frame $\mathcal{M}^i$ in the stream of differences S_m is segmented out in a set M^i of connected blobs B_j^i. Then a greedy deep first search is carried out taking into account two factors: The next chosen blob B_j^i within the set M^i is the largest; and the next interframe blob B_k^{i+1} chosen, within the space-time analysis, is the one with largest overlap.

background and the numerical instability present at the moment to compute optical flow. There has been many studies related to the coupling of detection and tracking, specially with the use of 3-D models of vehicles[9,18]. For instance, Leibe *et al.* [11] search for the globally optimal set of spatio-temporal trajectories which provides the best explanation for the current image while satisfying the constraints that no two objects may occupy the same physical space nor explain the same image pixels at any point in time. In their analysis, they use spatio-temporal volumes created with event cones to compute the trajectories. The use of 3-D models may be explained due the facility to introduce *a priori* knowledge about the vehicles geometry. Lou *et al.*[14] fit wire-frame parameters of translation and rotation to the observed data. This may prove to be useful in the presence of partial occlusion. The processes of recognition and tracking create a synergetic effect to increase the performance of both[5], extending the static image recognition approaches to dynamic scene analysis. The extraction of the trajectory is usually completed with the use of a Kalman filter [6,13]. One important problem present when tracking vehicles is the presence of shadows. To cope with them, Kato *et al.* present a car tracker based on a Hidden Markov Model/Markov Random Field (HMM/MRF)-based segmentation method that is capable of classifying each small region of an image into three different categories: vehicles, shadows of vehicles, and background. In this line of research, Hsieh *et al.*[7] uses the constraints provided by the lane lines to remove shadows, specially when they grow perpendicular to the lanes, improving the analysis of vehicles characteristics.

Recently, the shift in computer vision from static images to video sequences has focused research on the understanding of action or behavior. In [2], Bobick and Davis introduced a view-based approach to the representation of action called temporal templates. This feature consists on computing motion-differencing measures over image sequences. In this strategy, it is computed how the pixels have changed rather than how they have moved. Then a threshold is used to distinguish strong evidence of motion. Temporal templates have been mainly used to study human movement as a whole [3] or for specific human parts, such as facial recognition [23], gait recognition [12], and hand recognition [10]. In this document, we introduce a method to extract the vehicles trajectories from temporal templates spanned over a short period of time. Zhong *et al.*[25] used these templates to characterize events and detect when an unusual one appears. In our case, we study these streams to figure out the conditions under which they can be used to extract the trajectory of moving vehicles, exploiting temporal and spatial information encoded in the templates. This is specially interesting for avenues and crossroads where the vehicles are moving most of the time and, in many cases, cover much of the visual field. In the next section, we define the streams of differences. Then in §3, we detail the way space-time analysis is performed and how trajectories are computed. Following, in §4, we show some experimental results computed on a real vehicular intersection. Finally, we conclude summarizing our findings and pointing out future lines of research.

2   Temporal Templates

The detection of motion is a fundamental step in many computer vision systems. In some cases, an image stream $\mathcal{S} = \{\ldots, I_i, I_{i+1}, \ldots\}$ is used to compute a model of the background B[4,15,17]. Then, subsequent frames are subtracted from the background image to compute the moving objects. This process has the objective of highlighting distinctive features that can be tracked easily. Some other strategies involve looking for highly distinctive features directly before proceeding to track them. In this work, we develop a strategy where motion manifest itself over short periods of time before direct analysis is carried out. This is different to some strategies [1], where the objective is to find the most salient partitions of the spatio-temporal graph formed by the image sequence. Motion information is represented as streams of differences. Firstly, the sequence of images is divided in chunks of fixed time-length. Then, the interframe difference is computed. A threshold is applied to this difference to find out the significative changes within the scene.

Given a sequence of images $\mathcal{S}$, we select chunks of images with fixed time-length S. There is a trade off in the selection of the time span. On the one hand, it should be long enough to capture significative motion within the scene. Yet, on the other hand, it should be short enough to allow for quick processing of the information in the incoming stream. The current chunk is denoted by $S = \{I_0, I_1, \ldots, I_m\}$. The motion is detected applying a threshold to the difference between each consecutive pair of images I_i and I_{i+1} in S. A simple way to estimate automatically this threshold consists on analyzing the distribution of differences and assume that it follows a Gaussian process $\mathcal{N}(\mu, \sigma)$, with mean μ and standard deviation σ. The motion in a pair of images is denoted by the binary map

$$\mathcal{M}_i(\mathbf{x}) = \begin{cases} 1 & \text{if } \| I_{i+1}(\mathbf{x}) - I_i(\mathbf{x}) \| < \lambda, \text{ for } i = 0, \ldots, m-1, \\ 0 & \text{otherwise.} \end{cases} \tag{1}$$

where λ is an arbitrary and predefined threshold. Finally, a stream of differences is denoted as $S_m = \{\mathcal{M}_0, \mathcal{M}_1, \ldots, \mathcal{M}_{m-1}\}$, where each $\mathcal{M}_i \in S_m$ is a binary image that signals motion under the threshold λ, labeled by the time stamp i. The temporal templates are extracted out of the original image stream. The differences are added together without losing the time stamp for each individual interframe difference (see Fig. 1).

3   Space-Time Connectivity Analysis

The temporal templates record the impression of motion of the objects as they displace. For our spatio-temporal analysis, we apply the greedy deep first search [20]. An illustration of the process is given in Fig. 2. Each frame $\mathcal{M}^i$ in the stream of differences S_m contains a set M^i of $n(i)$ blobs $M^i = \{B_1^i, \ldots, B_{n(i)}^i\}$. Out of M^i, we select the blob with the largest number of pixels $\mathcal{N}(B_j^i)$. From the following frame M^{i+1} in the stream of differences, it is selected the blob

---

Algorithm 1. SPACE-TIME CONNECTIVITY ANALYSIS

Require: $S_m = \{\mathcal{M}_0, \mathcal{M}_1, \ldots, \mathcal{M}_{m-1}\}$, the temporal template
Ensure: $T = \{T_1, \ldots, T_t\}$ the set of trajectories.

1: Let $z \leftarrow 0$
2: **repeat**
3:     $j \leftarrow 0$
4:     **repeat**
5:         Let $i \leftarrow j$
6:         Let $M^i = \{B_1^i, \ldots, B_{n(i)}^i\}$ be the set of blobs that made up the i-th frame $\mathcal{M}^i$ in S_m
7:         **repeat**
8:             Select B_j^i, the blob with the largest number of pixels $\mathcal{N}(B_j^i)$ in the set M^i
9:             Select B_k^{i+1}, the blob in M^{i+1} with the largest intersection $q = \mathcal{N}(B_j^i \cap B_k^{i+1})$ with B_j^i
10:             Add B_j^i to T_z
11:             Remove B_j^i out of M^i, $M^i \leftarrow M^i - B_j^i$
12:             $i \leftarrow i + 1$
13:         **until** the intersection is null, $q = 0$, or we arrive at the end of the stream, $i = m$
14:         Add B_j^i to T_z
15:         Remove B_j^i out of M^i, $M^i \leftarrow M^i - B_j^i$
16:         $z \leftarrow z + 1$
17:     **until** No more blobs are left to be analyzed $M_j = \emptyset$
18:     $j \leftarrow j + 1$
19: **until** No more trajectories remain to be tracked, $j = m$

B_k^{i+1} with the largest overlap $\mathcal{N}(B_j^i \cap B_k^{i+1})$. We remove B_j^i out of the set M^i. This procedure continues in the direction of the time flow using B_k^{i+1} instead of B_j^i and M^{i+2} instead of M^{i+1} until the end of the sequence is reached with frame M_{m-1}. At that point, we go back to the first set M^0 in the streams of differences sequence and start it all over with the remaining blobs, applying the same criteria as before. The process is further clarified in the algorithm 1.

Depending on the rate of change related to image acquisition, global luminance changes may affect the temporal templates. However, in our case, most of these changes are related to clouds passing by and hence the camera frame acquisition rate is able to cope with its perceived effects. Quite the opposite happens with reflections which occur in one or a few consecutive frames. In this case, the temporal connectivity analysis allow us to discard its effects. In any case, the image rate acquisition must be fast enough, i.e., there must be temporal overlapping for each moving object. For the purposes of this paper, the perceived vehicle overlapping and the analysis of occlusions are not considered.

Finally, the trajectories are computed using the centers of the blobs in the temporal template. A Kalman filter, for a constant value[24] with emphasis in the measurement uncertainty, is used to smooth the result.

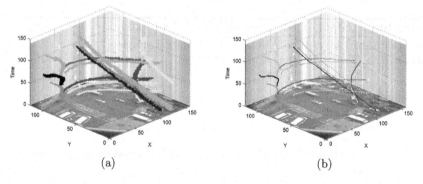

(a)   (b)

Fig. 3. Extracting Trajectories. (a) The streams of differences represent the spatiotemporal displacement of moving vehicles. (b) Our algorithm extracts the trajectories using connectivity analysis on the temporal templates.

4   Results

To test the algorithm described in the previous section, we used an image sequence composed of 220,492 frames, took from a camera located at the top of a 28 m tower which monitors a vehicular intersection. The sequence lasted for about 5 hours and 13 minutes. The image sequence was took and processed offline for verification purposes. The recording frequency was about 16 frames per second. Each image frame in the sequence of images has a resolution of 240 rows × 320 columns and 8 bits per pixel to describe the grayscale. Each temporal template embrace ten seconds of video. In all the experiments, we used a

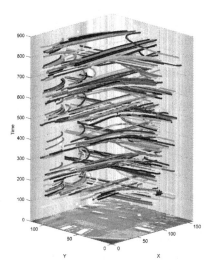

Fig. 4. Long Term Identification of the Trajectories. In this illustration 15 minutes, out of the 5 hours 13 minutes, of operation are shown. Note the repetitive pattern generated when the traffic lights switches on and off. Each traffic light cycle last for about two minutes in this particular crossroads.

desktop PC equipped with a Pentium IV processor clocked at 3.02 GHz with hyperthreading, one GB of RAM, and 80 GB in hard disk memory. The algorithms were programmed in Matlab version 7.6.

The temporal templates allow us to detect the vehicles trajectories without the need to construct a background model or detect and track moving objects. In Fig. 3(a), we show the result for a particular temporal template where the blobs differences are plotted in a spatiotemporal diagram. In Fig. 3(b), we show the results where each individual blob centroid has been chosen and a Kalman filter has been applied to smooth the result. These results reflect the short term behavior of the algorithm to identify the trajectory of vehicles. In Fig. 4 it is illustrated the long term behavior of the algorithm. For illustrative purposes, we show only 15 minutes, out of the 5 hours 13 minutes, of operation. Note the repetitive pattern generated when the traffic lights switches on and off. Each traffic light cycle last for about two minutes in this particular crossroads.

5   Conclusion

In this document, we introduce an algorithm to extract the trajectories of vehicles as they move on a vehicular intersection. The algorithm is particularly suitable for this kind of applications where on the one hand the objects move across the visual field and there is not much time left for complex analysis. The computed result can be fed into other stages of processing involving the detection of unusual activity, extraction of routes from trajectories, and so on. The scheme we propose, based on the analysis of temporal templates, is sound, reliable, and less complex than other alternatives such as the estimation of a model of the background, extraction the moving objects and tracking of their motion throughout the image sequence.

In the future, we aim to asses the set of constraints that warranty the successful extraction of moving objects trajectories. That is, to research into the required sequence time length, and sampling time frequency to assure a reliable computing of the trajectory.

References

1. Beymer, D., McLauchlan, P., Coifman, B., Malik, J.: A Real-Time Computer Vision System for Measuring Traffic Parameters. In: IEEE Conference on Computer Vision and Pattern Recognition, pp. 495–501 (1997)
2. Bobick, A., Davis, J.: An Appearance-Based Representation of Action. In: IEEE International Conference on Pattern Recognition, vol. 1 (1996)
3. Bobick, A., Davis, J.: The Recognition of Human Movement using Temporal Templates. IEEE Transactions on Pattern Analysis and Machine Intelligence 23(3), 257–267 (2001)
4. Chen, S.C., Shyu, M.L., Peeta, S., Zhang, C.: Spatiotemporal Vehicle Tracking: The Use of Unsupervised Learning-Based Segmentation and Object Tracking. IEEE Robotics & Automation Magazine 12(1), 50–58 (2005)
5. Foresti, G.L., Murino, V., Regazzoni, C.: Vehicle Recognition and Tracking from Road Image Sequences. IEEE Transactions on Vehicular Technology 48(1), 301–318 (1999)
6. Gardner, W.F., Lawton, D.T.: Interactive Model-Based Vehicle Tracking. IEEE Transactions on Pattern Analysis and Machine Intelligence 18(11), 1115–1121 (1996)
7. Hsieh, J.W., Yu, S.H., Chen, Y.S., Hu, W.F.: Automatic Traffic Surveillance System for Vehicle Tracking and Classification. IEEE Transactions on Intelligent Transportation Systems 7(2), 175–187 (2006)
8. Hu, W., Xiao, X., Xie, D., Tan, T., Maybank, S.: Traffic accident prediction using 3-D model-based vehicle tracking. IEEE Transactions on Vehicular Technology 53(3), 677–694 (2004)
9. Kim, Z., Malik, J.: Fast Vehicle Detection with Probabilistic Feature Grouping and its Application to Vehicle Tracking. In: IEEE International Conference on Computer Vision, vol. 1, pp. 524–531 (2003)
10. Kumar, S., Kumar, D.K., Sharma, A., McLachlan, N.: Visual Hand Gestures Classification using Temporal Motion Templates. In: International Conference on Multimedia Modelling (2004)
11. Leibe, B., Schindler, K., Cornelis, N., Van Gool, L.: Coupled object detection and tracking from static cameras and moving vehicles. IEEE Transactions on Pattern Analysis and Machine Intelligence 30(10), 1683–1698 (2008)
12. Liu, J., Zheng, N.: Gait History Image: A Novel Temporal Template for Gait Recognition. In: IEEE International Conference on Multimedia and Expo., pp. 663–666 (2007)
13. Lou, J., Tan, T., Hu, W.: Visual Vehicle Tracking Algorithm. Electronics Letters 38(18), 1024–1025 (2002)

14. Lou, J., Tan, T., Hu, W., Yang, H., Maybank, S.J.: 3-D Model-Based Vehicle Tracking. IEEE Transactions on Image Processing 14(10), 1561 (2005)
15. Magee, D.R.: Tracking Multiple Vehicles using Foreground, Background and Motion Models. Image and Vision Computing 22(2), 143–155 (2004)
16. Makris, D., Ellis, T.: Finding Paths in Video Sequences. In: British Machine Vision Conference (2001)
17. Maurin, B., Masoud, O., Papanikolopoulos, N.: Tracking All Traffic: Computer Vision Algorithms for Monitoring Vehicles, Individuals, and Crowds. IEEE Robotics & Automation Magazine 12(1), 29–36 (2005)
18. Morris, B., Trivedi, M.: Learning, Modeling, and Classification of Vehicle Track Patterns from Live Video. IEEE Transactions on Intelligent Transportation Systems 9(3), 425–437 (2008)
19. Piccardi, M.: Background Subtraction Techniques: A Review. In: IEEE (ed.) IEEE International Conference on Systems, Man and Cybernetics, vol. 4, pp. 3099–3104 (2004)
20. Russell, S., Norvig, P.: Artificial Intelligence: A Modern Approach. Prentice-Hall, Englewood Cliffs (1995)
21. Shi, J., Tomasi, C.: Good Features to Track. In: IEEE Conference on Computer Vision and Pattern Recognition (CVPR 1994), Seattle (June 1994)
22. Stauffer, C., Grimson, W.: Learning Patterns of Activity using Real-Time Tracking. IEEE Transactions on Pattern Analysis and Machine Intelligence 22(8), 747–757 (2000)
23. Valstar, M., Patras, I., Pantic, M.: Facial action unit recognition using temporal templates. In: 13th IEEE International Workshop on Robot and Human Interactive Communication, 2004. ROMAN 2004, pp. 253–258 (2004)
24. Welch, G., Bishop, G.: An introduction to the Kalman filter. Technical Report TR 95-041, University of North Carolina at Chapel Hill, Department of Computer Science, Chapel Hill, NC 27599-3175 (1995)
25. Zhong, H., Shi, J., Visontai, M.: Detecting Unusual Activity in Video. In: IEEE Conference on Computer Vision and Pattern Recognition, vol. 2, pp. 819–826 (2004)

Robust Detection and Tracking of Moving Objects in Traffic Video Surveillance

Borislav Antić[1], Jorge Oswaldo Niño Castaneda[2], Dubravko Ćulibrk[1], Aleksandra Pižurica[2], Vladimir Crnojević[1], and Wilfried Philips[2,*]

[1] Faculty of Technical Sciences, University of Novi Sad, Serbia
{Borislav.Antic,Vladimir.Crnojevic}@ktios.net, alef.tau@gmail.com
[2] Deptartment for Telecommunications and Information Processing,
Ghent University, Belgium
{Jorge.Nino,Aleksandra.Pizurica,Wilfried.Philips}@telin.ugent.be

Abstract. Building an efficient and robust system capable of working in harsh real world conditions represents the ultimate goal of the traffic video surveillance. Despite an evident progress made in the area of statistical background modeling over the last decade or so, moving object detection is still one of the toughest problems in video surveillance, and new approaches are still emerging. Based on our published method for motion detection in the wavelet domain, we propose a novel, wavelet-based method for robust feature extraction and tracking. Hereby, a more efficient approach is proposed that relies on a non-decimated wavelet transformation to achieve both motion segmentation and selection of features for tracking. The use of wavelet transformation for selection of robust features for tracking stems from the persistence of actual edges and corners across the scales of the wavelet transformation. Moreover, the output of the motion detector is used to limit the search space of the feature tracker to those areas where moving objects are found. The results demonstrate a stable and efficient performance of the proposed approach in the domain of traffic video surveillance.

Keywords: Traffic video surveillance, Object tracking, Moving object detection.

1 Introduction

The area of video surveillance has attracted a lot of attention of the image processing community during the last two decades. The algorithms for detection of moving objects and their tracking, developed within this prolific area, can be used to observe people in large waiting rooms, shopping centers, hospitals, campuses or monitor vehicles inside/outside cities, on highways, bridges, in tunnels etc. In spite of the tremendous progress made in this area, the ultimate goal of creating an efficient and robust system capable of working in stringent real-world conditions has not been achieved yet.

* This research has been supported in part by EUREKA!4160 Project.

J. Blanc-Talon et al. (Eds.): ACIVS 2009, LNCS 5807, pp. 494–505, 2009.
© Springer-Verlag Berlin Heidelberg 2009

There are many visual effects that impair performances of the algorithms for visual motion detection and tracking. Some of them, such as periodic background motion, flicker, gradual illumination changes or slight shadows, have been successfully characterized by some complex statistical models of the background. They aim at building an adequate stochastic model explaining the observed pixel behavior and predicting the future pixel values. A relatively recent survey by Piccardi [1] cites some popular techniques for background subtraction and comments on some of their advantages and disadvantages.

One of the simplest statistical approaches defined by Wren *et al* [2] treats every pixel as an independent Gaussian random variable completely characterized by its mean value and variance (or covariance matrix in case of multi-valued images). The existence of periodic motion in the background (e.g. swaying trees, moving escalators, sea waves) or periodic illumination (e.g. flickering fluorescent light or TV/monitor screen) are not fully described with only one Gaussian. In order to represent multi-modal pixel distributions, Stauffer and Grimson [3] proposed the use of the mixture of Gaussians (MoG) statistical model. Each pixel is modeled typically with 3 to 5 Gaussians, whose mean values, variances and weights are learned in unsupervised fashion. Value of a pixel in the latest frame is used for updating the existing Gaussians in the mixture, or it is used for creating a new Gaussian when the discrepancy between pixel value and MoG model is too large.

As a more flexible approach to learning pixel's probability density functions (pdf), Elgammal *et al* [4] proposed to use kernel density estimation (KDE). They noticed that histograms of pixel values calculated over spans of few hundreds of frames drastically change over time if video sequence contains some impairing visual effects, e.g. sporadic background motion. Instead of using all frames to learn the pixel's statistical model, Elgammal *et al* use pixel values from last several tens or hundreds of frames as kernel positions in the KDE model. They also check current pixel value against KDE models of pixel's neighbors, as a way to exploit statistical correlations among adjacent pixels.

More principled way to introduce spatial correlations among neighboring pixels is a single joint domain-range KDE model of Sheikh and Shah [5], that successfully models static and dynamic parts of the background. According to this approach, position of each kernel in the joint domain-range space is defined by pixel's location and value, but the kernel's domain and range bandwidths are kept constant throughout the space. The use of adaptive anisotropic kernels in joint domain-range space, proposed by Antic and Crnojevic [6], more realistically models probability density function, especially in transient zones around image edges and corners. Despite their great modeling power, KDE-based background models do not meet the expectations for real-time operation, due to their high requirements for computer memory and computational time.

All the statistical learning algorithms discussed by now operate on pixel's spectral characteristics (intensity or color vector). Li *et al* [7] suggest that better performance is attained if, in addition to spectral, spatial (gradient vector) and temporal (color co-occurrence) features are included in the feature set. In their elaborate Bayesian framework, spectral and spatial features are used for representing stationary backgrounds, while temporal features are more useful for characterizing dynamic (nonstationary) backgrounds. Mittal and Paragios [8] consider variable-bandwidth kernel density estimation for modeling dynamic backgrounds. They utilize three components of a normalized color space and two additional optical flow components to build a higher dimensional feature space that better captures complex behavior of dynamic backgrounds. New approaches, such as one carried out by Crivelli et al [9], try to exploit spatial context for joint motion detection and background estimation.

Our experimental work in the area of traffic surveillance reveals that sometimes extremely harsh conditions can occur and violate the premises of the statistical regularity and predictability of background pixels. Some of the effects that most severely deteriorate normal motion detection are abrupt illumination changes, specular light reflections, dark shadows and CCTV camera's regulatory mechanisms, such as automatic iris, exposure and white balance. This sort of effects is very hard to model statistically, but more appropriate approach is to calculate frame difference and classify pixels as foreground if their absolute difference is significant. However, two well-known drawbacks of frame difference method, as noticed by Collins et al [10], are foreground aperture and ghost appearance. Former problem relates to foreground misses that occur in poorly-textured parts of foreground objects, that give small temporal differences in spite of their apparent movement. Latter problem relates to false foreground detections that are found on those places in the image that were previously occupied by the object, but are now free. In their attempt to solve these problems, Kameda and Minoh [11] propose to use double differences between frames t and $t-1$, and between $t-1$ and $t-2$, and classify as foreground only pixels having both differences significant. In order to suppress ghosts, Collins et al [10] use double differences between frames t and $t-1$ and between t and $t-2$, but they also keep using a background model to mitigate the aperture problem.

In paper [12], we propose a novel multiresolution differencing method, that outperforms existing methods in terms of higher precision and recall metrics. This method applies double differencing framework on detail images generated by a non-decimated wavelet transformation, with the optimal statistical test to detect motion-related outliers in the difference images. Obtained motion detector shows high resistance to gradual or sudden illumination changes, light reflections, shadowing and CCTV camera's effects.

A new wavelet-based approach to robust feature extraction and tracking in the framework of Lucas and Kanade is described in this paper. Algorithms for feature tracking originate from popular techniques for computing dense optical flow [13]. They include methods by Horn and Schunck [14], Lucas and Kanade [15], Black and Anandan [16], and Szeliski and Couglan [17]. A crucial part of each feature tracking algorithm is feature selection, i.e. selection of local patches (windows) that are eligible for accurate tracking. To solve this problem, Moravec [18] and Thorpe [19] propose the use of windows with high standard deviations in the spatial intensity profile, Marr et al [20] prefer to use crossings of the

Laplacian of the image intensities, and Kitchen and Rosenfeld [21] and Dreschler and Nagel [22] choose corner features based on the first and second derivatives of the image intensity function. Shi and Tomasi [23] define a feature detector based on a moment matrix of the first and second order derivatives. The same moment matrix is used in the Lucas-Kanade tracking algorithm.

This paper uses the non-decimated wavelet transformation for selection of robust features for Lucas-Kanade tracking, and also makes use of wavelet differencing method for motion detection [12] to limit the search space of the Lucas-Kanade tracker. The non-decimated wavelet transformation, once calculated for the task of moving object detection, is reused for feature selection, which significantly reduces the amount of computations. The use of wavelet transformation for selection of robust features for tracking is also motivated by the fact that actual edges and corners in the images show persistence across scales in the wavelet transformation, while noisy features fade away as the scale increases. The system for robust detection and tracking of moving objects, described in this paper, is primarily intended to be used in traffic surveillance where most of the illumination and camera related impairing effects are encountered.

The paper is organized as follows. Section 2 provides information on all stages important to our algorithm for robust detection and tracking. Experimental results are given in section 3 and conclusions in section 4.

2   Robust Detection and Tracking of Moving Objects in Traffic Surveillance

The block diagram of the system for moving object detection and tracking applicable in traffic surveillance scenarios is shown in Fig. 1. Instead of relying on complicated statistical background models for detection of moving objects, we opted for the more robust concept of frame differencing set in the non-decimated wavelet transformation domain [12]. This approach provides better resilience to the disturbing phenomena of real-life traffic surveillance system. Multiresolution image representation given by the wavelet coefficients on multiple scales, can be conveniently used for finding image locations with persistent variations across several scales. By using inter-scale products of wavelet coefficients, we show that it is possible to discern image features with high relevance to the later Lucas-Kanade feature tracking [15]. Multiresolutional motion detection results, obtained through the optimal thresholding of wavelet coefficient differences, are used to detect new moving objects entering the scene. Beside this, motion maps are effectively constraining the local search in Lucas-Kanade feature tracking. The benefits of this constraint are twofold: 1) computational time is reduced, and 2) the risk of tracker's drift away is also reduced. The Subsection 2.1 provides more details on optimized wavelet differencing method for moving object detection, while the Subsection 2.2 describes a new approach to feature selection and tracking.

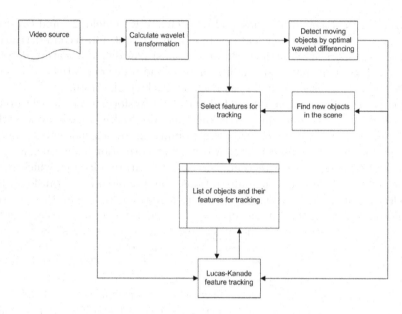

Fig. 1. Block diagram of the proposed algorithm for robust detection and tracking of moving objects in traffic surveillance

2.1 Optimized Wavelet Differencing Method for Moving Object Detection

The motivation for multiresolutional motion detection, as well as detailed explanation how to exploit wavelet representation for this purpose, has been given in the paper [12]. It has been found that most of the information necessary to separate out moving objects from video sequences is contained in the detail images. This fact has its justification in human visual system, that also uses multiresolutional details in images to fully understand the scene. Lowpass images contain most of the disturbing effects whose impact on performances of the surveillance algorithms has already been discussed. For this reason the scaling coefficients produced on the coarsest scale of wavelet transformation are not included in further analysis.

In order to obtain detail images on several scales, the non-decimated wavelet transformation is applied to the frames of a video source. This type of wavelet decomposition has been used extensively in other areas of image processing, where its real-time performance has already been proven (e.g. through an efficient FPGA implementation [24]).

Detection of moving objects starts with temporal differencing of wavelet coefficients Δw. If the signal component of a wavelet coefficient has not changed between two time instances due to the lack of motion, the wavelet difference Δw will contain only noise. In other cases, as a result of motion, the wavelet differences will contain both signal and noise components. Due to the sparsity of signal-bearing wavelet differences, they can be regarded as outliers in the distribution of all wavelet differences at the given level. In order to detect these outliers, modified z-score is calculated by the formula

$$z = 0.6745 \times \frac{|\Delta w|}{MAD} \tag{1}$$

where the MAD statistics refers to the median of absolute deviations about the median of the wavelet differences, so it is given by $MAD = median\{|\Delta w_{x,y}|\}$. The usage of MAD here stems from its application as a robust estimator of standard deviation [25].

Determination of the optimal threshold value for modified z-score is carried out in [12]. It has been done by jointly maximizing precision and recall measures on several frames that were chosen for training and equipped with the ground truth data. The obtained threshold value equals 12, but the performance of the threshold detector does not change significantly in the vicinity of this value.

Elimination of ghosting effects proceeds in a similar manner to Kameda and Minoh [11]. A pixel is marked as foreground only if there has been a significant change of wavelet coefficient value at that location during three successive frames. This means that wavelet differences Δw calculated at the moments t and $t - 1$ both have to be significant.

2.2 Lucas-Kanade Optical Flow Tracker

In many surveillance applications, the detection of moving objects is not sufficient, but their identification and tracking is desired. The tracker that we propose here is based on the Lucas-Kanade [15] approach, but is built in such a way to reuse the resources from the available moving object detector.

Lucas-Kanade [15] approach minimizes the sum of squared intensity differences between two consecutive windows. An underlying assumption is that given the small inter-frame motion, the current window can be approximated by a translation of the past one. It is also assumed that the image intensities in the translated window can be written as those in the original window plus a residue term that depends almost linearly on the translation vector. As a result of these approximations, it is possible to write a 2×2 linear system where the displacement vector between the two windows is the unknown variable. Iterating the basic solution of the algorithm in a Newton-Raphson fashion reduces the errors introduced by the approximations.

Given two consecutive frames I and J in a sequence, let us consider an image point $\mathbf{u} = [u_x \ u_y]^T$ in image I. The goal of the feature tracking is to find the location $\mathbf{v} = \mathbf{u} + \mathbf{d} = [u_x + d_x \ u_y + d_y]^T$ in image J, such as $I(u) = J(v)$. The vector $\mathbf{d}$ is known as the optical flow at $[x \ y]^T$, which is defined as being the vector that minimizes the residual function ϵ:

$$\epsilon(\mathbf{d}) = \epsilon(d_x, d_y) = \sum_{x=u_x-w_x}^{u_x+w_x} \sum_{y=u_y-w_y}^{u_y+w_y} (I(x,y) - J(x + d_x, y + d_y))^2 \tag{2}$$

where w_x and w_y are the two integers that define the integration window. To solve the *aperture* problem [26], we use the pyramidal implementation of the Lucas-Kanade feature tracker described in [27].

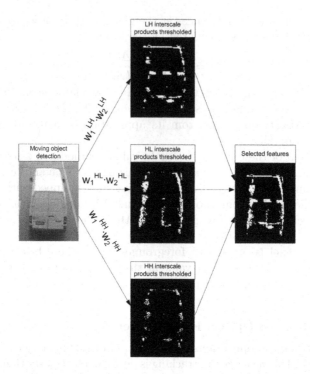

Fig. 2. Feature selection for tracking. Interscale products of each wavelet sub-band are thresholded, resulting in a horizontal (LH), vertical (HL) and diagonal (HH) features for tracking.

In the Lucas-Kanade tracker, a probabilistic dynamic model with constant velocity between frames is assumed for the image position (x, y) of each feature being tracked. This model is represented by

$$X_k = 2X_{k-1} - X_{k-2} + V_k \tag{3}$$

$$Y_k = X_k + W_k \tag{4}$$

where X_k denotes the estimated position at frame k, Y_k is the measured position at frame k (given by the Lucas-Kanade optical flow tracker). V_k is a zero-mean Gaussian noise to be present in the object moving process, and W_k is also a zero-mean Gaussian noise, present during the optical flow calculation and independent of V_k.

The tracking problem can be seen as a Maximum a Posteriori formulation:

$$\arg\max\{p(X_k|Y_k)\} = \arg\max\{p(Y_k|X_k)p(X_k)\} \tag{5}$$

thus given the image observations, the tracking result is the state with the highest posterior probability.

(a)   (b)

(c)   (d)

Fig. 3. The result of qualitative comparison of different methods for moving object detection at the moment of sudden change of CCTV camera's iris. This event occurs at 1840th frame of the *Bridge* traffic surveillance video. (a) The original frame, (b) Mixture of Gaussians model, (c) Bayesian model by Li *et al*, (d) Optimal wavelet differencing method.

The specific part of our algorithm, which differs from the commonly used Lucas-Kanade trackers is the use of wavelets for feature selection and the use of detected motion maps. We have two reasons for using wavelets in feature selection: Firstly, the wavelet decomposition behaves as an edge detector, where large wavelet coefficients appear only at the positions of image discontinuities, such as edges and corners, that we wish to detect and track. Secondly, because of the motion detector module, we already have the wavelet coefficients available.

The simplest approach would be to threshold the magnitude of the wavelet coefficients, but in order to improve robustness to noise, we first make interscale correlations and then apply a threshold to these interscale products. This method has been used by several authors for edge detection [28]. In this way we detect edge components in vertical, horizontal and diagonal directions, throughout three interscale product matrices, which are then merged in one to be fed into the Lucas-Kanade tracker, as illustrated in Fig. 2.

The finding of optimal features to track is hereby reduced to the choice of the threshold for the interscale products of the wavelet coefficients. One can either use threshold optimization to find this value [28] or select a given percentage of the largest products. We use the latter strategy here. During tracking,

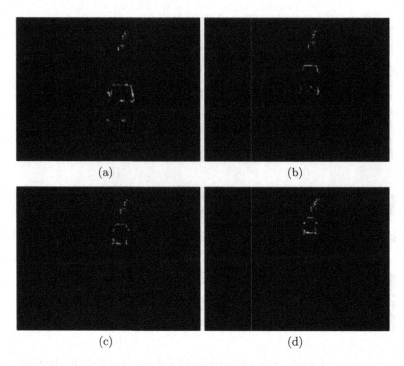

Fig. 4. Detection of features for tracking in several frames of *Bridge* traffic surveillance sequence. Feature detection is done by thresholding wavelet interscale products. (a) 1610th frame (b) 1615th frame (c) 1620th frame (d) 1625th frame.

Lucas-Kanade tracking algorithm searches for the corresponding features between frames, but only those found within the motion detection map are kept. In this way, errors in the calculated feature displacement vectors are reduced and a better tracking performance is achieved.

3   Experimental Results

In our experimental setup we have included demanding traffic surveillance sequences generated in a real world traffic surveillance system. The selected test sequences demonstrate some impairing visual effects that were already discussed in this paper (rapid illumination changes, shadows, image sensor blooming, automatic iris control etc.).

Fig. 3 shows the results of qualitative comparison of different methods for moving object detection at the moment of sudden change of CCTV camera's iris because of the appearance of a white bus in the scene. The second picture illustrates the result of the Mixture of Gaussians (MoG) model. The model was initialized with standard parameter values given in the original paper by Stauffer and Grimson [3], except for the learning rate that was given a rather high value of 0.1. High learning rate implies that background model can faster

(a)   (b)

(c)   (d)

Fig. 5. Results of the proposed algorithm for feature tracking, showing excellent performance on several frames of *Bridge* traffic surveillance sequence. (a) 1610th frame (b) 1615th frame (c) 1620th frame (d) 1625th frame.

integrate sudden changes of image intensities. In spite of this, detected moving object is not contained in a single connected component, and there are many false detections in the corners of the image. The third picture is the output of motion detector developed by Li *et al*, that uses standard parameter setups given in their paper [7]. The pixels' intensity change was drastic and Bayesian model could not cope with it, thus producing a huge number of false detections. The last picture shows the result of optimal wavelet differencing method [12], that uses three-level wavelet decomposition and Haar wavelet base. Although the aperture problem is still present due to bus' uniform texture, final motion detection map nicely depicts the actual shape of the bus. The operation in harsh conditions demonstrates a robustness of the wavelet differencing based motion detection.

Fig. 4 shows the regions where wavelet based features for tracking are found throughout several frames of the *Bridge* traffic surveillance sequence. In Fig. 5, the performance of the Lucas-Kanade tracker throughout several frames is presented. A cluster of features that corresponds to a part of moving object is tracked. The bounding box around the selected object remains stable during the tracking. This sequence as well as more tracking results can be found at http://telin.ugent.be/~jonino/seqsacivs/

4   Conclusion

This paper proposes a novel method for robust detection and tracking in traffic surveillance. The method includes a robust wavelet-based algorithm for motion detection, and proposes a new procedure for wavelet-based feature extraction and tracking. The use of wavelet differencing method for motion detection allows for robust operation in the presence of various impairing effects of real world surveillance systems, such as rapid illumination changes, dark shadows and CCTV camera's control mechanisms. The paper describes an efficient approach to motion segmentation and detection of features for tracking, that uses the same non-decimated wavelet transformation for both purposes. Moreover, the paper provides a principled way to reuse the output of the motion detector for limiting the search space of the feature tracker, thus reducing the computational burden. A robust and efficient algorithm has been demonstrated on demanding videos produced by real world traffic surveillance systems.

References

1. Piccardi, M.: Background subtraction techniques: a review. In: IEEE International Conference on Systems, Man and Cybernetics, vol. 4, pp. 3099–3104 (2004)
2. Wren, C., Azabayejani, A., Pentland, T.D., Pfinder, A.: Real-time tracking of the human body. IEEE Transactions on Pattern Analysis and Machine Intelligence 19, 780–785 (1997)
3. Stauffer, C., Grimson, W.: Learning patterns of activity using real-time tracking. IEEE Trans. Pattern Analysis and Machine Intelligence 22, 747–757 (2000)
4. ElGammal, A., Duraiswami, R., Harwood, D., Davis, L.: Background and foreground modeling using nonparametric kernel density estimation for visual surveillance. Proc. of the IEEE 90(7), 1151–1163 (2002)
5. Sheikh, Y., Shah, M.: Bayesian modeling of dynamic scenes for object detection. IEEE Trans. Pattern Anal. Mach. Intell. 27(11), 1778–1792 (2005)
6. Antic, B., Crnojevic, V.S.: Joint domain-range modeling of dynamic scenes with adaptive kernel bandwidth. In: Blanc-Talon, J., Philips, W., Popescu, D., Scheunders, P. (eds.) ACIVS 2007. LNCS, vol. 4678, pp. 777–788. Springer, Heidelberg (2007)
7. Li, L., Huang, W., Gu, I., Tian, Q.: Statistical modeling of complex backgrounds for foreground object detection. IEEE Trans. Image Processing 13, 1459–1472 (2004)
8. Mittal, A., Paragios, N.: Motion-based background subtraction using adaptive kernel density estimation, pp. 302–309 (2004)
9. Crivelli, T., Piriou, G., Bouthemy, P., Cernuschi-Frías, B., Yao, J.F.: Simultaneous motion detection and background reconstruction with a mixed-state conditional markov random field. In: Forsyth, D., Torr, P., Zisserman, A. (eds.) ECCV 2008, Part I. LNCS, vol. 5302, pp. 113–126. Springer, Heidelberg (2008)
10. Collins, R., Lipton, A., Kanade, T., Fujiyoshi, H., Duggins, D., Tsin, Y., Tolliver, D., Enomoto, N., Hasegawa, O.: A system for video surveillance and monitoring (2000)
11. Kameda, Y., Minoh, M.: A human motion estimation method using 3-successive video frames. In: ICVSM, pp. 135–140 (1996)

12. Crnojevic, V., Antic, B., Culibrk, D.: Optimal wavelet differencing method for robust motion detection. In: IEEE International Conference on Image Processing (2009)
13. Barron, J., Fleet, D.J., Beauchemin, S.: Performance of optical flow techniques (1992)
14. Horn, B.K.P., Schunck, B.G.: Determining optical flow, pp. 389–407 (1992)
15. Lucas, B.D., Kanade, T.: An iterative image registration technique with an application to stereo vision (darpa). In: Proceedings of the 1981 DARPA Image Understanding Workshop, April 1981, pp. 121–130 (1981)
16. Black, M.J., Anandan, P.: The Robust Estimation of Multiple Motions: Parametric and Piecewise-Smooth Flow Fields. Computer Vision and Image Understanding 63(1), 75–104 (1996)
17. Szeliski, R., Coughlan, J.: Spline-based image registration. Int. J. Comput. Vision 22(3), 199–218 (1997)
18. Moravec, H.: Obstacle avoidance and navigation in the real world by a seeing robot rover
19. Thorpe, C.E.: Fido: vision and navigation for a robot rover. PhD thesis, Pittsburgh, PA, USA (1984)
20. Marr, D., Ullman, S., Poggio, T.: Bandpass channels, zero-crossings, and early visual information processing. J. Opt. Soc. Am. 69(6), 914–916 (1979)
21. Kitchen, L., Rosenfeld, A.: Gray-level corner detection. Pattern Recognition Letters 1(2), 95–102 (1982)
22. Dreschler, L., Nagel, H.H.: Volumetric model and 3d-trajectory of a moving car derived from monocular tv-frame sequences of a street scene. In: Proc. of the 7th IJCAI, Vancouver, Canada, pp. 692–697 (1981)
23. Shi, J., Tomasi, C.: Good features to track. In: 1994 IEEE Computer Society Conference on Computer Vision and Pattern Recognition. Proceedings CVPR 1994, pp. 593–600 (1994)
24. Katona, M., Pizurica, A., Teslic, N., Kovacevic, V., Philips, W.: Fpga design and implementation of a wavelet-domain video denoising system. In: Blanc-Talon, J., Philips, W., Popescu, D.C., Scheunders, P. (eds.) ACIVS 2005. LNCS, vol. 3708, pp. 650–657. Springer, Heidelberg (2005)
25. Pizurica, A., Philips, W.: Estimating the probability of the presence of a signal of interest in multiresolution single- and multiband image denoising. IEEE Transactions on Image Processing 15(3), 654–665 (2006)
26. Shimojo, S., Silverman, G.H., Nakayama, K.: Occlusion and the solution to the aperture problem for motion. Vision research 29(5), 619–626 (1989)
27. Bouguet, J.Y.: Pyramidal implementation of the lucas kanade feature tracker: Description of the algorithm (2002)
28. Zhang, L., Bao, P.: Edge detection by scale multiplication in wavelet domain. Pattern Recogn. Lett. 23(14), 1771–1784 (2002)

Vehicle Tracking Using Geometric Features

Francis Deboeverie, Kristof Teelen, Peter Veelaert, and Wilfried Philips

Ghent University - Image Processing and Interpretation/IBBT,
St-Pietersnieuwstraat 41, B9000 Ghent, Belgium
University College Ghent - Engineering Sciences,
Schoonmeersstraat 52, B9000 Ghent, Belgium
Francis.Deboeverie@ugent.be, Kristof.Teelen@hogent.be,
Peter.Veelaert@hogent.be, Wilfried.Philips@ugent.be

Abstract. Applications such as traffic surveillance require a real-time
and accurate method for object tracking. We propose to represent scene
observations with parabola segments with an algorithm that allows us to
fit parabola segments in real-time to edge pixels. The motion vectors for
these parabola segments are obtained in consecutive frames by a matching technique based on distance and intensity. Furthermore, moving rigid
objects are detected by an original method that clusters comparable motion vectors. The result is a robust detection and tracking method, which
can cope with small changes in viewpoint on the moving rigid object.

1 Introduction

Object tracking is the problem of identifying and following image elements moving across a video sequence automatically. It has attracted much attention due
to its many applications in computer vision, including surveillance, perceptual
user interfaces, augmented reality, smart rooms, driver assistance, medical imaging and object-based video coding. Since many applications have real-time requirements, very low computational complexity is a highly desirable property.
However, also accuracy is very important. Thus, it is of interest to develop an
object tracking framework that can address all of these diverse requirements.

This research concentrates on the detection and the tracking of rigid objects
based on shape and intensity descriptions of their geometric features. As an example in this paper, we select the detection and tracking of vehicles with parabola
segments. A large number of studies have been devoted to vehicle detection and
tracking. Shan et al. [1] suggested an unsupervised algorithm learning discriminative features of matching road vehicles. Xiong et al. [2] examined real-time
vehicle tracking by combining a colour histogram feature with an edge-gradient-
based shape feature under a sequential Monte Carlo framework. Wang et al. [3]
extended the standard mean-shift tracking algorithm to an adaptive tracker by
selecting reliable features from colour and shape-texture cues according to their
descriptive ability. Using the shape for image understanding is a growing topic in
computer vision and multimedia processing and finding good shape descriptors
and matching measures is the central issue in these applications. Xu et al. [4]

J. Blanc-Talon et al. (Eds.): ACIVS 2009, LNCS 5807, pp. 506–515, 2009.
© Springer-Verlag Berlin Heidelberg 2009

proposed a shape descriptor of planar contours which represents the deformable potential at each point along a contour. Ferrari et al. [5] presented a family of scale-invariant local shape features formed by chains of connected roughly straight contour segments, and their use for object class detection. The difficulties that these methods have to face are mainly viewpoint and illumination changes, which in some applications have to be addressed in real time.

We propose detection and tracking of vehicles with a compact feature, the Parabola Edge Map (PEM), which describes parabola segments in an edge map. This paper provides parabola-based coding and matching techniques to integrate geometrical and structural features in a template matching method. We use motion vectors to describe the motion of parabola segments, which are matched one-to-one by a technique that considers both geometric distance and intensity profile similarity. Moving vehicles are detected and tracked by a cluster algorithm for sets of comparable parabola motion vectors.

The PEM approach has the advantages of geometric feature-based approaches, such as invariance for illumination and low memory requirements. A more important advantage of PEM is that it allows template matching. To represent objects, we need few parabola segments, which leads to stable and reliable feature sets. Even more, many parabola segments correspond to physically meaningful features. In addition, we will show by experimental results that our method is stable for small angle and scale changes, which is advantageous in the tracking of vehicles in bends.

This paper is organized as follows. First, we briefly indicate how to compute a PEM for a gray level image. In the following sections, we present the basic steps in our algorithm for the tracking of parabola segments over different frames in an image sequence by introducing a matching cost for individual parabola segments, and a clustering method for groups of moving parabola segments. The different steps in our algorithm, presented in these subsequent sections, are illustrated by an example application, where vehicles are tracked in the images of a still camera on a parking lot. Finally, we evaluate our method and conclude our paper in section 5 and 6.

2   Parabola Segmentation

The basic step of our method is the interpretation and description of an image edge map by geometric primitives. In previous work [6], we have shown that the approximations of edge maps by second order polynomials is a useful and elegant representation for both non-rigid and rigid structures. Our feature representation, the Parabola Edge Map (PEM), integrates structural information and spatial information by grouping pixels of an edge map into parabola segments.

Each image is preprocessed by a local average filter to reduce noise, before computing an edge map with the Canny edge detector. The Canny edge detector is more suitable than the Sobel operator, because it results in thin edges of one pixel thickness and is less sensitive to noise. Digitized curves are obtained from the edge map by a simple boundary scan algorithm. To obtain parabola segments, we use an incremental linear-time fitting algorithm for curve segmentation which is based on constructive polynomial fitting [7]. The output of the fitting algorithm is a list of parabola segments that approximate the edge map with an L_∞ user-specified threshold. The approximation is of the form $x = f(y)$ and $y = g(x)$, depending on which direction yields the smallest fitting cost. The features are restricted to be parabola and are represented by three parameters.

In figure 1, we show the PEM for one of the figures in the sequence of the example application in our experiments.

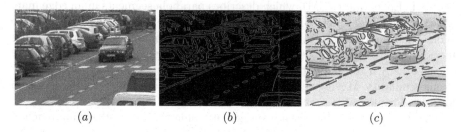

(a)   (b)   (c)

Fig. 1. Figure (a) shows an original image from the sequence of our example application. Figure b and c shows the edge map and the resulting PEM, respectively. The actual value for the threshold on the fitting cost is 2 pixels throughout our experiments.

3   Motion Vectors for Parabola Segments

The tracking technique for the parabola segments in the consecutive frames is based on a matching method for individual parabola segments using both distance and intensity information [6]. Let $M_0 = \{m_{01}, \ldots, m_{0f}, \ldots, m_{0u}\}$ and $M_1 = \{m_{11}, \ldots, m_{1g}, \ldots, m_{1v}\}$ be two sets of parabola segments from consecutive frames, where for each parabola segment the first index i is a time indicator, with each frame at $t-i$, and the second index is the index of the parabola segment in the set. The matching cost of two different parabola segments is a combined function of position, shape and intensity. To obtain position, rotation and scale independency, m_{0f} and m_{1g} are compared under $k + 1$ different viewing angles $\psi_k = 0, \pi/k, 2\pi/k, \ldots, (k-1)\pi/k$ and $\psi_\perp$.

For each viewing angle ψ_k, the shape dissimilarity function D_{ψ_k} is

$$D_{\psi_k}(m_{0f}, m_{1g}) = \sqrt{(d_k^{par} \sigma_k^{par})^2 + (d_k^{per})^2}, \tag{1}$$

where d_k^{par} is the average of the parallel distances measured along the viewing orientation ψ_k, σ_k^{par} denotes the variance of the distances, and d_k^{per} is the minimum distance measured perpendicular to the viewing orientation.

The intensity dissimilarity function I_{ψ_k} in the viewing orientation ψ_k, is defined as

$$I_{\psi_k}(m_{0f}, m_{1g}) = \sqrt{(i_k^{cv} \sigma_k^{cv})^2 + (i_k^{cc} \sigma_k^{cc})^2}, \tag{2}$$

where i_k^{cv} and σ_k^{cv} are the average differences in average intensity and the variance for the differences in intensity at the convex sides of the parabola segments, respectively. i_k^{cc} and σ_k^{cc} are defined similarly at the concave side.

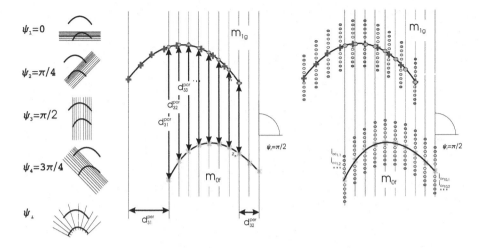

Fig. 2. The computation of the dissimilarity measures for two parabola segments for different viewing angles ψ_k. In this figure, we illustrate the computation of D_{ψ_3} and I_{ψ_3}.

We look for a one-to-one match for each of the parabola segments in the current frame by a minimization of the dissimilarities D_{ψ_k} and I_{ψ_k} between two segments m_{0f} and m_{1g} over all ψ_k. An example of matching parabola segments in two consecutive frames is shown in figure 3, corresponding parabola segments are indicated with the same colour.

The motion vector $\overrightarrow{v_{0fg}}(p_{0fg}, \Delta x_{0fg}, \Delta y_{0fg})$, at $t = 0$ for the unique parabola correspondence pair $\{m_{0f}, m_{1g}\}$ is then defined by three parameters,

- a location indicator $p_{0fg} = c_f(x, y)$, with $c_f(x, y)$ the center point of the segment m_{0f};
- a movement along the x-axis $\Delta x_{0fg} = d_k^{par} \cos \psi_k$;
- and a movement along the y-axis $\Delta y_{0fg} = d_k^{par} \sin \psi_k$;

(a)   (b)

Fig. 3. The matching parabola segments in two consecutive frames of the sequence

4   Motion Registration with Parabola Segments

Now the individual motion vectors for the parabola correspondence pairs must be grouped so that we can define the motion of the objects composed of clusters of parabola segments.

For every parabola segment m_{tf} in the current frame $t = 0$, we construct a chain $C_f = \{(m_{0f}, m_{1g}), (m_{1g}, m_{2h}), \ldots, \}$ of parabola correspondences over maximum the last Q_m frames, i.e. we look in each previous frame for the single best matching parabola segment. If there is no correspondence in a previous frame, the chain is broken. For each chain, we collect the motion vectors $\overrightarrow{v_{tfg}}$ for all $Q < Q_m$ correspondence pairs in the chain, with $t = 0, 1, \ldots, Q-1$. We denote this set of motion vectors by S_f for the parabola segment chain C_f. S_f is characterized by three parameters $(p_{S_f}, \Delta x_{S_f}, \Delta y_{S_f})$:

- a location parameter $p_{S_f} = p_{0fg}$;
- an average movement Δx_{S_f} along the x-axis over the last Q frames, i.e.

$$\Delta x_{S_f} = \frac{1}{Q} \sum_{t=0}^{Q-1} \Delta x_{tfg}; \tag{3}$$

- and an average movement Δy_{S_f} along the y-axis over the last Q frames,

$$\Delta y_{S_f} = \frac{1}{Q} \sum_{t=0}^{Q-1} \Delta y_{tfg}. \tag{4}$$

Among the advantages of using the chain of parabola segments are, first, a smoothing effect on the trajectory of the object, i.e. of the individual parabola clusters, second, longer chains get more weight in the computations of the cluster parameters, and third, we could introduce a learning parameter for a more advanced foreground/background segmentation algorithm.

In a first step we do foreground/background segmentation as followos: we verify whether the parabola segment m_{0f} is actually moved during the last Q frames. Therefore we check whether its average length $\sqrt{(\Delta x_{S_f})^2 + (\Delta y_{S_f})^2}$ is higher than a preset threshold T. In our experiments, we choose $T = 0.5$, so that we only take those parabola segments into account which are sufficiently moving. Otherwise, the parabola segment is assigned to the set of background parabola segments of the current scene.

In the second step we cluster the moving parabola segments into individually moving objects. The criteria for clustering are:

- the segments are in each others neighbourhood, temporally and spatially,
- the segments are moving with the same velocity,
- and in the same direction.

Initially, there are no clusters, so the first parabola segment chain C_1 defines a new cluster ω_1 in the cluster set Ω. The cluster ω_1 has center point $p_{\omega_1} =$

p_{S_1}, an average movement along the x-axis $\Delta x_{\omega_1} = \Delta x_{S_1}$ and an average movement along the y-axis $\Delta y_{\omega_1} = \Delta y_{S_1}$, i.e. it has a cluster motion vector $\overrightarrow{v_{\omega_1}}(p_{\omega_1}, \Delta x_{\omega_1}, \Delta y_{\omega_1})$.

For each new chain C_f, we verify whether it belongs to an existing cluster ω_n from the set of clusters $\Omega = \omega_1, \ldots, \omega_j, \ldots, \omega_n$. Otherwise, C_f defines a new cluster ω_{n+1}. C_f belongs to a cluster ω_j when it satisfies three conditions.

1. The Euclidean distance R_{fj} from p_{S_f} to the current cluster center point p_{ω_j} must be below the user specified radius R.
2. The parabola segments in a cluster must move with the same velocity. When including C_f with movements Δx_{S_f} and Δy_{S_f}, we can compute the new average movement along the x-axis as

$$\Delta x_{\omega_j}^{new} = \frac{m \Delta x_{\omega_j}^{old} + \Delta x_{S_f}}{m + 1}. \tag{5}$$

with m the number of parabola segments in the cluster ω_n. Similar, we compute $\Delta y_{\omega_j}^{new}$, the new average movement along the y-axis.

After inclusion, the variance σ_{lj}^2 of the lengths for all S_r in the cluster ω_j must be below V_l, i.e.

$$\sigma_{lj}^2 = \frac{1}{m+1} \sum_{r=1}^{m+1} (\sqrt{(\Delta x_{S_r})^2 + (\Delta y_{S_r})^2} - \sqrt{(\Delta x_{\omega_j}^{new})^2 + (\Delta y_{\omega_j}^{new})^2})^2 < V_l. \tag{6}$$

3. The parabola segments in one cluster must move in the same direction. Therefore, the variance $\sigma_{\gamma j}^2$ of all directions for all S_r in the cluster ω_j must be below V_γ, i.e.,

$$\sigma_{\gamma j}^2 = \frac{1}{m+1} \sum_{r=1}^{m+1} (\tan^{-1} \frac{\Delta y_{S_r}}{\Delta x_{S_r}} - \tan^{-1} \frac{\Delta y_{\omega_j}^{new}}{\Delta x_{\omega_j}^{new}})^2 < V_\gamma. \tag{7}$$

When C_f satisfies the requirements for more than one cluster, the combination $aR_{fj} + b\sigma_{lj}^2 + c\sigma_{\gamma j}^2$ is minimized. When C_f is added to the cluster ω_j, we update its motion vector $\overrightarrow{v_{\omega_j}}$, i.e. its center point and its average movements along the x- and y-axis as defined above.

Figure 4(a) shows an example of a detected cluster of moving parabola segments, there the parabola are indicated in red, while the background parabola are green. In Figure 4(b) the minimal enclosing bounding box is defined for a cluster op parabola segments.

The main direction in which the vehicle moves can also be detected in the histogram in Figure 4(c), in which the directions for all S_r in the bounding box of Figure 4(b) is shown. There are 32 bins in the histogram, so the width of each bin is $\frac{\pi}{16}$. The average direction of the cluster corresponds to the position of the peak in the histogram.

The cluster translation distance can also be estimated from the histogram of the lengths for all S_r in the bounding box, projected perpendicular on the axis

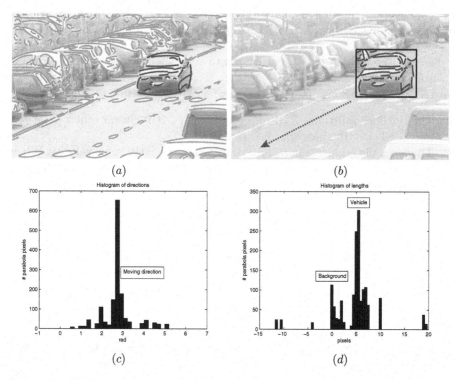

(a) $\quad\quad\quad\quad\quad\quad\quad\quad\quad\quad$ (b)

(c) $\quad\quad\quad\quad\quad\quad\quad\quad\quad\quad$ (d)

Fig. 4. Figure (a) shows a detected cluster of moving parabola segments, the parabola segments are indicated in red, while the background parabola segments are green. The minimal enclosing bounding box is defined in Figure (b). The histograms of directions and lengths from the parabola segment chains in the red cluster are shown in Figure (c) and Figure (d), respectively.

of the main direction. The width of the bins is 0.5 pixels in the histogram of Figure $4(d)$. The first blob is caused by background parabola segments, due to the representation of the rigid object by a bounding box, i.e. there are also some background parabola segments included.

5   Evaluation

The presented methods were evaluated on different video sequences. The algorithm presented in section 4 for the detection of clusters of moving parabola, was tested on a sequence recorded in a tunnel, where vehicles are regularly passing by in the camera view. An example is given in Figure 5 (a). Of the 70 moving vehicles in the sequence, our method extracted 68.

The accuracy of the algorithm for clustering computation was used and evaluated on the example application in which a sequence shows a car driving in one lane. Our methods are evaluated, by comparison to ground truth data, which is

(a)   (b)

Fig. 5. Figure (a) shows an application example of tunnel surveillance. Figure (b) shows an example of occluding parabola clusters.

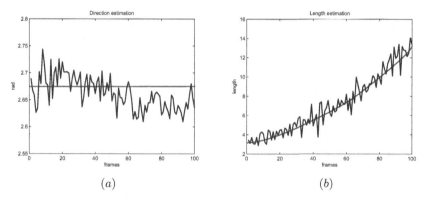

(a)   (b)

Fig. 6. Graphs (a, b) illustrate the accuracy by which the ground truth was estimated by the cluster transformation computation method for the trajectory indicated in Figure 4 (b)

manually created by indicating the trajectory of the car throughout the image sequence. To assess the accuracy of the direction estimation, we compute the RMSE of the estimated direction against the ground truth. The RMSE is 0.07 radials, when computed over 100 frames. The RMSE for the length estimation is 0.4 pixels. The graphs are shown in Figure 6.

The tracking algorithm for clusters of parabola also proves the work in situations where the visual appearance of the objects is radically changing throughout the video sequence. An example is given in Figures 7 (a) and (b), where the vehicle takes a turn, and our method succeeds in tracking the changing parabola.

Our method is still up for improvement, e.g. one of the problems not completely solved at the moment is occlusion. When part of the object gets obscured by other objects, we cannot keep track of the parabola clusters. An example is

Fig. 7. Tracking parabola clusters in which the parabola appearance significantly changes throughout the sequence

shown in Figure 5 (b). In our experience throughout experiments, a minimal percentage of the object surface must be visible for our method to work. A possible solution could be offered by a linear prediction of the object's position and size using previous parameters of the affine transformation, computed when a sufficient part of the object is still visible.

6   Conclusion

In this work, we present a real-time robust method for object tracking with geometric features. We propose a novel method to detect and track vehicles with parabola segments. The parabola segments are first obtained by an algorithm that allows to fit the segments in real-time to edge pixels, and then related in consecutive frames by a matching technique based on distance and intensity. Clustering of the resulting comparable motion vectors leads to the detection and tracking of individual rigid objects.

References

1. Shan, Y., Sawhney, H.S., Kumar, R.(T.): Unsupervised Learning of Discriminative Edge Measures for Vehicle Matching between Nonoverlapping Cameras. IEEE Trans. Pattern Analysis and Machine Intelligence 30(4) (April 2008)
2. Xiong, T., Debrunner, C.: Stochastic Car Tracking With Line- and colour-Based Features. IEEE Trans. on Intelligent Transportation Systems 5(4) (Decemeber 2004)
3. Wang, J., Yagi, Y.: Integrating color and shape-texture features for adaptive real-time object tracking. IEEE Trans. on Image Processing 17, 235–240 (2008)
4. Xu, C., Liu, J., Tang, X.: 2D Shape Matching by Contour Flexibility. IEEE Trans. Pattern Analysis and Machine Intelligence 31(1) (January 2009)

5. Ferrari, V., Fevrier, L., Jurie, F., Schmid, C.: Groups of Adjacent Contour Segments for Object Detection. IEEE Trans. Pattern Analysis and Machine Intelligence 30(1) (January 2008)
6. Deboeverie, F., Veelaert, P., Teelen, K., Philips, W.: Face Recognition Using Parabola Edge Map. In: Blanc-Talon, J., Bourennane, S., Philips, W., Popescu, D., Scheunders, P. (eds.) ACIVS 2008. LNCS, vol. 5259, pp. 994–1005. Springer, Heidelberg (2008)
7. Veelaert, P., Teelen, K.: Fast polynomial segmentation of digitized curves. In: Kuba, A., Nyúl, L.G., Palágyi, K. (eds.) DGCI 2006. LNCS, vol. 4245, pp. 482–493. Springer, Heidelberg (2006)
8. Deboeverie, F., Veelaert, P., Philips, W.: Parabola-based Face Recognition and Tracking. In: Proceedings of ProRISC, pp. 308–313 (2008)

Object Tracking by Non-overlapping Distributed Camera Network

Pier Luigi Mazzeo, Paolo Spagnolo, and Tiziana D'Orazio

Istituto di Studi sui Sistemi Intelligenti per l'Automazione, C.N.R.
Via G. Amendola 122/D 70126 Bari, Italy
{mazzeo,dorazio,spagnolo}@ba.issia.cnr.it
http://www.issia.cnr.it/

Abstract. People Tracking is a problem of great interest for wide areas video surveillance systems. In these large areas, it is not possible for a single camera to observe the complete area of interest. Surveillance systems architecture requires algorithms with the ability to track objects while observing them through multiple cameras. We focus our work on multi camera tracking with non overlapping fields of view (FOV). In particular we propose a multi camera architecture for wide area surveillance and a real time people tracking algorithm across non overlapping cameras. In this scenario it is necessary to track object both in intra-camera and inter-camera FOV. We consider these problems in this paper. In particular we have investigated different techniques to evaluate intra-camera and inter-camera tracking based on color histogram. For the intra-camera tracking we have proposed different methodologies to extract the color histogram information from each object patches. For inter-camera tracking we have compared different methods to evaluate the colour Brightness Transfer Function (BTF) between non overlapping cameras. These approaches are based on color histogram mapping between pairs of images of the same object in different FOVs. Therefore we have combined different methodology to calculate the color histogram in order to estimate different colour BTF performances. Preliminary results demonstrates that the proposed method combined with BTF outperform the performance in terms of matching rate between different cameras.

1 Introduction

The specific problem we address in this paper is the surveillance over wide-areas such as an airport, the downtown of a large city or any large public area. Surveillance over these wide areas consists of the search for suspicious behavior as persons loitering, unauthorized access, or persons attempting to enter a restricted zone. Currently, these surveillance tasks are accomplished by human operators who continually observe monitors to detect unauthorized activity over many cameras. Recent researches have demonstrated that the attention level drastically drops after few hours, so it becomes highly probable that suspicious activity would go unnoticed by a human operator. A computer vision system,

J. Blanc-Talon et al. (Eds.): ACIVS 2009, LNCS 5807, pp. 516–527, 2009.
© Springer-Verlag Berlin Heidelberg 2009

however, can monitor both immediate unauthorized behavior and long-term suspicious behavior. The system would then alert a human operator for a closer look. In most cases, it is not possible for a single camera to observe the complete area of interest because sensor resolution is finite and structures in the scene limit the visible areas.

In realistic scenarios, surveillance systems which cover large areas are composed by multiple cameras with non overlapping FOVs. In this paper we investigate on the feasibility of different techniques to evaluate intra-camera and inter-camera tracking based on color histogram. As first step we have evaluated different techniques to extract the color histogram from each foreground patches. After that, we have implemented tracking algorithms that by applying inter camera appearance matching are able to track people across multiple view separated by blind regions. We have compared different methods to evaluate the color Brightness Transfer Function (BTF) between non overlapping cameras. These approaches are based on the color histogram mapping between pairs of images of the same object in different FOVs. The experimental results show how the calculated transfer function, combined by different color histogram extraction approach, essentially improves the matching rate between non overlapped regions.

The remaining of this paper is organized as follows. In section 1.1 we give a brief overview of related work. The approaches for people tracking across non overlapping cameras are summarized in section 2. The color histogram extraction and tracking approaches are described in section 2.1. The sections 2.2 and 2.3 describe the multi-cameras correspondence detection and the multi-cameras people tracking approach. In section 3 we report the results obtained on some video sequences acquired with two cameras placed in different rooms.

1.1   Related Work

Most of the approaches presented in literature suppose the use of calibrated cameras and the availability of a site model. In [1] the conformity in the traversed paths of people and car is used to establish correspondence among cameras. The algorithm learns this conformity and hence the inter-camera relationships in the form of multivariate probability density of spacetime variables (entry and exit locations, velocities, and transition times) using kernel density estimation. To handle the appearance change of an object as it moves from one camera to another, the authors demonstrate that all brightness transfer functions from a given camera to another camera lie in a low dimensional subspace. This subspace is learned by using probabilistic principal component analysis and used for appearance matching. In [3] particle filters and belief propagation are combined in a unified framework. In each view, a target is tracked by a dedicated particle-filter-based local tracker. The trackers in different views collaborate via belief propagation so that a local tracker operating in one view is able to take advantage of additional information from other views. In [4] a target is tracked not only in each camera but also in the ground plane by individual particle filters. These particle filters collaborate in two different ways. First, the particle filters in each camera pass messages to those in the ground plane where the multi-camera information is integrated by intersecting the targets principal axes. This largely relaxes the dependence on precise foot positions when mapping targets from images to the ground plane using homographies. Secondly, the fusion results in the ground plane are then incorporated by each camera as boosted proposal functions. A mixture proposal function is composed for each tracker in a camera by combining an independent transition kernel and the boosted proposal function.

Kalman filters are used in [5] to robustly track each targets shape and motion in each camera view and predict the targets track in the blind region between cameras. For multi-camera correspondence matching, the Gaussian distributions of the tracking parameters across cameras for the target motion and position in the ground plane view are computed. Matching of targets across camera views uses a graph based track initialization scheme, which accumulates information from occurrences of target in several consecutive frames of the video. Geometric and intensity features are used in [7] to match objects for tracking in a multiple calibrated camera system for surveillance. These features are modelled as multivariate Gaussians, and the Mahalanobis distance measure is used for matching. A method to match object appearances over non-overlapping cameras is presented in [8]. In his approach, a brightness transfer function (BTF) is computed for every pair of cameras. Once such a mapping is known, the correspondence problem is reduced to the matching of transformed histograms or appearance models. However, this mapping, i.e., the BTF varies from frame to frame depending on a large number of parameters that include illumination, scene geometry, exposure time, focal length, and aperture size of each camera. Thus, a single pre-computed BTF cannot usually be used to match objects for moderately long sequences. An unsupervised approach to learn edge measures for appearance matching between non-overlapping views has been presented in [9]. The probability of two observations from two cameras being generated by the same or different object is computed to perform the matching. The main constraint of this approach is that the edge images of vehicles have to be registered together. Note that this requirement for registering object images could not be applicable for non-rigid objects like pedestrians. A Cumulative Brightness Transfer Function (CBTF) is proposed [10] for mapping color between cameras located at different physical sites, which makes use of the available color information from a very sparse training set. A bi-directional mapping approach is used to obtain an accurate similarity measure between pairs of candidate objects. An illumination-tolerant appearance representation, based on online k-means color clustering algorithm is introduced in [11], which is capable of coping with the typical illumination changes occurring in surveillance scenarios. A similarity measurement is also introduced to compare the appearance representation of any two arbitrary individuals. In [12] the distortion function is approximated as general affine and the object appearance is represented as a mixture of Gaussians. Appearance models are put in correspondence by searching a bijection function that maximizes a metric for model dissimilarity.

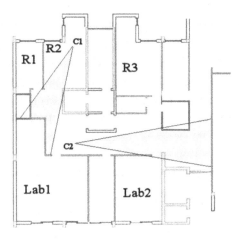

Fig. 1. The cameras configuration inside our office building

A common characteristic of the above related works is that the knowledge of model sites and particular camera positions in various scenarios allow the usage of geometrical and temporal constraints on the entry/exit areas of the image. In this way the appearance matching among different cameras is carried out on a sets of individuals that are candidate by their positions to be observed by distributed cameras.

2 Tracking in Multiple Cameras with Disjoint Views

The focus of this paper is the investigation of a multi-camera tracking system with non overlapping cameras. Two cameras C1 and C2 are arranged in two different places of a corridor as shown in figure 1. The cameras' field of views cover different non-overlapping areas. People observed in camera C2 can take a path across camera C1 turning right or also turning left in the Lab1 without entering the C1 field of view. In the same way people coming from the Lab1 are observed in camera C1 without passing trough the camera C2. The task of the multi-camera tracking algorithm is to establish correspondence across cameras finding which tracks belong to the same object. Because of the cameras' positions, it is not always possible to use space time constraints between the locations of the exits and entrances between the cameras. People can take many paths across C1 and C2, producing the same observations in the two cameras. For this reason in this paper we want to investigate the feasibility of a multi-camera tracking algorithm that relies just on the appearances of the objects in the two cameras. Anyway, the lack of entry/exit constraints renders more difficult the association task. Considering that the color distribution of an object can be fairly different when it moves in a single camera, matching appearances between different cameras is still more difficult, then it is necessary to find out the transformation that maps the appearance of an object in one camera with its appearance in the other camera. In this paper we considered a training phase during which known objects pass trough both the cameras and their appearances is used to estimate a Brightness Transfer Function (BTF). During this phases we tested two different BTFs, ie. the mean BTF and the cumulative BTF. In the testing phase the object matches were carried out choosing those that produced the lowest values of the Bhattacharya distance between the color histograms of the considered person in one camera with all the possible persons that had travelled through the second camera.

2.1 Color Histogram Extraction and Tracking

The implemented tracker models the appearance of the target object using color histogram. The task of finding the same object from the foreground region in current frame is formulated as follows: the color histogram feature is assumed to have a density function, while a candidate region also had a color histogram feature distributed by a certain density. The problem is to find a candidate region whose associated a density is most similar to the target density. A Bhattacharraya coefficient measure is used as metric between the distribution. We have implemented different method to extract the color histogram from the foreground patches, in order to eliminate noise and possible shadow from the object patch. One or more elliptic masks are used to reach this aim. The ellipse parameter (major and minor axis) are based on the patch dimension and on the distance of the object from the camera. Basing on the person position in the FOV we have estimated, using a mapping function, his body measure in the foreground patches. In this way we try to build the elliptic masks in order to catch more useful information possible. In order to obtain discriminant color histogram we discard any possible part of the patch that could be confuse the distribution of the histogram. In this way the ellipses are drawn to cover the most part of the people body (we cut the head of the person and his eventual shadow as shown in figures 2(b), 3(b)). In particular we have compared different combination of these masks (see pictures 2(b), 2(c), 2(e), 2(f), 3(b), 3(c), 3(e), 3(f)) in order to evaluate their performance.

2.2 Establishing Correspondence Across Multiple Cameras

The correspondence problem occurs when an object enters the FOV of a camera. We need to determine if the object is already being tracked by another camera or it is a new object in the environment. Many approaches are possible to evaluate the brightness transfer function among different cameras. In this paper we compare a mean BTF approach with the cumulative BTF proposed in [10]. Suppose an object O enters the camera C1. In figure 2 we show some images of the tracks of two persons in the camera C1, while in figure 3 the same persons are observed by the camera C2.

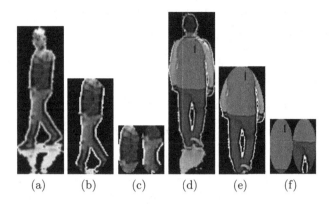

Fig. 2. Six images of two persons in the camera C1. a) Foreground patch extracted of the first person; b) Elliptic mask of the first person; c) Double Elliptic masks of the first person; d) Foreground patch extracted of the second person; e) Elliptic mask of the second person; f) Double Elliptic masks of the second person.

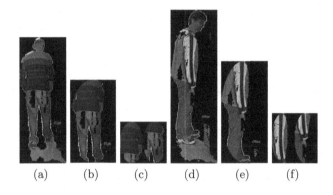

Fig. 3. Six images of two persons in the camera C2. a) Foreground patch extracted of the first person; b) Elliptic mask of the first person; c) Double Elliptic masks of the first person; d) Foreground patch extracted of the second person; e) Elliptic mask of the second person; f) Double Elliptic masks of the second person.

We evaluated the three channels RGB histograms for each image in the tracks of the camera C1. We did the same also for the tracks in the camera C2. The histograms are generated using all the 256 bins for each channel. We want to estimate a BTF $f_{1,2}$ between the cameras C1 and C2 such that, for each couple of images (i_1, j_2), given the brightness values $B^{i_1}(k)$ and $B^{j_2}(k)$ we have $B^{j_2}(k) = f_{1,2}(B^{i_1}(k))$ where $k = 0, .., 255$ represents the number of bins, $i_1 = 1, .., M$ represents the number of images in the camera C1 tracks, $j_2 = 1, .., N$ the number of images in the camera C2 tracks. In order to evaluate the BTF $f_{1,2}$ we collected a total on $N + M$ histograms obtained on the N images tracked in the camera C1 and on the M images of the same person tracked in the camera

C2. We denote the histograms obtained in the two cameras with H_{i_1} and H_{j_2} respectively. For each possible couple of histograms (i_1, j_2) we evaluated the brightness transfer function

$$f_{i_1 j_2}(B^{i_1}(k)) = B^{j_2}(k) \tag{1}$$

using the inverted cumulative histogram, that is

$$f_{i_1 j_2}(B^{i_1}(k)) = H_{j_2}^{-1}(H_{i_1}(B^{j_2}(k))) \tag{2}$$

and finally the mean BTF (referred in the following section as MBTF) $\overline{f}_{1,2}$

$$\overline{f}_{1,2} = \sum_{i_1=1}^{M} \sum_{j_2=1}^{N} f_{i_1 j_2} \tag{3}$$

We evaluated also a cumulative BTF (CBTF) as proposed in [10]. The generation of the CBTF involves an amalgamation of the training set before computing any BTFs. An accumulation of the brightness values is computed on all the training images of the camera C1 obtaining a cumulative histogram $\widehat{H}_1$. The same is done for all the corresponding training images of the camera C2 obtaining $\widehat{H}_2$. The CBTF $\widehat{f}_{1,2}$ is

$$\widehat{f}_{1,2}(B^1(k)) = \widehat{H}_2^{-1}(\widehat{H}_1(B^2(k))) \tag{4}$$

also in this case evaluated by using the inverted cumulative histogram.

2.3 Multi-camera Tracking Using BTFs

In order to solve the multi-camera people identification problem we have to choose among a set of possible correspondence hypotheses the one that produces the best match. Anyway, since our camera configuration allows people to enter into one camera field of view without passing through the other camera, we consider also the problem of finding a proper method to discard false matches. The common method to match person appearances is by estimating the similarity between color histograms. Let be $\{H_{k_1}^1, H_{k_2}^1, ... H_{k_{N_k}}^1\}$ the N_k histograms of the k-th person in the camera C1. Suppose that we have $k = P$ persons moving in the camera C1. When a new observation is taken in the camera C2 we have to decide either if it could be associated with one among the P persons moving in the camera C1 or if it is a new person entering the scene. For each person in the camera C1, i.e. $k = 1, .., P$, we evaluated the mean color histograms among the N_k observations of the k-th person obtaining the mean histograms $\overline{H}_k^1$. Anyway the mean histograms cannot be compared with those obtained by the camera C2 unless the transformation with the BTFs are applied. By using the BTFS described in the previous section we projected the K mean histograms in the new space as follows

$$\breve{H}_k^{12} = \overline{f}_{1,2}(\overline{H}_k^1) \tag{5}$$

where $\breve{H}_k$ represents the new histogram obtained using the mean BTF described in equation 3 and

$$\tilde{H}_k^{12} = \widehat{f}_{1,2}(\overline{H}_k^1)$$ (6)

is the transformation by using the CBTF described in 4. Let be $H_{l_1}^2$ the histogram of the first observation in the camera C2. We evaluated the similarity between couple of histograms by using the well known Bhattacharya distance (Sim_B). The association is done with the k-th person that produces the minimum distance, i.e.

$$min_k(Sim_B(H_{l_1}^2, H_k^{12})$$ (7)

3   Experimental Results

Different experiments were carried out to test the multi-camera tracking algorithm. The scenario was composed by two cameras located in two different points of our office. We used two wireless Axis IP camera with 640x480 color jpg resolution with an acquisition frame rate of 10 frames per second. The topology of this camera network is shown in figure 1, while two images acquired by the two cameras are shown in figures 4(a) and 4(b). Note that the illumination conditions and color quality vary greatly between these views.

We have divided the experiments in two different parts. In the first part we evaluate different kind of method to extract the color histogram from each foreground patch. In the second part we have evaluated different approaches to establish the correspondence across the disjoint views.

In both parts we have used the same data set. Our data-set consisted of synchronized mjpeg videos acquired simultaneously by two different cameras containing six persons. The patches data come from a single camera object detection method described in [13]. The data set were obtained by extracting people from the entire FOV of each camera. We didn't consider any geometrical constraint on the exiting and entering areas of people moving in the scenario.

(a) Camera 2 Field of view   (b) Camera 1 Field of view

Fig. 4. Frames from both camera views. The same person walks from camera 1 to camera 2.

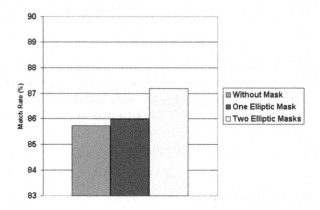

Fig. 5. A comparison of the matching success in the same FOV (Intra-camera) using different color histogram extraction method

We carried out different experiments using sets of samples as follows:

- First experiment: six individuals giving 889 appearance sample (coming from the same FOV) are used as testing data in order to evaluate the performance of different color histogram extraction methods (See section 2.1)
- In the second experiment we need a training and a testing data set: three individuals giving 561 appearance samples in both views were used in the training step, while four individuals with 493 appearance samples in both views were used in testing step (Note that in this case we added one person in the training phase and the test set remained unchanged);

In the figure 5 the results relative to the intra-camera histogram color tracking are presented. As explained in section 2.1 we have evaluated two different approaches to estimate the color histogram from extracted people patches. The similarity, between color histogram features belonging to different foreground patch, has been measured by means of Bhattacharyya distance. The lowest value of these distance among the patch and all the possible candidates (six different persons in the same FOV) determines the tracking association. It is possible to notice how the two elliptic masks approach gives better result in term of match rate. By using mask with two ellipses, in fact, it is possible to preserve the color histogram spatial information. In this way, the upper body and lower body color histograms of each patch are compared with the correspondent parts of another person (see figure 3(f), 3(c)). Results confirm that this color histogram extraction approach discriminates better among the different possible individual candidates.

In the figure 6, the results relative to the tracking across different cameras, are shown. The experiments consist of a training phase and a testing phase. During the training phase we supposed that the correspondence between the same object in the different cameras' FOV were known and this information was used to calculate the Mean Brightness transfer function (MBTF) and the Cumulative Brightness Transfer Function (CBTF). In the testing phase the correspondences between cameras were computed using the Bhattacharya distance, and the correct match was associated with the lowest value of these distances (see equation 7) among all the possible couple of candidates.

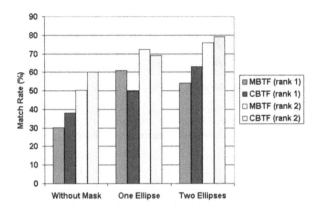

Fig. 6. A comparison of the matching success rate in establishing correspondence across cameras using varying color histogram extraction method and different Brightness Transfer Function Estimation (BTF)

As it can be noticed, in the testing phase we considered four individuals that were present in both views.

As explained in section 2.2 we tested two different approaches to calculate the BTFs between the two cameras: the MBTF and the CBTF. In order to compare these methods we used a uni-directional comparison using the Bhattacharya distance as similarity measure. For each individual we converted his RGB histograms into the target region color space (i.e. from camera 1 to camera 2). They have been compared against all individuals observed in this region. In particular we estimated the mean color histogram for the same individual in each view and we compare each converted histogram against it.

In figure 6 we report both the rank1 and rank2 results indicating the presence of the correct match as the highest and the second highest similarity score respectively. As the figure shows both methods had quite similar behaviors in term of match rates but it is possible to note that the CBTF outperform MBTF in the rank1 and rank2 results (we matched the histogram also against the mean histogram of the individual contained in the training set). Only in the case of the one elliptic mask approach MBTF gives better results than CBTF (the difference is very narrow). However the overall performances confirmed that CBTF retained more color information than MBTF and produced a more accurate mapping function. In the same figure the different color histogram extraction approaches are also compared, even in this figure the match rate shows that

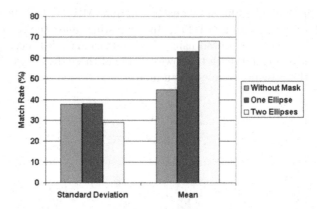

Fig. 7. Mean and standard deviation of the matching rate using different color extraction method to establish the correspondence between the two cameras

the two elliptic masks method gives the best results. This it what we expect for the reason explained in the first part of this section. Finally figure 7 shows the mean and standard deviation of the different color histogram extraction method estimated in both part of the experiment. Even these values demonstrate that double elliptic masks give the greatest mean score with the lowest standard deviation. This confirm that double elliptic masks method maps the data among the different six people classes better than the others.

4   Conclusions and Future Work

In this paper we have investigated on the feasibility of multi camera tracking algorithms based on the appearance similarity. We have considered two non overlapping cameras inside an office building. In this paper we have investigated the reliability of appearance similarity methods to track people in the same FOV and among two different FOVs. We evaluated different color histogram extraction approaches with different elliptic masks. Obtained results showed that using these masks improve overall results in terms of matching rate. We also compared two different Brightness Transfer Functions, ie. the MBTF and the CBTF. Experiments demonstrated quite similar behaviors of the two methods when the simple association problem has to be solved.

Future work will be addressed on the study of new methodologies for more reliable appearance matching. Since the people appearances can be similar in some parts of the body and differ in other parts we are thinking to apply different methodologies based on the extraction of graphs of patch histograms and use different weights in the correspondence matches in order to consider different reliability of the body parts and highlight only the significant differences among the people appearances.

References

1. Javed, O., Safique, K., Rasheed, Z., Shah, M.: Modeling inter camera space-time and apperacnce relationships for tracking across non-overlapping views. Computer Vision and Image Understanding 109, 146–162 (2008)
2. Javed, O., Shafique, K., Shah, M.: Appearance modeling for tracking in multiple non-overlapping cameras. In: CVPR, vol. 2, pp. 26–33 (2005)
3. Du, W., Piater, J.: Data Fusion by Belief Propagation for Multi-Camera Tracking. In: The 9th International Conference on Information Fusion (2006)
4. Du, W., Piater, J.: Multi-Camera People Tracking by Collaborative Particle Filters and Principal Axis-Based Integration. In: Yagi, Y., Kang, S.B., Kweon, I.S., Zha, H. (eds.) ACCV 2007, Part I. LNCS, vol. 4843, pp. 365–374. Springer, Heidelberg (2007)
5. Chilgunde, A., Kumar, P., Ranganath, S., WeiMin, H.: Multi-Camera Target Tracking in Blind Regions of Cameras with Non-overlapping Fields of View. In: BMVC 2004, Kingston, September 7-9 (2004)
6. Javed, O., Rasheed, Z., Alatas, O., Shah, M.: Knightm: a real time surveillance system for multiple overlapping and non-overlapping cameras.
7. Cai, Q., Aggarwal, J.K.: Tracking human motion in structured environments using a distributed camera system. IEEE Trans. Pattern Anal. Mach. Intell. 2(11), 1241–1247 (1999)
8. Porikli, F.: Inter-camera color calibration using cross-correlation model function. In: IEEE Int. Conf. on Image Processing (2003)
9. Shan, Y., Sahwney, H.S., Kumar, R.: Unsupervised learning of discriminative edge measures for vehicle matching between nonoverlapping cameras. In: IEEE Conf. on Computer Vision and Pattern Recognition (2005)
10. Prosser, B., Gong, S., Xiang, T.: Multi-camera Matching using Bi-Directional Cumulative Brightness Transfer Functions. In: British Machine Conference 2008 (2008)
11. Madden, C., Cheng, E.D., Piccardi, M.: Tracking people across disjoint camera views by an illumination-tolerant appearance representation. Machine Vision and Application 18, 233–247 (2007)
12. Jeong, K., Jaynes, C.: Object matching in disjoint cameras using a color transfer approach. Machine Vision and Application 19, 443–455 (2008)
13. Mazzeo, P.L., Spagnolo, P., Leo, M., D'Orazio, T.: Visual Players Detection and Tracking in Soccer Matches. In: IEEE Fifth International Conference on Advanced Video and Signal Based Surveillance. AVSS 2008, pp. 326–333 (2008)

Relational Dynamic Bayesian Networks to Improve Multi-target Tracking

Cristina Manfredotti and Enza Messina

DISCo,
Università degli Studi Milano-Bicocca

Abstract. Tracking relations between moving objects is a big challenge for Computer Vision research. Relations can be useful to better understand the behaviors of the targets, and the prediction of trajectories can become more accurate. Moreover, they can be useful in a variety of situations like monitoring terrorist activities, anomaly detection, sport coaching, etc.

In this paper we propose a model based on Relational Dynamic Bayesian Networks (RDBNs), that uses first-order logic to model particular correlations between objects behaviors, and show that the performance of the prediction increases significantly. In our experiments we consider the problem of multi-target tracking on a highway where the behavior of targets is often correlated to the behavior of the targets near to them. We compare the performance of a Particle Filter that does not take into account relations between objects and the performance of a Particle Filter that makes inference over the proposed RDBN.

We show that our method can follow the targets path more closely than the standard methods, being able to better predict their behaviors while decreasing the complexity of the tracker task.

1 Introduction

The goal of *multi-target tracking* is that of finding the tracks of an unknown number of moving targets from noisy observations. A track is defined as a path in space-time traveled by a target. Each path can be seen as a sequence of positions (or "states") that need to be estimated at each time (for online problems).

From the state of a target at time t a typical tracker initially *predicts* the future position of the target given the knowledge about the current state; once measurements about the state at time $t + 1$ are acquired, these are *filtered* to improve the prediction. The filtering step consists in "correcting" (this step is also called *correction*) the prediction given the measurement taking into account the noise introduce by the measurement instrument and the un-precision of the prediction step. In multi-target tracking, measurements or observations are relative to a series of different targets that in general are not directly distinguishable. The problem then becomes more difficult as we have to deal with *data association* between each observation and its target. A multi-target tracking at this step has to "associate" each prediction to its own measurement before filtering the

J. Blanc-Talon et al. (Eds.): ACIVS 2009, LNCS 5807, pp. 528–539, 2009.

prediction. An error in this task can have a very large impact on the tracker's performance; for example, two different objects might be mistaken one for another, or the tracker might erroneously believe that an object left the scene when in fact it did not (or viceversa).

To tackle this complexity we propose to exploit relations among objects. We seek to take advantage of the fact that objects that stand in some relationship together often exhibit a similar behavioral pattern: for example, while tracking vehicles on a highway, if at a given point a car slows down, the cars behind are likely to slow down as well. This fact could be used by the model to more accurately predict cars' positions and their behavior.

In this paper we will use a *Probabilistic Relational Model* [1] to monitor relations between moving objects in the scene. We will develop a transitional model that uses the notion of relations between objects to predict future state carefully, improving the performance of the tracker itself.

The paper is organized as follows. In the next section we explain the tracking problem, then introduce the concept of *relations* in tracking and review some related works and discuss their limitations. We next introduce the probabilistic model we used to model transition probabilities and before concluding and introducing some future works, we give some preliminary results.

2   The Tracking Problem

In (single object) tracking the tracker's objective is to identify and follow a moving object in the scene. In this section, we review the standard tracking problem. The following models form the basic components used by a tracker to reason about the scene:

- the **state transition model**, which describes the evolution of the state with time, and
- the **measurement model**, which relates (potentially noisy) measurements to the state.

Generally these models are available in a probabilistic form and the system itself can be represented by a *Dynamic Bayesian Network* [2] (DBN) where the inter-slice distribution represents the state transition model given by the pdf $p(x_{t+1}|x_t)$ and the intra-slice distribution represents the measurement model $p(z_t|x_t)$. It is appropriate to think of measurements (z_t) as noisy projections of the state (x_t).

In this environment, the *belief* of the state is calculated as the probability distribution over the state variable x_t conditioned on all past measurements $z_{1:t}$:

$$bel(x_t) = p(x_t|z_{1:t}) \tag{1}$$

The belief fo the state is taken after the acquisition of the measurement z_t. The prediction step is done before the acquisition of the measurement:

$$\widetilde{bel}(x_t) = p(x_t|z_{1:t-1}) \tag{2}$$

There $\widetilde{bel}(x_t)$ predicts the state at time t based on the previous belief, before incorporating the measurements at time t. Calculating $bel(x_t)$ from $\widetilde{bel}(x_t)$ is called *correction* (or *filtering*) and is the last step of a tracking algorithm.

The most general algorithm for calculating beliefs is given by the Bayesian filter algorithm that calculates the belief distribution from measurements data in a recursive way. For each x_t it:

- computes $\widetilde{bel}(x_t)$ from $bel(x_t)$

$$\widetilde{bel}(x_t) = \int p(x_t|x_{t-1})bel(x_{t-1})dx_{t-1} \tag{3}$$

- and updates the believe according to the measurements:

$$bel(x_t) = \eta p(z_t|x_t)\widetilde{bel}(x_t) \tag{4}$$

where η is a normalization constant.

Parametric (or Gaussian) filters are the earliest tractable implementations of Bayesian filters, based on the idea that beliefs are represented by multivariate normal distributions. Non-parametric filters, instead, can deal with any kind of distributions.

In this paper we want to accurately model the transitional process by taking advantage from the relations between objects; the model we develop is well suited for a non-parametric filter: we will use a particle filter to track moving objects.

3   Relations in Multi-target Tracking

Multi target tracking involves complex scenes with several target objects. Given their complexity, it is quite natural to think about exploiting the relations among targets. For example, an object movement might constrain the possible movements of the other objects nearby. In fact, objects in relationship often exhibit a similar behavioral pattern. If we are able to *track* the relations (monitoring the objects that take part in it) we can also leverage the prediction of the next state. For example, we can rule out conjoint behaviors that are not consistent with relationship.

Representing and reasoning about relations can be useful in two ways:

- *Relations can improve the efficiency of the tracking.* The information contained in the relationships can improve the prediction, resulting in a better final estimation of the behavior.. Also the *data association* task can become more precise, reducing the possibilities of errors. (in this paper, we focus on this objective).
- *Monitoring relations can be a goal in itself.* This is the case in many activities like traffic prediction or consumer monitoring, anomaly detection or terrorist activity recognition.

We will discuss this more in detail with an example.

3.1 Example

Consider several vehicles traveling on a one-lane highway; several highway entrances and exits are present at constant distance (we will call it d) along the highway. We want to track the vehicles, which are moving non-deterministically so that the future speed - and thus future position - cannot be exactly predicted by knowing the current state. As we have a limited number of possibly faulty and noisy sensors, we want to exploit the information that we can acquire from recognizing common behaviors due to relations. In this simple but representative scenario, a car is modeled by the following attributes:

- Color: red, green, pink
- Size: small, big
- Position: (x, y). The y-coordinate is in the direction of the highway.
- Speed
- Direction

Moreover, the n-th entrance (exit) is located at coordinates $y = (n-1)d$. One of every three exits is restricted, for safety reason, to small vehicles (for $n = 3, 6, 9, ..$).

The goal is to be able to track *relations* between the moving objects. In this way, we can readily find correlations between different objects' behaviors. For example, a vehicle moving at very high speed will eventually have to slow down if the cars in front are moving substantially slower. Or we might want to monitor which cars are likely to be traveling together. In this case we can make use of the following relations:

- *Before(X, Y)*: X's position is just before Y's according to y-coordinate. Denoting by $Y.y$ the y-coordinate of Y's position, we have $Y.y - t < X.y < Y.y$, where t is a constant, and there is no car Z such that $X.y < Z.y < Y.y$.
- *SameDirection(X, Y)*: X has the same direction of Y according to y-coordinate.
- *TravelingTogether(X, Y)*: X and Y are traveling together, so they have the same departure and arrival, and they travel as close as possible.

Relations can be exploited for the data association task. In this example, if there are many objects, data association can be a difficult problem, for example, due to the presence of prospective biases; or cars with similar features (size and color) could switch position between two sensor measurements, etc. If we know that there are two *RED BIG* cars that are traveling together, and from the sensor we identify the position of three RED BIG cars, two next to one another, and one apart, we can immediately associate the two observations of the two cars that are traveling together and the one observation to another car.

We need to specify a prior for the model's variables. For the speed, it is easy to imagine that the probability of slowing down $p_{speed}^{slowdown}$ depends on the location, and it is reasonable to assume it is higher near exits. For simplicity we consider only two prior values p_{low} and p_{high}. For points far from an exit, the value is p_{low}. We also need to account of the type of the exit (whether it is restricted to small vehicles).

- If the car is near to an exit and it is allowed to exit (either the car is small or the exit is not restricted) then the probability of slowing down $p_{speed}^{slowdown}$ is p_{high}
- else the probability of slowing down $p_{speed}^{slowdown}$ is p_{low}

The relation $TravelingTogether(X, Y)$ does not have a precise definition based on the other variables (as it was the case for the relation $Before$). In other words, unless we have some explicit external information about who is traveling with whom, we need to infer this relation from the scene, and reasoning about our *beliefs* that two cars are traveling together. Of course, we would need a training data-set to set the prior.

A sample prior definition of this belief probability might be the following, expressing that two cars are very likely to be traveling together if they have the same size and color and enter at the same entrance in temporal proximity:

- if cars X and Y entered from different entrance, $bel(together(X, Y)) = p_{together} = 0$
- if cars X and Y enter from the same entrance within a time-slice T, $bel(together(X, Y)) = p_{together} = q$ where q is the fraction of pairs of cars that entered from this entrance in the data-set that are traveling together
- if cars X and Y has the same size and color, and they have entered from the same entrance within a time-slice T, $bel(together(X, Y)) = p_{together} = q_{high}$, with $q_{high} \gg q$.

As we need to update this belief during the tracking, we can design a set of rules to model increased or decreased evidence about the fact that car X and car Y are traveling together.

- if car X exits but not Y, $bel(together(X, Y)) = p_{together} = 0$ (two cars that have different destinations are not traveling together)
- if the distance between X and Y exceeds a threshold, $bel_t(together(X, Y)) = k*bel_{t-1}(together(X, Y))$ with $k < 1$ (the probability decreases exponentially with respect to the number of time steps in which they are quite far away)
- if the distance between X and Y remains within a threshold for a time period T, the belief increases

Furthermore for this relation ($TravelingTogether(X, Y)$) we can state some "rules of thumb" expressing the correlation between objects in the same relation.

- If X and Y are traveling together, once X speeds up then Y speeds up (respectively slows down)
- If X and Y are traveling together, once X exits the highway then Y exits too

In short, the observation that two vehicles are behaving similarly, produces evidence that they are in relation (traveling together), but once we are quite sure that two vehicles are traveling together we can use this belief to predict that they will behave similarly into future. We can then anticipate the behavior of all components of the group, and reason with the rules that we have for other variables and relations.

  – If a group of cars, containing at least one big vehicle, is traveling together and
    the next exit is restricted to small vehicles, then the probability of slowing
    down near the exit for each car in the group will be p_{low}.

Moreover, studying relations can be useful to better predict future positions. If
car A is before car B and they are going in the same direction (i.e, *Before(A,B)*
holds and SameDirection(A,B) holds) and A slows down, the probability of B
slowing down increases.

   To be consistent with our terminology, we can include the relations as part of
a global scene's *state*. Then, we need to specify a transitional model for relations,
that usually can be very simple. For instance we can say that no group of vehicles
traveling together ever breaks up on the way - so the relation does not change (or,
instead we can introduce a probability of breaking up). For the *Before* relation,
its estimation is based on the estimation of the position, so we can directly derive
it from the cars positions beliefs.

   The types of relationships we have seen in this example are very valuable
cues for tracking, and their explicit representation can be an advantage. These
relations can be modeled and express easily. Equally importantly we can easily
and compactly model how changes in a relationship change our state prediction
(as in the case that a car slows down, the car before is probably going to slow
down as well). In the rest of this paper we will discuss how to model relations
for multiple targets tracking with Relational Dynamic Bayesian Networks.

3.2   Related Works

The most successful algorithm for multi-target tracking is the *multiple hypothesis*
tracker (MHT) [3]. In MHT, each hypothesis associates past observations with a
target and, as a new set of observations arrives, a new set of hypotheses is formed
from the previous hypotheses. In this algorithm the decision to form a new track
or remove an existing one is delayed until enough observations are collected and
the algorithm returns the hypothesis with the highest posterior. In contrast, our
model is an online tracker. Various heuristics have been developed to overcome
the computational complexity of MHT, its main disadvantage [4], [3], but all
of them sacrifice the optimality of the algorithm while remaining instable in an
environment with a lot of moving objects. Furthermore, the running time at each
step of the algorithm cannot be bounded easily, making it difficult to deploy in
a real-time surveillance system. In [5] a Markov Chain Monte Carlo (MCMC) is
used to deal with data association in a multiple-target tracking problem. MCMC
is a general technique to generate samples from a distribution by constructing
a Markov Chain which has the sampled distribution as stationary distribution.
A Kalman Filter is used to estimate the state of each target and its covariance.
Once a measurement is obtained, a MCMC based method is used to sample the
moves (like splitting a track or merging two tracks) that can be done on the set
of tracks to maximize the posterior pdf of the tracks given the measurements.
This MCMCDA approach is extended in [6] to relational structures. In [6] the
concept of class is used to develop an inference system able to deal with a large

number of related objects. Notice that in this case the objects are *related* but not *in relationship*: they belong to the same class, but there is not explicit representation of the relationship that could exist between them.

In the example given in the previous subsection, the approach presented in [6] would take into account the fact that the tracked objects are all cars and, for this reason, it will assign to them the same transitional model or, if the system is able to distinguish between a small car and a big car this approach will assign different transition models to the two categories (classes) of objects. But this system would not be able to distinguish their behaviors in the proximity of an exit because no relations with the environment are considered. While they could solve this by introducing knowledge about the environment into each transition model, their system could not account for interaction between objects such as those we described above: it would expect a higher speed for a car behind a slowing vehicle, or it might assume the possible departure of a member of a convoy, causing prediction errors. In the model proposed by Milch et.al. each object will have been assigned its own parameters for a common transition model that does not change with variation in the parameters of other vehicles' transitional model.

4   Modeling Behaviors with RDBNs

Relational Dynamic Bayesian Networks. (RDBNs) represent probabilistic dependencies in a dynamic relational domain by extending DBNs to first-order logic (FOL). Suppose the measurements in our example domain are obtained by a video camera. The positions of the targets are the only available measurement but many relations between targets can be inferred from these measures. We propose the inclusion of these relations as predicates of a target in its class to better explain the behavior of a moving target with respect to other objects (moving or not).

In Figure 1, a class for our (simplified) domain is showed. From two successive positions of each car it is possible to compute its direction and, from its

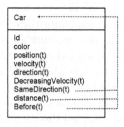

Fig. 1. A possible representation for the class car. Some attributes can be static (as the color), some others can depend on the time (like its velocity and direction). In the example there are also two relationships: *SameDirection*, that says which cars have the same direction of the considered car and *Before* that says which car is immediately in front the considered car.

actual position, which vehicle is behind it. This information will be useful on computing a more precise model able to deal with behaviors that depend on other target's behaviors (in this paper we implement and experiment especially the "slow down" behavior).

We have now to define what we mean with *state, transition model* and *sensor model* for this domain.

- We define as state the set of vectors (p_t^i, v_t^i) for all objects i in the scene, where p_t^i is the position of object i at time t and v_t^i is its speed. For each i $x_i = (p_t^i, v_t^i)$ is the state of the object i.
- For each car j in the scene the transitional model is defined as a Gaussian distribution with mean $\mu_t = A\mu_{t-1} + \epsilon$ where ϵ is a white noise and A is a matrix defined as follows:
  - if $\exists\, i$ such that $Before(i, j)$ holds and $v_{t-1}^i < v_{t-2}^i$ then

$$A = \begin{pmatrix} 1 & 0 & (1 + \frac{r}{1+d})dt & 0 \\ 0 & 1 & 0 & (1 + \frac{r}{1+d})dt \\ 0 & 0 & 1 & 0 \\ 0 & 0 & 0 & 1 \end{pmatrix} \qquad (5)$$

  where r is the ratio between the deceleration at time t of the front car and its speed at the time $t - 1$ and d is the distance between the two cars. We expect the car behind to decelerate as much as the car in front, with the distance acting as discount factor (the further away, the less need to slow down). In the experiments we used $r = \frac{v_t^i - v_{t-1}^i}{v_{t-1}^i}$.

  - otherwise

$$A = \begin{pmatrix} 1 & 0 & dt & 0 \\ 0 & 1 & 0 & dt \\ 0 & 0 & 1 & 0 \\ 0 & 0 & 0 & 1 \end{pmatrix}. \qquad (6)$$

- The sensor model for position is given by:

$$p(z_t|x_t) = \frac{1}{\sqrt{2\pi}\sigma} exp\{\frac{\|z_t, x_t\|^2}{2\sigma^2}\} \qquad (7)$$

  which assumes that the position measured is Gaussian distributed around the true position.

In particular, the transition model presented so far can be graphically described as in Figure 2, where the dependencies between the state of two different cars are explained by the relations that can exist between them given by their relational structure.

The conditions in the transition model can be represented by a *First Order Probabilistic Tree* (FOPT) which can be viewed as a combination of first-order trees [7] and probability estimation trees [8].

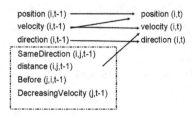

Fig. 2. A possible relational transition model for the example given

A FOPT replaces a vector of probabilities with a tree structure, where leaves represent probabilities of entire sets of objects and nodes represent all combination of the propositional attributes. A FOPT encapsulates an ordered set of probabilistic First Order rules that give the posterior pdf of an event. An example of FOPT for our application is given in figure 3.

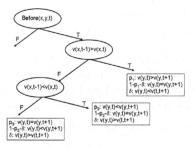

Fig. 3. A possible FOPT for the example given. Intuitively, if for two cars (x and y) $Before(x, y)$ holds and the velocity of x decreases ($v(x, t-1) > v(x, t)$), there is a high probability p_1 that also the velocity of y will decrease.

The proposed model is suitable for other kinds of relations like "being on the right/left" of another target.

5   Implementation and Experiments

In this section we present some preliminary results using a RDBN to model the transition probability of a tracking algorithm. We compare the results obtained by the use of a Particle Filter algorithm that implements our relational model to the ones obtained by the use of a Particle Filter that makes use of a a transition model that does not take into account relations.

5.1   The Particle Filter Algorithm

The Particle Filter (PF) algorithm [9] is a Monte Carlo method that forms the basis for most sequential Monte Carlo filters developed over the past decades.

It is a technique for implementing a recursive Bayesian filter by Monte Carlo simulations. The key idea is to represent the required posterior density function by a set of random samples with associated weights and to compute estimates based on these samples and weights. As the number of samples becomes very large, this Monte Carlo characterization becomes an equivalent representation to the usual functional description of the posterior pdf, and the PF approaches the optimal Bayesian estimate [10].

Let $\{x_{1:k}^i, \omega_k^i\}_{i=1}^{N_s}$ denote a *random measure* that characterizes the posterior pdf $p(x_{1:k}|z_{1:k})$, where $\{x_{1:k}^i, i = 1, ..., N_s\}$, is a set of support points with associated weights $\{\omega_k^i, i = 1, ..., N_s\}$, and $x_{1:k} = \{x_j, j = 1, ..., k\}$, is the set of all states up to time k. The weights are normalized such that $\sum_i \omega_k^i = 1$. Then, the posterior density at time k can be approximated as

$$p(x_{1:k}|z_{1:k}) \approx \sum_{i=1}^{N_s} \omega_k^i \delta(x_{1:k} - x_{1:k}^i). \tag{8}$$

We therefore have a discrete weighted approximation to the true posterior, $p(x_{1:k}|z_{1:k})$. The weights are chosen using the principle of *importance sampling*.

At each iteration, one could have samples constituting an approximation to $p(x_{1:k-1}|z_{1:k-1})$ and want to approximate $p(x_{0:k}|z_{1:k})$ with a new set of samples.

The PF algorithm, thus, consists of recursive propagation of the weights and support points as each measurement is received sequentially.

5.2 Experiments

In our experiments we compare the performance (defined as the ability to generate tracks as close as possible to the true trajectory) of two PFs, one that uses our relational transition model (RTM) and the other that uses a transition model that does not take into account relations (TM). The transitional model used in the latter algorithm is a transitional model based on the matrix A (Eq. 6) without the relations. The relational model is the one above. In both cases, Data Association was implemented using a simple algorithm that associates at each prediction the nearest measure obtained (in a certain distance range). The first time that it happen that no measurement is near enough, it assumes the measure to be the prediction itself, the second time it make the track "dying".

Results are obtained on a data set of 3 objects (Obj) moving in a one-dimensional path, each of them starting at the same time and going for 50 time steps. The data set is characterized by the fact that at a certain time step the object that leads the line slows down and afterwards the others have to slow down as well.

The RTM at each step, for each car checks if the distance with the car before is lower than a given threshold and if the car before slowed down at the previous time step, in that case it computes the prediction of the next state using (Eq. 5). The results are compared through their average error only for those steps in which the relational model (Eq. 5) has been used. For each of the measurements which the relational model has been used we have computed the distance between the corrected state (i.e, the filtered position given the measurement) and the true state. When the tracks has been completely processed, we computed the average of these distances along each track obtaining the average error. We iterated this process 100 times for each of the two methods (RTM and TM) and at the end of the simulations the average of the average distances over the 100 iterations has been calculated. We compare the results for number of particles (M) equal to 100 and 1000 and values of the variance of the sensor model (σ crf. Eq. 7) equal to 0.1, 0.3, 0.5, 1, 1.5, 2 and 3.

The error for the first car is not significant because to track it the system would never use the relational hypothesis. The average errors for the other two cars are reported in the following table:

	$M = 100$		$M = 1000$			$M = 100$		$M = 1000$	
	RTM	TM	RTM	TM		RTM	TM	RTM	TM
$\sigma = 0.1$					$\sigma = 0.3$				
Obj1	37.02	40.95	38.51	30.08	Obj1	7.26	10.87	4.00	5.17
Obj2	35.05	39.69	35.33	33.91	Obj2	11.57	19.42	8.23	12.36
Obj3	34.31	37.57	37.69	34.79	Obj3	12.98	20.88	8.32	15.90
$\sigma = 0.5$					$\sigma = 1.0$				
Obj1	3.49	3.26	2.36	3.17	Obj1	2.65	2.93	2.23	2.63
Obj2	6.34	8.50	3.68	4.95	Obj2	5.40	6.18	3.56	4.19
Obj3	6.43	9.52	3.62	5.92	Obj3	5.18	6.09	3.42	4.57
$\sigma = 2.0$					$\sigma = 3.0$				
Obj1	3.01	3.84	2.76	3.37	Obj1	3.94	4.25	3.62	3.97
Obj2	6.04	6.68	5.42	6.02	Obj2	6.14	6.91	5.96	6.74
Obj3	5.29	6.82	4.94	5.94	Obj3	5.63	6.86	5.75	6.38

From the obtained results we can conclude that on average our method tracks the real state more precisely than a standard method. However, the two trackers has been coded in the same way, using the same Data Association and the same Importance Sampling Approach; the computational time averaged over 100 iterations of the two trackers using 100 particles is for the PF that uses the Relational Model 1.61 s and the other takes 0.1 seconds less.

We can finally conclude that the method presented has shown to be more effective in terms of precision of tracking without being more computational demanding than a standard tracker.

6   Conclusion

In this paper we proposed the use of relations to model particular correlations between entities, aimed at improving multiple targets tracking. A RDBN has been used to represent the dependencies between objects attributes, scene's elements and the evolution of state variables over time. Preliminary results has shown the effectiveness and efficiency of the method proposed in a simple environment.

Our future works, now, is looking at modeling more complex behaviors as the ones that present relationships with the environment (for example, tracking the relationship "traveling together" in our highway scenario). Our aim in the future is to include relationships in the state: this means to maintain probabilistic beliefs about uncertainties that must be tracked. Probably in this case a new tracking algorithm would be necessary.

Another aspect we would like to explore is the application of these models to other domains such monitoring traffic flows, detection of unattended goods, consumer monitoring and so on.

Acknowledgements

We would like to thanks prof. Craig Boutilier for his invaluable suggestions. We would also like also to mention that RDBNs were first presented in a paper by S. Sanghai, et al. in 2005, that was recently retracted by the authors.

References

1. Friedman, N., Getoor, L., Koller, D., Pfeffer, A.: Learning Probabilistic Relational Models. In: IJCAI, pp. 1300–1309 (1999)
2. Murphy, K.: Dynamic Bayesian Networks: Representation, Inference and Learning. Computer Science Division, University of California, Berkeley (2002)
3. Reid, D.: An algorithm for tracking multiple targets. IEEE Transactions on Automatic Control (1979)
4. Cox, I.J., Hingorani, S.L.: An efficient implementation of Reid's multiple hypothesis tracking algorithm and its evaluation for the purpose of visual tracking. IEEE Transactions on Pattern Analysis and Machine Intelligence (1996)
5. Oh, S., Russell, S., Sastry, S.: Markov chain Monte Carlo data association for general multiple-target tracking problems. In: 43rd IEEE Conference on Decision and Control, 2004. CDC (2004)
6. Milch, B., Russell, S.J.: General-Purpose MCMC Inference over Relational Structures. UAI (2006)
7. Blockeel, H., De Raedt, L.: Top-Down Induction of First-Order Logical Decision Trees. Artif. Intell. 101(1-2) (1998)
8. Foster, J.: Provost and Pedro Domingos: Tree Induction for Probability-Based Ranking. Machine Learning 52(3) (2003)
9. Doucet, A., Defreitas, N., Gordon, N.: Sequential Monte Carlo Methods in Practice (2001)
10. Arulampalam, S., Maskell, S., Gordon, N.: A tutorial on particle filters for online nonlinear/non-Gaussian Bayesian tracking. IEEE Transactions on Signal Processing (2002)

Multiple Human Tracking in High-Density Crowds

Irshad Ali and Matthew N. Dailey

Computer Science and Information Management
Asian Institute of Technology,
Bangkok, Thailand
Irshad.Ali@ait.ac.th,
mdailey@ait.ac.th

Abstract. In this paper, we present a fully automatic approach to multiple human detection and tracking in high density crowds in the presence of extreme occlusion. Human detection and tracking in high density crowds is an unsolved problem. Standard preprocessing techniques such as background modeling fail when most of the scene is in motion. We integrate human detection and tracking into a single framework, and introduce a confirmation-by-classification method to estimate confidence in a tracked trajectory, track humans through occlusions, and eliminate false positive detections. We use a Viola and Jones AdaBoost cascade classifier for detection, a particle filter for tracking, and color histograms for appearance modeling. An experimental evaluation shows that our approach is capable of tracking humans in high density crowds despite occlusions.

Keywords: Human detection, head detection, pedestrian tracking, crowd tracking, AdaBoost detection cascade, particle filter.

1   Introduction

As public concern about crime and terrorist activity increases, the importance of public security is growing, and video surveillance systems are increasingly widespread tools for monitoring, management, and law enforcement in public areas. Since it is difficult for human operators to monitor surveillance cameras continuously, there is a strong interest in automated analysis of video surveillance data. Some of the important problems include pedestrian tracking, behavior understanding, anomaly detection, and unattended baggage detection. In this paper, we focus on *pedestrian tracking*.

The pedestrian tracking problem is very difficult when the task is to monitor and manage large crowds in gathering areas such as airports and train stations. There has been a great deal of progress in recent years, but still most state-of-the-art systems are inapplicable to large crowd management situations because they rely on either background modeling [1,2,3], body part detection [3,4], or body shape models [5,6,1]. These techniques make it impossible to track large numbers of people in very crowded scenes in which the majority of the scene

J. Blanc-Talon et al. (Eds.): ACIVS 2009, LNCS 5807, pp. 540–549, 2009.
© Springer-Verlag Berlin Heidelberg 2009

is in motion (rendering background modeling useless) and most of the humans' bodies are partially or fully occluded. Under these conditions, we believe that the *human head* is the only body part that can be robustly detected and tracked, so in this paper we present a method for tracking pedestrians by detecting and tracking their heads rather than their full bodies.

Our system assumes a single static camera placed a sufficient height that the heads of people traversing the scene can be observed. For initial detection we use a standard Viola and Jones Haar-like AdaBoost cascade [7], and for tracking we use a particle filter [8,9] for each head that incorporates a simple motion model and a color histogram-based appearance model.

Although this basic approach works very well in many cases, it suffers from two major issues: 1) shadows and other objects often cause false head detections, and 2) tracked heads are frequently lost due to partial or full occlusion. To address these issues, we introduce a *confirmation-by-classification* method that, on each frame, first uses the Viola and Jones classifier to confirm the tracking result for each live trajectory, then eliminates any live trajectory that has not been confirmed for some number of frames. This process allows us to minimize the number of false positive trajectories without losing track of heads that are occluded for a short period of time.

In an experimental evaluation with our current implementation, we find that on cheap hardware, the system requires approximately 2 seconds per frame to process a 640×480 video stream containing an average of 35.35 individuals per frame using 20 particles per head. We achieve a hit rate of 76.8% with an average of 2 false positives per frame. To our knowledge, this is the largest-scale human tracking experiment performed thus far, and the results are extremely encouraging. In future work, with further algorithmic improvements and run time optimization, we hope to achieve robust, real time pedestrian tracking for even larger crowds.

2   Human Head Detection and Tracking

In this section we first provide a summary of our tracking algorithm and then provide the details for each step. A block diagram is shown in Fig. 1.

2.1   Summary

1. Acquire input crowd video V.
2. In first frame v_0 of V, detect heads. Let N_0 be the number of detected heads.
3. Initialize trajectories T_j, $1 \leq j \leq N_0$ with initial positions $x_{j,0}$.
4. Initialize occlusion count O_j for each trajectory to 0.
5. Initialize the appearance model (color histogram) h_j for each trajectory from the region around $x_{j,0}$.
6. For each subsequent frame v_i of input video,
   (a) For each existing trajectory T_j,
      i. Use motion model to predict the distribution $p(x_{j,i} \mid x_{j,i-1})$, over locations for head j in frame i, creating a set of candidate particles $x_{j,i}^{(k)}, 1 \leq k \leq K$.

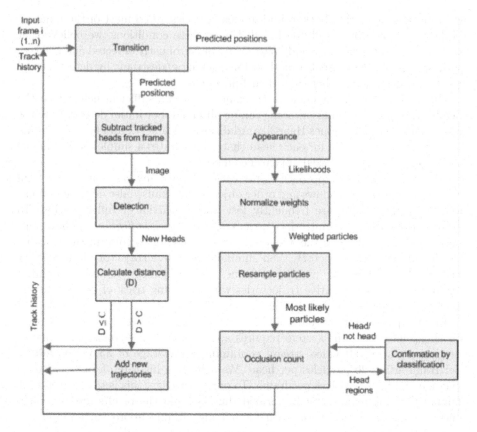

Fig. 1. Block diagram of the tracking algorithm. D is the distance between a newly detected head and a the nearest predicted location, and C is a threshold (in pixels) less than the width of the tracking window.

    ii. Compute the color histogram $h^{(k)}$ and likelihood $p(h^{(k)} \mid x_{j,i}^{(k)}, h_j)$ for each particle k using the appearance model.

    iii. Resample the particles according to their likelihood. Let k^* be the index of the most likely particle.

    iv. Perform confirmation by classification: run the head detector on the location $x_{j,i}^{(k^*)}$. If the location is classified as a head, reset $O_j \leftarrow 0$; else increase $O_j \leftarrow O_j + 1$.

    v. If O_j is greater than threshold, remove trajectory j.

 (b) Search for new heads in frame v_i and compute the Euclidean distance $D_{j,k}$ between each newly detected head k and each existing trajectory T_j. When $D_{j,k} > C$ for all j, where C is a threshold (in pixels) less than the width of the tracking window, initialize a new trajectory for detection k.

2.2   Detection

For object detection, there are many possibile algorithms; we use the Viola and
Jones technique [7,10]. We train an AdaBoost cascade using Haar-like features
off line. Then, at run time, we use the classifier in two ways, 1) as a detector,
running a sliding window over the image at the specific range of scales expected
for the scene, or 2) as a confirmer, to check whether the maximum likelihood
head position predicted by the particle filter is sufficiently head-like to continue
tracking.

2.3   Particle Filter

For tracking we use a particle filter [8,9]. The particle filter is well known to
enable robust object tracking (see e.g. [11,12]). We use the standard approach
in which the uncertainty about an object's state (position) is represented as a
set of weighted particles, each particle representing one possible state. The filter
propagates particles particles from frame $i-1$ to frame i using a motion model,
computes a weight for each propagated particle using a sensor or appearance
model, then resamples the particles according to their weights. The initial distribution for the filter is centered on the location of the object the first time it
is detected. Here are the steps in more detail:

1. **Predict:** we predict $p(x_{j,i} \mid x_{j,i-1})$, a distribution over head j's position in
   frame i given our belief in its position in frame $i-1$. The motion model is
   described in the next section.
2. **Measure:** for each propagated particle k, we measure the likelihood $p(h^{(k)} \mid
   x_{j,i}^{(k)}, h_j)$ using a color histogram-based appearance model. After computing
   the likelihood of each particle we treat the likelihoods as weights, normalizing
   them to sum to 1.
3. **Resample:** we resample the particles to avoid degenerate weights. Without
   resampling, over time, the highest-weight particle would tend to a weight of
   one and the other weights would tend to zero. Resampling removes many
   of the low weight particles and replicates the higher-weight particles. We
   thus obtain a new set of equally-weighted particles. We use the resampling
   technique described in [13].

2.4   Motion Model

Our motion model is based on a second-order auto-regressive dynamical model.
The autoregressive model assumes the next state y_t of a system is a function of
some number of previous states and a noise random variable ϵ_t:

$$y_t = f(y_{t-1}, y_{t-2}, ..., y_{t-p}, \epsilon_t).$$

In particular, we assume the simple second-order linear autoregressive model

$$x_{j,i} = 2x_{j,i-1} - x_{j,i-2} + \epsilon_i$$

in which ϵ_i is distributed as a circular Gaussian.

2.5   Appearance Model

Our appearance model is based on color histograms. We compute a color histogram h_j in HSV space for each newly detected head and save it to compute particle likelihoods in future frames. To compute a particle's likelihood we use the Bhattacharyya similarity coefficient between model histogram h_j and observed histogram $h^{(k)}$ as follows, assuming n bins in each histogram:

$$p(h^{(k)} \mid x_{j,i}^{(k)}, h_j) \propto e^{-d(h_j, h^{(k)})},$$

where

$$d(h_j, h^{(k)}) = 1 - \sum_{b=1}^{n} \sqrt{h_{j,b} h_b^{(k)}}$$

and $h_{j,b}$ and $h_b^{(k)}$ denote bin b of h_j and $h^{(k)}$, respectively. A more sophisticated appearance model based on local histograms along with other information such as spatial or structural information would most likely improve our tracking performance, but we currently use a global histogram computed over the entire detection window because of its simplicity.

2.6   Confirmation-by-Classification

To reduce tracking errors, we introduce a simple confirmation-by-classification method, described in detail in this section.

Recovery from Misses. Due to occlusion and appearance variation, we may not detect all heads in the first frame or when they initially appear. To solve this problem in each image, we search for new heads in all regions of the image not predicted by the motion model for a previously tracked head. Any newly detected head within some distance C of the predicted position of a previously tracked head is assumed to be associated with the existing trajectory and ignored. If the distance is greater than C, we create a new trajectory for that detection. We currently set C to be 50% of the width of the detection window.

Reduction of False Detections. Shadows and other non-head objects in the scene tend to produce transient false detections and tracking errors. In order to prevent transient false detections from being tracked through time, we use the head detector to confirm the estimated head position for each trajectory and eliminate any trajectory not confirmed for some number of frames. To implement this, we use a trajectory occlusion count. When head j is first detected and its trajectory is initialized, we set the occlusion count $O_j = 0$. After updating the head's position in frame i, we confirm estimated position through detection. Occlusion counts of trajectories not confirmed through classification are incremented, and occlusion counts of confirmed trajectories are reset to $O_j = 0$. Any trajectory that is not confirmed for some threshold number of frames is eliminated.

Tracking through Temporary Occlusion. The occlusion counting scheme just described also serves to help track a head through a partial or full occlusion. When a tracked head becomes partially or fully occluded, it will typically fail the confirmation by classification test, in which case we increase the trajectory's occlusion count. So long as an occlusion is brief and the motion model is not severely violated, the trjactory can be recovered in a subsequent frame.

3 Experimental Evaluation

3.1 Training Data

To train the Viola and Jones Haar-like AdaBoost cascade detector, we cropped 4325 heads from videos collected from various places and scaled them to 20×20 pixels. We also collected 2200 negative images. The detailed training parameters are given in Table 1. The training process required about 72 hours on an Intel Pentium 4 2.8GHz with 2GB RAM. We used the OpenCV `haartraining` utility to train the classifier.

Table 1. Head detector training parameters

Parameters	Values	Description
npos	4235	Number of positive samples
nneg	2200	Number of negative samples
nstages	20	Number of training stages
minhitrate	0.995	Minimum hit rate per stage (99.5%)
maxfalsealarm	0.5	Maximum false alarm rate per stage (50%)
mode	All	Use the full set of both upright and 45 degree rotated features
width, height	20	Training image patch width and height
boosttypes	DAB	Discrete AdaBoost.

3.2 Test Data

To evaluate our algorithm, we captured a video at 640×480 pixels and 30 frames per second at the Mochit light rail station in Bangkok, Thailand. A sample frame is shown in Figure 2. We then hand labeled the locations of all heads at least 20×20 pixels in the first few frames and a sample of the subsequent frames with gaps to test long tracking. We labeled a total of 40 frames containing a total of 1414 heads, for an average of 35.35 heads/frame. To evaluate our algorithm we compare the tracked heads with the hand-labeled ground truth and determine number of correctly tracked heads, missed heads and false positives.

Our algorithm is designed to track heads in high density crowds. The performance of any tracking algorithm will depend upon the density of the crowd. In order to characterize this relationship, we introduce the simple crowd density measure

$$\text{Crowd density} = \frac{\text{Total number of pixels in all individuals' bounding boxes}}{\text{Total number of pixel in the frame}}.$$

Fig. 2. A sample frame from the Mochit station dataset

According to this measure, the highest crowd density in our test sequence is 0.63, which is higher than that of any publicly-available pedestrian tracking video database.

Since the publicly available pedestrian tracking databases only contain low density crowds, a direct comparison of our high-density tracking results with other researchers' low-density tracking results is unfortunately not possible. We have also attempted to run the publicly available pedestrian tracking implementations on our data, but they fail due to different assumptions about the data. In any case, to encourage other researchers to attempt tracking the pedestrians in our data set, we make the data available at http://www.cs.ait.ac.th/ mdailey/headtracking/acivs09-5950.zip.

3.3 Implementation Details

We implemented the system in C++ with OpenCV without any special code optimization. Our approach relies mainly on object detection without a need for background subtraction. Our algorithm can thus track both moving and static humans in the scene. We detect heads and create initial trajectories from the first frame and then track heads from frame to frame. Further implementation details are given in the following sections.

Trajectory Initialization and Termination. We use the head detector to find heads in the first frame and create initial trajectories. To detect when new heads appear in subsequent frames, we also run the detector to search for heads in regions of each frame not predicted by the motion model for some existing trajectory. We first try to associate new heads with existing trajectories; when this fails for a new head detection, a new trajectory is initialized from the current frame. Any head trajectory in the "exit zone" (close to the image border) for which the motion model predicts a location outside the frame is eliminated.

Identity Management. It is also important to assign and maintain object identities (IDs) automatically during tracking. We assign a unique ID to each trajectory during initialization. The tracking and confirmation-by-classification processes maintain the object ID during tracking. Trajectories that are temporarily lost due to occlusion are reassigned the same ID on recovery to avoid identity changes.

(a) Frame 2.   (b) Frame 10.

(c) Frame 17.   (d) Frame 22.

Fig. 3. Sample tracking results on the Mochit test video. Red rectangles indicate estimated head positions, and green rectangles indicate ground truth head positions.

3.4   Results

There were an average 35.35 individuals per frame over the 40 hand-labeled ground truth frames, for a total of 1414 heads. We used 20 particles per trajectory. The average correct tracking rate was 76.8%, with 2.05 false positives per frame and 8.2 missing heads per frame. The processing time was approximately 2 seconds/frame for a frame size of 640×480 on an Intel Pentium 4 2.8GHz with 2GB RAM. A few sample frames with tracking results are shown in Figure 3. Using a smaller frame size, a faster machine, parallelization or a GPU or multi-core CPU, and/or code-level optimization, we expect that the processing time could be reduced significantly. Detailed results are shown in Table 2.

Table 2. Tracking Results

Total Heads	Tracked	False Positives	Missed
1414	1086 (76.8%)	82 (2.05/frame)	328 (8.2/frame)

Finally, to determine the difficulty of our data set in comparison to other existing pedestrian tracking datasets, we compared the density of our dataset with the CAVIAR dataset [14] and the Campus Plaza sequence [1], using the method described in Section 3.2. The results of the comparison are shown in Table 3.

Table 3. Crowd density comparison results

Mochit	CAVIAR [14]	Campus Plaza [1]
0.63	0.27	0.23

4   Discussion and Conclusion

Tracking people in high density crowds such as the one shown in Figure 2 is a real challenge and is still an open problem. In this paper, we propose a new algorithm based on a combination of head detection, appearance-based tracking with a particle filter, and confirmation-by-classification. Our experimental results demonstrate the promise of the method. It is particularly encouraging that the particle filter works well with a very small number of particles (20).

To further understand the performance of the algorithm, we examined the errors it makes on our test set more closely. We found that most of the missed heads were those which were partially or fully occluded. We also found that most of the false detections were shadows or human body parts other than heads. A few false detections arose from background features such as holes in the ground.

In future work we plan a more extensive evaluation of the method and improvements in the appearance model using other image features such as contours.

Acknowledgments

We thank Tao Zhao for providing the Campus Plaza sequence to us. Irshad Ali was supported by a graduate fellowship from the Higher Education Commission (HEC), Pakistan.

References

1. Zhao, T., Nevatia, R., Wu, B.: Segmentation and tracking of multiple humans in crowded environments. IEEE Transactions on Pattern Analysis and Machine Intelligence 30(7) (2008)
2. Wu, B., Nevatia, R.: Detection and tracking of multiple, partially occluded humans by bayesian combination of edgelet based part detectors. International Journal of Computer Vision 75(2), 247–266 (2007)
3. Wu, B., Nevatia, R., Li, Y.: Segmentation of multiple, partially occluded objects by grouping, merging, assigning part detection responses. In: IEEE Conference on Computer Vision and Pattern Recognition, CVPR (2008)
4. Andriluka, M., Roth, S., Schiele, B.: People-tracking-by-detection and people-detection-by-tracking. In: IEEE Conference on Computer Vision and Pattern Recognition (CVPR), pp. 1–8 (2008)
5. Ramanan, D., Forsyth, D.A., Zisserman, A.: Tracking people by learning their appearance. IEEE Transactions on Pattern Analysis and Machine Intelligence 29(1), 65–81 (2007)
6. Zhao, T., Nevatia, R.: Tracking multiple humans in crowded environment. In: Proceedings IEEE Conference Computer Vision and Pattern Recognition, vol. 2 (2004)
7. Viola, P., Jones, M.: Robust real time object detection. International Journal of Computer Vision (IJCV) 57, 137–154 (2001)
8. Isard, M., Blake, A.: A mixed-state condensation tracker with automatic model-switching. In: IEEE International Conference on Computer Vision, pp. 107–112 (1998)
9. Doucet, A., de Freitas, N., Gordon, N.: Sequential Monte Carlo Methods in Practice. Springer, New York (2001)
10. Viola, P., Jones, M.: Rapid object detection using a boosted cascade of simple features. In: IEEE Conference on Computer Vision and Pattern Recognition (CVPR), pp. 511–518 (2001)
11. Kang, H.G., Kim, D.: Real-time multiple people tracking using competitive condensation. Pattern Recognition 38, 1045–1058 (2005)
12. Martnez, S.V., Knebel, J., Thiran, J.: Multi-object tracking using the particle filter algorithm on the top-view plan. In: European Signal Processing Conference, EUSIPCO (2004)
13. Rui, Y., Chen, Y.: Better proposal distributions: Object tracking using unscented particle filter. In: IEEE Conference on Computer Vision and Pattern Recognition (CVPR), vol. 2, pp. II786–II793 (2001)
14. CAVIAR: Data set, http://homepages.inf.ed.ac.uk/rbf/CAVIARDATA1

3D Face Alignment via Cascade 2D Shape Alignment and Constrained Structure from Motion

Yunshu Hou, Ping Fan, Ilse Ravyse, and Hichem Sahli

Research Group on Audio Visual Signal Processing (AVSP)
Vrije Universiteit Brussel, Department ETRO,
Pleinlaan 2, 1050 Brussel
{yhou,pfan,icravyse,hsahli}@etro.vub.ac.be

Abstract. In this paper, we consider fitting a 3D wireframe face model to continuous video sequences for the tasks of simultaneous tracking of rigid head motion and non-rigid facial animation. We propose a two-level integrated model for accurate 3D face alignment. At the low level, the 2D shape is accurately extracted via a regularized shape model relied on a cascaded parameter/constraint prediction and optimization. At the high level, those already accurately aligned points from the low level are used to constrain the projected 3D wireframe alignment. Using a steepest descent approach, the algorithm is able to extract simultaneously the parameters related to the face expression and to the 3D posture. Extensive fitting and tracking experiments demonstrate the feasibility, accuracy and effectiveness of the developed methods. A performance evaluation also shows that the proposed methods can outperform the fitting based on an active appearance model search and can tackle many disadvantages associated with such approaches.

1 Introduction

Fitting a 3D facial model to an image sequence of a face allows recovering the face pose, its shape, and the facial appearance. The recovered information can then be used in many applications, among others one can cite: facial motion capture for animating a synthetic avatar, facial expression analysis and/or synthesis, realistic character animation in 3D computer games, and very low bitrate model based video coding. Moreover, such recovered information could also be used for the automatic classification of the so called action Units of Ekman & Friesen [1], which represent the muscular activity that produces momentary changes in facial appearance. Considering all these applications, the main requirements of model fitting algorithms are accuracy, i.e. accurate feature extraction and rigid head motion and non-rigid facial animation, and the efficiency of the fitting algorithms.

Automatic three-dimensional rigid and non-rigid motion parameters estimation from monocular video sequences is a very challenging problem in computer vision literature. For facial images, the proposed techniques can be divided into

J. Blanc-Talon et al. (Eds.): ACIVS 2009, LNCS 5807, pp. 550–561, 2009.

two classes, namely, *facial features based techniques*, and *combined facial texture and features techniques*. The former techniques use local texture to track feature points, which are then used to guide the three-dimensional motion estimation [2,3,4,5,6,7]. The latter techniques need to build-up the detailed three-dimensional face model of both shape and texture, and then align the model into the current sequence to obtain the proper shape, motion and texture parameters that best simulate the current face appearance [8,9,10,11].

In *facial features based techniques* there are two steps: two dimensional facial feature points extraction and three dimensional motion inference based on extracted facial feature points. For the feature points extraction there exist many methods in the literatures like Kanade-Lucas-Tomasi Tracker (KLT) [12] and Active Shape Model (ASM) [13], readers are referred to [14] for the details. For three-dimensional motion parameters inference given the tracked feature points, there are two typical ways: factorization based Structure From Motion (SFM) [15,16,17] and recursive model based SFM [3,18]. Generally, factorization based techniques work quite well for rigid motion models, however for nonrigid motion the two steps factorization (first rigid followed by nonrigid) often have poor estimation performance. Such approach refines the estimation using bundle adjustment or random samplings techniques [17], and hence requires the entire sequence. In recursive model based techniques there exist two ways: simultaneous rigid and nonrigid motions estimation [10] and sequential rigid and nonrigid motions estimation [11].

In *combined facial texture and features techniques* the approaches generally require a large database for the training of both 3D shape model and 3D texture model, which is computationally expensive [9] because of the required 'warping' of the texture while aligning the model and the huge model parameters to be estimated. It has been also reported, that direct texture-based motion parameters estimation may not produce precise point localization compared to *feature-based techniques*, especially for face contours and key facial components; however it can achieve better overall robustness and have gained much attention from model based coding research groups [10].

In face analysis literature there exist another important class of approaches such as Active Contour Models (ACM) [19], Active Shape Models (ASM) [13], Bayes Tangent Shape Models (BTSM) [20], Active Appearance Models (AAM) [21] and their extensions ([22,23,24,25,26,27]). The ASM-like techniques (ACM, ASM and BTSM) fall into *facial features based techniques*, and the AAM-like methods fall into *combined facial texture and features techniques*. In [20] BTSM is proposed to greatly improve the facial feature extraction. In [22] the same idea is generalized to multi-view face alignment and in [23] into 3D face alignment. In [26] and [27] two most advanced face alignment algorithms are proposed. Recently 3D AAM is more popular [25,24]. In [24] the bilinear active appearance model is proposed to simultaneously model facial appearance variations caused by pose, identity and expression. In [25] the asymmetry issue is modeled into AAM to further improve the facial alignment preciseness.

Even though the current facial analysis techniques have yielded significant results, their success is limited by the conditions imposed by many real applications such as precisely tracking person-adapted features, taking into account scene variations (illumination changes and facial expressions) and the computation efficiency. Having in mind that, using a learned overall 3D texture model together with a 3D shape model is computationally expensive, and may produce less precise point localization in key facial components [9], in this paper we propose to replace the time consuming 3D texture 'warping' with 2D image operations as constraints for the 3D model estimation. More precisely, we use an extension of the 2D facial feature extraction method of [14], which relies on a cascaded parameter prediction and optimization, to obtain a precise features tracking on a face image sequence. Then a parameterized 3D wire-frame model, the candide-3 model [28], is automatically fitted to these extracted 2D facial features by expressing a least-squares minimization problem to optimize the semantic and compact parameters of the 3D model.

The remainder of the paper is organized as follows. Section 2 summarizes the whole structure of the proposed monocular three dimensional face motion analysis system and section 3 gives the problem formulations. Section 4 describes the two dimensional constrained shape estimation technique and Section 5 describes the three dimensional rigid and nonrigid motion estimation algorithm. Finally, in Section 6 extensive experimental results are discussed and some conclusions are drawn in Section 7.

2   System Overview

The following notations have been adopted in the proposed system (we omit the subscript t):

- For each input frame I_t, we consider the following sets of feature points:
  - $\mathbf{s} = \{s_i\}_{i=1}^{L=83} = (s_1^x, s_1^y, \ldots, s_L^x, s_L^y)^t$, the coordinates of the L feature points on the 2D image, depicted as black dots in figure 1;
  - $\mathbf{s}^c = \{s_i^c\}_{i=1}^{C=6}$, a subset of $\mathbf{s}$ corresponding to the facial component points, being the eyes and mouth corners, depicted as green crosses in figure 1;
  - $\mathbf{s}^{3D} = \{s_i^{3D}\}_{i=1}^{M=55}$, a subset of $\mathbf{s}$ corresponding to an extended set of facial component points around eyes, brows, nose, upper/lower lips and profile, as indicated in red dots in figure 1;
- The Candide 3D shape wireframe model is given by the coordinates of the 3D vertices $P_i(X, Y, Z), i = 1 \ldots N, N = 113$ and can be expressed by a $3N$-vector $\mathbf{g} = (X_1, Y_1, Z_1, \ldots, X_N, Y_N, Z_N)^t$;
- the estimated 2D head pose, output of the low-level steps, is denoted $\hat{\gamma} = (\hat{s}, \hat{\theta}, \hat{t}_x, \hat{t}_y)^t$ where s is the 2D image plane scaling, θ rotation and t_x, t_y translation, respectively;
- the estimated 3D face model parameters are denoted $\mathbf{c} = (\omega, \mathbf{t}, \alpha)^t$ where α denotes facial animation parameters, ω, the 3D rotation parameters, and $\mathbf{t}$, the 3D translation parameters.

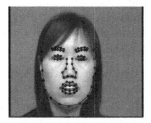

Fig. 1. Considered facial feature points

In this paper, we sequentially infer from each image frame, the dynamic behavior of a 3D face model. We propose a two-level integrated model for accurate 3D face alignment. At the low level, the 2D face shape is accurately extracted via the following cascaded processing: (i) kernel-based face detection and tracking, resulting in the detection and tracking of the facial region and its 2D pose $\hat{\gamma}_t$ [29]; (ii) accurate eye and mouth corners detection and tracking using the KLT Tracker [14], augmented with 2D head pose constraints and the open/close dynamics of eye/mouth, resulting in a set of eye/mouth landmarks, denoted as $\mathbf{s}_t^c$; (iii) full shape landmarks, $\mathbf{s}_t$, detection and tracking, as well as refinement of the head pose $\hat{\gamma}_t$, using the Constrained Shape Model (CSM) of [14]. The high level module considers (iv) the correspondence of a subset $\mathbf{s}_t^{3D}$ of $\mathbf{s}_t$ and the 3D vertices of the Candide model to solve an SFM problem resulting in the 3D rigid motion of the head and the 3D nonrigid facial deformations, being the parameter vector $\mathbf{c}_t$.

3   Problem Formulation

We adopt the Candide-3 model as the basis model in our study [28]. This 3D deformable wireframe model was first developed for the purpose of model-based image coding and facial animation and has exhibited many desirable properties in tracking applications. The 3D shape of this wireframe model is directly recorded in coordinate form. It is given by the coordinates of the 3D vertices $P_i, i = 1 \ldots N$, where $N = 113$ is the number of vertices. Thus, different face shapes and animations up to a global scale can be fully described by a $3N$-vector, $\mathbf{g}$, the concatenation of the 3D coordinates of all vertices P_i:

$$\mathbf{g}(\sigma, \alpha) = \bar{\mathbf{g}} + \mathbf{S}\sigma + \mathbf{A}\alpha \tag{1}$$

where

- $\bar{\mathbf{g}}$ is the *mean shape* of the model;
- $\mathbf{S}$ is the *shape unit matrix*, the columns of which are the selected *shape unit vectors* (SUV) from the candide model;
- $\mathbf{A}$ is the *animation unit matrix*, the columns of which are the selected *animation unit vectors* (AUV) from the candide model;

- column vector σ is the shape control parameters (sp) describing the overall 3D face shape difference between person;
- and column vector α is the animation control parameters (ap) representing the facial expression within the same person.

In this study, we use 13 modes (SUV) for the *shape unit matrix* and 7 modes (AUV) for the *animation unit matrix*. The selected 7 AUVs and corresponding animation parameters (ap) are: AUV6 Eyes closed (ap1), AUV3 Brow lowerer (ap2), AUV5 Outer brow raiser (ap3), AUV0 Upper lip raiser (ap4), AUV11 Jaw drop (ap5), AUV2 Lip stretcher (ap6) and AUV14 Lip corner depressor (ap7). Unlike the reduced model used in [30] the full Candide model used in our system facilitates us to estimate face shape variation between people and hence to track person-adapted features more precisely.

In summary, the *3D facial model parameters* in the proposed system is given by a 26-dimensional vector $\mathbf{c}$:

$$\mathbf{c} = (\sigma, \alpha, \omega, \mathbf{t}) \tag{2}$$

where $\omega = (\omega_X, \omega_Y, \omega_Z)^t$ and $\mathbf{t} = (t_X, t_Y, \beta t_Z)^t$ represent the rotation and translation i.e. the rigid head motion.

Given a video sequence depicting a moving head/face, we would like to recover, for each frame, the 3D head pose $(\omega, \mathbf{t})$, and the facial actions encoded by the facial control vector (σ, α). In other words, we would like to estimate the vector $\mathbf{c}$ (equation 2) at time t given the current observed data, denoted $\hat{\mathbf{u}}$. In the proposed system we use the extracted 2D facial feature points as observed data $\hat{\mathbf{u}}$, which can be seen as function of the *3D facial model parameters* $\mathbf{c}$:

$$\mathbf{u} = \mathbf{u}(\mathbf{c}) \tag{3}$$

where the 3D-2D points correspondence is directly obtained from the projection of the 3D candide model by a central projection model [3]. Then the 3D Model fitting can be defined as:

$$\tilde{\mathbf{c}} = \arg\min_{(\mathbf{c})} \sum_{i \in N} \|\mathbf{u}^i(\mathbf{c}) - \hat{\mathbf{u}}^i\|^2 \tag{4}$$

where $\mathbf{u}^i(\mathbf{c})$ is the i-th point of the projected parameterized 3D candide model and $\hat{\mathbf{u}}^i$ is the corresponding observed 2D facial feature point.

4   Two Dimensional Constrained Shape Estimation

Given a sequence $I(t)$, the task of 2D facial feature points extraction and tracking is to locate a number of L facial feature points $\mathbf{s}(t)$ on the 2D image for each frame. In BTSM [20], applying PCA analysis on a set of training shapes to model the 2D face shape variation due to the nonrigid motion and shape difference between people, the face shape $\mathbf{s}$ (here we omit t for simplification) can be expressed as:

$$\mathbf{s}(\mathbf{p}) = W(\bar{\mathbf{s}}_T + \mathbf{Q}\mathbf{b}; \phi) \tag{5}$$

where $\bar{\mathbf{s}}_T$ is the mean shape vector of a set of aligned face training shapes after Generalized Procrustes Analysis (GPA) [31], called the *tangent shape space*, $\mathbf{Q}$ is the shape basis matrix, $\mathbf{b}$ is a vector of tangent shape parameters, and $W(.; \phi)$ is a global similarity transformation from the tangent shape space to the image space with parameters ϕ. The 2D shape parameters are denoted as $\mathbf{p} = (\phi, \mathbf{b})$.

To find the 2D shape parameters $\mathbf{p}$ for a given image I, an iterative searching algorithm is usually used in ASM/BTSM: (i) find an observed shape $\mathbf{y}$ by locally finding the best nearby match of the pre-learned local texture model for each point; (ii) optimize the shape parameters $\mathbf{p}$ based on new matched points. In the second step, we optimize the following energy function:

$$E(\mathbf{p}|\mathbf{y}) = \Delta_y^T \Sigma_{\mathbf{y}}^{-1} \Delta_y + \lambda \cdot \mathbf{b}^T \Sigma_{\mathbf{b}}^{-1} \mathbf{b} \qquad (6)$$

where $\Delta_y = \mathbf{s}(\mathbf{p}) - \mathbf{y}$ is the difference between the estimated shape $\mathbf{s}(\mathbf{p})$ and the observed shape $\mathbf{y}$, $\Sigma_{\mathbf{y}}^{-1}$ is the image noise covariance matrix, $\Sigma_{\mathbf{b}}^{-1}$ is the covariance matrix of the tangent shape, and λ is a regularization factor.

In this work, we use the Constrained Shape Model (CSM) of [14], where several extensions to the BTSM have been made:

- to find the observed shape $\mathbf{y}$, CSM uses state-specific statistical adaptive local texture model [7, 32] instead of the pre-learned Principle Component Analysis (PCA) based local texture model;
- state-specific model based KLT used to track the eyes/mouth corners, $\mathbf{s}^c$;
- the estimated 2D face pose $\hat{\gamma}$, from a kernel based face region tracking, are transformed into the same reference frame as $W(.; \phi)$ to obtain $\hat{\phi}$;

As a result the energy function to be optimized in CSM [14] is:

$$E(\mathbf{p}|\mathbf{y}) = \Delta_y^T \Sigma_{\mathbf{y}}^{-1} \Delta_y + \lambda \cdot \mathbf{b}^T \Sigma_{\mathbf{b}}^{-1} \mathbf{b} + \lambda_c \cdot \Delta_c^T \Sigma_{\mathbf{c}}^{-1} \Delta_c + \lambda_\phi \cdot \Delta_\phi^T \Sigma_\phi^{-1} \Delta_\phi \qquad (7)$$

where $\mathbf{y}$ is the observed shape via state-specific statistical adaptive local texture model, $\Delta_c = \mathbf{s}^c(\mathbf{p}) - \hat{\mathbf{s}}^c$ is the difference of the estimated corners $\mathbf{s}^c(\mathbf{p})$ (of $\mathbf{s}(\mathbf{p})$) from current model with respect to the tracked corners $\hat{\mathbf{s}}^c$, $\Delta_\phi = \phi - \hat{\phi}$ is the difference of the estimated global similarity transformation ϕ from the current model with respect to the global similarity transformation $\hat{\phi}$, the covariance matrices $\Sigma_{\mathbf{c}}^{-1}$ and Σ_γ^{-1} models the uncertainty of the tracked corners and the estimated global similarity transformation respectively, and λ_c and λ_ϕ, the regularization factors. The energy function is optimized using EM algorithm. The details about the parameter settings and optimizations are refereed to [14]. The output of this phase is the set of facial landmarks, $\mathbf{s}_t^{3D}$, used in Equation 4.

5   Three Dimensional Model Fitting

Inference framework. For solving equation 4 we use a Gauss Newton algorithm. Suppose we have the initial guess of the model parameter $\mathbf{c}^*$, which can be set to the previous frame model parameter, an optimal solution $\tilde{\mathbf{c}}$ is obtained iteratively:

$$
\begin{cases}
\mathbf{c}_0 = \mathbf{c}^* \\
\mathbf{c}_{k+1} = \mathbf{c}_k \\
\quad +[\mathbf{J}^T\mathbf{J}]^{-1}\mathbf{J}(\mathbf{u}(\mathbf{c}_k) - \hat{\mathbf{u}})
\end{cases}
\tag{8}
$$

where $\mathbf{J} = \frac{\partial \mathbf{u}(\mathbf{c})}{\partial \mathbf{c}}$ stands for the Jacobian of $\mathbf{u}$ to $\mathbf{c}$. Two stopping criterias are being used: the number of iterations and the difference between successive iterations.

Simultaneously rigid and nonrigid motion estimation. The rigid and nonrigid motions are being independent to each other, it is straightforward that we can estimate them simultaneously. Here the $M = 55$ feature points of the set $\mathbf{s}^{3D}$ is used. Consequently the objective function is formulated as:

$$
(\tilde{\omega}, \tilde{\mathbf{t}}, \tilde{\alpha}) = \underset{(\omega,\mathbf{t},\alpha)}{\arg\min} \sum_{i=1}^{M} \|\mathbf{u}^i(\omega, \mathbf{t}, \alpha) - \mathbf{s}^{3D,i}\|^2
\tag{9}
$$

Sequentially rigid and nonrigid motion estimation. In this case we first infer the rigid motion parameters using

$$
(\tilde{\omega}, \tilde{\mathbf{t}}) = \underset{(\omega,\mathbf{t})}{\arg\min} \sum_{i=1}^{M} \|\mathbf{u}^i(\omega, \mathbf{t}) - \mathbf{s}^{3D,i}\|^2
\tag{10}
$$

and then, after compensation we estimate the nonrigid motion parameters as:

$$
\tilde{\alpha} = \underset{(\alpha)}{\arg\min} \sum_{i=1}^{M} \|\mathbf{u}^i(\alpha) - \mathbf{s}^{3D,i}\|^2
\tag{11}
$$

where $\mathbf{u}^i(\alpha)$ stands for the i-th point of the projected facial feature after the application of the updated rigid parameters $(\tilde{\omega}, \tilde{\mathbf{t}})$.

Initialization. Initialization is a very important task in building an automatic facial analysis system. However, it is often ignored by pervious publications. In our proposed system we use a two-step approach to make the full automatic 2D and 3D model initialization. In the first step, the face region is detected considering elliptical shape of the skin regions in the image and then γ_0 is obtained. Using the average face shape structure, corner extraction techniques automatically extract the eyes and mouth corners, constrained by iris and mouth detection results. The CSM approach, of Section 4, is used to detect the full shape $\mathbf{s}$ and hence $\mathbf{s}^{3D}$. In the second step, Equation 4 is solved using as initial value, $\mathbf{c}_0$ set as follows: γ_0 is used to set the initial values of ω_Z, t_X and t_Y, assuming the orthographic projection; t_Z can be initialized with proportional to the focal length; ω_X and ω_Y can be set to zero if we assume the near frontal view; and σ, α are set to zero.

6   Experimental Results

In the following we illustrate qualitative and quantitative results of the proposed 2D/3D facial motion estimation system, using simulated and real data.

6.1 Constrained 2D Shape Estimation

For the 2D shape estimation the Constrained Shape Model (CSM) approach as described in section 4 [14], has been compared to the original BTSM [20]. Fig. 2 depicts tracking results on a sequence of images ('pcm') recorded in our facilities, which is used later to illustrate 3D model fitting. Table 1, shows the mean shape error, estimated as the mean euclidian distance between the detected shape points and 12 manually selected points. As it can be seen CSM method outperforms the BTSM in terms of robustness and preciseness.

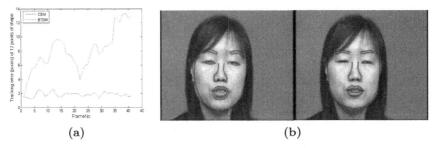

(a)   (b)

Fig. 2. 'pcm' sequence: Shape Model Tracking error BTSM v.s. CSM

Table 1. Tracking Error CSM v.s. BTSM

	BTSM		CSM	
sequence	mean	variance	mean	variance
pcm	8.25	2.88	1.59	0.31
claire	3.21	1.86	1.26	0.17

6.2 3D Fitting and Parameters Estimation

Equation (3) has been used to synthesize simulated face shapes both in 2D and 3D, where the motion parameters are manually pre-defined curves. Figure 3, depicts the rigid motion estimation results (R), and the non rigid motion (N), using simultaneous estimation (Fig 3(i)), and the sequential estimation (Fig. 3(ii)), respectively, for non noisy data.

Fig. 3 reveals that both simultaneous and sequential estimations are precise, however the simultaneous estimation is better than the sequential one in term of the smoothness of the estimated parameters, measured by a zero mean error of all parameters.

To examine the robustness to noise of the the motion estimation approach, we have imposed a gaussian noise on the 2D measurements, with variance of $(0,1,3,5,10,30)$ pixels. Even when the 2D measurement noise level is up to 30 pixels, the mean error of the recovered 3D parameters are still small, where the typical error of t_x and t_y are below 0.5; t_z below 9; the roll is below $0.01(1^o)$; the yaw and pitch are below $0.025(2^o)$; and the errors of the nonrigid motion

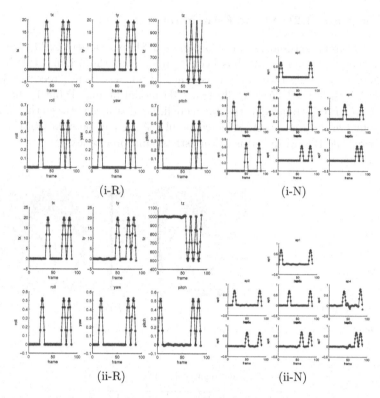

Fig. 3. Simulated data: Rigid (R) and non rigid (N) parameters recovered by (i) Simultaneous and (ii) Sequential estimation, using non noisy data. The blue curve is the ground truth and the red dots are the estimations.

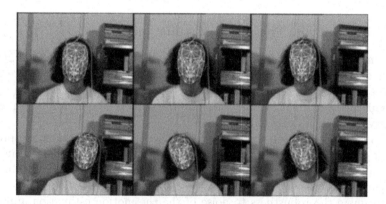

Fig. 4. 3-D Fitting results

parameters are about 0.1 (the nonrigid motion parameter vary from -1 to +1). The absolute error of t_z is a little bit high, which is due to the simulated data. The true value of t_z is from 500 to 1000, which means the relative error of t_z is about 1% to 2%. Moreover, for the nonrigid motion parameters estimation, the simultaneous and the sequential estimations have the same performance.

To quantitatively evaluate the 3D rigid motion estimation, we used 3 sequences from [33] provided with ground truth motion parameters. In order to have common reference for both ground truth and estimated parameters, the first frame has been set as reference frame, to which all the data are related. Figure 4 shows, for every 40 frames, the 3D fitting results, and Figure 5 shows the estimated (in dotted line) and ground-truth (in solid line) motion parameters (tx, ty, tz, roll, yaw, pitch from left to right, from top to down).

One can notice that the estimated parameters have the same behavior as the ground truth, however, it was not possible to evaluate the estimation error, as we do not have a reference frame for the ground truth 3D motion. Finally to illustrate the fitting, tracking and parameters estimation results, Figure 6 depicts the 3D fitting results on an in house recorded sequence (left), and a

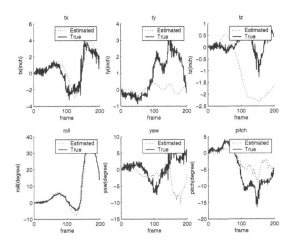

Fig. 5. 3D rigid motion parameters evaluation

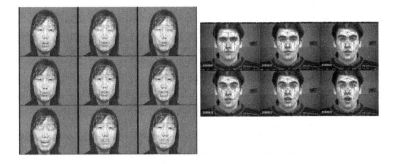

Fig. 6. Three-dimensional face alignment results

sequence from the CMU Facial Expression Database [34] (right). As it can be seen, the proposed 3D non-rigid motion estimation approach works well with this type of image sequences, especially for sudden eye close, and exaggerative facial expressions. The extracted 3D facial model parameters **c** contain meaningful information for emotion analysis and visual media production.

7   Conclusions

Our contribution lies in many aspects: we proposed a monocular three dimensional face sequence analysis system which performs the automatic adaptation of a 3D model to a face sequence. The proposed approach has indeed the ability to estimate face shape variation between people, face expression variation and relative rigid motion to the camera under the hypothesis of the best matching to 3D face shape projection. In fitting the 3D model, both the simultaneous estimation and the sequential estimation are used and compared and our experimental results show that compared to sequential estimation simultaneous estimation provides good estimates for both large three-dimensional rigid motions and subtle facial nonrigid motions. What's more we have proposed a full automatic 2D/3D model initialization method and our 3D tracking algorithm can work 25 fps in modern notebook.

References

1. Ekman, P., Friesen, W.: Facial Action Coding System. Consulting Psychologists Press, Palo Alto (1977)
2. Metaxas, D., Terzopoulos, D.: Shape and nonrigid motion estimation through physics-based synthesis. IEEE Transactions on PAMI 15, 580–591 (1993)
3. Azarbayejani, A., Pentland, A.: Recursive estimation of motion structure and focal length. IEEE Transactions on PAMI 17, 562–575 (1995)
4. Sarris, N., Grammalidis, N., Strintzis, M.G.: Fap extraction using three-dimensional motion estimation. IEEE Transactions on CSVT 12, 865–876 (2002)
5. Lowe, D.G.: Fitting parameterized three-dimensional models to images. IEEE PAMI 13, 441–450 (1991)
6. Xiao, J., Baker, S., Matthews, I., Kanade, T.: Real-time combined 2d+3d active appearance models. In: Proceedings of the IEEE CVPR, vol. 2, pp. 535–542 (2004)
7. Dornaika, F., Davoine, F.: On appearance based face and facial action tracking. IEEE Transactions on CSVT 16, 1107–1124 (2006)
8. Pighin, F., Szeliski, R., Salesin, D.H.: Resynthesizing facial animation through 3d model-based tracking. In: Proceedings of the ICCV, pp. 143–150 (1999)
9. Blanz, V., Vetter, T.: Face recognition based on fitting a 3d morphable model. IEEE PAMI 25 (2003)
10. Li, H., Roivainen, P., Forchheimer, R.: 3d motion estimation in model-based facial image coding. IEEE Transactions on PAMI 15, 545–555 (1993)
11. Li, H., Forchheimer, R.: Two-view facial movement estimation. IEEE Transactions on CSVT 4, 276–287 (1994)
12. Shi, J., Tomasi, C.: Good features to track. In: CVPR, pp. 593–600 (1994)

13. Cootes, T.F., Taylor, C.J., Cooper, D.H., Graham, J.: Active shape models - their training and application. CVIU 61, 38–59 (1995)
14. Hou, Y., Ravyse, I., Sahli, H., Zhang, Y., Zhao, R.: Robust shape-based head tracking. In: Blanc-Talon, J., Philips, W., Popescu, D., Scheunders, P. (eds.) ACIVS 2007. LNCS, vol. 4678, pp. 340–351. Springer, Heidelberg (2007)
15. Tomasi, C., Kanade, T.: Shape and motion from image streams under orthography: A factorization method. IJCV 9, 137–154 (1992)
16. Brand, M., Bhotika, R.: Flexible flow for 3d nonrigid tracking and shape recovery. In: Proceedings of CVPR, vol. 1, pp. 315–322 (2001)
17. Shan, Y., Liu, Z., Zhang, Z.: Model-based bundle adjustment with application to face modeling. In: Proceedings of the ICCV, pp. 644–651 (2001)
18. Essa, I.A., Pentland, A.P.: Coding, analysis, interpretation, and recognition of facial expressions. IEEE Transactions on PAMI 19, 757–763 (1997)
19. Blake, A., Isard, M.: Active Contours. Springer, Heidelberg (1998)
20. Zhou, Y., Gu, L., Zhang, H.: Bayesian tangent shape model: estimating shape and pose parameters via bayesian inference. In: Proceedings of CVPR, pp. 109–116 (2003)
21. Cootes, T.F., Edwards, G.J., Taylor, C.J.: Active appearance models. In: Proceedings of ECCV, vol. 2, pp. 484–498 (1998)
22. Zhou, Y., Zhang, W., Tang, X., Shum, H.: A bayesian mixture model for multi-view face alignment. In: Proceedings of CVPR, vol. 2, pp. 741–746 (2005)
23. Gu, L., Kanade, T.: 3d alignment of face in a single image. In: Proceedings of CVPR, pp. 1305–1312 (2006)
24. Gonzalez-Mora, J., De la Torre, F., Murthi, R., Guil, N., Zapata, E.L.: Bilinear active appearance models. In: ICCV, pp. 1–8 (2007)
25. Dedeoglu, G., Kanade, T., Baker, S.: The asymmetry of image registration and its application to face tracking. IEEE Transactions on PAMI 29, 807–823 (2007)
26. Liang, L., Xiao, R., Wen, F., Sun, J.: Face alignment via component-based discriminative search. In: Forsyth, D., Torr, P., Zisserman, A. (eds.) ECCV 2008, Part II. LNCS, vol. 5303, pp. 72–85. Springer, Heidelberg (2008)
27. Gu, L., Kanade, T.: A generative shape regularization model for robust face alignment. In: Forsyth, D., Torr, P., Zisserman, A. (eds.) ECCV 2008, Part I. LNCS, vol. 5302, pp. 413–426. Springer, Heidelberg (2008)
28. Ahlberg, J.: Candide-3: An updated parametrized face. Technical Report LiTH-ISY-R-2326, Linköping Univ. (2001)
29. Ravyse, I., Enescu, V., Sahli, H.: Kernel-based head tracker for videophony. In: ICIP 2005, vol. 3, pp. 1068–1071 (2005)
30. Dornaika, F., Davoine, F.: Simultaneous facial action tracking and expression recognition using a particle filter. In: Proceedings of ICCV, pp. 1733–1738 (2005)
31. Goodall, C.: Procrustes methods in the statistical analysis of shape. J. R. Statist. Soc. B., 285–339 (1991)
32. Ross, D., Lim, J., Lin, R.S., Yang, M.H.: Incremental learning for robust visual tracking. International Journal of Computer Vision 77, 125–141 (2008)
33. Cascia, M.L., Sclaroff, S., Athitsos, V.: Fast, reliable head tracking under varying illumination: An approach based on robust registration of texture-mapped 3d models. IEEE Trans. PAMI 22 (2000)
34. Kanade, T., Cohn, J., Tian, Y.L.: Comprehensive database for facial expresison analysis. In: Proceedings of AFGR, pp. 46–53 (2000)

Carotenoid Concentration of Arctic Charr (*Salvelinus Alpinus L.*) from Spectral Data

J. Birgitta Martinkappi, Jukka Kekäläinen, Yevgeniya Shatilova,
and Jussi Parkkinen

University of Joensuu, PL 111, 80101 Joensuu
{birgitta.martinkauppi,jussi.parkkinen}@cs.joensuu.fi,
jukka.kekalainen@cc.joensuu.fi,
evgenikka.joensuu@gmail.com

Abstract. The most striking feature of Arctic Charr (*Salvelinus alpinus L.*) is the red abdomen area during the mating season. This colouration is assumed to be related to the vitality, nutritional status, foraging ability and generally health of the fish – an important knowledge to fisheries and researchers. The colouration should be assessed numerically, and the amount of pigment (carotenoid) causing the colour should be known for quality evaluation of the fish. Especially the carotenoid amount is thought to be directly connected to the investment of the individual since carotenoids are energetically costly. To assess this amount, we investigate the relationship between chemical and spectral data. We also tested a simple model for approximating carotenoid content from spectral measurements. The preliminary results indicate a reasonable good correlation between these two data.

Keywords: Arctic Charr (*Salvelinus alpinus L.*), carotenoid, spectral data, chemical analysis.

1 Introduction

Arctic Charr (*Salvelinus alpinus L.*) is a fish species which population is greatly reduced in the recent decades in Finland due to environmental changes and other factors [1-2]. The fish is farmed in fisheries and individuals are restocked in their natural habitats making quality of the fish a significant factor to be followed. To determine quality (vitality and health) of the fish, an important feature seems to be its colouration. This suggests use of spectral based methods for evaluations.

A striking colouration feature of Arctic Charr is its red abdomen especially colourful in the mating season [3] which is assumed to be related to its genetic quality: Generally the pigments causing the red, orange and yellow colouration in animals are carotenoids [4]. Since animals cannot synthesize carotenoid compounds, the capacity to produce carotenoid-based colouration is linked to ability to acquire carotenoids from food (e.g. [5]). Therefore, expression of carotenoid-based colours may be condition dependent trait indicating the nutritional status and foraging ability of the bearer. For this reason carotenoid-based ornaments are often important signals in the mate

J. Blanc-Talon et al. (Eds.): ACIVS 2009, LNCS 5807, pp. 562–570, 2009.

choice in many animals and these colour patterns are often used for attracting potential mates, so that in many species more intensely coloured individuals are more attractive (e.g. [6-8]).

The colouration of Arctic Charr is caused by carotenoid called astaxanthin [3]. The saturation of the red abdomen varies substantially between different Charr individuals. We assume here that the saturation of the red ornaments greatly depends on the concentration of the carotenoid pigments in the skin. Therefore, our main goal is to study whether there can be found a correlation between chemical based pigment analysis and spectral colourimetric data.

The advantages of the proposed spectral based method over chemical analysis are its speed, non-contactness and applicability for large amount of samples. Since the method can be imaging it is possible to study ornamentation and variations within a sample. To get the precise estimate of carotenoid concentration, a chemical pigment analyses are usually needed. However, the chemical analyses for measuring the pigment concentrations are typically quite slow due to dissolution and extraction of the pigments which makes it inappropriate for large number of samples. The time required for analysis can take even several days. It also requires certain minimum size for the sample. Therefore, spectral based concentration estimation is highly sought-after and if reliable, would be highly applicable in many other areas.

The proposed method's novelty lies on spectral imaging on the fish skin and combining it with actually measured chemical data (see also [9]). Some papers have considered the relationship between spectra and pigments (see e.g. [10-11]) but they have not done the actual chemical analysis. For fish, there have been demonstrated correlations between colour and CIE Lab like for example in [12]: a colour component (a* of CIE Lab) has been shown to be positively correlated with carotenoids in muscle of salmonoids. An overview of colour and VIS spectroscopy is can be found in [13] (especially for fish freshness and other qualities of fish fillets and muscles). Use of spectral imaging for parasite detections is studied in [14]. Stien et. al. [15] proposed an automated analysis tool for trout cutlets. In Martinkauppi et al., [16], a system was introduced for monitoring the evaluation of Arctic Charr health using its colouration using RGB images. Other studies have inspected other aspects: recognition of fish ([17, 18]), fish detection and classification ([19, 20]) growth ring detection ([21, 22]), fish freshness sensor ([23]), 3D visualization of fish ([24]), and reporting anomalies in fish ([25]).

2 Arctic Charr Samples and Data

Frozen skin samples were prepared from the red abdomen area of Charr. The sizes of the samples were approximately 10 mm x 10 mm which is acceptable for chemical pigment analysis. The total number of samples was 30 and their colour range varied from pale pinkish to bright red to dark reddish brown.

All samples were subjected to spectral measurement, RGB imaging and chemical analysis. An example of RGB images of skin samples is shown in Fig. 1. Since the fish is a natural object it exhibit variations of surface colour. Before the spectral imaging the samples were set on a white kitchen paper.

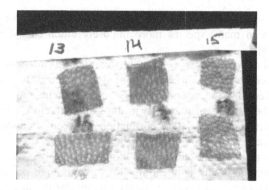

Fig. 1. The Arctic Charr skin samples were imaged with a Nicon digital camera. The RGB image above displays 6 samples with bright reddish colours. Variations in colour uniformity are easy to observe.

2.1 Spectral Measurements

The spectral imaging of Arctic Charr samples was done with ImSpector V10E line scanning spectral camera. Spectral images of fish were taken from 400 nm to 1000 nm by 5 nm steps. The image is formed from lines scanned at different position of the target moved by the sliding sledges. The setup is shown in Fig. 2.

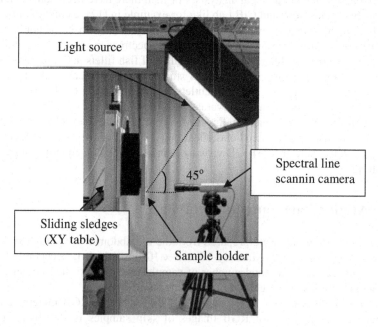

Fig. 2. The spectral imaging system with approximately 45° geometry

Spectral cameras measure the light reflected from the object (colour signal). To get the reflectance of the object the illumination effects should be eliminated for each wavelength. This can be done by the following standard procedure: measuring the white reflectance under the given conditions and using it as a divisor for the other data:

$$R(\lambda) = C(\lambda)/C_w(\lambda) \,, \tag{1}$$

where

R = reflectance of the object,
λ = wavelength,
C = colour signal, and
W = white.

Eq. (1) produces data in the range of 0-1 from which it can be scaled to 0-100 or other ranges.

An example of measured data is shown in Fig. 3. The image on the left shows the sRGB reproduction of spectral data. Some variations are still observable even if the spatial resolution is not as high as in Fig. 1. This lower resolution act as a smoothing filter for the data but this is not so detrimental since the chemical analysis produce only one value for each sample. The middle image displays a single sample which spectral data is presented on the right image. The fish spectral values vary significantly even inside the sample, and this makes it challenging to combine these results with the results of the chemical analyses.

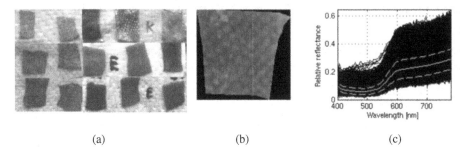

(a)   (b)   (c)

Fig. 3. The colour of the red abdomen area varies greatly between individual Arctic Charr as shown in sRGB reconstruction in (a). The variation is large even within one sample as demonstrated in sRGB images in (b). All the spectra of this sample and the corresponding mean and standard deviation spectra are plotted in (c).

2.2 Chemical Analysis

The skin samples were subjected to the chemical analysis to extract carotenoid pigments after RGB and spectral imaging. Unlike the spectral measurements, the chemical analysis destroys the sample permanently. The extraction was done with a method suggested by Scalia et al. [3]: 1) weighting of fish skin, 2) dissolving carotenoid astaxanthin from fish skin in acetone, 3) filtering them under reduced pressure, and 4) determining the concentration of astaxanthin from the extract using a special formula:

$$C=A(470)*V*T*10/(2350*W*1000), \tag{2}$$

where

C	= concentration of astaxanthin,
A(470)	= absorption at 470 nm,
V	= volume of the extract,
T	= dilution factor,
2350	= extinction coefficient of carotenoid at hexane (1 %, 1cm), and
W	= weight.

This method produces one value for the whole sample so the information about colour variation within the sample is lost. The reliability of the analysis was tested with the reference and it was found acceptable. However, the analysis did not work well on all samples: some samples required more than one dissolving for extracting the carotenoids.

3 Methods for Approximating Carotenoid

The objective of this study was to found out whether it is possible to predict the carotenoid concentration of the skin by means of the spectral data. Since the chemical analysis of carotenoid produces a single number and thus can be considered as an average concentration, the spectral data over the whole sample is averaged for testing a simple model.

Although the samples were imaged in the range of 400 – 1000 nm the selection of possible wavelengths was limited: the carotenoid approximation part is going to be used as a part of a system in which the spectral data is estimated from RGB images. Thus the selected wavelengths should be in the range which can be transformed from the RGB of a camera. It might be possible to use also directly the RGB values for approximation but the problem is that different spectra produces similar RGB values. No specific requirements for precision were settled for the carotenoid estimation.

The model to be tested was selected analysis of ratio between two spectra wavelength. This kind of model has been used by Chappelle et al. to examine the concentrations of soybean leaves [26]. Another research (Blackburn [27], especially the pigment specific simple ratio) suggested the 470 nm wavelength for carotenoid estimation as an optimal individual wavelength due to absorption characteristics of carotenoids at the blue region. Since the fish get their carotenoids from food (e.g. [5]) this was selected as a factor for the model. The second selected wavelength was 800 nm in the red area based as suggested in [27]. Based on these two papers, the model to be tested is

$$R800/R470=R(800 \text{ nm})/R(470 \text{ nm}). \tag{3}$$

The wavelength ratio in Eq. (3) is of course not the only possible choice but it was selected for this paper for testing the possible correlation. Blackburn [27] has tested this carotenoid index of tree leaves but it did not work very well. The quality of the results was evaluated using correlation coefficient r and coefficient of r^2 determination [28]. The first metric measures the relationship while the second one examines the predictability between the variables.

4   Results

First, the mean, median and standard deviation values were calculated to spectral data. We also calculated relative standard deviation in which the standard deviation is divided by the corresponding mean values. The results can be seen in Fig. 4. The mean and median spectra resemble each other and the standard deviation seems to be reasonable for natural Arctic Charr. The standard deviation and mean values indicate that the relative variation is largest at the blue and green end of the spectra. This may further indicate that the wavelength in this areas contain more information about the pigment concentration.

Table 1. Statistical evaluation of results

Metric	Value
Correlation coefficient r	0.7280*
Coefficient of determination r^2	0.5310

*a 95% confidence interval ranging 0.5-0.86.

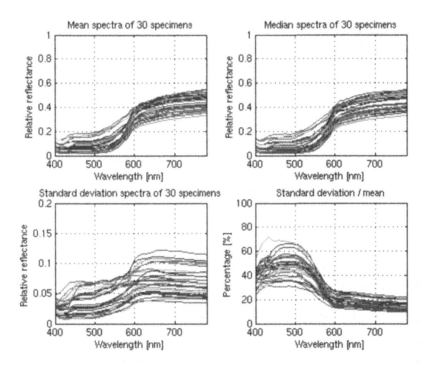

Fig. 4. Mean, median, standard deviation and standard deviation vs. mean metrics were applied on spectral data

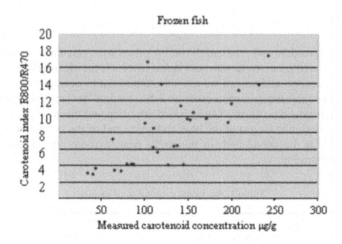

Fig. 5. The carotenoid concentration versus carotenoid-index R800/R470 indicates linear correlation

The spatial and textural information is of course lost by using mean spectra. Since the whole sample is used without removing any part, the average is influenced e.g. by the structure like fins or highlights. However, the goal of this paper is to investigate if there is a correlation between optical and chemical results. In further research, a more complex model will be applied and especially the effect of surface structure will be taken into account.

Fig. 5 shows the results from plotting the carotenoid concentration against the carotenoid index R800/R470. Although there are variations, the shape of the relationship can be assumed to be a straight line or linear as a starting point. It is also clear that some samples are outliers. This can be due to several factors like structure of surface (fins) or faulty chemical analysis.

Next the correlation coefficient and coefficient of determination were applied on the data. The results are shown in Table 1. They also indicate that even this simple method can be used to approximate the carotenoid content from the spectral data. Of course, the results are valid only for frozen fish since the freeze changes chemical properties.

5 Conclusions

We have studied spectral and chemical results for samples of Arctic Charr. The objective of the study was to find out whether there can be found a link between these two results.

A simple model was applied as a starting point and the findings indicate a possible positive correlation between chemical and spectral results. It worked surprisingly well when taking into account the properties of the used data. There were some outliers but given that the samples were derived from living organisms with naturally highly variable colouration, problems in chemical analysis and use of mean spectra, this is not surprising.

For future research, we are going to test a more complex model. It might be also reasonable to exclude some of clearly wrong data like highlights or discoloured scales since these do not contribute to carotenoid content. A more complex model might be able to separate carotenoid and melanin components. In addition, different ratios and wavelengths need to be evaluated to find out the best combination.

Acknowledgments. We thank Anne Ryynänen and Teija Zetterberg for their help.

References

1. Urho, L., Lehtonen, H.: Fish species in Finland. Riista- ja kalatalous - selvityksiä 1B/2008 Finnish Game and Fisheries Research Institute, Helsinki (2008), http://www.rktl.fi/julkaisut/j/419.html.
2. Primmer, C.R., Aho, T., Piironen, J., Estoup, A., Cornuet, J.-M., Ranta, E.: Microsatellite analysis of hatchery stocks and natural populations of arctic charr, Salvelinus alpinus, from the Nordic region: implications for conservation. Hereditas 130, 277–289 (1999)
3. Scalia, S., Isaksen, M., Francis, G.W.: Carotenoids of the arctic charr, Salvelinus alpinus L. J. Fish Biology 34(6), 969–970 (1989)
4. Fox, D.L.: Animal biochromes and structural colours. University of California Press, Berkeley (1976)
5. Badyaev, A.V., Hill, G.E.: Evolution of sexual dichromatism: contribution of carotenoid-versus melanin-based coloration. Biological Journal of the Linnean Society 69(2), 153–172 (2000)
6. Milinski, M., Bakker, T.C.M.: Female sticklebacks use male coloration in mate choice and hence avoid parasitized males. Nature 344, 330–333 (1990)
7. Olson, V.A., Owens, I.P.F.: Costly sexual signals: are carotenoids rare, risky or required? Trends in Ecology & Evolution 13(12), 510–514 (1998)
8. Zahavi, A.: The cost of honesty. J. Theoretical Biology 67(3), 603–605 (1977)
9. Shatilova, Y.: Color Image Technique in Fish Research, Master thesis, University of Joensuu (2008)
10. Tsumura, N., Nakaguchi, T., Ojima, N., Takase, K., Okaguchi, S., Hori, K., Miyake, Y.: Image-Based Control of Skin Melanin Texture. Applied Optics 45(25), 6626–6633 (2006)
11. Ojima, N., Tsumura, N., Akazaki, S., Hori, K., Miyake, Y.: Application of Image-Based Skin Chromophore Analysis to Cosmetics. J. Imaging Science and Technology 48(3), 222–226 (2004)
12. Rønsholdt, B.: Can carotenoid content in muscle of salmonids be predicted using simple models derived from instrumental color measurements? Aquaculture Research 36(5), 519–524 (2005)
13. Olafsdottir, G., Nesvadba, P., Di Natale, C., Careche, M., Oehlenschläger, J., Tryggvadóttir, S.V., Schubring, R., Kroeger, M., Heia, K., Esaiassen, M., Macagnano, A., Jørgensen, B.M.: Multisensor for fish quality determination. Trends in Food Science & Technology 15(2), 86–93 (2004)
14. Heia, K., Sivertsen, A.H., Stormo, S.K., Elvevoll, E., Wold, J.P., Nilsen, H.: Detection of Nematodes in Cod (Gadus morhua) Fillets by Imaging Spectroscopy. J. Food Science 72(1), E011–E015 (2007)
15. Stien, L.H., Manne, F., Ruohonen, K., Kause, A., Rungruangsak-Torrissen, K., Kiessling, A.: Automated image analysis as a tool to quantify the colour and composition of rainbow trout (Oncorhynchus mykiss W.) cutlets. Aquaculture 261, 695–705 (2006)

16. Martinkauppi, B., Doronina, E., Piironen, J., Jääskeläinen, T., Parkkinen, J.: Novel system for semiautomatic image segmentation of arctic charr. J. Electronic Imaging 16(3) (2007) 033012-1–8

17. Lee, D.-J., Schoenberger, R.B., Shiozawa, D., Xu, X., Zhan, P.: Contour matching for a fish recognition and migration-monitoring system. In: Harding, K.G. (ed.) Two- and Three-Dimensional Vision Systems for Inspection, Control, and Metrology II. Proc. SPIE, vol. 5606, pp. 37–48 (2004)

18. Chambah, M., Semani, D., Renouf, A., Courtellemont, P., Rizzi, A.: Underwater color constancy: enhancement of automatic live fish recognition. In: Eschbach, R., Marcu, G.G. (eds.) Color Imaging IX: Processing, Hardcopy, and Applications. Proc. SPIE, vol. 5293, pp. 157–168 (2003)

19. Chen, H.-H.: A feasibility study of using color indexing for reef fish identification. In: Proc. OCEANS, vol. 5, p. 2566 (2003)

20. Tidd, R.A., Wilder, J.: Fish detection and classification system. J. Electronic Imaging 10(1), 283–288 (2001)

21. Hickinbotham, S.J., Hancock, E.R., Austin, J.: S-Gabor channel design for segmentation of modulated textures. In: 6th International Conference on Image Processing and Its Applications, vol. 2, pp. 591–595 (1997)

22. Guillaud, A., Benzinou, A., Troadec, H., Rodin, V., Le Bihan, J.: Parameterization of a multiagent system for roof edge detection: an application to growth ring detection on fish otoliths. In: Dougherty, E.R., Astola, J.T. (eds.) Nonlinear Image Processing XI. Proc. SPIE, vol. 3961, pp. 196–207 (2000)

23. Hammond, J.M., Mlsna, T., Smith, D.J., Fruhberger, B.: Fish freshness sensor. In: Shaffer, R.E., Potyrailo, R.A. (eds.) Internal Standardization and Calibration Architectures for Chemical Sensors. Proc. SPIE, vol. 3856, pp. 88–96 (1999)

24. Rheingans, P., Marietta, M., Nichols, J.: Interactive 3D visualization of actual anatomy and simulated chemical time-course data for fish. In: Proc. IEEE Conference on Visualization, pp. 393–396 (1995)

25. Orlov, A.M.: Rare events of cyclopia and melanism among deepwater snailfishes (Liparidae, Scorpaeniformes). In: Proc. MTS/IEEE Conference and Exhibition OCEANS, vol. 2, pp. 864–869 (2001)

26. Chappelle, E.W., Kim, M.S., McMurtrey, J.E.: Ratio Analysis of Reflectance Spectra (RARS): an algorithm for the remote estimation of the concentrations of chlorophyll A, chlorophyll B, and carotenoids in soybean leaves. Remote Sensing of Environment 39(3), 239–247 (1992)

27. Blackburn, G.A.: Quantifying chlorophylls and carotenoids from leaf to canopy scales: An evaluation of some hyper-spectral approaches. Remote Sensing of Environment 66(3), 273–285 (1998)

28. Statistic 2, Correlation. Internet WWW-page,
    http://mathbits.com/mathbits/TISection/Statistics2/correlation.htm (11.12.2008)

Quality of Reconstructed Spectrum for Watermarked Spectral Images Subject to Various Illumination Conditions

Konstantin Krasavin[1,2], Jussi Parkkinen[2], Arto Kaarna[3], and Timo Jaaskelainen[4]

[1] Nokia Corporation, P.O. Box 1000, FI-33721 Tampere, Finland
Konstantin.Krasavin@nokia.com
[2] University of Joensuu, Department of Computer Science,
P.O. Box 111, FI-80101 Joensuu, Finland
Jussi.Parkkinen@cs.joensuu.fi
[3] Lappeenranta University of Technology, Department of Information Technology,
P.O. Box 21, FI-53851 Lappeenranta, Finland
Arto.Kaarna@lut.fi
[4] University of Joensuu, Department of Physics,
P.O. Box 111, FI-80101 Joensuu, Finland
Timo.Jaaskelainen@joensuu.fi

Abstract. Digital imaging continues expansion to various applications. Spectral images are becoming more popular as one field of digital imaging. In this study we utilize a watermarking method for spectral images, based on the three-dimensional wavelet transform. We study the influence of watermarking process to illuminated watermarked images. In particular, we focus on how the watermarking effects to the spectrum of restored images. The experiments were performed on a large dataset of 58 spectral images. The experiments indicate that using the proposed watermarking method the quality of reconstructed image depends more on illumination and embedding strength controller than compression, with respect to $L^*a^*b^*$ color difference.

Keywords: Spectral images, watermarking, wavelets.

1 Introduction

Image watermarking is an emerging method for supporting intellectual properties in digital media [1]. If the human visual system is used for measuring the embedding quality then it is rather easy to define embedding procedures that provide robust watermarking without visual changes in the image. This is the case for most of the color images.

Spectral color imaging is an imaging method, where color of an object is represented more accurately than in the traditional RGB images. For spectral images the requirements set by the various applications may be diverse. Again, for visual assessment watermarking is easy. For classification applications it might be too risky to modify the original, measured spectra through watermark embedding. The same

J. Blanc-Talon et al. (Eds.): ACIVS 2009, LNCS 5807, pp. 571–576, 2009.

applies to the lossy compression of spectral images. Now, the utilization of spectral images is spreading to various areas and the requirements for storing and transmitting the data must be solved. Lossless compression provides lower compression ratios comparing to lossy compression. This means that lossy methods with high compression ratios are required in practice. Even though the watermarking is modifying the original content of the image, the intellectual rights should be somehow managed.

This study confesses the requirements of the reality and as such, provides a practical approach to watermark embedding. We embed a gray-scale watermark in spectral images in the three-dimensional wavelet transform domain like in [6] and extensively analyze the method and draw some general conclusions. In particular, in this study we evaluate how well a color spectrum is preserved during watermarking, compression and illumination attacks.

The size of image database is 58 spectral images [5]. This is a rather large database in this domain, since spectral images are still not too easy to acquire. The properties of the watermarking on a large set of spectral images are studied.

2 Watermark Embedding and Extracting

Spectral images are three-dimensional signals with two spatial dimensions and a spectral dimension. The spatial dimensions contain the visual information, and the spectral dimension presents the reflectance spectrum connected to each pixel. Thus, spectral image watermarking in a three-dimensional transform domain is a natural choice.

The embedding procedure follows the method described in [3]. The watermark is embedded in the 3D wavelet transform domain. First, a three-dimensional wavelet transform of the spectral image is computed. Then, a two dimensional wavelet transform of the watermark is computed. The spatial size of the watermark is equal to the spatial size of the transformed block of the image. The transformed values of the watermark are added to the values of the transformed block B_{wt} of the spectral image, resulting to the watermarked block:

$$B_{wt,wm} = B_{wt} + \alpha W_{wt} .$$

(1)

where α is a weighting coefficient that controls the strength of the watermark. The larger the multiplier α is, the better the watermark survives from attacks, but at the same time the signal to noise ratio for the watermarked image is decreasing.
The spectral image is reconstructed by the inverse 3D DWT now containing the watermark.

Watermark extraction is an inverse operation to the embedding procedure. The three-dimensional wavelet transform is calculated both for the original image and watermarked image. Then, the difference of the watermarked image $I_{wt,wm}$ and the original image I_{wt} and in the transformed domain contains the watermark:

$$W_{wt,r} = I_{wt,wm} - I_{wt} .$$

(2)

Knowing the bands where the watermark pixels were embedded, the watermark $W_{wt,r}$ in the transform domain can be reconstructed by collecting the corresponding values. Then the 2D inverse wavelet transform will finally output the reconstructed watermark W_r.

3 Lossy Compression

We study the robustness of the embedded watermark in the PCA-wavelet compression attack. The original spectral images were watermarked, and then watermarked spectral images were compressed in a lossy manner with the following procedure. To reduce the spectral dimension, principal component analysis (PCA) was applied to spectral images. The compression was achieved by selecting only a limited number of principal components to reconstruct the image. The resulting principal images were compressed with the wavelet-based SPIHT method [4]. Spectral image were reconstructed by multiplying the restored principal images by the corresponding principal vectors.

4 Illumination

The viewing conditions change the perceptual color of the spectrum. External illumination can be compensated through combining the spectra of the image with the spectrum of the illumination. A standard set of light sources was used to illuminate the spectral images: A, B, C, D50, D65, F2, F8, F11.

We evaluated illumination after watermarking as an illumination attack. The original spectral image is watermarked, and then multiplied by the illumination vector, and then the resulting image is compressed. The watermark is extracted from the reconstructed image and compared to the original watermark.

5 Experiments

The proposed embedding procedure was applied to watermarking. In the experiments, 58 spectral images were watermarked and then compressed with different bit rates. The embedded watermark was extracted from the reconstructed watermarked images. S-CIELAB color difference was calculated between the original image and the reconstructed watermarked image. For the extracted watermark, the correlation coefficient between the original and extracted watermark was calculated.

The original spectral images had different number of the bands and different spatial sizes. We normalized all the images before watermarking, in order to have a constant spatial size and a constant number of bands. The spatial size of the normalized spectral images was 256x256 pixels. The number of bands was 32. As a watermark we used a gray-scale image with a spatial size of 128x128 pixels.

The compression procedure described above was applied to the watermarked images. We used 8 principal components of the spectral image and wavelet compression with bit rate [4 1 0.5 0.25 0.015625] bits per pixel, which result to compression ratios [16, 64, 128, 256, 4096].

In these experiments we focus on illumination after watermarking as an illumination attack. In the experiment we wanted to find a reasonable range for the watermark's strength controller α. A large value would mean strong embedding and thus, it would yield to a visible error in the watermarked image. A small value would result to weak embedding and thus to fragile watermarking. As such, robust watermarking

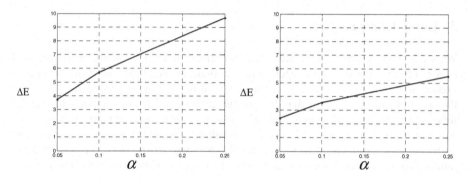

Fig. 1. Color differences between reference and watermarked image under illumination. CIELAB ΔE, left, S-CIELAB ΔE, right.

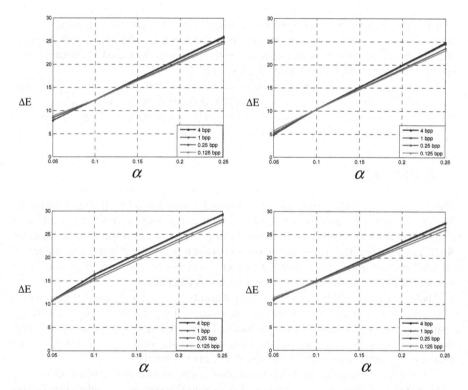

Fig. 2. Color difference for watermarked compressed image after illumination, S-CIELAB. Light sources A, B, C, D50 (from left to right, top to bottom).

means relatively strong embedding without visible or otherwise annoying errors in the watermarked image. In this experiment we used a large set of spectral images, but the results were averaged to define only one common value of α for all images.

5.1 Illumination After Watermarking

For the watermarked images, the signal to noise ratios and color difference ΔE in $L^*a^*b^*$ color space were calculated. ΔE measure between original and watermarked image under illumination is shown in Fig.1 as a function of α.

The original image, multiplied by corresponding illumination vector has been used as a reference. The results are averaged over all spectral images.

As can be seen from Fig.1, watermarking strength controller α has strong effect to calculated color difference.

Next, we utilize lossy compression attack with different bit rate. The original image is watermarked, compressed and then illuminated. The reconstructed image is compared to a reference image. The original image, multiplied by corresponding illumination vector has been used as a reference. The results are averaged over all spectral images.

Experiment results for light sources A, B, C, D50 are shown in Fig.2, and for the light sources D65, F2, F8, F11 are shown in Fig.3.

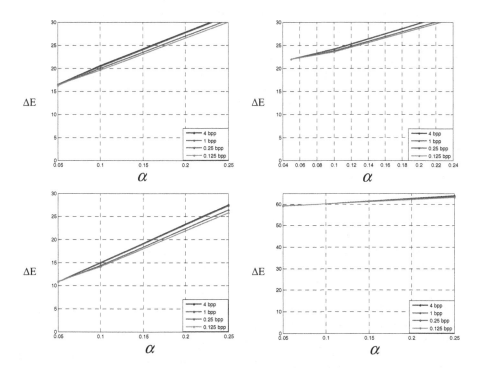

Fig. 3. Color difference for watermarked compressed image after illumination, S-CIELAB. Light sources D65, F2, F8, F11 (from left to right, top to bottom). Note the scale difference for "F11" case.

6 Discussion and Conclusions

We considered a technique for embedding a watermark into a spectral image. We embedded the gray-scale watermark in a spectral image in the three-dimensional wavelet transform domain. The properties of the watermarking on a large set of spectral images were studied. Especially we studied how well the color spectrum is preserved for different illumination conditions.

The quality of reconstructed spectral images in terms of S-CIELAB ΔE, depends more on illumination and on parameter α then compression. For all light sources, except F11, the color difference grows almost linearly with parameter α. The range of proposed α is not suitable for peaky illuminants as F11 is.

The experimental results support the conclusions made in [6]. For the illuminants A, C and D50 the reconstructed spectrum does not significantly different. For the illuminants D65, F2, F8 the color difference grows almost linearly depending on light source. The illumination changes the spectrum remarkably especially for F11. For Illuminant B, the color difference is smallest.

Using $L^*a^*b^*$ color difference as a measure for quality of reconstructed spectrum for watermarked and illuminated images has shown that most disturbance in spectrum is caused by watermarking and illumination processes. Compression does not disturb the spectrum significantly. In this sense, the watermarked and illuminator-compensated images allow various compression without producing much new errors. This is valid for the proposed range of α.

Evaluating of quality of watermarking for spectral images is not obvious task due to different image purposes comparing to ordinary RGB images. Experiment results for ΔE values for watermarked and illuminated images are greater then commonly accepted range for RGB images. For spectral images, ΔE values can be used as guidance for selecting parameter α depending on image purpose.

References

1. Ingemar, J., Cox, M.L., Miller, J.A.: Bloom: Digital Watermarking". Academic Press, San Diego (2002)
2. Hordley, S., Finalyson, G., Morovic, P.: A multi-spectral image database and its application to image rendering across illumination. In: 3rd International Conference on Image and Graphics, pp. 394–397 (2004)
3. Kaarna, A., Parkkinen, J.: Digital Watermarking of Spectral Images with Three-Dimensional Wavelet Transform. In: Scandinavian Conference on Image Analysis, pp. 320–327. Göteborg, Sweden (2003)
4. Said, A., Perlman, W.A.: A new, fast, and efficient image codec based on set portioning in hierarchical trees. IEEE Transactions on Circuits and Systems for Video Technology 6(3), 243–250 (1996)
5. Infotonics Center Joensuu: Spectral Image Database, http://ifc.joensuu.fi
6. Krasavin, K., Parkkinen, J., Kaarna, A., Jaaskelainen, T.: Robustness of Watermarking Spectral Images with 3D Wavelet Transform Subject to Various Illumination Conditions. In: CGIV 2008/MCS 2008, Terrassa, Spain (2008)

Compression of Remote Sensing Images for the PROBA-V Satellite Mission

Stefan Livens and Richard Kleihorst

VITO Flemish Institute for Technological Research,
Boeretang 200, B-2800 Mol, Belgium
{stefan.livens,richard.kleihorst}@vito.be
http://www.vito.be/

Abstract. We investigate compression of remote sensing images with a special geometry of non-square pixels. Two fundamentally different data reduction strategies are compared: a combination of pixel binning with near lossless compression and a method operating at higher compression rates. To measure the real impact of the compression, the image processing flow upto final products is included in the experiments. The effects on sensor non-uniformities and their corrections are explicitly modeled and measured. We conclude that it is preferable to apply higher compression rates than to rely on pixel binning, even if the derived images have lower resolutions.

Keywords: remote sensing, data reduction, image compression.

1 Introduction

We study the compression of the remote sensing images to be captured by the PROBA-V satellite. The data volume of raw images needs to be significantly reduced before transmission to earth. The quality of the resulting images, both in terms of radiometric and geometric properties, needs to be as high as possible, because the images will be used for scientific purposes. The on-board data handling is limited by memory and processing constraints [1].

The imaging system is quite complex and results in a special geometry of the raw images. The pixels at various positions within one image correspond to very different sizes on ground and the size also depends on the direction. From these, images will be derived with yet different geometries and lower resolutions.

Two fundamentally different data reduction strategies are considered and compared. The *compression flow* is based on compression with moderately high compression ratios. The *binning flow* starts with aggregation of the values of 3 vertically adjacent pixels into an average value. This process will be called *pixel binning*. The resulting images are compressed with a very low compression ratio. We will compare the results of both methods by investigating the errors they induce on the derived imagery called *products* and propose a preferred strategy.

J. Blanc-Talon et al. (Eds.): ACIVS 2009, LNCS 5807, pp. 577–586, 2009.

2   Remote Sensing Image Generation

2.1   Characteristics of the PROBA-V Imaging System

PROBA-V is a remote sensing micro-satellite being designed for global monitoring of vegetation [2]. It will offer daily global coverage of all land masses for latitudes above 35° (two-daily coverage for lower latitudes). From an altitude of 800 km, it will make 26 near-polar orbits per day. To achieve global coverage, it has to cover a wide swath of 2250km. Swath is defined as the strip of the surface of the earth seen by the sensor at once.

To achieve the corresponding wide angular field of view (total FOV = 101°), an optical design was chosen consisting of three identical camera systems: one central camera pointing downwards, and two side cameras pointing left and right. Each camera has an equal FOV, but the side cameras cover a larger portion of the swath (875km. vs. 500km.), as depicted in fig. 1.

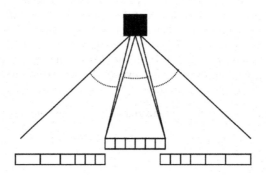

Fig. 1. Wide swath covered by 3 cameras with equal FOV

Each camera contains a set of push-broom (line) sensors to image 4 spectral bands. The BLUE, RED, and near infrared (NIR) sensors have 6000 pixel wide arrays in the across-track direction (horizontal, perdendicular to the movement of the satellite). The image in the along-track (vertical) direction is built up with continuous imaging during the flight.

For the central camera, this results in imaging with a ground sampling distance (GSD) of 100m in the across-track direction. GSD is the distance between two adjacent pixels measured on ground The imaging over time is adapted to match this so that the pixel size in the along-track direction is also 100m. However, the side cameras view the earth under larger angles. As a result, the GSD varies from 100m near the central camera to 300m at the far sides.

The short wave infrared (SWIR) spectral band has an 3000 pixel wide array with pixels that are twice as large. Its larger pixels have a similar geometry: square pixels (200m by 200m) gradually changing to 200m by 600m for the side camera images.

2.2   Remote Sensing Processing Chain

The data as captured by the cameras needs to go through a processing chain in order to derive useful remote sensing images called *products* [3]. To obtain the best possible results, the quality of the final output needs to be kept in mind during the design of every processing step [4]. Main steps of the PROBA-V user segment processing chain include at least geometric and radiometric corrections, resolution conversion and projection to a particular grid.

Two main product families will be generated. The first has a ground resolution of 300m, the best resolution achievable over the whole input field. The other product family will be generated with a ground resolution of 1km. This offers less detail, but its data size is more manageable and it is directly compatible with earlier products from the VEGETATION image archive [5].

2.3   Data Reduction

The image data volume captured by the PROBA-V platform during continuous operational imaging is much larger than the capacity for data transmission allows. Several measures are taken to reduce this problem. Images are only collected over land, and imaging of polar regions is omitted. Still, an very significant reduction is to be achieved by on-board data reduction [6]. The strategy can consist of 2 stages: binning and compression.

The compression relies on the CCSDS image compression algorithm, a well recognized standard for space applications [7]. It is based on wavelet decomposition of images. It splits the image into a low pass subimage and 3 high pass subimages, representing details in 3 different directions. The process is repeated on the low pass image, thus generating a tree-like multiresolution image representation. This is well suited to compression because most of the image energy is packed into the low pass subimages. The reduction of information can be done gradually by reducing the accuracy of representing various subimages.

The CCSDS algorithm allows compression upto exact defined quality or data size. Closely related to general frequency space image compression techniques such as JPEG2000 [8], it was shown to be better suitable to the type of images under study here [9]. CCSDS offers many options to steer the compression. One important choice is the selection of the wavelet function. We use the Integer (Reversible) 9/7M DWT (one of the recommended choices). As an integer wavelet, it has low computational complexity and allows true lossless compression. In our experiments we will use the TER implementation of the CCSDS algorithm [10].

2.4   Binning and Aliasing

Binning is considered only in the along-track direction. However, the high quality optical system is designed for optimal resolution in the direction demanding the highest resolution (across flight), with a similar resolution in the other direction. Therefore, high-frequency components are present on the sensor before binning and resampling.

For practical reasons, binning is implemented as a simple square hat filter adding adjacent pixels. Therefore, the high-frequency part of the signal will cause aliasing. A significant amount of the signals will be folded back and appear as false low-frequency artifacts in the binned image. These cannot be removed by post-processing and thus will also appear in the final images. The filters used in wavelet based compression techniques have a much larger span and correspond to a more narrowband filter in the frequency domain. Using them instead of a simple binning filter will significantly eliminate aliasing effects.

3 Methods

3.1 Binning Flow

The binning flow consists of a combination of binning and compression. Binning is averaging the data of several pixels and combining them to a single value. First binning of 3 pixels in the vertical direction is performed for all spectral bands except the SWIR. Next, lossy compression is applied with low compression ratios. The data flow is drawn schematically in figure 2.

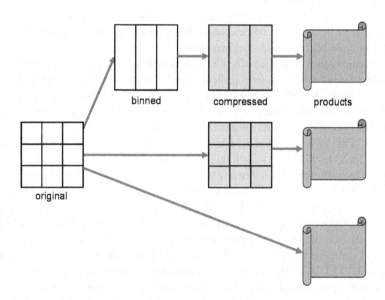

Fig. 2. Data reduction flows. Top: binning flow, middle: compression flow, bottom: ideal flow without data redcution.

The total data reduction is the product of the binning factor (3) and the CR. The reduction proposed per band is summarized in table 1. The lower resolution SWIR band uses about 10 %, the other bands about 30 % of the data budget. The BLUE channel is compressed more becasue it contains less detail and is less critical to most users. The compression on the NIR channel is slightly reduced.

Table 1. Proposed compression ratios for the different bands and cameras

Band	Camera	Binning	CR	Reduction	Raw Fraction	Compr. Fraction
BLUE	all	3	3,6	10,8	30,8 %	20,3 %
RED	all	3	2,4	7,2	30,8 %	30,5 %
NIR	all	3	1,8	5,4	30,8 %	40,7 %
SWIR	center	1	2,4	2,4	2,6 %	2,5 %
SWIR	side	1	1,8	1,8	5,1 %	6,7 %

3.2   Compression Flow

Binning is omitted and the data flow becomes very simple as shown in figure 2. To achieve the same amount of data reduction, the CR need to be increased by a factor of 3. The numbers of table 1 are easily modified: the binning is no longer in use and the CR numbers become equal to the total reduction numbers. Instead of near lossless compression, we now have lossy compression with fairly high compression rates. The effect of this change is a key point of this study.

The set of CR for the different bands was established for near lossless compression with binning and experimentally determined to give an optimal balance of errors for the different bands. The modification to 3× higher values yields a usable set of CR. It is however likely that this configuration is not optimal. We expect that when reinvestigating compression effects, the CR of the different bands can be improved to achieve better overall results within the data budget.

3.3   Measuring the Effect of Data Reduction on Product Quality

The main concern of goal is to retain good radiometry in the products. The data reduction alters the information available to the ground processing which impacts the quality of the derived products. To evaluate this, we need to compare actual products with a reference product. As reference we take an *ideal* product, directly generated from the original data as captured by the sensors. This corresponds to the trivial flow depicted at the bottom of figure 2. Note that during normal operation of the satellite, it would be possible to switch off the compression and generate ideal products (downlink bandwidth permitting).

The quality should be measured by the error on products because only then it reflects the impact of the data reduction on the whole system. Investigating the errors caused by a single reduction step (e.g. compression step only) cannot achieve this and yields less relevant results.

The deviation of an actual product from a theoretical ideal product is be measured using the Root Mean Square Error (RMSE):

$$RMSE = \sqrt{\frac{1}{n} \sum_{x=1}^{n} (F_{actual}(i) - F_{ideal}(i))^2}$$

where F_{actual} and F_{actual} are the pixel values at position i in both products. The RMSE values are most strongly influenced by the pixels with large errors.

The images have a bit depth of 12 bit but do not necessarily contain 12 bits of meaningful data. The least significant bits are expected to contain only noise. In earlier tests, it was shown that is is better to reduce the bit depth after than before compression, even if this implies higher compression rates. Still, it is most meaningful to calculate the RMSE for the 10 most significant bits only. Except for very small errors, when quantization errors play a role, RMSE for different bit depths are easy to convert, in general and for the case of 12 to 10 bits:

$$RMSE_b = 2^{b-a}.RMSE_a$$

$$RMSE_{10} = RMSE_{12}/4$$

3.4   Interaction of Data Reduction with Product Generation Steps

In the experiments, we use a simplified processing chain that only contains the essential steps that most strongly interact with the data reduction. We consider:

- *preprocessing*: including correction of sensor non-uniformity.
- *resolution conversion* without changing the spatial sampling.
- *projection* to the actual output grid.

Resolution conversion (without changing the actual sampling) is performed to filter out high spatial frequency data, unwanted for the generation of a lower resolution product It has a big impact and therefore needs to be included. The low pass filtering is implemented using fractional averaging on the original data grid, so that a moving average with the size of the product ground sampling distance is performed.

For an original image on a $100m \times 100m$ grid, the averaging needed for a $300m \times 300m$ product is a simple 3×3 flat averaging filter. For the side cameras, the original grid changes to become a $100m \times 100m$ at the very edge. For this grid, a 3×1 flat averaging filter is appropriate. For the 1km products, we use 9×9 and 9×3 flat averaging filters for the center and sides.

The actual projection involves spatial resampling by means of bicubic interpolation. It mixes values from different input pixels and thus interacts with the data reduction. Results of some initial tests showed that this has only a minor effect on the results provided the filtering step was carried out well. Therefore projection was omitted in further tests.

3.5   Non Uniformity Corrections

The individual pixels of a line sensor can have slightly different sensitivities which creates artificial high frequency content (stripes in along track direction). Defective pixels can be seen as a special case of non-uniformity. The patterns in the images make compression more difficult.

Due to limited computing resources on-board of the satellite, non-uniformities are corrected at the start of the ground processing, after decompression. The data reduction flows including uniformity corrections are depicted in fig 3. The artificial adding of non-uniformities to the original images is obviously only performed in the simulations and not in real data processing.

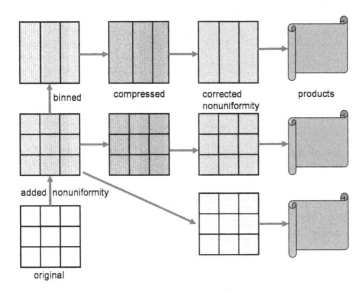

Fig. 3. Data reduction flows including non unfiformity corrections. Top: binning flow, middle: compression flow, bottom: ideal flow.

3.6   Custom Directional Compression

Different subbands represent the different directions in the image (horizontal, vertical and diagonal). In the CCSDS compression scheme, they are all assigned weights that determine the importance given to the subbands. The weights can be adjusted using *custom subband weighting* [7], thus tuning the compression to preserve details differently depending on the direction.

A standard set of weights (see fig. 4) is used by default. This set makes the transform approximately unitary, so each subband has equal importance in rate-distortion sense. This choice leads to the lowest errors if the quality is to be measured directly on the compression output.

However, as explained in section 3.3, we are interested in product quality. In order to achieve the lowest product errors, a different treatment of directional features can be advantageous for following reasons:

– for the side cameras, original image pixels do not represent square areas but have a larger ground horizontal (along-track) sampling distance. The product generation processing then becomes highly assymetric.
– sensor non-uniformity leads to high frequency patterns in the horizontal direction that need to be maximally retained to avoid erroneous non-uniformity corrections.
– the binning flow also reduces more information the vertical direction.

We investigated this and achieved assymetrical compression with a special set of coeficients shown in figure 4. Initial results indeed show better detail preservation in the horizontal direction. However, details in the other directions deteriorate

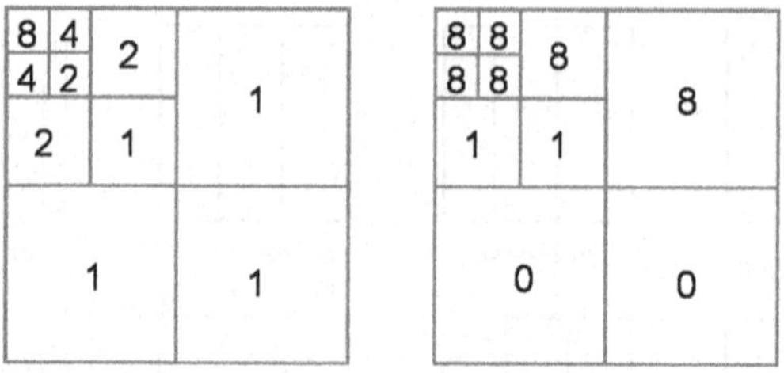

Fig. 4. Schema of directional weighting coeficients. Left: standard weights, Right: custom directional weights.

considerabily compared to standard compression. As a result, the overall RMSE became higher. Most likely, a more subtle differentation of the directional importance is needed to achive better results. This is still under investigation.

4   Experiments and Results

4.1   Data Reduction Flow Test

We performed tests on a set of 30 representative 12 bit images, 10 of each spectral band (RED, BLUE and NIR). We applied the binning flow and compression flow with appropriate CR according to table 1. The resulting images were filtered using the filters described in Section 3.4 to represent the 300m and 1km products generated from the center and the far sides of the images. The so-called *ideal products* were generated directly from the original data, without any compression, but using the same filtering.

Resulting $RMSE_{10}$ values are reported in 2. The binning flow produces $3 \times$ larger errors than the compression flow. For the compression flow, errors on the side are much larger than for the center because less averaging is performed. For the binning compression, the error increases much less because horizontal (across-track) details are preserved better.

It could be useful to differentiate the compression between the center and the side cameras, similar to what is foreseen for the SWIR images. Interestingly, the errors for the BLUE channel are much lower. Compression could still be increased for this channel.

4.2   Non Uniformity Test

The data flows including non-uniformity corrections were described in Section 3.5. The non-uniformities are present in the images to be compressed. While an earlier study showed no issues with low CR, we now investigate much higher CR. We use 2 typical images (BLUE and RED), apply a typical non-uniformity profile and then follow both data reduction flows. Finally the non-uniformity is corrected. In practice, non-uniformity profiles can be determined quite accurately by averaging over many measurements of uniform scenes. Therefore it is reasonable to assume perfect knowledge of the profile in our experiments.

Table 2. RMSE caused by data reduction for the various products

Band	Flow	CR	300m side	300m center	1km side	1km center
BLUE	binning	3,6	6,07	5,25	2,37	1,81
BLUE	compression	10,8	1,00	0,67	0,38	0,28
RED	binning	2,4	8,33	7,25	1,99	1,58
RED	compression	7,2	2,92	1,68	0,86	0,56
NIR	binning	1,8	14,21	12,23	3,33	2,64
NIR	compression	5,4	4,86	2,97	1,56	1,03

Table 3. RMSE caused by data reduction flows including non-uniformity corrections

Product method	300m side BLUE	300m side RED	300m center BLUE	300m center RED	1 km side BLUE	1 km side RED	1 km center BLUE	1 km center RED
binning								
no NUC	0,73	6,69	0,62	5,42	0,19	1,52	0,20	1,13
NUC	0,78	6,70	0,65	5,43	0,24	1,52	0,21	1,13
compression								
no NUC	0,45	3,38	0,30	1,79	0,15	0,92	0,15	0,57
NUC	0,95	3,43	0,46	1,81	0,29	0,94	0,21	0,58

Resulting RMSE values for the various products versus the ideal versions are listed in 3. In all cases, the non-uniformities lead to larger errors. For the binning flow, the differences are small. The compression results deteriorate more. Differences are quite large in the BLUE image. This represents a worse case example: BLUE images contain less detail so that the non uniformity radically alters the image. The CR is also the highest for BLUE. The RED band example on the other hand is a quite dense scene, where the same non uniformity applied has a much smaller impact. Overall, the symmetric compression gives the best results. For the BLUE images the binning method gives comparable, sometimes slightly better results.

5   Conclusion

We investigated the effects of on board data reduction for the PROBA-V remote sensing satellite. The quality measured on final products (both 300m and 1km) showed that the binning flow gives rise to large errors compared to ideal products. Much lower errors can be obtained with a data reduction based on compression only.

The effects of compressing data that was affected by sensor non-uniformities, and correcting for these non-uniformities afterwards were also studied. The binning flow is not very sensitive to this. The compression flow can suffer from increased errors due to non-uniformities. However its overall results are still better than those of the binning flow.

Taking into account the results ans the issue of aliasing for the binning flow, we conclude that the compression flow is the best choice for the PROBA-V imagery. For optimal results, the compression ratios should be revised within the current data budget. Typically, lower compression would be preferred for the side cameras, while for the BLUE band, compression could be increased.

References

1. Yu, G., Vladimirova, T., Sweeting, M.: Image compression systems on board satellites. Acta Astronautica 64(9-10), 988–1005 (2008)
2. Mellab, K.: Small Satellite Technology to Monitor the Global Earth: The PROBA V Mission. In: 33st International Symposium on Remote Sensing of Environment (ISRSE 33), Stresa, Italy (2009)
3. Benhadj, I., Dierckx, W., Dries, J., Duhoux, G., Heyns, W., Nackaerts, K., Sterckx, S., Van Achteren, T.: System performance simulation, calibration and data processing for the Proba-V mission. In: Sensors, Systems, and Next-Generation Satellites XIII, SPIE Europe Remote Sensing, Berlin, Germany (2009)
4. Mostert, S., Kriegler, E.: Implementing an image processing system for the next generation Earth observation sensors for the SUNSAT 2 micro-satellite programme. Acta Astronautica 56(1-2), 171–174 (2005)
5. Dries, J.: The SPOT VEGETATION and PROBA-V User Segments. In: 33st International Symposium on Remote Sensing of Environment (ISRSE 33), Stresa, Italy (2009)
6. Serra-Sagrista, J., Auli-Llinas, F.: Remote sensing data compression. In: Computational Intelligence For Remote Sensing. Studies in Computational Intelligence, vol. 133, pp. 27–61. Springer, Germany (2008)
7. CCSDS: Image data Compression, Recommendation for Space Data System Standards. CCSDS 122.0-B-1, Blue book Issue 1 (2005)
8. Algarni, D.A.: Compression of Remotely Sensed Data Using JPEG. In: International Archives of Photogrammetry and Remote Sensing, pp. 24–28 (1997)
9. CCSDS: Image data Compression, Informational Report. CCSDS 120.1-G-1, Green book (2007)
10. GICI group: TER user manual, Dept. of Information and Communication engineering, Universitat Autonoma Barcelona (2007)

Estimating Color Signal at Different Correlated Color Temperature of Daylight

Paras Pant, Pesal Koirala, Markku Hauta-Kasari, and Jussi Parkkinen

Department of Computer Science and Statistics, University of Joensuu,
P.O. Box: 111, FI-80101, Joensuu, Finland
{paras.pant,pkoirala,mhk,jussi.parkkinen}@cs.joensuu.fi

Abstract. Color signal changes with change in illuminant information. This study focuses on estimating color signals at different Correlated Color Temperature (CCT) of daylight. We selected a set of color signals at different CCT of daylight for estimation. An experiment was conducted by generating color signals from 24 color samples of Macbeth Color Checker and 1645 daylight spectral power distributions (SPD), where CCT ranges from 3757K to 28322K. By uniform sampling of this, we collected 84 color signals from each color samples and combined them to form a training dataset. Principal Component Analysis (PCA) has been applied on the selected training dataset to find the basis vectors and the number of color signals needed for estimation. We apply the Wiener estimation with different order of polynomials to estimate the color signal of color samples. Interestingly, good estimation of all 1645 color signals of given color sample from Macbeth color chart is obtained by selecting five best CCT color signals of that given color sample and with association to its third order polynomial. However, the results from high order polynomials yield to significant errors on Wiener estimation.

Keywords: PCA, Wiener Estimation, CCT, Color Signal, RMSE.

1 Introduction

Accurate estimation of color signals at different Correlated Color Temperature (CCT) is needed in different fields of study in color science. Color Signal is defined as the product of surface reflectance and spectral power distribution (SPD) of illumination. To estimate color signals some researchers focused on defining the surface reflectance from low dimensional models [11] [4] . For example, Stigell et al. [11] estimated the spectral reflectance from RGB image. For this estimation, the authors used reflectance spectra from 24 color samples of Macbeth color checker as prior knowledge and applied Wiener estimation method with different order of polynomials [11]. Likewise, David et al. [4] has approximated the surface reflectance and illuminant spectral information by low dimensional linear model. In their work, the authors used two mode linear models with prior information from surface reflectance of 462 munsell chip by Kelly and illumination information (CIE standard illumination A, B, C and blackbody radiant

J. Blanc-Talon et al. (Eds.): ACIVS 2009, LNCS 5807, pp. 587–597, 2009.

at 3K, 4K, 5K, 9K) to get good results in estimation. In addition Lópeze et al. [10] worked on the recovery of the best skylight SPD with optimum combination of sensors, and studied the recovery method, linear basis and matrix size from colorimetric and spectral metric viewpoint. For high dimensional spectral data recovery, Koirala et al. [13] [12] studied the surface reflectance prediction for all viewing direction in multi-angle measurement for purlesent and metallic sample. In their study, the authors computed the number of primary angles needed for prediction by Principal Component Analysis (PCA) base reconstruction. Then, they used PCA based prediction and Wiener estimation method based prediction to predict the spectral information in all viewing angles.

We are estimating the color signal at different CCT, first of all we need to know the CCT of the given illumination SPD as a prior knowledge. Different research works have been conducted to define the SPD of the illuminant and its corresponding CCT values. Judd et al. [1] have studied the spectral distribution of typical daylight as a function of CCT and a method to calculate the SPD of illuminant from 4800K to 10000K CCT was defined. Furthermore, Hernández et al. [9] [5] have collected and analyzed the SPD of natural daylight illumination and studied its CCT. Furthermore, a graphical method of finding CCT using the RGB diagram was developed [6]. Similar diagram was proposed by Kelly [6] [2]. Robertson [2] developed a numerical method to calculate CCT. He uses a technique of interpolation between isotemperature lines. For computing isotemperature lines Mori's method is used [6]. Judd was the first to propose and compute isotemperature line for evaluation of correlated color temperature [6]. Other different methods have been reviewed in [5]. We used the method purposed in [5] to calculate the CCT for the daylight SPD.

In our study, we estimated the color signals of color samples at different CCT of daylight ranging from 3757K to 28322K with a predefined set of best color signals at different CCT. We determined the best number of CCT color signals needed for our estimation and its basis information by applying PCA. Different researchers [3] [7] [8] agrees that much spectral information is retained by the first 3 basis functions of PCA for data reconstruction. They also confirmed that for efficient reconstruction more than 3 basis functions are needed. In our estimation we studied up to 8 basis functions and selected only the first five basis functions for the estimation of the best CCT color signal. The estimation of the color signal of a color sample over the whole illumination range is made by the selection of few best CCT color signals and using Wiener estimation [11] [12] method combined to PCA results.

2   Data Preparation

Daylight SPD were measured in Granada, Spain at different time of the day during two years period [9]. This spectral information ranges from 370 nm to 800 nm, at every 5 nm steps. We took 1645 daylight SPD with CCT ranging from 3757K to 28322K. We store them in an increasing order of CCT. This spectral information was linearly interpolated to get information between 420 nm to 721

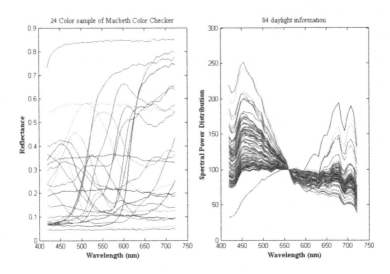

Fig. 1. Reflectance spectra of each patch of color checker and SPD of Daylight illumination in training dataset

nm at every 7 nm steps. We measured 24 reflectance spectra of Macbeth Color Checker in Fig. 2, from 420 nm to 721 nm at every 7 nm steps. The Color signal $S(\lambda)$ is computed for each individual color sample against 1645 daylight spectra as in Eqn. (1). Then we selected 84 color signals of each color sample by uniform sampling of CCT. The set of 84 color signals of individual sample were combined together and used as training dataset. The reflectance spectra of 24 color samples and daylight spectra used in training set are shown in Fig. 1.

$$S(\lambda) = \int_{\lambda} R(\lambda) I(\lambda) \tag{1}$$

where $S(\lambda)$ is the color signal, $R(\lambda)$ is the sample reflectance and $I(\lambda)$ is the illuminant information.

Fig. 2. Macbeth Color Checker

3 Methodology

3.1 Principal Component Analysis

In this study, we apply PCA on our training dataset to obtained the basis information of color signals at different CCT. The basis information gives the direction, where the dataset variance is the largest. The dataset is then projected towards this direction. PCA is used for dimensionality reduction of the given dataset. This dimensionality reduction causes a loss of information during reconstruction. The information loss is inversely proportional to the chosen number of basis vectors. At First in PCA, it is preferable to compute the mean subtracted data of training dataset [12]. We have color signals of m different color samples taken at k wavelengths for n different numbers of CCT. The training dataset is arranged in two dimensional matrices as in Eqn. (2).

$$S = \begin{bmatrix} s_1(T_1) & \cdots & s_m(T_1) \\ \vdots & \ddots & \vdots \\ s_1(T_n) & \cdots & s_m(T_n) \end{bmatrix} \tag{2}$$

Where $s_i(T_j)$ is the color signal in all wavelength of ith sample at j^{th} CCT. The size of the matrix S is $n \times N$ where N is $m \times k$.

The Correlation matrix C for the color signals is shown in Eqn. (3)

$$C = \frac{1}{N} \sum_{i=1}^{n} s_i s_i^T = \frac{1}{N} S S^T \tag{3}$$

where $[]^T$ is the transpose and N is $m \times k$. If S is the mean subtracted dataset correlation matrix C is defined as the covariance matrix.

Given the correlation matrix C, we solve the Eqn. (4) to get the Eigen values σ and Eigen vectors v. As results, we get two $n \times n$ matrix's, where we have n Eigen values and n Eigen vectors also termed as basis vectors.

$$Cv = \sigma v \tag{4}$$

The columns of matrix v are the basis vectors v_i and the diagonals of the matrix σ are the Eigen values σ_i which gives the variance in dataset. The basis vectors were arranged in a decreasing order of variance. The first basis vector v_1 gives the direction, where the variance of the dataset is the largest. The second basis vector v_2 gives the direction of maximum variance making orthogonal to v_1 and so on. We computed the inner product information as in Eqn. (5), taking p numbers of v_i basis vectors ($p \leq n$) and $i=1,2,..n$. This process describes also the data reduction process carried out by PCA taking the first p basis vectors.

$$IP = v^T S \tag{5}$$

where $[]^T$ represents the transpose. The basis vectors v is represented in Eqn. (6)

$$v = \begin{bmatrix} v_1(T_1) & \cdots & v_m(T_1) \\ \vdots & \ddots & \vdots \\ v_1(T_n) & \cdots & v_m(T_n) \end{bmatrix} \tag{6}$$

By linear combination of the first p basis vectors and the inner product information IP, the reconstruction of the color signals in training dataset was carried out as described in Eqn. (7).

$$S_r = vv^T \times S = v \times IP \tag{7}$$

where S_r represents the reconstructed color signals. Different research works agreed that seven or eight basis vectors are needed for good reconstruction [3] [7]. The number of basis vectors also depends on the fidelity value F set for the reconstruction. Fidelity value F is computed from the Eigen values σ as in Eqn. (8).

$$F = \left[\sum_{i=1}^{p} \sigma_i / \sum_{i=1}^{n} \sigma_i \right] \times 100 \tag{8}$$

In Eqn. (8) the numerator is the cumulative sum of variance depending on p ($p \leq n$) number of basis vectors. Denominator is the total sum of variance. The accuracy in reconstruction of training dataset is tested with the first p number of basis vectors. We computed fidelity value in percentage and spectral metric errors on reconstruction with p basis vectors successively.

Our aim is to estimate the color signals for all CCT of individual color samples by a set of best CCT color signals. The first p number of basis vectors used on reconstruction gives the numbers of CCT color signals set for estimation [13]. But, we need to estimate the inner product information for this set of best CCT color signals which is unknown. This problem was solved by selecting the test samples color signals at best CCT and the first p basis vectors of training dataset corresponding to the best CCT [13]. Selection of best CCT color signals is discussed in section 3.3.

Let $t = (t_1, t_2, t_3 \ldots, t_p)$ be the best CCT we obtained. These best CCT should be a part of the available CCT of the training dataset. We computed the new inner product information IP_b from the set of best CCT color signals as in Eqn. (9).

$$IP_b = \begin{bmatrix} v_1(t_1) & \cdots & v_p(t_1) \\ \vdots & \ddots & \vdots \\ v_1(t_p) & \cdots & v_p(t_p) \end{bmatrix}^T \begin{bmatrix} S_1(t_1) \\ \vdots \\ S_p(t_p) \end{bmatrix} \tag{9}$$

where $S_i(t_j)$ is $S_i(t_j) = \left[s_i^{420}(t_j), \ldots s_i^{721}(t_j) \right]$, i is the index of basis vector at j CCT.

The estimation of the color signal for all CCT range in the test sample is achieved by solving Eqn. (10) [13].

$$S_e = v \times IP_b \tag{10}$$

where v is the p numbers of basis vectors calculated in Eqn. (4).

3.2   Wiener Estimation

In spectral imaging, Wiener estimation provides good results in estimation of dataset with prior knowledge [11] [12]. The estimation of color signal is mathematically represented in Eqn. (11); the estimation matrix G maps the data from low to high dimension.

$$S_{est} = G \times t \qquad (11)$$

where S_{est} is the estimated color signal of test datasets, G is the estimation matrix and t is the inner product information computed from the best CCT in Eqn. (9). The size of matrix S_{est} is $n \times N$, G is $n \times p$ and t is $p \times N$. For individual sample estimation N is $1 \times k$. The estimation matrix G is computed for different order of polynomials [11] [12] such that it minimizes the square error between the original and the estimated color signals.

We implemented the method discussed in [11] to compute the estimation matrix using prior knowledge of the test dataset and the inner product information calculated for the best CCT color samples. The results of estimation has been tested with first to fifth order of polynomial combined with a selection of two to five best CCT color signals.

3.3   Selection of Best CCT Color Signal

The numbers of basis vectors used for reconstruction of training dataset by PCA gives the numbers of CCT color signal needed for estimation of test dataset [13]. We computed the best one, two and three CCT color signals from the available CCT color signals in our training dataset by combination as define in Eqn. (12). From each combination sets we calculate the mean error. We consider the combination with the minimum mean error value as the best CCT Color signal.

As the number of selection of CCT color signals increases from three to four, the process of combination becomes computationally slower and expensive to find best CCT. Thus, for the selection of four and five best CCT color signals, we uniformly sampled the numbers of CCT in training dataset, and run the combination process. We computed the mean error for these combinations. The set which gives minimum estimation mean error in all samples dataset is selected as the best CCT color signal. All together we computed five best CCT sets. The number of combination of t best CCT color signals from n CCT color signal of training dataset is defined in Eqn. (12)

$$\binom{n}{t} = \frac{n!}{(n-t)!n!} \qquad (12)$$

where ! stands for factorial.

From the best CCT we computed as described above, we calculate the corresponding color signals. For two color signals, the CCTs are 6890K and 11406K. For three color signals, the CCTs are 5502K, 9203K and 9732K. For four color signals, the CCTs are 3757K, 5735K, 6053K and 8368K. For five color signals, the CCTs are 5903K, 9009K, 9732K, 12631K and 16824K. Here K stands for color temperature in Kelvin absolute scale.

4   Error Measures

To see the difference between the original and the estimated color signals, we used different spectral metrics measures: Goodness of Fit coefficient (GFC) and Root Mean Square Error (RMSE). In GFC measure the difference value is computed as given in Eqn. (13)

$$GFC = \frac{\left| \sum_j S_m(\lambda_j) S_e(\lambda_j) \right|}{\sqrt{\left| \sum_j [S_m(\lambda_j)]^2 \right|} \sqrt{\left| \sum_j [S_e(\lambda_j)]^2 \right|}} \tag{13}$$

where $S_m(\lambda_j)$ is the original and $S_e(\lambda_j)$ is the estimated color signals at wavelength λ_j. GFC values ranges from 0 to 1, with 1 corresponding to an exact duplicate of $S_m(\lambda)$ and considered as the best spectral fit. For basic colorimetric accuracy $GFC \geq 0.995$ is required. Good colorimetric result and spectral fit is obtained with $GFC \geq 0.999$ and GFC value ≥ 0.9999 is considered as the excellent spectral fit for the colorimetric results [9].

RMSE measures the loss of information, as the squared error loss. RMSE is computed from taking the square root of the mean squared error and is defined as in Eqn. (14).

$$RMSE = \sqrt{\frac{1}{N} \sum_{i=1}^{N} (S_m - S_e)^2} \tag{14}$$

where S_m and S_e are respectively the original and the estimated color signals and N is the number of wavelength λ.

5   Results

Our work is based on 24 color samples, having each 1645 numbers of color signals at different CCT of daylight, i.e. 24×1645 color signals. From this dataset we selected 84 color signals by uniform sampling to form the training dataset, i.e. 24×84 color signals. PCA based reconstruction is applied to find the number of the basis vectors required for a good reconstruction and to retain much information of the training dataset. The corresponding fidelity in percentage, RMSE and GFC error during the reconstruction are given in Table 1. The reconstruction results are classified according to the selection of basis vectors from the first to the first eights. The result shows that the first basis vector retains the most information from the training dataset. However, the first three basis vectors are needed in reconstruction to retain enough information, which gives the fidelity percentage ≥ 99.9 and the GFC ≥ 0.999 which is considered as a good spectral fit [9] for all the training samples. The Table. 1 shows that RMSE decreases and that GFC value and fidelity value increase. Thus, for better results more than three basis vectors are required.

As discussed in reference [13] the number of basis vectors used for reconstruction gives the numbers of the primary angles needed for prediction, we used

Table 1. Fidelity value(F) and Reconstruction Error(RMSE,GFC) with different numbers of basis vectors in reconstruction of training dataset. μ is mean error and σ is standard deviation.

Basis Vectors	Fidelity F	RMSE μ	σ	GFC μ	σ
1st	98.285	4.221	2.494	0.992148	0.008816
1st and 2nd	99.597	1.768	1.586	0.998442	0.003306
1st to 3rd	99.965	0.613	0.337	0.999837	0.000192
1st to 4th	99.988	0.335	0.235	0.999947	0.000108
1st to 5th	99.996	0.203	0.117	0.999982	2.88E-05
1st to 6th	99.998	0.146	0.087	0.99999	2.31E-05
1st to 7th	99.999	0.118	0.062	0.999994	1.02E-05
1st to 8th	99.999	0.100	0.054	0.999996	7.93E-06

Table 2. Mean error (μ) and standard deviation (σ) in estimation of color signal of all test dataset taking best CCT set two to five color signal and order of polynomials *P2, P3, P4* and *P5*

which stands for second, third, fourth and fifth order of polynomials.

Best CCT in Kelvin (K)	Order of Polynomials							
	P2		P3		P4		P5	
	μ	σ	μ	σ	μ	σ	μ	σ
6890,11406	1.347	0.891	1.074	0.620	0.934	0.500	1.259	0.624
5502,9203,9732	0.404	0.243	0.287	0.155	0.265	0.144	2.342	0.204
3757,5735,6053,8368	0.281	0.183	0.192	0.106	1.334	0.419	7.011	0.758
5903,9009,9732,12631,16824	0.182	0.103	0.130	0.065	0.679	0.261	6.903	0.688

the same theory to get the number of CCT color signals (or sets) needed for estimation. We computed the best CCT color signals needed for estimation as discussed in section 3.3. In Table. 2, the best combination sets for 2 color signals to 5 color signals are used to verify the results of estimation with different order of polynomials in Wiener estimation. Fig. 5 shows the mean RMSE distribution of the whole test dataset. In Fig. 5, rows corresponds to RMSE distribution for selection of two to five best CCT color signals, where as columns are for two to five orders of polynomial. RMSE result in Table. 2 and Fig. 5 shows that, the accuracy of estimation improves with the increase in the numbers of best CCT color signals from two to five. Similarly, the results improve with the increase in order of polynomials up to the third order. Three best CCT color signals are needed to have mean RMSE value less than 1. With 5 best CCT and third order of polynomials we get the best estimation result for the test dataset. By increasing the order of polynomials to fourth and fifth order with 4 and 5 best CCT estimation results are not improved but rather decreased. From above results, we consider that the third order of polynomials to be the best order of polynomial for Wiener Estimation in our estimation of color signal at different CCT.

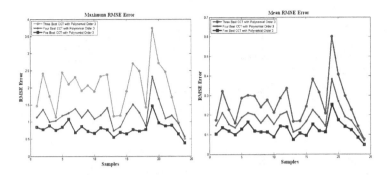

Fig. 3. Maximum RMSE and Mean RMSE in individual Color Sample at three different set (three to five) of CCT and third order of polynomial

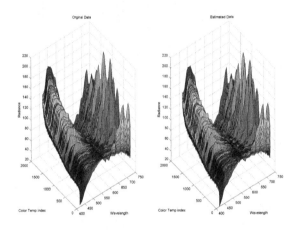

Fig. 4. Characteristics of color signal of color sample nineteen (white) before and after estimation

Furthermore we analyzed the third order of polynomials for an individual color sample for three four and five best CCT combinations. For this individual color sample, the Fig. 3 visualizes the mean and maximum RMSE in the three different cases. This Fig. 3 shows, results of estimation are improved with increases in best CCT numbers. The most error is obtained in sample number 19 though the results are improved with increase in best CCT. The characteristics curve of color signals of color sample 19 before and after estimation, which have relative maximum error than other samples is shown in Fig. 4. The estimation for this color sample is made with three CCT color signals for the third order of polynomials.

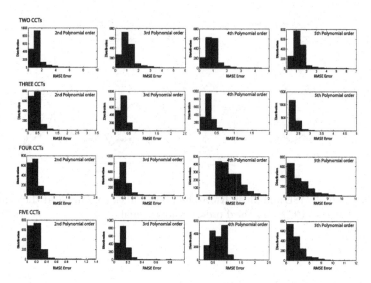

Fig. 5. RMSE distribution in 2 to 5 different set of best CCT with 2 to 5 order of polynomials, for all estimated color sample

6   Conclusion

Estimation method for color signal at different CCT is presented, with selection of minimum numbers of best CCT color signals. The proposed method used wiener estimation combined to PCA for estimation. Proposed approach gives good results of estimation and helps to identify the numbers of CCT color signal needed. As a future work dataset will be increased to incorporate the wide range of illumination information in nature. The optimization method for selection of best CCT will be studied such that further more numbers of best CCT color signals can be computed efficiently in low computational time.

Acknowledgments. We would like to thank Prof. Hernández-Andrés and Color Imaging lab, Department of optica, University de Granada, Spain for supports and providing Daylight Spectral Power Distribution information for this research work.

References

1. Judd, D.B., McAdam, D.L., Wyszecki, G.: Spectral Distribution of Typical Daylight as a Function of Correlated Color Temperature. J. opt. Soc. Am. 54, 1031–1040 (1964)
2. Robertson, R.: Computation of Correlated Color Temperature and Distribution Temperature. J. Opt. Soc. Am. 58, 1528–1535 (1968)
3. Parkkinen, J.P.S., Hallikainen, J., Jaaskelainen, T.: Characteristic spectra of Munsell colors. J. Opt. Soc. Am. A 6(2), 318–322 (1989)

4. Marimont, D.H., Wandell, B.A.: Linear models of surface and illuminant spectra. J. opt. Soc. Am. 9, 1905–1913 (1992)

5. Hernández-Andrés, J., Lee Jr., R.L., Romero, J.: Calculating correlated Color temperature across the entire gamut of daylight and skylight Chromaticites. Applied Optics 38(27), 5703–5709 (1999)

6. Wyszecki, G., Stiles, W.S.: Color Science Concepts and methods, Quantitative Data Formula, 2nd edn. Wiley Interscience Publication, USA (2000)

7. Chiao, C.-C., Cronin, T.W., Osorio, D.: Color signals in natural scenes: characteristics of reflectance spectra and effects of natural illuminants. J. Opt. Soc. Am. A 17(2), 218–224 (2000)

8. Laamanen, H., Jaaskelainen, T., Parkkinen, J.P.S.: Comparison of PCA and ICA in color recognition. In: Proc. SPIE 4197, pp. 367–377 (2000)

9. Hernández-Andrés, J., Romero, J., Nieves, J.L., Lee Jr., R.L.: Color and spectral analysis of daylight in southern Europe. J. Opt. Soc. Am. A 18(6), 1325–1335 (2001)

10. Lópeze-Álvarez Miguel, A., Hernández-Andrés, J., Valero Eva, M., Romero, J.: Selection Algorithm, Sensor, and linear Basis for optimum spectral recovery of skylight. J. Opt. Soc. Am., A 24(4), 942–956 (2007)

11. Stigell, P., Miyata, K., Hauta-Kasari, M.: Wiener estimation method in estimating of spectral reflectance from RGB images. Pattern Recognition and Image Analysis 17, 233–242 (2007)

12. Koirala, P., Hauta-Kasari, M., Parkkinen, J., Hiltunen, J.: Reflectance Prediction in Multi-Angle Measurement by Wiener Estimation Method. In: 16th color imaging conference, Portland, Oregon, USA, November 10-15, pp. 221–226 (2008)

13. Koirala, P., Hauta-Kasari, M., Parkkinen, J., Hiltunen, J.: Accurate reflectance prediction in multi-angle measurement, CGIV 2008, MCS 2008. In: 4th European Conference on Colour in Graphics, Imaging, and Vision, Terrassa, Spain, June 9-13, pp. 489–493 (2008)

Local Color Descriptor for Object Recognition across Illumination Changes

Xiaohu Song, Damien Muselet, and Alain Trémeau

Lab Hubert Curien, Université Jean Monnet
- 18 rue Benoît Lauras, 42000 Saint-Etienne, France
{xiaohu.song,damien.muselet,alain.tremeau}@univ-st-etienne.com
http://www.univ-st-etienne.fr

Abstract. In the context of object recognition, it is useful to extract, from the images, efficient local descriptors that are insensitive to the illumination conditions, to the camera scale factor and to the position and orientation of the object. In this paper, we propose to cope with this invariance problem by applying a spatial transformation to the local regions around detected key points. The new position of each pixel after this local spatial transformation is evaluated according to both the colors and the relative positions of all the pixels in the original local region. The descriptor of the considered local region is the set of the new positions of three particular pixels in this region. The invariance and the discriminating power of our local descriptor is assessed on a public database.

Keywords: object recognition, local descriptor, spatial normalization, discriminating power.

1 Introduction

Object recognition consists in finding among a database of target images those which represent the same object as this represented in a query image. In this paper, we consider that the objects are in cluttered scenes and can be partially occluded. Furthermore the representations of the same object in a target and a query images can be different because of the following variations (See Fig. 1):

- variations in illumination conditions,
- scale changes,
- variations in object 2D position and orientation,
- slight variation in object 3D orientation ($< 20^o$).

In this context, global descriptors have shown their limits and it is highly recommended to extract local descriptors to characterize the images. Thus, the classical systems of object recognition follow the three-step approach: *i*) detection of keypoints [2], *ii*) description of the local region around each detected keypoint [3] and *iii*) comparison of the sets of the query and target descriptors. Since we concentrate on the definition of an effective local color descriptor, the steps *i*) and *iii*) will not be studied in this paper.

J. Blanc-Talon et al. (Eds.): ACIVS 2009, LNCS 5807, pp. 598–605, 2009.

Example prototype images.

Example input test images.

Fig. 1. These images come from the Simon Fraser University Database [1] available at http://www.cs.sfu.ca/~colour/data

For such a setting, SIFT descriptor [4] is shown to provide better recognition rates than many alternatives [3]. The idea of this descriptor is to characterize local regions with relative gradient directions. Indeed, the relative direction of the gradient is almost insensitive to illumination changes, scale changes and 2D object pose. However, it has been noticed that the SIFT descriptor is sensitive to object 3D orientation (object viewpoint) [5]. Furthermore, with SIFT approach, 128 values are required for each local region in order to obtain good recognition rates and we know that the size of each local descriptor directly affects the time processing of the online comparison step.

Consequently, in this paper, we propose a new local descriptor which is

- not based on gradient directions in order to be more invariant in case of object 3D orientation modification,
- very compact since only 18 values are required to provide very good recognition rates,
- invariant to most photometric and radiometric variations.

The main idea of our approach consists in applying a spatial transformation to the local regions around detected keypoints so that the new position of each pixel after this local spatial transformation is a function of both the colors and the relative positions of all the pixels in the original local region. Furthermore, in order to be compact, the descriptor of the considered local region is the set of the new positions of only three particular pixels in this region. Thus, this descriptor takes into account the colors of the pixels and the spatial interactions between all the pixels of the considered local region. This explains its high discriminating power.

The second section of this paper presents the spatial transformation applied to each local regions. The invariance of the transformation according to photometric variations is treated in the third section and the compact descriptor is presented in the fourth section. In the fifth section, the improvement of our approach with respect to classical ones is assessed on a public database.

2   Local Spatial Transformation

In this section, we consider images acquired under the same illumination since photometric invariance is treated in the following section. Considering the local region around one detected keypoint, the approach consists in applying a geometrical transformation to the pixels of this region, from the image space to a 2D canonical destination space.

This kind of transformation has been introduced in [6] as a preprocessing step for image comparison and was applied on global images. For this purpose, the idea is to define a destination space whose axis are associated with color components and not with spatial position. Since a 2D-space is required, the red and green components of the RGB space have been chosen in [6].

In this paper, we propose to extend this global approach to local regions and to increase the number of canonical destination spaces. Indeed, we propose to take into account the interactions between every two of the three RGB color components, i.e. we consider the three red-green, red-blue and green-blue destination spaces.

Thus, a pixel P_i characterized by the color $\{c_i^R, c_i^G, c_i^B\}$ and the 2D-position $\{x_i^I, y_i^I\}$ in the original image space I will be associated with the 2D-position $\{x_i^{D_j}, y_i^{D_j}\}$ in the destination space D_j such as $x_i^{D_1} = c_i^R$, $y_i^{D_1} = c_i^G$, $x_i^{D_2} = c_i^R$, $y_i^{D_2} = c_i^B$ and $x_i^{D_3} = c_i^G$, $y_i^{D_3} = c_i^B$. This means that the destination positions of a pixel are deduced from its color components $\{c_i^R, c_i^G, c_i^B\}$ and not from its position $\{x_i^I, y_i^I\}$ in the original image space. The size of each destination space is $L \times L$ where L is the number of levels used to quantize the color components.

Thus, considering one destination space D_j, each pixel P_i of a local region is associated with two 2D-coordinates $\{x_i^I, y_i^I\}$ and $\{x_i^{D_j}, y_i^{D_j}\}$ which are its positions in the image space I and in the destination space D_j respectively. As explained by Lowe [4], the affine transformation from the image space to the destination space can be written as:

$$\begin{bmatrix} m_{j1} & m_{j2} \\ m_{j3} & m_{j4} \end{bmatrix} \begin{bmatrix} x_i^I \\ y_i^I \end{bmatrix} + \begin{bmatrix} t_{jx} \\ t_{jy} \end{bmatrix} = \begin{bmatrix} x_i^{D_j} \\ y_i^{D_j} \end{bmatrix} \tag{1}$$

where t_{jx} and t_{jy} are the translation parameters and the m_{ji} are the rotation, scale and stretch parameters.

Slight variations in object 3D orientation can be approximated by 2D rotation and translation when we work with local regions. So we propose to eliminate the stretch parameter of the transformation and keep only the 2D-rotation, translation and scale parameters. Thus we set $m_{j3} = -m_{j2}$ and $m_{j4} = m_{j1}$. Indeed, the descriptor presented in the fourth section is all the more discriminant as we reduce the number of degrees of liberty of this transformation.

Consequently, we have to estimate four parameters m_{j1}, m_{j2}, t_{jx} and t_{jy} for each destination space, and for this purpose, we rewrite the equation (1) as:

$$\begin{bmatrix} x_i^I & y_i^I & 1 & 0 \\ y_i^I & -x_i^I & 0 & 1 \\ & \cdots & & \\ & \cdots & & \end{bmatrix} \begin{bmatrix} m_{j1} \\ m_{j2} \\ t_{jx} \\ t_{jy} \end{bmatrix} = \begin{bmatrix} x_i^{D_j} \\ y_i^{D_j} \\ . \\ . \\ . \end{bmatrix} \tag{2}$$

which can be written: $[Im] \times [T_{rj}] = [De]$.

This equation is based on the coordinates of one pixel but we can account all the pixels of the local region by adding lines in the matrices $[Im]$ and $[De]$.

Thus, the parameters of the geometric transformation can be estimated by the least-squares solution:

$$T_{rj} = [Im^T Im]^{-1} Im^T De. \tag{3}$$

The use of the least-squares solution method increases the discriminating power of the process. Indeed, the resulted destination position of a pixel depends not only on its color but also on the colors and the relative positions of the other pixels of the local region. Thus, considering two local regions characterized by the same color histograms but by different spatial color arrangements, the resulted normalized images will be different. This characteristic is very interesting in the context of object recognition.

3   Photometric Invariance

In this section, we consider that the images to compare have been acquired under different illumination conditions. Therefore, a color normalization is added.

Unlike the classical approaches which model the color variations in case of illumination changes by linear transformations, Finlayson proposed a non-linear transformation based on the rank measures of the pixels [7]. The color images I are decomposed into color component images I_R, I_G and I_B in which the pixels Pi are characterized by their red ($c^R(P_i)$), green ($c^G(P_i)$) and blue ($c^B(P_i)$) levels, respectively. Next, within each color component image I_k, the pixels P_i are sorted in increasing order of their levels and characterized by their rank measures expressed as

$$RM^k[I](P_i) = \frac{Card\{P_j \in I / c^k(P_j) \leqslant c^k(P_i)\}}{Card\{P_j \in I\}} \tag{4}$$

Finlayson assumed that these rank measures are invariant to illumination changes and showed that this normalization is equivalent to three $1D$-histogram equalizations. Because of the non-linearity of this normalization, this approach provides better results than previous classical approaches [7].

Consequently, we propose to modify the destination spaces D_1, D_2, and D_3 into D_1', D_2' and D_3' so that their axis are the rank measures of the pixels rather than their levels, i.e, the axis of D_1', D_2' and D_3' are (RM^R, RM^G), (RM^R, RM^B) and (RM^G, RM^B). The transformation from the image space I to the invariant space D_j is called the jth "Invariant Spatial Transformation" (IST_j). We consider two images which represent the same object under different illumination conditions, different poses and different scales. Then, we consider one local region in each image so that these two regions represent the same part of the object. If we apply the IST_j to each of these regions, we should obtain the same results, i.e. the new positions of the pixels representing the same elementary surfaces should be the same in the D_j' spaces. We will verify it in the next section.

4   Compact Color Descriptor (CoCoD)

As we have already said, the subject of the paper is the definition of a new efficient local descriptor. This step comes after the keypoint detection step, which we are not treating there. So we assume that the keypoint detection has already been processed and that for each image, we have a set of keypoints characterized by their position, scale and orientation. The local region associated with a keypoint is constituted by all the pixels which are in the circle whose center position is the keypoint position and whose radius is the keypoint scale. Once the local regions have been detected, we propose to determine the IST_j, $j = \{1, 2, 3\}$ associated with each of them.

Images a) and b) of figure 2 represent the same object with different poses, scales and illumination. We have drawn the local regions around two detected keypoints in each image. These keypoints have been detected thanks to the SIFT approach and provide good results in this case.

The images c) and e) (d) and f) respectively) show the results of the application of the IST_1 on the two local regions of image a) (b), respectively). We could have also shown the results with IST_2 and IST_3 for which the conclusions are the same. We can see that the results are similar for the corresponding regions despite illumination, scale and pose variations.

These resulted images could be taken to characterize each region but we notice that the positions of three consecutive corners ("square mark", "triangle mark" and "circle mark" for example) are sufficient to characterize the local region.

Consequently, considering one local region in the original image, the application of IST_1 can be characterized by 6 values which are the 2D coordinates in D_1' of 3 consecutive corners of the corresponding square. So after applying IST_1, IST_2 and IST_3, the region is characterized by 18 values which are invariant across illumination, scale and pose variations.

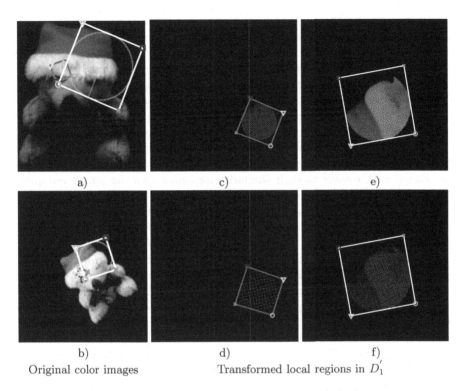

a)	c)	e)
b)	d)	f)
Original color images	Transformed local regions in D_1'	

Fig. 2. Invariant Spatial Transformation (IST_1)

5   Experimental Results

In this section, the Amsterdam Library of Object Images (ALOI) database [8] is used for testing. The Amsterdam database contains images of 1000 different objects under different poses and acquisition conditions and is available at http://staff.science.uva.nl/~aloi/. We propose to use different sets of images in order to assess the invariance of our compact descriptor. For each experiment, we use two sets of 1000 images. The first one is considered as the query set and the second one as the target set. The difference between the query and the target sets is either due to i) illumination conditions, ii) or to illumination conditions and scale variation iii) or to 3D object pose (object viewpoint).

Indeed, in the first experiment, the query set is composed of the images of the objects under illuminants having color temperature of 2175 K and the target set is composed of the images of the objects under illuminants having color temperature of 3075 K. In the second experiment, we just take the same sets but the scale of the images of the second set is four time lower than the scale of the images of the first set. In the third experiment, the images of the two sets have been acquired under the same illumination but the images of the first set represent the objects with $0°$ viewpoint and the images of the second set represent the objects with $20°$ viewpoint.

To illustrate the effectiveness of the proposed features in capturing object properties, we propose to use the same comparison approach as this used in [5]. The objects are characterized by densely sampling the image. The sampling is set in order to have around 60 keypoints in each image. Matching between images is straightforwardly performed by comparing the compact color descriptor (CoCoD) for each region of the query image against all regions in the target image and accumulating the best scores per query region. Regions were compared by calculating the euclidean distance between the respective 18-tuple CoCoD.

For searching, each of the 1000 images of the query set is compared with the 1000 images of the target set. For each recognition, the 1000 target images are ordered with respect to their similarity measures with the considered query image. When the first ordered target image represents the same object as the query image, the recognition is considered as successful.

In order to assess the efficiency of our approach, we propose to compare its recognition rate with those of classical approaches: two approaches are based on global invariant histograms, i.e. one histogram is extracted from each original color image and is normalized thanks to the greyworld normalization [9] or thanks to histogram equalizations [10]. These two global approaches has been shown to provide good recognition rates since the greyworld normalization provides the best results among 12 invariant methods [11] and the equalized histograms provide better results than the greyworld histograms [10]. The two other compared approaches (Wiccest [5] and SIFT [4]) are based on local invariant indexes and the reported recognition rates come from the paper [5].

Tables 1 and 2 indicate the percentage of successful object recognitions for these different methods.

By analyzing tables 1 and 2, we can notice that the local descriptors (SIFT, Wiccest and CoCoD) provide better results than global descriptors.

Table 1. Recognition rates in %. Illumination and scale variations.

Method	Rec. rate
Global color histograms [12]	9.5
Global greyworld histograms [9]	73.0
Global equalized histograms [10]	89.1
Wiccest [5]	73.0
SIFT [4]	97.4
CoCoD across illumination changes	99.9
CoCoD across illumination and scale changes	99.5

Table 2. Recognition rates in %. Viewpoint variations: $0°$ vs $20°$.

Method	Rec. rate
SIFT [4]	62.6
Wiccest [5]	90.3
CoCoD	86.1

Furthermore these tables show that our compact color descriptor provide almost perfect results across illumination and scale variation whereas it is composed of only 18 values. This shows that the used invariant spatial transformation is very discriminant to characterize local regions.

Finally, the results of the local descriptors such as Wiccest and CoCoD which are not based on gradient directions are higher than the results provided by the well-known SIFT.

6   Conclusion

In this paper, we have proposed a method to extract, from color images, local descriptors that are invariant to illumination conditions, scale factor and object viewpoint. The approach consists in determining, for each detected local region, an affine transformation from the image space to a 2D canonical destination space and to apply this transformation to three particular pixels of this local region. The destination spaces are designed so that each axis is associated with an invariant color component. Thus, the positions of the pixels after transformation depend on the colors and on the relative positions of all the pixels in the region. Experimental results show that the recognition rates provided by this approach are better than those provided by the most widely used schemes.

References

1. Barnard, K., Martin, L., Coath, A., Funt, B.: A data set for colour research. Color Research and Application 27, 147–151 (2002)
2. Li, J., Allinson, N.M.: A comprehensive review of current local features for computer vision. Neurocomput. 71, 1771–1787 (2008)
3. Mikolajczyk, K., Schmid, C.: A performance evaluation of local descriptors. IEEE Trans. Pattern Anal. Machine Intell. 27, 1615–1630 (2005)
4. Lowe, D.: Distinctive image features from scale-invariant keypoints. International Journal of Computer Vision 60(2), 91–110 (2004)
5. Geusebroek, J.: Compact object descriptors from local colour invariant histograms. In: British Machine Vision Conference, vol. 3, pp. 1029–1038 (2006)
6. Muselet, D., Trémeau, A.: Illumination invariant spatio-colorimetric normalization. In: Procs. of the Int. Conf. on Pattern Recognition, Tampa, Florida (2008)
7. Finlayson, G., Hordley, S., Schaefer, G., Tian, G.: Illuminant and device invariant colour using histogram equalisation. In: Procs. of the 9th IS&T/SID Color Imaging Conf., Scottsdale, USA, pp. 205–211 (2003)
8. Geusebroek, J.M., Burghouts, G.J., Smeulders, A.W.M.: The Amsterdam library of object images. Int. J. Comput. Vision 61, 103–112 (2005)
9. Gershon, R., Jepson, A.D., Tsotsos, J.K.: From [r,g,b] to surface reflectance: computing color constant descriptors in images. Perception, 755–758 (1988)
10. Finlayson, G., Hordley, S., Schaefer, G., Tian, G.Y.: Illuminant and device invariant colour using histogram equalisation. Pattern Recognition 38, 179–190 (2005)
11. Finlayson, G., Schaefer, G.: Colour indexing across devices and viewing conditions. In: Procs. of the 2nd Int. Workshop on Content-Based Multimedia Indexing, Brescia, Italy, pp. 215–221 (2001)
12. Swain, M.J., Ballard, D.H.: Color indexing. International Journal of Computer Vision 7(1), 11–32 (1991)

A New Method for Segmentation of Images Represented in a HSV Color Space

Dumitru Dan Burdescu, Marius Brezovan, Eugen Ganea, and Liana Stanescu

University of Craiova, Craiova,
Bd. Decebal 107, Romania
{burdescu_dumitru,brezovan_marius,ganea_eugen,
stanescu_liana}@software.ucv.ro

Abstract. This paper presents an original low-level system for color image segmentation considering the Hue-Saturation-Value (HSV) color space. Many difficulties of color image segmentation may be resolved using the correct color space in order to increase the effectiveness of color components to discriminate color data. The technique proposed in the article uses new data structures that lead to simpler and more efficient segmentation algorithms. We introduce a flexible hexagonal network structure on the pixels image and we extract for each segmented region the syntactic features that can be used in the shape recognition process. Our technique has a time complexity lower than the methods studied from specialized literature and the experimental results on Berkeley Segmentation Dataset color image database show that the performance of method is robust.

1 Introduction

There are multiple visual applications for image segmentation that gain more and more importance, and there are a wide range of computational vision problems that could use segmented images. However the problem of image segmentation remains a great challenge for computer vision. The importance of color image segmentation results from many fields that must use this technique.

In this paper we propose an original low-level system for color image segmentation. The segmentation task implements an efficient region based segmentation method that captures both certain perceptually important local and non-local image characteristics. The proposed feature-based segmentation method uses a flexible hexagonal network structure containing the image pixels in order to determine the color regions from the image and for a region the syntactic features which can give the signature of the region. Our segmentation method, unlike other methods that rely on detecting boundaries between regions, returns closed contours that are accurate polygonal approximation of simple or compound objects. We consider the HSV color space, which is the nearest color space for human color perception. Compared with native RGB color space for a digital images, the HSV is a more uniformly and the function for computing of the distance between two colors in HSV is a uniformly distributed function.

The paper is organized as follows: in Subsection 1.2 the determination of HSV color space components is introduced; Subsection 1.3 presents the method for construction of hexagonal structure on pixels image and the fundamental of image segmentation;

J. Blanc-Talon et al. (Eds.): ACIVS 2009, LNCS 5807, pp. 606–617, 2009.

Section 2 describes our algorithms for image segmentation; Section 3 presents our experimental results and Section 4 concludes the paper.

1.1 Related Work

There are many proposed techniques for color segmentation. In this section we consider some of the related work that is most relevant to our approach.

The segmentation process of a 2D image can be seen as containing three major steps [1]: preprocessing, feature color and texture extraction and decision. The first phase, which simplifies the image by reducing the image noise, typically involves image processing techniques such as median or morphological filtering. Several methods have been developed to improve this problem and very good results can be obtained using edge morphological filtering, as in [2] where a computationally efficient translation-invariant method is developed. In the feature extraction phase there are determined the pixel features that are necessary for partitioning the image. Depending on the used color space, the process of feature extraction can be as immediate as reading the RGB value of each pixel, or quite complex and computationally intensive, in cases of hybrid color space. Other than color features the texture features have also been recently introduced and have been demonstrated to be of importance in image segmentation [3]. Contour information can also be used as part of the feature space, to facilitate the formation of regions. Color features can be the RGB color values, as RGB was the initial choice for the segmentation process color space. The HSV color space has proven to be more appropriate on the human perception for the application of image segmentation. Transformation from RGB to HSV color space can be achieved through a non-linear transformation [4]. After the feature extraction phase is finished, a decision step must be involved to appropriately partition the feature space, this decision step being implemented via the application of a segmentation algorithm. Segmentation algorithms for 2D images may be divided primarily into homogeneity-based and boundary-based methods [5,6]. Homogeneity-based approaches rely on the homogeneity of spatially localized features such as intensity and texture. The boundary-based methods use gradient information in order to locate object boundaries. An important group of homogeneity-based segmentation methods includes split-based and merge-based methods. Combining these two types of methods, the split and merge technique applies a merging process to the partitions resulting from a split step. The watershed algorithms replace the rigid split and merge process and analyze an image as a topographic surface, thus creating regions corresponding to detected catchments basins [7]. The watershed algorithm proceeds in two steps. First, an initial classification of all points into regions corresponding to catchments basins is performed, by tracing each point down its path of steepest descent to a local minima. Then, neighboring regions and the boundaries between them are analyzed according to an appropriate saliency measure, such as minimum boundary height, to allow for merging among adjacent regions. The objective of the boundary-based methods is to locate the discontinuities in the feature space that correspond to object boundaries. Several edge detectors have been proposed, such as the Sobel, Prewitt, Roberts or Canny operators [8]. The Canny operator is probably the most widely used algorithm for edge detection in image segmentation techniques. By considering the boundary as a whole, a global shape measure is imposed, thus gaps are prohibited and overall consistency is emphasized. In [9], a different approach is proposed: a predictive coding scheme is employed to detect the direction of change in various image attributes and construct an edge flow field. By propagating the edge-flow vectors, the boundaries can be detected at image locations that encounter two opposite directions of flow. Hybrid color image segmentation based on HSV color space and a color histogram for K-Means clustering is proposed in [10]. Compared with the traditional K-Means clustering, the initialization of centroids and the number of cluster are automatically estimated. In addition, a filter for post-processing is introduced to effectively eliminate small spatial regions. The active contour technique consists in applying locally a velocity such that the initial contour evolves toward the contour of the object of interest. This velocity is derived from a characterization of the object formally written as a criterion to be optimized. Very popular in 2D image analysis, active contours have been generalized to curved surfaces only recently and use for feature extraction from 3D image [11].

1.2 Determination of the Color Space Representation

The methods that analyze the distribution of the pixel colors in a color space consider that each pixel in the color image is represented by a color point in a color space. The native color space for digital images is the (R, G, B) color space. Other color spaces can be used and the performance of an image segmentation procedure is known to depend on the choice of the color space. Unfortunately, there doesn't exist a color space which provides satisfying results for the segmentation of all kinds of images. We propose a color image segmentation approach by pixel clustering in a HSV color space. In the first step we determine the color components corresponding to the HSV color starting from RGB color space. There are different algorithms to compute HSV color space. The algorithm used in experiments follows the method described in [12]:

Algorithm 1. Transformation from RGB to HSV color space

   Input: The RGB color triplet (R, G, B)
   Output: The HSV color triplet (H, S, V)
1 $Max \leftarrow \max (R, G, B)$; $Min \leftarrow \min (R, G, B)$;
2 $V \leftarrow Max$; $S \leftarrow (Max - Min)/Max$;
3 **switch** *case* **do**
4   **case** *0*
5       $H \leftarrow 1 + (G\text{-}B)/(Max - Min)$;
6   **end**
7   **case** *1*
8       $H \leftarrow 3 + (B\text{-}R)/(Max - Min)$;
9   **end**
10   **case** *2*
11      $H \leftarrow 5 + (R\text{-}G)/(Max - Min)$;
12   **end**
13 **end**

In the second step we add filters for removing the image noise. This pre-processing step has a low computational time in the total time of the segmentation phase.

1.3 The Main Idea of Method

Our technique is based on a new utilization of pixels from the image that are integrated into a network type graph. We use a hexagonal network structure on the image pixels, as presented in Fig. 1. The vertices of the hexagonal network cover half of pixels from the image. The hexagonal structure represents a grid-graph, for each hexagon h in this structure there exist 6-hexagons that are neighbors in a 6-connected sense and the determination of indices for 6-hexagons neighbors having as input the index of current hexagon is very simple. The main advantage when using hexagons instead of pixels as elementary piece of information is the reduction of the time complexity of the algorithms. The list of hexagons is stored such as a vector of numbers $[1 \ldots N]$, where N, the number of hexagons, is determined based on the formula:

$$N = \frac{height - 1}{2} \times \left(\frac{width - width \mod 4}{4} + \frac{width - (width \mod 4) - 4}{4} \right) \quad (1)$$

with $height$ and $width$ representing the height and the width of the image.

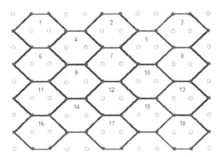

Fig. 1. The hexagonal structure on the image pixels

Each hexagon has associated two important attributes representing its dominant color and its gravity center. For determining these attributes we use eight pixels contained in a hexagon: the six pixels of the frontier, and the two interior pixels. The dominant color of a hexagon is the main vector color of all the eight colors of its associated pixels. We split the pixels of image into two sets, the set of pixels which represent the vertices of hexagons and the set of complementary pixels; the two lists will be used as inputs for the segmentation algorithm. The mapping of pixels network on the hexagons network is immediately and it is not time consuming in accordance with the following formula which determines the index for the first vertex of hexagon:

$$fv = 2 \times h + \frac{2 \times (h - 1)}{columnNb - 1} \quad (2)$$

where fv represents the index of the first vertex, $columnNb$ the column number of the hexagon network and h represents the index of the hexagon.

In the step of algorithm for the current hexagon we determine the 6-neigbors and for each neighbor we compute the color distance between the current hexagon and the current neighbor. In order to determine the distance between two colors in HSV color space, we use the following formula [13]:

$$d_{ij} = 1 - \frac{1}{\sqrt{5 \times [(v_i - v_j)^2 + (s_i cosh_i - s_j cosh_j)^2 + (s_i sinh_i - s_j sinh_j)^2]}} \qquad (3)$$

If the distance is less than a threshold then the current neighbor hexagon is marked as visited and is added to the current region of hexagons. The value of threshold is determined for each image in the pre-processing task with the formula:

$$threshold = \frac{sMedDist + devDist}{2} \qquad (4)$$

where $sMedDist$ is the mean value of the distances and $devDist$ is the standard deviation of the distances. In the final phase for each region determined in the segmentation process we compute the list of hexagons from the contour and the syntactic features that can be used in the shape recognition process.

2   Segmentation Algorithms

The proposed segmentation algorithms will produce a proper segmentation of pixels which are mapped on the hexagon network according to the definition of distance in HSV color space and the syntactic features for each region.

In the subsection 2.1 we explain the algorithm for determination of the list of color regions. To achieve this goal we built for each segmented image a list of components. The length of the list is given by the number of distinct colors which are found in image according to the distance computed with formula 3 and with a threshold computed with formula 4. Elements from the color list are members of one or more elements corresponding to the regions with the same color but distinct in the image space. For each sub-element we stored the associated list of hexagons and the first hexagon of this list, which is a hexagon from contour of region because we cross the hexagon network from left to right and from top to down. In the subsection 2.2 we expose the algorithm for the extraction of the contours of regions and the determination of the syntactic features. For each visual object from the image we detect the closed contour which is an accurate polygonal approximation. In the initial phase we choose the first hexagon as the current hexagon and we determine his neighbors with at least one neighbor in the exterior of

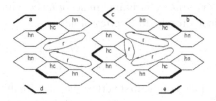

Fig. 2. The possible interconnections between three hexagons

the current region. In this way we decide if a hexagon is a contour hexagon and add it to the list. When the last hexagon found is the same with the first hexagon, the algorithm ends and there will be returned the list of hexagons which represents the close contour of current region. For this list we determine the syntactic characteristics that give how there are interconnected three by three the hexagons neighbors from the contour. In the Fig. 2 there are presented the 5 possible situations. For every possible situation we used for codification a letter $[a \ldots e]$. The hc represents the current hexagon, hn represents the hexagon neighbor and r signifies the interior of the current region. The algorithm returns a string with these letters which represent the signature of the object and can be used in shape recognition phase.

2.1 Algorithms for Determination of the List of Regions

In this subsection there are presented the algorithms for determining the list of salient regions from an image. These algorithms return a composed list corresponding to the salient colors from the input image, which is computed based on hexagonal network and the distance between two colors for HSV space color.

The procedure $sameVertexColour$ returns the color of a hexagon. This procedure has a constant execution time because all calls are constant in time processing.

Algorithm 2. Determination of the color for hexagon

Input: The current hexagon h_i
The colors list of pixels corresponding to the hexagonal network and colors list for complementary pixels of L_1 $L_1 = \{p_1, \ldots, p_{6n}\}, L_2 = \{p_1^c, \ldots, p_{6n}^c\}$
Output: The object $crtColorHexagon$
1 **Procedure** sameVertexColour $(h_i, L_1, L_2; crtColorHexagon)$;
2 * initialize $crtColorHexagon$;
3 * determine the colors for the six vertices of hexagon h_i;
4 * determine the colors for the two vertices from interior of hexagon h_i;
5 * calculate the mean color value $meanColor$ for the eight colors of vertices;
6 $crtColorHexagon.colorHexagon \leftarrow meanColor$;
7 $crtColorHexagon.sameColor \leftarrow$ true;
8 **for** $k \leftarrow 1$ **to** 6 **do**
9   **if** $colorDistance(meanColor, colorVertex[k]) > threshold$ **then**
10       $crtColorHexagon.sameColor \leftarrow$ false;
11   break;
12   **end**
13 **end**
14 **return** $crtColorHexagon$;

The procedure $expandColourArea$ presented in Algorithm 3 receives as input the two lists of colors pixels, the current hexagon, the current region index and the current color index, and returns the list of hexagons with the same color $crtRegionItem$.

Algorithm 3. Expand the current region

Input: The current hexagon h_i

The colors list of pixels corresponding to the hexagonal network and colors list for complementary pixels of L_1

$L_1 = \{p_1, \ldots, p_{6n}\}, L_2 = \{p_1^c, \ldots, p_{6n}^c\}$

The current region index $indexCrtRegion$ and the current color index $indexCrtColor$

Output: The list of hexagons with the same color $crtRegionItem$

1 **Procedure** expandColourArea $(h_i, V, L_1, L_2, indexCrtRegion, indexCrtColor;$ $crtRegionItem)$;

2 push(h_i);

3 **while** *not(empty(stack))* **do**

4      $h \leftarrow pop()$;

5   * determine the six hexagons neighbors $nHexagons$ for hexagon h;

6   **for** $k \leftarrow 1$ **to** 6 **do**

7   **if** *not(visit($nHexagons[k]$))* **then**

8              $crtColorHexagon \leftarrow$ sameVertexColour(L_1, L_2, h_i);

9   **if** $crtColorHexagon.sameColor$ **and** $colorDistance(crtColorHexagon.color,colors[indexCrtColor]) <$ $threshold)$ **then**

10   * add $nHexagons[k]$ to $crtRegionItem$;

11   * mark visit$(nHexagons[k])$;

12   push $(nHexagons[k])$;

13   **end**

14   **end**

15   **end**

16 **end**

Proposition 1. *The running time of the procedure expandColourArea is $O(n)$, where n is the number of hexagons from a region with the same color.*

Proof. In the loop WHILE we consider each hexagon h with the same color. All operations from block WHILE require only constant time. The code inside the WHILE loop is executed at most $|V|$ times, because in the worst case the entire image can represent a single region. The running time of the entire algorithm is therefore $O(n)$.

Proposition 2. *The running time of the procedure listRegions is $O(n^2)$, where n is the number of the hexagons network.*

Proof. Inside the loop FOR we consider each hexagon h from the hexagonal structure. All operations from the block FOR except the call of procedure *expandColourArea* require only constant time. The most consuming part is the expanding operation at line 21. The procedure *expandColourArea* is presented in Algorithm 3 and the time complexity is $O(n)$. The running time of the entire algorithm is therefore $O(n^2)$.

Algorithm 4. Determination of the segmentation list regions

Input: The vector corresponding to the hexagonal network $V = \{h_1, \ldots, h_n\}$
The colors list of pixels corresponding to the hexagonal network and colors list for complementary pixels of L_1
$L_1 = \{p_1, \ldots, p_{6n}\}, L_2 = \{p_1^c, \ldots, p_{6n}^c\}$
Output: A list of colors pixels, for each color we determine a list of regions
$\qquad C = \{\{c_1\}, \ldots, \{c_k\}\}, c_i = \{color, \{r_1, \ldots, r_p\}\}$

```
1  Procedure listRegions (V, L₁, L₂; C);
2  colourNb ← 0;
3  for i ← 1 to n do
4      * initialize crtRegionItem;
5      if not(visit(hᵢ)) then
6          crtColorHexagon ← sameVertexColour (L₁, L₂, hᵢ);
7          if crtColorHexagon.sameColor then
8              k ← findColor(crtColorHexagon.color);
9              if k < 0 then
10                 * add new color c_{colourNb} to list C;
11                 k ← colourNb++;
12                 indexCrtRegion ← 0;
13             else
14                 indexCrtColor ← k;
15                 indexCrtRegion ← findLastIndexRegion (indexCrtColor);
16                 indexCrtRegion++;
17             end
18             hᵢ.indexRegion ← indexCrtRegion;
19             hᵢ.indexColor ← k;
20             * add hᵢ to crtRegionItem;
21             expandColourArea (hᵢ, V, L₁, L₂, indexCrtRegion, indexCrtColor;
                   crtRegionItem);
22             * add new region crtRegionItem to list of element k from C
23         end
24      end
25  end
```

2.2   Algorithm for Determining the Contours of Regions

Proposition 3. *The running time of the procedure contourRegions is $O(n)$, where n is the number of hexagons from a region with the same color.*

Proof. Inside the loop WHILE we consider each hexagon h in the same color region. All operations inside this block require only constant time. The code inside WHILE is executed at most $|L|$ times, because in the worst case the region can be a single open curve line. The running time of the entire algorithm is therefore $O(n)$.

Algorithm 5. Determination of the contours of regions

Input: The list of hexagons from a region with same color $L = \{h_1, \ldots, h_n\}$
The current region index $indexCrtRegion$ and the current color index $indexCrtColor$
Output: The list of hexagons from contour of region

1 **Procedure** contourRegions $(L; L_c)$;
2 $firstHexagon \leftarrow h_1; finish \leftarrow$ false;
3 * initialize the stack of indices hexagons from contour;
4 push (h_1);
5 **while** *not(empty(stack))* **and** *not(finish)* **do**
6      $h \leftarrow$ pop();
7   * determine the six neighbors hexagons $nHexagons$ for hexagon h;
8   **for** $k \leftarrow 1$ **to** 6 **do**
9   **if** *not(visit(nHexagons[k]))* **and** *nHexagons[k] belong L* **then**
10   * determine the six neighbors hexagons $nNHexagons$ for hexagon
                $nHexagons[k]$;
11             $countExtHexagons \leftarrow 0$;
12   **for** $j \leftarrow 1$ **to** 6 **do**
13   **if** *not(nNHexagons[j] belong L)* **then**
14                     $countExtHexagons[k] \leftarrow 1$;break;
15   **end**
16   **if** $countExtHexagons = 1$ **then**
17   push($nHexagons[k]$);
18   * add $nHexagons[k]$ to list of hexagons from contour of current
                        region;
19   * mark visit($nHexagons[k]$);
20   **if** $nHexagons[k] = firstHexagon$ **then**
21   * add $firstHexagon$ to list of hexagons form contour of
                            current region;
22                         $finish \leftarrow$ true;break;
23   **end**
24   **end**
25   **end**
26   **end**
27   **end**
28 **end**

---

3 Experiments

We tested our method for image segmentation on a Berkeley Segmentation Dataset color image database (BSDB) [14]. The database contains two sets of images: a training set of 200 images and a test set of 100 images. For determining the over-segmentation and under-segmentation we reconstructed the initial image and we calculated the rapport between the pixels from the initial image and the pixels from the rebuilt image. In Figure 3 there are shown examples of segmentation images from BSDB.

Fig. 3. Images Segmentation Examples

The first column represents the extracted contours of the regions detected by the algorithms proposed in the new method. The second column represents the segmented images and the last column are the original images. After the segmentation, for each region it is known the list of pixel-hexagons and the HSV color of zone. Based on this information we rebuilt a copy for the original image and we calculated its number of pixels with the same color. In the processing phase, for each segmented image we saved the information corresponding to the number of pixels with the same color. We divided the images into regions based on seed-hexagons and determined the local number of pixels with the same color. The first hexagon of the network is the first seed-hexagon and the dimension of the regions, level - odd number, is given by the number of hexagons which can be found through the diagonal. For an image we defined the column number of the hexagon network, $columnNb$, as $(imageWitdh - imageWitdh \mod 4)/2$. The set of the hexagons from a region is determined starting from the seed-hexagon and adding the value $columnNb/2$; in this way we computed the indices of the hexagon from the first diagonal. After that, we used these indices in order to determine the hexagons on the secondary diagonals by adding /subtracting the value $(columnNb/2 - 1)$. The iteration process is finished when the number of hexagons from the current secondary diagonals is one. The indices from the last diagonal are used for determining the next seed-hexagon. The number of seed-hexagons depends on the level and it is computed with the following formula:

$$NSH = \frac{2 \times N}{level^2 + 1},\tag{5}$$

where NSH represents the number of seed-hexagons, N the total number of hexagons, and $level$ the number of hexagon from the diagonal. Starting from that information we defined a new error measure which quantifies the performance of an image segmentation algorithm. The number of pixels with the same color can be used as features because the segmentation method is a color-based segmentation. The formula used for establish segmentation error is:

$$error = \sum_{i=1}^{NHS} \frac{2 \times |N_i(r,g,b) - Nc_i(r,g,b)|}{level^2 + 1},$$ (6)

where $N_i(r,g,b)$ represents the number of pixels with the same color calculated for region i from the original image, and $Nc_i(r,g,b)$ represent the local number of pixels with the same color calculated for region i from the rebuilt image. By modifying the level value we determine the value of threshold for the classification of segmentation as being good. In Fig. 4 it is shown the correlation between threshold and level.

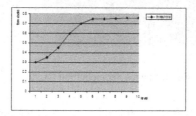

Fig. 4. The relationship between threshold and level

For the exact evaluation of the under-segmentation and over-segmentation case we used the modified formula 6 for determining if the image was split up into too few (under-segmentation) or too many regions (over-segmentation). We split the image in regions based on seed-hexagons and for each region we applied our segmentation method. After the reconstruction of the regions and number of pixels with the same color calculation we established the segmentation error with formula:

$$error_i = |N_i(r,g,b) - Nc_i(r,g,b)|,$$ (7)

where i is the index of region i. We compared the value of the error obtained with formula 4 with the maximum value of the errors vector for over-segmentation and with the minimum value of the errors vector for under-segmentation. We consider a good segmentation process if the error is between the values 0.4 and 0.65. Below the value 0.4 we obtain an over-segmentation, while over 0.65 we obtain an under-segmentation.

4   Conclusions

In this paper we presented a new method for image segmentation and extraction of the contours for regions. The novelty of our contribution concerns three aspects: (a) In order to minimize the running time we introduced a hexagonal structure based on the image pixels, that is used both in the image segmentation and contours extraction algorithms; (b) We proposed an efficient method for segmentation of color images based on HSV color space and for extracting syntactic features of contours regions; (c) We developed a fast method for extracting the contours of regions, which runs in polynomial time. The extracted syntactic features give the signature for the real objects from the image and will be used in the shape recognition process.

Acknowledgments. This research was partially supported by the Romanian National University Research Council under the PCE Grant No. 597.

References

1. Gonzalez, W.: Digital Image Processing, 2nd edn. Prentice Hall, Englewood Cliffs (2002)
2. Soille, P., Talbot, H.: Directional Morphological Filtering. IEEE Transactions on Pattern Analysis and Machine Intelligence 23 (November 2001)
3. Bashar, M.K., Matsumoto, T., Takeuchi, Y., Kudo, H., Ohnishi, N.: Unsupervised Texture Segmentation via Wavelet-based Locally Orderless Images (WLOIs) and SOM. In: Proceeding (398) Computer Graphics and Imaging (2003)
4. Makoto, M.: Mathematical Transform of (r,g,b) Colour Data to Munsell (h,s,v) Colour Data. SPIE Visual Communications and Image Processing, 1001 (1988)
5. Jacobs, D.: Robust and Efficient Detection of Salient Convex Groups. IEEE Transaction on Pattern Analysis and Machine Intelligence (1996)
6. Salembier, P., Marques, F.: Region-Based Representations of Image and Video: Segmentation Tools for Multimedia Services. IEEE Transaction on Circuits and Systems for Video Technology 9 (December 1999)
7. Beucher, S., Meyer, F.: The Morphological Approach to Segmentation: The Watershed Transformation. In: Mathematical Morphology in Image Processing. Marcel Dekker, New York (1993)
8. Canny, J.: Computational Approach to Edge Detection. IEEE Transaction Pattern Analysis and Machine Intelligence 8, 679–698 (1986)
9. Ma, W.Y., Manjunath, B.S.: EdgeFlow: A Technique for Boundary Detection and Image Segmentation. IEEE Transactions on Image Processing 9(8), 1375–1388 (2000)
10. Chen, T.W., Chen, Y.L., Chien, S.Y.: Fast Image Segmentation based on K-Means Clustering with Histograms in HSV Color Space. IEEE Multimedia Signal Processing (2008)
11. Krueger, M., Delmas, P., Gimel'farb, G.: Active Contour Based Segmentation of 3D Surfaces. In: Forsyth, D., Torr, P., Zisserman, A. (eds.) ECCV 2008, Part II. LNCS, vol. 5303, pp. 350–363. Springer, Heidelberg (2008)
12. Rogers, D.F.: Procedural Elements for Computer Graphics. McGraw-Hill, New York (1985)
13. Smith, J.R., Chang, S.F.: VisualSEEk: A Fully Automated Content-Based Image Query System. In: ACM Multimedia, Boston, MA (November 1996)
14. Fowlkes, C., Martin, D., Malik, J.: Learning Affinity Functions for Image Segmentation: Combining Patch-based and Gradient-based Approaches. In: Proc. of the IEEE Conference on Computer Vision and Pattern Recognition, Madison, Wisconsin, pp. 54–61 (2003)

Radar Imager for Perception and Mapping in Outdoor Environments

Raphaël Rouveure, Patrice Faure, and Marie-Odile Monod

Cemagref, TSCF Research Unit, BP 50085, 63172 Aubière, France
{raphael.rouveure,patrice.faure,marie-odile.monod}@cemagref.fr

Abstract. Perception remains a challenge in outdoor environments. Overcoming the limitations of vision-based sensors, microwave radar presents considerable potential. Such a sensor so-called K2Pi has been designed for environment mapping. In order to build radar maps, an algorithm named R-SLAM has been developed. The global radar map is constructed through a data merging process, using map matching of successive radar image sequences. An occupancy grid approach is used to describe the environment. First results obtained in urban and natural environments are presented, which show the ability of the microwave radar to deal with extended environments.

1 Introduction

In natural and extended environments, the perception process remains a critical point for many applications such as mobile robotics or environmental management. Optical sensors such as laser and camera are affected by dust, fog, rain, snow and ambient lighting conditions. In the microwave range, data can be acquired independently of atmospheric conditions and time of the day. Radar may then provide an alternative solution to overcome the shortcomings of laser, video or sonar sensors. Radar differs from other range sensors as it can provide complete power returns for many points down range. In addition it can cover a long range which makes it possible for a vehicle to have an efficient perception even with few and distant objects in the environment.

Because of its intrinsic characteristics, microwave radar is particularly well suited for outdoor applications and large scale mapping. It has been successfully used in numerous domains such as terrain imaging [1], target tracking [2], three-dimensional map building [3], vehicle localization and vehicle navigation [4]. Moreover, in recent years different simultaneous localization and mapping algorithms based on microwave radar sensor have been developed [5], [6].

In response to requirements related to the development of new applications e.g. agriculture [7], civil engineering [8] or rescue [9], we developed a small size radar perception system, easy to load onto a vehicle. We show its potentialities through a preliminary application in mapping of outdoor environment.

The principle and the main characteristics of the K2Pi radar are presented in Sect. 2. Sect. 3 describes the mapping algorithm, which is based on a map matching approach. The environment is described as an occupancy grid. A set of preliminary results, obtained in urban and natural environments, is presented in Sect. 4.

J. Blanc-Talon et al. (Eds.): ACIVS 2009, LNCS 5807, pp. 618–628, 2009.
© Springer-Verlag Berlin Heidelberg 2009

2 Description of the K2Pi Radar

For short-range distance measurements i.e. few hundreds meters, the classical pulse radar technique is not the best adapted solution because it imposes the use of fast and expensive electronics in order to obtain a proper precision. The K2Pi microwave radar (see Fig. 1) uses the frequency modulated continuous wave (FMCW) principle. In the range of some hundred meters, frequency modulation has the following advantages:

- low transmission power, as it is the mean power which limits the range
- transposition of the temporal variables into the frequency domain so that a very short delay time Δt is transformed into a broad variation of frequency Δf, easier to measure.

Fig. 1. General view of the K2Pi radar

The principle of FM CW radar consists to mix the emitted signal which follows a linear modulation waveform, with the received signal delayed after reflecting on the targets within the view of the antenna [10]. Let us consider a sawtooth modulation at frequency F_m over a range ΔF and a distribution of stationary targets at respective distances R_i. When the echo signal is heterodyned with a portion of the transmitted signal, a beat signal S_b will be produced [11]:

$$S_b = k \sum_i V_e V_{ri} \cos\left(2\pi \left(2\Delta F\, F_m\, \frac{R_i}{c} \right) t + \Phi_i \right). \tag{1}$$

V_e is the amplitude of the emitted signal, V_{ri} is the amplitude of the received signal from a target i and Φ_i a phase term. The light velocity is c and k is a mixer coefficient.

The rotating antenna achieves a complete 360° scan around the vehicle in one second. The range R_i to each target is determined by measuring the individual frequency components by the mean of a Fourier transform. A power spectrum is computed at each angle of sight, as illustrated in Fig. 2.

A so-called "panoramic radar image" covering 360° in the horizontal plane is carried out using a PPI (Plan Position Indicator) representation, which displays range of targets versus angle. Considering the combined effect of antenna rotation and vehicle motion (translation and rotation), one would observe intra-scan distortions on the final 360° image. To avoid such a trouble, two proprioceptive sensors are used to estimate the displacement of the vehicle and to take into account these distortions: an odometer

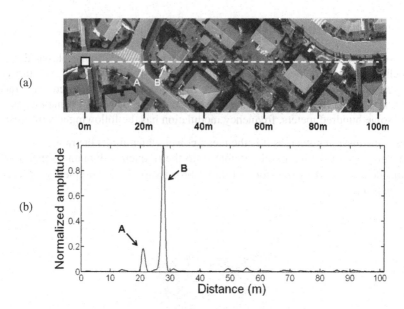

Fig. 2. Example of radar measurement in urban environment. (a) Aerial view. The white square indicates the position of the radar, the white dashed line the line of sight. Mark A: a hedge; mark B: a house. (b) The radar power spectrum.

to measure the longitudinal displacement of the vehicle and a gyrometer to measure the rotation of the vehicle. One measurement from the odometer and the gyrometer is carried out at each antenna rotation. The correction is computed in Cartesian coordinates. Therefore each radar acquisition is first transformed from polar coordinates into Cartesian coordinates. The trajectory of the vehicle is estimated for n turns of the antenna (n is related to the velocity of the vehicle) by assuming that the vehicle describes an arc of a circle with a constant velocity during one turn of the antenna (see Fig. 3). The motion equations of the vehicle are [12]:

$$
\begin{aligned}
x_{k+1} &= x_k + \Delta_k \cos\left(\psi_k + \omega_k/2\right) \\
y_{k+1} &= y_k + \Delta_k \sin\left(\psi_k + \omega_k/2\right) \\
\psi_{k+1} &= \psi_k + \omega_k
\end{aligned}
\tag{2}
$$

where (x_k, y_k) and (x_{k+1}, y_{k+1}) are the vehicle coordinates in the Cartesian space at time k and $k+1$, Δ_k and ω_k are the odometer and gyrometer measurements. ψ_k is the absolute direction, which is arbitrary set to 0.

Once the vehicle motion has been corrected, an anti-speckle filter is added. The speckle effect is a random amplitude modulation which exists in any radar image construction. Speckle noise reduction can be achieved either by spatial filtering or multilook filtering [13], [14], [15]. We chose the latter approach: n independent images of the scene are incoherently combined (by space-domain averaging) to produce a single final image.

It will be noticed that Doppler frequency introduced by moving targets is not considered here.

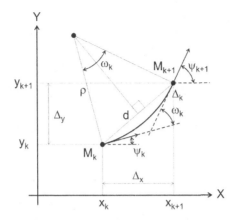

Fig. 3. Vehicle trajectory during one antenna turn

The overall diagram of the K2Pi radar process is presented in Fig. 4. The design of the K2Pi radar includes microwave components and electronic devices for emission and reception which are not detailed. Data acquisition and signal processing units are based on a Pentium M-2 GHz. Main characteristics of radar are described in Table 1.

Table 1. Characteristics of the K2Pi FMCW radar

Carrier frequency F_0	24 GHz
Transmitter power P_t	20 dBm
Antenna gain G	20 dB
Range	3-100 m
Angular resolution	1°
Distance resolution	1 m
Distance precision	0.02 m
Signal processing unit	104 PC – Pentium M – 2 GHz
Size (length×width×height) - Weight	27×24×30 cm - 10 kg

3   Map Construction with the R-SLAM Algorithm

The final purpose is to build a representation of the environment by associating successive panoramic radar images. The major interest in the so-called R-SLAM algorithm we developed is its ability to draw a map around the robot, i.e. localizing every targets in the environment. Another advantage is that it neither depends on the vehicle dynamics nor on the position of the radar on the vehicle. The global map is built with an incremental approach including two main steps (see Fig. 4):

a) map matching between the current radar scan and the previously constructed map, in order to estimate the inter-scan displacement
b) global map updating which includes the current radar image into the previously constructed map through a data merging process.

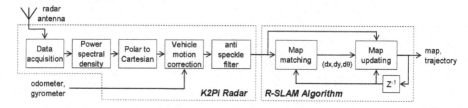

Fig. 4. General diagram of the radar imager

3.1 Map Matching

The image which is provided by the K2Pi radar can be considered as an occupancy grid (matrix of cells), dividing the area of interest in regular cells. Occupancy grids are powerful and flexible representation tools that capture the relevant scene aspects for radar-data interpretation [16], [17]. Each cell is related to a small area (20 cm × 20 cm), referenced by its coordinates (x, y) in an arbitrary plan. The occupation level of each cell is the power level of the reflected signal (i.e. the Radar Cross Section of the target).

Classical feature extraction and matching imply the need to recognize the same feature repeatedly during the map construction. This step is generally needed in order to detect persistent and reliable features in the scan. However, non-ambiguous target detection and identification based on radar signal interpretation are still open problems [18]. Radar power/range spectra contain a large amount of information mixed with various sources of noise, which makes detection and tracking of particular landmarks not a simple problem [5], [19]. Moreover, in poorly structured environment, clutter which is the noise backscattered by natural echoes such as the ground, must be taken into account because it may be the only available information. In such situations, a detection approach based on threshold selection will fail.

The main idea is to use the high density of radar data in a scan-matching technique which performs a 3D correlation (two translations and one rotation) between the current image B and the previously constructed map A. The first operation consists in a rotation of matrix B, followed by a 2D cross-correlation function between A and B. The result is the 3D cross-correlation matrix C:

$$C(i, j, k) = \sum_{m=0}^{(M_a-1)} \sum_{n=0}^{(N_a-1)} A(m,n) B_k^*(m+i, n+j)$$ (3)

where (M_a, N_a) and (M_b, N_b) are the respective dimensions of A and B, and B_k is the matrix B after rotation. The number and the values of rotations are set with the gyrometer's value.

The maximum of C will then give the displacement of the radar (translations and rotation) with a standard deviation equal to the peak magnitude at 3 dB. The localization accuracy is fixed by the size of the cell which is related to the radar resolution.

3.2 Global Map Updating

During the previous step the displacement of the radar has been estimated. Now the question is: how to superimpose the new image to the global map? The process faces an ambivalent situation:

– the necessity to take into account the new information from the current radar image,
– the necessity to preserve the information previously stored in the global map.

The principle retained in the data merging process is to consider that the probability for a target to appear in the map is proportional to the number of times it has been observed at the same place. If we denote P_i as the reflected power of the cell (x, y) in a previous image i, the corresponding cell in the global map is updated to the value M so that

$$M(x, y) = \left(\sum_{i=1}^{N} \alpha(d_i) P(x, y) \right) \Big/ N \qquad (4)$$

where N is the total number of images from the beginning to present and α a weighting coefficient. The coefficient α is related to the distance d_i between the radar and the cell coordinates (x, y) of the image i and also depends on intrinsic characteristics of the radar such as the size of the antenna beam. The global map is updated after each 360° scan and so increases as the new radar image is integrated.

The main advantage of this process is its robustness. The localization is indeed improved by using the global map which is the result of the best estimates from all previous observations. If only the latter scan were used in the first step (map matching) or with applying recursive algorithms, some situations may lead to a bad correlation result (e.g. obstacles disappearance from one scan to the next one).

4 Results

The K2Pi radar imager and the proprioceptive sensors have been loaded on to a vehicle from Cemagref Institute. The radar is positioned at the top of the vehicle (see Fig. 5). Data from the radar and proprioceptive sensors are acquired and stored in real time during the experiments. The R-SLAM algorithm has been implemented in Matlab language on a Quadri-Core 2.5 GHz Pentium PC with an off-line process. It takes 6 seconds to compute a radar image and to update the radar map.

Fig. 5. The K2Pi radar imager is loaded onto a Cemagref research vehicle used for on-road displacements

GPS data are simultaneously recorded with a second computer, in order to provide a data base for a later comparison. The GPS antenna was placed as close as possible to the radar antenna, and we consider in the following that they are at the same location.

4.1 Maps Construction

Two experiments are presented below. The first one (*trajectory 1*) was carried out in an urban area (Clermont-Ferrand University campus, France, latitude 45°45'37" N, longitude 3°06'33" E, elevation 408 m).

An aerial view is shown in Fig. 6(a). The vehicle moves with a mean velocity of 9.4 km/h (maximum velocity: 18.0 km/h). The overall length of the loop is 887 meters. White dots indicate the successive GPS positions. A total of 332 radar scans was stored and processed to work out the global map and trajectory (white dots) presented in Fig. 6(b). In this environment, most of detected elements are strong cooperative targets such as buildings, vehicles, urban lighting, metallic railings and poles. In some situations, this urban environment illustrates the "labyrinth" case where the horizon is very close to the vehicle.

In contrast, the second experiment (*trajectory 2*) was carried out in a vineyards area near Clermont-Ferrand, France (latitude 45°51'05" N, longitude 3°05'43" E, elevation 415 m). It is a natural and poorly structured environment, without any artificial construction such as a building in the range of the radar. The aerial image of the zone is presented in Fig. 7(a), and the GPS trajectory is superimposed with white dots. The vehicle moved along a distance of about 1063 m in the countryside. Its mean velocity was 8.2 km/h (maximum velocity: 13.0 km/h). A total of 463 radar images was stored and processed to work out the global radar map and trajectory (red dots) presented in Fig. 7(b). Most of the elements present within the area are slightly cooperative targets: trees, soil surfaces, vegetation, etc.

4.2 Trajectory Comparison

Beyond the immediate "visual quality" of the constructed radar maps, an important - but not simple- problem is related to the estimation of the quality of the final radar map. This problem can be addressed for example with a 2D correlation of radar maps with aerial photographs [20]. This approach is neither simple nor perfect because elements in a radar image and elements in an aerial photograph can not be immediately correlated: radar images are constructed considering a horizontal scanning of the environment, in contrast with aerial photographs which are based on a vertical scanning.

As the R-SLAM algorithm provides simultaneously a map and a localization within the map, the comparison between this estimated trajectory and a GPS trajectory can give some information about the quality of the map construction. But the comparison between GPS trajectory and radar estimated trajectory can not be immediately carried out. The first difficulty is that GPS measurements and radar acquisitions are asynchronous. The second problem is related to the absolute orientation of the radar map. The radar map orientation refers to the initial direction of the vehicle during the first radar scan. An additional problem is that the radar axis may be not perfectly aligned with the vehicle axis, introducing a bias in the radar absolute orientation which needs to be corrected.

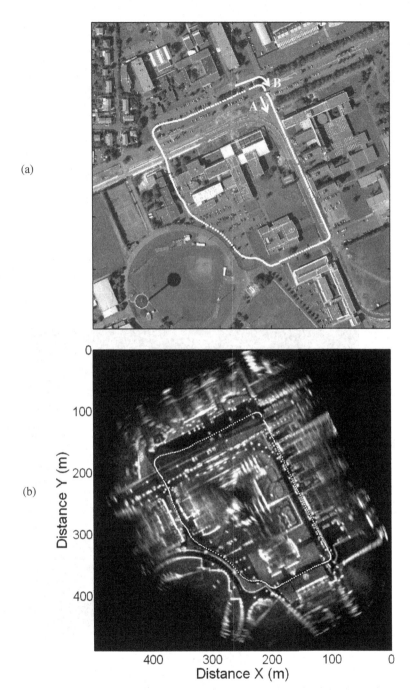

Fig. 6. Mapping of an urban environment. The loop is 887 meters long, and the mean velocity is 9.4 km/h. (a) Aerial image of the zone. White dots indicate GPS trajectory. Mark A: start of the trajectory; mark B: trajectory end. (b) Global radar map obtained and estimated trajectory (white dots). A total of 332 radar images was processed to work out the map and the trajectory.

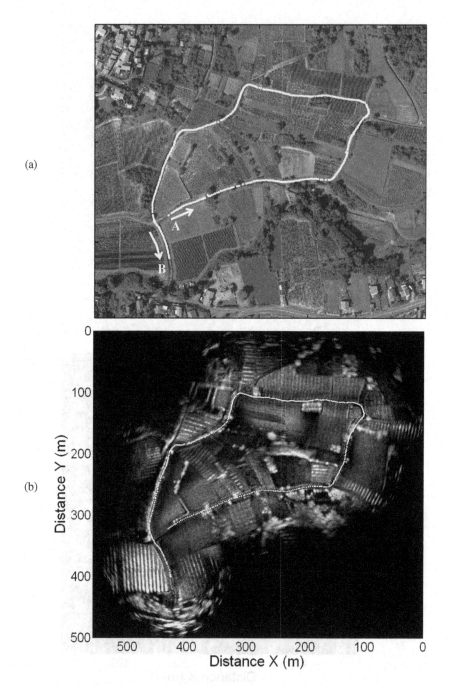

Fig. 7. Mapping of a natural environment. The loop is 1063 meters long, and the mean velocity is 8.2 km/h. (a) Aerial image of the zone. White dots indicate GPS trajectory. Mark A: start of the trajectory; mark B: trajectory end. (b) Global radar map obtained and estimated trajectory (white dots). A total of 463 radar images was processed to work out the map and the trajectory.

Considering these problems, the comparison between radar and GPS positioning based on a temporal synchronization is not possible, so we chose a spatial comparison. As the radar localization is built in a metric coordinate system, a localization correction is carried out by a rigid transformation (displacement and rotation) in order to minimize the mean squared error between GPS and radar estimated trajectories. The result of this rigid transformation for *trajectory 1* is presented in Fig. 8(a).

Once this correction is done, a distance is computed for each position of the radar (we implicitly consider that GPS information is correct). This distance corresponds to the projection of radar positions onto the GPS trajectory, assuming a linear displacement between two GPS points. Result for *trajectory 1* is presented in Fig. 8(b). For the whole trajectory, we obtain a mean absolute distance (MAD) of 0.92 meter, with a standard deviation of 0.60 meter.

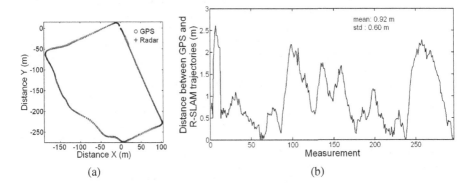

(a)   (b)

Fig. 8. Comparison between GPS trajectory and radar estimated trajectory in urban environment. (a) Superposition of GPS trajectory and radar estimated trajectory. (b) Distance between GPS and radar estimated trajectories. Mean of absolute error (MAE): 0.92 meter. Standard deviation error: 0.60 meter.

5   Conclusion

For outdoor environment perception, microwave radar is a sensor which presents a considerable potential, overcoming the limitations of vision-based sensors. In order to construct consistent maps of the chosen environment, the R-SLAM algorithm presented in this paper exploits all the richness of radar signal, avoiding the detection of particular landmarks. The algorithm builds simultaneously a map of the environment and a localization of the vehicle within the map, without using a global positioning system. The range of radar, combined with the R-SLAM algorithm performances, makes it possible to deal with extended and low structured environments. However, works remain to be done in validating the mapping, especially in a hilly environment. Current version of the K2Pi radar does not measure the radial velocity of targets, thus only static environments (without mobile elements) can be considered. In the case of dynamics scenes, taking into account moving elements remains an outstanding problem. Within the framework of the IMPALA project supported by the French Research Agency (ANR), a new radar imager will be designed to detect simultaneously moving elements in the environment.

References

1. Scheding, S., Brooker, G.V., Bishop, M., Maclean, A.: Terrain imaging and perception using millimeter wave radar. In: Proceedings of the 2002 Australasian Conference on Robotics and Automation, Australia (2002)
2. Brooker, G.: Millimeter Wave Radar for Tracking and Imaging applications. In: 1st International Conference on Sensing technology, New Zealand (2005)
3. Foessel, A., Bares, J., Whittaker, W.: Three dimensional map building with mmw radar. In: Proceedings of the 3rd International Conference on Field and Service Robotics, Finland (2001)
4. Clark, S., Durran-Whyte, H.: The design of a high performance mmw radar system for autonomous land vehicle navigation. In: Proceedings of the International Conference on Field and Service Robotics, pp. 292–299 (1997)
5. Jose, E., Adams, M.: Millimeter Wave RADAR Spectra Simulation and Interpretation for Outdoor SLAM. In: IEEE International Conference on Robotics & Automation, New Orleans, USA (2004)
6. Dissanayake, G., Newman, P., Durrant-Whyte, H.F., Clark, S., Csobra, M.: A solution to the simultaneous localization and map building (SLAM) problem. IEEE Transactions on Robotics and Automation 17(3), 229–241 (2001)
7. Fang, H., Fan, R., Thuilot, B., Martinet, P.: Trajectory Tracking Control of Farm Vehicles in Presence of Sliding. Robotics and Autonomous Systems 54(10), 828–839 (2006)
8. Bryson, L.S., Mayard, C., Castro-Lacouture, D., Williams, R.L.: Fully autonomous robot for paving operations. In: Conference Proceedings of the ASCE Congress, vol. 37 (2005)
9. Marques, C., Cristovao, J., Lima, P., Frazao, J., Ribeiro, I., Ventura, R.: RAPOSA: Semi-Autonomous Robot for Rescue Operations. In: IEEE/RSJ International Conference on Intelligent Robots and Systems (IROS), China (2006)
10. Skolnik, M.I.: Introduction to radar systems. Electrical Engineering Series. McGraw-Hill International Editions, New York (1980)
11. Monod, M.O.: Frequency modulated radar: a new sensor for natural environment and mobile robotics. Ph.D. Thesis, Paris VI University, France (1995)
12. Wang, M.: Localization estimation and uncertainty analysis for mobile robots. In: IEEE International Conference on Robotics and Automation, pp. 1230–1235 (1988)
13. Frost, V.S., Stiles, J.A., Shanmugan, K.S., Holtzman, J.C.: A model for radar images and its application to adaptive signal filtering of multiplicative noise. IEEE Transactions on Pattern Analysis and Machine Intelligence 4(2), 157–165 (1982)
14. Lee, J.S., Jurkevich, I., Dawaele, P., Wambacq, P., Oosterlinck, A.: Speckle filtering of synthetic aperture radar images: A review. Remote Sensing Reviews 8, 313–340 (1994)
15. Guoqing, L., Shunji, H., Hong, X., Torre1, A., Rubertone, F.: Study on speckle reduction in multi-look polarimetric SAR image. Journal of Electronics 16(1) (1999)
16. Martin, M., Moravec, H.: Robot Evidence Grids. Technical Report CMU-RI-TR-96-06, Robotics Institute. Carnegie Mellon University, Pittsburgh (1996)
17. Chandran, M., Newman, P.: Motion Estimation from Map Quality with Millimeter Wave Radar. In: IEEE/RSJ International Conference on Intelligent Robots and Systems (IROS), China, pp. 808–813 (2006)
18. Chen, Z., Samarabandu, J., Rodrigo, R.: Recent advances in simultaneous localization and map-building using computer vision. Advanced Robotics 21(3), 233–265 (2007)
19. Jose, E., Adams, M.: Relative RADAR Cross Section based Feature Identification with Millimetre Wave RADAR for Outdoor SLAM. In: IEEE/RSJ International Conference on Intelligent Robots and Systems (IROS), Japan (2004)
20. Brooker, G.: Correlation of Millimetre Wave Radar Images with Aerial Photographs for Autonomous Navigation of a UAV. In: 2nd International Conference on Sensing Technology, Palmerston North, New Zealand (2007)

Phantom-Based Point Spread Function Estimation for Terahertz Imaging System

Dan C. Popescu, Andrew Hellicar, and Yue Li

Wireless Technologies Lab
CSIRO ICT Centre, Marsfield NSW 2121, Australia

Abstract. We present a terahertz imaging system designed to operate in reflection mode and propose a method for estimating its point spread function. A phantom with known geometry is built, such as to generate a regular pattern with sharp edges under an ideal delta-like point spread function. The phantom is imaged with the terahertz system operating at 186 GHz. Several masking alterations applied to the beam pattern are also tested. The corresponding point spread functions are obtained by a deconvolution technique in the Fourier domain. We validate our results by using the estimated point spread functions to deblur the imaging results of a natural scene, and by direct comparison with a point source response.

1 Introduction

The last decade has seen a significant increase in the exploration of imaging techniques at terahertz frequencies, due on the one hand to the advent of new accessible laboratory based imaging technologies, and on the other hand to the unique properties of terahertz waves. These waves are capable of penetrating though clothes, packaging and plastic, while at the same time being nonionising, and therefore safe for humans. Application domains like security [1], medical imaging [2] and non-destructive testing [3] could benefit from developments in this area.

Imaging at wavelengths around the millimetre range poses a challenge to the resolution of the images that can be achieved, and a good knowledge of the imaging system's point spread function (PSF) is critical for improving image quality. Furthermore, if the point spread function can be modified in a controlled way, then this could pave the way to interesting developments related to superresolution and compressed sensing. The point spread function of a system could be estimated directly from the response of the system to a point-like source, but in practical situations an ideal point source may not be easy to generate. Approximations of point sources could take the form of recording beads in microscopy, quasars when calibrating astronomical instruments, or a pinhole into an opaque material for various optical systems. Most practical computational methods for the estimation of the point spread function are also system and application dependent, and fall into two categories: parametric and nonparametric methods. Parametric methods assume that the point spread function belongs to a given

J. Blanc-Talon et al. (Eds.): ACIVS 2009, LNCS 5807, pp. 629–639, 2009.

shape class, modelled by a small number of parameters, such as a confusion disk or a Gaussian, and then focus on finding a robust method for estimating the parameters [4], [5], [6], [7]. Nonparametric methods [8], [9] allow for the point spread function to be of any shape, although they may still impose some mild restrictions on it, such as not having a too large support.

In this paper, we present a terahertz imaging system architecture used for imaging in reflection mode, and propose a nonparametric method of determining its point spread function, based on the imaging of an object with known geometry. Some potential application areas of THz imaging in reflection mode include imaging of skin lesions and cancers, explosive detection under packaging and corrosion detection under paint. In section 2 we present the architecture of our experimental terahertz imaging system. In section 3 we describe the phantom used in our experiments and the alignment procedure. We present our point spread function estimation procedure and experimental results in section 4, and summarise our conclusions in section 5.

2   System Design

In the CSIRO Wireless Technologies Laboratory, we have designed a 186 GHz coherent imaging system. The system images by raster scanning a sample placed in the focused beam, which is quasi-optically coupled between a source and a detector. The system architecture can be modified, such that the system could scan in either transmission and reflection mode, depending on the setup of the quasioptical system. The diagram on the left hand side of Fig. (1) describes the system electronics used to achieve coherent detection. The input signal is generated by an RF source at 12 GHz and an LO source at 15.5 GHz. The RF source feeds a 12x multiplier chain which generates a 186 GHz signal. The LO

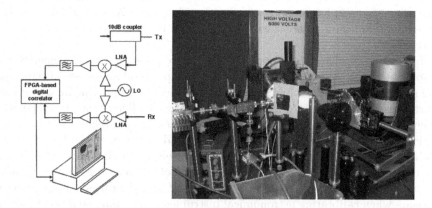

Fig. 1. Left: diagram of the system electronics. Right: a global view of the imaging system, showing the THz source, the silicon beam-splitter and the focusing mirrors, the target to be imaged which comprises the phantom, and the sensor.

source feeds a 4x multiplier chain resulting in a 47 GHz LO which is split and fed to 2 receive modules. Each receive module contains a LNA and a sub-harmonic mixer, which mixes the fourth harmonic of the LO with the input signal fed to the module. One mixer is fed a fraction of the source signal via a 10 dB coupler. The second mixer is fed a signal which is received after propagation through the imaging system. Both mixers IF output signals are then correlated together producing an in-phase and quadrature measurement, corresponding to the real and imaginary components of the measured signal.

A quasioptical system, which we describe below, is integrated into the system and constitutes the core of the reflection mode imaging architecture. The 186 GHz source signal passes through a silicon beam-splitter. Half of the power is lost, and half of it reaches mirror $M1$, which collimates the beam into mirror $M2$. $M2$ then focuses the signal onto the target. The signal which reflects off the target at the focal point returns to the beam-splitter through the same mirrors $M2$ and $M1$. Half of the reflected power is focused onto the receiver. This setup is shown schematically in the diagram at the left of Fig. (2). Images are acquired by mounting the sample to be imaged on an X/Y translation stage, at the focus of the system. A computer guided controller moves the translation stage and thus positions the object to be imaged in increments corresponding to the location of the pixels to be sampled. The in-phase and quadrature output measurements of the system are then stored in the computer. Typical images in our experiments were taken with pixels spacing of either 0.1 mm or 0.25 mm. Typical pixel acquisition times were around 120 ms/pixel. The major cause of the long imaging time is the dwell time of about 100 ms, necessary for stable positioning of the translation stage. The total integration time is 0.4 ms per pixel.

A top view of this quasioptical system appears on the right side of Fig. (2), with the THz source on the top side of the picture, the two parabolic mirrors in the centre, and the receiver on the right hand side of the picture; the beam-splitter is separating the source and the receiver.

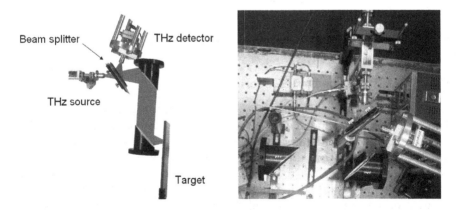

Fig. 2. Quasioptical system of with silicon beam-splitter and two parabolic mirrors

3 Phantom Design

A phantom representing a series of elevated concentric disks was manufactured out of aluminium, which has very good reflective properties. The radii of the disks (in mm) were: 5.0, 5.3, 5.9, 6.8, 8.0, 9.5, 11.3, 13.4, 15.8, 18.5 and 21.5 respectively, which follows a quadratic growth law. The rationale behind this particular design was to have strong edges at all orientations, and a pattern that would be easy to describe analytically, while still having a fair degree of variability with respect to the radial steps. In particular, we wanted to have at least the first annular ring thinner than the expected extent of the support for the point spread function. The depth step between consecutive disks was constant at 0.402 mm, corresponding exactly to a quarter-wavelength of our 186 GHz system, which translates to a half-wavelength in reflection mode. This meant that an ideal delta-like point spread function would return signals of approximately constant amplitude, and phase offsets of exactly π from adjacent disks. An optical image the aluminium phantom used in our experiments is shown in Fig. (3).

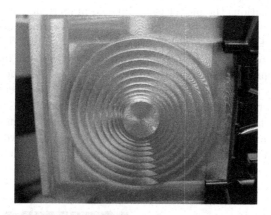

Fig. 3. Aluminium phantom, displaying a sequence of concentric disks, elevated in steps corresponding to a quarter of the wavelength

3.1 Ideal Phantom Data Generation

In order to generate the ideal phantom data, we firstly acquire the complex image data by scanning the aluminium phantom of Fig. (3), and then extract the phase data. From this phase data, we manually identify a number of points lying on the circumference of the outermost circle. The coordinates of those points are fed into a procedure of least squares circle-fitting algorithm, as described in [10]. The proposed procedure gives the best fitting n-dimensional sphere through a given set of points in $\mathbb{R}^n$. In particular for $n = 2$, the best fitting circle through the set of pints $\{(x_i, y_i), i = 1, 2, ...k\}$ results by firstly finding the vector $\mathbf{u} = [u_1, u_2, u_3]^T \in \mathbb{R}^3$ as the minimiser of $||B\mathbf{u} - \mathbf{d}||^2$, where d is the k-vector having component i equal to $x_i{}^2 + y_i{}^2$, and B is the $3 \times k$ matrix having column i equal to $[x_i, y_i, 1]^T$, for $i = 1, 2, ..., k$. This minimiser is:

$$\mathbf{u} = (BB^T)^{-1}B\mathbf{d} \qquad (1)$$

and then from Eq. (1) one finds the coordinates of the circle center as $(x_c, y_c) = (u_1/2, u_2/2)$ and the circle radius as $r = \sqrt{u_3 + (u_1^2 + u_2^2)/4}$. In practice, we found that identifying between 12 to 15 pairs of points on the outermost circle on the phantom was sufficient to get both the circle center and radius with sub-pixel accuracy (that is, feeding more points coordinates into the algorithm did not result in any significant variation.) The other inner circles are then easy to generate automatically, form the known dimensions of the phantom. The phase value on the first ring is set to be equal to the dominant value on the first ring, and the other values are set such as to follow the π-shift rule between adjacent rings. The amplitude value on the ideal phantom data is set constant, and equal to the value on the first ring on the amplitude image of the measured data. In Fig. (4) are shown the results of an original phase image from the complex image acquired using our system, the ideal phantom data generated using the circle-fitting algorithm described above and the knowledge of the phantom geometry, and their difference image. We can notice the very good alignment of the edges, the main noticeable differences being due to the thin inner annular ring having a radius below the wavelength.

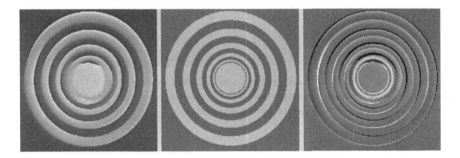

Fig. 4. Left to right: phase of the acquired complex phantom image, phase image generated using the circle fitting data and knowledge of the phantom geometry, and difference image

4   Point Spread Function Estimation

If an image $i(x, y)$ is captured with an imaging system having point spread function $p(x, y)$ in the presence of independent additive noise $n(x, y)$, then the resulting observed image $c(x, y)$ satisfies the equation:

$$c(x, y) = i(x, y) * p(x, y) + n(x, y) \qquad (2)$$

where $*$ denotes convolution. Because of the commutativity of the convolution operation, the roles of $i(x, y)$ and $p(x, y)$ are dual to each other, which means that

c and p can be used to estimate i (deblurring) or c and i can be used to estimate p (point spread function estimation). If there was no noise, either estimation would result from taking the Fourier transform of Eq. (2), and then applying a pointwise division of the resulting Fourier transforms, since the Fourier transform maps the convolution operator into the pointwise multiplication. For most practical imaging scenarios, though, the assumption of negligible noise is unrealistic. If noise is accounted for, then one can estimate either of the convolved components in terms of the other by using a Wiener filter [11]. The point spread function can be estimated from the equation:

$$P(u,v) = C(u,v)\frac{I^*(u,v)}{|I(u,v)|^2 + \frac{S_n(u,v)}{S_i(u,v)}} = C(u,v)\frac{I^*(u,v)}{|I(u,v)|^2 + \frac{1}{SNR(u,v)}} \quad (3)$$

where C, P and I denote the Fourier transforms of c, p and i, and S_i and S_n denote the power spectra of the i and n. In most practical situations, the inverse of the signal to noise ratio is difficult to measure or estimate accurately, and is often approximated by a constant s, leading to the simplified version of the Wiener deconvolution:

$$P(u,v) = C(u,v)\frac{I^*(u,v)}{|I(u,v)|^2 + s} \quad (4)$$

Fig. 5. Left to right: noise sample from our imaging system, white Gaussian noise having the same variance, generated with the Matlab *imnoise* function, and the corresponding Fourier spectra of the two noise samples

Fig. (5) shows a typical sample from the noise in our system, obtained by measuring the signal reflectance from air, against a sample of Gaussian white noise with the same variance. It can be seen that the characteristics of the two samples are similar, which justifies a flat spectrum approximation of noise. The spectrum of the ideal phantom response is also flat by design, as described in section 3. Therefore, the simplified Wiener filter model of Eq. (4) is suitable for our PSF estimation.

4.1 PSF Deconvolution

A scene consisting of the phantom described in section 3, a metal disk and a 50 cents coin of dodecagonal shape were imaged at 186 GHz, producing a complex-valued image. Fig. (6) shows the amplitude and phase images corresponding to this complex image. The phantom data was cropped out of the image of Fig. (6),

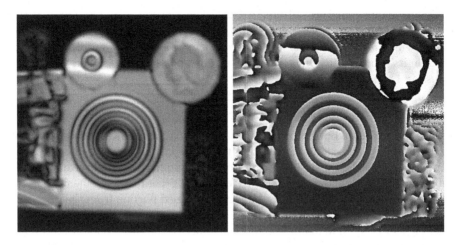

Fig. 6. Amplitude and phase images of a scene containing the phantom and a 50 cents coin, at 186 GHz

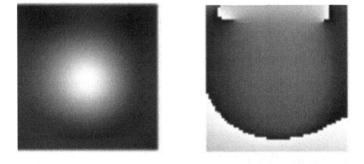

Fig. 7. Amplitude and phase images of complex point spread function

and then the algorithm described in subsection 3.1 has been applied to produce the ideal phantom data. Subsequently, the simplified version of the Wiener filter deconvolution of Eq. (4) has been applied to the measured and ideal phantom images, to produce a PSF estimation. For low values of the parameter s, the noise effects in the high frequencies become quite apparent. For high values of the parameter s, the noise effects are gradually eliminated and the estimated PSF stabilises to a constant shape with finite support of about 4 mm. We have found the optimal range for s by running a simulation test. We have convolved the ideal phantom data with a known point spread function, and added Gaussian noise of zero mean and variances between 0.01 and 0.03. We found that a Wiener filter deconvolution with the parameter s in the range between 10^6 and 10^7 returns very close reconstructions of the original point spread function. Within the same range of values for s, our experimental data returned a stable shape for the estimated point spread function of our system. The amplitude and phase of the estimated point spread function are shown in Fig. (7). The phase of the point spread function is almost flat all over the high intensity region of the PSF signal, which is in accordance with the expected phase variation of a Gaussian beam in its focal region. Our source and receiver horns were designed to produce Gaussian beams.

4.2   Deblurring Validation

We use the estimated point spread function, which has been calculated only on the basis of the phantom data, to deblur the entire image that contains the phantom, using again the Wiener deconvolution. The amplitude and phase data of the deblurred image are shown in Fig. (8). We notice a general improvement in sharpening of the details in the deblurred image. A zoomed portion from the images of Figs. (6) and (8), containing the coin area in those images, are shown in Fig. (9). Also shown in the same figure is an optical image of the coin, to allow for a more accurate assessment of fine features. One can see that the contour of the face and some features of the face are better represented in the deblurred image. The rim of coin, and the separating edge between the writing and the rim are more visible. Some elevated areas corresponding to letters start to show up, even though the exact patterns of letters remain indistinguishable. This is however to be expected, because the letters' fine details are smaller than the wavelength.

4.3   PSF from Masked Beam

We have also conducted our point spread function estimation on an imaging setup where we have partially blocked the incoming terahertz beam, in front of the beam-splitter. The main idea behind this experiment was to assess if we could

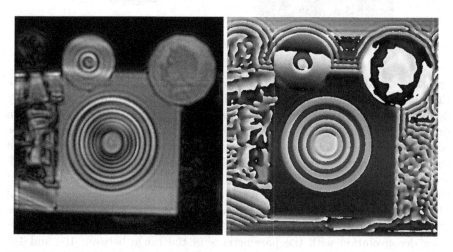

Fig. 8. Amplitude and phase of a deblurred complex image, using the estimated point spread function

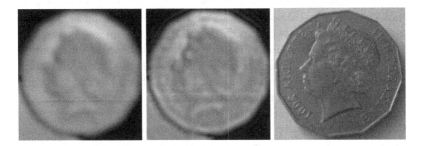

Fig. 9. Coin detail from the images in Figs. (6) and (8), and optical image of the coin

Fig. 10. Imaging setup corresponding to a vertical half-masked beam

Fig. 11. Amplitude images of two masked-beam point spread functions, corresponding to a vertical mask (top row) and horizontal mask (bottom row)

alter the beam pattern in a controlled way, in order to obtain several incoherent measurements of the same scene, with potential applications to superresolution and compressed sampling. Fig. (10) shows one instance of such a setup, where a vertical half of the beam has been blocked by a metal panel. The alignment of the panel was performed by gradually shifting the panel, until the measured power of the signal dropped to half of the value displayed without any blocking. Similar experiments have been conducted with a horizontal blocking of the beam, and with a diagonal one that cut two opposite square corners into the beam. In these experiments, a metal pinball of about 1.5 mm was also added to the scene. The pinball response approximates the response of a point source, and offers a direct, even if not very precise, indication of the point spread function's shape. In Fig. (11) are shown, from left to right, the point spread function estimations for the two imaging scenarios where the beam has been blocked vertically and horizontally, respectively. For each case, the point spread function estimated used our phantom based estimation is shown in a larger square, on the left, and the corresponding pinball response appears in a slightly smaller rectangle, immediately to the right. There is a remarkable consistency between the two types of estimations (and as expected, the pinball measurements appear a bit rougher.) The PSF pattern resulting from the vertical block is as expected a little bit more elongated in the horizontal direction, but unfortunately this elongation is only very slight. The expected vertical elongation in the vertical direction for the other pattern is minimal, almost nonexistent. Our point spread function estimation has allowed us to conclude that this particular beam-masking setup has failed to produce significantly altered imaging beam patterns, and turned out to be inferior to a setup of masking in the collimated part of the beam, which we have described in [12], in the context of a terahertz imaging system operating in transmission mode. In our future work we will investigate alternative masking strategies, in order produce less correlated point spread functions.

5   Conclusions

We have presented a terahertz imaging system, operating in reflection mode at 186 GHz, and a procedure for estimating its point spread function. A phantom with known geometry and sharp circular edges is imaged, and then a synthetic image, corresponding to a delta-like point spread function is aligned to this image. A Wiener filter type deconvolution is used to recover the point spread function. The point spread function obtained is validated by the deblurring of natural scenes obtained with the same system, and also by comparing it with pinball responses. The procedure also was used to estimate the point spread functions resulting from various masking alterations of the input terahertz beam, and we found that those alterations of the incoming beam only result in minor modifications of the PSF shape.

Acknowledgement

We acknowledge Carl Holmesby for manufacturing the phantom used in our experiments.

References

1. Kemp, M.C., et al.: Security Applications of Terahertz Technology. In: Proceedings of SPIE, vol. 5070 (2003)
2. Woodward, R.M., et al.: Terahertz Pulse Imaging of ex vivo Basal Cell Carcinoma. Journal Invest Dermatol. 120, 72–78 (2003)

3. Chen, C.H.: Ultrasonic and Advanced Methods for Nondestructive Testing and Material. World Pacific. 228 (2007)
4. Canon, M.: Blind Deconvolution of Spatially Invariant Image Blurs with Phase. IEEE Transactions on Acoustics, Speech and Signal Processing 24(1), 58–63 (1976)
5. Rajagopalan, A.N., Chaudhuri, S.: MRF model-based identification of shift-variant point spread function for a class of imaging systems. Signal Processing 76, 285–299 (1998)
6. von Tiedman, M., et al.: Image Adaptive Point-Spread Function Estimation and Deconvolution for In Vivo Confocal Microscopy. Microscopy Research and Technique 69, 10–20 (2006)
7. Sakano, M., Suetake, N., Uchino, E.: A Robust Point Spread Function Estimation for Out-of-Focus Blurred and Noisy Images Based on a Distribution of Gradient Vectors on the Polar Plane. Optical Review 14(5), 297–303 (2007)
8. Doukoglu, T.D., Hunter, I.W., Kearney, R.E.: Nonparametric two-dimensional point spread function estimation for biomedical imaging. Medical & Biological Engineering and Computing 31, 277–283 (1993)
9. Hall, P., Qiu, P.: Nonparametric Estimation of a Point-spread Function in Multivariate Problems. The Annals of Statistics 35(4), 1512–1534 (2007)
10. Coope, I.D.: Circle Fitting by Linear and Nonlinear Least Squares. Journal of Optimization Theory and Applications 76(2), 381–388 (1993)
11. Gonzales, R.C., Woods, R.E.: Digital Image Processing. Prentice Hall, Englewood Cliffs (2002)
12. Popescu, D.C., Hellicar, A.D., Li, L., Li, Y., Rosolen, G., Hislop, G.: Binary mask scanning for THz imaging. In: Proceedings of SPIE, Orlando, Florida, April 2009, vol. 7311(33), pp. 337–340 (2009)

Advanced Vision Processing Systems: Spike-Based Simulation and Processing

José-Antonio Pérez-Carrasco[1,2], Carmen Serrano-Gotarredona[2],
Begoña Acha-Piñero[2], Teresa Serrano-Gotarredona[1],
and Bernabe Linares-Barranco[1]

[1] Instituto de Microelectrónica de Sevilla (IMSE-CNM-CSIC)
Avenida Reina Mercedes, s/n. 41012, Seville, Spain
{jcarrasco,terese,bernabe}@imse.cnm.es
[2] Dpto. Teoría de la Señal, ETSIT, Universidad de Sevilla,
Avda de los descubrimientos, s/n. 41092, Seville, Spain
{cserrano,bacha}@us.es

Abstract. In this paper we briefly summarize the fundamental properties of spike events processing applied to artificial vision systems. This sensing and processing technology is capable of very high speed throughput, because it does not rely on sensing and processing sequences of frames, and because it allows for complex hierarchically structured neurocortical-like layers for sophisticated processing. The paper describes briefly cortex-like spike event vision processing principles, and the AER (Address Event Representation) technique used in hardware spiking systems. In this paper we present a simulation AER tool that we have developed entirely in Visual C++ 6.0. We have validated it using real AER stimulus and comparing the outputs with real outputs obtained from AER-based devices. With this tool we can predict the eventual performance of AER-based systems, before the technology becomes mature enough to allow such large systems.

1 Introduction

Artificial man-made machine vision systems operate in a quite different way from biological brains. Machine vision systems usually capture and process sequences of frames. This frame-based processing is slow, especially when many convolutions need to be computed in sequence for each input image or frame, such as in wavelet based processing. Biological brains do not operate on a frame by frame basis. In the retina, each pixel sends spikes (also called events) to the cortex when its activity level reaches a threshold. Very active pixels will send more spikes than less active pixels. All these spikes are transmitted as they are being produced, and do not wait for an artificial "frame time" before sending them to the next processing layer. Besides this frame-less nature, brains are structured hierarchically in cortical layers [1]. Neurons (pixels) in one layer connect to a projection-field of neurons (pixels) in the next layer. This processing based on projection-fields is equivalent to convolution-based processing [2]. This

J. Blanc-Talon et al. (Eds.): ACIVS 2009, LNCS 5807, pp. 640–651, 2009.

fact has been exploited by many researchers to propose powerful convolution based image processing algorithms [3][4]. However, convolutions are computationally expensive and it seems unlikely that software programs running on the fastest of today's computers could emulate the high number of convolutions that the brain might perform when fast vision processing is considered. A solution to this could be Address-Event-Representation (AER). AER is a promising emergent hardware technology that shows potential to provide the computing requirements of large frame-less projection-field based multi-layer systems. It is an event-based representation hardware technique for communicating events between layers of neurons in different chips. AER was first proposed in 1991 in one of the Caltech research labs [5][6], and a wide community of neuromorphic hardware engineers has used it since then. AER has also been used for auditory systems, competition and winner-takes-all networks, and even for systems distributed over wireless networks [7][8][9]. However, the high potential of AER has become even more apparent since the availability of AER convolution chips [10][11][12]. These chips, which can perform large arbitrary kernel convolutions (32x32 in [11]) at speeds of about 3×10^9 $connections/sec/chip$, can be used as building blocks for larger cortical-like multi-layer hierarchical structures, because of the modular and scalable nature of AER based systems. At present, only a small number of such chips have been used simultaneously [10], but it is expected that hundreds or thousands of such modular AER chips could be integrated in a compact volume. This would eventually allow the assembly of large cortical-like projection-field and event-based frame-less vision processing systems operating at very high speeds. The objective of this paper is to illustrate and to introduce the processing power of AER-based systems, based on the performance characteristics of already available AER hardware modules (chips), but through behavioral simulations. In spite of existing a lot of work developed in the study and simulation of the different layers in which the brain is structured [13][14], this work is not focused on simulating the biological aspects of the brain, but on simulating existing or possible hardware AER-based devices that are biologically inspired. To do this, we have developed an open AER simulator entirely in Visual C++ 6.0. With this tool we will be able to describe any AER module (including timing and non-ideal characteristics), and assemble large netlists of many different modules. This makes it possible to obtain a good estimation of the delays and processing power of the simulated systems. Furthermore, the AER behavioral simulator can be used to test new AER processing modules within large systems, and thus orient hardware developers on what kind of AER hardware modules may be useful and what performance characteristics they should possess. To validate the tool, we have used real AER stimulus obtained with an electronic motion-sensing retina [9][10] and we have simulated two real AER-based hardware implementations [10][11]. The outputs have been compared to those obtained with the real systems. Finally, in the last section we test the proposed tool with a single layer neural network based on AER for recognizing handwritten digits. In particular, we use the MNIST database [15] consisting of 70000 handwritten digits and provide a 91% of correct classification.

2   AER-Based Convolution

To illustrate how AER convolution is performed event by event (without frames)
consider the example in Fig. 1. Fig. 1(a) corresponds to a conventional frame
based convolution, where a 5x5 input image f is convolved with a 3x3 kernel h,
producing a 5x5 output image g. Mathematically, this corresponds to Eq. 1.

$$g(i,j) = \sum_m \sum_n h(m,n)f(i-m, j-n). \tag{1}$$

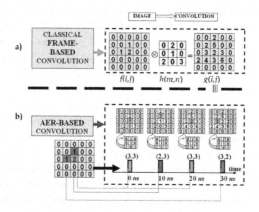

Fig. 1. *(a)*classical frame based and *(b)* AER-Based convolution processing

In an AER system, shown in Fig. 1, an intensity retina sensing the same
visual stimulus would produce events for 3 pixels only (those sensing a non-zero
light intensity). The pixel at coordinate (3,3) senses twice as much intensity as
pixels (2,3) and (3,2). The event frequency of address (3,3) will therefore be
twice that of pixels (2,3) and (3,2). In this particular case, the retina can send
a new event every 10ns. Thus, for this particular stimulus, after four events we
already have a valid representation of the stimulus and only 40ns are required
to transmit it. In a practical situation the two events of pixel (3,3) would be
separated by more than 20ns. Every time the convolution chip receives an event
from the retina chip, the kernel is added to the array of pixels (which operate as
adders and accumulators) around the pixel having the same event coordinate.
Note that this is actually a projection-field operation. In this way, after the four
retina events have been received and processed, the result accumulated in the
array of pixels in Fig. 1(b) is equal to that in Fig. 1(a). Additionally, in an AER
convolution chip, a fixed threshold level is defined for all pixels. Whenever a pixel
exceeds that level, it will generate an output event, and the pixel will be reset.
Consequently, events are generated, transmitted, and processed immediately,
without waiting for any frame timing constraints. In a more realistic situation,
the retina pixel values are higher and more events are sent per pixel. However,
note that more intense pixels have higher frequencies, and consequently their

events will start to come out earlier, and will be processed first. In general, more intense pixels are more information-relevant pixels (especially in contrast or motion retinae). In AER systems, since events are processed by a multi-layer cortical-like structure as they are produced by the sensor, it is possible to achieve successful recognition after a relatively small fraction of the total number of events are processed [16].

3   AER Simulator Tool

In the simulator proposed a generic AER system is described by a netlist that uses only two types of elements: instances and channels. An instance is a block that generates and/or produces AER streams. We have implemented a basic library of instances, and any user can easily modify them or add new ones. For example, a retina chip would be a source that provides an input AER stream to the AER system [9]. A convolution chip [10], [11], [12] would be an AER processing instance with an input AER stream and an output AER stream. For every input event at coordinate (x, y) a convolution map of a size specified by the user is added in the pixel array stored in the convolution module around the input event coordinate (Fig. 1). In a realistic situation, each pixel should be implemented as an integrate-and-fire neuron with a threshold and physical delays should be modeled. A splitter [10] would be an instance which replicates the events from one input AER stream onto several output AER streams. Similarly, a merger [10] is another instance which would receive as input several AER streams and merge them into a single output AER stream. Other developed instances are a winner-take-all module and a multiplier. Both instances will be described in the next sections. AER streams constitute the nodes of the netlist in an AER system, and are called channels. Channels represent point-to-point connections. Fig. 2 shows an example system. The system contains 7 instances and 8 channels. The netlist description is provided to the simulator through a text file. The ASCII file netlist corresponding to the example system is shown at the bottom in Fig. 2. Channel 1 is a source channel. Each source channel needs a line in the netlist file, starting with the key word sources, followed by the channel

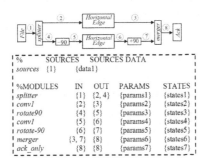

Fig. 2. Example AER-based system emulated by our simulation tool and its netlist ASCII file

number and the file containing its events. The following lines describe each of the instances, one line per instance in the network. The first field in the line is the instance name, followed by its input channels, output channels, name of a text file containing its parameters, and name of a text file containing its initial state. Each instance is described by a C++ function whose name is the name of the instance. The simulator imposes no restriction on the format of the parameters and state structures. This is left open to the user writing the code of the function of each instance. The simulator only needs to know the name of the files where these structures are stored. Channels are described by a list of events. Each element in the list has two components. The first one corresponds to information of one event and the second one is a pointer to the following event to be processed in the list. Each event has six components: 'x' and 'y', that represent the coordinates or addresses of the event, 'sign' represents its sign, 'tprereq' represents the time at which the emitter instance creates the event, 'treqef' represents the time at which the receiver instance processes the event, and 'tack' represents the time at which the receiver instance finally acknowledges the event. We distinguish between a pre-Request time and an effective Request time. The first one is only dependent on the emitter instance, while the second one requires that the receiver instance is ready to process an event request. This way, we can provide as source a full list of events which are described only by their addresses, sign, and times. Once an event is processed by the simulator, its final effective request and acknowledge times are established. Before starting the simulator, the events of the source channels have to be provided in an input text file (we have also implemented some tools to create these text files from real aer streams or from images). During the simulation, events in the channels are established. After the simulation, the user can visualize the computed flow of events in the different channels. The execution of the simulator is as follows. Initially the netlist file is read as well as all parameters and states files of all instances. Each instance is initialized according to the initial state of each instance. Then, the program enters a continuous loop that performs the following steps:

1. All channels are examined. The simulator selects the channel with the earliest unprocessed event (earliest pre-Request time). An event is unprocessed when only its pre-Request time has been established, but not its final Request time nor its acknowledge time.
2. Once a channel is selected for processing, its earliest unprocessed event is provided as input to the instance the channel is connected to. The instance updates its internal state. In case this event triggers new output events from this instance on its output channels, a list of new unprocessed events is provided as output. These output events are included by the simulator in the correct position of the respective channels, which at a later time should be processed by their respective destination instances. Finally, the simulator stores the new state for the instance under execution and goes back to 1.

4   Results for AER-Based Implementations

To validate the tool described above, we have implemented two simulations of two AER systems that had been previously built in hardware [10][11]. All the parameters describing the modules such us thresholds, forgetting ratio, kernels values, delays, array sizes, etc. have been chosen according to the specifications of AER devices [10][11] and adjusted to produce an output frequency in the same order as the input frequency of activity, as done in the physical implementations. Finally, we propose and simulate also an AER-based single layer neural network to detect hand-written digits from the MNIST database [15].

4.1   Detection and Tracking of Moving Circles with Different Radius

The first developed implementation was built to simulate the demostration system described in [10]. This system could simultaneously track two objects of different size. A block diagram of the complete system is shown in Fig. 3. The complete chain consisted of 17 pieces (chips and PCBs), and was intended to detect two solid circles of different radiuses on a rotating disc. The detection was implemented with two convolution chips programmed to detect circumferences of radius 4 pixels and 9 pixels, respectively. The AER scheme that we have used to emulate the detection system is that described in Fig. 4. The system receives as input the events captured by the electronic retina, the movement of a rotating disc with two solid circles of different radiuses. The captured data, available in data files, were previously converted to a valid format for our simulation tool. These events reach a convolution module programmed a kernel tuned to detect a circumference of a certain radius (convolution chip in Fig. 4). The output events describing the center of the circumference we want to detect are sent to a winner-take-all module. The output activity of this module responds only to the incoming addresses having the highest activity. We can implement the winner-take-all module using a convolution chip with a kernel that is positive in the center and negative in the rest of values and using the output activity from this chip as feedback to the input of the chip. The input frequency in each pixel belonging to each circumference was 266Hz, that is, 104312 events were produced in 4.5s when the kernel is tuned to detect the small circumference. We have obtained 1911 events at the output in total, all of them due to the pixel detecting the center of the circumference, which implies that this pixel produces events with a frequency of 266 Hz approximately. Note that AER streams are not represented by sequences of frames (as in conventional video). However, to show the results graphically, we have collected input and output events during time intervals of 33ms and show 2-D images. In Fig. 5 the four images in the left represent the images reconstructed with the hardware implementation (images were obtained with a java tool [10][11]). The gray values correspond to non-activity. Black values correspond to changes in intensity due to the motion sensing retina at the input and white levels at the bottom figures correspond to the pixels detecting the center of the moving ball at the output). The four images on the right correspond to the images obtained using our C++

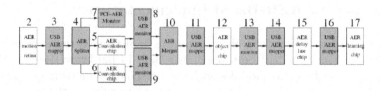

Fig. 3. Block diagram of the hardware implementation AER-based system to detect objects of different shape and size

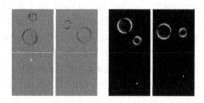

Fig. 4. Block diagram of the AER system developed to simulate the hardware implementation

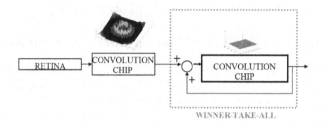

Fig. 5. *On the left*, input and output obtained with the hardware implementation. *On the right*, input and output obtained with the simulated implementation.

simulation tool. Black levels correspond to non-activity and white levels correspond to pixels producing activity.

4.2   Recognition of a Rotating Propeller Rotating at High Speed

The second experiment demonstrates the high-speed processing capabilities of AER based systems. It is the recognition and tracking of a highspeed S-shaped rotating propeller at 5000 rev/sec [11] and moving across the screen. At this speed, a human observer would not be able to discriminate the propeller shape and he would only see a moving ball across the screen. The propeller has a diameter of 16 pixels. The AER simulated system is again that shown in Fig. 4. This time, the convolution chip was programmed with a kernel to detect the center of the S-shaped propeller when it is in the horizontal position. In Fig. 6(a), the kernel is shown. In Fig. 6(b) and (c) we show the 2-D input (propeller) and output reconstructed images when we consider a $50\mu s$ interval of time collecting events

(1/4 of a rotating movement). In Fig. 6(d) and (e) we show the 2-D input and output images when we consider a 200ms interval of time collecting events (corresponding to one complete back-and-forth screen crossing). As it can be seen, only those pixels that detect the center of the propeller produce activity. The propeller is properly detected and tracked at every moment in real time. Note that using conventional frame-based image processing methods to discriminate the propeller is a complicated task, which requires a high computational load. First, images must be acquired with an exposure time of at least $100\mu s$ and all this must be performed in real time (the propeller is rotating at 5000 rev/sec). As done previously, all the parameters describing the modules were adjusted to produce an output frequency in the same order as the input frequency of activity (137 KHz), as done in the physical implementations [11].

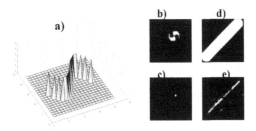

Fig. 6. *a)* Kernel used to detect the propeller, *b)* and *c)* input and output when we collect events during $50\mu s$, *d)* and *e)* input and output when we collect events during 200ms

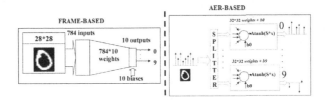

Fig. 7. Frame-based (on the left) and AER-based (on the right) implementation of a single layer neural network to detect digits of 28x28

4.3   Single Layer Neural Network

The last system that we have simulated is a single layer neural network trained with back-propagation [17]. When designing a pattern recognition system, one of the main problems is that the recognition accuracy is largely determined by the ability of the designer to come up with an appropriate set of features. This turns out to be a daunting task which, unfortunately, must be redone for each new problem. A possible solution to these problems is the use of neural networks [17]. Aimed to this, we have developed an AER-based system that emulates directly a frame-based a fully connected single layer neural network trained with back-propagation [17] and which is called Net-1. Net-1 is shown on the left of Fig. 7 with 10 sigmoid output units (7850 weights including the biases). The database MNIST [15] consisting of 70000 28x28 images of hand-written digits has been employed. 60000 are used for training and 10000 are used for testing purposes. Each pixel from one image constitutes an input to the network. Each output unit in the network computes a dot product between its input vector and its weight vector. This weighted sum, denoted xj for unit j, is then passed through a sigmoid squashing function (a scaled hyperbolic tangent) to produce the state of unit j, denoted by yj (Eq. 2):

$$yj = A \tanh(S * xj). \tag{2}$$

Where A is the amplitude of the function and S determines its slope at the origin. In the training phase, each weight is updated using backpropagation:

$$w_{ij} = w_{ij} - \epsilon \frac{\partial E}{\partial w_{ij}}. \tag{3}$$

Where w_{ij} is the weight that connects pixel i to output neuron j and E is the error at the output computed as:

$$E = \sum_j \frac{1}{2}(yj - dj)^2. \tag{4}$$

Where dj is the desired output for each input in unit j when using the training set. The same rule is used for the biases. After training the net, only the output neuron sensitive to the stimulus will produce positive activity at the output. A classification rate of 91% was obtained when we tested the net with the test images. On the left of Fig. 7 we show the frame-based implementation of the single layer neural network. In the figure, a digit corresponding to one training digit belonging to the MNIST database is supplied to the network and the output neuron sensitive to that input digit will reach a state of value '1'. The rest will have a value of '-1'. On the right part of Fig. 7 we show our AER-based scheme. This time, we do not have real AER input stimulus. However, our simulator proposed allows us to convert 2-D images into events. In this way, we have coded all the images in the MNIST database into events separated each other 10ns. Each flow of events corresponding to one digit is used as input to the system. When an event belonging to the input stimulus reaches a splitter module, it is replicated in each one of the ten output ports. Events travelling through one of this output ports come to a multiplier module. A multiplier module consists of an array with 784 weights and one bias value. When an event arrives to this module, its address is decoded and the weight specified with that address in the pixel array, which is stored in the module, is added to the state of the single neuron inside the module. If the state of the neuron reaches a certain positive or negative threshold, it produces a new output event positive or negative respectively. This event will be sent automatically to the output port. Then, the neuron resets

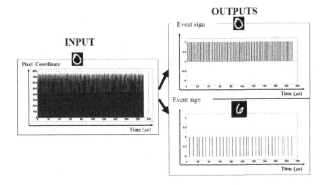

Fig. 8. Input and output events for neurons '0' and '6'

itself and it is initialized with the bias value specified inside each multiplier. All the weights and biases used in the implementation were computed with backpropagation using a frame-based scheme (this is not difficult because only one layer is involved). As an example, in Fig. 8 we show the input events when we used a version of digit '0'. For this input, in the same figure we show also the output events obtained for the neurons sensitive to input '0' and input '6' (the activity for the rest of neurons is quite similar). As it can be seen, output events are obtained automatically, without the need of waiting for the entire frame-time. In less that $3\mu s$ (note that duration of the input stimulus is almost $200\mu s$) since the first input event reached the system, we have output events indicating the correct detection of digit '0' (positive events). The rest of output neurons produce negative events, indicating that they are not sensitive to that stimulus. When we used the entire set of 10000 test images and converted them to events, we got a recognition rate of 91%. This rate is the same as the rate obtained in the net-1 frame-based implementation. It is obvious that AER allows for fast processing providing the good results that we had using classical frame-based methods but now in real time. In a real hardware implementation using AER modules we would be able to process input events at speeds going from 33 Mevents/sec to 3 Mevents/sec [11] when we use the maximum size for kernels allowed in convolution or multiplier chips. This implies that the real time recognition here simulated could be easily achieved by a real system and with aproximately the times here described. In the future, neural networks with more layers will be implemented in AER in order to achieve higher classification rates as those obtained (almost 100%) in recent frame-based schemes (LeNet-5 [18]).

5   Conclusions

In this paper, we have described a simulation C++ tool for AER-based systems. The tool is able to process around 20Kevents/sec. Hardware AER modules are able to process input events at speeds going from 33 Mevents/sec to

3 Mevents/sec [11]. However, in spite of the tool being slower than a physical hardware implementation, it will allow us to simulate complex and hierachically-structured systems before the available hardware technology allows it and without hardware cost. The AER-based simulation tool can be used to test new AER processing modules within large systems, and thus orient hardware developers on what kind of AER hardware modules may be useful and what performance characteristics they should possess. We have presented three implementations to validate our tool and the results show clearly the high speed and possibility of implementing complex processing systems that AER provides. With the three AER-based implementations we try to demonstrate the feasibility of AER technology when it is applied to real-time image processing. AER is able to process input stimulus in real time and to transmit the resulting activity in each layer to the following layers even without having finished collecting all the input events. It is also feasible to assemble multiple chips working in parallel so that complex processing and multiple convolutions can be done. The first two applications were intented to detect and track objects with different shape and size in real time. It can be observed that in the two implementations the processing has been always in real time and that the outputs were equal to those obtained with the hardware devices. The third application is an example of a single layer neural network to recognize hand-written digits in the MNIST database. Available AER devices allow us to implement simple but real-time architectures like the single layer neural network and with the times computed. In future implementations we want to develop more sophisticated and cortical-like multi-layer systems where the link between hardware AER implementations, bio-inspired processing and frame-based applications will become more apparent.

Acknowledgement

This work was supported in part by grant TEC-2006-11730-C03-01 (Samanta2) from the Spanish Ministry of Education and Science and grant P06-TIC-01417 (Brain System) from the Andalusian regional government. JAPC was supported by a doctoral scholarship as part of research project Brain System.

References

1. Shepherd, G.M.: The Synaptic Organization of the Brain, 3rd edn. Oxford University Press, Oxford (1990)
2. Rolls, E.T., Deco, G.: Computational Neuroscience of Vision. Oxford University Press, Oxford (2002)
3. LeCun, Y., Bengio, Y.: Convolutional Networks for Images, Speech, and Time Series. In: Arbib, M. (ed.) The Handbook of Brain Science and Neural Networks, pp. 255–258. MIT Press, Cambridge (1995)
4. Fasel, B.: Robust Face Analysis using Convolution Neural Networks. In: Proc. of the Int. Conf. on Pattern Recognition (ICPR 2002), Quebec, Canada (2002)
5. Sivilotti, M.: Wiring Considerations in Analog VLSI Systems with Application to Field-Programmable Networks, Ph.D. Thesis, California Institute of Technology, Pasadena CA (1991)

6. Mahowald, M.: VLSI Analogs of Neural Visual Processing: A Synthesis of Form and Function, Ph.D. Thesis, California Institute of Technology, Pasadena CA (1992)
7. Cauwenberghs, G., Kumar, N., Himmelbauer, W., Andreou, A.G.: An analog VLSI Chip with Asynchronous Interface for Auditory Feature Extraction. IEEE Trans. Circ. Syst. Part-II 45, 600–606 (1998)
8. Oster, M., Liu, S.-C.: Spiking Inputs to a Spiking Winner-Take-All Circuit. In: Weiss, Y., Schölkopf, B., Platt, J. (eds.) Advances in Neural Information Processing Systems (NIPS 2006), vol. 18, pp. 1051–1058. MIT Press, Cambridge (2006)
9. Lichtsteiner, P., Delbrück, T.: 64x64 AER Logarithmic Temporal D rivative Silicon Retina. Research in Microelectronics and Electronics 2, 202–205 (2005)
10. Serrano-Gotarredona, R., et al.: AER Building Blocks for Multi-Layers Multi-Chips Neu-romorphic Vision Systems. In: Weiss, Y., Schölkopf, B., Platt, J. (eds.) Advances in Neural Information Processing Systems (NIPS 2006), vol. 18, pp. 1217–1224. MIT Press, Cambridge (2006)
11. Serrano-Gotarredona, R., Serrano-Gotarredona, T., Acosta-Jiménez, A., Linares-Barranco, B.: A Neuromorphic Cortical Layer Microchip for Spike Based Event Processing Vi-sion Systems. IEEE Trans. on Circuits and Systems, Part-I 53(12), 2548–2566 (2006)
12. Serrano-Gotarredona, R., et al.: On Real-Time AER 2D Convolutions Hardware for Neu-romorphic Spike Based Cortical Processing. IEEE Trans. on Neural Networks 19(7), 1196–1219 (2008)
13. Serre, T., Wolf, L., Bileschi, S., Riesenhuber, M., Poggio, T.: Object recognition with cortex-like mechanisms. IEEE Transactions on Pattern Analysis and Machine Intelligence 29(3), 411–426 (2007)
14. Masquelier, T., Thorpe, S.J.: Unsupervised Learning of Visual Features through Spike Timing Dependent Plasticity. PLoS Comput. Biol. 3(2), e31 (2007)
15. The MNIST database, http://yann.lecun.com/exdb/mnist/index.html
16. Linares-Barranco, A., Jimenez-Moreno, G., Linares-Barranco, B., Civit-Ballcels, A.: On Algorithmic Rate-Coded AER Generation. IEEE Trans. on Neural Networks 17(3), 771–788 (2006)
17. Le Cun, Y., et al.: Backpropagation applied to handwritten zip code recognition. Neural Computation 1, 541–551 (1989)
18. Le Cun, Y., et al.: Gradient-based learning applied to document recognition. Proceedings of the IEEE 86(11), 2278–2324 (1998)

Self-assessed Contrast-Maximizing Adaptive Region Growing

Carlos S. Mendoza[1,*], Begoña Acha[1], Carmen Serrano[1],
and Tomás Gómez-Cía[2]

[1] Universidad de Sevilla
Av. de los Descubrimientos s/n
41092 Sevilla, Spain
[2] Grupo Unidad Clínica de Cirugía Plástica y Grandes Quemados
Hospitales Universitarios Virgen del Rocío de Sevilla
Avda Manuel Siurot, s/n
41013 Sevilla, Spain
{csanchez1,bacha,cserrano}@us.es, tgomezc@gmail.com

Abstract. In the context of an experimental virtual-reality surgical planning software platform, we propose a fully self-assessed adaptive region growing segmentation algorithm. Our method successfully delineates main tissues relevant to head and neck reconstructive surgery, such as skin, fat, muscle/organs, and bone. We rely on a standardized and self-assessed region-based approach to deal with a great variety of imaging conditions with minimal user intervention, as only a single-seed selection stage is required. The detection of the optimal parameters is managed internally using a measure of the varying contrast of the growing regions. Validation based on synthetic images, as well as truly-delineated real CT volumes, is provided for the reader's evaluation.

Keywords: CT, segmentation, region-growing, seed, muscle, bone, fat, surgical planning, virtual reality.

1 Introduction

One of the most promising applications of medical image computerized visualization is virtual reality surgical planning. Traditional surgical planning uses volumetric information stored in a stack of intensity-based images, usually from computerized tomography (CT) scanners. Based on a number of these image slices, surgeons build their own mental 3D model of the relevant tissues. This task is difficult, even for experienced surgeons. As a consequence, they can miss important information or draw incorrect conclusions due to anatomical variability, either of which can lead to suboptimal treatment strategy decisions [1].

* This work was supported by "Fundación Reina Mercedes" from "Hospital Universitario Virgen del Rocío" (Sevilla), and "Consejería de Salud de la Junta de Andalucía". Carlos S. Mendoza was supported by a doctoral scholarship financed by Universidad de Sevilla.

J. Blanc-Talon et al. (Eds.): ACIVS 2009, LNCS 5807, pp. 652–663, 2009.
© Springer-Verlag Berlin Heidelberg 2009

Using volumetric renderings of anatomical structures, and the appropriate virtual tools for basic surgical operations (like tissue excision and repositioning), the complexity of many plastic surgery interventions can be addressed prior to the actual physical procedure.

A main bottleneck for these computer environments is the delineation of the tissues involved, to such an extent that automated approaches become mandatory. Automatic segmentation is a fundamental problem exhaustively addressed in the literature. Any inaccuracies in the process can distort the simulated measures and surgical operations. In this paper we propose a novel segmentation strategy in the context of the development of a virtual surgical planning environment.

The environment under study was initially conceived for the simulation of head and neck reconstructive surgery, providing virtual tools for tissue excision and repositioning, tissue quantification and stereolithographic prototyping. In such a framework the need for proper delineation of diverse tissues like skin, fat, muscles, organs and bone becomes crucial. Although formerly relying on very simple segmentation methods like thresholding and simple region growing [2,3,4,5], only further developments in automatic segmentation approaches, deprived of user parameters, can remain useful for the clinical practitioners and surgeons. According to our on-field inquiries, only a seed-selection stage seems to be tolerated in such a non-technical environment. There is a strong restriction in the operating human time, so parameter selection becomes unaffordable.

In order to pay back the cost and burden of this virtual surgical planning platform development, a wide range of situations should be covered with the proposed technique. Most available physical resources, like imaging devices, should be compatible with the method, even ensuring backwards compatibility (for images acquired in the past). As a consequence neither resolution, contrast nor SNR specific standards can be expected. Further, no imaging protocol can be presumed, as related to patient positioning in the scanner, presence of radioactive contrast, body segment of the patient to be imaged and so on.

Few authors have referred to the issue of classifying a concrete set of tissues using a common method. In their work, Zhou et al. [6] developed a technique for skin, fat, muscle/organs and bone segmentation. Their approach consisted mainly of threshold selection except for bony tissue, for which they made use of a self-assessed adaptive region growing algorithm. Their threshold selection method, based on hierarchical discriminant analysis made assumptions on the histogram that turned out to be unaffordable in our less predictable context. Their strategy for bony tissue, that had been earlier proposed for bronchus segmentation by Law and Heng [7], computed the optimal adaptive threshold by detecting sudden increases in the segmented volume. Its main weakness is the need for an empirical range in this increase for distinguishing routinary growth from undesired leaking. This range would hardly be established in our more general problem. Apart from manual trial-and-error adaptive threshold selection [8], other self-assessed adaptive region growing strategies, outside our context of application, have been proposed in the past. In their work [9], Hojjatoleslami and

Kittler proposed a method based on finding the global maxima for two different contrast measures which they computed iteratively as intensity-decreasing pixels were added to the segmented region. The success of the assessment was founded on the assumption that maximal contrast occurred on region boundaries, which is a reformulation of approaches assuming that the variation of the gray values within regions is smaller than across regions, an inherent assumption in all region growing techniques [10]. Unfortunately, the exhaustivity of their per-pixel approach entailed very low computational efficiency. Revol-Muller et al. [11] used morphological measures to assess the multiplier of the adaptive range for region growing. Instead of computing their assessment function for every pixel addition to the region, they sampled the function for an evenly-spaced set of values.

In our method we propose an assessment function based on the evolving contrast of the region-growing sequence. This strategy allows for segmentation of images without a bimodal histogram requirement as opposed to the assessment measure proposed by Revol-Muller et al. [11]. To make this approach computationally feasible in 3D we produce only evenly-spaced samples of this function along the values of the multiplier for the adaptive ranges that extend around the iteratively estimated mean. We guarantee the sufficiency of the sampling resolution by setting it to a small percentage of the continuously updated standard deviation of the grown region. Globally, our goal is to provide fast automatic segmentation based only on a seed selection step. The results should be comparable to those obtained by manually-tuned region-growing approaches, in a very wide variety of imaging conditions.

2   Method

2.1   Tissue Model

Since our goal is providing a mechanism for segmentation of skin, fat, muscle/organs and bone tissues with minimal user intervention, we have established a model for these tissues that takes into account their intensity distributions in CT images.

First of all, we consider here only tissue segments that exhibit an inherent density and thus an average intensity in the image domain. We model then our object of interest as a connected region whose pixel intensities are sampled from a Gaussian distribution with unknown mean and standard deviation. We may presume that our tissues of interest are surrounded by other tissues derived from other, sometimes adjacent, intensity distributions, like other authors have stated [12]. Although common in the literature, this assumption for the intensities is rarely met in practice, in the sense that the intensity distributions of tissues are only approximately Gaussian. To deal with this inconvenience, and also with partial overlap of distributions between tissues, we propose the use of an assessment function that is to be evaluated along a sequence of region growing stages (region growing sequence).

2.2   Segmentation Algorithm

Normalization and Denoising. Since our method was conceived for images from a wide range of scanners and acquisition protocols, we decided to develop a normalizing stage that could account for such variability. As we will introduce later on, for the self-assessed region growing stage of the algorithm we require the input intensity dynamic range to be normalized with respect to some parameter estimates of the objective intensity distribution.

In the following equations N is a cubic neighborhood of radius R around the seed, x is a voxel position, $f(x)$ is the intensity for voxel at x, $\bar{f}_N$ is the mean intensity estimate in N and $|N|$ is the cardinality of N. Moreover, σ_{f_N} is the estimated standard deviation for intensities in N, K is a constant parameter, and $f(x)$, $f'(x)$ are the input and output intensities for the non-linear mapping described below.

$$\bar{f}_N = \frac{1}{|N|} \sum_{x_k \in N} f(x_k) \ , \tag{1}$$

$$\sigma_{f_N} = \sqrt{\frac{1}{|N|} \sum_{x_k \in N} \left(f(x_k) - \bar{f}_N \right)^2} \ , \tag{2}$$

$$f'(x) = \left(1 + \exp \left(-\frac{f(x) - \bar{f}_N}{\left(\frac{K\sigma_{f_N}}{3} \right)} \right) \right)^{-1} . \tag{3}$$

In a first step we proceed by maximum-likelihood (ML) estimation of the mean and standard deviation as in (1-2), and then perform a non-linear normalization using a sigmoidal transfer function centered on the estimated mean as in (3). The width of the sigmoidal window extends $K\sigma$ around the center $\bar{f}_N$ of the mapping. For $K = 3$ the width of the window would be enough to map 99.7% of the samples, of a Gaussian distribution with similar mean and standard deviation. Greater values of K ensures robust mapping for the estimated distribution. The sigmoidal mapping has been chosen because of its smoothness, and its ability to focus the output dynamic range on a given input intensity range of interest.

Finally, we perform non-linear denoising using an in-slice bidimensional median filter with kernel radius Γ. Other denoising schemes would be valid, always keeping in mind that edge preservation is crucial in our approach. We chose to use bidimensional median filtering because it is as fast as using a smoothing kernel, and preserves edges better than most linear filtering techniques.

Self-Assessed Region Growing. Departing from a normalized version of the image under study, whose intensities lie in the range $[0, 1]$, and a manually provided seed, we perform the self-assessed contrast-maximizing algorithm, for which a generic iteration is described in the following steps:

1. Update multiplier $k_i = k_0 + i\Delta k$
2. Compute, in last iteration grown region R_{i-1}, ML estimates for the mean (available from last iteration) and standard deviation $(\bar{f}'_{R_{i-1}}, \sigma_{f'_{R_{i-1}}})$

3. For every candidate voxel $x_{c_{i-1}}$ being 26-connected to R_{i-1}, $x_{c_{i-1}} \in R_i$ if

$$f'\left(x_{c_{i-1}}\right) \in \left[\bar{f'}_{R_{i-1}} \pm k_i \sigma_{f'_{R_{i-1}}}\right] \tag{4}$$

4. Compute the assessment function $O_i\left(\bar{f'}_{R_i}, \bar{f'}_{P_i}\right)$ using the intensity average $\bar{f'}_{R_i}$ in R_i and the intensity average $\bar{f'}_{P_i}$ in the external perimeter P_i of R_i according to (1) and the following eqs.:

$$P_i = \{x_{c_i}\} \cap R_i^{\,C} , \tag{5}$$

$$O_i\left(\bar{f'}_{R_i}, \bar{f'}_{P_i}\right) = \left| \frac{\bar{f'}_{P_i} - \bar{f'}_{R_i}}{\bar{f'}_{P_i} + \bar{f'}_{R_i}} \right| \tag{6}$$

5. If O_{i-1} was a local maximum, when compared to O_{i-2} and O_i (only when $i \geq 2$), then the algorithm stops and the output is R_{i-1}. Otherwise another iteration takes place

Of all aforementioned parameters only k_0 and Δk are critical for the performance of the algorithm. k_0 affects computational efficiency requiring a greater number of iterations before a local maximum of $O\left(\bar{f}_{R_i}, \bar{f}_{P_i}\right)$ is found. Therefore it should be set to the largest possible value that guarantees that only a small percentage of tissue intensity samples are included in the first iteration, in order not to miss the first local maximum. In what concerns Δk, the choice must guarantee that the assessment function is being sampled adequately in order to detect its local variations. Since the estimates for the mean and standard deviation are continually updated as the region grows, the estimates become increasingly close to the theoretical values. We argue that setting Δk below one tenth of 3 (which is the theoretical value multiplying the standard deviation of a Gaussian distribution for 99.7% of its samples to be included in a range of that width around the mean) is enough for the segmentation process to be able not to miss the available local maxima of the assessment function. This postulate is supported by our experimental results.

3   Results

We have implemented our algorithm using open source medical image processing libraries, more precisely the Insight Toolkit for algorithm development, and the command line executable module infrastructure provided by 3DSlicer for fast prototyping, calibration, evaluation, and manual segmentation on real images for further validation [13]. The algorithm that we will validate, and that was finally implemented in the virtual reality platform that motivated its development, uses the following parameter values: $R = 2, K = 12, \Gamma = 1, k_0 = 1$ and $\Delta k = 0.1$.

For validating our algorithm we have proposed several experiments, based on synthetic as well as real images. In their inspiring work, Udupa et al. [14] proposed a methodology for the validation of medical volume segmentation algorithms. For a segmentation algorithm to be proven useful it has to demonstrate its accuracy (quality of results), precision (parameter independence) and efficiency (human and computational times).

Accuracy is evaluated in terms of False Positive and False Negative Volume Fraction ($FPVF$ and $FNVF$). $FPVF$ compares the number of voxels assigned to the object which actually belong to the background, with the number of voxels which compose the background. $FNVF$ quantifies the number of voxels assigned to the background, which actually belong to the object, as compared to the number of voxels in the object. To produce such a comparison a true delineation of the object must be available. This ground-truth can be accomplished either by manual human-expert segmentation; or creating synthetic images, corrupting them with simulations of typical acquisiton artifacts, and then performing segmentation on the result.

$$FPVF = \frac{|\text{Segmented Region} - \text{True Region}|}{|\text{Entire Volume} - \text{True Region}|} \ , \tag{7}$$

$$FNVF = \frac{|\text{True Region} - \text{Segmented Region}|}{|\text{True Region}|} \ , \tag{8}$$

where $|\cdot|$ indicates again cardinality and subtracting means performing a set intersection with the complement of the subtrahend.

Precision is evaluated according to the so-called precision quotient (PR). Precision can be computed in terms of inter/intra-operator variability and inter-scanner variability. Since our method relies on only a seed selection procedure, and is supposed to work for a variety of acquisition devices, we decided to compute precision for inter-seed variability. This variability is accounted for by comparing the resulting segmentation from differently placed seeds.

$$PR = \frac{|\text{Segmentation 1} \cap \text{Segmentation 2}|}{|\text{Segmentation 1} \cup \text{Segmentation 2}|} \tag{9}$$

Several seeds can be used so that (9) is computed for all possible combinations of outputs, and then averaged to obtain a more representative measure.

Efficiency relates to the segmentation performance time, human as well as computational time. According to Udupa et al. [14], it is extremely hard to provide an efficiency measure that proves useful when comparing different methods. One possible way of summing up all efficiency factors is related to the economic cost of usage for an algorithm. Human time is much more expensive than computer time. In our method, usage is designed to be extremely simple, and reduces to placing one pin point on the desired object. For that reason we have computed here only computational times for the execution of our algorithm.

3.1 First Experiment: Constant-Valued Spheres

To validate the claim that our contrast-based assessment function accurately detects homogeneous-intensity regions, we have created synthetic volume images and corrupted them with some typical CT acquisition artifacts. We have created a 3D volume composed by two ideal tissues, with constant intensity. The first tissue is shaped as a ball centered in the image domain, with radius $r = 20$ voxels. The second tissue is the background which extends to a final image domain with

Table 1. Computed measures for constant-valued spheres

$FPVF$	$2.46 \cdot 10^{-4} \pm 1.06 \cdot 10^{-4}$
$FNVF$	0.0205 ± 0.0313
PR	0.925 ± 0.0413
$t_c(\mathrm{s})$	72.6 ± 40.8

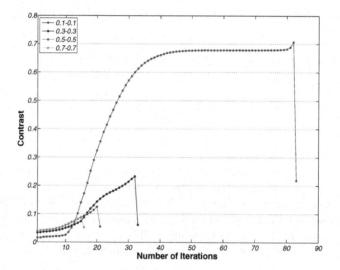

Fig. 1. Contrast evolution for some constant-valued spheres

Fig. 2. Synthetic volume slice, segmentation and reconstruction

size $512 \times 512 \times 100$ voxels. We argue that this simple phantom is enough to test the effect of artifacts on boundary detection as long as connectivity is preserved. Our method depends only on connectivity and intensity shifts, so the precise shape of the tissue is irrelevant as long as it is connected.

For simulating CT acquisition, we proceed by blurring the image (accounting for partial volume effect) and adding Gaussian noise. Blurring was performed using a Gaussian smoothing kernel with width σ_b. Zero-mean Gaussian noise is generated with standard deviations σ_n. We produce segmentations for all combinations for $\sigma_b \in [0.1, 0.9]$ in increments of 0.2, and $\sigma_n \in [0.1L, 0.7L]$ (with L the absolute intensity difference between the two tissues) in increments of 0.2.

From all the segmentations we compute $FPVF$ and $FNVF$. The average value for these measures is provided in Table 1. For a representative case ($\sigma_b = 0.5$, $\sigma_n = 0.5$), we have computed PR for all possible combinations of three different seeds, selected randomly inside the region of interest. The average PR is presented in Table 1. For efficiency evaluation, computational time t_c has been computed and averaged across all images. Notice in Table 1 how the obtained values for $FPVF$ and $FNVF$ are close to zero, indicating very high segmentation fidelity. PR is close to 1, indicating weak dependence on seed placement. Times show great variance due to the iterative nature of the algorithm.

For illustrative purposes we have included in Fig. 1 a graphical representation of the evolution of the assessment function as the algorithm iterates. Notice how the fall after the peak decreases as noise and blurring increase.

Also, in Fig. 2 we can see a slice of the generated volume for the case 0.5-0.5 and also a surface reconstruction of the segmented region. Notice the good results facing noise with standard deviation as high as half the intensity difference between the two tissues.

3.2 Second Experiment: Continuous-Valued Spheres

For this experiment we produced a similar synthetic image, only now the intensity inside the ball varies from 0 to 1 proportionally to the Euclidean distance from the center of the voxel to the center of the ball. The intensity value for the background was set to 1. In this scheme, no clear boundary is available, because we wanted to prove that our method does not require abrupt intensity changes for boundaries to be detected. We corrupted the image only with Gaussian noise of standard deviation $\sigma_n = 0.1, 0.3$ and 0.5. We computed the same accuracy and efficiency measures, as well as precision for the case $\sigma_n = 0.3$. Due to the nature of the values in the regions, seeds must be placed close to the center in order for the condition (which is inherent to any region growing approach) of greater variance across than inside regions to be met [10]. According to Table 2, the results for this extremely subtle boundary are still acceptable. $FPVF$ and $FNVF$ stay somewhat close to 0, and PR value is close enough to 1 as to support the claim of low seed location dependence. Time has increased due to the greater variance of the segmented tissue, which forcer the algorithm to perform more iterations.

Table 2. Computed measures for continuous-valued spheres

$FPVF$	$4.12 \cdot 10^{-4} \pm 4.44 \cdot 10^{-4}$
$FNVF$	0.191 ± 0.110
PR	0.930 ± 0.0176
$t_c(s)$	257 ± 12.9

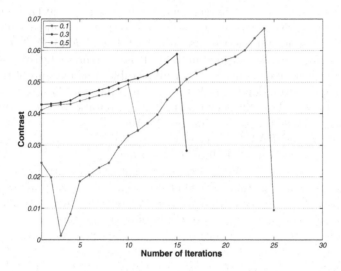

Fig. 3. Contrast evolution for some continuous-valued spheres

Fig. 4. Synthetic volume slice, segmentation and reconstruction

For Fig. 3 we can observe the same effect as in Fig. 1. Notice the increased roughness in these curves as compared to those in Fig. 1. This is due to a greater influence of noise on consecutive iterations of the region growing sequence, due to the non-constant intensity of the tissue.

We present in Fig. 4 again a slice of the generated volume for the case 0.5 and its segmentation reconstruction. The quality of the segmentation is pretty good even for extremely dim boundaries. This proves that our method detects not only intensity shifts, but also intensity evolution shifts.

3.3 Third Experiment: Real CT Images

For this last experiment we have produced automatic segmentations for 10 real CT images for the tissues described (skin, muscle/organs, fat and bone). The testing set proceeds from all different scanners involved in our clinical setting. As explained above, validation of real CT images requires manual segmentations provided by a clinical expert. In our application context this manual segmentation process can be extremely time-consuming, or even intractable, due to the

Table 3. Computed measures for real CT images

$FPVF$	$9.2 \cdot 10^{-3} \pm 1.75 \cdot 10^{-3}$
$FNVF$	0.151 ± 0.0815
PR	0.733 ± 0.171
$t_c(\mathrm{s})$	156.0 ± 36.2

lack of tissue localization. Just to give an example, manual segmentation of muscular tissue implies manually avoiding all blood vessels and fat traces, for up to 500 slices. For this reason we have computed our accuracy and precision metrics from just 20 slices in 10 cases.

Moreover, the manual accuracy of the segmentation is bounded by human perceptual limitations presenting considerable inter-subject variability, and we (the authors and the clinical practitioners) have observed that in many cases poorer results in accuracy are related to incomplete manual segmentations, rather than incomplete automatic segmentations. Let us say then, that the quality of the segmentation is *at least* as good as the presented results.

For the results presented in Table 3, all segmentations have been used for accuracy and efficiency assessment, and one particular segmentation and several seeds for precision. While $FPVF$ stays very low, ensuring self-contained segmented regions, $FNVF$ is still reasonably close to 0. Precision is not as good as for the synthetic images, due to the more complex shape of the segmented regions, which produce a slightly greater dependence on seed placement. Computational time ranges between 2 or 3 minutes, which implies a great reduction as compared to previous trial-and-error parameter tuning, according to non-technical users' opinions.

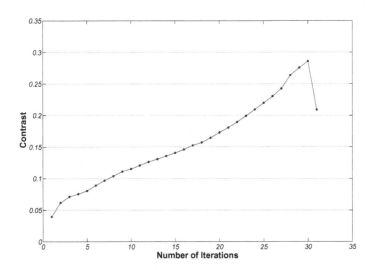

Fig. 5. Contrast evolution for real CT segmentation

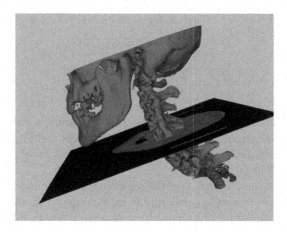

Fig. 6. Real CT volume slice and surface model for performed segmentation of bone tissue

Again illustration for contrast evolution and a rendering of the resulting segmented volume are presented in Figs. 5 and 6. All results were obtained from a single seed selection in each image.

4   Concluding Remarks, Limitations and Future Work

Considering the numeric results for the experimental validation we consider our approach successful in solving the particular needs for which it was conceived. The algorithm has been integrated in the reference platform and prevents from previous trial-and-error segmentation, which was very time-consuming according to its users. Its greatest advantage is thus the absence of tuning parameters and ability to produce nice results for a wide set of acquisition devices.

Its most significant limitation to this region growing approach has to do with the fact that connectivity is sometimes too weak as a requirement for some regions of interest, as they may be connected to other similar intensity regions. For this reason a future improvement for the technique could be incorporating some morphological limitations to the growth of the region in order to impose some degree of *stiffness*, to avoid flooding towards undesired regions. This improvement could make the algorithm useful in greater variety of situations (individual organs, tumors...).

References

1. Reitinger, B., Bornik, A., Beichel, R., Schmalstieg, D.: Liver surgery planning using virtual reality. IEEE Comput. Graph. Appl. 26(6), 36–47 (2006)
2. Zucker, S.W.: Region growing: Childhood and adolescence. Computer Graphics and Image Processing 5(3), 382–399 (1976)

3. Sivewright, G.J., Elliott, P.J.: Interactive region and volume growing for segmenting volumes in MR and CT images. Medical Informatics 19(1), 71–80 (1994)

4. Sekiguchi, H., Sano, K., Yokoyama, T.: Interactive 3-dimensional segmentation method based on region growing method. Systems and Computers in Japan 25(1), 88–97 (1994)

5. Suárez, C., Acha, B., Serrano, C., Parra, C., Gómez, T.: Virsspa- a virtual reality tool for surgical planning workflow. International Journal of Computer Assisted Radiology and Surgery 4(2), 133–139 (2009)

6. Zhou, X., Kamiya, N., Kara, T., Fujita, H., Yokoyama, R., Kiryu, T., Hoshi, H.: Automated recognition of human strucure from torso CT images, pp. 584–589 (2004)

7. Law, T.Y., Heng, P.A.: Automated extraction of bronchus from 3d CT images of lung based on genetic algorithm and 3d region growing, vol. 3979 (2000)

8. Adams, R., Bischof, L.: Seeded region growing. IEEE Trans. Pattern Anal. Mach. Intell. 16(6), 641–647 (1994)

9. Hojjatoleslami, S.A., Kittler, J.: Region growing: A new approach. IEEE Trans. Image Process. 7(7), 1079–1084 (1998)

10. Haralick, R.M., Shapiro, L.G.: Image segmentation techniques. Computer Vision, Graphics, & Image Processing 29(1), 100–132 (1985)

11. Revol-Muller, C., Peyrin, F., Carrillon, Y., Odet, C.: Automated 3d region growing algorithm based on an assessment function. Pattern Recognition Letters 23(1-3), 137–150 (2002)

12. Jian, W., Feng, Y., Ma, J.L., Sun, X.P., Jing, X., Cui, Z.M.: The segmentation and visualization of human organs based on adaptive region growing method, pp. 439–443 (2008)

13. Pieper, S., Lorensen, B., Schroeder, W., Kikinis, R.: The NA-MIC Kit: ITK, VTK, pipelines, grids and 3d slicer as an open platform for the medical image computing community, vol. 2006, pp. 698–701 (2006)

14. Udupa, J.K.: Multiple sclerosis lesion quantification using fuzzy-connectedness principles. IEEE Trans. Med. Imag. 16(5), 598–609 (1997)

Convex Hull-Based Feature Selection in Application to Classification of Wireless Capsule Endoscopic Images

Piotr Szczypiński and Artur Klepaczko

Technical University of Lodz, Institute of Electronics
ul. Wolczanska 211/215, 90-924 Lodz, Lodz
{pms,aklepaczko}@p.lodz.pl

Abstract. In this paper we propose and examine a Vector Supported Convex Hull method for feature subset selection. Within feature subspaces, the method checks locations of vectors belonging to one class with respect to the convex hull of vectors belonging to the other class. Based on such analysis a coefficient is proposed for evaluation of subspace discrimination ability. The method allows for finding subspaces in which vectors of one class cluster and they are surrounded by vectors of the other class. The method is applied for selection of color and texture descriptors of capsule endoscope images. The study aims at finding a small set of descriptors for detection of pathological changes in the gastrointestinal tract. The results obtained by means of the Vector Supported Convex Hull are compared with results produced by a Support Vector Machine with the radial basis function kernel.

Keywords: Wireless capsule endoscopy, feature selection, convex hull, support vector machines.

1 Introduction

Wireless capsule endoscopy (WCE) becomes more and more frequently used diagnostic technique of digestive system disorders. This is mainly due to its ability for visualization of the human small intestine, while being non-invasive and thus less traumatic for a patient when compared to other diagnostic methods. However, interpretation of a video sequence produced by the capsule endoscope demands signigicant effort and remains a time consuming procedure. This research aims at development of a system that would allow automatic recognition of WCE video frames containing potentially abnormal patterns appearing on the gastrointestinal tract's internal surface.

The adopted approach utilizes texture analysis to numerically describe anatomical structures viewed in the endoscopic images. It is assumed that texture parameters enable automatic discrimination between normal and pathologically altered tissues. The main problem which arises here is the multidimensional feature space generated by texture analysis. In the literature ([1,2]), one can find several approaches to texture description. Due to the versatile nature of

J. Blanc-Talon et al. (Eds.): ACIVS 2009, LNCS 5807, pp. 664–675, 2009.
© Springer-Verlag Berlin Heidelberg 2009

WCE images, it is difficult to arbitrarily choose a particular model as the best matching one. More reasonably, one should calculate many texture features and then select their most discriminative subset. However, as it will be shown, texture parameter vectors representing objectively different classes may be distributed evenly throughout the whole feature space in the endoscopic images domain. Accurate separation of features becomes feasible only when nonlinear decision boundaries are constructed.

In this study it is proposed to select relevant texture parameters using a measure which respects a possibility of encapsulating all vectors from one chosen pathology type by a convex hull. Simultaneously, vectors representing other classes should remain outside the hull. The main motivation for such an approach is to minimize the rate of false negative errors committed by the classifier. Since the process of convex hull construction largely depends on data vectors lying closest to the decision boundary, the proposed method hereafter shall be referred to as Vector Supported Convex Hull (VSCH). The method not only identifies significant parameters, but it also determines a classification rule based on the mathematical definition of the best found convex hull.

The remainder of this paper is structured as follows. Section 2 reviews the main aspects of the WCE imaging technique. The notion of texture analysis and the software tools used in this research are described in Sect. 3. Details of the proposed VSCH method are presented in Sect. 4. In the experimental part (Sect. 6), efficiency of VSCH is tested in comparison with the feature selection method based on the Support Vector Machines algorithm (recalled in Sect. 5) on a sample set of WCE images. Finally, Sect. 7 concludes.

2   Capsule Endoscopy

Wireless capsule endoscopy (WCE) [3,4], is a technique that facilitates the imaging of the human gastrointestinal system including small intestine. The WCE system consists of a pill-shaped capsule (cf. Fig. 1a) with built-in video camera, light-emitting diodes, video signal transmitter and battery, as well as a video signal receiver-recorder device. The wireless capsule endoscope used in this study produces color images of the internal lumen (cf. Fig. 1b). The images cover a circular 140° field of view. A patient under investigation ingests the capsule, which then passes through the gastrointestinal tract. When the capsule goes through the small bowel it is propelled by peristaltic movements. The capsule transmits video data at a rate of two frames per second for approximately 8 hours. Investigation of the recorded video is performed by a trained clinician. It is a tedious task that usually takes more than an hour. The video interpretation involves viewing the video and searching for abnormal-looking entities like bleedings, erosions, ulcers, polyps and narrowed sections of the bowel.

There is a need for automatic methods which would aid in the investigation process, either by reduction of the time spent on the process or by focusing the attention of the clinician on medically relevant video fragments. Several research groups have recently reported methods for gastro-intestinal tract segmentation

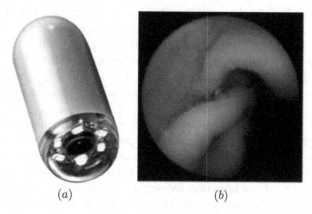

(a)   (b)

Fig. 1. Wireless capsule endoscope (a) and an example image (b)

into sections. In [5,6] image color and texture descriptors defined by the MPEG-7 standard are used for topographic segmentation of the gastro-intestinal (GI) tract into sections. A similar approach has been presented in [7,8,9], where the color and texture descriptors are used for image classification and pylorus detection. Another classification procedure is presented in [10]. Image features, such as image intensity, contrast, and selected geometrical parameters, are extracted from WCE video frames. By comparison of feature vectors computed for nearby frames, video fragments presenting contractions can be detected. Authors demonstrate that fragments with contractions are of particular interest. Another approach is to obtain an image of the bowel surface [11] by preprocessing the video. Such an image, a bowel map, enables to quickly get an overview of the entire recording in terms of completeness and quality. The map also facilitates the identification of abnormal areas and focuses the efforts on relevant ones.

In the presented approach we presume that image regions containing different pathologies and various aspects of normal mucosal appearance also differ in terms of color and texture descriptors. Such descriptors can be computed and then used for differentiation of image contents.

3   Texture Analysis

A texture is a visualization of complex patterns composed of spatially organized, repeated subpatterns, which have a characteristic, somewhat uniform appearance. The local subpatterns within an image are perceived to demonstrate specific brightness, color size, roughness, directivity, randomness, smoothness, granulation, etc. A texture may carry substantial information about the structure of physical objects. In medical images it may characterize the structure of human tissues or organs. Consequently, textural image analysis is an important issue in image processing and understanding in medical applications. To perform such analysis, mathematically defined texture properties are computed.

In our study we use MaZda 4.7 software [12,13] for textural feature computation. The software is capable of conducting a quantitative analysis of texture within arbitrarily selected regions of interest (ROI) and can provide an interpretation of the computed results. There are three categories of feature computation approaches that MaZda utilizes: statistical (based on image histogram, gradient, co-ocurrence matrix, run-length matrix), model-based (implementation of the autoregressive model) and image transform (based on the Haar wavelet). MaZda may be used to compute textural descriptors based on color components of a color image, such as Y, R, G, B, U, V, I, Q, color saturation and hue. The textural features computed for different color components can be combined to obtain a comprehensive characterization of a colored texture. Therefore, feature vectors computed by MaZda may include over a thousand elements per individual region of interest. Such a large number of features, creating several-hundred-dimensional spaces, are not easy to handle by statistical analysis or by classifiers.

4   Vector Supported Convex Hull Method

Since the main problem is to find a way of discriminating between various image classes, the Vector Supported Convex Hull Method aims at two objectives. The first is to reduce the dimensionality of the vector space by optimizing the number of vector features. This goal is achieved by selection of such subsets of features, which present best discrimination ability among other feature subsets. Usually only a limited number of features carry relevant information needed for discrimination and other features are redundant for classification. The profit of such selection is that redundant features are not calculated, which saves computation time.

The second objective of the VSCH method is to propose a way for vector classification. The method produces a number of conditions - inequalities, which define a region of vectors as belonging to the class of interest. Thus, rules for classification are formulated throughout these inequalities.

VSCH is a discriminant analysis method of supervised learning for reduction of vectors dimensionality and data classification. It aims at finding a subspace in feature vector space and produces a classification rule to separate the two classes. To explain the concept of VSCH let us assume input data consist of two sets (classes) of feature vectors in an n-dimensional space. All the features are real numbers and the feature vector space is also real. We search for a k-dimensional subspace $(k < n)$ such that vectors of the set number one form a cluster surrounded by vectors of the set number two (cf. Fig. 2).

$$\Theta \subset \Omega; \Theta \in \mathcal{R}^k; \Omega \in \mathcal{R}^n; k < n. \tag{1}$$

Let us consider a convex hull of set one in a k-dimensional subspace of feature vectors space $(k < n)$. The convex hull can be found by solving a system of equation (2) and inequality conditions (3).

$$\mathbf{B}^T \mathbf{x}_\Theta + b_0 = 0 \tag{2}$$

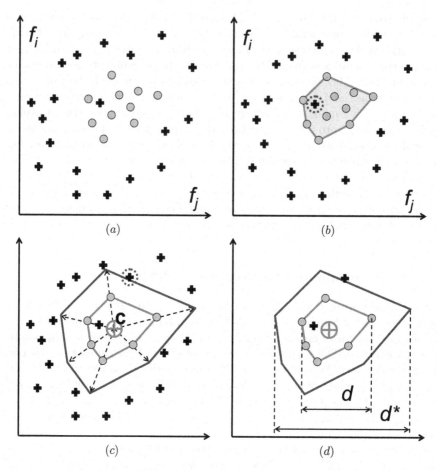

Fig. 2. Illustration of convex hull method in 2D space (k=2)

$$\mathbf{B}^T \mathbf{x}_\Theta + b_0 \leq 0. \tag{3}$$

Equation (2) defines a hyperplane in k-dimensional space. The equation (2) is solved for $k+1$ number of linearly independent vectors belonging to class number one. $\mathbf{B}$ is a versor of a hyperplane and parameter b_0 are unknowns. There are two solutions of (2) per each subset of $k + 1$ vectors, since versor $\mathbf{B}$ may point toward the inside or outside of the convex hull. The boundary of the convex hull is then defined by such solutions, which in addition satisfy inequality (3) for all the vectors belonging to class one.

Now we define a coefficient Q_1. It is the number of vectors belonging to the second class, which also belong to the convex hull built on class number one. It is the number of vectors of the second class satisfying inequality (3) defining the convex hull. The example in Fig. 2b shows one such vector. Therefore, in the case presented in the figure the $Q_1 = 1$. Generally, the lower the value of Q_1, the better class separation for the analyzed Θ subspace. The next step is to find a centroid **c** of the convex hull. Then the convex hull is isotropically scaled up (cf. Fig. 2c) around the fixed centroid **c** of the convex hull. The scaling is given by Eq. 4.

$$\mathbf{x}_{\Theta}^* = a(\mathbf{x}_{\Theta} - \mathbf{c}) + \mathbf{c}. \tag{4}$$

The parameter a defines a space enlargement. It is a maximum scaling factor for which Q_1 does not increase. Now we define a Q_2 coefficient which is equal to reciprocal of a (cf. Fig. 2d also).

$$Q_2 = a^{-1} = \frac{d}{d^*}. \tag{5}$$

Since, a is larger than 1, the coefficient Q_2 is a fraction. On the other hand coefficient Q_1 is an integer number equal or higher than 1. Now, we combine the two coefficients and define a comprehensive Q coefficient as:

$$Q = Q_1 + Q_2. \tag{6}$$

The Q specifies discriminative power of k-dimensional feature space. The lower value of the Q indicates the analyzed Θ subspace has better class separability. The algorithm for feature space reduction based on VSCH method was implemented. The algorithm searches through all the 1D, 2D and 3D feature subsets (Θ subspaces) and computes Q coefficient for each subset. For further analysis and classification purpose such subset is chosen, which exposes the lowest Q coefficient. The algorithm also produces rules of classification. The rules are given in form of inequalities (3). The inequalities define boundaries obtained by scaling-up the convex hull by factor of $a/2$.

In many medical applications it is crucial not to overlook any indications of pathology. Such indications usually are later verified by medical experts and may be rejected. If they are mistakenly rejected by an automatic method, an expert may never notice the pathology. Therefore, it is important to find methods characterized by a minimal false negative error. The VSCH method reveals a property which is particularly useful in biomedical image analysis.. The method produces classification rules, for which (for the training set vectors) the false negative error is equal to zero. The minimization of false positive errors is a secondary goal, and is achieved directly by minimization of the Q_1 coefficient.

The VSCH can be compared with other method utilizing convex hull, the Nearest Convex Hull (NCH) classifier [14]. However, the NCH still requires radial basis function kernels in cases illustrated in Fig. 2. In contrast, the VSCH exploits natural ability of convex hull for separation of radially distributed vectors. Moreover, the NCH is not applicable for feature selection task.

5   Support Vector Machines

The proposed VSCH method presumes specific distribution of vectors. Similar concept underlies a well established classification algorithm – Support Vector Machine (SVM) with the radial basis function (RBF) kernel [15], which produces spherical shape of a decision boundary between two different classes. Thus, it is reasonable to evaluate VSCH performance in comparison with the SVM-RBF classifier. For the need of the comparative study reported below, SVM-RBF was employed for both feature selection and classification tasks.

The SVM itself is a linear classification algorithm. The constructed decision hyperplane is defined as

$$y(\mathbf{x}) = b + \sum_{\alpha_i \neq 0} \alpha_i y_i \mathbf{x}_i \cdot \mathbf{x}, \qquad (7)$$

where parameters α_i and b together with the support vectors $\mathbf{x}_i$ determine location and orientation of the separating hyperplane. The learning procedure involves solving a constrained quadratic optimization problem which leads to determination of α_i coefficients, whose values are non-zero only for those vectors in a training sample which lie closest (on either side) to a decision boundary. It must be noted, that SVM algorithm constructs a hyperplane which defines the largest margin between different data vectors classes in a particular feature subspace. In this aspect, the VSCH method behaves similarly to SVM.

Another attractive property, which SVM possesses, allows its easy extension to non-linearly separable cases. The dot product ($\cdot$) in (7) can be replaced by the kernel function which corresponds to the dot product of data vectors non-linearly transformed into higher dimensional feature space. It is expected, that this hypothetical multidimensional space already allows linear discrimination of different classes. The main problem which arises here is to find appropriate transformation of the input data set. This reduces to choosing a kernel function for calculation of the dot product. Apart from the mentioned radial basis function, defined as

$$k(\mathbf{x}_i, \mathbf{x}_j) = \exp(-\gamma \|\mathbf{x}_i - \mathbf{x}_j\|^2). \qquad (8)$$

The polynomial kernel constitute frequent alternatives:

$$k(\mathbf{x}_i, \mathbf{x}_j) = (\mathbf{x}_i \cdot \mathbf{x}_j + 1)^n. \qquad (9)$$

From the reasons outlined above, in this research Eq. (8) was chosen. However, even if the general form of the kernel function is known, it still needs to be adjusted to the specific properties of a given data set. The value of γ coefficient cannot be determined automatically and several trials must be made before a trained classifier gains its discriminative power. In principle the larger γ is, the better accuracy on a training set is observed. On the other hand, there appears a risk of overfitting when the value of γ becomes too large. Hence, in every experiment one must find a good trade-off between error rate obtained for a training set and generalization capabilities of a trained SVM.

6   Experiment

To assess effectiveness of the VCSH method the following experiment was devised. Fifty images showing case of excessive ulceration were selected out of three

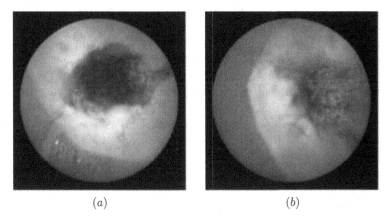

(a)   (b)

Fig. 3. Examples of class one (ulceration)

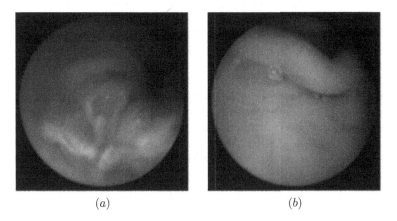

(a)   (b)

Fig. 4. Examples of class two (normal appearance of mucosal surface)

Fig. 5. Overlapping circular regions used in the study

video files obtained for three different patients (cf. Fig. 3). Regions of ulceration (regions of interest) were manually depicted within the images. For reference, 200 images showing normal appearance (cf. Fig. 4) of mucosal surface were randomly chosen from other ten videos. Then all the selected images were divided into circular overlapping subregions, each of 2009 pixels area (cf. Fig. 5).

For images showing ulcerations, textural features were computed within circular subregions enclosed within the depicted regions of ulceration. For other images textural features were computed within circular subregions enclosed within the image field of view. Features were computed by means of MaZda program. Feature vectors included histogram descriptors computed for 14 various color channels as well as gradient, co-ocurrence matrix, run-length matrix, autoregressive model and Haar wavelet transform descriptors computed for image brightness (together over 300 features per region).

The number of vectors obtained was over 400 for class one (ulceration) and over 4800 for class two (normal). After that, training and testing sets were assembled. Training set was composed of 109 vectors of class one and 258 vectors of class two. Testing set was composed of 100 vectors of class one and 100 vectors of class two. In both cases vectors were picked randomly from the set of all the produced vectors. Then, VSCH and SVM methods were applied for attribute subset selection and data classification purpose. In both applications the goal of feature selection was to find a pair of features with the highest discrimination ability given the methods criteria. Feature space exploration was performed using exhaustive search. This eliminates the impact of local optima of criterion function or randomness associated with heuristic strategies such as genetic algorithm or sequential search methods [16,17,18].

Based on the training set, the VSCH method selected a pair of features computed from hue and green color components of the image. They are the mean value of the hue component (X_Mean) and a tenth percentile of the green

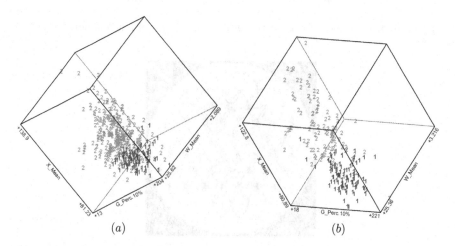

(a)   (b)

Fig. 6. Distributions of the training (a) and the testing (b) vectors in the feature subspace found by VSCH

Table 1. Classification results

		FPR [%]	Specificity	FNR [%]	Sensitivity
VSCH	Training set	9.3	0.907	0.0	1.000
	Testing set	7.0	0.930	6.0	0.940
SVM	Training set	4.3	0.958	6.4	0.936
	Testing set	5.0	0.950	9.0	0.910

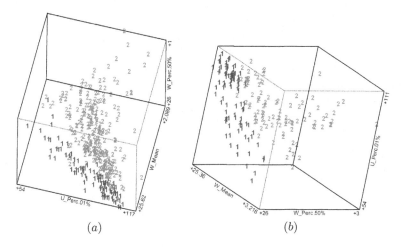

(a)   (b)

Fig. 7. Distributions of the training (a) and the testing (b) vectors in the feature subspace found by SVM-RBF

component (G_Perc.10%) computed within the image region. Fig. 6a presents distribution of the training set vectors within feature space of X_Mean, G_Perc. 10% and additional W_Mean (mean of brightness normalized U component). Fig 6b presents distribution of the testing set vectors within the feature space.

In the case of SVM-based analysis the resulting attribute subspace also consisted of two first-order-histogram features calculated for color components of the images (W_Perc.50% and U_Perc.01%). Scatter plots of the training and testing data vectors in the reduced feature space are depicted in Fig. 7. The classification specificity, sensitivity, false positive rate and false negative rate computed for both selection methods are presented in Table 1.

7 Results Discussion and Conclusions

Analysis of the obtained results leads to the following conclusions. First of all, the performed experiments confirm that texture analasysis provides a practical numerical description of the WCE images. It is possible to accurately classify different types of visualized tissues basing on the selected, most relevant texture parameters. Among the calculated attributes, color component features appear to be the best at discriminating ulceration and normal regions.

Secondly, the error rates as well as accuracy measures viewed in Table 1 are comparable for both tested approaches to feature selection. The VSCH method appears to be overoptimistic when predicting the False Negative Ratio (FNR) on the training set. This results directly from the very nature of the algorithm which aims at construction of a convex hull arround all vectors from a chosen pathology class. However, despite the observed increase in FNR calculated for the testing set, it is still lower than the score obtained for the SVM-based method. In the case of the latter, cost-sensitive learning should be applied to improve its performance with respect to positive class vectors misclassified as negatives. As it has already been mentioned, missing an image that contains important diagnostic information implies consequences that are potentially more dangerous for a patient. The False Positive Ratio (FPR) is not as important – a diagnostician allways has a chance to disregard images wrongly marked as containing pathologies. The proposed VSCH method ensures the desired behaviour without any explicit weighting of error types.

Eventually, usage of SVM involves problem-specific parameterization of a kernel function. Frequently, one must experiment with several values of power exponents (both in polynomial or radial basis functions) before a final choice can be made. On the other hand, VSCH is a non-parametric method and does not require any fine-tuning to solve particular tasks. Moreover, it does not require any feature space standardization. Also any other linear transformation of feature space has no influence on the result produced by the method.

The presented results constitute a preliminary study on classification of WCE images basing on their texture paramaters. This research shall be continued in order to further validate the proposed approach to feature selection. Furhter experiments are planned with the use of new sample images, possibly representing more than two classes.

Acknowledgments. This work was supported by the Polish Ministry of Science and Higher Education grant no. 3263/B/T02/2008/35. The second author is a scholarship holder of the project entitled "Innowacyjna dydaktyka bez ograniczen – zintegrowany rozwoj Politechniki Lodzkiej – zarzadzanie Uczelnia, nowoczesna oferta edukacyjna i wzmacnianie zdolnosci do zatrudniania, takze osob niepelnosprawnych" supported by the European Social Fund.

References

1. Haralick, R.: Statistical and structural approaches to texture. IEEE Proceedings 67(5), 768–804 (1979)
2. Tuceryan, M., Jain, A.: Texture Analysis. In: The Handbook of Pattern Recogntion and Computer Vision, pp. 207–248. World Scientific Publishing Co., Singapore (1998)
3. Iddan, G., Meron, G., Glukhowsky, A., Swain, P.: Wireless capsule endoscopy. Nature 405(6785), 417–418 (2000)
4. Swain, P., Fritscher-Ravens, A.: Role of video endoscopy in managing small bowel disease. GUT 53, 1866–1875 (2004)

5. Coimbra, M., Campos, P., Cunha, J.: Extracting clinical information from endoscopic capsule exams using mpeg-7 visual descriptors. In: The 2nd European Workshop on the Integration of Knowledge, Semantics and Digital Media Technology, EWIMT 2005, pp. 105–110 (2005)

6. Coimbra, M., Cunha, J.: Mpeg-7 visual descriptors–contributions for automated feature extraction in capsule endoscopy. IEEE Transactions on Circuits and Systems for Video Technology 16(5), 628–637 (2006)

7. Mackiewicz, M., Berens, J., Fisher, M., Bell, G.: Colour and texture based gastrointestinal tissue discrimination. In: Proceedings of the IEEE International Conference on Acoustics, Speech and Signal Processing, ICASSP, May 2006, vol. 2, pp. 597–600 (2006)

8. Mackiewicz, M., Berens, J., Fisher, M.: Wireless capsule endoscopy video segmentation using support vector classifiers and hidden markov models. In: Proceedings of the International Conference on Medical Image Understanding and Analyses (June 2006)

9. Li, B., Meng, M.H.: Ulcer recognition in capsule endoscopy images by texture features. In: 7th World Congress on Intelligent Control and Automation, WCICA 2008, June 2008, pp. 234–239 (2008)

10. Vilarinao, F., Kuncheva, L.I., Radeva, P.: Roc curves and video analysis optimization in intestinal capsule endoscopy. Pattern Recogn. Lett. 27(8), 875–881 (2006)

11. Szczypinski, P., Sriram, R.D., Sriram, P., Reddy, D.: A model of deformable rings for interpretation of wireless capsule endoscopic videos. Medical Image Analysis 13(2), 312–324 (2009)

12. Szczypinski, P., Strzelecki, M., Materka, A., Klepaczko, A.: Mazda - a software package for image texture analysis. Computer Methods and Programs in Biomedicine 94, 66–76 (2009)

13. Szczypinski, P.: (2009), http://www.eletel.p.lodz.pl/MaZda (Visited: April 2009)

14. Nalbantov, G., Groenen, P., Bioch, J.: Nearest convex hull classification. Econometric Institute Report EI 2006-50 Revision_Date: Erasmus University Rotterdam, Econometric Institute (January 2007)

15. Vapnik, V.: The Nature of Statistical Learning Theory. Springer, New York (1995)

16. Blum, A.L., Langley, P.: Selection of relevant features and examples in machine learning. Artificial Intelligence 97, 245–271 (1997)

17. Kohavi, R., John, G.H.: Wrappers for feature subset selection. Artificial Intelligence 97, 273–324 (1997)

18. Pudil, P., Somol, P.: Current feature selection techniques in statistical pattern recognition. In: Kurzynski, M., Puchala, E., Wozniak, M., Zolnierek, A. (eds.) Computer Recognition Systems. Advances in Sof. Computing, vol. 30, Springer, Heidelberg (2005)

Pattern Analysis of Dermoscopic Images Based on FSCM Color Markov Random Fields

Carlos S. Mendoza*, Carmen Serrano, and Begoña Acha

Universidad of Sevilla
Av. de los Descubrimientos s/n
41092 Sevilla, Spain
{csanchez1,cserrano,bacha}@us.es

Abstract. In this paper a method for pattern analysis in dermoscopic images of abnormally pigmented skin (melanocytic lesions) is presented. In order to diagnose a possible skin cancer, physicians assess the lesion according to different rules. The new trend in Dermatology is to classify the lesion by means of pattern irregularity. In order to analyze the pattern turbulence, lesions ought to be segmented into single pattern regions. Our classification method, when applied on overlapping lesion patches, provides a pattern chart that could ultimately allow for in-region single-texture turbulence analysis. Due to the color-textured appearance of these patterns, we present a novel method based on a Finite Symmetric Conditional Model (FSCM) Markov Random Field (MRF) color extension for the characterization and discrimination of pattern samples. Our classification success rate rises to 86%.

1 Introduction

In the last two decades a rising incidence of malignant melanoma has been observed. Because of a lack of adequate therapies for metastatic melanoma, the best treatment is still early diagnosis and prompt surgical excision of the primary cancer. Dermoscopy (also known as epiluminescence microscopy) is an in vivo method that has been reported to be a useful tool for the early recognition of malignant melanoma [1]. Its use increases diagnostic accuracy between 5 and 30% in clinical visual inspection [2].

Currently available digital dermoscopic systems offer the possibility of computer storage and retrieval of dermoscopic images. Some systems even display the potential for Computer Assisted Diagnosis (CAD) [3,4]. As diagnostic accuracy with dermoscopy has been shown to depend on the experience of the dermatologist, CAD systems will help less-experienced dermatologists and provide a lower impact for inter-subject variability.

* The authors would like to thank Dr. Amalia Serrano for providing and classifying dermatoscopic images used in this work, that has been funded by project FIS05-2028. Carlos S. Mendoza is also funded by a doctoral scholarship provided by Universidad de Sevilla.

J. Blanc-Talon et al. (Eds.): ACIVS 2009, LNCS 5807, pp. 676–685, 2009.
© Springer-Verlag Berlin Heidelberg 2009

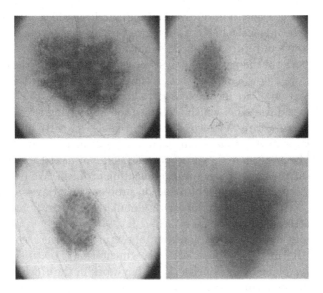

Fig. 1. Examples of the patterns under study. Reticular, globular, cobblestone and homogeneous patterns (respectively).

Most technical papers developing methods to automatically classify dermatological images are based on the ABCD rule (Asymmetry, Border irregularity, Color variation, Diameter greater than 6mm or growing). Frequently, such papers present an approach to cover one or several letters of the rule, that is, some are based on detecting Asymmetry [5,6], Borders [7,8,9,10], Color [11,12] or Diameter [12].

One of the key ideas of this paper is that it is not focused on detecting specific features in the images to cover the four letters of the ABCD rule, but instead follows the new tendency in Dermatology: to look for specific patterns in the lesions which can lead physicians to an assessment, by means of the so-called pattern *turbulence* analysis [13]. Before any pattern turbulence or irregularity can be analyzed, a previous requirement is lesion segmentation into single-pattern regions. The different patterns that can be found inside a lesion are: reticular; globular; cobblestone; homogeneous; starburst; and parallel [14]. In their article, Tanaka et al. [13] extracted different features for texture description of abnormal skin pigmentation samples. Unfortunately their study does not provide a list of principal features, preventing from further extensions towards a pattern segmentation method. Our contribution consists in a thorough description of a particular modelization [14] which, relying on a great classification success rate for as many as four of the existing melanocytic patterns, ultimately provides a framework for pattern map creation. Thus, further developments on pattern segmentation inside lesions, could be exploited for malignancy assessment using turbulence analysis. In this work we take Serrano et al. a couple steps forward. We segment the lesion from healthy skin, which was done manually in their work.

Also we perform classification on overlapping patches, which allows for future segmentation schemes. Last but not least, we provide a charting method which set the foundations of future turbulence analysis.

In order to perform the pattern analysis procedure to classify the dermoscopic image samples, we follow a model-based technique. In such methods, image classification is treated as an incomplete data problem, where the value of each pixel is known, and the label which identifies the underlying texture is missing. Additionally, textures are modeled as random fields, an MRF in our case, and their classification is posed as a parameter estimation problem. Once the parameters have been estimated, we propose a Gaussian model for the extracted parameters treated as features in our classification problem. We proceed then to classification solving an energy optimization problem in a Bayesian framework. In this initial study we will deal only with globular, reticular, homogeneous and cobblestone patterns, as can be seen in Fig. 1.

In our case, one important characteristic of texture patterns is color. Panjwani et al. develop MRF models for unsupervised segmentation of textured color images considering inter-plane dependencies [15]. They work in the RGB color space, a perceptually non-uniform space. Kato et al. [16] use a combination of grey-level based texture features and color instead of direct modeling of color textures. The color features are calculated in the $L^*u^*v^*$ color space. Tab et al. present a multiresolution color image segmentation algorithm [17]. Regarding to the MRF model for colored textures, they assume channel conditional independence and they use the YUV color space.

Regarding the use of MRF in segmentation/classification of dermoscopic images not much is available in the literature. To the best of our knowledge, only Gao et al. [18] present something related. The MRF technique is poorly explained, and they use the first plane of the PCT (Principal Component Transform) of the dermoscopic images, that is, is a grey-level version of MRF modeling. But, in any case, their ultimate goal is to tell lesion from healthy skin, which is not our aim.

In this paper we describe an MRF model-based classification framework, performed in the $L^*a^*b^*$ color space. We consider inter-channel dependencies explicitly in our approach.

2   Model-Based Classification Algorithm

For textured images, the theory based on Markov Random Fields (MRF) is an important field, which has been developed extensively in the last decades. MRF theory provides a convenient and consistent way for modeling context-dependent entities such as image pixels and correlated features [19].

In this paper we present a supervised method of classification. We are going to classify the following patterns: reticular, globular, cobblestone, and homogeneous. A training set with images individually representing each pattern is available, and the problem to be solved consists in, when presenting a lesion with a specific pattern, classifying it as the correct class it belongs to. The training set is formed by 50×50 color images, each one representing one specific realization of the four different patterns. Therefore, prior to texture classification the lesion will be segmented from the background (healthy skin). Then, the segmented area will be analyzed by classification of overlapping neighborhoods of size 50×50 according to the described training. Thus, a pattern chart is obtained as first approach towards pattern segmentation in melanocytic lesions.

In order to do that, we perform an MRF-based texture modeling, where each of the four textures appearing in the training set is assumed to be a different MRF, each element in the training set a different realization of the texture it belongs to, and the patches present in the lesions to be classified are assumed to be realizations of one of the four corresponding MRFs. To model a texture class is to specify the corresponding probabilities or Gibbs clique potential parameters of the underlying MRF. The following step is to classify the overlapping texture patches available in the segmented lesion, which consists in the extraction of texture features for each patch, and the design of a consistent decision rule. In MRF texture modeling, texture features correspond to MRF parameters and feature extraction is equivalent to parameter estimation [19]. In this supervised approach, the classification is performed using training data that will establish reference features.

The lesion segmentation has been performed by applying an Otsu thresholding and a post-processing step consisting in morphological dilation.

2.1 Texture Model

As suggested in Xia et al. [20], each separate texture is considered as a random field G, defined on a $W \times H$ rectangular lattice, where W and H represent the patch size (in our case $W = H = 50$). The lattice is denoted by $S = \{(i,j) : 1 \leq i \leq W, 1 \leq j \leq H\}$, which is indexed by the coordinate (i,j). The color values are represented by $G = \{G_s = g_s : s \in S\}$, where $s = (s_i, s_j)$ denotes a specific *site* and the random variable G_s represents a color pixel in the $L^*a^*b^*$ color space. An observed patch $g = \{g_s : s \in S\}$ is an instance of G. It can be described by a finite symmetric conditional model (FSCM) [21] as follows

$$g_s = \mu_s + \sum_{t \in \eta_g} \beta_{s,t}[(g_{s+t} - \mu_{s+t}) + (g_{s-t} - \mu_{s-t})] + e_s \ , \tag{1}$$

where $\eta_g = \{(0,1),(1,0),(1,1),(-1,1)\}$ is the set of shift vectors corresponding to the second order neighborhood system, μ_s is the mean of the pixels in the sample, $\{\beta_{s,t} : t \in \eta_g\}$ is the set of correlation coefficients associated with the set of translations from every site s, and $\{e_s\}$ is a stationary Gaussian noise sequence with variance σ_s^2.

The scope of our paper is to classify 50×50 pixel images into 4 possible patterns, that is, we have to assign the whole image to a specific label. Therefore, each image will be assigned one out of four possible patterns by polling the resulting classification for each of its forming patches. Each patch will be characterized by a unique parameter vector, calculated for the whole extent of the patch. It is important to note that pixels take values in a 3D (three-dimensional) space, generating a vector where each component is a color coordinate in the $L^*a^*b^*$ color space. Therefore, the parameter vector f is formed by 18 components.

2.2 $L^*a^*b^*$ Color Space

The $L^*a^*b^*$ color space is considered as a perceptually uniform color space transform, that means that distances calculated in this space correspond to difference as the human visual system perceives.

Chen et al [22] showed that applying the K-L (Karhunen-Love) transform to one hundred test images in $L^*a^*b^*$ coordinates, the principal eigenvector in CIE $L^*a^*b^*$ coordinates is very close to the vector $(1, 0, 0)^T$, and the other two eigenvector are primarily in the a^*b^* plane of the $L^*a^*b^*$ color system. That means that we can consider the L^* component as not correlated with the a^*b^* coordinates.

2.3   Parameter Estimation

In order to estimate the parameters, we follow the least-squares estimation method [23,24]. For each patch we get the following parameter estimations

$$\hat{\beta} = \left[\sum_{s \in N^I} Q_s Q_s^T\right]^{-1} \left[\sum_{s \in N^I} Q_s g_s\right] , \tag{2}$$

$$\sigma^2 = \frac{1}{|N^I|} \sum_{s \in N^I} \left[g_s - \hat{\beta}^T Q_s\right]^2 , \tag{3}$$

$$\mu = \frac{1}{|N|} \sum_{s \in N} g_s . \tag{4}$$

where Q_s is a column vector defined by $Q_s = [g_{s+t} + g_{s-t} : t \in \eta_g]$ with dimensions $(4 \times 1 \times 3)$ because g_s is a 3D color pixel, N is the set of all the sites belonging to the window where the parameters are calculated (the whole patch) and N^I is the interior subset of N. Because we are processing color images, the dimensions of the parameters are $(4 \times 1 \times 3)$ for $\hat{\beta}$, (1×3) for σ^2 and (1×3) for μ. In summary, the parameter vector has 18 components as it has been described in Sect. 2.1.

2.4   Feature Model

The Gausian mixture is typically an appropriate model for the components of the feature vector in most classification problems, where those components f are continuous valued. After training with 50 patches of size 50×50 of each one of the four pattern classes, we assume that the six parameters obtained from L^* component are independent from the twelve parameters calculated from the a^* and b^* components. Therefore, the f is decomposed into two parameter vectors:

$$f_L = (\mu_L, \sigma_L^2, \beta_{L,t} : t \in \eta_g) , \tag{5}$$

$$f_{ab} = (\mu_a, \mu_b, \sigma_a^2, \sigma_b^2, \beta_{a,t}, \beta_{b,t} : t \in \eta_g) \ , \tag{6}$$

each one following a Normal mixture distribution $N(M_{i,\lambda}, \Sigma_{i,\lambda})$ with mean $M_{i,\lambda}$ and covariance matrix $\Sigma_{i,\lambda}$ for $i \in \{L, ab\}$. The variable λ represents the pattern class, $\lambda \in R = \{1, 2, 3, 4\}$.

$$N(M_{i,\lambda}, \Sigma_{i,\lambda}) = \frac{\exp\left(-\frac{1}{2}(f_i - M_{i,\lambda})\Sigma_{i,\lambda}^{-1}(f_i - M_{i,\lambda})^T\right)}{\sqrt{(2\pi)^n |\Sigma_{i,\lambda}|}}, \tag{7}$$

where n is the dimension of the parameter vector ($n = 6$ for f_L and $n = 12$ for f_{ab}).

2.5 Optimization

As our images consist of overlapping patches containing patterns out of four different classes (reticular, cobblestone, homogeneous and globular), each patch will be assigned to a unique label λ, which is an instance of a random variable Λ, taking values from a finite set $R = \{1, 2, 3, 4\}$. We assume that each texture pattern occurs with the same probability in a pigmented lesion. Therefore the Λ variable is uniformly distributed. In order to find the optimum label for the patch under study, we apply the *maximum likelihood (ML)* criterion instead of the *maximum a posteriori probability (MAP)* criterion, as we assume that the prior information of the label is uniform:

$$\hat{\lambda} = argmax_{\lambda \in \Lambda} P(F_L = f_L, F_{ab} = f_{ab} | \lambda) \ . \tag{8}$$

Assuming independence between f_L and f_{ab} (according to Sect. 2.2):

$$P(F_L = f_L, F_{ab} = f_{ab} | \lambda) = P(F_L = f_L | \lambda) P(F_{ab} = f_{ab} | \lambda) \ . \tag{9}$$

The ML problem given by (8) can then be solved by minimizing the following energy:

$$\begin{aligned}
\hat{\lambda} &= \min_{\lambda \in \Lambda} \{E_G(f_L, \lambda) + E_G(f_{ab}, \lambda)\} \\
&= \min_{\lambda \in \Lambda} \left\{ \left[(f_L - M_{L,\lambda})^T \Sigma_{L,\lambda}^{-1} (f_L - M_{L,\lambda}) + \ln\left((2\pi)^6 |\Sigma_{L,\lambda}|\right) \right] \right. \\
&\quad \left. + \left[(f_{ab} - M_{ab,\lambda})^T \Sigma_{ab,\lambda}^{-1} (f_{ab} - M_{ab,\lambda}) + \ln\left((2\pi)^6 |\Sigma_{ab,\lambda}|\right) \right] \right\} \ , \tag{10}
\end{aligned}$$

that takes into account the Gaussian multivariate parameters obtained in the training and compares them with the parameter vectors obtained for the patch under study. We have a database with images classified by a dermatologist as belonging to one of the four possible patterns. Therefore a unique classification of the whole lesion is needed. In the preceding sections we have classified each overlapping 50×50 patch inside the lesion into a pattern class.

3   Experimental Results

The proposed algorithm has been tested on a database containing 9 dermato-scopic images displaying each one a different kind of pattern, adding up to a total of 36 images. All the images were acquired with the same, callibrated der-moscope Fotofinder Schuco International London Limited. The images are of size 767×576 and have been classified by a physician as globally belonging to one of the four patterns in our training set. Since the available lesions contain only sam-ples of one single class, the overall quality of the classification will be measured using the percentage of lesions assigned to the right global pattern available in each lesion. As training, we have employed 50 50×50 different patches for each of the 4 possible textures. Considering the small size of the available database, 5 patches were extracted from every lesions. For the classification of the patches inside a lesion, only patches from the other lesions were used for training.

The segmented area was analyzed in 50×50 overlapping neighborhoods ac-cording to the method described above. The average success rate is summarized in Table 1. Notice the good results for the first three pattern classes. Mediocre results for globular pattern are probably due to varying degree of globule scale in the available database. We expect this figure to rise as soon as we can have a greater database with representative cases for all patterns.

Table 1. Classification Results

Pattern	Success rate	Robustness
Reticular	1.00	0.65
Cobblestone	1.00	0.84
Homogeneous	0.89	0.82
Globular	0.56	0.80
Average	0.86	0.78

The robustness measure in Table 1 takes into account the percentage of prop-erly classified patches inside the globally successfully classified lesion. The lower value for reticular lesions indicate that the classifier encountered many non-reticular patches inside the reticular lesions. After carefully observing our retic-ular lesions, we conclude that in fact globally reticular lesions tend to contain fuzzy areas that are not strictly reticular. We plan to incorporate this knowledge into future developments.

Figure 2 shows an example of a pattern chart. The chart, when compared with the lesion, illustrates the fact that subtle irregularities in the single-texture claimed lesion, provide alternative pattern labellings, thus revealing the potential of the overlapping-patches analysis technique. This suggests that the computed robustness would be higher for truly single-textured lesions.

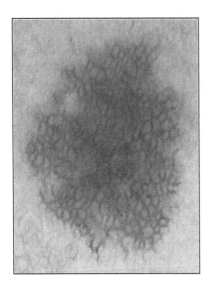
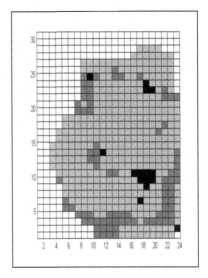

Fig. 2. Example for a reticular lesion. The grid on the right represents the labeling of the patches in the lesion on the left. Gray levels evolve from white to black according to the following order: Healthy skin, Reticular, Cobblestone, Homogeneous(absent in this example) and Globular. Notice how subtle irregularities are detected in the chart creation.

4   Conclusions, Discussion and Future Work

In this paper we have presented a novel pattern description technique based on MRF modeling. The main singularity of the paper is the methodology followed to analyze the dermoscopic images. To the best of our knowledge, except for [13,14], the references in the literature mostly apply the ABCD rule in order to classify the lesion. In this paper, we introduce a new methodology to create a chart of the patterns distribution in melanocytic lesions. In this work we improve those works. We segment the lesion from healthy skin, which was done manually in their work. Also we perform classification on overlapping patches, which allows for future segmentation schemes. Last but not least, we provide a charting method which set the foundations of future turbulence analysis.

For doing the analysis of the color textured pattern, we model the image as a FSCM model, and calculate a feature vector with the estimated parameters of the model. We make use of the $L^*a^*b^*$ color space and suppose independence between the parameters extracted from the L^* channel and the ones calculated from the a^* and b^* channels. To classify, we apply the ML criterion to maximize the conditional probability.

The starbust pattern was not analyzed in this paper because its description implies segmentation in itself, as its main discriminative characteristic from the rest of patterns is located in the border of the starbust lesion, and not in a particular pattern inside the lesion [14]. Regarding parallel pattern, we are currently working on spatially invariant descriptors that can possibly respond in the same manner to parallel pattern with different orientations.

The next step towards malignancy assessment passes by true texture segmentation, rather than charting, and ultimately by ulterior analysis of single-pattern regions. The search for texture turbulence abnormalities, might eventually lead to a computer-aided diagnosis (CAD) system with clinical application.

Further on, we plan to develop a series of subjective experiments in order to properly convey the perceptual sensations that dermatologists evaluate when clinically assessing malignant melanocytic lesions. This is a necessary step towards automatic diagnosis, and is by no means a resolved topic.

References

1. Stolz, W., Braun-Falco, O., Bilek, P., Landthaler, M., Burgdorf, W.H.C., Cognetta, A.B.: Color Atlas of Dermatoscopy. Blackwell Wissenschafts-Verlag, Berlin (2002)
2. Westerhoff, K., McCarthy, W.H., Menzies, S.W.: Increase in the sensitivity for melanoma diagnosis by primary care physicians using skin surface microscopy. British Journal of Dermatology 143(5), 1016–1020 (2000)
3. Binder, M., Kittler, H., Seeber, A., Steiner, A., Pehamberger, H., Wolff, K.: Epiluminescence microscopy-based classification of pigmented skin lesions using computerized image analysis and an artificial neural network. Melanoma Research 8(3), 261–266 (1998)
4. Schmidt, P.: Segmentation of digitized dermatoscopic images by two-dimensional color clustering. IEEE Transactions on Medical Imaging 18(2), 164–171 (1999)
5. Schmid-Saugeon, P., Guillod, J., Thiran, J.P.: Towards a computer-aided diagnosis system for pigmented skin lesions. Computerized Medical Imaging and Graphics 27(1), 65–78 (2003)
6. Stoecker, W.V., Li, W.W., Moss, R.H.: Automatic detection of asymmetry in skin tumors. Computerized Medical Imaging and Graphics 16(3), 191–197 (1992)
7. Erkol, B., Moss, R.H., Stanley, R.J., Stoecker, W.V., Hvatum, E.: Automatic lesion boundary detection in dermoscopy images using gradient vector flow snakes. Skin Research and Technology 11(1), 17–26 (2005)
8. Lee, T.K., Claridge, E.: Predictive power of irregular border shapes for malignant melanomas. Skin Research and Technology 11(1), 1–8 (2005)
9. Grana, C., Pellacani, G., Cucchiara, R., Seidenari, S.: A new algorithm for border description of polarized light surface microscopic images of pigmented skin lesions. IEEE Transactions on Medical Imaging 22(8), 959–964 (2003)
10. Golston, J.E., Moss, R.H., Stoecker, W.V.: Boundary detection in skin tumor images: An overall approach and a radial search algorithm. Pattern Recognition 23(11), 1235–1247 (1990)
11. Stanley, R.J., Moss, R.H., Stoecker, W.V., Aggawal, C.: A fuzzy-based histogram analysis technique for skin lesion discrimination in dermatology clinical images. Computerized Medical Imaging and Graphics 27(5), 387–396 (2003)
12. Tommasi, T., Torre, E.L., Caputo, B.: Melanoma recognition using representative and discriminative kernel classifiers. In: Beichel, R.R., Sonka, M. (eds.) CVAMIA 2006. LNCS, vol. 4241, pp. 1–12. Springer, Heidelberg (2006)
13. Tanaka, T., Torii, S., Kabuta, I., Shimizu, K., Tanaka, M.: Pattern classification of nevus with texture analysis. IEEJ Transactions on Electrical and Electronic Engineering 3(1), 143–150 (2008)

14. Serrano, C., Acha, B.: Pattern analysis of dermoscopic images based on markov random fields. Pattern Recognition 42(6), 1052–1057 (2009)
15. Panjwani, D., Healey, G.: Results using random field models for the segmentation of color images of natural scenes, pp. 714–719 (1995)
16. Kato, Z., Pong, T.C.: A markov random field image segmentation model for color textured images. Image and Vision Computing 24(10), 1103–1114 (2006)
17. Tab, F.A., Naghdy, G., Mertins, A.: Scalable multiresolution color image segmentation. Signal Processing 86(7), 1670–1687 (2006)
18. Gao, J., Zhang, J., Fleming, M.G., Pollak, I., Cognetta, A.B.: Segmentation of dermatoscopic images by stabilized inverse diffusion equations, vol. 3, pp. 823–827 (1998)
19. Li, S.Z.: Markov Random Field Modeling in Image Analysis. Springer, Tokyo (2001)
20. Xia, Y., Feng, D., Zhao, R.: Adaptive segmentation of textured images by using the coupled markov random field model. IEEE Transactions on Image Processing 15(11), 3559–3566 (2006)
21. Kashyap, R.L., Chellappa, R.: Estimation and choice of neighbors in spatial-interaction models of images. IEEE Transactions on Information Theory IT-29(1), 60–72 (1983)
22. Chen, Y., Hao, P.: Optimal transform in perceptually uniform color space and its application in image retrieval, vol. 2, pp. 1107–1110 (2004)
23. Manjunath, B.S., Simchony, T., Chellappa, R.: Stochastic and deterministic networks for texture segmentation. IEEE Transactions on Acoustics, Speech, and Signal Processing 38(6), 1039–1049 (1990)
24. Manjunath, B.S., Chellappa, R.: Unsupervised texture segmentation using markov random field models. IEEE Transactions on Pattern Analysis and Machine Intelligence 13(5), 478–482 (1991)

A 3D Statistical Facial Feature Model and Its Application on Locating Facial Landmarks

Xi Zhao, Emmanuel Dellandréa, and Liming Chen

Université de Lyon, CNRS
Ecole Centrale de Lyon, LIRIS, UMR5205, F-69134, France
{xi.zhao,emmanuel.dellandrea,liming.chen}@ec-lyon.fr

Abstract. 3D face landmarking aims at automatic localization of 3D facial features and has a wide range of applications, including face recognition, face tracking, facial expression analysis. Methods so far developed for 2D images were shown sensitive to lighting condition changes. In this paper, we propose a learning-based approach for reliable locating of face landmarks in 3D. Our approach relies on a statistical model, called 3D Statistical Facial feAture Model(SFAM) in the paper, which learns both global variations in 3D face morphology and local ones around the 3D face landmarks in terms of local texture and shape. Experimented on FRGC v1.0 dataset, our approach shows its effectiveness and achieves 99.09% of locating accuracy in 10mm precision. The mean error and standard deviation of each landmark are respectively less than 5mm and 4.

Keywords: 3D face, statistical model, learning, landmarking.

1 Introduction

3D face has emerged recently as a major solution in face processing and analysis to deal with pose and lighting variations [2]. While 3D face models are theoretically reputed to be insensitive to lighting condition changes, they still require to be pose normalized and correctly registered for further 3D face processing and analysis. As most of the existing registration techniques assume that some 3D face landmarks are available, a reliable localization of these facial feature points is capital.

Face landmarking has been extensively studied for 2D facial texture images, including appearance-based, geometric-based and structure-based approaches [1]. An interesting approach is 2D statistical models such as the popular Active shape model (ASM) [13] or Active Appearance Model [12] which drives statistical analysis both on facial appearance and structure. Training images were warped into shape-free patches based on manual landmarks. Variance of these landmarks and shape-free images were analyzed to create a joint PCA model. In fitting the model, the current residuals between the model and the target image were measured to predict changes to the current parameters leading to a better fit. However, these approaches, while working on 2D facial texture images, inherit the sensitivity to lighting condition changes and are thus hard to generalize

J. Blanc-Talon et al. (Eds.): ACIVS 2009, LNCS 5807, pp. 686–697, 2009.

on other context. A very interesting work is the constrained local model (CLM) [14] which proposes to learn variations of local patches instead of the ones on global appearance.

Works on 3D face landmarking are rather recent. Conde [3] calculate the spin images based on 3D face mesh and use support vector machine classifiers to locate the nose tip and inner eye points. In [7], nose tip and nose saddles are detected thanks to a local calculation of the curvature surface. Xu [4] define the 'effective energy' describing local surface feature, and design a hierarchical filtering scheme to filter both this feature and a local shape statistical feature. SVM is then used as a classifier to locate nose tip, which reaches 99.3% of correct detection rate. Nose tip is also detected in [5] by applying a generalized Hough Transform. In [6], descriptors representing local shape are calculated from inner product of points and their local plane normal. The search for nose tip and inner corner of eyes are based on matching these descriptors with ones from training, constrained by a graph model. In [8][21][22], authors try to best embed a priori knowledge on 3D face morphology, making use of 3D geometry-related information (curvature, shape index, etc.), thus enabling rather accurate prominent face shape features such as the nose tip or inner corner of eyes. Their localization precision unfortunately decreases for other facial feature points, depending on how specific their local geometrical shape is. Moreover, the number of feature points that can be located by these approaches is very limited, making further face analysis hard, such as feature-point-based facial expression recognition. There also exist some learning-based approaches in 3D face landmarking. The most remarkable one is the 3D morphable face model proposed by Volker Blanz and Thomas Vetter [15], which permits a dense correspondence between a statistical 3D morphable model and an input 3D face scan through an optical flow analysis. However, the matching between the 3D morphable face model and a 3D face scan requires a manual initialization or several face landmarks that we propose to detect automatically in this paper. In a recent work [20], Dibeklioglu et al. proposes a statistical modeling of local features around each face landmarks by a mixture of factor analysers(MoFA) in order to determine the most likely location for each landmark separately. This model produces one likelihood map for each landmark which needs to be further analyzed at a fine level for accurate landmark localization.

In this paper, we propose a statistical learning-based approach for 3D face landmarking. Taking advantage of 3D data, our 3D Statistical Facial feAture Model(SFAM)learns both global variations in 3D face morphology and local ones in terms of texture and shape around each landmark. For training the model, we manually labeled 15 landmarks for each frontal 3D face. Some preprocessing is first conducted to enhance the quality of face scans and normalize unnecessary variations such as head pose and face scale. Our SFAM is constructed from the learning dataset by applying PCA both to global 3D face morphology, local texture and shape around each landmark of the training data. By varying control parameters in SFAM, we can generate different 3D partial face instances which consist of local face regions with texture and shape, structured by a global 3D morphology. Once the model constructed, SFAM is applied to locate landmarks on a new 3D face scan by computing correlation between SFAM and the new face. Our work can be considered as a natural extension of the morphable 3D face model [15] and the constrained local model (CLM) [14] in that we propose to learn at the same time global variations of 3D face morphology and the local ones in terms of texture and shape around each landmark.

The paper is organized as follows: section 2 describes the building process of our model. Section 3 presents the algorithm to apply SFAM to locate feature points on a new face scan. Section 4 discusses the experimental results on the model building and localization of feature points using FRGC v1 dataset. Finally we conclude this paper and propose some future work directions in section 5.

2   Creating SFAM

The approach by SFAM is analysis by synthesis. Training 3D faces are first preprocessed (subsection 2.1) before the statistical modeling of global variations in 3D face morphology and the local ones in terms of texture and shape around each landmark (subsection 2.2). New partial 3D faces can then be synthesized from the learnt model (subsection 2.3).

2.1   Preprocessing Training Faces

3D face scans are sometimes corrupted by noises, so that spikes and holes appear on faces. We detect spikes by checking the discontinuity of points and remove them by median filter. Holes are located by morphological reconstruction [17] and filled by cubic interpolation.

Although faces are scanned from the frontal view, there still remain variations in head pose and position which may disturb the learning of global variations in 3D face morphology. They may further intrude on local shape variations which also need to be learnt properly in our approach. To compensate for intrusion by face position variations, all the gravity centers of the faces are translated into the origin of the coordinate system. To compensate for disturbance introduced by head pose variations, we use Iterative Closest Point (ICP) algorithm [19] to align all faces.

As illustrated in Fig. 1a, a set of 15 salient landmarks, including nose tip and corners, inner and outer eye corners, mouth corners, are manually labeled in the training set. We set a threshold on the Euclidean distance in x, y dimensions to define the local regions around each landmark. Points within all the 15 regions on a face are sampled by saving their 3D coordinates and intensity values. However, the number of sampled points in these regions varies depending on the face scale. In order to normalize this scale variation, a uniform grid with a fixed size is associated with each landmark. As illustrated in fig. 1b,c, each grid has its associated landmark of coordinates (x, y) as its center. x (resp. y) values in the grid are spaced by 1mm per column along X axis (resp. per row along Y axis); the z values (resp. intensity values) are interpolated from range values of sampled points (resp. the intensities of sampled points),

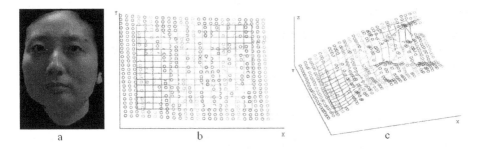

Fig. 1. Manually labeled landmarks(a) and scale normalization in a local region associated to the left corner of the left eye from two viewpoints(b,c). Circles are the sampled points from the 3D face model and the grid composed of the interpolated points. The interpolation is also performed for intensity values.

2.2 Modeling the Morphology and Local Feature

After the preprocessing of the training faces, we concatenate a vector X of the 3D coordinates in Eq.1 of all the landmarks, thus describing the global morphology of a 3D face :

$$X = (x_1, y_1, z_1, x_2, y_2, z_2, ..., x_N, y_N, z_N)^T \qquad (1)$$

Where N is the number of landmarks, e.g. 15 in this paper.

We further generate two vectors G, Z as in Eq.2, 3 by concatenating intensity and range values on all grids on a face (m is the number of interpolated points collected from all the 15 grids). G is further normalized such that its values (g_i) have zero mean and unit variance in order to reduce illumination variations. All the Z vectors thus describe variations of local shapes around each landmark while the G vectors the variations of local texture.

$$G = (g_1, g_2, ..., g_m)^T \qquad (2)$$

$$Z = (z_1, z_2, ..., z_m)^T \qquad (3)$$

Principal Component Analysis(PCA) is then applied to the training datasets X, Z, G to construct three linear models in preserving 95% variations in global morphology, local texture and shape:

$$S = \bar{S} + P_s b_s \qquad (4)$$

$$g = \bar{g} + P_g b_g \qquad (5)$$

$$z = \bar{z} + P_z b_z \qquad (6)$$

where $\bar{S}$, $\bar{g}$, $\bar{z}$ are respectively the mean morphology, mean normalized intensity and mean Z value while P_s, P_g, P_z respectively the three sets of modes of morphology, intensity and range variation, b_s, b_g, b_z the sets of parameters controlling respectively 3D morphology, local intensities and local shapes. All individual components respectively in b_s, b_z and b_g are independent. We further suppose all these b_i-parameters, where $i \in (b_s, b_z, b_g)$ are Gaussian distribution with zero mean and the standard derivation ρ.

2.3   Synthesizing Instances from a New Face

Given the parameters b_s , we can use Eq. 4 to generate a 3D morphology instance. It can be further rotated or translated by a 3D rotation matrix R and translation vector T.

Given a new face, the closest points from the morphology instance to the face are first computed. Based on these points, we then obtain vectors G and Z in Eq. 2, 3 through the same process as we did in the training phase. They are further used to estimate b_g and b_z, as follows:

$$b_g = P_g^T (G - \bar{g}) \tag{7}$$

$$b_z = P_z^T (Z - \bar{z}) \tag{8}$$

In limiting b_i to the range $\pm 3\sigma$, any b_i, $i \in (b_g, b_z)$, exceeding its boundary is replaced by its closest boundary. Then we can generate texture and shape instance $\hat{G}$ and $\hat{Z}$ by Eq. 5, 6 using these constrained b_g and b_z. The morphology, local texture and local shape instances compose a partial face instance.

3   Locating Landmarks

Once learnt, the previous SFAM can be used to locate face landmarks. By comparing partial face instances with different local regions on an input face, we can select the most similar match and thereby locate the face landmarks.

Given a 2.5D face, we first compensate for the variations in head pose and location using ICP algorithm as we did in the training phase. The locating procedure is as follows:

1. Start with the mean morphology model S which amounts to set all b_s to zeros in the morphology model of SFAM, Eq. 4.
2. Find the closest points X' to the morphology model S on the input face.
3. Synthesize texture and shape instances $\hat{G}$, $\hat{Z}$ as described in section 2.3.
4. Local regions around points in X' are sampled with a greater threshold and interpolated as in section 2.1, creating a set of G', Z'.
5. Compute intensity and shape correlation meshes as in Fig. 2 by correlating $\hat{G}$, $\hat{Z}$ respectively with G, Z, different part of G', Z' on local regions, as in Eq. 9,
6. Optimize b_s to reach the maximum value of f in Eq. 10 on both correlation meshes by Nelder-Meade simplex algorithm [16].

$$F_G = \sum_{i=1}^{N} \left\langle \frac{G_i}{\|G_i\|}, \frac{\hat{G}_i}{\|\hat{G}_i\|} \right\rangle, F_Z = \sum_{i=1}^{N} \left\langle \frac{Z_i}{\|Z_i\|}, \frac{\hat{Z}_i}{\|\hat{Z}_i\|} \right\rangle \tag{9}$$

Where $\langle \cdot, \cdot \rangle$ is the inner product and $\|\cdot\|$ is the L^2 norm, N is the number of feature points.

$$f(b_s) = F_G + F_Z \tag{10}$$

In order to ensure the morphology instance is plausible, we also limit b_s within the boundary of $\pm 3\sigma$. All trespassing b_s is replaced by the its closest boundary.

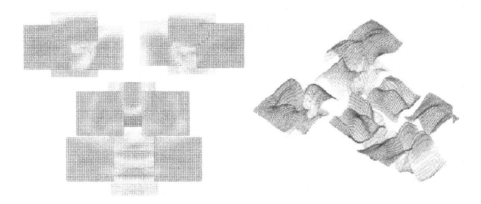

Fig. 2. A response mesh from two viewpoints. F_Z is the Z value of every point on the mesh, describing the similarity of shape instance from SFAM and local shape on the given face.

4   Results and Discussion

The data set we used is FRGC v1.0 [23], which contains 953 faces from 227 people. As illustrated in Fig. 1a, we manually labeled the 15 landmarks on all faces as ground truth for learning SFAM and testing the localization algorithm. They are available to the public for research purpose on demand. In our experiment, the whole dataset was first cleaned in filtering out several badly captured face models, further divided into the training parts (452 faces) and testing parts(462 faces), subjects in the training set being different from those in the testing set.

4.1   Results on SFAM

Fig. 3 illustrates the first two modes of face morphology in SFAM at their left and right ending variance(-3σ,3σ), namely -3std and +3std. The first mode mainly controls the variance in face size, while the second one the horizontal variations in the faces.

The texture model describes the texture in local regions on a face. Fig. 4 also illustrates the first two modes at(-3σ,3σ). We can see that the first mode mainly control the variance around ocular regions, while the second mode mainly is about the variance around nasal regions.

The shape model can generate different shapes in local regions on a face. In Fig. 5, we can see that both modes control the shape variance around ocular regions. However, the first mode contains more variance in nasal shape.

4.2   Results on Landmarking

The testing results of locating landmarks by SFAM are shown in Fig. 6. Errors are calculated as the 3D Euclidean distance between an automatic landmark and manual one. For accumulative precision, our model can localize 99.09% cases in

First mode from -3std(left) to 3std(right)

Second mode from -3std(left) to 3std(right)

Fig. 3. First two modes for the morphology model

Table 1. Mean and deviation of individual landmarks errors

	lcle	rcle	ucle	lwcle	lcre	rcre	ucre	lwcre	lsn	nt	rsn	lcm	cul	cll	rcm
Mean	4,31	3,27	3,13	3,05	3,37	3,94	3,08	2,96	4,36	4,56	4,72	4,05	3,22	4,28	4,01
Deviation	2,05	1,41	1,41	1,39	1,52	2,11	1,56	1,42	3,73	2,51	2,12	2,07	1,67	2,26	2,06

The index of points is the abbreviation of the legend in Fig. 6.

10mm precision and almost 100% in 20mm precision for all landmarks. The right corner of left eye is located with a 100% accuracy in precision 7mm. The right corner of right eye and right corner of nose fail to achieve 100% accuracy within precision 20mm, one case failed in each case.

Table 1 shows the mean and deviation of each landmark locating errors. Their mean errors are all less than 5mm, indicating the accuracy of SFAM. All deviations are less than 4, indicating the reliability of SFAM. Some locating examples is shown in Fig. 7.

The time to locate landmarks on a 3D face is expensive in two steps: the one on sampling and normalization, and the one on the optimization of morphology parameters. Roughly one thousand of iterations are performed in the optimization

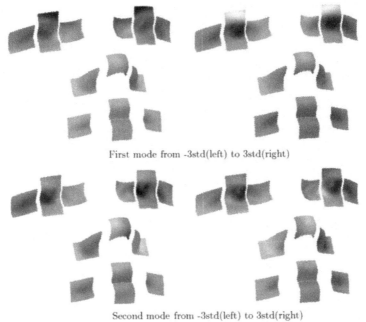

Fig. 4. First two modes for the texture model

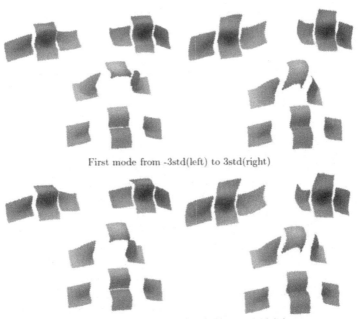

Fig. 5. First two modes for the shape model

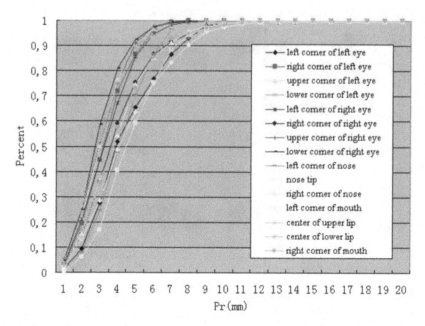

Fig. 6. Precision curves for individual landmarks(right)

procedure. In total, 15 minutes in average are required by SFAM to finish the landmark locating for each face with a P4 2Ghz processor.

4.3   Discussion

The previous experimental results has demonstrated the effectiveness of our statistical model 'SFAM' which applies a 'analysis by synthesis', driving a global face morphological analysis with a local one based on texture and shape. It allows to synthesize unseen partial face instances for further usages, e.g. facial expression recognition, etc.

Compared with others 3D landmarking algorithms[8][21][9][10][11][18][20], our SFAM-based localization has three strong points: first, we locate a bigger number of feature points; second, we enjoy a high precision with reliability; third, we can easily extend SFAM to locate more feature points, such as pupils, corners of eye brow or face edges, provided a corresponding learning data set.

Using the same data set and also a statistics methods in landmarking, [20] reported an accuracy rate of around 99% for nose tips and inner eye, around 90% for the outer eyes and mouth corners within around 19mm precision(3 pixels precision on a reduced face texture with the reduction rate 8:1 in the paper. The average 3D distance between pixels are 0.8mm in FRGCv1). Compared to this result, our localization deals with more feature points (15 instead of 7) with better accuracy. In [21], authors located 7 points, nose tips, corners of eyes and mouth also in the same dataset. The mean accuracy for these points are around 6.0mm to 10mm, while ours are around 3mm to 5mm with much smaller

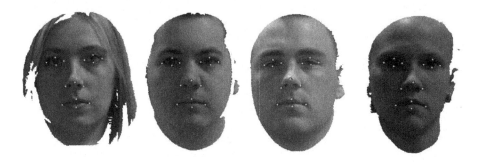

Fig. 7. Landmarking examples

standard derivation. We also have 11 people to do landmarks works on 10 faces, and calculate the mean errors and standard deviation of their manual landmarks compared with the mean landmarks. The mean of 15 landmarks errors on 10 faces is 2.49mm and the standard deviation is 1.34, while our approach achieves 3.75mm and 2.01.

5 Conclusion

We have proposed in this paper a 3D statistical facial feature model which learns global 3D face morphology from the overall geometrical structures by 3D face landmarks over learning 3D face scans, as well as texture and shape in local regions around each landmark. Once constructed, such a model allows synthesizing new 3D partial faces and can be further applied to locate landmarks on a new 3D face scan. Testing on the FRGCv1 data set, we have achieved 99.09% cases in 10mm precision and almost 100% in 20mm precision for all feature points. The results on average and standard deviation of feature points' errors further validate the accuracy and reliability of our method. In our future work, we will apply SFAM to other problems, in particular 3D facial expression recognition.

Acknowledgement

This work is partly supported by the ANR under the project Omnia under the grant ANR-07-MDCO-009 and the ANR FAR3D project under the grant ANR-07-SESU-004.

References

1. Ali Salah, A., Cinar, H., Akarun, L., Sankur, B.: Robust Facial Landmarking for Registration. Annals of Telecommunications 62(1-2), 1608–1633 (2007)
2. Bowyer, K.W., Chang, K., Flynn, P.: A Survey of Approaches and Challenges in 3D and Multi-Modal 3D+2D Face Recognition. Journal of Computer Vision and Image Understanding 101(1), 1–15 (2006)

3. Conde, C., Serrano, A.: 3D Facial Normalization with Spin Images and Influence of Range Data Calculation over Face Verification. In: IEEE Computer Society Conference on Computer Vision and Pattern Recognition, pp. 20–26 (2005)

4. Xu, C., Tan, T., Wang, Y., Quan, L.: Combining Local Features for Robust Nose Location in 3D Facial Data. Pattern Recognition Letters 27(13), 1487–1494 (2006)

5. Bevilacqua, V., Casorio, P., Mastronardi, G.: Extending Hough Transform to a Points Cloud for 3D-Face Nose-Tip Detection. In: Huang, D.-S., Wunsch II, D.C., Levine, D.S., Jo, K.-H. (eds.) ICIC 2008. LNCS (LNAI), vol. 5227, pp. 1200–1209. Springer, Heidelberg (2008)

6. Huertas, M.R., Pears, N.: 3D Facial Landmark Localisation by Matching Simple Descriptors. In: Proceedings of the International Conference on Biometrics: Theory, Applications and Systems, pp. 1–6 (2008)

7. Chang, K.I., Bowyer, K.W., Flynn, P.J.: Multiple Nose Region Matching for 3D Face Recognition under Varying Facial Expression. IEEE Transactions on Pattern Analysis and Machine Intelligence 28(10), 1695–1700 (2006)

8. D'House, J., Colineau, J., Bichon, C., Dorizzi, B.: Precise localization of landmarks on 3d faces using gabor wavelets. In: Proceedings of the International Conference on Biometrices: Theory, Applications, and Systems, pp. 1–6 (2007)

9. Faltemier, T.C., Bowyer, K.W., Flynn, P.J.: Rotated profile signatures for robust 3d feature detection. In: Proceedings of the International Conference on Face and Gesture Recognition (2008)

10. Xua, C., Tana, T., Wang, Y., Quanc, L.: Combining local features for robust nose location in 3D facial data. Pattern Recognition Letters 27(13), 1487–1494 (2006)

11. Colbry, D., Stockman, G., Anil, J.: Detection of Anchor Points for 3D Face Verification. In: Proceedings of Computer Vision and Pattern Recognition - Workshops, p. 118 (2005)

12. Cootes, T.F., Edwards, G.J., Taylor, C.J.: Active appearance models. IEEE Transaction on Pattern Analysis and Machine Intelligence 23(6), 681–685 (2001)

13. Cootes, T.F., Taylor, C.J., Cooper, D.H., Graham, J.: Active shape models - their training and application. Computer Vision and Image Understanding 61, 38–59 (1995)

14. Cristinacce, D., Cootes, T.F.: Automatic Feature Localisation with Constrained Local Models. Journal of Pattern Recognition 41(10), 3054–3067 (2008)

15. Blanz, V., Vetter, T.: A morphable model for the synthesis of 3D faces. In: Proceedings of the 26th Annual Conference on Computer Graphics and interactive Techniques, pp. 187–194 (1999)

16. Nelder, J.A., Mead, R.: A simplex method for function minimization. Computer Journal 7, 308–313 (1965)

17. Soille, P.: Morphological Image Analysis: Principles and Applications, pp. 173–174. Springer, Heidelberg (1999)

18. Jahanbin, S., Bovik, A.C., Choi, H.: Automated facial feature detection from portrait and range images. In: Proceedings of IEEE Southwest Symposium on Image Analysis and Interpretation (2008)

19. Zhang, Z.: Iterative point matching for registration of free-form curves and surfaces. International Journal of Computer Vision 13(2), 119–152 (1994)

20. Dibeklioglu, H., Salah, A.A., Akarun, L.: 3D Facial Landmarking under Expression, Pose, and Occlusion Variations. In: Proceedings of the International Conference on Biometrics: Theory, Applications and Systems, pp. 1–6 (2008)

21. Lu, X., Jain, A.K.: Automatic feature extraction for multiview 3D face recognition. In: Proceedings of the Internationl Conference on Face and Gesture Recognition, pp. 585–590 (2006)
22. Szeptycki, P., Ardabilian, M., Chen, L.: Automatic and precise 2.5D face landmarking. Technical Report, LIRIS (2009)
23. Phillips, P.J., Flynn, P.J., Scruggs, T., Bowyer, K.W., Chang, J., Hoffman, K., Marques, J., Min, J., Worek, W.: Overview of the Face Recognition Grand Challenge. In: Proceedings of the IEEE Computer Society Conference on Computer Vision and Pattern Recognition, vol. 1, pp. 947–954 (2005)

Behavioral State Detection of Newborns Based on Facial Expression Analysis

Lykele Hazelhoff[1,2], Jungong Han[1],
Sidarto Bambang-Oetomo[1,3], and Peter H.N. de With[1,2]

[1] University of Technology Eindhoven, The Netherlands
[2] CycloMedia Technology B.V., Waardenburg, The Netherlands
[3] Maxima Medisch Centrum, Veldhoven, The Netherlands

Abstract. Prematurely born infants are observed at a Neonatal Intensive Care Unit (NICU) for medical treatment. Whereas vital body functions are continuously monitored, their incubator is covered by a blanket for medical reasons. This prevents visual observation of the newborns during most time of the day, while it is known that the facial expression can give valuable information about the presence of discomfort.

This prompted the authors to develop a prototype of an automated video survey system for the detection of discomfort in newborn babies by analysis of their facial expression. Since only a reliable and situation-independent system is useful, we focus at robustness against non-ideal viewpoints and lighting conditions. Our proposed algorithm automatically segments the face from the background and localizes the eye, eyebrow and mouth regions. Based upon measurements in these regions, a hierarchical classifier is employed to discriminate between the behavioral states sleep, awake and cry.

We have evaluated the described prototype system on recordings of three healthy newborns, and we show that our algorithm operates with approximately 95% accuracy. Small changes in viewpoint and lighting conditions are allowed, but when there is a major reduction in light, or when the viewpoint is far from frontal, the algorithm fails.

1 Introduction

Prematurely born infants are observed in a Neonatal Intensive Care Unit (NICU) for medical treatment. These babies are nursed in an incubator, where their vital body functions such as heart rate, respiration, blood pressure, oxygen saturation and temperature are continuously monitored. To avoid excessive light exposure which may disturb sleep and thereby lead to discomfort, the incubator is covered by a blanket to reduce the intensity of light. The disadvantage of this practice is that visual observation of the newborn during most of the time is impaired. In this respect, pain and discomfort of the patient that cannot be observed by the monitoring of vital functions may pass unnoticed. The awareness that early treatment of pain and discomfort is important for the future development, is presently growing and this motivated us to develop a prototype for an automated video observation system that can detect pain and discomfort in newborn babies.

J. Blanc-Talon et al. (Eds.): ACIVS 2009, LNCS 5807, pp. 698–709, 2009.
© Springer-Verlag Berlin Heidelberg 2009

Discomfort on newborns can be detected by analysis of the facial expression [1]-[3]. Especially the appearances of the eyes, eyebrows an mouth are reported to be important facial features for detecting the presence of discomfort and pain. This has resulted in the development of scoring systems to assess the level of discomfort, based on the facial expression and physiological parameters. The scoring systems allow early alerting of caretakers when a patient suffers from pain or discomfort, so that appropriate actions can be taken in time.

So far, only one automatic video-surveillance system [4]-[5] for sick newborn infants has been developed. In this system, images of a large number of newborns are photographed during different situations: during a painful procedure (heel lance) and during other, non-painful, situations. Then, after manual rotation and scaling, pixel-based classifiers, such as Linear Discriminant Analysis and Support Vector Machines, are applied for classification of the facial expression. Although the results are acceptable, we consider this approach not robust enough to handle fluctuating, non-ideal situations, including varying lighting conditions and situations where the baby face is partly covered by plasters or tubing.

Because of this lack of robustness, we explore the design of a discomfort detection system, and describe a pilot system with the following properties. First, the detection of discomfort will be based on analyzing important facial regions, such as eyes, eyebrows and mouth, in an automated way. With this information, we detect the behavioral state of the newborn. Second, varying, non-ideal data-capturing situations are an integral part of the design considerations of this system in order to realize sufficient robustness. Third, for the time being, we omit practical conditions such as the visibility of plasters and tubes in the data, and use recordings of young infants under regular conditions. However, we do incorporate other practical situations, such as changes in lighting conditions and viewpoint, which typically lead to suboptimal conditions for video analysis.

The remainder of this paper is organized as follows. In Sect. 2, the requirements and algorithm overview are given, Sect. 3 explains the algorithmic steps, in Sect. 4 the experiments and results are described, followed by the conclusions in Sect. 5.

2   Requirements and Algorithm Overview

Let us first discuss some system requirements, which have an impact on the algorithm design. Experts indicate that an automatic system is desired. The system should be robust against varying capturing conditions and the camera should be of limited size, preferably placed outside the incubator. Furthermore, we want the system to be extensible for the type of computing tasks to be carried out. The computational part of the system should be designed with reasonable efficiency, both in size and computation, as it is placed in the vicinity of the incubator.

We have translated the above system aspects into an efficient processing architecture, from which the system overview is displayed in Fig. 1. An image containing the face region in front of a background is the input and the recognized state

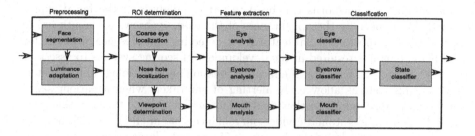

Fig. 1. System overview of the discomfort detection system

represents the output of the system. The four primary modules of the system are briefly described here and further detailed in the next section.

1. *Preprocessing*: From the input image, the face region is extracted using skin-color information. Afterwards, a lighting-compensation step is applied.
2. *Region-of-interest determination*: Within the face region, the eye and nose-hole positions are estimated. Based on the obtained locations, the Region Of Interest (ROI) is extracted automatically around all important facial components. Besides this, also the viewpoint is determined.
3. *Feature extraction*: Within the determined ROI, features are extracted from each important facial component.
4. *Classification*: A hierarchical classifier is employed to detect the behavioral state, based on the extracted features.

3   Algorithm Description

3.1   Preprocessing

From the input image, the face region is segmented from the background using skin-color information. To this end, a Gaussian skin-color model is applied in a loose way and the largest skin-colored blob is selected as face region. False face pixels are avoided by constraining the background during the recordings.

The lighting conditions are mainly non-uniform, especially in the hospital environment. To allow optimal detection results, all skin pixels should have about the same luminance value. Therefore, a lighting-compensation step is applied, aiming at removal of luminance differences within the extracted face region.

Fig. 2 illustrates both applied preprocessing steps.

3.2   Region of Interest (ROI) Determination

The ROI around the target facial components eyes, eyebrows and mouth can be defined in case the face orientation is known. This orientation is fixed in case the eyes and nostrils are localized, a process that is described in this subsection.

In literature, eyes are found using different methods. It is reported that the eyes have relatively low luminance and red intensity values [6]-[7], are elongated

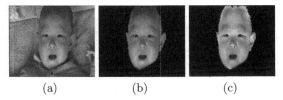

(a)   (b)   (c)

Fig. 2. Illustration of the consecutive preprocessing steps. (a): input image; (b): face segmentation; (c): result after luminance adaptation.

and are located in edge-filled areas [8]. Due to the large variability in the luminance channel Y around the eyes, the absolute gradient sum will also be large. This gradient sum G, operating in a region S around a pixel (x, y), is defined as:

$$G(x, y) = \sum_{x', y' \in S} |Y(x, y) - Y(x', y')|. \tag{1}$$

Combination of all above-mentioned clues with the assumption that the face is approximately upright, results in multiple eye candidates. The candidates are matched pair-wise to obtain the coarse position of both eyes. Afterwards, a coordinate system is defined, with the y-axis intersecting both eye centers. The described steps are portrayed by Fig. 3 (a)-(c).

The nostrils are identified in a predefined search region along the x-axis. The large luminance differences around the nostrils result in large absolute gradient sum values. By applying an adaptive thresholding technique, the nose line, defined as the line just below the nostrils and parallel to the y-axis, is found. The ROI around the eyes, eyebrows and mouth can be identified based on both the coarse eye positions and the nose line. This is shown in Fig. 3 (d)-(e).

In order to gain robustness against viewpoint deviations, information about the horizontal viewpoint is extracted. This is important for cases where the viewpoint is not frontal, but slightly panned, resulting in an asymmetrical view where one face half is better visible than the other. Therefore, we extract the widths w_l, w_r of the left and right eyebrow area, respectively, as viewpoint indicator and transform these widths to weights η_l, η_r for both face halves, defined as:

$$\eta_l = \begin{cases} 0 & \frac{w_l}{w_l + w_r} < 0.3, \\ 1 & \frac{w_l}{w_l + w_r} > 0.7, \\ 2.5 \cdot \left(\frac{w_l}{w_l + w_r} - 0.3 \right) & \text{else,} \end{cases} \tag{2}$$
$$\eta_r = 1 - \eta_l.$$

These weights can be used during the classification phase. It is experimentally found that in case one face side has a width ratio of about 30%, classification on that side becomes unreliable.

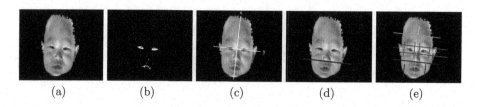

(a)   (b)   (c)   (d)   (e)

Fig. 3. Steps for ROI determination. (a): input image; (b): eye candidates; (c): coordinate system defined on obtained eye positions. (d): nose line; (e): determined ROIs.

3.3 Feature Extraction

The feature-extraction process is performed on the extracted ROIs, and is designed for robustness against viewpoint, lighting conditions and occlusions.

Eye Region. Within the eye region, a gradient-like operator is applied and the eye mask is obtained using an adaptive thresholding technique. This technique aims at selecting pixels with a 'large' gradient, where 'large' is defined based on the mean and maximum gradient at the same image row. Small noise regions are removed and a filling operation is performed to obtain the final eye mask. From this mask, the eye mask heights at $\frac{1}{3}$ and $\frac{2}{3}$ of the computed mask width are extracted as indication for the eye aperture size. Because the mask can be too wide under certain lighting conditions, the found height is decreased until the luminance value differs at least 20% from the vertical line-average. Fig. 4 illustrates the eye-region analysis process.

Eyebrow Region. In literature, the eyebrows are usually identified by their low luminance value [13]. However, we have found that the contrast between brow and skin is rather small for newborns, making the luminance value a poor discriminator under various lighting conditions. Therefore, we obtain the eyebrow mask in a different way. First, we apply the following empirically determined gradient operator:

$$X\left(x,y\right) = \left(R\left(x,y\right) - R\left(x+\delta,y\right)\right) - 0.5\cdot\left(G\left(x,y\right) - G\left(x-\delta,y\right)\right)$$
$$-0.5\cdot\left(G\left(x,y\right) - G\left(x-\delta,y\right)\right). \tag{3}$$

In this equation, x and y correspond with the coordinate system defined above; parameter δ is used with a value of 10. Afterwards, the same adaptive thresholding technique as used within the eye region is applied. On the acquired eyebrow mask, a three-point 'gravity' model is fitted, similar to [12]. The model points a, b and c (see Fig. 5 (c)) are extracted from the mask as the vertical center points at $\frac{1}{6}$, $\frac{1}{2}$ and $\frac{5}{6}$ of the mask width, where a is defined as the point closest to the nose. From these points, the cosine rule is applied to extract the angles between the vertices and the y-axis and between both vertices. As additional feature, a linear line piece is fitted through the eyebrow mask to estimate the dominant orientation of the eyebrow. Fig. 5 visualizes this process (without the latter line model).

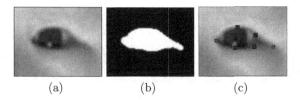

Fig. 4. Illustration of the eye investigation process. (a): input ROI; (b): eye mask; (c): extracted horizontal eye borders (red) and eye heights at $\frac{1}{3}$, $\frac{2}{3}$ of the eye width (blue).

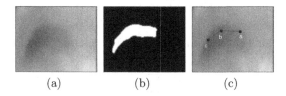

Fig. 5. Illustration of the eyebrow investigation procedure. (a): input ROI; (b): eyebrow mask; (c): fitted model, with a, b and c the model parameters.

Mouth Region. Lip-color information is often applied for mouth analysis and lip contour extraction [14]-[15]. However, for newborns, the lip color is not very clear, especially not for the upper lip. Therefore, we employ a gradient-based method for lip detection. First, to distinguish between lip and surrounding skin, a suitable color transformation is adopted from [14], which equals:

$$O = R + B - 6 \cdot G. \tag{4}$$

The same gradient-like operator is applied to signal O as within the eye region. A fixed threshold is used to remove small noise regions; the value of this threshold is not critical. Also regions with low edge densities are discarded. In the resulting mask, the blob corresponding to the upper lip has a negative value, while the blob corresponding with the lower lip is positive valued. The vertical projection histogram is employed to determine both vertical lip borders and the position of the line between both lips. The lip corners can be found on this line by combining luminance intensity, absolute gradient sum and parameter O. After this, a quadratic model is fitted on the lip blobs, using the determined lip corners and middle line. With A being the model height and w the relative distance between both lip corners, the model satisfies the relation:

$$M(w) = A \cdot \min(0.9, -4(w - 0.5)^2 + 1), \tag{5}$$

for $0 \leq w \leq 1$. The top and bottom borders of the lip mask are found by fitting model M (indicated as a white dotted contour in Fig. 6 (e)). The best fitting parameters A for both lips are extracted as features. Since the lip thickness can vary, these features cannot discriminate between a slightly open and a closed mouth. Therefore, we detect the mouth cavity, i.e. an area with both a low

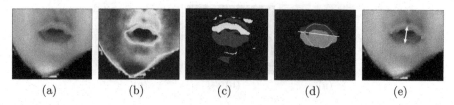

| (a) | (b) | (c) | (d) | (e) |

Fig. 6. Visualization of the mouth analysis process. (a): input ROI; (b): signal O; (c): filtered gradient map, negative values are shown in yellow, positive values in red; (d): segmented lips, lip corners (green) and fitted model (yellow); (e): extracted mouth height (white) and mouth corner points (green).

luminance and a high saturation value [16]. We calculate the following function in the mouth area Q:

$$\epsilon(x) = \sum_{\substack{y \\ x,y \in Q}} \frac{S(x,y)}{Y(x,y)}, \tag{6}$$

where S, Y correspond to the saturation and luminance signals, respectively. Within the mouth area, the average of ϵ is computed at each line. The maximum average value is extracted as the third feature. The mouth-region analysis-process is displayed in Fig. 6.

Summarizing, from the determined ROIs, the following features are extracted. Within the eye regions, the eye height is extracted at two locations. From the eyebrow area, three angles are extracted from a fitted model, together with the linear regression coefficient. From the mouth region, the distance between lip and inter-lip line is estimated for both lips, together with a measure for the presence of the mouth cavity.

3.4 Behavioral State Classification

Determining the facial expression based on the above-mentioned features is similar to feature-based emotion classification, which is a major topic in literature. Different classification techniques are common, including k-Nearest Neighbors (kNN) [9], Support Vector Machines [10] and Neural Networks [11]-[12]. In the target environment, not all facial components are always visible and not all features can be extracted reliably at all time instants. Moreover, we have also extracted information about the visibility of both face sides. This makes classification based on the aforementioned techniques difficult and impractical. Therefore, instead of using one overall classifier, we propose a *hierarchical* classification method, as depicted in Fig. 7. This method is able to handle the visibility information and is extensible to both the use of additional facial features and the inclusion of other reliability information.

For the individual components, we have defined a discrete number of states: the eyes can be closed, open or wide open, the eyebrows can be normal or lowered, and the mouth can be closed, open or wide open. At the lowest classification level (*component level*), a kNN classifier is used to detect the component states, where

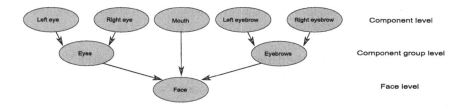

Fig. 7. Schematic overview of the hierarchical classifier

the k neighbors form evidence for a certain state. Each classifier is trained with 25 examples per state, all inferred from one newborn. Whereas a number of features consist of a measured distance on the face, these features are divided by the distance between both eye centers to obtain scale invariance.

At the medium classification level (*component group level*), the states of symmetric components (e.g. both eyes) are combined. In this step, the state for which most evidence is present is chosen. The extracted visibility fractions η_l, η_r are used to weight the evidence from the left and right components. This method assumes that both symmetric components have the same behavior; an assumption that is confirmed by medical personnel, which have experienced that for newborns the facial expression is always symmetric.

At the final classification level (*face level*), a rule-based classifier is applied to combine the component group states and detect the facial expression. Our prototype discriminates between the facial expressions corresponding to the behavioral states discomfort, awake and sleep. Note that this approach of using individual components which together contribute to a classification, is essentially the same as the pain-scale approaches reported in medical literature [2]-[3].

4   Experiments and Results

The above-described algorithm is tested on recordings of three different, healthy newborns. The age of the newborns varied from a few weeks up to a few months. A standard digital camera with at a resolution of 720×576 pixels is used, where the optical zoom is applied to focus on the infants' face. Since discomfort as defined in medical literature [1]-[3] is not common for healthy newborns, we aim at detection of a specific type of cry, with a facial expression close to the expression of medical discomfort. The target expression consists of closed or just opened eyes, a wide open mouth and lowered eyebrows.

The total of 40 sequences is grouped into two different classes. Class I contains normal situations, with a near low-frontal viewpoint and reasonable lighting conditions (21 sequences). Class II consists of sequences with non-frontal viewpoints and poor lighting conditions (19 sequences). Since two newborns already were aged a few months, they were able to make large movements. Due to the caused motion and compression artifacts, not all frames are suitable for analysis. Furthermore, if adjoining frames are too similar, a representative example selection is made. Thus, from each shot of each sequence, a number of significantly differing key frames are evaluated.

4.1   Class I: Normal Lighting Conditions With a Frontal Viewpoint

The presented system is first evaluated for images with a near-low frontal viewpoint, where the nostrils are clearly visible, and with acceptable lighting conditions. We address the results of the feature extraction process, component-level classifiers and complete system independently.

The feature points are extracted reliably in most cases, although small shadows and reflections can cause the features to be detected a few pixels from the optimal location. In case the eyes are stiffly closed, the coarse eye localization process can fail, causing the algorithm to abort. Also, for one of the newborns, the eyebrows were too light, and a shadow is detected as brow. Doctors indicate that this is typical for some newborns. However, in case of discomfort the eyebrows bulge, causing dark horizontal shadow lines. This enables detection of discomfort even when the brows themselves are not visible. Furthermore, for the somewhat older newborn, hair and eyelashes interfere with the eyebrows and eyes. This caused a slightly higher eye-height for closed eyes, thereby leading to misclassifications.

The results of the component-level classifiers are shown in Table 1. For the eyebrows only the results for clearly visible brows are listed; undetected brows are marked as *undefined*. As a result of using a discrete number of states, borderline cases can cause classification errors, since the feature values corresponding to a borderline case vary a little per newborn. Whereas this difference especially occurs for the *wide open* states, we expect that this deviation can be corrected by using a newborn-dependent normalization-coefficient. At component group level, most of these errors are corrected for the eyes and eyebrows.

The classification results of the complete system are shown in Table 2. The classification result can be seen as promising: in each of the experiments, only a few situations (around 5%) are classified into a different state. Since the system operates on frame basis, misclassifications can be caused by transients such as

Table 1. Performance matrix of the component level classifier

Eyes	Found State:	Wide open	Open	Closed	Total
	Wide open	89	7	0	96
	Open	4	75	1	80
	Closed	0	12	54	66
Eyebrows	Found State:	Normal	Lowered	Undefined	Total
	Normal	86	4	16	106
	Lowered	1	27	0	28
Mouth	Found State:	Wide open	Open	Closed	Total
	Wide open	28	4	0	32
	Open	0	35	5	40
	Closed	0	5	44	49

Table 2. Performance matrix of the complete classification system

Found State:	Sleep	Awake	Discomfort	Total
Sleep	49	1	0	50
Awake	3	47	0	50
Discomfort	0	2	28	30

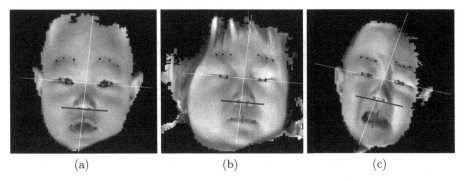

(a)   (b)   (c)

Fig. 8. Examples of extracted features for each of the three newborns. The white lines indicate the determined coordinate system; the horizontal line at the nose bottom corresponds to the obtained nose line. In (a) and (b), the newborns are shown during normal awake and sleep behavior, respectively. In (c), a discomfort situation is shown.

eye blinks. This can be solved by determining the state based on a window of e.g. 2 seconds, but since the newborns moved a lot especially during cry, this would reduce the amount of test data. With respect to cry, only one newborn showed the target type of cry during the recordings, but this situation occurred at various times in multiple sequences. The other newborns only showed normal behavior. Examples of investigated situations in Class I are displayed in Fig. 8.

4.2 Class II: Robustness to Lighting and Viewpoint Deviations

This class of test data has been explored to define difficult situations, classification problems etc., with the aim to outline future research directions. The tests focus on two major issues: lighting condition and viewpoint changes. Since this class only contains a few different samples per specific non-ideal situation, the test set contents would highly influence the results; therefore, no numerical results are given.

Various lighting conditions can be handled, and in many cases feature extraction for the eyes and mouth succeeds with small deviations from the expected values. However, it was found that feature extraction in the eyebrow area is sensitive to shadows and that reflections on the skin can cause improper skin-color segmentation and feature-extraction errors, e.g. when a part of the eyebrow is subject to the reflection. Fig. 9 shows investigated lighting conditions.

Viewpoint changes over the horizontal direction can be handled, unless there is no skin visible next to both eyes, disabling estimation of the eye positions.

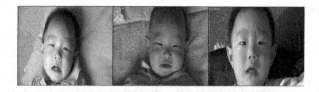

Fig. 9. Screenshots from evaluated sequences with different lighting conditions. For all three examples, the feature points can be extracted and classification can be performed.

Fig. 10. Screenshots from investigated sequences with different viewpoints. For all three examples, the feature points on the most important face side can be extracted.

Viewpoint deviations over the vertical direction are harder to handle: when viewing more from above, nostril detection is difficult, resulting in inaccurate ROIs. For large vertical deviations, the mouth cavity cannot always be found, since then either the palate or tongue is visible instead of the cavity. Note that the performance sensitivity in classification to vertical changes in viewpoint is partly explained by the measurement of a number of vertical distances on the face. Fig. 10 displays examples of investigated viewpoints.

5   Conclusions and Future Work

This paper has described a prototype system for automatic detection of the facial expression of newborns to estimate their behavioral state. In contrast with earlier work, we have developed a component-based approach with increased robustness against non-ideal viewpoints and lighting conditions. The system extracts features from the eye, eyebrow and mouth regions; a hierarchical classifier is employed to distinguish between the states sleep, awake and discomfort.

Tests on three healthy newborns show that our prototype system can be used for determination of the states of the above-mentioned facial components with an acceptable accuracy (approximately 88,2%). The obtained states are successfully combined to detect present discomfort, where normal situations, including light cries, are rejected. The system is able to determine the behavioral state with about 95% accuracy. When non-ideal viewpoints and poor lighting conditions are present, the system can still detect the facial states in many cases. Therefore, the algorithm is relatively robust against varying situations. An exploration with more extreme conditions has shown that vertical viewpoint changes and poor lighting conditions such as reflections can decrease the score and reliability of the system. However, since only one newborn showed all possible behavioral states and the total number of investigated newborns is small, we note that the reliability of the experiment is too limited for a real performance evaluation.

Application in a realistic hospital environment is not directly possible, since the system should then also be able to deal with skin-colored plasters, tubings in the nose and large horizontal viewpoint changes. These items are the main research topics for future work, together with newborn-independent classification and an extensive validation of our proposed approach.

References

1. Grunau, R.V.E., Craig, K.D.: Pain expression in neonates: facial action and cry. Pain 28(3), 395–410 (1987)
2. Stevens, B., Johnston, C., Pethryshen, P., Taddio, A.: Premature Infant Pain Profile: Development and Initial Validation. Clin. J. Pain 12(1), 13–22 (1996)
3. Chen, K., Chang, S., Hsiao, T., Chen, Y., Lin, C.: A neonatal facial image scoring system (NFISS) for pain response studies. BME ABC, 79–85 (2005)
4. Brahnam, S., Chuang, C., Shih, F.Y., Slack, M.R.: Machine recognition and representation of neonatal facial displays of acute pain. Artificial Intelligence in Medicine 36(3), 211–222 (2006)
5. Brahnam, S., Chuang, C., Sexton, R.S., Shih, F.Y.: Machine assessment of neonatal facial expressions of acute pain. Special Issue on Decision Support in Medicine in Decision Support Systems 43, 1247–1254 (2007)
6. Peng, K., Chen, L.: A Robust Algorithm for Eye Detection on Gray Intensity Face without Spectacles. Journal of Computer Science and Technology, 127–132 (2005)
7. Vezhnevets, V., Degtiareva, A.: Robust and Accurate Eye Contour Extraction. In: Proc. Graphicon, pp. 81–84 (2003)
8. Asteriadis, S., Nikolaidis, N., Hajdu, A., Pitas, I.: A novel eye-detection algorithm utilizing edge-related geometrical information. In: EUSIPCO 2006 (2006)
9. Sohail, A.S.M., Bhattacharya, P.: Classification of facial expressions using k-nearest neighbor classifier. In: Gagalowicz, A., Philips, W. (eds.) MIRAGE 2007. LNCS, vol. 4418, pp. 555–566. Springer, Heidelberg (2007)
10. Michel, P., Kaliouby, R.: Real time facial expression recognition in video using support vector machines. In: ICMI (2003)
11. Ioannou, S.V., Raouzaiou, A.T., Tzouvaras, V.A., Mailis, T.P., Karpouzis, K.C., Kollias, S.D.: Emotion recognition through facial expression analysis based on a neurofuzzy network. Neural Networks 18, 423–435 (2005)
12. Tian, Y., Kanade, T., Cohn, J.F.: Recognizing action units for facial expression analysis. IEEE Transactions on Pattern Analysis and Machine Intelligence 23(2), 97–115 (2001)
13. Chen, Q., Cham, W., Lee, K.: Extracting eyebrow contour and chin contour for face recognition. Pattern Recognition 40(8), 2292–2300 (2007)
14. Gomez, E., Travieso, C.M., Briceno, J.C., Ferrer, M.A.: Biometric identification system by lip shape, Security Technology (2002)
15. Leung, S., Wang, S., Lau, W.: Lip image segmentation using fuzzy clustering incorporating an elliptic shape function. IEEE Transactions on Image Processing 13(1), 51–61 (2004)
16. Gocke, R., Millar, J.B., Zelensky, A., Robert-Ribes, J.: Automatic extraction of lip feature points. In: Proc. of ACRA 2000, pp. 31–36 (2000)

Supervised Face Recognition for Railway Stations Surveillance

Maria Asuncion Vicente, Cesar Fernandez, and Angela M. Coves

Miguel Hernandez University,
Avenida de la Universidad s/n, 03203 Elche, Spain
{suni,c.fernandez,angela.coves}@umh.es
http://www.umh.es

Abstract. The feasibility of a supervised surveillance system for railway stations (or airports) is evaluated. Surveillance is based on suspicious recognition by means of video cameras. As the problem involves both face detection and face recognition, we have evaluated the best performing algorithms of these two areas. For face detection, we have selected the Viola-Jones algorithm; while for face recognition we have performed tests with an appearance based algorithm (PCA) and an interest-point based algorithm (SIFT). We have used both the AT&T database and the LFW database for our tests. The results obtained show that face detection works reliably and fast enough, but face recognition cannot cope with highly non-homogeneous images like those of LFW and requires parallel computing in order to work in real time. As a conclusion, supervised surveillance is feasible provided image homogeneity fulfils some minimum standards and parallel computing is used. Besides, interest-point based methods are more robust to image quality, so their use is encouraged.

Keywords: face detection, face recognition, surveillance.

1 Introduction

Surveillance has become necessary in airports as well as in railway stations and many other crowded places. Apart from the common luggage security checking, where the goal is to detect possible weapons, we propose to use face recognition techniques, the goal being to detect known suspicious persons.

Automated face recognition based on computer vision has been an area of research for the last twenty years, from Turk and Penland's initial developments [4]. Present face detection and face recognition algorithms have reached maturity, there are commercial systems available [8][10][13], and their performances are even comparable to those of humans [1]. The goal of the present paper is to check whether such performances are enough for a supervised surveillance scenario, where the computer vision systems issues alarms whenever a suspicious person is found. Such alarms would be supervised by a human, who should decide whether they are false alarms or not. Figure 1 shows the structure proposed for the system.

J. Blanc-Talon et al. (Eds.): ACIVS 2009, LNCS 5807, pp. 710–719, 2009.

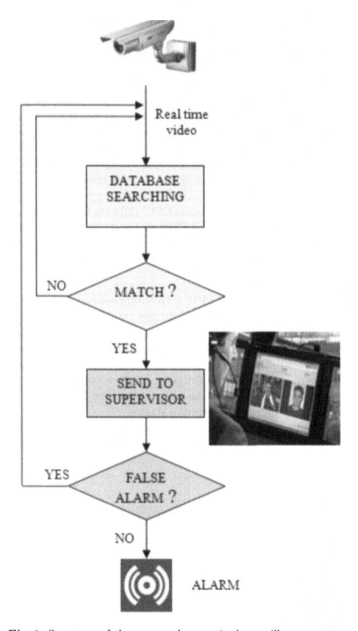

Fig. 1. Structure of the proposed supervised surveillance system

The viability of the system will be checked both in terms of processing speed and false recognition rates. The main ideas are: 1) to process images fast enough as to cope with the flow of persons in a railway station; 2) to keep false acceptances (undetected suspicious) at a very low level and 3) to keep false rejections (false alarms) at a low enough level so that a human supervisor can handle them.

2   Databases Selected for the Evaluation

We have performed a search among all the face databases available (an exhaustive list can be found in [11]) in order to select those more appropriate for testing our application.

Most databases have been obtained in controlled conditions (the subjects keep always the same distance from the camera, the backgrounds are uniform, the illumination is controlled, etc). Some examples are [9], [12] or [15]. Such databases are not appropriate, since their scenarios are very different to the ones that can be found in a railway station. However, we have use the well-known AT&T database ([9]) as a baseline for our comparisons of recognition rates.

Among the non-controlled databases, LFW (labeled faces in the wild, [14]) is more appropriate for our needs. In LFW, all images have been obtained from the World Wide Web, under almost unlimited different lightings, backgrounds, etc. We have used such database for our tests, although we have found several limitations:

- The proposed test scheme for LFW is to obtain comparison results for images corresponding to subjects not used during training (i.e. the goal is to infer whether two images correspond to the same person or not, when no images of any of these two persons have been used during training). Such evaluation strategy is not valid for our application, where the goal is to check whether an image corresponds to a certain person, whose training images have been made available to the system. As a conclusion, we have used LFW but we have developed a different evaluation strategy.
- The number of images per subject is not homogeneous. Such a number ranges from 530 to just one image (figure 2 shows the distribution of the database,

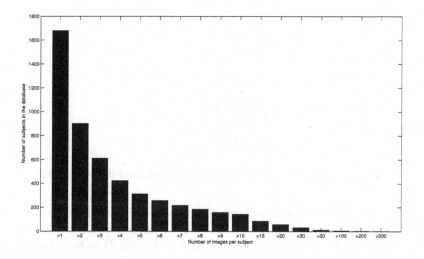

Fig. 2. Distribution of LFW database

excluding those 4069 subjects with only one image). We have used for our tests only subjects with ten or more images (158 out of 5749 subjects), and we have only used the first ten images for each subject in order not to bias the classifiers (that would be the case if most of the test images corresponded to only one person).

- Only face recognition can be tested (and not face detection) as all images have been preprocessed with a face detection algorithm (Viola-Jones, [7]). We have used different image datasets for face detection tests.

3   Face Detection and Face Recognition Algorithms Tested

Among the face detection algorithms, the most widely used is the Viola-Jones detector [7]. We have selected such algorithm for our tests.

Concerning face recognition, there are mainly two options: either to use a global description of the faces or a local description, based on interest points. We have selected one algorithm for each of these two options:

- Global description: we have selected PCA (principal component analysis, [4]), as it is the simplest method, with comparable results to other more complex methods (we have shown the equivalence of ICA and PCA in one of our previous papers [5]]).
- Local description: we have used SIFT (scale invariant feature transform) descriptors [3], and DOG (difference of Gaussians) detector. We follow our own strategy for measuring similarity between faces with such descriptors (a detailed description can be found in our previous paper [6])

4   Results Obtained

4.1   Face Detection

In order to measure the processing time required by the face detection algorithm, we performed experiments with images of different sizes and with different number of faces in them. Our intention was to obtain relationships between image size and processing time and between number of faces present and processing time. Five different images (shown in figure 3), each one at five different resolutions, were used for the experiment. The experiments were performed on a standard PC (Intel Quad Core 2.0 GHZ processor, 2 GB RAM) running Windows, and the results were averaged over 3 repetitions of the experiment. The results obtained are shown in figure 4 (average values plus maximum and minimum time for each experiment).

On one side, it becomes clear that, for a fixed image size, processing time depends on the particular image being processed, but the number of faces present in the image is not the key factor. Comparing the first two images of figure 3, both with only one face, processing time seems to be dependent on the complexity of the background.

Fig. 3. Images used for processing time experiments

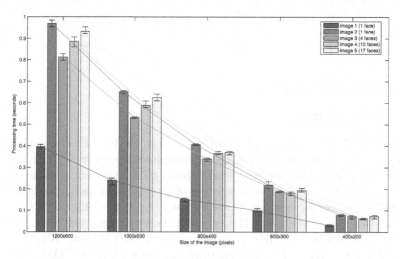

Fig. 4. Processing time required by the Viola-Jones face detector

On the other side, as expected, processing time is highly affected by image size. There is a quadratic relationship that recommends using small sized images for our system.

However, image size cannot be reduced over a certain limit, due to the decrease in the detection rate of the algorithm. A further test was performed in order to

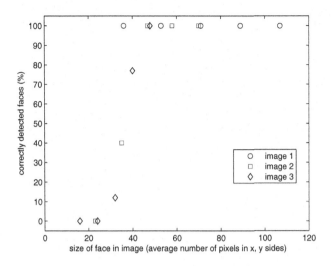

Fig. 5. Detection accuracy vs. face size (in pixels)

fix the limit in image size. In this test, we used the same images of the previous experiment, and we measured the detection errors at different resolutions. Figure 6 shows the results obtained: in the top image (1200x600), faces have an average width and height of 49 pixels; in the middle figure (1000x500) such average is 41 pixels; and in the bottom image such average is 33 pixels (we measure the side of the square output by the Viola-Jones algorithm). As a conclusion, in order to reliably detect faces, they should be described by at least 40x40 pixels. However, a few missing faces do not represent a problem for our application, since every person approaching the railway platforms will appear in more than one image (even if images are captured at a relatively slow rate).

Let us assume that the face size is fixed to approximately 40x40 pixels. Considering that the camera may not be perfectly centered in the person of interest, a much wider area must be covered by the camera. Thus, the image size should be at least ten times in width and five times in width the face size; that is 400x200. The average time required to process a 200x400 image, as shown in figure 4, is 63 ms.

4.2   Face Recognition

For face recognition tests, we have used both the AT&T and the LFW database. In particular, we have used a subset of LWF where there are ten images per subject, as we mentioned in section 2 (there are 158 subjects in such subset). Thus, both databases (AT&T and LFW) share a common structure: ten images per subject.

These ten images per subject are split in two separate sets: a training set composed of the first four images and a test set composed of images five to ten.

Fig. 6. Example of detection rate reduction for small face sizes

Such scenario may be similar to the one found in a real application, where every suspicious person may be represented in the system database by four images.

We have tested both the processing speed and the reliability of both the PCA-based method and the SIFT-based method.

Processing speed is highly related to the size of the database: every image taken by the system in real time has to be compared to images of all suspicious present in the database. For our tests, LFW database includes 158 subjects and AT&T database includes 40 subjects. We have performed experiments with both databases in order to evaluate how database size influences processing time.

The results in terms of processing speed are shown in table 1. It must be taken into account that the detection time (an average of 63 ms, as detailed in the previous section) must be added to the recognition time shown in the table.

Table 1. Face recognition processing time

Database	Number of subjects	Training images per subject	Total comparisons	Average PCA processing time (seconds)	Average SIFT processing time (seconds)
AT&T	40	4	160	0.19	0.84
LFW	158	4	632	0.73	3.2

As expected, processing time increases linearly with database size for both methods (PCA and SIFT). The PCA-based algorithm could be used without problems at a rate of 1Hz, even with large databases. On the other hand, the SIFT-based algorithm would only be applicable with large databases by parallelizing the comparisons. Such parallel computing is straightforward: every image captured by the camera may be sent to a set of processors or computers, each one in charge of comparing the image to up to 40-50 suspicious (4 processors will be required for a database similar in size to the LFW database used in our tests).

Reliability has been tested in terms of ROC (receiver operating curve). From the total of 10 images per subject, 4 of them were used as training data and the remaining 6 images were used for testing. For every test image, distance to all training images (160 for the AT&T database and 632 for the LFW database) were measured, and the minimum distance was kept as the best match.

Such strategy represents a nearest neighbor approach for face recognition. A different strategy was also tested: we averaged the distance to all training images of every subject and kept the minimum average as the best match. Recognition rates were lower for both databases and both methods (PCA and SIFT), so we discarded this strategy.

Figure 7 shows the results obtained with both databases and both methods. The first conclusion that can be drawn is that LFW is a much more demanding database for face recognition. The relatively poor results obtained with LFW imply that, in order to reliably apply the surveillance method presented in this paper, image quality (in terms of resolution, lighting and subject pose) must fulfill a minimum standard. In this sense, an ideal placement for cameras may be in walkthrough metal detectors.

As a second conclusion, the SIFT-based method has proved to be more robust to low quality images (particularly concerning homogeneity in terms of lighting, pose and background). Since PCA and SIFT results are similar for the ORL database, SIFT clearly outperforms PCA for the LFW database. We have focused on the SIFT results for evaluating the performances that could be obtained in a real application.

In a supervised surveillance application, every alarm (every possible suspicious detected by the system) must be checked by a human (the person in front of the computer screen). If the security level is high, most alarms will actually be false alarms. System feasibility can be evaluated in terms of the frequency of false alarms at a certain security level.

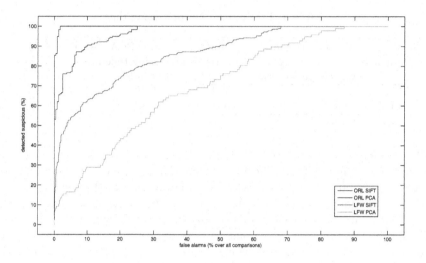

Fig. 7. ROC curves for SIFT method (AT&T and LFW databases)

If we assume that the maximum frequency for false alarms that a human supervisor can handle is around 1 false alarm per minute (handling a false alarm is as easy as comparing the real time image with the stored images for the suspicious), and supposing that the system works in real time at 1Hz (with parallel computing, if needed), it can be concluded that false alarm rate should be as low as 1/60 or 1.67%. Having a look at figure 7, such false alarm rate represents a 100% recognition rate for suspicious for the AT&T database, but only a 41% recognition rate for the LFW database (a 59% of suspicious will be undetected). These results imply that image quality should be higher than that of the LFW database for a reliable application of this surveillance system.

However, a recognition rate of 100% is not completely necessary in this application. If images are captured at a rate of 1Hz, every suspicious will appear in more than one image, thus being more probable their correct recognition (even with the poor results obtained in the LFW database, the probability of being undetected in four images would be 0.59^4, which gives 12.1% undetected suspicious).

5   Conclusions

The main conclusion is that supervised surveillance for railway stations (or airports) is feasible at the present state of the technology in face detection and recognition. However, some points must be taken into account: first, parallel computing may be required for large databases (above 50 suspicious); second, the placement of the cameras has to be carefully planned, the walkthrough detectors being the ideal placement.

Concerning face detection, Viola-Jones method is reliable enough even for low quality images, provided every face is represented by at least 40x40 pixels. Besides, the algorithm is fast enough for a real time application.

Concerning face recognition, interest-point or local based methods (like SIFT) seem to outperform global or appearance based methods (like PCA), particularly when the homogeneity of the images is not assured. Future work will be focused in other face recognition algorithms, like those based on AAM (active appearance models, [2]).

Acknowledgments. This project has been supported by the *Ministerio de Fomento*, project $S129/08$.

References

1. Phillips, P.J., Scruggs, W.T., O'Toole, A.J., Flynn, P.J., Bowyer, K.W., Schott, C.L., Sharpe, M.: FRVT 2006 and ICE 2006 Large-Scale Results, www.frvt.org
2. Cootes, T.F., Edwards, G.J., Taylor, C.J.: Active Appearance Models. IEEE Transactions on Pattern Analysis and Machine Intelligence 23(6), 681–685 (2001)
3. Lowe, D.G.: Distinctive Image Features from Scale-Invariant Keypoints. International Journal of Computer Vision 60(2), 91–110 (2004)
4. Turk, M., Pentland, A.: Eigenfaces for Recognition. J. Cognitive Neuroscience 3(1), 71–86 (1991)
5. Vicente, M.A., Hoyer, P.O., Hyvarinen, A.: Equivalence of Some Common Linear Feature Extraction Techniques for Appearance-Based Object Recognition Tasks. IEEE Transactions on Pattern Analysis and Machine Intelligence 29(5), 896–900 (2007)
6. Fernández, C., Vicente, M.A.: Face recognition using multiple interest point detectors and SIFT descriptors. In: 8th IEEE International Conference on Automatic Face and Gesture Recognition (2008)
7. Viola, P., Jones, M.: Robust real-time object detection. International Journal of Computer Vision (2002)
8. Animetrics, http://www.animetrics.com/Products/AnimetricsFIMS.php
9. AT&T, The Database of Faces (formerly "The ORL Database of Faces"), http://www.cl.cam.ac.uk/research/dtg/attarchive/facedatabase.html
10. Betaface, http://www.betaface.com
11. Face Recognition Homepage, http://www.face-rec.org
12. FRAV2D, http://www.frav.es/databases/FRAV2d/
13. L-1 Identity Solutions, http://www.l1id.com/
14. Label Faces in the Wild, http://vis-www.cs.umass.edu/lfw/
15. Yale Face Database, http://cvc.yale.edu/projects/yalefaces/yalefaces.html

Person's Recognition Using Palmprint Based on 2D Gabor Filter Response

Abdallah Meraoumia, Salim Chitroub, and Mohamed Saigaa

Signal and Image Processing Laboratory,
Electronics and Computer Science Faculty, USTHB,
P.O. Box 32, El Alia, Bab Ezzouar, 16111, Algiers, Algeria
Ameraoumia@Gmail.com, S_Chitroub@Hotmail.com, Saigaa12@Yahoo.fr

Abstract. Palmprint recognition is very important in automatic personal identification. The objective of this study is to develop an efficient prototype system for an automatic personal identification using palmprint technology. In this work, a new texture feature based on Gabor filter is proposed. First, the region of interest was filtering by 2D Gabor filter, then, the principal lines, wrinkles, and ridges, are extracted using a simple thresholding of the complex magnitude of the filtred ROI, Latterly, the candidate was found by matching process. We have tested our algorithm scheme over several images taken from a palmprint database collected by hong kong polytechnic university. The testing results showed that the designed system achieves an acceptable level of performance.

Keywords: Biometrics, Identification, verification, Palm authentication, Palmprint, Gabor filters.

1 Introduction

A biometric system is a pattern recognition system that recognizes a person based on a feature vector derived from a specific physiological or behavioural characteristic that the person possesses. Biometric system has been actively emerging in various industries for the past few years, and it is continuing to roll to provide higher security features for access control system [1]. Fingerprints, Iris, Voice, Face, and Palmprints are the different physiological characteristics used for identifying an individual. Palmprint-based personal identification (Palmprint technology), as a new member in the biometrics family, has become an active research topic in recent years. Palmprint is the palms of the human hands contain pattern of ridges and valleys much like the fingerprints. The area of the palm is much larger than the area of a finger and, as a result, palmprints are expected to be even more distinctive than the fingerprints [2]. Since palmprint scanners need to capture a large area, they are bulkier and more expensive than the fingerprint sensors. Human palms also contain additional distinctive features such as principal lines and wrinkles that can be captured even with a lower resolution scanner, which would be cheaper.

Different line extraction techniques are already proposed which includes edge detection techniques, line tracing techniques. However, these principal lines are

J. Blanc-Talon et al. (Eds.): ACIVS 2009, LNCS 5807, pp. 720–731, 2009.
© Springer-Verlag Berlin Heidelberg 2009

not sufficient to represent the uniqueness of each individuals palmprint because different people may have similar principal lines on their palmprints [3]. This paper presents the extraction of features like palm lines and texture present on the palm. Gabor filter technique is used for extracting the texture features.

The remainder of this paper is organized as follows : in section 2, we will introduce the system overview. The model of ROI (Region Of Interest) extraction is discussed in section 3. Section 4 presents the feature extraction technique. In section 5 we will discuss the similarity matching used. Experimental results are provided and commented in section 6. Finally, the conclusions and future work are drawn in the last section.

2   System Overview

Fig. 1 is an overview of typical biometric system. It can be divided into two modules [4]: (i) enrollment and (ii) authentication (verification or identification). The enrollment module scans the palmprint of a person through a sensing device and then stores a representation (called template or feature) of the palmprint in the database. The verification module is invoked during the operation phase. The same representation which was used in enrollment phase is extracted from the input palmprint and matched against the template of the claimed identity to give a "yes/no" answer. On the other hand, an identification system matches the input palmprint with a large number of palmprints in the database and as a result, palmprint classification "accepted/rejected" is effective only in an identification system and is not an issue in a verification system.

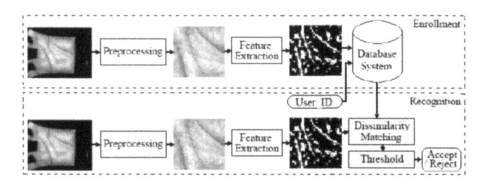

Fig. 1. Architecture of an authentication system

3   Extraction of ROI

The palm area (ROI) has to be located before further feature extraction. With referencing to the locations of the gaps between fingers, the palm is duly rotated and the maximum palm area is then located. Then the ROI is converted to

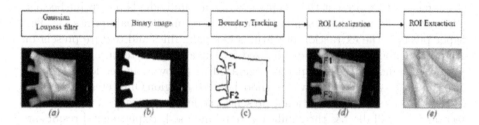

Fig. 2. Various steps in a typical region of interest extraction algorithm. *(a)* The filtered image, *(b)* The binary image, *(c)* The boundaries of the binary image and the points for locating the ROI pattern, *(d)* The central portion localization, and *(e)* The preprocessed result (ROI).

a fixed size (128 × 128 pixels) so that all of the palmprints conform to a same size. The ROI extraction method applied in our system is based on the algorithm described in [5]. We have summarized ROI extraction algorithm as follow : First, Apply a lowpass filter, such as Gaussian smoothing, to the original palmprint image. A threshold, Tp, is used to convert the filtred image to a binary image, then, the boundary tracking algorithm used to obtain the boundaries of the binary image. This boundary is processed to determine the points F_1 and F_2 for locating the ROI pattern and, based on the relevant points (F_1 and F_2), the ROI pattern is located on the original image. Finally, the ROI is extracted. The preprocessing steps are shows in Fig. 2.

4   Feature Extraction

A 2D Gabor filter is applied to the region of interest (ROI) in the grey level image to enhance the principal lines.

4.1   2D Gabor Filter

Gabor filter is traditional choice for obtaining localized frequency information. They offer the best simultaneous localization of spatial and frequency information [6]. In the spatial domain, a 2D Gabor filter is a Gaussian kernel function modulated by a sinusoidal plane wave. The even symmetric 2D Gabor filter has the following general form in the spatial domain:

$$gw2D(x, y, \theta, u, \sigma) = \frac{1}{2\pi\sigma^2} \exp\{-\frac{x^2 + y^2}{2\sigma^2}\} \exp\{2\pi i u(x\cos\theta + y\sin\theta)\} \quad (1)$$

Where x and y are the coordinates of the filter, u is the frequency of the sinusoidal wave, σ is the gaussian envelope and θ is the orientation. Here, the optimized values for the Gabor filter parameters such as $u = 0.001$ and $\sigma = 1$ have chosen after testing with different values at an orientation of $45°$.

4.2   Feature Vector

The response of a Gabor filter to an image is obtained by a 2D convolution operation. Let $I(i, j)$ denote the image (ROI) and $gw2D(i,j,\theta,u,\sigma)$ denote the response of a Gabor filter with frequency u and orientation θ. f_θ (feature) is obtained as :

$$f_\theta(i,j) = \sum_{x=1}^{N_f} \sum_{y=1}^{N_f} gw2D(x, y, \theta, u, \sigma) I(i - x, j - y) \qquad (2)$$

where I is the input image, f_θ is the feature at θ orientation, and $N_f \times N_f$ is the size of the Gabor filter mask. Equation (3) will give the overall magnitude of these real and imaginary part of the feature,

$$F_\theta = \sqrt{Re(f_\theta)^2 + Im(f_\theta)^2} \qquad (3)$$

The feature (magnitude) should be binarized by a proper threshold value. It is important to find the proper threshold value in order to separate the lines from

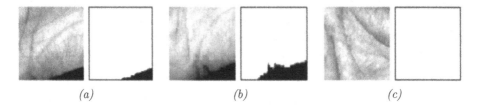

(a)   (b)   (c)

Fig. 3. Sample ROIs extracted and the corresponding masks

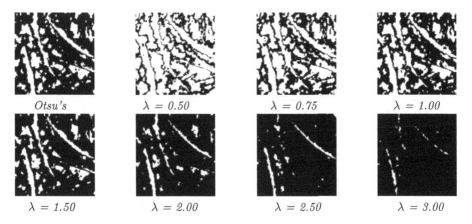

Fig. 4. The binary features at different $T_\theta(\lambda)$ (varying the λ) and the Otsu's threshold for a region of interest image from the PolyU database

palm. For the method, to find the threshold value, we employed thresholding by Otsu's and thresholding at level T_θ obtained as :

$$T_\theta(\lambda) = \lambda * mean(F_\theta) \tag{4}$$

where λ is a positive number and $mean(F_\theta)$ find mean value of the $N \times N$ feature. The threshold, T_θ, is used to convert this feature to a binary feature. The input to a thresholding operation is the feature F_θ . In the simplest implementation, the output is a binary image representing the segmentation. Black pixels correspond to background and white pixels correspond to foreground (or vice versa). In simple implementations, the segmentation is determined by a single parameter known as the intensity threshold. In a single pass, each pixel in the feature is compared with T_θ. If the pixel's intensity is higher than the T_θ, the pixel is set to, say, white in the output. If it is less than the T_θ, it is set to black. Mathematically, this transformation can be represented as :

$$\Psi(i,j) = \begin{cases} 1, & \text{if } F_\theta(i,j) \geq T_\theta; \\ 0, & otherwise \end{cases} \tag{5}$$

To remove such redundant information from the image (the user does not place his/her hand correctly and some nonpalmprint pixels will be included in the images), we generate a mask, M, to identify the location of the nonpalmprint pixels, Fig. 3 showing sum ROI patterns and the corresponding masks. An example of a binarized features for the image Fig. 3.c obtained in this manner is shown in Fig. 4.

5   Matching Process

Given two sets of features originating from two palmprints, the objective of the feature matching system is to determine whether or not the prints represent the same palm. The matching phase typically defines the similarity (distance) metric between two palmprint representations and determines whether a given pair of representations is captured from the same palm (mated pair) based on whether this quantified (dis)similarity is greater (less) than a certain (predetermined) threshold. The ranges of the vertical and horizontal translations are defined from -4 to 4. As the result, our palmprint matching process can handle different translation. The minimum D_o value obtained from the translated matchings is considered to be the final matching score.

5.1   Hamming Distance

The criterion for similarity/disimilarity is to minimize the score (distance) between the input feature Ψ_2 and the stored feature Ψ_1. The difference between the features is labeled "Hamming Distance". A simple XOR operation between the corresponding pair of features provides this Hamming Distance. Hamming distance does not measure the difference between the components of the feature vectors, but the number of components that differ in value. We can define the hamming distance D_o [7] as,

$$D_o = \frac{\sum_{i=1}^{N}\sum_{j=1}^{N} M(i,j) \cap \Psi_e(i,j)}{\sum_{i=1}^{N}\sum_{j=1}^{N} M(i,j)} \tag{6}$$

$$M(i,j) = M_I(i,j) \cap M_S(i,j) \tag{7}$$

$$\Psi_e(i,j) = \Psi_1(i,j) \oplus \Psi_2(i,j) \tag{8}$$

Where D_o is the hamming distance, Ψ_1 (Ψ_2) is the input (stored) feature, M_I (M_S) is the input (stored) mask, $\oplus$ is the exclusive OR operator (XOR), $\cap$ is the AND operator, and $N \times N$ is the size of the features. The value D_o lies between 0 and 1, inclusive, with 1 meaning that the two features are independent and 0 meaning they are completely identical.

5.2   Decision Module

The final step in the authentication process is the accepted/rejected decision based on the security threshold. This security threshold is either a parameter of the matching process or the resulting score (Hamming Distance is compared with the threshold value to make the final decision).

$$Decision = \begin{cases} D_o \leq threshold & \Rightarrow \quad \text{Accepted;} \\ D_o > threshold & \Rightarrow \quad \text{Rejected;} \end{cases} \tag{9}$$

The pre-defined threshold, for decision, value also separates "false" and "right" results. The error rate of a system can be determined as a function of threshold when varying the threshold in an experiment. A threshold value is obtained based on equal error rate criteria where false rejection rate FRR and false acceptance rate FAR are equal.

6   Experimental Evaluation

6.1   Test Palmprint Database

We experimented our approach on Hong Kong Polytechnic University (PolyU) palmprint database [8]. This database contains 100 classes. The resolution of the original palmprint images is 384×284 pixels taken with 75 dpi. Where six samples from each person were collected in two sessions; three samples were captured in the first session and the other three in the second session. The average interval between the first and the second collection was two months. The palmprint images are aligned and the central part of the image, whose size is 128×128, is automatically segmented to represent the region of interest (ROI) of the palmprint, the lighting conditions in the two sessions clearly result to variation of visual texture of the images. Three samples are used to set up the database and the other samples are used for testing the recognition rate.

6.2   Error Rates

To evaluate the system performance, we have used the two well-known measurements [9], that are FRR and FAR. FAR is the rate at which the system accepts a non-authenticated user. FRR is the rate of rejection of a genuine user by the system. Another performance measurement is obtained from FAR and FRR which is called total success rate (TSR). It represents the verification (identification) rate of the system.

$$FRR = \frac{Number\ of\ rejected\ genuine\ claims}{Total\ number\ of\ genuine\ accesses} *100\ [\%] \tag{10}$$

$$FAR = \frac{Number\ of\ accepted\ imposter\ claims}{Total\ number\ of\ imposter\ accesses} *100\ [\%] \tag{11}$$

$$TSR = (1- \frac{FAR + FRR}{Total\ number\ of\ accesses}) *100\ [\%] \tag{12}$$

However, these numbers are non-zero and depend on the security threshold. If the threshold is lower, then the false rejection is important and the false acceptance is less. Otherwise, if the threshold is higher, then the false rejection is less and the false acceptance is important.

6.3   Threshold Selection for Binarization

A series of experiments were carried out using the palmprint database. After the feature, F_θ, is formed, the values of F_θ is compared to a threshold, T_θ, to determine if a lines exists or not. The problem we address is as follows : Given N features, F_θ, we want chosen the λ such that the total success rate (TSR) is maximized. In the experiment, to determine λ, the imposter distribution and genuine distribution are generated by 150 and 3675 comparisons, respectively. A graphical relationship between the total success rate (TSR) and λ can be

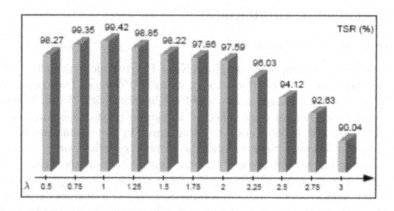

Fig. 5. Relationship between the total success rate and the λ

established (see Fig. 5). It is clear that the system achieved a maximum *TSR* when the λ parameter equal to 1.00. It is interesting to note that the total success rate of the system under the Otsu's threshold is equal to 86.67 %. It is concluded that the system performance under λ-thresholding ($\lambda = 1 \Rightarrow TSR = 99.42$ %; $\lambda = 0.75 \Rightarrow TSR = 99.35$ %) is a very efficient and yields better results than Otsu's-thresholding.

6.4   Results And Discussion

Palmprint Verification: To obtain the performance of the proposed method, the feature of each testing palmprint is compared with each feature in the database. The Receiver operating characteristic (*ROC*) curve is a way to visualize the tradeoff between the genuine acceptance rate (*GAR*) and *FAR* for a particular classifier.

For the database, a total of 44850 matchings were performed. The probability distribution for genuine (correct) matches was estimated with 750 matches and the imposter distribution was estimated with 44100 matches. Fig. 6.*a* and Fig. 6.*c* shows the two distributions for $\lambda = 0.75$ and $\lambda = 1.00$. Our proposed method gets better performance, it can achieve an Equal Error Rate (*EER*), which corresponds to $FAR = FRR$, of 6.13 % for $T_p = 0.459$ and the maximum $TSR = GAR = 93.87$ % for $\lambda = 0.75$, and an *EER* of 3.19 % for $T_p = 0.426$ and the maximum $TSR = GAR = 96.81$ % for $\lambda = 1.00$. The system performance at all thresholds can be depicted in the form of *ROC* curve, see Fig. 6.*b* and Fig. 6.*d* for $\lambda = 0.75$ and $\lambda = 1.00$. The performance of the proposed method under different the threshold, Tp, which control the false accept rate and the false reject rate is shown in ***Table 1***.

Table 1. Verification Rate

λ	Threshold	FAR (%)	FRR (%)	TSR (%)
	0.440	0.342	9.467	99.505
0.75	**0.459**	**6.133**	**6.133**	**93.867**
	0.462	15.00	5.733	85.155
	0.400	0.138	7.600	99.737
1.00	**0.426**	**3.191**	**3.191**	**96.809**
	0.430	6.277	3.867	93.764

Palmprint Identification: An identification system examines whether the user is one of enrolled candidates. The biometric feature of unknown user is presented to the system and the system will try to match the user with all the enrolled candidates in the database, thus the match is 1 to N. In our experiment, three sample of each person was used as inputs for identification. During the experiments, the Ψ feature of each image was extracted and matched. Two experiments were done in order to test the identification performance of the system, we setup

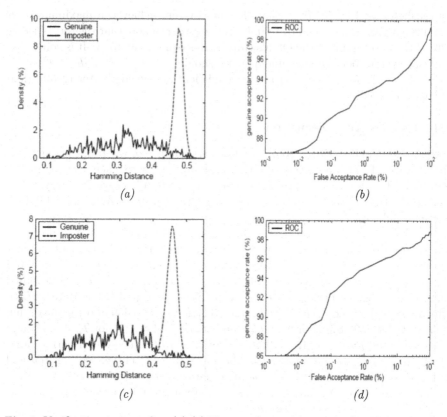

Fig. 6. Verification test results. *(a),(c)* The genuine and impostor distribution with λ = 0.75 and λ = 1.00, respectively, and *(b),(d)* The receiver operating characteristic curve with $\lambda = 0.75$ and $\lambda = 1.00$.

two registration databases for $N = 50$ and 100. None of palmprint images in the testing database are contained in any of the registration databases.

• *Experiment 1:*   In the first experiment, we found the performance of the biometric system with a database size $N = 50$. The results expressed as a *GAR*, vary, depending on the *FAR*. Fig. 7.*a* and Fig. 7.*c* presents the two distributions for $\lambda = 0.75$ and $\lambda = 1.00$. Fig. 7.*b* and Fig. 7.*d* shows the dependency of *GAR* on the *FAR* values. Our identification system can achieve an *EER* of 0.65 % for $T_p = 0.44$ and the maximum *GAR* = 99.35 % for $\lambda = 0.75$, and an *EER* of 0.58 % for $T_p = 0.40$ and the maximum *GAR* = 99.43 % for $\lambda = 1.00$.

The developed system is expected to give higher accuracy. However, it can safely be concluded that the new method yields much better identification results compared with some methods for palmprint identification. It is also better than the contour-based method in [10], which had an equal error rate of about 2.5 %. The system was tested with different thresholds and the results is shown in *Table 2*.

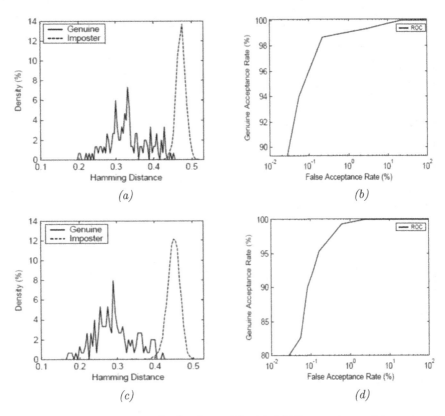

Fig. 7. Identification test results (50 Person's). *(a),(c)* The genuine and impostor distribution with $\lambda = 0.75$ and $\lambda = 1.00$, respectively, and *(b),(d)* The receiver operating characteristic curve with $\lambda = 0.75$ and $\lambda = 1.00$.

Table 2. Identification Rate (50 person's)

λ	Threshold	FAR (%)	FRR (%)	TSR (%)
	0.432	0.109	1.333	99.843
0.75	**0.442**	**0.654**	**0.654**	**99.346**
	0.452	3.374	0.000	96.758
	0.390	0.163	4.667	99.660
1.00	**0.402**	**0.575**	**0.575**	**99.425**
	0.416	2.395	0.000	97.699

- *Experiment 2:* In the second identification experiment, the database size is $N = 100$. From Fig. 8 our identification system can achieve an EER of 1.62 % for $T_p = 0.45$ and the maximum $GAR = 98.38$ % for $\lambda = 0.75$, and an EER of 1.05 % for $T_p = 0.41$ and the maximum $GAR = 98.95$ % for $\lambda = 1.00$. The proposed scheme works very well at suppressing the false identification. These results

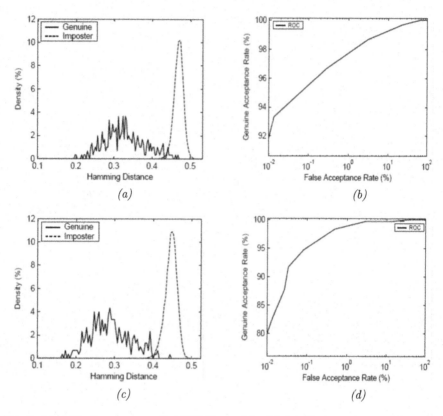

Fig. 8. Identification test results (100 Person's). *(a),(c)* The genuine and impostor distribution with $\lambda = 0.75$ and $\lambda = 1.00$, respectively, and *(b),(d)* The receiver operating characteristic curve with $\lambda = 0.75$ and $\lambda = 1.00$.

are encouraging and the scheme will be tested on a much larger database. The performance of the proposed method under different the threshold, Tp, which control the false accept rate and the false reject rate is shown in **Table 3**.

Table 3. Identification Rate (50 person's)

λ	Threshold	FAR (%)	FRR (%)	TSR (%)
	0.422	0.014	6.667	99.855
0.75	**0.446**	**1.624**	**1.624**	**98.376**
	0.456	7.192	0.667	92.937
	0.378	0.047	8.333	99.789
1.00	**0.414**	**1.050**	**1.050**	**98.951**
	0.416	1.859	0.333	98.172

7   Conclusion and Future Work

A palmprint identification system has been developed in this work. 2D Gabor filter technique used to represent a palmprint image using its texture feature, and apply a normalized hamming distance for the matching measurement. The performance of the biometric system is measured in terms of *FRR* and *FAR*. The experimental results, show that in our palmprint database of 300 palmprint images from 50 different palms, we can achieve high *TSR* (96.81 %) and low *FAR* (3.19 %) verification rates, which is comparable with all other palmprint recognition approaches. For 1-to-50 identification, our system can operate at a 0.58 % FAR and a reasonable 99.43 % GAR. For 1-to-100 identification, our system can operate at a 1.05 % FAR and a reasonable 98.95 % GAR. This result is also comparable with other hand based biometrics, such as hand geometry and fingerprint verification [11], [12], [13]. These results are encouraging to combine the proposed palmprint feature with other texture feature measurements such as texture energy to achieve higher performance.

References

1. Varchol, P., Levicky, D.: Using of Hand Geometry in Biometric Security Systems. Radio Engineering 16(4) (December 2007)
2. Li, F., Leung, M.K.H., Yu, X.: Palmprint Identification Using Hausdorff Distance. In: International Workshop on Biomedical Circuits & Systems, BioCAS 2004 (2004)
3. Roberts, C.: Biometric Technologies - Palm and Hand (May 2006)
4. Jain, A.K., Ross, A., Prabhakar, S.: An Introduction to Biometric Recognition. IEEE Transaction 14(1) (January 2004)
5. Zhang, D., Kong, W., You, J., Wong, M.: On-line Palmprint Identification. IEEE Trans. on PAMI 25(9), 1041–1050 (2003)
6. Kong, W.K., Zhang, D.: Palmprint Texture Analysis On Low Resolution Images For Personal Authentication. IEEE Trans. on Pattern Analysis and Machine Intelligence (2002)
7. Chen, Y., Dass, S.C., Jain, A.K.: Localized Iris Image Quality Using 2-D Wavelets. In: Zhang, D., Jain, A.K. (eds.) ICB 2005. LNCS, vol. 3832, pp. 373–381. Springer, Heidelberg (2005)
8. The Hong Kong Polytechnic University, PolyU Palmprint Database biometrics, http://www.comp.polyu.edu.hk/
9. Connie, T., Teoh, A., Goh, M., Ngo, D.: Palmprint Recognition with PCA and ICA, Palmerston North (November 2003)
10. Pang, Y., Andrew, T.B.J., David, N.C.L., Hiew, F.S.: Palmprint Verification with Moments. Journal of WSCG 12(1-3) (2004); ISSN 1213-6972, WSCG 2004, February 2-6, 2003, Plzen, Czech Republic
11. Dai, Q., Bi, N., Huang, D., Zhang, D., Li, F.: M-Band Wavelets Application To Palmprint Recognition Based On Texture Features. In: International Conference on Image Processing, ICIP (2004)
12. Wang, Y., Ruan, Q.: Kernel Fisher Discriminant Analysis for Palmprint Recognition. In: The 18th International Conference on Pattern Recognition, ICPR 2006 (2006)
13. Wu, X.-Q., Wang, K.-Q., Zhang, D.: Palmprint Recognition Using Fisher's Linear Discriminant. In: Proceedings of the Second International Conference on Machine Learning and Cybemedcs, Wan, November 2-5 (2003)

Retina Identification Based on the Pattern of Blood Vessels Using Angular and Radial Partitioning

Mehran Deljavan Amiri, Fardin Akhlaqian Tab, and Wafa Barkhoda

Department of Electrical and Computer Engineering
University of Kurdistan, Sanandaj, Iran
deljavan@ieee.org, f.akhlaqian@uok.ac.ir, w.barkhoda@ieee.org

Abstract. This paper presents a new human identification system based on features obtained from retina images using angular and radial partitioning of the images. The proposed algorithm is composed of two principal stages including feature extraction and decision making. In the feature extraction stage, first all of the images are normalized in a preprocessing step. Then, the blood vessels' pattern is extracted from retina images and a morphological thinning process is applied on the extracted pattern. After thinning, two feature vectors based on the angular and radial partitioning of the pattern image are extracted from the blood vessels' pattern. The extracted features are rotation and scale invariant and robust against translation. In the next stage, the extracted feature vectors are analyzed using 1D discrete Fourier transform and the Manhattan metric is used to measure the closeness of the feature vectors to have a compression on them. Experimental results on a database, including 360 retina images obtained from 40 subjects, demonstrated an average true identification accuracy rate equal to 98.75 percent for the proposed system.

1   Introduction

The recent advances in digital technology and increasing security concerns cause a requirement to use intelligent person identification systems based on the human's biological features. Biometric is the science of recognizing the identity of a person based on the physical or behavioral attributes of the individual. The popular used biometric features in identification purposes are fingerprint, face, facial thermo-gram, iris, retina, palm print, hand geometry, gait, ear, voice, signature, teeth, hand vein, etc. These features are unique in every individual and can be used as identification tools [1, 2, 4, 3]. Among these features, retina may provide higher level of security due to its indigenous robustness against imposture. Uniqueness of retina comes from uniqueness of blood vessels' pattern distribution at the retina. From the other hand, the retina pattern of each person undergoes less modification during his life. Therefore, we can say that the retina pattern is a good candidate to be used in identification systems. The retina pattern of each person can be identified even among genetically identical twins [5].

Several researches on retina identification have been reported in the literature [6,7,8]. The first retina based identification system named EyeDentification 7.5 was introduced by EyeDentify Company in 1976 [6]. In [7] Xu et al. obtained vector curve of blood vessels' skeleton using the green channel gray-scale retina images. They defined a set

J. Blanc-Talon et al. (Eds.): ACIVS 2009, LNCS 5807, pp. 732–739, 2009.

of feature vectors for each image including feature points, directions, and scaling factor. Although they have reached a good recognition result, but the major drawback of their method is its computational cost, since a number of rigid motion parameters should be computed for all possible correspondences between the query and enrolled images in the database. Ortega et al. [8] used a fuzzy circular Hough transform to localize the optical disk in the retina image. Then, they defined feature vectors based on the ridge endings and bifurcations from vessels obtained from a crease model of the retinal vessels inside the optical disk. For matching, they used a similar approach as in [7] to compute the parameters of a rigid transformation between feature vectors which gives the highest matching score. This algorithm is computationally more efficient with respect to the algorithm presented in [7]. However, the performance of the algorithm has been evaluated using a very small database including only 14 subjects. Recently, Tabatabaee et al. [9] presented a new approach for human identification using retina images by localizing the optical disk using Haar wavelet and active contour model and they used it for rotation compensation. Then, they used Fourier-Mellin transform coefficients and complex moment magnitudes of the rotated retinal image for feature definition. Finally, they applied a fuzzy C-means clustering for recognition and tested their approach on a database including 108 images of 27 different subjects.

Chalechale et al. have introduced a sketch-based method for image similarity measurement using angular partitioning (AP) [10,11]. In their method, a hand-drawn rough black and white query sketch is compared with an existing database of full color images. Although, this method have been proposed for natural and hand-drawn images retrieval, but it could be modified to be used in other image matching systems. In this paper, we are going to propose a new approach for identifying retina images based on angular and radial partitioning (RP) of images. The identification task in the proposed system is invariant form the most of the common affine transformations (e.g. rotation, scale changes and translation). The proposed system eliminates any constraint regarding the shape of the objects and the existence of any background. Also, segmentation and object extraction are not needed in this approach. So, the computational complexity of the image matching algorithm is low and the proposed system is suitable for secure human identification especially in real-time applications.

The rest of this paper is organized as follows: Section 2 introduces the angular and radial partitioning briefly. Section 3 presents the proposed system. The feature extraction procedure and decision making process is discussed in this Section. In Section 4, some details about the simulation of the proposed algorithm are given and experimental results of are presented in this Section. Finally, Section 5 concludes the paper.

2 Angular and Radial Partitioning

Chalechale et al. [10, 11] have defined angular partitions (slices) in the surrounding circle of the image I. The angle between adjacent slices is $\varphi = 2\pi/K$, where K is the number of angular partitions in the image (see Figure 1). Any λ slices rotation of a given image, with respect to its center, moves a pixel at slice S_i to a new position at slice S_j where $j = (i + \lambda) \bmod K$, for $i, \lambda = 0, 1, 2, ...K - 1$. They used the number of edge points at each slice of the image to represent the slice feature.

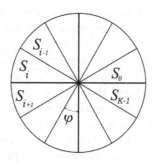

Fig. 1. Angular partitioning partitions the image into K successive slices

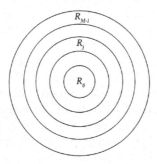

Fig. 2. Radial partitioning partitions the image into M concentric circles

$$f(i) = \sum_{\theta=\frac{i2\pi}{K}}^{\frac{(i+1)2\pi}{K}} \sum_{\rho=0}^{R} I(\rho, \theta)$$

R is the radius of surrounding circle of the rotated image. The feature extracted above will be circularly shifted when the image I is rotated $\tau = l2\pi/K$ radians in counter-clockwise direction ($l = 0, 1, 2, ...$).

It can be shown that for an image I and a rotated version of it, I_τ, using $1D$ discrete Fourier transform (DFT) of $f(i)$ and $f_\tau(i)$ and based on the property $|F(u)|=|F_\tau(u)|$ we can use the $\{|F(u)|\}$ and $\{|F_\tau(u)|\}$ as the rotation invariant features in images I and I_τ [10, 11].

The radial partitioning, partitions a given image I into the multiple concentric radial partitions (circles). The number of circles could be adjusted in the applications to reach the best performance (see Figure 2). During the rotation process for a given image with respect to its center, the local information of the image at each circle (e.g. the number of edge points, gray levels histogram, neighborhood information, etc.) are not changed.

To increase the delicacy of the extracted features in this paper, a combination of the AP and the RP was used in feature extraction. The details of the feature extraction process will be discussed in Section 3.

3   The Proposed System

Similar to the most of the pattern recognition algorithms, the identification task in the proposed system can be divided into two stages: 1- Feature extraction. 2- Decision making. The following subsections describe the details of steps.

3.1   Feature Extraction

The overview of feature extraction process in the proposed system is depicted in Figure 3. This process is done for every enrolled and query images. As Figure 3 shows, the feature extraction stage consists of some steps. In the preprocessing step, first, to achieve translation invariant features, the extra margins of the input image are cropped and the bounding box of retina is extracted from the input image. Also, to achieve the scale invariancy, the cropped image is normalized to $J \times J$ pixels (see Figure 4 (b)). At the next step, the pattern of the blood vessels' in the retina image should be detected. There are several vessels' pattern detection algorithms in the literature. Here we adopted a similar approach as in [12] to reach the vessels' pattern (see Figure 4 (c)). A morphological thinning procedure [13] is employed for thinning the vessels' pattern in the pattern image (see Figure 4 (d)). This task is based on the fact that usually there are thick lines in the pattern and thinning these lines helps to increase the performance of the system. At the next steps, two modes of feature extraction based on AP and RP are applied to the thinned pattern image in parallel (see Figures 4 (e) and 4 (f)). At each mode, first, the thinned pattern image is partitioned using the related partitioning method (AP or RP) and the number of pattern points is counted at each partition (slices in AP and circles in RP) as the partition feature. The results of these two parallel processes are two feature vectors (AP feature vector and RP feature vector) for each image. The resulting two vectors are the feature set of each image.

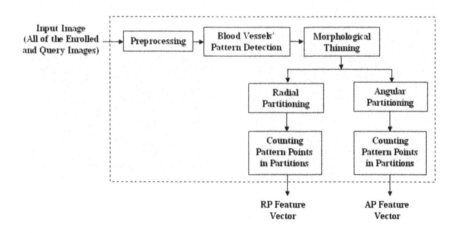

Fig. 3. The overview of the feature extraction process in the proposed system

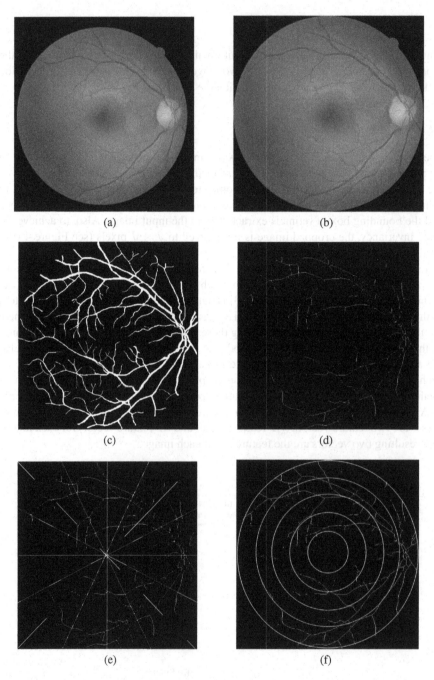

Fig. 4. (a). A sample retina image, (b) Preprocessed image, (c) The blood vessels' pattern, (d) Morphological thinned pattern, (e) Angular partitioning of the thinned pattern, (f) Radial partitioning of the thinned pattern

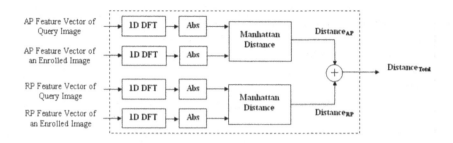

Fig. 5. Overview of the decision making stage

3.2   Decision Making

Similarity measurement is a key point in pattern recognition algorithms. One of the most important tasks in image based identification systems is search the image database to find an image or some images similar to a given query image. To compare the database's images and the query image, the feature vectors extracted from the database's images and from the query image are passed through a distance measurement metric to find out the degree of closeness. There are several metrics in the literature to measure the closeness of two feature vectors. The most common metrics among this family are the Manhattan and Euclidean metrics [14, 15, 16]. The weighted Manhattan and weighted Euclidean metrics are widely used for ranking in image retrieval [17, 18, 19].

As described in Section 3.1, in the proposed system, two feature vectors are extracted from every image (AP based and RP based feature vectors). To compare the feature vectors, first a 1D DFT is applied on each feature vector and the absolute value (Abs) of each DFT vector is calculated. As described in Section 2, this action is done to stultify the effect of rotation on the feature vectors and consequently results a rotation invariant identification system. Then, the Manhattan metric is used to measure the distance of feature vectors. Because of the existence of two feature vectors for each image, two Manhattan distances will be produce here. To have a total distance, the two Manhattan distances are combined with a simple summation (see Figure 5).

$$\text{Distance}_{Total} = \text{Distance}_{AP} + \text{Distance}_{RP}$$

The closest image in database to the query image is the one that have the minimum distance from the query image.

4   Experimental Results

The proposed system was fully software implemented and has been tested on a database including 40 retina images from DRIVE database [12]. To do the following experiments, the size of the preprocessed images was set to 512×512 ($J = 512$). To apply the AP on images, the angle of each partition was set to $5°$. Therefor each image is divided into 72 ($360°/5°$) slices and the *AP Feature Vector* have 72 elements (features). The number of circles in RP was chosen to be 8. So, the *RP Feature Vector* has 8 elements.

To produce test images (query images), each image in the database was rotated 8 times using various degrees to obtain 320 new query images. Table 1 shows the results of identification of the query images in the proposed system.

As the Table 1 shows, the proposed system has an average accuracy equal to 98.5 percent.

Table 1. Results for identifying query images

Rotation Degree	5	10	15	30	45	90	180	270	Mean
Accuracy (percent)	100	97.5	97.5	95	100	100	100	100	98.75

5   Conclusion

In this paper, a novel human identification system based on retina images was introduced. To identify a retina image, after normalizing it in a preprocessing step, the blood vessels' pattern was extracted from the retina image and a morphological thinning process is applied on the extracted pattern. Two feature vectors were extracted from the thinned pattern using angular and radial partitioning. To match the query image with the database, the feature vectors were analyzed using 1D discrete Fourier transform. The similarity between feature vectors was measured by Manhattan distance. The performance of the proposed system was evaluated using a database containing 360 images from 40 objects. Experimental results demonstrated an average true accuracy rate equal to 98.75 percent for the proposed system. Simplicity, low computational complexity, robustness against rotation, scaling and translation and high accuracy ration of the proposed approach, make it attractive for secure human identification systems and real-time applications. Further research will study the performance of the proposed identification approach against different geometric and non-geometric distortions and attacks.

References

1. Jain, A.K., Flynn, P., Ross, A.A.: Handbook of Biometrics. Springer, Heidelberg (2008)
2. Jain, A., Bolle, R., Pankanti, S.: Biometrics: Personal Identification in a Networked Society. Kluwer Academic Publishers, Dordrecht (1999)
3. Zhang, D.: Automated Biometrics: Technologies and Systems. Kluwer Academic Publishers, Dordrecht (2000)
4. Nanavati, S., Thieme, M., Nanavati, R.: Biometrics Identity Verification in a Networked World. John Wiley and Sons, Inc., Chichester (2002)
5. Tower, P.: The Fundus Oculi in Monozygotic Twins: Report of Six Pairs of Identical Twins. Archives of Ophthalmology 54(2), 225–239 (1955)
6. Hill, R.B.: Retinal identification. In: Biometrics: Personal Identification in Networked Society, p. 126. Springer, Berlin (1999)
7. Xu, Z.W., Guo, X.X., Hu, X.Y., Cheng, X.: The Blood Vessel Recognition of Ocular Fundus. In: Proc. 4'th Int. Conf. Machine Learning and Cybernetics (ICMLC 2005), Guangzhou, China, August 2005, pp. 4493–4498 (2005)

8. Ortega, M., Marino, C., Penedo, M.G., Blanco, M., Gonzalez, F.: Biometric Authentication Using Digital Retinal Images. In: Proc. 5th WSEAS Int. Conf. on Applied Computer Science (ACOS 2006), Hangzhou, China, April 2006, pp. 422–427 (2006)

9. Tabatabaee, H., Milani-Fard, A., Jafariani, H.: A Novel Human Identifier System Using Retina Image and Fuzzy Clustering Approach. In: Proc. 2nd IEEE Int. Conf. Information and Communication Technologies (ICTTA 2006), Damascus, Syria, April 2006, pp. 1031–1036 (2006)

10. Chalechale, A., Naghdy, G., Mertins, A.: Sketch-Based Image Matching Using Angular Partitioning. IEEE Trans. on systems, man. and cybernetics part a: systems and humans 35(1) (January 2005)

11. Chalechale, A., Naghdy, G., Mertins, A.: Sketch-based Image Retrieval Using Angular Partitioning. In: Proc. 3rd IEEE Int. Symp. Signal Processing and Information Technology (ISSPIT 2003), December 2003, pp. 668–671 (2003)

12. Staal, J., Abramoff, M.D., Niemeijer, M., Viergever, M.A., van-Ginneken, B.: Ridge-based Vessel Segmentation in Color Images of the Retina. IEEE Trans. Medical Imaging 23(4), 501–509 (2004)

13. Gonzalez, R.C., Woods, R.E.: Digital Image Processing. Addison-Wesley, Reading (1992)

14. Pass, G., Zabih, R.: Histogram Refinement for Content-based Image Retrieval. In: Proc. 3rd IEEE Workshop on Applications of Computer Vision, pp. 96–102 (1996)

15. Del Bimbo, A.: Visual Information Retrieval. Morgan Kaufmann Publishers, San Francisco (1999)

16. Jacobs, C.E., Finkelstein, A., Salesin, D.H.: Fast Multiresolution Image Querying. In: Proc. ACM Computer Graphics, SIGGRAPH 1995, USA, pp. 277–286 (1995)

17. Bober, M.: MPEG-7 Visual Shape Describtion. IEEE Trans. Circuits and Systems for Video Technology 11(6), 716–719 (2001)

18. Chalechale, A., Mertins, A.: An Abstract Image Representation Based on Edge Pixel Neighborhood Information (EPNI). In: Shafazand, H., Tjoa, A.M. (eds.) EurAsia-ICT 2002. LNCS, vol. 2510, pp. 67–74. Springer, Heidelberg (2002)

19. Won, C.S., Park, D.K., Park, S.: Efficient Use of MPEG-7 Edge Histogram Descriptor. Etri. J. 24(1), 23–30 (2002)

Author Index